FOURTH EDITION

Nursing Assessment & Health Promotion Strategies Through the Life Span

FOURTH EDITION

Nursing Assessment & Health Promotion Strategies Through the Life Span

Ruth Beckmann Murray, R.N., M.S.N., Ed.D.
Professor
Coordinator, Psychiatric/Mental Health Nursing Graduate Major
School of Nursing
St. Louis University
St. Louis, Missouri

Judith Proctor Zentner, R.N., M.A., C.F.N.P.
Director of Health Services
Corson Furniture Industries
Valdese, North Carolina

APPLETON & LANGE
Norwalk, Connecticut/San Mateo, California

0-8385-7006-2

Notice: The authors and publisher of this volume have taken care that
the information and recommendations contained herein are accurate and
compatible with the standards generally accepted at the time of publication.

Copyright©1989 by Appleton & Lange
A Publishing Division of Prentice Hall
©1985, 1979, 1975 by Prentice-Hall, Inc., Englewood Cliffs, N.J. 07632

All rights reserved. This book, or any parts thereof, may not be used or
reproduced in any manner without written permission. For information,
address Appleton & Lange, 25 Van Zant Street, East Norwalk, Connecticut 06855.

92 93 / 10 9 8 7 6 5

Prentice-Hall International (UK) Limited, *London*
Prentice-Hall of Australia Pty. Limited, *Sydney*
Prentice-Hall Canada, Inc., *Toronto*
Prentice-Hall Hispanoamericana, S.A., *Mexico*
Prentice-Hall of India Private Limited, *New Delhi*
Prentice-Hall of Japan, Inc., *Tokyo*
Simon & Schuster Asia Pte. Ltd., *Singapore*
Editora Prentice-Hall do Brasil Ltda., *Rio de Janeiro*
Prentice-Hall, *Englewood Cliffs, New Jersey*

Library of Congress Cataloging-in-Publication Data

Murray, Ruth Beckmann.
  Nursing assessment and health promotion strategies through the
life span / Ruth Beckmann Murray, Judith Proctor Zentner.—4th ed.
    p. cm.
  A combined rev. ed. of: Nursing assessment and health promotion
through the life span. 3rd ed. c1985.
  Includes bibliographies and index.
  ISBN 0-8385-7006-2
  1. Nursing. 2. Health promotion. 3. Human growth.
4. Developmental psychology. I. Zentner, Judith Proctor.
II. Murray, Ruth Beckmann. Nursing assessment and health promotion
through the life span. III. Murray, Ruth Beckmann. Nursing
concepts for health promotion. IV. Title.
  [DNLM: 1. Health Promotion—nurses' instruction. 2. Human
Development—nurses' instruction. 3. Nursing Assessment. WY 100
M983nb]
RT42.M8 1988
613—dc19
DNLM/DLC   88-22161
for Library of Congress   CIP

Acquisitions Editor: Marion Kalstein-Welch   Photos on pages 1, 103, 187, 383, and 567 are by H. Armstrong Roberts,
Production Editor: Karen Davis   by Gail B. Int Veldt, and from Ruth Murray.
Designer: Robert Kopelman

PRINTED IN THE UNITED STATES OF AMERICA

This book is dedicated to

Our students—for their inspiration
Our families—for their patience

Contributors

Mildred Heyes Boland, R.N., M.S.N.
Assistant Professor, Retired, College of
  Nursing
University of Arizona
Tucson, Arizona

Joyce Patricia Dees Brockhaus, R.N., Ph.D.
Child/Family/Marital Therapist (private
  practice)
Associate Clinical Professor, Department of
  Psychiatry
St. Louis University School of Medicine
St. Louis, Missouri

Robert Herold Brockhaus, Ph.D.
Professor, School of Business and
  Administration
St. Louis University
St. Louis, Missouri

Ellen K. Duvall, R.N., M.S. in Nursing, M.A.Ed.
Clinical Specialist in Oncology Nursing
Incarnate Word Hospital
St. Louis, Missouri

Dorothy Fox, R.N., Ph.D.
Professor, Department of Nursing
Madonna College
Detroit, Michigan

Mary Ellen Grohar-Murray, R.N., M.S.N., Ph.D.
Associate Professor of Medical-Surgical
  Nursing, School of Nursing
St. Louis University
St. Louis, Missouri

Joan Haugk, R.N., B.S.N., M.S.W.
In private counseling practice
St. Louis, Missouri

Ruth Ann Launius Jenkins, R.N., M.S.N., Ph.D.
Assistant Professor, Nursing of Children,
  School of Nursing
University of Missouri
St. Louis, Missouri

Ruth Murray, R.N., M.S.N., Ed.D.
Professor
Coordinator, Psychiatric/Mental Health
  Nursing Graduate Major, School of
  Nursing
St. Louis University
St. Louis, Missouri

Peggy H. McDowell, R.N., C.F.N.P., C.P.N.P.
President, Health for Industry, Inc.
Newton, North Carolina

Norma Nolan Pinnell, R.N., M.S.N.
 Instructor of Medical-Surgical Nursing,
  School of Nursing
 Southern Illinois University
 Edwardsville, Illinois

Eleanor Palermo Sullivan, R.N., Ph.D.
 Dean, Professor, School of Nursing
 University of Minnesota
 Minneapolis, Minnesota

Carolyn Samiezadi-Yazd, R.N., B.S.N.
 Staff Nurse
 Deaconess Hospital
 St. Louis, Missouri

Nina Kelsey Westhus, R.N., M.S.N.
 Clinical Nurse Specialist, Allergy/
  Immunology
 Cardinal Glennon Children's Hospital
 St. Louis, Missouri
 and
 Clinical Faculty, Nursing of Children,
  School of Nursing
 St. Louis University
 St. Louis, Missouri

Judith Proctor Zentner, R.N., M.A., C.F.N.P.
 Director of Health Services
 Corson Furniture Industries
 Valdese, North Carolina

Contents

Contributors	vii
Acknowledgments	xiii
To The Reader	xv
Introduction	xvii

PART I   INFLUENCES ON THE DEVELOPING PERSON AND FAMILY UNIT   1

Chapter 1   Sociocultural Influences on the Development and Health of the Person and Family   3
R. Murray, J. Zentner, and C. Samiezadi-Yazd

Key Terms	3
Definitions	4
Characteristics of Cultures	5
Comparison of Cultures	9
Socioeconomic Class Subculture	24
Influences of Culture on Health	31
Nursing Applications	31
References	37

Chapter 2   Environmental Influences on the Development and Health of the Person and Family   43
N. Pinnell, M. Grohar, R. Murray, and J. Zentner

Key Terms	43
Historical Perspective	44
Air Pollution	45
Water Pollution	48
Soil Pollution	51
Food Pollution	53
Noise Pollution	54
Surface Pollution	56
Occupational Hazards	59
Nursing Applications	61
References	70

Chapter 3   Spiritual and Religious Influences on the Person   77
J. Zentner, R. Murray, and E. Duvall

Key Terms	77
Definitions	78
World Religions	78
Hinduism and Sikhism	79
Buddhism, Jainism, and Shintoism	80
Confucianism and Taoism	81
Islam	82
Judaism	84
Christianity	86
Other Groups of Interest	89
North American Indian Religions	91
Other Considerations	92
Trends in Nonnative and Native American Religions	92
Nursing Applications	93
References	99

Part II   BASIC CONCEPTS RELATED TO THE DEVELOPING PERSON AND FAMILY UNIT   103

Chapter 4   The Family—Basic Unit for the Developing Person   105
R. Murray, J. Zentner, J. Brockhaus, R. Brockhaus, and E. P. Sullivan

	Key Terms	105
	Definitions	106
	Overview of Family Theoretical Approaches	108
	Purposes, Tasks, Roles, and Functions of the Family	108
	Family Adaptation	111
	Stages of Family Development	112
	Family Interaction	116
	Family Lifestyles and Childrearing Practices	123
	Nursing Applications for Health Promotion	127
	References	134
Chapter 5	**Overview: Theories of Human Development**	**137**
	R. Murray	
	Key Terms	137
	Current Biological Theories	138
	Current Ecological Theories	139
	Current Psychological Theories	140
	References	153
Chapter 6	**The Developing Person: Principles of Growth and Development**	**157**
	R. Murray, D. Fox, and J. Zentner	
	Key Terms	157
	Dimensions of Time	158
	Principles of Growth and Development	159
	General Assumptions About Behavior	159
	The Developing Person: Prenatal Influences and Stages	162
	Variables Related to Childbirth That Affect the Baby	175
	Early Childhood Variables That Affect the Person	177
	Sociocultural Factors That Influence the Developing Person	178
	Nursing Applications	181
	References	182

PART III	**THE DEVELOPING PERSON AND FAMILY: INFANCY THROUGH ADOLESCENCE**	**187**
Chapter 7	**Assessment and Health Promotion for the Infant**	**189**
	R. Murray, J. Haugk, R. Jenkins, N. Westhus, and J. Zentner	
	Family Deveopment and Relationships	189
	Key Terms	190
	Physiological Concepts	198
	Psychosocial Concepts	220
	Nursing Applications	225
	References	228
Chapter 8	**Assessment and Health Promotion for the Toddler**	**233**
	R. Murray, J. Zentner, and M. Grohar-Murray	
	Key Terms	233
	Family Development and Relationships	233
	Physiological Concepts	236
	Psychosocial Concepts	245
	Nursing Applications	253
	References	253
Chapter 9	**Assessment and Health Promotion for the Preschooler**	**255**
	R. Murray and J. Zentner	
	Key Terms	255
	The Preschooler	256
	Family Development and Relationships	256
	Physical Growth and Development	263
	Psychosocial Concepts	272
	Nursing Applications	286
	References	286
Chapter 10	**Assessment and Health Promotion for the Schoolchild**	**289**
	R. Murray, J. Zentner, and N. Pinnell	
	Key Terms	289

Contents

	Family Development and Relationships	290
	Physiological Concepts	293
	Psychosocial Concepts	304
	Nursing Applications	325
	References	325
Chapter 11	**Assessment and Health Promotion for the Adolescent and Youth**	**331**
	N. Pinnell, R. Murray, M. Grohar-Murray, and J. Zentner	
	Historical and Cultural Perspectives	331
	Key Terms	332
	Definitions	332
	Family Development and Relationships	333
	Physiological Concepts	335
	Psychosocial Concepts	344
	Adolescent Health Problems and Nursing Applications	355
	References	377
PART IV	**THE DEVELOPING PERSON AND FAMILY: YOUNG ADULTHOOD THROUGH DEATH**	**383**
Chapter 12	**Assessment and Health Promotion for the Young Adult**	**385**
	R. Murray, N. Pinnell, J. Zentner, and M. Grohar-Murray	
	Key Terms	386
	Family Development and Relationships	386
	Physiological Concepts	387
	Psychosocial Concepts	411
	Common Health Problems and Nursing Applications	427
	References	444
Chapter 13	**Assessment and Health Promotion for the Middle-Aged Person**	**457**
	R. Murray and J. Zentner	
	Key Terms	457
	Family Development and Interaction	458
	Physiological Concepts	467
	Psychosocial Concepts	476
	Nursing Applications	490
	Transition to Later Maturity	490
	References	490
Chapter 14	**Assessment and Health Promotion for the Person in Later Maturity**	**495**
	R. Murray, J. Zentner, N. Pinnell, and M. Boland	
	Key Terms	496
	Definitions	496
	Societal Perspectives	497
	Theories of Aging	498
	Family Development and Relationships	499
	Physiological Concepts	504
	Health Promotion and Health Problems	510
	Psychological Concepts	518
	Socioeconomic Concepts	526
	Federal Planning for the Aged in America	528
	Community Planning	530
	Nursing Applications	536
	References	539
Chapter 15	**Death, the Last Developmental Stage**	**545**
	R. Murray and J. Zentner	
	Key Terms	545
	Issues Related to Dying and Death	545
	Developmental Concepts of Death	547
	Behavior and Feelings of the Person Facing Death	551
	Nursing Applications	557
	References	564
PART V	**HEALTH PROMOTION PRINCIPLES AND STRATEGIES**	**567**
Chapter 16	**Basic Considerations in Health and Illness**	**569**
	R. Murray, N. Pinnell, and J. Zentner	
	Key Terms	569

Definitions of Health and Illness	569	
Variables That Affect Behavior and Health	573	
The Stress Response	576	
References	583	

Chapter 17 Health Promotion Strategies — 587
R. Murray, J. Zentner, and P. McDowell

Key Terms	588
Health Promotion: What Is It?	589
Definitions	589
Models Related to Health Promotion and Illness Behavior	590
Instruments to Assess Health Promotion and Illness Prevention Behaviors	591
Factors That Influence Health Promotion and Illness Prevention Behaviors	592
Health-Promoting Relationships	594
Communication to Promote Health	598
Health Education	601
Health Screening	606
Nutritional Recommendations	607
Exercise, Movement, and Rest Recommendations	607
Prevention of Illness and Injury	609
Stress Management	612
Sites for Health Promotion Nursing	625
New Horizons in Health Promotion: The Nurse Entrepreneur	626
References	626

Appendix I Review of Systems: Physical Assessment and Health History — 633

Appendix II Health Maintenance Procedures — 634

Appendix III Recommended Daily Dietary Allowances (RDA), National Academy of Sciences, Revised 1980 — 638

Appendix IV Major Sources and Functions of Primary Nutrients — 639

Appendix V Summary Comparison of Males and Females — 645

Index — 649

Acknowledgments

A book is the result of collaborative thinking and efforts on the part of many people; authors do not work in isolation.

We appreciate the feedback from students, colleagues, and reviewers; we have incorporated their ideas and maintained the basic direction of the book, based on their comments. We are grateful, also, to a number of people who have helped in manuscript preparation.

Our faithful secretary for each edition of the text, Sally Lehnert, again regularly produced typed material on short notice. Her conscientious work with handwritten materials is noteworthy. To our other typists, JoAnn Jenkins, Anne Willen, and Maxine Lax, who each also came to our rescue, we are grateful.

Without the assistance of Ruth's sister, Elizabeth Henry, the manuscript would not have been done on schedule. She lovingly and conscientiously gave over a week of her time to assist with paste-up of the updated reference lists, footnote numbering, and a variety of other such tasks. Rosemary Fields, a friend, joined us for a day in these efforts. Sharon Stecher, a graduate student, numbered pages and duplicated chapters, among other such tasks. All of their efforts made the finished product a reality.

Equally important was the support and assistance given by our families. Postal deliveries by Judy's husband Reid, and the words of encouragement by various family members enabled us in our work.

Our thanks, too, to the staff of Appleton & Lange, particularly Marion Welch, Executive Editor, and Karen Davis, Production Editor, who each gave valuable guidance and were our advocates at the publisher level.

Our thanks to manuscript reviewers for this edition: Catherine Graziano, R.N., M.S., Professor and Chairman, Salve Regina—The Newport College Department of Nursing, Newport, Rhode Island, and Linn Larson, R.N., M.N., Department of Psychosocial Nursing, University of Washington, Seattle, Washington.

Ruth Beckmann Murray
Judith Proctor Zentner

Organizational Chart

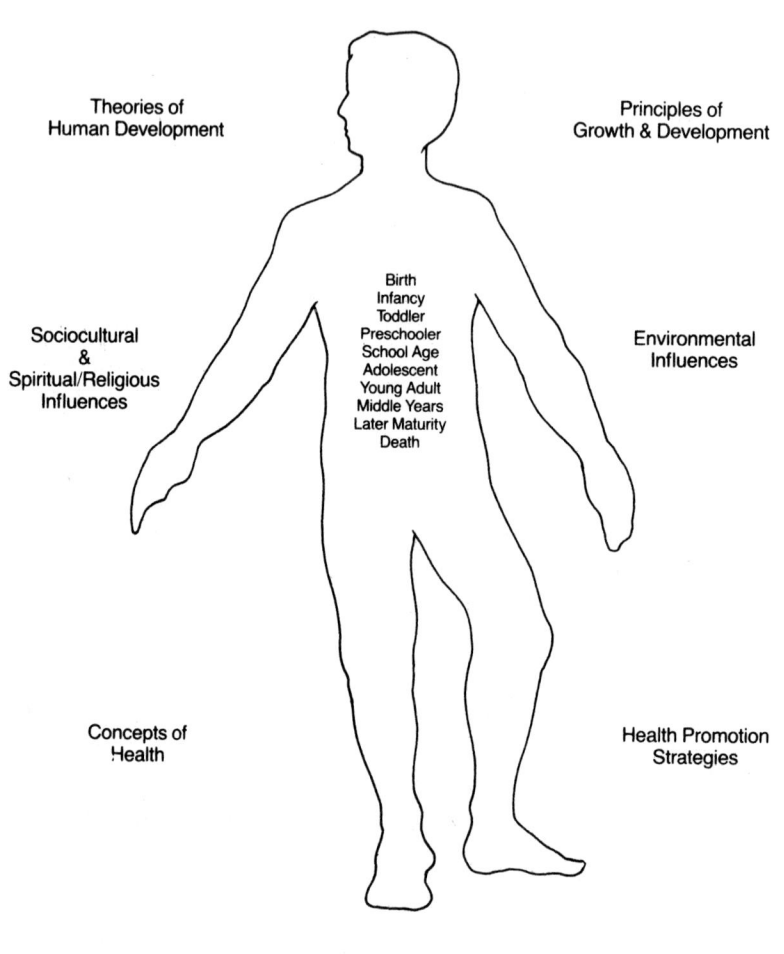

Theories of
Human Development

Principles of
Growth & Development

Birth
Infancy
Toddler
Preschooler
School Age
Adolescent
Young Adult
Middle Years
Later Maturity
Death

Sociocultural
&
Spiritual/Religious
Influences

Environmental
Influences

Concepts of
Health

Health Promotion
Strategies

The Family

To The Reader

We believe the nurse must consider the total health of the person and family. The physical, mental, emotional, sociocultural, and spiritual needs are interrelated. Increasingly your emphasis must be on comprehensive health promotion rather than on patchwork remedies.

These are the first two sentences in each of our previous editions. We are fulfilled to see our nursing emphasis dramatically followed our projection. As we have moved from young adults to middle-agers and as our children have moved from the preschool era to late adolescence, we have experienced a good deal of the life-span material as well as the comprehensive health promotion concept inclusion in nursing practice.

Now in the fourth edition we have decided to put the most important and up-to-date of this material under one cover. Thus, *Nursing Concepts for Health Promotion,* eds. 1, 2, and 3, and *Nursing Assessment and Health Promotion Through the Life Span,* eds. 1, 2, 3, are combined here as *Nursing Assessment and Health Promotion Strategies Through the Life Span,* 4th ed.

We do not cover many diseases, their treatment, or specific manual techniques. These are covered in many books that can be used in conjunction with this text. Instead we present knowledge of the highly complex normal and well person along with common health problems. Before you can understand the ill person and the family, you must understand the well person in the usual family and community setting. Only then can your assessment be thorough and your intervention individualized.

The use of he/she and her/him may seem awkward, but we believe in the importance of inclusive language. At times, we also use patient/client in our terminology, since some of the nursing responsibilities that we discuss are applicable to the ill, dependent person as well as to the well person who can participate actively in planning and care.

Before reading any chapters, you should orient yourself by studying the adjacent organizational chart which shows the many factors that must be considered in nursing for health promotion. Next, read the text introduction. You can gain further orientation by (1) reading the table of contents, (2) looking at the list of objectives which precedes each chapter, (3) glancing at chapter headings, and (4) noting the terms in boldface which are followed by their definitions.

We invite you to be an active participant as you read. Our ideas are presented with conviction and directness. But we want you to integrate and modify our ideas into your specific circumstances. Each of you will have to adapt this information to your setting—be it independent practice, health maintenance organization, hospital, clinic, or home.

Introduction

This text introduces you to the person and his family during the entire life span—from birth to death. Birth is considered the first developmental stage, death the last. Initially you will explore an overview of theories of human development, and the influences on the developing person. Finally, you will review basic concepts of health and health promotion strategies.

During the assessment a great deal of knowledge is needed. Not only is physiological knowledge necessary. The whole range of psychosocial circumstances affecting the person, of whatever age, whom you are assessing is equally important. These areas are addressed in this book. Major influences upon the person such as environment culture, religion, social class, and family are included. Relevant nursing diagnoses have also been added to each chapter.

Each person is unique. But the uniqueness often occurs in the predictable patterns discussed in this text. You can allay fears, give sound information, and make objective predictions with this knowledge. For example, a mother may be unduly distressed by the stubborn behavior of her toddler whom you are assessing. Your explaining that this behavior is characteristic of that age, with suggestions on how to deal positively with the behavior and what behavioral changes to expect in the future, can change a crisis into a workable situation. Also, your knowledge of normal mental and physical health at this and other developmental stages can help you detect deviations from the norm.

Your understanding of normal growth and development is used as a reference point not only for assessment but also for intervention measures appropriate to the person's or family's development. In this text, nursing intervention focuses on measures which maintain health as well as major points of care for common health problems.

Although nurses have always had to cope with death, usually it has been on a superficial basis. An in-depth study of the phases of dying, along with specific care measures, will enhance your ability to foster a naturalness about this last event in life.

FOURTH EDITION

Nursing Assessment & Health Promotion Strategies Through the Life Span

PART I

Influences on the Developing Person and Family Unit

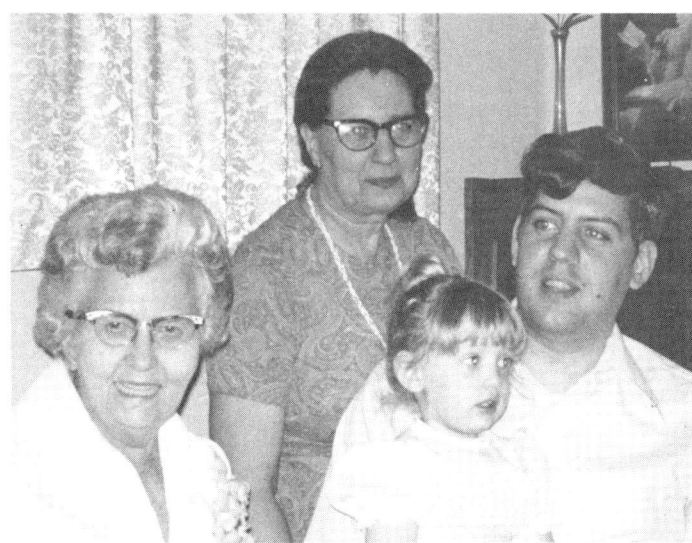

1

Sociocultural Influences on the Development and Health of the Person and Family

Study of this chapter will help you to

1. Define *culture* and *subculture* and describe various types of subcultures.
2. Discuss the general features of any culture and how they affect the persons under your care.
3. Identify the dominant cultural and social class values in the United States and how they influence you as a health care worker as well as the client and family.
4. Compare the cultural values of the traditional Greek, the Spanish-speaking American living in the southwestern United States, and the Japanese in relation to the family unit, male and female relationships, childrearing patterns, the group versus privacy, time orientation, work, and use of leisure, education, and change.
5. Contrast the attitudes toward health and illness of persons living in the main cultures of the United States, Greece, Spanish-speaking American-neighborhoods in the southwestern United States, Japan, and the Middle East.
6. Interview a person from another culture and contrast his/her values with those described in this chapter.
7. Discuss influences of culture and social class on the health status of the person and group.
8. Describe how knowledge of cultural and social class values and attitudes toward daily living practices, health, and illness can contribute to the effectiveness of your health care.
9. Discuss ways to meet the needs of another with cultural and social class values different from your own.
10. Apply knowledge about the teaching–learning process to a health education program for a person or family from another culture or social class.
11. Assess and care for a person or family from another culture and social class and identify your own ethnocentric tendencies.

KEY TERMS*

Culture	Ethic
Subculture	Evil eye
Ethnic	Poverty
Ethnicity	Acute
Regional culture	Chronic
Socioeconomic class	Transcultural nursing
Value system	Cultural relativity
Religious culture	Pluralistic society
Family culture	Ethnocentricity
Ritual	Mongolian spots
Status	Lactose intolerance
Dialect	Caring

When someone talks or acts differently from you, consider that to him you may also seem to talk or act differently. Many such differences are cultural and should be understood rather than laughed at or ignored.

The great divide between humans and animals is culture. Culture includes using language, art forms, and games to communicate with others; cooperating in problem solving; deliberately training children; developing unique interpretations; forming organizations;

---

*Throughout this book key terms are listed in the order that they appear in the chapter.

and making, saving, using, and changing tools. Humans are heir to the accumulation of wisdom and folly of preceding generations and, in turn, they teach others their beliefs, feelings, and practices. The patient/client, family, and you are deeply affected by the culture learned during the early years, often more so than by that learned later. An understanding of the cultural and socioeconomic class systems and their influence on development of behavior is essential to understanding yourself and the person under your care.

Definitions

Culture is the sum total of the learned ways of doing, feeling, and thinking, past and present, of a social group within a given period of time. These ways are transmitted from one generation to the next or to immigrants who become members of the society. **Culture** *is a group's design for living, a shared set of socially transmitted assumptions about the nature of the physical and social world, goals in life, attitudes, roles, and values.* **Culture** *is a complex integrated system that includes knowledge, beliefs, skills, art, morals, law, customs, and any other acquired habits and capabilities of the human being. All provide a pattern for living together.*

A **subculture** *is a group of persons, within a culture, of the same age, socioeconomic status, ethnic origin, education, or occupation, or with the same goals, who have an identity of their own but are related to the total culture in certain ways (77).* Mexican-Americans, Latinos or Spanish-speaking Americans, American Indians, and Afro-Americans (American Blacks) represent subcultures within the overall culture of the United States of America. Ethnic, regional, social-class, religious, and family subcultures also exist. A description of each follows.

The term **ethnic** *pertains to a group of people, racial or national, that possess common physical and mental traits as a result of heredity, cultural traditions, language or speech, customs, and common history.* **Ethnicity** *frequently refers to nationality (15).* In the United States, there are many European ethnic subcultures, for example, German, Italian, Polish, Slavic (representing a number of Slovakian countries), Scandinavian (Danish, Norwegian, Icelandic, Finnish, or Swedish), Swiss, French, Dutch, or Russian. There are also ethnic subcultures from the United Kingdom: English, Irish, Welsh, or Scotch.

Hispanic, referring to Spain, Hispania, or Spanish, is often *a term reserved for Latinos or Spanish or Latin Americans* who have low income, dark skins, or mixed ancestry, without identifying country of origin. Most of those who are called Hispanic speak Spanish or Portuguese. However, *among the Hispanic population there are wide differences in genetic background, culture, tradition, lifestyle, and health behavior, depending on culture of origin, ancestry, and current social class status. The person who is designated Hispanic or Latino may have come from Spain, Mexico, Puerto Rico, Cuba, Dominican Islands, or any Central American or South American country.* Those of Mexican-American origin constitute the largest group of Hispanics/Latinos. The term **Latino** has been coined in preference to the term Hispanic. For statistical purposes, specific birthplace should be recorded. *For a general discussion of culture in this text the term Spanish-speaking will be used (9).*

Regional culture *refers to the local or regional manifestations of the larger culture.* Thus the child learns the sectional variant of the national culture—for example, rural or urban, Yankee, Southern, Mid-western. Regional culture is influenced by geography, trade, and economics; variations may be shown in values, beliefs, housing, food, occupational skills, and language.

Socioeconomic class *is a cultural grouping of persons who, through group consensus and similarity of financial position or wealth, occupation, and education, have come to have a similar status, lifestyle, interests, feelings, attitudes, language usage, and overt forms of behavior.* The people belonging to this group meet each other on equal terms and have a consciousness of cohesion (77, 140). Socioeconomic class is not only economic in origin; other factors also contribute to superior status, such as age, sex, and personal endowment.

The more a class as a group becomes fixed, the more predictable is its patterns of attitudes and behavior. The child learns the patterns of his/her own class and the class attitude toward another class. The attitude patterns make up a culture's **value system,** *its concept of how people should behave in various situations as well as which goals they should pursue and how.* The value systems of the general culture and of the subculture or socioeconomic class may conflict at times.

Religious culture *also influences the person, for a religion constitutes a way of living and thinking and therefore is a kind of culture.* Religious influences on values, attitudes, and behavior are discussed in Chapter 3.

Family culture *refers to the family life, which is part of the cultural system.* The family is the medium through which the large cultural heritage is transmitted to the child. *Family culture consists of ways of living and thinking that constitute the family and sexual aspects of group life.* These ways include courtship and marriage patterns, sexual mores, husband–wife relationships, status of men and women, parent–child relationships, childrearing, responsibilities to parents, and attitudes toward unmarried women, illegitimate children, and divorce (54, 68).

The family gives the child status. The family name

gives the child a social position as well as an identity; the child is assigned the status of the family and the reputation that goes with it. Family status has a great deal to do with health and behavior throughout life because of its effect on self-concept (54, 68).

Family rituals are the collective way of working out household routines and using time within the family culture. **Ritual** *is a system of definitely prescribed behaviors and procedures and it provides exactness in daily tasks of living and has a sense of rightness about it.* The more often the behavior is repeated, the more it comes to be approved and therefore habitual. Thus rituals inevitably develop in family life as a result of the intimacy of relationships and the repetition of continuity of certain interactions. Rituals change from one life cycle to another—for example, at marriage, after childbirth, when children go to school, and when children leave home. Rituals are important in child development because

1. They are group habits that communicate ways of doing things and attitudes related to events, including family etiquette, affectionate responses between family members, organization of leisure time, and education for group adjustment.
2. They promote solidarity and continuity by promoting habitual behavior, unconsciously performed, which brings harmony to family life. Many rituals will continue to the next generation, increasing the person's sense of worth, security, and family continuity or identity.
3. They aid in maintaining self-control through disciplinary measures.
4. They promote feelings of euphoria, sentimentality, or well-being—for example, through holiday celebrations.
5. They dictate reactions to threat, such as at times of loss, illness, or death (54).

Family influences are dealt with more extensively in Chapter 4.

✔ In nursing consider the person's culture or subculture and standard rituals as you plan care.*

Characteristics of Culture

Culture as Learned

Culture has three basic characteristics. First, *culture is learned.* People function physiologically in much the same way throughout the world, but their behavior is learned and therefore relatively diverse. Because of culture, a child is ascribed or acquires a certain **status** *or position of prestige.* The child also learns or assumes certain **roles,** *patterns or related behaviors expected by others, and later by him/herself, that define behavior and adjustment to a given group.* The behavior, values, attitudes, and beliefs, learned within the culture become a matter of tradition, even though the culture allows choices within limits and may even encourage certain kinds of deviancy. The way in which a person experiences the culture and society and what he/she learns during development are of great significance. Culture determines the kinds of experiences the person encounters and the extent to which responses to life situations will be either unhealthy, maladaptive, and self-defeating, or healthy, adaptive, constructive, and creative (32, 125). What the person has learned from the culture determines how and what you will be able to teach him/her, as well as your approach during care.

Culture as Stable But Changing

The second characteristic of culture is that *it is subject to and capable of change in order to remain viable and adaptive, although it is basically a stable entity.* The culture of a society, like a human body, is dynamic but maintained at a steady state by self-regulating devices. *Stabilizing features are traditions and the ready-made solutions to life's problems* that are provided for the group, enabling the person to anticipate the behavior of others, predict future events, and regulate his/her life within the culture. *Everyone within the same culture does not behave in exactly the same way.* Yet, behavior, carefully defined by the culture, is difficult to change because of group pressure. Norms and customs that persist may have a negative influence on the group. Food taboos during illness and during pregnancy, pica, a high-animal-fat diet, or crowding of people into a common dwelling that provides an apt incubator for spread of contagious disease are examples (32).

A culture makes adaptation possible through its ideas, inventions, and customs. Together with physiological adaptive processes, culture is a powerful force. The human, for example, is able to live in a wide variety of climates because the body has adjusted gradually to permit survival. People also heat and cool the environment for comfort, control predators and parasites, and domesticate animals and plants for personal needs. We have constructed a variety of lifestyles and patterns of social relationships to guarantee our survival and to free ourselves from the limits of physical environments. Prescribed cultural norms are the most effective adaptive mechanisms that humans use:

---

*Throughout this book, content about nursing planning or intervention is interwoven in the chapter, in addition to the description in a specific section. The content related to intervention is indicated by a check mark (✔) for differentiation from content pertinent to assessment and nursing diagnosis.

they affect physical, social, and mental well-being; aid adaptation to diverse situations, environments, and recurring problems; and teach about other environments to which we may have to adapt. In addition, some adaptive modifications are achieved through genetic, physiological, and constitutional capacities that have been transmitted for generations through natural selection or cultural conditioning. Physical mutation or survival of the fittest may also promote permanent changes in a group if it enables the person to compete successfully and live, promoting adaptation.

Another stabilizing, limiting aspect of culture is the use of language. Although language forms vary from culture to culture, the terms for *mother* and *father* sound very much alike across cultural lines, perhaps because certain vocalizations are easy for a child to articulate and learn.

Learning cultural and family language is primarily by ear and can affect the child who learns better by sight. In addition, use of language is determined considerably by age and sex—for example, baby talk, child talk, adult talk, girl talk, and boy talk. Subcultural groups, particularly the family, differ in conversational mores—that is, permitted topics of conversation; proper situations for discussing certain topics, such as during mealtime or before bedtime; level of vocabulary used; reaction to new words used; number of interruptions permitted; who can be interrupted; and who talks most (54).

The meeting ground between cultures is in language and **dialect,** *a variety of a language spoken by a distinct group of people in a definite place.* All immigrants to the United States brought their own ethnic and cultural heritage and language. No doubt all had problems being acculturated to mainstream America, but generally their different lifestyles and accents were considered interesting and eventually accepted. Until recently Afro-Americans were the least accepted and understood group of "immigrants," brought to America by force and separated from their culture in Africa. They were expected to express their cultural and racial identity through the Caucasian culture and image of what it meant to be Black. Thus English was superimposed on the many African languages that were forced together. An artificial subculture characterized by Aunt Jemima and Uncle Remus was created.

With the movement of the Black American minority to express its identity, dialect, as well as other components of its subculture, has received attention (49, 50, 120, 196, 197). Understanding of the Afro-American subculture and dialect can help you to talk with, understand, and care for the person, just as an understanding of the subculture and dialect of any ethnic group enhances acceptance and care of that person. Non-Blacks often do not understand Black dialect. Although it often coincides with "standard American English," it has its own grammatical rules (and errors), slang, cadence, and intonation. Black dialect will vary from region to region and with the age, sex, and economic status of the user. Some Afro-Americans avoid using Black dialect, especially those more highly educated and in the higher social classes. And keep in mind that dialect usage changes, as all language usage changes, with time. A word that is first specific to a minority ethnic group can later be adopted by members of the mainstream culture.

Black dialect has words for which there are no analogies in "standard American English," such as the *hawk:* a severe, bone-chilling wind (originally blowing off the Great Lakes). The verbs *am, is,* and *are* are often omitted in dialect, being unnecessary for a complete sentence. The verb form *be* can indicate extended or repeated action, and *been,* completed or past action: "He be hurtin' " means "He has been in pain for some time." "He been hurtin' " means "He was in pain." A sentence without an auxiliary verb indicates an activity going on now that does not usually occur—for example, "She workin'." "She *be* workin' " indicates the person is doing the work she usually does. Possession can be expressed without the use of *'s*—for example, as in "my baby clothes," instead of "my baby's clothes." The letter *g* is commonly dropped as an end sound; two syllables may be shortened into one, and *th* pronounced like *v* or *d.* To avoid grammatical redundancy, the *s* is omitted in plural noun forms if some other word in the sentence indicates plural—for example. "She have three brother." *Man* may be used instead of the name of the person addressed or to convey emphasis. The word *ain't* can be used to negate verbs in the past tense: "Dey ain't like dat" can mean "They *didn't* like that" rather than "They *aren't* like that." An undifferentiated form of the possessive pronoun occurs—as in "He a nice girl."

▶ You will find a variety of regional dialects in the United States—for example, "Brooklynese"; southern mountain; "Tex-Mex" along the Texas–Mexico border; Texas cotton country; Missouri Ozarkian, and Pennsylvania Dutch. Language differences may give a false impression about the intelligence of the person, for some people have difficulty switching from dialect to "standard American English." Listen carefully to the language spoken, be accepting of the dialect, and validate meanings of words when necessary.

Von Bertalanffy (208) and others discuss how language emphasizes the values of a culture. For example, neither the language of the Nootka Indians on Vancouver Island nor that of the Hopi has a separate subject and predicate or parts of speech, as does English. These languages instead describe an event as a whole with a single term. He points out that Americans are complex, abstract, and fragmentary in their descriptions of the world around them. The Indo-European languages, of which English is one, emphasize time. Cultures using these languages keep records, use mathematics, do accounting, use clocks and calendars, and study archeology to learn of their historical past. In contrast, past, present, and future tenses do not exist in the Hopi language; the validity of a statement is not based on time or history but on "fact," memory, expectations, or customs. The Navaho language has little mention of clock time and instead emphasizes type of activity, duration, or aspects of movement. Moreover, von Bertalanffy shows how Indo-European languages, like English, describe nonspatial relationships with spatial metaphors—for example, *long* and *short* for duration; *heavy* and *light* or *long* and *short* for intensity; *rise* and *fall* for tendency. In the Hopi language psychological metaphors are used to name mental processes; for example, *heart* can be used for *think* or *remember*. Thus various cultures have different conceptualizations with which to perceive the same matter or reality. The kinds of conceptualizations influence the values, behavior, stability, and progress of a culture (208). Assessment of the person's intellectual ability must consider culture as well as age. People from non-Western cultures may learn differently and at a different rate because of different language and perceptual skills and value orientations (15). Most cultures are less technical and verbal than ours.

Analyses of the habits and practices of various peoples show that traditional language and behavior patterns practiced between parent and child within a culture are related to the interactions within that culture between employer and employee, among peers, and between nurse and patient, making for predictability and stability. Stability of culture promotes adaptability and economy of energy (125, 140).

Cultures also change, sometimes imperceptibly, so that norms, the usual rules for living, are modified to meet the group's needs as new life challenges arise. Cultures change primarily in response to technological innovation, by borrowing from another culture, or through mass media and education. For example, the harnessing of electrical power and the subsequent invention and use of electrical appliances and tools changed the way of life in the United States: in work, recreation, food preservation, communication, education, vocabulary, women's roles, health care, and the entire value system.

Cultures also change for other reasons:

1. Competition among groups for geographical regions in order to meet the members' sustenance and safety needs.
2. Use of deferred gains for members to induce them to work for the good of the culture, such as in communist countries.
3. Change in political leadership, such as in China, Russia, Iran, or Central America.
4. Increased scientific and industrial complexity.
5. Increased or decreased population growth.
6. Change in economic practices and standards, such as the change from feudalism to industrialism seen in some African and Asian countries.
7. Use of behavior modification techniques by groups in power.
8. Promotion of values, lifestyle, and products through mass media programming and advertisements (140).

Culture is continually shaped by forces and people outside our awareness. Toffler (205) describes how the United States is moving into a postindustrial society. He identifies some of the problem areas of such a society as

1. The need for more professional knowledge.
2. Greater expectations by the public.
3. More goods considered to be public goods.
4. Lack of measurements to show what is actually needed and thus where money and resources should be directed.
5. A changing demography with more urban concentration.
6. Increased life expectancy.
7. Changing values.

Toffler (205) has described the concept of "future shock," a force he predicted would ensure adaptational breakdown unless people came to grips with rapid social change. Toffler described the frequent shifting of families from one place to another, alterations in bureaucratic structures that may speedily engulf the worker in change, and diversity of options and continuing novelty in many life situations. The disposable, transient culture makes it difficult for people to establish roots or pass on culture as a guideline to future generations. Many of his predictions are now part of the norm in the United States. Not all people have adjusted to the continual rapid change.

Because of the "future shock syndrome," risk of illness can be predicted from the amount of change present. If a person is in the equivalent of the Alarm Stage of the stress syndrome continually, body defenses weaken. Extreme examples of persons caught in rapidly changing environments are the combat soldier, the disaster victim, the culturally dislocated traveler, the homeless, the migrant worker. Other examples include the aged who are uprooted and the person who moves from a rural to an urban environment.

Resulting problems in health care include: rising costs, maldistribution of health personnel and specialized services, and greater demand by the consumer for professional competence and accountability and more procedures for ensuring it (205).

When significant numbers of people begin to respond differently to one or more facets of a culture, this factor may cause others in the society to realize that a particular custom or norm is no longer useful. Such customs might pertain to marriage, burial, childrearing, or moral codes. If a group of people (or isolated persons) can consistently adapt while at the same time following the norm imperfectly, they may establish a new norm, which may be gradually adopted to others until it becomes the generally established pattern. Thus the culture and the people in it can be changed in spite of initial resistance. Such changes can have a positive or negative influence on health (125).

Each culture is a whole, but not every culture is integrated in the same way to the same extent. Some cultures are so tightly integrated that any change threatens the whole. Other cultures are characterized by traditional patterns that are easy to manipulate and change.

Cultural Components and Patterns

✓ The third characteristic of culture is that *certain components or patterns are present in every culture*, regardless of how "primitive" or "advanced" it may be (140). Understanding them can help you understand yourself, your patient/client and the health care system in which you work.

Communication Systems. The language itself or the complexities of mass media, computers, and satellites are the basis for interaction and cohesion between persons and a vehicle for the transmission and preservation of culture. In addition to vocabulary and word taboos, gestures, facial expressions, and voice qualities—intonation, rhythm, speed, pronunciation—vary among families or groups within a culture and carry specific meanings. Because millions of U. S. residents nightly watch television, it has become the most powerful cultural communication force in the United States today. Television could be used more effectively for mass health teaching, just as it is used now for mass advertising (140). Television is a powerful force in other countries as well.

Methods and Objects Used to Provide for Physical Welfare. Methods include getting food; establishing personal care habits; making, using, saving, and improving tools; and manufacturing. Objects include instruments and machines used to change land terrain for farming, home building, or industrialization, and equipment used to diagnose and test disease.

Means or Techniques of Travel and Transportation of Goods and Services. Travel and transportation are particularized to a culture. Whether walking, use of dog or horse, or a complex system of cars, trucks, railways, and airplanes, they will affect the person's ability to obtain health care, among other services and goods.

Exchange of Goods and Services. Exchange may occur through barter, trade, commerce, involve occupational roles, and affect work and payment in a health care system.

Forms of Property. Real estate and personal property are defined by the culture in terms of their necessity and worth. Respecting the person's property in the hospital or home shows that you respect him/her personally.

Sexual and Family Patterns. Patterns may vary considerably from culture to culture and affect how you care for and teach the person. Such patterns include wedding ceremonies, divorce proceedings, forms of kinships, guardianship roles, inheritance rights, the family's division of labor, and roles assigned men, women, and children.

Societal Controls and the Institution of Government. Controls include **mores,** *morally binding attitudes,* and **customs,** *long-established practices having the force of unwritten law.* Other controls include public or group opinion, laws, political offices and the organization of government, the regulation of time, and institutionalized forms of conflict within the society or between tribes, states, or nations, such as war. These factors all influence the health care system in which you work. Increasingly, the nurse must become familiar with the political system and skilled in using it for improving health care.

Artistic Expression. Architecture, painting, sculpture, music, literature, and dance are universal art forms, although what is considered art by one culture may not be so considered by another. Knowledge of these factors can be useful in therapy and rehabilitation.

Recreational and Leisure-Time Interests and Activities. These are defined by each cultural group, are essential for health and must be considered in the nursing history and in medical diagnosis.

Religious and Magical Ideas and Practices. These exist in the form of various beliefs, taboos, ethical codes, rituals, mythology, philosophy, or the organized institution of the church and serve to guide the behavior of a cultural group during health and illness.

Knowledge Basic to Survival and Expansion of the Group. In developed countries **science**, *systematized knowledge based on observation, study, and experimentation,* is basic to technological innovation and improving material living standards. Education has traditionally been considered a bridge that enables the person to move up in socioeconomic status in the United States. In modern Western cultures science is highly valued as a basis for health care. Medical science influences people biologically and socially. Less-developed countries also have a knowledge base; although it may be less scientific from our view, it is equally important.

Cultural Structuring of Basic Human Patterns. This includes rules for competition, conflict, cooperation, collaboration, and games. Also, the intimate habits of daily life, both personally and in groups, the manner in which one's house and body are perceived, and the many "taken-for-granted" activities between people are basically structured.

All the foregoing components and patterns influence and are influenced by adaptation to climate, use of natural resources, geography, sanitation facilities, diet, group biological and genetic factors, and disease conditions and health practices.

Comparison of Cultures

Cultural Values in the United States

Several orientations and value systems may be simultaneously present in a given society or culture, but only one orientation dominates over a given period of time. The following middle-class (or mainstream) orientation and values are dominant in the United States at present:

1. Speed, change, progress, activity, punctuality, and efficiency.
2. Personal achievement, occupational and financial success, and status consciousness.
3. Youth, beauty, health, self-reliance.
4. Science and the use of machines and various social institutions.
5. Materialism, consumerism, and use of disposable items.
6. Conformity to the group simultaneously with emphasis on rugged individualism and personal pleasure.
7. Competitive and aggressive behavior and exploitation of others rather than cooperation and contemplation.
8. Social and geographical mobility.
9. Pursuit of recreational activities, a leisure ethic.
10. Equality of people, but recognition of social differentiation and inequality based on personal abilities, education, and opportunity.
11. Future orientation; interest in long-term goals and willingness to defer immediate satisfaction (54, 140).

In the late 1980s, we see an increasing nostalgia for the apparent, though not necessarily real, serenity of past eras and for pastoral images. There is a return by some people in the United States to Victorian Age values, such as emphasis on family life, domesticity, and home as a haven; historic preservation; appreciation for Victorian architecture, and use of Victorian Age products—authentic or imitation. It is a way for the adult generation to expose their children to a way of life that neither young adults, adolescents, nor children have experienced (26).

In the past (and to some degree still now), the Puritan or Protestant ethic described by sociologist Max Weber was the prime influence on American culture, even for those Americans who were not Protestants. An **ethic** *is defined as an outlook or view made up of assumptions that are not often noticed and still less often questioned or tested.* These assumptions are blindly and passively accepted because they have been handed down from generation to generation and had their origins in an unimpeachable, but long forgotten, authority. With new knowledge, the assumptions are often found invalid, but assumptions about living undergo a slow process of change. The Protestant ethic encompasses a harsh, pessimistic view of the human race. It upholds the five following assumptions.

1. Man is basically imperfect and must struggle against imperfection.
2. Man was placed on earth to struggle and so struggle must be valued. Any sign of surrender or softness denotes weakness in the person and is bad.
3. Self-sacrifice and aspiring to good conduct are essential to overcome evil and gain personal salvation.
4. Emotions cannot be overtly expressed. Displaying anger is basically un-Christian. One should love one's neighbor, but expressing love openly is suspect, especially if related to sexuality, for sex is considered an animal pleasure and therefore a taboo topic. Even too intense an expression of nonsexual love can be a sign of weakness and one must be strong and self-controlled in order to struggle.

Anxiety must be avoided or denied, for it shows that the struggle is not going well.
5. The world is seen as useful to man and should provide for material satisfaction. Thus the exploitation of land, even ruthlessly, is acceptable. Mastery of the environment is emphasized. Conservation of natural resources is secondary, for the resources of the world (which are supposedly inexhaustible) were put there to be used (213).

Earlier in this century Puritanical values and rigid Christian morality upheld the tenet of God's judgment. A strong conscience was developed in fear of punishment and social disfavor. Society was stable because traditions were adhered to and proverbs were taken seriously. Hard work, plain living, thrift, self-control, responsibility, willpower, honesty, and initiative were emphasized. Family, gender, and community roles were clearly defined: father was the patriarch; mother was subservient to him; and children were obedient to all. Education also emphasized discipline, order, and obedience to authority. People were tradition-bound and hard-working, and they provided stability in society. Your understanding that many elderly and middle-aged persons still live by these values can help you better accept them and plan their care.

You need only look around at what Toffler calls our superindustrial society to realize that the Protestant ethic has lost its hold (205). Yet parts of this ethic are being revived by some of the growing fundamentalist religious groups.

The value system of the United States is worldly, in spite of its religious roots, for the most highly valued activities involve competitive, practical, secular pursuits rather than contemplation, devotion, cooperation, or esthetic satisfaction. Thus the ideal society, originally the Kingdom of God on earth, has for many people been secularized into a good society with ideals of liberty, justice, general prosperity, materialism and consumerism, and equality of opportunity (54).

The United States is undergoing major cultural shifts, according to Naisbitt (146), which include moving from:

1. Industrialization to an information society.
2. Forced technology to a combination of high technology and high touch or interaction.
3. Short-term to long-term considerations in business, the economy, health practices, and social services.
4. Centralization to decentralization of management and services.
5. Institutional to self-help practices.
6. Representative democracy to participatory democracy.
7. Use of hierarchies to the practice of networking (interacting with others), to solve problems and achieve goals.
8. Either/or to multiple options in solving problems or seeking services.

Several of these trends are important to nursing: the emphasis on an information society, the high technology/high touch in care, the long-term perspective, decentralization of services, use of self-help practices, use of networking, and seeking of multiple options.

Because of these cultural shifts, we see another phenomenon in the United States. There is an increasing number of a new class of migrant workers—mostly well-educated professionals and highly paid blue-collar workers who move around the country, following job relocations and business and economic trends. Frequent migrations prevent the family from establishing roots. Changing addresses may help the family and children be more flexible, if there is a strong family cohesion and identity, or it may create a sense of anomie, isolation, and identity diffusion. The family must realize that its problems will move with them, and often a change in lifestyle and higher cost of living awaits them in the new job/residential area. In the transition, there may be loss of friends, familiarity, and finances, and sometimes treasured items as well (7).

Other cultural lifestyles are often perceived as problematic by mainstream America. Various cultural groups may have values and behaviors or a lifestyle that are in conflict with the dominant values of society. For example, the American Indian values nature. Mainstream America believes that the environmental resources are to be used. A persistent sense of family responsibility is traditional to American Indians, for example. Although family members leave the reservation to find work, they are expected to return to visit relatives or for emergencies and lifecycle, or tribal, events. When the cultural values of sharing, cooperation, and mutual dependence conflict with the demands of a job, American Indians face a difficult choice. If the call to attend a funeral or help a sick relative comes when a worker cannot take time off, the decision may be to give up the job. Employers are not always understanding of the values underlying the behavior (91).

The Western movies showing the rampaging Indian on the Western Plains killing the American pioneer are not fully accurate; through the media attitudes have been shaped negatively. Most Caucasians in the United States can trace their ancestry to the White settlers of the 1600s, 1700s, and 1800s, immigrants who were escaping the brutality of feudal and industrial slavery, oppression, and wars in Europe. In turn, when they moved into the wilderness areas of this country, they were relatively helpless in the strange continent. In contrast to the movies, myths, and legends about the murderous American Indian, these early settlers survived because of the goodwill and assistance of various Indian people. That most American Indians, like most Caucasians, are peaceful and helpful to others must be taught to the public. The values of assistance to others; family harmony; gentleness to and love of the natural environment; inclusion in community roles and respect for and care of the elderly; cooperation instead of competition; among others, are values that would be useful for all of our society to learn and practice. The Indian tribes were quite ahead of our Women's Liberation Movement in many ways. For example, marriage customs do not treat women and children as property, and homosexuality has been better accepted (74).

For many second- and third-generation Latin or Spanish-speaking Americans, educational and socioeconomic advances have paralleled a reduction in the size of their households and the development of individual and family rather than community orientation. But for the majority, loyalty to the family and a preference for large kin groups that act as support networks are very strong. Thus the competitiveness against others that is part of the educational system is avoided; the children may not make the high grades in school that are likely to ensure continued educational and employment success.

Many non-Jewish, Caucasian U. S. ethnic cultures inherited work and family values from European Catholic peasant societies—values that seem to set family interests against individual achievement. Generations of underemployment, fear of losing what little wealth the family had managed to accumulate, and the constant struggle to feed ever-growing families encouraged European immigrants to favor economic security over risk taking (89).

The southern Appalachian person may have a value system that is almost on the opposite end of the continuum from the upper-middle-class professional as shown by Table 1–1 (95, 96).

Issues of violence are to this generation in the United States what the issue of sex was to the Victorian world. Today's young adults have grown up with the ever-present possibility of instantaneous death or permanent maiming by thermonuclear, chemical, or biological warfare agents. The threat and fear of violence are therefore constant facts of life. Fear of violence has led to a fascination with violence that further surrounds people with its symptoms. U. S. society is preoccupied with, almost mesmerized by, the violence of organized crime, urban rioting, and political assassinations. Violence on television and in the movies shows the potential for brutality and aggression in all (26, 140).

People react differently to constant exposure to violence: they may tolerate it, develop disease symptoms, project their own aggression onto others, develop a neurotic preoccupation with it, or act violently themselves in order to discharge rage. We see examples of each reaction in our society in the form of physical, emotional, and social illness.

Persad (157) discusses how concepts of aggression and dependency vary from culture to culture. In U. S. culture, aggression is regarded as an innate force that has survival value and that requires appropriate channels for its expression; it is considered an integral part of social success. If aggression is not dealt with appropriately, however the person becomes psychopathic. In some cultures, aggression is considered the result rather than the cause of psychopathy. Americans teach their children to be independent and emphasize the importance of the adolescent or young adult leaving home. Psychiatric therapy in the United States is often directed toward these goals. In traditional Oriental cultures, however, indirect communication, modesty, cooperation with the team, and conformity to the group are valued rather than assertiveness of the individual. Touch or physical contact between business colleagues is avoided. The young adults may be castigated for abruptly leaving home or striving for independence. Consideration for family elders is more important than one's desires to pursue personal goals. In our culture, a well-developed ego is considered necessary for maturity. In Oriental cultures, personal preoccupation with the ego is considered absurd. In the Saudi Arabian culture, behavior that is normal for the U. S. businessperson is considered offensive, such as abrupt or interrupting speech, asking about the man's wife, or emphasizing a time schedule (157).

Four Cultures: Greek, Spanish-American or Spanish-Speaking, Japanese, and Middle Eastern

Tables 1–2 through 1–8 contrast Greek culture, Spanish-speaking American culture in the southwestern United States, and Japanese culture. Although many nationality groups fit under Spanish-speaking and *each nationality group has its unique values and customs*, the values, norms, customs, and behaviors described in the following tables are applicable to people who have a Spanish background whether they are from Spain, Mexico, Puerto Rico, the Caribbean Islands, or Central or South America. There are variations in these values as the person or family is integrated into the mainstream American culture. Fur-

TABLE 1-1. Basic Values of Cultures with Selected Cultural Examples

VALUE	RANGE OF BELIEFS	EXAMPLE OF CULTURAL SUBCULTURAL GROUP ADHERING TO VALUE
Human nature (What is innate nature of man?)	• The person is basically *evil but capable of achieving goodness* with self-control and effort.	Puritan ancestors. Protestants of Pentecostal or Fundamentalist background. Appalachian subculture.
	• The person is a *combination of good and evil*, with self-control necessary but lapses in behavior understood.	Most people in the United States.
	• The person is basically *good*.	Some religious groups, such as Society of Friends; some philosophical groups, such as humanistic psychologists or members of Ethical Society.
Man-nature (What is relation of man to nature or supernatural?)	• The person is *subjugated to nature* and cannot change whatever is destined to happen.	Spanish-American culture. Appalachian subculture.
	• The person lives in *harmony with nature;* man-nature-supernatural exist as a whole entity.	Oriental cultures. Navaho Indian culture.
	• The person is to gain *mastery over nature;* all natural forces can be overcome.	Middle-and upper-class and highly educated people in the United States.
Time (What is temporal focus on human life?)	• *Past time* is given preference; most important events to guide life have happened in the past.	Historic China.
	• *Present time* is the main focus; people pay little attention to the past and regard the future as vague.	Spanish-American cultures. Appalachian subculture.
	• *Future* is the main emphasis, seen as bigger and better; people are not content with the present.	Educated, professional, and middle-class people in the United States
Activity (What is the main purpose in life?)	• *Being orientation.* The person is important just because he/she is and may spontaneously express impulses and desires.	Appalachian subculture. While no culture allows complete expression of impulses and all cultures must have some work done, the Mexican fiesta and Mardi Gras in New Orleans are manifestations of this value.
	• *Becoming-in-being orientation.* The person is important for what he/she is, but must continue to develop.	Most religious cultures. Native American subcultures.
	• *Doing orientation.* The person is important when he/she is active or accomplishing something.	Most people in the United States.
Relational (What is one's relation to other people?)	• *Individualistic relations.* These emphasize autonomy of the person; he/she does not have to fully submit to authority. Individual goals have primacy over group goal.	Most Gemeinschaft societies, such as folk or rural cultures. Yankee and Appalachian subcultures. Middle-class America, with emphasis on nuclear family.
	• *Collateral relations.* These emphasize that the person is part of a social and family order and does not live just for him/herself. Group or family goals have primacy.	Most European-American ethnic groups, especially Italian-American, Spanish-American culture. Native American tribal subcultures. Most cultures adhere to somewhat through sibling relations in family.
	• *Lineal relations.* These emphasize the extended family and biological and cultural relationships through time. Group goals have primacy.	Cultures that emphasize hereditary lines. Upper-class America. Oriental cultures. Middle-East cultures.
	• Relations are impersonal, focused on role behavior.	Business interactions, upper middle class, and those moving up the social ladder.

TABLE 1–2. A Comparison of Cultures: The Family Unit

COMPONENT	GREEK	SPANISH-AMERICAN	JAPANESE
Basis for Marriage	Social and family welfare. All of society patterned on family.	Family welfare central.	Value family and household lineage.
Type of Family System	Paternalistic. Extended family. Monogamy. Marriage bond strong.	Paternalistic. Extended. Monogamy. Marriage bond strong. Family cares for ill, needy.	Traditional value on authority of father and elderly. Family strongly identified with father. Subordinate position of women and arranged marriage still accepted by older generation. Home, family, children is focus of women.
Family Size	Want many children.	Large so parents not alone in old age.	Family planning, including use of abortion to control size in modern family.
Pattern of Interaction	Authoritarian; man dominant in conversation and decision making. Man head of house and disciplinarian. Sex roles traditional male and female. Mother powerful in own way; credited with sustaining child with moral strength. Children subordinate. Oldest son responsible for family if husband not present. Child not focus of family activity. No special activities for child, even birthday a time to wish family long happiness with child rather than focus on child. Family together most of time with child learning to enjoy adult behavior and anticipate adulthood. Peer contacts through family.	Authoritarian. Man head of house; woman subordinate socially. Sex roles traditional male and female. Child not sole focus of attention. Avoid admiration of child for fear of "evil eye." Child proud of home responsibilities. Age and authority figures highly respected. Family loyalty strong. Obedience emphasized. Family ties may extend beyond biological relatives, including godparents, the boss. Modesty about body care and functions and sexuality.	Family revered as an institution, but interrelationships lacking companionship and warmth. Major decisions made by family. Subordination of individual to family interest. Traditional autocratic family system stronger in rural areas, with eldest son inheriting family property and hesitant to rebel against father. Young generation choosing own marriage partner, establishing own household, and daughter-in-law gaining freedom from mother-in-law's dominance. Increasing premarital and extramarital sexual affairs.

thermore, values may be lived differently, outwardly, if the person resides in Greece, Mexico, or Japan rather than the United States. The Middle Eastern culture is described in the following section.

Yet much of the behavior of the third- or fourth-generation family or person from a country reflects the original cultural-ethnic values. That fact explains the differences among groups of people and should not be considered abnormal. Discussion centers on the family unit, male and female relationships, childrearing, the group versus privacy, time orientation, work and use of leisure time, education, and attitudes regarding change. The following discussion then compares the attitudes of U. S. residents toward health and illness with the corresponding attitudes in each of these cultures (1, 9, 11, 15, 23, 32, 58, 76, 84, 90, 114, 123, 131, 137, 139, 143, 148, 149, 156, 163, 178, 188, 190, 191, 198, 200).

✔ Table 1–1 summarizes Kluckhorn's presentation of five basic value questions, the range of beliefs derived from these questions, and examples of some (sub)cultural groups adhering to these beliefs (96). You may wish to assess your clients and their families according to these values as well as the characteristics presented in Tables 1–2 through 1–8. Although *neither a comprehensive study nor a stereotype of everyone in*

TABLE 1–3. A Comparison of Cultures: Childrearing Patterns

COMPONENT	GREEK	SPANISH-AMERICAN	JAPANESE
Process of Childbirth	Considered normal process, not to be feared.	Considered normal process. Husband little involved. Prefer woman's presence. Special practices surrounding process.	Considered normal process.
Philosophy of Childrearing	Effectiveness sought as parent, not as pal. Child raised to be strong, hard, firm, straight, for that is ideal personality. Wishes of elders put before child's wishes.	Effectiveness sought as parent, not as a pal. Child taught to do as parents do, to listen to parents' advice, learn from their experience, and not advance further than their parents.	Traditionally child to be dutiful, disciplined, responsible, respectful to elders. Young urban generations not bound as firmly by traditions.
Practices of Childrearing	Mother firm, not overprotective. Baby kept in straight position when carried or in bed. Follow rigid schedule, consistent.	Consistent traditional, faith in own judgment. Tradition of breast feeding needs reinforcement if in Anglo health care setting.	Mother enveloping child in warmth during early years, but when child older, relationship more distant. Oldest son reared differently from other brothers, and brothers from sisters, so every child aware of his/her place.
Responsibility for Child Care	Primarily mother, but older children involved in daily activities, including care of younger siblings. Attitude of love and responsibility among siblings; new baby not seen as competition.	Husband ultimately responsible as head of household. Any family member, including siblings and cousins, responsible at times.	Mother primarily, but all of family involved.
Discipline	Consistent. Obedience very important and taught to child at early age. Child praised when good and told when bad. Taught that it is important to be good and not shame family. Use group pressure to set limits on behavior.	Consistently correct child when behavior is bothersome and warned not to act in a way to provoke father. Instill fear of consequences. Pride in self-control and fear of being shamed instilled in child. Seldom told he/she is "good" or "bad."	Firm, consistent, lack strong emotional expression. Emphasis on responsibility, duty, loyalty, patience, and orderliness. Promote feeling of insecurity when do wrong.
Training of Child	Taught to value interdependence, cooperation. Sibling rivalry when new baby arrives but does not last long. Mother delighted with new baby but shares self equally with older child, including offer of free breast during feeding. Older child invited to share excitement about baby. Parents never clowning for child's amusement or giving many material things.	Taught to value interdependence, companionship. Little sibling jealousy. Freely show affection and attention. May use child as translator for family if they are not bilingual.	Taught to value interdependence but responsible for own behavior. Taught to carry out obligation regardless of personal cost and to control behavior to avoid personal shame and disgrace of group. Develop strong sense of responsibility, loyalty to family or work group. Poor communication between generations because of differences in experiences, education, language comprehension, and values fostering problems in modern society.

TABLE 1–4. A Comparison of Cultures: Interaction with Others Versus Privacy

COMPONENT	GREEK	SPANISH-AMERICAN	JAPANESE
Basic Values of Person and Behavior	Strong sense of self-esteem. Inner core of personality not to be exposed or shamed. Value equality, individuality. Aloneness not sought, but borne with fortitude. Pride in glorious past of Greece.	Anxiety about being alone and concern for people who are alone. Not considered proper to compete, push self forward in group through achievements. Better to submit than provoke anger in another. Self-restraint emphasized. Violence atypical.	Strong sense of self-respect and important to be treated respectfully by others. Privacy not valued, apparently unwanted, and seen as loneliness.
Personal Possessions	Value in shared living and sharing possessions, especially with family and friends.	Sharing of possessions. One's own house nebulous; frequent unannounced visiting among family and friends.	Possessions not highly valued. Shared living space and possessions in family.
Status of Person	Valued for what he/she is rather than position or achievement. Family unit valued, not individual.	Valued for what he/she is, depends on family. Child has mother and father's surname, respectively; hyphenated name common.	Belonging to right clique or faction important to status and future success. Try to join influential group at early age.
Interaction among Persons	Resented when treated impersonally, mechanically, or like a number on a chart. No word for "group," but born into group of family and friends. Extended family working together for benefit of each other. Units of cooperation retained from past, not created. Work to achieve common goal with those to whom he/she feels loyalty. Speech of much importance because it establishes interactions; expressive of feelings	Much neighborhood socializing, especially among women to borrow, help, consult, discuss, or exchange gifts. Interchange of gifts and services frequent. Accepting as gracious as giving, and person not satisfied until he/she has returned a gift to show appreciation; return gift not necessarily same kind or form. Strangers not completely accepted unless related to established family by marriage. Interdependence between family and close friends does not extend to broader community.	Suppression of emotion in many situations. Most docile with strong urge to conform. Pleasant, polite, correct but aloof behavior to others in all classes. Avoids handshake or body contact. Restrained, formal, hierarchal relationships in family, company, and political party rather than horizontal, comradely behavior. Ceremonious, at ease, and apologetic to acquaintances and friends but less so with strangers. Man unappreciative of domineering woman. Wish to avoid confrontation; strive to save face in conflictual situation.
Social Activities	Family basic social group. Circle of friends important. Enjoy social affiliations, great loyalty to all groups to which belong. Food important with social activities.	Few formalized social groups. Suspicious of outsiders. Dependency on others accepted. Family basic social group. Women thought of as one social group, men another. Remain close to own social group for job or marriage partner. Makes use of diplomacy, tact, concern, respect for other's feelings. May appear to agree when does not. Child may avoid eye contact or not verbalize feelings, out of deference to elder.	Fondness for crowds and physical proximity of people. Participation and spectator roles in social activities and sports enjoyed.

TABLE 1–5. A Comparison of Cultures: Time Orientation

COMPONENT	GREEK	SPANISH-AMERICAN	JAPANESE
Concept of Time	Present important but prepare for something in future that is sure part of the life. No automatic faith in future. Distasteful to organize activities according to clock. Life regulated by body needs and rhythms, daily pattern of light and dark, and seasons.	Present important but validated by past. Expect future to be like present. Perform with distinction in present rather than emphasize efficiency, quantity. Life not regulated by clock but by body needs and rhythms, light and dark, seasons, religious holidays.	Time neither an absolute nor objective category but a process—the changing of nature with man as part of it. Planning for future valued. Present considered important, and past priceless.
Use of Time	Time used spontaneously; not time conscious. Elastic attitude toward time; governed by cycles of nature. "Tomorrow" thought of as tomorrow, next week, or never. Activities and appointments usually not starting on time, but person not hurried.	Time used spontaneously; not time-conscious. Little emphasis on long-range planning. "Right now" means now or later. May arrive after scheduled appointment time.	Appreciation and effective use of time. Calmness and time for daily ceremony highly valued. Ceremony carried out in spite of rush of work.

these cultures, these comparisons indicate that subtle as well as obvious differences, along with some similarities, exist among different groups' values and behavior. *Understand that these cultural patterns will be followed by different persons in each culture to varying degrees*, denied by some, and not identified, yet taken for granted by others. Chapter 4 will discuss some of these values in relation to the family culture of the United States.

Middle-Eastern Culture*

More people from a number of Middle Eastern countries† are migrating to the United States because of political unrest in these countries and somewhat easier travel possibilities. Many first generation immigrants come here to study and then become permanent residents in America. These people strongly maintain their culture and religious values and practices; this makes them a unique set of clients to be cared for. Even though many of these clients identify with their country of origin, many also identify with a family, such as the Seyeds of Iran, or a city or a village they lived in, or a religion.

Roles. In Middle-Eastern countries, Islam is a dominant religion, and roles and families are also dictated by the religion of Islam, as well as by the culture of the country. Men tend to have earning positions in the household, and thus they either cannot or refuse to help with household duties. Women, on the other hand, tend to be in control of household affairs. These roles are divided but complementary. There are some women in the Islam culture who maintain professional roles through the performance of a professional job outside of the home. But in a traditional society and environment, roles tend to hold a status quo; the woman is at home and the man is the wage earner.

Muslim society tends to be paternalistic. Children carry throughout their entire life the last name of their father as their legal name. Even upon marriage, women will continue to maintain the last name of their father's family. Men have a great need to feel in control of situations relating to self and the family, and this may be viewed in Western culture as excessive control of the women or family members. The controlling male brings great compliance into the family system through his role of leader.

✔ Therefore, in the health care setting it is best to ask the man's permission or opinion when it relates to the family members. If this aspect is neglected, the man will feel insulted, and mistrust will develop in the relationship. In Western culture, this practice is viewed as a type of ownership by the man over his family. It is not viewed in this way by the Muslim. The man rather perceives this as protecting the family for which he is responsible. This protection can be especially seen with the new mother and baby. In the absence of the husband, the health care worker can communicate through

---
*This section is written by Caroline Samiezadi-Yazd, B.S.N.
† We are referring here to Lebanon, Syria, Jordan, Arabia, Egypt, Central Asia, Turkey, Afghanistan, Iran, and Palestine.

TABLE 1–6. A Comparison of Cultures: Work and Use of Leisure Time

COMPONENT	GREEK	SPANISH-AMERICAN	JAPANESE
Concept of Work	Work thought of as life, a joy and dignity, not drudgery. Work interrupted primarily for religious reasons, not as claim to idleness or leisure. Women as hardworkers as men. Tenacious and resourceful at making the best of what they have and coping with difficulty. Person not to be hurried but works efficiently at own pace.	Work considered inevitable part of daily life. Not done just to keep busy or earn more money if present needs met. No moral corruption in being idle. Work at own pace and no specially defined working hours if possible. Everyone expected to cooperate and do his/her part. Work shared to decrease loneliness. Work roles of sexes and age groups distinct but each aware of tasks performed by the other. Able to take over work roles of other family members. Child a part in work of home and family and feels important. No special rewards.	Enjoyment of work more important than money earned. Industriousness and hardwork emphasized. Strong ties between person, the job, and the company. Works hard for success. Job mobility frowned on; loyalty to company. Independence in work traditionally valued but younger workers adjusting to Western concept of employment. Seek perfection on job; high sense of responsibility for job; quiet achievement. Consensus management emphasized.
Concepts of Leisure	Leisure an attitude, a dimension of all life and work. Not confined to certain time but a continual expression of internal freedom, at work or rest.	Leisure synonymous with free time. No emphasis on leisure for own sake. Intersperse work with rest, socialize during work. Free time spent visiting.	Some leisure time used in solitude. Much leisure time spent in traveling with peers. Freer expression of emotion in recreational pursuits.

TABLE 1–7. A Comparison of Cultures: Education

COMPONENT	GREEK	SPANISH-AMERICAN	JAPANESE
Value on Education	Highly prized, especially professional education. Curiosity and creativity valued. Educated person accorded much respect. Use of creative intellect and being cultured citizen valued, but can be achieved through life's experiences and work as well as by education.	Learns that which interests him/her. Absent from school if learning little or if something more interesting going on elsewhere. Not seen as only way to achieve.	Respect for school and teacher. Education highly valued, with emphasis on scientific information. Parents involved in education. Eager to learn. Memorization emphasized. Believe in value of practical experience as well. Choice of college influences status in life. Much competition in education.
Educational Methods	Emphasize quickness, curiosity, cleverness, realism, reason. Education applied to matters of life.	No emphasis on excelling or competing against other family members for high grades or honors. Use of native language may interfere with success in school.	Educational reform by U. S. occupation after World War II counter to traditional methods: replaced rote memorization with progressive methods, de-emphasized moral training and unquestioning acceptance of authority, granted equal status to women, broadened opportunity for women.

TABLE 1—8. A Comparison of Cultures: Attitudes Regarding Change

COMPONENT	GREEK	SPANISH-AMERICAN	JAPANESE
Value of Change	Not valued for itself. Progress hoped for but not taken for granted. Change not necessarily bringing progress or improvement.	Change condemned simply because it is change. Patience and postponing personal desires emphasized. Appreciate gentle, approach. Little faith in progress or control over own destiny.	Physical world considered transient. Person appreciative but does not cling to things; thus change accepted.
Pace of Change	Deliberate.	Slow. Fearful or suspicious of change. Deliberate.	Able to adjust lifestyle to rapid economic, industrial, and urban changes.
Effect of Change	No value on unlimited progress. Wants what is better than present but what is known and can be achieved. A plan to an American synonymous with a dream to a Greek. Use material goods. Do not discard useful articles. Repair to maintain usefulness of object. Traditional Greek culture changing, becoming Westernized, affecting behavior of young.	Value system seen as constant. Feel many individuals not amenable to change by human endeavor. Adjust to environment. Use material goods to capacity. Generally remain near traditional home, maintaining stable relationships with people. Change in main culture affecting behavior of young, causing insecurity in elders.	Urgency of Western-like activity a new phenomenon. Breaking traditional patterns and solidarity, increased individualism, competition, and individual insecurity. Youth seeking new values to replace old dogmas. Parent generation generally revere authority of family and state—now rejected by younger generation.

the woman's father or father-in-law, a designated brother or uncle of the husband, or the mother or mother-in-law.

In the Middle East, a large portion of the traditional village female population is illiterate. Therefore, the role of mother and ability to bear and raise children is a major source of sense of self-esteem and identity. This affords one of the greatest opportunities for the woman to realize her potential as a person. Because women are very respected for their role as mother, children, even into adulthood, place their mother's needs as paramount. Often this is done before considering even the wife's or family's needs, which places an internal strain within the family structure.

Parenthood. Women do not practice contraception in the Middle East as in the West because the role of the female is to bear children. Many misconceptions center around conception, such as conception will not occur during breastfeeding. Misconceptions are held even by the most educated people. Arabs and Iranians may use abortion as a form of birth control, although it is not openly recommended or talked about, and is clearly prohibited by Islamic practice. Selective abortions are used in the case of an illegitimate child, as an attempt by the individual to maintain the society's integrity, since illegitimate children and unsanctioned sexual practices carry grave consequences with them (127).

Sexuality and childrearing practices differ from those of the West. Middle Eastern clients possess a feeling of fatalism; they do not plan for future events but rather leave them to the will of God. Many women do not seek prenatal care in the Middle East; only when the baby is ready to be born do they go to the hospital or call a midwife to come to the home for the birth. Many women do not plan the layette or select a name until after the infant is born. Traditional as well as modern Middle Eastern women tend to breastfeed for extended periods of time; it is written as a requirement in the Koran to breastfeed for 2 years (127).

Children in the Middle East are viewed not only as a commodity but also as a blessing to the family. They are something to be cherished; therefore, families invest a great deal emotionally into their children and tend to practice lenient discipline measures. Children are usually never physically hit or verbally abused. Rather they are distracted away from whatever they are doing that is bad and encouraged to do good things.

Many Middle Eastern clients tend to base the success of their parenthood not on the cognitive skills of children, but rather on the weight gain, health, and normality of their children. They do not accept deviation of health status in others compared to the normal population. This author knew a women from Kuwait who had a younger sister with Down's Syndrome. Upon introduction of her family, she said "This is my mother and this is my abnormal sister." She does not feel her sister is worthy enough to be called by her name.

🗸 *Need for Affiliation.* An important aspect of caring for Middle Eastern clients is to recognize their need for affiliation and belonging, which is central and critical to survival. The strength and importance of the individual is directly related to the family members and friends; family and friends are an integral part of life. Although men and women may be segregated, socialization is extensive. Middle Eastern people are known for their hospitality, and they emphasize family relations. Visiting between members of the extended family and their friends is a social obligation on all occasions, and children of all ages are included as part of the visits.

🗸 *Cleanliness.* Although Middle Easterners may live in crowded family situations within their homes, they use basic measures to insure cleanliness. In addition to the requirement of the client's body and clothes always being clean of any body secretions, most of these clients' homes are also required to be and are always being cleaned. The expression is very literal in Middle Eastern households, "You can eat off the floor," because the family does eat from the floor, as well as sit, lie down, and sleep on the floor. These homes generally have no furniture or are sparsely or very selectively furnished. When you walk into this home, you are required to remove your shoes in order to keep the carpet clean so events of the home may take place on a clean area. This produces for the Middle Easterner a definite feeling of separation between the external world and the internal world of their home.

🗸 *Health Care.* Muslims and Middle Eastern people often have home cures for common health problems. If it does not harm the client, let the person carry out the home or cultural remedies. It will serve to build trust in the relationship and show respect for the client. They believe that cures can be obtained through the use of home remedies, such as herbs, concentrated sugar preparations, and hot/cold foods. Although they believe in the superiority of Western medicines, they do not always trust it; therefore, they practice home remedy medicine side by side with modern Western medical practices. When prescribing medical treatment or dispensing medicine, these clients believe that intrusive measures are better and of more value than nonintrusive measures. For example, intravenous medication is better than that given intramuscularly; injections are better than pills, and colored pills are better than white ones. Another example of a cultural practice is that at the time of delivery, parents want to say a prayer in the newly born child's ears. Muslims believe that the first sounds a child hears should be from the Koran in praise and supplication to God. This practice does not hurt the baby, but allowing its practice will go a long way to build trust into the relationship with the parents and family.

🗸 In the health care setting, the extensive visiting by family and friends can become very difficult for the institution to accommodate because visiting is usually restricted by policy. But for the Middle Eastern client, this visiting becomes extremely important in how the person perceives the disease and adapts to it. Visiting should be allowed on a liberal basis. Visits from family members are also important because Middle Eastern clients do not expect personal care from health workers; the role of the family members is to physically care for the person who is in the hospital.

Communication. Islam dictates that family affairs remain family affairs and they are not affairs for the rest of the world. This can be seen in many situations, with modesty as one example. Women dress differently outside the home than they do inside the home. The body tends to be covered and only shows the face, hands, and feet. For the Muslim woman residing in the West, this manner of dress is usually modified but still retains the quality of conservative fashion.

🗸 Respecting the person's modesty during health care or implementation of procedures is essential. Because of modesty, there is a difference in the information that a person gives to various people. Very personal information is shared only with intimate contacts; nonintimate or general information can be shared with almost anyone. Thus, assessment must be done gradually and respectfully. Certain information may never be obtained.

Communication in the Middle East is an elaborate system. It can be either very intimate in terms of content and word usage, or it can be very stilted in terms of using only proper nouns and formal forms of verbs. The choice depends on whom you are talking to and the subject. The person may knowingly say the opposite of what he/she is thinking to avoid being rude. There are communication methods to avoid, especially in nonintimate conversations, because they are perceived as offensive and rude. First, outwardly showing anger or insulting someone is considered bad manners. Emotion can be shown with intimate persons but not with nonintimate contacts. Second, do not be abrupt or interrupt, especially with elders, when another is speaking. Third, in preliminary casual conversation that is part of business or professional association, do not ask the man (especially if the inquiring person is a man) about the female members of his family, including his wife, sisters, or daughters after they reach the age of puberty.

✔ As in all populations, communication and patient teaching become critical issues related to health outcome. Individuality should never be viewed as noncompliance. There are generally always reasons for the Muslim's behavior or choice of action. Not carrying out the health care worker's teachings does not mean the Muslim is being uncooperative. You should reassess the situation in terms of its cultural totality.

✔ *Language Barriers.* Interpreters or family members can be used to assist with teaching when the client's language is not known. However, family members may withhold information that they feel may be too threatening for the client to hear or is inappropriate to disclose about the client. If interpreters are used, they should be of the same language, religion, and the same country of origin. A mistake was made in one agency by having a female Muslim from Iraq translate in Arabic to a new Muslim mother from Arabia, without first having obtained the husband's consent. When the father of the baby discovered this arrangement for his wife to learn newborn care through the Iraqi woman, he became angry and would not allow the situation to take place. Involve family members when doing patient teaching and always attempt to involve both the husband and wife together in discussions. If in the event the health care worker needs to talk to the wife about her husband, extreme tact should be used at all times in the discussion.

✔ Language barriers can cause a great amount of misunderstanding to occur. Listen to the themes of the content being discussed rather than to the exact words being used. It can take many years for a foreign person to learn a language, and usually building a vocabulary is the most difficult part of any language mastery. As an example, this author's husband has been in the United States for 7 years and is a doctoral student as well as a college instructor; he still is learning vocabulary that I take for granted. Ironically, with many foreigners, even though their vocabulary is not strong, their grammar and word usage is perfect.

✔ When you do teaching with the individual or family, remember that the foreign person may appear to be understanding your communication when in reality he/she is not understanding what you are saying, in order to avoid embarrassment and save face. Some Middle Eastern persons are very good at convincing others that they know when in reality they do not understand enough to take responsibility for their own or their family's health needs or care. It is best in these situations, if a translator cannot be procured, to use short simple sentences containing easy-to-understand vocabulary. Speak slowly and clearly and rely more on nonverbal means of teaching. Although there may be cultural differences in body language, some nonverbal communication may express similar emotions, in any culture, such as fear, pain, or sadness. Teaching can also occur by physically moving the body of the person or showing what you want the person to learn by demonstrating on yourself. Pictures can be drawn to illustrate points of learning, or flash cards that are bilingual can be made to aid teaching. The cards should be bilingual so that the teacher and the learner each know what the card says and therefore have some basis for communication. These cards can be used at other times when translators or family are not available to communicate basic needs of the patient, such as on night shift when the patient wants to use the bathroom. Although this appears as a very simplistic means of communication, it can be very efficient and serve to decrease frustration and anxiety in both the client and health worker.

Differences in Values. Middle Eastern clients do not emphasize a time schedule; this Western value and practice is imposed on Middle Eastern people. Time factors for these people tend to be in terms of what is important at that moment rather than projecting rigidly into the future as to what is important.

✔ This can cause conflicts in a health care setting where tests or doctors' appointments are scheduled at particular times and the client does not feel it is a priority. The client may view taking a bath and being clean as more of a priority and that the test can wait or be rescheduled for later.

✔ Middle Eastern clients expect health care practitioners to find effective cures without asking many questions or using numerous diagnostic tests, which are often needed for a correct diagnosis. They believe if a doctor or nurse asks too many questions or orders too many tests that the practitioner is naive, lacks experience, should not be trusted, or is narrow in perspective and understanding. These clients prefer older male doctors, preferably heads of departments in their specialty area, rather than younger or female doctors. The exception is that a female obstetrician or gynecologist is preferred, in fact required, for a female client who is pregnant or has a gynecological disorder. Generally, Middle Eastern clients do not trust doctors completely because they feel doctors are too expensive, ask too many questions, and often lack experience.

↙ These clients prefer the same caretaker each day; the same caretaker increases trust and acceptance in the relationship and decreases suspicion of the health worker by the client and his/her family. Having the same caretaker also helps to decrease mistrust of the world of medicine that they really do not understand thoroughly. The nurse can capitalize on this situation by being the same caregiver and consistently offering help.

The Middle Eastern client believes that if somebody compliments the person about something that is good or of value, such as jewelry or a new baby, or even looks at it with admiration, this behavior will bring out the evil eye. The **evil eye** is a form of jealousy and mistrust of the admirer by the owner of the object being complimented.

↙ In the health care setting, avoid suspicion of the evil eye in Middle Eastern clients by directing compliments to the owner or to God (Allah), rather than to the object itself. Such action converts the possibility of the evil eye and misfortune into a blessing instead.

↙ *Legal Documents.* The last area of patient concerns is legal documents. It is recommended that birth certificates should be signed by both the father and the mother of the baby. The state vital statistic department in the United States feels the mother is the only one that it can be sure is a real parent of the child but this can be very insulting to a patrilineal father. By having both parents sign the birth certificate, the problem of the father being insulted would be remedied and both the state and family would have their interests met.

↙ Consent forms are generally not used in the Middle East. First the patient does not feel he/she has the knowledge to assume responsibility for health decisions and therefore leaves this responsibility for the doctor who has been trained to make these decisions. Secondly, in Islam, especially in front of witnesses, a man's word and agreement is considered binding and written documentation is therefore not necessary. When a consent form needs to be signed after an agreement has been made, it can be interpreted with mistrust and suspicion toward that doctor. To avoid this, one doctor found that, if the consent form was just presented in a nonpatient and institutionally-oriented, matter-of-fact way, mistrust was minimized, and patients carried through with the required procedures.

↙ *Religious Beliefs.* Middle Eastern clients may be Muslims, or they may adhere to other religions: lifestyle and health care practices will also be influenced by their religious beliefs. Chapter 3 discusses additional practices to be considered in the person's care, based on religious beliefs of the Middle Eastern client.

↙ Without your understanding of Middle Eastern culture, patients can be very frustrating to work with, but when you understand the culture and reasons for the cultural values, and realizes that these values have meaning for the individual, Middle Eastern clients become enjoyable and rewarding clients to work with. When you have established trust with the person and family, you will see other aspects of their lives open up to you. This new view can be rewarding.

Attitudes Toward Health and Illness

How health is identified, physically and emotionally, varies from culture to culture, as do ideas about the factors related to health and disease. American definitions are emphasized in Chapter 16.

U.S. Culture. Attitudes in the United States toward health are influenced considerably by society's emphasis on mastery of the environment as opposed to adjustment to it. Illness is seen as a challenge to be met by mobilizing resources: research, science, funds, institutions, and people. Americans tax themselves to finance health and welfare organizations and persons giving time and effort to these organizations are given special status by the community. Because independence is highly valued, the weak are expected to help themselves as much as possible. Self-care is emphasized. The strong help the weak as long as their problems are caused by events beyond their control; otherwise the physically, socially, or emotionally weak, deformed, or unsightly are devalued.

A person is evaluated on productivity or "doing good." Because the ability to be productive depends in part on health, individual health is highly valued. Health in the broadest sense is considered necessary for successful interaction with others, educational accomplishment, ability to work, leadership, childrearing, and capacity to use opportunities. Thus development of medical, nursing, and other health sciences and technology is considered important. The physical cause of illness is generally accepted. Only recently have the psychological and sociocultural causes of disease also been emphasized.

↙ The importance of health has been accentuated by industrialization, high-level technology, greater social controls, and mass communications, as well as by a high level of responsibility and stress placed on the person. Americans at times react to the complexities of society by retreating into ill health, physically, emotionally, or socially. Levels of pathology that could be tolerated in pre-industrial societies cannot be tolerated in complex modern life. Americans are more likely to interpret a person's difficulty in fulfilling social-role expectations as illness than would some other societies. Thus the person who is ill is less likely to be tolerated or kept in the family. When ill, the person is supposed to leave home, isolate self from the family, and be cared for in a strange place, the hospital, by strange people who are authorities on illness. One's capacity for meeting social role expectations is developed primarily through family socialization and education, but it is protected and restored through the health care system. The ill person is expected to want to return to normal roles and to leave behind the feelings of alienation, regression, and passivity that are part of the deviance of illness. The impersonal agency of the hospital exerts pressures that discourage staying dependent and ill.

Greek Culture. In Greece health is important and desired, but it is not a preoccupation. One should not pamper the self. Straight living gives a healthy body and so fortitude, hardness, and a simple standard of living are pursued. Excesses in living—in eating, drinking, or smoking—are avoided, and, in general, the level of public health is high. Because children are prized, their health needs take precedence over adults' needs. ✔ Going to bed is a sign of weakness except for recognized disease. People do not go to a doctor unless there is something seriously wrong; but then they expect the doctor, who is a father figure, to have the answers for their problems. Home remedies and the services of an herbalist are tried first as treatment. Prayers are said and vows are made. Illness is thought to arise from evil or magical sources that can be counteracted through magical practices. Entering the hospital is a last resort. The whole family is involved when the person is sick; each person has a specific role and a role gap exists during illness.

The organs of highest significance are the eyes, for they reflect the real person. Next in importance are the lips because of the words that come out of them. A girl's hair and a man's mustache are important symbols of sexual identity and attractiveness. The genital organs are not freely talked about but are respected for their reproductive functions. The body is meant to be covered and exposed only when necessary. Dress and ornamentation are essential to complete one's body image.

Childlessness is unfortunate and in the past the woman was held responsible. The woman dislikes any examination or treatment of the reproductive organs and will accept gynecological problems rather than seek medical care for fear fertility will be affected. Special care is given to the woman during pregnancy, when special regulations about hygiene, rest, activity, and a happy environment are followed.

The handicapped are not easily accepted because of the emphasis on a whole, strong, firm body. To be crippled, blind, or lame means that one is not a whole person, is dependent, and is unable to do anything for oneself.

The Greek-American adheres to some or many of the aforementioned values and practices, depending on closeness to cultural ties.

Spanish-American Culture. Attitudes among Spanish-Americans in the U. S. Southwest (or other Spanish-speaking people) are very unlike attitudes in mainstream America. The Spanish-American considers the self to be a whole person; thus "better health" has no meaning. Good health is associated with the ability to work and fulfill normal roles, for one gains and maintains respect by meeting one's responsibilities. Criteria of health are a sturdy body, ability to maintain normal physical activity, and absence of pain. The person does not have to have perfect health; as long as the family is around, he/she is all right. Thus preventive measures are not highly valued. The person does seek to care for self, however, through moderation in eating, drinking, work, recreation, and sleep, and by leading a good life.
✔ The Spanish-American believes that hardship and suffering are part of destiny and that reward for being submissive to God's will and for doing good will come in the next life. Ill health is accepted as part of life and is thought to be caused by an unknown external event or object, such as natural forces of cold, heat, storms, water, or as the result of sinning—acting against God's will. The Spanish-American, for example, thinks that one cause of illness is bad air, especially night air, which enters through a cavity or opening in the body. Thus a raisin may be placed on the cord stump of the newborn and surgery is avoided if possible; both practices help prevent air from entering the body. Avoiding drafts, keeping windows closed at night, keeping the head covered, and following certain postpartum practices have the same basis. Other causes of disease (according to Spanish-American beliefs) include overwork, poor food, excess worry or emotional strain, undue exposure to weather, uneven wetting of the body, taking a drink when overheated, and giving blood for transfusion. Underlying this thinking is the hot-cold theory of disease that stems from the Hippocratic humoral theory and was carried to the Western Hemisphere by the Spanish and Portuguese in the sixteenth and seventeenth centuries. Basically all diseases are classified as hot and cold. Arthritis is a cold disease and an ulcer is a hot disease, for instance. It is considered dangerous to be outdoors at night if one's body is warm. Pregnancy and menstruation are considered warm body states. The hot and cold theory of disease does not always refer to physical temperature or foodstuff, but also to the effects that certain sub-

stances have or are thought to have on the body. Beliefs about which foods are warm and cold vary from one geographic region and culture to another. For example, prenatal vitamins may be a hot food and will not be taken during pregnancy, a hot condition, unless swallowed with fruit juice, a cold food. All foods, herbs, medicines are classified as hot or cold. Avocado is a cold food and aspirin and corn meal are considered hot. A goal is to balance the body: a hot disease is cured with a cold food and a cold disease is cured with a hot food, herb, or medication. Thus aspirin could be taken for arthritis—which also fits into the Western medical system (9, 23, 149).

✔ **Evil eye,** *mal ojo, is a cause of disease that results when a person looks admiringly at the child of another.* Usually children are not openly admired, but precautions against illness include patting the child on the head or a light slap. (Do you know people in other subcultures with similar beliefs? Such causes are commonly stated when illness occurs.) A common illness, in this culture, *susto,* with symptoms of agitation and depression, results from traumatic, frightening experiences and may result in death. Psychosocial forces causing disease are also seen in *empacho,* a gastrointestinal disease that results from eating food that is disliked, or from overeating, or from eating hot bread. Disease may also result from organs or parts of the body moving from the normal position. Little attention is paid to colds, minor aches, or common gastrointestinal disorders.

✔ The role of the family is important in time of illness. The head of the house, the man, determines whether illness exists and what treatment is to be given. The person goes to bed when too ill to work or to move. Treatment from a lay healer is sought if family care does not help. The medical doctor is called only when the person is gravely ill; this is combined with visiting so the patient does not get the rest and isolation advised by health workers in the majority culture. The sick person does not withdraw from the group; doing so would only make him/her feel worse. Acceptance of present fate amounts to saying "If the Lord intends for me to die, I'll die." The discomfort of the present is considered, but not in terms of future complications. Being ill brings no secondary advantage of care or coddling. Communicable diseases are hard to control, for resistance to isolation is based on the idea that family members, relatives, and familiar objects cannot contaminate or cause illness. Taking home remedies, wearing special articles, and performing special ceremonies are accepted ways of getting and staying well. The person feels he/she will keep well by observing the ritual calendar, being brotherly, being a good Catholic and member of the community. If the health worker uses any procedure, such as an x-ray, it is considered to be the treatment and hence the person should be cured.

Accidents are feared because they disrupt the wholeness of the person. In addition, the Spanish-American fears surgery, the impersonality of the hospital and nurses, and any infringement on modesty.

✔ The hospital represents death and isolation from family or friends. The "professional" (Anglo) approach of the majority culture is regarded as showing indifference to needs and as causing anxiety and discomfort.

✔ Anthony-Tkach describes specific health care practices of the Mexican-American person or family and nursing implications, including for childbirth, childrearing, and prevention of communicable diseases. She also discusses customs related to use of folk medicine, use of surnames, and customs of interaction (9).

Japanese Culture. Attitudes in Japan toward health strongly reflect the belief in a body–mind–spirit interrelationship. Spiritual and temporal affairs in life are closely integrated; thus health practices and religion are closely intertwined, influenced considerably by the magicoreligious practices of Shinto, Japan's ancient religion. Bathing customs stem from Shinto purification rites, for example, and baths are taken in the evening before eating not only for cleanliness but for ceremony and relaxation as well.

There is a strong emphasis on physical fitness, an intact body, physical strength, determination, and long life. Self-discipline in daily habits is highly valued, as are the mental, spiritual, and esthetic aspects of the person. These traits remain equally important to the sick person.

✔ As a child, the person is taught to minimize reactions to injury and illness. Hence to the Westerner the sick person may appear stoic. Part of the reserve in expressing emotion and pain is also influenced by child-rearing and interaction practices, which emphasize correct behavior and suppression of emotion. Yet the sick person, as much as the well, expects to be treated with respect and resents being addressed abruptly or informally by first name. The person also resents people entering the hospital room without knocking. The Japanese male resents being dominated by women and he may feel uncomfortable with an American female nurse because he interprets her behavior as overbearing. The person is eager to cooperate with the medical care program but wishes to be included in planning and decisions regarding care. The so-called professional approach of the average U. S. health worker is likely to insult the average Japanese, although he/she may be too polite to say so.

✔ By studying life patterns of people in various cultures (especially those of patients for whom you care) and by taking into account the factors discussed in the following chapters on religion and family, you can better understand and handle varying levels of health, health problems, and attitudes toward care of different groups.

✔ You may obtain additional information about people from the following (sub)cultures and their specific nursing needs from references at the end of the chapter:

1. Afro-American (38, 39, 61, 75, 83, 135, 162, 170, 217, 222).
2. Amerian Indian (36, 74, 91, 97, 99, 151, 164, 165, 185, 211, 212, 214, 223, 224,).
3. Appalachian (64, 69, 91, 147, 169, 175, 183, 206, 219).
4. Eskimo (17, 21, 36, 53, 138).
5. German-American (40, 59, 166, 173, 182, 186).
6. Greek-American (15, 81, 114, 218).
7. Gypsy (8).
8. Irish-American (15, 226, 227).
9. Italian-American (15, 42, 100, 226, 227).
10. Japanese-American (1, 45, 76, 90, 130, 142, 148).
11. Jewish (15, 23, 58, 145, 149, 226).
12. Middle Eastern (10, 12, 14, 72, 79, 109, 110, 126, 127, 128, 129, 133, 215).
13. Migrant farmer (15, 152, 210).
14. Oriental American (25, 29, 36, 45, 46, 51, 67, 70, 108, 118, 144, 168, 190, 192, 200, 221, 225).
15. Polish-American (94, 111, 134, 180, 202).
16. Puerto Rican (45, 63, 106, 172).
17. Southeast Asian refugees (33, 65, 73).
18. Spanish-speaking (5, 9, 11, 28, 43, 55, 84, 87, 122, 123, 136, 139, 143, 162, 163, 178, 179, 188).
19. Vietnamese (100, 209).

Socioeconomic Class Subculture

Research about social stratification indicates that the person's class position is influenced by economic and social status and political power of the family and affects formation of values, attitudes, and lifestyle. Each class tends to have a more or less well-specified set of values and role expectations regarding practically every area of human activity: sex, marriage, male–female and parent–child responsibilities and behavior, birth, death, education, dress, housing, home furnishings, leisure, reading habits, occupational status, politics, religion, and status symbols. In turn, health status in the United States is closely linked to income level. Poor people are more likely to have poor health and chronic illness (80). Social class includes a group consciousness. Most persons can be objectively placed within a certain class (140), but they are sometimes accorded a status by others around them that might be different. Furthermore, they may see themselves at yet a different status level, based on race, sex, religion, ancestry, ethnic origin, or wealth in material goods. What seems natural and logical in determining status to some people may be rejected by others.

✔ As you gain general knowledge about values and lifestyles of people in various economic levels, realize also that no one person encompasses all that the literature describes. Knowledge about lifestyles is generally useful to a nursing practice, but *avoid the stereotyping of people* because of this knowledge.

Profile of Socioeconomic Levels

The Upper-Upper or Corporate Class. This class consists of a relatively small number of people who own a disproportionate share of personal wealth and whose income is largely derived from ownership. This group has both money and power and it can control how its assets are used as well as various other economic and political aspects of society. The decisions made by this group affect everyone else. Coles (35, 37) refers to them as the *affluent.* These are the people who have had lineage, inherited wealth, and power for several generations. They are acknowledged by the general public and themselves as leaders nationally and internationally. They feel obliged to tend their own financial and material resources well, to obtain the best possible education, and to take care of their health so that they can meet their obligation of giving of themselves personally and philanthropically to society (35, 37, 82). The affluent family, including the women and youth, participate in and contribute considerably to the community and society as a whole through financial contribution and volunteer activities to various social, welfare, health, and political organizations.

This person or family lives in an exclusive residential area in a house whose atmosphere is spatial and formal and that affords privacy from the masses. This person or family may own several estates in different areas of the country (or world) that are used in different seasons or for different purposes. The family may have a number of people to help it maintain its lifestyle, such as a maid, butler, gardener, and other staff members (35, 37, 82).

The children are reared by a governess or maid as well as by the parents. The mother usually is selective in her teaching, guiding, and care. Certain aspects of rearing are done only by the mother, others only by the maid. The children, like the parents, live with choices, for they have more animate and inanimate objects and possessions than others and many opportunities to follow the arts; to learn certain sports, such as horseback riding, tennis, swimming, or skiing; and to travel. But even the children know the importance and value of the objects and opportunities that surround them. They recognize the importance of self-control, behaviorally and in their various activities and sports. They seek privacy, reverie and disciplined activity even though in the public view. They are able to move smoothly from one activity to another without being *driven* to excel. Yet they expect to be competent at their chosen academic, recreational, and social pursuits (35, 37).

Although the upper class is adult oriented, children know at an early age that they are special and parents try to instill a feeling that the child must do well because he/she has special responsibilities to society on reaching adulthood. The child, like the parent, associates with others from the same class, observing the average person from the sidelines, never really understanding what life is like for the average citizen or why middle- or lower-class people live as they do. Although both adults and children take a lot for granted and feel entitled to the fine things in life, they feel a sense of responsibility and try to live up to their ideals. Destiny is abundance and limitless possibility. They are confident that life will be rewarding. Even crisis, such as illness or surgery, can be made into something basically pleasant, for the best of specialized health care professionals and comprehensive facilities can be obtained, and convalescence frequently involves a trip to and rest at a secluded place (35, 37, 82)

The Lower-Upper Class. This group consists of people whose wealth is more recently acquired and who have become well known (actors, famous doctors or lawyers, athletes) or they may be less famous but have large incomes, homes, and lifestyles that show off their money. They have social position and prestige because of what they *do*. The upper-upper class person has position and prestige because of *who* he/she is; the person does not lose them even if encountering financial setbacks. The lower-upper-class person may slide down into middle-class anonymity if wealth is lost. The lower-upper-class (or newly rich) person or family also has an abundance of possessions and opportunity, however, but may be less humble about or more self-conscious of it than the upper-upper-class person. Although this person or family may attend the same activities, travel to the same areas, or send the children to the same schools as the upper-upper-class family, this person or family is seen as different by the upper-upper class (35, 37, 98). Often a fine line separates the upper-upper and lower-upper classes in a community; such intangibles as social charm or likeability, family background, religion, value of residence, and schooling often make the difference. Money is only loosely related to social standing in many communities (32, 37). Both women and men of the lower-upper class are working—entering a profession, starting a business, or doing consultant work—for fun, for a sense of identity, to be worthwhile, to provide structure to the day or to life, to avoid the image of being intellectual (they are usually college educated), to avoid being important only through the spouse.

The Upper-Middle Class. This group is described as *those who are well off*. Income is high but varies, depending on occupation and geographical area. Each spouse is college educated and at least one is a professional—the average doctor, dentist, engineer, business manager, or lawyer. The main work of these people is intellectual instead of manual, requires professional training, and offers upward mobility. They live in a large house in the better part of town or suburb, may have a maid and often a gardener, have more than one car, travel nationally and sometimes abroad, may belong to a semi-elite country club, and frequently send the children to private schools and college (37, 98). Both family stability and community leadership are valued. The children have a number of opportunities educationally and culturally; in return, they are expected to be successful academically and socially. The children are often involved in a number of prestigious out-of-home activities and organizations, as are parents, and the children may actually have fewer home responsibilities than the upper-class child. Childrearing is permissive; children are given explanations instead of punishment. The parents will exert more direct influence on the child's schooling than will the middle or working class (24, 32, 37, 82).

The Middle Class. The middle class sometimes is divided in two categories. Those who reached the American dream and those who have a comfortable existence. Members of the *American dream* group have education above the high school level in a professional or specialized school and include business people with small or medium-sized enterprises who employ a few or many workers; self-employed business people, artists; skilled workers; office and sales workers; and public or private school teachers. Nurses and other professional health workers typically are in this class. These people have a special status because of education and occupation (many *work with* people), although they do not have much wealth. Typically they work in occupations that involve thinking rather than hard physical labor. They live in a pleasant residential section or suburb, in a nicely furnished house, have two cars, usually including a station wagon or four-wheel drive vehicle. The family eats out weekly and vacations annually. The middle-class family is usually a nuclear family, but it has linkages through kin for social and family goals. The family is active in community activities and organizations and pursues some sports or other leisure activities as a family unit, but the family members frequently go to separate activities several evenings a week. Members of the *comfortable existence* group tend to have less education and less material goods than the first group, but they live comfortably. They have more than the necessities and are somewhat active in the community (24, 54, 98, 201).

The middle class is child-oriented; family life often revolves around children and their interests. At work, the middle-class person typically deals with manipulation of symbols, ideas or interpersonal relationships, has to be self-directive, and must use initiative to get ahead. Thus, families (single- or two-parent) have high aspirations for children and take pride in their accomplishments. Parents emphasize education and value and encourage verbal and problem-solving skills (98). The middle (and upper) class(es) uses an elaborate code of speech, which is characterized by precision, differentiation of ideas, and extensive use of modifiers and clauses. Its verbosity may bury the meaning, and the abstractness of such speech causes lack of understanding among the working and lower classes (54). Parents teach the importance of hard work, self-reliance, thrift, patience, planning ahead, and postponing immediate rewards for later rewards. These parents are typically more responsive to the advice of experts and research results. They accept the advice of experts, since it is based on middle-class values and thus offers what they want. Thus the middle-class parent changes childrearing practices, perhaps several times on one child. The middle-class parents, because of education, are more likely to feel insecure in childrearing and view it as problematic. They discuss childrearing practices with neighbors and friends, consult the doctor, nurse, or child's teacher about what they are doing wrong (seldom do they see themselves doing anything right), and join various community organizations, such as the P.T.A., where they can learn even more about childrearing. Middle-class parents are consistently more concerned about the child's feelings and try to understand the dynamics of the child's behavior and mix discipline with permissiveness. Discipline is often in the form of withdrawal of privileges or of disapproval, threats, or appeals to reason. Punishment is based on the parent's interpretation of the child's intent behind his/her action. If the child loses control, he/she is punished; if the outburst represents a release of feeling, he/she is less likely to be punished. Additionally, the parent is more likely to feel and be supportive, accepting, and egalitarian to the child than is the working-class parent. The child is expected to be expressive verbally and emotionally, be happy and cooperative, confide in parents, want to learn, have self-control, share readily, be self-directive, and stay well and healthy (24, 54, 107, 201).

In the middle class, the man and wife do many activities together, and roles are not as sharply differentiated. Both parents are supportive of the children, especially of same-sexed children, and the father's role as disciplinarian is secondary to that of supportive figure. This is in accordance with his wife's wishes. Father tends to agree with the mother and plays a role close to that desired by her. The middle-class parent has greater stability of income and takes for granted much of what the lower class parent works hard to achieve. Thus, the parent is freer to give attention to the child (54, 82 201).

Overall the middle class uses the internist, family practice physician, and pediatrician for routine health care, but the services of specialists are used when indicated. The middle class respects health professionals and wants thorough and scientific diagnosis and treatment. Middle-class people see themselves as knowledgeable about health, but they appreciate and will try to use additional information. They tolerate, although they do not like, the high medical costs (32).

The Lower-Middle or Working Class. This group is often perceived as those who are *just getting by* (98). Generally both spouses have graduated from high school and both work as industrial or blue-collar workers, clerical or service workers, agricultural wage earners, technicians, skilled or semiskilled workers, as telephone operators or waitresses. Many working-class people work with things. The family rents either a small home with two or three bedrooms or an apartment and takes good care of its home and belongings, including an older car. It has some conveniences but may not own many luxuries. The family depends on the extended family instead of on social agencies for economic and emotional support and may be active in church but not active in the P.T.A. or other community organizations. The husband is typically head of the house and the woman is considered responsible for the home and child care. The family enjoys recreational activities as a family unit, such as bowling or movies, and eating at fast-service or local "home-style" restaurants (54, 98).

Members of the working class value patriotism, religion, authority, the work ethic, honesty, respectability, self-reliance, conformity, consumerism, competition, achievement, education, the home, saving for the future, and law and order. They believe people with money are not happy. They accept their position and are basically proud of their hard work and accomplishment, even with less education. They believe that on-the-job, collective action is important. They believe that the poor are lazy, deserve their poverty, and should not be given welfare. (A natural economic depression and forced unemployment are the only two causes for poverty without moral blame.) Being higher in the social scale than the poor and minorities gives them a social identity and a measure of social worth. They feel that equality of all people, including the poor, minorities, and women, is threatening and would pose problems of social adjustment. Another danger of equality is that friends or neighbors might surpass them. The present inequality allows the upper class or supervisors to be an elite group, to take care of people, to be friendly, helpful leaders. Equality of income would deprive people of their incentive to work. Working-class people are stable breadwinners, churchgoers, voters, and family men/women. They may have two jobs and little leisure. Leisure is usually focused on activities that help the person forget the life situation and work temporarily. Many do not like their jobs but fear not finding another; therefore they keep the job because of family responsibilities and the hold on respectability that the job brings. What they want most is a decent standard of living (54, 98, 140).

The working-class adult typically has less education, reads less, and is therefore less responsive to research results and the advice of experts. Further, expert advice usually is not relevant to this value system. Childrearing is taken for granted and is not perceived as something that you do with a preset plan, nor as something which is problematic—or to be discussed with others. These parents rely heavily on the extended family, retaining the traditional methods of parenting and keeping the same goals that they perceived in their homes and parents. Desirable characteristics in the child, according to the working-class parent, include the following: the child should be neat, clean, honest, obedient, respectful to parents, pleasant to adults, conform to externally imposed standards, trustworthy, and respect the rights of others (54, 62, 98, 140).

That the working-class parent has the above values and views on childrearing can be related to how he/she was raised and educated and the present occupational role. The working-class person typically deals with the manipulation of things; he/she is subjected to standardization and direct supervision and authority; and getting ahead depends on collective action rather than individual initiative. Congruence exists between the adult's occupational requirements and values about the behavior of children. The occupational experience affects the parent's concept of what is desirable behavior—on or off the job, for adults or children.

The working-class parent values conformity of behavior; he/she has learned to conform to get ahead. Thus he/she punishes nonconforming behavior, including what experts would call the natural curiosity of the child, as well as behavior which is extreme or disturbing. The preferred discipline technique is physical punishment rather than emphasis on reasoning typical of the preceding classes. The child should not break rules that are externally imposed, but should remain orderly and obedient. And so the child of the working-class parent is prepared for a position in society as an adult, and in the future as a parent will impose constraints on his/her children in much the same manner (54, 62, 98).

In the working class, work and social roles and the roles of mother and father are more sharply differentiated, and the man and woman lead separate social lives. The mother is the more supportive parent, wanting the father to help with discipline. Frequently, the father views himself as the economic provider but sees no reason to help shoulder the responsibility of childrearing. He thinks it is important that the child be taught not to transgress, and since mother has the primary responsibility for child care, discipline should also be her job. Because he is less involved in childrearing, the father also has less real authority and status in family affairs. In the process, the male and female children learn what it is to be a father and mother, and as adults, their expectations and behavior are influenced, at least some degree by what they unconsciously learned as children. If they have the opportunity of enough education and advantage to move up into the middle class, they may slowly change their values and childrearing practices as they outwardly imitate other middle-class parents around them. Yet very often, values do not change and even overt behavior is nearer to that of their parents than that of their newly found middle-class friends (54, 69, 98).

Health care is sought when the person is too sick to work; prevention is less emphasized than for the foregoing classes. They may try home or folk remedies first and then go to a general practitioner. The neighborhood health center will be used if one exists. Dental care is more likely to be neglected than other medical care. They respond well to an approach that is respectful, personable, prompt, and thorough. They do not understand why health care should be so costly and they may omit very expensive treatments or drugs whenever possible (32, 140).

The Upper-Lower Class. This group is perceived as those who are *having a real hard time.* The family is often only one step away from poverty and welfare. The person has fewer chances of acquiring education. Thus upper-lower-class people work at menial tasks, usually nonunion, but are proud to be working. These people may work as domestics, gardeners, hospital or school maintenance or cafeteria workers, junk collectors, garbage collectors, or street cleaners. Often neither husband nor wife has completed high school and sometimes one may not have completed junior high. The family lives in a substandard flat in an older building, usually with an absentee landlord. The family enjoys picnics in the park and other free diversions. The family's only long trips are for funerals of relatives (100). Often the upper-lower-class family had its beginning in lack of motivation for education, resulting in high school dropout for pregnancy or lack of academic success, an early parenthood, a poor first job, a rapid succession of children, or an early separation or divorce. As life progresses, the chance to advance becomes even less likely (32, 62, 98, 140).

The Poor. Poor people include those who are in acute poverty and those in chronic poverty. First, poverty has two definitions. **Poverty** *is having inadequate pre-tax money or source of income to purchase a minimum amount of goods and services.* **Poverty** *is also a power issue. It is the relative lack of an individual's access to and control over environmental resources.* Poverty reflects racial stratification and hopelessness and is seen in increasing homelessness and health problems that result from the conditions of poverty (132). The person or family in **acute poverty** *has reduced economic means because of given circumstances for a limited time* but anticipates being able to return to work and a better lifestyle. The person or family in **chronic poverty** *has a long family history of being unemployed and without adequate economic means and is unlikely to see much opportunity for improvement* (34, 153).

The lines are not always so clearly drawn, however. Because of the unemployment problems of the 1980s, more traditionally middle-class people are economically classified as poor. The single parent raising several children, although middle class by birth, may become acutely poor when a job is not available or a prolonged illness or other crisis occur (56). Currently, one in every five American children live in poverty (one in six Caucasian children; 40 percent of Hispanic children; 50 percent of Afro-American children). In the late 1980s, one child in every four is born into poverty. Poor children are often sick at birth, are more likely to suffer physical deformities and display mental deficiencies—either because of inadequate nutrition or poor prenatal and early child care. Seventy percent of poor children live with only one parent, often a teen and usually the mother. Among Afro-Americans, more than one-half of the children live with one parent. The child develops deep emotional scars, feeling low self-esteem, a sense of failure, mistrust of self and others, and anger. The older the child gets, the greater the difficulty. In school, he/she performs badly on tests and often drops out. Then the person is less employable, more susceptible to drug and alcohol abuse, more likely to serve a jail term, and more likely to have children who will repeat the cycle (3).

Some poor children will defy the odds, and through initiative, a strong will, defiance against their situation, good parenting, and an encounter with an extraordinary teacher or adult over the years will break out of the cycle.

Other people are joining the ranks of acutely poor in the 1980s because of governmental policies and economic trends. Some people work full-time but earn only minimum wage. Acutely poor families include the middle- or working-class family where both spouses work to maintain their standard of living, and one or both becomes unemployed. Or the main provider becomes unemployed; the second salary, once providing extras, is now inadequate. The longer the person is unemployed, the more difficult it becomes to find a job using specific educational or job skills. Unless the individual is willing to take any kind of job, there may be no available job. Another group of people, many of whom have joined the ranks of recent and acutely poor, is the small farmer. Having only the skills, the muscle, and knowledge involved in farming; having over-invested in the land and farm operation; and having lost money because of weather conditions and consequent poor crops, falling prices for grain and livestock, and increasing costs for machinery, land, seed, and fertilizer; the farm family, once able to provide for basic needs, may rather suddenly lose the farm land and home and everything in it. Homelessness and destitution may follow. In a rural area, economic losses to the farmer in turn affect the businessmen in small towns. The circle of poverty become larger. The elderly person who considered him/herself middle class or even affluent may now barely be able to pay for the essentials of life or may be living in poverty conditions. Reder (171) states that poverty among the elderly is more prevalent than among other adults, twice as high for elderly women as men. Elderly minorities and the very old, over 85 years, are especially vulnerable. The poverty rate for elderly Afro-Americans is three times higher than for elderly Caucasians; one of every four Spanish-speaking elderly are in poverty. In 1985, poverty levels had declined slightly from 1976 for Caucasians and Afro-Americans, but not for people of Spanish origin (161).

Although the poor or lower-class person has traditionally not finished high school, perhaps not even elementary school, and is an unskilled or semiskilled worker, often employed in temporary or seasonal jobs, the person with a doctorate degree may also be unemployed and living in poverty. Often the woman is better able to get a job than the man, but neither may have the necessary job skills for our competitive and technologically changing society. The poor person may live in a mixed residential area, on welfare in the city or rural area, or in an inner city or ghetto tenement infested by rats and roaches and without hot water. Recreation for the man may consist of talking with peers on the street corner or at a cheap bar, sitting alone in a park, or watching television. The woman's chief leisure activity may be attending church and visiting relatives. The family unit may be nuclear or extended and frequently there are a number of offspring (34, 98, 124, 171).

Much of the results of the research of the 1960s on people in the lower socioeconomic class and "the culture of poverty" reflected the bias or race of the researchers or focused on institutionalized populations or people in trouble, without reflecting on the many variables that influence people. Typically only negative traits were assigned to the poor person or family—traits at the opposite end of the continuum from the desired middle-class characteristics. The victim of social oppression and racism was blamed for his/her problems. Fortunately, later research findings give a more balanced view, which should help health workers to better understand and offer the same quality of care to the poor as to the middle and upper classes (34, 153). *Characteristics and behavior of the poor person or family is adaptive for the economic and social situation and constraints on lifestyles.*

Chilman's study (31) of the patterns of childrearing and family relationships of the very poor and the eventual effect upon the next generation of parents further validates what was described from Kohn's (98) and others' study (34, 54, 62, 92, 124, 153, 170). These characteristics include:

1. Misbehavior is regarded in terms of overt outcome; reasons for behavior are infrequently considered.
2. Lack of goal commitment, impulsive gratification, fatalism, lack of belief in long-range success result from effects of chronic poverty upon the person's motivations and lifestyle.
3. Communication between family members is more physical than verbal.
4. Families are frequently large; each member acts to get whatever gratification he/she can. Previously unmet needs in the parent causes self-centeredness; the parent is poorly equipped to meet the dependency needs of many children. The child, as adult, will be continuing the cycle of previously unmet needs and inability to gratify another as parent.
5. Mother is the chief child care agent; father is mainly a punitive figure. The milieu of the home is authoritarian, even though father may be frequently out of the home.
6. Discipline is harsh, inconsistent, and physical, makes use of ridicule, and is based on whether or not the child's behavior annoys the parent.
7. Aggressive behavior is alternately encouraged and restrained, depending primarily upon the consequences to the parent of the child's behavior. Such inconsistency causes the child to learn how to get away with certain behavior and does not teach impulse control.
8. Sex is viewed as an exploitative relationship. Questions about sex and sexual experimentation are met with a repressive, punitive attitude.

Parents often have low self-esteem (31). Studies by Coopersmith and Lidz (107) indicate that parents with low self-esteem provoke feelings of shame, guilt, defensiveness, decreased self-worth, and being bad in the child by overestimating his/her ability to conform, by inappropriately or forcefully punishing or restraining the child, denying necessities, and withdrawing love. Such childhood experiences cause low self-esteem in the child and these feelings continue into adulthood, so that as a parent, this individual inflicts the same feelings he/she suffered as a child.

Authoritarian or harsh childrearing practices, which may be a euphemism for discipline, have as their explicit objective the development of toughness and self-sufficiency for survival. Yet in spite of the authoritarian, direct approach, the parent is warm and expressive. An attachment exists between parent and child. In his/her own home the child is also likely to be expressive, although the child may seem restrained with strangers (34). The child is often given adult responsibilities early; he/she is not the focus of the family in the way that the middle-class child is. Everyone must fend more for self (27, 98).

Most minority and ethnic cultures value kinship ties and the emotional, social, and economic support that the extended family provides in contrast to dominant middle-class America, which values individualism and independence. Much visiting goes on between relatives in the lower and working classes; assistance is sought and appreciated. All get along better by sharing meager resources or by working together to gain resources. The grandmother (and grandfather if living) is valued as caretaker for the child if the mother works. But the grandmother is also valued because she is the carrier of the culture; she is wise and can teach the young a great deal. The grandparent also benefits from being valued as a person (27, 34, 98).

Ability to delay gratification appears related to the situation. If the minority person is being tested by a

White person or has experienced broken promises—either by the researcher or others—he/she does not delay gratification. That is, the person requests an immediate reward in the experiment instead of being willing to wait. Moreover, ability to wait is related to **internal locus of control,** *a feeling that the self has some control over events.* Frequently the poor person learns early that he/she is at the mercy of the system, whether the system is White, economic, educational, or health (27, 34). Then, too, if hungry, cold, or without necessities, small wonder that the person takes whatever possible to appease hunger or feel more comfortable. The child learns to delay gratification if he/she can trust that what is needed will be there when needed. The poor child may seldom have this opportunity because of economic problems in the family. If meager resources are used to meet today's needs, it is difficult or impossible to plan ahead, to save, or to anticipate that planning and saving have merit. The lower class is present-oriented, in contrast to the future perspective of middle and upper classes, because of necessity, cultural values, or inability to trust what is not tangible (34, 153).

✔ Often the poor person appears to need an authoritarian, directive approach. The poor person (or the parents) may work in a situation in which he/she takes orders; the poor person's expectancy is to be *told* rather than *invited to talk with* someone about his/her ideas, problems, tentative solutions, or insight. Or the person may not understand the health care worker's professional jargon but is too polite or fearful to ask for an explanation. Also, if previous attempts to share ideas were met with rejection or ridicule by parent, teacher, or health care worker, the person learned that it was safer not to respond. Finally, the poor person values action—getting something accomplished—more than words or promises (27, 34, 124, 132).

✔ Impaired verbal communication and problem-solving ability may be present, not because the poor person is cognitively deficient but for other reasons. Many ethnic or minority groups speak a dialect in the home; the child then has difficulty understanding standard English or being understood. Essentially the child must become bilingual to be successful in school (38). The poor person uses a restricted code that is characterized by short sentences, lack of specificity, and lack of subordinate clauses for elaboration of meaning. The poor person speaks directly to the point. Such language is said to be concrete and to indicate lack of abstract thinking. In contrast to the middle-class elaborate and sometimes vague speech, the speech of the poor class is logical and expressive. Thought is not buried in verbosity and vagueness. The blunt speech may be uncomfortable to listen to, both in words and ideas (31, 38, 176). The same words in professional and folk terminology may have a different meaning. For example, some Afro-Americans use the term "high blood" to mean that they believe there is too much blood in the body. Ingestion of large amounts of salty foods is believed to be helpful for an astringent effect. The health care professional must clarify that high blood pressure is different so that the person does not increase the hypertensive state further by excessive eating of salty foods (66).

Linguists have found that dialects do have grammatical structure (49, 50). Use of a dialect does not necessarily inhibit abstract thinking. The child must be taught problem solving and abstract thinking, however. If parents are seldom at home because of work, if the subculture values action more than words, if parents talk little with the child or brush aside questions, and if the child associates more with peers than with adults, he/she is not likely to be stimulated to try new speech forms or new thought patterns. School teachers try, but unfortunately they often have classes too large to give the needed individual instruction, to form a motivating relationship, or to assess fully what the child does not know. Parents often wish to help the child learn more; in fact, most poor parents repeatedly emphasize that their children must get an education so that they can achieve more than their parents did. Unfortunately, good intentions and admonitions are not enough. Poor parents often lack the education, energy, time, or resources to help the child advance educationally or even keep up minimally. The farther behind the child gets, the less the likelihood of ever catching up with cognitive skills. The cycle is repeated each generation. Yet most poor parents are receptive to suggestions on how to make the best possible use of their limited resources or what specific measures to follow to enhance the child's development (34, 38, 39, 91, 98).

There is a clear relationship between poverty and ill health. Long-term ill health may contribute to poverty. Poverty predisposes to certain illnesses or causes the person to suffer adverse consequences of illness. The ill child who is poor is less likely to attend school. The poor have less prenatal care, a higher infant and maternal mortality rate, and a higher number of deaths from accidents. Preventive measures are less likely to be carried out in the family; (193) children are less likely to be immunized.

The lower-class person defines self as ill when unable to work for days or weeks. The lower-class person first uses folk or home remedies when ill or may go to a cultural healer. Reluctantly, and only when absolutely necessary, does he/she enter the scientific health care system. The person in abject poverty may not go for professional, scientific care at all because of the lack of knowledge, money, transportation, or an inadequate sense of self-worth. The lower-class person is suspicious of the health worker or feels that there is a distance between the health worker and him/herself. These feelings can be overcome only by a gentle, respectful, courteous, prompt approach and straightforward speech. Although many people feel that much financial assistance is available for the poor and sick, such assistance is limited. Moreover, the poor person is unfamiliar with or unlikely to use community agencies wisely without your assistance. Because the poor person often does not have the resources to practice preventive physical or dental care, he/she may be very ill—even irreversibly—on entry to the health care system (13, 27, 32, 34, 124, 132).

Living in poverty takes its toll physically, emotionally, and mentally. The person who lives in chronic poverty is more likely to have behavioral characteristics opposite to the dominant culture because of not being involved with or learning from the dominant culture. Such behaviors, however, should not be viewed as innately bad, predetermined, irreversible, or the fault of the victims (34,199).

Influences of Culture on Health

Because every culture is complex, it can be difficult to determine whether health and illness are the result of cultural or other factors, such as physiological or psychological factors. Yet there are numerous accounts of the presence or absence of certain diseases in certain cultural groups and reactions to illness that are culturally determined.* Cultural influences may include food availability, dietary taboos, methods of hygiene, and effects of climate—all factors related to culture. Several examples of the influences of culture on health and illness follow. The examples are necessarily limited. The influence of other cultural folkways on health has been studied. Race, social class, ethnic group, and religion influence distribution of disease and death.

To determine the effect of ethnic group on respiratory disease occurrence, average annual sex, ethnic, and disease specific mortality rates for the period of 1969 to 1977 were calculated for New Mexico's American Indian, Hispanic, and Anglo populations. Incidence data were available for respiratory tract cancer. This study corroborates previous findings of reduced mortality from lung cancer in American Indians of both sexes and in Hispanic males. American Indian mortality from tuberculosis and from influenza and pneumonia was high. Hispanic males and American Indians of both sexes showed low mortality rates for chronic obstructive pulmonary disease (COPD). Differing cigarette usage is the most obvious explanation for the variations in COPD and lung cancer occurrence with ethnic groups (179).

✔ Culturally induced belief in magic can cause illness and death. The profound physiological consequences of intense fear, including inability to eat or drink, may be responsible. Yet there may be no physiological changes except in the terminal moments. If the behavior of friends and relatives—what they say or do—strongly reinforces the person's conviction of imminent death, the victim becomes resigned to fate and soon meets it (119).

Gomes and Carozos (71) describe the sudden death of a 21-year-old Mexican-American male following a **moldicion** (*hex*) uttered by his mother. Toxicology and drug screening were negative in autopsy; only chronic bronchitis was evidenced. There was no evidence of suicide. The mother admitted to having delivered a curse upon the son the evening before his death and that he trembled and sobbed all night. When she called an ambulance to take the son to a local hospital, he died enroute. The woman's husband died of a heart attack while crossing the street 10 days later. It was then that relatives and neighbors designated her as a *bruja* or witch. She blamed the local hospital for both deaths.

A culture's favored drink may have implications for health. Health workers in a remote Mexican village found that the only available beverage was an alcoholic drink made from the juice of a local plant. A safe water supply was brought in, but the people did not fare well on it. The local drink was a rich source of essential vitamins and minerals not otherwise present in the local diet. Thus although it may have appeared desirable to change a cultural pattern for certain health reasons, the unanticipated consequences proved detrimental to health in another way.

✔ *NURSING APPLICATIONS*

Importance of Cultural Concepts for Nursing

Mainstream Americans have not been adept at understanding people from other countries and cultures, although the United States has been an open society to foreigners and immigrants. Those of minority cultures in the United States and people from other lands typically, and of necessity, have carefully observed

---
*Refer to 2, 5, 8, 9, 11, 12, 13, 18–20, 22, 25, 27–29, 33, 43–46, 48, 51, 57, 58, 60, 64–66, 71, 73, 75, 78, 82, 85–88, 91, 93, 97, 99–105, 107–110, 112–119, 122, 124, 126–129, 131–133, 137, 139, 141–145, 149–150, 154–157, 163–165, 174, 177–179, 183, 184, 186, 187, 191–193, 195, 198, 200, 203, 204, 206, 207, 210, 211–217, 220, 221, 224–227

and become familiar with the maintream Caucasian culture in the United States.

Because of the rise of scientific medical practices and specialization, many consumers of health care in the United States are voicing a preference for caring behaviors and cultural practices. Especially the poor, middle-to-lower socioeconomic groups, and rural populations find the cosmopolitan approach to medical care too complex, too questionable, too difficult to understand and attain, and too expensive. Further, human dignity and normal developmental processes may be sacrificed in the process (103).

Transcultural (cross-cultural) nursing, developed by Madeleine Leininger in the mid-1960s, is increasingly a focus in nursing education and practice. **Transcultural nursing** *is the study and comparative analysis of different cultures/subcultures throughout the world in relation to caring, health, and illness, beliefs, values, and practices, so that this knowledge can be used in the nursing process to provide culture-specific and cultural-universal nursing care to people* (100–105). The goal is to develop a body of knowledge so that transcultural nursing concepts, theories, and practices are an integral part of nursing education, service, and research. Essential to practice is awareness of cultural values, sensitivity to different beliefs and practices, and the concept of **cultural relativity** (*behavior that is appropriate or right in one culture may not be so defined in another culture*) versus **ethnocentrism** (103).

Attitudes Related to Culture

If you live or work in a culture different from your own, you may suffer **cultural shock,** *the feelings of bewilderment, confusion, disorganization, frustration, and stupidity, and the inability to adapt to the differences in language and word meanings, activities, time, and customs that are part of the new culture.* An antidote for cultural shock is to look for similarities between your native and new cultures. In order to adapt to a new culture, be interested in the culture and be prepared to ask questions tactfully and to give up some of your own habits. Leininger and Weiss give a number of specific suggestions for adapting to another culture (100, 215).

In the United States, you are working in a **pluralistic society** *in which members of diverse ethnic, racial, religious, and social groups maintain independent lifestyles and adhere to certain values within the confines of a common civilization.* Knowledge of other cultures helps you examine your own cultural foundations, values, and beliefs, which, in turn, promotes increased self-understanding. But avoid **ethnocentricity,** *believing that your own ways of behavior are best for everyone.* For example, emphasizing daily bathing to a group who has a severely limited water supply is useless, for the water will be needed for survival. Recognize that your patterns of life and language are peculiar to your culture.

All people have some prejudice; it emerges in such expressions as "Those upper-crust people always . . ." or "Those welfare people never. . . ." Examine your thinking for unconscious prejudice, understand your own class background, and distinguish your values from those held by people under your care. Try to withhold value judgments that interfere with your relationship with the patient and with objective care. *There are too many unknown factors in people's lives to set up stereotyped categories.* A family may be in the middle class or upper class in terms of income, education, and goals, for example, and yet live in an upper-lower-class neighborhood because they refuse to emphasize material wealth. A farmer, according to our criteria, may be labeled upper-lower-class and yet regard him/herself very much a part of the middle class. A person who lives in an economically depressed section of the United States and is poor may have an adequate public education, a middle-class value system, and upper-class graciousness.

If you feel you are stooping by helping lower-class people, you may be labelled a "do-gooder" and be ineffective. Recognize the behavior of the lower class not as pathological but as adaptive for their needs. Realize, too, that not only the poor need your help. The upper-class person may need a great deal of help with care, health teaching, or counseling. Having money does not necessarily mean one is knowledgeable about preventive health measures, nutrition, and disease processes. Persons of all classes deserve competent care, clear explanations, and a helpful attitude.

The misinterpretation of behavior typical of a social class does not always go in one direction, from upper to lower. Suppose that you are a nurse with a working-class background whose patient is a 50-year-old corporation president, admitted for coronary disease, a member of the newly rich class. He/she seems obsessed with learning when he/she can resume professional duties, exactly how many hours can be worked daily, and chances for a recurrence. An understanding of his/her class position, along with possible motives, values, and status (which he/she feels must be maintained), will enable you to work with the seeming obsession rather than simply label him/her an "impossible patient."

Try to accept people as they are regardless of culture or social class. Picture the world from the eyes of others—those you care for. In this way, you can maintain your own personal standards without being shocked by theirs.

Assessment

Learning about another's cultural background can promote feelings of respect and humility as well as enhance understanding of the person and the family—needs, like and dislikes, behavior, attitudes, care and treatment approaches, and sociocultural causes of disease. According to Tripp-Reimer, Brink, and Saunders, a thorough cultural assessment guide would include the following components (207):

1. Values: Health, human nature, man–nature, time, activity, relational, and other.
2. Beliefs: Health (health maintenance, causes and treatment of illness), religious, other.
3. Customs: Communication (verbal and nonverbal), decision making, food/diet, grief/dying, religious, family roles, and sick role/patient.
4. Social structure: Family, political involvement, education, ethnic affiliation, physical environment, religion, use of economic resources, health care facilities, use of art and history, and cultural change.

Orque's Ethnic/Cultural System Framework shows how basic human needs are influenced by various aspects of a culture: (1) value orientation, (2) family life processes, (3) diet, (4) religion, (5) language and communication processes, (6) healing beliefs and practices, (7) the social group's interactive patterns, and (8) art and history of the social group (149).

Cultural differences should be anticipated not only in foreigners and first-generation immigrants but also in persons even further removed in time from their country and in persons from other regions within your country. The person's behavior during illness is influenced by cultural definitions of how he/she should act and the meaning of illness. Understanding this situation and seeking reasons for behavior help to avoid stereotyping and labeling the person as uncooperative and resistant just because the behavior is different. As you consider alternate reasons for behavior, care can be individualized. People from different cultural backgrounds classify health problems differently and have certain expectations about how they should be helped. If cultural differences are ignored, your ability to assess and help the patient/client and his/her ability to progress toward a personally and culturally defined health status may be hampered. You should be able to translate your knowledge of the health care system into terms that match the concepts of your patients/clients.

Knowledge about social classes and cultural groups may help explain late or broken agency appointments that result from fear or inferiority feelings, lack of transportation, or someone to care for the children at home rather than from lack of interest in health. The reservation American Indian, the poor Afro-American, or recent immigrant, for instance, may not be accustomed to keeping a strict time schedule or appointments if unemployed, for a strict clock time orientation is not valued as highly as in the industrialized work force. Take time to talk with the person and you will learn of his/her fears, problems, aspirations, and concern for health and family, and his/her human warmth.

As you assess the person, remember that people differ biologically, physically, and culturally (Table 1–9). Studies on biological baselines for growth and development or normal characteristics have usually been done on White populations. These norms may not be applicable to nonwhites. Biological features, such as skin color, body size and shape, and presence of enzymes, are the result of biological adjustments made by ancestors to the environment in which they lived (18, 150, 174).

Various physical differences are known to exist. **Mongolian spots,** *the hyperpigmented, bluish discoloration* occasionally seen in Caucasian neonates, are normal for many Asians, American Indians, and Afro-Americans. Type of ear wax varies and may determine the presence of ear disease in preschoolers. Dry ear wax is recessive and is found primarily in American Indians and Asians. Wet ear wax is found in most Afro-Americans and Caucasians. Also, people with dry ear wax have fewer apocrine glands and perspire less; they usually do not have as much body odor. Thus presence of body odor may be indicative of disease. Pelvic shape of the woman, shape of teeth and tongue, fingerprint pattern, blood type, keloid formation, and presence of the enzyme lactase vary among groups. Persons with certain blood types are more prone to certain illnesses (18, 150, 174). The adult who has **lactose intolerance** is *missing lactase, the enzyme for digestion and metabolism of lactose in milk and milk products.* The person becomes ill on ingestion of these foods. Symptoms include flatulence, distention, abdominal cramping, diarrhea, and colitis. Milk intolerance because of enzyme deficiency occurs in over 80 percent of Chinese, Japanese, and Eskimo adults and in 60 to 80 percent of Native American, Afro-American, Jewish, and Mexican-American adults. Only people of northern European Caucasian extraction and members of two African tribes tolerate lactose indefinitely and even some aged Whites will have lactose deficiency. Do not automatically teach everyone to drink milk. Calcium can be obtained in other ways: seafoods (cook fish to yield edible bones); leafy vegetables; yogurt, buttermilk, or aged cheese (lactose has been changed to lactic

TABLE 1-9. Assessment of Skin Color

CHARACTERISTIC	WHITE OR LIGHT-SKINNED PERSON	DARK-SKINNED PERSON
Pallor: Vasoconstriction present	Skin takes on white hue, which is color of collagen fibers in subcutaneous connective tissue.	Skin loses underlying red tones. Brown-skinned person appears yellow-brown. Black-skinned person appears ashen-gray. Mucous membranes, lips, nailbeds pale or gray.
Erythema, Inflammation: Cutaneous vasodilation	Skin is red.	Palpate for increased warmth of skin, edema, tightness, or induration of skin.
Cyanosis: Hypoxia of tissues	Bluish tinges of skin, especially in earlobes, as well as in lips, oral mucosa, and nailbeds.	Lips, tongue, conjunctiva, palms, soles of feet are pale or ashen gray. Apply light pressure to create pallor; in cyanosis tissue color returns slowly by spreading from periphery to the center.
Ecchymosis: Deoxygenated blood seeps from broken blood vessel into subcutaneous tissue	Skin changes color from purple-blue to yellow-green to yellow.	Obtain history of trauma and discomfort. Note swelling and induration. Oral mucous membrane or conjunctiva will show color changes from purple-blue to yellow-green to yellow.
Petechiae: Intradermal or submucosal bleeding	Round, pinpoint purplish red spots on skin.	Oral mucosa or conjunctiva show purplish-red spots if person has black skin.
Jaundice: Accumulated bilirubin in tissues	Yellow color in skin, mucous membranes, and sclera of eyes. Light-colored stools and dark urine often occur.	Sclera of eyes, oral mucous membranes, palms of hand and soles of feet have yellow discoloration.

acid during aging); or homemade soup (add vinegar to the water when cooking a soupbone to decalcify the bone). Most ethnic groups have adapted ways of cooking to ensure calcium intake from nondairy sources; listen carefully to their dietary descriptions. If the lactase-deficient person wishes to ingest considerable milk foods, an enzyme product to add to milk, called Lact-Aid, may be purchased from drug or health food stores (86, 158, 177). An acidophilus milk, which contains a controlled culture of lactobacillus acidophilus bacteria, is also easily digested.

Other biological variations exist. Susceptibility to disease varies with blood type. Rh-negative blood type is common in Caucasians, rarer in other groups, and absent in Eskimos. Myopia is more common in Chinese; color blindness is more common in Europeans and East Indians. Nose size and shape correlate with ancestral homeland. Small noses (seen in Asians or Eskimos) were produced in cold regions, high-bridged noses (common to Iranians and American Indians) were common in dry areas; and the flat, broad noses characteristic of some Blacks were adaptive in moist, warm climates (18, 150, 174).

If the person does not speak English as a first language, learn key words of his/her language. Use language dictionaries or a card file of key words.

Breach the language barrier so that your assessment is more accurate and care measures will be understood by the person. Muecke offers practical suggestions to overcome language differences (141).

To aid assessment, learn about the significant religious practices and the everyday patterns of hygiene, eating, types of foods eaten, sleeping, elimination, use of space, and various rituals that are a part of the person's culture. Interference with normal living patterns or practices adds to the stress of being ill. You will encounter and need to adapt care to the following customs: drinking tea instead of coffee with meals, eating the main meal at midday instead of in the evening, refusing to undress before a strange person, doing special hair care as described by Grier (75), avoiding use of the bedpan because someone else must handle its contents, maintaining special religious or ethnic customs, refusing to bathe daily, refusing a pelvic exam by a male doctor, moaning loudly when in pain, and showing unreserved demonstrations of grief when a loved one dies.

Folk medicine practices help the person gain a sense of control over his/her fate. Often the practice does no real harm but can be misinterpreted. For example, a Vietnamese mother used the ancient Chinese practice of cao gio ("scratching the wind") to care for her child's cold. In this practice, the child's chest or back is covered with mentholated oil and then rubbed with a coin or hard object. The striations left on the child's skin, while causing no harm or injury, were interpreted by a health care worker as signs of child abuse. The health care worker reported the family, as required by law, based on her perceptions. The parents were charged, and the father, in fear of jail term and in humiliation, hung himself (66). Be aware of possible folk medicine practices and their terminology, and explore these practices prior to making conclusions about the patient/client.

Some recent immigrants may adhere closely to traditional practices. Others may not. Your assessment cannot be based on assumption or stereotype. In a study by Sheppard of Chinese-American health beliefs and practices, the influence of ethnicity and of other variables was examined. The health behavior activities of exercise, religious practices, lifestyle, and illness behavior activities were reported to be Western in orientation by over 80 percent of the Chinese Americans. In the health behavior activities of dietary practices and the sick behavior measures, a mixture of Chinese and Western practices were reported by over 50 percent of the Chinese Americans. Chinese Americans described more Western practices the longer they lived in the United States. Four influencing variables, (1) the familiarity of the participant to the Western health care systems, (2) language, (3) occupation, and (4) religion, were significant to their described health beliefs, dietary practices, and sick behavior measures (187).

The nursing diagnoses in Table 1-10 may be applicable to your work with people in various cultures.

Intervention

Caring *is assistive, supportive, or facilitative actions toward another person or group with evident or anticipated needs in order to ameliorate or improve a human condition or lifeway* (103, 104). Nurses in different cultures tend to know and emphasize different care constructs such as support, comfort, and touch. Caucasian nurses in the United States, generally believe that care involves use of technological aids, medicines, and psychophysiological comfort measures. Generally, Caucasian and some non-Caucasian patients/clients agree. In several non-Western cultures, nurses and patients/clients perceive care as protective with a sociocultural emphasis. For example, nurses in Turkey and Israel emphasize restorative caring functions because of war activities. Samoan caregivers are expected to protect the person from breaking cultural or social rules in order to prevent illness or harm. Chinese nurses perceive surveillance and protection as dominant caring modes. Depending upon the culture, Leininger states that the concept *care* can mean (103-105):

TABLE 1-10. Selected Nursing Diagnoses Related to Transcultural Nursing[a]

PATTERN 5: CHOOSING
Ineffective Individual Coping
Decreased Conflict
Health Seeking Behaviors

PATTERN 6: MOVING
Altered Health Maintenance

PATTERN 7: PERCEIVING
Powerlessness

PATTERN 8: KNOWING
Knowledge Deficit

[a]Many of the NANDA nursing diagnoses are applicable to an individual in any culture, who is ill.
Source: NANDA Approved Nursing Diagnostic Categories, *Nursing Diagnosis Newsletter*, 15, no. 1 (Summer, 1988), 1-3.

Comfort	Restoration
Support	Direct Assistance
Attention	Helping the Dependent
Compassion	Tenderness
Touch	Trust
Love	Instruction
Stimulation	Succorance
Presence	Empathy
Protection	Medical/Technical
Surveillance	Assistance
Personalized Help	Maintaining Well-Being
Nurturance	
Stress Alleviation	

Respecting the person's need for privacy or need to have others continually around is essential. Understand that some patients or families will not be expressive emotionally or verbally. Respect this pattern, recognizing that nonverbal behavior is also significant. Be aware, too, that word meanings may vary considerably from culture to culture so that the person may have difficulty understanding you and vice versa. Be sure the gesture or touch you use conveys the message you intend. If you are unsure, avoid nonverbal behavior to the extent that you can.

A patient/client with a strict time orientation must take medicines and receive treatments on time or feel neglected. You are expected to give prompt and efficient, but compassionate, service to the patient and family. Time orientation also affects making appointments for the clinic and plans for medication routine or return to work after discharge and influences the person's ideas about how quickly he/she should get well. The person with little future-time orientation has difficulty planning a future clinic appointment or a long-range medication schedule. This person cannot predict now how he/she will feel at a later date and thinks that clinic visits or medicines are unnecessary if he/she feels all right at the moment.

For some patients/clients, the hurrying behavior of the nurse is distressing; it conveys a lack of concern and lack of time to give adequate care. In turn, the person expresses guilt feelings when it is necessary to ask for help. Although you may look very efficient when scurrying, you are likely to miss many observations, cues, and hidden meanings in what the person or family says.

Examine your own attitude about busyness and leisure in order to help others consider leisure as part of life. The disabled person, whose inability to work carries a stigma, must develop a positive attitude about leisure and may seek your help.

Your knowledge of cultures will enable you to practice holistic nursing care, including cultural values and norms in the nursing process. Holistic healing practices combine the best of two worlds: the wisdom and sensitivity of the East and the technology and precision of the West. Although holistic practitioners use conventional therapies in many cases, the emphasis remains on the whole person: physical, emotional, intellectual, spiritual, and sociocultural background. The focus is on prevention and overall fitness and on the individual taking responsibility for his/her own health and well-being. Multiple techniques are used to restore and maintain balance of body energy—the life force. These techniques include exercise, acupuncture, massage, herbal medicine, nutritional changes, manipulation of joints and spine, medications, stress management, and counseling. The nurse–client relationship is the key to holistic nursing care, for the person has come to expect a caring interaction from the healer. The curandera (herb healer) of the Spanish Southwest makes a tea from herbs, for example, and the patient slowly sips the tea. The pain is gone. The client's faith is a major factor in herbal cures—faith in God, the plants, and the curandera. The curandera also has faith in recovery as she shows caring, looks, listens, and heals.

Or the woman in labor who is a product of a parochial background with reliance on lay medical help and suspicious of the impersonal hospital and professional-looking nurses asks to have a knife placed under the bed to help "cut labor pains." While implementing scientific health care, you can be more prepared to act on this belief that psychologically helps the patient. Herbs used by various cultural groups are increasingly found to have medicinal value; they are chemically similar to drugs used by scientific practitioners.

You can incorporate indigenous folk medicine and practitioners into professional and scientific health care practices. The two are not automatically exclusive. For example, in one Navaho nursing care service, the medicine man is an active participant, and Navaho mothers are encouraged to use their infant cradle boards and to be home for the blessing ceremonies (103).

As you intervene, teach, or counsel, adjust your communication approach with and behavior toward the person from another cultural background, since people from most ethnic/racial groups feel uncomfortable initially when interacting with someone who is different. While you may be communicating in a way that is natural to you, someone from another culture may perceive that behavior as too forward or aggressive, too passive, or unempathic. While you cannot assume a different mask for each person you interact with, be aware that the client may misinterpret your well-intentioned behavior. Use general knowledge about a culture while you simultaneously see the individual and unique differences of people. Unfortunately, many nurses are not bilingual. The client who uses English as a second language may not either speak or understand English adequately for you to effectively assess, teach, or intervene in other ways.

In male-dominated households (Spanish-speaking, Asian, Middle Eastern), the male head of house must be included in all decisions and health teaching if you expect to solicit cooperation. In most such families and the Afro-American and Jewish families, there is also an older female relative such as an aunt, mother-in-law, or grandmother, who is the designated health care provider for that family. She must also be included in decision making and health teaching. Speaking to the important family elder with respect will gain you a staunch ally; the desired behavior change will almost certainly be assured (66).

Relations between the patient/client and the family may at times seem offensive or disharmonious to you. Differentiate carefully between patterns of behavior that are culturally induced and expected and those that are unhealthy for the persons involved.

The changing society may cause families to have a variety of problems. Be a supportive listener, validate realistic ideas, prepare the family to adapt to a new or changing environment, and be aware of community agencies or resources that can provide additional help. When a patient/client has no family nearby and seems alone and friendless, you may provide significant support.

Develop a personal philosophy that promotes a

feeling of stability in your life so that you, in turn, can assist the patient/client and family to explore feelings and to formulate a philosophy for coping with change. Toffler speaks about ways in which the person can learn to cope with rapid change. One important way is to develop some ritual or pattern in your personal life that you can practice regardless of where you are and thus maintain some sense of continuity and stability (205).

One way to have a lasting effect on the health practices of a different cultural group is through health teaching that includes a philosophy of prevention. Present-day China compared with China during the 1940s is an example of how public health standards can be effectively raised through an emphasis on prevention. Increasingly your role includes health education, as discussed in Chapter 17. Outsiders cannot make decisions for others, but people should be given sufficient knowledge concerning alternate behavior so that they can make intelligent choices themselves.

Various pressures interfere with attempts at health teaching. Behind poor health habits lie more than ignorance, economic pressure, or selfish desires. Motivation plays a great part in continuing certain practices even though the person has been taught differently by you. Motivation, moreover, is influenced by the person's culture, status, and role in that culture and by social pressures for conformity. Starting programs of prevention can be difficult when people place a low value on health, cannot recognize cause-and-effect relationships in disease, lack future-time orientation, or are confused about the existence of preventive measures in their culture. Thus preventive programs or innovations in health care must be shaped to fit the cultural and health profiles of the population. Long-range prevention goals stand a better chance of implementation if combined with measures to meet immediate needs. A mother is more likely to heed your advice about how to prevent further illness in her sick child if you give the child immediate attention.

Be mindful of how people view you. If they cannot understand you, if you threaten their values, or if they view you as an untouchable professional, you will not cross the cultural barrier.

You may also talk with members of the National Association of Hispanic Nurses, the American Indian/ Alaskan Indian Nurses Association, and the Black Nurses Association in order to gain information about how to give care that includes cultural values and customs.

Cannon, et. al. describe the importance of value clarification as you care for people from diverse cultures (30). The information in this chapter presents information that will aid you in the process of value clarification as well as in the nursing process with the person and family through the life span—as you promote health and care for the ill individual.

References

1. A "Superminority" Tops Out, *Newsweek* (May 11, 1987), 48–49.
2. Aeschleman, Dorothy, Guidelines for Cross-Cultural Health Programs, *Nursing Outlook*, 21, no. 10 (1973), 660–663.
3. Affluent America's Forgotten Children, *Newsweek* (June 2, 1986), 20–21.
4. Aichlmayr, Rita, Cultural Understanding: A Key to Acceptance, *Nursing Outlook*, 17, no. 7 (1969), 20–23.
5. Ailinger, Rita, A Study of Illness Referral in a Spanish Speaking Community, *Nursing Research*, 26, no. 1 (1977), 53–56.
6. Ali, Yousfi, transl., *The Holy Quran*.
7. America's New Migrant Workers, *Newsweek* (August 3, 1987), 34–35.
8. Anderson, Gwen, and Bridget Tighs, Gypsy Culture and Health Care, *American Journal of Nursing*, 73, no. 2 (1973), 282–285.
9. Anthony-Tkach, Catherine, Care of the Mexican-American Patient, *Nursing and Health Care*, 2, no. 8 (1981), 424–432.
10. Azzi, Robert, Saudi Arabia: The Kingdom and Its Power, *National Geographic* 158, no. 3 (1980), 286–344.
11. Baca, Josephine, Some Health Beliefs of the Spanish Speaking, *American Journal of Nursing*, 69, no. 10 (1969), 2172–276.
12. Beare, Patricia, Nursing Education Comes into Its Own in Saudi Arabia, *Nursing and Health Care*, 8, no. 5 (1987), 272–274.
13. Becher, Marshall, et al., A New Approach to Explaining Sick-Role Behavior in Low-Income Populations, *American Journal of Public Health*, 64, no. 3 (1974), 205–215.
14. Beeman, W. O., What Is (Iranian) National Character? A Sociological Approach, *Iranian Studies* (Winter, 1976), 22–48.
15. Bernadino, Stephanie, *The Ethnic Almanac*. Garden City, NY: Doubleday, 1981.
16. Billingsley, A., *Black Families and the Struggle for Survival: Teaching Our Children to Walk Tall*. New York: Friendship Press, 1974.
17. Birkert-Smith, K., *Eskimos*. New York: Crown Publishers, 1971.
18. Block, Bobbie, and Mary Hunter, Teaching Physiological Assessment of Black Persons, *Nurse Educator*, 6, no. 1 (1981), 24–27.
19. Bouws, Beth, Working with Albanian Families, *American Journal of Nursing*, 74, no. 5 (1974), 902–905.

20. Branch, Marie, and Phyllis Paxton, *Providing Safe Nursing Care for Ethnic People of Color*. New York: Appleton-Century-Crofts, 1976.
21. Briggs, J. L., *Never in Anger, Portrait of an Eskimo Family*. Cambridge, MA: Harvard University Press, 1970.
22. Brink, Pamela, ed., *Transcultural Nursing*. Englewood Cliffs, NJ: Prentice-Hall, 1976.
23. Brink, Pamela, Value Orientations as an Assessment Tool in Cultural Diversity, *Nursing Research*, 33, no. 4 (1984), 198–203.
24. Bronfenbrenner, Urie, The Split-Level American Home, in *Human Life Cycle*, ed. William Sze. New York: Jason Aronson, 1975, 179–191.
25. Brower, H. Terri, Culture and Nursing in China, *Nursing and Health Care*, 5, no. 1 (1984), 26–31.
26. Brown, Patricia, The Victorian Age Is Upon Us Again, *St. Louis Post-Dispatch*, July 1, 1987, Sec. F, pp. 4,6.
27. Bullough, Vern L., and Bonnie Bullough, *Health Care for the Other Americans*. New York: Appleton-Century-Crofts, 1982.
28. Cadena, Maxine, The Mexican-American Family and the Mexican-American Nurse, in *Family Health Care*, eds., Debra Hymovich and Martha Barnard. New York: McGraw-Hill, 1979.
29. Campbell, Teresa, and Betty Chung, Health Care of the Chinese in America, *Nursing Outlook*, 21, no. 4 (1973), 245–249.
30. Cannon, Rose, et al., A Values Clarification Approach to Cultural Diversity, *Nursing and Health Care*, 5, no. 3 (1984), 161–164.
31. Chilman, Catherine, Child Rearing and Family Relationship Patterns of the Very Poor, in *Human Life Cycle*, ed., William Sze. New York: Jason Aronson, 1975, 143–154.
32. Clemen-Stone, Susan, Diane Eigsti, and Sandra McGuire, *Comprehensive Family and Community Health Nursing* (2nd ed.). New York: McGraw-Hill, 1987.
33. Coakley, T. Anne, Paul Ehrlich, and Elaine Hurd, Southeast Asian Refugees: Health Screening in a Family Clinic, *American Journal of Nursing*, 80, no. 11 (1980), 2032–2036.
34. Cohen, Susan, et al., *Culture of Poverty Revisited*. New York: Mental Health Committee Against Racism, n.d.
35. Coles, Robert, The Children of Affluence, *The Atlantic Monthly*, September 1977, pp. 53–66.
36. ———, *Eskimos, Chicanos, Indians*. Boston: Little, Brown, 1978.
37. Coles, Robert, *Children of Crisis: Vol 5—Privileged Ones, The Well Off, and Rich in America*. Boston: Little, Brown, 1978.
38. Comer, James, *Beyond Black and White*. New York: Quadrangle Books, 1972.
39. ———, and Alvin Poussaint, *Black Child Care*. New York: Simon & Schuster, 1975.
40. Cook, H., *Cultural Policy in German Democratic Republic*. Paris: Unesco Press, 1975
41. Coopersmith, Stanley, *The Antecedents of Self Esteem*. San Francisco: W.H. Freeman, 1967.
42. Cordasco, Francesco, ed., *Studies in Italian American Social History*. Totowa, NJ: Rowman and Littlefield, 1975.
43. Darabi, Katherine, and Vilma Ortuz, Childbearing Among Young Latino Women in The United States, *American Journal of Public Health*, 77, no. 1 (1987), 25–28.
44. Davis, Mardell, Getting to the Root of the Problem, *Nursing '77*, 7, no. 4 (1977), 60–65.
45. Davitz, Lois, Y. Sameshima, and J. Davitz, Suffering as Viewed in Six Different Cultures, *American Journal of Nursing*, 76, no. 8 (1976), 1296–1297.
46. DeGracio, Rosario, Filipino Cultural Influences, *American Journal of Nursing*, 79, no. 8 (1979), 1412–1414.
47. DeLaguna, Frederica, *Voyage to Greenland*. New York: W.W. Norton, Inc., 1977.
48. Deutsch, Elizabeth, A Stereotype—or an Individual? *Nursing Outlook*, 19, no. 2 (1971), 106–108.
49. Dilliard, J., Negro Children's Dialect in the Inner City, *Florida FL Reporter*, Fall 1967.
50. ———, Non-Standard Negro Dialects: Convergence or Divergence? *Florida FL Reporter*, Fall 1968, pp. 9–12.
51. Dorio, Josephine, and Mary Nelson, China's Caring Is the Same, *Nursing Outlook*, 31, no. 2 (1983), 100–104.
52. Dorson, R., *American Folklores*. Chicago: The University of Chicago Press, 1977.
53. Dumond, Don E., *The Eskimos and the Aleuts*. London: Thames and Hudson, 1977.
54. Duvall, Evelyn and Brent Miller, *Marriage and Family Development* (6th ed). New Yorker: Harper and Row, 1984.
55. Ehling, M. B., The Mexican American (el chicano), in *Cultural and Childrearing*, ed. A. L. Clark. Philadelphia: F. A. Davis, 1981.
56. Ehrenreich, Barbara, and Karin Stallard, The Nouveau Poor, *The New Day*, 14, no. 4 (1982), 1.
57. Erkel, E. A., The Implications of Cultural Conflict for Health Care, *Health Values: Achieving High Level Wellness*, 4 (1981), 51–57.
58. *Ethnicity and Health Care*. New York: National League for Nursing, 1976.
59. Evans, R.J., *German Family Life*. London: Croom Helm, 1982.
60. Farhood, Laila, and Richard Day, Nursing Interventions in Wartime, *Journal of Psychosocial Nursing*, 24, no. 7 (1986), 25–29.
61. Feinman, Saul, Trends in Racial Self-Image of Black Children: Psychological Consequences of a Social Movement, *Journal of Negro Education*, 48, no. 4 (1979). 488–499.

62. Feldman, Saul, *Life Styles*. Boston: Little Brown, 1975.
63. Fitzpatrick, Joseph, *Puerto Rican Americans: The Meaning of Migration to the Mainland*. Englewood Cliffs, NJ: Prentice-Hall, 1971.
64. Flaskerud, Jacquelyn, Perceptions of Problematic Behavior by Appalachians, Mental Health Professionals, and Lay Non-Appalachians, *Nursing Research*, 29, no. 3 (1980), 140–149.
65. Floriani, Carol, Southeast Asian Refugees: Life in a Camp, *American Journal of Nursing*, 80, no. 11 (1980), 2028–2030.
66. Folk Medicine, *California Nursing Today* (January, 1986), 2, 13, 20.
67. Fraser, John, *The Portrait of a Chinese People*. New York: Summit Books, 1980.
68. Friedman, Marilyn, *Family Nursing: Theory and Assessment* (2nd ed.). Norwalk, CT: Appleton-Century-Crofts, 1985.
69. Glenn, Max, *Appalachia in Transition*. St. Louis: Bethany Press, 1970.
70. Gillette, Ned, Adventure in Western China, *National Geographic*, 159, no., 2 (1981), 174–192.
71. Gomez, Efran, and Ninfa Carazos, Was Hexing the Cause of Death. *American Journal of Social Psychiatry*, 1, no. 1 (April, 1981), 50–52.
72. Good, B. J., The Heart of What's the Matter, *Culture, Medicine, and Psychiatry*, 1 (1977) 25–58.
73. Gordon, Verona, Irene Matonsek, and Theresa Lang, Southeast Asian Refugees: Life in America, *American Journal of Nursing*, 80, no. 11 (1980), 2031–2036.
74. Graham, Judith, *Another Mother Tongue*. New York: Beacon Press, 1984.
75. Grier, Margaret, Hair Care for the Black Patient, *American Journal of Nursing*, 76, no. 11 (1976), 1781.
76. Grossberg, Kenneth A., ed., *Japan Today*. Philadelphia: Ishi Institute for Study of Human Issues, 1981.
77. Guralnik, David, ed., *Webster's New World Dictionary of the American Language* (2nd college ed.). New York: World, 1972.
78. Harris, Ralph, et al., The Child-Adolescent Blood Pressure Study: Distribution of Blood Pressure Levels in Seventh Day Adventist (SDA) and Non-SDA Children, *American Journal of Public Health*, 71, no. 12 (1981), 1342–1348.
79. Hathout, M., Comment on Ethical Crisis and Cultural Differences, *The Western Journal of Medicine*, 139, no. 3 (1983), 380–381.
80. Health in America Closely Linked to Income Level, *The Nation's Health* (October–November, 1985), 1, 15.
81. Hecker, Melvin, and Fenton Heike, eds., *The Greeks in America, 1528–1977*. Dobbs Ferry, NY: Oceana, Publishers, 1978.
82. Henry, Beverly, and Elizabeth Di Giacomo-Geffers, The Hospitalized Rich and Famous, *American Journal of Nursing*, 80, no. 8 (1980), 1426–1429.
83. Hill, R. *The Strengths of Black Families*. New York: Emerson Hall, 1972.
84. Hispanic Latino—What's In a Name? *American Journal of Public Health*, 77, no. 1 (1987), 15–17.
85. Holck, Susan, et al., Lung Cancer Mortality and Smoking Habits: Mexican-American Women, *American Journal of Public Health*, 72, no. 1 (1982), 38–42.
86. Hongladarom, Gail, and Millie Russell, An Ethnic Difference—Lactose Intolerance, *Nursing Outlook*, 24, no. 12 (1976), 764–765.
87. Horn, Beverly, Cultural Concepts and Postpartal Care, *Nursing and Health Care*, 2, no. 11 (1981), 516–517, 526–527.
88. Hostetler, J.A., *Amish Society*. Baltimore, MD: The John Hopkins University Press, 1974.
89. How Are Things in Your Neigbhorhood? *Graduate Woman* (March–April 1980), 17 ff.
90. How to Win Over a Japanese Boss, *Newsweek*, February 2, 1987, 46–48.
91. Hutchinson, Sarah, The American Indian Senior Citizens View of Women, *Bulletin of American Association of Social Psychiatry*, 1, no 3 (1980), 13–15.
92. Hutto, Ruth, Poverty's Children, *American Journal of Nursing*, 69, no. 10 (1969), 2166–2169.
93. Jacobson, Mark, Mary Mercer, Linda Miller, et al., Tuberculosis Risk Among Migrant Farm Workers on the Delmarva Peninsula, *American Journal of Public Health*, 77, no. 1 (1987), 29–31.
94. Kimball, Stanley, The Polish Presence in Illinois, *Alumnus—Southern Illinois University at Edwardsville*, Fall, 1986, 5–7.
95. Kluckhorn, Florence, Family Diagnosis: Variations in Basic Values of Family Systems, *Social Casework*, 32 (February-March 1958), 63–72.
96. Kluckhorn, Florence, and E. Strodtbeck, *Variations in Value Orientations*. New York: Row, Petersen, 1961.
97. Kniep-Hardy, Mary, and Margaret Burkhardt, Nursing the Navaho, *American Journal of Nursing*, 77, no. 1 (1977), 95–96.
98. Kohn, Melvin, Social Class and Parent-Child Relationships, in *Human Life Cycle*, ed. Wm. Sze. New York: Jason Aronson, 1975, pp. 541–553.
99. Kosko, Debra, and Jacquelyn Flaskerad, Mexican American Nurse Practitioner, and Lay Control Group Beliefs About Cause and Treatment of Chest Pain, *Nursing Research*, 36, no. 4 (1987), 226–231.
100. Leininger, Madeline, *Nursing and Anthropology: Two Worlds to Blend*. New York: John Wiley, 1970.
101. Leininger, Madeleine, *Transcultural Nursing: Concepts, Theories, and Practices*. New York: John Wiley, 1978.
102. Leininger, Madeline, *Transcultural Nursing*. New York: Masson, 1979.
103. Leininger, Madeline, Caring: A Central Focus of Nursing and Health Care Services, *Nursing and Health Care*, 1, no. 10 (1980), 135–143.

104. Leininger, Madeleine, *Care: The Essence of Nursing and Health*. Thorofare, NJ: Charles B. Slack, 1984.
105. Leininger, Madeleine, Transcultural Nursing: An Overview, *Nursing Outlook*, 32, no. 2 (1984), 72.
106. Leonard, Sister Margaret Ann, and Sister Carol Ann Joyce, Two Worlds United, *American Journal of Nursing*, 71, no. 6 (1971), 1152–1155.
107. Lidz, Theodore, *The Person: His and Her Development Throughout the Life Cycle* (2nd ed.). New York: Basic Books, 1983.
108. Lin, Yuen Chow, China: Health Care in Transition, *Nursing Outlook*, 31, no. 2 (1983), 94–99.
109. Lipson, J. G., and Afaf Meleis, Issues in Health Care of Middle Eastern Patients *The Western Journal of Medicine*, 139, no. 6 (1983), 854–861.
110. Lipson, J. G., and Afaf Meleis, Culturally Appropriate Care: The Case of Immigrants, *TCN*, 7, no. 3 (1985), 48–56.
111. Lopata, H., *Polish Americans*. Englewood Cliffs, NJ: Prentice-Hall, Inc., 1976.
112. Loughlin, B., Pregnancy in the Navajo Culture, *Nursing Outlook*, 13, no. 3 (1965), 55–58.
113. Lykins, Robert, Children of the Third Culture, *Kappa Delta Pi Record*, Winter, 1985, 39–43.
114. Lynn, F., An American Nurse Visits Two Mental Hospitals in Greece, *Nursing Outlook*, 14, no. 12 (1966), 50–53.
115. McCabe, Gracia, Cultural Influences on Patient Behavior, *American Journal of Nursing*, 60, no. 8 (1960), 1101–1104.
116. McEvoy, Larry, and Garland Land, Life Style and Death Patterns of the Missouri RLD's Church Members, *American Journal of Public Health*, 71, no. 12 (1981), 1350–1356.
117. McGregor, Frances, Uncooperative Patients: Some Cultural Interpretations, *American Journal of Nursing*, 67, no. 1 (1967), 88–91.
118. McKenzie, Joan, and Noel Chrisman, Healing Herbs, Gods, and Magic: Folk Health Beliefs Among Filipino-Americans, *Nursing Outlook*, 26, no. 5 (1977), 326–329.
119. MacDonald, Anne, Folk Health Practices Among North Coastal Peruvians: Implications for Nursing, *Image*, 13, no. 6 (1981), 51–56.
120. Malmstrom, Jean, Dialects—Updated, *Florida FL Reporter*, Spring-Summer 1969.
121. Mandel, Marjorie, Hard Times Displace the New Homeless, *St. Louis Post-Dispatch*, May 2, 1982, Sec. A., p. 7.
122. Manfredi, Maricel, Primary Health Care and Nursing Education in Latin America, *Nursing Outlook*, 31, no. 2 (1983), 105–108.
123. Martines, Edward, *The Mexican American*. Boston: Houghton Mifflin, 1973.
124. Mason, Diana, Perspectives on Poverty, *Image*, 13, no. 3 (1981), 82–88.
125. Mead, Margaret, *Cultural Patterns and Technical Change*. New York: The New American Library, Mentor Books, 1955.
126. Meleis, Afaf, The Arab American in the Health Care System, *American Journal of Nursing*, 81, no. 6 (1981), 1880–1883.
127. Meleis, Afaf, Arab American Women and Their Birth Experience *MCN*, 6, no. 3 (1981), 171–176
128. Meleis, Afaf, and A. R. Jansen, Ethical Crisis and Cultural Differences, *The Western Journal of Medicine*, 138, no. 6 (1983), 889–893.
129. Meleis, Afaf, and Catherine LaFever, The Arab American and Psychiatric Care, *Perspectives in Psychiatric Care*, 22, no. 2 (1984), 72–86.
130. Memorizing vs. Thinking, *Newsweek*, January 12, 1987, 60–61.
131. Millar, Wayne, and Thomas Stephens, The Prevalence of Overweight and Obesity in Britain, Canada, and the United States, *American Journal of Public Health*, 77, no. 1 (1987), 38–41.
132. Moccia, Patricia, and Diana Mason, Poverty Trends: Implications for Nursing, *Nursing Outlook*, 34, no. 1 (1986), 20–24.
133. Mohseni, M., and A. A. Alemi, A Causal Concept of Disease in an Iranian Community, *Journal Biosocial Science*, 10 (1978), 347–351.
134. Momatink, Yva, and John Eastcott, Poland's Mountain People, *National Geographic*, 159, no. 1 (1981), 104–129.
135. Monroe, Sylvester, Brothers, *Newsweek* (March 23, 1987), 54–85.
136. Moore, John, *Mexican-Americans*. Englewood Cliffs, NJ: Prentice-Hall, 1976.
137. Moore, L. G., P. W. VanArsdale, J. E. Glittenberg, et al., *The Biocultural Basis of Health Care*. St. Louis: C. V. Mosby, 1980.
138. Morgan, Lael, *And the Land Provides: Alaskan Natives in a Year of Transition*. Garden City, NY: Anchor Press/Doubleday & Co., 1974.
139. Moses, Marion, Viva in Causa, *American Journal of Nursing*, 73, no. 5 (1973), 843–848
140. Mott, Paul E. *The Organization of Society*. Englewood Cliffs, NJ: Prentice-Hall, 1976.
141. Muecke, Marjorie, Overcoming the Language Barrier, *Nursing Outlook*, 22, no. 4 (1970), 53–54.
142. Mummah, R., Sakaguchi San and I Had a Contract: A Nurse Helps a Patient Surmount Seemingly Insurmountable Setbacks, *Nursing '78*, 8, no. 12 (1978), 36, 38.
143. Murillo, N., The Mexican American Family, in *Chicanos: Social and Psychological Perspectives*, eds. C. A. Hernandez, M. J. Haug, and N. W. Wagner. St. Louis: C. V. Mosby, 1976.
144. Murphy, Patricia, Tuberculosis Control in San Francisco's Chinatown, *American Journal of Nursing*, 70, no. 5 (1970), 1044–1046.

145. Naimann, H., Nursing in Jewish Law, *American Journal of Nursing*, 70, no. 11 (1970), 2378–2379.
146. Naisbitt, J., *Megatrends*. New York: Warner Books, 1982.
147. Newman, Monroe, *The Political Economy of Appalachia*. Lexington, MA: D. C. Heath, 1972.
148. Norbury, Paul, ed. *Introducing Japan*. New York: St. Martin's Press, 1977.
149. Orque, Modesta, Bobbie Bloch, and Lidia Monrroy, *Ethnic Nursing Care: A Multi-cultural Approach*. St. Louis: C.V. Mosby, 1983.
150. Overfield, Theresa, Biological Variations: Concepts from Physical Anthropology, *Nursing Clinics of North America*, 12, no. 1 (1977), 19–26.
151. Page, Jake, Inside the Sacred Hopi Homeland, *National Geographic*, 162, no. 5 (1982), 607–629.
152. Park, Jeanne, Children Who Follow the Sun, *Today's Education* (January–February 1976) 53–56.
153. Parker, S., and R. J. Kleiner, The Culture of Poverty: An Adjustive Dimension, *American Anthropologist*, 72 (1970), 516–527.
154. Patrick, D., Y. Sittampalam, S. Somerville, et al., A Cross-Cultural Comparison of Health Status Values, *American Journal of Public Health*, 75, no. 12 (1985), 1402–1407.
155. Paynich, M., Cultural Barriers to Nurse Communication, *American Journal of Nursing*, 64, no. 2 (1964), 87–90.
156. Pedersen, P., J. Draguns, W. Lonner, J. Trible (eds.), *Counseling Across Cultures*. Honolulu, University of Hawaii Press, 1981.
157. Persad, Emmanuel, Some Cultural Factors in Psychiatric Training, *Canadian Mental Health*, 19, nos. 3–4 (1971), 11–15.
158. Pinkney, Alphonse, *Black Americans*. Englewood Cliffs, NJ: Prentice-Hall, 1975.
159. Pipes, Peggy, *Nutrition in Infancy and Childhood* (3rd ed.). St. Louis: Times Mirror/Mosby, 1985.
160. Poverty: Drain on Health Reaffirmed, *St. Louis Globe Democrat*, June 26, 1986, Sec A, p. 6.
161. Poverty Level Declines: Largest Drop Since 1976, *The Nation's Health* (October–November, 1985), 10.
162. Prather, Jeffrey L., *A Mere Reflection: The Psychodynamics of Black and Hispanic Psychology*. Ardmore, PA: Dorrance, 1977.
163. Prattes, Ora, Beliefs of the Mexican-American Family, in *Family Health Care*, eds. Debra Hymovich and Martha Barnard. New York: McGraw-Hill, 1973, pp. 128–137.
164. Primeaux, Martha, Caring for the American Indian Patient, *American Journal of Nursing*, 77, no. 1 (1977), 91–94.
165. ———, American Indian Health Care Practices, *Nursing Clinics of North America*, 12, no. 1 (1977), 55–65.
166. Prittie, T., *Germany*. New York: Time Incorporation, 1981.
167. Proctor, Pamela, Rich Women Who Work for Fun and Profit, *Parade* (January 23, 1977), 12–14.
168. Putman, John, China's Opening Door, *National Geographic*, 164, no. 1 (1983), 64–83.
169. Rafferty, M., *The Ozarks: Land and Life*. Tulsa, Oklahoma: The University of Oklahoma Press, 1980.
170. Rainwater, Lee, Crucible of Identity: The Negro Lower Class Family, in *Human Life Cycle*, ed. Wm. Sze. New York: Jason Aronson, 1975, pp. 109–142.
171. Reder, Nancy, In Search of Welfare Solutions, *The National Voter*, 37, no. 1 (May, 1987), 9–12.
172. Richards, Bill, The Uncertain State of Puerto Rico, *National Geographic*, 163, no. 4 (1983), 516–543.
173. Rippley, La Vern J., *The German-Americans*. Boston: Twayne Publishers, Division of G. K. Hall, 1976.
174. Roach, Lora, Assessment: Color Changes in Dark Skin, *Nursing '77*, 7, no. 1 (1977), 48–51.
175. Rohrbough, M.J., *The Trans-Appalachian Frontier*. New York: Oxford University Press, 1978.
176. Rose, Peter I., ed., *Nation of Nations: The Ethnic Experience and the Racial Crisis*. New York: Random House, 1972.
177. Rosenberg, Frances, Lactose Intolerance, *American Journal of Nursing*, 77, no. 5 (1977), 823–824.
178. Rubel, Arthur, Concepts of Disease in Mexican-American Culture, *American Anthropologist*, 62 (1960), 795–814.
179. Samet, Jonathan, et al., Respiratory Disease Mortality in New Mexico's American Indians and Hispanics, *American Journal of Public Health*, 70, no. 5 (1980), 492–497.
180. Sanders, I., and E. Morawska, *Polish American Community Life: A Survey of Research*. Boston: Boston University Press, 1975.
181. Sargis, Nancy, Judith Jennrich, and Kathleen Murray, Housing Conditions and Health: A Crucial Link, *Nursing and Health Care*, 8, no. 3 (1987), 335–338.
182. Schalk, Adolph, *The Germans*. Englewood Cliffs, NJ: Prentice-Hall, 1971.
183. Schmidt, Cheryl, Five Become a Team in Appalachia, *American Journal of Nursing*, 75, no. 8 (1975), 1314–1315.
184. Schneider, V., Letter from Lambarene, *American Journal of Nursing*, 65, no. 10 (1965), 128–130.
185. Schroeder, Albert, ed., *The Changing Ways of Southwestern Indians: A Historic Prospective*. Glorietta, NM: The Rio Grande Press, 1973.
186. Seidell, Jacob, Karel Bakx, Paul Deurenberg, et al., The Relation Between Overweight and Subjective Health According to Age, Social Class, Slimming Behavior, and Smoking Habits in Dutch Adults, *American Journal of Public Health*, 76, no. 2 (1986), 1410–1415.
187. Sheppard, Diane, Chinese American Health Beliefs and Practices and Influencing Variables. Unpublished paper presented at Fourteenth Annual Research Con-

ference, St. Louis University School of Nursing, St. Louis, MO, October 28, 1987.
188. Smith, Griffin, The Mexican Americans: A People on the Move, *National Geographic*, 157, no. 6 (1980), 780–808.
189. Smith, Mary, Transformation: A Key To Shaping Nursing, *Image*, 16, no. 1 (Winter, 1984), 28–30.
190. Sowell, Thomas, *Ethnic America: A History*. New York: Basic Books, 1981.
191. Spector, Rachel, E. *Cultural Diversity in Health and Illness*. New York: Appleton-Century-Crofts, 1978.
192. Stanley, Margaret, China: Then and Now, *American Journal of Nursing*, 72, no. 12 (1972), 2213–2218.
193. Starfield, Barbara, Child Health and Socioeconomic Status, *American Journal of Public Health*, 72, no. 6 (1982), 532–533.
194. Starting Out Poor: A World Called Desire, *Newsweek* (June 2, 1986), 23–24.
195. Stern, Phyllis, Solving Problems of Cross-Cultural Health Teaching: The Filipino Childbearing Family, *Image*, 13, no. 6 (1981), 47–50.
196. Stewart, W., Sociolinguistic Factors in the History of American Negro Dialects, *Florida FL Reporter*, Spring 1967.
197. ———, Continuity and Change in American Negro Dialects, *Florida FL Reporter*, Spring 1968.
198. Sue, D., *Counseling the Culturally Different: Theory and Practice*. New York: John Wiley, 1981.
199. Sullivan, Nancy, and Susan Fedem, Poverty's Drain on Health Reaffirmed, *St. Louis Globe-Democrat*, June 26, 1985, Sec. A, p. 6.
200. Tao-Kim-Hai, A., Orientals Are Stoic, in *Social Interaction and Patient Care*, eds. J. Skipper and R. Leonard. Philadelphia: J. B. Lippincott, 1965, pp. 142–155.
201. Tarshis, Barry, *The Average American Book*. Saddle Brook, NJ: American Book-Stratford Press, 1979.
202. The Face and Faith of Poland, *National Geographic*, 161, no. 4 (1982), Supplement.
203. Thiederman, Sondra, Ethnocentrism: A Barrier to Effective Health Care, *The Nurse Practitioner* (August, 1986), 52–59.
204. Thornton, J., Developing a Rural Nursing Clinic, *Nurse Educator*, no. 3, (Summer, 1983).
205. Toffler, Alvin, *Future Shock*. New York: Bantam Books, 1970.
206. Tripp-Reimer, Toni, and Mary Friedl, Appalachians: A Neglected Minority, *Nursing Clinics of North America*, 12, no. 1 (1977), 41–54.
207. Tripp-Reimer, Toni, Pamela Brink, and Judith Saunders, Cultural Assessment: Content and Process, *Nursing Outlook*, 32, no. 2 (1984), 78–82.
208. von Bertalanffy, Ludwig, *General System Theory*. New York: George Braziller, 1968.
209. Vuong, G. Thuy, *Getting to Know the Vietnamese*. New York: Frederick Unger, 1976.
210. Walker, G. M., Utilization of Health Care: The Laredo Migrant Experience, *American Journal of Public Health*, 69 (1979), 667–672.
211. Wallace, Louella Thornton, Patient Is an American Indian, *Supervisor Nurse* (May 1977), 22–23.
212. Wax, Murray, *Indian American: Unity and Diversity*. Englewood Cliffs, NJ: Prentice-Hall, 1971.
213. Weber, Max, *The Protestant Ethic and the Spirit of Capitalism*, trans. Talcott Parsons. New York: Charles Scribner's Sons, 1930; students' edition, 1958.
214. Weddle, D., Indian Pow-Wow, *Globe Democrat Sunday Magazine*, October 12, 1975, pp. 6–11.
215. Weiss, M. Olga, Cultural Shock, *Nursing Outlook*, 19, no. 1 (1971), 40–43.
216. White, Earnestine, Health and the Black Person: An Annotated Bibliography, *American Journal of Nursing*, 74, no. 10 (1974), 1839–1841.
217. ———, Giving Health Care to Minority Patients, *Nursing Clinics of North America*, 12, no. 1 (1977), 27–40.
218. White, Peter, To Be Indomitable, to Be Joyous: Greece, *National Geographic*, 157, no. 3 (1980), 360–393.
219. Wigginton, Eliot, *The Foxfire Books*, Vols. 1–5. Garden City, New York: Anchor Press/Doubleday, 1979.
220. Williams, Dennis, Black Problems Become White, *Newsweek*, August 18, 1986, 7.
221. Williams, Phoebe, A Comparison of Philippine and American Children's Concepts of Body Organs and Illness in Relation to Five Variables, *International Journal of Nursing Studies*, 15 (1978), 193–202.
222. Willie, Charles, The Black Family and Social Class, *The American Journal of Orthopsychiatry*, 44, no. 1 (1974), 50–60.
223. Wisdom of the Elders: Mississippi Choctaws, *AARP News Bulletin*, 27, no. 11 (December, 1986), 5.
224. Yuki, Trudy, Caring for the Urban American Indian Patient, *Journal of Emergency Nursing*, 7, no. 3 (1981), 110–113.
225. Zabilka, Gladys, *Customs and Culture of the Philippines*. Rutland, VT: Charles E. Tuttle, 1970.
226. Zborowski, Mark, Cultural Components in Response to Pain, in *Sociological Studies of Health and Sickness*, ed. Dorrian Apple. New York: McGraw-Hill, 1960, pp. 118–133.
227. Zola, Irving Kenneth, Culture and Symptoms: An Analysis of Patients Presenting Complaints, *American Sociological Review*, 31, (October, 1966), 615–631.

2

Environmental Influences on the Development and Health of the Person and Family

Study of this chapter will help you to

1. Explore the scope of environmental pollution, both outdoor and indoor, and the interrelationship of the different kinds of pollution with one another and with people.
2. Observe sources of air pollution in your community and identify resulting hazards to human health.
3. List types of water pollution and describe resultant health problems.
4. Describe substances that cause soil pollution and the effect of these substances on the food web as well as on other facets of health.
5. Discuss the types of food pollution and ways to prevent food contamination.
6. Listen to noise pollution in various settings and discuss its long-term effects on health.
7. Contrast the different types of surface pollution and resultant health problems.
8. Discuss health hazards that are encountered in the home and on the job and the major effects of these contaminants.
9. Discuss and practice ways that, as a citizen, you can reduce environmental pollution.
10. Discuss your professional responsibility in assessing for illness caused by environmental pollutants and in taking general intervention measures.
11. Demonstrate an ability to help establish a therapeutic milieu for a patient/client.

Key Terms

Perfect complete combustion
Perfect incomplete combustion
Carbon monoxide
Sulfur oxide compounds
Sulfur dioxide
Nitrogen oxide
Nitrogen dioxide
Particulate matter
Hydrocarbons
Acid rain
Radioactive substances
Radon
Pesticides
Food additives
Zoonoses
Sound overload
Decibels
Recycled
Hazardous waste
Pica
Teratogenic
Mutagenic
Therapeutic milieu

Although ecology is a well-publicized subject, often the physical environment in which we live is taken for granted and overlooked as a direct influence on people and their health. You may wonder why a unit discussing major influences on the developing person, family unit, and their health contains a chapter about humans and their environment. Yet where we live and the condition of that area—its air, water, and soil—determine to a great extent how we live, what we eat, the disease agents to which we are exposed, our state of health, and our ability to adapt. This chapter focuses primarily on noxious agents to which many people in the United States are exposed in the external environment. Because of the interdependence of people, only those living in isolated rural areas escape the unpleasant effects of our urban, technologically advanced society. Yet even the isolated few may encounter some kind of environmental pollution, whether through groundwater contaminated from afar, food shipped into the area, smog blown from a nearby city, or contaminated rain or snow.

🖙 Nursing in the past was concerned primarily with the patient's immediate environment in the hospital or home. Today nursing is extended to include assessment of the family and community as well as the individual. Intervention measures are directed toward promoting a healthy environment for the person and family, well or ill, and maintaining public health standards and federal regulations. Understanding some specific environmental health problems, their sources and effects, will enable you to function both as a citizen and as a professional nurse to help prevent or correct those problems. Teach about prevention of and effects from the pollutants described in this chapter as you care for people in the agency, home, or community.

Historical Perspective

The natural components of the environment were once considered dangerous. In most instances, people dealt successfully with any environmental problems encountered. In their quest to conquer nature, early people discovered fire and the wheel. Fire was essential to survival; but with its advent, natural or manmade sparks and pollutants were sent into the atmosphere—the beginning of environmental pollution.

The fire and the wheel played major roles in the early civilization and industrialization of the world. With the Industrial Revolution came many technological advances that gave people increased power and comforts. These advances also introduced artificial, chemical, and physical hazards into the environment. Soon after the start of the Industrial Revolution, the population of cities grew; disease spread with the crowding of people, and food distribution became more complex. It became apparent that the natural components of the environment were not as dangerous as the manmade components.

The entire environment has been and is a vital part of our existence. Human skill in manipulating the environment has produced tremendous benefits; but none has been without a price, the high price of pollution. Pollution of our environment is not only a health threat but also offends esthetic, spiritual, social, and philosophic values. Environmental pollution is a complex, significant problem requiring multiple solutions (Fig. 2–1).

Antipollution legislation in the United States can be traced back to the early 1900s. In 1906 the first federal Food and Drug Act was passed, and in 1914 drinking water standards were enacted to serve as guides for water supplied on interstate carriers. Congress passed the federal Water Pollution Control Act in 1948. Most of these legislative moves were poorly funded and supported, however, and so had little effect on growing pollution problems. Finally in the early 1960s Congress began taking a firm and leading role in combating environmental pollution. The Clean Air and Solid Waste Disposal Act of 1965 and the Clean Water Restoration Act of 1966 are examples of this attempt to fight pollution (47, 109). The United States Environmental Protection Agency (EPA) was created in 1970 to consolidate, strengthen, and coordinate federal efforts. Several important laws were passed after the formation of the EPA, for example, Clean Water Act (1972), Pesticides Control Act (1972), Safe Drinking Water Act (1974), Resource Conservation and Recovery Act (1976), and Toxic Substances Con-

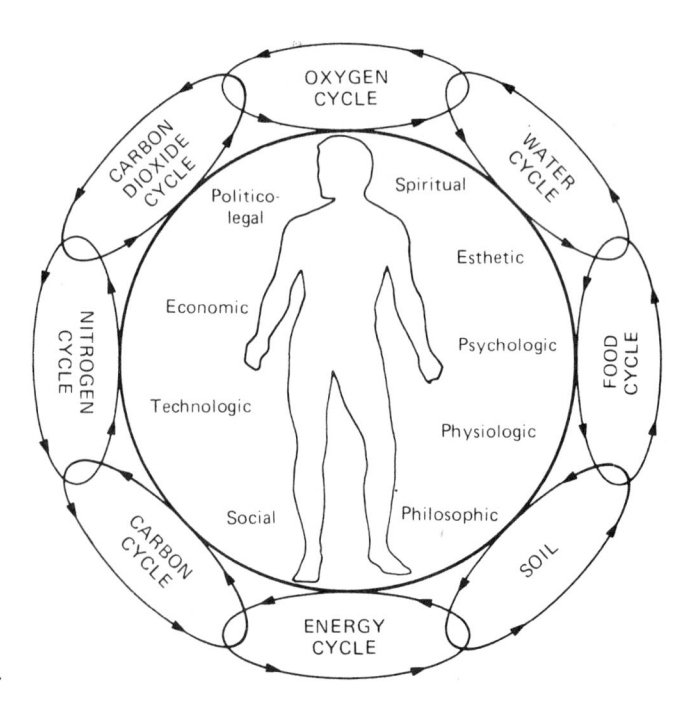

Figure 2–1. The Person's Interrelationship with the Environment.

trol Act (1976). The Toxic Substances Control Act was the first attempt to provide comprehensive regulation of potentially dangerous chemical substances. The Resource Conservation and Recovery Act gave the EPA the power to track hazardous wastes from generation site to final disposal (114, 135, 158).

Throughout the 1970s, the strengthening of existing laws and the enactment of new laws allowed the EPA to mandate and accomplish national goals. With the advent of the 1980s, however, the agency began to reverse some earlier decisions and delay implementation of some of their requirements (118, 119, 120, 138, 185). At present, the agency remains in a state of transition with many political, industrial, and environmental groups attempting to influence its decisions (30, 31, 96, 148, 151).

The following discussion is divided into categories of air, water, soil, food, noise, and surface pollution. Keep in mind, however, that these categories overlap. To illustrate, when a person inhales harmful particles from the soil that have become airborne, soil pollution becomes air pollution. And soil or surface pollution becomes water or food pollution if these harmful particles are swept into the water, consumed first by fish and then by people.

Air Pollution

> ... This most excellent canopy, the air, look you, this brave o'erhanging firmament, this majestical roof fretted with golden fire—why, it appears no other thing to me than a foul and pestilent congregation of vapors.
>
> *Hamlet* (II, ii, 314–315)

Problems of Air Pollution

Air pollution is not a new problem; people have known for centuries that air can carry poisons. Miners would take canaries with them into the mines—a dead bird meant the presence of lethal gas. Natural processes, such as forest and prairie fires, volcanic eruptions, or wind erosion, have long contaminated the air. Perhaps the most recent and most dramatic example of natural air pollution in the United States was caused by the 1980 eruption of Mount St. Helena in the state of Washington. Gases and dust from the volcano were spewed into the atmosphere, and local communities were covered with volcanic ash. Human activities, such as burning fossil fuels, surface mining of coal, incineration of solid wastes, or manufacturing processes, are recognized as sources of pollution. The current problem of toxic air pollution came sharply into focus in late 1984 when more than 2500 people died and as many as 100,000 were left with permanent disabilities as a result of a gas leak from a Union Carbide plant in India (229).

Air and water pollution act interchangeably; together they present a world problem. All people on the earth share the oceans and the air. Significant local pollution of either can greatly affect distant areas, especially if the oceans cannot, by the processes of precipitation, oxidation, and absorption, cleanse the atmosphere before harmful effects occur. Given enough time, the ocean can cleanse the atmosphere. But if the amount of pollution exceeds the ocean's capacity to neutralize the waste, then the harmful effects are dispersed into the atmosphere and we realize the effects by breathing contaminated air (21). Air pollution is most harmful to the very young, the very old, and persons with respiratory and cardiac disease.

Sources of Air Pollution

The five most common pollutants found in the air are carbon monoxide, sulfur oxides, nitrogen oxides, suspended particles, and hydrocarbons. The sources of these air pollutants vary and the effects on humans differ according to length and degree of exposure to the pollutant (Table 2–1).

Carbon Monoxide. A major cause of air contamination is imperfect or incomplete combustion. **Perfect or complete combustion** exists only in the chemistry books and is *the result of hydrogen and carbon uniting completely with oxygen, thereby relinquishing heat, water vapor, light, and carbon dioxide to the air.* **Imperfect or incomplete combustion** refers to *the additional liberation of carbon monoxide, sulfur oxides, and nitrogen oxides into the air.* Industry, forest fires, burning cigarettes, and motor vehicles are sources of **carbon monoxide,** *a colorless and odorless poisonous gas produced during the incomplete combustion of carbon.* The greatest source of carbon monoxide in our cities is the motor vehicle. Between 1975 and 1983, the level of carbon monoxide in the air decreased 33 percent (194). However, dangerous levels of carbon monoxide can accumulate in garages, tunnels, and heavy traffic. Research has shown that some people in New York City have blood concentration levels of 5.8 percent carbon monoxide as compared to the 1.5 percent considered safe (114). Carbon monoxide combines with the hemoglobin of red blood cells in place of oxygen and can produce a **hypoxic state,** *a decreased amount of oxygen* in the body. The severity of this state depends on the ratio of carbon monoxide to oxygen in the air inhaled. The deficiency of oxygen in the blood caused by carbon monoxide primarily affects respiration and the function of the brain and heart. Carbon monoxide in high concentra-

TABLE 2–1. Common Air Pollutants (20, 103, 135, 141, 158)

POLLUTANT	SOURCE	EFFECTS
Carbon monoxide	Car exhaust; forest fires; burning cigarette	Reduces O_2 levels in blood; contributes to photochemical smog
Sulfur oxides	Burning coal or oil containing sulfur	Irritation of mucous membranes of eyes, nose, and throat; injury to lungs; damage to plant life; contribution to corrosion
Nitrogen oxides	Burning fossil fuel	Increase in respiratory illness; irritation to mucous membranes; alteration in night vision
Suspended particles	Wind erosion; fires; incineration of solid wastes; surface mining	Respiratory diseases
Hydrocarbons	Toxic chemicals may also be windborn	Birth defects, neurological impairment, cancer
	Decomposition of organic matter; incomplete combustion of gasoline	Involved in formation of ozone and photochemical smog

tions can cause death: in small amounts it can cause dizziness, headache, fatigue, and impaired perception and thinking. Carbon monoxide pollution can be especially dangerous for persons who suffer from heart disease, respiratory disease, or anemia, for they already have a physiologically impaired oxygen-carrying capacity (217, 222), and for the fetus because it can cause retardation of growth and brain development.

Sulfur Oxides. When coal or oil-containing sulfur is burned by factories and power plants, the sulfur in the fuels is oxidized. These **sulfur oxide compounds** (*sulfur dioxide and sulfur trioxide*) pollute the air in many sections of the country. **Sulfur dioxide (SO_2)** *is a heavy, poisonous gas that causes a choking sensation when inhaled.* Sulfur trioxide (SO_3) reacts with water vapor to form a mist of **sulfuric acid** (H_2SO_4), *a heavy, corrosive, colorless liquid.* Between 1975 and 1983, the level of sulfur dioxide in the air decreased 36 percent; between 1983 and 1984, the amount of sulfur dioxide in the air increased 2 percent. This increase was directly related to the 7 percent increase in use of domestic coal during that time (1,194). World-wide it is estimated that more than 600 million people live in cities where average sulfur dioxide levels in the air are higher than safety guidelines set by the World Health Organization (170). Elevated levels of sulfur oxide have been linked to human illness and death. Irritation of the sensitive mucous membranes of the eyes, nose, and throat; injury to the mucous membranes that line the lungs, and aggravation of or precipitation of respiratory problems, such as bronchitis, may occur (135, 158). Besides directly affecting our health, sulfur dioxide and its by-product, sulfuric acid, indirectly jeopardize health by damaging plant life and contributing to rust on metals.

Nitrogen Oxides. Other gaseous end products are the **nitrogen oxides**. Approximately 95 percent of the annual emissions of **nitrogen oxides** *stem from burning fossil fuels:* 40 percent of the total from motor vehicles and other transportation modes; 30 percent from burning natural gas, oil, and coal in power plants; and 20 percent from industrial combustion of fossil fuels. **Nitrogen dioxide** (NO_2) initially composes only 10 percent of nitrogen emissions. However, complex chemical reactions in the air convert much of the nitric oxide to **nitrogen dioxide,** *a visible, red-brown, toxic, foul-smelling gas* (158). Between 1975 and 1983, the level of nitrogen dioxide in the air decreased 20 percent; between 1983 and 1984, a 2 percent increase was reported due to increased use of domestic coal (1, 194). Exposure to nitrogen dioxide causes irritation of the mucous membranes of the throat, altered night vision, and breathing difficulties. Research has also suggested that high levels of nitrogen dioxide may contribute to an increase in respiratory disease, cancer, and heart disease (158).

Suspended Particles. Another air contaminant is **particular matter,** *minute particles, such as dust, dirt, soot, smoke, aerosols, and fly ash.* Forty-three percent of suspended particle pollutants are produced by industrial processes while 39 percent by power and heating plants (141). Particulate matter, suspended in vapors and fumes, may hover for annoying and dangerous periods of time, depending on atmospheric conditions. These pollutants may soil surfaces, scatter or distribute light rays unevenly, and most dangerously, enter the lungs of people breathing the air. The severity of the lungs' response depends on the percentage of particulate matter or fumes and vapors in the air mixture and on pre-existing lung disease.

✔ Breathing asbestos particles can cause cancer and asbestosis. Asbestos was once widely used for fireproofing and insulating homes and public and private buildings. It was used in vinyl floor tiles and floorings, patching compounds and textured paints, shingles and siding, and appliances. Most of this use is now prohibited or regulated by EPA (Environmental Protection Agency) standards. However, this does not always protect the individual who unknowingly has items containing asbestos in the home or work place. When the asbestos material becomes damaged or starts to deteriorate, asbestos fibers are released into the air. In addition, particles are released into the atmosphere from the wearing of brake linings and clutch facings, manufacturing and fabricating facilities, and mining (158, 199, 216). Inhaled beryllium, used in making metal alloys, also is known to cause a debilitating form of lung infection (218).

✔ *Cigarette smoke* has been identified as an air pollutant, causing increased carbon monoxide content in the blood. In addition, numerous other chemicals make up the particulate matter in tobacco smoke. Tobacco smoke can produce cardiovascular, respiratory, and other symptoms in nonsmokers as well as smokers. Nonsmoking pregnant women exposed to tobacco smoke for at least 2 hours daily are twice as likely to deliver a low birthweight infant as pregnant women not exposed to smoking. Second-hand smoke can produce respiratory disease and cancer in the nonsmoker as well as smokers. Sufficient exposure to any type of particulate pollution may lead to pulmonary emphysema (186, 222, 225) (a condition in which the alveoli of the lungs become distended or ruptured).

Hydrocarbons. **Hydrocarbons** *(volatile organic compounds) are compounds that consist of only hydrogen and carbon.* About 85 percent of the hydrocarbons found in the atmosphere come from natural sources, including forests, coal, gas, and petroleum fields, and decomposition of organic matter. Incomplete combustion and evaporation of gasoline from motor vehicles account for most of the emissions caused by human activities. Industrial and chemical manufacturing processes also contribute to this form of pollution. Hydrocarbons appear to have little direct effect on plants or animals but are involved in atmospheric reactions that form secondary air pollutants (135, 158).

Nitrogen oxides and hydrocarbons react in the presence of sunlight to produce ozone, photochemical smog, and peroxylacetyl nitrate. **Ozone** *(triatomic oxygen O_3) is a pungent, colorless, toxic gas.* In the upper atmosphere, ozone forms a protective barrier that prevents excessive ultraviolet light from reaching the earth. In the lower atmosphere ozone is *formed in the air by chemical reactions between nitrogen oxides and hydrocarbons (volatile organic compounds),* such as the vapors of gasoline and chemical solvents. These reactions are stimulated by sunlight and produce a type of *photochemical smog.*

✔ Ozone is a dangerous pollutant. Ozone affects the eyes, the respiratory tract, and the nervous system; it produces eye irritation, respiratory distress, irritation of the mucous membranes of the nose and throat, exhaustion, headaches, and decreased tolerance to physical exercise. School-age children, the elderly, and individuals with chronic heart and lung diseases are the most severely affected by ozone. New research has also found that ozone can impair the immune system of animals and damage crops. (114, 191, 208, 209).

✔ *Peroxylacetyl nitrate* (PAN) is damaging to plants and causes leaf mottling and reduced growth, which affects the food supply. *Photochemical smog* was first noted in the Los Angeles area. Since then, it has frequently been observed in many other cities. Photochemical smog produces some of the same effects on humans as ozone—eye irritation, lung damage, and decreased tolerance to physical activity (158, 169).

The EPA has developed the Pollutant Standards Index (PSI) as a means of reporting daily air pollution concentrations. The PSI converts the pollutant concentrations measured in a community's air to a number on a scale of 0 to 500. Intervals on the PSI scale are related to the potential health effects of the daily measured concentrations of the five major pollutants previously described. The intervals and terms used to describe the air quality levels are as follows: 0 to 50, good; above 50, moderate; above 100, unhealthful; 200 to 299, very unhealthful; 300 and above, hazardous (203).

✔ When the pollution index is over 100, individuals with existing heart or respiratory ailments should reduce physical exertion and outdoor activity.

Four additional air pollution problems should be mentioned: (1) depletion of the upper atmosphere ozone layer, (2) increasing levels of atmospheric carbon dioxide, (3) acid rain, and (4) radioactive substances. As noted, a small layer of ozone surrounds the earth and blocks much of the ultraviolet radiation from reaching the earth's surface. The ozone layer is in danger of being depleted by the continued use of fluorocarbons (freon) and chlorofluoromethanes that release chlorine into the stratosphere to combine with ozone. The continued use of fluorocarbon-propelled aerosol products and supersonic transport planes would add to that danger (185).

✔ In Caucasians, short-wavelength ultraviolet sunlight is thought to cause melanoma and nonmelanoma skin cancer that would increase in incidence if there were a reduction of the ozone layer (49, 175).

Increasing Carbon Dioxide. The *atmospheric content of carbon dioxide* has increased by 15 percent in the past century. CO_2 is added to the atmosphere by burning fossil fuels. The increased level of atmospheric CO_2 alters the heat balance of the earth. Sunlight is allowed to pass through the CO_2 but the radiation of heat away from the earth is slowed, producing what is known as the greenhouse effect. Such changes might eventually result in polar ice caps melting, flooding of large coastal plain areas, and disruption of food production (10, 60). Some scientists fear the opposite may occur—the refrigerator effect. The CO_2 concentration would eventually prevent the sun's rays from reaching earth and cooler temperature would occur, again affecting food production and health factors (114).

Acid Rain. **Acid rain** *is the end product of chemical reactions that begin when sulfur dioxide and nitrogen oxides enter the atmosphere from coal-oil, and gas-burning power plants, iron and copper smelters, and automobile exhausts.* These gases undergo changes and eventually react with moisture to form sulfuric acid and nitric acid. One-half to two-thirds of the pollution falls as acid rain or snow; some of the remainder is deposited as sulfate or nitrate particles that combine with dew and mist to form dilute acids (61). Most of northeastern United States and parts of Ontario, Quebec, Nova Scotia, and Newfoundland, as well as portions of the upper Midwest, the Rocky Mountains, and the West Coast, now receive strongly acidic precipitation (56, 57, 80, 227). The United Kingdom, continental Europe, and central Soviet Union have reported environmental damage from acid rain or snow. Although the full effect on the environment is not understood as yet, increased acidity in soil, streams, or ponds can be documented. Certain freshwater ecosystems are particularly sensitive to acid; fish, frogs, and certain aquatic plants die. Acid rain leaches compounds out of soil, damaging the root systems of plants. Forests die. Crops are damaged. With continued episodes of acid rain, limestone and marble statues and buildings are dissolved, and homes and other structures weather more quickly (3, 140, 198). It will be years before the full effect of acid precipitation is known. At present, the only solution is to decrease the emissions of sulfur and nitrogen oxide to the atmosphere.

✓ *Radioactive Substances.* **Radioactive substances** *are produced by mining and processing radioactive ore and by nuclear-fission and radiation procedures* used in industry, medicine, and research. Pollution from radioactive materials poses a serious threat to our ability to reproduce and to our gene structure. It is also related to an increase in leukemia and other cancers, as demonstrated in persons working with radioactive materials over long periods without adequate safeguards and in survivors of Hiroshima and Nagasaki. A small fraction, 1 to 3 percent, of all cancers in the general population is attributable to natural radiation. Occupational irradiation produces an increase over the natural incidence (24, 64, 219).

Indoor Air Pollution

Recent air samplings in new energy-efficient homes have shown that many pollutants are more concentrated indoors than out. Nitrogen dioxide and carbon monoxide accumulate when gas stoves and kerosene heaters are burning. **Radon,** *a natural radioactive gas produced by the decay of uranium 238*, seeps into basements through cracked floors and diffuses out of brick and concrete building materials. Formaldehyde escapes into the air from foam insulation, particle board, and furniture made of plywood.

✓ Formaldehyde gas in newly insulated homes has reached concentrations high enough to cause dizziness, rashes, nosebleeds, and vomiting. Indoor radon may be contributing to thousands of lung cancer cases each year (58). Particles, such as dust, soot, ash, or cigarette smoke, may be inhaled into the lungs. Many household products, such as cleansers, drain openers, or paint removers, have toxic ingredients and cause respiratory irritation, as well as eye or skin irritation on contact. Some are carcinogenic when fumes or particles are inhaled over time (18, 111). Fungi and bacteria from humidifiers and air conditioning systems may cause allergies or Legionnaire's disease and aggravate asthma.

Indoor air pollution can be controlled by several measures: proper venting of gas stoves, heaters, and wood stoves, painting over materials that emit radon and formaldehyde, and daily airing of the house. Houseplants, especially spider plants, can be used to absorb air pollutants in the home.

✓ All forms of air pollution are physically irritating and present a potential hazard to our long-range health either by direct harm to the mucous membranes of the respiratory tract or by the indirect effects of continuously breathing contaminated air. Only in becoming aware of these factors as personal health threats will we seriously consider alternatives to using two or three cars, seek to know the serious hazards in our jobs, become concerned about houses downwind from an industrial site or the amount of ultraviolet light we receive, and use natural products instead of chemicals for many household tasks.

Water Pollution

Pollution of the water from the natural processes of aquatic animal and plant life, combined with manmade waste, constitutes another hazard to the delicate state of human health. Man-made water pollution has two major origins, *point sources* and *nonpoint sources*. Point sources are those that discharge pollutants from a well-defined place, such as outlet pipes of sewage treatment plants and factories. Nonpoint sources consist of runoff from city streets, construction sites, farms, and mines.

Types of Water Pollution

The most common water pollutants are common sewage, pathogenic organisms, plant nutrients, synthetic chemicals, inorganic chemicals, sediment, radioactive substances, oil, and heat.

Common Sewage. Traditional waste from domestic and industrial sources or sewage is a significant problem because oxygen is required to render this waste harmless. This waste thus uses up oxygen needed by aquatic plant and animal life. With increasing amounts of sewage, the problem is even more serious because of the inability of the water to deal successfully with the waste. When bacteria in the water can no longer decompose the waste, widespread aquatic death results. Waste will then accumulate, and the water will become useless as a personal or industrial resource.

✔ *Pathogenic Organisms.* These pollute water when sewage carrying these bacteria enter a river, lake, or stream. A human or animal drinking this water can become ill. Occasionally a whole community or area may be negatively affected if a large source of water becomes contaminated with diseased microbes. Although medical science has made major strides in the prevention and treatment of these diseases, it is still possible for outbreaks of infectious gastroenteritis and hepatitis, typhoid fever, giardiasis, cholera, or other infectious diseases to occur. Migrant farm workers and persons living in rural and urban fringe areas where population density is high or public utilities are limited are at greater risk from this form of pollution (5, 8, 60).

Plant Nutrients. Nutrients that nourish plant life, especially phosphates and nitrates, are produced by sewage, industrial wastes, and soil erosion. These nutrients are not easily removed by treatment centers because they do not respond to the usual biological processes. Moreover, treatment centers may inadvertently change these substances into a more usable mineral form that stimulates excessive plant growth. This increased growth of bacteria and algae becomes a problem by interfering with treatment processes, marring the landscape, producing an unpleasant odor and taste in the water, and disturbing the normal food web in a body of water. Because humans depend on many lower forms of life for food, this process could eventually affect their well-being (Fig. 2–2).

✔ *Synthetic Chemicals.* Those that are used in everyday household chores, especially chemicals found in detergents, pesticides, and other cleaning agents, affect the water. They may be poisonous to aquatic life even in small proportions. When resistant to local treatment measures, they can produce an unpleasant taste and odor in the water. The extent of the long-term problem is not known, but the possibility of human poisoning over a long period by the consumption of small doses of these chemicals taken in drinking water cannot be ignored. This problem is discussed later in the chapter.

Inorganic Chemicals. These are mineral substances from mining or manufacturing processes that can destroy land animals (including people) and aquatic life when ingested. Industries sometimes improperly and illegally empty large quantities of toxic materials into sources of local water supply. This group of pollutants corrodes water-treatment equipment and makes waste treatment an even more expensive problem.

Sediment. Particles of dirt or sand resulting from soil erosion have been identified as a significant water pollutant. Soil particles suspended in water interfere with the penetration of sunlight and therefore reduce photosynthesis of aquatic plants and animals (158). When sediment settles out, it covers food sources on the bottom of lakes and streams, smothers bottom-dwelling organisms, disrupts the reproductive cycle of fish and other organisms, fills streams, and prevents natural reservoirs from filling during rainy seasons. Because of its sheer volume, sediment also increases the cost of water treatment.

Radioactive Material. Natural or synthetic radioactive material can contaminate water. Potential sources of radioactive pollutants in water include waste from nuclear power plants, industrial or research facilities using radioactive materials, or uranium mines (158). Incidence of stomach cancer among Navaho Indians is four times the national average, probably because half of the nation's supply of uranium was mined in or near the Navaho Reservation during the 1950s and 1960s. Water, and in turn food supplies, have been contaminated with radioactive material; uranium tailings remain even though the mines are closed (180).

Oil. Oil found in natural water is usually the result of man's deliberate actions, not from accidents.

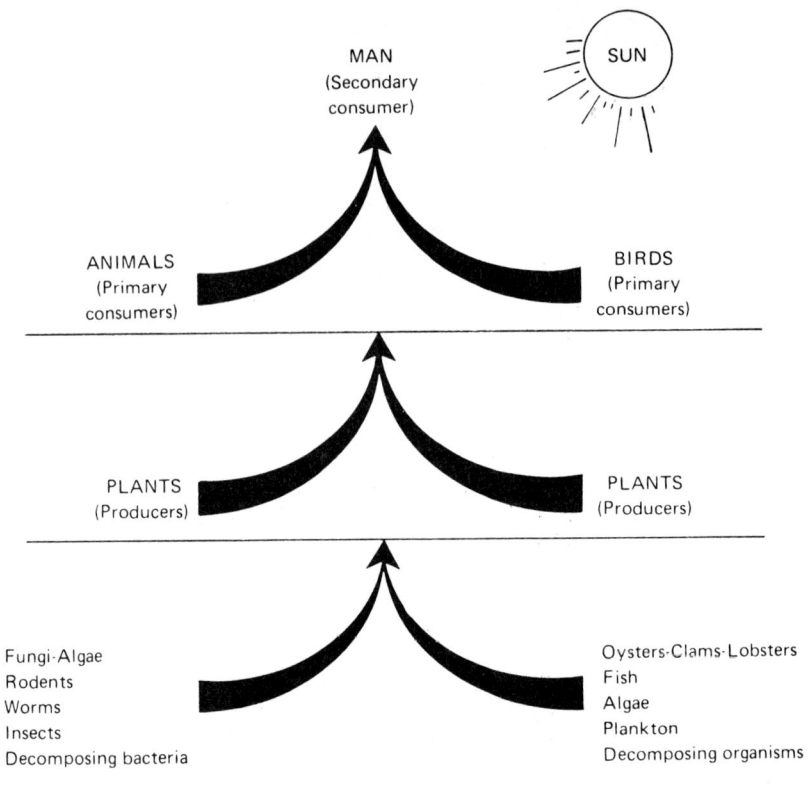

Figure 2-2. Food Web.

Accidental spills account for only 10 to 14 percent of all oil spilled into the ocean. The rest is from natural seepage, dumping of waste oil, flushing of ships' bilges, and discharging oil from refineries. Numerous biological effects result from the presence of oil in natural waters: contact with the oil ruins the waterproofing and insulating qualities of birds; oil contaminates or destroys the natural food of birds, and residuals from the oil are being found in the food web of humans (10, 158).

Heat. This becomes a problem because it reduces the ability of the water to absorb oxygen. If significant amounts of water are heated through industrial use, the water becomes less efficient in providing oxygen for aquatic life and in assimilating waste. Even more dangerous, the ecological balance of lakes and rivers can be permanently upset through prolonged alteration of water temperature. The food that people eat either comes directly from water or has fed on aquatic life somewhere in the food web. Faced with an expanding world population, we must increasingly be aware of the significance of every organism in the food web (Fig. 2-2) and its relationship to us.

One of the most frightening results of water pollution is the threat to the oceans. The collective discharges of the world's nations and the practice of ocean dumping of sewage sludge may permanently pollute the oceans. The Ocean Dumping Act was amended in 1977 so that ocean dumping would not be allowed after December 31, 1981. Yet ocean dumping of solid, semisolid, or liquid waste generated by municipal wastewater treatment plants not only continues but is also increasing. When the act was amended in the 1970s, most people were concerned about the environment. In the 1980s, the major concern has become the cost of enforcing environmental standards. Continued research on the effects of deep ocean dumping and the development of a waste management plan for coastal areas and pretreatment techniques that reduce the danger of sewage sludge should be continued before major investments in other forms of disposal are made (187).

Problems in Water Purification

The common denominator of all major water pollution is called **biologic oxygen demand (BOD),** *which is the amount of free oxygen that extraneous substances absorb from water* (135). The natural water purification process involves the action of bacteria using oxygen to decompose organic matter. If too much waste is dumped into a given body of water, this natural cleansing process cannot take place, or at least does not take place fast enough. Further, once the water in the underground aquifer is contaminated, it is nearly impossible to guarantee a safe water supply.

The ultimate problem of water pollution stems from our using natural resources in greater and greater amounts because of additional industrialization, population growth, a greater dependence on appliances, and a subsequent increase in the need for sewage disposal. The problem of dissolving waste has put a strain on waste-disposal systems. Even excessive amounts of treated waste now obstruct the waterways. Current engineering research is attempting to solve some of the problems of water pollution by developing different types of waste-disposal systems.

✔ When water contains pollutants in ever-increasing amounts, it becomes a threat to human health. At present, the quality of water service for countless people must be improved; many inhabitants of rural areas and small towns obtain their drinking water from polluted sources. In several areas of the United States, wastewater is being used for irrigation. Although this water is considered safe for human use it may contain low levels of organic chemicals which may be harmful following long-term ingestion. This water is not meant for drinking purposes; however, indirect human consumption does occur when surface waters are used for water supply (48, 103, 224). Keeping drinking water separate from water for other uses would help conserve water supplies and ensure greater purity, for water used for other purposes could be refiltered with less expense (139).

✔ Pollution of marshes and shorelines has severely impaired breeding habitats for many types of shellfish and deep-water species, thereby subsequently affecting the nation's food supply. Polluted water cannot be used for recreational purposes; backpackers, campers, swimmers, windsurfers, and waterskiers have all felt the impact of water pollution. In addition to the health risk, the odor of decay and the unsightliness of polluted water destroy the beauty of any natural setting.

✔ Misuse of our water has far-reaching consequences, threatening people all over the world from every age group and culture. We must take definite personal responsibility for stopping needless pollution of the water by exercising careful personal use of agents that can ultimately destroy it and by using legal procedures to prevent undue dumping of wastes into lakes, rivers, and streams. Some health problems associated with contaminated water would be eliminated via proper legislation, and needless sickness and death could be avoided. Such legislation as the Clean Water Act of 1987 and the revised Safe Drinking Water Act of 1986, which promote water quality standards and impose a system of control on all sources of pollution, are effective and worthy of support. More importantly, the health of future generations and their chance to enjoy the beauty, taste, and power of the water depend on those of us who are so carelessly polluting it. Water, like oxygen, is essential to life, development, and health.

Soil Pollution

As early as 1950 the federal Food and Drug Administration announced that the potential health hazards of compounds containing chlorinated hydrocarbons, such as dichloro-diphenyl-trichloroethane (DDT), had been underestimated (109). The Federal Environmental Pesticide Control Act, passed in 1972 and amended in 1975 and 1978, requires that all pesticide products sold or distributed in this country must be registered with the United States Environmental Protection Agency (210).

Substances used to kill weeds, rats, mice, worms, fungi, and insects are called **pesticides.** Soil pollution can occur as a result of excessive or improper use of pesticides (insecticides, herbicides, fungicides) or crop fertilizers. Many chemicals used in these preparations are highly toxic and can remain in the soil for long periods of time without being degraded, thus setting the stage for pollution of food, water, and, ultimately, people.

Farmers are the largest users of pesticides, but they are also used by industry: federal, state, and local governmental agencies; and individual people in their homes and gardens. Actual toxic effects of the different compounds vary and some effects occur before the chemicals reach the soil. Vertebrates usually will not suffer acute poisoning from these substances except through accidental ingestion, direct skin contact, or inhalation of the dust or spray of the more toxic pesticides.

✔ Workers in pesticide manufacturing plants, agricultural workers, and commercial pest-control operators applying the chemicals to crops or soil can all inhale pesticide dust or spray. Inhalation exposure can occur in a subtle manner at times—for example, by inhaling the dust from storage bags during the filling and emptying process or from cultivated soil previously treated with pesticides. Symptoms occurring as the result of such exposure may not be attributed to the pesticides. Therefore many episodes of acute poisoning go undiagnosed. Direct skin contact can occur when solutions are spilled accidentally or when the moist spray touches exposed skin (28, 110, 113). An occupational history aids early diagnosis of such problems.

Effects of Soil Pollution

✔ Reports from epidemiological studies conducted in Iowa, California, Central and South America, and Mexico indicate that various acute illnesses and physiological changes were observed in farmers and migrant workers handling agricultural chemicals. Such effects on the central nervous system as forgetfulness, decreased attention and interest span, hyperirritability, anxiety, depression, nervousness, and insomnia have been reported. Skin diseases, eye and respiratory conditions, and digestive disorders have also been identified. Sterility and birth defects in humans and animals and leukemia and various cancers in farmworkers and their children are increasing as a result of exposure to pesticides and herbicides used in agriculture and production of fruits and vegetables. In some instances, these problems occurred after a single exposure to a toxic chemical (126, 195, 211, 222). Reproductive problems, birth defects, and increased risk of cancer are also associated with low-level, chronic exposure to some pesticides (14). This exposure may come from inhalation of the pesticide, skin contact, by ingestion of food and water containing residues, and contact with contaminated equipment. Some pesticides are known to be central nervous system stimulants or depressants or cholinesterase inhibitors (133). Some affect blood cells and other body enzymes (126).

Pesticides have an immediate toxic effect on birds, bees, and rodents, thus curtailing the necessary agents of cross-pollination and insect destruction, which, in turn, can affect the food supply. Surface water may be contaminated during spraying or dusting; or rain may wash pesticides or fertilizers into streams and lakes, again affecting food supply. Earthworms are capable of concentrating toxic chemicals from the soil and storing these chemicals in their fatty tissues. Because earthworms provide food for other animals that are also capable of concentrating these chemicals, they may prove to be an important source of undesirable chemical residues in higher animals and humans (42, 126).

The Environmental Protection Agency's pesticide control program has three major components: registration of pesticides, training of pesticide applicators, and monitoring and research. All pesticides must be registered with the Agency before being marketed. The Agency approves labeling and sets maximum safe levels for pesticide residues in human and animal food. The EPA has developed an applicator training program, certifying individuals permitted to apply restricted-use pesticides. In addition, the Agency sponsors research on pesticides and monitors pesticide levels in the environment. Both acute and long-term pesticide effects are considered in the epidemiological studies (218).

In spite of the EPA's efforts, evidence indicates that EPA receives insufficient funding, and standards are not being followed; long-term effects are yet unknown. According to a report from the National Research Council of the National Academy of Sciences, industrial wastes are being dumped on or pumped into the earth's crust and few studies are being done to determine whether the sites are safe. It may be possible to contain wastes safely and to lessen toxicity in wastes in the natural systems of the earth if the chemical nature of the waste and the geologic nature of the disposal area are understood. Geological mapping is needed as a guide to safe disposal sites and for research on reactions between chemicals and rock or soil, fracture patterns in rocks, fluid flow, and hydrodynamics of deep basins (85).

The widespread contamination by dioxin in Missouri in 1983 following massive flooding illustrates the complexity and extent of the problem. Chemicals were used without awareness of harmful effect. Unregulated use of chemicals and dumping of various chemicals by industries had occurred for some time and had only become apparent later. Furthermore, chemicals did not remain where originally used or dumped. Flood waters, underground water, and wind transported chemicals or their residues from one soil site to another. People are now learning that their past and present symptoms and diseases are related to or caused by hazardous pollutants in the environment to which they did not know they were being exposed (167).

Dioxin, for example, is considered the most toxic synthetic compound known to science. A complex organic chemical compound, it is insoluble in water but dissolves in organic solvents mixed with water. It is strongly attracted to lipids: fatty tissues in the body, oils, or related lipid substances. It becomes strongly attached to soil particles. The chemical remains in lipids or soil for many years and during a flood or soil erosion can move through water with solvents, soil particles, or colloids to which it is attached. Dioxin is also part of many other chemical compounds—for example, chlorophenols, herbicides, and the antiseptic hexachlorophene. It can be generated by incineration of industrial, commercial, and municipal wastes that contain chlorinated aromatics, chlorophenols, or PCBs.

✔ It produces a wide range of harmful effects in humans and animals, including:

1. Fatal liver damage
2. Birth defects
3. Spontaneous abortions and sterility
4. Many types of cancer
5. Nerve and brain damage
6. Disturbed enzyme production
7. Reduced immunity to infections

8. Chloracne, a disfiguring and painful affliction of the skin
9. Damage to the urinary, genital, and gastrointestinal tracts, the thymus and spleen

Many effects are chronic and long term (167).

Dioxin is not only a problem for residents along rivers outside of St. Louis, the scene of much publicity in 1983. Dioxin is a contaminant in Agent Orange, the herbicide sprayed in Vietnam. Many U. S. service personnel and their families were exposed, and are suffering a variety of health problems. Where else dioxin contamination may be found is not yet known (167).

Food Pollution

Some of the same chemicals found in pesticide preparation are used as **food additives**. These purposely used additives are not designed to be toxic but rather *to preserve, improve, and protect nutritional value*. The average person in the United States consumes approximately three pounds of these additives every year. Artificial flavors and colors make up 80 percent of all chemicals used in our food; preservatives, sweeteners, and thickeners, a total of 11 categories of substances, make up the rest of the additives (68, 104). However, determining their potential health hazard over a life span is difficult. Certain food additives interfere with intestinal mucosa absorptive ability and therefore affect availability of nutrients and drugs. Also, some nontoxic substances or chemicals used as food additives are metabolized into toxic substances in the body. Adverse reactions to synthetic flavors and colors include gastrointestinal, respiratory, neurological, skeletal, and skin disorders. Removal of artificial flavors and colors from the diet has been found to reduce hyperkinesis and certain learning disabilities in 50 percent of the children with these disorders (2, 50, 68, 226). Under certain physiological conditions nitrites used to inhibit bacterial growth in processed foods can combine with certain amines to form chemicals that are potentially mutagenic and carcinogenic (68).

Unexpected side effects due to *antibiotic and hormone residues from drugs given to animals for growth promotion and disease prevention* have resulted. In people these residues have resulted in (1) allergy and increased drug toxicity or resistance to pathogens when the *same* family of antibiotics is later administered therapeutically and (2) change of normal bacterial flora in a body area so that invasion by pathogens is more likely, causing infection or disease (23). Synthetic estrogen diethyl-stilbestrol (DES) was used in cattle feed to promote rapid weight gain. Studies have linked DES to increases in a rare genital tract tumor in young women whose mothers were given DES while pregnant. As a result of these studies, use of DES has been restricted. An attempt to ban its use and the use of other sex hormones as feed supplements is underway (68).

A considerable amount of *pesticides* are ingested by most families in the United States, from fruits and vegetables grown in Mexico and the United States where large amounts of chemicals are used repeatedly to control insects, weeds, rodents, and other agricultural pests. The U. S. consumer wants to purchase fruits and vegetables that are without blemish and appear as perfect as a picture. Blight, rust, fungus, or other causes of discoloration can most quickly be controlled by chemical application. However, the farmers are caught in a pesticide treadmill. Each year it takes more and different poisons to accomplish the same task, and insects continue to produce hybrid strains that are resistant to the chemicals. Even those banned by the Environmental Protection Agency in the United States are likely to be used in other countries, usually shipped by U. S. chemical manufacturers. Examples of disease-producing chemicals that contaminate foodstuffs include:

1. Chlordane.
2. Toxaphine.
3. 2,4-D.
4. DBCP.
5. Paraquat (a small amount on the skin causes asphyxiation).
6. EDBC (a fungicide which breaks down into a potent carcinogen ETU).
7. Aldicarb (methyl isocyanate which converts to hydrogen cyanide gas, which killed and injured people at Bhopal, India).
8. Parathion (an organophosphate pesticide so lethal that a tablespoon on the skin is fatal).

The pesticide market is so large that production is estimated to equal one pound of chemicals annually for every person—men, women, and children—on earth. While DDT, chlordane, Dieldren, and 2,4, 5-T are banned in the United States and Europe, they are sold to many developing countries which are increasingly a source of some of our food products. People in Third World countries do not know how to use chemicals to avoid widespread contamination, and the number of deaths and injuries attributed to agrichemicals in those countries is increasing. For example, in rural Brazil, DDT levels ten times that considered safe have been found in mother's milk. Ten percent of that population suffers symptoms of mild chronic poisoning. Levels of DDT 90 times higher than that in U. S. milk has been found in milk sold in Guatemala. Stomach and colon cancer have increased five times in

African countries where large amounts of agrichemicals have been used. Drinking paraquet has become a popular form of suicide in Sri Lanka and Central and South America, although careless handling causes the most deaths of agricultural workers. In addition to causing human misery, the pesticides and herbicides are ravaging the ecosystems by killing birds, plants, and marine life.

Pesticide use could be reduced greatly by using better agricultural techniques, such as:

1. Crop rotation.
2. Intercropping, alternating small plots of different plants.
3. Avoid monocropping—planting huge fields of only one crop season after season.
4. Polyculture—diversifying species within the same crop type.
5. Providing habitat for beneficial insects.
6. Selecting plants for their resistance to pests.
7. Timing planting of crops to avoid pest attacks or to plant them in their optimal climate.
8. Development of biological controls; some insects and pests are natural predators on other insects and pests.
9. Developing improved hardware for safer application when pesticides and herbicides are applied (126).

Often the problem of a toxin remaining in the food chain remains even after a toxic chemical has been banned because they bioaccumulate in the environment. Chlordane, used widely in the Midwest in the 1970s as a soil insecticide for corn, was banned for that use because studies showed it produced cancer. However, it was allowed until recently to remain in the market as a termiticide. Through groundwater contamination, it has accumulated in the sediments of rivers and lakes. In the spring of 1987, residents of Missouri and other nearby states that receive river flow from Missouri were warned not to eat fish from a number of the Missouri rivers and lakes because the fish were contaminated with chlordane (133).

In St. Louis, Missouri, and the surrounding area, the soil, and thereby the water and air, remain contaminated from the processing of uranium oxide for the world's first nuclear reaction 45 years ago. There are several radioactive waste sites in the St. Louis metropolitan area. Nearby people live and children play without knowledge of the radioactive levels, the impending danger, or the long-term effects in health development. Only recently have the sites and their potential dangers become known (97).

This is not too different from what residents of the Great Lakes regions recently learned: that 37 million people who live near the Great Lakes have as much as 20 percent higher levels of toxic chemicals in their bodies than other U. S. residents. Over the years they have ingested many toxins (benzine, hexachloride, PCBs, DDT, toxaphene, mercury) from contaminated water and fish (1).

Nor do we know the effects on present and future generations of the 900 identified leaking hazardous waste sites in the United States. Other sites, as yet unidentified, may be contaminating soil, and in turn, water, food, and air (1).

Other food pollution hazards are *radioactive materials,* such as strontium 90, which has been traced in milk; mercury found in swordfish; worms; and mold, which may be present without noticeable change in the food's appearance, taste, or smell. Food handlers may introduce their infectious diseases into food by touching it or the equipment with soiled hands or by coughing onto it. Prolonged storage of highly acidic foods in aluminum cookware or aluminum foil may cause more aluminum than usual to enter the body. Using unlined copper utensils for cooking or storing food may also be harmful (77). Food sources may become contaminated by the chemicals and metals used in fertilizers and pesticides. In the future, diseases from **food additives** may assume as much significance in humans as do the **zoonoses,** *diseases transmitted between animals and humans,* such as trichinosis, brucellosis, tuberculosis, psittacosis, salmonellosis, typhus, roundworms, and rabies.

Because of the endless contamination possibilities from bacteria, toxins, viruses, parasites, and protozoa, the Food and Drug Administration and the Department of Agriculture enforce laws passed by Congress, impose various regulations of their own, and, in general, monitor the food industry nationwide. Various state and local authorities also attempt to regulate standards within their respective jurisdictions (21, 231). Yet these agencies cannot possibly determine every breach of regulation.

Astute observations must be made about standards in the food store. Demanding to know the growing, cleansing, processing, and handling procedures is not out of line. Reporting suspected breaches is your responsibility for health.

Noise Pollution

Sensory stimulation plays a major role in psychological and physiological development and is therefore directly related to physical and mental health. Sound is but one form of sensory stimulation. **Sound overload,** *unwanted sound that produces unwanted effects,* as well as sound deprivation, can be hazards to health (47, 175, 207).

✔ **Sound overload** can produce temporary or permanent hearing loss by affecting the tympanic membrane and by slowly deteriorating the microscopic cells that send sound waves from the ear to the brain. The effects produced on each person's hearing vary, depending on the sound intensity and pitch, the location of the source in relation to the person, the length of exposure, and the person's age and history of previous ear problems. Surveys have shown that at least 20 million Americans have measurable hearing deficits and still another 16 million are exposed to occupational noise levels capable of producing permanent hearing loss (128, 200, 205).

One means of determining the potential hazard of any sound is to measure its loudness. *The measurement of sound loudness is stated in* **decibels.** The faintest audible sound is designated 1 decibel; ordinary conversation, measured at 40 to 60 decibels, is considered adequately quiet. The Environmental Protection Agency identifies 55 decibels as the level above which harmful effects occur. Studies have shown that moderately loud sounds of 75 to 80 decibels, such as those produced by a clothes washer, tabulating machine, or home garbage-disposal unit, can be discomforting to human ears and can, over a period of time, produce temporary or permanent hearing loss. Here are examples of common sound pollutants and their decibel readings.

	DECIBELS
Vacuum cleaner	72
Dishwasher	76–96
Minibike	76
Loud street noise	80–100
Heavy city traffic	90–95
Food blender in home	93
Pneumatic hammer	95
Air compressor	95
Power lawnmower	95
Farm tractor	98
Outboard motor	102
Jet flying over at 1000 feet	103
Riveting gun	110
Motorcycle	115
Live rock music	120
Jet plane at takeoff	150
Rocket engine	180

Sound louder than 130 decibels, such as that produced by a nearby jet plane, gunshot blast, or a rocket at the launching pad, may cause actual pain (59, 195, 204–206). Persons who work regularly with any of the machines listed should realize the potential long-range effects of such noise levels.

The Noise Control Act was passed in 1972 and amended in 1978 as the Quiet Communities Act. Under this act the Environmental Protection Agency set noise emission standards for transportation vehicles and products that are major sources of noise. The Act also provides for research into the psychological and physiological effects of noise on people. State and local governments have been given primary responsibility for enforcing these standards (132).

Effects of Noise Pollution

✔ Sound overload affects everyone at some time by intruding on privacy and shattering serenity. It can produce impaired communication and social relationships, irritability, chronic headache, depression, fatigue, and tension, in addition to hearing loss. Research indicates that less obvious physiological changes can also occur. These changes include involuntary responses in the digestive, cardiovascular, endocrine, and nervous system. They can produce blood vessel constriction, pallor, dilated pupils and visual disturbance, increased and irregular heart rate, hypertension, headache, gastrointestinal spasm with nausea and diarrhea and eventual peptic ulcer, hyperactive reflexes, and muscle tenseness. These responses do not subside immediately but continue up to five times longer than the actual noise. Noise has also been associated with elevated blood cholesterol levels, atherosclerosis, and accident proneness (38, 59, 166, 195, 222).

We do not adapt to excessive sound, as was once thought; we learn to tolerate it. Even when a person is asleep, noise cannot be shut out completely. We are exhausted by our efforts to remain asleep in the midst of this external stimuli. Perhaps being aware of these environmental stress factors can aid in reducing or coping with them (59, 220, 222).

✔ Although not every harmful form of sound can be avoided, certain measures, such as wearing protective ear coverings, shortening exposure time, having regular hearing examinations, and seeking immediate medical attention for any ear injury or infection, will decrease the possibility of permanent damage or hearing loss. Noise can be brought under control without excessive cost. You can educate the public about the hazards of excess noise and ways to reduce noise in the home environment. Some suggestions to reduce noise are: hang heavy drapes over windows closest to outside noise sources, use foam pads under blenders and mixers, use carpeting in areas of heavy foot traffic, use upholstered instead of hard-surfaced furniture, and install sound absorbing ceiling tile in the kitchen.

✔ The hospital, considered a place to recuperate and rest, may actually contribute to symptoms because of the noise levels in certain areas. One study showed that noise levels in infant incubators, the recovery room, and acute care units were high enough to act as a stressor and stimulate the hypophyseal-adrenocortical axis. Peripheral vasoconstriction affecting blood pressure and pulse, threats to hearing loss in patients receiving aminoglycosidic antibiotics, and sleep deprivation were noted. Noise pollution in the operating room, causing vasoconstriction, pupil dilation, fatigue, and impaired speech communication, has also been found (166).

Surface Pollution

Until the mid-1960s, U. S. residents were not concerned with problems of waste disposal or recycling. Raw materials were plentiful and the open-dump method of disposal was convenient and economical. In the early 1970s, however, people became more concerned with the decreasing supply of natural resources and the health problems created by open dumps.

The Solid Waste Disposal Act was passed by Congress in 1965. The primary focus of this act was on the disposal of waste, not collection or street cleaning. In 1970 Congress passed the Resource Recovery Act, which shifted the emphasis of federal involvement from disposal to recycling, resource recovery, and the conversion of waste into energy. Subsequent laws, such as the Resource Conservation and Recovery Act of 1976, have been passed to facilitate further the safe disposal of waste (129, 218).

The total quantity of solid waste is large and increasing. Over 4 billion metric tons of solid household, municipal, industrial, agricultural, and mineral wastes are produced yearly in the United States (28, 174). The waste-disposal system of an average city must accommodate about 14.5 kilograms of refuse per day for every family of four (204). Most present disposal methods for this waste pollute land, air, or water. We can see this pollution everywhere: in open air, foul-smelling dumps, smoking incineration centers, junkyards, and poorly covered landfills.

Solid-Waste Disposal Methods

Solid waste is discarded in four basic ways: (1) open dumps, (2) sanitary landfills, (3) incineration, and (4) salvage.

Open Dumps. The open dump (now illegal in most states) is the oldest, most convenient, and most economical method. It creates many health problems, however, and is esthetically undesirable. Dumps serve as breeding grounds for rodents, flies, and other insects, such as cockroaches; they also attract seagulls, notorious as thieves and literers. Houseflies carry poliomyelitis, tuberculosis, diarrhea, dysentery, hepatitis, and cholera. Rats carry plague, tapeworm, Rocky Mountain spotted fever, and rat-bite fever. Water running off from these dumps pollutes local streams and lakes. Rain and surface water can seep through the wastes and pollute underground water. Any attempt to burn the surface waste in the dumps emits large quantities of foul-smelling fumes that increase air pollution and thus respiratory problems among local inhabitants. Dumps also invite accidents and fires, in addition to lowering the value of surrounding property (109, 195).

Landfills. When handled properly, landfills can be economical, sanitary, and esthetically acceptable. These areas should be placed far from water sources. Even with this precaution, underground or surface water may become polluted. The waste should be quickly covered to avoid foul smells, spontaneous combustion, breeding of rats and flies, and scavenging by rodents (195, 199, 201).

Incineration. Approximately 80 percent of household solid wastes are combustible and therefore suitable for incineration. Decentralized incineration is usually poorly controlled and it frequently produces gaseous emissions and particulates that pollute the air and damage our health. Central incineration conducted by federal, state, or local governmental bodies is expensive, although necessary for large urban areas. The controlled-combustion process used in these centers prevents the emission of harmful gases and uses the byproduct, heat, for an energy source. Through incineration the volume of waste can be reduced to one-fifth of its original bulk. The remaining material can be removed to landfills or compressed for use in soil conditioners or construction material (21).

Salvage. The composition of solid waste has changed in past years; today it includes larger amounts of paper, plastics, aluminum cans, and other packaging and wrapping materials. Many such materials will not decompose or rust; therefore they present new problems in disposal. If these products are *salvaged,* they can be **recycled,** *treated by mechanical, thermal, or biological means so that they can be used again*, thus promoting resource recovery and reuse (23, 29, 163).

Hazardous-Waste Disposal

The Environmental Protection Agency has defined **hazardous waste** as *discarded material that may pose a threat or hazard to human health or the environment.* These wastes can be solids, liquids, sludges, or gases. They are toxic, ignitable, corrosive, infectious, reactive (react with air, water, or other substances, resulting in explosions and toxic fumes), or radioactive (44). According to EPA estimates, the United States generates about 250 million tons of hazardous waste annually (213).

Hospitals, medical research laboratories, mining operations, service stations, retailers, and householders contribute in small amounts to hazardous-waste production. The Armed Forces with their obsolete explosives, herbicides, and nerve gases contribute significantly to the total volume. Most hazardous wastes generated, however, come from manufacturing industries. According to the Environmental Protection Agency, only about 10 percent of the hazardous waste currently generated is disposed of in an environmentally sound manner. The rest threatens our water and air quality and our water and land ecosystems. The EPA estimates that if available recycling and resource recovery technologies were used, the production of hazardous wastes could be reduced by as much as 20 percent (44).

An example of the problems associated with hazardous-waste disposal can be found in the small community of Wilsonville, Illinois. In 1977, Wilsonville residents learned that a national disposal firm was burying dirt contaminated with polychlorinated biphenyls, a cancer-causing substance, in a landfill near their town. After a long legal battle, the landfill was closed and the hazardous wastes were to be removed. Removal of the waste did not begin until late 1982. Because the company has no way of disposing of the material completely, it was transferred to a landfill in the Midwest (76). Thus a task that will take several years to complete will decrease the danger at Wilsonville but may pose a threat to another community. In an attempt to prevent such happenings and to protect U. S. citizens from the dangers of hazardous waste, The Comprehensive Environmental Response, Compensation and Liability Act was passed in 1980. One objective of this act was to establish a fund—Superfund—for the purpose of responding to emergency situations involving hazardous substances and of performing remedial cleanups. In 1986, a new Superfund was established and the program strengthened (214).

Nuclear Waste

One type of hazardous-waste product that has attracted considerable attention is radioactive waste. Some fission products that must be stored are cesium-137, strontium-90, iodine-131, and plutonium-239. Some decay rapidly in hours or days while others require thousands and millions of years to lose their radioactive potency (212). No satisfactory method of permanent disposal has been developed; the cost and fear of leakage from the storage area have been stumbling blocks.

The use of nuclear energy or power produced by fission reactors has called much concern and debate among the people of the United States. The concerns center around two major issues: the long-term disposal of radioactive wastes and the safety of the actual reactors.

When a utility shuts down a reactor at the end of its period of usefulness, the utility is faced with the problem of what to do with intensely radioactive materials. At present, only three means of disposal exist: dismantlement of the reactor with the debris shipped to a burial site, entombment of the reactor in a concrete structure, and protective storage that would prevent public access for 30 to 100 years. Even though nuclear power is a quarter-century old, the problem of safe disposal of radioactive waste is not solved (137).

The seriousness of problems associated with the safety of nuclear reactors for generating electricity is well illustrated by the following highly publicized event. In Pennsylvania, in March 1979, an accident occurred at the nuclear reactor site known as Three Mile Island. In retrospect, the accident was preventable and was less severe than originally reported. Residents near the site, however, were exposed to the radioactive isotope xenon-133, which has a half-life of approximately 5 days. The radiation release has the potential for causing the death, by cancer, of less than one person in the next 30 or 40 years (106). The major health effect of the accident appears to have been on the mental health of the people in the region. The fear, anger, and confusion felt by the Three Mile Island community are shared nationally and internationally. The majority of citizens now have serious second thoughts about the safety and reliability of nuclear power (106, 153). Diminishing resources lead to the need for alternative energy sources, such as coal and the sun. The problems in this area must be explored.

Hospital Waste

The amount of solid waste being produced by hospitals should be a primary concern to health workers. The average citizen accumulates and disposes of over 6 pounds of solid waste daily whereas the average hospital patient accumulates over 25 pounds daily. Hospitals add over 170,000 tons of pathological materials yearly to the waste load (201). This increase in hospital wastes can be attributed to the increase in disposable products: syringes, needles, surgical supplies, styrene dishes and utensils, various plastic products, linens, uniforms, and medication containers. Many hospitals use disposable products because they are considered cheaper, easier to store, and less likely to produce cross-infection. Yet hospitals often fail to consider the cost or inconvenience of transporting or discarding large quantities of these contaminated objects. Much of a hospital's solid waste, often contaminated by infectious organisms, is removed to open dumps or sanitary landfills without proper initial sterilization, thus spreading pathogens to land, water, and air (112). Most hospital workers do not consider the implications of casually using disposable items (188).

✔ One study conducted in an urban area with 16 participating hospitals revealed that the nurse influences decisions regarding the purchase of patient care items more than any other hospital worker. If these decisions are largely your responsibility, know how much trash your hospital creates, where the waste goes, the decontamination procedures used before disposal, the cost of disposal, why your agency uses disposable products, and how much your agency contributes to environmental pollution. Form an interdepartmental committee, perhaps of administrators, nurses, doctors, and patients. Report your findings to them and together consider all the advantages and drawbacks of various products. Consider cost, convenience, infection control, and quality. Give each new product a careful clinical trial and adopt it for use only after careful consideration about contributions to patient care. Avoid using disposable items if nondisposables will do the job as well. Pass this information on to the patients and families. Encourage health workers in homes to demonstrate and teach proper disposal of such items as syringes and dressings, especially at this time of increasing incidence of infectious diseases, including AIDS. Work to reduce the huge volume of solid waste that is taking space and depleting natural resources (91). And work for disposal of infectious wastes in non-air-polluting incinerators, which many cities and hospitals do not have.

The effectiveness of nonpolluting incinerator conversion of trash into hot gases, which then transforms water into steam, has been demonstrated for over 10 years by St. Louis University Hospital, St. Louis, Missouri. The Hospital's incinerator conversion project, which heats and cools the entire St. Louis University Medical Center and also sterilizes all hospital equipment, received national attention at the U. S. Department of Energy's Technology Transfer 80's Program. The Hospital received a national award for the project from the Department of Energy in November, 1984.

Lead Poisoning

Lead is another surface pollutant. We inhale lead as an air pollutant and ingest traces of lead daily through a normal diet. Because lead wastes increased during the past century, particularly from industry and automobile use, exposure and intake into the body have multiplied. Consequently, the rate of absorption by soft tissue exceeds the rate of excretion or storage by bone (26, 40, 223). Lead gasoline additives, nonferrous smelters, and battery plants are the most significant contributors to atmospheric lead levels. Transportation sources contribute about 80 percent of the annual emissions of lead (217). However, with the change in composition of gasoline, the National Center for Disease Control reports an average 36.7 percent decrease in blood levels of lead (114, 217). A problem is controlling the lead exposure that occurs from drinking or eating from or storing food in improperly lead-glazed earthenware or ceramic ware, consuming lead-contaminated "moonshine," or working in or living near industries where lead exposure is not controlled (105). Two-thirds of the lead found in canned foods comes from solder. This source of lead constitutes one-third of the lead that the average person ingests from food (32).

✔ Individuals who work in areas with high lead levels show evidence of chronic lead poisoning. Persistent abdominal pain is the cardinal symptom in adults. They also exhibit fatigue, nervousness, and sleep disturbances as well as cognitive deficits and peripheral neuropathy. Kidney damage occurs slowly and may not be detected until two-thirds of the kidney function is destroyed. The male workers have a decrease in the quantity and quality of sperm, and the female workers have an increased risk of fetal damage and/or abortion (74).

✔ Another urgent problem arises when young children, mainly in urban slums, form the *habit of eating nonfood substances, including peeling paint, plaster, or putty containing lead. This behavior is called* **pica**. The precise cause of pica is not completely understood, but it may be related to nutritional, cultural, and emotional factors. Acute or chronic lead poisoning, an insidious disease, results from this eating pattern and is a major source of brain damage, mental deficiency, and behavior problems. The pathological changes that occur affect the nervous, renal, and hematopoietic systems. Kidney damage is usually reversible, but chronic lead poisoning in childhood may lead to gout or kidney disease later in life. Damage to the hematopoietic system is evident by the reduction in the number and quality of red blood cells produced, thus leading to severe anemia. The most serious effects are on the nervous system. The mortality rate from lead encephalopathy (disease of the brain) is 5 percent. Of the children who survive acute lead poisoning, 40 percent have convulsive disorders and another 20 percent have significant neurological deficits (39, 78, 155, 156).

Studies show the following trends:

1. Blood lead levels are higher in Afro-Americans than Caucasians among all socioeconomic and urbanization levels.
2. Young children from both Afro-American and Caucasian families with incomes under $6000 have a significantly higher prevalence of elevated blood lead than those from households with incomes of $6000 or more.
3. Almost one-fifth of Afro-American children from low-income families, the group with the highest proportion of elevated blood lead levels, should be referred for medical follow-up.
4. Mean blood lead level in young children increases with the degree of urbanization where they live (78).

✔ Although there seems to be a trend toward reduced lead screening, child health programs should consider routine screening of all children from 1 to 5 years of age. Reduction of leaded gasoline and establishment of auto-emissions standards set by the EPA have been steps in the right direction, for the mean blood level in the United States fell significantly between 1976 and 1980 (78).

Occupational Hazards

✔ Increasingly we learn of the health hazards that many workers face daily at their jobs. Monotony, paced work, and performance pressures are major sources of stress in many jobs and can contribute to disease pathology. The muscle strains, backaches, fractures, burns, eye injuries, and other accidental emergencies are taken for granted by the public. But workers may not suffer the consequences of the hidden environmental hazards—the chemicals or radiation they work with directly or indirectly—until years later. Often in the past the etiology of the physical illness remained unsolved. Not only do miners and factory workers become ill because of their work environment, hospital workers also may suffer. Those who work regularly with certain anesthetics, for example, may develop cancer, leukemia, or lymphoma. Those who work with high levels of radiation risk sterility or defective offspring if adequate protection is not maintained. Nurses may suffer infections, back and muscle injuries, varicose veins, and any of the other physical or emotional effects of stress.

The Occupational Safety and Health Act of 1970, the Coal Mine Health and Safety Act of 1969, and the Toxic Substances Control Act of 1976 are some of the laws passed by Congress that have been responsible for making occupational safety and health a public health concern rather than a private matter. Through these laws the federal government works to prevent work-related accidents and disease, to correct hazardous working conditions, to promote good health for working men and women, and to improve compensation. The Occupational Safety and Health Act established the Occupational Safety and Health Administration, which conducts inspections of industries to force compliance and research to establish the hazardous levels of various chemicals. Relatively few of the many chemicals in industry have been researched, but the standards, as well as prevention and treatment measures, are published periodically in *The Federal Register*, which can be obtained from the Department of Labor.

✔ The Act has forced industries to become more active in seeking health services for employees and has assisted the occupational health nurse to offer additional services related to disease prevention and education of employees (165). Health screening is also being emphasized, for contamination from some substances can be detected early enough to prevent disease. In one community where smelter employees were manifesting symptoms of nerve damage, for example, high levels of arsenic were found in the urine, fingernails, and hair (176). Earlier screening could have prevented arsenic poisoning.

It takes about two decades for health effects of industry to be evident. In the 1940s, Louisiana had a large petrochemical industry. In the 1950s and 1960s, a higher cancer incidence was being documented. About that time, companies moved from the North to the mouth of the Mississippi River to avoid property taxes and costs associated with pollution regulation. Pesticides, chlorine, rubber, antifreeze, detergents, plastics, and a variety of chemicals were manufactured. In 1986, Louisiana ranked third in the United States in chemical production, after New Jersey and Texas. There has been an increasing death rate from cancer in each of those states, surpassing other industrial states (20).

✔ To promote early screening and prevent long-term effects of noise pollution on hearing, *The Federal Register* publishes updated guidelines on occupational hearing conservation. Basically each hearing program must consist of five parts:

1. Employee education. Each employee must be told the significance of the program.
2. An analysis of the noise in the workplace, now required every 2 years or as noise levels change.
3. Engineering and administrative controls. The environmental noise must be altered if possible.
4. Audiometric testing. All employees exposed to 85 decibels or more (over a period of 8 hours) must be tested yearly as well as on preemployment.

5. Personal protective equipment. A variety of hearing protectors must be available.

Along with these guidelines are specific requirements for those who administer and interpret tests, circumstances under which tests are administered, and the instruments for measuring noise levels and hearing (179).

Another group of health hazards related to a large industry in the United States is cosmetics, including aerosol preparations, hair dyes, and feminine sprays, which increasingly are related to skin and other diseases, including cancer. As with other occupational chemicals, effects of the use of these products are usually not known until years after their regular usage (222). The World Health Organization estimates that 75 to 85 percent of all cancers are environmentally caused. No one knows how much occupational factors contribute to these causes (228).

Laryngeal cancer has been found among workers exposed to asbestos, cutting oil, wood dust, grease, and oil; among workers in the paper, metal, construction, leather, food, and textile industries; and among barbers, sheet metal workers, electricians, and naphthalene cleaners (51).

Often occupational hazards are taken for granted. They are seen as part of the job. Employees in laundry and dry cleaning establishments, for example, suffer hazards of excess heat, humidity, and noise; falls and accidents from slipping on wet floors; back injury and muscle strains from lifting; and circulatory problems from standing. Janitorial workers may have contact with dangerous chemicals in cleaning agents. Asthma is an occupational hazard for animal workers, veterinarians, farmers, bakers, carpenters, welders, and many other workers.

Industrial nurses and safety engineers emphasize wearing protective clothing and using protective equipment. Yet there are problems. The employee may not want to be bothered with cumbersome protective clothing. Or the protective clothing and equipment given to a female worker may be too large and heavy, thus ill-fitting and not protective, for it is designed for the male employee. (However, a few companies do specialize in protective clothing designed for females.) Hard hats, safety shoes and gloves, and ear muffs that fit improperly may actually contribute toward an accidental injury.

To compound the problem of prevention, length of exposure to an industrial substance often determines if it will cause disease. The amount of exposure to the worker often depends on the production phase involved. Additionally, each substance appears likely to produce disease, such as cancer, in a specific body part; such information becomes available after workers become ill. Sex is also a factor, for some substances affect the reproductive organs of the female (or fetus) but do not affect the male. Some substances do not affect the male reproductive organs, but the father's genes may contribute to fetal damage.*

Each year an estimated 10,000 American workers die of work-related injuries. In 1980, women comprised 43 percent of the American workforce; they were more likely than men to work in certain industries and occupations (retail trade, personal services, and professional and related services) and less likely than men to work in others (agriculture, mining, construction, and transportation). The risks men and women workers face, therefore, can be expected to differ (34).

In a review of death certificates of 348 Texas women whose death resulted from injury at work, the median age of the women at death was 37 years, with a range of 17 to 92 years. This resulted in a premature loss (death before age 65) of 9,078 potential years of life. Homicide was the leading cause of death (53 percent), followed by injuries from motor vehicles, falls, fires and flames, machinery or tools, explosions, and other causes. Injuries from firearms caused 70 percent of the homicides. The remaining homicides were caused by injuries from cutting or piercing instruments, strangulation, drowning, and other means. The retail trade industry had the highest workplace homicide rate. Three retail trade subindustries had especially high workplace homicide rates: gasoline service stations, food-bakery-and-dairy stores, and eating-and-drinking places. Of the occupations, female drivers of heavy trucks had the highest fatal occupational injury rate, with motor vehicle incidents accounting for 89 percent of their fatal injuries. Three occupations had markedly elevated workplace homicide rates: stock handlers and baggers, food counter and fountain workers, and supervisors and proprietors in sales occupations. Of the 85 confirmed workplace homicides, 47 percent occurred during robberies, 7 percent during arguments between victims and customers, 21 percent under other known circumstances, and 25 percent under unknown circumstances. The offenders were either of unknown relationships or strangers to the victims in 71 percent of the homicides; spouses or other intimate acquaintances in 16 percent of the homicides; customers in 8 percent of the homicides; and co-workers in 5 percent homicides. Injuries from firearms caused 81 percent of the confirmed workplace homicides. Similar results have been found

---

*Information about health hazards for women employees and preventive or corrective measures is available from the Woman's Occupational Health Resource Center, American Health Foundation, 320 East 43rd Street, New York, NY, 10017.

in studies in Wisconsin and Maryland. However, these studies probably underestimate fatal occupational injuries of women (34).

Studies of causes of occupationally related death in California and Texas showed a higher percentage of homicides, particularly for police, security guards, taxi drivers, and supervisors or clerks in gas stations, waiters in food and dairy stores and eating and drinking places. In California, homicide rates for females were highest among service occupations (eating/drinking places). Firearms accounted for 77 percent of all work-related homicides. Workers of 65 years or older were at higher risk for homicide than younger workers. Homicides are more likely to occur between 3 P.M. and 3 A.M. (33, 99).

✔ Controlling exposures of high-risk individuals and developing strict standards for reducing such exposures, such as handgun control laws, might greatly reduce assaults and prevent senseless loss of life in the workplace. Employees in food-bakery-and-dairy stores are a high-risk group. The number of homicide-related robberies in convenience stores can be reduced by: making the cash register area more visible from the street; making it known that as little money as possible is kept in the cash register; the use of a drop safe into which, at night, all bills of value greater than $1 are placed; and keeping the store clean of potential hiding places. Bulletproof barriers between the driver and passenger compartments in taxicabs, enclosed cashier booths in gasoline service stations, and protective vests for law-enforcement officers and private-security personnel are other possible techniques to prevent workplace homicides. However, the extent to which these techniques are already practiced and their efficacy at preventing these homicides is unknown (33, 99).

Hazards of the factory or mine can extend beyond the workplace and endanger the workers' families and other residents of the community. Workers carry out dust particles on skin and clothing; wind currents also deposit particles. Even if workers shower before leaving work, the total removal of all dust particles of some chemicals or elements is difficult. As a result, some communities become well known for a high incidence of certain types of cancer or skin or respiratory disease.

✔ Knowing that the worker may come in contact with a variety of harmful substances and that presenting symptoms may often seem unrelated to the occupation should help you be more thorough and careful in assessment. Also, as a citizen you can work for enforcement of preventive measures for known hazards and for continued research.

Table 2–2 summarizes common industrial agents (various substances, elements, or chemicals) and their major known effects. Refer to the references at the end of the chapter for more information (18, 20, 27, 39, 40, 51–53, 64, 75, 84, 86, 97, 100, 105, 116, 122–124, 133, 143, 149, 150, 157, 164, 176–178, 182, 188, 189, 228, 233).

Excessive heat, cold, humidity, sunlight, noise and/or vibration are health hazards in many occupations. Examples are listed below. These hazards are further aggravated by smoking or alcohol or drug abuse (143).

Agriculture	Gasoline station
Airlines	attendant
Auto mechanics	Highway/street workers
Construction	Laundry
Cosmetology	Lumbering/sawmill
Dry cleaning	operations
Exterminators	Meat butchering/
Factory assembly	wrapping
line production	Mining
Firefighting	Painting
Fisherman	Police/security guard
Forestry	Postal workers
Foundry/smelter	Shipping industry
Gardener/nursery	Shipyard workers
	Transportation
	Welding
	Wood workers

Other occupational hazards exist for women and men. Clerical and other workers who regularly use video display terminals and computers have higher stress-related illnesses, more eyestrain, and greater emotional burnout (176).

✔ *NURSING APPLICATIONS*

Personal Responsibility

Consider the environment, the various social institutions, and the population as a complex of interacting, interdependent systems. Environmental problems are a concern to everyone and are of equal consequence to every part of the world. Each of us shares the earth and so we are all responsible for its well-being. Environmental pollution is our collective fault and requires our collective solutions. In the United States alone, discarded materials amount to billions of tons yearly and the quantity is growing annually.

A fourfold environmental protection system is useful for continuously identifying, analyzing, and controlling environmental hazards:

1. Surveillance—maintaining an awareness of what people and industries are doing to the air, water, and land, and of the effect of these actions on health; monitoring exposure.

TABLE 2—2. Effects of Some Common Industrial Agents Upon the Worker

AGENT	TYPE OF INDUSTRY OR OCCUPATION	BODY AREA AFFECTED
ACETALDELHYDE	Chemical. Paint.	All body cells, especially brain and respiratory tract.
ACETIC ANHYDRIDE	Textile.	Exposed tissue damage, especially eye and respiratory tract. (ulceration, irritation).
ACETYLENE	Welding. Plastic. Dry Cleaning.	Respiratory tract asphyxiant. Explosive, especially when combined with certain substances.
ACROLEIN	Chemical.	Skin. Eye. Respiratory tract.
ALLYL CHLORIDE	Plastic.	Skin. Respiratory tract. Kidney.
AMMONIA	Chemical. Leather. Wool. Farmers. Refrigeration Workers.	Eyes. Skin. Respiratory tract (ulceration, irritation.)
ANESTHETIC GASES (Leakage from equipment, exhalation of patients)	Surgical Nurses. Medical. Hospital. Dental. Veterinary Workers.	Reproductive organs (spontaneous abortions, infertility, congenital abnormalities and cancer whether male or female exposure). Neurological system (drowsy, irritable, headache). Respiratory tract (infections, cancer).
ANILINE	Paint. Rubber.	Skin. Hematopoietic system.
ARSENIC	Mines. Smelters. Leather. Chemical. Oil Refinery. Ship Builders. Insecticide Makers and Sprayers. Pottery Workers. Agriculture.	Skin (ulcerations, cancer). Lung, liver (cancer). Neurological damage. Reproductive system (birth defects, chromosome alterations).
ASBESTOS	Brake Mechanics. Mines. Textiles. Insulation. Paint. Sheet Metal Workers. Shipyard Workers. Construction. Plastics. Pipe Fitters. Maintenance Workers.	Respiratory tract (cancer, asbestosis, bronchitis, emphysema). Gastrointestinal tract (cancer). More harmful to people who smoke.
BENZENE	Rubber. Chemicals. Explosives. Paints and Paint Strippers. Shoemakers. Dye Users. Office Workers. Chemists. Hospital Workers. Solvent Cleaner Users. Coke Oven Workers. Furniture Finishers. Artists.	Skin. Liver. Brain (carcinogenic). Hematopoietic system (anemia, leukemia). Reproductive system (chromosome mutations in males, menstrual irregularities, stillbirths).
BERYLLIUM	Foundry. Metallurgical. Aerospace. Nuclear. Household Appliance. Production. Metal Cans. Shipbuilding.	Skin and eye (inflammation, ulcers). Respiratory tract (acute inflammation and berylliosis—chronic lung infection). Systemic effects on heart, liver, spleen, kidneys.
BUTYL ALCOHOL	Lacquer. Paint.	Eye. Skin. Respiratory tract.
CADMIUM	Smelters. Storage Battery Workers. Silver Industry. Plastics. Dental. Pigment Makers. Artists. Electrical Workers. Households (silver cleaner, ice cube trays).	Gastrointestinal tract (irritation, cancer). Reproductive system (deceased sperm, impotence).
CARBON DISULfIDE	Rubber. Viscose Rayon Workers. Plastics. Soil Treaters. Wax, Glue or Resin Makers. Medical. Laboratory Workers. Agriculture.	Gastrointestinal. Heart. Liver. Kidney. Brain. Reproductive system (deceased sperm, decreased libido, impotence, infertility, menstrual changes, stillbirth, spontaneous abortion).
CARBON TETRACHLORIDE	Solvent. Dry Cleaning. Paint. Chemical Laboratory. Household (fire extinguishers).	Skin. Gastrointestinal. Liver. Kidney. Bladder. Brain. Respiratory tract (irritation and carcinogen).
CHEMOTHERAPY (Antineoplastic) MEDICATIONS	Medical. Nurses.	Skin and cornea (irritation, ulcers). Reproductive system (fetal damage, cancer). Liver and other organs (may be carcinogenic). (Some need special handling. Effects vary with specific agent.)

TABLE 2–2. Continued

AGENT	TYPE OF INDUSTRY OR OCCUPATION	BODY AREA AFFECTED
CHLORINE	Industrial Bleaching. Laundry. Chemical Industries. Swimming Pool Maintenance.	Eyes. Respiratory tract and skin (irritation, ulcerations, infections, cancer). Skin discoloration orange.
CHLOROFORM (Chlorinated hydrocarbons)	Chemical. Plastics. Dry Cleaners. Drug Workers. Electronic Equipment Workers.	Heart degeneration. Liver. Kidney. Reproductive system (infertility male and female).
CHROMIUM	Chrome Plating. Chemical. Industrial Bleaching. Glass and Pottery. Linoleum Makers. Battery Makers. Metal Cans and Coatings.	Irritating to all body cells. Skin. Eye. Respiratory tract (cancer, ulcerations). Liver. Kidney.
CLEANING AGENTS, SOLVENTS	Maintenance Workers. Painters. Households.	Respiratory tract (irritation, allergy, asthma, cancer). Eyes (irritation, ulcers). Skin (ulcers, dermatosis, cancer).
COAL COMBUSTION PRODUCTS (Soot, tar, coal tar products)	Gashouse Workers. Asphalt, Coal Tar or Pitch Workers. Coke Oven Workers. Mines. Plastics. Roofers. Waterproofers. Metal Coating Workers. Ship Building.	Skin. Respiratory tract. Gastrointestinal tract. Scrotum, urinary tract, bladder (carcinogenic to all areas). Hyperpigmentation of skin.
COTTON, FLAX, HEMP, LINT	Textile.	Respiratory tract (byssinosis-chest tightness, dyspnea, cough, wheezing; chronic bronchitis). Cigarette smokers especially affected.
CREOSAL	Chemical. Oil Refining.	Denatures and precipitates all cellular protein. Skin. Eye. Respiratory tract. Liver. Kidney. Brain.
DICHLOROETHYL ETHER	Insecticide. Oil Refining.	Respiratory tract.
DIMETHYL SULFATE	Chemical. Pharmaceutical.	Eye. Respiratory tract. Liver. Kidney. Brain.
DYES	Dyeworkers.	Urinary bladder (cancer).
ETHYLENE OXIDE	Hospital Workers (sterilization). Workers Using Epoxyresins.	Skin. Eyes (infection, ulcers, burns). Neurological system (drowsy, weak). Leukemia. Lymphoma. Respiratory tract (dyspnea, cyanosis, pulmonary edema, cancer). Gastrointestinal tract (vomiting, cancer). Reproductive organs (chromosome damage, spontaneous abortion, fetal damage, infertility male and female).
EXHAUST FUMES	Mechanics. Gas Station and Garage Workers.	Respiratory tract. Urinary bladder (cancer).
FORMALDEHYDE	Laboratory Workers. Medical (Cold Sterilization). Mechanics. Textile. Home Insulators. Mobile Home Owners. Households (wet-strength paper towels, permanent press clothing, foam insulation).	Liver, lung, skin (infection, ulcers, cancer). Eye, nose, throat (irritation). Neurological system (headache, fatigue, memory loss, nausea). Reproductive tract (gene mutation).
FUNGUS, PARASITES, MICROORGANISMS	Food. Animal. Outdoor Workers. Clinical Laboratory Workers.	Skin. Respiratory tract (infection, including hepatitis B).
GERMICIDAL AGENTS	Health Care Workers. Maintenance/Cleaning Workers.	Skin (contact allergy, dermatosis).
HYDROGEN CHLORIDE	Meat Wrappers.	Respiratory tract (irritation and asthma).
IRON OXIDE	Mine, Iron Foundry. Metal Polishers and Finishers.	Respiratory tract (cancer).
LEAD	Auto. Smelters. Plumbing. Paint. Metallurgical. Battery Workers. Paint. Plumbers. Plastics. Pottery. Ceramics. Gasoline Station Attendants. Electronics. Manufacture. Shipbuilding. Shoemakers. Households. Exposure in 120 Industries.	Hematopoietic, cardiovascular (hypertension). Liver. Kidney. Central nervous system and brain (behavioral change). Muscles. Bone. Gastrointestinal tract.

TABLE 2–2. Effects of Some Common Industrial Agents Upon the Worker—Continued

AGENT	TYPE OF INDUSTRY OR OCCUPATION	BODY AREA AFFECTED
LEAD (continued)		Reproductive system (chromosome mutation, causes fetal damage or spontaneous abortion during first trimester of pregnancy, infertility male and female, stillbirth, impotency, menstrual irregularities).
LEATHER	Leather. Shoe.	Nasal cavity and sinuses. Urinary bladder (carcinogenic).
LYE	Households (drain openers, oven and other cleaners).	Eyes (corneal ulceration). Skin (ulcerations). Respiratory tract (irritation).
MANGANESE	Mine. Metallurgical. Welders. Shipbuilding.	Respiratory tract. Liver. Brain.
MERCURY	Electrical and Laboratory Workers. Dye makers. Explosives. Drug Workers. Plastics. Paint. Pesticide Workers. Households. Exposure in 80 Different Types of Industries.	Toxic to all cells. Skin (ulcers, dermatosis, hyperpigmentation). Respiratory tract. Liver. Brain damage. Reproductive system (infertility male and female, spontaneous abortions, birth defects). Exposure of pregnant women causes congenital defects and retardation in child.
METHYLENE CHLORIDE	Paint Removers.	Respiratory tract (irritant, carcinogen).
MICA	Rubber. Insulation.	Respiratory tract.
NICKEL	Metallurgical. Smelter. Electrolysis Workers.	Skin. Respiratory tract (infection and cancer).
NITRIC ACID	Chemical Industries. Electroplaters. Jewelers. Lithographers.	Skin (ulcerations, orange discoloration). Eye (ulcerations.)
NITROBENZENE	Synthetic Dyes.	Skin. Hematopoietic system. Brain.
NITROGEN DIOXIDE	Chemical. Metal.	Eye. Respiratory tract. Hematopoietic system.
ORGANOPHOSPHATES (Pesticides)	Agriculture. Pesticide Manufacturers and Sprayers. Exterminators.	Reproductive system (congenital anomalies). Brain dysfunction and neurological damage (memory loss, disorientation, ataxia). Liver and kidney (cancer). Respiratory tract (infections, cancer).
PENTA-CHLOROPHENOL	Wood Preservatives Industry.	Liver. Kidney. Nervous system.
PETROLEUM PRODUCTS	Rubber. Textile. Aerospace. Workers in Contact with Fuel Oil, Coke, Paraffin, Lubricants. Dry Cleaning.	Skin. Respiratory tract. Scrotum (carcinogenic to each). Dermatosis. Hyperpigmentation to skin.
PHENOL	Plastics.	Corrosive to all tissue. Liver. Kidney. Brain. Skin (ulceration).
POLYURETHANE	Plastics and Most Other Industries.	Respiratory tract (asthma, cancer). Dermatosis.
PRINTING INK	Printers.	Respiratory tract (irritation). Urinary bladder (cancer).
RADIATION	Health Care Workers. Doctors, Nurses, Dentists, Radiologists, and X-Ray Technicians (diagnostic, fluoroscopy, treatment, isotopes). Physical Therapists (diathermy). Microbiologists and Laboratory Technicians (electron microscope). Office Workers (some types of computers and office machines). Radar Systems (police, weather, airport workers). Nuclear Generating Stations. AM, FM, TV Broadcasting Stations. Atomic Workers. Food Workers. Fiber Workers. Households (microwave ovens, some computers).	Reproductive system (chromosome irritation, sterility in men and women, birth defects, impotence, cancer). Hematopoietic system (leukemia). Thyroid (cancer). Other body systems, bone and skin (cancer).

TABLE 2–2. Continued

AGENT	TYPE OF INDUSTRY OR OCCUPATION	BODY AREA AFFECTED
RUBBER DUST	Rubber.	Respiratory tract (chronic disease, cancer). Dermatosis.
SILICA	Mine. Foundry. Ceramic or Glass Production.	Respiratory tract (silicosis, pneumoconiosis, emphysema).
TALC DUST	Mine.	Respiratory tract (cancer). Calcification of pericardium.
TETRAETHYL LEAD	Chemical.	Hematopoietic system. Brain.
THALLIUM	Pesticide. Fireworks or Explosives	Skin. Respiratory and gastrointestinal tracts. Kidney. Brain.
TOLUENE	Metal Coatings. Rubber. Paint. Clerical Workers. Printers. Cosmetologists. Plastics.	Skin. Respiratory tract. Liver. Hematopoietic system. Brain (may cause drunken state and accidents). Reproductive system (infertility, birth defects, chromosome damage in male).
TRICHLORETHYLENE	Chemical-Metal Degreasing. Contact Cement. Paint. Plastics. Upholstery Cleaners.	Skin. Liver. Kidney. Brain (carcinogen).
VINYL CHLORIDE	Plastic. Rubber. Insulation. Organic-Chemical Synthesizers. Polyvinyl-Resin Makers.	Skin. Respiratory tract (asthma). Cancer in the liver, kidney, spleen and brain. Reproductive system (chromosome mutation, stillbirth, spontaneous abortion). Exposure of pregnant woman to polyvinyl chloride causes defective fetus.
WOOD PRODUCTS	Furniture.	Respiratory tract (asthma).

2. Development of criteria for the detection of pollution; detection.
3. Research, including data from various records.
4. Compliance—getting local government and industry to accept and implement new standards (53, 109, 164).

Citizen Role. An informed public can help establish such a system, but the financial support and legislative and administrative guidance of federal, state, and local governments seem to be the most feasible solutions. Encourage your local, state, or federal government officials to pass legislation that would protect the environment, for example, installation of scrubbers in factories to decrease the release of sulfur dioxide, use of low-sulfur or "washed" coal, and installation of antipollution devices on automobiles and air crafts.

The Resource Conservation and Recovery Act of 1976 (PC 94-580) provides for recycling of our natural resources, safe disposal of discarded materials, and management of hazardous wastes, those that contribute to increased mortality or pose a substantial present or potential threat to human health or environment. But these goals are not possible without individual effort. Refer to Table 2–3 for disposal of hazardous products.

As a citizen, you should conserve natural resources to the best of your ability and learn about the environmental pollution in your own area. Remember that metallurgical and chemical companies are the greatest source of hazardous waste. Campaign for minimized waste and for safe disposal of unavoidable waste. Encourage the development of additional burial sites for long-term safety as well as the monitoring of present sites for escape of wastes (174).

Lifestyle Changes. Quiet surroundings are a natural resource, too. Make your own quieter through personal habits. Help plan for local recreation sites that offer natural surroundings. Campaign for adequate acoustical standards in homes, apartments, hospitals, and industrial buildings, and for noiseless kitchen equipment. Participate in local government planning to decrease town and city noise in relation to transportation routes, zoning, and industrial sites.

Avoid unnecessary use of water, electricity, and fuel. Do not litter. Buy beverages in returnable bottles and save cans and papers for recycling. Most cities have aluminum recycling points for beverage cans, gutters, siding, furniture, or household items for your use.

Use undyed paper products. Avoid high-phosphate detergents and aerosols. Do not carelessly dispose of

TABLE 2–3. Common Toxics and How to Dispose of Them

PRODUCT	DANGER	DISPOSAL
• Pest-control chemicals (insecticides; mothballs, flea and roach powder, weed killer)	Poisonous carcinogenic	Offer leftovers to a nursery or garden shop, or local business. Pesticides may be accepted by a chemical waste company or county agricultural agency.
• Oil-based paints	Flammable	Call your local health department, ask if it has a policy for disposal of paint (some agencies have free clean-up days). Paint you cannot use can go to a neighbor, friend, or local organization or theatre group.
• Solvents (paint thinner, turpentine, rust remover, nail polish remover, and furniture stripper)	Flammable and poisonous; respiratory, eye and skin irritant	Use them up or give them away. Paint thinner can be reused by letting the liquid sit (in a closed jar) until paint particles settle out. Strain off and reuse the clear liquid. Wrap the residue in plastic and put in trash.
• Waste motor oil	Poisonous if ingested	Recycle at a gas station or auto service center.
• Car batteries	Corrosive to skin and eyes	Check area gas stations. Some will take old batteries. A few even offer cash for them.

used batteries, used engine oil, or empty pesticide containers. Walk or bicycle instead of driving a car when feasible. Avoid cigarette smoking in closed, crowded areas. Avoid contact with pesticides by thoroughly scrubbing or peeling foodstuffs and, if possible, maintain your own garden without use of pesticides.

Do not burn leaves; contribute to a natural resource—soil—by composting plants or organic content in garbage. Plant a rooftop or patio garden to contribute to the oxygen cycle. Limit the number of pet animals.

Support for Conservation. Join citizens' crusades for a clean environment or a conservation organization and attend workshops given by the Cancer Society, Sierra Club, Conservation Foundation, and League of Women Voters to learn more about problems, preventive measures, and means of strengthening legislation. Support antipollution and noise-control laws. Be an involved citizen!

The various national wildlife organizations are studying the environment and alerting citizens about hazardous wastes and toxins in the environment. These organizations, such as National Wildlife Federation, Audubon Society, Sierra Club, Nature Conservancy, and Coalition for the Environment in St. Louis have worked closely with Congress and state legislators to pass protective legislation, have held public hearings to initiate protective measures, and have conducted citizen education. Often neither the legislators nor the citizens are as attentive as they should be. Support to this type of organization and to legislative efforts is important as a citizen. In the process, you are contributing to the health of your family, your community, and your nation.[†]

Professional Responsibility

Although nursing responsibilities have been interwoven throughout this chapter, consider that your primary responsibilities are detection through thorough assessment, making suggestions for intervention, and health teaching.

Assessment and Diagnosis. Screening for occupational diseases resulting from exposure to contaminants is most accurately done by occupational health nurses and physicians rather than by employees in corporate medical groups (233). Increasingly there are improved radiologic and blood chemistry diagnostic tests to de-

---

[†] For more information on specific measures for wasting less and practicing ecologically sound living, see Saltonstall, *Your Environment and What You Can Do About it* (161) and the booklets published by the United States Department of Labor and the Environmental Protection Agency that are listed in the references.

tect diseases that are related to the occupation, including a blood test to detect pesticide contamination. Keep abreast of medical advances (189, 233).

You can play a significant role in the early detection of lead poisoning, for example. Assessment of a child's health should include observation for physical signs, such as tremors, abdominal discomfort, decreased appetite, and vomiting, as well as questions related to a pica behavior. Ask the mother about her child's interest in play, ability to get along with playmates, coordination, and level of developmental skill attainment. Phrase your questions and comments carefully, in a nonjudgmental manner, so that the mother will not feel that her fitness as a parent is being judged. If the persons for whom you are caring live in unsatisfactory, low-income housing, work for improvement through local legislation. Emphasis must be placed on repair and deleading of dwelling places, not just on moving the present dweller to a new house or apartment. You can encourage the formation of screening and case-finding programs, already started in many cities, and you can assist with their activities. Be as thorough in assessment as possible. An example of questions usually not asked on standard health history forms that you could use in assessment of the employed client is presented in Table 2–4. Table 2–5 refers to nursing diagnoses.

Intervention. Health teaching and advocacy can increase client and community awareness and contribute to prevention of illness from pollutants or hazards.

Natural or manmade chemical pollution in soil, water, and food products can produce various adverse effects, ranging from slight health impairments to death. Higher-than-normal concentrations of nitrates in water, for example, can cause acute methemoglobinemia (a type of anemia) in infants (128, 136). Although local public health officials are responsible for maintaining safe nitrate levels in the water supply, your responsibilities are to aid in the education of the public concerning the health hazards of such pollutants and to use the epidemiological method in your work. Be

TABLE 2–4. Occupational History Form

1. Occupational History (start with last job first).

	COMPANY	DATE EMPLOYED	JOB
(a)			
(b)			
(c)			
(d)			

2. In these jobs, have you ever been exposed to:
   Excessive radiation or radioactive material? _____
   Excessive noise? _____ Excessive heat or light? _____

3. Have you worked in dusty trades? _____
   With any specific chemicals? _____
   In any vapors or fumes _____
   If your answer is yes to any questions in (2) and (3), please elaborate. _____

4. Has a job ever made you "sick"? _____ If so, which job? _____
   Explain how you were sick. _____

5. Have you ever worn any protective equipment or a specific support? _____
   If so, what? _____

6. Have you ever had a serious work injury? _____ If so, please describe.

7. Have you had several minor work injuries? _____ If so, please describe.

8. Have you ever applied for, or received, workers' compensation? _____

9. Have you ever had a pension for disability? _____

TABLE 2–5. Selected Nursing Diagnoses Related to Environmental Considerations[a]

PATTERN 1: EXCHANGING	PATTERN 6: MOVING
Potential for Injury	Altered Health Maintenance
PATTERN 3: RELATING	PATTERN 7: PERCEIVING
Social Isolation	Powerlessness
PATTERN 5: CHOOSING	PATTERN 8: KNOWING
Health Seeking Behaviors	Knowledge Deficit

[a]Many of the NANDA nursing diagnoses are applicable to the person who is ill as a result of environmental pollution or hazards, or occupational causes.
Source: NANDA Approved Nursing Diagnostic Categories, *Nursing Diagnosis Newsletter*, 15, no. 1 (Summer, 1988), 1–3.

aware of such symptoms as fatigue, listlessness, and sleepiness that may indicate an untoward reaction to this particular form of pollution.

Another dangerous problem associated with chemical pollution is its possible carcinogenic effect (as seen on Table 2–2). Incidence of specific forms of cancer can be higher or lower, depending on exposure to specific compounds, a common example being the high incidence of lung cancer in the United States and England because of heavy tobacco use. Be aware and knowledgeable of the incidence of chemically produced cancer in your particular locale. Health teaching can then be directed at trying to eliminate or control the responsible carcinogenic chemical. Radiation is also carcinogenic. Encourage the use of protective clothing and sunscreen lotions to prevent overexposure to the sun. Prevent overexposure to ionizing radiation by making certain that unnecessary x-rays are not taken, by keeping a record of the frequency of x-rays, and by using a lead shield when x-rays are given.

The biochemical response to chemical pollution or radiation can influence the cells in various ways. **Teratogenic** (*producing malformations*) and **mutagenic** (*producing hereditary changes*) are two such changes in cells. Be aware that these changes can occur in both the client and the health care worker who are exposed to radiation. Genetic counseling might be indicated for couples who have been exposed to radiation. Citizens should know of the possibility for dealing effectively and therapeutically with biochemical changes, whether prenatally or in any stage of growth and development (70).

In 1977, the National Institute for Occupational Safety and Health (NIOSH) issued a document, "The Right to Know: Practical Problems and Policy Issues Arising From Exposure to Hazardous Chemicals and Physical Agents in the Workplace." It proceeded from the premise that workers have a right to know about risks to which they have been exposed. For political and economic reasons, and because of constraints from the Department of Health and Human Services, NIOSH officials were reluctant to create a regulation based on the document. However, pressure from workers, consumer and conservation groups, and unions persisted.

Under the Hazardous Communication Rule passed in 1983, workers must be informed about any hazardous chemicals to which employees are exposed in the workplace. However, the Rule is limited: it covers only manufacturing companies, and employers may claim a chemical is a trade secret and release the name only to a health professional who has a right to know. Health care professionals, the unions, and conservation and consumer groups will need to continue to advocate for all workers so that the Rule will be applied in a broader perspective (11, 160). Stromberg (183) discusses recent legislation that regulates the workplace and carcinogenic agents, benefits to workers, and the nurse's role. Her information may be useful to you.

As a professional and as a citizen, you can encourage officials and consumers in your community to develop innovative technologies to cope with the hazardous effects of aspects of our current lifestyle. For example, the city of Muskegan, Michigan, constructed an innovative facility that recycles wastewater so that it can be used safely and economically to irrigate farmland. Sewage residues given conventional treatment becomes more toxic with each step. Wastewater and sewage residues that are gradually percolated through natural soil filters uses fewer chemicals to treat sewage and generates less sludge. The resulting water residues are high in plant nutrients and can be recycled as fertilizer. Land treatment facilities use energy only for pumping, allow communities to reuse water, and can make money for the community (107).

Join the Nurses Environmental Health Watch, a nonprofit organization formed in 1979, with chapters in 39 states. The organization seeks to educate nurses and the public about current issues influencing health and the environment, including environmental toxins and pollutants, nuclear energy and energy alternatives, resource recovery and recycling, chemical and biological welfare, and occupational hazards for nurses. A quarterly newsletter, *Health Watch*, includes items about national and local activities and resources on environmental issues. Educational forums are sponsored by local chapters.

In the past 100 years, disease and death have been reduced because of preventive public health measures in the form of environmental control, such as water and waste management, rodent and insect control, development of housing codes. Now we are again faced with problems and diseases that have an environmental impact. Prevention can begin with informed consumer groups who have educational and work projects as their goals. It can begin with your responsibility for the patient's environment.

The Patient's/Client's Immediate Environment

Besides a feeling of responsibility for the community and physical environment in which the patient lives, you also have a responsibility for that individual's immediate environment while receiving health care. The patient's *surroundings should constitute a* **therapeutic milieu** *free of hazards and conducive to recovery, physically and emotionally.*

The patient's surroundings should be clean and adequately lighted, ventilated, and heated. Precautions should always be taken to prevent injury, such as burns from a hot-water bottle. Falls should be prevented by removing obstacles from walking areas and having the person wear well-fitted shoes and use adequate support while walking. Lock the bed or wheelchair while the patient is moving to and from them. Be sure that electrical cords and scatter rugs are not so placed that the patient could fall. Wipe up spilled liquids immediately. Use sterile technique and proper handwashing methods to ensure that you bring no pathogenic organisms to the patient. Avoid excessive noise from personnel and equipment to the degree possible.

The esthetic environment is also important for rest. Arrange articles on the bedside table in a pleasing manner if the patient is unable to do so. Keep unattractive equipment and supplies out of sight as much as possible. Electrical equipment should be in proper repair and function. Minimize offensive odors and noise. Place the person's bed or chair by a window or door so that the person can watch normal activity rather than stare at the ceiling and walls. As a nurse, involve yourself in making the entire ward as well as the patients' rooms look pleasing. Consider color combinations and the use of drapes, furniture, clocks, calendars, pictures, and various artifacts to create a more homelike atmosphere. The committee in charge of decorating and building should include at least one nurse. You may need to volunteer to ensure that nursing and, indirectly, patients are represented in such programs.

The patient's surroundings should not only be safe and attractive, but the emotional climate of the unit and entire institution affects patients and staff as well. The patient and family are quick to respond and react to the attitudes and manner of the staff. Here are some questions you might ask yourself. How do I treat delivery workers who bring gifts and flowers to patients? Do I participate in the joy such remembrances bring to the patient? Do I help arrange the flowers into a pleasant pattern or just stick them quickly into whatever can be found? Do I treat visitors as welcome guests or as foreign intruders? The emotional climate should radiate security and acceptance. A warmth should prevail that promotes a sense of feeling of trust, confidence, and motivation within the patient as he/she and the staff work together to cope with problems. The emotional relationship between the patient and the health care staff should help the patient reach the goal of maximum health.

In a truly **therapeutic milieu** the staff also feel a sense of harmony among themselves. There are mutual trust and acceptance between staff and supervisors, and supervisors recognize work well done by the staff. As a result, staff feel motivated to continue to learn and to improve the quality of patient care. Staff members are not likely to give individualized, comprehensive, compassionate care in an agency where they are not treated like individuals or where their basic needs are not met.

Be aware of environmental pollution in the health care environment. "No Smoking" should be the rule not only when oxygen is in use but also in any health care setting. Often the conference or dining rooms or lounges for health care workers are polluted with cigarette or cigar smoke and ashtrays are full. It is difficult to teach a client the adverse effects of smoking and nicotine when an odor of cigarette smoke hangs on the uniform. Moreover, health care workers will benefit from practicing what they teach others. Health care workers and clients may also come in contact with agents listed in Table 2–2. Constant vigilance is necessary to detect harmful agents and prevent or reduce their usage. Early assessment of harmful effects to reduce the symptoms and proper interventions for dermatoses, allergens, or other symptoms is essential.

There are times when the treatment for the client may also affect the health care worker—for example, radiotherapy. Proper precautions should be taken to protect the worker from excess exposure and to protect any body areas of the client that should not be exposed. Constant monitoring of the dosage and duration of exposure to radiation, whether from a portable x-ray machine or a radium implant, is essential.

When the following safety rules are adhered to, nurses can be assured of personal safety:

1. Quantities of radioactive materials used in *diagnostic* tests are very small and do not constitute a health hazard.
2. If a patient has had *therapeutic* doses of radioisotope, he/she becomes potentially dangerous, and strict precautions should be observed. The hazard

varies with the type and dosage of the isotope used and the circumstances of the particular patient. Avoid radiation exposure as much as possible and avoid contamination from radioactive body fluids.
3. Check the patient's chart as to the type of isotope given and its dosage.
4. Special orders are usually written for each patient in respect to handling contaminated linens, utensils, and other sources of contamination.
5. Contaminated materials should be kept in containers specified by the radiologist.
6. Nursing care should be given adequately, but the time element is important; the radiologist should prescribe the time that can safely be spent with the patient. Follow the principle that the farther one is away from the source of radiation, the less the danger (inverse square law).
7. Hands should be kept clean; wash thoroughly after caring for the patient under radioisotope treatment.
8. Rubber gloves should be worn to handle contaminated objects. Never touch the face; be sure to wash the gloved hands thoroughly before removing the gloves.
9. In case of a patient's death, either the radiologist or the physician (or both) should be notified and their directions specifically followed.
10. Never touch a dislodged radium needle. The radiologist should be called at once if it seems to be out of place.

Patients who are receiving radiotherapy should be assessed for the following side effects (232):

1. Malaise, weakness, fatigue, headache.
2. Redness, edema, itching, denuding, and atrophy of skin.
3. Inflammation, dryness, pain, and impaired physiological function of mucous-lined areas of the body, including the oral cavity, esophagus, and vagina. Alterations in taste are common.
4. Sloughing of epithelial cells in various body areas, such as the esophagus, stomach, intestine, and genitourinary tract, resulting in ulceration, chronic inflammation, pain, necrosis, and impaired physiological functions of the organ system affected (vomiting, diarrhea, cystitis).
5. Depression of bone marrow, resulting in reduced white and red blood cells and platelets, which, in turn, causes infections, anemia, and hemorrhagic tendencies.
6. Inflammatory and fibrotic damage to the lungs and heart, causing pneumonitis, pericarditis, and occasionally myocarditis.
7. Temporary or permanent loss of hair, depending on dosage and duration of exposure.

Intervention for these side effects includes skin and mouth care; dietary modifications; use of mild analgesics, antiemetics, and antidiarrheal drugs; and reverse isolation technics. Refer to a medical-surgical text for specific interventions for the patient who is suffering side effects from radiotherapy.

If you are caring for a person in the home, you are limited in the amount of change you can make. You can point out such hazards as electrical cords in the walking area, however. You can make suggestions for furniture rearrangement if you think that the person could function more easily with the change. You can put a clock in sight, pull the drapes, or put needed materials within the patient's reach if feasible.

Specific ways of meeting the patient's environmental needs also differ for various developmental stages. The components of a therapeutic milieu are different for the baby than for the middle-aged man. However, a safe, secure environment, physically and psychologically, must be present for both. Accurately determining the factors that make up the environment and making appropriate changes may be the first step in promoting health.

It is past time for all of us to ask ourselves some basic questions. How much energy and natural resources do we need to sustain life, to maintain the high standard of living in the United States? How much are we willing to pay for benefits that will not poison us with side effects? How does population growth affect the use and abuse of natural resources? Will strictly controlled energy allocation be necessary because people refuse to abide by suggested limits? Must people continue to grow up with strontium-90 in their bones, DDT in their fat, and asbestos in their lungs? What more can each of us do personally and professionally to maintain a health-fostering environment?

References

1. A Nation Troubled by Toxins, *National Wildlife*, 25, no. 2 (1987), 33–40.
2. Additives at Fault in Hyperactivity, *Science News*, 117, no. 13 (1980), 199, 204.
3. Alexander, Peter, et al., *Biology*. Morristown, NJ: Silver Burdett, 1986.
4. Anderson, A.C., G.R. Hodges, and J.S. Reed, Needlestick and Puncture Wounds: Definition of the Problem, *American Journal of Infection Control*, 8, no. 4 (1980), 101–106.
5. Arbab, Donna, and Louise Weidner, Infectious Diseases and Field Water Supply and Sanitation Among Migrant Farm Workers, *American Journal of Public Health*, 76, no. 6 (1986), 694–695.
6. Arms, Karen, and Pamela Camp, *Biology* (3rd ed.). Philadelphia: Saunders College Publishing, 1987.

7. Back Injury—the Money Side: Problems of Getting Compensation, *Nursing Times* (November 7, 1974), 1728–1729.
8. Baker, Dean, Giardia! *National Wildlife*, 23, no. 5 (1985), 19–21.
9. Barlett, Donald, and James Steele, *Forevermore: Nuclear Waste in America*. New York: W.W. Norton, 1985.
10. Barrett, James, Peter Abramoff, Krishna Kumaran, et al., *Biology*. Englewood Cliffs, NJ: Prentice-Hall, 1986.
11. Bayer, Ronald, Notifying Workers at Risk: The Politics of the Right-to-Know, *American Journal of Public Health*, 76, no. 11 (1986), 1352–1356.
12. Bergen, Jane, and Merilyn Reeves, Safety on Tap, *The National Voter*, 37, no. 1 (1987), 13–17.
13. Begley, Sharon, The Greater, *Newsweek* (March 16, 1987), 76–77.
14. Begley, Sharon, Silent Spring Revisited, *Newsweek* (July 14, 1986), 72–74.
15. Begley, Sharon, The Silent Summer, *Newsweek* (June 23, 1986), 64–66.
16. Berman, J., L. Desi, M.L. Levin, et al., Tuberculosis Risk for Hospital Employees: Analysis of a Five-Year Tuberculin Skin Testing Program, *American Journal of Public Health*, 71, no. 11 (1981), 1217–1222.
17. Bernstein, Robert, Henry Falk, Douglas Turner, et al., Nonoccupational Exposures to Indoor Air Pollutants: A Survey of State Programs and Practices, *American Journal of Public Health*, 74, no. 9 (1984), 1020–1023.
18. Beware Sick-Building Syndrome, *Newsweek* (January 7, 1985), 58–60.
19. Bowman, R.A., and M. Heins, What the SNA's are doing . . . in Tennessee, *American Journal of Nursing*, 82 (1982), 583–584.
20. Brown, Michael, The Toxic Cloud, *Greenpeace*, 12, no. 4 (1987), 17–23.
21. Brubaker, Sterling, *To Live on Earth*. New York: New American Library, 1972.
22. Bryen, M., H. Cerr, and M. Gregg, An Outbreak of Nonparenterally Transmitted Hepatitis B, *Epidemiology for the Infection Control Nurse*. St. Louis; C.V. Mosby, 1978.
23. Burton, Lloyd, and Hugh Smith, *Public Health and Community Medicine for the Allied Medical Professions* (2nd ed.). Baltimore: Williams & Wilkins, 1975.
24. Cancer: The Environmental Connection, *Science Challenge*, 5, no. 3 (1982), 3–11.
25. Chanlett, Emil, D. Rogers, and G. Hurst, The Necessity for Environmental Health Planning, *American Journal of Public Health*, 63, no. 4 (1973), 341–344.
26. Chisolm, Julian, Lead Poisoning, *Scientific American*, 244, no. 2 (1971), 15–23.
27. Choi-Lao, A., Trace Anesthetic Vapors in Hospital Operating Room Environments, *Nursing Research*, 30, no. 3 (1981), 156–160.
28. Cimino, J., Health and Safety in the Solid Waste Industry, *American Journal of Public Health*, 65, no. 1 (1975), 38–46.
29. Clark, Matt, The Garbage Health Scare, *Newsweek* (July 20, 1987), 56.
30. Clean Air Legislation Likely in this Congress, *Chemecology*, (March 1987), 6.
31. Clean Water Act Passes Over Veto, *Chemecology* (March 1987), 8.
32. Corwin, Emil, On Getting the Lead Out of Food, *FDA Consumer*, 16, no. 2 (1982), 19–21.
33. Davis, Harold, Workplace Homicides of Texas Males, *American Journal of Public Health*, 77, no. 10 (1987), 1290–1293.
34. Davis, Harold, Patricia Honchar, and Lucina Suarez, Fatal Occupational Injuries of Women, Texas 1975–84, *American Journal of Public Health*, 77, no. 12 (1987), 1524–1527.
35. de L.G. Solbe, J.F. (ed.), *Effects of Land Use on Fresh Waters: Agriculture, Forestry, Mineral Exploitation, Urbanization*. West Sussex, England: Ellis Horwood, 1986.
36. Dewailly, Eric, Claude Poirier, and Francois Meyer, Health Hazards Associated with Windsurfing on Polluted Water, *American Journal Public Health*, 76, no. 6 (1986), 690–91.
37. Dilday, R.C., What the SNA's Are Doing . . . in Georgia, *American Journal of Nursing*, 82, (1982), 581–582.
38. Dobrzanski, T., and T. Rychta, Cattell's 16 Personality Factors and Biochemical Responses to Occupational Noise Exposure, *Poland's Archives of Medicine*, 58, no. 5 (1977), 427–435.
39. Drummond, A.G. Lead Poisoning in Children, *Journal of School Health*, January 1981, pp. 43–47.
40. Duffus, John M., *Environmental Toxicology*. New York: John Wiley, 1980.
41. Durso-Hughes, Katherine, and James Lewis, Problems in Recycling Hazardous Waste, *Environment*, 24, no. 2 (1982), 14 ff.
42. Edwards, Clive, Soil Pollutants and Soil Animals, *Scientific American*, 220, no. 4 (1969), 88–99.
43. Eisenbud, Merril, *Environmental Radioactivity: From Natural, Industrial, and Military Sources*. Orlando: Academic Press, 1987.
44. Elliott, B., and E. Williams. Help for the Helper—An Employee Assistance Program, *American Journal of Nursing*, 82 (1982), 586–587.
45. Ensor, B.E., and L.V. Jefferson. Help for the Helper—Confronting a Chemically Impaired Colleague, *American Journal of Nursing*, 82 (1982), 574–577.
46. Ensor, B.E., What the SNA's Are Doing . . . in Maryland, *American Journal of Nursing*, 82 (1982), 581.
47. Epstein, Samuel, and Lester Brown, *Hazardous Waste in America*. San Francisco: Sierra Publications, 1982.
48. Fattal, Badri, Yohanan Wax, Michael Davies, et al., Health Risks Associated with Wastewater Irrigation:

An Epidemiological Study, *American Journal of Public Health*, 76, no. 8 (1986), 977–979.
49. Fears, Thomas, J. Scott, and M. Schneiderman, Skin Cancer, Melanoma, and Sunlight, *American Journal of Public Health*, 66, no. 5 (1976), 461–464.
50. Feingold, Ben, Hyperkinesis and Learning: Disabilities Linked to Artificial Food Flavors and Colors, *American Journal of Nursing*, 75, no. 5 (1975), 797–803.
51. Flanders, W., and Kenneth Rothman, Occupational Risk for Laryngeal Cancer, *American Journal of Public Health*, 72, no. 4 (1982), 369–372.
52. Freidman, Tracy, Staying at Home Can be Dangerous to Your Health, *Common Cause* (June, 1982), 13–17.
53. Froines, John, Cornelia Dellenbaugh, and David Wegman, Occupational Health Surveillance: A Means to Identify Work-Related Risks, *American Journal of Public Health*, 76, no. 9 (1986), 1089–1096.
54. Galvin, David, and Sally Toteff, Toxics on the Home Front, *Sierra*, 71, no. 5 (1986), 44–48.
55. Gearing Up to Deal with Radon; Action Begun on Risk in Homes, *The Nation's Health*, September 1986, 1,7.
56. Gibbons, Don, Acidic Confusion Reigns, *Science Quest*, 55, no. 1 (1982), 10–15.
57. Glass, Norman R., et al., Effects of Acid Precipitation, *Environmental Science and Technology*, 16, no. 3 (1982), 162A–169A.
58. Gold, Michael, Indoor Air Pollution, *Science '80*, 1, no. 3 (1980), 30–35.
59. Goldsmith, John, and Erland Johnson, Health Effects of Community Noise, *American Journal of Public Health*, 63, no. 9 (1973), 782–793.
60. Gottfried, Sandra, et al. *Biology* (4th ed.). Englewood Cliffs, NJ: Prentice-Hall, 1987.
61. Graves, C.K., Rain of Troubles, *Science '80*, 1, no. 5 (1980), 75–79.
62. Green, Margaret, et al., An Outbreak of Watermelon-Borne Pesticide Toxicity, *American Journal of Public Health*, 77, no. 11 (1987), 1431–1434.
63. Greene, S.B., Frequency of Hospitalization Among Hospital Employees and Their Families, *American Journal of Public Health*, 71, no. 9 (1981), 1021–1025.
64. Griffin, Melanie, Setting the Record Straight on Nuclear Power Safety, *Sierra* (March–April, 1986), 23–27.
65. Grisham, Joe, ed., *Health Aspects of the Disposal of Waste Chemicals*. New York: Pergamon Press, 1986.
66. Gross, Rosalind, *Child Resistant Packages for Pesticides*. Washington, DC: U. S. Environmental Protection Agency, Office of Pesticide Programs, 1985.
67. Guralnik, David, ed., *Webster's New World Dictionary of the American Language* (2nd college ed.). New York: World Publishing, 1972.
68. Guthrie, Frank, and Jerome Perry, *Introduction to Environmental Technology*. New York: Elsevier North-Holland, 1980.
69. Hallenbeck, W.H., *Pesticides and Human Health*. New York: Springer-Verlag, 1985.
70. Hamilton, Michael, ed., *The New Genetics and the Future of Man*. Grand Rapids, MI: William B. Eerdmans, 1972.
71. Haque, Rizwanul, ed., *Dynamics, Exposure and Hazard Assessment of Toxic Chemicals*, Ann Arbor, MI: Ann Arbor Science Publishers, 1980.
72. Harakal, B.M., What the SNA's Are Doing . . . in Ohio, *American Journal of Nursing*, 82, 1982, 582–583.
73. Harrison, W.L., R.C. Hoever, and W.C. McCormick, Pilferage of Controlled Substances in Hospitals, *American Journal of Hospital Pharmacy*, 38, 1981, 1007–1010.
74. Hattis, Dale, Robert Goble, and Nicholas Ashford, Airborne Lead: A Clearcut Case of Differential Protection, *Environment*, 24, no. 6 (1982), 14–20.
75. *Hazardous Waste and Toxic Substances*. Chicago: U. S. Environmental Protection Agency-Region 5, Office of Public Affairs, Summer 1985.
76. Hazelwood, Mary, Wilsonville: What Went In, Must Come Out, *Alton Evening Telegraph*, October 9, 1982, Sec. B, p. 8.
77. Henderson, Doug, Cookware as a Source of Additives, *FDA Consumer*, 16, no. 2 (1982), 11-B.
78. Hickey, Susan, Report: Lead Poisoning Worse Than Predicted, *The Nation's Health*, 12, no. 10 (1982), 7.
79. Hileman, Bette, Acid Disposition, *Environmental Science and Technology*, 16, no. 6 (1982), 323A–327A.
80. ———, Carbon Dioxide Buildup: The Greenhouse Effect, *Environmental Science and Technology*, 16, no. 2 (1982), 90A–93A.
81. Hornblower, Margot, How Dangerous is Acid Rain? *National Wildlife*, (June/July 1983).
82. Hudson, M.P., et al., Back Pain Research, *Nursing Times*, May 14, 1981, 857–858.
83. Illinois Environmental Protection Agency, *Ozone, Smog, and You*, Springfield, IL: Office of Public Information, (Summer 1987).
84. *Indoor Air Pollution and S. 1198 Fact Sheet*. Washington, D.C.: Consumer Federation of America, 1985.
85. Industrial Wastes and the Earth, *The Nation's Health*, 12, no. 10 (1982), 7.
86. Inh, Ruay-Wang, and Nabih Asal, Mortality Among Laundry and Dry Cleaning Workers in Oklahoma, *American Journal of Public Health*, 74, no. 11 (1984), 1278–1280.
87. In Defense of Survival, from Lake to Sea, *Greenpeace*, 11, no. 2 (1986), 7–18.
88. Isler, C., The Alcoholic Nurse: What We Try to Deny, *National Clearinghouse for Alcohol Information* (n.d.), 1–5.
89. Jaffe, S., Help for the Helper—First-Hand Views of Recovery, *American Journal of Nursing*, 82 (1982), 578–579.
90. Jefferson, Linda V. and Barbara E. Ensor, Help for the

Helper: Confronting a Chemically-Impaired Colleague, *American Journal of Nursing*, 82, no. 4 (1982), 574–587.
91. Jennings, Betty, and Susie Gudermuth, Hospital Solid Waste: A Challenge for Nurses, *Missouri Nurse*, 47, no. 2 (1973), 5–7.
92. Johnson, Leland, *Biology* (2nd ed.), Dubuque, Iowa: Wm. C. Brown, 1987.
93. Jones, J.W., Attitudinal Correlates of Employee Theft of Drugs and Hospital Supplies Among Nursing Personnel, *Nursing Research*, 30, no. 6 (1981), 349–351.
94. Judge Upholds NYC Health Code Ban on Holding Patients for X-ray, *American Journal of Nursing*, 81, (1981), 1788–1791, 1907–1908.
95. Karlen, Neal, Nuclear-Powered Murder? *Newsweek* (November 4, 1985), 29.
96. Karlen, Neal, Pollution: Now the Bad News, *Newsweek* (April 8, 1985), 26.
97. Kaufman, Stephen, Radioactive Wastes in St. Louis: The Waste Pile Grows to 45 Years High, *Alert*, 18, no. 1 (1987), 4, 8.
98. Knowles, R.S., and J.E. Virden, Handling of Injectable Antineoplastic Agents, *British Medical Journal* (August 30, 1980), 589–591.
99. Kraus, Jess, Homicide While at Work: Persons, Industries, and Occupations at High Risk, *American Journal of Public Health*, 77, no. 10 (1987), 1285–1289.
100. Krokosky, Nancy, Black Lung and Silicosis, *American Journal of Nursing*, 85, no. 8 (1985), 883–886.
101. Kryter, Karl, *The Effects of Noise on Man* (2nd ed.). Orlando: Academic Press, 1985.
102. Lapham, Sandra, Richard Hopkins, Mary White, et al., A Prospective Study of Giardiasis and Water Supplies in Colorado, *American Journal of Public Health*, 77, no. 3 (1987), 354–355.
103. Legge, Allan, and Sager Krupa, *Air Pollutants and Their Effects on the Terrestrial Ecosystem*. New York: John Wiley, 1986.
104. Lehmann, Phyllis, What Are Those Additives in Food? *Consumer's Research Magazine*, 65, no. 3 (1982), 13–17.
105. Levine, R., et al., Occupational Lead Poisoning, Animal Deaths and Environmental Contamination at a Scrap Smelter, *American Journal of Public Health*, 66, no. 6 (1976), 548–552.
106. Lewis, Harold, The Safety of Fission Reactors, *Scientific American*, 242, no. 3 (1980), 53–65.
107. Licht, Judy and Jeff Johnson, Sludge is an Awful Thing to Waste, *Sierra* (March–April, 1986), 29–32.
108. Likens, Gene, Richard Wright, James Galloway, et al., Acid Rain, *Scientific American*, 241, no. 4 (1979), 43–51.
109. Linton, Ron, *Terracide*, Boston: Little, Brown, 1970.
110. Lippman, Morton, and Richard Schlesinger, *Chemical Contamination in the Human Environment*, New York: Oxford University Press, 1979.
111. Lipske, Mike, How Safe Is the Air Inside Your Home? *National Wildlife*, 25, no. 3 (1987), 35–39.
112. Litsky, Warren, Joseph Martin, and Bertha Litsky, Solid Waste: A Hospital Dilemma, *American Journal of Nursing*, 72, no. 10 (1972), 1841–1847.
113. Long, Keith, Pesticides: An Occupational Hazard on Farms, *American Journal of Nursing*, 71, no. 4 (1971), 740–743.
114. Mader, Sylvia, *Biology: Evolution, Diversity, and the Environment* (2nd Ed.). Dubuque, Iowa: Wm. C. Brown, 1987.
115. Maki, D.G., and R.D. McCormick, Epidemiology of Needle Stick Injuries in Hospital Personnel, *American Journal of Medicine*, 70, (1981), 928–932.
116. Mancino, D.J., Radiation in the Nurse's Workplace, *Imprint*, 30, (1983), 35–39.
117. Marine Pollution Threatens Water Bodies and Human Health, *The Nation's Health*, (July 1987), 8.
118. Marshall, Eliot, Turnabout on EPA Lead Rules, *Science*, 217, no. 4561 (1982), 711.
119. ———, EPA May Allow More Lead in Gasoline, *Science*, 215, no. 4538 (1982), 1375–1378.
120. ———, The Senate's Plan for Nuclear Waste, *Science*, 216, no. 4547 (1982), 709–710.
121. Marshall, G., Don't Be Shocked, *Nursing Times*, 77, no. 17 (1981), 721–722.
122. Mattia, Michael A., Hazards in The Hospital Environment: Anesthesia Gases and Methylmethacrylate, *American Journal of Nursing*, 83, no. 1 (1983), 73–76.
123. Mattia, Michael A., Hazards in the Hospital Environment: The Sterilants, Ethylene Oxide and Formaldehyde, *American Journal of Nursing*, 83, no. 2 (1983), 241–243.
124. Mattia, Michael A., and Sheila Blake, Hospital Hazards: Cancer Drugs. *American Journal of Nursing*, 83, no. 5 (1983), 758–762.
125. Mayberry, J.F., and R.G. Newcombe, Are Nurses at an Increased Risk of Developing Inflammatory Bowel Disease? *Digestion*, 22, (1981), 150–154.
126. McCormick, John, Diet for a Poisoned Planet, *Greenpeace*, 12, no. 3 (1987), 17–20.
127. McGrath, James, and Charles Barnes, *Air Pollution—Physiological Effects*. New York: Academic Press, 1982.
128. McKee, William, ed., *Environmental Problems in Medicine*, Springfield, IL: Charles C Thomas, 1974.
129. Melosi, Martin, Waste Management: The Cleaning of America, *Environment*, 23, no. 8 (1981), 6 ff.
130. Melville, Mary, Risks on the Job: The Worker's Right to Know, *Environment*, 23, no. 9 (1981), 12–20, 42–45.
131. Miller, Stanton, Is This the Last Word on Love Canal? *Environmental Science and Technology*, 16, no. 9 (1982), 500A–501A.
132. Miller, Maurice, and Carol Silverman, eds., *Occupa-

132. *tional Hearing Conservation*. Englewood Cliffs, NJ: Prentice-Hall, 1984.
133. Miller, Michael, Chlordane in Missouri, *Alert*, 18, no. 1 (Spring 1987), 1, 6–7.
134. Moses, Evelyn, and Aleda Roth, Nursepower: What Do Statistics Reveal About the Nation's Nurses, *American Journal of Nursing*, 79, no. 10 (1979), 1745–1756.
135. Nathanson, Jerry, *Basic Environmental Technology: Water Supply, Waste Disposal and Pollution Control*. New York: John Wiley, 1986.
136. Newberne, Paul, ed., *Trace Substances and Health*. New York: Marcel Dekker, 1976.
137. Norman, Colin, A Long-Term Problem for the Nuclear Industry, *Science*, 215, no. 4531 (1982), 376–378.
138. Norris, Ruth, Toxic Waste: EPA's Misleading List of 114 'Worst' Sites, *Audubon*, 84, no. 1 (1982), 106–108.
139. Okum, Daniel, Drinking Water for the Future, *American Journal of Public Health*, 66, no. 7 (1976), 639–643.
140. On the Trail of Acid Rain, *National Wildlife*, 25, no. 2 (1987), 8–12.
141. Otto, James, and Albert Towle, *Modern Biology* (11th ed.). New York: Holt, Rinehart and Winston, 1985.
142. Osborn, P., Employee Health Service in a Hospital, *Supervisor Nurse*, 10, no. 10 (1979), 40–42.
143. Ossler, Charlene, Men's Work Environments and Health Risks, *Nursing Clinics of North America*, 21, no. 1 (1986), 25–36.
144. Pantelick, E., et al., Hepatitis B Infection in Hospital Personnel During an Eight Year Period, *American Journal of Medicine*, 81, no. 4 (1981), 924–927.
145. Passive Smoke Is Workplace Risk, *The Nation's Health*, July, 1987, 13.
146. Peakall, David, Pesticides and the Reproduction of Birds, *Scientific American*, 222, no. 4 (1970), 72–78.
147. Pechter, Kerry, How Stressful Is Your Job, *Prevention* (September, 1983), 60–64.
148. Pocket Veto Kills Water Bill, *Chemecology*, (December 1986/January 1987), 3.
149. Precautionary Measures in the Preparation of Antineoplastics, *American Journal of Hospital Pharmacy* (September, 1980), 1184–1186.
150. Pretty Poison, *City of St. Louis Weekly Health Letter* (August 28, 1987), 1.
151. Proposed Water Rules Unjustified, CMA says, *Chemecology*, (April, 1986), 7.
152. Puetz, B.E., Who Cares for the Care-Givers?, *Occupational Health Nursing*, 29, no. 10 (1981), 34–37.
153. Purcell, Arthur, Three Mile Island's Three Fateful Dates . . . and the Fate of Nuclear Energy, *Science Digest*, 87, no. 4 (1980), 44–48.
154. Raistrick, A., Nurses with Back Pain—Can the Problem Be Prevented? *Nursing Times*, May 14, 1981, 853–856.
155. Raloff, J., Childhood Lead: Worrisome National Levels, *Science News*, 121, no. 5 (1982), 88.
156. Reed, Jane, Lead Poisoning: Silent Epidemic and Social Crime, *American Journal of Nursing*, 72, no. 2 (1972), 2181–2184.
157. Reich, S.D., Pharmaceutics: Antineoplastic Agents as Potential Carcinogens—Are Nurses and Pharmacists at Risk? *Cancer Nurse*, 4, no. 6 (1981), 500–502.
158. Revelle, Roger, Carbon Dioxide and World Climate, *Scientific American*, 247, no. 2 (1982), 35–43.
159. Ritchie, Ingrid, and Robert Lehmen, Formaldehyde-related Health Complaints of Residents Living in Mobile and Conventional Homes, *American Journal of Public Health*, 77, no. 3 (1987), 323–327.
160. Rule Finalized Last November: Suit Challenges OSHA Limits on Workers' Right to Know Hazards, *The Nation's Health* (July, 1984), 1, 5.
161. Saltonstall, Richard, *Your Environment and What You Can Do About It: A Citizens' Guide*, New York: Walker and Company, 1970.
162. Schultz, Cathleen, Sulfite Sensitivity, *American Journal of Nursing*, 86, no. 8 (1986).
163. Seldman, Neil, and Jon Huls, Waste Management: Beyond the Throwaway Ethic, *Environment*, 23, no. 9 (1981), 23–25.
164. Seligman, P., W. Halperin, R. Mullan, et al., Occupational Lead Poisoning in Ohio: Surveillance Using Workers' Compensation Data, *American Journal of Public Health*, 76, no. 11 (1986), 1299–1302.
165. Serafini, Patricia, Nursing Assessment in Industry, *American Journal of Public Health*, 66, no. 8 (1976), 755–760.
166. Shapiro, R., and T. Berland, Noise in the Operating Room, *New England Journal of Medicine*, 287 (December 14, 1972), 1236–1237.
167. Shaeffer, Mark, Alert on Dioxin (a series of articles), *Alert Newsletter—Coalition for the Environment*, 13, no. 1 (1983).
168. Siegel, Lenny, High-Tech Pollution, *Sierra*, (November/December, 1984), 58–64.
169. Slesnick, Irwin, et al., *Biology*, Glenview, IL: Scott, Foresman, 1985.
170. 600 Million Live in Cities with Air Pollution Risk, The Nation's Health, (July, 1987), 9.
171. Smith, Dorothy, Patienthood and Its Threat to Privacy, *American Journal of Nursing*, 69, no. 3 (1969), 509–513.
172. Smith, R. Jeffrey, How Safe Is Niagara Falls? *Science*, 217, no.. 4562 (1982), 809.
173. ———, The Risks of Living Near Love Canal, *Science*, 217, no. 4562 (1982), 808–810.
174. Solid Waste Disposal—A Long Standing Public Health Problem Comes of Age, *American Journal of Public Health*, 67, no. 5 (1977), 419–420.

175. Some Cancers May Increase Due to Ozone Depletion, *The Nation's Health*, 12, no. 6 (1982), 7.
176. Stellman, Jeanne, Occupational Health Hazards of Women—An Overview, *Preventive Medicine*, 7 (1978), 281–293.
177. Stellman, Jeanne, *Women's Work, Women's Health: Myths and Realities*. New York: Pantheon Press, 1978.
178. Stellman, Jeanne, The Effects of Toxic Agents on Reproduction, *Occupational Health and Safety*, April 1979, 36–43.
179. Stewart, Andrew P. Oral presentation at an Industrial Hearing Conservationist Training Course, November 10–12, 1982, Carrboro, NC.
180. Stomach Cancer in Navahos and Uranium Link Suspected, *The Nation's Health*, July, 1987, 9.
181. Stranahan, Susan, Living in the Shadows of Poisonous Air, *National Wildlife*, 25, no. 5 (August–September, 1987), 31–33.
182. Strobino, B., J. Kline, and Z. Stein, Chemical and Physical Exposure of Parents: Effects on Human Reproduction and Offspring, *Early Human Development*, 1, no. 4 (1978), 371.
183. Stromberg, Marilyn, Carcinogens: Are Some Risks Acceptable? *American Journal of Nursing*, 86, no. 7 (1986), 815–817.
184. Study Cites Needle Disposal as Risk for Hospital Employees, *Hospital Infection Control*, September, 1980, 105–106.
185. Sun, Marjorie, EPA Relaxes Hazardous Waste Rules, *Science*, 216, no. 4543 (1982), 275–276.
186. Surgeon General's Report Cites Hazards in Passive Smoking, *The Nation's Health* (January, 1987), 1, 13.
187. Swanson, R.L., and M. Devine, Ocean Dumping Policy, *Environment*, 24 no. 5 (1982), 14–20.
188. Technology Produced Occupational Hazards for Nurses, *The American Nurse* (April, 1987), 7–8.
189. Test Can Detect Pesticide Poisoning in Farmers, *St. Louis Post-Dispatch*, February 1, 1987, Sec C, p. 12.
190. The Clean Water Act: Amendments of 1987, *Environment Reporter*, 18, no. 19 (September 4, 1987).
191. The Earth's Ozone, *Chemecology*, 16, no. 8 (1987), 1–3.
192. The New High-Style Hospital, *Newsweek* (July 28, 1986), 82–83.
193. Toner, Mike, Pollution Fighters Take to the Trees, *National Wildlife*, 25, no. 1 (1987), 39–40.
194. Troubling Times with Toxics, *National Wildlife*, 24, no. 2 (1986), 29–36.
195. Turk, Amos, Janet Wittes, Jonathan Turk, et al., *Environmental Science* (2nd ed.). Philadelphia: W.B. Saunders, 1978.
196. Uehling, Mark, Radon Gas: A Deadly Threat, *Newsweek*, (August 18, 1986), 58–61.
197. United States Department of Labor, Occupational Safety and Health Administration, *Handling Hazardous Wastes*, Washington, D.C.: U. S. Government Printing Office, 1975.
198. United States Environmental Protection Agency, *Acid Rain Facts*. Washington, D.C.: U. S. Government Printing Office, January 1984.
199. ———, *Asbestos Fact Book*. Washington, D.C.: Office of Public Affairs, May 1986.
200. ———, *Environment Midwest*. Chicago: Region V, 1981.
201. ———, *The Hazardous Waste System*. Washington, D.C.: Office of Solid Waste, June 1987.
202. ———, *The Invisible Problem*. Washington, D.C.: Office of Public Affairs, October 1986.
203. ———, *Measuring Air Quality*. Washington, D.C.: Office of Public Affairs, July 1978.
204. ———, *Noise and Its Measurement*. Washington, D.C.: Office of Public Affairs, February 1977.
205. ———, *Noise and Recreational Vehicles*. Washington, D.C.: Office of Public Affairs, December 1976.
206. ———, *Noise Around Our Homes*, Washington, D.C.: Office of Public Affairs, February 1977.
207. ———, *Noise at Work*, Washington, D.C.: Office of Public Affairs, February 1977.
208. ———, *Ozone Fact Sheet*. Washington, D.C.: Office of Public Affairs, July 1987.
209. ———, *Ozone in the Lower Atmosphere: A Threat to Health and Welfare*. Washington, D.C.: U. S. Government Printing Office, December 1986.
210. ———, Pesticides and the Consumer, *EPA Journal*, 13, no. 4 (1987), 2–47.
211. ———, *Pollution and Your Health*. Washington, D.C.: Office of Public Affairs, May 1976.
212. ———, *Radioactive Wastes*, Washington, D.C.: Office of Public Affairs, 1976.
213. ———, *Solving the Hazardous Waste Problem*. Washington, D.C.: Office of Solid Waste, November, 1986.
214. ———, *Superfund: Looking Back, Looking Ahead*. Washington, D.C.: Office of Public Affairs, April, 1987.
215. ———, *The New Superfund: What It Is, How It Works*. Washington, D.C.: U. S. Government Printing Office, August 1987.
216. ———, *Toxics Information Series: Asbestos*. Washington, D.C.: Office of Pesticides, and Toxic Substances, April 1980.
217. ———, *Trends in the Quality of the Nation's Air—A Report to the People*. Washington, D.C.: Office of Public Awareness, October 1980.
218. ———, *Your Guide to the Environmental Protection Agency*. Washington, D.C.: Office of Public Awareness, December 1980.
219. Upton, Arthur, The Biological Effects of Low-Level Ionizing Radiation, *Scientific American*, 246, no. 2 (1982), 41–49.

220. Van Sickle, Derek, *The Ecological Citizen.* New York: Harper & Row, 1971.
221. Vietmeyer, Noel, Plants That Eat Pollution, *National Wildlife,* 23, no. 5 (1985), 10–11.
222. Waldbott, George, *Health Effects of Environmental Pollutants* (2nd ed.). St. Louis: C.V. Mosby, 1978.
223. Waldron, Harry, and D. Stofen, *Sub-Clinical Lead Poisoning.* New York: Academic Press, 1974.
224. Wastewater Recycling and Reuse, *American Journal of Public Health,* 76, no. 8 (1986), 960–961.
225. Weber, A., C. Jermini, and E. Grandjean, Irritating Effects on Man of Air Pollution Due to Cigarette Smoke, *American Journal of Public Health,* 66, no. 7 (1976), 672–676.
226. Weiss, Bernard, et al., Behavioral Responses to Artificial Food Colors, *Science,* 207, no. 4438 (1980), 1487–1488.
227. West, Susan, Acid from Heaven, *Science News,* 117, no. 5 (1980), 76–78.
228. WHO: Most Cancers Are in the Developing World, *The Nation's Health,* 11, no. 12 (1981), 18.
229. Whitaker, Mark, 'It was Like Breathing Fire...', *Newsweek,* (December 17, 1984), 26–32.
230. Wilson, Richard, Gasoline Vapor Controls: Pros and Cons, *EPA Journal,* (April, 1987), 23–25.
231. World Health Organization, *Health Hazards of the Human Environment,* Geneva: Office of Publications and Translation, World Health Organization, 1972.
232. Yasko, J., *Care of the Client Receiving Radiation Therapy: A Self-Learning Module for the Nurse Caring for the Client with Cancer.* Reston, VA: Reston Publishing Company, 1982.
233. Zoloth, S., et al., Asbestos Disease Screening by Non-Specialists: Results of an Evaluation, *American Journal of Public Health,* 76, no. 12 (1986), 1392–1395.

3

Spiritual and Religious Influences on the Person

Study of this chapter will enable you to

1. Define the terms *religious* and *spiritual* and the connotations of each.
2. Contrast the major tenets of Hinduism, Sikhism, Buddhism, Jainism, Shintoism, Confucianism, Taoism, Islam, Judaism, Christianity, and Native North American Indians.
3. Compare the major tenets of the various branches of Christianity: Roman Catholicism, Eastern Orthodoxy, various Protestant denominations, other Christian sects.
4. Gain an overview of the variety of religions in the United States.
5. Discuss how religious beliefs influence lifestyle and health status in the various religious groups and subgroups.
6. Identify your religious beliefs, or lack of them, and explore how they will influence your nursing practice.
7. Discuss your role in meeting the spiritual needs of client and family.
8. Describe specific nursing measures that can be used to meet the needs of persons with different religious backgrounds.
9. Work with a patient who has religious beliefs different from your own or refer the client to an appropriate resource.

Until an illness occurs, the person may give no thought to the meaning of his/her life or spiritual beliefs. But when he/she feels vulnerable and fearful of the future, solace is sought. Religion can provide that solace.

A patient sneezes. You say "God bless you." Why? Perhaps unconsciously you are coordinating the medical-

Key Terms

Religion
Spiritual dimension
Hinduism and Sikhism
Buddhism, Jainism, and Shintoism
Confucianism and Taoism
Islam
Judaism
Christianity
   Roman Catholicism
   Greek/Eastern Orthodox faith
   Protestantism
   Seventh Day Adventists
   Church of Jesus Christ of Latter-Day Saints
   Jehovah's Witnesses

Christianity (cont.)
   Church of Christ, Scientist
   Society of Friends
   Unity School of Christianity
   Mennonites
   Amish
   Moravians
   Waldenses
   Neo-Pentecostalism
Shamanism
Agnostic
Atheistic
Cults
Devil or Satan worship
Spiritual distress

physical with the religious-spiritual. But you may feel afraid to work professionally with the combination. This fear comes in part from the long-lived schism between science and religion.

The attitude that medical science is superior to the spiritual or to religion has affected us all. Yet spiritual dimensions and religion are there as they always have been. Each culture has had some organization or priesthood to sustain the important rituals and myths of its people. Primitive man combined the roles of physician, psychiatrist, and priest. The Indian medicine man and the African witch doctor combine magic with religion; with their herbs, psychosuggestion, and appeals to the gods, they realize that man is a biopsychospiritual being (87).

I had the cancer patient visualize an army of white blood cells attacking and overcoming the cancer cells. Within two weeks the cancer had diminished and he was rapidly gaining weight. He is alive and well today (18).

Is this a priest or a faith healer talking? No, this is a prominent tumor specialist talking in the late 1980s. An internationally known neurosurgeon says, "In a very real sense, medicine is now—as it has always been—faith healing." Dr. Elisabeth Kübler-Ross, internationally known for studies of dying, states that there is definitely life after death (41). Thus some health workers are trying to reunite the biopsychospiritual being.

The 1980s have shown an increased awareness of the link between health and religion and the subject is being discussed more openly.

Definitions

Religion is defined on various levels: *a belief in a supernatural or divine force that has power over the universe and commands worship and obedience; a system of beliefs; a comprehensive code of ethics or philosophy; a set of practices that are followed; a church affiliation; the conscious pursuit of any object the person holds as supreme* (29). *In short, religion signifies that a group of people have established and organized practices that are related to spiritual concerns.*

This definition, however, does not portray the constancy and at times the fervency that can underlie religious belief. In every human there seems to be a **spiritual dimension,** *a quality that goes beyond religious affiliation, that strives for inspiration, reverence, awe, meaning, and purpose even in those who do not believe in any god. The spiritual dimension tries to be in harmony with the universe, strives for answers about the infinite, and especially comes into focus as a sustaining power when the person faces emotional stress, physical illness, or death. It goes outside a person's own power.*

✔ In the midst of our specialized health care you have an opportunity to go beyond the dogma to bring together the biopsychospiritual being through the study of the religions and religious symbols of your patients/clients. And those are world religions, not your personal or country's basic religion. Mass media, rapid transportation, and cultural exchanges have nullified the provincial approach.

World Religions

Studying world religions poses a semantic difficulty in that an expression in the Chinese-based religion of Confucianism may have no equivalent in the English language. Thus language has dictated what people think, how they act, and how their religious beliefs are carried out (52).

Concepts, however, are often basically the same but are rephrased in each religion's own linguistic style. The saying "Love one another as I have loved you" will appear to the Hindu as "This is the sum of religion, do not unto others what causes pain to you"; to the Taoist as "Return goodness for hatred"; and to the Muslim as "No one is a believer unless he desires for his brother what he desires for himself."

Each religion also has other characteristics in common:

1. Basis of authority or source(s) of power.
2. A portion of scripture or sacred word.
3. An ethical code that defines right and wrong.
4. A psychology and identity so that its adherents fit into a group and the world is defined by the religion.
5. Aspirations or expectations.
6. Some ideas about what follows death.

The major world religions can be divided into categories in an attempt to group characteristics even further (52). The *alpha* group includes Christianity, Judaism, and Islam. All adhere to a Biblical revelation of a supernatural, monotheistic God. People in these religions are "doers." They obey because God commands; they make covenants with God for protection; they have a historical fixed scripture that is canonized for public use, and they often proselytize. Into the *gamma* group go Taoism,★ Confucianism, and Shintoism. In these religions people believe either that everything is in the being of God or that there is no Godhead (still a definite belief). These people try to be in harmony with the world around them. Their most immediate concern is in relationships with others. Scripture is a family affair. They can be characterized as simple in faith, spontaneous, and straightforward in feelings of affection for people, flowers, and birds. The final grouping is the *beta* group, which includes Buddhism and Hinduism. These religions have their roots in Indian soil and teach that everything is in the being of God. Adherents are interested in "being" rather than "doing." They have a collective literature for private devotion. Control of mind and body is desired, as some of the yoga practices show. The beta and gamma groups do not define God as clearly as the alpha group. The beta and gamma groups look inside themselves for answers: common sense rather than commands from God determines good.

★Pronounced "dowism."

The following discussion presents a more detailed insight into each major world religion through personality sketches. Each person has a fictitious name and represents not a single person but a composite of knowledge gained from the authors' interviewing, reading, and personal experience. Although these personalities are presented as acting and thinking in a certain way, remember that the person's culture, family background, and personality affect how that person lives out a religious experience. Thus a particular Hindu and a given Roman Catholic may be more in agreement religiously than two Lutherans. You cannot make generalizations about a religion from knowing a single follower.

HINDUISM AND SIKHISM

Rama tells us that nothing is typically **Hindu** and that anyone who puts religion in neat packages will have difficulty comprehending his outlook. Rama is named after Ramakrishna, the greatest Hindu saint of the nineteenth century. The history of Rama's religion goes back to approximately 1500 BC, when the **Vedas**—*divine revelations*—were written. His main religious texts are the **Upanishads**, *or scriptures*, and the **Bhagavad Gita**, *a summary of the former with additions. The most expressive and universal word of God is* **Om**, *or* **Aum**— providing the most important auditory and visual symbol in Rama's religion.†

Rama speaks of some of the worship popular in India today: of the family and local deities; of the trinity—**Brahma**, *the creator;* **Vishnu**, *the preserver and god of love;* and **Shiva**, *the destroyer*.

Rama tells of his own shrine in his home where, in the presence of various pictures of **incarnations** (*human forms of God*) and with incense burning, he meditates. He also thinks of Buddha, Muhammed, and Jesus as incarnations and sometimes reads from the scriptures inspired by their teachings, although they represent other major religions.

In spite of this vast array of deities and the recognition that all religions are valid, Rama believes in one universal concept—**Brahman**, *the Divine Intelligence, the Supreme Reality*. Rama believes all paths lead to the understanding that this "reality" exists as part of all physical beings, especially humans. Rama's entire spiritual quest is directed toward uniting his *inner and real self*, the **atman**, with the concept of Brahman. So although Rama has gone through several stages of desire—for pleasure, power, wealth, fame, and humanitarianism—the last stage, his desire for freedom, for touching the infinite, is his main goal.

Rama is interested in health and illness only as a guide to this goal. He feels that the human love for the body is a cause for illness. He says, for example, that we overeat and get a stomachache. He views the pain as a warning—in this case, to stop overeating. He does not oppose medical treatment if absolutely necessary, but he feels that medicine can sometimes dull the pain and then the person overeats again, thus perpetuating the cause of the problem. Medical or psychiatric help, Rama says, is at best transitory. The cause of the pain must be rooted out.

In order not to dwell on physical concerns, Rama strives for moderation in eating as well as in other bodily functions. He considers only the atman as real and eternal, the body as unreal and finite. The body is a temple, a vehicle, no more. He tries to take care of it so that it will not scream at him because of overindulgence or underindulgence. Rama is a vegetarian. He feels that meat and intoxicants would excite his senses too much. Yet the Hindu diet pattern is flexible; definite rules are not set. If Rama is sick, he tries to bear his illness with resignation, knowing its temporary nature. He believes that the prayer of supplication for bodily cure is the lowest form of prayer whereas the highest form is devotion to God. To him, death and rebirth are nearly synonymous, for the atman never changes and always remains pure. He compares the atman to the ocean: as ocean water can be put into various containers without changing its nature, so can the atman be put into various physical and human containers without changing its nature.

Thus if death is imminent, Rama believes that the body, mind, and senses weaken and become lifeless but that the never-changing atman is ready to enter into a new form of life, depending on the person's knowledge, deeds, and past experiences. Full acceptance of death is encouraged. Death is a friend to be faced bravely, calmly, and confidently.

Rama says that as a devotee of God he is following a *training course* called **yoga**. As a preliminary, however, he must establish certain moral qualifications. He must strive for self-control, self-discipline, cleanliness, and contentment. He must avoid injury, deceitfulness, and stealing. His overwhelming desire to reach God can be implemented through one or a combination of the four yoga paths: (1) **inana yoga** through *reading and absorbing knowledge*, (2) **bhakti yoga** through the *devotion of emotion and love*,

---

† See the symbol at the beginning of this section. A transliteration of the script is *a, u. m*. It is written in English as *Om,* or *Aum. Om, God,* and *Brahman* are synonymous and mean a *consciousness* or *awareness* rather than a personified being.

(3) **karma yoga** through *work dedicated to God,* and (4) **raja yoga** through *psychological experiments on oneself.* Rama combines the first three by reading and memorizing portions of the ancient scriptures, by meditating daily at his shrine, and by dedicating the results of his professional work to God.

Rama mentions that various forms of yoga have spread around the world to form hybrid groups with varied purposes. One branch that has appeared in medical centers is **hatha yoga,** meaning *sun and moon,* symbolizing an inner balance that is achieved through *muscle and breathing exercises.* Ultimately the body is prepared for meditation through these exercises.

From the bhakti emphasis comes **Sikhism.** Founded by Nanak who was born in 1469. The Sikhs had nine other gurus, or spiritual mentors, who sequentially taught that God was the one and only reality. The fifth guru compiled the scripture. Starting as a pacifist group, the Sikhs evolved to warriors.

Also from bhakti influence has come the **Hare Krishna** movement in the United States, starting in 1965 when A. C. Bhaktivedanta came to New York City. The first Krishna temple was established on the Lower East Side (19). Rama reports that there are now reportedly 150,000 Krishnas in the United States, almost all of them converts from Catholicism, Judaism, or Protestantism. At New Vrindaban Krishna community in Moundsville, West Virginia, a palace has been built solely by community members. It contains $500,000 worth of gold, silver, onyx, marble, stained glass, teak, and crystal chandeliers. In contrast, the lifestyle is austere: work, study, and praise beginning about 3:30 A.M., no meat eating, no stimulants, no intoxicants, and no sex except for procreation (43).

For Rama, religion is not something to be picked up and put down according to a schedule or one's mood. It is a constant and all pervading part of his life and the life of his country. India's literature and art are witness to this fact.

↙ If you give nursing care to someone with Rama's background, consider how the religious beliefs will influence your approach. Be accepting if the person seems to minimize bodily ills. Keep in mind the view of the body as only a vehicle to carry the atman and the belief that the desire for bodily cure is a low form of prayer. Yoga training, emphasizing self-control and devotion to God through reading and meditation, may cause the person to seek help from inner resources and the literature of Hinduism rather than from medication or consultation with staff. Providing an atmosphere conducive to this practice will be appreciated. Should death seem imminent, remember that death is perceived as a rebirth. The person will want rebirth to have as much dignity as possible.

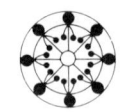

BUDDHISM, JAINISM, AND SHINTOISM

Umeko Sato is a member of the *Buddhist sect* **Soka Gakkai.** This sect is now a powerful religion in Japan, with a government party, a university, and a grand temple representing it. Now 57 years old, this organization that composes 10 percent of Japan's population, known previously as a militant proselytizer, has toned down this phase and is living more graciously with other sects and creeds. Based on the **Lotus Sutra,** *part of the Buddhist scriptures,* its doctrine advocates the three values of happiness: profit, goodness, and beauty. Sato is attracted by the practicality of the teaching, the mottoes that she can live by, the emphasis on small group study, and present world benefits, especially healing.

Although Sato's beliefs at some points seem in direct contrast to the original Buddhist teachings, she is happy to explain the rich multireligious tradition that her family has had for generations. She emphasizes that she is affected by the **Confucian** emphasis on the family unit, by Christianity's healing emphasis, by **Shintoism,** the state religion of Japan until 1945, and by Buddhism, which originated about 600 BC in India with a Hindu named Siddhartha Gautama.

Currently about 90 percent of Japan's 120 million people adhere both to Buddhism and to Shintoism, although the nation has never been known to be devout. Less than 1 percent are Christian. Another small religious group is known as **Jainism.** The "Jains" hark back to the sixth century BC, about the same time as Buddha. All are members of a fourfold congregation: monks, nuns, laymen and laywomen. They all take vows which guide them in all aspects of daily life.

Gautama, shortly after a historic enlightenment experience during which he became the Buddha, preached a sermon to his followers and drew on the earth a wheel representing the continuous round of life and death and rebirth. Later eight spokes were added to illustrate the sermon and to provide the most explicit visual symbol of Buddhism[‡] today. Sato repeats Buddha's four noble truths: (1) life is disjointed or out of balance, especially in birth, old age, illness, and death; (2) the cause of this imbalance is ignorance of one's own true nature; (3) removal of this ignorance is attained by reaching **Nirvana,** *the divine state of release, the ultimate reality, the perfect knowledge* via (4) the eightfold path.

The eight spokes of the wheel represent the eightfold path used to reach Nirvana. Sato says that followers subscribe to right knowledge, right intentions,

---

[‡] See the symbol at the beginning of this section.

right speech, right conduct, right means of livelihood, right effort, right mindfulness, and concentration. From these concepts has arisen a moral code that, among other things, prohibits intoxicants, lying, and killing of any kind (which explains why Buddhists are often vegetarians). She further explains that the Mahayana branch of Buddhism took hold in Japan as opposed to the Theravada branch. The **Theravada branch** emphasizes an intellectual approach through wisdom, man working by himself through meditation and without ritual. The **Mahayana branch** emphasizes involvement with mankind, ritual, petitionary prayer, and concern for one's sibling. Sato feels that the Mahayana branch provides the happier philosophy of the two and she tells of the ritual of celebration on Gautama's birthday. But most Japanese believe in **Amitabha Buddha,** a god rather than a historical figure, who in replacing the austere image of Gautama as a glorious redeemer, one of infinite light. Also, the people worship **Kwannon,** a goddess of compassion.

Sato explains that she cannot omit mention of the one austere movement within the Mahayana branch, the **Zen sect.** Taking their example from Gautama's extended contemplation of a flower, Zen followers care little for discourse, books, or other symbolic interpretations and explanations of reality. Hours and years are devoted to meditation, contemplation of word puzzles, and consultation with a Zen master. In seeking absolute honesty and truthfulness through such simple acts as drinking tea or gardening, the Zen student hopes to experience enlightenment.

Sato next turns to her former state religion, **Shintoism.** While Buddhism produced a solemnizing effect on her country, Shintoism had an affirmative and joyous effect. Emperor, ancestor, ancient hero, and nature worship form its core. Those who follow Shintoism, she says, feel an intense loyalty and devotion to every lake, tree, and blossom in Japan as well as to the ancestral spirits abiding there. They also have a great concern for cleanliness, a carryover from early ideas surrounding dread of pollution in the dead.

Sato says that her parents have two god shelves in their home. One contains wooden tablets inscribed with the name of the household's patron-deity and a symbolic form of the goddess of rice, as well as other texts and objects of family significance. Here her family performs simple rites, such as offering a prayer or a food gift each day. In a family crisis, perhaps an illness, the family conducts more elaborate rites, such as lighting tapers or offering rice brandy. The other god shelf, in another room, is the Buddha shelf; and if a family member dies, a Buddhist priest, the spiritual leader, performs specified rituals there.

Sato strongly emphasizes that if illness or impending death causes a family member to be hospitalized, another well family member will stay at the hospital to bathe, cook for, and give emotional support to the patient. Sato feels that recovery largely depends on this family tie. If death occurs, Sato will be reminded of the Buddhist doctrine teaching that death is a total nonfunction of the physical body and mind and that the life force is displaced and transformed to continue to function in another form. Every birth is a rebirth, much as in the Hindu teaching, and rebirth happens immediately after death, according to some Buddhists. Others believe that rebirth occurs 49 days after death, during which time the person is in an intermediary state. The difference in quality of death, birth, and existence depends on whether the person lived a disciplined or undisciplined life.

Buddhist religion teaches the living how to die well. The elderly, or feeble, are to prepare themselves mentally for a state that would be conducive for a good rebirth. The person is to remain watchful and alert in the face of death, to resist distraction and confusion, to be lucid and calm. Distinct instructions are given in what to expect as life leaves the body, as the person enters an intermediary state, and as Nirvana is about to occur.

So although Sato has grasped a new religious path for herself, her respect for tradition remains.

✔ In giving care to a person with Umeko Sato's background, be aware of the varied religious influences on life. The sect's emphasis on the here and now rather than on the long road to Nirvana may place a high value on physical health so that the person can benefit from the joys and beauty of this life. The person may readily voice impatience with the body's dysfunction. You can also respond to the great concern for cleanliness, the desire to have family nearby, and the need for family rites that are offered for the sick member. Should a family member be dying, you may see some ambivalence. The family member may want to prepare himself or herself in the traditional way while someone with Sato's background, with emphasis on present world benefits and healing, may deny that there is a valid preparation for death.

CONFUCIANISM AND TAOISM

Wong Huieng is a young teacher in Taiwan simultaneously influenced by **Taoism,** *the romantic and mystical,* and **Confucianism,** *the practical and pragmatic.* To provide insights into these Chinese modes of thinking, although it is more representative of Taoism, Wong Huieng uses the yin-yang symbol.[§] The symbol

---

[§] See the symbol at the beginning of this section.

is a circle, representing **Tao** or *the absolute,* in which two tear shapes fit perfectly into one another, each containing a small dot from the other. Generally yang is light or red, and yin is dark. Ancient Chinese tradition says that everything exists in these two interacting forces. Each represents a group of qualities. Yang is positive or masculine—dry, hot, active, moving, and light. Yin is feminine or negative—wet, cold, passive, restful, and empty. For example, fire is almost pure yang and water almost pure yin—but not quite. The combination of yin and yang constitutes all the dualisms a person can imagine: day–night, summer–winter, beauty–ugliness, illness–health, life–death. Both qualities are necessary for life in the universe; they are complementary and, if in harmony, good. Yang and yin energy forces are embodied in the body parts and affect food preferences and eating habits.

Huieng translates this symbol into a relaxed philosophy of life: "If I am sick, I will get better. Life is like going up and down a mountain; sometimes I feel good and sometimes I feel bad. That's the way it is." Though educated, she is not interested in climbing up the job ladder, accumulating wealth, or conquering nature. Her goal is to help provide money to build an orphanage in a natural wooded setting.

Huieng thinks of death as a natural part of life, as the peace that comes when the body is worn out. She admits, however, that when her father died, human grief took hold of her. Before his death, her mother went to the Taoist temple priest and got some incense that was to help cast the sickness from his body. After death, they kept his body in the house for the required time, 49 days. The priest executed a special ceremony every 7 days. Her mother could cry only 1 hour daily, 2:00 until 3:00 in the morning. Now her mother talks through the priest to her father's ghost. Although Huieng regards this practice as superstitious and thinks that painting a picture of a lake and mountain is a more fitting way to erase her grief, she looks at the little yellow bag, containing a blessing from the priest, hanging around her neck, and finds it comforting if not intellectually acceptable.

Now Huieng turns to her practical side and talks about **Confucius,** the first saint of the nation. Although **Lao-tzu,** *the founder of Taoism,* is a semi-legendary figure said to have vanished after he wrote the bible of Taoism, **Tao-te-ching,** Confucius has a well-documented existence.

Confucius, born in 551 BC, wrote little. His disciples wrote the **Analects,** *short proverbs, embodying his teachings.* He is revered as a teacher, not as a god. Huieng does not ask him to bless her but tries to emulate him and his teachings, which she has heard since birth. The temple in his memory is a place for studying, not for praying. And on his birthday, a national holiday, people pay respect to their teachers in his memory.

Five important terms in Confucius' teaching are **Jen,** *a striving for goodness within:* **Chun-sui,** *establishing a gentlemanly/womanly approach with others;* **Li,** *knowing how relationships should be conducted and having respect for age;* **Te,** *leading by virtuous character rather than by force;* and **Wen,** *pursuing the arts as an adjunct to moral character.* Huieng stresses that in *Li* are the directives for family relationships. So strongly did Confucius feel about the family that he gave directives on proper attitudes between father and son, elder brother and junior brother, husband and wife. Also, Huieng feels she cannot harm her body because it was given to her by her parents. Her concept of immediate family includes grandparents, uncles, aunts, and cousins. Her language has more words for relationships between relatives than the English language does.

✔ Huieng feels that in caring for her body, she cares for her family, the country, and the universe. Essentially, to her, all people are family.

✔ Important in your understanding of a person with Wong Huieng's background is the dualism that exists in such thinking. Acceptance of the particular version of mysticism and practicality, and of the yin and yang forces that are seen as operating within self, will help in building a foundation of personalized care.

✔ The person may have more respect for older than younger staff members and may respond well to teaching. There may be a strong desire to attain and maintain wellness. These factors are directly related to the religious teaching; you can use them to enhance care.

ISLAM*

Omar Ali is **Muslim,** a member of Islam, the youngest of the major world religions. This faith, with its Arabic coloring and tenacious monotheistic tradition, serves as a bridge between Eastern and Western religions. "There is no God but Allah; Muḥammed is His Prophet"# provides the key to Omar's beliefs. He must say this but once in his life as a requirement, but he will repeat it many times as an affirmation. Muslims believe in a final judgment day when everyone will be judged and either sent to Paradise or to the fire of hell depending on how justly they lived their lives

---

*A portion of this section was contributed by Caroline Samiezadi-Yazd, R.N., B.S.N.

#These words are a translation of the sacred calligraphy in the symbol shown at the beginning of this section. The prophet's name is sometimes spelled *Muhammad.*

according to God's Laws. They believe everyone, except children before the age of puberty, are responsible for their own good and bad actions and deeds and that no one can intercede on behalf of another.

Omar has also been influenced by the 3000-year-old **Zoroastrianism,** *which is a religion of pre-Islamic Iran,* but flourishes in Bombay today. Likewise, it was a monotheistic religion even though dualism was also espoused.

Omar is an Egyptian physician whose religious tradition was revealed through Muhammed, born approximately AD 571 in Mecca, then a trading point between India and Syria on the Arabian peninsula. Hating polytheism and paganism in any form, and influenced by Judaism and Christianity, Muhammed wrote *God's revelation to him* in the **Quran,**‡ *scriptures* that to Omar confirm the truths of the Jewish-Christian Bible. Omar believes in the biblical prophets, but he calls Muhammed the greatest—the Seal of Prophets.

Through the *Quran* and the **Hadith,** *the traditions,* Omar has guidelines for his thinking, devotional life, and social obligations. He believes he is a unique individual with an eternal soul. He believes in a heaven and hell and while on earth he wants to walk the straight path.

✔ To keep on this path, Omar prays five times a day: generally on rising, at midday, in the afternoon, in the early evening, and before retiring. Articles needed are water and a prayer rug. Because the *Quran* emphasizes cleanliness of body, Omar performs a ritual washing with *running* water over the face, arms, top of head, and feet before each prayer. Omar explains that in the bedridden patient this requirement can be accomplished by pouring water out of some sort of receptacle. If a Muslim's entire body is considered ritually unclean, he must wash the entire body. If water is unavailable or the person cannot bathe, then clean soil may be used in place of the ritual washing. After this the Muslim needs either a ritually clean cloth or a prayer rug and a clean place to pray. Then, facing Mecca, Omar goes through a series of prescribed bodily motions and repeats various passages in praise and supplication.

Omar also observes **Ramadan,** a fast month,¶ during which time he eats or drinks nothing from sunrise to sunset; after sunset he takes nourishment only in moderation. He explains **fasting** (abstinence from eating) as a discipline aiding him to understand those with little food. At the end of Ramadan, he enters a festive period with feelings of goodwill and gift exchanges. The sick, the very old, pregnant and lactating mothers, children, and Muslims who require the ingestion or injection of substances throughout the day hours are exempt without penalty from practice of this belief.

Omar has made one pilgrimage to Mecca, another requirement for all healthy and financially able Muslims. He feels the experience created a great sense of brotherhood, for all the pilgrims wore similar modest clothing, exchanged news of followers in various lands, and renewed their mutual faith. The twelfth day of the Pilgrimage month is the **Feast of Sacrifice,** (*Eida-Fita*) when all Muslim families kill a lamb in honor of Abraham's offering of his son to God.

In line with the *Quran*'s teaching, Omar does not eat pork (including such items as bologna, which might contain partial pork products), gamble, drink intoxicants, use illicit drugs, or engage in religiously unlawful sexual practices such as premarital sex, homosexuality, or infidelity. He worships no images or pictures of Muhammed, for the prophet is not deified. Nor does he hang or display pictures of any Prophet or any God or worship statues or religious symbols. He gives a portion of his money to the poor, for Islam advocates a responsibility to society.

Omar mentions that parts of the basic Islam faith are used by a United States-based group called the Black Muslims (Nation of Islam). Known to have stringent, seclusionist rules, the Black Muslims have taken some new positions since 1976 and seem to be moving toward more orthodox Islam. Members may now get politically involved; membership is open to Whites; dress codes have changed; and some of the myths about the American founder, W. D. Fard, have been erased.

✔ Omar outlines the ideas of his religion as it applies to his profession. He feels that he can make a significant contribution to health care, but that essentially what happens is God's will. Submission to God is the very meaning of Islam. This belief produces a very fluid feeling of time and sense of fatalism. Planning ahead for a Muslim is not a value as it is in Western culture; to defy God's will brings on the evil eye.

✔ Muslim patients are excused from religious rules, but many will still want to follow them as closely as possible. Even though in a body cast and unable to get out of bed, a patient may want to go through prayers symbolically. The person might also recite the first chapters of the *Quran*, centered on praise to Allah, which are often used in times of crises. Family is a great comfort in illness and praying with a group is strengthening, but the Muslim has no priest. The relationship is directly with God. Some patients may seem fatalistic, completely resigned to death, whereas others, hoping it is God's will that they live, cooperate

---

‡ Sometimes spelled *Koran.*
¶ Coming during the ninth month of the Muslim year, always at a different time each year by the Western calendar, and sometimes spelled *Ramazan.*

vigorously with the medical program. Muslims do not discuss death openly because if they did, the patient and family may lose all hope and the patient could die as a result. Instead, Muslims tend to communicate grief in gradual stages rather than immediately and all at once. Further, they make it a point never to let the affected person lose hope. The family, even in the gravest of situations, will not attempt to prepare for the death even when it is imminent. After death, a body must be washed with running water and the hands folded in prayer. Muslims do not perform autopsies, embalmment, or use caskets for burials. Instead, they wrap a white linen cloth around the dead person and then place the body into the ground facing Mecca. Knowledge of these attitudes and traditions can greatly enhance your care.

JUDAISM

Seth Lieberman, strongly influenced by the social-concern emphasis in Judaism, is a psychiatrist. In the Jewish community each member is expected to contribute to others' needs according to his/her ability. Jews have traditionally considered their community as a whole responsible for feeding the hungry, helping the widowed and orphaned, rescuing the captured, and even burying the dead. Jewish retirement homes, senior citizens' centers, and medical centers are witness to this philosophy.

Seth cannot remember when his religious instruction began—it was always there. He went through the motions and felt the emotion of the Sabbath eve with its candles and cup of sanctification long before he could comprehend his father's explanations. Book learning followed, however, and he came to understand the fervency with which his people study and live the law as given in the **Torah,** *the first five books of the Bible;* and in the **Talmud,** *a commentary and enlargement of the Torah.* His *spiritual leader is the* **rabbi.** His spiritual symbol is the *menorah.**

His own *entrance into a responsible religious life and manhood* was through the **Bar Mitzvah,** a ceremony which took place in the synagogue when he was 13. (Girls are also educated to live responsible religious lives, and a few congregations now have a similar ceremony, the **Bas Mitzvah,** for girls.)

Although raised in an *Orthodox* home, Seth and his family are now *Reform.* And he mentions another group, the *Conservatives.* The **Orthodox** believe God gave the law; it was written exactly as He gave it; it should be followed precisely. **Reform** *Jews believe the law was written by inspired men* at various times and therefore is subject to reinterpretation. Seth says he follows the traditions because they are traditions rather than because God demands it. **Conservatives** *are in the middle,* taking some practices from both groups. Overriding any differences in interpretation of ritual and tradition is the fundamental concept expressed in the prayer "Hear, O Israel, the Lord our God, the Lord is One." Not only is He one, He loves His creation, wants His people to live justly, and wants to bless their food, drink, and celebration. Judaism's double theme might be expressed as "Enjoy life now, and share it with God." Understandably, then, Seth's religious emphasis is not on an afterlife, although some Jewish people believe in one. And although Jews have had a history of suffering, the inherent value of suffering or illness is not stressed. Through their observance of the law, the belief of their historical role as God's chosen people, and their hope for better days, Jews have survived seemingly insurmountable persecution.

Seth works with physically, emotionally, and spiritually depressed persons. He feels that often the spiritual depression is unnoticed, misunderstood, or ignored by professional workers. He cites instances in which mental attitudes have brightened as he shared a common bond of Judaism with a client.

✔ He offers guidelines for working with a Jewish person in a hospital or nursing home. Although Jewish law can be suspended when a person is ill, the patient will be most comfortable following as many practices as possible.

✔ Every Jew observes the **Sabbath,** *a time for spiritual refreshment, from sundown on Friday to shortly after sundown on Saturday.* During this period Orthodox Jews may refuse freshly cooked food, medicine, treatment, surgery, and use of radio, television, and writing equipment lest the direction of their thinking be diverted on this special day. An Orthodox male may want to wear a **yarmulke** *or skullcap* continuously; use a *prayerbook called* **Siddur,** and use **phylacteries,** *leather strips with boxes containing scriptures,* at weekday morning prayer. Also, the ultra-Orthodox male may refuse to use a razor because of the Levitical ban on shaving.

Some Orthodox Jewish women observe the rite of **Mikvah,** an *ancient ritual of family purity.* From marriage to menopause (except when pregnant) these women observe no physical-sexual relations with their husbands from 24 hours before menstruation until 12 days later when a ritual immersion in water renders them ready to meet their husbands again.

Jewish dietary laws have been considered by some

---

*See the symbol at beginning of this section. The seven-branched candelabrum stands for the creation of the universe in 7 days; the center light symbolizes the Sabbath; and the candlelight symbolizes the presence of God in the Temple.

scholars as health measures: to enjoy life is to eat properly and in moderation. The Orthodox, however, obey them because God so commanded. Food is called **treyfe** (or treyfah) if it is *unfit* and **kosher** if it is *ritually correct*.

✔ Foods forbidden are pig, horse, shrimp, lobster, crab, oyster, and fowl that are birds of prey. Meats approved are from those animals that are ruminants and have divided hooves. Fish approved must have both fins and scales. Also, the kosher animals must be healthy and slaughtered in a prescribed manner. Because of the Biblical passage stating not to soak a young goat in its mother's milk, Jews do not eat meat products and milk products together. Neither are the utensils used to cook these products ever intermixed, nor the dishes from which to eat these products.

✔ Guidelines for a satisfactory diet for the Orthodox are as follows:

1. Serve milk products first, meat second. Meat can be eaten a few minutes after milk, but milk cannot be taken for 6 hours after meat.
2. If a person completely refuses meat because of incorrect slaughter, encourage a vegetarian diet with protein supplements, such as fish and eggs, considered neutral unless prepared with milk or meat shortening.
3. Get frozen kosher products marked Ⓤ, K, or *pareve*.
4. Heat and serve food in the original container and use plastic utensils.

Two important holy days are *Rosh Hashanah* and *Yom Kippur*. **Rosh Hashanah,** *the Jewish New Year,* is a time to meet with the family, give thanks to God for good health, and renew traditions. **Yom Kippur,** *the day of atonement,* a time for asking forgiveness of family members for wrongs done, occurs 10 days later. On Yom Kippur, Jews fast for 24 hours, a symbolic act of self-denial, mourning, and petition. **Tisha Bab,** *the day of lamentation,* recalling the destruction of both Temples of Jerusalem, is another 24-hour fast period. **Pesach** or **Passover** (8 days for Orthodox and Conservative, 7 days for Reform) *celebrates the ancient Jews' deliverance from Egyptian bondage.* **Matzo,** *an unleavened bread,* replaces leavened bread during this period.

✔ The Jewish person is preoccupied with health. Jews are future-oriented and want to know diagnosis, how a disease will affect business, family life, and social life. The Jewish people as a whole are highly educated, and although they respect the doctor, they may get several medical opinions before carrying out a treatment plan.

✔ While family, friends, and rabbi may visit the ill, especially on or near holidays, they will also come at other times. Visiting the sick is a religious duty. And although death is final to many Jews except for living on in the memories of others, guidelines exist for this time. When a Jewish person has suffered irreversible brain damage and can no longer say a **bracha,** *a blessing to praise God,* or perform a **mitzvah,** *an act to help a fellow,* he/she is considered a "vegetable" with nothing to save. Prolonging the life by artificial means would not be recommended. But until then the dying patient must be treated as the complete person he/she always was, capable of conducting his/her own affairs and entering into relationships.

✔ Jewish tradition says never to leave the bedside of the dying person, which is of value to the dying and the mourners. The dying soul should leave in the presence of people and the mourner is shielded from guilt of thinking that the patient was alone at death or that more could be done. The bedside vigil also serves as a time to encourage a personal confession by the dying, which is a *rite de passage* to another phase of existence (even though unknown). This type of confessional is said throughout the Jewish life cycle whenever one stage has been completed. Confessional on the deathbed is a recognition that one cycle is ending and that another cycle is beginning. Recitation of the *Shema* in the last moments before death helps the dying to affirm faith in God and focus on the most familiar rituals of life.

✔ Death, being witnessed at the bedside, helps to reinforce the reality of the situation. Immediate burial and specified mourning also move the remaining loved ones through the crisis period. (Note, however, that if a Jew dies on the Sabbath, he cannot be moved, except by a non-Jew, until sundown.) After the burial, the mourners are fed in a meal of replenishment called *se'udat havra'ah*. This step symbolizes the rallying of the community and the sustenance of life for the remaining. Also, Jews follow the custom of sitting *shiva* or visiting with remaining relatives for 1 week after the death (39).

✔ Judaism identifies a year of mourning. The first 3 days are of deep grief; clothes may be torn to symbolize the tearing of a life from others. Seven days of lesser mourning follow, leading to 30 days of gradual readjustment. The remainder of the year calls for remembrance and healing. During that year a prayer called the mourner's *Kaddish* is recited in religious services. It helps convey the feeling of support for the mourner (39). At the annual anniversary of death, a candle is burned and special prayers said.

So from circumcision of the male infant on the eighth day after birth to his deathbed, and from the days of the original menorah in the sanctuary in the wilderness until the present day, the followers of Judaism re-enact their traditions. Because many of these traditions remain an intrinsic part of the Jew while striving to maintain or regain wellness, the preceding guidelines offer a foundation for knowledgeable care.

CHRISTIANITY

Beth Meyer, a *Roman Catholic*, Demetrius Callas, an *Eastern Orthodox*, and Jean Taylor, a *Protestant*, are Christian American nurses representing the three major branches of Christianity. Although Christianity divided into Eastern Orthodox and Roman Catholic in AD 1054, and the Protestant Reformation provided a third division in the sixteenth century, these nurses share some basic beliefs, most importantly that Jesus Christ as described in the Bible is God's son. Jesus, born in Palestine, changed "BC" to "AD." The details of His 33 years are few, but His deeds and words recorded in the Bible's New Testament show quiet authority, loving humility, and an ability to perform miracles and to visit easily with people in varied social positions.

The main symbol of Christianity is the cross,* but it signifies more than a wooden structure on which Jesus was crucified. It also symbolizes the finished redemption—Christ rising from the dead and ascending to the Father in order to rule with Him and continuously pervade the personal lives of His followers.

Christians observe **Christmas** *as Christ's birthday;* **Lent** *as a season of penitence and self-examination preceding* **Good Friday,** *Christ's crucifixion day;* and **Easter,** *His Resurrection day.*

Beth, Demetrius, and Jean rely on the New Testament as a guideline for their lives. They believe that Jesus was fully God and fully man at the same time, that their original sin (which they accept as a basic part of themselves) can be forgiven, and that they are acceptable to God because of Jesus Christ's life and death. They believe God is three persons—the Father, the Son, and the Holy Spirit (Holy Ghost), the last providing a spirit of love and truth.

Beth, Demetrius, and Jean differ in some worship practices and theology, but all highly regard their individuality as children of God and hope for life with God after death. They feel responsible for their own souls, *the spiritual dimension of themselves*, and for aiding the spiritual needs of their patients.

Roman Catholicism, according to Beth, is a religion based on the dignity of man as a social, intellectual, and spiritual being, made in the image of God. She traces the teaching authority of the church through the scriptures: God sent His Son to provide salvation and redemption from sin. He established the Church to continue His work after ascension into heaven. Jesus chose apostles to preach, teach, and guide. He appointed Saint Peter as the Church's head to preserve unity and to have authority over the apostles. The mission given by Jesus to Saint Peter and the apostles is the same that continues to the present through the Pope and his bishops. Beth notes that in the last several years, women in the Roman Catholic Church, both nuns and laywomen, are speaking out more on issues and are asking for more recognition and respect as God's spokespeople.

Beth believes that the seven *Sacraments* are gracegiving rites that give her a share in Christ's own life and help sustain her in her efforts to follow His example. The Sacraments that are received once in life are Baptism, Confirmation, Holy Orders and usually Matrimony.

✔ Through **Baptism** *the soul is incorporated into the life of Christ and shares His divinity*. Any infant in danger of death should be baptized, even an aborted fetus. If a priest is not available, you can perform the sacrament by pouring water on the forehead and saying, "I baptize thee in the name of the Father, of the Son, and of the Holy Spirit." The healthy baby is baptized some time during the first weeks of life. Adults are also baptized when they convert to Catholicism and join the church.

Confirmation *is the sacrament in which the Holy Spirit is imparted in a fuller measure to help strengthen the individual in his/her spiritual life.* **Matrimony** *acknowledges the love and lifelong commitment between a man and a woman.* **Holy Orders** *ordains deacons and priests.*

The Sacraments that may be received more than once are Penance (Confession), the Eucharist (Holy Communion), and the Anointing of the Sick (Sacrament of the Sick). Beth feels that **Penance,** *an acknowledgment and forgiveness of her sins in the presence of a priest*, should be received according to individual need even though it is required only once a year by church law. The Mass, often called the **Eucharist** is the liturgical celebration whose core is the sacrament of the Holy Eucharist. Bread and wine are consecrated and become the body and blood of Christ. The body and blood are then received in Holy Communion.

✔ The Eucharist is celebrated daily and all Roman Catholics are encouraged to participate as often as possible; they are required by church law to attend on Sundays (or late Saturdays) and specified holy days throughout the year unless prevented by illness or some other serious reason.

✔ Beth is glad that the Anointing of the Sick has been modified and broadened and explains the rite to patient and family to allay anxiety. Formerly known as

---

*See the symbol at the beginning of this section.

Extreme Unction or the last rites, this sacrament was reserved for those near death. Now **Anointing of the Sick,** *symbolic of Christ's healing love and the concern of the Christian community,* can provide spiritual strength to those less gravely ill. Following anointing with oil, the priest offers prayers for forgiveness of sin and restoration of health. Whenever possible, the family should be present to join in the prayers.

✔ If the patient is dying, extraordinary artificial measures to maintain life are unnecessary. At the hour of death the priest offers communion to the dying person by means of a special formula. This final communion is called *Viaticum*. In sudden deaths the priest should be called and the anointing and Viaticum should be administered if possible. If the person is dead when the priest arrives, there is no anointing, but the priest leads the family in prayers for the person who just died.

Beth divides the Roman Catholic funeral into three phases: the **wake,** *a period of waiting* or vigil during which the body is viewed and the family is sustained through visiting; the **funeral mass,** *a prayer service* incorporated into the celebration of the Mass; and the **burial,** *the final act* of placing the person in the ground. (This procedure may vary somewhat, for some Catholics are now choosing cremation.) The mourners retain the memory of the dead through a Month's Mind Mass, celebrated a month after death, and anniversary masses. Finally, the priest integrates the liturgy for the dead with the whole parish liturgical life.

✔ Beth is convinced that her religious practice contributes to her health. She feels that the body, mind, and spirit work together and that a spirit rid of guilt and grievances, and fortified with the strength of Christ's life, has positive effects on the body. She believes that suffering and illness are allowed by God because of our disobedience (original sin), but that they are not necessarily willed by God or given as punishment for personal sin.

✔ While in the hospital, a Roman Catholic may want to attend Mass, have the priest visit, or receive the Eucharist at bedside. (Fasting an hour before the sacrament is traditional, but in the case of physical illness, fasting is not necessary). Other symbols that might be comforting are a Bible, prayer book, holy water, a lighted candle, crucifix, rosary, and various relics and medals.

The Greek Orthodox Faith is discussed by Demetrius. The Eastern Orthodox Church, the main denomination, is divided into groups by nationality. Each group has the **Divine Liturgy,** *the Eucharistic service,* in the native language and sometimes in English also. Although similar in many respects to the Roman Catholic, the Eastern Orthodox have no pope.

The seven sacraments are followed with slight variations. Baptism is by triple immersion: the priest places the infant in a basin of water and pours water on the forehead three times. He then immediately confirms the infant by anointing with holy oil.

✔ If death is imminent for a hospitalized infant and the parents or priest cannot be reached, you can baptize the infant by placing a small amount of water on the forehead three times. Even a symbolic baptism is acceptable, but only a living being should receive the sacrament. Adults who join the church are also baptized and confirmed.

The **unction of the sick** has never been practiced as a last rite by the Eastern Orthodox; *it is a blessing for the sick*. Confession at least once a year is a prerequisite to participation in the Eucharist, which is taken at least four times a year; at Christmas, at Easter, on the Feast Day of Saint Peter and Saint Paul (June 30), and on the day celebrating the Sleeping of the Virgin Mary (August 15).

Fasting from the last meal in the evening until after **Communion,** another term for the Eucharist, is the general rule. Other fast periods include each Wednesday, representing the seizure of Jesus; each Friday, representing His death; and two 40-day periods, the first before Christmas and the second before Easter.

✔ Fasting to Demetrius means avoiding meat, dairy products, and olive oil. Its purpose is spiritual betterment, to avoid producing extra energy in the body and instead think of the spirit. Fasting is not necessary when ill. Religion should not harm one's health.

Demetrius retains the Eastern influence in his thinking. He envisions his soul as blending in with the spiritual cosmos and his actions as affecting the rest of creation. He is mystically inclined and feels insights can be gained directly from God. He tells of sharing such an experience with a patient, Mrs. A., also Greek Orthodox.

Mrs. A. had experienced nine surgeries to build up deteriorating bones caused by rheumatoid arthritis. She faced another surgery. On the positive side, the surgery promised hope for walking; on the negative, it was a new and risky procedure. Possibly she would not walk; possibly she would not live. Demetrius saw Mrs. A. when he started working at 3:30 P.M. She was depressed, fearful, and crying. Later, at 6:30 P.M., he saw a changed person—fearless and calm, ready for surgery. She explained that she had seen Jesus in a vision, and that He said, "Go ahead with the surgery. You'll have positive results. But call your priest and take Communion first." Demetrius called the priest, who gave her Communion. She went into surgery the next day with supreme confidence. She now walks.

✔ In addition to Communion, other helpful symbols

are prayer books, lighted candles, and holy water. Especially helpful to the Orthodox are **icons,** *pictures of Jesus, Mary, or a revered saint.* Saints can intercede between God and the person. One of the most loved is **Saint Nicholas,** *a third-century teacher and father figure* who gave his wealth to the poor and became an archbishop. He is honored on Saint Nicholas Day, December 6, and prayed to continuously for guidance and protection.

Every Sunday morning Demetrius participates in an hour-long liturgy. Sitting in an ornate sanctuary with figures and symbols on the windows, walls, and ceiling, facing the tabernacle containing the holy gifts and scripture, Demetrius finds renewal. He recites "I believe in one God, the Father Almighty, Maker of Heaven and Earth, and of all things visible and invisible. And in one Lord Jesus Christ, the only begotten Son of God."

Protestantism is divided into many denominations and sects. Jean Taylor is a member of the *Church of God* (Anderson, Indiana). She identifies the church by its headquarters because there are some 200 independent church groups in the United States using the phrase "Church of God" in their title. Her group evolved late in the nineteenth century because members of various churches felt that organization and ritual were taking precedence over direction from God. They banded together in a drive toward Christian unity, toward a recognition that any people who followed Christ's teachings were members of a universal Church of God and could worship freely together.

This example speaks of one of the chief characteristics of Protestantism: the insistence that God has not given any one person or group of persons sole authority to interpret His truth to others. Protestants use a freedom of spiritual searching and reinterpretation. Thus new groups form as certain persons and their followers come to believe that they see God's teaching in a new and better light. Jean feels that reading the Bible for historical knowledge and guidance, having a minister to teach and counsel her, and relying on certain worship forms are all important aids. But discerning God's will for her life individually and following that will are her ultimate religious goals.

Jean explains that she "accepted Christ into her life" when she was 8 years old. This identified her as personally following the church's teaching rather than just adhering to family religious tradition. A later experience, in which the Holy Spirit gives the person more spiritual power and discernment, is called *sanctification.*

Jean defines her corporate worship as free liturgical, with an emphasis on congregational singing, verbal prayer, and scripture reading. A sermon by the **minister,** *the spiritual leader,* may take half the worship period. As with many Protestant groups, two sacraments or ordinances are observed: (1) baptism (in this case, **believer's** or **mature baptism** *by total immersion into water*) and (2) Communion. To Protestants, the bread and wine used in Communion are symbolic of Christ's body and blood rather than the actual elements. One additional ordinance practiced in Jean's church and among some other groups is **foot-washing,** *symbolic of Jesus washing His disciples' feet.* These ordinances are practiced with varied frequencies.

✔ Because of the spectrum of beliefs and practices, defining Protestants, even within a single denomination or sect, is almost impossible. Some Protestant groups, retaining their initial emphasis on individual freedom, have allowed no written creed but expect members to follow an unwritten code of behavior. Jean does suggest some guidelines, however. She lists some of the **main Protestant bodies** in the United States, beginning with the most formal liturgically and sacramentally, the *Protestant Episcopal* and *Lutheran* churches. The in-betweens are the *Presbyterians, United Church of Christ, United Methodists,* and *Disciples of Christ (Christian Church).* The liturgically freest and the least sacramental are the *Baptists* and *Pentecostals.*

Among these groups, some of the opposing doctrines and practices are as follows: living in sin versus living above sin; predestination versus free will; infant versus believer's baptism; and loose organization versus tightly knit organization. Some uphold **fundamental precepts,** *holding to the Scriptures as infallible* whereas others uphold **liberal precepts,** *using the Scriptures as a guide, with various interpretations for current living.*

✔ With this infinite variety, Jean feels that learning the individual beliefs of her Protestant patients is essential. When and if a patient wants Communion; if an infant should be baptized; and what will be most helpful spiritually to the patient—these factors are learned by careful listening. Generally Jean feels that prayer, a scriptural motto such as "I can do all things through Christ who gives me strength," or a line from a hymn can give strength to a Protestant. Some patients will also want anointing with oil as a symbolic aid to healing.

✔ Jean has discovered that there are wide differences in Protestantism, sometimes even within the same denomination, about the theology and rituals of death. Some Protestant theologies have come to grips with the realities and meaning of death; others block authentic expression of grief by denying death and focusing on "If you are a Christian, you won't be sad."

✔ Some Protestants view death as penalty and punishment for sins; others see death as a transition when the soul leaves the body for eternal reward; and still others view death as an absolute end. All agree that death is a biological and spiritual event, a mystery not fully comprehended.

Rituals surrounding death vary widely. Some churches believe that the funeral service with a closed casket or memorial service with no casket present is more of a testimony to the joy and victory of Christian life than the open-casket service. Others believe that death is a reality to be faced instead of denied and that viewing the dead person promotes the grief process and confrontation with death in a Christian context.

Jean believes that, for most Protestants, the minister represents friendship, love, acceptance, forgiveness, and understanding. His presence seems to help the dying face death with more ease. She also feels that Protestants are becoming more active in ministering to the bereaved through regularly scheduled visits during the 12 to 18 months after the funeral, although there are no formal rituals.

Other Groups of Interest

Practices or beliefs unique to certain groups should be part of every health worker's knowledge.*

✓ **Seventh-Day Adventists** rely on Old Testament law more than do other Christian churches. As in Jewish tradition, the Sabbath is from sundown Friday to sundown Saturday. And like the Orthodox Jew, the Seventh-Day Adventist may refuse medical treatment and the use of secular items, such as television, during this period and prefer to read spiritual literature. Diet is also restricted. Pork, fish without both scales and fins, tea, and coffee are prohibited. Some Seventh-Day Adventists are **lacto-ovo-vegetarians:** *they eat milk and eggs but no meat.* Tobacco, alcoholic beverages, and narcotics are also avoided. Because Adventists view the body as the "temple of God," health reform is high on their list of priorities and they sponsor health institutes, cooking schools, and food-producing organizations. They have pioneered in making foods for vegetarians, including meat-like foods from vegetable sources. Worldwide they operate an extensive system of over 4000 schools and 400 medical institutions and are active medical missionaries (55, 78). Much of their inspiration comes from Ellen G. White, a nineteenth-century prophetess who gave advice on diet and food and who stressed Christ's return to earth.

The **Church of Jesus Christ of Latter-Day Saints** (**Mormons**) takes much of its inspiration from the **Book of Mormon,** *translated from golden tablets found by the prophet Joseph Smith.* The Mormons believe that this book and two others supplement the Bible. Every Mormon is an official missionary. There is no official congregational leader, but a **seventy** and a **high priest** *represent successive steps upward in commitment and authority.*

The Articles of Faith of the Church of Jesus Christ of Latter-day Saints, as given by Joseph Smith, include statements of belief:

1. God and His Son, Jesus Christ, and the Holy Ghost.
2. The same organization that existed in the Primitive Church.
3. Worship of God according to personal conscience while obeying the law of the land.
4. People being punished for their own sins and not for Adam's transgression.
5. All people being saved, repentance, and obedience to the laws and ordinances of the Gospel.
6. Being honest, true, chaste, benevolent, virtuous, hopeful, persistent, and doing good to all people.

Specific Mormon beliefs are that the dead can hear the Gospel and can be baptized by proxy. Marriage in the temple seals the relationship for time and eternity. After a special ceremony in the temple, worthy members receive a white garment. This garment, continuously worn under the clothes, has priesthood marks at the navel and at the right knee and is considered a safeguard against danger. The church believes in a whole-being approach and provides education, recreation, and financial aid for its members. A health and conduct code called "Word of Wisdom" prohibits tobacco, alcohol and hot drinks (interpreted as tea and coffee) and recommends eating, though sparingly and with thankfulness, herbs, fruit, meat, fowl, and grain, especially wheat.

✓ The Mormon believes that disease comes from failure to obey the laws of health and from failure to keep the other commandments of God. However, righteous persons sometimes become ill simply because they have been exposed to microorganisms that cause disease. They also believe that by faith the righteous sometimes escape plagues that are sweeping the land and often, having become sick, the gift of faith restores the obedient to full physical well-being.

Statistics indicate that the Mormon population succumbs to cancer and diseases of the major body systems at a much lower rate than the general population in this country. The death rate for patients suffering from cancer is less than 50 percent that of the general population; 50 percent less for those with diseases of the nervous, circulatory, and digestive systems; 33 percent less for kidney diseases, and 10 percent less for those with respiratory diseases. Mental

---
*See *Nursing '77,* December 1977, pp. 64–70, for more detailed study.

illness occurs only half as often among Mormons as among the general population (61).

✔ An explanation for these differences from the norm might be that the Mormons literally believe that the body is the "temple of God." And they have programs of diet, exercise, family life, and work to help that "temple" function at optimum level.

✔ Although the two groups just discussed—the Seventh-Day Adventists and the Mormons—generally accept and promote modern medical practices, the next two groups hold views that conflict with the medical field. The first group, **Jehovah's Witnesses**, refuses to accept blood transfusions. Their refusal is based on the Levitical commandment, given by God to Moses, declaring that no one in the House of David should eat blood or he would be cut off from his people, and on a New Testament reference (in Acts) prohibiting the tasting of blood. Jehovah's Witnesses in need of surgery may be fortunate enough to be near a surgeon who uses no blood transfusions because of reduced operating time. Other surgeons are becoming more willing to do surgery without using blood, using intravenous fluids like the body's fluid composition instead. The new plasma expanders can also be used.

Masulis discusses the ethical dilemmas facing the nurse and other health care professionals when caring for the child of a family who are Jehovah's Witness. She believes the Jehovah's Witness argument against receiving blood transfusions (ingesting blood) (Genesis 9:3–6; 1 Samuel 14:31–35; Acts 15:19–21, 28–29) is based on false analogy. Transfused blood does not function as food and is not equivalent to ingested blood (46).

Every Jehovah's Witness is a minister. Members meet in halls rather than in traditional churches and they produce massive amounts of literature explaining their faith.

✔ The second group, **Church of Christ, Scientist (Christian Scientists)**, turn wholly to spiritual means for healing. Occasionally they allow an orthopedist to set a bone if no medication is used. Parents do not allow their children to get a physical examination for school; to have eye, ear, or blood pressure screening; or to receive immunizations. In addition to the Bible, Christian Scientists use as their guide Mary Baker Eddy's *Science and Health with Key to the Scriptures*, originally published in 1875. The title of this work indicates an approach to wholeness and those who follow its precepts think of God as Divine Mind, of spirit as real and eternal, of matter as unreal illusion. Sin, sickness, and death are unrealities or erring belief. Christian Scientists do not ignore their erring belief, however, for they have established nursing homes and sanitoriums, the latter recognized in the United States under the federal Medicare program and in insurance regulations. These facilities are operated by trained Christian Science nurses who give first-aid measures and spiritual assistance.

✔ A Christian Science graduate nurse must complete a 3-year course of training at one of a number of accredited sanitoriums. The training includes, among other subjects, classes in basic nursing arts, care of the elderly, cooking, bandaging, nursing ethics, care of reportable diseases, and theory of obstetrical nursing. The training is nonmedical and in the work of a Christian Science nurse no medication is administered. The nurse supports the work of the **practitioner**, *who devotes full time to the public practice of Christian Science healing*. Healing is not thought of as miraculous but as the application of natural spiritual law.

The practitioner helps people apply natural spiritual law. Such a person is not a clergyman and does not necessarily hold special church office. Becoming a practitioner is largely attained through self-conducted study and a short course of intensive study from an authorized teacher of Christian Science, but daily study, prayer, application, and spiritual growth are the foundation of practice. The practitioner will treat anyone who comes for help and is supported, like other general practitioners, by patients' payments.

✔ A Christian Scientist who is in a medical hospital has undoubtedly tried Christian Science healing first, may have been put there by a non-Scientist relative, or may be at variance with sacred beliefs. If brought in while unconscious, the person would want to be given the minimum emergency care and treatment consistent with hospital policy. The person may also appreciate having a Christian Science practitioner called for treatment through prayer.

Yet sometimes the Christian Scientist person or family may feel so desperate about personal or a loved one's health status that they seek traditional medical care—sometimes too late. The article by Case (13) describes how a Christian Scientist family, following their traditional beliefs and guidance of the sect elders, sought medical care too late to save the life of their son. The parents describe their anguish as they learned that earlier antibiotic treatment for bacterial meningitis could have saved their son's life, while Christian Science practitioners had no effective care measures. They also discuss the conflicts and guilt related to leaving Christian Science and seeking spiritual solace elsewhere. They also discuss appreciation of the nonjudgmental and supportive approach of the nursing and medical team as they rendered treatment, explained, and tried to save the son's life.

Two more groups of special interest because of their positive personal and health emphasis are the **Unity School of Christianity** and the **Society of Friends (Quakers)**. While most Roman Catholics acknowledge the earthly spiritual authority of the Pope and most Protestants regard the Bible as their ultimate authority, the *Friend's* authority resides in direct experience of God within the self. A Friend obeys the **light within,** *the* **inner light** *or the* **divine principle;** *this spiritual quality causes the Friend to esteem self and listen to inner direction.*

✔ All Friends are spiritual equals. Without a minister and without any symbols or religious decor, unprogrammed corporate worship consists of silent meditation with each person seeking divine guidance. Toward the end of the meeting, people are free to share their inspiration. The meeting closes with handshaking. Always interested in world peace, Friends have been instrumental in establishing organizations that work toward human brotherhood and economic and social improvements resulting in better health. Friends have staffed hospitals, driven ambulances, and served in medical corps, among numerous other volunteer services.

✔ The **Unity School of Christianity** believes that health is natural and that sickness is unnatural. Followers think illness is real but they believe it can be overcome by concentrating on spiritual goals. Late in the nineteenth century, Charles and Myrtle Fillmore started this group after studying, among other religions, Christian Science, Quakerism, and Hinduism. Thus it blends several established concepts in a new direction. Today Unity Village in Missouri has a publication center that publishes several inspirational periodicals, is beautifully landscaped and open for guests to share in the beauty, and houses its real force, Silent Unity. **Silent Unity** *consists of staff who are available on a 24-hour basis to answer telephone calls, telegrams, and letters from people seeking spiritual help.* They offer prayer and counseling to all faiths with no charge.

Some religious groups have retained lifestyle and geographical solidarity as well as theological unity. These groups originated in other countries and immigrated to America.

The **Mennonites,** for example, some of whom settled in Pennsylvania, are part of a group called the Pennsylvania Dutch, who are of German, rather than Dutch or Holland descent. The Mennonites generally emphasize plain ways of dressing, living, and worshipping. They do not believe in going to war, swearing oaths, or holding offices that require the use of force. Many of them farm the land or are inclined toward service professions. They are well known for their missionary efforts. Another group, the **Amish,** is a split from the Mennonite family.

A group with northern headquarters in Bethlehem, Pennsylvania, and southern headquarters in Winston-Salem, North Carolina, are the **Moravians.** These people have also been noted for their missionary work. A restored Moravian village is open for touring in Winston-Salem and during Christmas and Easter special services are shared with non-Moravian friends.

The **Waldenses,** a Presbyterian group, have their headquarters in Rome but largely populate the town of Valdese, North Carolina. Each summer an outdoor drama portrays their pilgrimage to freedom.

Neo-Pentecostalism

Another facet of Christianity in the United States is Neo-Pentecostalism. This is not a group but a trend or phenomenon that has gained support from small groups in all major denominations—some Roman Catholics, Presbyterians, and Lutherans—as well as from those churches traditionally closer to the Pentecostal spirit.

✔ The heart of the Pentecostal spirit is an enthusiastic personal relationship with Christ. Those who are a part of this trend tell about getting out of dead, organized religion or of getting out of a religious tradition that no longer has meaning. They are anxious to share their insights. The hallmark of this experience is "speaking in tongues" or "glossolalia." Christians trace this experience back to the first century AD. In 1914, however, the phenomenon became institutionalized with the organization of the Pentecostal Assembly of God Church. This group placed its emphasis of a right relationship with God on glossolalia. Three other Pentecostal denominations have come into being: Church of God (Cleveland, Tennessee), Foursquare, and United Evangelical Brethren (16).

Neo-Pentecostalism is thought of as the *renewed interest in glossolalia; it is sometimes called the Charismatic Movement.*

Just what is **glossolalia?** Oral Roberts describes it as the *prayer language of the spirit;* he feels that it is a release of thoughts so deep within the person that ordinary words do not suffice. Sounds made by the person are not in any known language and the conscious mind, through prayer, should interpret the glossolalia after the experience so that the person can use the gained insight in everyday living (62).

North American Indian Religions

The **American Indian religion** developed for years with very little influence from outside the continent. Power, supreme being, guardian spirits, totems, fasting, visions, **shamanism** (*belief in priest who can influence good and evil spirits*), myth telling and ritualism are all part of a varied and colorful system. Furthermore, the location of the group influenced the belief system. Indians of the Far North, Northeast Woodlands, Southeast Woodlands, Plains, Northwest Coast, California and the Intermountain Region, and the Southwest make up the main divisions.

Yet, all groups have certain features in common: (1) **spirit world**—a *dimension that permeates life but is different;* (2) **Supreme Being**—*God who represents other lesser deities;* (3) **culture hero**—*a spirit who competes with the Great Spirit, and who sometimes is a trickster;* (4) *spirits and ghosts such as atmospheric spirits (wind) or underworld powers (snakes);* (5) *guardian spirits acquired by visions seen during fasting;* (6) *medicine men and medicine societies;* (7) *ritual acts such as the Sun Dance;* (8) *prayers and offerings.*

✔ Harmony or spiritual balance is what North American Indians want to achieve in their relations with the supernatural powers.

✔ When caring for an American Indian, it will be wise to obtain access to the spiritual leader from that particular region and his/her tribe. Many healing rituals are kept a secret, so the health care worker can be most effective by making the appropriate connection, rather than by trying to intervene in the belief system.

Other Considerations

Agnosticism and Atheism

✔ This chapter has concentrated so far on worship of God, the divine or other positive spirits, with an emphasis on traditional teaching. Some people live by ethical standards, considering themselves either **agnostic**, *incapable of knowing whether God exists,* or **atheistic**, *believing that God does not exist.*

Cults

In the 1970s various *cults* gained publicity. Some older cults are based on fundamental religions, but they are unique in their own way. The Snake People, for example, incorporate the holding of snakes into their services. Newer cults have arisen from communal groups whose goals are stated as religious. Some cults spring from the philosophy and schedule of a self-chosen leader who entices youth in search of identity from their parents and formalized church. The youth involved may evolve into robots; parents have had to "kidnap" their children in order to get them home and "deprogram" them in order to recognize their original personalities (23).

✔ You may be involved in the long-term therapy of such a youth. Attention has focused on cults that are attracting not only the young but also the elderly. There are thought to be 2000 cults throughout the world with a membership of 3 million (60).

Devil or **Satan Worship** is also practiced as a cult. One young man spoke of how he became a precocious student of Satan. He read dozens of books on Satan as "Light-Bearer, the strongest and wisest angel in heaven, robbed of his rightful worship by a jealous God." He spoke of putting a hex on others, drinking ghoulish concoctions, and being obsessed with certain rites as he moved through the hierarchy to priesthood (88).

✔ Counselors and psychiatrists, as well as some ministers and priests, have had to deal with devil possession in treating clients. Although we do not often speak in these terms in our scientific age, devil possession is a recurring theme in patients' self-diagnosis and one that you should listen for with the new wave of interest in psychic occultism and witchcraft, and their various practices.

Summary of American Religions

The Encyclopedia of American Religions (1978, two volumes) by J. Gordan Meltan would be a good addition to the reference shelf in any health care facility in the United States. It is the first reference work to gather detailed information on all 1200 American religions from the well-known to the lesser cults. This work encompasses all religionists from mystical Hassidic Jews, metaphysicians, psychics, and witches to believers in the imminent end of the world, magic, and UFOs, as well as traditional Catholics, Lutherans, and Methodists. The author places all 1200 groups into 18 families (50) with common heritages and lifestyles and identifies these familes as

Liturgical	Liberal
Reformed-Presbyterian	Holiness
Pietist Methodist	European Free Church
Pentecostal	Independent Fundamentalists
Baptist	
Adventist	Latter Day Saints
Communal	Metaphysical
Psychic and New Age	Magick
Eastern	Middle Eastern
Lutheran	

Trends in Nonnative and Native American Religions

Only when Christianity combines its beliefs with the already existing beliefs of other religions does the blend have a chance of working. For example, Mormonism and Charismatics have had the most impact on native American religion, and since the 1960s, these groups have become more visible on Indian Reservations. Likewise, the Peyote Religion in which the followers eat the peyote cactus, have added some Christian content such as God, Mary, Jesus, and heavenly angels—all with Indian symbolism.

In churches across the country, what formerly was known as "voodoo" is now called "spiritualism" and is testimony to blending of African and Catholic traditions.

In another trend, religion is being thought of by mainline Americans as a private affair. People may have strong personal beliefs but not want to rely on established institutions to control their religious life. Also, more religious programming is brought into the home, car, or work, via television, VCR, tapes, radio and compact discs. People can listen in almost any setting via headphones without disturbing others.

Also families may be meeting their needs in nontraditional ways. One family of four—two parents and two children—decided, at a family conference, that their historical church was not providing an adequate spiritual diet for them. Rather than all look for another church together, they decided to pursue what was developmentally and spiritually appropriate for each. In time, one child joined the Methodist Church, the other child an Interdenominational Church, one parent a Charismatic Church, and the other parent an Episcopal Church.

Another trend can be seen on university and college campuses. In spite of talk of the cynical and materialistic 1980s, a fervency of religious spirit has been funneled through such groups as Inter-Varsity and Campus Crusade for Christ as well as mainline Catholic, Muslim, Jewish, and Methodist groups.

NURSING APPLICATIONS

You can use the foregoing—basic beliefs, dietary laws, and ideas of illness, health, body, spirit, mysticism, pragmatism, pain, death, cleanliness, and family ties—as a *beginning*. Even more basic than understanding these concepts is respecting your patient as a person with spiritual needs who has a right to have these needs met, whether he/she has formal religious beliefs. No one will respect your spiritual aid if you do not appear competent and thoughtful in your work. You are not expected to be a professional spiritual leader, for which lengthy training and experience would be required. You can, however, aid patients. You are the transition, the key person between the patient and spiritual help.

If you feel inadequate, you may want to imitate several nurses who also felt the same. They decided that they could not meet the spiritual needs of others because they had not met—or even identified—their own. They had a series of discussions focusing on their own needs and used the book *Spiritual Care: The Nurses Role* (24), along with the accompanying workbook (72). When they had a clear vision of their own value system and made plans to meet their own needs, they could begin to focus on others. They also discussed appropriate and inappropriate spiritual intervention and learned to be comfortable making appropriate referrals when they felt that their lack of time or expertise did not allow them to intervene (7).

Also, by one of the same authors is *The Spiritual Needs of Children* (73) and *Spiritual Dimensions of Mental Health* (74), both excellent guidebooks.

CASE STUDY

Consider the following case of a man with spiritual needs.

Jason Smith is a 40-year-old, middle-class, Caucasian bank president. He lives in a small town with his wife and four children. He also deals in real estate, works with civic and Roman Catholic church groups, and is developing an advertising company. He seems constantly busy. He discusses business over lunch and competes with friends when playing golf or tennis.

One evening he started vomiting and defecating blood and learned, after being hospitalized locally, that he had a bleeding duodenal ulcer. He was then taken in an ambulance to a metropolitan hospital 200 miles away, where a specialist successfully performed a partial gastrectomy, surgical removal of part of the stomach.

For the first time in his life, Jason was stopped. He was away from family and friends and was confined. Good and bad memories flooded his mind. He began to evaluate his activities, his emphasis on material gain and competition, how his children were growing so fast, how his religious activities were superficial, and how, without skilled surgery, he might have died.

At first he tried being jovial with the staff in order to strike out these new and troubling thoughts. But he could not sleep well. He was dreaming about death in wild combinations with his past life. He began to mention these dreams, along with questions about how the surgery would affect his life span, diet, and activities. He mentioned a friend who seemed severely limited from a similar surgery. He also said he was worried about the problems his teenagers were beginning to face and about his own ability to guide them properly.

The staff members never forced Jason to express more than he wished but answered the questions that were medically based and asked him if he would like to see the chaplain, since his own priest was not available. Jason agreed. An appointed nurse then informed the chaplain of Jason's physical, emotional, and spiritual history to date. In the course of several sessions the chaplain helped Jason work through a revised philosophy of life that put more emphasis on spiritual values, family life, and healthy use of leisure.

Assessment

Although you can learn a great deal by picking out points in case studies, remember that they provide only a basis. You will have to accept each patient's individual spiritual development. For example, the sacraments have a very different meaning to Jason than to a child. To a 10-year-old, the meaning of baptism might be carrying an ugly little baby on a pillow to the front of the church, pouring water on its head, and trying to believe that the baby emerges as a beautiful child of God. An adolescent or young adult caught up in sorting out various facets of learned idealism and trying to fit them into more realistic daily patterns may temporarily discard religious teaching. He/she may reject the guidance of a spiritual leader because the latter is associated with the parents' beliefs; yet the adolescent is nevertheless searching and needs guidance. An elderly person suffering the grief of a recently lost mate may repeatedly question how a God of love could allow this loss. Some physiologically mature people are not religiously mature; they may expect magic from God. The spiritually maturing individual experiences the fruits of faith in God in behavioral terms of love, trust, and security. The external spiritual stimuli of God's word, sacraments, and relationships with other believers create an inner peace and love through which the person experiences God within and then reaches out to others in supporting relationships.

Furthermore, realize that people can use the same religious terms differently; *saved, sanctified, fell out, slain by the spirit*, and *deathbed conversion* all connote religious experiences. You should listen carefully and you may have to ask questions to determine accurately the individual person's meaning.

Spiritual beliefs and beliefs about purpose in life, and life after death are important dimensions of high-level wellness. Beliefs are related to feelings about self-worth, goals, interactions with others, philosophy of life, interpretations of birth, life events, and death. The value and meaning of life is not judged by its length, but by the purpose for which the person lives, the principles by which they live, the reflection about a being greater than self, the love and joy obtained from relationships with others. All of these factors may directly affect health status. An open-ended spiritual assessment guide has been developed by Young (92), and is designated to have the person describe various facets of religious beliefs and spirituality.

Assessment for spiritual needs for any client, not just the terminally ill or dying, should be part of the nursing history. Four areas of concern can be covered later in the interview, as part of psychosocial assessment, if necessary, and after the patient/client feels safe with the nurse. These areas are:

1. The person's concept of God or deity.
2. The person's source of strength and hope.
3. The significance of religious practices and rituals.
4. The perceived relationship between spiritual beliefs and current state of health.

During this part of the assessment, be prepared for any answer. The agnostic or atheist may answer with as much depth and meaning, from his/her perspective, as someone with a specific religious background. The person who is part of a formal religion may not answer freely, reserving such conversation for the spiritual leader, or hesitating until the nurse is better known to the client.

When determining medical background, such as drug or food allergies, you could also ask about religious dietary laws, special rituals, or restrictions that might be an important part of the patient's history. Recording and helping the patient follow beliefs could speed recovery.

Perhaps you could share with the chaplain the responsibility for asking some of the following questions as you give patient care. No specific set of questions will be right for every patient, but the following questions might draw helpful responses as you make a nursing assessment-diagnosis in the spiritual realm.

1. Who is your God? What is He/She/It like? (Or, what is your religion? Tell me about it.)
2. Do you believe that God or someone is concerned for you?
3. Who is the most important person to you? Is that person available?
4. Has being sick (what has been happening to you) made any difference in your feelings about God? In the practice of your faith? If it has, could you explain how it has changed?
5. Do you feel that your faith is helpful to you? If it is, how? If it is not, why not?
6. Are there any religious beliefs, practices, or rituals that are important to you now? If there are, could you tell me about them? Can I help you carry them out by showing you where the chapel is? By telling the dietary department about your vegetarian preference? By allowing you specific times for prayer or meditation?
7. Is there anything that would make your situation easier? (Such as a visit from the minister, priest,

rabbi, or chaplain? Someone who would read to you? Time for reading your religious book or praying? Someone to pray with you?)
8. Is prayer important to you? (If so, has being sick made a difference in your practice of praying?) What happens when you pray?
9. Do you have available religious books or articles, such as the Bible, prayer books, phylacteries, or crucifix, that mean something to you?
10. What are your ideas about illness? About life after death?
11. Is there anything especially frightening or meaningful to you right now?
12. If these questions have not uncovered your source of spiritual support, can you tell me where you do find support (78)?

Be sure to look for the patient's strengths, not weaknesses. And remember that you must not preach or reconstruct. Allow the patient to assume his/her own spiritual stance.

Because your relationship with the patient may be of short duration, be sure to document well the results of this interview. And later, when you or others care for the patient, you should watch for religious needs that may be expressed through nonreligious language. You must again let the patient know what options are open for spiritual help. If you hide behind busyness and procedures, you may lose a valuable opportunity to aid in health restoration.

Your greater understanding of social-class and cultural differences gleaned from Chapter 1 should help you comprehend some of the religious differences. For instance, a poor Protestant American who has grown up with the barest survival materials, who has no economic power, no money for recreation, no hope for significant gain, and no positive attitude about this life may center his/her whole being in the church. It provides as best it can for his/her emotional, recreational, and spiritual needs. When the person sings about heaven in terms of having beautiful clothes, a crown, and a mansion, he/she is singing with a much different meaning than the wealthy Protestant American who is really more concerned about mansions *here* than *over there*.

In a wider sense, an Egyptian Christian and an American Christian, although voicing the same basic beliefs, will differ in their approaches to religion. The Egyptian, influenced by the Islamic attitudes of his/her country might say, "No matter what happens, it's God's will. I can do no more about it." The American Christian may be more influenced by the individual drive to guide his/her life, a philosophy so prevalent in this culture. Another cultural difference centers on the influence of the family with an ill member. The Egyptian, accustomed to having family and friends around nearly constantly, will expect a continuation of such activity during illness. Their presence provides spiritual and emotional support. The American, more mobile and used to the American hospital system of limiting visitors in number and time, may be better able to detach self from the emotional and religious support given by the presence of family.

Religion influences behavior and attitudes toward:

1. Work—whether you work to expiate sin, because it is there to do, or because of a conviction that it is a God-given right and responsibility.
2. Money—whether you save money to deny yourself something, do installment buying, buy health insurance, consider money the root of all evil, or believe that it is to be used for the betterment and development of persons and society.
3. Political behavior—ideas about the sanctity of the Constitution, effects of Communism, importance of world problems, spending abroad versus spending for national defense, school or residential desegregation, welfare aid, and union membership.
4. Family—kinds of interaction within the family, honoring of parents or spouse, children, or siblings.
5. Childrearing—interest in the child's present and future, attitudes toward punishment or rewards for behavior, values of strict obedience as contrasted with independent thinking, or how many children should be born.
6. Right and wrong—what is sin, how wrong is gambling, drinking, birth control, divorce, smoking, and abortion (5).

Consider how essentially the same situation can be diversely interpreted by two teenagers of different faiths. One, a fundamentalist Protestant, may spend an evening dancing and playing cards and suffer crushing guilt because she participated in supposed sinful acts. The other, a Jewish teenager, may participate in the same activities and consider it a religiously based function. Your knowledge of and sensitivity to such differences are important, for essentially similar kinds of decisions—right and wrong as religiously defined—will be made about autopsy, cremation, and organ transplants. (See reference 37 for additional information.) Furthermore, although religious bodies may hand down statements on these issues, often the individual person will alter the group's stand while incorporating individual circumstances into the decision.

Ideally, religion provides strength, an inner calm and faith with which to work through life's problems. But you must be prepared to see the negative aspect. To some, religion seems to add guilt, depression, and confusion. Some may blame God for making them ill, for letting them suffer, or for not healing them in a prescribed manner. One Protestant felt she had made a contract with God: if she lived the best Christian life she could, God would keep her relatively well and free from tragedy. When an incurable disease was diagnosed, she said, "What did I do to deserve this?" Another Protestant, during her illness, took the opposite view of her contract with God. She said "I wasn't living as well as I should and God knocked me down to let me know I was backsliding."

Healing, too, has varied meanings. Some will demand that God provide a quick and miraculous recovery whereas others will expect the process to occur through the work of the health team. Still others combine God's touch, the health workers' skill, and their own emotional and physical cooperation. Some will even consider death as the final form of healing.

Sometimes you must deal with your own negative reactions. Your medical background and knowledge may cause you to be dismayed at some religious practices. For instance, how will you react as you watch a postoperative Jehovah's Witness patient die because she has refused blood? How will you react to a Christian Scientist patient who, in your opinion, should have sought medical help a month ago to avoid present complications? Here is one response given by a Christian Science nurse: "People can be ruined psychologically by going against a long held belief. They may live and get better physically, but will suffer depression, guilt, and failure in not holding to their standard." Basically they prefer to die. Should you dictate otherwise? You may need to think through and discuss such situations with a spiritual leader.

Nursing Diagnosis

The spiritual needs of the patients have become a part of the evolving nursing diagnosis system of classification. **Spiritual distress,** *when the person experiences or could experience a disturbance in the belief system that is his/her source of strength,* is the main diagnostic category. This problem may be related to not being able to practice spiritual rituals or may be caused by a conflict between the spiritual beliefs and the health regimen (56). *As nurses become more attuned to this situation, perhaps meeting the patient's spiritual needs will not be unattached from other care.* At the same time, the spiritual dimensions must be thought of as something in addition to the psychosocial dimension. Specific measures need to be taken for spiritual care, which are not necessarily included in psychosocial care. One study showed that nursing educators were using only psychosocial intervention for spiritual care (55).

Intervention

Spirituality is an integral part of holistic health. Spiritual support to the ill and dying person can be given in various ways. Your warmth, empathy, and caring human relationship are essential. Respect for the person's belief, willingness to discuss spiritual matters, and providing for rituals and sacraments of religion are important. Be open to religious and philosophical beliefs other than your own. Some nurses may be uncomfortable discussing spiritual matters, yet it is for the patient/client that the nurse will try to overcome personal reluctance to discuss spiritual concerns, just as nurses have worked to overcome reluctance to discuss sexuality concerns. Often, the intimacy of spiritual concerns are discussed by the patient/client during the intimacy of physical care. Helping the person ask questions and seek solutions does not mean that you have to supply the answers.

The nurse who has struggled with personal spiritual needs, beliefs, and concerns, including the thought of her/his own death, can better help another work through concerns and needs. Being aware of sources for spiritual growth and support is important for self and the patient/client. Knowledge about various religions and of their spiritual leaders and about cultures and the related values can prepare you for providing spiritual support.

Be alert to subtle clues which indicate desire to talk about spiritual matters, need for expressions of love and hope, desire for your silent presence, acceptance of behavior when the patient/client labels self as bad.

These are certain norms for providing spiritual care that must be followed:

1. Do not impose personal beliefs on patients/clients or families. A sickbed or deathbed is not a proper time for proselytizing.
2. Respond to the person out of his/her own background. Use knowledge about that background, but avoid acting in stereotypes. (For example, all Catholics believe _____ or all Hindus do _____.)
3. If you cannot give the spiritual support being asked for by the person, get someone who can.

For too long there has been no communication between the nurse and the chaplain. You can fill that gap. Nurse and chaplain rapport can mean that the *whole* person is served rather than segmented parts. Chaplains are especially helpful to clients, as well as to nurses, when they assist with the expression of anger, death, and the expression of grief (21). Nurse and chaplain, however, need to know what to expect from each other; there is no substitute for talking about these expectations and agreeing on strategies.

The following chart lists nine combinations of behavior that call for conferring with or referring to a spiritual leader, unless contraindicated by the care plan:

1. Withdrawn, sullen, silent, depressed.
2. Restless, irritable, complaining.
3. Restless, excitable, garrulous, wants to talk a lot.
4. Shows by word or other signs undue curiosity, anxiety, about self.
5. Takes turn to worse, critical, terminal.
6. Shows conversational interest, curiosity in religious questions, issues, reads Scriptures.
7. Specifically inquires about chaplain, chapel worship, Scripture.
8. Has few or no visitors, has no cards, flowers.
9. Has had, or faces, particularly traumatic or threatening surgical procedure.

With all these aspects to consider, a team approach that includes the patient–family, health workers, and chaplain or other spiritual leader is imperative. Because Americans want weekends away from the job, the weekend hospital staff often has double responsibility. Furthermore, weekends are when most people attend corporate worship. Preparing the patient for chapel service, or seeing that the Sabbath ritual is carried out, puts a special responsibility on you, the nurse.

Validate the appropriateness of proposed interventions with the patient/client, for example, ask if the person wishes you to pray with him/her about the concerns that have been voiced. The person can then accept or reject your offer.

If a patient is confined to a room, you can simply prepare a worship center or shrine by arranging flowers, prayer book, relics, or whatever other objects have spiritual meaning.

You should keep one or more calendars of various religious holidays. The Eastern Orthodox Easter usually does not coincide with the Roman Catholic and Protestant Easter. Jewish holidays usually do not fall on the same dates of the Western calendar in successive years. Remember, also, that holidays are family days and that ill people separated from the family at such times may be especially depressed.

Maintaining a list of available spiritual leaders, knowing when to call them, and knowing how to prepare for their arrival are other important responsibilities. If a patient cannot make the request, consult with the family. One woman said, "If my sister sees a priest, she will be sure she is dying." Once a health worker took the initiative to call an Eastern Orthodox priest who, unfortunately, represented the wrong nationality; the patient's main source of comfort was to have come from discussion and prayers in the native language. Sometimes the family needs reassurance and guidance from the chaplain. You can suggest this option.

As you prepare the patient and the setting for a spiritual leader, help create an atmosphere that reflects more than sterile procedure. Privacy has previously been emphasized by drawing curtains and shutting doors. Although acceptable to some, this approach may produce a negative response in others. Perhaps more emphasis should be given to cheerful surroundings: sunshine, flowers, lighted candles, openness, and participation by family and staff in at least an introductory way. Perhaps the patient and spiritual leader could meet outdoors in an adjoining garden. The Shintoist and Taoist would especially benefit from the esthetic exposure. If the patient is a child on a prolonged hospitalization, a special area might be designated for religious instruction.

Brief the spiritual leader on any points that might provide special insight and be sure that the patient is ready to receive him/her. Prepare any special arrangements, such as having a clean, cloth-covered tray for Communion. Guard against interruption by health workers from other departments who may be unaware of the visit. Finally, incorporate the results of the visit into the patient's record.

Many will benefit from the sacraments, the prayers, Scripture reading, and counseling given by the spiritual leader, but others will want to rely on their own direct communication with God. The Zen Buddhist, Hindu, Muslim, and Friend might be in the latter category. All may wish reading material, however. Most will bring their sacred book with them, but if they express a desire for more literature, offer to get it. Some hospitals furnish daily and weekly meditations as well as copies of the King James Version of the Bible (which recently has been updated). Or you might suggest the Bible paraphrased in modern language by Kenneth Taylor, called *The Living Bible* (Tyndale House, 1971). The same edition is available as *The Children's Living Bible* (Tyndale House, 1972) with appropriate illustrations. *The Way* (Tyndale House, 1972) has the same wording as *The Living Bible* with guidelines and illustrations for youth. The *Amplified Bible* (Zondervan Publishing House, 1965) is especially good for translating the original Greek into comparable English meaning. The *New International Version* (Zondervan Bible Publishers, 1978) was a new translation which resulted from over 100 scholars working from the best available Hebrew, Aramaic, and Greek texts.

Occasionally it may be helpful to give Scripture references for various stated spiritual needs. For example, reference to love and relatedness can be found in Psalm 23; reference to forgiveness in Matthew 6:9–15; reference to meaning and purpose in Acts 1:8.

A positive interfaith magazine is *Guideposts* (Guideposts Associates). A novel with religious insights is *Christy* (Avon Books, 1968) by Catherine Marshall. A spiritually based autobiography is *Joni* (World Wide Publication, 1976) by Joni Eareckson. A delightful biography about a spiritually mature preschool-school-age child is *Mister God, This Is Anna* (Ballantine Books, 1974) by Fynn. *In Search of God: The Story of Religion* by Marietta Maskin is written for youth but is also recommended for adults who work with youth. Do not overlook the opportunity to share the ministry of books.

If you feel comfortable doing so, you can at times say a prayer, read a Scripture, or provide a statement of faith helpful to the patient. If you do not feel comfortable in providing this kind of spiritual care, you can still meet the patient's spiritual needs through respectful conversation, listening to the patient talk about beliefs, referral to another staff member, or calling one of the patient's friends who can bolster his/her faith. If spiritual leaders are not available, you could organize a group of health workers willing to counsel with or make referrals for patients of their own faiths.

Shared prayer, if it is accepted by the patient/client, counteracts the loneliness of illness or dying by offering the person intimacy with a Supreme Being and another person without the need for confession. It can be a means of bringing both human and divine love. It holds transcendent qualities and conveys both present and future hope. Prayer can focus on the conditions or emotions that the patient/client is unable to talk about, allowing the person to handle the matter or vent in another way. Prayer should promote closeness, through closed eyes and hands that touch. Prayer should not strip the person of defenses. Nor should prayers be recited as a way to avoid the person or avoid questions raised by the person.

Use of life review can foster developmental, emotional, and spiritual maturity (not only in the elderly and dying person). Encourage the person to reminisce about past life experiences. Memories can be pleasurable or painful, but recalling them with a skilled listener can help resolve those ridden with shame, guilt, anger, or other feelings. Past sources of strength can also be identified, and sometimes they are useful in the present situation.

Several authors describe how counseling and mental and spiritual methods can be combined to help the patient/client heal hurtful or traumatic memories, for-

TABLE 3—1. Practices Rated Helpful by Individuals in the Judeo-Christian Religion to Establish and/or Maintain a Relationship with God

USING RELIGIOUS LITERATURE	CATHOLICS		N	PROTESTANTS		N	JEWS		N
Reading from the Bible by yourself.	21	(68%)	31	48	(98%)	49	23	(92%)	25
Reading from the Bible with others.	18	(56%)	32	48	(96%)	50	20	(83%)	24
Discussing Bible passages with others.	21	(66%)	32	50	(100%)	50	23	(96%)	24
Reading from religious writings of people of your religious group or denomination.	22	(71%)	31	45	(92%)	49	20	(87%)	24
Reading religious books, magazines, and/or religious newspapers	29	(83%)	35	45	(92%)	49	21	(88%)	24
USING PRAYER									
Praying silently, using your own words.	37	(100%)	37	48	(96%)	50	25	(100%)	25
Praying silently, using written or memorized prayers.	36	(95%)	38	7	(14%)	49	11	(69%)	16
Praying aloud with your religious leader.	31	(91%)	34	44	(90%)	49	23	(85%)	27
Praying aloud when a group of your faith is listening and praying with you.	29	(85%)	34	46	(94%)	49	21	(84%)	25
Praying aloud when you are alone.	31	(84%)	37	48	(98%)	49	16	(64%)	25
Praying aloud with one or two others.	22	(65%)	34	46	(94%)	49	12	(48%)	25
Praying aloud when people not of your faith are in the vicinity and may overhear you.	10	(33%)	30	35	(73%)	48	8	(33%)	24
ATTAINING SPIRITUAL SUPPORT WITH HELP OF OTHERS									
Listening to me talk through my problems.	33	(97%)	34	47	(94%)	50	19	(76%)	25
Reading Bible passages to me.	13	(41%)	32	44	(88%)	50	4	(20%)	20
Praying with me.	28	(78%)	36	47	(98%)	48	12	(52%)	23
Saying prayers for me (when I was not with the person).	36	(95%)	38	47	(94%)	50	12	(48%)	25

3 Spiritual and Religious Influences on the Person

give self or others, work through unresolved grief, promote healing within self, and establish healthier relationships with others. Both non-Christian and Christian nurses may find these articles helpful (64, 70, 80).

The atheist is not to be neglected because he/she does not profess a belief in God. He/she has the same need for respect as anyone else and may need you to listen to fears and doubts. The person does not need your judgment.

Moreover, just as health teaching is often omitted for health workers who are patients, so is spiritual guidance often omitted for spiritual leaders who are patients. You must recognize that each person, regardless of religious stand or leadership capacity, may need spiritual help.

Various groups refuse medical or hospital treatment for illness, including members of Fundamentalist or Holiness groups, Jehovah's Witnesses, Amish, and Christian Scientists. Realize that if adults refuse treatment for themselves or their children, they are not deliberately choosing death. They are rejecting something objectionable, based on their beliefs. If at all possible, offer acceptable alternative treatments. Jehovah's Witnesses accept intravenous normal saline, Ringer's lactate, dextrose, Haemaccel, and hydroxyethyl starch solution. Members of rural Fundamentalist sects and the Amish are often willing to go to chiropractors and will allow physicians to set fractures and suture lacerations. Nurses may teach nutritional therapy or various stress management or relaxation techniques (44). Sometimes parents will accept the services of a home health nurse although they refuse hospital and formal medical treatment.

Although a hospital setting has been used as a point of reference throughout this chapter, you can improvise in your setting—nursing home, school, industry, clinic, home, or other health center—in order to provide adequate spiritual assistance.

Evaluation

Exactly what constitutes spiritual intervention needs further research. In an attempt to identify which practices are used by individuals to establish or maintain a relationship with God, three groups within the Judeo-Christian religion completed a 23-item questionnaire. The questionnaire listed 16 practices that individuals in the Judeo-Christian religion might do to establish or maintain a relationship with God; study participants were asked to check if the practice was "helpful" or "not helpful" to them. The questionnaire focused on religious practices that do not require the clergy. The three groups, one Protestant, one Catholic, and one Jewish, were randomly selected from

TABLE 3–2. Nursing Interventions Rated Helpful

HAVING A NURSE:	CATHOLIC	N	PROTESTANT	N
• Read to me Bible passages I have chosen.	15 (75%)	20	36 (88%)	41
• Read or recite Bible passages of the nurse's choice.	12 (55%)	22	31 (78%)	40
• Listen to me talk through my problems.	22 (92%)	24	32 (80%)	40
• Pray with me at my bedside.	20 (83%)	24	37 (93%)	40
• Tell me that the nurse is praying for me (when not with me).	23 (96%)	24	36 (92%)	39

churches and synagogues listed in the Yellow Pages of a Midwestern city. The Protestant church so selected was Pentecostal and the Jewish synagogue was Orthodox. At least 25 individuals from each group completed the questionnaire.

Table 3–1 lists the practices from the questionnaire and the number and percentage of subjects that identified the practice "helpful" from each of the three groups.

Subjects who had had contact with nurses were also asked if they believed a nurse could be helpful to them in establishing or maintaining a relationship with God. Only 5 of 24 Jewish subjects responded "yes." One subject added the comment, "No one, nurse or otherwise, can help in my relationship with God." However, 42 (91%) of the Protestant respondents and 26 (72%) of 36 Catholic respondents checked "yes." The subjects indicating a nurse could be helpful were asked to rate "helpful" or "not helpful" to five possible nursing interventions. The Catholic and Protestant responses are in Table 3–2.

This study is limited by the small number of subjects in each of the three groups. The responses, however, can give direction for more investigation to other Catholic, Protestant, and Jewish groups. Additional studies also need to determine which practices are helpful to individuals in hospitals, hospices, and nursing homes.

References

1. Abbott, Walter M., and Joseph Galleger, eds., *The Documents of Vatican II*. New York: The America Press, 1966, pp. 37–39, 158, 363.

2. Allport, Gordon, *The Individual and His Religion*. New York: Macmillan, 1961, pp. 24–27.
3. Anderson, Harry, and Ellen Williams, God Goes Back to College, *Newsweek* (November, 1986), 10–16.
4. Berkowitz, Philip, and Nancy Berkowitz, The Jewish Patient in the Hospital, *American Journal of Nursing*, 67, no. 11 (1967), 2335–2337.
5. Bossard, J., and E. Boll, *The Sociology of Child Development* (4th ed.). New York: Harper & Row, 1966.
6. Butler, Richard, The Roman Catholic Way in Death and Mourning, in *Concerning Death: A Practical Guide for the Living*, ed. Earl Grollman. Boston: Beacon Press, 1974, pp. 101–118.
7. Buys, Ann, Discussion Series Sensitizes Nurses to Patient's Spiritual Needs, *Hospital Progress*, 62 (October 1981), 44–45.
8. Caillat, Collett, Jainism, in *The Encyclopedia of Religion*, 7, ed. Mircea Eliade. New York: Macmillan, 1987, pp. 507–514.
9. Campbell, Teresa, and Betty Chang, Health Care of the Chinese in America, *Nursing Outlook*, 21, no. 4 (1973), 245–249.
10. Carpenito, Lynda Juall, *Nursing Diagnosis: Application to Clinical Practice*. Philadelphia: J. B. Lippincott, 1983, pp. 451–466.
11. Carson, Verna, Meeting the Spiritual Needs of Hospitalized Psychiatric Patients, *Perspectives in Psychiatric Care*, 18, no. 1 (1980), 17–20.
12. Carson, Verna Benner, et al. The Effect of Didactic Teaching on Spiritual Attitudes, *Image: Journal of Nursing Scholarship*, 18, no. 4 (1986), 161–164.
13. Case, Ramona, We Let Our Son Die, *Journal of Christian Nursing*, 4, no. 2 (1987), 4–8.
14. Conrad, Nancy L., Spiritual Support for the Dying, *Nursing Clinics of North America*, 20, no. 2 (1985), 415–426.
15. David, Rod, Behind the Voodoo Mask, *America*, pp. 29–35, n.d.
16. DeVol, Thomas, Ecstatic Pentecostal Prayer and Meditation, *Journal of Religion and Health*, 13, no. 4 (1974), 285–288.
17. Dixon, Dorothy, *World Religions for the Classroom*, West Mystic, CT: Twenty-Third Publications, 1975.
18. Doctors Use Psychic Tools for Healing, *St. Louis Globe-Democrat*, September 30, 1975, Sec. A, p. 12.
19. Eck, Diana, *Roots in Who Are They?* Los Angeles: The Bhaktivedanta Book Trust, 1982.
20. Eich W., When is Emergency Baptism Appropriate?, *American Journal of Nursing*, 87, no. 12 (1987), 1680–1681.
21. Eickhoff, Alice, The Chaplain-Nurse Relationship, *Nursing Management*, 13, no. 3 (1982), 25–26.
22. Ellis, Donelda, Whatever Happened to the Spiritual Dimension? *The Canadian Nurse*, September 1980, 42–43.
23. Enroth, Ronald, *Youth, Brainwashing, and the Extremist Cults*. Grand Rapids, MI.: Zondervan Publishing House, 1977.
24. Fish, Sharon, and Judith Allen Sheely, *Spiritual Care: The Nurses Role*. Downers Grove, IL: Inter-Varsity Press, 1978.
25. Fleeger, Rebekah, and Judy Van Heukelein, The Patient's Spiritual Needs—A Part of Nursing Diagnosis, *The Nurses Lamp*, 28, no. 4 (1977).
26. Glustrom, Simon, *When Your Child Asks: A Handbook for Jewish Parents*. New York: Block Publishing, 1959.
27. Gordon, Audrey, The Jewish View of Death: Guidelines for Mourning, in *Death, the Final Stage of Growth*, ed. Elizabeth Kubler-Ross. Englewood Cliffs, NJ: Prentice-Hall, 1975, pp. 44–51.
28. Guoli, Gherardo, Zorastrianism, in *The Encyclopedia of Religion*, 15th ed. Mircea Eliade, New York: Macmillan, 1987, pp. 579–591.
29. Guralnik, David, ed., *Webster's New World Dictionary of the American Language* (2nd college ed.). New York: World Publishing, 1972.
30. Hackney, E. J., personal letter on Zen Buddhism, January 19, 1973.
31. Hover, Margot, If a Patient Asks You to Pray With Him, *RN* (April, 1986), 17–18.
32. Hultkrantz, Ake, North American Religions: An Overview, in *The Encyclopedia of Religion*, 10, ed. Mircea Eliade. New York: Macmillan, 1987, pp. 526–535.
33. Impoco, Jim, Japanese Religious Group Changing, *Hickory Daily Record*, December 16, 1987, Sec. D, p. 13.
34. Jordan, Merle, The Protestant Way in Death and Mourning, in *Concerning Death: A Practical Guide for Living*, ed. Earl Grollman. Boston: Beacon Press, 1974, pp. 81–100.
35. Jorgensen, Joseph G., Modern Movements, *The Encyclopedia of Religion*, 10, ed. Mircea Eliade, New York: Macmillan, 1987, pp. 541–544.
36. Kepler, Milton, The Religious Factor in Pediatric Care, *Clinical Pediatrics*, 9, no. 3 (1970), 128–130.
37. —, Human Values in Medicine: Some Helping Organizations, *Journal of the American Medical Association*, 15, no. 3 (1973), 305–307.
38. Kertzer, Milton, *What Is a Jew?* (rev. ed.). New York: Macmillan, 1969.
39. Kushner, Harold, *When Bad Things Happen to Good People*. New York: Schocken Books, 1981.
40. Lang, Bruce, The Death that Ends Death in Hinduism and Buddhism, in *Death, The Final Stage of Growth*, ed. Elizabeth Kubler-Ross. Englewood Cliffs, NJ: Prentice-Hall, 1975, pp. 52–57.
41. Life After Death? 'Beyond Shadow of Doubt,' Psychiatrist Says, *St. Louis Globe-Democrat*, November 15–16, 1975, Sec. A, p. 15.
42. Luce, Henry R., ed., *The World's Great Religions*. New York: Time, 1957.

43. Marshall, Gary, Growing up in Krishna, *Parade: St. Louis Post-Dispatch*, February 24, 1980, pp. 4–10.
44. Martin, JoAnn, A Home Health Responds: Seek Understanding, *Journal of Christian Nursing*, 4, no. 2 (1987), 10–16.
45. Marty, Martin E., Native Americans, *Christian Churches in the United States*, 1985, pp. 114–115.
46. Masulis, Karen, When Parents Refuse Treatment for Their Children, *Journal of Christian Nursing*, 4, no. 2 (1987), 10–16.
47. McConkie, Bruce R., *Mormon Doctrine*. Salt Lake City: Bookcraft, 1966.
48. McGilloway, Olly, and Freda Myco (eds.), *Nursing and Spiritual Care*. London: Harper and Row, Limited 1985.
49. Mead, Frank, *Handbook of Denominations in the United States* (4th ed.). Nashville: Abingdon Press, 1965.
50. Melton, J. Gordon, *The Encyclopedia of American Religions*, I & II. Wilmington, NC: McGrath, 1978.
51. Munley, A. *The Hospice Alternative: A New Context for Death and Dying*. New York: Basic Books, 1983.
52. Okamoto, Abraham, Religious Barriers to World Peace, *Journal of Religion and Health*, 15, no. 1 (1976), 26–33.
53. Petersen, Mark, *A World of Wisdom*. Salt Lake City: Church of Jesus Christ of Latter-Day Saints, n.d.
54. Piepgras, Ruth, The Other Dimension: Spiritual Help, *American Journal of Nursing*, 68, no. 12 (1968), 2610–2613.
55. Piles, C., *Spiritual Care a Part of the Nursing Curriculum: A Descriptive Study*, St. Louis, MO.: St. Louis University, 1980. (Unpublished Master's Thesis).
56. Piles, C., *Scripture References Related to Spiritual Needs*, Spiritual Care Workshop, St. Louis University, 1986.
57. Pill, Robert, The Christian Science Practitioner, *Journal of Pastoral Counseling*, 4, no. 1 (1969), 39–42.
58. Porath, Thomas, Humanizing the Sacrament of the Sick, *Hospital Progress*, 53, no. 7 (1972), 45–47.
59. Prophet or Plagiarist? E.G. White, *Time* (August 2, 1976), p. 43.
60. Religious Cults and the Elderly, *Information on Aging*. Institute of Gerontology at Wayne State University, Michigan, July 1982, p. 2.
61. Richards, LeGrande, *A Marvelous Work and a Wonder*. Salt Lake City: Deseret Book Company, 1975.
62. Roberts, Oral, *A Daily Guide to Miracles*. Tulsa: Pinoak Publications, 1975.
63. Rosten, Leo, ed. *Religions in America* (rev. ed.). New York: Simon & Schuster, 1963.
64. Rush, Beverly, Healing A Hidden Grief," *Journal of Christian Nursing*, 3, no. 2 (Summer, 1986), 10.
65. Russell, Douglas L., personal letter on Christian Science beliefs and practices, December 1, 1975.
66. Ryan, Juanita, The Neglected Crisis, *American Journal of Nursing*, 84, no. 10 (1984), 1257–1258.
67. Sachen, Karen L. and Verna J. Carson, Responding to the Spiritual Needs of the Chronically Ill, *Nursing Clinics of North America*, 22, no. 3 (1987), 603–611.
68. Satprakashananda, Swami, ed., *The Use of Symbols in Religion*. St. Louis: The Vedanta Society, 1970.
69. Saunders, E. Dale, *Buddhism in Japan*. Philadelphia: University of Philadelphia Press, 1964, pp. 265–286.
70. Seamonds, David, Healing of Memories: What Is It? Is It Biblical? *Journal of Christian Nursing*, 3, no. 2 (Summer, 1986), 4–9.
71. Schutzius, Mary Jane, Missing Voices of Women in our Church, *Probe*, 25, No. 4 (1987), 1.
72. Shelly, Judith Allen, *Spiritual Care Workbook*. Downer's Grove, IL: Inter-Varsity Press, 1978.
73. ———, *The Spiritual Needs of Children: A Guide for Nurses, Parents and Teachers*. Downer's Grove, IL: Inter-Varsity Press, 1982.
74. Shelly, Judith Allen and Sandra D. John, *Spiritual Dimensions of Mental Health*. Downer's Grove, IL: Inter-Varsity Press, 1983.
75. Singh, Khushwant, Sikhism, in *The Encyclopedia of Religion*, 13, ed. Mircea Eliade. New York: Macmillan, 1987, pp. 315–320.
76. Slimmer, Lynda, Helping Students to Resolve Conflicts Between Their Religious Beliefs and Psychiatric-Mental Health Treatment Approaches, *Journal of Psychiatric Nursing and Mental Health Services*, 18 (July 1980), 37–39.
77. Smith, Huston, *The Religions of Man*. New York: Harper & Row, 1965.
78. Stoll, Ruth, Guidelines for Spiritual Assessment, *American Journal of Nursing* 79, no. 9 (1979), 1574–1577.
79. Suzuki, D. T., E. Fromm, and R. DeMartino, *Zen Buddhism and Psychoanalysis*. New York: Grove Press, 1960, p. 5.
80. Tawless, June, Visualizing the Healer, *Journal of Christian Nursing*, 3, no. 2 (Summer, 1986), 12–14.
81. Thomas, David M., Religion as a Family Life-Style, *Marriage and Family Living Magazine*, 1979, 1–4.
82. Those Who Preserve the Ritual Bath, *St. Louis Post-Dispatch*, January 9, 1977, Sec. H, p. 3.
83. Tinney, James, S., Black Muslims, *Christianity Today*, 20 (March 12, 1976), 51–52.
84. Ujhely, Gertrud, On Being Possessed by the Devil, *Perspectives in Psychiatric Care*, 10, no. 5 (1972), 202–209.
85. *Unity School of Christianity*. Unity Village, MO: Unity School of Christianity, n.d.
86. Utt, Richard, *The Builders: A Photo Story of Seventh-Day Adventists at Work Around the World*. Mountain View, CA: Pacific Press Publishing Association, 1970.
87. Walker, H. B., Why Medicine Needs Religion, *International Surgery*, 56, no. 8 (1971), 37B–40B.
88. Warnke, Michael, When Evil Fights Back, *Guideposts*, November 1972, 22–25.
89. Wasson, Elgin, personal letter and paper from Christian

Science Committee on Publication for Missouri, January 8, 1973.
90. Wilson, John, *Religion in American Society*. Englewood Cliffs, NJ: Prentice-Hall, 1981.
91. Wood, Verna, personal letter on Religious Society of Friends, January 29, 1973.
92. Young, R. C., *Community Nursing Workbook: Family as Client*. Norwalk, CT: Appleton-Century-Crofts, 1982, pp. 189–190.

Personal Interviews

93. Andrews, Constantine, pastor, St. Nicholas Greek Orthodox Church, St. Louis, January 26, 1973.
94. Bregman, Alan, rabbi, Temple Israel, St. Louis, January 27, 1973.
95. Crump, Ronald, pastor, Rock Hill Church of God, St. Louis, January 30, 1973.
96. Danker, William, professor of world mission, Concordia Seminary St. Louis, January 26, 1973.
97. Dickes, Hans, a seventy in the Church of Jesus Christ of Latter-Day Saints, St. Louis, January 20, 1973.
98. Gowing, Peter, regional professor, Southeast Asia, Graduate School of Theology, Singapore, January 10, 1973.
99. Griswell, John, pastor, Seventh-Day Adventist Central Church, St. Louis, January 31, 1973.
100. Guirguis, Youssef, and Laila Guirguis, Egyptian Christians, January 13, 1973.
101. Katsarus, Georgia, Greek Orthodox, January 19, 1973.
102. Khalifa, Saeed, Soheir Eltoumi, E. Z. Eltoumi, Mohammed Ahmed, and Fatma Ahmed, Egyptian Muslims, January 13, 1973.
103. Kimelman, Dr. Nathan, Mrs. Nathan Kimelman, Dr. Harry G. Mellman, and Jane Tarlow, American Jews, January 29 and February 2, 1973.

PART II

Basic Concepts Related to the Developing Person and Family Unit

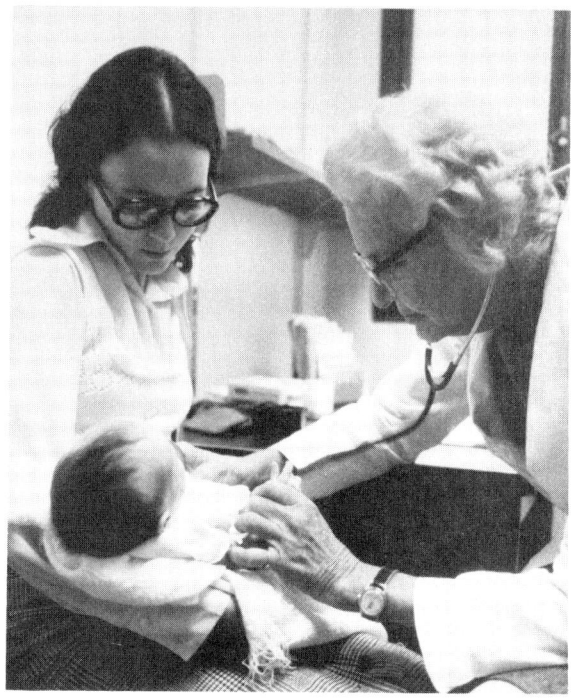

4

The Family—Basic Unit for the Developing Person

Study of this chapter will enable you to

1. Define *family* and discuss the family as a system and the implications for the developing person.
2. Summarize theoretical approaches for studying the family.
3. Describe the purposes, tasks, roles, and functions of the family and their relationship to the development and health of its members.
4. Describe family adaptive mechanisms and their purposes.
5. List stages of family life and developmental tasks for the establishment, expectancy, parenthood, and disengagement phases.
6. Discuss your role in helping the family achieve its developmental tasks.
7. Relate the impact of feelings about the self and childhood experiences on later family interaction patterns.
8. List and describe the variables affecting the relationship between parent and child and general family interaction, including single-parent, step-parent, and adoptive families.
9. Identify ways in which your family life has influenced your present attitudes about family.
10. Discuss the influence of twentieth-century changes on family life and childrearing practices.
11. Predict how a changing culture may affect the development and health of the family system.
12. Explore your role in promoting physical and emotional health of a family and assess community services that might assist you.
13. Assess and work with a family to enhance its welfare while simultaneously giving health care to one of its members.

Key Terms

Family	Establishment stage
Nuclear	Expectant stage
Extended	Couvade Syndrome
Patrifocal/Patriarchal	Parenthood stage
Matrifocal/Matriarchal	Disengagement stage
Reconstituted/Blended	Family interaction
Roles	Dyads
Physical functions	Single parent family
Affectional functions	Stepparent family
Social functions	Single state
Personality	Family cultural
Adaptive responses	pattern
in the family	Fourth trimester

It's an uncanny feeling—to suddenly know that I am answering my son's question with the same words—even the same tone—as my father used with me 30 years ago.

Even though I have a happy, successful marriage, two loving children, a nice home, and a profession in which I feel competent, I constantly fight a feeling of inferiority. A contributing factor must be that my parents never encouraged or complimented me. When I took a test, they emphasized the 2 wrong, not the 98 right.

I always admired my aunt. If my cousin, her son, had told her he wanted to build a bridge to the moon, she would have furnished the nails.

These three people are speaking of aspects of a social and biological phenomenon that is often taken for granted: the family. So strongly can this basic unit affect our development and health that we may live successfully or unsuccessfully because of its influence. Much that the person learns about loving, coping, and the various aspects of life is first learned in the family unit.

Between society and the individual person, the family exists as a primary system and social group, for most people share many of life's experiences with the family. Thus the family has a major role in shaping the person; it is a basic unit of growth, experience, adaptation, health, or illness.

This chapter is not an exhaustive study of families or family life. Rather, it is an overview of the various forms, stages, and functions of contemporary American families and of how nursing can use this knowledge. Although various aspects of the family are discussed separately, keep in mind that family purposes, stages of development, developmental tasks, and patterns of interaction are all closely interrelated, all influenced by historical foundations, and all continually evolving into new forms. Thus the family should be viewed as a system, affected by the culture, the environment, religious-spiritual dimensions, and other variables, which in turn effects the person and society.

Definitions

Family. The **family** *is a small social system and primary reference group made up of two or more persons "living together" who are related by blood, marriage, or adoption or who are living together by agreement over a period of time.* The family unit is *characterized by face-to-face contact, bonds of affection, love, loyalty, harmony, simultaneous competition and mutual concern, a continuity of past, present, and future, shared goals and identity, and behaviors and rituals common only to the specific unit* (45, 48, 85). With the family, the person can usually let down his/her guard and be more himself/herself than with other people. The family is comprised of a permanent household (or cluster of households), that persists over years or decades, and that is characterized by value, role, and power structures; communication patterns; affective, socialization, family coping, and health care functions; and developmental stages and tasks (29, 75). Internal and external structures exist in a family. Internal structure includes family composition, rank order, subsystems, and boundary. External structure includes culture, religion, social class status and mobility, environment, and extended family. Instrumental function refers to how routine activities of daily living are handled. Expressive function refers to nonverbal and verbal communication patterns, problem solving roles, control aspects, beliefs, alliances, and coalitions (85).

Healthy families are characterized by (1) a sense of togetherness that promotes capacity for change; (2) a balance between mutual and independent action on the part of family members; (3) availability of nurturance and resources for growth and sustenance; (4) stability and integrity of structure; (5) **adaptive functioning**; and (6) mastery of developmental tasks leading to interdependence, progressive differentiation, and transformation to meet the requisites for survival of the system (60, 73, 85).

In this stressful time, families may have difficulty in maintaining these characteristics. Your support, teaching, and counseling may assist them in maintaining health.

Family Composition. The family takes several forms. The family may be **nuclear** (*mother, father, child*), **extended** (*nuclear plus other relatives of either or both spouses live together*), **patrifocal** or **patriarchal** (*the man has the main authority and decision-making power*), **matrifocal** or **matriarchal** (*the woman has the main authority*), or **reconstituted/blended** (*one divorced or widowed adult with all or some of his/her children and a new spouse with all or some of his/her children, so that parents, stepparents, children, and stepchildren live together.*) Or the family may be made up of siblings, especially in middle or late life, homosexuals, friends in a commune, or a male and female living together without being married. The family may be symbolically duplicated in the work setting: a woman may be perceived as a grandmother, mother, or sister, or a man may be perceived as a grandfather, father, or brother to an employee. The family member who is dead or missing may remain clearly in the other members' memory; they may refer to the person on special occasions. Or the deviant of the family—the alcoholic or runaway—may influence other family members to act in an opposite manner.

The family may also be a series of separate but interrelated families. The middle-aged parents are helping the adolescent and young adult offspring to be emancipated from the home while simultaneously caring for increasingly dependent parents and sometimes up to four pairs of grandparents and older aunts and uncles as well. All related family members may not live under the same roof (in fact, they never did in America), but the extended family exists psychologically—in spirit. Often the responsibility is nearly overwhelming to the middleagers, who may have little time or resources to spend on themselves. The conflict inherent in having to care for a number of relatives and in-laws can contribute to marital disharmony as well as poor relationships between the generations. The middle-ager's caregiving role will be discussed in Chapter 13.

The elderly person is sometimes aware of such a situation and will try to make minimal demands. Often he/she feels that more attention is deserved and may make extra demands or chastise the middle-aged offspring for not doing more for elder family members.

A real entity is psychic life of the family; the

TABLE 4–1. Summary of Four Family Theories/Approaches

DEVELOPMENTAL THEORY

Compilation of several frameworks

Family defined as a series of interacting personalities, intricately organized into paired positions (father, husband, daughter, sister). Norms for reciprocal relations prescribe role behavior for each position. Predictable natural history designated by stages.

Person is a member of group; each new member adds to complexity of interaction.

- *Study family* in terms of role behaviors for each family life stage, with the changing ages of each person; study quality and type of interaction as age and member composition of family changes.
- *Focus:* Analysis of developmental needs and tasks of each family life-cycle stage; analyze family behaviors and changing developmental tasks and role expectations in terms of increasing complexity; analyzing children, parents, and family unit as a whole. Cultural influences at each stage of family life cycle considered.

STRUCTURAL-FUNCTIONAL THEORY

Family defined as social system open to outside influences and transactions, maintaining boundaries by responding to demands of system or acting under family constraints, passively adapting to external forces rather than acting as an agent of change in itself.

Person is seen as reactive, fulfilling roles, and having status in the social system.

- *Study family* in relation to other social structures or social systems and in terms of roles.
- *Focus:* Determine how family patterns related to other institutions and overall society; study family functions (reproductions, socialization of children, provision of physical needs, economics).

INTERACTIONAL THEORY

Rejection of role theory and psychodynamic theory

Family defined in terms of individual members, a unity of interacting personalities with assigned position and roles, expectations, and norms of behavior; seen as closed unit with little relationship to outside institutions, associations, or cultures.

Person is seen as fulfilling roles and as an interacting being.

- *Study family* in terms of overt interactions, fulfillment of interacting roles.
- *Focus:* Analysis of roles, interstatus relations, authority matters, action-taking communication processes, conflicts, problem solving, decision making.

ROLE THEORY

Life is structured according to roles that are ascribed or assumed by the person in interaction with others; roles learned through socialization.

Family defined in terms of members' role interaction.

Roles contribute in the following way to the family unit; Roles:

1. Circumscribe behavior.
2. Define social position, responses, expectations.
3. Influence group associations.
4. Are purpose of interaction.
5. Provide norms for the family/group.

Person is seen in terms of roles, which are specialized or shared, and depend on gender, age, social norms, status, complementarity. Roles and change through development and negotiation, which depends on flexibility, stability, and congruence of expectations.

- *Study family* in terms of role interactions, differentiation and allocation, role change, and role strain.
- *Focus:* Analysis of role reciprocity, complementarity and strain.

Role reciprocity—mutual exchange; sharing effects decision making and cohesion; personal and family needs met; high mutual dependence in division of labor; potential for growth; commitment to family and reducing conflict.

Role complementarity—family members differentiate and define roles in relation to each other; opportunity for growth; sometimes not a sense of mutual gratification; can confirm identity of one at expense of other; if rigid roles—transitions are difficult.

TABLE 4–1. Summary of Four Family Theories/Approaches—Continued

ROLE THEORY (CONT.)

Role strain occurs when individuals have difficulty meeting others or own expectations and the obligations of the role; and is manifested as:
1. *Role conflict*—unclear, incomplete, contradictory elements in role; performing one role makes it impossible to perform another; conflicting norms.
2. *Role overload*—must consider impact of distribution of power; the greater the control over negotiation of roles, the more person can avoid role strain; person with less power assumes more unwanted burdens; person with more power has less dependency needs and can make role demands.

extended family affects thoughts and actions, provides sustenance, and contributes to identity. Present day mobility of people, ease of communication over distance, freedom to evolve and think independently, freedom to develop in ways less restricted by strong or rigid ethnic or cultural mores, and ease of transportation allow families in the United States to be geographically distant yet emotionally close, and often quite involved with each other—to the point of giving assistance.

The mass media presents a picture of family life dissolving in the United States. Although the divorce rate is approximately 50 to 70 percent, most divorced people remarry. Because of longer life expectancy and the young age at which people marry, the young couples of today enter and remain in marriage longer than did their grandparents. Family authorities estimate that the divorce rate, extremely high in the 1970s and early 1980s, may begin to decline by the 1990s. People are beginning to realize that divorce does not necessarily improve life; the allure of creativity, growth and expanding oneself emotionally through divorce is not necessarily realistic (57).

Overview of Family Theoretical Approaches

There are several theoretical approaches to the study of families: developmental, structural-functional, interactional, and role theories. These approaches are summarized in Table 4–1. Refer to several references at the end of the chapter for more extensive explanation (1, 2, 26, 29, 75, 83).

Purposes, Tasks, Roles, and Functions of the Family

Although the institution of the family is being scrutinized and predictions are made that it may pass into oblivion, the family has demonstrated throughout history that it is a virtually indestructible institution. Family structure, roles, and responsibilities have always been influenced by technology and the resulting social changes. But technological advances alone do not determine family structure and function. Family systems are endlessly adaptive and very resistant to outside pressure. In a society where objects are often disposable and people feel uneasy and dispensable, they seek secure relationships. The family can be a source of security.

The U.S. family has passed through major transitions. The family was once a relatively self-contained, cohesive domestic work unit; it has become a group of persons dispersed among various educational and work settings. Various agencies have absorbed many purposes once handled solely by the family group. Schools educate; hospitals care for the sick; mortuaries prepare the dead for burial; churches give religious training; government and private organizations erect recreational facilities; nursing homes care for the aged; and various manufacturing firms bake, can, or bottle food and make clothes.

Purposes and Tasks of the Family

When the family changed from a production unit to a consumption unit, it also lost some degree of authority to regulate its members' behavior. The emphasis is now on democratic sharing, togetherness, the child's potential as an individual, and the fun aspects of parenthood. Enjoyment and relaxation in every human relationship are considered important. Technology is seen as the reason for this view, and the way to attain the happy state, but the person who believes too strongly in what technology can accomplish may have unrealistic expectations about living and thus undergo considerable stress in marriage and child-rearing.

Yet the family is still considered responsible for the child's growth and development and behavioral outcomes; indeed, the family is a cornerstone for the child's competency development. Because the family is strongly influenced by its surrounding environment as well as by the child itself, the family should not bear full blame for what the child is or becomes. Few parents deliberately set out to rear a disturbed, handicapped, or delinquent offspring, although such failures occur (70).

The family is expected to perform the following *tasks:*

1. Provide for physical safety and economic needs of its members and obtain enough goods, services, and resources to survive.
2. Create a sense of family loyalty and a mentally healthy environment for the family's well-being.
3. Help members to develop physically, emotionally, intellectually, and spiritually, as well as to develop a personal and family identity.
4. Foster a value system built on spiritual and philosophical beliefs and the cultural and social system that is part of the identity.
5. Teach members to communicate effectively their needs, ideas, feelings, as well as respect for each other.
6. Provide social togetherness simultaneously with division of labor, patterning of sexual roles, and performance of family roles with flexibility and cooperation.
7. Reproduce and socialize the child(ren), inculcating values and appropriate behavior, providing adult role models, and fostering a positive self-concept and self-esteem in the child(ren).
8. Provide relationships and experience within and without the family that foster security, support, encouragement, motivation, morale, and creativity.
9. Help the members to cope with crises and societal demands.
10. Maintain authority and decision making, with the parents representing society to the family as a whole and the family unit to society.
11. Promote integration into society and the ability to use social organizations for special needs when necessary.
12. Release family members into the larger society—school, church, organizations, work, and politics.
13. Maintain constructive and responsible ties with the neighborhood, school, and local and state government (1, 9, 23, 53, 85).

The family often has difficulty in meeting these tasks and needs assistance from external resources. The family's ability to meet its tasks depends on the maturity of the adult members, the support given by the social system—nursing and health care, educational, work, religious, social, welfare, governmental, and leisure institutions. The family that is most successful as a unit has a working philosophy and value system that is understood and lived, uses healthy adaptive patterns most of the time, can ask for help and use the community services available, and develops linkages with nonfamily units and organizations (23).

Roles of the Family

The family apportions **roles,** *prescribed behaviors in a situation,* in a way similar to society at large (48). In society, there are specialists who enforce laws, teach, practice medicine, and fight fires. In the family, there are also such performance roles: breadwinner, homemaker, handyman (or handywoman), the expert, political advisor, chauffeur, and gardener. There are also emotional roles: leader, nurturer, sustainer, protector, healer, arbitrator, scapegoat, jester, rebel, dependent, "sexpot," and "black sheep." Members may fill more than one role. The fewer people there are to fulfill these roles, as in the nuclear family, the greater the number of demands placed on one person. If a member leaves home, someone else takes up his/her role. Any member of the family can satisfactorily fulfill any role in either category unless he or she is uncomfortable in that role. The man who is sure of his masculinity will have no emotional problems diapering a baby or cooking a meal. The woman who is sure of her femininity will have no trouble gardening or taking the car for repair. Today, many men and women no longer are restricted to carrying out only traditional gender roles. They enjoy sharing roles, working together to get the tasks done without worrying about what is man's or woman's work.

The emotional response of a person to the role he/she fulfills should be considered. Someone may perform the job competently and yet dread doing it. The man may be a carpenter because his father taught him the trade, although he wants to be a music teacher. Changes in performance roles also necessitate emotional changes—for example, in the man who takes over household duties when his wife becomes incapacitated.

The child learns about emotional response to roles in the family while imitating adults. The child experiments with various roles in play and eventually finds one that is emotionally comfortable. The more pressure put on the child by the parents to respond in a particular way, the more likely that child is to learn only one role and be uncomfortable in others, as evidenced by the athletic champion who may be a social misfit. The child becomes less adaptive socially and even within the family as a result.

Exercising a capacity for a variety of roles, either in actuality or in fantasy, is healthy. The healthy family is the one in which there is opportunity to shift roles intermittently with ease (48). Through these roles family functions are fulfilled.

Functions of the Family as a Social System

The family is a system. It functions as a unit to fulfill its purposes, roles, tasks. It provides shelter, stability, security, and a setting for nurturance and growth. It is a safe place to experiment with the dynamics and role behaviors required in a system. It has an energy that provides a support system for individual members. As the social system changes, the family system must also adapt if it is to meet individual needs and prepare its members to participate in the social system.

The organization of a family system is hierarchal, although it may not be directly observable. The usual family hierarchies are built on kinship, power, status, and privilege relationships that may be related to individual characteristics of age, sex, education, personality, health, strength, or vigor. We can infer a hierarchy by observing each person's behavior and communication. For instance, who talks first? Last? Longest? Who talks to whom? When? Where? About what? If one family member consistently approaches the staff about the patient/client's health care, he/she probably holds an upper position in the family and has the task of being "expert." Your attempt to communicate with family members may meet with resistance if the communication inadvertently violates the family communication hierarchy (59).

Hierarchal relations in the family system determine the role behavior of family members. These hierarchal role relationships typically have great stability and ordinarily family members can be counted on to behave congruently with their roles. When there are differences in behavior from situation to situation, they are almost inevitably in response to the family's expectations for that particular situation or circumstance (59). Families develop a system of balanced relationships. When one member leaves the family or experiences a change, such as illness, other family members must adapt as well. Roles and relationships are based on reciprocal interaction, each member of the family contributing to the total unit in a unique and functional way. If a member should fail to meet the expectations of the roles established by his or her position in the hierarchy for the moment, the remaining members of the family generally react by using pressure (for example, persuasion, punishment, argument, being ignored) on the "deviant" person (59). Ackerman states that all family functions can be reduced to two basic ones: (1) ensuring the physical survival of the species and (2) transmitting the culture, thereby ensuring essential humanness. The union of mother and father, of parent and child, forms the bonds of identity that are the matrix for the development of this humanness (1).

Physical Functions of the family are met by the parents *providing food, clothing, and shelter, protection against danger, provision for bodily repairs after fatigue or illness, and by reproduction.* In "primitive" societies these physical needs are the dominant concern. In Western societies many families take them for granted (1, 48).

Affectional Functions are equally important. Although many traditional family functions, such as education, job training, and medical care, are being absorbed by other agencies, *meeting emotional needs and promoting adaptation and adjustment are still two of the family's major functions*. The family is the primary unit in which the child tests emotional reactions. Learning how to reach and maintain emotional equilibrium within the family enables him/her to repeat the pattern in later life situations. The child who feels loved is likely to contract fewer physical illnesses, learn more quickly, and generally have an easier time growing up and adapting to society (1, 48).

Satir believes a healthy family has five dominant attitudes:

1. No distinctions are made about worth of people; all members are perceived as equal.
2. All persons are seen as unique and developing.
3. When a disturbing situation arises, members understand that many factors were involved—people were not simply trying to be difficult.
4. Members accept that change is continuous.
5. Members freely share their thoughts and feelings with a minimum of blame and feel good about each other and themselves (67).

Other important attitudes are

1. The feeling of unity between man and woman and a separateness from their families of origins so that interfamily interference with the marriage is avoided.
2. An ability to invest in the marriage to a greater degree than in other relationships.
3. A feeling of balance or complementarity, for perfect equality is probably impossible.
4. A movement from a romantic "falling in love" to a warm, loving, companionable, accepting relationship.
5. An ability to maintain variety and frequent interactions with each other (67).

Social Functions of the modern family include *providing social togetherness, fostering self-esteem and a personal identity tied to family identity, providing opportunities for observing and learning social and sexual roles, accepting responsibility for behavior,* and *supporting individual creativity and initiative.* The family actually begins the indoctrination of the infant into society when it bestows a name and hence a social position or status in relation to the immediate and kinship-group families. Simultaneously, each family begins to transmit its own version of the cultural heritage and its own family culture to the child. Because the culture is too vast and comprehensive to be transmitted to the child in its entirety and all at once, the family selects what is to be transmitted. In addition, the family interprets and evaluates what is transmitted. Through this process, the child learns to share family's values (1, 48, 70).

Thus socialization is a primary task of the parents, for they teach the child about the body, peers, family, community, and age-appropriate roles as well as language, perceptions, social values, and ethics. The family also teaches about the different standards of responsibility society demands from various social groups. For example, the professional person, such as a physician, nurse, or lawyer, those in whom people confide and to whom they entrust their lives and fortunes, are held more accountable than the farmer or day laborer. There is also a difference in the type of contact that society has with a particular group: for example, the mail or milk deliverer does not enter the home, but the exterminator is free to enter a home and look into every corner.

The parent generation educates by literal instruction and by serving as models. Thus the child's **personality,** *a product of all the influences that have and are impinging on him/her,* is greatly influenced by the parents (45).

Family Adaptation

Adaptive responses in the family *represent the means by which it maintains an internal equilibrium so that it can fulfill purposes and tasks, deal with stress and crisis, and allow for growth of individual members.* Some capacity for functioning may be sacrificed in order to control conflict and aid work as a unit. But the best functioning family keeps anxiety and conflict within tolerable limits and maintains a balance between effects of the past and new experiences. Just as other social systems adapt, so must the family system (29).

Ideally, the family achieves equilibrium by talking over problems and finding solutions together. Humor, nonsense, shared work, and leisure all help relieve tension. The family members know that certain freedoms exist within their confines that are not available elsewhere.

Successful and happy families define their most important priority as the spouse and the family; the business or career of both or either one of the partners comes second. Children may come second before the business or career; hobbies and volunteer activities are further removed priorities. Each spouse needs to serve as a comforter, listener, companion, and counselor to the other, to be supportive and fully committed, and to avoid being negative. That does not mean one person is a doormat, for each are supportive to the other. The spouses may wish to set aside one night a week, or a month, to be only with each other, sharing uninterrupted time and activity. Each parent may wish to have a day date with each child monthly, spending time together at lunch, shopping, or in some mutually favorite activity (69).

Yet even the most stable family will briefly use the following behaviors to cope with stress, which, in turn, promotes more stress. However, these mechanisms are not overused in healthy families (41, 48).

Adaptive Mechanisms in Family Life

Family conflict can be avoided or minimized through scapegoating, coalitions, withdrawal of emotional ties, fighting, use of family myths, reaction formation, compromise, or designation of a family healer. Two or more of these mechanisms may be used within the same family. If these mechanisms are used exclusively, however, they become defensive and are unlikely to promote resolution of the conflict so that the same issue will arise repeatedly (41, 48).

Scapegoating or Blaming. This involves labeling one member as the cause of the family trouble and is expressed in the attitude, "If it weren't for you. . . ." Or one member may offer himself as a scapegoat to end an argument by saying, "It's all my fault." Such labeling controls the conflict and reduces anxiety, but it prevents communication that can get at the root of the problem. Growth toward resolution of the problem is prohibited.

Coalitions or Alliances. These may form when some family members side together against other members. Antagonisms and anger result. Eventually the losing party tries to get control.

Withdrawal of Emotional Ties. Loosening the family unit and reducing communication may be used to handle conflict, but then the family becomes rigid and mechanized. Family members are also likely to seek affection outside the family so that the home becomes a hotel with everyone superficially nice. In some families there is no show of emotion, for such emotion signifies loss of control or giving in to unacceptable impulses.

Repetitive Fighting. Verbal abuse, physical battles, loud complaints, curses, or accusations may be used to relieve tension and allow some harmony until the next round. The fight may have the same theme each time stress hits the family. The healthy family allows some "blowing up" as release from everyday frustrations, but it does not make a major case out of every minor incident or temporary disagreement.

Family Myths or Traditional Beliefs. These can be used to overcome anxieties and maintain control over others. Such statements are as follows: "Children are seen, not heard." "We can't survive if you leave home." "Talking about feelings will cause loss of love." In contrast the healthy family members encourage growth and creativity rather than rigid control.

Reaction Formation. This is seen in a family in which there is superficial harmony or togetherness. Traumatic ideas are repressed and transformed into the opposite behavior. Everybody smiles but nobody loves. No one admits to having any difficulties. Great tension is felt because true feelings are not expressed.

Resignation or Compromise. Temporary harmony may occur when someone gives up or suppresses the need for assertion, affection, or emotional expression in order to keep peace. The surface calm eventually explodes when unmet needs can no longer be successfully suppressed.

Designation of One Person as Family Healer or Umpire. This involves using a "wise one" (most often in the extended family), or a minister, storekeeper, bartender, or druggist to arrange a reconciliation between dissenting parties. Part of the dynamics sometimes underlying the helper role is that the referee gets great satisfaction from finding someone worse off than self. The healer feels a sense of heightened self-esteem or omnipotence. A variant of the healer role is that of family "protector." Here one person takes on all the stresses in order to save other members stress or conflict. One person ends up fighting the battles for everyone else in the family.

To remain adaptive, families maneuver to secure compliance of all members with the family rules through verbal and nonverbal communication to each other. Usually one member is designated as the one who must maintain a specific pattern of dependent behavior, sometimes negative or unhealthy, in order to keep all other family members comfortable. If the designated member tries to change behavior and become more independent, he/she receives no support. The feedback received is that he/she is disrupting the status quo and the other family members are uncomfortable. Thus sick behavior will be maintained at the expense of the development of the designated person and of the family.

Signs of strained or destructive family relationships include:

1. Lack of understanding and communication between spouses.
2. Each family member alternately acting as if the other did not exist or harassing through arguments.
3. Lack of family decision making.
4. Parents' possessiveness of the children or the mate.
5. Children's derogatory remarks to parents or vice versa.
6. Extreme closeness between husband and his mother or family or the wife and her mother or family.
7. Parent being domineering about performance of household tasks.
8. Few outside friends for parents or children.
9. Scapegoating or blaming each other for difficulties.
10. High level of anxiety or insecurity present in the home.
11. Lack of creativity.
12. Pattern of immature or regressive behavior in parents or children. (29, 80, 85).

You may find yourself in the role of family healer. Help the family to develop harmonious ways of coping and avoid the protector or omnipotent role. The text by Kramer gives in-depth information pertinent to assessment of and intervention with families (41).

Stages of Family Development

Like an individual, the family has a developmental history marked by predictable crises. The developmental crises are normal, but they are also disturbing or frightening because each life stage is a new experience. The natural history of the family is on a continuum: from marriage or cohabitation; choosing whether to have children; rearing biological or adoptive offspring, if any; and releasing children into society to establish homes of their own. In later life the aging parents or grandparents are a couple once again, barring divorce or death. The nurturing of spouse or children goes on simultaneously with a multitude of other activities: work at a job or profession, managing a household, participation in church and community groups, pursuit of leisure and hobbies, maintaining friendships and family ties. Or the person may decide to remain single but live with a person of the same or opposite sex; then the purposes, tasks, and roles of family life must also be worked out.

Initial or Establishment Stage

Courtship and engagement precede establishment of the family unit. Developmental tasks to be accomplished during this courtship period include: contending with partner-selection pressures from parents; giving over autonomy while retaining some independence; preparing for marriage, including a mutually satisfying sex life, and becoming free of parental domination. In the **establishment stage,** *the couple establish a home of* their own; their main psychological tie is no longer with family of orientation (parental family). They commit themselves to living together, usually through marriage. [Readiness for marriage in U. S. society is discussed in relation to young adulthood in Chapter 12.] They must work out patterns of communication, daily living, sexual relations, a budget, and a philosophy of life. Relationships with family and friends are also different after marriage and must be worked out (23, 49, 80).

Today families may choose to have no children, one child and adopt, or one, two, or three children instead of a larger family. Some women feel that motherhood is not necessary for fulfillment. Certainly the man's chief fulfillment is not necessarily from fatherhood. Some people are wise enough to know that children do not automatically bring happiness to a marriage. Children bring happiness to parents who want them and who are selfless enough to become involved in the adventure of rearing them. Children bring trauma to a troubled marriage.

Limitation of family size and birth spacing yield substantial family health benefits. Certain associations in death, disease, and disability are apparent. Maternal deaths increase when maternal age is below 20 or above 40 years and after the third pregnancy for women of all age groups except those over 40. Increased maternal disease, obstetrical complications, maternal deaths, and postnatal mortality occur with six or more pregnancies. Unwanted pregnancy increases maternal disease and death, especially if the pregnancy is terminated by illegal abortion that results in infection or hemorrhage. Other effects of unwanted pregnancy include excessive nausea and vomiting, spontaneous abortion, toxemias, complications of labor and delivery, emotional illness prenatally or postnatally, marital friction, and divorce. Infant mortality rate increases for birth order above three in the lower social class and rises among women under 17 years of age. The safest years for a normal delivery are between ages 20 and 29. Infants of youngest mothers of highest parity are at greatest risk for disease and death regardless of social class. Mothers are less likely to have premature or low-birth-weight, and therefore healthier infants when spacing is greater than 2 years but less than 6 years (70).

The establishment phase ends when the woman becomes pregnant or when the couple work out their living patterns and philosophy of life (which may include a decision not to have children).

The Expectant Stage

During the **expectant stage** or *pregnancy*, which is a development crisis, many domestic and social adjustments must be made. The couple (or the single mother and her significant others) are learning new roles and gaining new status in the community. Attitudes toward pregnancy and the physical and emotional status of the mother and father (as well as of significant others) will affect parenting abilities. Now the couple thinks in terms of family instead of a pair. They explore beliefs about childrearing and plan for the expanded family in terms of space, budget, and necessary supplies (23).

The woman may initially dislike being pregnant because it interferes with her personal plans or she may feel proud and fulfilled. Sexual desire may either increase or decrease. She may be more or less interested in her surroundings. Usually she is more preoccupied with herself, her new feelings, and changing body image, and she experiences fantasies and fears regarding the baby and the childbirth experiences.

The man experiences a variety of feelings on learning of the pregnancy, feelings that change during the pregnancy. The reality of the pregnancy increases with time. One study showed that 70 percent of the men experienced ambivalent feelings initially, but fatherly feelings developed. The men also felt guilty about the wife's pregnancy and her physical symptoms, anxious and depressed about their own adequacy, proud of their virility, and fearful of approaching the wife sexually. Concerns identified by fathers were as follows: caring for the infant, adequacy as a father, financial security, and concern related to the baby's effect on the marital dyad (36, 43, 45, 47).

Early and thorough prenatal care for the woman is essential. Both the woman and the man may experience similar physical and emotional symptoms, such as nausea, indigestion, backache, distention, irritability, and depression. Symptoms may result from hormonal changes or feelings about the pregnancy in the woman. In the man they are part of the **couvade syndrome**, *which may be a reaction based on identification with or sympathy for the woman, ambivalence or hostility toward the pregnancy, or envy of the woman's childbearing ability*. The physical symptoms, complex feelings, and changes in body image that accompany pregnancy are described by several authors (18, 20, 38 55, 64, 65, 70).

Major decisions for the couple are whether to attend childbirth preparation classes and whether the man should be present in the labor and delivery rooms. The woman may feel eager to have the man with her or she may fear that he will think of her as sexually unattractive or be repulsed. The man may be curious about what is happening and want to attend his child's birth, or he may feel guilty about not wanting to when he feels others expect him to be there. He may be embarrassed about his wife's behavior and appearance during labor and delivery, or he may fear that he cannot cope with the childbirth event if present. Sexual fantasies triggered by labor and delivery may threaten the man who has tenuous emotional equilibrium. If the man has considerable unconscious conflicts or a weak self-image as a man, he may wish not to be involved in childbirth preparation, labor, or delivery. Some men and women cannot participate in childbirth preparation classes and should not be made to feel guilty about their decision. Participation may not enhance the couple's self-esteem and may create additional emotional crisis. Participation in Lamaze classes and childbirth does not change the woman's perception of her partner as ideal man, husband, or father, but it does improve her self-image as ideal woman, wife, and mother (36). In addition, the woman is more likely to be in good physical condition for labor if she has had preparation.

Although the woman needs extra "mothering" from the partner (or others) during pregnancy, the man also needs extra attention and nurturing or he may be unable to continue to support the mother-to-be emotionally (36). You can listen to the woman's and man's concerns and help them understand that what they are experiencing is normal. Various teaching aids explaining pregnancy and what to expect during the birth experience are also useful. Your care should be family centered, directed toward both parents-to-be. You can help the woman to gain maternal feelings and the man to see the importance of his role as provider as well as nurturer.

The man must be prepared for fathering just as the woman is for mothering. Fathers also go through the five operations (mimicry, role play, fantasy, introjection-projection-rejection, and grief work) identified by Rubin as necessary to attain the maternal role (64).

For additional information about prenatal influences on the mother and baby, see chapters 6 and 7. Information about parenting and developmental tasks for the expectancy phase is also presented in Chapter 12. Several authors give further information on the fathers' reactions and responsibilities (27, 33, 43, 45, 47, 70).

Parenthood Stage

With the **parenthood stage** or *birth of a child*, the couple assume a status that they will never lose as long as each has memory and life—that of parent. The *stages of parenthood* are:

1. Anticipatory stage. The woman is pregnant and the couple are learning the new roles and perceptions associated with pregnancy discussed earlier.
2. Honeymoon stage. The time following birth when the parents feel excited about the new relationship but also uncertain about the meaning of parental love. A parent–child attachment is being formed. During this time difficult adjustments need to be made. Because the parents lose sleep, husband–wife intimacy diminishes and there is less freedom for the couple to follow their own interests.
3. Plateau stage. The years during the child's development when the parents are active in the role of mother and father. During this time the parents deal with problems in the family, community, church, school and immediate social sphere. They are concerned with family planning, socialization and education of the child, and participating in community organizations.
4. Disengagement stage. The termination of the parent–child family unit that occurs when the last child marries or leaves home permanently and the parents let go of their major childrearing responsibilities to allow the offspring to be autonomous (62, 63).

Americans value creativity and individuality; thus no set patterns of parenthood exist. Parents rely on their own uniqueness, wisdom, and skills, how their parents raised them, or on books. Youth are poorly prepared to make the transition to parenthood. Yet how parents treat a child is the single most important influence on the child's physical, emotional, and cognitive development and health.

The couple may accept the idea of parenthood but reject a particular child because of the child's sex, appearance, time of the birth in their life cycle, or the child's threatening helplessness. Or the couple may reject the idea of parenthood but genuinely love the baby who was unplanned. Often parents have difficulty because pregnancy, childbirth, and parenting are romanticized in our society, and the romantic ideal differs considerably from the reality of 24-hour responsibility and submersion of their personal desires for many years to come.

How the parents care for and discipline the child is influenced considerably by the parents' own maturity; how they were cared for as children (as shown by studies on child abuse); their feelings about self; culture, social class, and religion (see Chapters 1 and 3); their relationship with each other; their perceptions of and experiences with children and other adults; their values and philosophy of life; and life stresses that arise. Moreover, the historical eras in which the parents were reared and are now living in and the prominent social values of each era subtly influence parental behavior.

Each critical period in the child's development reactivates a critical period in the parent. Demands made on the parent vary with the age of the child. The infant needs almost total and constant nurturance. Some parents thrive during this period and depend on each other for support. Other parents feel overwhelmed by the infant's dependency because their own dependent needs are stimulated but unmet. The baby's cry and behavior evoke feelings of helplessness, dependency, and anger associated with their unacceptable dependency needs and feelings, and then guilt and fatigue. The toddler struggles with individuality and autonomy, exploring and vacillating between dependency and independency. At this stage the child is intense and often unreasonable in demands and refusal to obey commands. The parents may enjoy this explorative, independent behavior of the child, even though the toddler leaves the parent feeling tired and frustrated. Or the primitive behavior of the child may stimulate primitive impulses in the parent, who may feel threatened by the will of the toddler. The parent who has difficulty controlling angry impulses may find the toddler's temper outbursts totally unacceptable. Parents who have difficulty caring for the dependent infant may do very well with the independent preschooler or adolescent or the reverse may be true. The parent may be able to resolve personal conflicts and move to a more advanced level of integration as he/she works with the developing child or the parent may be unable to cope with the aroused feelings (6).

Some parents feel that they must possess a child and will try to fit that child into a mold—their image. Other parents see their task of parenthood as stewards—to be a guide, helping friend, standard setter for the child. They invest themselves in the creative potentialities of their young—nurturing, educating, and protecting the child. They love but do not smother; guide but do not control; discipline but do not punish; offer freedom but do not abandon. They see the child as a lamp to be lit rather than a vessel to be filled (7, 49).

Parents who possess their children feel that they have the right to dictate the terms of their child's life. Then the child has only half a life; parental need to control is greater than real love for child. Too much pressure is placed on the growing child, disturbing his/her emotional development (7, 49).

Just as detrimental are the parents who abandon the child to rear itself, parents who spend too little time with and give too little affection to the child. Such children spend considerable time with television and peers; they learn that the adult world does not want them. In one study children who spent most of their time with peers were more influenced by the lack of the parents' presence, attention, and concern than by the attractiveness of the peer group. The peer-oriented child held negative views of self and peer group and expressed dim views of the future. The peer-oriented children rated parents lower in both expression of affection and support and in exercise of discipline control than did children who spent more time with adults. Peer-oriented children reported engaging in more antisocial behavior, such as doing something illegal, playing hooky from school, or lying (7, 49).

Parents should rethink their priorities when they have children. Parents need to invest time in such a way that it brings quality to their relationship with the child. Children need the encouragement of doing things and talking through things with adults (7, 49).

Developmental tasks for *the couple*, which are reworked with the birth of each child, are to:

1) Provide for the physical and emotional needs of the child, conveying love and security freely regardless of the child's appearance or temperament.
2) Reconcile conflicting roles—wife–mother, husband–father, worker–homemaker or family man, and parent–citizen.
3) Accept and adjust to the demands and stresses of parenthood, learning or relearning basics of child care, adjusting personal routines and needs to meet the child's needs, and trying to meet the spouse's needs as well.
4) Provide opportunities for the child to master competencies expected for each developmental stage, to allow the child to make mistakes and learn from them, to restrict the child reasonably and consistently for safety, and to attain the emotional developmental tasks described by Erikson (25).
5) Share responsibilities of parenthood and together make necessary adjustments in space, finances, housing, lifestyle, and daily routines that are healthy for the family (meals, sleep).
6) Maintain a satisfying relationship with spouse—emotionally, sexually, intellectually, spiritually, and recreationally—while maintaining a personal sense of autonomy and identity.
7) Feel satisfaction from being competent parents and the parenting experience but maintain contacts with relatives and the community.
8) Provide socialization experiences to help the child make the emotional shift from family to peers and society so that the child can become a functioning citizen.
9) Refine the communication system and relationships with spouse, children, and others and permit offspring to be autonomous after leaving home (23, 53).

Other authors also describe the reactions, roles, and responsibilities involved in parenting (1, 6, 7, 9, 32, 41, 43, 45, 47, 49, 50, 61, 67, 69, 70, 85).

As the children mature and leave home, the parents must rework their self-concepts as parents and people in order to take on new roles, responsibilities, and leisure activities so that the last stage of parenthood, disengagement, can be accomplished. You can assist the couple in meeting developmental tasks.

Disengagement Stage of Parenthood

Sometimes the last or **disengagement stage** *when children leave and the partners must rework their separateness*, does not last too long. The young adult who is unemployed, a college dropout, or divorced may return home to live. The aged parents or other relatives may be unable to continue to live independently and then are included in the household of middle-aged offspring. Consequently, the tasks, functions, roles, and hierarchical relationships of the family must be reworked. Space and other resources must be reallocated. Time schedules for daily activities may be reworked. Privacy in communication, use of possessions, and emotional space must be ensured. Old parent–child conflicts, ideas about who is boss and how rules are set and discipline accomplished may resurface and should be discussed and worked through. These families can benefit from counseling; your guidance may be crucial. The middle-age family is more fully discussed in Chapter 13.

Fox (28) offers the following suggestions to adult children and their parents to make living together more harmonious.

1. Remember what it was like when a new baby came home. No matter how beloved the child, disruptions are bound to occur. Realize that another relative's homecoming will be the same.
2. Everyone involved should remember whose house it is.
3. Realize that no matter how many years sons or daughters have been away, family procedures do not change. Mom may still be critical. Dad may be the constant advice-giver. Expect it.
4. Talk about resentments. Discuss problems if you think it will help.
5. Parents may say offspring are grown up. But that does not mean they believe it. Still, they cannot exert the same authority with a 30- or 40-year-old as with a youngster.
6. Offspring and elderly parents need to be flexible. It's unfair to expect the middle-agers who are the "hosts" to change their household and life routines too much.
7. Even if parents refuse money, adult offspring should insist on paying something, no matter how minimal. Otherwise the offspring are reinforcing the idea that parents are taking care of them. Elderly parents can also contribute financially most of the time.
8. When grandchildren are involved, set rules about who is in charge. To decrease dependency, babysitters should be hired when possible. Then family members do not feel obligated or constrained.
9. Determine length of the adult offspring's stay. It need not be a precise date, but future plans about leaving the home should be explicitly stated.
10. Both adult offspring and older relatives should share responsibilities if possible. But do not upstage mom or dad; for example, if mom loves cooking, do not make her feel useless by taking over in the kitchen.
11. Space permitting, privacy is important. The relative who has lived on his or her own is probably used to time and space alone.
12. Middle-agers should resist meddling in the affairs of either offspring or parents. They can advise. But grown offspring need to think for themselves and older relatives expect to make their own decisions.
13. Realize that the living situation may be temporary. Living together may not be ideal for anyone. But some parents and offspring or middle-agers and their parents become closer during such periods (28).

Family Interaction

Family interaction *is a unique form of social interaction based on a set of intimate and continuing relationships. It is the sum total of all the family roles being played within a family at a given time* (23). Families function and carry out their tasks and lifestyles through this process.

Family therapists, psychiatrists, and nurses are giving increased attention to the emotional balance in family **dyads** or *paired role positions*, such as husband and wife or mother and child. They have noted that a shift in the balance of one member of the pair (or of one pair) alters the balance of the other member (or pair). The birth of a child is the classic example (49). Dyads and emotional balance also shift in single-parent and step-parent families (41, 61, 66, 85).

Interaction of the husband and wife, or of the adult members living under one roof, is basic to the mental, and sometimes physical, health of the adults as well as to the eventual health of the children. Two factors strongly influence this interaction: (1) the sense of self-esteem or self-love of each family member and (2) the different socialization processes for boys and girls (7).

4 The Family—Basic Unit for the Developing Person

Importance of Self-Esteem

The most important life task for each person—to feel a sense of self-esteem, to love and have a positive self-image—evolves through interaction with the parents from the time of birth onward and, in turn, affects how the person interacts in later life with others, including spouse and offspring.

The adult in the family who lacks self-acceptance and self-respect is not likely to be a loving spouse or parent. Behavior will betray feelings about self and others because he/she will perceive no automatic acceptance and little love from others in the family. Because perception of an event is the person's reality, such a person in turn reacts in ways designed to defend self from the rejection that he/she *thinks* will be received: he/she may criticize, get angry, brag, demand perfection from others, or withdraw. In this way, he/she builds up self, the emotional reasoning being: "I may not be much, but others are worse." Such behavior is corrosive to any relationship but particularly one as intimate as the family's. Because of overt behavior, those intimate with him/her are not likely to appreciate or respond to the basic needs for love, acceptance, and respect. Indeed, the common responses to such behavior are counterattack or withdrawal, which, in turn, perpetuate the other's negative behavior. To remain open and giving in such situations is difficult for the mate but may be the only way to elevate the other's self-esteem. Perhaps only then can he/she reciprocate loving behavior. You can help family members realize the importance of respecting and loving one another and help them work through problems stemming from the low self-esteem of a family member (7).

Influence of Childhood Socialization

The second crucial influence on interaction between adults in the family is the difference in socialization processes for boys and girls. These differences are so embedded in the U. S. social matrix that until recently they had gone nearly unnoticed. There is a different social source for self-love in boys and girls. The girl is loved simply because she exists and can attract, as shown by the admiration pretty little girls receive. The girl is also taught to be subtle, for such behavior is part of her attraction. The boy is loved for what he can do and become; he must prove himself. Boys, especially from school age on, are given less recognition than girls for good looks and much recognition for what they can do. A boy learns to be direct, to brush aside distractions (sometimes including a woman's voice, for most disciplining will come from the mother and female schoolteachers and can be perceived as nagging after a while), and to get to the essence of things (7).

These concepts of what is appropriate boy and girl behavior are taught early and continue to affect heterosexual interactions throughout life. In traditional courtship, for example, the boy is expected to be in charge, to be dominant, to prove himself; the girl is expected to attract, to be passive. In marriage, however, these expectations cause problems, for the man is proving himself largely through his work, and this aspect of his earlier courtship behavior is now less visible to his wife. If the woman does not understand the dynamics of his behavior, she is likely to feel rejected and unloved, thinking she can no longer attract him. If the wife is also working, the husband may think of her as a competitor and work harder to keep his self-esteem. His physical self, including his involvement in lovemaking, is very much intertwined with his social, professional, and financial self, and failure in one is likely to cause feelings of failure in the total self, affecting his sense of masculinity, sexuality, and personhood (7).

All these facts are compounded by the shift in balance between the man and woman found in modern marriage, especially with the advent of the women's liberation movement. The husband often labors under the illusion that he enjoys the rights and responsibilities inherent in a patriarchal family system. Yet he must recognize the qualifications and drive for independence, the basic humanness, of his wife. You can help the couple to recognize the effect of their early socialization on their behavior and expectations and to work through misunderstandings. Help parents to overcome sexual stereotypes so that they do not inflict them on their children. Carmichael's book *Nonsexist Childrearing*, may be helpful (17).

Variables Affecting Interaction Between the Child and Adult

Long before the child learns to speak, sensory, emotional, and intellectual exchanges are made between the child and other family members. Through such exchanges, and later with words, the child receives and tests instructions on how to consider the rights of others and how to respond to authority. The child also learns how to use language as a symbol, how to carry out certain routines necessary for health, how to compete, and what goals to seek. The games and toys purchased for and played with the child, the books selected and read, and the television programs allowed can provide key learning techniques.

The child's spontaneity can evoke in the adult fresh ways of looking at life long buried under habit and routine. The child says "It's too loud, but my earlids won't stay down" or "I want one of those little red olives with the green around" or "Give me that eraser with the handle." The child can also recreate for the adult the difficulty of the learning process: "Is it today, tomorrow, or yesterday? You said when I woke up it would be tomorrow, but now you call it 'today.'"

Family interaction for the child and adult is also affected by the ordinal position and sex of the children, as well as by the presence of an only child or of multiple births, such as twins, of an adoptive child, or stepchild.

Parents tend to identify with their children and to treat them according to how they were treated as children. A parent can identify best with the child who matches his/her own sibling position. A man from a family of boys may not know how to interact with a daughter and may not empathize with her. In the process of identifying with the parent, the child picks up many of the parent's characteristics, especially if the child is the oldest or lone child. For example, the oldest boy may be dependent instead of independent if his father was the youngest sibling and retained his dependent behavior into adulthood. Using family constellation theory, Toman describes features of each child in a family, based on sex and ordinal position, how the child feels about and interacts with people, and which ordinal position spouse he/she will most happily marry (78).

Ordinal Position of the Child. Birth order is important to development (45, 48, 78). Siblings have an important influence on each other. The first-born, who is an only child until the second one comes along, may enjoy some advantages in achievement of intellectual superiority and perspective about life, including a greater sense of responsibility. He/she has more contact with adults and is the sole recipient of attention for a time. He/she becomes dominant over younger siblings. Secondborn boys with an older sister are more feminine than those with an older brother. The younger children benefit from the parents' experience with childraising and from having older siblings to imitate. Lastborns are also more sociable, possibly to ensure acceptance by older siblings or to gain parental attention. The lastborn may be more dependent. The middle child is likely to become caught between the jealousy of the older child and the envy of the younger, who may form a coalition against him/her. But he/she learns double or triple roles and is prepared for more kinds of relationships in adulthood. If two siblings are more than 6 years apart, they tend to grow up like only children (78).

The Only Child. This child may feel more loneliness but develops more rapidly and may seem older and more serious than peers who have siblings. He/she lacks the opportunities siblings could provide. Thus he/she usually does not share feelings and experiences with someone close, or cope with jealousy and envy from rivals in the home, or learn intimately about ways of the opposite- or same-sexed peers. The only child learns less about compromising with peers, sharing adult attention, and erecting strong defenses against the feelings displaced on him/her by adults and peers. He/she may prefer adults; the usual ways of relating and behavioral tactics do not work with peers.

Children are the logical targets for fulfilling many of the parents' frustrated ambitions and needs. In a large family these yearnings and aspirations can be parceled out among a number of children, but when there is only one child, this child can sense the parents' manipulation and expectations. Thus the only child tends to be a peacemaker if he/she and the parents are the only household members. He/she is inadvertently brought into the parents' conflicts and is forced to help maintain harmony and preserve equilibrium in the household (48, 78).

In a family with only one child, there are few people to fulfill the many roles of a family; thus more is demanded of each member. The only child may be forced prematurely to assume roles for which he/she is ill equipped. The child may become deft at performing adult tasks and roles, but self-confidence in the capacity to do so may be uncertain (48, 78).

The only child sometimes has special problems on becoming a parent, seeing in the child a longed-for brother or sister. The danger in the situation is that the child is also a rival for the spouse's attention. On reaching adolescence, the offspring may then pose a threat to the parent's own adult roles, and the parent may unconsciously become overly competitive (48, 78). Yet the only child is now regarded as an answer for the parents who want the parenting experience but who also want time to fulfill their own careers.

Certainly the only child can develop into a wholesome, well-adjusted person. The qualities of being more serious, assertive, responsible, independent, curious, and able to entertain self, and find satisfaction in personal pursuits frequently develop because of parental and home demands. These demands can enhance abilities to be a mature, capable adult. The greater opportunities available for adult contact, beginning at home, develop the only child's creativity, language skills, planning abilities, and intellectual potential. He/she has a high need to achieve and prefers the novel or complex. Firstborn and only children, such as Cary Grant, Brooke Shields, Martha Collins, Ted Koppel, Joe Montana, John Updike, Isaac Newton, Franklin Roosevelt, Emile Zola, Herbert Spencer, Rainer Maria Rilke, and some of the American astronauts, rank high on the roster of outstanding leaders, artists, and scientists.

As you counsel parents who plan for or have only

one child, emphasize the need for peer activity and the danger of too much early responsibility and pressure.

The Family with a Large Number of Children. The family with more than 3 or 4 children is less frequently seen now than in the past. The last-born child may be less wanted than the first or middleborn, although parents feel more skilled and self-confident in rearing the younger children. Large families have advantages. Of necessity, the children learn thrift and conservation of resources and material goods. Members know the hot water supply is not unlimited, that food is not to be wasted, and that toys and clothing can be recycled. Children learn to share time, space, and possessions. The children learn to do for themselves and each other; they learn responsibility. In a loving home, they have not only their parents', but also siblings', love, a listening ear, respect, support, compassion, and help. If the parent does not have time to read to the 3 year old, the older sibling does. He/she gains more experience in reading, gains increased self-esteem from being helpful, and learns responsibility and caring. Each child learns cooperation, compromise, and tolerance, and how to handle peer pressure. The effort, work, expense, self-denial of having a large family can be offset by the rewards of watching children grow and develop, and by a sense of contribution to the generations to come (45, 49, 74).

▶ Your teaching and support can influence how well parents cope with responsibility of a large family.

Multiple Births. Twins, or other multiple births, have considerable impact on family interaction. If ovulation has been inhibited with contraceptive pills, multiple births are more likely once this method stops being used (70). The needs and tasks of these parents will differ from the parents who have a single birth.

▶ Your suggestions and support can influence how well the parents cope with their responsibility.

Because multiple births are often premature, the first 4 or 5 months are very demanding on the parents in terms of the amount of energy and time spent in child care; this means that the parents have less energy and time for each other or other children. The mother should have help for several months if possible—from the husband, a relative, friend, or neighbor. Financial worries and concern about space and material needs may also intrude on normal husband–wife relationships or on relationships with other children.

Although books discourage the mother of twins from breast-feeding or using alternate breast-and-bottle-feeding, the mother may be able to breast-feed both twins successfully, by alternating breast with bottle feedings. The babies will not necessarily be poor breast-feeders with this arrangement.

▶ You can suggest shortcuts in, or realities about, care that will not be detrimental to twin babies and that will give the parents more time to enjoy them. A diaper service, for example, is well worth the investment, for 1000 diapers may be used in a month's time. The parents should not be made to feel guilty if they are not as conscientious with two babies as they would be with one. Each can be given a total bath every other day instead of daily. Heating bottles before feeding is not necessary. The parents should try to avoid getting so wrapped up in meeting the babies' physical needs that resentment, anger, or excessive fatigue creep in. Multiple offspring should be fun as well as work.

▶ Encourage the parents of twins (or multiple offspring) to perceive the babies as individuals and to consider the long-term consequences of giving them similar-sounding names, dressing them alike, having doubles of everything, and expecting them to behave alike. Tell parents about the U.S. national organization, Mothers of Twins, whose local branch can be a place to share feelings and ideas and gain practical suggestions. In the United Kingdom, there is a Twins Clubs Association, a self-help organization with local chapters that provide educational and advocacy services.

Multiple-birth children are likely to be closer than ordinary siblings. These children have lived with each other from before birth on, so experiences are different from that of having various aged siblings. Parents often force one to be older and one to be younger in behavior; it is difficult for the one to play role of "older" because neither has the advantage of extra years of experience over the other, who is developmentally on the same level. With paternal twins, authority preference of parents tends to determine what age-ranks the girl and the boy will be ascribed. In contrast, identical twins meet the world as a pair; it is difficult to imagine life without each other. It takes longer to separate in adolescence and childhood (they may not, emotionally or physically). Each tends to seek multiple birth persons as friends or mates.

They soon learn about the extra attention resulting from their birth status and may take advantage of the situation. Interaction between them is often complementary; for example, one twin may be dominant and the other submissive. Each learns from reinforcement of his/her experiences about the advantages of the particular role chosen. They learn to resist control by others and to manipulate others by acting alike and "in collusion." They do not have to manage conflicts with parents or others alone.

Siblings of a multiple birth tend to be more detached from other siblings, even parents, than each other. Twins may each receive less parental affection and communication because parents have less time to devote to each child. Thus twins are often slower to talk and many have a slower intellectual growth unless parents work to prevent it (49, 50, 70).

Gender of the Child. Gender also influences development within the family (45). In most cultures a higher value is placed on male than on female children. Actually, in some cultures only a boy's birth is welcomed or celebrated and the family's status is partially measured by the number of sons. Or a family with several girls and no boys may perceive another baby girl as a disappointment. The girl may discover this attitude in later years from overhearing adult conversations and she may try to compensate for her sex and gain parental affection and esteem by engaging in tomboy behavior and later assuming masculine roles.

If a boy arrives in a family that hoped for a girl, he may receive pressure to be feminine. He may even be dressed and socialized in a feminine manner. If the boy arrives after a family has two or three girls, he will receive much attention but also the jealousy of his sisters. He will grow up with three or four "mothering" figures (some may be unkind) and in a family more attuned to feminine than to masculine behavior. Developing a masculine identity may be more difficult for him, especially if there is no male nearby with whom to relate. In spite of being pampered, he will be expected by his family to be manly. The boy may feel envious of his sisters' position and their freedom from such great expectations.

The girl who arrives in a family with a number of boys may also receive considerable attention, but she may have to become tomboyish in order to compete with her brothers and receive their esteem. Feminine identity may be difficult for her.

You can help parents understand how their attitude toward their own sexuality and their evaluation of boys and girls influence their relationship with their children. Emphasize the importance of encouraging the child's unique identity to develop.

The Adopted Child. The adopted child may suffer some problems of the only child. In addition, the adopted child may have to work through feelings about rejection and abandonment by the biological parents versus being wanted and loved by the adoptive parents. The child should be told that he/she is adopted as early as the idea can be comprehended. Usually by the preschool years he/she can incorporate the idea of being a wanted child.

Adopted children bring their own genes, birth experiences, biological family ties, and often an extensive life history, to their adoptive family. The adoptive family is not the same as a biological family. Both adoptive parents and adopted children tend to feel they have less control over their situation than other families. Adoptive parents and adopted children are both likely to have experienced a sense of loss. It is not unusual for the adoptive child to seek his/her own biological parents in late adolescence or young adulthood, even when the adoptive parents are truly considered the parents. This search may be a threat to adoptive parents, or they may feel secure enough to even assist the offspring in the search.

The adoptive parents' personal qualifications, their marital harmony, their love of the child, their acceptance of the child as is, and the child's having friends are major determinants of the child's adjustment and development. Factors not predictive of adjustment are socioeconomic status, occupational status, presence or absence of biological siblings, age of parents, health of adopters, religion, or prior experience with children (19, 70).

Definition of "suitable" adoptive parents has been liberalized. Adoption agency requirements of age, marital status, race, and mother's employment status are more flexible. The adoptive parent may be a man. Additionally, today's couples consider adoption even if they have their own children. Some believe they have a responsibility and enough love to provide a home for an existing child rather than add to the total population. Others are single persons who want to offer love and security to a child.

Social and legal changes have affected the kinds of children in need of adoption. Earlier adoption agencies served mainly Caucasian unmarried mothers who saw adoption as the only alternative for their babies. Today fewer infants are available because there is greater social acceptance of out-of-wedlock births; more unmarried mothers keep their babies. Contraceptives and abortions have also reduced the number of unwanted infants. A different category of adoptable children has grown in size, however. These children with "special needs" have at least one of the following characteristics: over age 5; Black, biracial; or physically, emotionally, or cognitively handicapped. Increasingly, state legislatures terminate parental rights in the case of children in long-term foster care who have remained unvisited and ignored by their biological parents and when the likelihood of the child's returning to his/her own home is minimal. New legislation has allowed abused children to become eligible for adoption (11–13, 22, 24, 30, 82).

Because of fewer available children in the United States, families are more likely to consider adopting a foreign child. Foreign adoption raises cultural, social, interracial, and emotional issues for the adoptive parents, their families and friends, and the specific community. Warren (82) discusses issues and concerns, qualifications, and the process.

✔ Additional information is available from International Concerns Committee for Children, 911 Cypress Drive, Boulder, Colorado, 80303 (82).

In spite of more liberal definitions of adoptability, the number of people applying to adopt a child, homes approved, placements made, and adoptions completed declined compared to the number of available children. Thus an increasing number of older children need permanent placement.

✔ You may have an opportunity to educate adults about the opportunity for adopting an older child with special needs or to work with adoptive parents, who also have needs.

Adoption of a child with special needs involves four phases: (1) commitment of adults and child, (2) honeymoon or placement period, (3) storm period, and (4) adaptation and adjustment. The phases do not abruptly begin and end; each phase builds on the preceding phase and sometimes reversals occur. The phases, along with thoughts, emotions, and activities accompanying each phase, are summarized in Table 4–2. The adoptive process can terminate at any point. If termination is necessary, both sides—the family and child—need help to understand what happened and to understand that no *one person* is responsible. Future

TABLE 4–2. The Adoptive Process

PHASES	THOUGHTS AND EMOTIONS	ACTIVITIES
• Commitment of Adult(s) and Child(ren):	*Adult(s)* make general decision to adopt (stage 1), leading to decision to adopt specific child(ren) (stage 2).	*Adult(s)* prepare for adoption through dialogue with helpful people/agencies, and sometimes attend sessions on adoption given by adoption agency.
"Courting Stage"	*Child(ren)* express desire for adoption (stage 1), leading to decision on specific family (stage 2).	*Child(ren)* are counseled for potential adjustment by adoption agency staff. Visits are arranged and made between potential family—child(ren). All members involved (including existing children in family) get to know each other.
• Placement: "Honeymoon Period"	*Parent(s)* are on an "emotional high"; excitement.	Household routines are altered to accommodate child(ren). Limit-setting is minimal. Parent(s) meet child(ren)'s whims.
(Child[ren] come to live with parent[s].)	*Chid(ren)* are excited but somewhat scared. "Can I trust these people?" "Will they send me away when I don't act my best?"	*Child(ren)* put on best behavior. Sometimes parent(s)' show of affection for child(ren) is not accepted because of child(ren)s' past negative parenting.
• "Storm Period"	*Parent(s)* are tired of permanent house guest(s), feel anger, disappointment, guilt, and displace these feelings on each other and the child. They may wish the child would leave.	*Parent(s)* treat child(ren) or other family members with decreasing tolerance for behavior not in family norm.
	Child(ren) can no longer keep up good behavior but want to be loved and accepted.	*Child(ren)* may have tantrums, run away, try to reject parents before they reject him/her.
	Parent(s) may feel sense of failure. They may have expected too much of themselves and child(ren), and now may strike out at each other and other family members. Spouses may be jealous of time and energy mate gives to child(ren).	If the outcome is positive, the *parent(s)* will use problem solving, limit setting with flexibility, sense of humor, ongoing empathy and caring, supportive others, and community resources.
	Child(ren) may think, "They don't want me. What's going to happen to me?" and may live with anticipatory grief, fears of rejection, and insecurity based on past hurts. Parent(s) and child(ren) test each other.	
• Adaptation and adjustment phase (Equilibrium occurs.)	All feel they can live and work together; mutual trust is growing; family feels fused as a unit and able to handle frustrations and crises.	Parent(s) are consistent with child(ren). *Parent(s)* and *child(ren)* can attend to outside interests without threatening family status.
	Child(ren) feel good about self, feel love and acceptance.	

adoption procedures are enhanced if proper guidance is given with the first failure (11–13).

Stresses to adoptive families include the following:

1. Worry about child's heredity.
2. Parents choose to be, hence, are highly motivated to give parenting, and thus will invest considerable expense and time.
3. The parents see themselves as chosen group because someone thought they should be good parents; the chosen group idea leads to problems, such as difficulty in setting limits, increased stress in parenting role, and oversensitivity to problems in child.
4. Infertile couples may have feelings of hostility or inferiority that are projected on child; the child is a constant reminder of inability to conceive.
5. Adopted child or adolescent may project normal feelings of anger onto "adoptive" parents; parents may think normal developmental problems are a fact of adoption.
6. If one child is adopted and one is biological, favoritism, insufficient rewards to adoptive child, or competition between children may result.
7. Sanctions and regards for role performance differ from biological parents; e.g. the company may not have maternity leave for adoptive parents; there is little emotional support for adoptive parents in society.
8. Role autonomy is lacking. Adoptive parents need someone to agree that they will be good parents but need someone else to bear a child. These requirements inject dependence into a role considered to be independent, which may undermine parental confidence.
9. Community or school attitudes may be negative; one's "own" child is spoken of as biological child. The child encounters these attitudes of distinguishing between "real" and "adoptive," which undermines the sense of belonging and can drive a wedge between parents and child (11, 13, 14, 30, 41, 42, 56, 81).

What was once viewed as a process which ended when the adoption decree was granted is now recognized as a condition which affects those involved throughout their lives. It is a permanent change in legal status. Adoption is a unique way of building families. These families are different from other families because of the circumstances that bring people to adoption, and because of the way adoption continues to affect their lives.

Adoptive parents, adoptive children, and adoptive family dynamics are different from birth parents, birth children, and birth family dynamics. Sometimes these differences generate problems within a family, and sometimes the adoption becomes the focus of other conflicts or unresolved family issues. Any time there are problems in an adoptive family, the significance of the adoption needs to be considered. Changes in the nature of adoptions have meant that more adoptive families have been seeking professional assistance, and that professionals are having to consider the kinds of services the families may need, and how to deliver them. Table 4–3 summarizes intervention

TABLE 4–3. Intervention Guidelines for Adoptive Families

- Conventional treatment may not work well with adoptive families.
- Adoptive parents need validation as parents and of their decision to adopt.
- Adoptive parents must be included in therapeutic interventions in order to further empower them, and to reinforce the adoptive commitment.
- In treating child-rooted problems, often the job will be to help parents modify their expectations.
- A child cannot successfully mourn the past and integrate it into the present circumstances if preoccupied with emotional survival. Developing a sense of safety and security is of paramount importance.
- Child-rooted barriers can come from unfinished emotional business, attachment disorders, or poor preparation for adoption.
- Adult-rooted barriers may stem from unfinished business, marital problems or individual pathologies.
- Environmental barriers include lack of support or active disapproval from the extended family or the broader community.
- Any assessment is only useful if the assessed family accepts it as valid.
- In deciding to terminate an adoption which is not working, one must be committed to preserving the family's integrity, yet open to the removal of the child as a viable option.
- When an adoption is terminated, avoid judgment about reasons for its failure. Plans for adoption of another child should not be made until grief of the loss is resolved.

guidelines for therapy with adoptive families (10, 11, 13, 14, 22, 30, 41, 42, 56).

The Stepchild. The stepchild grieves and mourns the loss of a biological parent from death or divorce and must also deal with problems associated with integration into a new family unit. The stepchild may have conflicting feelings of loyalty to the natural parent and to the stepparent, thinking that acceptance of the stepparent is rejection of the natural parent. The stepchild may also feel rejected by his/her remarried natural parent, seeing the stepparent as a rival for the parent's attention. More on the stepparent family follows in the next section.

Family Lifestyles and Childrearing Practices

There is no single type of contemporary U. S. family, but the lifestyles of many correspond to the factors discussed in this section, including family structure, family cultural pattern, and the impact of the twentieth century. These factors, in addition to those already discussed, influence family interaction and so understanding them will assist you in family care.

Family Structure

Childrearing and family relationships are influenced primarily by family structure. The biological and reproductive unit considered typical in the United States is the mother–father–child group. Ordinarily the parents are married, have established a residence of their own, are viewed (along with their children) as an integral social unit, and live in an intimate, monogamous relationship. Emphasis in U. S. marriage is on pursuit of love in a romanticized way and on individual happiness rather than on family bonds, as in many other cultures. Yet kinship ties are usually recognized on both sides of the family.

In many situations, however, a child may grow up in a family that differs from the typical one. An aunt, uncle, or grandparent may be a continuing member of the household unit; one or the other parent may be absent because of death, divorce, illegitimacy, military service, or occupation involving travel.

The Single-Parent Family is increasingly common in numbers. Families in which only one parent is living full time with offspring are called single-parent families. Although death and illegitimacy may cause the family to have only one parent, divorce of the natural parents is the more common reason. In most cases, these families have undergone a major change in lifestyle. A parent may have died either suddenly or after a long illness. If the parents are divorced, the family may have experienced considerable disruption prior to the breakup. These families—and society—may ignore the changed family structure, for they do not fit the traditional social norm, thereby putting even more stress on people attempting to deal with the situation.

In many healthy persons, emotional attachment to a dead or divorced spouse, with recurrent episodes of painful grief, may remain many years. Mourning in later life may be qualitatively different from in earlier life, (may be more prolonged and more difficult to complete; related to less flexibility in aging, more rigid ego, and enormity of loss) (spouse, identity, peer and family relations, sex companionship, style of living, routines and habits, economic security). The attachment for the spouse, lost either through divorce or death, which lasts for many years may be unknown to even the closest friends or family of the survivor. Yet most mourners resolve their loss and become involved in life in new ways and with new people. The loss also offers an opportunity for personal development (19, 70).

In the single-parent family the children may experience grief for the absent parent, guilt for their real or imagined part in the loss, shame for the change in their family structure, and fear about what changes the future may bring. Roles are changed. Each person may need to assume additional responsibilities and tasks. Parents may change their lifestyles. Mother may go to work or school, for instance; father may move into an apartment; or both parents may begin dating. An adolescent may serve as a parent substitute to younger siblings, or other children may assume new household tasks. The initial task of this family is to accept its family structure as a workable option for family living.

✔ Often an open discussion of the changed lifestyle along with support from relatives, friends, and other single-parent families, enhances the problem-solving abilities of these persons. Occasionally some family members may need professional help if they exhibit symptoms of more extreme dysfunction, grieving, or prolonged "acting-out" behaviors.

The Reconstituted, Complex, Blended, or Stepparent Family is also common. *The remarriage of a divorced or widowed parent with children may form a composite family unit known as the* **reconstituted, complex, blended,** *or* **stepparent family.** The "wicked stepmother" myth pervades our culture; in addition, the common usage of the word "stepchild" denotes inferior status. These families may be formed in a variety of ways: a mother with children may remarry; a father whose children visit may remarry; either of the new parents may have an ex-spouse or children from a previous marriage (children add stepsiblings) and, to complicate this family even more, the remarried couple may decide to have children of their own. In-laws and several sets of grandparents complete the picture. This family is now a far cry from the typical nuclear family and the interaction becomes increasingly complex.

When a couple marries for the second time and either or both have children from a previous marriage, the new husband and/or wife becomes an instant stepparent. This addition of children to a couple's life differs from the situation of first-marriage couples, whose children are added at a slower pace. Additionally, the myth that familial love occurs via the marriage ceremony is common.

Adjustment to a new, unique family unit is the major task of the stepfamily. New members cannot be assimilated with an existing family; instead a new family unit is formed. New rules, customs, and activities must be developed. Conflictual values and family ghosts must be resolved.

All members of this new family bring a history of life experiences, relationships, and expectations to the stepfamily. Conflict often occurs when the values and rules of individuals or the former single-parent family differ from those of the second.

Conflicts about raising stepchildren can be the most explosive issue in remarriages. The partners must realize they will not receive instant love from the stepchildren. In fact, the child may never be affectionate toward the stepparent; the divided loyalty between the birth parent and stepparent may be unresolvable. And the adult may not really feel affection for the stepchild either, in spite of wanting to. Time must be spent between adult and child: it takes time and shared activity to build a trusting, caring relationship. Parents or children should not expect too much too fast. The stepparent should avoid criticism of or competition with the birth parent; a new niche must be fashioned. The stepparent should reach out to the child even if rejection is present, be fair and honest in interactions, create time and space that is designated for only the stepchild. Discipline problems are best handled at first by the birth parent; later regulations and rules can be applied by either partner. Since most children are part of a single-parent home before they merge into a stepparent home, they are not likely to relinquish roles easily. Lastly, partners should focus on their marriage relationship and present an undivided front to the children.

In time family members develop agreement about what is "right." Such agreement may include the "correct" church to attend, the "right" time for dinner, and how birthdays are to be celebrated. Open communication between members is essential if decisions that are livable for all members are to be made.

In addition to adjusting in the family, stepfamilies must adjust to expectations of the outside world. Often differences in the reconstituted family are ignored because the family appears to be intact. Feelings of frustration, inadequacy, and isolation in family members stem from expectations that they feel as close to one another as blood relatives are expected to. The absent parent may still be an active influence in the original family. For instance, a divorced father may still contribute to his children's support and spend time with them on a regular basis, but they may be living with a stepfather. Even a deceased parent is remembered, not always accurately, and sometimes the stepparent is compared to the memory.

The child's ability to work through these feelings is influenced by age, sex, level of development, adaptive capabilities, and the understanding and support received from significant adults. He/she may need professional help to work through the difficulties of integration into a new family structure.

The stepfamily, like the single-parent family, needs to accept and be accepted as a combination of persons living together in a unique family unit. It is a potentially stressful situation that requires flexibility and adaptability of its members. Yet this family offers many opportunities for growth and friendship through the differing experiences of its members.

In early 1983 there were about 25 million stepparents in the United States. Increasing numbers of children in America have at least one stepparent. In response to the growing number of these families, support groups, such as the National Stepfamily Association, operate to help these families face their unique situations. In spite of the old adage that children are flexible and can "bounce back," the trauma of divorce is second only to death. Often the problems that arise in the second marriage are more devastating than earlier ones. The children now know that the original parent will not return and they are faced with a new parent whom they often initially neither want nor accept emotionally. Counseling groups have started in schools, courts, and private practice to help these children (31).

Yet the stepfamily, like the single-parent family, needs to accept itself and be accepted as a combination of persons living together in a unique family unit. It is predicted that by 1990 these two groups will constitute more than 50 percent of U. S. families (31, 66). Even though frequently the complexity of the stepfamily or single-parent unit is initially a stressful situation, the members, through flexibility and adaptability, can offer many opportunities for growth and friendship.

Other Structures. Another type of family structure has been termed *Apartners*. Instead of getting married, a couple, who may have children by a previous marriage, choose to maintain separate residences, take care of their own children, professional lives, and everyday affairs but share special times with each other on a regularly scheduled basis. Personal time and freedom, coupled with intimacy, are what the participants say they seek. Homosexual couples may also have this arrangement, often because of social constraints rather than choice.

The Single State (never married, separated, divorced, widowed) is another family structure. Today in the United States there are more singles who have chosen singlehood. Some would apply family developmental tasks to this person, however it is no longer considered necessary to marry and bear children to be fulfilled and accomplished. The single state can promote development of creativity, object ties, and healthy narcissism through:

1. Privacy—being able to think and create in a peaceful atmosphere without interruption.
2. Time—to travel, cultivate talents and interests, entertain and be entertained, follow intellectual pursuits.
3. Freedom—being able to choose and make decisions, form friendships, use time as desired, depend on self, to have a healthy narcissism.
4. Opportunity—to extend borders of friendship, develop skills and knowledge, enjoy geographic moves or job mobility and success; the single person is often preferred for certain jobs/positions (19, 70).

Yet, singlehood is not always happy for the never-married, separated, widowed, or divorced. It can be lonely. There can be too much unoccupied time and resulting depression. There can be too much space and freedom, and the inability to make decisions. The silence of the home upon entry from a day's work may be overwhelming. There may be a need to talk and to share, both joys and stresses, as well as daily routine events, and no one who really wants to be contacted, or who responds other than in his/her own narcissistic way. There may be financial concerns or unwise use of money because of prior lack of opportunity with financial affairs. Others may expect the single person to always be available to help because he/she "has no family or obligations," but the single person may have difficulty receiving help in return—or even in asking for it. It is as if society expects the single person to manage everything alone. The person is a nonentity until someone needs something, and the single person is seen as available. In like manner, the single person may be taken advantage of by home repairmen, by businesses, by acquaintances who pose as lovers, by someone seeking an object interaction sexually. There may be places the single person cannot go because of cultural restrictions. Our society is couple-oriented. Special holidays and anniversary dates can be especially painful. The person may be alone and forgotten by friends who are busy with their families; or even in a crowd of merrymakers, and in spite of a smiling face, the person may feel isolated and alone (19).

Your acceptance, support, validation, teaching are crucial in promoting health in the single person.

Family Size

Family size is related to distinctive patterns of family life and child development. Most children in the United States are members of a small family system—that is, one with three children or less.

The small family system has the following features: (1) emphasis is on planning (the number and the frequency of births, the objectives of childrearing, and educational possibilities); (2) parenthood is intensive rather than extensive (great concern is evidenced from pregnancy through every phase of childrearing for each child); (3) group actions are usually more democratic; and (4) greater freedom is allowed individual members. The child or children in the small family usually enjoy advantages beyond those available to children in large families of corresponding economic and social level, including more individual attention. On the other hand, these children may retain emotional dependence on their parents, grow up with extreme pressure for performance, and retain an exaggerated notion of self-importance.

The **large family**, generally thought of as one with six or more children, is not a planned family as a rule. Parenthood is commonly extensive rather than intensive, not because of less love or concern but simply because parents must divide their attention more ways. In the very large family emphasis is on the group rather than on the individual member. Conformity and cooperation are valued above self-expression. Discipline in the form of numerous and stringent rules is frequently stressed and there is a high degree of organization in the activities of daily living (19). Or if parents lack initiative and use their resources unwisely, disorganization may exist. For additional information see the section on The Family with a Large Number of Children, page 119.

Family Cultural Pattern

The ways of living and thinking that constitute the intimate aspects of family group life are the **family cultural pattern** (20). The family transmits the cultural pattern of its own ethnic background and class to the child, together with the parents' attitudes toward other classes.

Within the national cultural pattern of the United States, significant variations have been found in family cultural patterns and social systems (9). In Millstadt, Illinois, for instance, the German farm family provides a distinctive social system with cultural features distinct from its Italian neighbors across the river in St. Louis. The Maine Yankee and the North Carolina rebel may speak the same language, but the meanings of the words used may be quite different because of regional variables. Thus how families rear their children will depend on ethnic group and class, region, nation, and historical period.

Influence of Twentieth-Century Changes

The Shift in This Century from an Agrarian to a Complex Technological Society. This has produced dramatic changes for the U.S. family (37). A greater percentage of children now survives childhood than in 1900 and a higher percentage of mothers survives childbirth. Marriage, on the average, occurs at an earlier age than in former generations. Fewer children are born to most parents and they are spaced closer together. Middle-aged couples now have more time together after their children are grown and leave home. And because of an increased life expectancy, families now have more living relatives than formerly, especially elderly relatives (23).

Other Trends Are Related to Living in a Complex Industrial Society. Families live primarily in urban areas. More women work outside the home. The U.S. woman who formerly stayed home and was the "homemaker" has also gone through several changes. Once homemaking took a good deal of time. Now modern conveniences make tasks easier. The woman who stays home today concentrates more on "mothering." Her outside activities may include volunteer work, so she can control her hours, feel she has prime time at home but yet is contributing outside the family unit. Family members are becoming better educated. Family incomes are increasing and acquisition of personal housing and equipment comes earlier in the marriage. Greater individual freedom exists. Sexual mores are changing, with trial and serial marriages.

The emphasis on the family-kinship group has been replaced by acceptance of the nuclear or other types of family. Because Americans are so mobile and are increasingly living in smaller homes or in apartments, many ties with kin other than the immediate family are loosened or at least geographically extended. Sometimes close friends become "the family." Yet many Americans strengthen kinship ties through letters, telephone calls, and holiday and vacation visits. Religious influences affect family ties. Jews, with their many family traditions, are generally more embedded in a network of relatives than White Protestants are.

Rapid Change. This is a fact that families must acknowledge. Medical, pharmacological, and scientific advances in birth technology and all areas of health, the increased number of single-parent families, the growing emphasis on the civil and economic rights of minority groups, and the women's liberation movement are only a part of the cultural expansion of this century. As people live longer, more older people will divorce, remarry, or cohabitate. Those who lack healthy emotional roots within their nuclear families, who have few or no kinship ties, who cannot adjust to rapid change, and who have little identity except as defined by job and income are more likely to become depressed, alcoholic, unfaithful to mate, or divorced (48). Today's changing social environment makes it increasingly difficult for a parent to be certain of his identity. How, then, is he to provide emotional roots for the child?

U.S. Childrearing Practices. There is no one traditional national pattern, only the general concern that children develop "normally." Parents are encouraged through culture, education, and the mass media to use whatever the dominant childrearing theory is at the time. At the turn of the century, the dominant theory reflected the prevailing scientific belief in the primacy of heredity in determining behavior. In the early 1900s, child care emphasized the importance of environment, and by the midthirties Freudian Psychoanalytic Theory had gained ascendency. Today Neo-Behavioristic theories are prominent. With each new wave of "knowledge," parents are bombarded by conflicting reports and condemnation of previous practices. Often the change in theory application occurs during the same parental generation so that parents do not trust their own judgment and considerable inconsistency results. The inconsistency, rather than the theory, probably creates the main problems in childrearing. Sometimes parents strive to avoid rearing their children as they were reared, but nevertheless do so unwittingly because of the permanency of enculturation. Children are often given approval and disapproval for their behavior and told they are "good" or "bad." This practice, along with inconsistency and other factors, contributes to competition and sibling rivalry.

Father's Role. The father's role is being reconsidered and he is more active in child care (43, 47). Still, the mother is primarily responsible for the crying baby and young child care. The infant is often unconsciously trained in privacy, individualism, and independence by being left alone in the crib or playpen much of the time. There is still, unfortunately, the fear of "spoiling" the infant if he/she is held too much or responded to spontaneously. Thus the infant may develop behavioral extremes in order to get needs met.

He/she is being given the foundation to later stand out, push forward, to compete and achieve.

Then when the children are old enough to be out of the home, parents often strive to do things for their children and center their activities around their children's activities. Work responsibilities are not necessarily demanded, but there is subtle pressure for the children to repay by pleasing the parents through use of talents, organizational achievements, or honors won. Because of the small size of the nuclear family, the school-age child or adolescent may spend more time with peers than with family members. And because of the youth idealization of our culture, seniority does not invoke special respect for the older person (parent). The childrearing parent must offer more than age if he/she wants to maintain control.

A growing trend is for children to be cared for by day-care centers or babysitters who are usually not relatives. What happens if the mother and parent-surrogate differ greatly about childrearing practices? The child generally acknowledges the authority of parents, or at least the mother, but parent-surrogates affect him/her nevertheless. Any adult who is with the child reinforces behavior in the child that conforms to the adult's own standard of behavior. The child conforms to the adult's desires in order to gain approval. If the parent-surrogate acts in a way contrary to the values of the parents, both parents and child are likely to be distressed.

✔ NURSING APPLICATIONS FOR HEALTH PROMOTION

The family as the basic unit for the developing person cannot be taken for granted. Although family forms have changed and will continue to change, each person, in order to develop healthfully, needs some intimate surroundings of human concern. "No man is an island."

You will frequently encounter the entire family as your client in the health care system, regardless of the setting. You may be asked to do family-centered care, to nurse the patient and the family, or to do "family therapy." Yet you will not be able to carry out the nursing process with the family even minimally unless you understand the dynamics of family living presented in this chapter.

Rapid change, increasing demands on the person, technological progress, and other trends mentioned seem to isolate people. A glance at one vanishing symbol of American family life—the front porch—can illustrate this point. What happened to the porch where the family used to gather? Where mother sat when the evening dishes were done? Where father rested after a day's work? Where toddlers rode their kiddie cars? Where Susie got her first kiss? Where neighbors stopped to chat? The porch has been converted into a private patio in the back of the house and is used briefly when the family can force themselves to leave the air-conditioned comfort of indoors. Susie and her boyfriend are gone in his car. Father is absorbed in his TV programs. Mother cannot hear the toddler calling because the dishwasher, clothes washer, dryer, and garbage disposal block out all human sounds. The older children are carpooled to separate activities.

You cannot call back the front-porch era. Nor do all families live with the foregoing luxuries and isolated from each other. But you should understand that many families are not even aware of the forces that are pulling them apart. More than ever, they need one place in their living where they can act without self-consciousness, where the pretenses and roles demanded in jobs, school, or social situations can be put aside. The living center should be a place where communication takes place with ease; where each knows what to expect from the other; where a cohesiveness exists that is based on nonverbal messages more than verbal; and where a person is accepted for what he/she is. The family may need your help in becoming aware of disruptive forces, of their maladaptive patterns, and of ways to promote an accepting home atmosphere.

In doing a family assessment, ask questions related to achieving the developmental tasks that were described earlier. Also, determine communication patterns and relationships, family health, access to health care, occupational demands and hazards, religious beliefs and practices, childrearing practices, participation in the community, and support systems. When you work with the family unit, the information in Table 4–4 will help you to assess the family's lifestyle and needs.

You can help families understand some processes and dynamics underlying interaction so that they, in turn, learn to respect the uniqueness of the self and of each other. Certainly members in the family need not always agree with each other. Instead they can learn to listen to the other person, about how he/she feels and why, accepting each person's impression as real for self. This attitude becomes the basis for mutual respect, honest communication, encouragement of individual fulfillment, and freedom to be. There is then no need to prove or defend the self.

Once the attitude "We are all important people in this family" is established, conflicts can be dealt with openly and constructively. Name calling and belittling are out of place. Families need to structure time together; otherwise individual schedules will allow them less and less time to meet. Parents need to send consistent messages to their children. To say "Don't smoke" while immediately lighting a cigarette is hardly effective.

TABLE 4-4. Family Assessment Tool

MEETING OF PHYSICAL, EMOTIONAL, AND SPIRITUAL NEEDS OF MEMBERS

Ability to provide food and shelter
- Space management as regards living, sleeping, recreation, privacy
- Crowding if over 1.5 persons per room
- Territoriality or control of each member over lifespace
- Access to laundry, grocery, recreation facilities
- Sanitation including disposal methods, source of water supply, control of rodents and insects
- Storage and refrigeration
- Available food supply
- Food preparation, including preserving and cooking methods, (stove, hotplate, oven)
- Use of food stamps and donated foods as well as eligibility for food stamps
- Education of each member as to food composition, balanced menus, special preparations or diets if required for a specific member

Access to health care
- Regularity of health care
- Continuity of caregivers
- Closeness of facility and means of access such as car, bus, cab
- Access to helpful neighbors
- Access to phone

Family health
- Longevity
- Major or chronic illnesses
- Familial or hereditary illnesses, such as rheumatic fever, gout, allergy tuberculosis, renal disease, diabetes mellitus, cancer, emotional illness, epilepsy, migraine, other nervous disorders, hypertension, blood diseases, obesity, frequent accidents, drug intake, pica
- Emotional or stress-related illnesses
- Pollutants that members are chronically exposed to, such as air, water, soil, noise, or chemicals that are unsafe to health

Neighborhood pride and loyalty

Job access, energy output, shift changes

Sensitivity, warmth, understanding between family members
- Demonstration of emotion
- Enjoyment of sexual relations
  - Male: Impotence, premature or retarded ejaculation, hypersexuality
  - Female: Frigidity (inability to achieve orgasm), enjoyment of sexual relations, feelings of disgust, shame, self-devaluation; fear of injury, painful coitus
    Menstrual history, including onset, duration, flow, missed periods and life situation at the time, pain, euphoria, depression, other difficulties

Sharing of religious beliefs, values, doubts
- Formal membership in church and organizations
- Ethical framework and honesty
- Adaptability, response to reality
- Satisfaction with life
- Self-esteem

CHILDREARING PRACTICES AND DISCIPLINE

Mutual responsibility
- Joint parenting
- Mutual respect for decision making
- Means of discipline and consistency

Respect for individuality
Fostering of self-discipline
Attitudes toward education, reading, scholarly pursuit
Attitudes toward imaginative play
Attitudes toward involvement in sports
Promotion of gender stereotypes

COMMUNICATION

Expression of a wide range of emotion and feeling
Expression of ideas, concepts, beliefs, values, interests
Openness
Verbal expression and sensitive listening
Consensual decision making

SUPPORT, SECURITY, ENCOURAGEMENT

Balance in activity
Humor
Dependency and dominance patterns
Life support groups of each member
Social relationship of couple: go out together or separately; change since marriage mutually satisfying; effect of sociability patterns on children

GROWTH-PRODUCING RELATIONSHIPS AND EXPERIENCES WITHIN AND WITHOUT THE FAMILY

Creative play activities
Planned growth experiences
Focus of life and activity of each member
Friendships

RESPONSIBLE COMMUNITY RELATIONSHIPS

Organizations, including involvement, membership, active participation
Knowledge of and friendship with neighbors

GROWING WITH AND THROUGH CHILDREN

Hopes and plans for children
Emulation of own parents and its influence on relationship with children
Relationship patterns: authoritarian, patriarchal, matriarchal
Necessity to relive (make up for) own childhood through children

UNITY, LOYALTY, AND COOPERATION

Positive interacting of members toward each other

SELF-HELP AND ACCEPTANCE OF OUTSIDE HELP IN FAMILY CRISIS

4 The Family—Basic Unit for the Developing Person

Times of communication are especially necessary when children are feeling peer pressure; children, moreover, should be praised for what they do right rather than reprimanded for what they do wrong. Children need structure but should be told the reason for the structure if old enough to comprehend. As you help the family achieve positive feelings toward and interaction with one another, you are also helping them to fulfill their tasks, roles, and functions. Review the adaptive mechanisms of families described in this chapter.

The person's health problems, especially emotional ones, may well be the result of the interaction patterns in childhood or present family. Knowledge of the variables influencing family interaction—parents' self-esteem and upbringing, number of siblings, the person's ordinal position in the family, cultural norms, family rituals—all will help you assist the person in talking through feelings related to past and present conflicts. Sometimes helping the person understand these variables in relation to the spouse's upbringing and behavior can be the first step in overcoming current marital problems.

You are a nurse, not a specialized family counselor, although with advanced preparation you could do family therapy. But you can often sense lack of communication in a family. Through use of an empathic relationship and effective communication, teaching, and crisis therapy, you can encourage family members to talk about their feelings with one another and assist in the resolution of their conflicts. Help them become aware of the need to work for family cohesiveness just as they would work at a job or important project. Refer them to a family counseling service if the problems are beyond your scope. Your work with them should also help them better use other community resources, such as private family or psychiatric counseling or family and children's services. Table 4–5 lists pertinent *nursing diagnoses*.

One family self-help resource that does not use the traditional "medical model" (wait until problems surface and then intervene) but rather the "educational model" (learn new information and skills while basically well) is called Family Clusters. Devised by Margaret Sawin and first used in 1970, the Family Cluster is a group of four or five complete family units (including blended, single-parent, cohabitation, or the traditional unit) who contract to meet together over an extended period of time for shared educational experiences that concern relationships within their families. Where available, it provides a positive approach and affirms family members because a commitment is made for all persons—no matter what their age—to have both power and input into the cluster. Training to lead family clusters is available. For more information, write to Family Clustering, Inc., PO Box 18074, Rochester, NY 14618 (68).

Your knowledge of the family life cycle, with developmental tasks to be performed at each stage, provides a foundation for learning the specifics of sequential development. This combined knowledge will help you in assessing the status of the family and the individual person in planning care, in intervention, and in objectively evaluating your effectiveness.

One liability in working with families of various social classes and cultures may be *you*. For example, if you come from a middle-class U. S. background, that fact will affect your opinions about what constitutes family life. Your attitude toward nonconforming families or unconventional living arrangements may interfere with your objectivity and thus with your ability to assist some families. You will need to go through your own maturation process of learning

TABLE 4–5. Selected Nursing Diagnoses Related to Family Nursing[a]

PATTERN 2: COMMUNICATING	PATTERN 6: MOVING
Impaired Verbal Communication	Diversional Activity Deficit
	Impaired Home Maintenance Management
PATTERN 3: RELATING	Altered Health Maintenance
Impaired Social Interaction	Ineffective Breastfeeding
Social Isolation	Altered Growth and Development
Altered Role Performance	
Altered Parenting	PATTERN 7: PERCEIVING
Potential Altered Parenting	Chronic Low Self-Esteem
Sexual Dysfunction	Situational Low Self-Esteem
Altered Family Processes	Personal Identify Disturbance
Parental Role Conflict	Unilateral Neglect
Altered Sexuality Patterns	Hopelessness
PATTERN 4: VALUING	Powerlessness
Spiritual Distress	
	PATTERN 8: KNOWING
PATTERN 5: CHOOSING	Knowledge Deficit
Ineffective Individual Coping	
Impaired Adjustment	PATTERN 9: FEELING
Defensive Coping	Dysfunctional Grieving
Ineffective Denial	Anticipatory Grieving
Ineffective Family Coping: Disabling	Potential for Violence: Self-Directed or Directed at Others
Ineffective Family Coping: Compromised	Post-Trauma Response
Family Coping: Potential for Growth	Anxiety
Decisional Conflict	Fear
Health Seeking Behaviors	

[a]Many of the NANDA nursing diagnoses are applicable to the ill individual in the family unit.
Source: NANDA Approved Nursing Diagnoses Categories, *Nursing Diagnosis Newsletter*, 15, no. 1 (summer, 1988), 1–3.

that your way is not always the best or only way. The process is difficult. The book by Kramer (41) gives insights helpful to the person who is working with families.

Role of the Nurse in Well-Baby Care

You may care for well babies and mothers in a variety of settings—the clinic, hospital, home, or doctor's office. Your actions contribute significantly to their health.

Prenatal Care. Prenatal care to the mother and her partner may include physical assessment, teaching healthful practices for mother and baby, listening to mother vent frustrations or share fears, counseling her during periods of depression or uncertainty, and sharing her happy feelings about becoming a mother. You may conduct childbirth classes for mother and father so that they can better understand changes occurring in the mother as well as the nutrition and hygiene necessary during pregnancy; know what to expect during labor, delivery, and postpartum; and prepare for an active role during birth. An obstetric nursing book will give adequate detail to help you do prenatal assessment and care as well as intrapartal and postpartal assessment and intervention.

If the mother-to-be is unwed, you may also try to work with the father-to-be if both are willing. The father-to-be needs help in talking about his feelings and needs to support her, if they are compatible. He may also seek sex education.

To help the unwed parents, as well as break the cycle for future generations, we must gain a better understanding of the unwed father. Do not perceive him as irresponsible or having taken advantage of an innocent girl. The relationship between the unwed mother and the father is not necessarily a hit-and-miss affair but often meaningful to both. If the parents-to-be are adolescents, they realize that a new life has been created as a result of their actions. They want to act in a responsible way. They are concerned about the child's well-being (43, 47, 70).

The unwed father can be encouraged to stand by the unmarried mother. Often he feels proud of fathering; he has proven his masculinity. The long-term consequences of having a child are such, however, that alternate solutions regarding the future of the child should be thoroughly explored with and by both partners. Alternatives include marriage, placing the child for adoption, or assumption by either parent or the grandparents of the responsibility for caring for and rearing the child. The man needs help in understanding how and why he became a father and the serious implications for the mother, the child, and himself.

Adolescents may admit that their sexual experiences were unsatisfactory, leaving them depressed, guilty, and scared. The good relationship with the girlfriend may have begun to deteriorate when sexual relations were started. Pregnancy comes as a shock to both. They know about contraceptives, but their use may have been sporadic, if at all, for some people believe that the spontaneity and sincerity of the sexual act are lessened when prepared for (43, 47, 70).

Sex education must relate to the values of interpersonal relations and concern for others if it is to be successful. The implications and responsibilities of sexual behavior need to be discussed with the teenagers. The difference between teenage love and a more mature relationship between people who are ready to meet the problems and responsibilities of adulthood should be discussed (43, 47, 70).

Parents of the unwed father must be involved in helping their son; communication between the boy and parents should be reestablished. In addition, parents should assert themselves in helping the boy take responsibility for his actions and assist the boy in the case of marriage (43, 47, 70).

Efforts to prevent unwed pregnancies must be directed to improving and strengthening family life and developing a better respect for the father's role in the family. Many unwed fathers come from female-dominated homes or from homes in which the father is absent or inadequate in his role (43, 47, 70).

Fathers can help adolescent sons by talking with and listening to them, by being slow to judge, by taking them to the job so the youth can see how the father earns a living, by being a role model in relating maturely to the spouse and other women. Fathers can create an atmosphere in which the sons will want to talk about emerging sexual feelings and experiences (43, 47). If the adolescent son comes from a home where no father is present, the mother can work at listening to and discussing problems and feelings with the son. She may also be able to foster a bond between the son and another male member of the family.

Childbirth Education Classes. If you conduct childbirth education classes, try to interview each couple in their home early in the pregnancy, by the fourth month if possible, to observe their relationship and determine their response to pregnancy. Their response may be different and more honest in their own home than in class. During the classes include opportunities for men, as well as women, to talk about the problems they feel are uniquely theirs, their feelings, or the commonality of the couvade syndrome. Provide anticipatory guidance about the couvade syndrome. Avoid pushing the father into participation and provide support for him. Focus childbirth education on the known benefits to the baby and parents and not on overromanticized and dramatic statements about improved marital relationships. Educate both parents about family planning so that future pregnancies can be mutually planned. Refer either partner, or both, to psychological counseling when necessary, especially if antisocial behavior is seen or if there has been fetal loss.

Labor. During labor you do necessary physical care, but you may also act as a coach for the mother, or you may support the father as he assists his wife. Flexibility in hospital routines for obstetrical patients is usually possible and contributess to the parents' sense of control. In fact, negative feelings about traditional hospital deliveries have become so widespread that home deliveries are increasing in many cities, often attended by a granny midwife instead of a professional doctor or nurse–midwife.

The physician and nurse or nurse–midwife can work as a team with the expectant couple. In some facilities the nurse–midwife assumes primary responsibility for the family unit. Whenever a mother delivers, she has the right to capable, safe care by qualified caretakers. Home deliveries can be carefully planned and safe. And hospital deliveries can be more home-like. Maternity centers now provide families anticipating a normal childbearing experience with antepartum care that is educational in nature; labor and delivery in a home-like setting (but with adequate equipment) with discharge to home whenever it is safe for mother and baby, probably within 12 hours after delivery; and follow-up care by public health nurses in the home during the postpartum course. The labor-delivery rooms can be designed to accommodate the presence of the father or family during delivery and be less traumatic (cold, with intense lights) for the newborn. Following birth, the infant can remain with the mother, the newborn's physical exam can be done in her presence with the father present as well. Childbirth should be a positive, maturing experience for the couple. Expectant parents have the right and responsibility to be involved in planning their care with the health team and to know what is happening. Cultural beliefs should be recognized, respected, and accommodated whenever possible. A positive childbearing experience contributes to a healthy family unit.

Delivery Methods. These are changing in some centers as doctors and midwives follow the trend set by Dr. Leboyer in France. The delivery room lights are dimmed; people speak softly or whisper; the infant is placed on the mother's abdomen in order to maintain body temperature and the prebirth curved position of the spine; the baby is massaged by mother and doctor; and the cord is not cut immediately. The baby is placed in warm water. Precautions are taken when necessary, but apparently delivery does not have to be so traumatic for the baby (44, 70).

Postpartum Period. In the early postpartum period assess mother and baby and give the mother physical care and assist her as necessary even if she looks well and able. "Mother" the mother (15, 64, 65). Arrange the environment and hospital routines to enhance bonding between mother and baby. Listen to the mother's concerns; answer her questions; support her maternal behavior. In a nonthreatening way, teach the mother how to handle her baby. Help her begin to unlearn preconceived ideas about the baby and herself and perceive herself and the baby positively. Give her special assistance if she is breast-feeding. After the initial "taking-in" period of having received special care and attention, the mother moves to the "taking hold" stage, where she is able to care for the child (64, 65).

The interaction between the infant and primary caretaker is crucial. The mothering person helps the baby feel secure and loved, fosters a sense of trust, provides stimulation, reinforces certain behavior, acts as a model for language development, and trains the baby in basic learning strategies. In turn, maternal behavior is influenced by baby's cries, coos, smiles, activity, and gazes, as well as by how well baby's behavior meets the mother's expectations.

Your significant contribution to the family unit is to promote attachment between parents and baby, encourage continuing contacts between the family and health professionals so that adequate health and illness care are received, and encourage parents to meet the baby's needs adequately. You can help the parents feel good about themselves and the baby.

You can be instrumental in continuing new trends in care to make the hospital or clinic environment more homelike while providing safe, modern care.

Continued Care in the Fourth Trimester

During the **fourth trimester,** the 6 or 8 weeks after delivery, the mother needs assistance with child care and an opportunity to regain her former self physically and emotionally. Father also needs support as he becomes involved in child-care responsibilities (58). In the nuclear or single-parent family the parent(s) may struggle alone. Visits by a home health nurse may be useful. Some communities have a crisis line for new parents. You may be able to suggest services or help the parent(s) think of people who could be helpful.

As you assess the mother's functioning, consider her physical and emotional energy, support systems, and current level of parenting activity. If she does not appear to be caring adequately for the child, assess for anemia, pain, bleeding, infections, lack of food or sleep, drug use, or other medical conditions that would interfere with her activity level and feelings of caring. Depression and postpartum blues are difficult to differentiate. In depression the mother is immobilized and forgets basic care, but with postpartum blues she may cry but care for the baby's physical needs.

The new mother usually has enough energy to do only top-priority tasks—eating, sleeping, baby care, and essentials for other family members. A house that is too clean is a danger signal that she is neglecting the baby, herself, or both (8).

The mother's support system is crucial for her energy maintenance, physical as well as emotional. She needs direct support and assistance with daily tasks, plus moral support, a listener, a confidant. Support comes from personal and professional sources—the partner, parents, friends, other relatives, and the nurse, doctor, social worker, or pastor. Negative attitudes from others can drain emotional energy.

Bishop's (8) and Campbell's and Smith's (16) guides to assess parenting feelings and adequate mothering may be helpful. Actual parenting skills can be manifested in various ways: touching, cuddling, a tender, soft voice tone, and loving gazes. Ability to obtain adequate medical care is typical of the caring parent; lack of use of medical services for the baby indicates a poor mother–child relationship. Additional information about parents' feelings and the parenting process are described in Chapter 7, pp. 192-197.

If the baby is progressing in normal fashion, focus on the mother's needs and concerns. Help her find nonprofessional support systems that can assist her when the professional is unavailable or that can help with child care. In addition to concern over child care, we must help the mother grow developmentally. Helping her stay in good physical and emotional health ensures better parenting.

Working with Families Who Have Child Born Prematurely or with Defect. Prematurity accounts for 50 percent of neonatal mortality and premature infants who survive contribute significantly to the number of physically, intellectually, and emotionally handicapped children in the United States. Complications of prematurity include major and minor physical abnormalities, general motor incoordination, short attention span, distractibility and hyperactivity, difficulty separating from parents, preoccupation with the body, and scholastic underachievement (50, 70).

The last complications may be more related to an early disturbed mother–child relationship than to the prematurity, perinatal complications, or the child's birth defects. Typically the infant is rushed to the nursery after birth, thereby preventing physical or eye contact between mother and baby. The mother is often isolated from other mothers; professionals and family may avoid conversation about the baby. Mother often sees the baby in the premature or intensive care nursery at a distance and only indistinctly; or the baby may have been transported to a children's hospital at some distance so that visiting the baby after her discharge is difficult. The mother may have no opportunity to form any attachment feelings unless nursing staff foster the involvement in child care to the extent possible and keep her informed of baby's condition and progress. The baby who finally comes home to the parents may be a stranger for whom the mother has no maternal response or commitment. Additionally, the mother has developed little confidence in her mothering abilities and no caretaking regimen.

Behavior patterns in parents that strongly suggest a disturbed parent–child relationship and future problems in parenting the premature or defective child include the following behaviors:

1. Unable to talk about guilt feelings, fears, and their sense of responsibility for the child's early arrival, with each other or others.
2. Demonstrate no visible anxiety about the baby's condition, deny the reality, or displace anxiety onto less threatening matters.
3. Make little effort to secure information about the baby's condition.
4. Consistently misinterpret or exaggerate either positive or negative information about the baby and display no signs of hope as baby's condition improves.
5. Receive no practical support or help from family or friends, and community resources are lacking.
6. Unable to accept and use help offered.

You may be instrumental in promoting certain procedures that can be used by hospital personnel to promote parent–child relationship:

1. Permit the mother to see and touch the baby as soon as possible, preferably in the delivery room. Or transfer the baby to the mother's room in a portable incubator if the baby remains in the same hospital.
2. Permit the mother to become involved in baby's care as soon as possible. Take the mother to the premature care unit, teaching her to use the necessary aseptic technique in order to touch, care for, and visit with the baby.
3. Provide an atmosphere that encourages questions.
4. Encourage parents to talk with each other, family members, and friends—using others for support.

5. Recognize that parents' excessive questions, demands, and criticisms are a reaction to stress and not personal attacks on the professional worker or hospital.
6. Do not offer reassuring cliches or comforting statements too quickly. Encourage parents to cry, to face the reality of the situation.
7. Do not pressure parents to talk about their feelings all at once, but avoid using the excuse of "not wanting to probe" to avoid talking with them.
8. Encourage the mother to express breast milk if she wishes; the breast milk can be taken to a breast-milk bank and used for the infant. When the baby is sucking well, the mother can help bottle-feed the baby until the baby is strong enough to breast-feed.
9. Arrange for father to visit the baby prior to discharge, calling him about baby's progress at intervals when he is unable to visit.
10. Encourage the parents to handle the baby and do baby's care prior to discharge; teach about baby care as necessary while the parents are engaged in care of their baby.

Refer also to Chapter 7, pp. 226 to 228, for additional information.

Parent Education

To combat the problems associated with the high adolescent birthrate, some junior and senior high schools are establishing creative programs in parenthood education. Some hospitals and health clinics are initiating specialized prenatal and postnatal services for the adolescent mother and her at-risk infant. You can initiate nontraditional programs in your own community.

Cincinnati General Hospital established an innovative program to help adolescent mothers become more effective parents. The adolescent mother who decides to keep her baby needs all the family and outside help she can get. She fears that whatever personal ambitions she has will be thwarted by the baby. Unmarried and unprepared for employment, she finds it almost impossible to make her own way in the world. Anger, frustration, and ignorance hamper her ability to attach to and appropriately care for the baby. Repeated pregnancies, child neglect and abuse, and welfare dependency often occur (4).

Shaw also describes the formation of a mother's group, consisting of women of various ethnic origins in a lower-income bracket, whose purpose was to provide parent education and support and foster talking about feelings (71). Hiemstra gives suggestions on how to educate parents to use community resources (34).

Your work with the mother may prevent maternal deprivation, insufficient interaction between mother and child, conditions under which the deprivation or even abuse develops, as well as negative effects on the child's development.

Work with Adoptive Families

You can help the adoptive parents in their adjustment. Assure them that attachment develops over time. Help them think through how and when to tell the child that he/she is adopted so that the child understands and is not traumatized. Help the parents anticipate how they will help the child cope when the child is taunted by peers about being adopted. Help them realize that the adopted child will probably seek answers to many questions when he/she gets older. Who were the parents? Their cultural, racial, or ethnic background? Their ages, occupations, interests, appearance? Why was he/she relinquished? What are the medical facts surrounding heredity and birth? Help parents realize that these questions do not mean that the child does not love them. Various articles supply information on adoption procedures, stresses encountered, and how to make adoption a success (11–14, 22, 24, 30, 40, 42, 56, 81, 82). Refer also to pages 120 to 123.

Work with Single-Parent or Reconstituted Families

The guidelines already discussed will be useful to you as you help the single-parent or reconstituted family adjust to its situation. The single-parent family can be referred to a local chapter of Parents Without Partners if the person seeks support from peers. Do not rush in with answers for these families until you have heard their unique problems. Acknowledge their strengths; help them formulate their own solutions. Often a few sessions of crisis therapy will be sufficient. Several references give further information (2, 31, 37, 60, 66, 80, 83, 85). Refer also to pages 123 to 124.

Family Care Throughout the Life Cycle

You may be called on to assist families as they meet various developmental crises throughout the life cycle: school entry of the child, the adolescent period, children leaving home, divorce, retirement, death of a member. Your goal is health promotion and primary prevention. Your intervention early in the family life cycle may help establish a positive health trend in place of its negative counterpart. The care you give to young parents lays the foundation for their children's health.

References

1. Ackerman, Nathan, *Diagnosis and Treatment of Family Relations*, New York: Basic Books, 1972.
2. Andolfi, Maurizio, *Family Therapy: An Interactional Approach*. New York: Plenum Press, 1979.
3. Andrews, Ernest, *The Emotionally Disturbed Family*. New York: Jason Aronson, 1974.
4. Badger, E., D. Burns, and B. Rhoads, Education for Adolescent Mothers in a Hospital Setting, *American Journal of Public Health*, 66, no. 5 (1976), 469–472.
5. Bell, Alan, Martin Weinberg, and Sue Hammersmith, *Sexual Preference: Its Development in Men and Women*. Bloomington, IN: Indiana University Press, 1981.
6. Benedek, Theresa, Parenthood During the Life Cycle, in *Parenthood: Its Psychology and Psychopathology*, eds. E. J. Anthony and T. Benedek. Boston: Little, Brown, 1970, pp. 185–206.
7. Bettelheim, Bruno, *A Good Enough Parent: A Book on Child-Rearing*. New York: Alfred A. Knopf, 1987.
8. Bishop, Barbara. A Guide to Assessing Parenting Capabilities, *American Journal of Nursing*, 76, no. 11 (1976), 1784–1787.
9. Bossard, James, and Eleanor Boll, *Sociology of Child Development* (4th ed.). New York: Harper & Row, 1960.
10. Bowlby, J., The Making and Breaking of Affectional Bonds, *British Journal of Psychiatry*, 130, (March, 1977), 201–210.
11. Brockhaus, Joyce, and Robert Brockhaus, Adopting an Older Child—The Emotional Process, *American Journal of Nursing*, 82, no. 2 (1982), 288–291.
12. Brockhaus, Joyce P., Adopting a Child with Special Needs: The Legal Process, *American Journal of Nursing*, 82, no. 2 (1982), 291–294.
13. Brockhaus, Joyce P., Foster Care, Adoption, and the Grief Process, *Journal of Psychiatric Nursing and Mental Health Services.*, 20, no. 9 (1982), 9–16.
14. Brodzinsky, D.M., D.E. Schechter, A.M. Braff, et al. Psychological and Academic Adjustment of Adopted Children, *Journal of Consulting & Clinical Psychology*, 52 (1984), 869–878.
15. Brown, Marie, and Joan Hurlock, Mothering the Mother, *American Journal of Nursing*, 77, no. 3 (1977), 439–441.
16. Campbell, S., and J. Smith, Postpartum: Assessment Guide, *American Journal of Nursing*, 77, no. 7 (1977), 1179.
17. Carmichael, Carrie, *Nonsexist Childraising*. Boston: Beacon Press, 1977.
18. Clinton, Jacqueline, Expectant Fathers at Risk for Couvade, *Nursing Research*, 35, no. 5 (1986), 290–294.
19. Colarusso, Calvin, and Robert Nemeroff, *Adult Development*. New York: Plenum Press, 1981.
20. Coleman, Arthur, and Libby Coleman, *Pregnancy: The Psychological Experience*. New York: Herder and Herder, 1972.
21. David, Miriam, and Elaine Doye, First Trimester of Pregnancy, *American Journal of Nursing*, 76, no. 12 (1976), 1945–1948.
22. Dunn, Linda (ed), *Adopting Children with Special Needs: A Sequel*. Washington, D.C.: North American Council on Adoptable Children, 1983.
23. Duvall, Evelyn, and Brent Miller, *Marriage and Family Development* (6th ed.). New York: Harper and Row, 1984.
24. Edwards, M.P., and F.E. Boyd, Adoption for Adolescents, *Child Welfare*, 54, no. 4 (1975), 298–299.
25. Erikson, Erik, *Childhood and Society* (2nd ed.). New York: W. W. Norton, 1963.
26. Fife, B., A Model for Predicting the Adaptation of Families in Medical Crisis: An Analysis of Role Integration, *Image*, 17, no. 4. (1985), 108–112.
27. Fogg, Susan, New Views on Child Rearing Make Room for Daddy, *Washington Post–Sunday Times*, November 30, 1980, p. 26.
28. Fox, Tom, Tips on Making the Reunited Family Work, *St. Louis Globe–Democrat*, January 31, 1980, reprinted in *LTC Notes:* The Catholic Health Association, 11, no. 2 (1981), 2–3.
29. Friedman, Marilyn, *Family Nursing: Theory and Assessment* (2nd ed.). Norwalk, CT.: Appleton-Century-Crofts, 1985.
30. Gil, O., and B. Jackson, *Adoption and Race: Black, Asian, and Mixed-Race Children in White Families*. New York: St. Martin's Press, 1983.
31. Gardner, Richard, *Psychotherapy with Children of Divorce*. New York: Jason Aronson, 1976.
32. Gordon, Thomas, *Parent Effectiveness Training*. New York: Peter H. Wyden, 1970.
33. Greenberg, Martin, and Norma Morris, Engrossment: The Newborn's Impact Upon the Father, *American Journal of Orthopsychiatry*, 44, no. 4 (1974), 520–531.
34. Hiemstra, Roger, Educating Parents in the Use of the Community, *Adult Leadership*, 23, no. 3 (1974), 85–88.
35. Horowitz, J., and B. Perdue, Single Parent Families, *Nursing Clinics of North America*, 12, no. 3 (1977), 503–512.
36. Hott, Jacqueline, The Crisis of Expectant Fatherhood, *American Journal of Nursing*, 76, no. 9 (1976), 1436–1440.
37. How to Stay Married, *Newsweek* (August 24, 1987), 52–57.
38. Hrobsky, Diane, Transition to Parenthood: A Balancing of Needs, *Nursing Clinics of North America*, 12, no. 3 (1977), 457–468.
39. Hughes, Cynthia, An Eclectic Approach to Parent Group Education, *Nursing Clinics of North America*, 12, no. 3 (1977), 469–480.
40. Jewett, Claudia L., *Helping Children Cope with Separation and Loss*. Cambridge, MA: The Harvard Common Press, 1982.

41. Kramer, Jeannette, *Family Interfaces: Transgenerational Patterns*. New York: Brunner/Mazel, 1987.
42. Krementz, Jill, *How It Feels to Be Adopted*. New York: Alfred Knopf, 1982.
43. Lamb, Michael, *The Father's Role*. New York: John Wiley, 1986.
44. LeBoyer's Babies, *Science News*, January 22, 1977.
45. Lidz, Theodore, *The Person: His and Her Development Throughout the Life Cycle*. (2nd ed.) New York: Basic Books, 1983.
46. Lubic, Ruth, Developing Maternity Services Women Will Trust, *American Journal of Nursing*, 75, no. 10 (1975), 1685–1688.
47. Lynn, David, *The Father: His Role in Child Development*. Monterey, CA: Brooks/Cole Publishing, 1974.
48. Messer, Alfred, *The Individual in His Family: An Adaptational Study*. Springfield, IL: Charles C Thomas, 1970.
49. Minuchin, Salvador, *Family Kaleidoscope*. Cambridge, MA: Harvard University Press, 1984.
50. Moshman, David, John Glover, and Roger Bruning, *Developmental Psychology*. Boston: Little, Brown, 1987.
51. Murphy, Susan, Family Study and Nursing Research, *Image*, 18, no. 4 (1986), 170–173.
52. Obrzut, Lee, Expectant Father's Perceptions of Fathering, *American Journal of Nursing*, 76, no. 9 (1976), 1440–1442.
53. Otto, H. A., Criteria for Assessing Family Strengths, *Canada's Mental Health*, 6 (1966), 257.
54. Petze, C. Health Promotion for the Well Family, *Nursing Clinics of North America*, 19, no. 2 (1984), 229–237.
55. Perdue, B., J. Horowitz, and F. Herz, Mothering, *Nursing Clinics of North America*, 12, no. 3 (1977), 491–502.
56. Plumey, Jacqueline Hornor, *Successful Adoption*. New York: Harmony Books, 1982.
57. Portrait of Divorce in America, *Newsweek* (February 2, 1987), p. 78.
58. Rising, Sharon, The Fourth Stage of Labor: Family Reintegration, *American Journal of Nursing*, 74, no. 5 (1974), 870 ff.
59. Robbins, Margaret, and Thomas Schacht, Family Hierarchies, *American Journal of Nursing*, 82, no. 2 (1982), 284–286.
60. Roberts, C., and S. Feetham, Assessing Family Functioning Across Three Areas of Relationships, *Nursing Research*, 31, no. 4 (1982), 231–235.
61. Rosenthal, Kristine, and Harry Keshet, *Fathers without Partners*. Totowa, NJ: Rowman and Littlefield, 1981.
62. Rossi, Alice, Transition to Parenthood, *Journal of Marriage and Family*, 30 (1968), 26–39.
63. ———, Transition to Parenthood, in *Human Life Cycle*, ed. Wm. Sze. New York: Jason Aronson, 1975, pp. 515–529.
64. Rubin, Reva, Attainment of the Maternal Role, Part 1: Processes, *Nursing Research*, 16, no. 3 (1967), 237–245.
65. ———, Attainment of the Maternal Role: Part II—Models and Referrants, *Nursing Research*, 16, no. 4 (1967), 342–346.
66. Sager, Clifford, et al., *Treating the Remarried Family*. New York: Brunner/Mazel, 1983.
67. Satir, Virginia, Love, Understanding, Communication Are Vital Elements of Family Health, *Parameters*, 4, no. 3 (1979), 8–10.
68. Sawin, Margaret, Learning Through Family Clusters, *The Christian Home*, (December–February 1980–81), p. 10.
69. Schuller, Arvella, The Family Comes First, *Possibilities* (May–June, 1987), 17–28.
70. Schuster, Clara Shaw, and Shirley Smith Ashburn, *The Process of Human Development: A Holistic Life–Span Approach* (2nd ed.). Boston: Little, Brown, 1986.
71. Shaw, Nancy, Teaching Young Mothers Their Role, *Nursing Outlook*, 22, no. 11 (1974), 695–698.
72. Sklar, Kathryn, Who Is Minding the Children? *Graduate Woman*, 70, no. 2 (1982), 12–13.
73. Smilkstein, G., The Cycle of Family Function: A Conceptual Model for Family Medicine, *Family Practitioner*, 11 (1980), 223.
74. Smith, Sara, Big Families Can Be Happy, Too, *Newsweek*, January 14, 1985. 12–13.
75. Terkelson, K., Toward a Theory of the Family Life Cycle. In E. Carter and M. McGoldrich (eds.), *The Family Life Cycle: A Framework for Family Therapy*. New York: Gardner Press, 1980, pp. 21–52.
76. Thistleton, Kristin, The Abusive and Neglectful Parent: Treatment Through Parent Education, *Nursing Clinics of North America*, 12, no. 3 (1977), 513–524.
77. Toffler, Alvin, *Future Shock*. New York: Random House, 1970.
78. Toman, Walter, *Family Constellation* (3rd ed.). New York: Springer, 1976.
79. Visher, Emily, and John Visher, *Step Families: A Guide to Working with Step Parents and Step Children*. New York: Bruner/Mazel, 1979.
80. Wachtel, Ellen, and Paul Wachtel, *Family Dynamics in Individual Psychotherapy: A Guide to Clinical Strategies*. New York: The Guilford Press, 1986.
81. Ward, M., Parental Bonding in Older Child Adoptions, *Child Welfare*, 40, no. 1 (1981), 24–34.
82. Warren, Andrea, Adopting a Foreign Child, *Better Homes and Gardens*, 63, no. 10 (1985), 25–27.
83. Whall, Ann, *Family Therapy Theory for Nursing: Four Approaches*. Norwalk, CT: Appleton-Century-Crofts, 1986.
84. Williams, Dennis, Black Problems Become White, *Newsweek* (August 18, 1986), 7.
85. Wright, L., and M. Leahey, *Nurses and Families: A Guide to Family Assessment and Intervention*. Philadelphia: F.A. Davis, 1984.

5

Overview: Theories of Human Development

Study of this chapter will assist you to

1. Identify major theoretical perspectives for understanding the developing person.
2. Describe some physiological theories about aspects of the developing person.
3. Identify major psychological developmental theorists, according to their views about the developing person.
4. Compare major concepts of First, Second, and Third Force theorists.
5. Discuss ecological theory as it applies to the developing person.
6. Apply concepts from at least three theories of development in care of the client/patient.

Key Terms

Heterozygous	Superego
Homozygous	Ego Ideal
Polygenic inheritance	Conscience
Neurotransmitters	Conscious
Ecology	Preconscious
Anomie	Unconscious
System	Anxiety
Social system	One Genus Postulate
Open system	Prototaxic mode
Linkage	of experiencing
First Force	Parataxic mode
Second Force	of experiencing
Third Force	Syntaxic mode
Neo-Behaviorist	of experiencing
Shaping	Concept of anxiety
Classical conditioning	Self-system
Behavior	Mandala
Learning	Modeling
Operant conditioning	Maturational
Transfer	Learning
Positive reinforcement	Equilibration
Negative reinforcement	Assimilation
Behavior modification	Accommodation
Id	Adaptation
Instinctual forces	Schema
Pleasure principle	Phenomenal field
Ego	Self-actualization
Reality principle	

In the past, human development was considered something that just happened. Children at first were seen as little adults, only weaker and less capable. Gradually children were seen as different, not only in proportion, but in needs and characteristics. Until the twentieth century, the study of child development and advice on how to care for children was not based on the scientific method but rather on biases and folklore.

During the eighteenth century, scientific, religious, economic, and social trends combined to foster the study of child development. The "nature versus nurture" argument began: The child was considered either the product of heredity or environment. With the rise of Protestantism, which emphasized self-reliance, independence, and responsibility for self and others, adults began to feel more responsible for how the child developed into an adult. With the Industrial Revolution, the family changed from a clan-like group to the nuclear family and children became more visible and more important to their parents. In turn, parents concentrated more intensely on their offspring. Education was provided for children and teachers became important in the child's development. As the spirit of democracy filtered into the home, parents became more uncomfortable about autocratic attitudes toward and discipline of children. Eventually the science of **psychology,** *the study of human behavior*, led people to understand themselves better by learning more about child behavior. By the nineteenth century, all these forces had come together, and the study of the child was more common and systematic. Yet, the study of child development was not based on the variety or sophistication of theory that was to evolve during the twentieth century (57).

The study of development, which began with study of the child, expanded in the beginning of the twentieth century to include adolescence as a transitional period of life. In the early twentieth century, the study of the aged person began. By the midtwentieth century, as more people were living longer, the study of aging and the aged person became popular. The study of young adulthood and middle age as developmental periods is a phenomenon of the past two decades. Now in the last quarter of the twentieth century, the focus is on the study of human development through the life span.

Persons continue to develop or undergo change—physically, emotionally, cognitively, spiritually, and socially—throughout the life span. Dying is seen as the last developmental phase, the final attempt to come to terms with self, others, and life in general. The study of the changes made by the individual and the family unit throughout the life span is the focus of this book. By learning more about ourselves and others, including how people respond to surrounding influences to meet basic needs, we hope to help people become better able to meet their individual potential, and, in turn, create a better world.

Theories that are used to explain the developing person and the person's behavior use either a biological, ecological-social, or psychological basis. Although we shall focus on the psychological theories, a brief explanation of biological and ecological-social theories will be given. The psychological theories will be divided according to their emphases—behaviorism, analytic, cognitive, and humanistic. Theorists who focus on these various psychological theories have been grouped according to similarity of theories.

✔ Keep in mind that any theory explains an aspect of the person. The whole person is best understood when several theories are combined to explain the person's total development. The theories have been developed by one or several methods for studying people.

Current Biological Theories

Research on the physiological basis for behavior has gained sophistication with our advancing technology in studying the brain and nervous system, endocrine functions, and physiological responses in a variety of situations. These findings are having an impact on current beliefs about health, normality, and development. In the following discussion, theories related to genetic, biochemical, and neurophysiological factors will be briefly covered. For comprehensive study, refer to references listed at the end of the chapter (41, 49). Also, Chapter 6 discusses physiological factors that effect the person, as do Chapters 7 through 14.

Genetic Factors

Understanding of the role of genetic factors has been derived historically from studies focusing on pedigree descriptions, incidence of abnormalities in generations of families, and more recently in direct visual examination of chromosomes and biochemical analyses of genetic material and enzymatic processes (49).

The Mendelian Law of Inheritance states that a dominant gene for a trait or characteristic in at least one parent will cause, on the average, one-half of the children to inherit it. If both parents have the dominant gene, three-fourths of their children will inherit the trait. When the trait is attributed to a recessive gene, the offspring does not inherit it unless the gene was received from both parents. If the gene was received from only one parent, the offspring is not affected but will probably pass on the gene to the child (the grandchild). If the spouses are **heterozygous** for a recessive gene (*both received the same gene type from only one of their parents*), then one-fourth of the children will probably be affected. If the spouses are **homozygous** for the recessive gene (*the same gene type was received from both of their parents*), then all the children will probably inherit the trait or characteristic (41, 57).

The Mendelian law explains the occurrence of many physical traits, such as eye color or height, and may explain certain physiological characteristics as well. However, the Mendelian law does not fully explain emotional or mental development and does not cover social or spiritual development. Rather, **polygenic inheritance,** *the combination of many genes acting together to produce a behavioral characteristic,* is believed to be a factor if certain characteristics or behavioral defects occur. Environmental effects contribute to the person's development of genetic potential from the moment of conception (36, 41, 57). Environmental variable are discussed in greater detail in Chapter 2.

Biochemical Factors

Research on the relationship between biochemical factors and behavior involves the areas of neurochemistry and hormones.

Neurochemistry is implicated in some behavioral development. The amount of biogenic amines, especially the **neurotransmitters,** *chemicals involved in transfer or modulation of nerve impulses from one cell to another,* appears to be related to mood. Catecholamines, including adrenalin, noradrenaline, dopamine, and serotonin, are important neurotransmitters in the brain and are involved in such emotional states as arousal, fear, rage, pleasure motivation, exhilaration, sleep, and wakefulness (41). Such behavior, in turn, affects reactions of others, especially parents to the child, and the child's moods may affect child-rearing behavior.

Hormonal factors, based on changes in the endocrine system during stress, or endocrine system disorders, may contribute to certain behavior. Steroid hormones are increased during stress behavior, which in turn may interfere with normal developmental processes physically and cognitively (49). Research findings indicate that higher thought processes influence physiological reactions as well as the subjective experience of emotional states (40, 49).

Neurophysiological factors mediate all physiological processes and behavior via the nervous system; however, neurophysiological factors in behavior and personality development are inconclusive. Some specific motor and speech functions and various sensations in different body parts can be traced to specific brain areas. There are also large areas of the cerebral cortex that do not have localized functions (41).

Maturational Factors

The maturational view emphasizes the emergence of patterns of development of organic systems, physical structures, and motor capabilities under the influence of genetic and maturational forces. Because of an inherent predisposition of the neurological, hormonal, and skeletal-muscular systems to develop spontaneously, physiological and motor development occurs in an inevitable and sequential pattern in children throughout the world. The growth of the nervous system is critical in this maturation, unless the normal process is inhibited by severe environmental, physiological, and emotional deprivation. Gesell, Ilg, and Ames (26) did extensive longitudinal studies in a large number of individuals from birth to 16 years of age from 1922 to 1946, which was instrumental in determining developmental sequences. Research by others since then has confirmed and added to their studies (41).

Biological Deficiencies

Biological stressors such as certain kinds of foods, lack of food, medications, or lack of sleep, may change behavior and the course of development. These factors are discussed further in Chapters 6 and 12.

Current Ecological Theories

Ecology is *an emerging science that is concerned with the community and the total setting in which life and behavior occur.* A basic ecological principle is that the continuity and survival of a person depends on a deliberate balance of factors influencing the interactions between the family or person and the environment.

Family is dependent on the resources and groups in the community to survive and continue its own development as well as to nurture adequately development of offspring. Further, climate, terrain, and natural resources affect family lifestyle and development and behavior of family members. The neighborhood may adversely affect development, especially if the person is reared in a family that lives in a deteriorating neighborhood or in an area with poor schools, inadequate housing, and high crime rate. Excessively crowded housing may create stresses within the family that contribute to sleep deprivation, bickering, incest, or other abuse, which, in turn, affects developmental progress in all spheres of the person. Job loss because of a changing community, and the resultant financial problems, may affect health-care practices and nutrition and, in turn, physical growth and emotional security.

Urbanization, rapid social changes, social stressors, discrimination, unemployment, poor housing, inadequate diet and health care, poverty, feelings of **anomie** (*not being part of society*), and negative self-image all contribute to stress and developmental difficulties in the vulnerable, immature person or in one without an adequate support system (57).

Sociological variables, including family socioeconomic level and position in the community, and the prestige related to birth, race, age, cultural ties, and power roles all affect development, behavior, and adaptation of the person and family. Certain behaviors may be expected from a person because of age, sex, race, religion, or occupation. The individual may experience role conflicts and developmental problems when there are discrepancies between norms and values and the demands of age, gender, occupation, or religion (49).

Cultures vary in their definitions of normal and abnormal behavior; cross-cultural comparisons of developmental norms are difficult. Theorists in each culture describe their research findings about normal child or adult characteristics or behavior based on norms of their culture and their cultural bias. For example, cognitive impairment in the elderly is rare in cultures that revere their elderly or where people live only 20 or 30 years. What might be indicative of homosexuality in our culture, such as men embracing, is considered normal man-to-man behavior in the Arab world.

Some authors believe that minorities must be evaluated by different psychological criteria than those used for Caucasians. They cite adaptive personality traits that Afro-Americans have adopted to survive in white society (49).

Geographical moves may create many adjustments

for the person as he or she attempts to meet norms of the new community. Developmental problems or dysfunctional behavior may occur among those who migrate (49). Persons who move often as children may never form chumships or close relationships later in adulthood. However, the mobile family and individual do learn coping skills that help them adjust to unfamiliar or stressful situations.

✓ Some professionals, as well as lay people, think abnormal behavior results from individual failure. In this view, an individual's psychological problems are the result of some personal circumstance such as deficient achievement of developmental tasks, immaturity, character defect, or maladjustment (49). An alternate view is to see the individual problems as stemming from social causes. The broad economic, political, cultural, and social patterns of the nation and particular subcultures can be viewed as determinants of individual developmental responses. Then the community is the place to begin making changes if individual dysfunction is to be decreased (49). Chapters 1, 2, and 4 discuss cultural, environmental, and family variables, and Chapters 7 through 14 present the interrelationship of these variables on the person.

A Systems Perspective: General Systems Theory Applied to Behavior

General Systems Theory. First proposed by von Bertalanffy, this presents a comprehensive, holistic, and interdisciplinary view. This theory proposes that the family, individual, various social groups, and cultures are systems. Nothing is determined by a single cause or explained by a single factor (83). Nothing can be studied as a lone entity; be it the environment; various sociocultural components; political–legal, religious, educational, and other social institutions or organizations; the person, family, group, or community; or the health-care delivery organization. All have interrelating parts, and all components interact with each other (2, 7).

A **system** *is an assemblage of interdependent parts, persons, or objects that are united by some form or order into a recognizable unit and that are in equilibrium* (2, 7, 50, 83).

People satisfy their needs within social systems. The **social system** *is a group of people joined cooperatively to achieve common goals, using an organized set of practices to regulate behavior* (7). The person occupies various positions and has defined roles in the social system. The person's development is shaped by the system; in turn, people create and change social systems (2, 50). The elements or components that are common to all systems are presented in Table 5–1. A given entity is not a system unless these characteristics are present (2, 7, 50, 83).

All living organisms—every person—is an open social system. An **open system** *is characterized by the ability to exchange energy, matter, and information with the environment to evolve into higher levels of heterogeneity, organization, order and development* (2). Physically, there is a hierarchy of components such as cells and organ systems. Emotionally, there are levels of needs and feelings. Cognitively, a person has memories, knowledge, and cognitive strategies. Socially, the person is in a relative rank in a hierarchy of prestige roles such as boss, worker, adult, or child. Although internal stimuli are at work, such as those governed by the nervous and endocrine systems, outer stimuli also affect the person. The boundaries or environment—such as one's skin, the limits set by others, social status, home, and community—influence the person's needs and goal achievement. To remain healthy, the person must have feedback: The condition of the skin tells about temperature control; an emotional reaction signifies a sense of security, a job well done, or a failure; a pain signifies malfunction or injury. In turn, the person influences the external world through his or her developmental behavior. A constant exchange of energy and information must exist with the surrounding specified environment if the system is to be open, useful, and creative. If this information or energy exchange does not occur, the system becomes closed and ineffective.

Other social systems are the family; church; economic; politico-legal, educational institutions; and health care agencies.

Linkage *occurs when two systems exchange energy across their boundaries* (2). Industry, the church, or the health agency, for example, draws energy from its linkage to the family. In return, industry is willing to contribute to family welfare funds, United Fund, mental health campaigns, or ecological improvements. The church maintains its role as prime defender of family stability. The health agency sets standards of health care.

Current Psychological Theories

A number of psychological theories have been formulated to explain human development, behavior, and personality. This discussion is not meant to be exhaustive. A current model to help understand behavior and its underlying reasons and the approaches to working with people is to categorize the schools of thought (and the different theorists) under either First, Second, or Third Force theories. There are significant differences between these *different theories or schools of thought* (**Force**) in terms of their beliefs about human behavior and the perspectives from which their observations are made.

TABLE 5-1 Elements/Characteristics of a System

ELEMENT	DEFINITION/EXAMPLE
Parts	*The system's components which are interdependent units.* None can operate without the other. Change in one part affects the entire unit.
	The person as a whole system, is made up of physical, emotional, mental, spiritual, and social aspects. Physically, he/she is made up of the body systems—neurological, cardiovascular, and so on. The health agency is one part of the health care system, and it, in turn, is made up of parts: the physical plant, employees, clients, departments that give services.
Attributes	*Characteristics of the parts,* such as temperament, roles, education, age, or health of the person.
Information/Communication	*Sending of messages and feedback, the exchange of energy,* which varies with the system but is essential to achieve goals.
Boundary	*A barrier or area of demarcation that limits or keeps a system distinct from its environment* and within which information is exchanged.
	The skin of the person, home of the family, or walls of the health agency are boundaries. The boundary is not always rigid. Relatives outside the home are part of the family. The boundary may be an imaginary line, such as the feeling that comes from belonging to a certain racial or ethnic group.
Organization	*The formal or informal arrangement of parts to form a whole entity so that the organism or institution has a working order that results in established hierarchy, rules, or customs.*
	The person is organized into a physical structure, basic needs, cognitive stages, and achievement of developmental tasks. Hierarchy in the family or health agency provides organization that is based on power (ability to control others) and responsibility. Nursing care may be organized into primary or team nursing, which is a way of differentiating services. The specialization of medical practice is also a way of organizing care. Organization in an institution is also maintained by norms, roles, and customs that each member must follow.
Goals	*Purposes of or reasons for the system to exist.* Goals may be long term or short term. Goals include survival, development, and socialization of the individual member of the family, or contributions to society.
Environment	*The social and physical world outside the system, boundaries, or the community in which the system exists.*

The **First Force** *is identified with the Behaviorist and Neo-Behaviorist schools of psychology,* whose focus is the stimulus–response link. Behaviorism views the person as an object or as a technical being. Technology is viewed as no different from the human and may be viewed as superior. The **Second Force** *was originally identified with Psychoanalytic Theory, both Freudian and Neo-Freudian (NeoAnalytic), but has been expanded to include cognitive and developmental theorists.* The **Third Force** *was first identified with humanistic psychology and now includes existential and phenomenological theorists.*

Although the three Forces, and families of theorists within each Force, will be discussed separately, a theorist who is considered in one of the families may disagree with another theorist from the same family. For example, some behaviorists would disagree with B. F. Skinner on some points. Further, no theorist or group of theorists has all the answers about human behavior. Yet the theorists within one Force hold certain ideas in common about development and behavior. This classification of theorists can assist you in synthesizing and using the main ideas of several theorists who hold similar views about the person and in realizing that often theorists who sound very different in their theory may be stating basically similar concepts.

Theorists that are mentioned in the following chapters are discussed under the First, Second, and Third Forces. The discussion about theorists is not comprehensive; no effort has been made to include all theorists that fall under any of the Forces.

First Force Theory

Overview. First Force theorists are Behaviorists who adhere to stimulus–response conditioning theories. This scientific approach to the study of the person generalizes results from animal experiments to people. The **Neo-Behaviorists**—*contemporary Behav-*

ioral theorists and the theorists in this school who have changed their ideas—obtain data for laws of behavior by observing the human's behavioral response to stimuli. The person is considered in terms of component parts. The focus is on isolated, small units of behavior or parts of behavioral patterns that are objectively observed and analyzed from the perspective of nonmental, physiological associations.

View of the Human. The person is seen as an object, a reactive organism responding mechanically, automatically, involuntarily, overtly, and quantitatively to past conditioning and present situations. The person is regarded as a product of learning. The person has sensory input and, in turn, acts to reduce a need; there is a natural tendency and drive to satisfaction. The person is acted on or reinforced by the environment, which causes learning and predictable behavior (10, 34).

Because the focus is on physiological processes and identifiable aspects of the person, subjective, unobservable, unique, and inner aspects of the human are denied or dismissed as illusory. Undesirable behavior is removed from the person by **shaping,** *setting up the situation so that the person acts in a desired way and then is rewarded for the desired behavior* (10, 34, 57).

First Force Theorists

Early Theorists. Ivan Pavlov, a Russian physiologist, laid the foundations for the Behavioral School in the nineteenth century through his study of salivation and flow of digestive juices in dogs. His experiments established **classical conditioning,** *whereby an unconditioned or new stimulus is presented with a stimulus that is already known just prior to the response to the conditioned familiar stimulus. The organism learns to respond to a new stimulus in the same way it responded to a familiar stimulus.* Associations are shifted from one stimulus to another, with the same response being made to the substituted stimuli (33, 57).

John B. Watson is considered the founder of Behaviorism. His experiments showed that fears and phobias could result from classical conditioning in childhood and could, in turn, be unlearned in adulthood (36). He emphasized physiological associations and connections in understanding physiological processes.

✔ Some present-day relaxation methods used by health-care providers are based on classical conditioning. The client is trained to respond to a therapist's direction by relaxing a muscle group; music is then played while the therapist gives directions for relaxing. Later the person is able to respond automatically by relaxing when music plays (34, 36). Classical conditioning is also used in the Lamaze preparation for childbirth. Emotions are believed by Behaviorists to arise from body changes or to be learned through classical conditioning. Emotions arise in the present situation, based on past learning that is associated with the present event. For example, a person likes men with beards because he/she learned this response during childhood as a result of associating beards with a kindly bearded grandfather.

Skinner: Operant Conditioning Theory

Skinner is well known for his Operant Conditioning Theory that uses animal studies and builds on the theories of Watson and Thorndike. According to Skinner, **behavior** *is an overt response that is externally caused and is primarily controlled by its consequences.* The environmental stimuli will determine how a person alters behavior and responds to people or objects in the environment. Feelings or emotions are the accompaniments or result, not the cause of behavior. Innate or hereditary reflexes activate the internal glands and smooth muscles, but reflexive behavior accounts for little of human behavior (34, 75, 78).

Learning is *a change in the form or probability of response as a result of conditioning.* **Operant conditioning** *is the learning process whereby a response (operant) is shaped and is made more probable or frequent by reinforcement.* **Transfer** *is an increased probability of response in the future.* Responses or a set of acts are called operant because they operate on the environment and generate consequences. The important stimulus is the one immediately *following* the response, not the one preceding it. Operant conditioning occurs in most everyday activities, according to Skinner. People constantly cause others to modify their behavior by reinforcing certain behavior and ignoring other behavior. During development people learn to balance, walk, talk, play games, and handle instruments and tools because they are reinforced after performing a set of motions, thereby increasing the repetition of these motions. Social and ethical behaviors are learned as people are reinforced to continue them through their reinforcing of others for the same behaviors. Operant reinforcement improves the efficiency of behavior, whether the behavior is appropriate or inappropriate. Any attention, even if negative, reinforces response to a stimuli (34, 75, 77, 78).

Positive reinforcement *occurs when the presence of a stimulus strengthens a response;* **negative reinforcement** *occurs when withdrawal of a stimulus strengthens the tendency to behave in a certain way.* A positive reinforcer is food, water, or a smile. A negative reinforcer consists of removing painful stimuli. Skinner's theory emphasizes positive reinforcement (34, 78).

✔ Application of Skinner's theory is threefold. His

theory, when applied to clinical and classroom problems, is called *behavior modification.* When applied to courses of study, it is called *programmed learning.* When applied to correction of physiological problems, it is called *biofeedback* (41, 78). As a nurse, you may use each of these applications in client care and teaching.

Behavior modification *is the deliberate application of learning theory and conditioning, thereby structuring different social environments to teach alternate behaviors and to help the person gain control over behavior and environment.* Shaping also achieves behavioral change. **Shaping** *is the gradual modification of behavior by breaking complex behavior into small steps, and reinforcing each small step that is a closer approximation to the final desired behavior.*

✔ In behavior modification the behavior must first be reinforced each time it occurs. Reinforcement can be gradually tapered off until the behavior is learned. Behavior that has been maintained by an intermittent schedule of reinforcement or partial reinforcement is highly resistant to extinction (78). For example, the child learns to talk not only through imitation of others but because of parental approval, love, and verbal responses that serve as rewards or reinforcement.

✔ Sometimes aversive methods, for example, seclusion, are used to change behavior. The purpose is not punishment but time out, as in allowing a tantrum to run its course without accidental reinforcement and without triggering similar behavior in other people. Strategies of punishment and deprivation, which are standard techniques in child rearing, are examples of using Skinner's principles of behavior modification. Some parents do not question sending a child to bed without a meal as punishment, and parents may even be criticized by other parents if they do not spank their children for naughty behavior.

✔ Operant conditioning is used in many situations: (1) to replace undesirable behaviors of normal or developmentally disabled children; (2) to reduce abnormal or self-destructive behavior; (3) to train parents, teachers, probation officers, and nurses to be more efficient in their roles; (4) to reduce specific maladaptive behaviors such as stuttering, tics, poor hygiene, or messy eating habits; and (5) to control physical symptoms through biofeedback.

Cybernetic Principles. These take respondent and operant conditioning one step further to account for the continuous adjustment and modification necessary in learning complex, goal-directed behaviors. The learner becomes a control system between the stimulus and the response. The Cybernetic Theory of Learning suggests that learning results from the dynamic interaction between input (stimulus information), output (learner's response), and information feedback. Feedback modifies input, which, in turn, alters output.

While each of the Behaviorists' theories sheds some light on learning complex motor skills, none accounts for the higher cognitive processes. Advocates of cognitive learning principles argue that the learner's ability to organize and process task-related information systematically is the critical variable in performing complex motor behaviors. It is this ability that enables the person to interact with a dynamic environment in carrying out decision-making skills.

In order to reconcile the objectivity of behaviorism with the flexibility of cognitive principles, researchers are turning toward information-processing models of behavior. Such models address the concepts of information (in its technical sense), uncertainty, and redundancy. The amount of information that a given event generates or feeds back depends on how complex the event is and how likely or unlikely it is that the event will occur again. The amount of information that an event generates is directly proportional to its complexity and is inversely proportional to the probability of its occurrence. If an event is redundant, its uncertainty is reduced. Redundancy results in improvement, due to practice. No single theory alone can account successfully for the many complicated processes involved in the acquisition and application of complex skills. Each theory offers some guiding principles regarding learning and teaching (57).

Second Force Theory

Overview. Second Force theorists include those who adhere to Psychoanalytic, Neoanalytic, and Cognitive Learning theories. These theorists generally believe data for study about the person come from within the developing person, observation of interpersonal relationships, and knowledge of the impact of social units, norms, and laws on the person. Data from early development are used to understand present behavior and goal direction. This group of theorists studies the person more comprehensively and as a social being, using experimentation, objective observation, and self-report methods. Second Force theorists give us a helpful view of causation and provide a way of dealing with developmental and behavioral problems (49).

View of the Human. Knowledge of genetics, developmental levels, effects of internal stimuli, unconscious processes, social relationships, and environmental context are all employed to understand the person.

Reality is external and interpersonal—what people agree on. The person is a social organism with a developmental past on which to build and a level of readiness that influences or contributes to learning and behavior. The person has maturational and social needs that affect development, learning, and behavior; he/she seeks social role satisfaction and reacts to social values and symbolic processes. The person internalizes societal rules to gain approval, can understand cause and effect relationships and complex abstract issues, is capable of insight and emotions, and initiates action and makes choices. The goal of behavior is seen as reduction of symbolic or internal needs or tension (49).

The goal of developmental guidance and discipline is to help the person become an adaptive, effective social being, aware of and responsive to social reality and patterns. The person has to learn and follow socially prescribed values, customs, and norms to fit into society as an effective and well citizen. Development, learning, and behavior are also influenced strongly by the person's developmental level, personal history, cognitive processes and intellect, and intrapsychic processes (49).

Emphasis is on the person, even in the young years, understanding self and his/her behavior. Increased insight promotes development and maturation. If the person is not ready to learn or change behavior, the parent, teacher, or another acts as an external motivator or facilitator of readiness to change. Rewards are given through approval, affiliation, and various verbal and nonverbal methods. Learning and behavior change also are self-reinforcing to the person (49).

Second Force Theorists

Second Force theorists are numerous and can be divided into those with a psychodynamic perspective and those with a cognitive perspective. The *psychodynamic theory or perspective* is then divided into two groups: Psychoanalytic (Freud) and Neo-Analytic (Jung [40], Adler [58], Rank [58], Horney [35], Fromm [21], Sullivan [80], Erikson [13], and Berne [3, 5]). Freud is the Analytic theorist discussed in this section; Sullivan, Erikson, and Jung are the Neo-Analytic theorists presented. The Neo-Analytic theorists reinterpreted Freud's Psychoanalytic Theory in formulating their theories. Sullivan further developed new emphases in his Interpersonal Theory: (1) Causation of behavior was seen as the result of dyad (mother–child) relationships, and (2) development continued into adulthood. Erikson, in his Epigenetic Theory, expanded understanding of normal developmental stages and tasks through the life span, emphasized sociocultural influences to a greater degree, and saw the person as capable of emotional growth throughout life. Kohlberg's Theory of Moral Development is also discussed in this section.

The *cognitive theory or perspective* includes a number of theorists. Some have combined or modified concepts from behavioral and psychodynamic theories with an emphasis on cognitive processes to learn adaptive, satisfying behavior and to gain control over personal life. Such theorists are A. Bandura (Social Learning Theory) (4) and J. Piaget (Theory of Cognitive Development) (62–64).

In addition to the Second Force theorists who emphasize that people develop in sequential stages, other current "stage" theorists are George Vaillant (82), Roger Gould (29), Gail Sheehy (73), and Daniel Levinson (48). Their concepts and theories are referred to in Chapters 12 and 13, on young adulthood and middle age.

Psychodynamic Perspective. The psychodynamic perspective is concerned with the inner and unconscious processes of the person—drives, needs, motivations, feelings, and conflicts. Past developmental experiences are important in the causation of behavior and for achieving present developmental tasks and maturity. Most of the Neo-Analytic theorists have paid little attention to biology. Because thoughts and feelings are not directly observable, these theorists infer them from overt behavior (49).

Freud: Psychoanalytic Theory. Sigmund Freud, a Viennese neurologist, developed Psychoanalytic Theory, the first psychological theory to include a fully developed explanation of abnormal behavior. He gave biological factors little emphasis but used the medical model of emphasizing pathology and symptoms.

Freud's theory of personality seems complicated because it incorporates many interlocking factors. Major components are psychic determinism; psychic structures of id, ego, and superego; primary and secondary process thinking; the conscious-unconscious continuum; libido or psychic energy; behavior; anxiety and defense mechanisms; and psychosexual development. Some of his theory will be discussed here and referred to in the chapters on childhood.

The psychic structures of the person are id, ego, and superego. **Id** is *the structure of personality that is an unorganized reservoir of psychic energy* and furnishes energy for the operation of the other two structures, the ego and superego. The *id*, present at birth, discharges tension and consists of **instinctual forces,** *biological drives and impulses that must be satisfied for survival*. The id operates on the **pleasure principle,** *seeking immediate gratification and avoidance of discomfort* (18).

The **ego** is *the part of the personality that establishes relations with the environment through conscious perception, feeling, and action and serves to control impulses* *from id and demands of superego.* The ego operates on the **Reality Principle**, *whereby external conditions are considered and immediate gratification is delayed for future gains that can be realistically achieved.* Besides mediating between the demands of the id and superego, the ego controls access of ideas to the conscious, appraises the environment and external reality, uses various mechanisms to help the person feel safe emotionally, and guides the person to acceptable behavior. The ego also directs motor and cognitive functions (18).

Superego is the third personality structure to be formed, beginning in the preschool years. *It represents internalized moral code, rules, and norms of society, which restrain expression of instinctual drives in the person and prevent disruption of society.* The superego is not necessarily an accurate representation of cultural norms and parental prohibitions, but it is the child's interpretation of these norms and prohibitions. The superego, if well internalized, is active in directing the person's thoughts, feelings, and actions. The superego is made up of two systems: the ego ideal and the conscience. The **ego ideal** *corresponds to those aspects the parents feel are morally good and behavior or achievements to which the person aspires.* The **conscience** *corresponds to those aspects considered morally bad and is responsible for guilt feelings.* The superego can either reward or punish the ego or person's consciousness; the restrictions and fears stemming from the superego may be unrealistic and rigid (20, 49).

These three systems operate and interact as the structure of personality that Freud described in the conscious-unconscious continuum. Id is unconscious; ego and superego are both conscious and unconscious (20).

The **conscious** includes *all aspects of mental life that are currently in awareness or easily remembered.* The **preconscious** is *the element of mental life that can be remembered with help but is not currently at the level of awareness.* **Unconsciousness materials** are *those thoughts, feelings, actions, experiences, and dreams that are not remembered, are very difficult to bring into consciousness, and are not recognized if one is told of them.* The existence of the unconscious is inferred from behavior. Psychic energy is channeled by conscious and unconscious forces that are not always in harmony. The greater the degree of intrapsychic conflict, the greater the likelihood that mental events remain unconscious. The greater the unconscious conflict, the greater the vulnerability to anxiety (16, 20).

Anxiety is *the response of tension or dread to perceived or anticipated danger or stress and is the primary motivation for behavior.* There are two types of anxiety-provoking situations. Anxiety may be caused by excessive stimulation that the person cannot handle, of which birth is the prototype experience. Anxiety may also rise from intrapsychic or unconscious conflicts, unacceptable wishes, unknown or anticipated events, superego inhibitions and taboos, and threatened loss of self-image. If anxiety cannot be managed by direct action or coping strategies, the ego initiates unconscious defenses by warding off awareness of the conflict, to keep the material unconscious, to lessen discomfort, and to maintain the self-image. Because everyone experiences psychological danger, the use of defense mechanisms clearly is not a special characteristic of maladaptive behavior. Such mechanisms are used by all people, either singly or in combination, at one time or another, and are considered adaptive (17, 19, 49). Commonly used ego adaptive (defense) mechanisms are described throughout the text in relation to the developmental era during which they arise.

Freud proposed five stages of psychosexual development and contended that personality was formed by age 5 years (16, 49). The following stages in psychosexual development, each resolved in turn, are referred to throughout the text.

1. *The oral stage.* During the first year of life, satisfaction is obtained primarily through the erogenous zone of the mouth. Security is the greatest need. Pleasure comes through eating and sucking. Weaning is a major conflict in this period.
2. *The anal stage.* For the second and third years of life, the anus is the site of tension and sensual gratification. Excretory processes, retentive (holding back) and expulsive (forcing out), are experienced as pleasurable, particularly as these functions come under the child's control.
3. *The phallic stage.* In the fourth and fifth years energy is centered in the genital region. Masturbation, fantasy, play activities, experimentation with peers, and questioning of adults about sexual topics are indicative behaviors. The stage is labeled *phallic* because the penis is presumed to be the main object of interest: to the little girl who is envious (according to Freud), or to the little boy who is constantly fearing castration for unconscious desires to experience sexual gratification with mother. This represents the major conflict and has been termed the *Oedipal Complex.* Resolution occurs when the child identifies with the parent of the same sex.
4. *The latency period.* After about the sixth year, the child's sexual urges are dormant until their reawakening at puberty. During this period energy is channeled into school, home, and organizational activities, hobbies, and relationships with peers.
5. *The genital stage.* At puberty, the adolescent becomes sexually mature and energy is centered again on the genital area.

Freud's ideas about psychosexual development are undoubtedly the most controversial aspect of his theory. Although many theorists agree that childhood experiences are very important in personality development, many reject Freud's assertions about childhood sexuality and the Victorian and stereotyped ideas about men and women (49).

Psychoanalytic Theory has been criticized for many reasons (see an objective critique by Graves [30]). In contrast, Greenberg and Fisher have reviewed the thousands of scientific studies done worldwide to check the validity of Freud's ideas and have found that Freud's model of personality development and behavior is supported by other studies (31). His theory continues to influence twentieth-century thought and research, especially in western cultures, in relation to development and therapy of the ill person (32).

Major Neo-Analytic Theorists. Neo-Freudians or Neo-Analysts follow Freud's theory in general but disagree with or have modified some of the original propositions. They maintain the medical model and share the view of intrapsychic determinism as the basis for external behavior. Some take into account the social and cultural context in which the person lives. Harry Stack Sullivan (80), Erik Erikson (13), and Carl Jung (38–40) will now be described briefly; Sullivan and Erikson are referred to throughout the text.

Sullivan: Interpersonal Theory of Psychiatry

Harry Stack Sullivan (80) formulated the Interpersonal Theory of Psychiatry. The theory focus is on relationships between and among people, in contrast to Freud's emphasis on intrapsychic sexual phenomena and Erikson's focus on social aspects. Experiences in major life events are the result of either positive or negative interpersonal relationships. Personality development is largely the result of the mother–child relationship, childhood experiences, and interpersonal encounters. There are two basic needs: satisfaction (biological needs) and security (emotional and social needs). Biological and interpersonal needs are interrelated. How biological needs are met in the interpersonal situation will determine sense of satisfaction and security and will provide avoidance of anxiety (80).

Sullivan utilized the following biological principles to understand the person's development:

1. *Principle of communal existence:* A living organism cannot be separated from the necessary environment to survive. For example, the embryo must have the correct intrauterine environment to live and the baby must have love and human contact to become socialized or human.

2. *Principle of functional activity:* Functional or physiological activities and processes affect the person's interaction with the environment.
3. *Principle of organization:* The person is systematically arranged physically and emotionally and within societies, and this organization enables function (80).

An important principle for the study and care of people is the **One Genus Postulate** *that states we are all more simply human than otherwise—hence more similar than different in basic needs, development, and in the meaning of our behavior* (80).

Sullivan postulated that people experience events in the following three modes. The differences between these modes are due to the crucial role of language in experience and development (80) and are described further in Chapters 7, 9, and 10.

1. **Prototaxic Mode of Experiencing** *refers to experiences that occur in infancy before language symbols are acquired or to the first time a person experiences an event that is difficult to describe in words.*
2. **Parataxic Mode of Experiencing** *refers to experiences characterized by symbols used in a private (autistic) way and encompasses fantasy, magical thinking, and lack of cause and effect thinking that is seen in children and adults.*
3. **Syntaxic Mode of Experiencing** *refers to experiences of preadolescence, adolescence, and adulthood characterized by consensual validation, whereby persons communicate with each other using language or symbols that are mutually understood.* This mode of experiencing begins during the chum stage in the school-age child or thereafter.

Sullivan implied that the need to avoid anxiety along with the need to gratify basic needs are the primary motivations for behavior. His **Concept of Anxiety** *states that anxiety has its origin in the prolonged dependency of infancy, urgency of biological and emotional needs, and how the mothering person meets those needs. Anxiety is the result of uncomfortable interpersonal relationships, is the chief disruptive force in interpersonal relationships, is contagious through empathic feelings, and can be relieved by being in a secure interpersonal relationship* (80).

The **self-system** *is the internal organization of experiences that exists to defend against anxiety and to secure necessary security.* One aspect of the self-system is known as *good-me, bad-me, and not-me* (80), which refers to feelings about the self that begin to form in infancy. Sullivan's developmental stages are described in Chapters 7 through 14, in relation to each developmental era.

Erikson: Epigenetic Theory of Personality Development

Erik Erikson (13) formulated the Epigenetic Theory, based on the principle of the unfolding embryo: Anything that grows has a ground plan out of which parts arise. Each part has its time of special ascendancy until all parts have arisen to form a functional whole. Thus, each stage of development is the base for the next stage.

His theory explains step-by-step unfolding of emotional development and social characteristics during encounters with the environment. Erikson's psychosexual theory enlarges on Psychoanalytic Theory because it (1) is not limited to historical era, specific culture, or personality types, (2) encompasses development through the life span and is universal to all people, and (3) acknowledges that society, as well as heredity and childhood experiences, influences the person's development (13).

The following are basic principles of his theory, based on cross-cultural studies.

1. Each phase has a specific developmental task that is to be achieved or solved. These tasks describe the order and sequence of human development and the conditions necessary to accomplish these, but actual accomplishment is done at an individual pace, tempo, and intensity.
2. Each psychosexual stage of development is a developmental crisis because there is a radical change in the person's perspective, shift in energy, and an increased emotional vulnerability. During this peak time the potential in the personality comes in contact with the whole environment and the person has some degree of success in solving the crucial developmental task of the specific era. How the person copes with the task and crisis depends on previous developmental strengths and weaknesses.
3. The potential inherent in each person evolves if given adequate chance to survive and grow. Anything that distorts the environment essential for development interferes with evolvement of the person. Society attempts to safeguard and encourage the proper rate and sequence of the unfolding of human potential so that humanity is maintained.
4. Each developmental task is redeveloped, reworked, and redefined in subsequent stages. Potential for further development always exists.
5. Internal organization is central to development. Maturity increases as the tasks of each era are accomplished, at least in part, in proper order (13).

Erikson proposed eight stages of development and described the developmental task of crisis for each stage. These are described in Chapters 7 through 14, in relation to each developmental era.

Jung's Theory

Carl Jung (14, 40, 79), another Neo-Analytic theorist, proposed the following assumptions about personality structure:

1. The **ego** or **consciousness** includes *awareness of self and the external world.*
2. The **persona** is the *image or mask presented to the outer world*, depending on the roles of the person.
3. The **shadow** consists of *traits and feelings that cannot be admitted to the self;* it is the opposite of ego or self-image.
4. The **anima** and **animus** in the personality *refer to the characteristics traditionally considered feminine and masculine.* Each person has both characteristics or is androgynous or bisexual with the feminine, nurturing, feeling side and the masculine, logical, assertive side. Socialization forces the person to overemphasize gender characteristics so that the opposite aspect of the person is not usually fully developed.
5. The unconscious is made up of two layers:
   (a) The **personal unconscious** is unique, *contains all the repressed tendencies and feelings that build over the lifetime,* and *includes the shadow and some of the anima or animus.*
   (b) The **collective unconscious** is *inherited and shared by all humankind and is made up of archetypes, or innate energy forces and organizing tendencies.* Archetype images are unknowable and are found in myths, art, dreams, and fantasies throughout the world and include the image of Earth Mother, Wise Old Man, death, the witch, rebirth, God. The archetypes influence the nature and growth of other parts of the personality. These are essentially unknowable, like instincts or innate perceptual tendencies.
6. Self is the most important archetype, our unconscious centeredness, wholeness, and meaning. It is an inner urge to balance and reconcile the opposing aspects of our personalities, represented in drawings of **mandalas,** *figures in which all sides are perfectly balanced around a center point.*
7. **Individuation** is the unattainable goal pursued by the self, which *involves finding the unique way, achieving a measure of psychic balance while separating self from societal conformity* to goals and values.
8. There are two basic personality types or tendencies:
   (a) **Introversion** refers to being *inner-reflective, caught up in one's inner state, fears, hopes and feelings.* The introvert hesitates in relationships, is more secure in his/her inner world,

and takes pleasure in activities that can be done alone.
(b) The **extrovert** confidently *engages in direct action and starts interactions with others.* The extrovert moves outward toward the world and prefers activities with people (14, 40, 79).

To Jung, life is a series of periods identified by different energy uses. Early childhood years were not emphasized in this developmental theory. The first period, until age 35 or 40, is a time of outward expansion. Maturational forces direct the growth of the ego and unfolding of capacities. After age 40, the person undergoes a transformation and looks for meaning in his activities. With increasing age, there is increasing reflection. Late thirties and early forties were seen as important in life transition; this was seen as a time when energy from youthful interests was channeled to cultural and spiritual pursuits (40). Jung's theory will be referred to again in the chapters on adulthood.

The Cognitive Perspective

Cognitive psychology deals with the person as an information processor and problem solver. The cognitive perspective is concerned with internal processes but emphasizes how people attempt to acquire, interpret, and use information to solve life's problems and to remain normal or healthy. It emphasizes conscious processes, present thoughts, and problem-solving strategies. The cognitive perspective has grown out of new directions in learning and psychodynamic theories. Some present-day learning theorists are becoming increasingly interested in what goes on within the person between the application of a stimulus and the response, and some current psychodynamic theorists are focusing on thinking and problem solving as well as on feelings and emotions. Relationships among emotions, motivations, and cognitive processes are being studied. Overlap between the cognitive perspective and other approaches is becoming more evident (41, 57).

Bandura: Social Learning Theory

Albert Bandura's Social Learning Theory (4) states that learning occurs without reinforcement, conditioning, or trial-and-error behavior since people can think and anticipate consequences of behavior and act accordingly. This theory emphasizes (1) the importance of vicarious, symbolic, and self-regulatory processes in psychological functioning; and (2) the capacity of the person to use symbols, represent events, analyze conscious experience, communicate with others at any distance in time and space, and plan, create, imagine, and engage in foresightful action. The person does not simply react to external forces: He/she selects, organizes, and transforms impinging stimuli and thus exercises some influence over personal behavior. There is a continuous, reciprocal interaction between cognitive, behavioral, and environmental determinants (4).

Human nature is characterized as a vast potentiality that can be fashioned by direct and vicarious experience into a variety of forms of development and behavior, within biological limits. The level of psychological and physiological development restricts what can be acquired at any given time (4).

The person may be motivated by ideas or fantasies of future consequences or by personal goal-setting behavior. If the person wants to accomplish a certain goal, and there are distractions from the task, the person visualizes how he/she will feel when the goal is attained. People respond evaluatively to their own behavior and tend to persist until the behavior or performance meets the goal (4).

Bandura proposes that learning occurs through **modeling,** *imitation of another's behavior.* According to his theory, much of our daily behavior is learned by modeling. Imitation is one of the most effective forms of learning. Babies learn to speak by imitating the sounds of their parents; older children learn a number of behaviors by watching the teacher, parent, or peers. People learn how to be normal or abnormal. Maladaptive behavior arises from modeling when the child imitates abnormal parental behavior. Bandura's research also shows the power of watching television on people's behavior, and that for some people the model of aggressive behavior will cause later acting-out behavior (4). This is discussed further in Chapter 10.

Piaget: Theory of Cognitive Development

Jean Piaget (62–64) formulated the Theory of Cognitive Development. The bulk of his research was concerned with the child's thinking at particular periods of life and with studying differences among well children of a specific age. A great amount of empirical data was used in developing the theory. He believed that development is neither **maturational,** an unfolding of the innate growth process, nor **learning,** an accumulation of experiences. Rather, development is an active process resulting from **equilibration,** an internal force that is set in motion to organize thinking when the child's belief system develops sufficiently to contain self-contradictions (62–64).

Four factors interact within the person to stimulate mental development:

1. Maturation of the nervous and endocrine systems which provides physical capabilities.
2. Experience involving action, with a consequent discovery of properties of objects.
3. Social interaction with opportunity to observe a wide variety of behaviors, gain direct instruction, and to receive feedback about individual performance.
4. An internal self-regulation mechanism that responds to environmental stimuli (64).

Intelligence is an adaptive process by which the person modifies and structures the environment to fit personal needs and also modifies self in response to environmental demands.

By interaction with the environment, the person constructs reality by assimilation, accommodation, and adaptation. **Assimilation** *is taking new and content experiences into the mind or cognitive structure.* **Accommodation** *is the revising, realigning, and readjusting of the cognitive structure to take into account the new content.* **Adaptation** *is the change that results from the first two processes.* Piaget emphasizes the innate, inborn processes of the person as the essential force to start the process of equilibration or cognitive growth. Cognitive development proceeds from motor activity to interaction with the wider social world, and finally to abstract ideas. Development is seen as solidly rooted in what already exists, and it displays a continuity with the past. Adaptations do not develop in isolation; all form a coherent pattern so that the totality of biological life is adapted to its environment. The theory focuses on development of intellectual capacities with little reference to emotional or social development (62–64, 84).

The thinking process is explained by schematic mental structures of pictures formed in response to stimuli. A **schema** *is a cognitive structure, a complex concept encompassing both motor behavior and internalized thought processes. A schema involves movement of the eyeballs, paying attention, and the mental picture that is formed as a result of the sensory process.* Thinking eventually involves using combinations of mental pictures, forming concepts, internalizing use of language or subvocal speech, drawing implications, and making judgments. When these internal actions become integrated into a coherent, logical system, they are considered logical operations. The schemata that are developed and the specific levels of function are unique to each person and in turn structure future learning. Learning is determined by (1) what is observed, (2) whether new information is fit into old schematic accurately or in a distorted way, and (3) how much increase in competence results from the encounter or experience (62–64).

Piaget divided human development into four periods: Sensorimotor, Preoperational, Concrete Operations, and Formal Operations. In each stage the person demonstrates interpretation and use of the environment through certain behavior patterns. He/she incorporates and restructures the previous stage and refines ability to perceive and understand. Suggested ages for each stage are indicated, but innate intellectual ability and environmental factors may cause variation. These periods are discussed with development of the infant, toddler, preschooler, schoolchild, and adolescent.

Kohlberg: Theory of Moral Development

Lawrence Kohlberg formulated a Theory of Moral Development. Because moral development is related to cognitive and emotional development as well as to societal values and norms and is divided into stages by Kohlberg, he can be identified with Second Force theorists (44, 46).

Moral reasoning focuses on ten universal values: punishment, property, roles and concerns related to affection, roles and concerns related to authority, law, life, liberty, distribution of justice, truth, and sexual behavior. A conflict between two or more of these universal values necessitates a moral choice and its subsequent justification by the individual, requiring systematic problem solving and other cognitive capabilities.

↙ Development of moral judgment is stimulated whenever (1) the educational process intentionally creates cognitive conflict and disequilibrium so that the person can work through inadequate modes of thinking, (2) when the person has opportunity for group discussion of values and can participate in group decision making about moral issues, and (3) the person has opportunity to assume responsibility for the consequences of behavior (45).

Kohlberg theorized that a person's moral reasoning process and behavior develop through six stages. Each stage is derived from a prior stage and is the basis for the next stage. *Each moral stage is based or dependent on the reason for behavior* and shows an organized system of thought by which the person is consistent in the level of moral judgment. The person is considered to be in a specific stage when the same level of reason for action is given at least half the time. More advanced logical thinking is needed for each successive moral stage. One criterion of moral maturity, the ability to decide autonomously what is right and caring, is lacking in the Preconventional and Conventional Levels because in each level the person is following the commands of authority figures. If the person's cognitive stage is at Concrete Operations, according to Piaget, the person is limited to the Preconventional or Conventional Levels of moral reasoning. Even the person in Formal Opera-

TABLE 5–2. Progression of Moral Development

LEVEL	STAGE
Preconventional: *The person is responsive to cultural rules of labels of good and bad, right or wrong. Externally established rules determine right or wrong actions.*	I. *Punishment and Obedient Orientation* Fear of punishment, not respect for authority, is the reason for decisions, behavior, and conformity. Good and bad are defined in terms of physical consequences to the self from parental, adult, or authority figures. The person defers to superior power or prestige of the person who dictates rules. (*"I'll do something because you tell me, and to avoid getting punished."*) Average age: Toddler to 7 years. II. *Instrumental Relativist Orientation* Conformity is based on egocentricity and narcissistic needs. The person's decisions and behavior are usually based on what provides satisfaction, out of concern for self: Something is done to get something in return. Occasionally the person does something to please another for pragmatic reasons. There is no feeling of justice, loyalty, or gratitude. These concepts are expressed physically. (*"I'll do something if I get something for it or because it pleases you."*) Average age: Preschooler through school age.
Conventional: *The person is concerned with maintaining expectations of the family, group, nation, or society. A sense of guilt has developed and affects behavior. The person values conformity, loyalty, and active maintenance of social order and control. Conformity means good behavior or what pleases or helps another and is approved.*	III. *Interpersonal Concordance Orientation* A. Decisions and behavior are based on concerns about others' reactions; the person wants others' approval or a reward. The person has moved from egocentricity to consideration of others as a basis for behavior. Behavior is judged by the person's intentions. (*"I'll do something because it will please you or because it is expected."*) B. An empathic response, based on understanding of how another person feels, is a determinant for decisions and behavior. (*"I'll do something because I know how it feels to be without; I can put myself in your shoes."*) Average age: School age through adulthood. Most American women are found to be in this stage. IV. *Law-and-Order Orientation* The person wants established rules from authorities, and the reason for decisions and behavior is that social and sexual rules and traditions demand the response. The person obeys the law just because it is the law or out of respect for authority and underlying morality of the law. The law takes precedent over personal wishes, good intentions, and conformity to group stereotypes. (*"I'll do something because it's the law and my duty."*) Average age: Adolescence and adulthood. Most men are found in this stage; 80 percent of adults do not move past this stage.
Postconventional: *The person lives autonomously; defines moral values and principles that are distinct from personal identification with group values. He/she lives according to principles that are universally agreed on and that the person considers appropriate for life.*	V. *Social Contract Legalistic Orientation* The social rules are not the sole basis for decisions and behavior because the person believes a higher moral principle applies, such as equality, justice, or due process. The person defines right actions in terms of general individual rights and standards that have been agreed on by the whole society but is aware of relativistic nature of values and opinions. The person believes laws can be changed as people's needs change. The person utilizes freedom of choice in living up to higher principles but believes the way to make changes is through the system. Outside the legal realm, free agreement and contract are the binding elements of obligation. (*"I'll do something because it is morally and legally right, even if it isn't popular with the group."*) Average age: Middle-age or older adult. Only 20 percent, or less, of Americans achieve this stage. VI. *Universal Ethical Principle Orientation* Decisions and behavior are based on internalized rules, on conscience rather than on social laws, and on self-chosen ethical and abstract principles that are universal, comprehensive, and consistent. The rules are not concrete moral rules but instead

TABLE 5–2. Continued

encompass the Golden rule, justice, reciprocity, and equality of human rights, and respect for the dignity of human beings as individual persons. Human life is inviolable. The person believes there is a higher order than social order, has a clear concept of civil disobedience, and will use self as an example to right a wrong. The person accepts injustice, pain, and death as an integral part of existence but works to minimize injustice and pain for others. ("*I'll do something because it is morally, ethically, and spiritually right, even if it is illegal and I get punished, and even if no one else participates in the act.*")
Average age: Middle-age or older adult. Few people attain or maintain this stage. Examples of this stage are seen in times of crisis or extreme situations.

---

tions may not be beyond the Conventional Level of moral maturity. Kohlberg found that 50 percent of late adolescents and adults are capable of Formal Operations thinking, but only 10 percent of these adults demonstrated the Post-Conventional Level in stages 5 and 6. Thus the person moves through stages, but few people progress through all six stages. Table 5–2 shows the three levels and six stages (45). Moral development will be discussed in relation to each developmental era in Chapters 7 through 14.

Third Force Theory

Overview. Third Force theorists include those who are proponents of Humanistic Psychology, Existential Psychology, and Phenomenological Psychology. Humanistic and existential psychologies acknowledge the dynamic aspect of the person but emphasize the impact of environment to a greater degree. They seek to answer the following questions: What are the possibilities of the person? From these possibilities, what is an optimum state for the person? Under what conditions is this state most likely to be reached? These disciplines strive to maximize the individuality and developmental potential of the person (12, 52, 54).

Because all behavior is considered a function of the person's perceptions, data for study of the person are subjective and come from self-reports, including (1) feelings at the moment about self and the experience, (2) meaning of the experience, and (3) personal values, needs, attitudes, beliefs, behavioral norms, expectations. Perception is synonymous with meaning. The person has many components—physical, physiological, cognitive, emotional, spiritual, cultural, social, and familial—and cannot be adequately understood if studied by individual components. The person is also affected by many variables, both objective and subjective. All behavior is pertinent to and a product of the phenomenal or perceptual field of the person at the moment of action. The **phenomenal field** *is the frame of reference and the universe as experienced by the person at the specific moment (the existential condition)* (10, 12, 28, 53).

View of the Human. The person is viewed as an unique whole individual, in dynamic interaction with the environment, and in the process of becoming. In addition, the person is seen as holistic, more than the sum of the parts. The person is constantly growing, changing, expanding perceptual processes, learning, developing potential, and gaining insights. Every experience affects the person, depending on the perceptions. The person is never quite the same as he/she was even an hour or day earlier. The goals of the creative being are growth, feeling adequate, and reaching the potential. The person is active in pursuing these goals. Basic needs are the maintenance and enhancement of the self-concept and a sense of adequacy and self-actualization (10, 12, 28, 51, 53).

Reality is internal; the person's reality is the perception of the event rather than the actual event itself. No two people will view a situation in exactly the same way. Various factors affect perception (1) the sensory apparatus and central nervous system of the person, (2) time for observation, (3) opportunities available to experience events, (4) the external environment, (5) interpersonal relationships, and (6) self-concept. What is most important to the person is what is happening to the self at a given time. The person is aware of social values and norms but lives out those values and norms in a way that have been uniquely and personally defined (12, 53).

Perceptions are crucial in influencing behavior. Of all the perceptions that exist for the person, none is more important than those held about the self and the personal meaning and belief related to a situation. Self-concept is learned as a consequence of meaningful interactions with others and the world and has a high degree of stability at its core, changing only with time and opportunity to try new perceptions of self.

The truly adequate person sees self (and others)

as having dignity, integrity, worth, and importance. Only with a positive view of self can the person risk trying the untried or accepting the undefined situation. The person can become self-actualized only through the experience of being treated as an adequate person by significant others. This person is open to all experiences, develops trust in self, and dares to recognize feelings, live life fully, and express uniqueness. The person feels a sense of oneness with other people, depending on the nature of previous contacts.

Third Force Theorists. The theorists of the Third Force include the humanists Abraham Maslow (Theory of Motivation and Hierarchy of Needs) (51–53) and Carl Rogers (Theory on Self-Concept and Client-Centered Therapy) (68–70). Other humanistic theorists include Arthur Combs (12), Donald Snygg (12), Sidney Jourard (37), and Rollo May (54). Humanistic nursing as a framework has been developed by Josephine Paterson and Loretta Zderad (60). Although found as a thread in other nursing models, including Neuman's Health Care Systems Model (59), humanism is the basis for the views of Hildegard Peplau (61), Dorothy Johnson (66), and Martha Rogers (71). Only Maslow will be discussed in this chapter. References at the end of the chapter give information on other theorists who have contributed to nursing.

Maslow: Theory of Motivation and Hierarchy of Needs. Abraham Maslow originated the term *Third Force* to show the perspectives of creativity and potential for freedom in the person, aspects he felt were neglected in psychoanalytic and learning theories. Maslow studied normal people and mental health (28), in contrast to other developmental and personality theorists. One of his most important concepts is **self-actualization,** *the tendency to develop potentialities and become a better person*, and the need to help the person achieve the sense of self-direction implicit in self-actualization. Implicit in this concept is that people are not static but are always in the process of becoming different and better (28, 51–53).

✔ The needs that motivate self-actualization can be represented in a hierarchy of relative order and predominance. The basic needs, always a consideration in patient/client care, are as follows (28, 51–53):

1. *Physiological needs* include oxygen, water, food, temperature control, elimination, shelter, exercise, sleep, sensory stimulation, and sexual activity. These needs cease to exist as active means of determining behavior when satisfied, re-emerging only if they are blocked or frustrated.

2. *Safety needs* include shelter, security, dependency, consistency, stability, fairness, structure, order, and limits; maintenance of predictable environment; protection from immediate or future danger to physical well-being; freedom from fear, anxiety, and chaos; and a certain amount of routine.

3. *Love and belonging needs* derive from societal factors and include identification with significant others, acceptance, love, and affection from and affiliation with others; recognition and approval; companionship; and group interactions. Love is not synonymous with sexual needs, but sexual needs may be motivated by a need for love and affection.

4. *Self-esteem and esteem from others* are concerned with being a worthwhile person and an awareness of individuality. Included are needs for self-respect; respect for and from others; awareness of personal uniqueness; a sense of confidence, dignity, achievement, competence, independence, prestige, status, and success; and recognition from others for accomplishments.

5. *Self-actualization needs* include self-fulfillment; ongoing emotional and spiritual development; desire to attain standards of excellence; reaching individual potentialities; using talents; being productive, creative, and having peak experiences. Self-actualization involves experiencing fully, vividly, with full concentration, and without self-consciousness. The person accepts self and others and identifies with their problems.

6. *Knowledge and understanding needs* involve curiosity; a desire to know as much as possible; attraction to the mysterious, unknown, and unexplained; a desire to understand, systematize, organize, analyze, to look for relations and meanings; and a desire to construct a value system. The person who cannot meet these needs feels bored, apathetic, self-hate, depressed, and loses interest in life, self, and others.

7. *Aesthetic needs* include beauty, harmony, and order and are expressed in efforts to make the surroundings as attractive as possible, as well as in art, music, literature, dance, or other creative forms.

Maslow's study of self-actualizing people refutes Freudian Theory that the human unconscious or id is only bad or dangerous. In self-actualizing people the unconscious is creative, loving, and positive (28).

✔ Although Maslow ranked these basic human needs from lowest to highest, they do not necessarily occur in a fixed order. The physiological and safety needs (deficiency needs), however, are dominant and must be met before higher needs can be secured. Personal growth needs are those for love and belonging, self-esteem and recognition, and self-actualization. The highest needs of self-actualization, knowledge, and aesthetic expression may never be as fully gratified as those at lower levels. Individual growth and self-fulfillment are a continuing, lifelong process of becoming (28, 52). ✔ For the person to be motivated toward self-actualization, there must be freedom to speak, to pursue creative potential, and to inquire; an atmosphere of justice, honesty, fairness, and order; and environmental stimulation and challenge (28). Many have trouble moving toward self-actualization because of the environment in which they live. For example, socialization practices may hinder women in using fully their intellectual abilities. Men may be inhibited from expressing emotions of tenderness, love, or need of others by cultural norms. Deprivation of growth needs results in feelings of despair and depression and a sense that life is meaningless (28, 51–53).

References

1. Almy, M., E. Chittenden, and P. Miller, *Young Children's Thinking: Studies of Some Aspects of Piaget's Theory*. New York: Teachers College Press, 1967.
2. Anderson, Ralph, and I. Carter, *Human Behavior in the Social Environment*. Chicago: Aldine, 1974.
3. Babcock, Dorothy, Transactional Analysis, *American Journal of Nursing*, 76, no. 7 (1976), 1152–1155.
4. Bandura, Albert, *Social Learning Theory*. Morristown, N.J.: General Learning Press, 1971.
5. Berne, Eric, *Transactional Analysis in Psychotherapy*. New York: Grove press, 1961.
6. Bernie, Rosemarian, and Wilbert Fordyce, *Behavior Modification and the Nursing Process*. St. Louis, Mo.: C. V. Mosby, 1973.
7. Berrien, Kenneth, *General and Social Systems*. New Brunswick, N.J.: Rutgers University Press, 1968.
8. Buhler, Charlotte, The Course of Human Life as a Psychological Problem, *Human Development*, 11 (1968), 184–200.
9. Carruth, Beatrice, Modifying Behavior through Social Learning, *American Journal of Nursing*, 76, no. 11 (1976), 1084–1086.
10. Carter, Susan, The Nurse Educator: Humanist or Behaviorist? *Nursing Outlook*, 26, no. 9 (1978), 554–557.
11. Claggett, M. S., Anorexia Nervosa: A Behavioral Approach, *American Journal of Nursing*, 80 (1980), 1471–1472.
12. Combs, Arthur, and Donald Snygg, *Individual Behavior: A Perceptual Approach to Behavior*. New York: Harper & Row, 1959.
13. Erikson, Erik, *Childhood and Society*, 2nd ed. New York: W. W. Norton, 1963.
14. Fordham, Frieda, *An Introduction to Jung's Psychology*. Baltimore: Penguin Books, 1966.
15. Freud, Anna, *The Ego and the Mechanisms of Defense*. London: Hogarth Press, 1937.
16. Freud, Sigmund, *A General Introduction to Psychoanalysis*. New York: Simon & Schuster, 1935.
17. ———, *The Problem of Anxiety*. New York: W. W. Norton, 1936.
18. ———, *Ego and the Id*. London: Hogarth Press, 1947.
19. ———, *Inhibitions, Symptoms, and Anxiety*. London: Hogarth Press, 1948.
20. ———, *Outline of Psychoanalysis*. New York: W. W. Norton, 1949.
21. Fromm, Eric, *The Art of Loving*. New York: Harper & Row, 1963.
22. Furth, H. G., and H. Wachs, *Thinking Goes to School: Piaget's Theory in Practice*. New York: Oxford University Press, 1975.
23. Gelman, David, Finding the Hidden Freud, *Newsweek*, November 30, 1981, 64–70.
24. Gesell, Arnold, *The First Five Years of Life*. New York: Macmillan, 1940.
25. Gesell, Arnold, and Frances Ilg, *The Child From Five to Ten*. New York: Harper & Brothers Publishers, 1946.
26. Gesell, Arnold, Frances Ilg, and Louise Ames, *Youth: The Years From 10 to 16*. New York: Harper & Brothers Publishers, 1956.
27. Gesell, Arnold, Frances Ilg, Louise Ames, and J. Rodell, *Infant and Child in the Culture of Today; The Guidance of Development in Home and Nursery School*. New York: Harper & Row, 1974.
28. Goble, Frank, *The Third Force: The Psychology of Abraham Maslow*. New York: Grossman, 1970.
29. Gould, R., The Phases of Adult Life: A Study in Developmental Psychology, *American Journal of Psychiatry*, 129, no. 5 (1972), 521–531.
30. Graves, Joy, Psychoanalytic Theory. A Critique, *Perspectives in Psychiatric Care*, 11, no. 3 (1973), 114–120.
31. Greenberg, Roger, and Seymour Fisher, Testing Dr. Freud, *Human Behavior*, 7, no. 9 (1978), 28–33.
32. Hartmann, Heinz, *Essays on Ego Psychology*. New York: International Universities Press, 1964.
33. Heidbreder, Edna, *Seven Psychologies*. Englewood Cliffs, N.J.: Prentice-Hall, 1961.
34. Hilgard, Ernest, and Gordon Bower, *Theories of Learning*, 4th ed. Englewood Cliffs, N.J.: Prentice-Hall, 1975.
35. Horney, Karen, *The Neurotic Personality in Our Time*. New York: W. W. Norton, 1937.
36. Jones, Franklin, Karl Garrison, and Raymond Morgan, *The Psychology of Human Development* (2nd ed.). New York: Harper & Row, 1985.
37. Jourard, Sidney, *Disclosing Man to Himself*. New York: D. Van Nostrand, 1968.

38. Jung, Carl, *Modern Man In Search of a Soul*. New York: Harcourt, Brace, and World, 1933.
39. Jung, Carl, *The Undiscovered Self* (transl. by R. F. C. Hall) New York: Mentor Books, 1958.
40. Jung, Carl, Psychological Types, in *Collected Works of Carl G. Jung*, Vol. 6, ed. G. Adler, et al. Princeton, N.J.: Princeton University Press, 1971.
41. Kaluger, George, and Merien Kaluger, *Human Development: The Span of Life* (3rd ed). St. Louis: Times Mirror/Mosby, 1984.
42. Kolhberg, Lawrence, Moral Education in Schools, *School Review*, 74 (1966), 7.
43. Kohlberg, Lawrence, A Cognitive Developmental Approach to Moral Education, *The Humanist*, 1 (November–December, 1972), 15 ff.
44. ———, *Recent Research in Moral Development*. New York: Holt, Rinehart & Winston, 1977.
45. Kohlberg, L., The Cognitive-Developmental Approach to Moral Education, in *Readings in Moral Education*, ed. Peter Scharf. Minneapolis, MN: Winston Press, 1978, pp. 36–51.
46. Kohlberg, Lawrence, and Elliot Turiel, Moral Development and Moral Education, in *Psychology and Education Practice*, ed. G. S. Lesser. Chicago: Scott, Foresman, 1971.
47. LeBow, M., Applications of Behavior Modification in Nursing Practice, in *Progress in Behavior Modification*, 2, eds. M. Hersen, R. M. Eisler, and P. M. Miller. New York: Academic Press, 1976.
48. Levinson, Daniel, *The Seasons of a Man's Life*. New York: Ballantine Books, 1978.
49. Lidz, Theodore, *The Person: His and Her Development Throughout The Life Cycle* (2nd ed.). New York: Basic Books, 1983.
50. Loomis, C. P., *Social Systems*. New York: D. Van Nostrand, 1960.
51. Maslow, Abraham, *Towards a Psychology of Being*, 2nd ed. New York: D. Van Nostrand, 1968.
52. ———, *Motivation and Personality*, 2nd ed. New York: Harper & Row, 1970.
53. ———, *The Farther Reaches of Human Nature*. New York: Viking Press, 1971.
54. May, Rollo, *Psychology and the Human Dilemma*. New York: D. Van Nostrand, 1967.
55. Middleton, Joan, Existentialist as Helper? *Canadian Psychiatric Nursing*, 20, no. 3 (1979), 7–8.
56. Morgan, J., Behavioral Treatment of Obesity: The Occupational Health Nurse's Role, *Occupational Health Nursing*, 6 (1984), 312–314.
57. Moshman, David, John Glover, and Roger Bruning, *Developmental Psychology: A Topical Approach*. Boston: Little, Brown, 1987.
58. Munroe, Ruth, *Schools of Psychoanalytic Thought*. New York: Holt, Rinehart & Winston, 1955.
59. Neuman, Betty, The Betty Neuman Health-Care Systems Model: A Total Person Approach to Patient Problems, in *Conceptual Models for Nursing Practice* (2nd ed), eds. Joan P. Riehl and Callista Roy. New York: Appleton-Century-Crofts, 1980.
60. Paterson, Josephine, and Loretta Zderad, *Humanistic Nursing*. New York: John Wiley, 1976.
61. Peplau, Hildegarde, *Interpersonal Relations in Nursing*. New York: G. P. Putnam's Sons, 1952.
62. Piaget, J., *The Origins of Intelligence in Children*. New York: W. W. Norton, 1963.
63. ———, *Six Psychological Studies*. New York: Random House, 1967.
64. Piaget, J., and B. Inhelder, *The Psychology of the Child*. New York: Basic Books, 1969.
65. Quinn, Susan, *A Mind of Her Own: The Life of Karen Horney*. New York: Summit Books, 1987.
66. Riehl, Joan, and Sister Callista Roy, Theory and Models, in *Conceptual Models for Nursing Practice* (2nd ed.), eds. Joan Riehl and Callista Roy. New York: Appleton-Century-Crofts, 1980.
67. Rimm, R. C., J. C. Masters, *Behavior Therapy Techniques and Empirical Findings*. New York: Academic Press, 1979.
68. Rogers, Carl, *Client-Centered Therapy*. Boston: Houghton-Mifflin, 1951.
69. ———, *On Becoming a Person*. Boston: Houghton-Mifflin, 1961.
70. ———, A Theory of Personality, in *Theories of Psychopathology*, ed. T. Millan. Philadelphia: W. B. Saunders, 1973.
71. Rogers, Martha, *An Introduction to the Theoretical Basis of Nursing*. Philadelphia: F. A. Davis, 1970.
72. Scott, A., The Value and Practical Use of Behavior Modification Programmes: A Nurse's Viewpoint, *Australian Journal of Mental Retardation*, 4, (1977), 14–17.
73. Sheehy, Gail, *Passages*. New York: Bantam Books, 1977.
74. Skinner, B. F. *The Behavior of Organisms*. New York: Appleton-Century-Crofts, 1938.
75. Skinner, B. F., *Walden Two*. New York: Macmillan, 1948.
76. Skinner, B. F., *Science and Human Behavior*. New York: Macmillan, 1953.
77. ———, *Beyond Freedom and Dignity*. New York: Alfred A. Knopf, 1971.
78. ———, *Cumulative Record* (3rd ed.). New York: Appleton-Century-Crofts, 1972.
79. Storr, Antony, *The Essential Jung*. Princeton, N.J.: Princeton University Press, 1983.
80. Sullivan, Harry Stack. *The Interpersonal Theory of Psychiatry*. New York: W. W. Norton, 1953.
81. Thompson, Clara, The Different Schools of Psychoanalysis, *American Journal of Nursing*, 57, no. 10 (1957), 1304–1307.
82. Vaillant, G., The "Normal Boy" in Later Life: How

Adaptation Fosters Growth, *Harvard Magazine*, 6 (1977), 234–239.
83. Von Bertalanffy, Ludwig, *General System Theory*. New York: George Braziller, 1968.
84. Wadsworth, Barry, *Piaget's Theory of Cognitive and Affective Development* (3rd ed.). New York: David McKay, 1984.
85. Wolpe, J., *Practice of Behavior Therapy* (2nd ed.), New York: Pergamon Press, 1979.

6

The Developing Person: Principles of Growth and Development

Study of this chapter will help you to

1. Define growth, development, and related terms.
2. Explore general insights into and principles of human behavior.
3. Discuss various influences that have an effect on the developing person: prenatal variables involving father, mother, and fetus; variables related to childbirth; early childhood variables, including child abuse; sociocultural experiences; and environmental factors.
4. Relate information in this chapter to yourself as a developing person.
5. Use information from this chapter when assessing the person through the life span.
6. Teach the person and family about factors that influence development of self or offspring, when appropriate.

Key Terms

Social Time
Historical time
Cohort
Norms
Growth
  Incremental growth
  Replacement growth
  Hypertrophy
  Hyperplasia
Development
Developmental task
Maturation
Biological Age
Chronological Age
Learning
Critical periods
Physical competencies
Cognitive competencies
Emotional competencies
Social competencies
Principle of Development Toward Self-Knowledge and Autonomy
Principle of Differentiation
Cephalocaudal Principle
Proximodistal Principle
Bilateral Principle
Principle of Asynchronous Growth
Principle of Discontinuity of Growth Rate

Chromosomes
Genes
Ovum
Zygote
Gametes
Meiosis
Follicle
Ovulation
Germinal Stage
Embryonic Stage
Fetal Stage
Conceptus
Anemia
Pica
Teratogen
Teratogenesis
Folklore
Anoxia
Prematurity
Hormone
Integration
Regulation
Morphogenesis
Socialization
Vulnerable and resilient children
Child abuse
Sexual molestation
Emotional abuse
Neglect
Maternal deprivation
Failure to thrive
Perceptual deprivation

Developmental theory, which discusses the person throughout the life span, centers around certain principles of and influences on the person's growth and development. While growth and development are usually thought of as a forward movement or a kind of adding on, such as increase in height and weight or the self-actualizing personality, the model can also apply to reversal, decay, deterioration, or death. Three kinds of reversals occur: (1) loss of some part, such as occurs with catabolism (changing of living tissue into wastes or destructive metabolism), (2) purposefully changing behavior when it is no longer useful, and (3) death (45, 67, 80).

Growth and development are generally characterized by the following: (1) direction, goal, or end state, (2) identifiable stage or era, (3) forward progression, so that once a stage is worked through, the person does not return to the same position, (4) increasing specialization, (5) causal forces that are either genetic or environmental, and (6) potentialities and capabilities for various behaviors, and achievements (45, 67, 80).

Dimensions of Time

Lifetime or chronological age is frequently used as an index of maturation and development but is only a rough indicator of the person's position on any one of numerous physical or psychological dimensions. Further, the society is a reference point for understanding the behavior; what is appropriate for a 14-year-old in one society is not in a different society (69).

Social time or *social expectations of behavior for each age era* is not necessarily synchronous with biological timing. Neither chronological age nor maturational stage is itself a determinant of aging status but only signifies the biological potentiality upon which a system of age norms and age grading can operate to shape the life cycle (69).

Historical time shapes the social system, and the social system creates a changing set of age norms and a changing age-grade system which shapes the person's life cycle. **Historical time** *refers to a series of economic, political, and social events that directly shape the life course of the person as well as long-term processes,* such as industrialization and urbanization, that create the social–cultural context and changing definitions of the phases of the life cycle (69).

A group of people born at a certain calendar time (**cohort**) have, as a group, a particular background and demographic composition, so that most of the people of that specific age or generation will have similar experiences, level of education, fertility and childrearing patterns, sexual mores, work and labor force participation patterns, value systems, leisure patterns, religious behavior, consumer behavior, and ideas about life generally (69).

Social time is prescribed by each society, in that all societies rationalize the passage of lifetime, divide life into socially relevant units, and transform calendar or biological time into social time. Thus age grading occurs; the life cycle consists of a succession of formally age-graded, descriptive norms. Duties, rights, and rewards are differentially distributed to age groups. In societies where division of labor is simple and social change is slow, a single age-grade system becomes formalized, and family, work, religious, and political roles are allocated. A modern, complex, rapidly changing society, which has several or overlapping systems of age status, has some tasks and roles that are tied to chronological age and some that are more fluid or less defined. In every society, there is a time to be a child and dependent, a time to be educated to whatever level is needed, a time to go to work, to marry, to have a family, to retire, and to die. The members of the society have a general consensus about these age expectations and norms, although perceptions may vary somewhat by age, sex, or social class. Thus, there is some pressure to conform. If the person engages in the tasks earlier or later than others in the society, he/she is considered deviant. Patterns of timing can play an important role with respect to self-concept and self-esteem, depending on the person's level of awareness about his/her fit to social age norms and the rigidity in the culture. The young are more likely to deny that age is a valid criterion by which to judge behavior. The middle-aged and old, who see greater constraints in the age-norm system than do the young, have learned that to be off time involves negative consequences. Many of the major marks in the life cycle are ordered and sequential, are social rather than biological, and their time is socially regulated (69).

The life course dimension is indexed by chronological age which serves as an indicator of the person's experience, including age-related organic changes affecting physical and mental functioning, and including the probability of certain psychological and social experiences (69).

This book is organized along chronological lines, whereby the life cycle is divided into different time periods, rather than having content organized around a topical approach. We have divided the person into the following chronological stages: the prenatal period (from the moment of conception to birth); infancy (birth to 1 year); toddlerhood (1 to 3 years); preschool (3 to 6 years); school years (6 to 12 years); adolescence (12 to 25 years); young adulthood (25 to 45 years); middle age (45 to 65 years); and late maturity (65 years and over). These divisions are somewhat arbitrary as it is difficult to assign definite ages since individual lives are not marked off so precisely. In discussion of stage theories, such as those of Freud, Erikson, and Piaget, we use the theorists' own age ranges, and the same reservations apply to them.

The study of development is not merely a search for facts about people at certain ages. The study involves finding *patterns* or *general principles* that apply to most people most of the time.

People are often at one level in one area of development and at another level in another area. For example, a 11-year-old girl may have begun to menstruate—an activity that marks her physical transition from childbirth to puberty—before she has outgrown many childish feelings and thoughts. A 48-year-old man who took several years to find his career direction, who married in his thirties, and who became a father in his forties may in many important psychological ways be in the young adulthood period. On the other hand, his 49-year-old neighbor who settled early on a professional direction and into family life may already be a grandfather and may act and feel more like a middle-aged man. Furthermore, individual differences among people are so great that they enter and leave these age periods at different times of life. People are aware of their own timing and are quick to describe themselves as "early," "late," or "on time" regarding developmental tasks.

Ideal **norms,** *standards or expectancies,* for different behaviors vary among different groups of people. The entire life cycle is speeded up for the poor and working class, who tend to finish their education earlier than middle- or upper-class people, to take their first jobs sooner, marry younger, have children earlier, reach the peak of their careers earlier, and become grandparents earlier. These differences are related to financial needs that make it imperative for poor and working-class people to get paying jobs earlier in life. People from more affluent backgrounds can pursue their educations for a longer time, can use young adulthood to explore options, and can delay becoming financially independent and beginning a family (27, 45, 80).

Principles of Growth and Development

Definitions

Certain words are basic to understanding the person and are used repeatedly. They are defined below for the purposes of this book.

Growth *refers to increase in body size or changes in structure, function, and complexity of body cell content and metabolic and biochemical processes up to some point of optimal maturity* (45, 80). Growth changes occur through incremental or replacement growth. **Incremental growth** *refers to maintaining an excess in growth over normal daily losses from catabolism, seen in urine, feces, perspiration, and oxidation in the lungs.* Incremental growth is observed as increases in weight or height as the child matures. **Replacement growth** *refers to normal refills of essential body components* necessary for survival (35). For example, once a red blood cell (erythrocyte) has entered the cardiovascular system, it circulates an average of 120 days before disintegrating, when another red blood cell takes its place (35). Growth occurs through **hypertrophy,** *increase in the size of cellular structures,* and **hyperplasia,** *an increase in the number of cells* (35). Growth during the fetal and infancy periods is achieved primarily through hyperplasia, which is gradually replaced by hypertrophic growth. Each body organ has its own optimal period of growth. Body tissues are most sensitive to permanent damage during periods of the most rapid hyperplastic growth.

Development *is the patterned, orderly, lifelong changes in structure, thought, or behavior that evolve as a result of maturation of physical and mental capacity, experiences, and learning and result in a new level of maturity and integration* (45, 67, 93). Development should permit the person to adapt to the environment by either controlling the environment or controlling responses to the environment. Developmental processes involve interplay among the physiological characteristics that define the person; the environmental forces, including culture, that act on him/her, and the psychological mechanisms that mediate between them. Psychological processes include the person's perception of self, others, and the environment, and the behaviors he/she acquires in coping with needs and the environment. Development combines growth, maturation, and learning and involves organizing behavior (23).

Developmental task *is a growth responsibility that arises at a certain time in the course of development, successful achievement of which leads to satisfaction and success with later tasks.* Failure leads to unhappiness, disapproval by society, and difficulty with later developmental tasks and functions (23).

Maturation *refers to the emergence of genetic potential for changes in form, structure, complexity, integration, organization, and function* (80).

Biological age *is the level of physical growth and development.* **Chronological age** *is the time since birth and is not always identical to biological age.*

Learning *is the process of gaining specific knowledge or skill and acquiring habits and attitudes as a result of experience, training, and behavioral changes.* Maturation and learning are interrelated. No learning occurs unless the person is mature enough to be able to understand and change his/her behavior (80).

General Assumptions About Behavior

C. Buhler is a developmental theorist whose thinking in the early 1900s influenced a number of present well-known personality and developmental theorists.

Buhler (7) described the person's life course as having a definite basic structure and direction or goals. These structures and goals are evident in the biological life cycle and in psychological development. The structure and phasic organization of the person's life, with its properties and potentials, determines the person's goals, and is influenced by environmental circumstances, time limits, personal characteristics, and society's assignment of roles.

In Buhler's theory, life is divided biologically into a nonreproductive phase (first 15 years, approximately), a reproductive phase from about 15 to 45 years, and then a decline and loss in the reproductive ability, first in the female and then in the male (after middle age for the woman and in old age for the man). Onset of reproductive ability, from puberty to 25 years, is followed by a peak period for reproductive ability and stationary growth (25 to 45 years). A period of gradual decline follows (7).

Psychological development is not parallel to biological development because (1) psychological development is continuous, and (2) there is no exact parallel between the two aspects of life so far as tasks or goals are concerned. Psychological and mental development may be behind biological development, is generally independent of physical or biological factors, and extends beyond reproductive abilities. The psychological system develops in a maturational order and is influenced by learning and the impact of emotional experiences. Abilities, aptitudes, motives, and goals contribute to personality development (7).

The following statements may not be proven by strict scientific study, but they have been observed so regularly that they seem to be true.

The *person is a unified but open system* made up of the components of body, mind, feelings, and spirit, which are, in turn, continually influenced by the environment. The person, in turn, influences the environment (45, 67, 80, 92).

All *persons are similar and have the same basic needs, but they are also unique in* following and expressing their own developmental patterns. The *One Genus Postulate states that people are more similar than different simply because they are all Homo sapiens* (92).

The *person is a unifed whole.* Thus, understanding the whole person is not possible through study of isolated components of the person (77).

The *person's life process evolves irreversibly;* the person cannot totally return to something he/she was developmentally (46, 77). Nevertheless, the past influences the person to some degree whether or not he/she is aware of the influence, and it sets the direction for present and future patterns of behavior (46, 92).

The *person responds as a total organism at any given moment to events, persons, or objects* in terms of personal perception, needs, and expectations (46).

Each person is a social being who has the capacity to communicate and react to other people and the environment. Thus, the person can function in the social system and its various institutions such as family, school, and church (46).

The *person cannot understand the self without understanding others, and he/she cannot understand others without understanding the self.* Understanding the past and the parents helps to understand the self, since developmental patterns of the parents are repeated in the child (92).

Culture and society determine guidelines for normal progression of development and behavior patterns. What is normal in one ethnic or racial group may be considered deviant or undesirable in another. Further, deviation from normal may occur in all or only certain areas of function. The child may show abnormally slow development in one area and unusually accelerated or a mature quality in another. Yet, in spite of these differences, the child may be perceived generally by others as a normal person, depending on the degree of deviance.

Throughout life the person strives to reach optimal physical and emotional potential, barring great interferences. An inner drive or motivation propels him/her onward to meet the various developmental tasks. The person tries all types of adaptive behavior when interferences occur. He/she may regress to work through unsolved problems from the past. Once a need is met or a goal is accomplished, the person is free to move on to new arenas of behavior (27, 92).

General Principles of Development

The following statements apply to the overall development of the person:

Childhood is the foundation period of life. Attitudes, habits, patterns of behavior and thinking, personality traits, and health status established during the early years (the first 5) determine to a large extent how successfully the person will continue to develop and adjust to life as he/she gets older. Early patterns of behavior persist throughout life, within the range of normalcy (27, 28, 80).

Development follows a definable, predictable, and sequential pattern and occurs continually through adulthood. All persons progress through similar stages, but the age for achievement varies, since achievement depends on inherent maturational capacity interacting with the physical and social environment. The different areas of growth and development—physical, mental, emotional, social, and spiritual—are interrelated, proceed together, and affect each other; yet, these areas mature at their own pace. The stages of development overlap, and the transition from one stage to another is rather gradual (27, 28, 80, 92).

Growth and development are continuous, but they occur in spurts rather than in a straight upward direction. At times the person will appear to be at a standstill or even regress developmentally.

Growth is not necessarily accompanied by behavior change. As the child matures, he/she retains earlier ways of behaving, although there will be a developmental revision of habits. For example, the high-activity infant becomes a high-activity toddler or adult, but the object of the activity changes from diffuse interests to concentrated play to work. The young child's temperament is a precursor of later behavior, although the person is adaptable and changes throughout life.

Critical periods *in human development occur when specific organs and other aspects of a person's physical and* *psychosocial growth undergo marked rapid change and the capacity to adapt to stressors is underdeveloped.* During these critical periods, when tremendous demands are placed on the person, the individual has an increased susceptibility to adverse environmental factors that may cause various types and degrees of negative effects. For example, implantation is a critical period, and at certain times during pregnancy certain substances are more likely to damage fetal structures (81). During adolescence the rapid physical growth may negatively affect social relationships or feelings about self. Middle or old age may be other critical periods.

If appropriate stimuli and resources are not available at the critical time or when the person is ready to receive and use particular stimuli for the development of a specific psychomotor skill, the skill may be more difficult to learn later in the developmental sequence. However, learning of any psychomotor skill is also influenced by sociocultural factors; the extent to which any skill is influenced by genetics, environmental opportunity, cultural and family values and patterns, and emotional status is not fully known.

Mastering developmental tasks of one period is the basis for mastering the next developmental era, physically and emotionally. Certain time periods exist when the task can be best accomplished and the task should be mastered then; if the time is delayed, the person will have difficulty in accomplishing the task. Each phase of development has characteristic traits and a period of equilibrium when the person adjusts more easily to environmental demands and a period of disequilibrium when he experiences difficulty in adjustment. Developmental hazards exist in every era. Some are environmental and interfere with adjustment; others come from within the person (23, 27, 39, 68, 72, 92).

Progressive differentiation of the self from the environment results from increasing self-knowledge and autonomy. The young child first separates as an object apart from mother. Gradually he/she becomes less dependent emotionally on the parents. As the child matures into adulthood, an increase in cognitive development enables more control over behavior. The person can think and act on his/her own and become more and more autonomous (28, 80).

The developing person acquires simultaneously competencies in four major areas: physical, cognitive, emotional, and social. **Physical competency** *includes various motor and neurological capacities* to attain mobility and manipulation and care for self physically. **Cognitive competency** *includes learning how to perceive, think, solve problems, and communicate thoughts and feelings* which, in turn, affect emotional and social skills. **Emotional competency** *includes developing an awareness and acceptance of self as a separate person, responding to other people and factors in the environment because others have been responsive to him/her, coping with inner and outer stresses, and becoming increasingly responsible for personal behavior.* **Social competency** *includes learning how to affiliate securely with the family first and then with various people in various situations.* These four competencies constantly influence one another. Health of one domain or the extent of competency affects the other domains or competencies. Lack of care or stimulation in any one area inhibits development of the other three areas. Repetition and practice are essential to learning. Rewarded behavior is usually repeated (67). The person optimally utilizes personal assets, inner resources, competencies, and abilities to keep energy expenditures at a minimum while focusing toward the achievement of a goal (80).

Readiness and motivation are essential for learning to occur. Hunger, fatigue, illness, pain, and the lack of emotional feedback or opportunity to explore inhibit readiness and lower motivation.

Many factors contribute to the formation of permanent characteristics and traits, including the child's genetic inheritance, undetermined prenatal environmental factors, family and society when he/she is an infant and young child, nutrition, the physical and emotional environment, and the degree of intellectual stimulation in the environment.

Progressive differentiation of the self from other people and the environment, **the Principle of Development Toward Self-Knowledge and Autonomy,** is made apparent with the individual's increasing self-awareness and emergent self-concept. The young child achieves increasing ability to perceive himself/herself as an initiator of action on the environment and an increasing ability to regulate his/her own behavior, to think and act in an individual and unique way, and to become more autonomous. The ability to be autonomous and interdependent is reworked throughout life (45).

Principles of Growth

There are several principles of growth emphasized in the following pages, but the primary determinant of normal growth is the development of the central nervous system, which, in turn, governs or influences other body systems.

The **Principle of Differentiation** *means that development proceeds from (1) simple to the complex; (2) homogeneous to heterogeneous; and (3) general to specific* (67). For example, movement from *simple to complex* is seen in mitotic changes in fetal cell structures as they undergo cell division immediately following ovum fertilization by a sperm (35). All human embryos are anatomically female for the first 6 weeks of life; only through the action of specific hormones does the male embryo develop between the sixth and twelfth weeks of life (67). Differentiation from simple to complex motor skill is seen after birth as the baby first waves his/her arms and then later learns to control finger movements. The general body configuration of male and female at birth tends to be much more similar than during late adolescence, thus indicating *movement from homogeneity to heterogeneity* (67). The mass of cells in the embryo is at first homogeneous, but the limbs of the 5-week-old embryo show considerable differentiation as the elbow and wrist regions become identifiable and finger ridge indentations outline the progressive protrusion of future fingers from the former paddle-shaped arm bud (35). *General to specific* development is observed in motor responses, which are diffuse and undifferentiated at birth and become more specific and controlled later. Baby first moves the whole body in response to a stimuli; later, he/she reacts with a specific body part (80). The behavior of the child becomes more specific to the person or situation with increasing age.

The **Cephalocaudal, Proximodistal, and Bilateral Principles** *all indicate that major physical and motor changes invariably proceed in three bipolar directions.* **Cephalocaudal** *(head to tail) means that the upper end of the organism develops with greater rapidity than and before the lower end of the organism.* Increases in neuromuscular size and maturation of function begin in the head and proceed to hands and feet. For example, a comparison of pictures of a 5-week-old embryo during a period of several days clearly shows the extensive head growth, caused mainly by development of the brain, accompanied by further oblongation of the body structure from head to tail. Further, auditory, visual, and other sensory mechanisms in the head develop sooner than motor systems of the upper body. At the same time, the arm buds, first appearing paddle shaped, continue to change in shape and size more rapidly than do the lower limbs. After birth, the infant will be able to hold the head erect before being able to sit or walk (80). **Proximodistal** *(near to far)* means that growth progresses from the central axis of the body toward the periphery or extremities. **Bilateral** *(side to side)* means that the capacity for growth and development of structures is symmetrical (67); growth that occurs on one side of the body occurs simultaneously on the other.

The **Principle of Asynchronous Growth** *focuses on developmental shifts at successive periods in development.* A comparison of pictures of persons of different ages indicates that the young child is *not* a "small adult"; the proportional size of head to chest and torso to limbs of younger and older persons is vastly different. Length of limbs in comparison to torso length is smaller in the infant than the schoolchild and greater in the aged than the adolescent because of the biological changes of aging (67, 80).

The **Principle of Discontinuity of Growth Rate** *refers to the different rate of growth changes at different periods during the life span* (67). The *whole* body does not grow as a total unit simultaneously. Instead, various structures and organs of the body grow and develop at different rates, reaching their maximum at different times throughout the life cycle. For instance, in its rudimentary form the heart and circulatory system begin to function during the third week of embryonic life, continue to mature slowly compared to the rest of the body, and after the age of 25 years remain fairly constant in size (67, 80). Before birth the head is the fastest growing body part. The brain grows and develops according to a different pattern; this vital organ grows very rapidly during fetal life and infancy, reaching 80 percent of its maximum size at the age of 2 years. Full growth is seen at about 6 years of age (67, 80). Body growth is rapid in infancy and adolescence and relatively slow during school years.

All body systems normally continue to work in unity throughout the life span. Some physiological characteristics, such as oxygen concentration in the blood, remain fairly stable throughout life. Others, such as body temperature, undergo minor changes, depending on age, hormonal balance, or time of day. Some characteristics change markedly during the life cycle, such as pulse rate and fluid intake that are affected by changes in body surface, organ size, or maturity (80). Age-related changes occur at varying chronological periods. Structural deterioration usually precedes functional decline. Some organs and systems deteriorate more rapidly than others. In late life the capacity for adaptation changes and finally decreases. Prior to death, decline or deterioration usually affects most structural and many functional centers in the aged person (67).

The study of growth and development processes must focus on the complete continuum of the life cycle—from conception through death—to acquire a comprehensive understanding of the complexity of these processes and how these principles are activated throughout the life span.

The Developing Person: Prenatal Influences and Stages

Heredity

Genetic information is transmitted from parents of offspring through a complex series of processes. Twenty-three pairs of chromosomes in the human germ cells divide into two gametes by meiosis, giving to each of these mature germ cells (female ovum and male spermatazoon) one-half the genetic material necessary for producing a new individual. The specific hereditary information is carried on the chromosomes by thousands of genes, but the expression of gene characteristic is not a preprogrammed, unchangeable process (35).

Further, hereditary factors do not by themselves fully determine what the person will become. Innate characteristics and environmental forces are closely related. Genetic endowment in respect to any trait may be compared to a rubber band. The rubber band may remain unstretched because of environmental influences, causing potential to remain dormant. Or the rubber band may be stretched fully, causing the person to excel beyond what seems his/her potential. The person in later maturity, for example, has had many years of changing environmental influences; what he/she has become is no doubt an expression of innate genetic potential and environmental supports, and the widsom to take advantage of both.

Embryological development and principles of genetics affecting body structure and function are complex. A number of references provide additional information (35, 39, 45, 67, 68, 72, 75, 80, 81, 93).

The Beginning

The cell, the basis for human life, is a complex unit. Refer to an anatomy or physiology text for review of cell structure and function. This chapter will present a brief overview of the prenatal period as the beginning of life. For in-depth study of the biological differences of the male and female, the reproductive process, including fertilization and development of the unborn child in utero, inheritance patterns, and the processes of labor and delivery, refer to an anatomy and physiology or developmental text and to a maternity nursing text (35, 39, 45, 67, 72, 80, 81).

All body cells have 22 pairs of rod-shaped particles, nonsex **chromosomes** (*autosomes*), and a pair of sex chromosomes. The biological female has two X chromosomes; the biological male has one X and one Y chromosome. The 46 chromosomes each contain about 20,000 *segments strung out like lengthwise beads* called **genes**. The genes, apparently located according to function, are made up of DNA (deoxyribonucleic acid), which possesses the information that determines the makeup and specific function of every cell in the body. The genes play a major role in determining hereditary characteristics (80, 81, 93).

According to the Jacob-Monod (42) hypothesis, there are three different types of genes. Only one type is directly responsible for growth. The other two regulate genetic activity as a result of information from the rest of the reproductive cell. These synthesizing genes do not automatically perform the processes contained in their genetic code; their function is to be sensitive to environmental conditions within the cell. Thus gene expression is affected by the prevailing cellular environment of the fetus and the uterine environment, which are active in determining the structure and organization of each fetal system (42). Variation in the human results from common factors, such as cross-over of genes in a variety of combinations, mutations, unusual sexual configurations, and other abnormalities in genetic process (35, 81). Many chromosomal defects can now be diagnosed.

The female reproductive cycle is more regular and is easier to observe and measure than is the male reproductive cycle (19). In contrast to the normal menstrual cycle, spermatogenesis normally occurs in cycles that continuously follow one another.

About 14 days after the beginning of the menstrual period fertilization may occur in the outer third of the Fallopian tube. The sperm cell from a male penetrates and unites with an **ovum** (*egg*) from a female to form a *single cell* **zygote.** The sperm and ovum, known as **gametes** (*sex cells in half cells*), are produced in the reproductive system through **meiosis,** a *specialized process of cell division and chromosome reduction* (35, 81).

A newborn girl has about 400,000 immature ova in her ovaries; each is in a **follicle,** *small sac.* **Ovulation,** *the expelling of an ovum from a mature follicle in one of the ovaries*, occurs about once every 28 days in a sexually mature female.

Spermatozoa, much smaller and more active than the ovum, are produced in the testes of the mature male at the rate of several hundred million a day and are ejaculated in his semen at sexual climax (orgasm). For fertilization to occur, at least 20 million sperm cells must enter a woman's body at one time. They enter the vagina and try to swim through the **cervix** (*the opening to the uterus*) and into the Fallopian tube. Only a tiny fraction of those millions of sperm cells makes it this far. More than one may penetrate the ovum, but only one can fertilize it to create a new human. The sex of the baby is determined by the pair of sex chromosomes; the sperm may carry either an X or Y chromosome, resulting in either a girl (XX zygote) or a boy (XY zygote). Thus, the man determines the sex of the baby (35, 67, 81).

Spermatozoa maintain their ability to fertilize an egg for a span of 24 to 72 to 90 hours; ova can be fertilized for about 24 hours. Thus, there are about 72 to 90 hours during each menstrual cycle when conception can take place. If fertilization does not occur, the spermatozoa and ovum die. Sperm cells are devoured by white blood cells in the woman's body; the ovum

Table 6—1. Summary of the Sequence of Prenatal Development

GERMINAL STAGE

Time Period After Fertilization	Developmental Event
30 hr	First division or cleavage occurs.
40 hr	Four-cell stage occurs.
60 hr	**Morula,** *a solid mass of 12 to 16 cells;* total size of mass not changed because cells decrease in size with each cleavage to allow morula to pass through lumen of Fallopian tube. Ectopic pregnancy within Fallopian tube occurs if morula wedged in lumen.
3 days	Zygote has divided into 32 cells, travels through Fallopian tube to uterus.
4 days	Zygote contains 70 cells. Morula reaches uterus, forms a **blastocyst,** *a fluid-filled sphere.*
4½ to 6 days	Blastocyst floats in utero. **Embryonic disk,** *thickened cell mass from which baby develops,* clusters on one edge of blastocyst. Mass of cells differentiates into two layers: (1) **Ectoderm,** *outer layer of cells* that become the epidermis of skin, nails, hair, tooth enamel, sensory organs, brain and spinal cord, cranial nerves, peripheral nervous system, upper pharynx, nasal passages, urethra, and mammary glands; (2) **Endoderm,** *lower layer of cells* that will develop into gastrointestinal system, liver, pancreas, salivary glands, respiratory system, urinary bladder, pharynx, thyroid, tonsils, lining of urethra, and ear.
6 to 7 days	**Nidation,** *implantation of zygote* into upper portion of uterine wall, occurs.
7 to 14 days	Remainder of blastocyst develops into the following: (1) **Placenta,** *a multipurpose organ connected to the embryo by the umbilical cord* that delivers oxygen and nourishment from the mother's body and absorbs the embryo's body wastes, combats internal infection, confers immunity to the unborn child, and produces the hormones that (a) support pregnancy, (b) prepare breasts for lactating, and (c) stimulate uterine contractions for delivery of the baby. Placenta circulation evidenced by 11 to 12 days. (2) **Umbilical cord,** *a structure that contains two umbilical arteries and an umbilical vein and connects embryo to placenta.* Approximately 20 inches long and 1½ inches in diameter. Rapid cell differentiation occurs. (3) **Amniotic sac,** *a fluid-filled membrane that encases the developing baby,* protecting it and giving it room to move.
2 to 8 weeks	Period during which embryo firmly establishes uterus as home and undergoes rapid cellular differentiation, growth, and development of body systems. This is a **critical period** *when embryo is most vulnerable to deleterious prenatal influences.* All developmental birth defects occur during **first trimester** (*3 months*) of pregnancy. If embryo is unable to survive, a **miscarriage** or **spontaneous abortion,** *expulsion of conceptus from the uterus,* occurs.
15 days	Cranial end of elongated disk has begun to thicken.
16 days	**Mesoderm,** *the middle layer,* appears and develops into skin dermis, tooth dentin, connective tissue, cartilage, bones, muscles, spleen, blood, gonads, uterus, and excretory and circulatory systems. Yolk sac, which arises from ectoderm, assists transfer of nutrients from mother to embryo.
19 to 20 days	Neural fold and neural groove develop. Thyroid begins to develop.
21 days	Neural tube forms, becomes spinal cord and brain.
22 days	Heart, the first organ to function, initiates action. Eyes, ears, nose, cheeks, and upper jaw begin to form. Cleft palate may occur if defective development.
26 to 27 days	Cephalic portion (brain) of nervous system formed. Leg and arm buds appear. Stubby tail of spinal cord appears.
28 days	Crown to rump length, 4 to 5 mm.
30 days	Rudimentary body parts formed. Limb buds appear. Cardiovascular system functioning. Heartbeat 65 times per minute; blood flow through tiny arteries and veins. Lens vesicles, optic cups, and nasal pits forming. By end of first month, new life has grown more quickly than it will at any other time in life. Swelling in head where eyes, ears, mouth, and nose will be. Crown to rump length, 7 to 14 mm (¼ to ½ inches).
31 days	Eye and nasal pit developing. Primitive mouth present.
32 days	Paddle-shaped hands. Lens vesicles and optic cups formed.
34 days	Head is much larger relative to trunk. Digital rays present in hands. Feet are paddle shaped. Crown to rump length, 11 to 14 mm.
35 to 38 days	Olfactory pit, eye, maxillary process, oral cavity and mandibular process developing. Brain has divided into three parts. Limbs growing. Beginning of all major external and internal structures. Crown to rump length, 14 to 16 mm.

Table 6–1. Continued

Time Period After Fertilization (Cont.)	Developmental Event (Cont.)
40 days	Elbows and knees apparent. Fingers and toes distinct but webbed. Yolk sac continues to (1) provide embryological blood cells during third through sixth weeks until liver, spleen, and bone marrow assume function; (2) provide lining cells for respiratory and digestive tracts; (3) provide cells that migrate to gonads to become primordial germ cells.
42 days	Crown to rump length, 21 to 23 mm.
50 days	All internal and external structures present. External genitalia present but sex not discernible; yolk sac disappears, incorporated into embryo.
55 to 56 days	Eye, nostril, globular process, maxilla and mandible almost completely formed. Ear beginning to develop.
8 wk	Stubby end of spinal cord disappears. Distinct human characteristics. Head accounts for half of total embryo length. Brain impulses coordinate function of organ systems. Facial parts formed, with tongue and teeth buds. Stomach produces digestive juices. Liver produces blood cells. Kidney removes uric acid from blood. Some movement by limbs. Weight, 1 g. Length, less than 1 inch.
FETAL STAGE	
9 to 40 wk	Remainder of intrauterine period spent in growth and refinement of body tissues and organs.
9 to 12 wk	Eyelids fused. Nail beds formed. Teeth and bones begin to appear. Ribs and vertebrae are cartilage. Kidneys function. Urinates occasionally. Some respiratory-like movements exhibited. Begins to swallow amniotic fluid. Grasp, sucking, and withdrawal reflexes present. Sucks fingers and toes in utero. Makes specialized responses to touch. Moves easily but movement not felt by mother. Reproductive organs have primitive egg or sperm cells. Gender distinguishable. Head one-third of body length. Weight, 30 g (1 oz). Length, 3 to 3½ inches at 12 wk.
13 to 16 wk	Much spontaneous movement. Sex determination possible. **Quickening,** *fetal kicking or movement,* may be felt by mother. Moro reflex present. Rapid skeletal development. Meconium present. Uterine development in female fetus. **Lanugo,** *downy hair,* appears in body. Head one-fourth of total length. Weight, 120 to 150 g (4 to 6 oz). Length, 8 to 10 inches.
17 to 20 wk	New cells exchanged for old, especially in skin. Quickening occurs by 17 wk. Vernix caseosa appears. Eyebrows, eyelashes, and head hair appear. Sweat and sebaceous glands begin to function. Skeleton begins to harden. Grasp reflex present and strong. Permanent teeth buds appear. Fetal heart sounds can be heard with stethoscope. Weight, 360 to 450 g (12 oz to 1 lb). Length, 12 inches.
21 to 24 wk	Extrauterine life, life outside uterus, is possible but difficult because of immature respiratory system. Fetus looks like miniature baby. Mother may note jarring but rhythmic movements of infant, indicative of hiccups. Body becomes straight at times. Fingernails present. Skin has wrinkled, red appearance. Alternate periods of sleep and activity. May respond to external sounds. Weight, 720 g (1½ lb). Length, 14 inches.
25 to 28 wk	Jumps in utero in synchrony with loud noise. Eyes reopen. Respiratory-like movements. Respiratory and central nervous systems sufficiently developed; some babies survive with excellent and intensive care. Assumes head-down position in uterus. Weight, 1200 g (2½ lb).
29 to 32 wk	Begins to store fat and minerals. Testes descend into scrotal sac in male. Reflexes fully developed. Thumb sucking present. Mother may note irregular, jerky, crying-like movements. Lanugo begins to disappear from face. Head hair continues to grow. Skin begins to lose reddish color. Can be conditioned to environmental sounds. Weight, 1362 to 2270 g (3 to 5 lb). Length, 16 inches.
33 to 36 wk	Adipose tissue continues to be deposited over entire body. Body begins to round out. May become more or less active because of space constriction. Increased iron storage by liver. Increased lung development. Lanugo begins to disappear from body. Head lengthens. Excellent chance of survival if born. Weight, 2800 g (6 lb). Length, 18 to 20 inches.
37 to 40 wk	Organ systems operating more efficiently. Heart rate increases. More wastes expelled. Lanugo and vernix caseosa disappear. Skin smooth and plump. High absorption of maternal hormones. Skull and other bones becoming more firm and mineralized. Continued storage of fat and minerals. Ready for birth. Weight, 3200 to 3400 g (7 to 7½ lb). Length, 20 to 21 inches. Baby stops growing about 1 wk before birth.

passes through the uterus and vagina in the menstrual product (35, 67, 81).

Multiple births may occur. Twins occur in about one of 86 births. Occasionally two ova are released within a short time of each other; if both are fertilized, **fraternal** (*dizygotic, or two-egg*) twins will be born. Created by different eggs and different sperm cells, the twins are no more alike in their genetic makeup than other siblings. They may be of the same or different sex. If the ovum divides in two after it has been fertilized, **identical** (*monozygotic, or one-egg*) twins will be born. At birth these twins share the same placenta. They are of the same sex and have exactly the same genetic heritage; any differences they will later exhibit are due to the influences of environment, either before or after birth. Other multiple births—triplets, quadruplets, and so forth—result from either one or a combination of these two processes (80, 81, 93).

Multiple births have become more frequent in recent years due to the administration of certain fertility drugs that spur ovulation and often cause the release of more than one egg. The tendency to bear twins appears to be inherited and more common in some families and ethnic groups than in others. Twins have a limited intrauterine space and are more likely to be premature and of low-birth-weight. They are therefore at greater risk for survival at birth (81).

After either single or multiple fertilization the zygote travels to the uterus for implantation or imbedding in the uterine wall. Progesterone secretion has prepared the uterus for the possible reception of the fertilized ovum. The continued secretion of ovarian estrogen and progesterone develops the uterus for the 9-month nurturance of the developing embryo and fetus in pregnancy. Continued secretion of estrogen during this period increases the growth of the uterine muscles and eventually enlarges the vagina for the delivery of a child. Continued secretion of progesterone during pregnancy serves to keep the uterus from prematurely contracting and expelling the developing embryo before the proper time. In addition, progesterone prepares the breast cells in late pregnancy for future milk production (81).

Stages of Prenatal Development

Life in utero is usually divided into three stages of development: germinal, embryonic, and fetal. The **germinal stage** *lasts about 10 days to 2 weeks after fertilization*. It is characterized by rapid cell division and subsequent increasing complexity of the organism, and its implantation in the wall of the uterus. The **embryonic stage**, *from 2 to 8 weeks*, is the time of rapid growth and differentiation of major body systems and organs. The **fetal stage**, *from 8 weeks until birth*, is characterized by rapid growth and changes in body form caused by different rates of growth of different parts of the body (81).

The fetus is a very small but rapidly developing human being, who is influenced by the maternal and external environment, and to whom the mother responds, especially when fetal movement begins. Table 6–1 summarizes some major milestones in the sequence development of the **conceptus,** *the new life that has been conceived*. However, it is *difficult to be precise about the exact timing* (28, 35, 67, 80, 81, 93).

Maternal Age as a Prenatal Influence

✔ Age of mother and number of previous pregnancies affect the health of the fetus. If the woman has had three or more pregnancies before the age of 20, the baby is less likely to be healthy. Pregnancy during the teen years is more frequently associated with prematurity and infant illness (72). Risk for the infant is least when the mother is in her twenties (67, 72, 81). The woman who becomes pregnant after age 35 may increase her risk of delivery complications and problems in the neonate. These problems include prematurity, low-birth-weight, Down's Syndrome, birth defects, and fraternal twinning (39, 81). The more pregnancies the woman has had, the greater the risk to the infant. Maternal physiology cannot support many pregnancies in rapid succession, and as age increases the ability to cope with the stresses of pregnancy decreases (39, 67, 81).

Prenatal Endocrine and Metabolic Functions as Prenatal Influences

Fetal growth and development are dependent on maternal endocrine and metabolic adjustments during pregnancy. The placenta helps to provide necessary estrogens, progesterone, and gonadotropin to sustain pregnancy and trigger other endocrine adjustments that involve primarily the pituitary, adrenal cortex, and thyroid. Fetal endocrine function is regulated independently from the mother, but endocrine drugs given to the mother may produce undesirable effects on the fetus (35, 39, 45, 81, 93).

Animal research indicates that later sexual characteristics and behavior may be affected by administration of or presence or absence of sex hormones during fetal development. This is the first critical period for sexual differentiation. Although the fetus has a chromosomal combination denoting male or female, the fetus must be exposed to corresponding hormones during pregnancy. If the male fetus is insensitive to androgen (a masculinizing hormone) and exposed to large amounts of estrogen (a feminizing hormone), the child may possess many female characteristics (67, 81, 93). Testicular inductor substance causes production of fetal androgens that suppress anatomical precursors of the oviducts and ovaries, and, in turn, cause the male genital tract to develop during the seventh to twelfth weeks. The male embryo's testosterone offsets the maternal hormone influences. Unless androgens are present, the external genitalia of the fetus will appear female regardless of chromosomal pattern. Estrogens are released in the genetically female embryo and are necessary for the fetus to develop female genitalia. Likewise, inspection of the external genitalia of a newborn female may show abnormal fusion of the labia and enlargement of the clitoris caused by an androgen agent taken by the mother early in her pregnancy (81).

The second critical period for sexual differentiation occurs just before or after birth, when sex typing of the brain may occur. Testosterone may influence the hypothalamus, so that a noncyclic pattern for release of pituitary hormones, the gonadotropins, will occur in males and a cyclic pattern of gonadotropic release will occur in females (93).

Fetal and placental growth, nourishment, waste excretion, and total function are dependent on the adequacy of the mother's blood system. Inadequate hemoglobin or red blood cells interfere with fetal function (35, 81).

✔ The diabetic mother is at high risk. Apparently the mother's hyperglycemia stimulates the fetal pancreas to overproduce insulin in fetal life and is responsible for increased fat in and size of the baby. The metabolic stress of fetal hyperinsulinism apparently contributes to increased anomalies, e.g., obesity of the newborn (39, 93). Many fetal metabolic defects can now be diagnosed (81, 93).

Maternal Nutrition

Nutrition is one of the most important variables for fetal health and prevention of prenatal and intrapartal complications. Scientists know that at least 60 nutrients are basic to the maintenance of healthy growth and development (73). Lack of these nutrients over a period of time may depress appetite, encourage disease, and retard growth and development, including causing mental retardation. If the mother's nutritional state is not adequate, the fetus is deprived of nutrients (81).

✔ *Caloric* and *protein* intake are of particular importance: Calories are implicated in cell multiplication, and protein is thought to be primarily related to enlargement of these cells. Therefore, failure of the cells to receive sufficient protein and calories during critical periods of growth can lead to slowing down and ultimate cessation of the ability of these cells to enlarge, divide, and develop specialized functions. Lack of protein also affects later intellectual performance. Further, sufficient calories from fats and carbohydrates are needed so that protein is not used for energy. On the other hand, an excessive intake of protein and calories may produce excessive fat storage cells that do not disappear and may contribute to later obesity (22, 72).

✔ Caloric requirements for the pregnant woman are about 300 calories higher than for the nonpregnant woman, contributing to a total weight gain of about 25 pounds. If the woman has not gained at least 10 pounds by 5 months' (20 weeks') gestation, she is at risk for delivery of an ill child. Low maternal weight at conception and little weight gain during pregnancy are associated with birth of a child who is underweight for gestational age and prone to development hazards. The overweight woman jeopardizes the fetus if she tries to lose weight during pregnancy; the effects of ketoacidosis, which results from calorie limitations, have been associated with neuropsychologic defects in the infant (22, 65, 73).

✔ Protein requirements are 1.5 grams per kilogram daily for the pregnant woman, compared to the usual 1.0 gram per kilogram daily (73).

✔ Mineral intake, especially calcium and phosphorus, follows protein as the next most essential requirement. Calcium is mostly deposited in the infant during the last month of gestation; a good supply must be stored from the early months of pregnancy to meet this demand and minimize depletion of maternal reserves. Supplementation with 30 to 60 milligrams of ferrous iron during the last 3 to 4 months of pregnancy is beneficial in building and protecting maternal reserves and preventing iron deficiency anemia, which predisposes to underweight and congenital defects in the newborn. Salt should not be restricted unless edema develops.

✔ Folic acid supplementation helps to prevent anemia. Additional iodine prevents inadequate physical and mental growth (22, 73). Further information on diet for the pregnant woman, including the vegetarian, is found in Chapter 12.

An adequate intake of vitamins acquired through foods affects normal metabolism. Although supplementary vitamins may be prescribed by the physician or purchased over the counter, natural foods are the best source of vitamins (22, 73). This recommendation is supported by a 1986 study of vitamin C (ascorbic acid) health practices and mortality (26).

✔ Maternal malnutrition, which is usually related to a lifetime of inadequate nutrition in the mother, has an adverse effect on the child and grandchildren generations. The fetal central nervous system is the structure most damaged; impaired intelligence performance results later in life (2).

✓ Effects of inadequate nutrition are most severe for the pregnant adolescent who herself has growth requirements and for the mother with accumulated effects of several pregnancies, especially closely spaced ones. Nutritional deficiencies of the mother during her own fetal and childhood periods contribute to structural and physiological difficulties in supporting a fetus. Improvement of the pregnant woman's diet when she has previously been poorly nourished does not appreciably benefit the fetus. The fetus apparently draws most of its raw materials for development from maternal body structure and lifetime reserves (65, 72). You have a significant role in teaching proper nutrition to children and adolescents.

✓ Socioeconomic level significantly affects the mother's nutritional status. Regardless of ethnic or cultural background, families who are relatively affluent tend to choose more foods from the Basic Four food groups and eat a better balanced meal. However, studies comparing mothers with deficient and adequate diet have not compared for other variables often associated with dietary deficiency, such as extreme stress, poverty, and deprived socioeconomic class (22, 28, 61, 87).

In a study on Guatemala newborns, it was found that the birth weight was significantly affected by the number of supplemental calories ingested by the mother during pregnancy, but not by the supplemental protein intake (22). Stein and associates also failed to find any improvement in birth weight attributed specifically to a protein-enriched supplemental diet (88). Length of gestation was increased with a corresponding increase in birth weight of infants born to mothers who were placed on a balanced protein–calorie supplementation; the same results were not found in the high-protein-only supplementation. In fact, some mild short-term psychological adverse affects occurred in the later group (79). The implications of these results are uncertain; further studies are needed.

Anemia as a Prenatal Influence

The effects of maternal anemia on the fetus are less clear than on the mother. **Anemia** *denotes a decrease in the oxygen-carrying capability of the blood*, which is directly related to a reduction in hemoglobin concentration. Anemia, regardless of its etiology, has been associated with spontaneous abortion, prematurity, low-birth weight, and fetal death—even in mild cases (hemoglobin 8 to 11 g) (66). A direct relationship between anemia and fetal distress has not been established, unless the anemia of the mother is severe (hemoglobin less than 6 g).

✓ The common association of anemia and inadequate maternal nutritional intake with lower educational levels and socioeconomic background is prominent in the literature (66, 75).

✓ Iron Deficiency Anemia (IDA) accounts for 75 percent of all the anemias diagnosed during pregnancy (66). The iron requirements of pregnancy are considerable; close to 800 mg, of which 300 mg go to the fetus and placenta and 500 mg are used to expand the maternal hemoglobin mass (100). IDA (as well as underweight and congenital defects) develops unless adequate replacement of these and other natural maternal iron losses occur. The developing fetus may not suffer severe ill effects of the mother's decreased iron supply if its own hemoglobin production is maintained at a normal level, that is, if the placental source of iron is of sufficient amounts for the fetus to establish and continue normal hemoglobin levels (75).

✓ Sickle Cell Anemia in the mother, associated with sickle cell disease seen predominantly in the Black population, may show a number of negative effects on the developing fetus. Changes in the mother's pathophysiological state may lead to intrauterine growth retardation, premature labor, a reduction of 250 to 500 g in average birth weight, and even stillbirth related to the "sickling" or clumping of malshaped erythrocytes within the placental vascular system (39, 66, 75).

Pica as a Prenatal Influence

✓ **Pica** *is eating nonfood substances*, such as clay, unprocessed flour, cornstarch, coal, soap, toothpaste, mothballs, petrol, tar, paraffin, wood, plaster, soil, chalk, charcoal, and cinders. Pica is common in children and women of all cultures who are hungry, poor, malnourished, and desire something to chew (39). Sometimes secrecy or superstitious beliefs accompany this habit. Some people, such as Black inhabitants in the southern part of the United States and their descendants, believe that eating red and white clay overcomes the chances of disfigured offspring. Pica is usually associated with iron deficiency; whether anemia is the cause or effect is unknown. Certainly pica interferes with normal nutrition by reducing appetite (39, 73).

Environmental Hazards to the Fetus: Teratogenic Effects

Teratogens. A **teratogen** *is an agent that interrupts normal development and causes malformations*. **Teratogenesis** *means development of abnormal structures* (39).

✓ Prominent environmental factors that have the potential of damaging the fetus include radiation, some food additives, various pollutants, chemical interactions, nicotine from smoking tobacco, pica, drugs, alcohol, maternal and paternal infections, and maternal stress. The timing of fetal contact with a specific teratogen is a crucial factor. For instance, a teratogen introduced into the system of an embryo between 3 and 8 weeks of gestation, when principal body systems are being established, is likely to do much more harm than if it came in contact with the same conceptus during the third or eighth months. During the implantation period, when the fertilized ovum lies free within the uterus and uses uterine secretions as its nutrition source, teratogens can kill the embryo (16, 67, 74, 93). Even during the third trimester fetal cerebral vascular reaction to certain teratogens can be detrimental (12–14, 16).

There is no evidence that congenital malformations will always be produced when a teratogen is present, for the embryo has the inherent capacity to replace damaged cells by newly formed cells. Once implantation has occurred (7 or 8 days after fertilization), the embryo undergoes very rapid and important transformations for the next 4 weeks. The sequence of embryonic events shows that each organ (brain, heart, eye, limbs, and genitalia) undergoes a critical stage of differentiation at precise times. During these individual critical periods the embryo is highly vulnerable to teratogens, producing specific gross malformations. A substance can have adverse effects on the central nervous system but not on normal development of limbs. A teratogen may cause a variety of gross anomalies; a few show a preferential action on specific organs. For example, thalidomide anomalies are characterized by skeletal malformations; no other form of growth retardation is noted (16, 39, 76, 81, 93).

A complicated interplay exists among the father, mother, offspring, and teratogen. In addition to the critical period or developmental stage and genetic susceptibility, the degree to which a teratogen causes abnormalities depends on its dosage, absorption, distribution, metabolism, the physical state of the mother, and excretion by the separate body systems of mother and fetus. A teratogen that enters a mother's system also enters the system of her developing child, meaning that the so-called *placental barrier* is practically nonexistent (16, 67).

External Environmental Factors. Prenatally, environmental factors such as high level of noise, radiation from multiple sources at work, or ultraviolet rays from the sun or sunlamp, and pollution of air, water, and food, are increasingly shown as important for the newborn. Certain trace metals and normal exposure to radiation produce teratogenic effects although they may be undetectable (89, 93).

✔ Occupational hazards include transfer of drugs and chemicals from the male to the female during intercourse—an action which later can negatively affect fertilization or implantation, or, if already pregnant, can have teratogenic effects on the developing person. For example, decreased sperm count and infertility are related to paternal exposure to Diabromochloropapane (DBCP). Paternal exposure to toxic agents is most likely to result in male infertility or spontaneous abortions. Anesthetic gases, vinyl chloride exposure, chloroprene, or other hydrocarbons have all been connected to spontaneous abortions. Lead present in the environment directly increases sperm abnormalities, induces male infertility, and facilitates spontaneous abortion through either affected sperm or indirect contamination (18, 89).

Agent Orange, named for the orange strip wrapped around 11 million gallons shipped and sprayed in Vietnam, is composed of 2,4,5-T and other chemicals including dioxin. Dioxin, a widely publicized, highly toxic substance is believed to be responsible for the many adverse effects of exposure to Agent Orange experienced by Vietnam veterans, such as chloracne, latent extreme fatigue, liver damage, and joint pain in back, hips and fingers, plus increases in spontaneous abortions and congenital malformations—spina bifida, cleft lip, and neoplasms. A major study commissioned by the U.S. government is now underway to explain the linkage of Agent Orange to reproductive problems encountered by veterans and the presence of abnormalities in their offspring (18, 89, 97).

Smoking Tobacco. Smoking is associated with decreased maternal pulmonary function and with an increased incidence of abnormal bleeding during pregnancy (33, 88). Adverse effects of maternal smoking on the fetus extend to the categories of both morbidity and mortality (32, 36, 48, 96). Although many of the hazards of smoking are well publicized, it is estimated that nearly half the women who seek prenatal care classify themselves as "smokers" (33).

The prevalence of smoking has decreased more among Caucasian than Afro-American pregnant women, and among those who are at least 20 years of age and are more educated. Unmarried mothers are much more likely to smoke than their counterparts. Although smoking is perceived as a threat to normal growth and development patterns, research indicates that women who quit smoking during pregnancy are likely to resume the habit after delivery (48).

✔ The average reduction in birth weight increases as the number of cigarettes smoked daily increases. Nicotine, along with many other components of cigarette smoke, such as Cotinine, passes through the placenta and directly affects the fetus. Although it affects many systems of the developing person, the primary target is the cardiovascular system (39). Nicotine transferred to the fetus by the mother's smoking of one cigarette is enough to lower the fetal pH and oxygen tension in its blood and decrease fetal oxygen (48). Furthermore, the carbon monoxide that crosses the placenta attacks the fetal hemoglobin, reducing the oxygen tension at the capillary level which then induces hypoxia in the fetus (48).

✔ Carbon monoxide is believed to be responsible for many cases of growth retardation later observed in offspring of smoking mothers (39, 48). Additionally, slight retardation in learning skills—reading and mathematics specifically—has been identified by researchers who conducted an extensive study on several thousand children between 7 and 11 years whose mothers had smoked during pregnancy (48).

✔ Additionally, infants of smoking mothers have significantly more hospital admissions with the diagnosis of bronchitis or pneumonia in comparison to infants of nonsmoking mothers (36). Children of heavy smokers (ten or more cigarettes per day) have poorer physical and social development than offspring of light or nonsmokers (48).

✔ Based on the abundance of evidence pointing to the damaging effects of smoking to both mother and fetus, total avoidance of smoking during pregnancy is now a major medical recommendation (75). Maternal cigarette smoking and heavy caffeine use, both during and after pregnancy, are linked to increased rates of infantile apnea (96). For males, cigarette advertisements continue to link smoking with virility. However a growing body of research links smoking with reduced sperm count. Large doses of marijuana smoke produce the same effect (18).

Drug Hazards to the Fetus: Teratogenic Effects

Drugs Cross the Placenta. Many drugs cross the placenta to the fetus from the mother's blood. The placenta acts like a sieve, not a barrier. Thus, no drugs, whether obtained by prescription or over the counter, should be taken during pregnancy unless it is medically prescribed as necessary for the mother (76). Pritchard and MacDonald stress two basic points: (1) With rare exception, any drug that exerts a systemic effect in the mother will cross the placenta to reach the embryo or fetus; (2) If an essential drug is administered during pregnancy, the advantages to be gained must clearly outweigh any risks inherent in its use (75). Physicians prescribe fewer drugs to pregnant women now than in the past; a drug is prescribed only if withholding it would cause a more serious consequence for the mother than its adverse effects on the fetus.

✔ *Aspirin (acetylsalicylic acid) and Darvon (propoxyphene hydrochloride)* cross the placenta and should be avoided. Medications containing salicylates, including in combination with caffeine and phenacetin, are associated with an increased incidence of anemia, hemorrhage, prolonged gestation, perinatal mortality, and low-birth weight (38, 76, 93).

✔ *Some antibiotics* are teratogenic and should be given cautiously during pregnancy (74). Some women are plagued by urinary tract and other rather common types of bacterial infection during gestation. The question of safety of the embryo and fetus is raised when medications are prescribed to alleviate these medical problems. Penicillin has been used extensively during pregnancy and appears to be harmless to the embryo and fetus (4, 11, 16, 74, 93). *Sulfonamides* are relatively safe but should be avoided during the last few weeks of pregnancy because of risk of neonatal hyperbilirubinemia. On the other hand, tetracycline therapy causes minor tooth defects, discoloration of the deciduous teeth, and distortion of bone growth (76, 81). Streptomycin and other aminoglycosides are also excluded as drugs of choice because their use can result in deafness (76). Information available pertaining to placental transmission of antimicrobial agents is yet incomplete, although it is known that the period of maximum teratogenicity lasts until the ninth week of gestation (11, 76).

✔ Offspring of males or females with epilepsy show an increased rate of birth defects, some of which result from the anticonvulsant drug Phenytoin and some of which may be due to the epilepsy itself. In the male, lowered sexual potency, decreased fertility, and sperm with decreased motility and abnormal structural changes have been identified (18).

✔ *Most cytotoxic drugs* used in the treatment of maternal cancer are known to cross the placenta, as do many of the other drugs discussed here. These agents may cause abortion or fetal anomalies if taken during the first trimester. However, no ill effects on the fetus have been reported in cases where the drugs were administered to the mother during the remainder of the pregnancy (34, 75, 76). Furthermore, the circulating cancerous cells of the mother appear not to invade or harm the developing embryo and fetus. The study of cytotoxic drugs and their potential effects on mother and infant continues. In the male, research indicates that some cancer chemotherapy agents damage the sperm; sperm banking prior to therapy or perhaps artificial insemination of mates are available options.

✔ *Hormones* may also have a deleterious effect on the fetus. Taking sex hormones or oral contraceptives either just before or during pregnancy may harm the developing fetus (39, 75, 76, 81, 89). Spontaneous abortion and cardiovascular defects in the newborn have been reported. A delayed consequence has been observed in adolescents or young women who develop vaginal or cervical cancer, which may be fatal. Adolescent and young adult female offspring of women who received diethylstilbestrol (DES) during the first trimester of pregnancy to prevent miscarriage are more likely to develop such cancers or show changes in vaginal tissue or vaginal and cervical structures. Daughters of women who were administered DES in the 1950s should have regular pelvic examinations. Sons of women who received DES may experience sterility and testicular abnormalities and cancer. Corticosteroids, e.g., prednisone, are other hormones that pass through the placental barrier and may cause adverse effects to the fetus (39, 75, 76, 81, 89).

✔ The diabetic mother should take the hormone insulin; oral antidiabetic drugs are not recommended due to risk of neonatal jaundice and hypoglycemia (76).

✔ *Drug Abuse and Addiction.* During pregnancy drug abuse and addiction continues to manifest iself as a major psychosocial and physical problem for both mother and child. Wager and Keith (99) note that prior to 1968 only a few published reports documented this complication of pregnancy. Now substances commonly abused during pregnancy, taken individually or in combination, are known to have multiple effects on the developing person, the outcome of pregnancy as well as neonatal neurobehavior (99). Infants exposed to addictive drugs in utero are at risk for a higher rate of congenital malformations and perinatal mortality (16, 18, 19, 74, 89).

These drugs include amphetamines, barbiturates, cocaine, (includes "crack," a potent and purified version), Placidyl (ethchlorvynol), heroin, Demerol (meperidine hydrochloride), methadone, morphine, Talwin (pentazocine hydrochloride), Darvon (propoxyphene hydrochloride), PCP (phencyclidine, known as "angel dust"), THC (tetrahydrocannabinos or marijuana), and methamphetamine (53, 99). Drugs that act on the central nervous system are often lipophilic and of relatively low-molecular weight characteristics which facilitate crossing the so-called placental–fetal blood–brain barrier (16). Some drugs can be metabolized by the fetal liver and placenta; however these metabolites are water soluble (81). A high incidence of maternal nutritional deficiency and anemia is also associated with drug use (39, 65).

✔ Clinical assessment for substance abuse should include an evaluation of physical appearance, a nursing history, and a substance abuse interview. The patient's/client's demeanor, neatness, cleanliness, and affect may give subtle or overt clues. Urine samples of mothers are effective to screen for ingestion of illicit drugs; alcohol breath tests are appropriate to check maternal alcohol levels at periodic intervals.

✔ Low-birth-weight, short gestation, and major malformations occur more often among offspring of marijuana users (53). Numerous adverse effects of maternal drug addiction reported in the literature are summarized by Wager and Keith: prematurity, low-birth weight and accelerated weight loss in the newborn period, depressed Apgar scores at birth, chromosomal abnormalities, and neuromotor abnormalities (99).

✔ Addictive drugs, such as heroin, codeine, and morphine in the mother's blood, are related to a high incidence of obstetric complications: toxemia, abruptio placenta, spontaneous abortion, stillbirth, premature and breech delivery, and postpartal hemorrhage (resulting in part from poor prenatal care) (81, 99). Of the three drugs, cocaine in its various forms is the most devastating.

✔ Chasnoff and associates (12–15) explain that cocaine acts peripherally to inhibit nerve conduction and prevent norepinephrine uptake at the nerve terminals, producing increased norepinephrine levels with subsequent vasoconstriction and a concomitant abrupt rise in blood pressure.

✔ Placental vasoconstriction also occurs, decreasing blood flow to the fetus with an increase in uterine contractility. In the neonate, tachycardia and hypertension are clearly associated with cerebrovascular hemorrhage. CT scan of the neonate may confirm presence of acute focal cerebral infarction.

✔ A generation of children, exposed to cocaine in the fetal state, have an abnormally high incidence of "severe" physical and emotional problems. These children have a higher incidence of: (1) learning difficulties; (2) severe impairments in motor movement, including simple movements like eating and dressing; (3) irritability; (4) tremors; (5) sensitivity to sounds; and (6) various personality–social difficulties. Many of these children have been born to middle class and wealthy parents, a group increasingly using cocaine (17).

✔ The Brazelton Neonatal Behavioral Assessment Scale is recommended to evaluate normality of responses to environmental stimuli (39). The specific pattern of symptoms is dependent on (1) the type, amount, and combination of drugs used by the mother, (2) the length of time between drug exposure and delivery, and (3) the fetal ability to metabolize the drug (99). Neurological signs (the first to appear within 24 hours following birth) include tremors, hyperirritability, hyperactivity, shrill cry, fever, "hard to hold" or a failure to mold to the holder's body, and possible convulsions. Respiratory involvement shows signs of rapid, irregular breathing, excessive secretions and nasal congestion, intermittent cyanosis, and periods of apnea. Gastrointestinal signs include disorganized sucking behavior with poor closure of lips around nipple, appearance of being very hungry, sensitive gag reflex, vomiting and regurgitation, and loose stools and diarrhea. Cardiovascular signs may include tachycardia and hypertension. Of these, Wager and Keith explain that the following are the four primary clinical considerations of Neonatal Withdrawal Syndrome: (1) prolonged tachypnea and respiratory alkalosis; (2) extreme hyperactivity; (3) decreased ability to orient and visualize; and (4) disturbed REM sleeping patterns. Newborns may require up to 40 days of treatment during the withdrawal phase (99). The limited ability of the newborn to metabolize and eliminate these fat-soluble drugs may be responsible for postponement of withdrawal symptoms for 2 to 4 weeks in some infants (32).

✔ The child of a cocaine-addicted mother is likely to demonstrate permanent physical and mental damage due to fetal anoxia and/or fetal/neonatal strokes (cerebrovascular hemorrhages) (12, 17). Long-term effects in the child of the heroin-addicted mother include the following characteristics: lower weight and shorter height than normal for age and lower scores on perceptual and learning tests (93).

✔ Intrauterine growth retardation—an actual reduction in the number of cells in organs of the passively addicted fetus—is believed to be due to the nutritional deficiencies associated with the maternal drug lifestyle (39). Observed chromosomal damage related to low Apgar readings requires more research. Neuromotor anomalies consist of decreased visual orientation: irregular sleep patterns—disorganized rapid eye movement (REM) periods and absence of "quiet sleep"; nonnutritive sucking; hyperactivity and impaired attention span; and a disturbed motor development with varying patterns (99). The decreased ability to orient to auditory and visual stimuli can have extensive effects on later character development and learning behaviors (39). Disrupted REM sleep patterns also directly affect the child's personality development (41).

✔ Withdrawing the addicted woman prior to delivery causes the fetus to experience withdrawal distress caused by visceral vasoconstriction affecting circulation to the uterus. Intrauterine death may occur. The infant is born with drug addiction and experiences withdrawal symptoms in 2 to 4 days.

Fetal, maternal, paternal, and environmental factors all interact to produce neonatal withdrawal syndrome, which is actually a diverse collection of signs and symptoms demonstrated in the newborn (39, 81).

✔ *Mood Altering or Psychotropic Drugs.* These drugs, administered prior to and during pregnancy, are to be avoided when possible because of their reported untoward effects on the developing person. Such drugs ingested by the mother before conception or between conception and implantation are known to produce chromosomal anomalies in the embryo (39, 76, 93). Minor tranquilizers and antidepressants can produce damaging effects, depending on the critical period of fetal development when the drug is circulated within the mother's system. For instance, thalidomide shows its teratogenic effects when ingested between days 28 and 42 of pregnancy (93). If psychotropic drugs are taken late in pregnancy, the neonate is likely to suffer drug toxicity, hypothermia, respiratory depression, hypotonia, convulsions, and withdrawal symptoms (76). Newborns of mothers who had taken lithium have been described as hypotonic, listless, and floppy (76). For treatment of stress-related illnesses in males, Tagamet (cimetidine) and Azulfidine (sulfasalazine) may temporarily suppress sperm production up to nearly 50 percent (18, 19).

✔ Drug abuse in the father may also act as a teratogen. For example, marijuana abuse may cause chromosomal breaks in the father and contribute to fetal risk (90). Animal studies indicate that morphine-dependent and methadone-dependent males father offspring having decreased birth weight, increased stillbirth rates, and, increased neonatal mortality rates (18).

✔ *Alcohol.* Alcohol ingested before or during pregnancy serves as another common cause of abnormal changes in the fetus (36, 39, 47, 56, 60, 88, 91, 100). Alcoholic beverages should be avoided; drinking as little as 3 ounces of liquor daily increases the chances of congenital defects (56), low-birth weight, preterm delivery, stillbirth, abruptio placenta, or spontaneous abortion (88). Alcoholism in the father may inhibit spermatogenesis and also act as a teratogen that contributes to chromosomal breaks or damaged genes, resulting in spontaneous abortion or birth defects. It is common for alcoholic men and women to be married, with each contributing to the development of Fetal Alcohol Syndrome (discussed below) to some degree (89). Even abstinence during the gestation period seems to be "too little too late" for infants born to mothers who have had a history of heavy alcoholic intake prior to conception (56). The affected newborn may suffer many of the signs and symptoms described in Neonatal Withdrawal Syndrome due to maternal drug-related consumption. The term in this case is fetal alcohol syndrome (FAS). Fetal alcohol syndrome due to the excessive ingestion of alcohol causes the following characteristics: low-birth weight; small head; flat facial profile or deformity; ear and eye abnormalities; poor motor coordination; disturbed sleep patterns; extra digits; and heart defects (39, 44, 56, 60, 75, 88, 91, 93). Research conducted by Jones and associates indicates that perinatal mortality is abnormally high, impaired fine and gross motor development is continued as the surviving child matures, and the incidence of mental retardation is abnormally high when evaluated at age 7 (44). Isouh and others add that the younger the mother at the onset of alcoholism, the higher the incidence of speech and language problems in the offspring (41). These children who suffer the effects of maternal alcoholic intake via FAS have been found to be more prone than the average child to acquiring both classifications of bacterial infections—minor and life threatening (72). Lesser defects may occur in the offspring (10 percent risk of FAS) when the mother engages in moderate social drinking or when the woman drinks an average of 1 to 2 ounces of absolute alcohol daily in the months prior to pregnancy. Heavy paternal drinking may also be a factor in FAS (48, 60, 80). Growth is retarded throughout childhood, and mental and motor capabilities appear limited for life. FAS may rank second only to German measles as a cause of congenital disorders (56).

Effects of Folklore as a Prenatal Influence

✔ **Folklore** *can be defined as strong beliefs about certain facets of or influences on basic aspects of life.* Most cultures, especially those that adhere less to scientific thinking, define certain desirable or forbidden activities for the pregnant woman. These superstitions, however, are often believed, feared, or unconsciously practiced even by well-educated or professional people, although they might not confess that they believe in them. The commonly experienced fear of giving birth to an abnormal infant causes the pregnant woman, or even the father-to-be, to act in ways that would otherwise be rejected or opposed. The more tightly the woman is bound by her culture, the more she follows the rules or taboos surrounding food, hygiene, activity, and contacts with other people. Many cultures emphasize that the woman should look at pleasant sights, think positive thoughts, eat certain foods, and pursue certain leisure activities to ensure a healthy, happy, talented child. Cultures usually emphasize that unhappy thoughts, aggressive actions, certain foods, unpleasant sights, or unusual or strenuous activity should be avoided to prevent bearing a sick, deformed, or dead baby. Often folklore practices do not interfere with scientific practices; therefore, you should not ridicule or try to convince the mother to drop these practices since the resulting conflict she feels internally or from her culture may have adverse health effects. Further, folklore often evolves so that the pregnant woman is protected from hazards or given extra care which, in turn, meets her needs emotionally and physically (39).

✔ Various references are available to give you further information about specific folklore that affects prenatal care (28, 39, 92, 100).

Maternal Infections: Hazardous Influence on the Fetus

✔ The pregnant woman is more susceptible to infections. The placenta cannot screen out all infectious organisms; therefore, infectious diseases in the vaginal region can travel up to the amniotic sac and penetrate its walls and infect the amniotic fluid. Diseases that have a mild effect on the mother may have a profound effect on the fetus, depending on gestational age (28, 39).

Acquired Immune Deficiency Syndrome (**AIDS**) is transmitted from mother to fetus at some point near the actual birthing process; the exact mode of transmission is not clearly understood. Women who are infected with the HTLV III/LAV virus and women who are at risk for infection (intravenous [IV] drug users, Haitian-born, partner of IV drug users, partner of bisexual man) place the unborn fetus in serious jeopardy (71).

✔ The majority of AIDS cases in the pediatric age range (up to 13 years) are the result of acquiring the HTLV III/LAV virus perinatally from infected mothers. Transmission of the virus through breast milk has also been reported. Other modes include transfusion, either prenatally or postnatally. The ELISA blood screen for HTLV III/LAV has not presumably significantly reduced the likelihood of acquiring AIDS by transfusion. Records indicate that the earliest year of birth for children with perinatally acquired AIDS was 1977; the earliest transfusion of blood known to have infected a child with HTLV III/LAV was 1978 (78).

✔ Except for Kaposi's sarcoma, clinical manifestations of AIDS in newborns are different than those observed in adults. These differences make the task of identifying and managing infected offspring just that more difficult. Conditions such as failure to thrive, *Candida* infections, generalized lymphadenopathy, diarrhea, and bacterial infections (bacteremia, pneumonia, otitis media) persist over time in AIDS-infected infants. Diagnosis of AIDS may take several months and includes intensive blood analysis with particular attention to significant changes in T-lymphocyte activity. Prognosis for infants of less than 1 year is bleak (71, 78).

The following text is highly recommended as a source on the pathology and transmission of AIDS in children and adults: *AIDS Modern Concepts and Therapeutic Changes*. Samuel Broder (ed.), New York: Marcel Dekker (1987).

Another example of maternal infection is *rubella* (German measles) during the first 3 months of pregnancy.

✔ Rubella may go unnoticed by the mother but it may cause serious congenital anomalies in the eyes, heart, or brain—and death. About 1 in 600 children is born with congenital rubella (1, 28, 39, 80, 98).

↙ To minimize or prevent clinical features of the disease, large doses of gamma globulin are generally administered to nonimmunized pregnant women who have been exposed to rubella. Immunization of all female children prior to puberty can effectively retard the spread of rubella. The vaccine should never be administered to pregnant women; the rubella vaccine virus will cross the placenta just as the wild (community-acquired) rubella virus (1). The rubella vaccine is actually a live-virus vaccine containing a strain of rubella virus that has been somewhat altered. Therefore, women who (1) are at risk, (2) are not aware of being pregnant, and (3) agree to prevent conception for a 3-month period should be vaccinated according to the U.S. Public Health Service Advisory Committee on Immunization Practices (98).

↙ Galash and others report that small-for-date births are a fetal complication of maternal rubella. The fetus suffers an abnormal decrease in the absolute number of cells in most organs due to the viral interference with cell multiplication. The virus also causes adverse changes in the small blood vessels of the developing fetus and does profuse damage to the placental vascular system as well, thus interfering with the fetus's blood flow and oxygenation (30).

↙ *Rubeola* ("long mealses") is also associated with congenital defects. Viruses causing mumps, smallpox, scarlet fever, and viral hepatitis may be related to formation of anomalies in utero, and during the last month of pregnancy they may cause a life-threatening fetal infection (4, 39, 81).

↙ *Maternal syphilis* causes severe adverse effects, such as congenital syphilis, brain damage, spontaneous abortion (miscarriage), or stillbirth. Adequate treatment prior to the eighteenth week of pregnancy prevents syphilis in the fetus, since the fetus appears relatively immune to syphilis, compared to other diseases, in early pregnancy. Symptoms at birth include lesions of the skin and mucous membranes, coryza, anemia, and localized septicemia. Or the child may appear healthy at birth with symptoms appearing in 2 to 6 weeks. Occasionally, symptoms may not appear for 2 years (28, 39, 72). Treatment of the mother also ensures treatment of the ill fetus because penicillin readily crosses the placenta. Other antibiotics are available for those persons who are allergic to penicillin, such as erythromycin (39, 76).

↙ *Maternal gonorrhea* and other less-known types of sexually transmitted disease have varying degrees of negative effects on the mother and her offspring. These conditions are receptive to antibiotic treatments (32, 39, 76).

↙ *Herpes simplex* of the genital area is increasing in incidence. Thus the prevention and treatment of *perinatal herpes simplex* (type II) is of great public concern. Its primary source is maternal in nature in that genital herpes infections are sexually transmitted; consequently, affected women are mainly in the child-bearing age group (1, 6). The majority of genital infections are asymptomatic and difficult to recognize on clinical examination, thus making the identification of a mother whose fetus is in jeopardy very difficult (20, 39).

↙ Unlike rubella, which readily crosses the placenta, the potential hazards of herpes simplex generally await the unsuspecting fetus in the maternal cervix or lower genital tract. The virus invades the uterus following the rupture of membranes or contact is made with the fetus during the normal vaginal birth descent. Cesarean section is the delivery of choice if the infection has been diagnosed as a means of protecting the fetus from contamination (75).

↙ Congenital and neonatal herpes simplex viral infections often prove lethal (1). A mortality rate of 60 percent, plus serious central nervous system and eye damages have been identified in half the survivors. Because drug therapeutic measures taken thus far to cure the mother and newborn have proven ineffective, research in prevention and treatment of the infectious disease continues.

↙ Another dangerous infection is *cytomegalic inclusion disease* (CID), which is caused by one of the herpes viruses, and occurs in 1 to 2 percent of pregnant women and about half their babies. Cytomegalic inclusion disease may go undetected in the mother and in the young child because the disease is asymptomatic; but laboratory analysis of infant cord blood detects the virus (81). The disease in the newborn is characterized by microcephaly, impaired growth, impaired intellectual ability, impaired hearing, enlarged liver and spleen, hemolytic anemia, and fracture of long bones (72, 81).

↙ A *parasitic disease, toxoplasmosis,* is acquired by human contact with cat feces or eating inadequately cooked food that contains the parasitic cysts. Transplacental transmission occurs during acute infection of the mother, but the disease causes congenital liver and brain damage, and can result in convulsions, blindness, and mental retardation. The infected mother can be treated with medication, which probably reduces fetal damage. However, pregnant women who are not immune should be advised to not handle cats, cat feces, or litter boxes (81).

Fetal Infection as a Prenatal Influence

↙ Intrauterine fetal infection due to group B *Streptococcus* probably occurs with greater frequency than is clinically diagnosed (8). In the most serious of cases the clinical signs—apnea, respiratory distress, and shock—emerge at birth or within a few hours (5). Evidence points to the passage of this infectious agent through the fetal membranes that were previously thought to be effective in blocking such an invasion. Only penicillin is indicated for use as an antibiotic since no severe allergic reaction to the fetus or newborn has been reported (32).

Immunologic Factors as a Prenatal Influence

✓ The fetus is immunologically foreign to the mother's immune system; yet, the fetus is sustained. Selected antibodies of measles, chicken pox, hepatitis, poliomyelitis, whooping cough, and diptheria are transferred to the fetus. The resulting immunity lasts several months after birth. Antibodies to dust, pollen, and common allergens do not transfer across the placenta (39).

✓ The most commonly encountered interference with fetal development is incompatibility between maternal and infant blood factors, resulting in various degrees of circulatory difficulty for the baby. This problem is more complex than the commonly known Rh incompatibility. When a fetus's blood contains a protein substance, the Rh factor (Rh-positive blood), but the mother's blood does not (Rh-negative blood), antibodies in the mother's blood may attack the fetus and possibly bring about jaundice, spontaneous abortion, stillbirth, anemia, heart defects, mental retardation, or death. Usually the first Rh-positive baby is not affected adversely, but with each succeeding pregnancy the risk becomes greater. A vaccine can be given to the Rh-negative mother within 3 days of childbirth or within 3 days of abortion that will prevent her body from making Rh antibodies. Babies affected by the Rh syndrome can be treated by repeated blood transfusions (81). Indepth information can be attained from a physiology or obstetrics text (35, 39, 81).

Maternal Emotions as a Prenatal Influence

✓ The physical–psychological interdependence between mother and fetus continues to be studied; effects of the mother's elation, fear, and anxiety on the behavior and other developmental aspects of the baby are poorly understood. Anxiety, for instance, produces a variety of physiological changes in the person because of activation of the hypothalamus and the sympathetic division response of the autonomic nervous system, which stimulates the adrenal medulla to produce adrenaline. Adrenaline, in turn, stimulates the anterior lobe of the pituitary to produce adrenocorticotropic hormone (ACTH), which activates the adrenal cortex to release cortisone. The results are: increased heart rate, constriction of peripheral vessels, dilation of coronary vessels, decrease in gastrointestinal motility, changed carbohydrate and protein metabolism, which also affects many body functions and changes in the adrenocortical hormonal system (35). These changes occurring in the pregnant woman contribute to hyperactivity of the fetus because increased maternal cortisone is secreted and enters the blood circulation, crossing the placenta to the fetus (35, 39, 80). Because the fetus experiences only the consequences and not the cause of the emotion itself, the experience may mean nothing to the fetus (54). However, some studies indicate that maternal fear and anxiety induce the same sensations in the fetus. Animal studies indicate that stress-producing situations influence the fetus, causing changes in emotional states and also in learning activity after birth (28). Studies indicate that the human fetus responds with increased activity to loud noises in the environment (67). Maternal stress, therefore, may be considered a teratogen resulting in physical and psychological alterations of the developing person before and following birth.

✓ Maternal anxiety reactions are also related to physiological responses of pregnancy, such as nausea and vomiting, backaches, and headaches which, in turn, affect the fetus.

✓ The woman who begins pregnancy with inadequate psychic reserves is especially vulnerable to stresses and conflicting moods that accompany pregnancy (39). However, maternal emotionality during pregnancy has not been correlated with specific mother–child behavioral interaction.

Birth Defects Transmitted by the Father

✓ Genes of both mother and father, as well as the prenatal maternal environment, may cause birth defects. Genetic mutations in sperm occur in less than 1 percent of the population. Mutations may be caused by exposure to irradiation, infection, drugs, and chemicals. These mutations occur more frequently as a man ages and may be responsible for various inborn disorders and congenital anomalies (80, 93). For males, this "cut-off" is 45 years of age; risks for chromosome abnormalities may double when the male is 55 years or older (19). Refer also to Chapter 2 for additional information on birth defects transmitted by the father, with a focus on Table 2–2.

Variables Related to Childbirth That Affect the Baby

Medications

✓ Analgesics and general anesthetics during childbirth cross the placental barrier, affecting the newborn for days after delivery. Respiration after birth is negatively affected; artificial resuscitation may be needed for severe respiratory depression. Motor skills are also less adept and more crying irritability is seen after birth (39, 72). Local anesthetics also indirectly affect the fetus by reducing blood flow to the uterus and thus affecting the fetal heart rate (39, 81).

✔ Childbirth without drugs was first introduced in 1914 by Grantly Dick-Read. He was followed by Dr. Fernand Lamaze. In recent times, the natural childbirth method has become popular both to mother and father, as they can both actively participate in the birth of their child. During natural childbirth classes, parents learn about the physiology of pregnancy and childbirth, exercises that strengthen the mother's abdominal and perineal muscles, and techniques of breathing and relaxation during labor and delivery. The father acts as encourager and coach throughout the prenatal classes and during labor and delivery, so that the birth experience is shared between the couple. Equally of benefit is the child who comes into the world without any ill effects of medication. Refer to literature from the American Society for Psychoprophylaxis in Obstetrics and obstetric nursing texts for more information on prepared childbirth.

Method of Delivery

✔ In the early 1970s, F. LeBoyer, a French obstetrician, developed a less traumatic method of delivering the baby by reducing intensity of new stimuli—light, gravity, and coolness. Lights are dim, only essential talking is allowed, and baby is placed on mother's abdomen until the cord stops pulsating (3 to 5 minutes). During this time the baby's back is gently massaged to simulate uterine contractions. Baby is wrapped in a warm blanket and placed to mother's breast after the cord is cut. Baby is quieter and more alert as a result (39).

Inadequate Oxygenation

✔ **Anoxia,** *decreased oxygen supply,* and increased carbon dioxide levels may result during delivery. Some degree almost routinely occurs from compression of the umbilical cord, reduced blood flow to the uterus, or placental separation. Fortunately, newborn babies are better able to withstand periods of low oxygen than are adults. Other causes of asphyxia, however, such as drug-induced respiratory depression or apnea, kinks in the umbilical cord, wrapping of the cord around the neck, very long labor, or malpresentation of the fetus during birth, have more serious effects. Longitudinal studies over 7 years of anoxic newborns revealed lower performance scores on tests of sensorimotor and cognitive–intellectual skills and personality measures than for children with minimal anoxia at birth. Anoxia is also the principal cause of perinatal death and a common cause of mental retardation and cerebral palsy (39, 81).

Premature Birth

Prematurity may have long-term consequences for the child. **Prematurity** *is defined as the infant born at gestational age of 37 weeks or earlier, combined with birth weight of less than 2,500 grams or 5½ pounds.* Risk of death is greater in premature babies.

✔ Later developmental and behavioral problems may also be correlated with prematurity, such as physical and mental retardation and hyperactivity (39, 72). Treatment of the premature neonate in sterile, precisely controlled incubators causes the absence of environmental and sensory stimuli, which also contributes to retardation (39, 72). Research shows 5 minutes of gentle rubbing hourly throughout the 24-hour day for 10 days showed positive effects immediately and later for infants in isolettes: they were more active and gained weight faster, and 7 months later they performed better on tests of motor development while appearing healthier and more active than control children (49, 50).

✔ The small-for-date or low-birth-weight (less than 5½ pounds) infant may not be premature. This distinction has been made in the last 10 to 15 years. Previous studies did not distinguish between these two factors.

✔ The following factors contribute to a higher risk of low-birth weight babies: (1) mother is underweight before pregnancy; (2) gaining less than 21 pounds during pregnancy; (3) lack of prenatal care; (4) mother's age is 16 years or younger or, 35 years or older; (5) the mother smoked during pregnancy, and (6) the mother used addicting drugs or alcohol during pregnancy (34). Complications that affect low-birth-weight babies include breathing difficulties, jaundice, anemia, low blood sugar, and poor regulation of body temperature. Later, behavior problems may be manifested (59).

✔ A sixfold increase in the risk of low-birth-weight is associated with financial problems existing during the pregnancy, irrespective of the variables of race, poor health habits, and complications during pregnancy (2). A study of low-birth weight children born to disadvantaged families showed that those who had received sensory stimulation in the nursery and additional sensorimotor stimulation from their mothers throughout the first year of life performed better on tests of intellectual and sensorimotor development at the end of the year than the children who had not received extra stimulation (80).

✓ Premature children differ from full-term infants in a number of ways, including sleep patterns, which are poorly organized with poorly differentiated sleep states. Shorter and less regular periods of each sleep state are exhibited and may persist beyond infancy. Because more growth hormone is released during sleep, disturbed sleep patterns in the premature may affect physical growth and size generally (81).

Early Childhood Variables That Affect the Person

Nutrition

✓ Nutrition can exert an important influence on growth and development, especially if nutritional deficiency diseases occur. Unfortunately, minimum, optimum, and toxic levels of nutrients are not well researched to date. However, inadequate nutrition may slow normal growth and apparently causes permanent effects of low intellectual ability. As much as 30 percent of the brain's neurons may never be formed if protein intake is inadequate during the second trimester of pregnancy or the first 6 months of life. Children who suffer starvation do not catch up with growth norms for their group, although later in life adequate nutrition and socioemotional support help to offset the differences (72, 73).

✓ Obesity in childhood is more likely to be related to eating patterns than to genetics, according to a study of weight differences between infants of obese and nonobese foster mothers. The babies weighed 4½ pounds at birth and entered the foster home at 3½ weeks of age. Children cared for by obese foster parents also became obese. The mean weight of all children of obese mothers was heavier at all ages than for children of nonobese mothers. The obese baby may become the obese adult; infant weight correlates with adult weight independently of other factors considered (65, 72, 73).

✓ Even breast feeding is not completely safe. Many drugs ingested by the mother are excreted in human milk. (Several authors discuss drugs and their effects [16, 76, 89].) The newborn is susceptible to foreign substances because the body's principal detoxifying mechanisms are not functional, the enzyme system is immature, and kidney function is incompletely developed (81). Media reports indicate that pesticides in food and other environmental pollutants unknowingly ingested by the mother are excreted in human milk.

Stress

✓ Stress related to emotional and sensory deprivation causes undesirable physical, emotional, and intellectual effects (39, 84–86). Some studies of the effects of mild physical stress on infants and rats reveal increased physical height, faster weight gain, and greater resistance to disease; however, variables for these studies appear to be poorly controlled and the studies are primarily anecdotal (28, 80). Other studies show that severe stress, discomfort, or pain cause the infant to perceive less external stimuli and to distort perceptions. Less tolerance for stress develops (67).

Effects of Practice on Neuromuscular Development

✓ Effects of exercise or practice on developing early motor skills remain contradictory in reports. Apparently certain motor behavior appears when the body has the neuromuscular maturity for that behavior; practice of the behavior prior to its natural appearance does little to speed up long-term development, although it may appear that the child can do an activity earlier. Unpracticed children catch up, often doing the same activity in research studies only a few days later (67).

Endocrine Function

Mediation of hormones is crucial to the child and person throughout life. *A* **hormone** *is a chemical substance produced by an endocrine gland and carried by the bloodstream to another part of the body (the target organ) where it controls some function of the target organ.* The major functions of hormones include (1) integrative action, (2) regulation, and (3) morphogenesis. **Integration,** *permitting the body to act as a whole unit in response to stimuli,* results from hormones traveling throughout the body and reaching all cells of the body. For example, the response of the body to epinephrine during fright is generalized. Estrogen, although more specific in its action, affects overall bodily function. **Regulation,** *maintaining a constant internal environment or homeostasis,* results from all the hormones. The regulation of salt and water balance, metabolism, and growth are examples. In **morphogenesis,** *the rate and type of growth of the organism,* some hormones play an important part (43).

Growth hormone (GH) or *somatotropic hormone* (STH), secreted by the anterior pituitary gland and regulated by a substance called growth-hormone-releasing-factor (GHF) produced in the hypothalamus, affects morphogenesis by promoting the development and enlargement of all bodily tissues that are capable of growing. Growth hormone has three basic effects on the metabolic processes of the body: (1) protein synthesis is increased; (2) carbohydrate conservation is increased; and (3) use of fat stores for energy is increased.

✔ Growth hormone is secreted in spurts instead of at a relatively constant rate. The lowest concentrations of plasma GH are found in the morning after arising; the highest concentrations occur between 60 and 90 minutes after falling asleep at night. The peak of GH is clearly related to sleep; thus the folk belief that sleep is necessary for growth and healing has been supported (35, 45, 67, 80, 93).

Sociocultural Factors That Influence the Developing Person

Cultural and Demographic Variables

✔ Culture, social class, race, and ethnicity of the parents variously affect the person from the moment of conception: foods eaten by the pregant woman; prenatal care and childbirth practices; child-rearing methods; expected patterns of behavior; language development and thought processes during childhood and adulthood; and health practices. However, the person will demonstrate some behaviors outside the cultural norm. If the child's parents are from a different ethnic or social background from most citizens of the area, the child may learn to talk, act, and think differently from most people. Conflict results between the person and the representatives (people and institutions) of the main culture, which, in turn, affects the child's ongoing development and care. Refer to Chapter 1 for in-depth discussion.

✔ The health care given to the child by the parents is related to sociocultural status. For example, in urban areas parents of children who are adequately immunized are likely to have the following characteristics: (1) they perceive childhood diseases as serious; (2) they know about the effectiveness of vaccination; (3) they are older; (4) they are better educated; (5) they have smaller family size (number of children); (6) they read newspapers, listen to radio or television promotions of immunizations, and respond to these community educational efforts; and (7) they are likely to be Caucasian. Inadequately immunized children in urban areas were found in families in which the parents are young, poor, minimally educated, and non-White with a large number of children. The parents do not perceive childhood diseases as serious, do not know about the effectiveness of vaccines, or do not pay attention to health education in the mass media (45, 67).

All the advantages of inheriting a good brain can be lost if the child does not have the right environment in which to develop it. Animal and human studies demonstrate that lack of physical or social stimulation has an effect on later behavior and development. For example, studies comparing rats raised in a stimulus-deprived environment and stimulus-rich environment showed that rats that had things to keep them interested, amused, and challenged had a greater number of neurons than the other rats, and their brain cells were richer in biochemical content. Studies on rats also show that, although there cannot be an increase in the number of neurons after brain-cell division has stopped, the neurons that already exist can grow 15 percent larger and form more associations when the rat is given extra stimulation after being deprived. Thus the deprived rat can catch up in intellectual capacities.

✔ The same seems to be true of humans, as demonstrated by Korean and Vietnamese children who were adopted by American parents. In a new, loving environment they improved in all spheres of behavior and intelligence (67).

Socialization Processes

Socialization *is the process by which the infant is transformed into a member of a particular society and learns the roles appropriate to sex, social class, and ethnic group or subculture* (69).

All humans experience socialization, the shaping of the person into a socially acceptable form, especially during the early years of life. Thus, heritage and culture are perpetuated. The newborn is a biological organism with physical needs and inherited characteristics. These will be socialized or shaped along a number of dimensions: emotional, social, cognitive/intellectual, perceptual, behavioral, and expressive. During the period of socialization, various skills, knowledge, attitudes, values, motives, habits, beliefs, needs, interests, and ideals are learned, demonstrated, and reinforced. Various people are key agents in the socialization process: parents, siblings, relatives, peers, teachers, and other adults. Certain forces will impinge on the person and interact with all that the individual is and learns; these forces include culture, social class, religion, race/ethnicity, the community, the educational system, mass media, and various organizations. Certain factors may limit or enhance the socialization process: age, gender, rate and stage of development, general constitution, and innate intelligence. Integration of all the various individual and socializing forces will form the adult character, personality traits, role preferences, goals, and behavioral mode (69).

Socialization is a lifelong process of social learning or training through which the person acquires knowledge, skills, attitudes, values, needs, motivations, and cognitive, affective, and conative patterns that relate to the sociocultural setting. The success of the socialization process is measured by the person's ability to perform in the roles he/she attempts, and to respond to rapid social change and a succession of life tasks (69).

The life cycle is seen as a succession of roles and changing role constellations. A certain order and predictability of behavior occurs over time as the person moves through the given succession of roles. The person learns to think and behave in ways consonant with the roles to be played; performance in a succession of roles leads to predictable personality configurations (69).

Community Support System

✔ *Community relationships* influence primarily the parents, but they also influence the child. An emotional support system for the parents, physical and health-care resources in the community, and social and learning opportunities that exist outside the home promote the child's development and prepare him or her for later independence and citizenry roles. If the parents are unable to meet the child's needs adequately, other people or organizations in the community may make the difference between bare survival and eventual physical and emotional normalcy and well-being.

✔ Cultures vary in the degree to which the new mother is given help. For example, in India the mother is assisted with child care and is allowed to do nothing except care for her baby for 40 days after delivery. Several decades ago mothers in the United States were hospitalized for 10 or 12 days, and the family helped at home for another couple weeks or so. Now the mother is sent home after 24 to 72 hours, often to assume total child care.

✔ Physical health of the baby and emotional health of the mother in the months following delivery depend on whether or not she had assistance with infant care during the first month after delivery (72).

Family Factors

The family structure, developmental level and roles of family members, their health and financial status, their perception of baby, and community resources for the family influence the child's development and well-being. The child learns to behave differently, and as an adult will have different values and expectations if he/she is reared in a single-parent, nuclear, extended, matrifocal, or patriarchal family, or in a poor or wealthy family. The number of siblings, their sexes, and birth order influence how the child is treated and perceives self. The stresses on and crises within the family determine how well the child is cared for from birth, how and what is taught to the child, discipline measures, and how he/she looks at life. The family's presence or absence of work, leisure, travel, material comforts, habits of daily living, and the facade put on for society all affect the child's self-concept, learning, physical well-being, and eventual lifestyle. Refer to Chapter 4 for more information.

Spitz (84, 85) studied four different child-rearing situations to determine the effect on the young child. Children from professional, urban homes had the highest developmental quotient initially, and it stayed high. Children living in an isolated fishing village with poor nutrition, housing, hygiene, and medical care had a low developmental quotient in the first 4 months, and it remained low. Children born to delinquent women and reared in a penal institution by their mothers had a lower development quotient initially than children in the fishing village, but they gained slightly. Children from a Latin, urban background who were raised in a foundling home had an initial high developmental quotient, but the score was lowest of the groups studied at the end of the first year.

✔ The children in the foundling home had been given minimal mothering by overworked nurses. The presence of the mother is sufficient to compensate for lack of material objects. The lack of development was related to lack of human stimulation, since deterioration of the child was arrested if he/she were removed from the foundling home at 1 year of age.

✔ The mother has traditionally been credited with having the most effect on the child, whether the outcome was good or bad. However, researchers now acknowledge the importance of father and the effect of the father's presence or absence on the developing child (52, 58). The stability and strength of attachment between the child and family will largely determine the degree to which he/she will become a self-confident, productive citizen. The long-term emotional and physical environments are the most crucial variables in the child's measured performance at 10 years. A positive environment overcomes negative perinatal influences; a negative environment may have lasting effects (67).

Vulnerable and Resilient Children. Both kinds of children develop within the same family system. Siblings, brought up under chaotic situations, with alcoholic or drug-using parents, or in impoverished circumstances, do not all develop the same personality traits. One becomes physically or emotionally ill, while the sibling thrives. There is no single set of qualities or circumstances that characterize such resilient children, but they are different from their vulnerable siblings from birth. **Resilient children** appear to be *endowed with innate characteristics that insulate them from the pain of their families and allow them to reach out* *to some adult who provides crucial emotional support.* These children typically have the ability to use some talent or personality traits to draw some adult to them as a substitute parent. Also these children seemed to recover quickly from stressors (95). Resilient children differ from their siblings. From birth, these children are more alert to their surroundings. By 1 year of age, trust had been established with their mothers. There has been warm and secure relationships with the mother, regardless of other circumstances. By age 2, even when abused or neglected, these children are more independent, easy going, enthusiastic for activities, and able to tolerate frustration. By age 3½, the resilient children are more cheerful, flexible, and persistent in the face of stress or failure. They show ability to seek help from adults (95).

The children closest emotionally to the distressed parent are most likely to show signs of distress. These children are more likely to be self-derogatory, anxious, depressed, and physically ill. However, hardships can leave even the resilient children with psychological scars, although they tend not to become emotionally disabled. Even apparently well-adjusted, successful resilient children may pay a subtle psychological cost. In adolescence, they are more likely to cling to a moralistic outlook. In intimate relationships, they are apt to be disagreeable and judgmental. They tend to be constricted and overcontrolled. If the disturbed parent is of the opposite gender, the resilient person is often emotionally distant in intimate relationships; breaking off relationships as they become more intimate. Some seek partners with problems, with the idea of rescuing or curing them (95).

Child Abuse. This is a negative influence on the developing person. It is currently an epidemic, and children are suffering more serious and brutal injuries. Parents who abuse their children are from every race, color, creed, ethnic origin, and economic level (8). As a nurse, you are crucial in preventing child abuse through your assistance to parents. **Child abuse** *is a pattern of abnormal parent–child interactions and attacks over a period of time that results in nonaccidental injuries to the child physically, emotionally, or sexually or from neglect.* Other terms are *battered child* or *maltreatment syndrome.* Abused children range in age from neonate through adolescence.

✔ You may be the first health worker to encounter such a child in the community. Be alert for signs of child abuse as you assess the injured or ill child. Nonaccidental physical injury includes multiple bruises or fractures from severe beatings, poisonings; or overmedication; burns from immersion in hot water or lighted cigarettes, excessive use of laxatives or enemas; and human bites. The trauma to the child is often great enough to cause permanent blindness, scars on the skin, neurological damage, subdural hematoma, and permanent brain damage or death. **Sexual molestation,** *exploitation of the child for the adult's sexual gratification,* includes rape, incest, exhibitionism to the child, or fondling of the child's genitals. **Emotional abuse** *includes excessively aggressive or unreasonable parental behavior to the child,* placing unreasonable demands on the child to perform above his/her capacities, verbally attacking or constantly belittling or teasing the child, or withdrawing love, support, or guidance. **Neglect** *includes failure to provide the child with basic necessities of life* (food, shelter, clothing, hygiene, or medical care), *adequate mothering, or emotional, moral, or social care* (8, 24, 25, 37, 38, 57, 70, 82). The parents' lack of concern is usually obvious. Abandonment may occur. In all forms of abuse, the child frequently acts fearful of the parents or adults in general. The child is usually too fearful to tell how he or she was injured.

There are a number of characteristics of the potentially or actually abusive parent(s). Typically, the abuser manifests the following characteristics: (1) young in age; (2) emotionally unstable, unable to cope with the stress of life or even usual personal problems; (3) insufficiently mothered, rejected, or abused as a child; (4) lonely, few social contacts, isolated from people; (5) unable to ask for help, lack of friends or family who can help with child care; (6) does not understand the development or care needs of children; (7) living through a very stressful time, such as unemployment, being abused by the spouse, or poverty; (8) personal emotional needs previously unmet; difficulty in trusting others; (9) angered easily; negative self-image and low self-esteem; (10) no one from whom to receive emotional support, including partner; (11) expects the child to be perfect and to cause no inconvenience; (12) may perceive the child as different, too active, or too passive, even if the child is normal or only mildly different. Sometimes the child has mild neurological dysfunction and is irritable, tense, and difficult to hold or cuddle. The child may have been the result of an unwanted pregnancy, or premature, or have a birth defect. Usually only one child in a family becomes the scapegoat for parental anger, tension, rejection, and hate. The child who does not react in a way to make the parent feel good about his/her parenting behavior will be the abused one (24, 25, 38, 57, 70, 72, 80).

✔ *Prolonged Separation.* Separation of over 3 months from a mothering person leads to serious consequences, because from about 3 to 15 months of age the presence of a consistently loving caretaker is essential. Physical and intellectual growth is impaired, and the baby will not learn to form and maintain trust or a significant relationship. He/she will either withdraw or seek precociously to adapt by getting attention from as many people as possible. Death may result even with the best possible physical care (72, 82, 85).

Maternal Deprivation or Failure to Thrive. These are the terms used to describe infants who have insufficient contact with a mothering one and who do not grow as expected in the absence of an organic defect (72, 84, 85). These infants may be institutionalized or have a parent who does not exhibit affectionate maternal behavior. Deprivation during the second 6 months occurs when a previously warm relationship with the mother is interrupted. This deprivation is more detrimental to the child than the lack of a consistent relationship during the first 6 months. Another cause for failure to thrive is **perceptual deprivation**, *lack of tactile, vestibular, visual, or auditory stimuli*, resulting from either organic factors or the lack of mothering (80). Touch and cuddling are essential for the infant; the skin is the primary way in which baby comes to know self and the environment.

Although damage to the child from maternal deprivation may be severe, not every deprived child grows up to be a delinquent or a problem adult. Some infants who have lacked their mother's love appear to suffer little permanent damage. The age of the child when deprived or abused, the length of separation or duration of abuse, the parent–child relationship before separation or in later childhood, care of the child by other adults during separation from the parents, and the stress produced by the separation or abuse all affect the long-range outcome.

Spiritual Factors

Religious, philosophical, and moral insights and practices of the parents (and of the overall society) influence how the child is perceived, cared for, and taught. These early underpinnings—or their lack—will continue to affect the person's self-concept, behavior, and health as an adult, even when he/she purposefully tries to disregard these early teachings. Refer to Chapter 3 for more information.

Macroenvironmental Factors That Influence the Developing Person

The overall environment of the region in which the person lives, as well as in the home, affect development and health. The climate the person learns to tolerate, water and food availability, emphasis on cleanliness, demands for physical and motor competency, social relationships, opportunities for leisure, and inherent hazards depend on whether the child lives on a farm or in the city, on the seacoast or in a semiarid region, in the cold north or sunny south, in a mining town or a mountain resort area. Added to these effects are the hazards from environmental pollution that affect all societies, whether it is excrement from freely roaming cattle or particles from industrial smokestacks. No part of the world is any longer uncontaminated by pesticides; all parts have disease related to problems of waste control. On a more immediate level, the size, space, noise, cleanliness, and safety within the home will affect the person's behavior and health and the home environment he/she will eventually build.

Further discussion of effects of the macroenvironment on the person's health can be found in Chapter 2.

NURSING APPLICATIONS

Your support, assistance, and teaching with the pregnant woman and her significant support system will contribute to more nurturing parenting. Refer to texts on obstetrical and maternal–child nursing for additional information about nursing care of the woman during pregnancy, labor and delivery, and after delivery. Information is also given in Chapters 2, 7 through 11, and 17 that can be shared with the pregnant woman and parents for health promotion.

Consider the principles of growth and development as you assess people in different developmental eras. Carefully assess pregnant women to determine whether they are at risk because of any of the negative influencing factors. A helpful screening system for the woman prenatally and intrapartally and for the neonate has been devised (72). Help those who are at risk to get the care necessary to prevent fetal damage and maternal illness. Consider also the sociocultural and religious backgrounds and the lifestyle of the person you are caring for so that you do not overlook or misinterpret factors that are significant to the pregnant woman and her family.

Teach potential parents about the many factors discussed in this and following chapters that can influence the welfare of their offspring. Be aware of community services, such as genetic screening and counseling, family planning, nutritional programs, prenatal classes, counseling for prevention of child abuse, as well as medical services. Join with other citizens in attempts to reverse environmental and child abuse hazards.

Your role with the child-abusing parent and the abused child is a significant one. To help parents and child, you must first cope with your own feelings as you give necessary physical care to the child or assist parents in getting proper care for the baby. Often parents who feel unable to cope with the stresses of childrearing will repeatedly bring the child to the emergency room for a variety of complaints or minor, vague illnesses or injuries. Be alert to the subtle message; talk with the parent(s) about himself or herself, the management of the child, feelings about parenting and the child, and who helps in times of stress. Establish rapport; act like a helpful friend; convey a feeling of respect for them as people (which may be difficult if you feel that the child abuser is a monster). Avoid asking probing questions too quickly; do not lecture or scold the parent about his or her childrearing methods. Help parents to feel confident and competent in any way possible. If possible, form a "cool mothering" relationship with the parent(s), that is, make yourself consistently available but do not push too close emotionally. Often the mother responds well to having a grandmotherly person (usually a volunteer) spend time with her in the home. In a sense, the grandmotherly person is mothering the mother, but she is also assisting with a variety of household chores, giving the mother time to spend with her baby while unharried by demands of other children or household tasks. The grandmotherly person can also be a model on how to approach, cuddle, and discipline the child. Both you and the volunteer can share information about normal child behavior and developmental characteristics appropriate for age; the parent may expect the 6-month-old to obey commands. Convey that consistency of care is important. Realize that the parent will need long-term help in overcoming the abusive pattern. After a relationship has been formed, the abusing parent(s) may benefit from joining a group such as Parents Anonymous, where the problems of being a child abuser can be resolved and the information about normal development can be learned.

To avoid driving the parent away from potential help or becoming more abusive to the child, use the principles of therapeutic communication and crisis intervention discussed in Chapter 17. In your zeal to protect the child, intervene sensibly with the parents and the child to avoid further harm and to avoid disrupting any positive feelings that might exist between parents and child. Foster home care is not necessarily the answer; foster parents are sometimes abusive, too. Rapid court action may antagonize parents to the point of murdering the child or moving to a different geographical location where they cannot receive help. Refer the parents to Parents Anonymous, a self-help parent's group that exists in some large cities, or to other local self-help crisis groups. For more information, refer to the "Symposium on Child Abuse and Neglect," *Nursing Clinics of North America*, 16, no. 1, March, 1981 (37, 51, 57, 83).

Further, cooperate with legal, medical, and social agencies to help the parent(s) and to prevent further child abuse—and possible death or permanent impairment of the child. Child abuse is against the law in every state, and every state has at least one statewide agency to receive and investigate suspected cases of child abuse. Any citizen or health worker can anonymously report a case of child abuse to authorities without fear of recrimination from the abuser. An investigation by designated authorities of the danger to the child is carried out shortly after reporting; the child may be placed in a foster home or institution by court order if the child's life is threatened. The goal of legal intervention is to help the parents and child, not to punish (51, 57).

Unless the problem of child abuse can be curbed, many of today's children will become the next generation of abusing parents.

Mothers and children constitute about two-thirds of the population in any society (17). They are worth caring for physically and emotionally because of their worth to the future of the society.

References

1. Amstey, M. S., Specific Viral Infections: Rubella, Herpes Simplex, Varicella-Zoster, in *Gynecology and Obstetrics*, ed. J. J. Sciarra. Philadelphia: Harper & Row, 1982.
2. Binsacca, Donald, Factors Associated with Low Birth Weight in an Inner-City Population: The Role of Financial Problems, *American Journal of Public Health*, 77, no. 4 (1987), 585–586.
3. Blumenthal, Sol, L. Bergner, and F. Nelson, Low Birth Weight of Infants Associated with Maternal Heroin Use, *Health Services and Mental Health Administration*, 88, no. 5 (May, 1973), 416–422.
4. Bobitt, J. R., Specific Bacterial Infections: Group B Streptococcus and Listeria, in *Gynecology and Obstetrics*, ed. J. J. Sciarra. Philadelphia: Harper & Row, 1982.
5. Brill, Norman, Emotional Abuse of Children, *American Journal of Psychiatry*, 1, no. 2 (1981), 41.
6. Brunell, P. A., Prevention and Treatment of Neonatal Herpes, *Pediatrics*, 66, no. 11 (1980), 5.
7. Buhler, C., The Developmental Structure of Goal Setting in Group and Individual Studies, in *The Course of Human Life*, eds. C. Buhler and F. Massarik. New York: Springer-Verlag, 1968.
8. Campbell, J. E., and J. Humphreys, *Nursing Care of Victims of Family Violence*. Reston, VA: Reston, 1984.
9. Castleman, M., Toxics and Male Infertility, *SIERRA* 70, no. 2 (1985), 49–52.
10. Center for Disease Control, USDHHS, Recommendations for Assisting in the Prevention of Human T-Lymphotrophic Virus Type III/Lymphadenopathy-Associated Virus and Acquired Immunodeficiency Syndrome, *MMWR*, 34 (December 6, 1987), 721–726, 731–732.

11. Charles, D., Placental Transmission of Antibiotics, in *Gynecology and Obstetrics*, ed. J. J. Sciarra. Philadelphia: Harper & Row, 1982.
12. Chasnoff, I. J., M. E. Bussey, R. Savich, et al., Clinical and Laboratory Observations: Perinatal Cerebral Infarction and Maternal Cocaine Use, *The Journal of Pediatrics*, 108, no. 3 (1986), 456–459.
13. Chasnoff, I. J., W. J. Burns, S. H. Schnoll, et al., Cocaine Use in Pregnancy, *New England Journal of Medicine*, 313 (September 12, 1985), 666–669.
14. Chasnoff, I. J., Perinatal Effects of Cocaine, *Contemporary OB/GYN*, (May, 1987), 163–179.
15. ———, Cocaine and Pregnancy, *Childbirth Educator*, (Winter, 1986–87), 37–42.
16. ———, Drug use in Pregnancy: Mother and Child, *MTP Press*, 1986.
17. Cocaine Babies May Have Long Lasting Effects, *The Nation's Health*, (May–June, 1986), 9.
18. Cohen, F. L., Paternal Contributions to Birth Defects, *Nursing Clinics of North America*, 21, no. 1 (March, 1986), 51–66.
19. Cohen, F. L., Clinical Genetics in Nursing Practice, Philadelphia: J. B. Lippincott, 1984.
20. Committee on Infectious Diseases: Fetus and Newborn, Perinatal Herpes Simplex Virus Infections, *Pediatrics*, 66, no. 7 (1980), 1.
21. Davis, R. M., Current Trends in Cigarette Advertisement and Marketing, *The New England Journal of Medicine*, 316 (12) (March 1987), 725–733.
22. Delgado, H., et al., Maternal Nutrition—Its Effects on Infant Growth and Development and Birthspacing, in *Nutritional Impacts on Women*, eds. S. S. Moghissl and T. N. Evans, Hagerstown, Md.: Harper & Row, 1977.
23. Duvall, Evelyn, and Brent Miller, *Marriage and Family Development* (6th ed). New York: Harper & Row, 1984.
24. Elmer, Elizabeth, *Children in Jeopardy: The Study of Abused Minors and Their Families*. Pittsburgh: University of Pittsburgh Press, 1962.
25. ———, Child Abuse: The Family's Cry for Help, *Journal of Psychiatric Nursing*, 5, no. 4 (1967), 338ff.
26. Enstrom, J. E., L. E. Kanim, and L. Breslow, The Relationship Between Vitamin C Intake, General Health Practices, and Mortality in Alameda County, California, *American Journal of Public Health*, 76, no. 9 (September 1986), 1124–1129.
27. Erikson, Erik, *Childhood and Society* (2nd ed.). New York: W. W. Norton, 1963.
28. Freiberg, Karen, *Human Development: A Life Span Approach* (3rd ed.). Monterey, Calif.: Wadsworth Health Sciences Division, 1987.
29. Fried, P. A., Marijuana Use by Pregnant Women and Effects on Offspring: An Update, *Neurobehavioral Toxicology and Teratology*, 4 (1982), 451–454.
30. Galash, R. P., B. Larsen, and M. J. Ohm, Infection in Maternal-Fetal Medicine: An Overview, in *Gynecology and Obstetrics*, ed. J. J. Sciarra. Philadelphia: Harper & Row, 1982.
31. Garn, S. M., M. Johnson, S. A. Ridella, et al., Effects of Maternal Cigarette Smoking on Apgar Score, *American Journal of Disabled Children*, 135, no. 6 (1981), 503–506.
32. Giacoia, G. P., and S. Yaffe, Perinatal Pharmacology in *Gynecology and Obstetrics*, ed. J. J. Sciarra., New York: Harper & Row, 1982.
33. Giesler, C. F., and J. R. Webster, Jr., Pulmonary Disease in Pregnancy, in *Gynecology and Obstetrics*, ed. J. J. Sciarra. Philadelphia: Harper & Row, 1982.
34. Give Your Baby the Gift of a Great Start, *City of St. Louis Weekly Health Letter* (October 9, 1987), 1.
35. Guyton, A., *Human Physiology: Normal Functions and Mechanisms of Disease* (3d ed.). Philadelphia: W. B. Saunders, 1982.
36. Harlap, Susan, and A. Davis, Infant Admissions to Hospital and Maternal in First and Second Trimesters, *Lancet*, 2, no. 7 (1980), 1973.
37. Hayes, Patricia, The Long-Term Treatment of Victims of Child Abuse, *Nursing Clinics of North America*, 16, no. 1 (1981), 139–147.
38. Helberg, June, Documentation in Child Abuse, *American Journal of Nursing*, 83, no. 2 (1983), 236–239.
39. Holmes, Janine, and Lana Magiera, *Maternity Nursing*. New York: Macmillan, 1987.
40. Irwin, M. H. K., *The Cocaine Epidemic*, Public Affairs Pamphlet No. 633. Public Affairs Committee. 381 Park Avenue South, New York, NY 10016. (1985), 1–29.
41. Isouh, S., et al., Fetal Alcohol Syndrome Revisited, *Pediatrics*, 68, no. 10 (1981), 475.
42. Jacob, J., and J. Monad, Genetic Regulatory Mechanisms in the Synthesis of Proteins, *Journal of Molecular Biology*, 3 (1961), 318–356.
43. Jankowski, C. B., Radiation and Pregnancy, *American Journal of Nursing*, 86, no. 3 (1986), 260–265.
44. Jones, K. L., and D. W. Smith, The Fetal Alcohol Syndrome, *Teratology*, 12 (1975), 1.
45. Kaluger, George, and Meriem Kaluger, *Human Development: The Span of Life* (3rd ed.). St. Louis: Times Mirror/Mosby, 1984.
46. King, Imogene, *Toward a Theory of Nursing: General Concepts of Human Behavior*. New York: John Wiley, 1971.
47. Klein, J., P. Shrout, Z. Stein, et al., "Drinking During Pregnancy and Spontaneous Abortion. *Lancet*, 2, no. 7 (1980), 1976.
48. Kleinman, J. C., and A. Kopstein, Smoking During Pregnancy, *American Journal of Public Health*, 77, no. 7 (July 1987), 823–825.
49. Kramer, L., and M. Pierpont, Rocking Waterbeds and Auditory Stimuli to Enhance Growth of PreTerm Infants, *Journal of Pediatrics*, 88, (February, 1976), 297–299.

50. Kramer, Marlene, I. Chamorro, D. Green, et al., Extra Tactile Stimulation of the Premature Infant, *Nursing Research*, 24, no. 5 (September-October, 1975), 324–334.
51. Kreitzer, Margaret, Legal Aspects of Child Abuse: Guidelines for the Nurse, *Nursing Clinics of North America*, 16, no. 1 (1981), 149–161.
52. Lamb, Michael, *The Father's Role*. New York: John Wiley, 1986.
53. Levin, Shari, et al., The Association of Marijuana Use With Pregnancy, *American Journal of Public Health*, 73, no. 10 (1983), 1161–1164.
54. Liley, A. W., The Fetus as a Personality, *Australia-New Zealand Journal of Psychiatry*, 6 (1972), 99ff.
55. Links Cancer to Testes to Mother's Drug, *St. Louis Post Dispatch*, March 11, 1983, p. 11.
56. Little, R. E., A. Streissgoth, H. M. Barr, et al., Decreased Birth Weight in Infants of Alcoholic Women Who Abstained During Pregnancy, *Journal of Pediatrics*, 96, no. 6 (1980), 974.
57. Ludwig, Stephen, A Multi-disciplinary Approach to Child Abuse, *Nursing Clinics of North America*, 16, no. 1 (1981), 161–165.
58. Lynn, David, *The Father: His Role in Child Development*. Monterey, Calif.: Brooks/Cole Publishing, 1974.
59. Make Yours 5.5, *City of St. Louis Weekly Health Letter*, (September 18, 1987), 1.
60. Marbury, Martin, et al., The Association of Alcohol Consumption with Outcome of Pregnancy, *American Journal of Public Health*, 73, no. 10 (1983), 1165–1168.
61. Mare, Robert, Socioeconomic Effects on Child Mortality in the United States, *American Journal of Public Health*, 72, no. 6 (1982), 539–547.
62. Mead, Margaret, and N. Newton, Conception, Pregnancy, Labor, and the Puerperium in Cultural Perspective, *Review of Medical Psychology*, 4, (1962), 22ff.
63. Mercer, Ramona, A Theoretical Framework for Studying Factors That Impact on Maternal Role, *Nursing Research*, 30, no. 2 (1981), 73–77.
64. Miller, Georgia, A Theoretical Framework for Nursing Research in Child Abuse and Neglect, *Nursing Research*, 30, no. 2 (1981), 73–83.
65. Mitchell, Helen, et al., *Nutrition in Health and Disease* (17th ed.). New York: J.B. Lippincott, 1982.
66. Morrison, S. C., Anemia Associated with Pregnancy, in *Gynecology and Obstetrics*, ed. J. J. Sciarra. Philadelphia: Harper & Row, 1982.
67. Moshman, David, John Glover, and Roger Bruning, *Developmental Psychology*. Boston: Little, Brown, 1987.
68. Mussen, P., J. Conger, J. Kagan, and A. Huston, *Child Development and Personality* (6th ed.). New York: Harper & Row, 1984.
69. Neugarten, Bernice, Adaptation and the Life Cycle, *The Counseling Psychologist*, 6, no. 1 (1976), 16–20.
70. Olson, Robert, Index of Suspicion: Screening for Child Abuse, *American Journal of Nursing*, 76, no. 1 (January, 1976), 108–110.
71. Parks, W. P., and G. B. Scott, An Overview of Pediatric AIDS: Approaches to Diagnosis and Outcome Assessment, in *AIDS: Modern Concepts and Therapeutic Challenges*, ed. Samuel Broder. New York: Marcel Dekker, 1987.
72. Pillitteri, Adele, *Child Health Nursing: Care of the Growing Family* (3rd ed.). Boston: Little, Brown, 1987.
73. Pipes, Peggy, *Nutrition in Infancy and Childhood* (3rd ed.). St. Louis: Times Mirror/Mosby, 1985.
74. Porter, J. B., J. Hunter-Mitchell, H. Jick, et al., Drugs and Stillbirth, *American Journal of Public Health*, 76, no. 12 (1986), 1428–1430.
75. Pritchard, J. A., and P. C. MacDonald, *Williams Obstetrics* (16th ed.). New York: Appleton-Century-Crofts, 1980.
76. Rao, J., and R. Arulappu, Drug Use in Pregnancy: How to Avoid Problems, *Drugs*, 22, no. 11 (1981), 33, 409–414.
77. Rogers, Martha, *The Theoretical Basis of Nursing*. Philadelphia: F. A. Davis, 1970.
78. Rogers, M. F., P. A. Thomas, E. T. Starcher, et al., Acquired Immunodeficiency Syndrome in Children: Report of the Center for Disease Control National Surveillance, 1982 for 1985, *Pediatrics*, 79, no. 6 (1987), 1008–1012.
79. Rush, D., Z. Stein, and M. Susser, A Randomized Controlled Trial of Prenatal Nutritional Supplementation in New York City, *Pediatrics*, 65, no. 4 (1980), 683.
80. Schuster, Clara Shaw, and Shirley Smith Ashburn, *The Process of Human Development: A Holistic Life-Span Approach* (2nd ed.). Boston: Little, Brown, 1986.
81. Sciarra, J. J., ed., *Gynecology and Obstetrics*. Philadelphia: Harper & Row, 1982.
82. Scipien, G.M., Barnard, M.A., Howe, J., et al., *Comprehensive Pediatric Nursing* (3rd ed.). New York: McGraw-Hill, 1986.
83. Smith, Janis, Care of the Hospitalized Abused Child and Family: A Framework for Nursing Intervention, *Nursing Clinics of North America*, 16, no. 1 (1981), 127–137.
84. Spitz, Rene, Hospitalism, in *The Psychoanalytic Study of the Child, Vol. 1*. New York: International University Press, 1945.
85. ———, Hospitalism: The Genesis of Psychiatric Conditions in Early Childhood, in *Human Life Cycle*, ed. William Sze. New York: Jason Aronson, 1975, pp. 29–43.
86. ———, and K. M. Wolf, Anaclitic Depression: An Inquiry into the Genesis of Psychiatric Conditions in Early Childhood, in *The Psychoanalytic Study of the Child, Vol. 2*. New York: International University Press, 1946, pp. 313–342.
87. Starfield, Barbara, Child Health and Socioeconomic

88. Stein, Zena, and Jennie Klein, Smoking, Alcohol, and Reproduction, *American Journal of Public Health*, 73, no. 10 (1983), 1154–1156.
89. Stellman, J. M., The Effects of Toxic Agents on Reproduction, *Occupational Health and Safety*, April, 1979, 36–43.
90. Stenchover, Morton, Fetal Risks from Paternal Medication, *Journal of American Medical Association*, 211 (February 23, 1970), 1382.
91. Streisswitt, A. P., and R. A. LaDuc, Psychological and Behavioral Effects in Children Prenatally Exposed to Alcohol, *Alcohol World*, 10, no. 1 (Fall, 1985), 6–12.
92. Sullivan, Harry S., *Interpersonal Theory of Psychiatry*. New York: W. W. Norton, 1953.
93. Tanner, J.M., *Foetus into Man: Physical Growth from Conception to Maturity*. London: Open Books, 1978.
94. Taylor, Philip, et al., Polychlorinated Biphenyls: Influence on Birthweight Gestation, *American Journal of Public Health*, 74, no. 10, (1984), 1153–1154.

(Preceding entry, continued from previous page:) Status, *American Journal of Public Health*, 72, no. 6 (1982), 532–533.

95. Thriving Despite Hardship: Key Childhood Traits Identified, *The New York Times* (October 13, 1987), Sec. I, 19.
96. Toubas, P., et al., Effects of Maternal Smoking and Caffeine Habits on Infantile Apnea: A Retrospective Study, *Pediatrics*, 78 (July, 1986), 159–163.
97. Theiler, P., A Vietnam Aftermath, *Common Cause Magazine* (November–December 1984), 29–34.
98. United States Public Health Service Advisory Committee on Immunization Practices, Revised Recommendations on Rubella Vaccine, *Pediatrics*, 65, no. 6 (1980), 6.
99. Wager, G., and L. Keith, Drug Addiction in Pregnancy, in *Gynecology and Obstetrics*, ed. J. J. Sciarra. Philadelphia: Harper & Row, 1982.
100. Warren, K., Alcohol and Related Birth Defects, *Alcohol World*, 10, no. 1 (Fall, 1985), 4–5.
101. Whiting, B., ed., *Six Cultures: Studies of Childrearing*. New York: John Wiley, 1963.

PART III

The Developing Person and Family: Infancy Through Adolescence

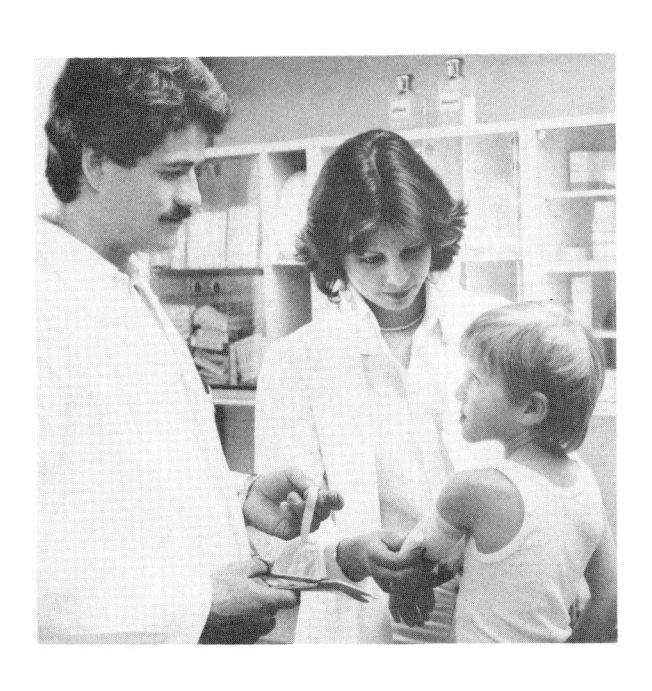

7

Assessment and Health Promotion for the Infant

Study of this chapter will help you to

1. Define terms and give examples of basic developmental principles pertinent to the neonate and infant.
2. Discuss the crisis of birth for the family, factors that influence parental attachment and family response, and your role in assisting the family to adapt to this crisis and perform their developmental tasks.
3. Describe the adaptive physiological changes that occur at birth.
4. Assess the neonate's physical characteristics and the manner in which psychosocial needs begin to be filled.
5. Contrast and assess the physiological, motor, cognitive, linguistic, emotional, and social characteristics and adaptive mechanisms of the infant at 3, 6, 9, and 12 months.
6. Discuss and assess the nutritional, sleep, movement, and play needs and patterns and sexuality development of the infant.
7. Interpret the immunization schedule and other safety and health promotion measures for a parent.
8. Discuss your role in assisting parents to foster the development of trust and a positive self-concept as well as to nurture the infant physically.
9. State the developmental tasks for the infant and behavior which indicates that these tasks are being met.
10. Compare parental behavior toward the infant who thrives with parental behavior toward the infant who fails to thrive.
11. Discuss your role in promoting parental attachment and preventing maternal deprivation and child abuse.
12. Begin to implement appropriate intervention measures with parents and baby after delivery and during the first year of life.

This chapter discusses the normal growth and development of the baby during the first year of life, baby's effect on the family, the family's influence on baby. Measures to promote his/her welfare that are useful in nursing practice and which can be taught to parents are described throughout the chapter.

In this chapter, the term **neonate**, or **newborn**, *refers to the first 4 weeks of life;* **infant** *refers to the first 12 months.* **Mother** *or* **parent(s)** *are the terms used to denote person(s) responsible for the child's care and long-term welfare.*

You can refer to an embryology and obstetrical nursing book for detailed information on fetal development, prenatal changes, and the process of labor and delivery. This chapter builds on information presented in Chapters 4 and 6 and focuses on the developmental tasks of the infant and family after birth.

Family Development and Relationships

The coming of the child is a **crisis**, *a turning point in the couple's life in which old patterns of living must be changed for new ways of living and new values* (59, 60, 75, 106) The crisis may first be felt by the woman as she recognizes body changes and new emotional responses. The crisis may relate to losing the slim figure; determining how long she can work if she is in a career or profession, and whether or not she can balance working and child rearing; making spatial changes in the home or moving to a new home to accommodate the baby; and balancing the budget to meet additional expenses. The crisis will be less if the baby is wanted than if the couple had planned on having no children. But having a baby is always a crisis—a change.

Key Terms

Neonate/Newborn	Hydrocele
Infant	Hernia
Mother (Parent(s))	Imperforate anus
Crisis	Spina bifida
Attachment	Amblyopia
Bonding	Colic
Engrossment	Stools
Binding-in	Colostrum
Identification	Weaning
Claiming	Phenylketonuria (PKU)
Polarization	Immunizations
Psychological abuse, battering, or maltreatment	Herd immunity
	Diaper dermatitis (rash)
	Atopic dermatitis
Autistic behavior	Seborrheic dermatitis
Anterior fontanel	Oral candidiasis (Thrush)
Posterior fontanel	
Caput succedaneum	Constipation
Cephalohematoma	Iron deficiency anemia
Acrocyanosis	Roseola infantum
Lanugo	Psychosocial development
Vernix caseosa	
Milia	Intelligence
Hemangiomas	Cognitive behavior
Mongolian spots	Speech awareness
Jaundice	Speech
Physiological jaundice	Language
Desquamation	Undifferentiated cry
Umbilical cord	Cooing
Circumcision	Babbling
Phimosis	Lalling
Brown fat	Autistic
Surfactant	Basic trust
Meconium	Mistrust
Reflex	Body image
Consummatory	Self-concept
Avoidant	Adaptive mechanisms
Exploratory	Symbolization
Social	Condensation
Attentional	Incorporation
Microganthia	Displacement
Ptosis	Sexuality

"Your life will never be the same again." A starry-eyed expectant couple often hears this phrase. Being caught up in the romantic adventure of pregnancy, these words may fall on deaf ears. What do these words really imply?

With the advent of parenthood, a couple is embarking on a journey from which there is no return. To put it simply, parents cannot quit. Most losses in today's world are reversible. If one loses the marriage partner, one can remarry; if one loses a job, one can find a new position. But one cannot assume an "I'll-try-it" attitude toward parenthood. The child's birth brings a finality to many highly valued privileges and a permanence of responsibilities.

The young couple who has enjoyed an intense relationship suddenly finds a not-always-so-welcome onlooker and intruder. Gone for many years are sleeping late on Saturday mornings, last-minute social invitations or plans for a weekend trip, spontaneous sex, quiet meals by candlelight, an orderly house, and naps when desired. Of course, some of these activities can still be accomplished but never as freely as before. What was previously taken for granted now becomes a luxury. The "childhood" of parents comes to a screeching halt as the infant's needs take precedence.

Going to work, to visit friends, or even to shop is no easy task. Even a few hours away from home means making sure you have everything baby needs—bottle, food, pacifier, a few toys, a clothing change, and more than enough diapers. In addition to this armful, an infant seat or stroller must also be packed. By the time baby is dressed and everything is packed, Mom may want a nap more than anything else. Making sure baby has on a dry diaper before the final exit through the door becomes more important than the finishing touches of makeup or putting on the special jewelry for the outfit. If there are several small children to care for in addition to baby, the planning and effort are compounded and older brothers and sisters can help with various tasks only to a certain point.

The intensity of the newcomer's demands may call for massive changes in lifestyle. Life changes have been correlated with illness susceptibility in the Social Readjustment Scale by Holmes and Rahe (60). When enough life changes occur within a year and add up to more than 300 points, trouble may lie ahead. In one survey, 80 percent who exceeded a score of 300 became pathologically depressed, had heart attacks, or developed other serious ailments (59). Changes that may be connected with the addition of a family member total up to an ominous 397, as the table on the following page shows (59, 60).

Whether perceived as positive or negative, change always involves a sense of loss of the familiar, for the way it used to be. The vacuum created by the loss is a painful one and one for which parents are usually ill-prepared. The couple's life will never again be "normal" as they once knew it, but together the family now needs to find a "new normal."

↙ If pregnancy and parenting create a crisis for a couple who want a baby, they are even more upheaving for the adolescent or for the woman who is the single-parent family—either unmarried or, if married, left by the husband or father to face pregnancy, birth, and

Pregnancy	40
Sex difficulties	39
Gain of new family member	39
Change in financial state	38
Change in number of arguments with spouse	35
Trouble with in-laws	29
Wife begins or stops work	26
Change in living conditions	25
Revision of personal habits	24
Change in recreation	19
Change in church activities	19
Change in social activities	18
Change in sleeping habits	16
Change in number of family get-togethers	15
Change in eating habits	15
	397

childrearing alone. This adolescent/woman needs the support of and help from at least one other person during this period. A parent, relative, or friend, can be a resource. Often the support and help of a number of people are needed. As a nurse, you may be the primary source of support. Your empathetic listening, acceptance, practical hints for better self-care and baby care, and general availability can make a real difference in the outcome of the pregnancy and in the mother's ability to parent—and in her ability to handle future crises. Referral to other resources and self-help groups, such as C.O.P.E., Coping with Overall Parenting Experience, and Parents without Partners, or to a counselor may also be of great help to the mother.

The Growth and Development of Parents

Most people are not prepared either intellectually or emotionally for family life. Further, creating and maintaining a family unit are difficult in today's society. Many occupations demand travel, frequent change of residence, as well as working on Sundays and holidays, the traditional family days. The rapid pace of life and available opportunities interfere with family functions. The close-knit interdependence of the old family unit is being replaced with a group of individuals whose lives seem merely thrown together.

Expectations for self and others have increased. For example, the woman may be striving for success in several areas. No longer is being a wife and mother enough: A woman is exhorted to have a career as well. All these expectations conflict with a strong family life, for children demand becoming other-centered instead of self-centered.

In spite of today's difficulties in maintaining a family unit, the norm still exists to have children. Thus many couples wander rather naively into the developmental crisis of parenthood. In a culture in which adolescence may last until the mid-twenties, most young people are just getting used to being called Ma'am or Sir when suddenly they become Mom and Dad. Thus, along with the developmental tasks of finding identity and intimacy may be superimposed the task of being generative as well.

"Pregnancy is preparation . . . birth is the event . . . parenting is a process" (35). Becoming a parent involves grieving the loss of one's own childhood and former lifestyle. The person has to be in touch with and be able to express and work through feelings of loss before he or she can adapt and move on to a higher level of maturation. Being aware of the tremendous influence of parents on their children's development, parents may feel challenged to become the best persons they are capable of being. New parents may need to develop a confidence that they do not feel, an integrity that has been easy to let slide, and values that can tolerate being scrutinized. To grow and develop as a parent, the person needs to make peace with his/her past so that unresolved conflicts are not inflicted on the child.

After a baby joins the family, a number of problems must be worked through. The mother must deal with the separation from a symbiotic relationship with the baby. The reality of child care and managing a household may be a disillusionment after exposure to the American ideals inculcated by the mass media and advertising.

✔ One of the potential problem areas that you can explore with parents is that of reestablishing a mutually satisfying sexual relationship, which is not a simple physiological process but has intricate psychological overtones for man and woman. You may also need to address the couple's desire for family planning (see Table 12-2 in Chapter 12 for information on contraceptive measures). Sexual relationships usually decrease during pregnancy, childbirth, and postpartum. By 6 weeks after birth the woman's pelvis is back to normal; lochia has ceased; involution is complete; and physically she is ready for an active sex life. But the mother may be so absorbed in and fatigued by the challenges and responsibilities of motherhood that the father is pushed into the background. Father may feel in competition with baby, resenting baby and his wife.

Either one may take initiative in renewing the role of lover, in being sexually attractive to the other. The woman can do this by getting a new hairdo or stylish clothes for the now slimmer outward figure. Inwardly, she can strengthen flabbly perineal muscles through prescribed exercise. Patience on the part of the husband is also necessary, for if an episiotomy was done before delivery, healing continues for some time and the memory of pain in the area may cause the woman involuntarily to tense the perineal muscles and wish to forego intercourse. Happy couples who have a sound philosophy and communication system soon work out such problems, including the fact that the baby's needs will sometimes interrupt intimacy. For couples whose earlier sex life was unsatisfactory and who do not work together as a team, such problems may be hard to surmount. The woman may prolong nursing, complain of fatigue, ill health, or pain. The man may find other outlets (38).

✔ Husband and wife must reestablish effective communication so that they can share feelings of pride, joy, anxiety, insecurity, and frustrations of early parenthood; avoid eclipsing their marriage by the new family roles, and understand the involvement of the multiple roles of mate, parents, and persons. Your support, suggestions, and assistance in helping the couple seek and accept help from family and friends fosters their ability to manage.

Given the whole realm of stresses and life changes associated with a baby's birth, it is understandable that at least initially parenting is at best a bittersweet experience. Parents feel strong ambivalences and what Angela Barron McBride calls "normal crazy" thoughts and feeling toward this child whom they have together created (86).

✔ The following stress factors may be used in your assessment to predict the likelihood of postpartum difficulties:

1. Primapara (woman having her first baby).
2. No relatives available for help with baby care.
3. Complications of pregnancy in family history.
4. Husband's father dead.
5. Wife's mother dead.
6. Wife ill apart from pregnancy.
7. Wife ill during pregnancy.
8. Wife's education higher than that of her parents.
9. Husband's education higher than that of his parents.
10. Wife's education incomplete.
11. Husband's occupation higher than that of his parents.
12. Husband's occupation higher than that of his wife's parents.
13. Husband often away from home.
14. Wife has had no previous experience with babies (48).

Postpartum difficulties are also more likely if the parent is an adolescent or has suffered child abuse. The more past and present stresses, the more difficulty the woman has in coping with the postpartum experience (48).

Parenting is a risky process. It involves facing the unknown with faith, because no one can predict the outcome when the intricacies of human relationships are involved. Parents grow and develop by taking themselves and their child one day at a time and by realizing the joy that can be part of those crazy, hectic early weeks and months. The feelings of joy and involvement increase as the parent-child attachment is cemented.

Because establishing this attachment is crucial to the long-term nurturing of the child and parental interest in the child, the process will be explored in depth to assist you in assessment and intervention.

Infant–Parent Attachment

Attachment is a *close and reciprocal relationship between two people that involves contact and close proximity and endures through time.* **Bonding** usually refers to the *initial maternal feeling and attachment behavior immediately following delivery.* **Engrossment** is a term used to describe the *father's initial paternal response to the baby.* Table 7–1 outlines the optimal behaviors of the infant, mother, and father in the typical order of progression in establishing this initial tie (12, 17, 18, 19, 34, 49, 62, 113, 115, 116, 135). The extent to which these behaviors are shown will depend on how much contact is permitted by the hospital or staff between parents and baby.

✔ Some research shows that all mothers do not initially follow the sequence of handling that is described in most of the literature and in Table 7–1. Some mothers initially use palms or arms to handle the infant and then their fingers to explore the infant. Often mothers simultaneously use fingers and palms and then arms and trunk to explore and hold the baby. These differences should be considered in assessment of maternal bonding and attachment (136, 137).

The state of the infant is a strong predictor of the relative frequency with which fathers display interactional behavior, affection, and comfort toward the infant. Very young crying infants are comforted or shown affectional behavior. Fathers are most likely to stimulate by touch those infants who are awake but not crying. Fathers are as likely to talk in a stimulating manner to crying as noncrying and to sleeping as awake infants. Perhaps fathers perceive talking to be less soothing to crying infants than touch and less disturbing than touch to sleeping infants. Infant state behaviors are strongly related to affectional paternal

TABLE 7–1. Infant–Parent Attachment Behaviors

INFANT	MOTHER	FATHER
Reflexly looks into mother's face, establishes eye-to-eye contact or "face tie"; molds body to mother's body when held.	Reaches for baby; holds high against breast-chest-shoulder area; handles baby smoothly.	Has great interest in baby's face and notes eyes.
Vocalizes and stretches out arms in response to mother's voice.	Talks softly and in high-pitched voice, and with intense interest to baby. Puts baby face-to-face with hers (en face position). Eye contact gives baby sense of identity to mother.	Desires to touch, pick up, and hold baby. Cradles baby securely. Shows more fingertip touching and smiling to male baby. Has more eye contact with infant delivered by forceps or cesarean section.
Roots, licks, then sucks mother's nipple if in contact with mother's breast; cries, smiles.	Touches baby's extremities, examines, strokes, massages, and kisses baby all shortly after delivery. Puts baby to breast if permitted.	Looks for distinct features; thinks newborn resembles self. Perceives baby as beautiful in spite of newborn characteristics.
Reflexly embraces, clambers, clings, using hands, feet, head, and mouth to maintain body contact.	Calls baby by name; notes desirable traits; expresses pleasure toward baby; attentive to reflex actions of grunts and sneezes.	Feels elated, bigger, proud after birth. Has strong desire to protect and care for child.

Note: Similar behaviors are seen with a premature baby but the timing will vary.

responses, indicating that new fathers begin early to read and respond to infant cues (66)

✔ Studies in bonding and attachment have been done primarily on middle-class, reasonably well-educated Caucasians. Bonding and attachment behaviors, especially for the male, could be different in other racial and cultural groups. Some cultures emphasize the mother as caretaker of the infant; the bond or attachment between father and child is less overt and may be emphasized later in childhood.

✔ The first hour after birth seems to be a critical time for stimulating attachment feelings and bonding in the parents, since then the baby tends to have eyes open, gazes around, has stronger sucking reflexes, cries more, and shows more physical activity than in subsequent hours (49).

In addition to causing an increased alertness in the baby, effective maternal–infant bonding can promote baby's physical health: Transference of maternal nasal and respiratory flora to baby may prevent him from acquiring hospital strains of staphylococci; maternal body heat is a reliable source of heat for the newborn; and regular breast feedings can pass on the antibodies IgA and T and B lymphocytes to baby to protect against enteric pathogens (69, 106).

Binding-in is the term Rubin (115, 116, 118) uses to *describe the maternal–child relationship as a process which is active, intermittent, and accumulative over a period of 12 to 15 months*. Maternal identity is essential for the binding-in process, and both maternal identity and binding-in are either enhanced or inhibited by the infant's behavior and society. The process involves (1) identification of the infant by the mother as part of self and belonging to self; (2) claiming the child as her own emotionally and physically; (3) polarization or separating the infant from the unity of self and fetus.

Maternal binding-in is stimulated by fetal movements and the physical needs of the newborn. After birth, fantasies about the child are replaced by an object to see, touch, hear, smell, and care for, which organizes maternal behavior and attitudes. Sex, size, and condition of the infant are critical to the maternal response. Complete **identification** *occurs when the mother knows by looking, touching, hearing, or smelling that the child is well or unwell, hungry or satisfied, comfortable or in distress.* **Claiming** *occurs with the mother's commitment to the child in labor and delivery and is seen in the pleasure with the birth of the child.* Claiming also occurs by association with significant others in the social environment who claim the infant and her. **Polarization,** *separating from the symbiotic relationship with the fetus, begins with labor and delivery.* Gradually the woman realizes the baby is not inside of her. The infant is held, nurtured, and compared to self and family members but is increasingly seen as a separate, unique individual, and less as an extension of self and her own body image. Family life is reorganized; the baby is included in family activities. Over the period of the first year the mother can let go of the child as he/she gains motor, social, and emotional competence. The psychological loosening allows the mother to also give the child more physical space (115, 116, 118).

Motherly Feelings Do Not Necessarily Accompany Biological Motherhood. Various factors affect the mother's attachment and care taking. Variables that are difficult or impossible to change include the woman's level of emotional maturity, how she was reared, what her culture encourages her to do, relationships with her family and partner, experience with previous pregnancies, and planning for and events during the course of this pregnancy (34, 62, 69, 106, 115, 117).

✔ *Deterrents to adequate mothering* include the mother's own immaturity or lack of mothering, stress situations, fear of rejection from significant people, loss of a loved one, financial worries, lack of a supportive partner, and even the gender and appearance of the child. Separating mother and infant the first few days of life, depersonalized care by professionals, rigid hospital routines, and too early discharge from the hospital without adequate help also interfere with establishing attachment and maternal behaviors (19, 34, 51, 62, 69). Assess for these deterrents. Your nurturing of the mother and helping her seek additional help may offset the negative impact of these factors.

✔ *Parenting skills* can be manifested in various ways. While eye contact, touch, and cuddling are important, love can be shown by a tender, soft voice and loving gazes. Observe other indications of warm parenting feelings:

1. Calls the baby by name.
2. Expresses enjoyment of the baby and indicates that the baby is attractive or has other positive characteristics,
3. Looks at the baby and into baby's eyes.
4. Talks to the baby in a loving voice.
5. Takes safety precautions for the baby.
6. Responds to the baby's cues for attention or physical care.

✔ Note the methods of relating to and holding the infant that would indicate the *mother's difficulty in establishing attachment:*

1. Maintains little or no eye contact with baby.
2. Does not touch baby, or picks up baby at times to meet her own needs.
3. Does not support baby's head.
4. Holds baby at a distance, at arm's length, loosely, or not at all.
5. Appears disinterested in baby, preoccupied with something else when baby is present, and has a flat, fixed facial expression or unconvincing smile in response to your enthusiasm about baby.
6. Perceives baby as unattractive or looking like someone she dislikes.

7. Talks or coos to baby little or not at all.
8. Has passive response when baby brought to her; allows baby to be placed in her arms rather than reaching out to baby.
9. Calls baby "it" rather than saying "my baby" or calling baby by name.
10. Notes defects or undesirable traits in baby, even if baby is normal, or is convinced baby is abnormal.
11. Avoids talking about baby, even when someone else initiates the topic.
12. Expresses dissatisfaction with or revulsion about care of baby.
13. Ignores baby's communications of cries, grunts, sneezes, and yawns.
14. Gets upset when baby's secretions, feces, or urine touch her body or clothes; perceives care of baby as revolting.
15. Readily gives baby to someone else.
16. Does not take adequate safety precautions with baby, for example, in relation to diapering, feeding, covering baby, or baby's movements.
17. Handles the baby roughly, even after the baby has eaten or vomited.
18. Gives inappropriate responses to baby's needs such as over-or underfeeding, over- or under-handling.
19. Thinks baby does not love her.
20. Expresses dislike of self, finds attribute in baby that is disliked in self.
21. Complains of being too tired to take care of baby.
22. Expresses fears that baby might die of a minor illness (13, 17, 33, 34, 115, 116).

✔ You may not observe all these behaviors in the mother, but a combination of several should alert you to actual or potential difficulty with being a parent.

✔ Three components must be present before child abuse occurs: (1) the parents must have the potential for abuse; (2) there must be a special child; and (3) there must be a crisis or series of crises. The cycle of abuse can be prevented or treated by intervening with one of these components (88).

Parents Anonymous, a nationwide organization of and for adults with child abuse problems, recognizes 6 forms of child abuse: (1) physical abuse, (2) physical neglect, (3) emotional abuse, (4) emotional neglect, (5) verbal abuse, and (6) sexual abuse (88).

✔ Be aware of the parent who has such *difficulty with attachment that maltreatment or abuse of the child results*. Types of abuse, signs and symptoms of the abused child, and characteristics of the child who suffers abuse, neglect, or material deprivation, and characteristics of the abusing parent are presented in Chapter 6. Chapter 4 also describes characteristics and behaviors of the parent who has difficulty with parenting.

Garbarino, et al. (44) describe types of psychologi-

Table 7-2 Parental Behaviors Characteristic of Psychological Maltreatment

Rejecting	Refuses to accept the child's attachment behavior or spontaneous overtures.
	Refusal to return smiles and vocalizations.
Isolating	Denies child the experience of enduring patterns of interaction.
	Leaves the child in its room unattended for long periods.
	Denies access to the child by interested others.
Terrorizing	Exposes the child consistently and deliberately to intense stimuli or frequent change of routine.
	Teases, scares, or gives extreme or unpredictable response to child's behavior.
Ignoring	Fails to respond to infant's spontaneous behavior that forms basis for attachment.
	Does not respond to infant's smiles, vocalizations, or developing competence and changing skill.
Corrupting	Reinforces bizarre habits.
	Creates alcohol or drug addictions.
	Reinforces the child for oral sexual contact.

cal abuse, battering, or maltreatment. *Psychological abuse, battering or maltreatment is a deliberate pattern of attack by a parent or an adult in a child's development status, sense of self, or social competence.*

✓ Table 7-2 presents parental behaviors that are characteristic of psychological abuse or maltreatment. As a result of maltreatment, the child becomes vulnerable to negative forces in the broader social environment, does not develop a sense of trust, and becomes emotionally, socially, and sometimes physically, ill (44).

✓ Garbarino, et al. discuss strategies and tools for identification and intervention with the family, individual child, and institutional network of social services (44).

✓ Helberg gives specific criteria for documentation of child abuse (56).

✓ Switzer describes legal definitions of child abuse in various states, who is required to report and reporting procedures, the legal effects of failure to report in various states, and confidentiality issues (134).

✓ The article by Mittleman et al. shows pictures of subtle as well as obvious abuse and gives detailed and specific description for clues that will assist you in assessing the child (94).

Fatherly Feelings Do Not Necessarily Accompany Fatherhood. Bonding and attachment feelings in the father appear related to various factors: general level of education, participation in prenatal classes, gender of infant, role concept, attendance at delivery, type of delivery, early contact, and feeding method for baby (12, 17, 49, 135).

Support from the mother is most effective in reducing stress levels in expectant fathers; support from others is critical only if the expectant woman cannot be supportive. This may be because intimacy and self-disclosure for men is maintained primarily in the partner relationship. For the expectant woman, support from both the partner and others is critical in coping with stress, perhaps because women are socialized to value and depend on social relations to a greater extent than men (24).

Father is increasingly recognized as an important person to the infant and young child, not only as a breadwinner but also as a nurturer. Lack of a father figure can cause developmental difficulties for the child. Just as the mother is not necessarily endowed with nurturing feelings, the father is not necessarily lacking nurturing feelings. Some fathers seem to respond better to this role than their spouses.

The man who nurtures his children may meet some resistance in a society in which this role is sometimes considered unmanly, although social attitudes are changing. One father who was taking the basic child-raising responsibilities while his wife pursued the major family career was ostracized when he appeared at a meeting calling for "scout mothers." No women sat with him until he initiated conversation explaining why he was there. Occasionally the mother herself cannot understand when the father seems to cherish the nurturing role. She feels that her position is threatened, her husband is not acting "as a man," or he loves the children more than he loves her. Actually, the man who is allowed to express these feelings often simultaneously develops an even closer feeling for his wife.

Development of attachment between parent and baby continues through infancy. It involves emotional, cognitive, and socialization processes: loving through cuddling, touching, stroking, kissing, cooing and talking to, laughing, playing with, and reinforcing and teaching baby. Such contact should be consistent and done while caring physically for baby. The touching, cooing, talking and laughing can also be focused on baby while mother is preparing a meal, doing a household task, or waiting in a grocery line. Mother's voice across the room can also soothe and contributes to attachment.

✔ *Personalizing Nursing Care in Order to Promote Attachment.* Call the child, mother, and father by their names during your care. Inquire about the mother's well-being; too often all the focus is on the baby. She is in a receptive state and needs to be emotionally and physically cared for. Father may also need nurturance before he can show caring and be helpful to mother and baby. Every minute of contact must be well used. Make favorable comments about the infant's progress. Compliment the mother on her intentions or ability to comfort, feed, or identify her baby's needs. Speak of the pleasure baby shows in response to the parent's ministrations. Reassure parents that positive changes in baby are a result of their care, and avoid judgmental attitudes or guilt statements. Encourage both parents to cuddle, look at, and talk to the baby; if necessary, demonstrate how to stroke, caress, and rock baby. Encourage parents to be prompt and consistent in answering the infant's cry. Encourage parents to rely on their own values and judgment, to trust their feelings, and to take action and responsibility for them. Parents will learn that baby is tougher than he/she looks.

✔ As you support, teach, and counsel, the following *interventions can promote mother–infant attachment and optimal infant stimulation.*

1. Assist mother soon after birth in gaining confidence in her ability to respond effectively to baby's cry through recognizing the meaning of the cry and using soothing measures, such as rocking, redundant sounds, or swaddling.
2. Explain the infant's interactive abilities during the early puerperium and help the mother develop awareness of her own initial effective responses to the newborn's behavior.
3. Explain the basis of early infant learning as the discovery of associations, connections, and relationships between self and repeated occurrences. Explore how to provide variety and a gradually increasing level of stimuli complexity: Sights, sounds, smells, movements, positions, temperatures, and pressure all provide learning opportunities and opportunities for emotional, perceptual, social, and physical development.
4. Call attention to baby and those behaviors that indicate developmental responsiveness, such as reflex movements, visual following, smiling, raising chin off bed, rolling over, and sitting alone. Pupil dilation in the presence of another person or a valued object begins about 4 weeks of age. During the first few weeks of life, baby prefers the human face to other visual images.
5. Differentiate between contact stimulation and representative behaviors present in fetal life. Pressure and touch sensation are present a few months before birth; thus the newborn responds well to touch and gentle pressure. Rooting and hand–mouth activity occur in fetal life and is a major adaptive activity after birth.
6. Emphasize the importance of visual and auditory skills for developing social behaviors during the first 2 months of life (119).
7. Encourage mutual eye contact between mother and baby; all infant's efforts to vocalize should be reinforced. Eye contact between the dyad increases during the first 3 months of life and is soon accompanied by other social responses—smiling and vocalization.
8. Encourage regular periods of affectionate play when the infant is alert and responsive. Mother may pick up and hold the baby close, encourage visual following and smiling, and talk to the infant, repeating sounds. Rhythm and repetition are enjoyed. Often baby is most alert after a daytime feeding.
9. Promote awareness in other family members of baby's competencies so that they can also respond to and reinforce the infant.

✔ You can inform the nursing team about progress in the mother–infant interaction process to assist other members with assessment and intervention. Riesch suggests that information relative to the infant's interactional potential and the maternal behaviors that support and enhance that potential should be included in all standard plans of maternal–neonatal nursing care (110).

✔ *Several tools are designed to help you assess baby, mother, and mother's attitude toward* baby as you continue their care (13, 20, 29, 33). The *Neonatal Behavioral Assessment Scale* points out unique characteristics and strengths of the neonate (20). For example, you can demonstrate to the parents how the newborn can follow the direction of the mother's soft high-pitched voice as she moves from the line of baby's vision.

✔ The *Neonatal Perception Inventory* gauges how the mother feels about the infant through how she feels about herself. Other inventories that question the mother about her perception of the baby are *The Average Perception Inventory* and *Your Baby*. These are completed at 1 and 2 days' postpartum and two inventories are repeated again in 1 month along with the *Degree of Bother Inventory*. If the infant is not perceived as better than average and if the degree of bother index is too high, psychiatric problems in the child may be predicted (23, 34). *The Blank Infant Tenderness Scale* can be used to measure mother's perceptions of infant tenderness needs and ability to give physical and emotional nurturance (15). The

Dyadic Interaction Code is a tool for studying over time the interaction process between mother and newborn. There is rhythmicity in the mother–infant interaction, associated with synchronous interactions, heightened levels of positive affect, and extended periods of attention. The baby who is preterm, not healthy, or suffering from congenital anomalies may not be as responsive to the mother, thus interrupting rhythmicity and attachment (31).

✔ Bishop describes an extensive assessment tool that can be used to assess the mother's physical and emotional energy, support systems available to the mother, and the mother's current level of parenting activity. The tool is used for several visits, combining repeated observations and interviews, to obtain an accurate and comprehensive assessment (13). As you pinpoint problems by means of these inventories, you should be able to intervene or direct the parents to a helpful resource.

✔ Incorporate the parents' cultural beliefs, values, and attitudes into your nursing care and modern health-care practices whenever possible. Maintaining important cultural traditions is one way to individualize care. Satz gives specific examples of how she incorporated the values of the Navajo in promoting attachment (121). Specific traditions may extend to naming or bathing the baby, prenatal and postnatal care of mother, how to hold or dress baby, inclusion or exclusion of father from the delivery, and roles of various family members. Be sensitive to the preferences of clients who represent a culture different from your own. Listen to and observe carefully their requests. Listen to what is not said but is implied. Suggest rather than advise or direct when you teach.

✔ Listen attentively for information and signs that give you clues to the parents' feelings about themselves, where they are in their own developmental growth, who they rely on for strength, their ideas about child discipline, and their expectations of the new child. As you see weaknesses or gaps in necessary information, you can instruct. If your approach is right, the parents will recognize you as a helpful friend. Mothers are receptive to your information as well as your reinforcement of the mother's mothering skills.

✔ While you are helping parents with discharge planning, remember that soon the complete focus on mother–father–new baby will be gone. Other roles will be reestablished: husband, wife, employer or employee, student, daughter, son, friend. The new parents will have to allow for all aspects of their personalities to function again. Baby will have to fit in.

✔ While you are caring for baby, you will no doubt feel great satisfaction. However, remember that the child belongs to the parents; this is not *your* baby.

Do not become so involved that through your actions you push aside the parents and cause them to feel ineffective.

Baby's Influence on Parents

Some babies have a high-activity level and warm up easily to the parent; some are quiet, withdrawn, with a low-activity level; and various other mixtures of activity level and temperament exist. The infant's dominant reaction pattern to new situations manifests an innate temperament, and the temperament affects the reactions of others, especially the parents. They in turn will mold baby's reaction pattern (106).

It is easy to love a loveable baby, but parents have to work harder with babies who are not highly responsive. You should assess the reactions between baby and parents, since the style of child care that will develop has its basis here. A highly active mother who expects an intense reaction may have a hard time mothering a low-activity, quiet baby, because she may misinterpret the baby's behavior, feel rejected, and in turn reject the child. Baby will be denied the stimulation necessary for development. If the mother is withdrawn, quiet, unexpressive, and has a high-activity baby, she may punish baby for normal energetic or assertive behavior and ignore the bids for affection and stimulation. The child needs to feel his/her behavior will produce an effect or he/she will stop contacting the parents. Extreme parental rejection or lack of reaction causes emotional illness and **autistic behavior,** *characterized by self-absorption, isolation from the world, obsession with sameness, repetitive behavior, and lack of language communication with others* (11). An assertive child may become controlling with an indecisive mother and not learn that others also have needs and rights. If baby is controlled by mother, he/she cannot develop trust, independence, or ability to cope with persons on equal terms.

✔ Help parents understand the mutual response between baby and themselves. All parents feel incompetent and despairing at times when they are unable to understand the child's cues and meet needs, but if self-confidence is consistently lacking, the parent's despair may turn to anger, rejection, and abuse.

Expansion of Intrafamily Relationships

Grandparents-to-be and other relatives frequently become more involved with the parents-to-be, bringing gifts and advice, neither of which is necessarily desired. Yet their gifts and supportive presence can be a real help if the grandparents respect the independence of the couple, if the couple has resolved their earlier adolescent rebellion and dependency conflicts, and if the grandparents' advice does not conflict with the couple's philosophy or the doctor's advice. The couple and grandparents should collaborate rather than compete. Grandparents should be reminded not to take over the situation, and the couple's autonomy should be encouraged in that they can listen to the various pieces of advice, evaluate the statements, and then as a unit make their own decision. In addition, parents should refrain from expecting the grandparents to be a built-in babysitter and to rescue them from every problem. Grandparents usually enjoy brief rather than prolonged contact with baby care. For the single parent, the grandparents or other relatives can be a major source of emotional and financial help, as well as providing help with child care.

✔ You may assist the parent(s) in working with grandparents—resolving feelings of either being controlled or not adequately helped, understanding grandparents' feelings, accepting help, and avoiding excessive demands.

✔ In some cultures the maternal grandmother has a major role in care of the pregnant and postpartum daughter and in care of the infant. The grandmother may give advice about nutrition, self-care, or baby care to the daughter; the advice may be contrary to scientific and medical knowledge and practices. Establish rapport with the grandmother as well as the pregnant woman/mother. Respect the role of the grandmother. Often the advice she gives is culturally based: The practices have maintained the group for centuries. The practices may be carried out along with modern-day health and medical practices. If the advice is truly harmful to the mother or baby, then your rapport, nonjudgmental approach, and well-timed, low-key teaching to the grandmother may help her to accept the teaching you direct to the pregnant woman/mother. Indeed, if either or both grandparents are considered the head of the household, direct your attention initially to them and direct your teaching to them. Initial or exclusive focus on their daughter is likely to alienate them so that they discontinue coming for care or become resistive and not allow their daughter to carry out your teaching.

Physiological Concepts

The Neonate—Physical Development

The neonatal period of infancy includes the critical transition from parasitic fetal existence to physiological independence. The normal newborn will be described in the following pages; references 79, 80, 106, and 126 will be used. Transition begins at birth with the first cry. Air is sucked in to inflate the lungs. Complex chemical changes are initiated in the cardiorespiratory system so that the baby's heart and lungs can assume the burden of oxygenating the body. The foramen ovale closes during the first 24 hours; the ductus arteriosus closes after several days. For the first time, baby experiences light, gravity, cold, and firm touch.

The newborn is relatively resistant to stress of anoxia and can survive longer in an oxygen-free atmosphere than an adult. The reason is unknown, as are the long-term effects of *mild* oxygen deprivation (10, 106).

Appearance. The newborn does not match the baby ads and may be a shock to new parents. The misshapen head, flat nose, puffy eyelids, and often undistinguished eye color, discolored skin, large tongue and undersized lower jaw, short neck and small sloping shoulders, short limbs and large rounded abdomen with protruding umbilical stump which remains to 3 weeks, and bowed skinny legs may prove very disappointing if the parents are unprepared for the sight of a newborn. The head, which accounts for one-fourth of the total body size, appears large in relation to the body.

The **anterior fontanel,** *a diamond-shaped area at the top of the front of the head,* and the **posterior fontanel,** *a triangular-shaped area at the center back of the head,* are often called **soft spots.** These unossified areas of the skull bones, along with the suture lines of the bones, allow the bones to overlap during delivery and also allow for expansion of the brain as they gradually fill in with bone cells. The posterior fontanel closes by 2 or 3 months; the anterior fontanel closes between 8 and 18 months. These soft spots may add to the parents' impression that the newborn is too fragile to handle (80).

✔ Reassure the parents that the newborn, while in need of tender, gentle care, is also resilient and adaptable. The head and fontanels can be gently touched without harm, although strong pressure or direct injury should be avoided. Reassure them also that the baby will soon take on the features of the family members and look more as they expected.

Head Circumference. Measurement of circumference is important in assessing the speed of head growth to determine if any abnormalities, such as too rapid or too slow growth, are present. The measurement is taken over the brow just above the eyes and across the posterior occipital protuberance. This standard measure of head size averages about 14 inches or 35 centimeters at birth, but variations of one-half inch are common. Chest circumference is usually about an inch less than head size (106). Parents should be prepared for molding of the skull during vaginal delivery; **caput succedaneum,** *irregular edema of the scalp* which disappears about the third day; or for **cephalohematoma,** *a collection of blood beneath the fibrous covering of the skull bones,* usually the parietal. Obstruction of the nasolacrymal duct is also common, and the excessive tearing and pus accumulation usually clears up when the duct opens spontaneously in a few months.

The baby's characteristic position during this period is one of flexion, closely imitating the fetal position, fists tightly closed, arms and legs drawn up against the body. The baby is aware of disturbances in equilibrium and will change position, reacting with the Moro reflex.

↙ *Apgar Scoring System.* The physical status of the newborn is determined with the Apgar tool one minute after birth and then 5 minutes later. The newborn's respirations, heart rate, muscle tone, reflex activities, and color are observed. A maximum score of 2 is given to each sign, so that the score could range from 0 to 10, as indicated by Table 7–3. A score under 7 means that the newborn is having difficulty adapting, needs even closer observation than usual, and may need life-saving intervention.(125).

↙ In addition to using the Apgar score, assessment includes estimating gestational age in order to utilize parameters other than weight to assess an infant's level of maturity. By considering *both birth weight* and *gestational age,* you can categorize infants into one of several groupings. Problems can then be anticipated and, if present, be identified and treated early. Assessment can be done as early as the first day of life, and should be done no later than the fifth day of life since external criteria, such as hip abduction, square window, dorsiflexion of foot, and size of breast nodules change after 5 to 6 days of life. If the neonate is examined on the first day of life, he/she should be examined again before the fifth day to detect neurological changes. The score can be affected by asphyxia or maternal anesthesia.

↙ To assess gestational age, two sources can be used: The *Dubowitz Guide to Gestational Age Assessment* includes an examination of ten neurological and eleven external signs (37). *Colorado Clinical Estimation of Gestational Age-A Guide* includes obstetrical data, physical and neurological criteria, and defines when certain characteristics should be present. For best results, assess the infant according to both. Add scores together; the sum of the scores will correlate with a certain gestational age in weeks. Plot the baby's weight and gestational age in weeks on the Colorado Growth Chart. This will place the infant in one of nine categories based on *age* and *weight.*

Skin. The skin is thin, delicate, and usually mottled, varies from pink to reddish, and becomes very ruddy when the baby cries. **Acrocyanosis,** *bluish color of the hands and feet,* is the result of sluggish peripheral circulation that occurs normally only a few days after birth. **Lanugo,** *downy hair of fetal life,* most evident on shoulders, back extremities, forehead, and temples, is lost after a few months and is replaced by other hair growth. The *cheesy skin covering,* **vernix caseosa,** is left on for protective reasons; it rubs off in a few days. **Milia,** *tiny white spots which are small collections of sebaceous secretions,* are sprinkled on the nose and forehead and should not be squeezed or picked; they will disappear. **Hemangiomas,** *pink spots* on the upper eyelids, between eyebrows, on the nose, upper lip, or back, may or may not be permanent. **Mongolian spots,** *slate-colored areas* on buttocks or lower back in Black, Oriental, or Mediterranean babies, fade without treatment. If a birth-mark is present, parents should be assured it is not their fault. **Jaundice,** *yellowish discoloration of skin,* should be noted. If it occurs during the first 24 hours of life, it is usually caused by blood incompatibility between mother's and baby's blood and requires medical investigation and possibly treatment. **Physiological jaundice** normally appears about the third or fourth day of life because the excess number of red blood cells present in fetal life which are no longer needed are undergoing hemolysis, which in turn causes high levels of bilirubin (a bile pigment) in the bloodstream. The jaundice usually disappears in about 1 week when the baby's liver has developed the ability to metabolize the bilirubin.

TABLE 7–3. Assessment of the Newborn: Apgar Scoring System

SIGN	0	1	2
1. Heart rate	Absent	Below 100 per min	Above 100 per min
2. Respirations	Absent	Slow, irregular	Cry; regular rate
3. Muscle tone	Flaccid	Some flexion of extremities	Active movements
4. Reflex irritability	None	Grimace	Cry
5. Color	Body cyanotic or pale	Body pink, extremities cyanotic	Body completely pink

If bilirubin levels are excessively high, the neonate is place under full-spectrum lights (phototherapy) to promote bilirubin breakdown. The baby's eyes must be covered during phototherapy.

✔ Parents should be reassured about these and other conditions of the skin that normally occur. Foot or hand prints are made for identification, since these lines remain permanently. **Desquamation,** *peeling of skin,* appears in 2 to 4 weeks.

Umbilical Cord. *The bluish-white, gelatinous structure that transports maternal blood from placenta to fetus* is the **umbilical cord.** It is cut 1½ to 3 inches from baby's abdominal wall. Because of the high water content, the stump of the cord dries and shrinks rapidly, losing its flexibility by 24 hours after birth. By the second day, it is a very hard yellow or black (blood) tab on the skin. Slight oozing where the cord joins the abdominal wall is common and offers an excellent medium for bacterial growth.

✔ The area should be cleaned with cotton balls and alcohol several times daily until the cord has dropped off (6 to 14 days), and for 2 or 3 days after the cord falls off when the area is completely healed. Parents should be taught this procedure.

Circumcision. *The surgical removal of the foreskin,* **circumcision,** is done almost automatically on newborn males. In contrast to past ideas, this is a painful procedure for the baby, as shown by the cry (102). The same reasons are given by people in different cultures either to do or not to do circumcision. These reasons include:

1. Sign of manhood
2. Cultural norms
3. Sexuality concerns
4. Hygienic/cosmetic/comfort concerns
5. Biblical or religious mandate
6. Prevention of later genitourinary problems
7. Medical advice

The main difference among various cultural groups related to circumcision is the issue of pain. Some people believe the procedure is not harmful or even very painful to infants; others believe it is traumatic and dangerous (53). While it is part of religious ritual for the Jewish male, most families have the boy circumcised to facilitate hygiene of the penis and decrease the risk of penile cancer.

✔ Although there are risks to circumcision, these complications occur infrequently. Irritation and infection can occur. Hemorrhage is the most common complication, requiring sutures or pressure dressings that can cause scarring, deformity, or phimosis. If the physician is not skilled, various surgical mishaps may occur. Although rare, septicemia with osteomyelitis, pulmonary abscess, and death may occur. Physicians are now questioning the necessity of circumcision. Good hygiene provides the same medical benefits without the risk of surgery and the pain (36, 102). Parents may feel they have no choice about circumcision. Discuss the procedure with them, so that their action is based on information. Further, you may share that the American Academy of Pediatrics states there are no medical indications for circumcision. However, urologists report that a small percentage of uncircumcized males develop genitourinary infections, inflammation of the glans, or *phimosis (tightening of the foreskin)* (36).

Weight, Length, and Head Circumference. In newborns these provide an index to the normality of development, and measurements should be accurate. *The average birth weight* of Caucasian male infants in America is 7½ pounds (3400 grams) and for girls is 7 pounds (3180 grams). Newborn infants of Afro-American, Indian, and Oriental groups are smaller, on the average, at birth (101). The factors maternal age, parity, lifestyle, and the woman's previous state of nutrition also influence birth weight. In all instances, female babies tend to be somewhat smaller than males. Shortly after birth the newborn loses weight, up to 10 percent of birth weight, due to water loss, and parents should be told that this is normal prior to a steady weight gain which begins in 1 or 2 weeks. Tissue turgor shows a sense of fullness because of hydrated subcutaneous tissue (80, 106).

Average length. American infants at birth is just under 20 inches (50.8 cm). Boys range from 19 to 21 inches (48.2 to 53.3 cm); girls average slightly less. The bones are soft, consisting chiefly of cartilage. The back is straight and curves with sitting. The muscles feel hard and are slightly resistant to pressure (80, 106).

Ethnic differences for weight, length, head circumference, and other measurements have been noted in Anglo and Mexican-American children ages 48–56 weeks. The Mexican-American child has shorter stature and greater weight for length than the Anglo child, with greater chest circumference, subscapular skinfolds, and estimated body fat, with no difference by gender. Head circumference is greater for males than females in both ethnic groups but greater in Anglo than Mexican-American children. Thigh circumference is greater in Mexican-Americans than Anglos and in females than in males (72).

Other Characteristics. Several other characteristics are also normal and resolve themselves shortly after birth: swollen breasts which contain liquid in boys and girls; swollen genitalia with undescended testicles in the boy; and vaginal secretions in the girl, caused by maternal hormones. Genitalia size varies for boys and girls. Urine is present in the bladder and the baby voids at birth.

Vital Signs. In the newborn, vital signs are not stable. *Respiratory efforts* at birth are most critical and immediate adaptations must occur to counter the decreasing oxygen level and increasing carbon dioxide level in the blood. Causes of respiratory initiations may include physical stimulation of the birth process, the sudden change in baby's environment at birth, the exposure to firm touch, and the cool air. If mother were medicated during labor or if the baby is premature, the respiratory center of the brain is less operative and baby will have more difficulty with breathing. *Respirations* range from 50 to 80 per minute during the first hour after birth and then decrease to 30 to 60 per minute. Respirations are irregular, quiet, and shallow and may be followed by a 5- to 10-second pause in breathing intermittently (125).

Body temperature ranges from 97 to 100° Fahrenheit (F) (36.1 to 37.7° Celsius (C)) because (1) the heat-regulating mechanism in the hypothalamus is not fully developed; (2) shivering to produce heat does not occur; (3) there is less subcutaneous fat; and (4) heat is lost to the environment by evaporation, conduction, convection, and radiation. At birth, amniotic fluid increases temperature loss by evaporation from the skin; thus diligent efforts to dry the skin are necessary. The wet newborn can lose up to 200 calories of heat per kilogram per minute (90 calories/minute is the maximum the adult can lose). If the room is cool and the baby is placed in contact with cold objects, heat loss occurs by convection, radiation, and conduction.

✔ Thus, baby should be placed next to mother's abdominal skin or breasts initially and then wrapped well in blankets before being placed in a warm crib. Several mechanisms occur to help the newborn conserve heat: (1) vasoconstriction by which constricted blood vessels maintain heat in the inner body; (2) flexion of the body to reduce total amount of exposed skin (the premature does not assume a flexion of the extremities onto the body); (3) increased metabolic rate, which causes increased heat production; and (4) metabolism of adipose tissue that has been stored during the eighth month of gestation. This *adipose tissue* is called **brown fat** because it *is brown in color from a rich supply of blood vessels and nerves,* and it is unique in that it *aids adaptation to the stress of cooling.* Brown fat, located between the scapulae around the neck, behind the sternum, and around the kidneys and adrenal glands, accounts for 2 to 6 percent of the neonate's body weight and is metabolized quickly (125).

✔ Body temperature of the baby normally drops 1 to 2°F immediately after birth, but in a warm environment begins to rise slowly after 8 hours. Thus prevention of heat loss, especially during the first 15 minutes, is crucial to adaptation to extrauterine life (125). Also, babies who have lost excessive amounts of heat cannot produce surfactant as well. (**Surfactant** is a *thin lipoprotein film that reduces surface tension of the alveoli and allows them to expand [125].*)

Heart rate ranges at birth from 100 to 160 beats per minute because of the immature cardiac regulatory mechanism in the medulla. The heart rate may increase to 170 to 180 beats per minute when the newborn cries and drop to 90 during sleep. The pulse rate gradually decreases during the first and subsequent years (125).

Blood pressure may range from 40 to 50 millimeters of mercury (mm Hg) systolic, depending on cuff size or the instrument used for measurement. By the end of the first month, blood pressure averages 80/40 (125).

Meconium. *The first fecal material* is sticky, odorless, and tarry. This **meconium** is passed from 8 to 24 hours after birth. Transitional stools for a week are loose, contain mucus, are greenish-yellow and pasty, and have a sour odor. There will be two to four stools daily. If the neonate takes cow's milk, the stools will become yellow and harder and average one to two daily.

Reflex Activity. This is innate or built in through the process of evolution and develops while the baby is in utero. **Reflex** *is an involuntary, unlearned response elicited by certain stimuli,* and it indicates neurological status or function (106, 125, 126). Individual differences in the newborn's responses to stimulation are apparent at birth. Some respond vigorously to the slightest stimulation; others respond slowly, and some are in between. Several types of reflexes exist in the neonate and young infant; consummatory, avoidant, exploratory, social, and attentional. **Consummatory reflexes** *promote survival through feeding, such as rooting and sucking.* **Avoidant reflexes** *are elicited by potentially harmful stimuli* and include the Moro, withdrawing, knee jerk, as well as sneezing, blinking, or coughing. **Exploratory reflexes** *occur when infants are wide awake and are held upright so that their arms move without restraint.* The visual object at eye level elicits both reaching and grasping reflexes. **Social reflexes,** *such as smiling, promote affectionate interactions between parents and infants* and thus have a survival value. Crying in response to painful stimuli, loud noise, food deprivation, or loss of support; quieting in response to touch, low, soft tones, or food; and smiling in response to changes

TABLE 7-4. Assessment of Infant Reflexes

REFLEX	DESCRIPTION	APPEARANCE/DISAPPEARANCE
Rooting	Touching baby's cheek causes head to turn toward the side touched.	Present in utero at 24 wk; disappears 3 to 4 mo; may persist in sleep 9 to 12 mo.
Sucking	Touching lips or placing something in baby's mouth causes baby to draw liquid into mouth by creating vacuum with lips, cheeks, and tongue.	Present in utero at 28 wk; persists through early childhood; especially during sleep.
Bite	Touching gums, teeth, or tongue causes baby to open and close mouth.	Disappears 3 to 5 mo when biting is voluntary, but seen throughout adult years in comatose person.
Babkin	Pressure applied to palm causes baby to open mouth, close eyes.	Present at birth; disappears in 2 or 4 mo.
Pupillary Response	Flashing light across baby's eyes or face causes constriction of pupils.	Present at 32 wk of gestation; persists throughout life.
Blink	Baby closes both eyes.	Remains throughout life.
Moro or Startle	Making a loud noise or changing baby's position causes baby to extend both arms outward with fingers spread, then bring them together in a tense, quivery embrace.	Present at 28 wk of gestation; disappears 4 to 7 mo.
Withdrawing	Removes hand or foot from painful stimuli.	Present at birth, persists throughout life.
Colliding	Moves arms up and face to side when object is in collision course with face.	Present at birth or shortly after; persists in modified form throughout life.
Palmer Grasp	Placing object or finger in baby's palm causes his fingers to close tightly around object.	Present at 32 wk of gestation; disappears 3 to 4 mo replaced by voluntary grasp at 4 to 5 mo.
Plantar Grasp	Placing object or finger beneath toes causes curling of toes around object.	Present at 32 wk of gestation; disappears 9 to 12 mo.
Tonic Neck or Fencing (TNR)	Postural reflex seen when infant lies on back with head turned to one side; arm and leg on the side toward which he/she is looking are extended while opposite limbs are flexed.	Present at birth; disappears about 4 mo.
Stepping, Walking, Dancing	Holding baby upright with feet touching flat surface causes legs to prance up and down as if baby were walking or dancing.	Present at birth; disappears about 2 to 4 mo. With daily practice of reflex, infant may walk alone at 10 mo.
Reaching	Hand closes as it reaches toward and grasps at object at eye level.	Present shortly after birth if baby is upright; comes under voluntary control in several months.
Orienting	Turning head and eyes toward stimulus of noise, accompanied by cessation of other activity, heartbeat change, and vascular constriction.	Present at birth; comes under voluntary control later; persists throughout life.
Attending	Fixing eyes on a stimulus that changes brightness, movement, or shape.	Present shortly after birth; comes under voluntary control later; persists throughout life.
Swimming	Placing baby horizontally, supporting him under abdomen, causes baby to make crawling motions with his arms and legs while lifting head from surface, as if he were swimming.	Present after 3 or 4 days; disappears about 4 mo; may persist with practice.
Trunk Incurvation	Stroking one side of spinal column while baby is on his abdomen causes crawling motions with legs, lifting head from surface, and incurvature of trunk on the side stroked.	Present in utero; then seen about third or fourth day; persists 2 to 3 mo.
Babinski	Stroking bottom of foot causes big toe to raise while other toes fan out and curl downward.	Present at birth; disappears about 9 to 10 months. Presence of reflex later may indicate disease.
Landau	Suspending infant in horizontal, prone position, and flexing head against trunk causes legs to flex against trunk.	Appears about 3 mo; disappears about 12 to 24 mo.
Parachute	Sudden thrusting of infant downward from horizontal position causes hands and fingers to extend forward and spread as if to protect self from a fall.	Appears about 7 to 9 mo, persists indefinitely.
Biceps	Tap on tendon of biceps causes biceps to contract quickly.	Brisk in first few days, then slightly diminished; permanent.
Knee Jerk	Tap on tendon below patella or on patella causes leg to extend quickly.	More pronounced first 2 days; permanent.

in brightness, comforting stimuli, or escape from uncomfortable stimuli are examples of innate reflexes that can be modified by experience and that persist throughout life. **Attentional reflexes,** including orienting and attending, *determine the nature of the baby's response to stimuli* and have continuing importance through development (106).

↙ The nervous system of the newborn is both anatomically and physiologically immature, and reflexes should be observed for their presence and symmetry. These reflexes are described in Table 7–4 (106, 125, 126, 143)

Sensory Abilities. The newborn has more highly developed sensory abilities than was once supposed. Apparently, a moderately enriched environment, one without stimulus bombardment or deprivation, is best suited for sensory motor development. Even premature babies placed in a stimulus-rich environment until discharged from the hospital learn more quickly and are healthier at 4 months than premature babies who lived in the traditional environment (71, 106).

↙ The infant's use of the senses, innate abilities, and environment lay the ground work for intellectual development. Studies show that 20 minutes of extra handling a day will result in earlier exploring and grasping behavior by the infant. He/she is very sensitive to touch and vestibular (rocking, holding upright) stimulation; cutaneous and postural stimulation is necessary for development of the nervous system, skin sensitivity, and emotional health (71).

↙ The first impressions of life, security, warmth, love, pleasure, or lack of these, come to the infant through touch. Knowledge of the people around him/her, initially of mother, is gradually built from the manner in which baby is handled. He/she soon learns to sense mother's self-confidence and pleasure as well as her anxiety, lack of confidence, anger, or rejection. These early touch experiences and the infant's feelings through them apparently lay the foundation for feelings about people thoughout life. Extra kinesthetic stimulation daily results in a baby who is quieter, gains weight faster, and shows improved socioemotional function and ability to cope with stress.

↙ *Sensitivity to pain, pressure, and temperature* extremes are present at birth; pain is shown by a distinct cry (87). The baby is especially sensitive to touch around the mouth and on the palms and soles. Females are more responsive to touch and pain than males (80). The newborn reacts diffusely to pain since he/she has little ability to localize the discomfort because of incomplete myelinization of the spinal tracts and cerebral cortex (106, 126). However, the baby's response to pain increases each day in the neonate period. Visceral sensations of discomfort, such as hunger, overdistention of the stomach, passage of gas and stool, and extremes of temperature, apparently account for much of the newborn's crying. At first the cry is simply a primitive discharge mechanism that calls for help. He/she wails with equal force regardless of stimulus. In a few weeks baby acquires subtle modifications in the sound of the cry that provide clues to the attentive parent about the nature of the discomfort so response can be adjusted to the baby's need (106).

Characteristics of newborn vision are:

1. Acuity—clarity of vision at a specific distance (8 to 20 inches).
2. Fixation—ability to direct eyes at same point in space for specific time (4 to 10 seconds).
3. Discrimination—demonstrated preference for particular sizes, shapes, colors, or patterns; discriminates large from small and intensity of color.
4. Conjugation—ability of the eyes to move together; frequency of refixation is more frequent for newborn.
5. Scanning—ability to move eyes over the visual field and focus on satisfying image.
6. Accommodation—adjustment of eyes for distance; the preferred distance is 8 inches up to 1 month of age; at 4 months, ability to adjust is on adult level (82).

The *visual abilities* of the newborn are apparent as he/she tracks or visually follows large moving objects beginning a day after birth. Central vision is adequate for fixation and coordinated binocular eye movements. Infants prefer less complex stimuli and large pictures or objects. The eyes are as sensitive to changes in light intensity as adult eyes. Because eye movements are not yet fully coordinated and the neonate's eyeball is shorter than that of the adult, the newborn cannot focus on objects unless they are held about 8 to 20 inches from his/her face. The infant maintains contact with the environment through visual fixation, scanning, and tracking and pays more attention to stimuli from the face than to other stimuli. The newborn looks at mother's face while feeding, and while sitting upright follows the path of an object, crying if it comes too close to his/her face. He/she appears to have innate depth perception, can define stripe and edge, and correlates touch with sight (79, 82, 106, 126). He/she apparently sees colors and prefers black and white to red, orange, or yellow. The newborn looks longer at colors of medium intensity (yellow, green, pink) than at bright (red, orange, blue) or dim (gray, beige) colors. Pupils respond sluggishly to light and although bright lights may cause discomfort, they will not injure vision.

↙ Parents should be reassured that the antibiotic ointment or solution correctly placed in baby's eyes at birth will not damage vision but prevents blindness if the mother should have an undetected gonorrheal infection. Teach parents that baby needs eye contact as well as opportunity to see the human face and a variety of changing scenes and colors. A mirror or chrome plate that reflects light and objects and rotating the bed helps the baby use both eyes, avoiding one-sided vision. Hang cardboard black and white mobiles, especially those that make sound, and have them within the reach of baby's kicking feet. Later the infant enjoys other colors and designs that are within grasp. By age 2 months, baby can see the ceiling and decorations on it. As baby grows older the crib should be low enough that he/she can see beyond the crib (79, 82).

Hearing is developed in utero when the fetus is exposed to internal sounds of mother's body. Hearing is blurred the first few days of life because fluid is retained in the middle ear, but hearing loss can be tested as early as the first day (79). The neonate cannot hear whispers but can respond to voice pitch changes. A low pitch quiets; a high pitch increases alertness. Baby responds to sound direction—left or right—but responds best to mother's voice and to sounds directly in front of his/her face (106). Baby often sleeps better with background songs or a tape recording of mother's heartbeat (120).

Differentiation of sounds and perception of their source will take some time to develop, but there are startle reactions. By 4 weeks the baby is more likely to respond to mother's voice than to loud noise.

The presence of congenital (born deaf) hearing loss is more common than ordinarily understood. It is believed that approximately 1½ to 3 percent of infants born in the United States each year have a hearing loss severe enough to require special education or help. Table 7–5 is a guide for parents and health-care professionals to check for hearing ability in the neonate and infant (29).

Taste and smell are not highly developed at birth, but acid, bitter, salt, and sweet substances evoke a response. Taste buds for sweet are more abundant in early than late life. Breathing rhythm is altered in response to fragrance, showing some ability to smell (79, 106, 126).

Neonates differ in their appearance, size, function, and response. Girls are more developmentally advanced than boys and Afro-Americans are more than

TABLE 7–5. Checklist to Detect Hearing In Infancy

From Birth to 2 Weeks Old *Does Baby:*	*From 2½ Months to 6 Months Old* *Does Baby:*
Jump or blink when there is a sudden loud sound.	Always coo with pleasure when you start to talk
Stop crying when you start to talk	Turn eyes to the speaker
Seem aware of your voice	Know when father comes home and wriggles in welcome (if awake)
Stir in sleep when there is continuous noise close by	Startle when you bend over the crib after awakening
Jump or blink when there is a sudden soft click, as a light switch or a camera click when the room is otherwise quiet	Seem to enjoy a soft musical toy (e.g., a crib musical toy)
Stop sucking momentarily when there is a noise or when you start to talk	Cry when exposed to sudden, loud unexpected noise
Look up from sucking or try to open eyes when there is a sudden noise	Stop movements when a new sound is introduced
	Try to turn in the direction of a new sound or a person who starts to talk
From 2 Weeks to 10 Weeks Old *Does Your Baby:*	Make many different babbling sounds when alone
Stop crying when you talk to him/her	Try to "talk back" when you talk
Stop movements when you enter the room	Start wriggling in anticipation of a bottle when you start preparing it (if the baby is awake and the preparation is out of sight, as the refrigerator door opening, etc.)
Seem aware of your voice	Know own name (smiles, turns, or otherwise gives an indication)
Sleep regardless of noises	
Waken when the crib or bassinet is touched	
Respond to comforting only when held against mother or familiar caretaker	
Cry at sudden loud noises	
Blink or jerk at sudden loud noises	

Note: If the child is hearing impaired or deaf, a source of information about treatment facilities and of other educational materials for parents can be obtained from Galludet College, Washington, D.C.

Caucasians. The most accurate assessment is made by comparing the neonate against norms for the same sex and race (106, 126).

Special Considerations in Physical Assessment of the Neonate

✔ When a newborn is examined, the primary concerns are neurological status, congenital deformities, and metabolic disturbances. Any history of hereditary diseases, as well as pregnancy and delivery information, is essential. See Table 7–4, because reflex status indicates neurological and some congenital deformities. The following are particular aspects to check when physically assessing the neonate (61, 106, 126, 131, 132).

A small chin, called **micrographia**, may mean that the neonate will experience breathing difficulties since the tongue can fall back and obstruct the nasopharynx.

Ear position is important as there is a strong association between low-set ears and renal malformation or in a chromosomal aberration such as Down's Syndrome.

Discharges from the eye may be due to chemical irritation or to ophthalmic neonatorum from gonorrhea in the mother. A mongoloid slant in a Caucasian infant may suggest a chromosome abnormality.

Ptosis *(drooping)* of the eyelids should be a cause of concern. Drooping eyelids reduce the amount of light entering the retina and can decrease development of sight.

Conjunctival hemorrhage is usually of no significance. An infant lid retractor may be used to view the fundus if the muscles of the newborn keep the eyelids closed.

The *nose* should be patent. Flaring of the nostrils usually represents respiratory distress. A thick bloody discharge from the nose suggests congenital syphilis.

The *mouth* should be inspected for cleft lip and cleft palate. Although spitting up is common in the newborn, projectile vomiting is not. The newborn should have very little saliva, and tonsillar tissue should not be present at birth.

The *chest* and *abdomen* are considered a unit in the newborn. The anterior—posterior (AP) diameter is usually equal to the transverse diameter. Wide set nipples may indicate Turner's syndrome, a genetic disorder. Smaller breasts which contain liquid are not uncommon in both male and female. The breath sounds in the infant are bronchovesicular. If heart murmurs exist, they are usually best heard over the base of the heart rather than at the apex.

The *umbilical cord* should have two arteries and one vein. Auscultation of bowel sounds should precede palpating for masses, an extremely important procedure in the newborn.

The *genitalia* are examined for deformities. The testes should be palpated in the scrotum, although sometimes they are still undescended. A **hydrocele**, *a collection of watery fluid in the scrotum or along the spermatic cord*, and **hernia**, *a protrusion of part of the intestine through the abdominal muscles*, are common findings in males.

A bloody or mucous vaginal discharge may be present in girls. Fused labia is a serious anomaly, but simple adhesion may be due to inflammation.

Rectal temperatures will rule out **imperforate anus** *(lacking normal anal opening)*.

The spine should be palpated for **spina bifida**, *a congenital neural tube defect characterized by anomaly in posterior vertebral arch*. Observation for symmetrical bilateral muscle movements of the hips and knees is essential. The *hips* should be examined for dislocation by rotating the thighs with the knees flexed.

Extremities should be noted for the right number of fingers and toes and bilateral movements, and position of hands and feet should be checked.

The Infant—Physical Development

Appearance. The growing infant changes in appearance as he/she changes size and proportion (106, 126). The face grows rapidly; trunk and limbs lengthen; back and limb muscles develop; and coordination improves. By 1 month of age baby can lift the head slightly when prone and hold the head up briefly when the back is supported. By 2 months the head is held erect, but it bobs when he/she is sitting unsupported.

Skull enlargement occurs almost as rapidly as total body growth during the first year and is determined mainly by the rate of brain expansion. From birth to 4 weeks, the head size increases to 14.75 inches (37.5 cm); at 3 months to 15.75 inches (39.5 cm); at 20 weeks to 16.5 inches (41 cm); and at 30 weeks to 17 inches (43 cm). By the end of the first year the head will be two-thirds of adult size (106, 126).

Physical Growth and Emotional, Social, and Neuromuscular Learning. These are concurrent, interrelated, and rapid in the first year.

The first year of life is one of the two periods of rapid physical growth after birth. (The other period is pre- and postpuberty.) Baby gains ⅔ ounce per day in the first 5 months and ½ ounce per day for the next 7 months. Birth weight doubles by 5 to 6 months and triples by 12 months. Baby grows about 1 foot in the first year (79, 80, 106).

Physical and motor abilities are heavily influenced by genetic, biological, and cultural factors, nutrition, maturation of the central nervous system, skeletal formation, overall physical health status, environmen-

TABLE 7–6. Assessment of Physical Characteristics of the Infant

1 TO 3 MONTHS	3 TO 6 MONTHS	6 TO 9 MONTHS	9 TO 12 MONTHS
Many characteristics of newborn, but more stable physiologically.	Most neonatal reflexes gone. Temperature stabilizes at 99.4°F (37.5 °C).		Temperature averages 99.7°F (37.7°C).
Heartbeat steadies at about 120 to 130 beats per min.		Pulse about 115 per min.	Pulse about 100 to 110 per min.
Blood pressure about 80/40; gradually increases.		Blood pressure about 90/60.	Blood pressure about 96/66.
Respirations more regular at 30 to 40 per min; gradually decreases.			Respirations 20 to 40 per min.
Appearance of salivation and tears.			
Weight gain of 5 to 7 oz (141.75 to 198.45 grams) per wk.	Weight gain of 3 to 5 oz (85.05 to 141.75 grams) per wk.		Weight gain of 3 to 5 oz (85.05 to 141.75 grams) per wk.
Weight at 8 to 13 lb (3629 to 5897 grams).	Weight at 15 to 16 lb by 6 mo. (6.8 to 7.3 kg).	Birth weight doubled by 6 mo.	Birth weight tripled; average 22 lb. (10 kg).
Head circumference increases 1 inch up to 16 inches (40 cm).	Head size increases 1 inch (2.54 cm).	Head size 17.8 inches (43.21 cm).	Head size increases slightly more, about ½ inch (18.3 inches or 45 to 46 cm).
Chest circumference 16 inches (40 cm).	Chest size increases over 1 inch (17.3 inches or 43 to 44 cm).	Chest circumference increases ½ inch (17.8 inches or 44 to 45 cm).	Chest circumference increases about ½ inch (18.3 inches or 45 to 46 cm).
Growth of 1 inch (2.54 cm) monthly.	Growth of ½ inch (1.27 cm) monthly.	Growth of ½ inch (1.27 cm) monthly.	Growth of ½ inch monthly; height 29 to 30 inches (72.5 to 75 cm), increased by 50% since birth.
TNR and Moro reflexes rapidly diminishing.	Most neonatal reflexes gone. Palmar reflex diminishing.		
Arms and legs found in bilaterally symmetric position.			
Limbs used simultaneously, but not separately.	Movements more symmetrical		
Hands and fingers played with.			
Clenched fists giving way to open hands that bat at objects.			
Reaches for objects.	Reaches for objects with accurate aim and flexed fingers.	Palmar grasp developed. Picks up objects with both hands.	
	Objects transferred from one hand to another by 6 mo.	Bottle held with hands.	
	Bangs with objects held in one hand.	Preference for the use of one hand.	
	Scoops objects with hands.		
	Begins to use fingers separately.	Probes with index finger.	
		Thumb opposition to finger (prehension).	Brings hands and thumb and index finger together at will to pick up small objects.
			Releases objects at will.
Can follow moving objects with eyes when supine. Begins to use both eyes together about age 2 months.	Binocular depth perception by about 5 mo.	Explores, feels, pulls, inspects, tastes, and tests objects.	Makes mark on paper.

TABLE 7–6. Continued

1 TO 3 MONTHS	3 TO 6 MONTHS	6 TO 9 MONTHS	9 TO 12 MONTHS
	Looks for objects when they are dropped.		
	Improving eye–hand coordination.	Hand–mouth coordination.	
		Feeds self cracker and other finger foods.	Eats with fingers; holds cup, spoon.
	Eruption of one or two lower incisors.	Begins weaning process.	Has six teeth, central and lateral incisors. Eruption of first molars about 12 mo.
Attends to voices.	Binaural hearing present.		
	Turns head to sound.		
Raises chin while lying on stomach at 1 mo.			
Raises chest while lying on stomach at 2 mo.			
Holds head erect in prone position at 3 mo.			
	Rolls over compeletely by 6 mo.		Rolls easily from back to stomach.
Sits if supported.	Sits with support at 4 mo.		
	Holds head steady while sitting.		
	Pulls self to sitting position.		
	Beings to sit alone for short periods.	Sits erect unsupported by 7 mo.	Sits alone steadily.
	Plays with feet.		Puts feet in mouth.
	Begins to hitch (scoot) backward while sitting.	Creeps or crawls by 9 mo.	Hitches with backward locomotion while sitting.
	Bears portion of own weight when held in standing position.	Pulls self to feet by holding onto support.	Sits from standing position without help.
	Pushes feet against hard surface to move by 3 or 4 mo.	Cruises (walking sideways while holding onto object with both hands) by 10 mo.	Stands alone for a minute.
			Walks when led by 11 mo.
		Begins to walk with help.	Walks with help by 12 to 14 mo.
			Lumbar and dorsal curves developed while learning to walk.
			Turning of feet and bowing of legs normal.
			Beginning to show regular bladder and bowel patterns; has one to two stools per day; interval of dry diaper does not exceed 1 to 2 hr.
			Not ready for toilet training.
Smiles at comforting person reflexly.	Smiles at person deliberately during interaction.	Experiences separation anxiety about 7 to 9 mo.	
			Begins to cooperate in dressing; puts arm through sleeve; takes off socks.
			Improves previously acquired skills throughout this period.

tal conditions, stimulation, and consistent loving care. Black infants mature ahead of Caucasian infants in motor skills, bone ossification, and walking. This is apparently due to genetic factors and has evolutionary adaptive value (79, 80, 106).

✔ Table 7–6 divides further developmental sequence into 3-month periods for specific assessment (46, 79, 80, 106, 126). *It is only a guide*, not an absolute standard. Great individual differences occur among infants, depending on their physical growth and emotional, social, and neuromuscular responses. Girls usually develop more rapidly than boys, although the activity level is generally higher for boys. Even with these cautions, the table can be a useful tool if you observe overall behavior patterns rather than isolated characteristics.

Nervous System. The nervous system is immature, but it continues the fetal pattern of developing a functional capacity at a rapid rate. Consistent stimulus of the nervous system is necessary to maintain growth and development, or function is lost and cannot be regained.

Under 4 months of age baby does not look for an object hidden after seeing it, and when the same object reappears, it is as if the object is a new object. The infant has no knowledge that objects have a continuous existence: The object ceases to exist when it is not seen (23, 104, 106, 126). The baby coordinates both eyes, and attends to and prefers novel stimuli. At 4 months he/she can focus for any distance and perceive shape constancy when the object is rotated at different angles (79). Infants look longer at patterned stimuli of less complexity than at stimuli that have more complex designs or no lines or contours and can detect change of pattern (79, 30). The infant is attracted by checkerboard designs, geometric shapes, and large pictures (circles, dots, and squares at least 3-inches high and with angles rather than contours) (79). Full depth perception develops about 9 months, when the images received in the central nervous system from the macula of each eye are integrated. Visual stimulation of both eyes simultaneously is necessary for the baby to develop binocular vision. Otherwise **amblyopia** *(lazy eye) develops, which is a gradual loss of the ability to see in one eye because of lack of stimulation of visual nerve pathways*, without damage to the retina or other eye structures. If visual stimulation is not lacking for too many weeks, the condition reverses itself. If one eye continues to do all the work for several months, blindness results in the other eye (106, 126).

During infancy, vital signs (temperature, pulse, respirations, and blood pressure) stabilize, as shown in Table 7–6.

Intersensory integration takes place in infancy; information from two sense modalities is interrelated. Four-month-old infants respond to relationships between visual and auditory stimuli that carry information about an object. Six-month-old infants look longer at television when both picture and sound are on than when only the picture is on. They look longer at patterns on television then other types of stimuli (79).

The haptic system is that body system pertaining to tactile stimulation. At birth all humans possess central nervous system ability to register and associate sensory impressions received through receptor organs in the skin and from kinesthetic stimuli that originate with neuromuscular stimulation from their contact with other humans. Sensory pathways subserving kinesthetic and tactile activities are the first to complete myelinization in infancy, followed by auditory and visual pathway myelinization.

✔ Touching the infant from birth on provides the basis for higher-order operations in the neurological, perceptual, muscular, skeletal, and cognitive systems. Each tactile act carries a physiological impact with psychological and sociocultural meaning. Much information is gained through discriminating one physical stimuli from another with the form or quality of touch changing the perception of the tactile experience. Tactile stimulation is essential for the beginning body image development, as well as other learning (95, 143). Encourage parents to stroke, massage, and cuddle baby; to talk and sing to baby; and to provide toys that have primary colors, different textures, and movement.

Endocrine System. This function begins to develop primarily in infancy and childhood; it is limited in fetal life. Thus the child is very susceptible to stress, including fluid and electrolyte imbalance, during the first 18 months of life because the pituitary gland and adrenal cortex do not function well together and the adrenal gland is immature. The pituitary gland continues to secrete growth hormone and thyroid-stimulating hormone (begun in fetal life), which influence growth and metabolism (126).

Respiratory Tract. These tissues remain small and relatively delicate and provide inadequate protection against infectious agents. Close proximity of the middle ear, eustachian tube, throat, trachea, and bronchi result in rapid spread of infection from one structure to the other. Mucous membranes are less able to produce mucus, causing less air humidification and warming, which also increases susceptibility to infection. The amount of dead air space in the lungs remains relatively large; more air must be moved in and out per minute than later in childhood; causing increased respiratory rate. By age 1 year the lining of the airway resembles that of the adult. Respiratory rate at rest decreases gradually during the first year (80 106, 126).

Gastrointestinal System. This matures somewhat after 2 to 3 months, when the baby can voluntarily chew, hold, or spit out food. Saliva secretion increases and composition becomes more adult-like. The stomach's emptying time changes from 2½ to 3 hours to 3 to 6 hours; by 3 months the stomach can hold 150 milliliters. Tooth eruption begins about 6 months and stimulates saliva flow and chewing. Peristaltic waves mature by slowing down and reversing less after about 8 months; then stools are more formed and baby spits up or vomits less. **Colic,** a term that indicates *daily periods of distress*, usually occurs between 2 to 3 weeks and 2 to 3 months and seems to have no remedy. X-rays taken of such infants show unusually rapid and violent peristaltic waves throughout the intestinal tract. These movements are normally set off by a few sucking movements. Gas pressure in the rectum is also three times greater than in the average infant (80, 106, 126). Some physicians believe colic is caused by a deficiency of vitamin K, A, or E. Some mothers find that changing formula and giving plain, low-fat yogurt helps reduce the pains. When small yogurt feedings do not help, vitamin A and E supplements have been found effective. Apparently, colic disappears as digestive enzymes become more complex, and normal bacterial flora accumulate as baby ingests a larger variety of food. By 2 months baby usually has two **stools** (*bowel movements*) daily. By 4 months there is a predictable interval of time between feeding and bowel movements. Breast-fed babies usually have soft, semiliquid stools that are light yellow in color. Breast-fed babies may vary more in the bowel movement pattern: the baby may have three or four watery stools a day or may go several days without a bowel movement. The stools of the formula-fed baby are more brown and formed. As the autonomic nervous system and gastrointestinal tract mature, interconnections form between higher mental functions and the autonomic nervous system; the infant's gastrointestinal tract responds to emotional states in self or of someone close to him/her (80, 106, 126)

Muscular Tissue. At birth, muscular tissue is almost completely formed; growth results from increasing size of the already existing fibers under the influence of the growth hormone, thyroxin, and insulin. As muscle size increases, strength increases in childhood. Muscle fibers need continual stimulation to develop to full function and strength (80, 106, 126).

Skin Structures. Structures typical of adult skin are present, but they are functionally immature; thus baby is more prone to skin disorders. The epidermal layers are very permeable, causing greater loss of fluid from the body. Dry, intact skin is the greatest deterrent to bacterial invasion. Sebaceous glands, which produce sebum, are very active in late fetal life and early infancy, causing milia and cradle cap, which go away at about 6 weeks. Production of sebum decreases during infancy and remains minimal during childhood until puberty, which accounts for the dry skin.
✔ Eccrine (sweat) glands are not functional in response to heat and emotional stimuli until a few months after birth, and function remains minimal through childhood. The inability of the skin to contract and shiver in response to cold or perspire in response to heat causes ineffective thermal regulation (80, 106, 126).

Kidney. Structural components are present; by 5 months tubules have adult-like proportions in size and shape. However, renal function is not mature until approximately 1 year of age; therefore the child is unable to handle increased intake of proteins, which is ingested if cow's milk is given too early (80, 106, 126).

Immunologic System. Components are present or show beginning development. The phagocytosis process is mature, but the inflammatory response is inefficient and unable to localize infections. The ability to produce antibodies is limited; much of the antibody protection is acquired from the mother during fetal life. Development of immunologic function depends on the infant's gradual exposure to foreign bodies and infectious agents (80, 106, 126).

Red Blood Cell and Hemoglobin Level. High at birth, this drops after 2 or 3 months and then gradually increases when erythropoiesis begins. Iron deficiency anemia becomes apparent around 6 months of age if the physiological system does not function adequately to sustain red blood cell and hemoglobin levels. By the end of infancy white blood cells, high at birth, decline to reach adult levels. Red blood cell and hemoglobin levels reach adult norms in late childhood (80, 106, 126)
✔ Increasingly, studies show that the health of the adult is influenced considerably by the person's health status in early life. Obesity, discussed in Chapters 10, 11, and 12, is an example. Blood pressure in adult years is apparently set by age 1 year; the mix of genetic

and environmental influences, such as diet, stress, and infections, is unknown. One measure of childhood onset of a tendency toward hypertension (high blood pressure) and a possible screening method are being sought in the enzyme kallikrein, released by the kidney and found in the urine. Kallikrein causes the release of materials that dilate blood vessels and is lowest in people with hypertension; kallikrein is also lower in Black children than in Caucasian children, even before a difference in their blood pressure is seen (101, 107).

Nutritional Needs

The feeding time is a crucial time for baby and mother: a time to strengthen attachment, for baby to feel love and security, a time for mother and baby to learn about self and each other, and a time for baby to learn about the environment.

Breast-Feeding. Breast-feeding of infants has come in and out of fashion, however, the American Academy of Pediatrics recommends breast-feeding for the first year of life. However, a large percent of infants are bottle-fed (147). In the past human milk was considered ideal because it is sterile, digestible, available, inexpensive, and contains the necessary nutrients except vitamins C and D and iron. Further, even in undernourished women the composition of breast milk is adequate, although vitamin content depends on the mother's diet (54, 74). Breast milk is all that baby needs the first 6 months of life. It contains higher levels of lactose, vitamin E, and cholesterol and less protein than cow's milk. The additional cholesterol may induce production of hormones required for cholesterol breakdown in adulthood. Breast milk has a more efficient nutritional balance of iron, zinc, vitamin E, and unsaturated fatty acids (107 146).

Because of the host-resistant factors in human milk, breast milk offers many advantages to the infant, including the premature infant. Immunoglobulins and antibodies to many types of microorganisms, especially those found in the intestinal tract, and enzymes that destroy bacteria are obtained from human milk. Living milk leukocytes, which further promote disease resistance, are also present in breast milk. Respiratory and gastrointestinal diseases and meningitis occur two to three times less frequently in breast-fed than bottle-fed babies. Breast-fed babies are also less prone to allergies. Human milk kept refrigerated in a sterile container (not pasteurized and not frozen) can be given to premature infants to prevent necrotizing enterocolitis, a frequently fatal bacterial invasion of the colon wall (80, 106, 146).

The mother's decision to either breast-feed or bottle-feed can be influenced by the obstetrician, pediatrician, hospital staff, husband, friends, and how her own mother fed her children. Or there may be no decision making at all. It may be assumed from the start that the mother will feed either one way or the other. Recently in the United States more Anglo women, both of lower and higher economic status, are returning to breast-feeding.

In the study by Scrimshaw (127), 82 percent of Mexican-American women planned to breast-feed for at least one month; 30 percent planned to breast-feed for over 6 months. Mexican-American women who were more acculturated were less likely to breast-feed. Women who were married or planning to be married, rather than unmarried women, were more likely to breast-feed. Women who were less anxious prenatally and in postpartum were more likely to breast-feed. Bottle-feeding, on the other hand, seemed more often a decision made by the woman herself. Reasons for not breast-feeding included no milk, pain, husband against breast-feeding, and dislike for the procedure. Fewer women plan to breast-feed if they plan to return to work soon, which is mandatory if the woman does not have economic support from the father or is not married.

The woman who works can be encouraged to breast-feed when at home, although in some work sites women could bring the baby so breast-feeding could be continued. The mother can be told of the benefits of breast-feeding to the baby and informed about community resources such as La Leche League.

Any woman is physiologically able to nurse her baby, with very rare exceptions (146). But childbirth, breast-feeding, and child rearing are sexual experiences for the woman. The woman's success in breast-feeding is related to other aspects of her psychosexual identity (22). She may choose not to breast-feed or to limit the lactation period because of personal preference, illness, or employment in a place where she cannot take baby with her. Further, in the United States, feelings of embarrassment, shame, guilt, and disgust about breast-feeding are still apparent, in spite of today's openness about the subject; often medical personnel convey these feelings to women who wish to breast-feed. In cultures in which breast-feeding is accepted, women breast-feed without difficulty. Mother keeps baby nearby day and night and feeds baby whenever he/she is hungry or needs comfort. Babies fed in this way seldom cry and are satisfied. In societies with a leisure class where women are objects of amusement and pleasure and technology is king, women are less likely to breast-feed or to have success if they try. Breast-feeding is a learned social behavior. A positive social support system is essential for the woman who breast-feeds, since fear of failure, embarrassment, anxiety, exhaustion, frustration, humiliation, anger, fear, or any stress-producing situation can prevent the effect of oxytocin and can block the flow of milk (22). The woman who really wants to breast-feed will develop the courage to do so as comfortably as possible when in public places.

✓ Preparation for breast-feeding begins during pregnancy. An adequate diet during pregnancy is an initial step toward successful lactation and breast-feeding. Teach the woman the importance and method of preparation. Atkinson is a helpful reference (5). The woman may also consult La Leche League literature.

During pregnancy the progesterone level is high, like just before menstruation. If a mother nurses after delivery, the pituitary gland secretes prolactin. The high levels of estrogen from the placenta which inhibited milk secretion during pregnancy are gone. As the baby sucks, the nipple is in the back of the mouth and the jaws and tongue compress the milk sinuses. These tactile sensations trigger the release of the hormone oxytocin from the pituitary gland which, in turn, causes the "let-down" response. The sinuses refill immediately and milk flows with very little effort to the baby. This is the crucial time to learn breast-feeding. Oxytocin also causes a powerful contraction of the uterus, lessening the danger of hemorrhage (1, 125).

✓ Every effort should be directed toward making breast-feeding a comfortable, uninterrupted time (26). Effective techniques for mother getting into a comfortable position, holding the baby, and putting the baby to nipple are described in La Leche League literature, obstetric nursing and other child care books, and in some booklets prepared by formula companies (1, 26, 58, 68, 86, 100, 106). Mother needs an encouraging partner or family member, knowledgeable and supportive medical personnel to assist, acquaintance with other successful nursing mothers, and hospital routines that allow the baby to be with her for feeding when the baby is hungry and her breasts are full. The mother should not automatically receive medication to stop lactation; the baby should not be fed in the nursery between breast-feedings. The mother whose milk does not let-down may need oxytocin, a period of relaxation, or perhaps a soothing liquid before feeding. She should, in any case, be encouraged to increase her fluid intake and meet the increased Recommended Dietary Allowances for lactating women (107, 146).

✓ The baby may be put to breast immediately after delivery and fed within 8 hours after birth to reduce hypoglycemia and hyperbilirubinemia (106, 126).

The first nourishment the baby receives after delivery from breast-feeding is **colostrum**, *a thin yellow secretion*. Colostrum is rich in carbohydrates, which the newborn needs, and serves as a laxative in cleaning out the gastrointestinal tract; apparently, colostrum fed immediately after birth triggers antibody production (1, 107, 146). Depending on how soon and how often the mother nurses, true milk comes in the first few days.

✓ The baby may nurse every hour or two at first, perhaps 15 to 30 minutes each time, but graduate to 3- to 4-hour intervals, obtaining more milk in shorter feeding sessions. If anxieties, excessive stimuli, and fatigue are dealt with appropriately, the mother's milk supply will increase or decrease to meet the demand. Alternating breasts with each feeding and emptying the breasts will prevent caking. The infant should grasp the areola completely to avoid excess pressure on the nipples. The large or active infant may need supplemental feeding in addition to breast milk, even when mother's supply is not compromised. However, usually extra formula or baby food is not necessary before the fourth month. Food in addition to breast milk (or formula) should be introduced by the end of the sixth month. If mother received ample amounts of iron during pregnancy, her baby's iron stores should last 4 to 12 months, even on an iron-poor diet (107, 146).

✓ Premature infants can breast-feed earlier and with less effort than bottle-feed, but they need time to learn to suck. Physiologically, breast-feeding is an advantage; premature infants suck for about 25 minutes at one time, but the longer feeding fills the stomach more slowly. The infant controls the pace of breast-feeding and also avoids gastric distention, in contrast to bottle-feeding and the caregiver controlling feeding pace, amount, and time (21).

✓ Breast-feeding the premature infant is possible and desirable and can be a rewarding option for the mother, as well as nutritionally and emotionally beneficial to the baby. Boggs and Rau (16) describe: (1) the specific procedure for pumping the breasts; (2) how the mother can maintain a milk supply; (3) ways to enhance the experience for the mother, baby, and intensive care nursery staff; and (4) continuation of breast-feeding after discharge.

Breast milk may not be so ideal as was once thought. Alcohol; nicotine; many medications, including laxatives and barbituates; and drugs and foreign substances, such as chemical pollutants and pesticides, pass into the milk and to the infant. Studies show that baby's exposure to the chemicals polybrominated byphenyl (PBB) and polychlorinated biphenyl (PCB) can occur through breast milk as well as in utero. PBB is used in fire-retardant materials as well as other products, and PCB is a semisynthetic, chlorinated, petroleum-derivative oil that is in so many products and pesticides that its contamination is now worldwide, including Antarctica. Although manufacture of PCB was stopped in 1979, residues remain. The breast-feeding mother can easily ingest these or other chemicals in food or water, and baby stores these chemicals in adipose and hepatic tissue since they are slowly excreted. Studies show that these chemicals (and perhaps others that are yet untested) produce a long-term effect of reduced scores on tests of attention, verbal ability, perceptual and perceptual-motor tasks, intelligence, and various other developmental abilities in the infant and young child. The immature and developing neurological function of the infant (and fetus) is likely to be more affected by such contamination than is the neurological function of the adult. Infants exposed to such chemical contamination are more prone to a variety of symptoms and illnesses in childhood (77, 98, 114, 124, 128).

🗸 Mother should be informed of these hazards to her baby if she breast-feeds so that she can avoid harmful substances if possible. Foods without preservatives or dyes can be purchased; some food can be homegrown by families if they wish to exert the effort and use space. All medications except essential ones should be avoided by the lactating woman; even prescribed medications should be taken with caution.

Weaning gradually, whether to a bottle or a cup, will lessen the discomfort of temporarily having a greater supply than demand. There are normal growth spurts during the first few months when baby may demand more milk, or mother may notice a lag as the infant's interests are directed more to the surroundings. She can assume that the infant is receiving enough milk if weight gain is normal, if he/she has six or more wet diapers a day, and if the urine is pale (80, 107, 146)

Commercial Formulas. These are similar to each other and to human milk, but they are not exactly the same. Most have a slightly higher renal solute load than does breast milk. Special formulas have been developed to meet the needs of infants with phenylketonuria, fat malabsorption, and protein hypersensitivity. Modular formula, made by Ross Laboratories, consists of a core of proteins and vitamins and minerals to which different carbohydrates and fats can be added in increasing amounts. Normal growth and development are possible without breast-feeding (107).

Higher protein intake from formula produces a higher BUN and serum or urine level of amino acids (except taurine). If soy protein isolate is used as a substitute for milk protein, it is supplemented with the amino acid methionine in the formula. Soy protein isolate formula supports growth similar to breast-fed babies except the preterm baby. Soy-based formulas are used for infants with lactose deficiency or galac-tosemia for the baby in a vegetarian family, or for the baby who is allergic to cow's milk—or regular formulas. Protein hydrolysate or meat-based formulas can be used for infants allergic to cow's milk or who have malabsorption problems (147). If the osmolality is too high, water is drawn from the tissue, causing dehydration. Necrotizing enterocolitis may also be more likely to result (147).

🗸 Infants should receive supplemental iron by 4 months of age, and preterm babies by 2 months. Iron-fortified formulas are the best source for formula-fed babies. Too high sodium level in the formula may cause transient elevation of blood pressure in neonates (107, 146, 147).

🗸 Teach parents that care must be taken if the bottle is heated; it is not essential to do so. Instruct the parents why baby bottles should preferably not be heated in the microwave. The bottle, nipple, and milk all become too hot and will cause oropharyngeal and esophageal burns. Further, the formula-filled disposable plastic liner of a commercial nurser may explode after removal of the heated bottle from the microwave, causing body burns. Wink compares human milk and formulas (147). This comparison is shown in Table 7–7.

Cow's Milk. Cow's milk is designed for another animal; thus it is not surprising that it varies considerably in composition from human milk. Cow's milk is unsuitable for the infant under 6 months of age. Cow's milk contains from two to three times as much protein as does human milk, and a much greater percentage of the protein is casein, which produces a large, difficult to digest curd. It is higher in saturated fats and lower in cholesterol than is human milk, but the total fat content is comparable. However, the butterfat is poorly absorbed. Cow's milk contains half as much total sugar as human milk, and also has galactose and glucose. Although it contains more sodium, potassium, magnesium, sulphur, and phosphorus than human milk, like human milk, it is a relatively poor source of vitamins C and D and iron. One striking difference between cow's milk and human milk is the calcium content: Cow's milk contains over four times as much calcium, and babies fed cow's milk have larger and heavier skeletons. Whether or not this is normal or better is debatable. Two percent or skim milk should not be fed to infants because they will not gain weight (107, 146, 147).

🗸 The baby needs about 100 to 150 milliliters of water per kilogram of body weight daily to offset normal fluid losses. Some of this is obtained through the milk, but hot weather, fever, diarrhea, or vomiting quickly leads to dehydration. Infants become dehydrated more quickly than adults because they have a smaller total fluid volume in the body compared to

Table 7–7. Comparison of Human Milk and Formula

NUTRIENT OR COMPONENT	HUMAN MILK	FORMULA (BY NATIONAL STANDARDS)
Protein	1.6 g/100 kcal; whey/casein ratio of 60:40	1.8 to 4.5 g/100 kcal; average 2.3 g/100 kcal; whey/casein ratio of 60:40.
Carbohydrates	Lactose 70 g/L (39% of calories)	Lactose, sucrose, corn syrup corn syrup solids, maltodextrins, or tapioca starch (40 to 50% of calories).
Fats	50% of calories	3.3 to 6 g/100 kcal; at least 300 mg/100 kcal must be linoleic acid, polyunsaturated fat (30 to 54% of calories). Butterfat of cow's milk excreted; soy, coconut, corn, oleo, safflower, or medium-chain triglyceride oils added.
Osmolality	300 milliosmoles/kg	400 milliosmoles/kg.
Iron	1 mg/L	0.15 mg/100 kcal.
Sodium		Higher than human milk.
Potassium		Higher than human milk.
Chloride		Same as human milk.

body size (107, 146). Water should be offered at least twice daily. Parents should know the signs of dehydration: dry, loose, warm skin; dry mucous membranes; sunken eyeballs and fontanels; slowed pulse; lower blood pressure and increased body temperature; concentrated, scanty urine; constipation, or mucoid diarrhea; lethargy; a weak cry. Any combination of these symptoms implies the need for medical treatment.

✓ *After the initial period of adjustment* (7 to 10 days after birth), the baby needs a daily average of 2.2 grams of protein and 117 calories per kilogram (or 36 per pound) of body weight to grow and gain weight satisfactorily. Moderate protein intake is apparently well utilized and increases growth. No specific fat requirement is set, but some fats are necessary because they contain essential fat-soluble vitamins, furnish more energy per unit than carbohydrates and protein, and contribute to diet palatability. Adequate vitamins and minerals, especially iron and fluoride, are essential. If the water supply is not fluorinated, supplementation should be given until 12 years of age to prevent dental caries. Recommendations for various ages can be found in Appendix III and in a nutrition text (107, 146).

✓ Mothers may frequently need instruction concerning times and methods of burping (bubbling) the baby to reduce gaseous content of the stomach during feeding, since the cardiac sphincter is not well developed (68). Young babies need to be bubbled after every ounce and at the end of a feeding. Later they can be bubbled halfway through and again at the end. The infant should be moved from a semireclining to an upright position while the feeder gently pats the back. Because a new infant's gastrointestinal tract is unstable, milk may be eructated with gas bubbles. Adequate bubbling should occur before the infant is placed into the crib to prevent milk regurgitation and aspiration. The infant should be positioned prone (on abdomen) or laterally.

✓ Although infants vary in the amount of formula they drink and their demand for food, knowledge of the following amounts and schedules will help the mother plan for feeding (106, 107, 146). During the first week the newborn needs six to eight feedings of 2 to 3 ounces every 3 to 4 hours. For the next 3 weeks the neonate averages 3 to 4 ounces every 4 hours. Orange juice is generally not recommended early in life because of the allergenic potential; a vitamin C-enriched noncitrus juice should be given to provide ascorbic acid. By 1 month, baby eats five to six times a day. By the time the baby is 2 or 3 months old, he/she sleeps through the night and needs five feedings of 4 to 6 ounces of milk daily. By this time he/she readily accepts cereal. Rice cereal is often given first. At age 4 or 5 months, baby eats five times daily of 5 to 7 ounces of milk and enjoys other foods gradually added, such as strained, cooked vegetables, meat, fruit, and egg yolk. Foods with soy or wheat flour and egg products are usually postponed until after 6 months of age to reduce chance of allergies. At age 6 or 7 months, the baby eats four or five times a day, drinks 7 to 8 ounces of milk each time, and enjoys finger foods, especially when teething begins. By 8 or 9 months, he/she drinks 8 ounces of milk with three meals of regular food, following the eating pattern of the family. Additional fluids are consumed throughout the day (107).

Solid Foods. There is no rigid sequence in adding solid foods to the infant's diet. Whatever solid food is offered first or at what time seems to be largely a matter of individual preference of the mother or of the pediatrician. Ideally, the infant's needs and developmental achievements, such as eye–hand–mouth coordination and fine pincer grasp, should be considered when introducing solids. A large, active baby may need cereal added to the diet at 2 months of age to satisfy hunger. A smaller, more lethargic baby may find it awkward to accept such supplements before 3 or 4 months.

✔ The mother or nurse introducing the baby to solid foods should make it a pleasant experience. The foods offered should be smooth and well diluted with milk or formula. The infant should not be hurried, coaxed, or allowed to linger more than 30 minutes. New foods should be offered one at a time and early in the feeding while he/she is still hungry.

✔ Because fetal iron stores may last up to 6 to 12 months and because of an increasing incidence of allergies in infants introduced to a variety of solids before 3 months, many physicians now recommend later introduction of solids. Many pediatricians are also concerned about early feedings because of the relationship between overfeeding and infant and adult obesity. Some even encourage a total milk diet as a nutritionally adequate diet during the first 6 months. Then, in the second 6 months they recommend offering a variety of chopped table foods. Developmentally a child of 6 to 7 months is ready to chew solids rather than ingest only thickened feedings, and readiness usually hastens acceptance of a new activity (107).

✔ Help the parents realize that when baby is first fed puréed foods with a spoon, he/she expects and wants to suck. The protrusion of the tongue, which is needed in sucking, makes it appear as if baby is pushing food out of the mouth. Parents misinterpret this as a dislike for the food, but it really is the result of immature muscle coordination and possibly surprise at the taste and feel of the new items in the diet. This reflex gradually disappears by 7 to 8 months. The baby should not be punished for spitting out food. Further, baby begins to exercise some control over the environment by pacing the feeding.

✔ When you or the physician suggests that the mother offer "table food" to the infant, ask what table food is in their home. Depending on the level of the household hygiene or the family food pattern, table food may or may not constitute an adequate or healthy diet. Family diet counseling may be necessary to ensure continued health of the family unit. Food supplies not only physical sustenance but also many personal and cultural needs. The introduction of foods characteristic of a culture provides the foundation for lifelong food habits as well as the basis for teaching a cultural pattern of eating.

✔ Infant nutritional status can be assessed by measuring head circumference, height, and weight. The fat baby, with a differential of two or more percentiles between weight and length, is more likely to become an overweight adult (42).

However, Shapiro (130) found that weight at birth or weight gain in infancy are not accurate predictors of obesity at 9 years. Small stature may indicate undernutrition, unless there is a genetic influence from small-sized parents. Signs of nutritional deprivation include smaller than normal head size, pale skin color, poor skin turgor, and low hemoglobin and hematocrit (42).

✔ Teach parents to avoid overfeeding—either milk or foods. Theories hold that babies who are fed more calories than they use daily develop additional fat cells to store unused energy sources. These fat cells proliferate in infancy and continue to replace themselves during childhood. Adults who were fat infants will have excess fat cells to fill through life and will have difficulty with weight control or will be obese. Another theory about the effect of infant feeding on adult weight is that eating patterns are difficult to change, especially if food symbolizes love, attention, or approval.

✔ In addition to discussing the food quantities, quality, and nutrients needed by the baby, help parents to realize that food is a learning experience. The baby gains motor control and coordination in self-feeding; he/she learns to recognize color, shape, and texture, use of mouth muscles stimulates speech movements, and he/she continues to develop trust with the consistent, loving atmosphere of mealtime.

✔ Unless you are an experienced mother, you may feel uncomfortable in teaching about feeding or other child care. Yet, you can share information gleaned from the literature, experiences of other mothers you have helped, and your own experiences if you have worked in the newborn nursery or helped a family member with a new baby. Do not tell the mother what method is best; give her the available information and then support her in *her* decision. Because feeding is one of the first tasks as a mother, she will need your guidance, assistance, and emotional support. You can offer suggestions, such as the posture that will assure a comfortable position for her as she cradles the baby in her arms, close to her body. Whether breast- or bottle-fed, the baby needs the emotional warmth and body contact. The bottle should never be propped because choking may result. Further, nursing-bottle mouth may develop; tooth decay is much higher in children when mothers use the bottle of milk, juice, or sugar water as a pacifier. The upper front teeth are most affected because liquids pool around these teeth when baby is drowsy or asleep (107).

✔ Mother–child contacts after birth are a continuation of the symbiotic prenatal relationship. The dependence of the baby on the mother and the reciprocal need of the mother for satisfaction from the child, proving her dependability and giving her confidence, are necessary to develop and continue the relationship. A successful feeding situation sets the foundation for the infant's personality and social development. It is the main means of establishing a relationship with another person and consequently the most basic opportunity to establish trust. Thus feeding is much more than a mechanical task. Your teaching attitude can convey its importance. If a father is going to be a primary nurturer, teach him the same way you would teach the mother.

Mercer (92) explored early psychophysiological mother–infant interaction using the tenderness and anxiety theorems of Harry Stack Sullivan. Maternal anxiety and perception were assessed and related to changes in healthy infant satiety, anxiety, and bottle-feeding behavior. Blood samples were obtained from the infants just before and 60 minutes after feeding for determination of glucose and cortisal. Formula consumption was also noted. An empathetic linkage exists in healthy postpartum mother–infant couples. The interaction of both a mother's transitory anxiety around feeding time and overall anxiety is associated with changes in her infant's satiety and anxiety levels and feeding behavior. Relatively low maternal anxiety at feeding time is associated with both increased formula intake and decreased postfeed cortisol, the latter being indicative of a feeling of security. Extremely low maternal anxiety or apathy (which can result from anxiety) around feeding time is associated with both decreased formula intake and increased postfeed cortisol, the latter reflecting a feeling of insecurity. Thus maternal anxiety levels are a threat physically and emotionally to the infant. A mother's perception of the infant tenderness needs is related to her prefeed and feed anxiety level. Increased maternal tenderness is associated with low maternal anxiety before and during infant feeding.

Weaning. *The gradual elimination of breast-feeding or bottle-feeding in favor of cup and table feeding* (weaning), is usually completed by the end of the first year. Baby shows signs of making this transition: Muscle coordination increases, teeth erupt, and he/she resists being held close while feeding. The two methods should overlap and allow baby to take some initiative and allow mother to guide the new method. Mother's consistency in meeting the new feeding schedule is important to development of a sense of trust.

The most difficult feeding to give up is usually the bedtime feeding because baby is tired and is more likely to want the "old method." After the maxillary central incisory teeth erupt, a night bottle should contain no carbohydrate to reduce decay in the deciduous teeth. During periods of stress the baby will often regress. Baby is also learning to wait longer for food and may object vigorously to this new condition.

✔ The need to suck varies with different children. Some children, even after weaning, will suck a thumb or use a pacifier (if provided). The baby should not be shamed for either of these habits because they are not likely to cause problems with the teeth or mouth during the first 2 years.

✔ Weaning coincides with a slower growth rate and will be accompanied by a decrease in appetite. Baby should not be forced to eat at the old rate during this period. Teach parents the meaning of baby's behavior and how to adapt to this new period of development.

Asian infant-feeding patterns differ from those of many other countries, including the dominant culture in the United States, the United Kingdom, and Europe. Some Asian-born immigrants have traditionally breast-fed the baby for one to three years, after which the child is fed a plain diet of rice, lentils, some vegetables, occasionally eggs, fish or fruit, and rarely meat. The Moslem parent, a vegetarian, cannot use, for religious purposes, commercially prepared baby food that has any meat product in it. They may occasionally eat animals slaughtered according to Moslem religious laws and rituals (meat is then classed as *halal*), but such meat is difficult to find in non-Moslem countries. Thus eggs and milk are primary sources of protein. If the diet for the weaned child is well planned, it can be adequate. Assess for steady weight gain, normal developmental behavior, healthy appearing hair, skin, teeth, and eyes, energy, ability to play and sleep, and infrequent colds or other infections. The main difference between Western and Asian infant-feeding practices seems to be lack of variety in diet and prolonged use of milk and certain baby foods (78).

Sleep Patterns

One of the most frequent concerns of a new mother is when, where, and how much baby sleeps. Awake, alert periods are altered by different types of feeding schedules.

The infant exhibits at least five states or levels of arousal: (1) regular or quiet sleep; (2) irregular, active, or rapid eye movement (REM) sleep; (3) quiet wakefulness; (4) active wakefulness; (5) crying; and (6) an indeterminate state of transition from one state of alertness to another (80, 106).

Every infant has a unique sleep pattern and no two babies—even if they are twins—have identical sleep habits. The following are some generalizations that can serve as a guide for the baby's first months. During regular or quiet sleep, eyes are closed, breathing is regular, and the only movements are sudden, generalized startle motions. Baby makes little sound. This is the low point of arousal; infant cannot be awakened with mild stimuli. During irregular, active REM sleep, baby's eyes are closed, breathing is irregular, muscles twitch slightly from time to time, and there are facial responses of smiles or pouts in response to sounds or lights. Baby may groan, make faces, or cry briefly. These are all normal patterns of an infant's sleep, and none of them requires attention(3). During quiet wakefulness, eyes are open; the body is more active; breathing is irregular; and there is varying spontaneous response to external stimuli. During active wakefulness, eyes are open; there is visual following of interesting sights and sounds, body movements, and vocalizations that elicit attention (80, 106).

The newborn and young infant spend more time in REM sleep than adults. In this state baby shows continual slow rolling eye movements on which are superimposed rapid eye movements. Additionally, respirations increase and are irregular and small muscle twitchings are seen (80, 106).

As the infant's nervous system develops, baby will have longer periods of sleep and wakefulness that gradually become more regular. By 6 weeks, baby's biological rhythms usually coincide with daytime and nighttime hours, and he/she will be sleeping through the night. Babies sleep an average of 16 to 20 hours a day for the first week. By 12 to 16 weeks these hours will be reduced to 14 or 15 a day. Usually this pattern will continue through the first year, with nap times getting shorter until the morning nap is eliminated. By 7 or 8 months, baby may sleep through the night without awakening. By the end of the first year, the baby may sleep 12 to 14 hours at night and nap 1 to 4 hours during the day (106, 126).

✔ Help parents understand that when a baby goes through the stage of separation anxiety about 8 months of age, bedtime becomes more difficult because he/she does not want to leave mother. Because the baby needs sleep, the parent should be firm about getting the child ready for bed. Prolonging bedtime adds to fatigue and separation fears. Caressing or singing softly while holding baby in a sleeping position in bed is calming; restraint is perceived as helpful rather than punitive. If the mother is available when the baby first awakes, he/she anticipates this pleasure, and sleep is associated with return of mother. If the baby awakes and cries during the night, the parent should wait briefly. Many times the crying will subside with the baby's growing ability to control personal anxiety feelings. Persistent crying indicates unmet needs and should be attended.

✔ Frequently a mother becomes concerned if baby sleeps too long during the day, perhaps 6 or 7 hours without a feeding. If this happens frequently, it may help to awaken the baby during the day for regular feedings and attempt to establish a better routine with longer sleeping periods at night. Occasional oversleeping is little cause for concern. The physical preparations for sleep ideally include a room and a bed for the baby, especially after the first few weeks. Sharing the parents' bed or room may lead to later sleep problems for the infant and can be detrimental to the husband-wife relationship. The infant should at least have a consistent place for sleeping (be it box, drawer, or crib) and a clean area for supplies. Sometimes baby does not seem to sleep enough. Some babies sleep less and remain healthy. Other babies have chronic sleeplessness, which may be due to allergy to cow's milk. A suitable milk substitute should be used, if so (67).

✔ A baby can sleep comfortably in an infant crib or bassinet during the first few weeks, but as soon as active arms and legs begin to hit the sides he/she should be moved to a full-sized crib. The crib slats should be no more than 2½ inches apart. There should be no pillows used. The crib should have a crib border placed at the bottom of the slats to prevent the head getting caught between the bars. It should be fitted with a firm, waterproofed, easy-to-clean mattress and with warm light covers loosely tucked in. The sides of the crib should fit closely to the mattress so that the infant will not get caught and crushed if he/she should roll to the edge. Thin plastic sheeting can cause suffocation and should never be used on or around the baby's crib. Teach these safety measures to the parents.

Play Activity

The infant engages in play with self: with the hands or feet, by rolling, getting into various positions, and with the sounds he/she produces. Baby needs playful activity from both mother and father to stimulate development in all spheres. Share the following information with parents.

✔ Certain toys are usually enjoyed at certain ages because of changing needs and developing skills. From birth to 3 months he/she needs colorful hanging toys that make sound—mobiles, rattles, bells, music boxes. From 3 to 6 months, baby needs toys to touch, grab, and mouth, such as large wooden and nonsplintering plastic beads, clothespins, empty spools, and soft, stuffed toys to feel and hold. From 6 to 9 months, motion toys and those that can be transferred from hand to hand are fun. Baby enjoys his/her image in the mirror; simple games with people, such as peek-a-boo and pat-a-cake; and out-of-door excursions. From 9 to 12 months, baby enjoys toys that pull apart, such as nesting, stack, or climbing blocks; boxes; mother's kitchen utensils; toys for bath and sand play to practice pouring, filling, and dumping; and cuddle toys for bedtime. The baby can remain satisfied playing with self for increasing amounts of time but prefers to have people around.

✔ Because much of baby's play involves putting objects into the mouth, a clean environment with lead-free paint is important. A small object that baby swallows, such as a coin, is passed through the digestive tract. However, small batteries used in cameras, calculators, and other electronic equipment may be hazardous if swallowed because they can rupture and release poisonous chemicals. Surgical removal may be necessary. Children gradually build up an immunity to the germs encountered daily on various objects. However, health may be threatened by that which goes unnoticed. Sitting and playing in dirt or sand contaminated by dioxin, other pesticides or herbicides, or radiation is dangerous to the developing physiological systems. Children's or parents' reading material, which can become play objects, may also be hazardous. The high lead content of the glossy color pages of magazines and newspaper inserts may account for some cases of lead poisoning in young children, who are eaters of the inedible. A study conducted by researchers at the Connecticut Agricultural Experiment Station revealed that the lead content of glossy paper printed in color—especially pages containing the color yellow—is so high that a child devouring a 4-inch square of it every day for 6 weeks could be at a critical stage of lead poisoning. While black-and-white newsprint, the comics, and the black-and-white magazine stock are scarcely recommended for snacking, their lead content is dramatically lower than that of the shiny, colored pages, the research showed. Ideally, the child does not eat paper; yet most children have been observed sucking or chewing on corners of magazines or pieces of paper (38).

✔ Toys need not be expensive, but they should be colorful (and without leaded paint), safe, sturdy, and easily handled and cleaned. They should be large enough to prevent aspiration or ingestion; they should be without rough or sharp edges or points, detachable parts, or loops to get around the neck, and some should make sounds and have moving parts.

✔ Baby needs an unrestricted play area that is safe, although use of a playpen is necessary for short periods. Excess restriction or lack of stimulation inhibits curiosity, learning about self and the environment, and development of trust. Therefore, baby should not wear clothing that is restraining, he or she should not be kept constantly in a playpen or crib, and he/she needs play objects and a loving parent who provides stimulating surroundings.

✔ Verzemnieks (140) discusses ways to stimulate sensory development of the hospitalized child during routine care measures, and common items in the hospital that can be used as toys, such as medicine cups, souffle cups, empty tape cylinders, and various boxes. She also lists common household items that can be used for toys in the home which can provide fun and stimulate creativity—more so than some of the expensive toys on the market.

✔ Parents should know the dangers of overstimulation and rough handling. Fatigue, inattention, and injury may result. The playful, vigorous activities that well-intentioned parents engage in, such as tossing the baby forcefully into the air or jerking the baby in a whiplash manner, may cause bone injuries or subdural hematomas and cerebrovascular lesions that could later cause mental retardation. Premature infants and male babies are twice as vulnerable as full-term girls, according to one study, because of the relative immaturity of their brains (106, 126).

Health Promotion and Health Protection

✔ In addition to measures already discussed, including the safety measures in the previous section on play activity, the following measures also promote health.

✔ At birth the neonate should have silver nitrate drops or ointment instilled in the eyes. Although less than 3 percent of mothers have gonorrhea, the possibility of blindness in the infant, along with the low cost and effectiveness of the treatment, makes this procedure mandatory (3).

✔ Injecting 1 mg of vitamin K is effective in preventing hemorrhagic disease, which is caused in 1 of 2000 to 1 of 3000 live births by a transient deficiency of Factor VIII production. Sickle cell screening can be obtained from in-cord blood (3).

✔ During the first week of life the infant should be screened for **phenylketonuria (PKU),** *an inborn metabolic disorder characterized by abnormal presence of phenylketone and other metabolites of phenylalanine in the urine.* Hypothyroid screening is also recommended for all newborns. Refer to Appendices I and II for a schedule of health screening measures for the infant.

Immunizations. Immunizations, *promoting disease resistance through injection of attenuated, weakened organisms or products produced by organisms* (50), are essential to every infant as a preventive measure. Before birth, baby is protected from certain organisms by the placental barrier and mother's physical defense mechanisms. Birth propels baby into an environment filled with many microorganisms. Baby has protection against common pathogens for a time, but as he/she is gradually exposed to the outside world and the people in it, further protection is needed through routine immunizations, available from private physicians or public health clinics.

✔ The infant needs the combination of diphtheria and tetanus toxoids and pertussis vaccine (DTP). The diphtheria bacillus is still prevalent, and the fully immunized person, protected against the disease, can acquire and transmit the disease as a carrier. Pertussis (whooping cough) is a serious disease for babies. Unimmunized children may have the disease, but the nonspecific manifestations often cause a delay in diagnosis. The infant needs oral polio vaccine which carries a risk of one case of paralytic polio in 9 million doses, a risk far less than that of the disease. The American infant should receive DTP at ages 2, 4, and 6 months and live oral polio vaccine (OPV) at 2 and 4 months, with an optional dose at 6 months. (45, 99, 129, 138). At 1 year the infant should be given a tine test to detect possible tuberculosis (3). Vaccination is essential to provide **herd immunity,** *immunity to all susceptible persons,* especially pregnant women in the first trimester (45).

✔ Parents should be told the importance of immunizations and should be helped to get them, for example, through flexible clinic hours or low-cost mass immunizations in a community. Parents should also keep a continuing record of the child's immunizations. Your teaching, encouragement, community efforts, and follow-up are vital.

✔ One study showed that a mailed reminder about the date for immunization of the 6-month-old infant increased the chances that baby would receive the scheduled immunization, especially in families that had a record of not keeping clinic appointments. Other nurses have found that a telephone reminder works well in getting mothers to return for well-baby immunizations (149).

✔ *Safety Promotion and Injury Control.* These are based on the understanding of infant behavior. Accidents are a major cause of death to children under 26 years of age. Risk factors that influence the occurrence of fatal childhood accidents include: (1) host factors such as age and sex; (2) environmental factors such as hazardous play equipment, flammable clothing, and accessible poisons; and (3) parental characteristics such as socioeconomic status (145).

The risk of a fatal accident among infants during the first year of life is directly related to the level of the mother's schooling for Caucasian as well as Afro-American children. Infants whose mothers completed 8 or fewer years of education had nearly double the rate of fatal accidents as infants whose mothers had some high school education in a study in North Carolina (145).

Epidemiological studies report that the main causes of death for the infant are drowning, suffocation by inhalation and/or ingestion of food or by mechanical means (in bed or cradle, by plastic bag), transport accidents, and falls (25). Contrary to common belief, the baby is not immobile: he/she will not necessarily stay where placed. Baby rolls, crawls, creeps, walks, reaches, and explores. And since he/she is helpless in water, the baby should never be left alone or with an unresponsible person while in water. The home and car have many often unnoticed hazards; the baby should never be left alone in either, and should never roam freely in the car while it is in motion. Parents should use an approved car infant seat or harness. Richi and Krzy (109) give a detailed description of various kinds of child car seats and restraints and the advantages of each. You can incorporate such information as you teach parents safety measures for their child. Baby's physical ability to move is developing, but he/she lacks reasoning ability, knowledge, experience, and self-control.

✔ Falls can be avoided if the parents or nurse are responsible for doing the following: (1) keeping crib rails up; (2) maintaining a firm grasp of the baby while carrying or caring for him/her and supporting the head during the first few months; (3) using a sturdy high chair and car infant seat or harness with fasteners in place (this is law in many states); and (4) having a gate at the top of the stairs or in front of windows or doors that are above the first story (106).

✔ Suffocation at home and in the health-care setting can be avoided by (1) removing any small objects that could be inhaled or ingested (safety pins, small beads, coins, toys, nuts, raisins, popcorn, balloons); (2) keeping plastic bags, Venetian blind cords or other cords out of reach; and (3) avoiding pillows in the crib or excessively tight clothing or bedcovers (80, 106).

✔ Burns can be avoided by: (1) placing the crib away from radiators or fireplaces; (2) using warm-air vaporizers with caution; (3) covering electrical outlets; (4) avoiding tablecloths that hang over the table's edge; (5) turning pot handles inward on the stove; (6) avoiding excessive sun exposure; and (7) avoiding smoking around the baby (80, 106).

✔ Encourage parents to take a first-aid course, one directed to cardiopulmonary resuscitation, preventing airway obstruction, and other home and family concerns, that enables them to recognize hazards and take appropriate measures to avoid injury to loved ones. Teaching parents about the child's normal developmental patterns will also enable them to foresee potential accidents and take precautions.

Common Health Problems: Prevention and Treatment

Dermatitis can be a problem in infancy. One of the most common is **diaper dermatitis** (*or* **rash**), *an inflammation of the skin covered by the diaper*. Urine, stool, and chemicals in detergents and soaps can all be causative factors. Bacterial, viral, or fungal infections or an underlying skin disorder can compound the problem.

✔ Teach parents that prevention lies in keeping the area free from urine and stool. Air should be allowed to circulate in the perineal area. Soap should be thoroughly removed from cloth diapers. Suspect the disposable diaper of irritation if nothing else can be traced. Treatment for mild inflammation includes applying a bland ointment after the diaper change. An aluminum acetate soak may be necessary for more severe inflammation with weeping. A prescription medication may be necessary if the dermatitis is fungal or bacterial (61).

Atopic dermatitis usually appears after 2 months of age and is a *chronic inflammatory disease of the skin characterized by itching*. It sometimes resolves by age 2 years. When it occurs in adulthood, it usually has different characteristics. Often the family has a history of allergic diseases. The dermatitis may progress from rough, red, nonelevated papules to weeping and crusting eruptions, often found on cheeks, scalp, around the neck, and on forearms and legs.

✔ Teach parents that prevention includes any precautions to avoid dry, itching, and irritated skin: (1) use warm instead of hot water for brief baths; (2) apply lotions that seal moisture into the skin (for example, Alpha-Keri); (3) use soft cotton for clothing and bedding; (4) keep fingernails short; and (5) rinse laundry well. During the active phase, prescription medication may be necessary to stop the itching and ensure healing (61).

Seborrheic dermatitis, *an oily, scaling condition occurring in areas with large numbers of sebaceous glands*, usually starts in infants on the scalp and is called "cradle cap."

✔ Teach parents that treatment consists of shampooing the hair with a nonprescription shampoo and massaging the scalp with a soft brush every other day until scales are gone, and then two times weekly. For persistent cases a shampoo such as Sebulex can be used, followed by massage (61).

Oral candidiasis or **thrush** *is a fungal infection found in the mouth of infants*. It is easily passed from a mother's or caretaker's hands to the baby's mouth. It can be passed from the mother's vagina during the birth process, and sometimes is passed to the mouth from the infant's own candidal diaper dermatitis. White, irregular plaques can be seen in the infant's mouth. When removed they leave an inflamed base.

✔ Treatment consists of an oral antifungal agent that is put in the infant's mouth by dropper. Prevention occurs by advising anyone who handles infants to wash his/her hands between each handling. Infants should not share clothing, pacifiers, or nipples. See that any infant contact who has fungal vaginitis is treated, as well as that candidal diaper dermatitis is treated (61).

Constipation, *difficulty in passing stools, excessive firmness of stool, and decreased frequency of defecation*, is sometimes a problem in infancy. Because the child has not yet learned how to withhold feces, the problem is usually related to dehydration or to an acute illness associated with decreased activity and appetite.

✔ Teach parents that a nonconstipating diet for an infant only on formula is difficult. Adding 2 tablespoons of dark corn syrup to 1 quart of the infant's formula helps. The infant must also be given water by bottle in addition to formula. An older infant who is eating fruits and vegetables may be helped with the addition of like food to the diet, especially prune preparations (61).

Iron deficiency anemia, a form of anemia associated with an *inadequate supply of iron for synthesis of hemoglobin*, is usually found in the infant who has a premature birth and who has been without supplemental iron or iron-fortified milk. Under these circumstances, the infant is usually anemic by 9 months of age. This anemia will be manifested by a hematocrit of less than 30 percent between the ages of 3 to 6 months and by a hematocrit of less than 33 percent from 6 months to 1 year. Pallor, lethargy, irritability, and anorexia are all possible symptoms of iron deficiency anemia, but more often it is symptomless and found in routine health maintenance screening.

✔ Teach parents that prevention for the premature infant is iron-fortified milk until 18 months of age or medicinal iron supplement from 2 to 18 months of age. Prevention for the full-term infant is the same except the medicinal iron supplement should be started at 3 months. Infants should eat iron-containing foods as soon as advisable (egg yolk, liver, turkey, dried fruit, beans). Treating the existing anemia will involve discontinuing whole cow's milk and substituting evaporated milk or commercial milk formula, eating iron-rich foods, and taking supplemental iron until the hematocrit reaches normal (61).

A little understood but fairly common benign disease of infancy is **roseola infantum**. The infant has a sudden high fever, usually lasting 3 to 4 days, with few other symptoms. When the fever subsides, a faint rash appears, mainly on the trunk and neck, and lasts 24 to 48 hours. There is no known prevention. Contagion and incubation periods are not known, and the only treatment is an antipyretic (61).

The incidence of *bronchitis* and *pneumonia* increases with the increasing number of cigarettes smoked by the mother, particularly in infants aged 6 to 9 months. In a prospective study of 10, 672 infants relating hospital admission during the first year of life to maternal smoking, findings supported the hypothesis that atmospheric pollution with tobacco smoke endangers the health of nonsmokers. Infants of smoking mothers had significantly more admissions for bronchitis or pneumonia and more injuries (52).

Psychosocial Concepts

The intellectual, emotional, social, and moral components can be combined into what is often referred to as **psychosocial development.** The separation of these facets of growth is artificial for they are closely interrelated. Similarly, psychosocial, physical, and motor development greatly influence each other. A level of physiological maturation of the nervous system must be present before environmental stimulation and learning opportunities can be effective in promoting emotional and cognitive development. In turn, without love and tactile, kinesthetic, verbal, and other environmental stimuli, some nervous system structures do not develop. Low-birth-weight and premature infants have neurological deficits that predispose to an increased risk for developmental delays, and they are apt to have behavioral styles that are more difficult to handle, which reduces maternal involvement and the stimulation needed for development (91).

Cognitive–Intellectual Development

Intelligence *is the ability to learn or understand from experience, to acquire and retain knowledge, to respond to a new situation, to solve problems.* It is a system of living and acting developed in a sequential pattern through relating to the environment. Each stage of operations serves as a foundation for the next (105). **Cognitive behavior** *includes thinking, perceiving, remembering, forming concepts, making judgments, generalizing, and abstracting.* Cognitive development is learning and depends on innate capacity, maturation, nutrition, gross and fine motor stimulation, touch, stimulation of all senses through various activities, language, and social interaction (79, 80).

Sequence in Intellectual Development. The sequence described by Piaget corresponds rather roughly in time span to those described for emotional development. The infant is in the sensorimotor period of cognitive development (104, 105, 141).

The infant arrives in the world with great potential for intellectual development, but at birth intellectual capacities are completely undifferentiated.

Stage One, the Reflex Stage, covers the neonatal period when behavior is entirely reflexive. Yet, all stimuli are being assimilated into beginning mental images through reflexive behavior and from human contact.

In *Stage Two, Primary Circular Reactions,* 1 to 4 months, life is still a series of random events, but hand–mouth and ear–eye coordination is developing. The infant's eyes follow moving objects; eyes and ears follow sounds and novel stimuli. Responses to different objects vary: He/she spends much time looking at objects in the environment and begins to separate self from them. Beginning intention of behavior is seen. For example, the 8-week-old infant can purposefully apply pressure to a pillow to make a mobile rotate, smile at familiar faces, and anticipate a routine such as diapering.

Stage Three, Secondary Circular Reactions, covers 4 to 8 months. Baby learns to initiate and recognize new experiences and repeat pleasurable ones. Intentional behavior is seen. Increasing mobility and hand control help him/her become more oriented to the environment. Reaching, grasping, listening, and laughing become better coordinated. Memory traces are apparently being established: Baby anticipates familiar events or a moving object's position. Habits developed in previous stages are incorporated with new actions. Baby will imitate another's behavior if it is familiar and not too complex.

Stage Four, Coordination of Secondary Schemata, is from 8 to 12 months. Baby's behavior is showing clear acts of intelligence and experimentation. Baby uses certain activites to attain goals. He/she realizes for the first time that someone other than self can cause activity, and activity of self is separate from movement of objects. He/she searches for and retrieves a toy that disappeared from view. Shapes and sizes of familiar objects are recognized, regardless of the perspective from which they are viewed. Because of the baby's increased sense of separateness, he/she experiences separation (eighth month) anxiety when the mothering figure leaves. Baby is more mobile; sitting, creeping, standing, or walking gives a new perception of the environment. Coordination of schema involves using one idea or mental image to attain a goal and a second idea or image to deal with the end result (46, 104–106, 126, 141).

🗸 Reaffirm with parents that they can greatly influence the child's later intellectual abilities by the stimulation they provide for baby, the loving attention they give, and the freedom they allow for baby to explore and use his/her body in the environment (34). There are many educational toys on the market, but common household items can be made into educational toys. For example, a mobile of ribbons and colorful cutouts will attract as much attention as an expensive mobile from the store. Unbreakable salt and pepper shakers or small cardboard boxes partly filled with rice, sand, or pebbles makes a good rattle (2).

Communication, Speech, and Language Development

Communication between people involves facial expressions, body movements, other nonverbal behavior, vocalizations, speech, and use of language. A newborn is ready to communicate if parents and caretakers know how to read the messages. The first communications are through eye contact, crying, and body movements.

Speech awareness begins before birth. In utero, the fetus hears a melody of language, equivalent to overhearing two people talk through the walls of a motel room. This creates a sensitivity that after birth provides the child with clues about sounds that accompany each other. If babies have been read to in utero, after birth they appear to prefer the sound of the stories they had heard in utero (100).

Speech is the *ability to utter sounds;* **language** refers to *the mother tongue of a group of people, the combination of sounds into a meaningful whole to communicate thoughts and feelings* (50). Speech development begins with the cry at birth, and the cry remains the basic form of communication for the infant. Baby's **cry** is **undifferentiated** for the first month; *the adult listener cannot distinguish between cries of hunger, pain, fear, and general unhappiness.* Parents learn to distinguish the meanings of different cries and grunts the baby makes in the first 2 or 3 months. At first, baby responds to both soothing and distressing stimuli with similar sounds. Then, other prespeech sounds are heard: (1) **cooing,** *the soft murmur or hum of contentment;* (2) **babbling,** *incoherent sounds made by playing with sounds;* (3) **lalling,** *the movement of the tongue with crying and vocalization* (50), such as m-m-m-; (4) *sucking sounds;* and (5) *gestures.* Cooing and babbling begin at 2 or 3 months. The number of sounds produced by babbling gradually increases, reaches a peak at 8 months, and gives way for true speech and language development. Smiles, frowns, and other facial expressions often accompany the baby's vocalizations, as well as gestures of reaching or withdrawing to convey feelings (79).

There is a biological basis for speech; the brain has amazing ability to process and interpret verbal expressions over an infinite range. However, parent–child interaction is essential for the child to learn language and conversation. Further, there is a critical period during which young children need environmental stimuli, or they will not learn to speak even when the sensory stimulation is exchanged for sensory deprivation (100).

At first vocalizations are reflexive; no difference exists between the vocalizations of hearing babies and deaf babies before 6 months of age. Later, vocalizations are self-reinforcing, that is, the baby finds pleasure in making and hearing his/her own sounds, and responses from others provide further reinforcement. Reinforcement when desired sounds are made, and when certain sounds are omitted, is necessary for the infant to progress to language development. The child must also hear others speak to further reinforce using the sounds and language of the culture. Effective mothers speak to their children frequently, even while they are doing their housework (79, 80).

By 9 months baby will have made every sound basic to any human language. The sounds made in infancy are universal, but when he/she learns the native language, the potential to say all universal sounds is lost (79, 100).

At every age the child comprehends the meaning of what others say more readily than he/she can put thoughts and feelings into words. In speech comprehension, the child first associates certain words with visual, tactile, and other sensations aroused by objects in the environment. Between 9 and 12 months, baby learns to recognize his/her name and the names of several familiar objects, responds to "no," and may occasionally obey the parent (79).

Baby tries to articulate words from the sounds heard. Words are invented such as "didi" to mean a toy or food. Language is **autistic;** *he/she associates meanings with sounds made by the self, but the sounds are not meaningful to others,* often even to the parents. By trial and error and by imitation, and as a result of reinforcement from others, the baby makes the first recognizable words, such as "Mama," "Dada," or "No," between 10 and 18 months of age. (If the correct sound is directed to the appropriate parent, the sound is reinforced, and the baby continues speech.) Words such as "Mama" and "Nana" are universal to babies in every culture because they result from the sounds the infant normally makes in babbling. By age 1 year baby has a vocabulary of approximately six words. He/she learns to associate meaning with an object, such as its name, size, shape, texture, use, and sound; then a word becomes a symbol or label for the object. Learning to speak involves pronouncing words, building a vocabulary, distinguishing between sounds like "*p*et" and "*p*at" or "*h*ear" and "*n*ear" and then making a sentence. The baby's first sentence usually consists of one word and a gesture (79).

✔ Teach parents that many factors influence speech and language development: innate intelligence, ability to hear, modification of the anatomic structures of the mouth and throat, sense of curiosity, parental verbal stimulation and interest, and encouragement to imitate others (79).

Emotional Development

Eight psychological stages in the human life cycle are described by Erikson (39). He elaborates on the core problems or crisis with which each person struggles at each of these levels of development. In addition to these problems, the child has other tasks to accomplish that relate to the psychosocial crisis, such as learning to walk. Emotional or personality development is a continuous process. No person succeeds or fails completely in attainment of the goal to be reached at a particular point in personality development.

Developmental Crisis. According to Erikson, the psychosexual crisis for infancy is trust versus mistrust (39). **Basic trust** *involves confidence, optimism, acceptance of and reliance on self and others, faith that the world can satisfy needs, a sense of hope or a belief in the attainability of wishes in spite of problems and without overestimation of results.* A sense of trust forms the basis for later identity formation, social responsiveness to others, and ability to care about and love others. A sense of trust may be demonstrated in the newborn and infant by the ease of feeding, the depth of sleep, the relaxation of the bowels, and the overall appearance of contentment. **Mistrust** is *a sense of not feeling satisfied emotionally or physically, an inability to believe in or rely on others or self.* It is characterized by lethargy, lack of weight gain, poor eating, excessive colic, lack of sleep, and failure to thrive. Later, predominant feelings and behaviors are pessimism, lack of self-confidence, suspicion and bitterness toward others, and antagonism. The person feels things will not turn out right; therefore, he/she withdraws or may be dependent, clinging, and easily hurt although he/she sets the self up to be hurt. In contrast, as the person gets older, he/she may bully others to be sure of coming out on top or behave in a controlling, sarcastic, aggressive manner. Sometimes mistrust is turned into pathological optimism; the person gambles on everything turning out all right, thinking nothing can go wrong.

✔ Security and trust are fostered by the prompt, loving, and consistent response to the infant's distress and needs as well as by the positive response to happy, contented behavior. You can teach parents that they do not "spoil" a baby by promptly answering the distress signal, his/her cry. Rather, they are teaching trust by relieving tension. Parents should understand the meaning they convey through such care as changing diapers. Even if the techniques are not the best, baby will sense the positive attitude if it exists. If the parents repeatedly fail to meet primary needs, then fear, anger, insecurity, and eventual mistrust result. If the most important people fail him/her, there is little foundation on which to build faith in others or self and little desire to be socialized into the culture. The world cannot be trusted. If the baby is abused, neglected, or deprived, he/she may suffer irreversible effects, as discussed in Chapter 6, pp. 180 to 181.

The infant who is in a nurturing, loving environment and who has developed trust is a happy baby most of the time. He or she is sociable and responsive to others. Attachment to the parent has been formed so that separation or stranger anxiety is experienced about 7 to 9 months of age and may extend to 10 to 12 months. After a time the infant will again respond to strangers. One study found that sociable babies have sociable mothers and that sociable, friendly babies score higher on cognitive tests than less sociable or mistrusting infants (133).

✔ The working mother may discuss her situation with you. Emotional development of the infant is not compromised by the working mother if she has time and energy to maintain consistent, loving, and stimulating responses when she is with baby. Quality of care rather than quantity of time is the essence of parenting and promoting emotional development. When work is not stressful and is a source of personal satisfaction for the mother, she is a more contented mother and gives the baby better care. The father's nurturance is also important, and often he is more involved in caring for the child when the mother works, which contributes to quality care. The lowest scores of adequate mothering are found in dissatisfied homemakers (80). Further, the effective mother does not devote the bulk of her day in the home to child rearing but instead designs an environment that is loving, adequately stimulating, and helpful to the child in gaining competency (79, 106).

✔ Because so many mothers work today, an important subject to discuss is child-care arrangements or babysitting services. Even if the parent does not work, some time away from the baby is rejuvenating and enhances the quality of parenting. Each parent has different ideas about how often, if at all, to leave the baby with a sitter. Discuss characteristics to consider in a sitter. Point out that parents will probably be most satisfied with a sitter whose child-rearing philosophy and guidance techniques coincide with theirs and who has had some child-care training or experience.

✓ The *sitter* should be physically and emotionally healthy, acquainted with the baby and the home, and like the baby. If possible, parents should keep baby with the same sitter consistently, especially around 7 or 8 months when he/she is experiencing separation anxiety. The sitter should have exact instructions about where the parents can be reached; special aspects of care; telephone numbers of doctor, police, and fire department; name and telephone number of another family member; and the telephone number of a poison control center, if nearby. As more mothers return to work shortly after childbirth, there will probably be an increasing trend toward infant daycare centers. Factors to consider in choosing day care services are discussed in Chapter 9, pp. 260 to 261.

Development of Body Image

Body image, *the mental picture of one's body*, includes the external, internal, and postural picture of the body, although the mental image is not necessarily consistent with the actual body structure. Included also are attitudes, emotions, and personality reactions of the individual in relation to his/her body as an object in space, with a distinct boundary and apart from all others and the environment. The body image, gradually formulated over a period of years, is included in the **self-concept** (*awareness of self or me*) *and derives from reactions of others to his/her body, perceptions of how others react, experiences with his/her own and other bodies, constitutional factors, and physiological and sensory stimuli (122).*

At birth the infant has diffuse feelings of hunger, pain, rage, and comfort, but no body image. Pleasurable sensations come mainly from the lower face, the mouth–nose area, which has considerable nerve innervation. At first, all the baby knows is self. Baby has the same attitude toward his/her body as toward other objects in the environment; the external world is an extension of self. Gradually, baby distinguishes his/her body from other animate and inanimate objects in the environment as he/she bites a hand, bangs the head, grasps and mouths a toy, and experiences visceral, visual, auditory, kinesthetic, and motor sensations (122).

A primitive ego or self-development begins at about 3 months. Weaning, contact from others, and more exploration of the environment also heighten self-awareness. As the child approaches the first birthday, there is some coordination of these sensory experiences which are being internalized into the motor body image. He/she is aware that some body parts give greater pleasure than other parts and that there are differences in sensation when his/her body or another object is touched (122).

✓ Without adequate somatosensory stimulation, there is impaired body image and ego development, as shown by studies of premature incubator infants who lacked rocking, stroking, and cuddling (14). The infant's initial experiences with his/her body, determined largely by maternal care and attitudes, are the basis for a developing body image and how he/she later likes and handles the body and reacts to others.

Adaptive Mechanisms

Adaptive mechanisms *are learned behavioral responses that aid adjustment and emotional development*. At first the baby cries spontaneously. Soon baby learns that crying brings attention; therefore, he/she cries when uncomfortable, hungry, or bored. Other tools besides crying used in adaptation are experimentation, exploration, and manipulation. Baby uses the body in various ways to gain stimulation. He/she grabs and plays with whatever is within reach, whether it is father's nose or a toy. By the end of infancy, emotions of anger, fear, delight, and affection are expressed through vocalization, facial expression, and gestures.

The young infant does not understand waiting. But as baby meets with security and feels a sense of tenderness from caretakers, he/she begins to wait a short time between feeling hunger pains and demanding food. And instead of immediately screaming when a toy cannot be reached, baby will persist in repeating the action that will get him/her to the object. The baby is beginning to respond to the expectations of others and adapt to the family's cultural patterns.

If, however, care does not foster trust, the infant constantly feels threatened. At first he/she cries and shows increased motor activity, perhaps expressing rage, but may eventually feel powerless and become apathetic.

Adaptive mechanisms in infancy are called *primary process*. Some of these rudimentary methods of handling anxiety are symbolization, condensation, incorporation, and displacement. **Symbolization** *occurs when an object or idea comes to stand for something else because of associated characteristics*. For example, taking milk from mother's breast satisfies hunger. Soon the act also means pleasurable body contact, emotional response, and security. **Condensation** *is the reverse process. Several objects are fused into a single symbol*. The word *toy*, for example, comes to represent a variety of objects. **Incorporation** *occurs when the representation of mother or other objects is taken into the self and becomes a part of the understanding* and is the basis for the child's separation anxiety or attachment to parents. **Displacement** *occurs when emotions are transferred from an original object to another*, such as from the mother to other family members or the babysitter (11, 139).

✔ Adaptive behavior is developed through structuring of the baby's potential. He/she needs a combination of freedom to explore and exercise with consistent, pleasant restraints for personal safety, which together enable learning of self-restraint. Constantly saying "No" or confining the child to a walker or playpen does not help the learning of adaptive behavior.

One study compared the temperament of very low-birth-weight infants to that of full-term infants at 6 and 12 months of age, assessed patterns of change in temperament from 6 to 12 months, and investigated effects of the neonatal experience on manifestations of temperament. The infants were free of congenital anomalies and appropriate for gestational age. At 6 months, the very low-birth-weight infants were significantly less adaptable and more intense than full-term infants. There were significantly more "difficult" and fewer "easy" infants in the study group. However, while at 12 months, the infants were less persistent than a full-term toddler, the behavioral style clusters of the children did not differ significantly from other toddlers. The social environment of the low-birth-weight infant plays an important role in the manifestation of childhood temperament as early as 6 months of age, but behavioral styles are modified during the first year of life with corrective nurturing (90).

✔ Findings of another study confirm other researchers' findings that environmental factors can assist or sabotage developmental progress in a child who was originally at biological risk. Developmental progress in very low-birth-weight infants may be more sensitive to subsequent environmental influences than it is to past perinatal insults. The impact of the environment appears to become more powerful as the child matures (123).

There are two possible explanations for this finding. One explanation concerns the infant's natural self-righting tendencies. The infant may be temporarily deflected off course by premature birth, prolonged hospitalization, and illness around the time of birth, but once exposed to an even minimally appropriate environment, natural self-righting mechanisms have the potential to bring him/her back into the maturational trajectory characteristic of their species. A second explanation lies in the view of human development; the infant is changing and growing within the context of a transactional, organismic milieu. Negative past events become less important as the child, the parents, and the environment influence one another. The child elicits and reinforces parental responses, and parental behaviors and characteristics support developmental gains. The quality of the home environment and the passage of time significantly affect the outcome (123).

Sexuality Development

Sexuality *may be defined as a deep, pervasive aspect of the total person, the sum total of one's feelings and behavior as a male or female, the expression of which goes beyond genital response.* Sexuality includes the attitudes that are necessary to maintain a stable and intimate relationship with another person. Sexuality culminates in adulthood, but it begins to develop in infancy (139).

Gender is determined at the moment of fertilization. Chromosome combination and hormonal influences affect sexual development prenatally, as discussed in Chapter 6. Sometimes mothers respond to the fetus in a gender-differentiated way: An active fetus is interpreted as a boy, a quiet one as a girl. Prenatal position, according to folklore, relates to sex: Boys are supposedly carried high and girls are carried low.

Gender or sex assignment occurs at birth. The parents' first question is usually "Is it a boy or a girl?" The answer to this question often stimulates a set of adjectives to describe the newborn: soft, fine-featured, little, passive, weak girl; robust, big, strong, active boy, regardless of size or weight. The name given to baby also reflects the parents' attitudes toward the baby's gender and may reflect their ideas about the child's eventual role in life. Mothers, however, engage in less sex-typing stereotypes than fathers (80).

✔ Occasionally external genitalia are ambiguous in appearance, neither distinctly male nor distinctly female. When this occurs, parents should be given as much support and information as possible to cope with the crisis; gender assignment based on chromosome studies or appearance should be made as soon as possible [57]).

The stereotypes about gender do have some basis in fact because at birth males tend to be larger and have more muscle mass, are more active, and are more irritable than girls. Females are more sensitive to auditory, touch, and pain stimuli (8, 84). At 3 weeks of age males are still more irritable and are sleeping less than females.

Initially, mothers seem to respond more to male infants than to female infants (perhaps because male infants have traditionally been more highly valued). But by 3 months this reverses, and mothers are thought to have more touch and conversational contact with female infants, even when they are irritable. This reverse may occur because mothers are generally more successful in calming irritable daughters than irritable sons (96).

By 5 months baby responds differently to male and female voices, and by 6 months he/she distinguishes mother from father and as distinct people. At 6 months the female infant has a longer attention span for visual for visual stimuli and better fixation to a human face, is more responsive to social stimuli, and prefers complex stimuli. The male infant has a better fixation response to a helix of light and is more attentive to an intermittent tone (8, 70, 84.)

Also, when the babies are 6 months old, mothers imitate the verbal sounds of their daughters more than their sons, and mothers continue to touch, talk to, and handle their daughters more than their sons. Throughout infancy and childhood, female children talk to and touch their mothers more, whereas boys are encouraged to be more independent, exploratory, and vigorous in gross motor activity (47).

Fathers tend to treat the baby girl more softly and the baby boy more roughly during the last 6 months of infancy. At 9 months baby girl behaves differently with her mother than with her father. She will be rougher and more attention seeking with her father (70).

By 9 to 12 months, baby responds to his/her name, an important link to gender and role. Research indicates that girl babies are more dependent and less exploratory by 1 year than boys because of different parental behaviors to each sex. Parents appear to reinforce sex-coded behavior already in infancy, so that gender role behavior is learned on the basis of parental cues (47).

Infants receive stimulation of their erogenous zones during maternal care. The mouth and lower face are the main erogenous zones initially, providing pleasure, warmth, and satisfaction. Both sexes explore their genitalia during infancy.

✔ Explore sexuality development with parents. Help them be aware of their behavior and feelings toward the boy or girl and develop ways to relate optimally to the child.

Developmental Tasks

Infancy is far from what some have assumed—a time for rigidly and mechanically handling the baby because he/she seems to have so little capability as an adapting human being. The following developmental tasks are to be accomplished in infancy:

1. Achieve equilibrium of physiological organ systems after birth.
2. Establish self as a dependent person but separate from others.
3. Become aware of the alive versus inanimate and familiar versus unfamiliar and develop rudimentary social interaction.
4. Develop a feeling of and desire for affection and response from others.
5. Adjust somewhat to the expectations of others.
6. Begin to manage the changing body and learn new motor skills, develop equilibrium, begin eye–hand coordination, and establish rest–activity rhythm.
7. Begin to understand and master the immediate environment through exploration.
8. Develop a beginning symbol or language system, conceptual abilities, and preverbal communication.
9. Direct emotional expression to indicate needs and wishes (35).

✔ Explore these tasks with parents. Help them realize specific ways they enable their baby to achieve these tasks.

✔ NURSING APPLICATIONS

Your role with the infant and family has been discussed with each section throughout this chapter. See Table 7–8 for some *nursing diagnoses* that may apply to the infant. You can also be instrumental in establishing or working with community agencies that assist parents and infants. You may be called upon to work with families who have adopted a child, or the single parent, or the reconstituted family who then has their own child (see also Chapter 4). You may work with a family whose child is not healthy or perfect or is

Table 7–8. Selected Nursing Diagnoses Related to the Infant[a]

PATTERN 1: EXCHANGING

Altered Nutrition: More than body requirements
Altered Nutrition: Less than body requirements
Altered Nutrition: Potential for more than body requirements
Potential for Infection
Potential for Injury
Potential for Suffocation
Potential for Poisoning
Potential for Trauma
Potential for Aspiration
Potential Impaired Skin Integrity

PATTERN 6: MOVING

Impaired Physical Mobility
Sleep Pattern Disturbance
Ineffective Breastfeeding
Altered Growth and Development

PATTERN 7: PERCEIVING

Sensory/Perceptual Alterations
Unilateral Neglect

PATTERN 9: FEELING

Pain
Anxiety

[a]Other of the NANDA diagnoses are applicable to the ill infant.
Source: NANDA Approved Nursing Diagnostic Categories, *Nursing Diagnosis Newsletter*, 15, no. 1 (1988), 1–3.

born prematurely. (see also Chapter 4). You may work with a family who experiences sudden death of the infant.

Establishment and Use of Community Resources for Continuity of Care

Some sources of help that may be found in your community are summarized in Table 7–9 (35).

In one large city, two maternity nurses identified a need for a local organization that would offer courses in parenting. In addition to course offerings, the organization now hosts discussion groups for expectant and new mothers and for parents of toddlers. Recently a "postpartum hot line" was started. The despair of couples who experience postpartum problems is pointed out repeatedly. For example, "This is Julie . . . We had our baby on the 14th. But (*tears*) you must have to be a pediatrician to be a mother. The baby is crying all the time; I don't know if I can continue to nurse her. . . . Everything is horrible!" (A home visit and a series of follow-up phone calls played a part in this mother's nursing her baby happily for 8 months [35].)

Instead of using referral to a community agency, a hospital may provide its own postpartal home-care services especially for mothers and babies who are discharged from the hospital in 12 to 24 hours after delivery. Jones describes how she set up such a service (65). Early discharge can have the advantages of treating mother and baby as well, not ill, reducing family separation time, and more directly involving father in care. Every woman or family, however, is not a candidate for early discharge. Prenatal preparation is necessary. Mother and baby must show no potential complications. Medical back-up care must be quickly available. Further, at times mother may get more rest and emotional support in the hospital than at home, depending on home and family conditions. In fact, visits by a nurse practitioner 1 hour daily for 3 days and then as needed for the first 2 weeks may *not* provide sufficient care (65). Or, the hospital may have a lay visitor program to assist the mother at home shortly after discharge (76).

Whenever visits are made in the home, assessment tools that can be used, if administered by a qualified person, are the *Denver Developmental Screening Test* (DDST), a general scale that measures personal and social skills, language, and gross and fine motor abilities (42), the *Infant Temperament Questionnaire* (ITQ), which addresses various areas of temperament and behavior (30) and the *Home Observation for Measurement of the Environment* (HOME) in which the home-rearing situation is assessed (28).

Care of the Premature and Congenitally Defective Baby

When the infant is born prematurely or with a congenital defect, the circumstances surrounding birth change. The anticipated joy is turned to fear, grief, and depression.

The major problem with the **premature infant** is that he/she is usually separated from the parents. Often the newborn is in an isolette on another hospital floor; sometimes he/she is transferred to another hospital. If the infant is in the same hospital, every possible opportunity for touch and eye contact should be given to the parents. (The parent can even hold the baby while the nurse gives a gavage feeding.) If the baby must stay in the premature nursery, arrange for the parents to view

TABLE 7–9. Community Resources for Parents

TYPE OF ASSISTANCE	RESOURCE/AGENCY
Classes on parenting, prenatal or postnatal care, Lamaze or psychoprophylaxis method of childbirth.	Junior or senior college, presenting nonacademic courses; hospital clinics; individual childbirth educators who are members of local and International Childbirth Education Association; crisis agencies such as Parent and Child, St. Louis: local Red Cross chapter; community health nursing services.
Breast-feeding information.	La Leche League.
Parent support.	Voluntary self-help agencies, such as Cesarean Support Group; Mother's Center; A.M.E.N.D. (A Mother Experiencing Neo-natal Death); St. Louis Association for Retarded Citizens; Local chapters for Sudden Infant Death Syndrome; Parent and Child, St. Louis; Association of Family Women; C.O.P.E. (Coping With Overall Parenting Experience, Boston, Mass.)
Crisis attendance or counseling.	Crisis hotlines such as Life Crisis Center or Parent and Child, St. Louis; Family and Children's Services; the clergy.

the baby at a time when he/she is most alert, for example, right before feeding time; help the parents feel welcome. A note similar to the following pinned to the crib can give parents much encouragement: "Hi Mom and Dad. I am so glad you could come to visit me. Signed, Patricia." Try to give as much information as possible to the parents about the baby's habits, strengths, and gains. This information could also be put in note form: "Dear Mom and Dad, I gained 2 whole ounces yesterday. This is a lot for my size. I'm also kicking my feet more. I think I will be a soccer player. I love you. Brian."

If the premature infant is in another hospital, father should be encouraged to visit the infant and to be the link between baby and the mother until she can visit. The father can explain the care the baby is getting, take photos of the baby to show his wife, and describe the daily gains. If you work in the premature nursery, and if the parents cannot visit, you can take the initiative to call the parents to describe how the baby is changing, the baby's schedule, and environment. The parents, in turn, can express their feelings.

Parents may find the book *Premature Babies: A Handbook for Parents* a helpful resource as they cope with anxieties about their premature child and prepare to give physical and emotional care (97).

The guidelines presented earlier on teaching the mother ways to stimulate her infant can also be taught to the mother of the premature—to be used whenever the baby's condition permits. Refer also to Chapter 4 for additional information.

LaRossa and Brown found that foster grandparents in the premature nursery can provide some of the nurturing, holding and tactile stimulation that the premature needs for normal development if the parents and grandparents cannot visit the nursery and participate in care (106).

Cultures vary in the care of the premature. Premature babies in some countries are placed with their mothers 2 to 3 hours after birth and are sent home soon after birth because of economic status of the parents, problems with cross- and nosocomial infections, and deep respect for natural processes. Anderson, et al. describe a program in Bogota, Columbia, that is designed to give optimal care to premature baby and mother after early discharge from the hospital. (4)

Parents of the **congenitally defective baby** will need the same considerations as parents of the premature infant. They should be encouraged to see their infant as soon as possible to avoid fantasies that are often worse than the anomaly. Show them the normal parts and emphasize the baby's positive features. Above all, show your acceptance of the infant: Hold, cuddle, and look at the infant as you talk to him. Give information about the anomaly and the possible prognosis. This is a difficult time for parents, and they will need ample time to express their grief, guilt, and worries. Your patience and support will be most helpful. Various references provide more in-depth information to be shared with parents pertinent to the specific disability (4, 27, 32, 57, 144). Refer to Chapter 4 for additional information on nursing practice with the family.

There are *ethical dilemmas* with care of the premature infant, especially if greatly preterm and very low-birth-weight, and with care of the infant that has a severe congenital anomaly.

Among the over 3 million babies born in this country annually, about 132,000 have congenital defects. Infants who, in 1960, would have had no chance for survival are today receiving care from health professionals armed with extensive knowledge and state-of-the-art technologies. In fact, among all babies born between the years 1970 and 1980, deaths during the neonatal period diminished by one-half. Many infants with multiple and serious handicaps can now survive anywhere from weeks to years, which raises questions about the cost of their care and the quality of their lives. The average cost for treating a baby in a neonatal ICU may be anywhere from $20,000 to $100,000, depending on the length of stay and treatment required (142).

The primary controversies of withholding treatment revolve around two questions: (1) should life-sustaining treatment be denied to any infant regardless of the infant's pathology, related handicaps, or suffering; and (2) if treatment is not considered appropriate in all cases, which infants should be denied it, on what grounds, and who should decide (142)?

Parents and members of the health-care and judicial systems continue to debate hotly the anticipated length and quality of many of those infants' lives. Some infants who are saved will continue to be a financial and care burden for their parents the rest of the parents', and the child's life.

The ethical, personal, and economic dilemmas posted by the use of life-sustaining technologies are considerable and have caused policymakers to consider withholding treatment from selected infants (142). Using high technology treatment methods may be experimentation and research, shrouded in the guise of treatment. The pivotal case of Baby Doe has come to exemplify just such an event. The case is discussed at length by Wakefield-Fisher (142).

It is suggested that nursing and medical associations establish joint committees to further clarify ethical issues and to suggest practices related to withholding life-sustaining treatment from infants. The associations could communicate recommendations to professionals, the Department of Health and Human Services, and hospital-based committees. Such action would align nurses and physicians, helping both groups understand and exchange information about the related issues. Direction from a joint committee could encourage providers to adopt a more uniform response to seriously ill infants in terms of standards of care (142).

Nurses increasingly have understanding of both the questions and legal and ethical responses related to withholding life-sustaining treatment from infants. Nurses must participate in the decision making over the next decade, based on adequate knowledge of the issue.

Care of the Family Experiencing Adoption and Infant Death

Mothers Who Adopt Out Their Newborns. These mothers are confronted with a crisis that involves bereavement. Ambivalence prevails during the prenatal period: love for baby, guilt about abandonment, and concern for his/her future. Therapeutic intervention begins prenatally by exploring with the mother the anticipatory grief, anger, depression, decisions about seeing the baby, and choice of postdelivery care. To promote bonding would be cruel, but the mother should have the opportunity—the reality—of holding and inspecting. To not recognize the infant is to deny the pregnancy; seeing the infant gives concrete focus to the mother's grief. A maternity nurse–specialist should consult the relinquishing mother on a scheduled basis to promote the woman's personal growth, self-respect, and dignity. Refer also to Chapter 4 for more information on the adoptive process and family.

Care of the Family Experiencing Infant Death

Parents Whose Infants Die. If the newborn dies, parents must work through the affectional–symbiotic bond developed within the mother in anticipation of the baby as perfect. Full expression of the grief, guilt, and anger is necessary. Many hospital practices tend to discourage these reactions by removing all evidence of the baby's existence. Nothing is left to confirm the reality of the baby's death. Parents should, if they desire, be permitted to view, touch, and hold their dead infant. Within the beliefs of the parents, some traditional bereavement service should be arranged to promote grieving and making the death real (69). Klaus suggests meeting with the parents three times after the death of the infant to assist them through normal mourning: right after birth, within the next 2 to 3 days before discharge, and in 3 to 6 months (69). During these visits you can effectively listen, encourage expression of feelings, and check for normalcy in the parents' feelings and reactions.

Although *Sudden Infant Death Syndrome (SIDS)* is at least as old as Biblical times, it did not become acceptable as a term to be used on death certificates until the early 1970s. Formerly it was called *crib death.* This disease is the primary cause of death in infants after the first week of life (106).

A typical case might be an apparently healthy infant, with possibly a slight cold, usually between the ages of 3 weeks and 7 months, who is put to bed and then found dead when the caretaker goes to check him/her. Usually the baby has not made a sound and there is no evidence of struggle.

Autopsy is the only means of making a diagnosis and may reveal widely diffuse petechiae across the pleura, minor inflammation of the upper respiratory tract, minor lung congestion and common viruses, or no unusual findings (106).

No one knows what causes SIDS but there are many theories: (1) The mild viral infection may affect nerves that affect lung activity; (2) inherent nerve deficit may affect the larynx, causing laryngospasm; and (3) there may be decreased carbon dioxide sensitivity or sleep apnea. Because there is no known cause, there is no known prevention (106), although close monitoring may aid prevention. Special monitoring devices to be used in the home can be purchased.

The thrust for the nurse is in helping the parents or caretakers deal with their guilt, grief, and future psychological balance. You should be able to direct these people to national or local help. National organizations are the following: Compassionate Friends, Box 1347, Oakbrook, IL, 60521; National Foundation for SIDS, 1501 Broadway, New York, NY, 10036; and National Sudden Infant Death Syndrome Foundation, 310 South Michigan Ave., Chicago, IL, 60604. In some health departments there are nurses who are designated to make visits for as long as needed. Luscombe describes a self-help group formed to assist parents with mourning, and feelings of guilt, failure, and isolation after their infant's death. Information about the group can be obtained by writing P.R.I.D.E., P.O. Box 95, Neptune, NJ, 07754 (83).

No matter what birth takes place—normal or abnormal—the family is going through a type of *rebirth*, in that their lives are forever changed by the event. Your guidance in this process may be felt for years.

References

1. A Guide to Counseling the Breast-feeding Mother. Columbus, Ohio: Ross Laboratories, 1980.

2. Alexander, Mary, Homemade Toys for Infants, *American Journal of Nursing*, 70, no. 12 (December, 1970), 2557–2560.
3. Allen, Donald W., Health Maintenance Procedures in Family Practice: A Critical Appraisal, *The Family Medicine Review*, 1, no. 3 (1982), 50, 53.
4. Anderson, Gene, Elizabeth Marks, and Vivian Wahlberg, Kangaroo Care for Premature Babies, *American Journal of Nursing*, 84, no. 7 (1984), 807–809.
5. Atkinson, Leslie, Prenatal Nipple Conditioning for Breastfeeding, *Nursing Research*, 28, no. 5 (1976), 267.
6. Avery, Gordon, et al. Examination of the Newborn Infant, *G. P.*, 37, no. 4 (1968), 78–94.
7. Baker, Susan, and Roberta Henry, *Parents' Guide to Nutrition: Healthy Eating from Birth through Adolescence*. Reading, MA: Addison-Wesley, 1986.
8. Bardwich, J., *Psychology of Women: A Study of Biocultural Conflicts*. New York: Harper & Row, 1971.
9. Barnard, Martha Underwood, Supportive Nursing Care for the Mother and Newborn Who Are Separated, *The American Journal of Maternal-Child Nursing*, 1, no. 2 (March/April, 1976), 107–110.
10. Berman, Lawrence, and Brian Saunders, Newborn Resuscitation, *Perinatology/Neonatology*, 4, no. 1 (1980), 22–31.
11. Bettelheim, Bruno, *A Good Enough Parent: A Book on Child-Rearing*. New York: Alfred A. Knopf, 1987.
12. Bills, Barbara, Enhancement of Paternal-Newborn Affectional Bonds, *Journal of Nurse-Midwifery*, 25, no. 5 (1980), 21–26.
13. Bishop, Barbara, A Guide to Assessing Parenting Capabilities, *American Journal of Nursing*, 76, no. 11 (November, 1976), 1784–1787.
14. Blaesing, Sandra, and Joyce Brockhaus, The Development of Body Image in the Child, *Nursing Clinics of North America*, 7, no. 4 (1972). 597–598.
15. Blank, Deidre, Development of the Infant Tenderness Scale, *Nursing Research*, 34, no. 4, (1985), 211–215.
16. Boggs, Kathleen, and Penelope Rau, Breastfeeding the Premature Infant, *American Journal of Nursing*, 83, no. 10 (1983), 1437–1439.
17. Bowen, Sheila, and Brent Miller, Paternal Attachment Behavior as Related to Presence at Delivery and Preparenthood Classes: A Pilot Study, *Nursing Research*, 29, no. 5 (1980), 307.
18. Bowlby, John, *Attachment and Loss: Vol. 1*. New York: Basic Books, 1969.
19. ———Disruption of Affectional Bonds and Its Effect on Behavior, *Canada's Mental Health Supplement*, no. 59 (January-February, 1969), 2–12.
20. Brazelton, Perry T., *The Neonatal Behavioral Assessment Scale*. Philadelphia: J. B. Lippincott, 1973.
21. Breast Is Best—For Premies Too, *American Journal of Nursing*, 87, no. 11 (1987), 1403–1404.
22. Brock, Datha, Social Forces, Feminism, and Breastfeeding, *Nursing Outlook*, 23, no. 8 (September 1975), 556–561.
23. Broussard, Elsie R., and Mariam Sturgeon, Further Considerations Regarding Maternal Perception of the First Born, in *Exceptional Infant: Studies in Abnormalities, Vol. 2*, ed. Jerome Hellmuth. New York: Brunner/Mazel, 1971.
24. Brown, Marie, Social Support, Stress, and Health: A Comparison of Expectant Mothers and Fathers, *Nursing Research*, 36, no. 2 (1986), 74–76.
25. Budnick, Lawrence, and David Ross, Bathtub Drownings in the United States, 1979–81, *American Journal of Public Health*, 75, no. 6 (1985), 630–633.
26. Burd, Ben, Encouragement Counts in Breast Feeding, *American Journal of Nursing*, 81, no. 8 (1981), 1491.
27. Butani, Pushpa, Reactions of Mothers to the Birth of an Anomalous Infant: A Review of Literature, *Maternal-Child Nursing Journal*, 3: (Spring, 1974), 59–76.
28. Caldwell, B., *Home Inventory for Infants*. Fayetteville, Ark.: Fayetteville Center for Development and Education, University of Arkansas, 1978.
29. Can Your Baby Hear? St. Louis: St. Louis Hearing and Speech Center, 1980.
30. Carey W. B., and S. C. McDevitt, A Review of the Infant Temperament Questionnaire, *Pediatrics*, 61 (1978), 735–738.
31. Censullo, Meredith, Barry Lester, and Joel Hoffman, Rhythmic Patterning in Mother-Newborn Interactions, *Nursing Research*, 34, no. 6 (1985), 342–348.
32. Christiansen, Roberta, Bea vandenBerg, Lucille Milkovich, et al., Incidence of Congenital Anomalies Among White and Black Live Births with Long-Term Follow-up, *American Journal of Public Health*, 71, no. 12 (1981), 1333–1341.
33. Clark, Ann L., Recognizing Discord Between Mother and Child and Changing it to Harmony, *The American Journal of Maternal-Child Nursing*, 1, no. 2 (March-April, 1976), 100–116.
34. ———, and Dyanne D. Affonso, Infant Behavior and Maternal Attachment: Two Sides of the Coin, *The American Journal of Maternal-Child Nursing*, 1, no. 2 (March-April, 1976), 94–99.
35. Cooksey, Nancy, *What Is Parent and Child/St. Louis . . . ?* December, 1976.
36. Doubts About Circumcision, *Newsweek*, March 30, 1987, 70.
37. Dubowitz, Lilly, and Victor Dubowitz, *A Clinical Manual: Gestational Age of the Newborn*. New York: Addison-Wesley, 1977.
38. Duvall, Evelyn, and Brent Miller, *Marriage and Family Development* (6th ed). New York: Harper and Row, 1984.
39. Erikson, Erik, *Childhood and Society* (2nd ed.). New York: W. W. Norton, 1963.

40. ———, *Toys and Reasons*. New York: W. W. Norton, 1977.
41. Federal Register, *Rules and Regulations*, 49 (January 12, 1984), 1651–1654.
42. Frankenburg, W. K., and J. B. Dodd, The Denver Developmental Screening Test, *Journal of Pediatrics*, 71 (1967), 181–191.
43. From Chain Saws to Baby Cribs: Agency Names Priority Hazards, *The Nation's Health*, 12, no. 6 (1982), 16.
44. Garbarino, James, Edna Guttmann, and James Seeley, *The Psychologically Battered Child: Strategies for Identification, Assessment, and Intervention*. San Francisco: Jossey-Bass, 1987.
45. General Recommendations on Immunizations, *Morbidity and Mortality Weekly Report*, 32, no. 1. Atlanta: U.S. Department of Health and Human Services Public Health Service Center for Disease Control, 1983, 1–17.
46. Gesell, Arnold, et al., *The First Five Years of Life*. New York: Harper Brothers, 1940.
47. Goldstein, Joseph, Anna Freud, and Albert J. Solnit, *Beyond the Best Interests of the Child*. New York: The Free Press, Macmillan, 1973.
48. Gordon, R. E., E. E. Kapostins, and K. K. Gordon, Factors in Postpartum Adjustment, *Obstetrics and Gynecology*, 25, no. 2 (1965), 158–166.
49. Greenburg, M., and N. Morris, Engrossment: The Newborn's Impact Upon the Father, *American Journal of Orthopsychiatry*, 44 (1974), 520–531.
50. Guralnik, David, *Webster's New World Dictionary* (2nd college ed.). New York: World Publishing, 1972.
51. Hall, Lynne, Effect of Teaching on Primiparas' Perceptions of the Newborn, *Nursing Research*, 29, no. 5 (1980), 317–321.
52. Harlap, Susan, and A. M. Davies, Infant Admissions to Hospital and Maternal Smoking, *Lancet*, 1 (March 30, 1974), 529–532.
53. Harris, Chandice, Cultural Values and the Decision to Circumcise, *Image*, 18, no. 3 (1986), 98–103.
54. Hartwick, Nanci, Infant Formula: A Threat to Third-World Babies, *Graduate Woman*, 75, no. 6 (1981), 26–31.
55. *Health United States, 1982*. Washington, D.C. U.S. Government Printing Office 1982, Publication # PHS 83–1232.
56. Helberg, June, Documentation of Child Abuse, *American Journal of Nursing*, 83, no. 2 (1983) 234–239.
57. Hill, Sharon, The Child with Ambiguous Genitalia, *American Journal of Nursing*, 77, no. 5 (May, 1977), 810–814.
58. Holmes, Janine, and Lana Magiera, *Maternity Nursing*. New York: Macmillan, 1987.
59. Holmes, Thomas H., and Minoru Masuda, Life Change and Illness Susceptibility, *Separation and Depression AAAS*, (1973), 161–186.
60. ———, and R. H. Rahe, The Social Readjustment Rating Scale, *Journal of Psychosomatic Research*, 2 (1967), 213–218.
61. Hoole, Axalla, Robert Greenberg, and C. Glenn Pickhard, *Patient Care Guidelines for Nurse Practitioners* (3rd ed.), Boston: Little, Brown, 1988.
62. Hurd, Jeanne Marie L., Assessing Maternal Attachment: First Step Toward the Prevention of Child Abuse, *Journal of Obstetric, Gynecologic, and Neonatal Nursing*, 4, no. 4 (July–August, 1975), 25–30.
63. Infant Formula is not Microproof, *American Journal of Nursing*, 85, no. 4 (1985), 358.
64. Jackson, Pat, When a Baby Isn't Perfect, *American Journal of Nursing*, 85, no. 4 (1985), 396–399.
65. Jones, Deloras, Home Early After Delivery, *American Journal of Nursing*, 78, no. 8 (1978), 1378–1380.
66. Jones, L. Colette, and Elizabeth Lenz, Father-Newborn Interaction: Effects of Social Competence and Infant State, *Nursing Research*, 35, no. 3 (1986), 149–153.
67. Kahn, A., et al., Insomnia and Cow's Milk Allergy in Infants, *Pediatrics*, 76 (December, 1985), 880–884.
68. Kelly, Paula, ed., *First Year Baby Care: An Illustrated Step-by-Step Guide for New Parents*. Deephaven, Minn.: Meadowbrook Press, 1983.
69. Klaus, M., and J. Kennell, *Maternal-Infant Bonding*. St. Louis: C. V. Mosby, 1976.
70. Kleeman, J., The Establishment of Core Gender Identity in Normal Girls," *Archives of Sexual Behavior*, 1 (1971), 103–116.
71. Kramer, Marlene, Ilta Chamorro, Dora Green, and Frances Knudtson, Extra Tactile Stimulation of the Premature Infant, *Nursing Research*, 24, no. 5 (September–October, 1975), 324–334.
72. Krantz, Linda, Comparison of Body Proportions of One-year Old Mexican American and Anglo Children, *American Journal of Public Health*, 71, no. 3 (1981), 280–282.
73. Krieger, L., Bill Offers Treatment Guidelines, *American Medicine News*, September 21, 1984.
74. Lactation and Composition of Milk in Undernourished Women, *Nutrition Review*, 33, no. 2 (1975), 42–43.
75. Lamb, Michael, *The Father's Role*. New York: John Wiley, 1986.
76. Lay Visitor Program Helps New Parents, *American Journal of Nursing*, 79, no. 3 (1979), 421.
77. Lazieh, Marie, The Breast Feeding Worker—Risk or Benefit, *Occupational Health Nursing*, 30, no. 11 (1982), 34–37.
78. Lee, Eluned, Asian Infant Feeding, *Nursing Mirror*, 160, no. 21 (May 22, 1985), 14–15.
79. Lerner, Richard, and David Hultsch, *Human Development: A Life-Span Perspective*. New York: McGraw-Hill, 1983.
80. Lidz, Theodore, *The Person: His and Her Development Throughout the Life Cycle* (2nd ed). New York: Basic Books, 1983.
81. Linley, Jayne, Screening Children for Common Orthopoedic Problems, *American Journal of Nursing*, 87, no. 10 (1987), 1312–1316.

82. Ludington-Hoe, Susan, What Can Newborns Really See? *American Journal of Nursing*, 83, no. 9 (1983), 1286–1289.
83. Luscombe, Kate. P.R.I.D.E.—Parents Resolving Infant Death Experiences, *Free Association '85*, 12, no. 3 (1985), 1–7.
84. Macoby, E., Sex Differences in Intellectual Functioning, in J. Bardwich, ed., *Readings on the Psychology of Women*, New York: Harper & Row, 1972, pp. 34–44.
85. Mama, Talk to Your Baby, *Newsweek*, November 2, 1987, 77.
86. McBride, Angela Barron, *The Growth and Development of Mothers*. New York: Harper & Row, 1973.
87. McDonald, Betsy, Heeding the Baby's Cry, *Washington University School of Medicine Outlook*, 24, no. 1 (1987), 17–19.
88. McKeel, Nancy, Child Abuse Can Be Prevented, *American Journal of Nursing*, 78, no. 9 (1978), 1478–1481.
89. McNees, Pat, Whole-Child Learning, *Parents* (July 1986), 97–100, 178.
90. Medoff-Cooper, Barbara, Temperament in Very Low-Birth-Weight Infants, *Nursing Research*, 35, no. 3 (1986), 139–142.
91. Medoff-Cooper, Barbara, and Barbara Schraeder, Developmental Trends and Behavioral Styles in Very Low Birth-Weight Infants, *Nursing Research*, 31, no. 2 (1982), 68–72.
92. Mercer, Deidre, Relating Mother's Anxiety and Perception to Infant Satiety, Anxiety, and Feeding Behaviors, *Nursing Research*, 35, no. 6 (1986), 347–361.
93. Mercer, Ramona, Theoretical Models for Studying the Effect of Antepartum Stress in the Family, *Nursing Research*, 35, no. 6 (1986), 339–346.
94. Mittelman, Roger, Hollace Mittelman, and Charles Wetu, What Child Abuse Really Looks Like, *American Journal of Nursing*, 87, no. 9 (1987), 1185–1188.
95. Montagu, A., *Touching: The Human Significance of the Skin*. New York: Columbia University Press, 1971.
96. Moss H., Sex, Age, and State as Determinants of Mother-Infant Interaction, in *Readings on the Psychology of Women*, ed. J. Bardwich. New York: Harper & Row, 1972, pp. 22–29.
97. Nance, Sherri, and Premature, Inc., *Premature Babies: A Handbook for Parents*. New York: Arbor House, 1980.
98. Nebert, Daniel, Janet Elashoff, and Kenneth Wilcox, Possible Effect of Neonatal Polybrominated Biphenyl Exposure on the Developmental Abilities of Children, *American Journal of Public Health*, 73, no. 3 (1983), 286–289.
99. O'Grady, Roberta, and Thomas Dolan, Whooping Cough in Infancy, *American Journal of Nursing*, 76, no. 1 (1976), 114–117.
100. Out of The Mouths of Babes, *Newsweek* (December 15, 1986), 84–86.
101. Owen, G. and A. Lubin, Anthropometric Differences Between Black and White Preschool Children, *American Journal of Diseases of Children*, 126 (1973), 168–169.
102. Owens, Mark, A Crying Need, *American Journal of Nursing*, 86, no. 1 (1986), 73.
103. Pearn, J., et al., Bathtub Drownings: Report of Seven Cases, *Pediatrics*, 64, no. 7 (1979), 68–70.
104. Piaget, Jean, *The Construction of Reality in the Child* (M. Cook, transl.). New York: Basic Books, 1954.
105. ———, *The Origins of Intelligence in Children*. New York: International University Press, 1952.
106. Pillitteri, Adele, *Child Health Nursing: Care of the Growing Family* (3rd ed.). Boston: Little, Brown, 1987.
107. Pipes, Peggy, *Nutrition in Infancy and Childhood* (3rd ed.). St. Louis: Times Mirror/Mosby, 1985.
108. Pridham, Karen, and Marc Hansoen, Helping Children Deal with Procedures in a Clinical Setting: A Developmental Approach, *Journal of Pediatric Nursing*, 2, no. 2 (1987), 13–21.
109. Richi, Frances, and Ronna Krzy, The Child In the Car: What Every Nurse Should Know About Safety, *American Journal of Nursing*, 83, no. 10 (1983), 1421–1424.
110. Riesch, Susan, and Sharlyn Munns, Promoting Awareness: The Mother and Her Baby, *Nursing Research*, 33, no. 5 (1984), 271–276.
111. Rising, Sharon Schindler, The Fourth Stage of Labor: Family Integration, *American Journal of Nursing*, 74, no. 5 (1974), 870–874.
112. Robertson, J., To Treat or Not to Treat Defection Newborns: Dilemma in Danville, *The Hastings Center Report*, 10 (1981), 5–8.
113. Robson, Kenneth, The Role of Eye-to-Eye Contact in Maternal-Infant Attachment, *Journal of Child Psychology and Psychiatry*, 8 (1976), 13–25.
114. Rogan, Walter, et al., Polychlorinated Biphenyls (PCBs) and Dichlorodiphenyl Dichloroethene (DDE) in Human Milk: Effects of Maternal Factors and Previous Lactation, *American Journal of Public Health*, 76, no. 2 (1986), 172–177.
115. Rubin, Reva, Attainment of the Maternal Role—Part I, *Nursing Research*, 16, no. 3 (1967), 237–245.
116. ———, Attainment of the Maternal Role–Part II, *Nursing Research*, 16, no. 4 (1967), 342–346.
117. ———, Cognitive Style in Pregnancy, *American Journal of Nursing*, 70, no. 3 (1970), 502–508.
118. ———, Binding-in in the Postpartum Period, *Maternal-Child Nursing Journal*, 6 (1977), 67–75.
119. Ruffing, Mary Ann, Mothering and Early Infant Stimulation, *Nursing Forum*, 18, no. 1 (1979), 69–79.
120. Salk, Lee, The Role of the Heartbeat in the Relations Between Mother and Infant, *Scientific American*, 228, (May, 1973), 24–29.
121. Satz, Karen, Integrating Navajo Tradition Into Maternal-Child Nursing, *Image*, 14, no. 3 (1982), 89–91.

122. Schilder, Paul, *The Image and Appearance of the Human Body*. New York: International University Press, 1951.
123. Schraeder, Barbara, Developmental Progress in Very Low-Birth-Weight Infants During the First Year of Life, *Nursing Research*, 35, no. 4 (1986), 237–242.
124. Schwartz, Edward, and William Rae, Effect of Polybrominated Biphenyls (PBB) on Developmental Abilities in Young Children, *American Journal of Public Health*, 73, no. 3 (1983), 277–281.
125. Sciarra, J. J., ed., *Gynecology and Obstetrics*. Philadelphia: Harper & Row, 1982.
126. Scipien, G. M., Barnard, M. A., Howe, J., and P. J. Phillips, *Comprehensive Pediatric Nursing* (3rd ed.). New York: McGraw-Hill, 1986.
127. Scrimshaw, Susan, et al., Factors Affecting Breastfeeding Among Women of Mexican Origin or Descent in Los Angeles, *American Journal of Public Health*, 77, no. 4 (1987), 467–470.
128. Seagull, Elizabeth, Developmental Abilities of Children Exposed to Polybrominated Biphenyls (PBB), *American Journal of Public Health*, 73, no. 3 (1983), 281–285.
129. Selekman, Janice, Immunization: What's It All About? *American Journal of Nursing*, 80, no. 8 (1980), 1440–1445.
130. Shapiro, Leona, et al., Obesity Prognosis: A Longitudinal Study of Children From Age 6 Months to 9 Years, *American Journal of Public Health*, 74, no. 9 (1984), 968–972.
131. Sherman, Jacques L., Jr., and Sylvia Fields, *Guide to Patient Evaluation* (3rd ed.). Garden City, N.Y.: Medical Examination Publishing, 1978.
132. Siffert, Robert S., Orthopedic Checklist for Neonates and Infants, *Hospital Practice*, 6, no. 1 (1970), 66–70.
133. Stevenson, Marguerite, and Michael Lamb, Effects of Infant Sociability and the Caretaking Environment on Infant Cognitive Performance, *Child Development*, 50, no. 2 (1979), 340–349.
134. Switzer, Jackqueline, Reporting Child Abuse, *American Journal of Nursing*, 86, no. 6 (1986), 663–664, 668.
135. Toney, Linnie, The Effects of Holding the Newborn at Delivery on Paternal Bonding, *Nursing Research*, 32, no. 1 (1983), 16–19.
136. Tulman, Lorraine, Mothers' and Unrelated Persons' Handling of Newborn Infants, *Nursing Research*, 34, no. 4 (1985), 205–210.
137. ———, Initial Handling of Newborn Infants by Vaginally and Cesarean Delivered Mothers, *Nursing Research*, 35, no. 5 (1986), 296–299.
138. U.S. Department of Health and Human Service, New Recommended Schedule for Active Immunization of Normal Infants and Children, *Morbidity and Mortality Weekly Report*. 35, no. 37 (September 165, 1986), 577–579.
139. Urdang, Laurence, and Helen Swallow, eds., *Mosby's Medical and Nursing Dictionary*. St. Louis: C. V. Mosby, 1983.
140. Verzemnieks, Inese, Developmental Stimulation for Infants and Toddlers, *American Journal of Nursing*, 84, no. 6 (1984), 749–752.
141. Wadsworth, Barry, *Piaget's Theory of Cognitive and Affective Development* (3rd ed.). New York: David McKay, 1984.
142. Wakefield-Fisher, Mary, Balancing Wishes with Wisdom: Sustaining Infant Life, *Nursing and Health Care*, no. 11 (1987), 517–520.
143. Weiss, Sandra. The Language of Touch, *Nursing Research*, 28, no. 2 (1979), 76–80.
144. Whaley, Lucille, and Donna Wong, *Nursing Care of Infants and Children* (3nd ed.). St. Louis: C. V. Mosby, 1987.
145. Wicklund, Kristine, Sheila Moss, and Floyd Frost, Effects of Maternal Education, Age, and Parity in Fetal and Infant Accident, *American Journal of Public Health*, 74, no. 10 (1984), 584.
146. Williams, Sue Rodwell, *Nutrition and Diet Therapy* (5th ed.). St. Louis: TimesMirror/ Mosby, 1985.
147. Wink, Diane, Getting Through the Maze of Infant Formulas, *American Journal of Nursing*, 85, no. 4 (1985), 388–392.
148. Yotema, Sharon, *Vegetarian Baby*. Ithaca N.Y.: Plenum, 1980.
149. Young, Seth, et al., Effectiveness of a Mailed Reminder on the Immunization Levels of Infants at High Risk of Failure to Complete Immunizations, *American Journal of Public Health*, 70, no. 4 (1980), 422–424.

8

Assessment and Health Promotion for the Toddler

Study of this chapter will help you to

1. Discuss the effects of family and toddler on each other, the significance of attachment behavior and separation anxiety, and the family developmental tasks to be achieved.
2. Explore with parents ways to adapt to the toddler while simultaneously they socialize the child and meet their developmental tasks.
3. Assess a toddler's physical and motor characteristics and related needs, including nutrition, rest, exercise, play, safety, and health protection measures.
4. Assess a toddler's general cognitive, language, emotional, and sexuality development.
5. Describe specific guidance and discipline methods for the toddler and the significance of the family's philosophy about guidance and discipline.
6. Discuss with parents their role in contributing to the toddler's cognitive, language, emotional, self-concept, and moral development.
7. Discuss the commonly used adaptive mechanisms which promote autonomy and your role in assisting parents to foster the development of autonomy.
8. State the toddler's developmental tasks and ways to help him/her achieve these.
9. Work effectively with a toddler and the family in the nursing situation.

In this chapter, development of the toddler and the family relationships are discussed. *Nursing responsibilities for health promotion of the child and family are discussed throughout the chapter.* The information in this chapter is the basis for care of the toddler and family in any setting.

Key Terms

Toddler stage
Separation anxiety
Protest
Despair
Denial
Myelinization
Accommodate
Hyperopia
Spider nevi
Mongolian spots
Cafe au lait spots
Bruises
Parallel play
Myopia
Astigmatism
Strabismus
Otitis media
Dental caries
Malabsorption syndrome
Impetigo
Pharyngitis
Acute non-specific gastroenteritis (diarrhea)
Varicella (chicken pox)
Reye's Syndrome
Rubella
Pinworms (enterobius vermicularis)
Juvenile hypertension
Parataxic mode
Egocentric
Syncretic speech
Telegraphic speech
Autonomy
Shame
Doubt
Anal stage
Self-concept
Self-system
    Good-me
    Bad-me
    Not-me
Primary identification
Regression
Suppression
Denial
Reaction formation
Projection
Sublimation
Discipline

Family Development and Relationships

The **toddler stage** *begins when the child takes the first steps alone at about 12 to 15 months and continues until about 3 years of age.* The family is very important during this short span of the child's life, as he/she acquires language skills, increases cognitive achievement, improves physical coordination, and achieves control over bladder and bowel sphincters. These factors lead to new and different perceptions of self and the environment, new incentives, and new ways of dealing with problems. Behaviorally, the toddler changes considerably between 15 months and 3 years, which in turn affects family relationships. Because of new skills, the child begins to develop a sense of independence, establishes physical boundaries between self and mother, and gains the sense of a separate, self-controlled being who can do things on his/her own.

The family of a toddler can be quiet and serene one minute and in total upheaval the next resulting from the imbalance between the child's motor skills, lack of experience, and mental capacities. One quick look away from the toddler can result in a broken object, a spilled glass of milk, or overturned dish. The toddler's quickly changing moods from tears to laughter or anger to calm combined with energy, sense of independence, and curiosity also account for parents' labeling their toddler a *terrible two*.

✔ Help parents realize this behavior is normal and necessary for maturation. Expecting, planning for, and trying to handle patiently each situation will reduce parent frustration.

The toddler is frequently jealous of younger siblings because of having to vie for the center of attention that was once his/her own; older siblings are resented because they are permitted to do things he/she cannot. Power struggles focusing on feeding and toilet training occur between parent and child. Family problems may also arise when the toddler's activities are limited because of parental anxieties concerning physical harm or because of their intolerance of the child's energetic behavior and unknowing infractions of societal rules.

✔ You can inform parents that their social teaching will likely center on cleanliness and establishing reasonable controls over anger, impulsiveness, and unsafe exploration.

The Influence of the Family

The chief molder of personality is the family unit, and home is the center of the toddler's world. Family life nurtures in the child a strong affectional bond, a social and biological identity, attitudes, goals, and ways of coping and responding to situations of daily life. The family life process also imparts tools, such as language and an ethical system in which the child learns to respect the needs and rights of others, and provides a testing ground before he/she emerges from home.

Parents with high self-esteem provide the necessary conditions for the toddler to achieve trust, self-esteem, and autonomy (self-control) through allowing age-appropriate behavior. Parents with low self-esteem provoke feelings of shame, guilt, defensiveness, decreased self-worth, and "being bad" in the child by overestimating the child's ability to conform, inappropriately or forcefully punishing or restraining the child, denying him necessities, and withdrawing love (11).

✔ Help parents work out their feelings about self in relation to the child. Changing parental attitudes are often evident. If the parent is delighted with a dependent baby and is a competent parent to an infant, the parent may be threatened by the independence of the toddler and become less competent. Some parents have difficulty caring for the dependent infant but are creative and loving with the older child. But if the parent's development was smooth and successful, if the inner child of the past is under control, and if he/she understands self, then parental behavior can change to fit the maturing child.

Attachment Behavior This is very evident during the toddler years. The symbiotic mother–child relationship is slowly being replaced by the larger family unit, but the toddler still needs mother close. The toddler shows attachment behavior by maintaining proximity to the parent. Even when out walking, the child frequently returns part or all the way to the parent to be reassured of the parent's presence, to receive a smile, to establish visual, and sometimes touch, contact, and to speak before again moving away (8).

Although attachment is directed to several close people, such as father, siblings, babysitter, and grandparents, it is usually greatest toward one person, mother. Attachment patterns do not differ significantly between children who stay home all day versus those who go to day-care centers, since attachment is related to the intensity of emotional and social experience between child and adult rather than to physical care and more superficial contact. Attachment is as great or greater if the mother shows warm affection less frequently than if she is present all day but not affectionate. In comparing children raised in Israeli *kibbutzim* to American children, both groups are equally attached to their parents although young children in the *kibbutzim* have a greater attachment to peers than do young American children because they depend more on peers for approval (6).

Separation anxiety, *the response to separation from mother,* intensifies at about 18 and 24 months. Anxiety can be as intense for the toddler as for the infant if the child has had a continuous warm attachment to a mother figure, since he/she thinks an object ceases to exist when it is out of sight. The child who is more accustomed to strangers will suffer less from a brief separation. When separated, the child experiences feelings of anger, fear, grief, and revenge. An apathetic, resigned reaction at this age is a sign of abnormal development. The child who is separated from the parent for a period of time, as with hospitalization, goes through three phases of *grief and mourning* as a result of separation anxiety, which may merge somewhat: protest, despair, and denial (8, 34).

During **protest**, *lasting a few hours or days, and seen for short or long separations, the need for mother is conscious, persistent, and grief laden. The child cries continually, tries to find her, is terrified, fears he/she has been deserted, feels helpless and angry that mother left him, and clings to her on her return.* If he/she is also ill, additional uncomfortable bodily sensations assault the toddler (8, 34). The child needs mother at this time.

Despair *is a quiet stage, characterized by hopelessness, moaning, sadness, and less activity. The child does not cry continuously but is in deep mourning. He/she does not understand why mother has deserted him/her. The child makes no demands on the environment nor responds to overtures from others, including at times the mother. Yet the child clings to her if permitted.* Mother may feel guilty and want to leave to relieve her distress, since she may feel her visits are disturbing to the child, especially when the child does not respond to her.

✔ Mother needs help in understanding that the reactions of her child and herself are normal and that the child desperately needs her presence (8, 34). If she can be present, you can promote family-centered care through your explanations to the mother and child, by not being rigid about visiting hours, by attending to mother's (or father's) comfort and needs, and by letting the parent help care for the child. Protests, in the form of toddler's screams and crying, will thus be less intense. Be accepting if a parent cannot stay with the child. Parents may live great distances from the hospital or have occupational or family responsibilities that indeed prevent them from visiting the child as often as they desire. The parent may also be ill or injured. Be as nurturing to the toddler as possible while the parent is away. Tell the toddler how much Mommy and Daddy love him/her and want to be present but cannot. If possible, have the parent leave an article with the child that is a familiar representation of the parent.

Denial, *which occurs after prolonged separation, defends against anxiety by repressing the image of and feelings for mother and may be misinterpreted for recovery.* The child now begins to take more interest in the environment, eats, plays, and accepts other adults. Anger and disappointment at mother are so deep that the child acts as if he/she does not need her and shows revenge by rejecting her, and sometimes even rejecting gifts she brings. To prevent further estrangement, mother should understand that the child's need for her is more intense than ever (8, 34).

✔ Continue the above interventions that promote family-centered care. Give mother (father) and child time together undisturbed by nursing or medical care procedures. Provide toys that help the child to act out the fears, anxiety, anger, and mistrust experienced during the hospitalization and separation. Encourage the parent to talk about and work through feelings related to the child's illness and absence from the family.

With prolonged hospitalization, the child may fail to discover a person to whom he/she can attach for any length of time. If the child finds a mother figure and then loses her, the pain of the original separation is re-experienced. If this happens repeatedly, the child will eventually avoid involvement with anyone, but invest love in self and later value material possessions more highly than any exchange of affection with people.

✔ Teach parents that immediate aftereffects of separation include changes in the child's behavior—regression, clinging, and seeking out extra attention and reassurance. If extra affection is given to the child, trust is gradually restored. If the separation has been prolonged, the child's behavior can be very changed and disturbed for months after return to the parents. The parent needs support in accepting the child's expressions of hostility and in meeting his/her demands. Counteraggression or withdrawal from the child will cause further loss in trust and regression.

Child abuse or maltreatment may begin, or be continued at this age. Sometimes by this developmental era, the child will have had several emergency room visits or several hospitalizations as a result of the abuse. Be alert to signs and symptoms of child abuse discussed in Chapters 4, 6, and 7.

Maltreatment of the young child is demonstrated by the behaviors described in Table 8–1 (18).

Family Developmental Tasks

The family with a toddler faces many new developmental tasks:

1. Meeting the spiraling costs of family living.
2. Providing a home that is safe, comfortable, and has adequate space.
3. Maintaining a sexual involvement that meets both partners' needs.
4. Developing a satisfactory division of labor.
5. Promoting understanding between the toddler and the family.
6. Determining whether or not they will have any more children.
7. Rededicating themselves, among many dilemmas, to their decision to be a child-bearing family (13)

✔ Help parents to be cognizant of these tasks. Encourage them to talk through concerns, feelings, and

Table 8-1. Parental Behavior Characteristic of Psychological Maltreatment

Rejecting	Excludes actively from family activites.
	Refuses to take child on family outings.
	Refuses to hug or come close to child.
	Places the child away from the family.
Isolating	Teaches the child to avoid social contact beyond the parent–child relationship.
	Punishes social overtures to children and adults.
	Rewards child for withdrawing from opportunities for social contact.
Terrorizing	Uses extreme gestures and verbal statements to threaten, intimidate, or punish the child.
	Threatens extreme or mysterious harm (from monsters or ghosts or bad people).
	Gives alternately superficial warmth with ranting and raging at the child.
Ignoring	Is cool and apathetic with child.
	Fails to engage child in daily activities or play.
	Refuses to talk to child at mealtimes or other times.
	Leaves child unsupervised for extended periods.
Corrupting	Gives inappropriate reinforcement for aggressive or sexually precocious behavior.
	Rewards child for assaulting other children.
	Involves the child sexually with adolescents or adults

Source: Reference (18).

practical aspects related to fulfilling these tasks. Refer them to a counselor or community agency if help is desired.

Physiological Concepts

Physical Characteristics

Appearance. The appearance of the toddler has matured from infancy. He/she has lost the roly-poly look of infancy by 12 to 15 months, with abdomen protruding, torso tilting forward, legs at stiff angles, and flat feet spaced apart. Limbs are growing faster than torso, giving a different proportion to the body. By 12 to 15 months, chest circumference is larger than head circumference. The child increasingly looks like a family member as face contours fill out with the set of deciduous teeth. By age 2, he/she has 16 teeth. Gradually the chubby appearance typical of the infant is lost; muscle tone becomes firmer as the fat storing mechanisms change. Less weight is gained as fat; more weight is gained from muscle and bone (24, 30, 39, 47).

Rate of growth. During toddlerhood, growth is slower than in infancy, but it is even and development follows the cephalocaudal, proximaldistal, and general to specific principles discussed in Chapter 6. Although the rate of growth slows, bone growth continues rapidly with the development of about 25 new ossification centers during the second year (54).

Between the first and second years, the average height increase is 4 to 5 inches (10 to 12 centimeters). Average height increase the next year is 2½ to 3½ inches (6 to 8 centimeters). Weight gain averages 5 pounds (2.27 kg) between the first and second years. Birth weight is quadrupled by age 2 years. The 2-year-old stands 32 to 33 inches (81 to 84 centimeters) and weighs 26 to 28 pounds (11 to 13 kilograms). At 30 months, average height is 36 inches (91.5 centimeters) and weight is about 30 pounds (13.6 kilograms). By age 2 years, the girl has grown to 50 percent of final adult height, by age 2½ the boy to 50 percent of adult height (24, 30).

Neuromuscular Maturation. Neuromuscular maturation and repetition of movements help the child further develop skills. **Myelinization,** *covering of the neurons with the fatty sheath called myelin*, is almost complete by 2 years. This enables the child to support most movement and increasing physical activity as well as to begin toilet training. Additional growth also occurs as a greater number of connections form among neurons and the complexity of these connections increases. Lateralization or specialization of the two hemispheres of the brain has been occurring; evidence of signs of dominance of one hemisphere over the other can be seen. The left hemisphere matures more rapidly in girls than in boys; the right hemisphere develops more rapidly in boys. These differences may account for language ability in girls and spatial ability in boys. Handedness is demonstrated and spatial perception is improving. (24, 39, 47). (Spatial ability will be complete about age 10). The limbic system is mature; sleep, wakefulness, and emotional responses become better regulated. Toddler responds to a wider range of stimuli and has greater control over behavior.

The brain reaches 80 percent of adult size by age 2 (24, 34). The growth of the glial cells accounts for most of the change (30, 39).

Motor Coordination. Increasing gross motor coordination is shown by leg movement patterns and by hand–arm movements. Spontaneous scribbles are followed by circular motions and then vertical and horizontal lines. The child enjoys handling a spoon and glass and feeding self, but he/she frequently spills fluid from a glass or tips food from a container. By 2 to 2½ years, the child throws a ball overhand. The child walks alone by 12 to 15 months. By 17 months, he/she walks backward and sideways. At first, stair steps are walked with help (20 months); by 2 years the child walks up and downstairs alone, holding onto a hand, wall, or rail. The child places both feet on each step before climbing to the next. By 28 months, he/she jumps off the floor with both feet. By age 2½ years, the child can balance on one foot and walk on tip toes. By 32 months the child can jump from a chair and pedal a tricycle. By 3 years, he/she is climbing upstairs, alternating the forward foot and jumping a distance of 10 to 12 inches (24, 30, 47).

Vision. Visual acuity and the ability to **accommodate,** *to make adjustments to objects at varying distances from the eyes,* are slowly developing. Vision is **hyperopic,** *farsighted,* testing about 20/10 at 2 years. visual perceptions are frequently similar to an adult's even though the child is too young to have acquired the richness of symbolic associations. The child's eye–hand coordination also improves. At 15 months he/she reaches for attractive objects without superfluous movements (24, 34).

Endocrine System. Endocrine function is not fully known. Production of glucagon and insulin is labile and limited, causing variations in blood sugar. Adrenocortical secretions are limited, but they are greater than in infancy. Growth hormone, thyroxin, and insulin remain important secretions for regulating growth (24, 34).

Respiratory System. Respirations average 20 to 30 per minute. Lung volume is increased and susceptibility to repiratory infections decreases as repiratory tract structures increase in size (34).

Circulatory System. The pulse decreases, averaging 105 beats per minute. Blood pressure increases, averaging 80 to 100 systolic and 64 diastolic. The size of the vascular bed increases, thus reducing resistance to flow. The capillary bed has increased ability to respond to hot and cold environmental temperatures, thus aiding thermoregulation. The body temperature averages 99°F (37.2°C) (24, 34).

Gastrointestinal System. Foods move through the gastrointestinal tract less rapidly, digestive glands approach adult maturity. Acidity of gastric secretion increases gradually. Liver and pancreatic secretions are functionally mature (34, 54).

Skin. The skin becomes more protective against outer invasion from microorganisms and it becomes tougher with more resilient epithelium and less water content. Less fluid is lost through the skin as a result. The skin remains dry because sebum secretion is limited. Eccrine sweat gland function remains limited. At this age, eczema improves and the frequency of rashes declines (34).

Urinary System. Renal function is mature; except under stress, water is conserved and urine is concentrated on an adult level (34, 54).

Immune System. Specific antibodies have been established to most commonly encountered organisms, although the toddler is prone to gastrointestinal and respiratory infections when he/she encounters new microorganisms. Despite environmental exposure, antibody IgC increases, IgM reaches an adult level, and IgA gradually increases. Lymphatic tissues of adenoids, tonsils, and peripheral lymph nodes undergo enlargement, partly because of infections and partly from growth. By age 3 years, the adenoid tissue reaches maximum size and then declines, whereas tonsils reach peak size around 7 years (17, 34, 54).

Blood Cell Components. Blood cell counts are approaching adult levels, although the hemoglobin and erythrocyte (red blood cell) count are lower. Sufficient iron intake is necessary to maintain an adequate erythrocyte level. Erythrocytes are formed in the bone marrow of the ribs, sternum, and vertebrae as in adulthood. During stress, the liver and spleen also form erythrocytes and granulocytes (40).

Development does not proceed equally or simultaneously in body parts and maturational skills. Sometimes a child concentrates so intently on one aspect of development (for example, motor skills) that other abilities (for example, toilet training) falter or regress. Illness or malnutrition may slow growth, but a catch-up growth period occurs later so that the person reaches the developmental norms. The brain is more vulnerable to permanent injury because destroyed cells are not replaced, although some brain cells may take over some functions of missing cells. Most children also show seasonal spurts in growth. Caucasians, for example, show more height increase in spring and more weight increase in fall (17). There are also cultural differences in growth and development. The Afro-American child develops motor skills at a greater pace than the Caucasian until age 3 years. The Afro-American child may be walking alone at 7 or 9 months, in contrast to 12 or 15 months. If all variables are controlled, the Afro-American child is also likely to be heavier and have more advanced skeletal development (24, 30).

✔ Discuss physical characteristics of the toddler with the parents to help them adjust to his/her changing competencies.

✔ Physical Assessment of the Young Child

The approach to the physical examination will be dependent on the age of the individual. Adequate time should be spent in becoming acquainted with the child and the accompanying parent. A friendly manner, quiet voice, and relaxed approach help to make the examination more fruitful. Hands should always be warmed before giving an examination, but especially so in the case of the child.

No assessment is complete without knowing the antenatal, natal, and neonatal history. When the child is old enough, let him/her tell what conditions surround the visit even if the message is only "stomach hurt."

Many times you will be learning about the young child from the mother, as well as learning about the mother's attitude. If other siblings are present, observe the interaction among the family members.

What are the mother's facial expressions? In what tone of voice does she talk? Does she look away or comfort the child if the child seems disturbed with a procedure?

What are the other siblings' reactions toward the toddler, the mother, and the health-care worker? What are the siblings' reactions in general?

Although the child may not talk much, general appearance can reveal much information. Does the child look ill or well? What is the activity level? Coordination? Gait, if walking? Reactions to parents, siblings, and examiner? Nature of cry, if present? Facial expressions (43, 44)?

Before 6 months of age the infant usually tolerates the examining table. Between 6 months and 3 to 5 years, most of the examination can be done from the mother's or caretaker's lap. After age 4 years much depends on the relationship established with the child.

The sequence of the examination with the young should be from least discomfort to most discomfort. Undressing can be a gradual procedure, since children are often shy about this process. Some examiners prefer to go from toe to head, or at least to start with auscultation, which is painless and sometimes fascinating to the child. It is best to leave the ears, nose, and mouth to the end, as these often initiate a negative response.

Generally, the temperature should be taken rectally during the first years of life. Through the age of 2 years, the head circumference is measured at its greatest width and plotted on a growth curve scale that is compared to the norm (43, 44).

Blood pressure should be taken with the cuff that will snugly fit the arm. The first reading is recommended at age 3 years. The inflatable bladder should completely encircle the arm but not overlap. Artificially high blood pressure results if the cuff is too narrow or too short (43, 44). Because this is a procedure that causes some discomfort and as it is important to get readings in a low-anxiety state, sensitive timing is needed to get desired results. It sometimes helps to make a game out of the procedure by allowing the toddler to help pump up the bulb or read the numbers on the gauge.

The skin can be examined for turgor by feeling the calf of the leg, which should be firm. **Spider nevi,** *pinhead-sized red dots from which blood vessels radiate,* are commonly found, as well as **Mongolian spots,** *large, flat black or blue-and-black spots.* One or two *patches of light brown, nonelevated stains,* called **cafe au lait spots,** are within normal findings, but more may be indicative of fibromas or neurofibromas. **Bruises** (*ecchymosis*) are not abnormal in healthy active children but their location is important. Bruises not on the extremities or on areas easily hit when falling may indicate child abuse, or excessive bruising may indicate blood dyscrasias (22, 43, 44).

Lymph nodes are palpable in almost all healthy young children. Small, mobile, nontender nodes often point to previous infection (43, 44).

When examining the head region, consider the following:

1. The auricles of the ears should be pulled back and down in young children and back and up in older children.
2. A complete hearing test with an audiometer should be done before a child enters school. Prior to that, the whisper technique or the use of a tuning fork is adequate.
3. A Snellen E chart can be used for testing visual acuity before the child knows the alphabet. Visual acuity at 3 years is 20/40 and at 4 to 5 years is 20/30.
4. Other aspects of the visual examination depend on the child's age and the suspected problem (for example, following surgery for congenital cataracts).
5. Teeth should be examined for their sequence of

eruption, number, character, and position (22, 43, 44).

When examining the thorax and lungs, remember that breath sounds of young children are usually more intense and more bronchial and expiration is more pronounced than in adults. The heart should be examined with the child erect, recumbent, and turned to the left. Sinus arrhythmia and extrasystoles can be benign and are not uncommon (22, 43, 44).

When standing, a child's abdomen may be protuberant; when lying down, it should disappear. The skilled examiner should be able to palpate both the liver and the spleen (43, 44).

When examining the male genitalia, the testicles should be examined while the male is warm and in a sitting position, holding his knees with heels on the seat of the chair or examining table. Without warmth and abdominal pressure, the testes may not be in the scrotum (22).

Examination of the female genitalia is basically visual unless a specific problem in the area has developed.

When examining the extremities, the examiner may note bowlegs, which are common until 18 months. Knock knees are common until about age 12 years. The toddler may appear flat-footed when first walking. All these characteristics are usually short term (22, 43, 44).

The neurological examination is conducted throughout and is not much different from the sequence in the adult examination; however, the appropriate maturation level must be kept in mind.

Nutritional Needs

The daily diet of a toddler should include one serving of meat or fish, an egg or cheese, two or more servings of green and yellow vegetables, at least two servings of fruit, cereal, and bread to meet caloric needs, butter or margarine, and a maximum of 1 quart of milk, preferably low fat to lower caloric and fat intake. Liver or another high-iron food should be served at least once a week. Toddler likes breads, sweets, mashed potatoes, milk, and snack foods; such a diet, if served exclusively, would impair health. Too much milk without adequate amounts of other foods is also undesirable because omission of meats and vegetables could lead to iron-deficiency anemia (35, 55).

Caloric needs are not high and increase slowly throughout the toddler period. Approximately 1000 calories per day are needed at age 1 year and only 1300 to 1500 calories are required by age 3 because the child is growing less rapidly than during infancy. Body tissues and muscles are growing; thus protein needs are not high, about 1 gram of protein per pound of body weight daily. Vitamin supplements are rarely needed if food intake is balanced in nutrients. (Refer to Appendix III.) Fluoride supplements are helpful in areas without fluorinated water (35, 55).

Food intake, or its refusal, is one way for the toddler to show increasing independence. Decreased food intake may result from a (1) slower growth rate; (2) short attention span and distractability by other stimuli; and (3) increased interest in the surroundings. However, how well the child eats is determined to a great extent by how parents manage mealtime, parental behavior toward food, and the atmosphere surrounding the meal.

✔ These are some suggestions to teach parents, to avoid having mealtime be a battleground: (1) serve food in small portions; (2) serve finger foods or cut food so that it can be eaten with the fingers; (3) let the child choose; it is not necessary for the toddler to sample every food served; and (4) do not include high carbohydrate foods, such as soda, candy, cake, or empty nutrition snack foods in the choice.

The toddler is a great imitator; he/she eats the kind of foods eaten by the parents. Parental pressure or reprimands when the child does not eat a particular food conveys anxiety or anger and reinforces not eating, either because of the negative attention received or the stress response felt by the child. Or the toddler may overeat, as parents overeat. If there is a high caloric intake, obesity may result. Weight gain between 1 and 2 years of age in girls is the earliest predictor age for obesity at age 9 (42).

✔ Teach parents about the nutritional needs and eating patterns of the toddler. Avoid serving too large a portion, which can be the beginning of overeating or cause refusal to eat all the food, with resultant conflict between parent and toddler. Average serving size for the child of 2 to 3 years is:

> Milk—6 oz (¾ glass)
> Juice—3 to 4 oz (⅓ to ½ cup)
> Meat—⅙ lb
> Egg—1 medium size
> Cereal 3 tbsp cooked, ½ c ready-to-eat
> Bread—½ slice
> Fruits and vegetables—½ of raw fruit, 1 to 2 tbsp cooked (35, 55).

✔ Malnutrition may lead to slower growth, tooth decay, lowered resistance to disease, and even death. Signs of malnutrition include abdominal swelling, lethargy, lack of attention to stimuli, lack of energy, diminished muscle strength and coordination, changes in skin color, and hair loss. Females appear to be better buffered against effects of malnutrition or illness than males. Malnutrition delays growth, but children have great recuperative powers if malnutrition does not continue too long. When nutrition improves, growth takes place unusually fast until norms for weight, height, and skeletal development are reached. For example, Korean children who suffered early malnutrition but were adopted and raised by American parents in homes providing good nutrition performed as well on intellectual tests as their American-born peers (35, 55).

✔ A hospitalized toddler frequently regresses; refusing to feed self is one manifestation. The child needs a lot of emotional support and to feel some kind of control over his/her destiny, that he/she is not totally helpless and powerless. A way of assuring some area of control is by permitting the child to choose foods and encouraging him/her to feed self.

Play, Exercise, and Rest

Play is the business of the toddler. During play he/she exercises, learns to manage the body, improves muscular coordination and manual dexterity, organizes the world by scrutinizing objects, and develops spatial and sensory perception. The child also releases emotional tensions as he/she channels unacceptable urges, such as aggression; translates feelings, drives, and fantasies into action; and learns about self as a person. Through play the toddler becomes socialized and begins to learn right from wrong.

The child has little interest in other children except as a curious explorer. Play is solitary and **parallel;** *he/she plays next to but not with other children.* There is little overt exchange, but there is satisfaction in being close to other children. Toddler is unable to share toys and is distressed by demands of sharing since he/she has a poorly defined sense of ownership. Toddler will play cooperatively with guidance, however.

Items that toddlers enjoy playing with include crayons and paints with paper for scribbling, large blocks, musical and sound toys, playdough and clay, jungle gyms, pounding toys, sandboxes, toy cars and trucks, picture books and magazines, cuddle toys, and the ever-favorite kitchen utensils. By the end of 2 years, most children imitate adults in dramatic play by doing such things as setting the table and cooking. When selecting play materials for the toddler, remember likes and dislikes and choose a variety of activities because the attention span is short. The toddler likes pull and push toys, pedal-propelled toys, and toys that can be opened and closed. He/she also enjoys being read to, turning book pages, and identifying pictures. (Safety and durability aspects of toys, as discussed in Chapter 7, must be considered.)

✔ Help parents understand the importance of play and safety. A relation exists between the quality of attachment between mother and baby and the quality of play and problem-solving behavior at 2 years of age. Toddlers who are securely attached at 18 months of age are more enthusiastic, persistent, cooperative, and able to share than if secure attachment has not developed. There is also more frequent and sophisticated interaction with peers at 3 years when secure attachment has formed in infancy (24). Discuss play patterns and toys with the parents.

✔ Help parents realize the importance of offering playthings that can transform into any number of toys, depending upon his/her mood and imagination at the time. The adult can be available or initially start a play activity with the child. However, the child should be encouraged to play independently, developing mastery, autonomy, and self-esteem in the process.

✔ Verzemnieks (51) describes developmental stimulation, play activities, and toys for the hospitalized child. Table 8–2 summarizes how play can be effectively used with the ill child.

Rest. Rest is as essential as exercise and play, and although a child may be tired after a day full of exploration and exerting boundless energy, bedtime is often a difficult experience. Bedtime means loneliness and separation from fun, family, and most important, the mother figure. The toddler needs an average of 10 to 12 hours of sleep nightly plus a daytime nap.

✔ Teach the following guidelines to parents for establishing a bedtime routine for the toddler:

1. Set a definite bedtime routine and adhere to it. If the child is overly tired, he/she becomes agitated and difficult to put to sleep.
2. Establish a bedtime ritual, including bath, a story, and a tucking-in routine. Begin about 30 minutes before bedtime. The tucking-in should be caring and brief.
3. If the child cries, which most children do briefly, go back in a few minutes to provide reassurance. Don't pick up the child or stay over 30 seconds. If the crying continues, return in 5 minutes and repeat the procedure. Thus, the parent can determine whether there is any real problem and the child feels secure.
4. If extended crying continues, lengthen the time to return to the child to 10 minutes. Eventually fatigue will occur, the cry will turn to whimpers, and the child will fall asleep.
5. The child should remain in his/her bed rather than sleep for all or part of the night with parents. Bedtime routine becomes a precedent for other separations. However, if the parents make an occasional exception, such as during a family crisis of major loss, trauma, or transition, or if the child is

ill, neither the marriage relationship nor the child's development will be hindered. It is important that the exception not become the routine.

6. As the child grows older, limit the number of times the child can get up, for any reason, after going to bed.

✔ Sleep problems during hospitalization may show up through restlessness, insomnia, and nightmares. Increasingly, hospitals are permitting parents to spend the night in the child's room to lessen fears and separation anxiety. Cuddling is still important to a toddler, especially if hospitalized. If a parent cannot remain with a frightened child, you can hold and rock him/her while he/she holds a favorite object.

Health Promotion and Health Protection

✔ *Routine Immunizations.* These remain a vital part of health care. The Centers for Disease Control estimate that only 65 percent of 2-year-olds in the United States are immunized (41). The toddler should receive a rubeola (long measles), rubella, and mumps (MMR) combined vaccine at 15 months; at 18 months he/she should receive a combined vaccine of diphtheria, tetanus, and pertussis (DTP) along with oral polio virus vaccine (OPV) to complete the primary series. The tine test is repeated at 3 years of age (19). The young child should be vaccinated against life-threatening *Haemaphilus influenzae* type B (Hb). The vaccine is recommended for all children who are 2 years of age or older, and for children 18 months or older in high risk groups, including children who attend day care (41, 50). If the parent refuses to have the child immunized for religious reasons, emphasize the need to prevent exposure to these diseases, if possible, and the importance of continued good hygiene and nutrition.

✔ Common health threats at this age are respiratory infections and home accidents. The causes for accidents are motor vehicles, burns, suffocation, drowning, poisoning, and falls. Accidents are the leading cause of death, and deaths from poisonings continue to increase. Situations outside the home—the yard, the street, the grocery cart—have greater hazard because today there is more contact with them. Commu-

Table 8–2. Using Play While Caring for the Child

During Physical Assessment	• Talk soothingly and calmly. Explain what you are doing as you do it. • Blow on the stethoscope. Ask child to imitate. • Have child listen to own heart beat with stethoscope. • Name body parts and touch them. "Foot, Here is my foot." "Where are your eyes?" "There are your eyes!" "Where is your nose?" Guide the child's hands to touch. • Use diversions—another toy, tickles (especially abdomen). • Play peek-a-boo: Cover your eyes, then child's. Hide your head with blanket, then child's head. When child covers own head, say, "Where's (name?)" Then delight in discovery. • Use body movement, exercising child's arms and legs rhythmically while doing assessment. • Sing a nonsense tune, or talk animatedly. • Talk about sensations; warm/cold, soft/rough, as sensations are presented. • Name body position: up/down, over. • Encourage child to do examination of doll, teddy bear, toy animal.
During Bathing	• Experiment with the properties of water in a small tub. Use items that float and sink—washcloth, plastic soap dish, paper cup, plastic lid, empty plastic cylinders or toys at child's cribside. Talk about what happens. • Identify body parts as you wash them. Give simple directions ("Close your eyes." "Raise your arms." "Wash your hair.") Be sure to praise all help. • Encourage child to "bathe" a doll, teddy bear, or toy animal.
During Feeding	• Place the child in high chair or walker when he/she can sit unsupported. Tie toy or utensil to high chair to facilitate retrieval. • Discuss the food: hot/cold, colors, textures, which utensils to use. • Use an extra spoon and cup: one for you, one for baby. • Experiment with food: fingerpaint with food on tray, make lines.
During Diagnostic Procedures	• Explain to the child what you plan to do and are doing. Be honest but gentle. • Tell the child it is all right to cry; comfort if child cries. • Set up situation so child can do procedure on doll or toy animal. While child is imitating, talk about how much it hurts. Cuddle and comfort the child, cooing, singing softly, rocking after the procedure. • Distract the child with empty dressing packages, encouraging crushing and listening to sounds. • Make the sounds and touch different parts of child's body. • Vocalize sounds related to procedure. Have child imitate you.

nicable diseases are less a health threat than parasitic diseases.

↳ *Safety Promotion and Injury Control.* These include child-proofing the home. Teach parents they can prevent injury from furniture by selecting furniture with rounded corners and a sturdy base, packing away breakable objects, and putting safety catches on doors. Prevent falls by avoiding hazardous waxing, discarding throw rugs, keeping traffic lanes clear, placing gates at tops of stairways and screens on the windows, and placing toys and favorite objects on a low shelf. Burns are prevented by blocking access to electrical outlets, heating equipment, matches, or hot water. Placing tools and knives high on the wall or in a locked cabinet can prevent lacerations or more serious injury.

↳ Parents may call you to help when their child has been injured or is ill. Know emergency care. A poison treatment chart is available from the National Poison Center Network, Children's Hospital, 125 DeSoto Street, Pittsburg, PA 15213. Many cities also have poison control centers to treat and give information to parents and professionals. The Red Cross is also a source of first-aid information. Teach parents to prevent poisoning through the following steps:

1. Purchase medication bottles that have safety-top closures.
2. Teach the child that medication and vitamins are not candy.
3. Keep medicines, polishes, insecticides, drain cleaners, bleaches, household chemicals, garage products, and other potentially toxic substances in a locked cabinet out of the child's reach.
4. Store nonfood substances in original containers with labels attached, not in food or beverage containers.
5. If you are interrupted while pouring or using a product that is potentially harmful, take it with you. The toddler is curious and impulsive and moves quickly.
6. Keep telephone numbers of the physician, poison control center, local hospital, and police and fire departments by the telephone.

↳ Thoroughly explore safety promotion with the parents since the following normal developmental characteristics make the toddler prone to accidents. He/she moves quickly and is impulsive. The inquisitive, assertive behavior helps him/her enjoy learning by touch, taste, and sight; but the curiosity can lead to hazards. The toddler enjoys playing with small objects which can be hazardous. He/she likes to attract attention; has a short attention span and unreliable memory; lacks judgment; has incomplete self-awareness; and imitates the actions of others.

Common Health Problems: Prevention and Treatment

The child must be carefully assessed for infections and other disease conditions because he/she lacks the cognitive, language, and self-awareness capacities to describe discomforts. Refer to Appendices I and II for a schedule of health screening measures for the toddler.

Visual Defects. These may occur and may be difficult to detect. Squinting or holding objects very close or far from the face are clues that vision is faulty. **Myopia**, *nearsightedness*, and **astigmatism,** *unequal curvature in the refractive surfaces of the eye that interferes with clear focusing*, are two common refractive errors. **Strabismus,** *(cross-eyes, wall eye), occurs because eye muscles cannot move the eyes in parallel or coordinated movements*. Early assessment is essential.

↳ Teach parents that prescribed eyeglasses correct myopia and astigmatism. Strabismus does not correct itself. The child will adjust by using only one eye; the other eye remains out of line and eventually loses visual function. The deviating eye can be brought back into binocular vision before age 6 years by having the child wear a patch over the better aligned eye to require the deviated eye to fixate, or by surgery to alter attachment of extraocular muscles. Correcting strabismus, as well as other visual problems, is important for learning as well as for maintaining a positive self-concept. Because strabismus affects the child's appearance, it can be psychologically as well as cognitively damaging. Further, no parent wants the child to grow up visually impaired in one eye when it could have been prevented (17, 34, 36)

↳ There is no accurate method available to tell the visual acuity of children under age 3 years, but using Allen cards can provide useful data and will seem like play for the child. Familiar objects, such as a birthday cake or horse, are on each card. The child should first become familiar with the cards, and you should know that he/she does recognize the objects. Test each eye by covering the opposite eye and flashing the pictures one by one as the child identifies the objects. Gradually back away from the child and record the maximum distance at which the child can identify the objects. Thirty feet represents the maximum distance at which a child this age should identify the objects; if a toddler identifies them at 15 feet, his/her vision is 15/30 (36).

Otitis Media. *An infection in the middle ear* is a common infection causing pain and fever. Sataloff gives detailed description of the types of otitis media, diagnosis, and treatment, as well as complications, including hearing loss (38).

Hearing Impairment. Mild *hearing loss* is frequently caused by middle-ear infections that accompany the common cold or ear trauma. Assessment of the child's auditory ability is crucial to prevent language, social, and learning problems. Signs of impaired hearing include inability to speak by 2 years, failure to respond to noises that are out of sight, or tilting the head while listening (17, 34).

✔ Encourage parents to obtain an early diagnosis. Educational treatment through lip reading and sign language during the toddler period prevents a later learning lag and psychological problems.

Dental Caries. These occur infrequently in children under 3 years, but rampant *tooth decay* in very young children is almost always related to excessive intake of concentrated sweets or prolonged bottle feedings at nap and bedtime (bottle mouth syndrome).

✔ The toddler should be weaned from the bottle or at least not allowed to fall asleep with it in his mouth (34). Teach parents that the adverse effects of bedtime feeding are greater than thumb sucking or the use of pacifiers. If deciduous teeth decay and disintegrate early, spacing of the permanent teeth is affected, and immature speech patterns develop. Discomfort is felt, and emotional problems may result and appearance is affected.

✔ Encourage parents to take the child for the first dental visit between 18 and 24 months. Suggestions to help prepare the toddler or young child for the first dental visit are:

1. Explain what a dentist is in simple, positive terms.
2. Play dentist at home to prepare the child for the client role.
3. Prepare him/her for being alone in the dentist's office.
4. Describe dental instruments and how they are needed by the dentist.
5. Explain what X-rays are and how they take pictures of the teeth.
6. Never bribe the child to visit that dentist or use a dental visit as a form of punishment.
7. Avoid passing on parental or adult fears to the child (46).

✔ Dental hygiene should be started when the first tooth erupts by cleansing the teeth with gauze or cotton moistened with hydrogen peroxide and flavored with a few drops of mouthwash. After 18 months the child's teeth can be brushed with a soft or medium toothbrush (34). Fluoride supplements are also believed to prevent caries.

✔ A child with discolored teeth, pain, dental infection, or chipping of the front teeth should be referred to a dentist immediately. Irritability, restlessness, appetite disturbances, and behavioral changes may indicate dental caries (34).

Other Conditions. A child with *lactose deficiency* will have a **malabsorption syndrome** or *lactose intolerance*. Because there is not enough of the enzyme lactose to digest milk, the child has chronic vomiting and diarrhea, abdominal discomfort or pain, flatulence, and is irritable, often sleeping poorly. Milk is tolerated only in small amounts. Soybean formula is tried initially and may be digested.

✔ One author described how she prepared a special formula in a blender that was a substitute for milk and milk products such as ice cream. After 5 weeks without symptoms, nonfat milk was introduced gradually in amount and number of feedings. The toddler was then able to tolerate some milk (16).

Another common problem usually caused by group A beta-hemolytic streptococci is **impetigo,** in which the *upper layers of skin have honey-colored, fluid-filled vesicles that eventually crust, surrounded by a red base.* Impetigo is often a complication of insect bites, abrasions, or dermatitis that become infected with the organism. Some impetigo is contagious, and since acute glomerulonephritis may follow, proper identification of these lesions and appropriate antibiotic therapy is recommended (22).

✔ Additionally, teach parents that fingernails should be trimmed to avoid spread of organisms via scratching. The toddler should have the lesions soaked and gently scrubbed three times a day to soften and remove crusts. Towels and clothing of the infected toddler should be kept and washed separately.

A problem that often begins in the toddler years is **pharyngitis,** *sore throat,* which involves *inflammation of the pharynx or tonsils, or both.* Usually the cause is viral, but sometimes it is caused by Group A beta-hemolytic streptococci, and rarely by *Mycoplasma pneumoniae* and *Corynebacterium diphtheriae. It is not possible to determine the cause of pharyngitis by clinical features alone* (22).

✔ A throat culture is needed to determine if the origin is due to group A beta-hemolytic streptococci. Because this organism has the potential to cause rheumatic fever, heart valvular disease, cervical lymphadenitis, otitis media, peritonsillar abscess, retropharyngeal abscess, sinusitis, and acute glomerulonephritis, proper identification and eradication of the organism with appropriate antibiotics are essential. For pharyngitis of any origin, antipyretic medication (if fever is present), warm saline gargles (if the older toddler can be taught this procedure), and increased fluid intake are in order (22). Other respiratory infections of a more severe nature may also occur. Consult a pediatric nursing text (54).

Acute nonspecific gastroenteritis or **simple diarrhea** is often preceded by vomiting and is an *inflammation of the gastrointestinal tract during which stools are more liquid and frequent than usual*. The cause is unknown. (In contrast, some gastroenteritis can be traced to a bacterial infection, side effects of oral antibiotics, and food poisoning.) The toddler must be watched for signs of dehydration such as sunken eyes, dry mucous membranes, decreased skin turgor, and weight loss (22).

✔ Treatment is varied but generally the current diet, especially milk, should be discontinued. Small amounts of clear liquids, such as cola (at room temperature and with the carbonation released), may decrease the vomiting tendency. These clear liquids should be alternated with an electrolyte solution such as Pedialyte. As diarrhea improves, easily absorbed foods, such as Jell-O or bananas, can be added. In a couple of days, simple solid foods, such as dry toast and plain baked potato, should be tolerated. Cereal, if given, should be mixed with water. Milk, cheese, and eggs should not be added until the previously suggested foods are tolerated well (22).

Varicella (chicken pox) is an *acute, highly contagious disease* caused by the varicella zoster virus for which no vaccine is yet available. The main characteristic is a rash consisting of lesions that appear in crops and in rapid succession (6 to 8 hours) going from a flat macule to a fluid-filled vesicle that crusts.

✔ You can determine that the lesion is chicken pox because it begins on the trunk and spreads peripherally. Sometimes the lesions are in the mouth. Lesion formation and resolvement usually last for 3 to 5 days. Other symptoms, in addition to itching, are a fever that may cause headache, general malaise, and loss of appetite. Teach parents that treatment is symptomatic. Fingernails should be kept short to reduce scarring from scratching. Such lotions as calamine may help dry the skin and reduce itching. Occasionally a prescription drug will be used to reduce intense itching. Fever may be treated with an antipyretic drug other than aspirin, which may be associated with the development of Reye's Syndrome. The child should be isolated as soon as possible and until the lesions have crusted. Complications are rare (22).

Reye's Syndrome is *a rare but sometimes fatal disease of children who have been administered salicylates to treat respiratory or gastrointestinal illness or chicken pox*. In one multicenter study, more than 90 percent of the children with Reye's Syndrome had taken aspirin. During 1981 to 1985, 1003 cases of Reye's Syndrome, with 291 deaths, were reported to the Communicable Disease Center in Atlanta, while in 1985, only 91 cases were reported, probably because of decreased use of aspirin for children. Of those who survive Reye's Syndrome, one-third are likely to have permanent brain damage (22).

✔ Teach parents to avoid use of aspirin with children and to substitute a nonsalicylate analgesic.

✔ **Rubella** *is a viral disease characterized by a rash of 3-day duration, along with lymph node enlargement*. When acquired postnatally it is mild. When acquired as a pregnant female, it is associated with a high degree of congenital malformations. To avoid the tragedy of malformation *every 15-month-old should have the rubella vaccine*. Exceptions are only those toddlers who are on immunosuppressive therapy, who have immunodeficiency disorders, or who have malignant disease (22).

Pinworms (enterobius vermicularis) *infest the intestinal tract and are the most common parasitic infestation in the United States*. Rare is the family with small children that escapes a bout with these slender, white, threadlike worms that average about 1 cm in length. Itching in the perianal region is the chief symptom. The cycle begins with oral ingestion of pinworm eggs. Eggs from the itching perianal region are picked up by the hands, especially of toddlers, and then are put in their mouth and onto hands of other persons, as well as onto toys, rugs, and clothes. As hands touch these objects and then go to the mouth, the infestation is multiplied. Once swallowed, the eggs pass through the intestinal tract in 15 to 28 days and hatch into larvae and then adult worms. At night, when the child is still, the mature female worms migrate from the anus to the perineum where they deposit thousands of eggs, thus completing the cycle that will begin again with scratching (22).

✔ Parents may be embarrassed to tell you about this infestation. Tell them that pinworms can be killed with a single dose of prescription medication. Usually all the symptomatic family members are treated at the same time. The real task, however, is stopping the cycle. Personal hygiene is extremely important, particularly handwashing before eating and after using the toilet. Careful washing of pajamas and bed sheets should be carried out after treatment. Favorite stuffed animals, chairs, and rugs often harbor the eggs and every effort should be made to cleanse properly these areas (22).

Juvenile hypertension has been defined as *sustained blood pressure levels above the 95th percentile on at least three measurements at different visits under circumstances where anxiety is minimized*. Another definition for children 3 to 12 years is *a diastolic pressure greater than 90 mm Hg* (29).

✔ If hypertension is suspected, a complete investigation is warranted by a specialist interested in hypertension in children. Tell parents that many children will respond to an overall cardiovascular health program. If at all possible, drug therapy will be avoided (29).

8 Assessment and Health Promotion for the Toddler

↳ Consult pediatric nursing texts for additional information on childhood illnesses and their assessment, care and prevention (34, 54).

Psychosocial Concepts

Cognitive Development

The intellectual capacity of the toddler is limited. The child has all the bodily equipment that allows for an assimilation of the environment, but he/she is just beginning intellectual maturity.

Learning occurs through several general modes: (1) natural unfolding of the innate physiological capacity; (2) imitation of others; (3) reinforcement from others as the child engages in acceptable behavior; (4) insight, gaining understanding in increasing depth as he/she plays, experiments, or explores; and (5) identification, taking into self values and attitudes like those he/she is closely associated with through use of the other modes (10, 20, 39).

The toddler experiences the world in a **parataxic mode,** *in that wholeness of experience and cause–effect relationships do not exist.* He/she experiences parts of things in the present; they are not necessarily connected events with past and future (45). Repeating simple and honest explanations—for example, why a certain tool works or why he/she should not play in the street—will eventually lead to understanding of cause and effect.

The toddler's attention span lengthens. He/she likes songs, nursery rhymes, and stories, even though he/she does not fully understand simple explanations of them. He/she can name pictures on repeated exposure. The toddler plays alone sometimes but prefers being near people.

Part of the toddler's learning is through imitation of the parents, helping them with simple tasks such as bringing an object, trying new activities on his/her own, ritualistic repetition of activity, experimenting with language, and expressing self emotionally. According to Piaget, the toddler finishes the Fifth and Sixth Stages of the Sensorimotor Period and begins the Preoperational Period at about age 2 (39, 52).

In the *Fifth Stage* (12 to 18 months), the child consolidates previous activities involving body actions into *experiments* to discover new properties of objects and events and achieve new goals instead of applying habitual behavior. Understanding of *object permanence, space perception,* and *time perception* can be observed in new ways. The child is aware that objects continue to exist even though they cannot be seen; he/she accounts for sequential displacements and searches for objects where they were *last* seen. Toddler manipulates objects in new and various ways to learn what they will do. For the first time, objects outside the self are understood as causes of action. Activities are now linked to internal representations or symbolic meaning of events or objects (memories, ideas, feelings about past events) (26, 52).

The *Sixth Stage of the Sensorimotor Period* (18 to 24 months) seems primarily a transitional phase to the Preoperative Period. Now the child does less trial-and-error thinking but uses memory and imitation to act as if he/she arrived at an answer. Toddler begins to solve problems, to foresee maneuvers that will succeed or fail, and to remember an object that is absent and search for it until it is found (26, 52)

In the *Preoperational Period* (2 to 7 years), thought is more symbolic; the child begins to arrive at answers mentally instead of through physical activity, exploration, and manipulation. Symbolic representation is seen in (1) the use of language to describe (symbolize) objects, events, and feelings, (2) the beginning of symbolic play (crossing two sticks to represent a plane), and (3) delayed imitation (repeating a parent's behavior hours later) (24). The toddler can understand simple abstractions, but thinking is basically concrete (related to tangible events) and literal. He/she is **egocentric** (*unable to take the viewpoint of another*); the ability to differentiate between subject and object, the real object and the word symbol, is not developed. He/she knows only one word for any object and cannot understand how the one word *chair* can refer to many different styles of chairs. If the flower is called *flower* and *plant,* the child will not understand that more than one word can refer to the same object. Concept of time is *now* and concept of distance is whatever can be seen. This level of learning will continue through the preschool era (26, 52).

Pushing children to read and write at an early age has not been shown to produce long-lasting positive effects. It may cause the child to lose initiative, curiosity, desire to use ingenuity, and ability to cope with ordinary life stresses. The child knows inside what he/she can do. If the parents whom the child looks to for support and guidance are manipulating him/her to meet their needs, the child may come to mistrust parents and self. Before parents put the child in a preschool that emphasizes formal academics, they should consider what the child is not learning from missed playtime. Play that is parallel to and cooperative with peers helps the child develop language, motor, cognitive, nonverbal, and social skills; positive self-esteem; a sense of worth as an individual; and unique problem-solving skills in the face of stress (31).

↳ Teach parents about this aspect of development. This period can be trying and should be tempered by supportive guidance and discipline: parents' saying what is meant, providing environmental stimulation, showing interest in the child's activities and talking and working with the child, reinforcing intellectual attempts, and showing a willingness to teach with simple explanations. Much of the intellectual development now depends on the achievements of infancy, how parents utilized the baby's potential, and the *quality* of parent–child interaction rather than the *amount* of time, per se, that is spent with the child (26). The child learns to enjoy learning, which forms the basis for later school achievement.

Language Development

Learning to communicate in an understandable manner begins during this era. Through speech the toddler will gradually learn to control unacceptable behavior, exchange physical activity for words, and share the view of reality held by society.

The ability to speak words and sentences is not governed by the same higher center that controls understanding. The child understands words before they are used with meaning, and some children develop adequate language comprehension but cannot speak (26).

There are various theories to explain language acquisition. While First Force Theory, Behaviorism or Learning Theory, explains some language learning through receiving reinforcement for imitation of language sounds, the number of specific stimulus–response connections that would be necessary to speak even one language could not be acquired in a lifetime. Nor does First Force Theory explain the sequence of language development, regardless of culture. However, learning principles can be used to modify acquired language deficits (24).

Interactionist Theory (Second Force Theory) is used by most theorists to explain language development. Language develops through interaction between heredity, maturation, encounters with people and environmental stimuli, and life experiences. Humans are biologically prepared for language learning but experience with the spoken word and with loving people who facilitate language acquisition is equally essential. Further, the child has an active role in learning language rather than a passive one. Adults modify their speech when talking to a child and the child is more attentive to simplified speech. Mothers and fathers use different conversational techniques to talk with the child, which, in turn, teaches language in a broader way (24).

Speech and language are major adaptive behaviors being developed during the second year. Speech enables the child to become more independent as well as to better make needs known. Speech is the mediation for thought processes. The greater the comprehension and vocabulary a child has, the further a child can go in cognitive processes. As the child and parents respond verbally and nonverbally to each other, the child learns attitudes and values as well as behaviors and ideas (24). The child first responds to patterns of sounds rather than to specific word sounds; if others speak indistinctly to the child, he/she will also speak indistinctly. The normal child will begin to speak by 14 months, although some children may make little effort to speak until after 2 years. By age 3, he/she may still mispronounce more than half the sounds (24).

The toddler speaks in the present tense initially, using **syncretic speech,** *where one word stands for a certain object, and has a limited range of sounds.* Single words represent entire sentences; for example, "go" means "I want to go." By 18 to 20 months he/she uses **telegraphic speech,** *2-to-4 word expressions,* that contains a noun and verb and maintains word order, such as "go play" and "go night-night." Variety on intonation also increases. A 2-year-old will introduce additional words and say "I go play" or "I go night-night." Conversation with parents involves contraction and expansion. The *child shortens into fewer words what the parent says but states the main message* (**contraction**); the *parent elaborates on, uses a full sentence, and interprets what the child says* (**expansion**). Expansion helps the child's language development (24). The toddler frequently says "no," perhaps in imitation of the parents and their discipline techniques, but may often do what is asked even while saying "no." Stuttering is common because ideas come faster than the ability to use vocabulary (24, 39).

Recognizable language develops sequentially. The first words a child learns are nouns of one syllable and then verbs that connote action. Adjectives, then adverbs, and other grammatical components are learned from 18 months on. The last area of language development is the use of pronouns. By age 3 the child has a vocabulary of hundreds of words. The toddler may learn 10 or more new words a week (20, 24, 39).

The toddler's speech is **autistic** because *vocalizations have specific meaning only to the child.* He/she plays with sounds and incorrectly produces the majority of consonant sounds.

Apparently, the child learns to speak in a highly methodical way, breaking down language into its simplest parts and developing rules to put the parts together. Moskowitz describes in detail how children proceed from babbling to one-word and two-word sentences, use of word order and plurals, use of negative sentences, and the importance of phonetics or a sound system (30). To communicate effectively, the child must learn not only the language and its rules, but also the use of social speech which takes into account the knowledge and perspective of another person (20). This begins in toddlerhood and continues to develop through childhood as the child gains interpersonal and social experiences.

✔ Teach parents that this is facilitated when they teach social language strategies to the child as they introduce him/her to life experiences. Through conversation with the family at mealtime and in other activities, vocabulary is enlarged, and the child learns family expressions that aid socialization. Mealtime provides a miniature society in which the toddler can feel secure in attempting to imitate speech. He/she gets positive reinforcement for speech efforts, especially for words that are selected, repeated frequently, and reinforced by eager parents. In addition, being talked to frequently throughout the day, being read to, and having an opportunity to explore the environment increase comprehension of words and rules of grammar as well as organization and size of vocabulary and use of word inflections (7).

✔ Language development requires a sense of security and verbal and nonverbal stimulation. For a child to speak, he/she must have a loving, consistent relationship with a parent or caretaker. Unless the toddler feels that this person will respond to his/her words, toddler will not be motivated to speak. The toddler may not talk when separated from mother, such as during hospitalization or the first day at day care. When being prepared for hospital procedures, the toddler needs simple and succinct explanations, with gestures pointing to the areas of the body being cared for, and verbal and physical displays of affection.

✔ If a child is delayed in speech, carefully assess the child and family. Causes may include deafness or the inability to listen, mental retardation, emotional disturbance, maternal deprivation, lack of verbal communication within the family and to the child, presence of twins, or parents' anticipating the needs of the child before he/she has a chance to communicate them.

✔ Verbal interaction, an environment with a variety of objects and stimuli, and freedom to explore are crucial to help the young child use his/her senses and emerging motor skills, and thereby necessary to learn during the Sensorimotor and Preoperational States (53).

Emotional Development

The toddler is a self-loving, uninhibited, dominating, energetic little person absorbed in self-importance, always seeking attention, approval, and personal goals. Sometimes toddler is cuddly and loving. At other times, he/she bites or pinches and looks almost happy, feeling no sense of guilt or shame. There is little self-control over exploratory or sadistic impulses. The toddler only slowly realizes that he/she cannot have everything desired and that some behavior annoys others. He/she experiments with abandon in the quest for independence, yet becomes easily frightened and runs to the parent for protection, security, reassurance, and approval.

Because the toddler still relies so much on the parents and wants their approval, he/she learns to curb the negativism without losing independent drives, to cooperate increasingly, and to develop socially approved behavior. Need for attention and approval is one of the main motivating forces in ego development and socialization.

The toddler often repeats performances and behavior that are given attention and laughed at; he/she likes to perform for adults and pleases self as much as the audience. He/she has a primitive sense of humor, laughs frequently, especially at surprise sounds and startling incongruities, and laughs with others who are laughing and at his/her own antics. Parents should give sufficient attention but not make the child show off for an audience, verbally or physically, and they should not overstimulate with laughter or games.

Developmental Crisis. The psychosexual crisis for the toddler is autonomy versus shame and doubt (14). **Autonomy** *is shown in the ability to gain self-control* over motor abilities and sphincters; to make and carry out decisions; to feel able to cope adequately with problems or get the necessary help; to wait with patience; to give generously or to hold on, as indicated; to distinguish between self, possessions or wishes and others', and to have a feeling of good will and pride. Autonomy is characterized by the oft-heard statement, "Me do it." Mastery accomplished in infancy sets the basis for autonomy.

Using negativism, even displaying temper, dawdling, and rituals; exploring even when parents object; developing language skills, saying "no" although he/she may do as asked; and increasing control over his/her body or situations are some apparent ways the toddler is demonstrating developing autonomy and maintaining a sense of security and control. Ritualistic behavior is normal and at a peak at 2½ years, especially at bedtime and during illness. Although autonomy is developing, emotions are still contagious. The toddler reflects others' behavior and feelings. For example, if someone laughs or cries, he/she will imitate for no apparent reason.

Shame and doubt are felt if autonomy and a positive self-concept are not achieved (14). **Shame** *is the feeling of being fooled, embarrassed, exposed, small, impotent, dirty, of wanting to hide, and rage against self.*

Doubt *is fear, uncertainty, mistrust, lack of self-confidence, and feeling that nothing done is any good and that one is controlled by others rather than being in control of self.*

✔ There is a limit to how exposed, dirty, mean, and vulnerable one can feel. If the child is pushed past the limit, disciplined, or toilet trained too harshly, he/she can no longer discriminate about self, what he/she should be and can do. If everything is planned and done *for* and *to* the child, he/she cannot develop autonomy. The toddler's self-concept and behavior will try to measure up to the expectations of parents and others, but there is no close attachment to an adult. Apathy and withdrawal may occur, or he/she may become defiant, excessively negativistic, physically overactive, and develop behaviors opposite to expectations. A low frustration tolerance and difficulty with eating, digestion, elimination, and sleep may be seen. Too much shaming does not develop a sense of propriety but rather a secret determination to get away with things. As an adult, he/she may become either too compliant, letting self be controlled and manipulated in spite of being angry about it; or he/she may become impulsive, stubbornly assertive, obstinate, or negativistic, have little sense of responsibility, and want to get away with things. The person may give up easily in all efforts, withdraw, be compulsive in behavior, hoard objects, or be either messy or overmeticulous.

✔ Discourage parents from creating an emotional climate of excessive expectations, criticism, blame, punishment, and overrestriction for the toddler because within the child's consciousness a sense of shame and doubt may develop that will be extremely harmful to further development. The child should not be given too much autonomy or he/she will feel all-powerful. When toddler fails to accomplish what he/she has been falsely led to believe could be achieved, the self-doubt and shame which result can be devastating. Aggressive behavior results if the child is severely punished, or if parents are aggressive (2). With the proper balance of guidance and discipline, the toddler gains a sense of personal abilities and thus has the potential to deal with the next set of social adjustments.

Toilet Training. This is a major developmental accomplishment and relates directly to the crisis of autonomy versus shame and doubt or to what Freudian theory calls the **anal stage.** The toddler is interested in the products he excretes. The toddler gradually learns to control bowel and bladder. Neuromuscular maturity, which occurs from 1 to 3 years, with bowel before bladder control, is necessary for regular, self-controlled evacuation (22).

There are many factors involved besides biological readiness, since the toddler's fears, goals, and conflicting wishes also influence this learning experience. Psychologically, toilet training is complex. Mother gives approval not only for defecating properly but also for withholding feces. The sensations of giving and withholding feces, imitation of parents and siblings, approval from family, and pride in the accomplishments hasten toilet training. Being forced to do the parents' will may cause problems of negativism.

✔ Bowel training is a less complex task than bladder training and should be attempted first. You can assist parents by alerting them to signs of readiness. The toddler shows readiness for bowel training when he/she defecates regularly and shows some signs of being aware of defecation, such as grunting, straining, or tugging at the diaper. It also helps if the child can speak, understand directions, and manipulate the clothing somewhat.

✔ Some toddlers, after defecation, cry and indicate distress until they are changed. Others do not indicate discomfort and will play with and smear feces. They are curious, explore, and see nothing shameful about such behavior. They have not learned the aesthetic and cultural connotations of feces being "dirty" and "smelly" and not an object for play. But since play with feces must be restricted because it is unsanitary and nonaesthetic, changing diapers immediately after defecation, using safety pins to keep the diaper on snugly, having well-fitted training pants, and showing parental disapproval are ways to prevent such play. In addition, encourage parents to provide opportunities for play and smearing with clay, sand, mud, paste, and finger paints to help the child develop natural potentials and divert instinctual urges into socially accepted behavior.

✔ Parents may demonstrate inordinate interest in this aspect of development, producing anxiety over bowel training with possible harmful physical effects, such as constipation, or psychological effects which result from trying to meet excessive demands. Be aware of the development problems associated with toilet training, but remember that elimination is a natural process. Teach parents to approach toilet training in a matter-of-fact and relaxed way, to expect some resistance, and not push the child or reflect anxiety. Every child by age 3 can carry on this task with some help as to where and how. Culturally, American society seems to demand that mothers begin toilet training somewhere around 2 years of age, but 2½ years would be soon enough (26). However, when younger parents follow the directions given in this chapter, grandma may defy them and secretly sit 1-year-old Suzie on the potty. Toilet training should not be started in turbulent periods, such as hospitalization of the toddler, homecoming of a new baby, absence of the main caretaker from home, or a family crisis. Even when started in a calm period, some regression is natural.

✔ Encourage the parents to have the child use a potty chair, since it is mechanically easier than the family toilet. Recommend that the child wear training pants and that training take place when disruptions in regular routine are at a minimum. The toddler should be praised for success.

Bladder training is more complex because the reflexes appropriate for bladder training are less explicit, neurological maturation comes later, and urination is a reflex response to bladder tensions and must be inhibited. Bladder control demands more self-awareness and self-discipline from the toddler and is usually achieved between the ages of 2½ and 3½ years when physiological development has progressed enough that the bladder can retain urine for about 2 hours. Waking hours and sleeping hours present two phases of control as well as differences in awareness of bladder function.

The series of events necessary for bladder training are that the toddler must first realize he/she is wet, then know he/she is wetting, next recognize impulses that tell that he/she is going to urinate, and finally control urinating until he/she is at the toilet (34).

✔ You may help the parents by explaining the process of urination. Make it clear to the parents that both boys and girls can sit down while urinating and that both may try to stand like daddy. Sleeping control will be effective when the child responds to bladder reflexes and not before. Cutting down on fluids and other devices to reduce enuresis, or bed wetting, are not effective in gaining reflex control.

✔ After waking control has been well established, sleeping control usually follows. Past 5 years, however, if nighttime control has not been achieved, there might be a physiological or psychological problem. Encourage medical attention if this problem persists, and consider possible emotional causes. Enuresis is discussed further in Chapter 9.

Body-Image and Self-Concept Development

Body Image. This development gradually evolves as a component of self-concept. The toddler has a dim self-awareness, but with a developing sense of autonomy, he/she becomes more correctly aware of the body as a physical entity and one with emotional capabilities. Toddler is increasingly aware of pleasurable sensations in the genital area as well as on the skin and mouth and is learning control of the body through locomotion, toilet training, speech, and socialization.

The toddler is not always aware of the whole body or the distal parts, and might even consider distal parts, such as the feet, as something apart from self. Toddler does not always know when he/she is sick, tired, or too hot, or when the pants are wet. The child also has difficulty realizing that body productions, such as feces, are separate from self; therefore, he/she may resist flushing the toilet. Toddler is not aware of the influences on his/her body but is aware of general feelings and thoughts, and increasingly of others' reactions to his/her body and behavior. For example, when the toddler is in control of the environment, the body feels good, wonderful, and strong. When things are not going well, if he/she cannot succeed, or is punished excessively, the child feels bad and shameful.

Self-Concept. This is also made up of the feelings about self, adaptive and defensive mechanisms, reactions from others, as well as one's perceptions of these reactions, attitudes, values, and many of life's experiences.

As the child incorporates approval and disapproval, praise and punishment, gestures which are kind and forbidding, he/she forms an opinion about self as a person. How the person feels about self is determined to a great degree by the reactions of others and in turn later determines how he/she views others. The young child is very aware of the gradient of anxiety—mild, moderate, or severe. He/she watches for signs of approval and disapproval from others in relation to self. Increasingly there is recall about what caused discomfort or anxiety. Experiences of discomfort are first with mother and then are generalized to other people, and much behavior becomes organized to avoid or minimize discomfort around others. Thus he/she gradually evolves adaptive and defensive behaviors and learns what to do to get along with others. The **self-system** gradually develops as *an organization of experiences that exists to defend against anxiety and to secure satisfaction* (45).

The various appraisals of others cause the child to form feelings of **good-me, bad-me,** or **not-me,** as the self-concept. The child is fully aware of reactions that convey approval, love, security, and because these make him/her feel good, **a concept of good-me** forms. *He/she likes self because others do, the basis of a positive self-concept.* Reactions of disapproval or punishment from significant adults increase the child's anxiety, and if this cycle continues, **bad-me,** *a negative self-concept,* results. If negative reaction is never-ending, the child may evolve defensive behaviors, such as denial, that prevent noticing the negative evaluations. Some appraisals from others evoke severe discomfort or panic; these *feelings and awareness of the situation are repressed and dissociated from the rest of the personality,* forming the **not-me part of the self.** *These are the ideas, feelings, or body parts that later seem foreign to the person.* For example, severe toilet training or punishing the child for masturbating or touching the genitals may be so traumatic and panic producing that he/she becomes almost unaware of the genital area. Later the person does not include the lower half of the body or the genital area in self-drawings or speak of sexual matters; he/she may be very inhibited about toileting, and a disturbed gender identity may be evident through behavior. The more feelings or life experiences that are dissociated, the more rigid the personality and the less aware of self he/she is in later life. Each person attempts to find ways to keep feelings of *good-me* and reduce the uncomfortable feelings elicited by the *bad-me* (45).

The direction of the self-concept and personality often follows the impetus given it in early childhood; the person remains fairly consistent in behavior and attitudes, although there are some changes throughout life as the person encounters new experiences and people. For example, if the young child internalizes feelings of being bad, unworthy, inadequate, perhaps because of race, color, or neighborhood, he/she will later have difficulty believing that he/she is good or competent, even when that is realistic. If the person has good, happy, adequate feelings about self because of childhood experiences, occasional failures will not dampen self-esteem or feelings of competence.

✔ The child's major caretaker should have a positive self-concept and feel good about being a mother (father). If others in the family or if society debase the mothering one, there is injury to the child's self-esteem. Thus the issue of equality of women becomes critical. Equality as a person, the importance of the mother and homemaker role, and the importance of women to society and to the work world are all critical to successful chidrearing. If the female caretaker doubts her own worth, is resentful of societal oppression, and has doubts about her own power and status, these negative feelings will be conveyed nonverbally to the child and will have a direct bearing on his/her sense of security and self-worth. This critical phase of development lies between 18 and 36 months (1).

✔ Be mindful of body-image and self-concept formation as you care for toddlers, for it determines their reaction. Only through repetitious positive input can you change a negative self-concept to one that is positive. By stimulating a positive self-image, you are promoting emotional health. Teach parents to provide an environment in which the child can successfully exercise skills, such as running, walking, and playing, and feel acceptance of his/her body and behavior. Help them realize that as autonomy develops so too will a more appropriate mental picture of his/her body and emotions.

Adaptive Mechanisms

Before the child is 2 years old, he/she is learning the basic response patterns appropriate for the family and culture; a degree of trust and confidence, or lack of it, in the parents; how to express annoyance and impatience as well as love and joy; and how to communicate needs.

The toddler begins to adapt to the culture because of **primary identification.** He/she imitates the parents and responds to their encouragement and discouragement. With successful adaptation, the child moves toward independence. Other major adaptive mechanisms of this era include repression, suppression, denial, reaction formation, projection, and sublimation (26).

Repression *unconsciously removes from awareness the thoughts, impulses, fantasies, and memories of behavior which are unacceptable to the self.* The *not-me* discussed earlier is an example and may result from child abuse. **Suppression** *differs from repression in that it is a conscious act.* For example, the child forgets that he/she has been told not to handle certain articles. **Denial** *is not admitting, even when warned, that certain factors exist,* for example, that the stove is hot and will cause a burn. **Reaction formation** *is replacing the original idea and behavior with the opposite behavior characteristics.* For example, the child flushes the toilet and describes feces as dirty instead of playing in them, thus becoming appropriately tidy. **Projection** *occurs when he/she attributes personel feelings or behaviors to someone else.* For example, if the babysitter disciplines toddler, he/she projects dislike for her by saying, "You don't like me." **Sublimation** *is channeling impulses into socially acceptable behavior rather than expressing the original impulse.* For example, he/she plays with mud, finger paints, or shaving cream instead of feces, which is socially unacceptable.

✔ Teach parents that the child's adaptive behavior is strengthened when he/she is taught to do something for self and permitted to make a decision *if that decision is truly his/hers to make.* If the decision is one that must be carried out regardless of the toddler's wish, it can best be accomplished by giving direction rather than by asking the child if he/she wants to do something.

Sexuality Development

Traditionally parents have handled sons and daughters differently during infancy, and the results began to be evident in toddlerhood.

Because parents encourage independent behavior in boys and more dependency in girls, by 13 months the boy ventures farther from mother, stays away longer, and looks at or talks to his mother less than does the girl. The girl at this age is encouraged to spend more time touching and staying near mother than is the boy. However, the separation process later seems less severe for girls. Perhaps boys should be touched and cuddled longer (26, 28).

Boys play more vigorously with toys than do girls, and they play more with nontoys, such as doorknobs and light switches. Yet, basically there is no sexual preference for toys, although parents may enforce a preference. A boy responds with more overt aggression to a barrier placed between him and his mother at 13 months of age than do girls. Boys show more exploratory and aggressive behavior than girls, and this behavior is encouraged by the father (26, 28). The female continues to be attentive to a wide variety of stimuli and complex visual and auditory stimuli. The female demonstrates earlier language development and seems more aware of contextual relationships, perhaps because of the more constant stimulation from the mother (5).

Society has traditionally been easy on girls in terms of achievement. If they excel, this is an added plus; if they do not, no one cares. Boys, however, are expected to achieve. As early as the toddler years this influence can be seen: Girls are allowed to be more dependent while boys are pushed to achieve. Attitudes, however, are changing about women's roles and abilities (45).

Imitation and observation of the same-sexed parent contribute to gender identity. The child by 15 months is interested in his/her own and others' body parts. Both male and female achieve sexual pleasure through self-stimulation, although girls masturbate less than boys (possibly because of anatomical differences) (4).

By 21 months the child can refer to self by name, an important factor in the development of identity. By 2 years of age, the child can categorize people into boy and girl and has some awareness of anatomical differences if he/she has had an opportunity to view them (4).

By the end of toddlerhood, the child is more aware of his body, body's excretions, and his/her actions, and he/she is able to be more independent in the first steps of self-care. Ability to communicate verbally expands to the point that he/she can ask questions and talk about sexual topics with parents and peers.

✔ Help parents to understand the developing sexuality of their child and to be comfortable with their own gender identification and sexuality so that they can cuddle the child and answer questions. Help them understand that a wide variety of play experiences will prepare the child for adult behavior and competence. They may talk through their concerns about a son becoming a sissy if he plays with dolls or wears mother's high heels in dramatic play. Help parents realize that a daughter playing with trucks does not mean she will become a truck driver.

Guidance and Discipline

Discipline *is guidance that helps the child learn to understand and care for self and to get along with others.* It is not just punishing, correcting, or controlling behavior, as is commonly assumed (26).

Everything in the toddler's world is new and exciting and meant to be explored, touched, eaten, or sat on, including porcelain figurines from Spain or boiling water. In moving away from complete dependency, the toddler demonstrates energy and drive, and requires sufficient restrictions to ensure physical and psychological protection and at the same time enough freedom to permit exploration and autonomy. Because mother must now set limits, a new dimension is added to the relationship established between mother and toddler. Before, mother met his/her basic needs immediately. Now with the toddler's increasing ability, freedom, and demands, the parent sometimes makes him/her wait or denies a wish if it will cause harm. The transition should be made in a loving, consistent, yet flexible manner so that the child maintains trust and moves in the quest for independence. Excessive limitations, overwhelming steady pressure, or hostile bullying behavior might cause an overly rebellious, negativistic, or passive child. Complete lack of limitations can cause accidents, poor health, and insecurity.

Mother is usually the main disciplinarian at this age, her approach is important. When the mother is under high acute or chronic stress, support and help from others is the most significant factor in reducing a negative discipline approach to the child(ren), regardless of the mother's age, education, or marital status (9).

Through guidance and the parent's reaction, the child is being socialized, learning what is right and wrong. Because the child cannot adequately reason, he/she must depend on and trust the parents as a guide for all activities. He/she can obey simple commands. Later, the child will be capable of internalizing rules and mores and will become self-disciplined as a result of having been patiently disciplined. Setting limits is not easy. Parents should not thwart the toddler's curiosity and enthusiasm, but they must protect from harm. Parents who oppose the toddler's desire of the moment are likely to be met with anything from a simple "no" to a temper tantrum.

✔ Teach parents the importance of constructive guidance and discipline. Temper tantrums result because the toddler hates being thwarted and feeling helpless. Once the feelings are discharged, the child regains composure quickly and without revenge. If temper tantrums, a form of negativism, occur, the best advice is to ignore the outburst; it will soon disappear. The child needs the parent's reaction for the behavior to continue. Belittling or beating the child does not help temper tantrums. If he/she is given more frustration than can be handled, fear, hostility, and anger mount, and the lack of verbal ability inhibits adequate outlet. Hence he/she strikes out, bites, or hits physically. Now toddler desperately needs mother's support, firm control and mediation. The parent's calm voice, expressing understanding of feelings, and introduction of an activity to restore self-esteem are important to teaching self-control.

✔ Because parents are sometimes confused about handling the toddler's behavior, you can assist them by teaching some simple rules:

1. Provide an environment in which the child feels respected.
2. Decide what is important and what is not worth a battle of will. For example, the child may not be wearing matched clothing but resists parental attempts to change. Avoid negativism and an angry scene by deciding that today it is all right for the child to wear an unmatched outfit.
3. Changing the mind, pursuing an alternate activity, or letting the child have his/her way is not giving in, losing face, being a poor parent, or letting the child be manipulative. When limits are consistent, changing a direction of behavior can be a positive learning experience for the child. The child is becoming aware of being a separate person, able to assert self and influence others.
4. Remove or avoid temptations, such as breakable objects within reach or candy that should not be eaten, in order to avoid having to repeatedly say "No."
5. Try not to ask open-ended questions for the child to decide about an activity when the decision is not really one the child can make.
6. Consider limits as more than restrictions but also as a distraction *from* one prohibited activity *to* another in which the child can freely participate. Distraction with alternatives or a substitute is effective with the toddler because attention span is short.
7. Reinforce appropriate behavior through approval and attention. The child will continue behavior that gains attention, even if the attention is punitive, because negative attention is better than none to the child.
8. Set limits consistently so that the child can rely on the parent's judgment rather than testing the adult's endurance in each situation.
9. State limits clearly, concisely, simply, positively, and in a calm voice. For example, if the child cannot play with a treasured object, he/she should not be allowed to handle it. Say "Look with your hands behind your back" or "Look with your eyes, not your hands" rather than "Don't touch."
10. Set limits only when necessary. Some rules promote a sense of security, but too many confuse the child.
11. Provide a safe area where the child is free to do whatever he/she wants to do.
12. Do not overprotect the child; he/she should learn that some things have a price, such as a bruise or a scratch.
13. Do not terminate the child's activity too quickly, tell him/her that the activity is ending (26, 39).

Each situation will determine the extent of firmness or leniency needed. The toddler needs grades of independence.

Moral—Religious Development

Birth through the toddler era might be termed the *prereligious stage*. This label does not deny religious influences but simply points out that the toddler is absorbing basic intellectual and emotional patterns regardless of the religious conviction of the caretakers. The toddler may repeat some phrases from prayers while imitating a certain voice tone or body posture that accompanies those prayers. The child only knows that when he/she imitates or conforms to certain rituals, affection and approval come which add to the sense of identification and security. The "good" and "bad" are defined in terms of physical consequences to self.

✔ Teach parents that the toddler can benefit from a nursery-school type of church program in which emphasis is on positive self-image and appropriate play and rest rather than on a lesson to be learned. Toddler also needs to have others to imitate who follow the rules of society, and he/she needs rewards and reinforcement for good or desirable behavior.

Developmental Tasks

Development tasks for the toddler may be summarized as follows:

1. Settling into healthy daily routines.
2. Mastering good eating habits.
3. Mastering the basics of toilet training.
4. Developing the physical skills appropriate to the stage of motor development.
5. Becoming a family member.
6. Learning to communicate efficiently with an increasing number of others (13).

The constantly sensitive situation of the toddler, gaining autonomy and independence—at times over-

Table 8–3. Selected Nursing Diagnoses Related to the Toddler[a]

PATTERN 1: EXCHANGING
Altered Nutrition: More than body requirements
Altered Nutrition: Less than body requirements
Altered Nutrition: Potential for more than body requirements
Potential for Infection
Potential for Injury
Potential for Suffocation
Potential for Poisioning
Potential for Trauma
Potential for Aspiration

PATTERN 2: COMMUNICATING
Impaired Verbal Communication

PATTERN 3: RELATING
Impaired Social Interaction

PATTERN 6: MOVING
Impaired Physical Mobility
Altered Growth and Development

PATTERN 7: PERCEIVING
Self Esteem Disturbance
Sensory/Perceptual Alterations
Unilateral Neglect

PATTERN 9: FEELING
Pain
Anxiety
Fear

[a]Other of the NANDA diagnoses are applicable to the ill toddler.
Source: NANDA Approved Nursing Diagnostic Categories, *Nursing Diagnosis Newsletter*, 15, no. 1 (1988), 1–3.

reaching and needing mother's help, at times needing the freedom from mother's protection—is one which you can help parents understand. The child's future personality and health will depend partially on how these many opportunities are handled now. Your role in teaching and support is critical.

✔ NURSING APPLICATIONS

Your role with the toddler and family has been discussed with each section throughout this chapter. Table 8–3 lists some *nursing diagnoses* that may apply to the toddler, based on assessments that would be accomplished from knowledge presented in this chapter. Interventions include your role modeling of caring behavior to the toddler and family, parent/family education, support, and counseling; or direct care to meet the toddler's physical, emotional, cognitive, and social needs.

References

1. Adams, P., What Women's Inequality Means to Children and Adolescents, *American Journal of Social Psychiatry*, 1, no 1 (April, 1981), 6–8.
2. Argyle, Michael, *The Psychology of Interpersonal Behavior*. Baltimore: Penguin Press, 1967.
3. Baker, Susan, and Roberta Henry, *Parents' Guide to Nutrition: Healthy Eating from Birth through Adolescence*. Reading, MA: Addison-Wesley, 1986.
4. Bardwich, J., *Psychology of Women: A Study of Biocultural Conflicts*. New York: Harper & Row, 1971.
5. ———, and E. Douvan, Ambivalence: The Socialization of Women, in *Readings on the Psychology of Women*, ed. J. Bardwich. New York: Harper & Row, 1972, pp. 52–58.
6. Bettelheim, Bruno, *A Good Enough Parent: A Book on Child-Rearing*. New York: Alfred A. Knopf, 1987.
7. Bossard, James H. S., and Eleanor Stoker Boll, *The Sociology of Child Development* (4th ed.). New York: Harper & Row, 1966.
8. Bowlby, John, *Attachment and Loss, Vol. I. Attachment*. New York: Basic Books, 1969.
9. Brandt, Patricia, Stress-Buffering Effects of Social Support on Maternal Discipline, *Nursing Research*, 33, no. 4 (1984), 229–235.
10. Carruth, Beatrice. Modifying Behavior Through Social Learning, *American Journal of Nursing*, 76, no. 11 (1976), 1804–1806.
11. Coopersmith, Stanley, *The Antecedents of Self-Esteem*. San Francisco: W. H. Freeman, 1967.
12. DiLeo, Joseph, *Children's Drawings as Diagnostic Aids*. New York: Brunner/Mazel, 1973.
13. Duvall, Evelyn, and Brent Miller, *Marriage and Family Development* (6th ed). New York: Harper & Row, 1984.
14. Erikson, Erik H., *Childhood and Society* (2nd ed.). New York: W. W. Norton, 1963.
15. Falkner, Frank, and J. M. Tanner (eds.), *Human Growth* (2nd ed.). New York: Plenum Press, 1986.
16. Feigenberg, Myrtle, and Judith Sotman, A Toddler with a Malabsorption Syndrome, *American Journal of Nursing*, 75, no. 6 (1975), 978–979.
17. Freiberg, Karen, *Human Development: A Life Span Approach* (3rd ed.). Monterey, Calif.: Wadsworth Health Sciences Division, 1987.
18. Garbarino, James, Edna Guttmann, and James Seeley, *The Psychologically Battered Child: Strategies for Identification, Assessment, and Intervention*. San Francisco: Jossey-Bass, 1987.
19. General Recommendations on Immunizations, *Morbidity and Mortality Weekly Report*, 32, no. 1. Atlanta: U.S. Department of Health and Human Services, Public Health Service Center for Disease Control, 1983, 4.
20. Gesell, Arnold, et al, *The First Five Years of Life*. New York: Harper & Brothers, 1940.

21. *Health in the United States*, Publication No. PHS 83-1232. Washington, D.C.: United States Government Printing Office, 1982.
22. Hoole, Axalla, Robert Greenberg, and C. Glenn Pickard, *Patient Care Guidelines for Nurse Practitioners* (3rd ed.). Boston: Little, Brown, 1988.
23. Jones, Franklin, Karl Garrison, and Raymond Morgan, *The Psychology of Human Development* (2nd ed.). New York: Harper & Row, 1985.
24. Kaluger, George, and Meriem Kaluger, *Human Development: The Span of Life* (3rd ed.). St. Louis: Times Mirror/Mosby, 1984.
25. Lamb, Michael, *The Father's Role*. New York: John Wiley, 1986.
26. Lidz, Theodore, *The Person: His and Her Development Throughout the Life Cycle*. (2nd ed.). New York: Basic Books, 1983.
27. Linley, Jayne, Screening Children for Common Orthopedic Problems, *American Journal of Nursing*, 87, no. 10 (1987), 1312-1316.
28. Macoby, E., Sex Differences in Intellectual Functioning, in *Readings on the Psychology of Women*, ed. J. Bardwich. New York: Harper & Row, 1972, pp. 34–44.
29. Missouri Hypertension Control Program/Bureau of Chronic Diseases, Questions—Answers. Jefferson City, Mo. (n.d.).
30. Moshman, David, John Glover, and Roger Bruning, *Developmental Psychology*. Boston: Little, Brown, 1987.
31. Murphy, Brenda, Pushing Up Baby. *Washington University School of Medicine Outlook*, 24, no. 3 (1987), 16.
32. New Evidence Links Reye's Syndrome and Aspirin, *The Nation's Health*, (May–June, 1987), 20.
33. Out of the Mouths of Babes, *Newsweek* (December 15, 1986), 84–86.
34. Pillitteri, Adele, *Child Health Nursing: Care of the Growing Family* (3rd ed.). Boston: Little, Brown, 1987.
35. Pipes, Peggy. *Nutrition in Infancy and Childhood* (3rd ed.). St. Louis: Times Mirror/Mosby, 1985.
36. Potter, Diana, ed., *Assessment*. Springhouse, Pa.: Intermed Communications, 1982.
37. Pridham, Karen, and Marc Hansoen, Helping Children Deal with Procedures in a Clinic Setting: A Developmental Approach, *Journal of Pediatric Nursing*, 2, no. 2 (1987), 13–21.
38. Sataloff, Robert, and Cynthia Colton, Otitis Media: A Common Childhood Infection, *American Journal of Nursing*, 81, no. 8 (1981), 1480–1483.
39. Schuster, Clara Shaw, and Shirley Smith Ashburn, *The Process of Human Development: A Holistic Life-Span Approach* (2nd ed.). Boston: Little, Brown, 1986.
40. Scipien, G. M., Barnard, M. A., Howe, J., et al, *Comprehensive Pediatric Nursing* (3rd ed.). New York: McGraw-Hill, 1986.
41. Selekman, Janice, Immunization: What's It All About?, *American Journal of Nursing*, 80, no. 8 (1980), 1440–1445.
42. Shapiro, Leona, et al., Obesity Prognosis: A Longitudinal Study of Children From age 6 Months to 9 Years, *American Journal of Public Health*, 74, no. 9 (1984), 968–972.
43. Sherman, Jacques L., Jr., and Sylvia Fields, *Guide to Patient Evaluation* (3rd ed.). Garden City, N.Y.: Medical Examination Publishing, 1978.
44. Silver, Henry II, C. Henry Kempe, and Henry Bruyn, *Handbook of Pediatrics* (12th ed.). Los Altos, Calif.: Lange, 1977.
45. Sullivan, Harry S., *Interpersonal Theory of Psychiatry*. New York: W. W. Norton, 1953.
46. Taking Care of Toddlers' Teeth, *Health Scene*, Fall, 1987, 11.
47. Tanner, J. M., *Foetus into Man: Physical Growth from Conception to Maturity*. London: Open Books, 1978.
48. Turner, Jeffrey, and Donald Helms, *Lifespan Development* (3rd ed.). New York: Holt, Rinehart & Winston, 1987.
49. U.S. Department of Health and Human Service, New Recommended Schedule for Active Immunization of Normal Infants and Children, *Morbidity and Mortality Weekly Report*. 35, no. 37 (September 19. 1986), 577–579.
50. Vaccinating Children Against *H. Influenzae*," *American Journal of Nursing*, 85, no. 6 (1985), 642.
51. Verzemnieks, Inese, Developmental Stimulation for Infants and Toddlers, *American Journal of Nursing*. 84, no. 6 (1984), 749–752.
52. Wadsworth, Barry, *Piaget's Theory of Cognitive and Affective Development* (3rd ed.). New York: David McKay, 1984.
53. Webb, Patricia, Piaget: Implications for Teaching, *Theory Into Practice*, 19, no. 2 (1980), 93–97.
54. Whaley, Lucille, and Donna Wong, *Nursing Care of Infants and Children*. (3rd ed.). St. Louis: C. V. Mosby, 1987.
55. Williams, Sue, *Nutritional and Diet Therapy* (5th ed.). St. Louis: C. V. Mosby, 1985.

9

Assessment and Health Promotion for the Preschooler

Study of this chapter will help you to

1. Compare the family relationships between the preschool and previous developmental eras and the influence of parents, siblings, and nonfamily members on the preschooler.
2. Explore with the family the expected developmental tasks and ways to meet them.
3. Visit several day-care centers and nursery schools, compare their values and services to parents and child, and discuss necessary adaptation by the preschooler in each setting.
4. Assess physical, motor, mental, language, play, and emotional characteristics of a 3-, 4-, and 5-year-old.
5. Describe the health needs of the preschooler, including nutrition, exercise, rest, safety, and immunization, and measures to meet these needs.
6. Explore with parents their role in contributing to the preschooler's cognitive, language, self-concept, sexuality, moral-religious, and emotional development as well as physical health.
7. Discuss measures to diminish the trauma of hospitalization for this age group.
8. Explore with parents effective ways for communication with and guidance and discipline of the preschooler to enhance his/her development.
9. Describe the developmental crisis of initiative versus guilt, the adaptive mechanisms commonly used that promote a sense of initiative, and the implications of this crisis for later maturity.
10. Discuss the developmental tasks and your role in promoting achievement of these.
11. Work effectively with a preschooler in the nursing situation.

Key Terms

Preschool years
Peers
Oedipal/Electra Stage
Identification
Day-Care
Nursery school
Early school experiences
Montessori programs
Compensatory programs
Kindergarten
Siblings
Dyads
Active immunity
Passive immunity
Minor head injury
Minor Lacerations
Burns
   First degree
   Second degree
   Third degree
Encephalopathy
Strabismus
Diplopia
Amblyopia
Conjunctivitis
Acute Purulent Otitis
   Media
Urinary tract infection
Enuresis
Nonspecific
   vulvovaginitis
Measles
Concepts

Concept formation
Action space
Body space
Object space
Map space
Abstract space
Quantitative concepts
Concepts of causality
Animistic
Egocentric
Transductive logic
Absolute thought
Centering
Reversibility
Peer
Peer group
Physical activity
Dramatic play
Creative playthings
Quiet play
Permissive discipline
Overpermissive discipline
Anthropomorphism
Superego
Initiative
Guilt
Differentiation
Articulate
Integration
Introjection
Secondary identification
Fantasy

↙ In this chapter, development of the preschool child and the family relationships are discussed. *Nursing responsibilities for health promotion for the child and family are discussed throughout the chapter. The information regarding normal development and needs serves as a basis for assessment.* Your role will be to use information on assessment and health promotion in health education and counseling of families and in your care of the preschooler. You will find opportunity in many settings—the neighborhood, day-care center, church group, clinic, doctor's office, school, industrial setting, or hospital—to correct parents' misconceptions and validate their sound thinking about their child's development and the importance of the family's behavior for the child's emotional, physical, and social health. Principles of communication, health teaching, and crisis work also apply. Become active as a citizen to educate the public about needs of hospitalized children, promote needed legislation, or directly offset problems that affect children's health such as child abuse or lead poisoning. Promote quality day-care or preschool programs. The range of possible effective intervention is wide and will depend on your work setting and interest.

The Preschooler

The **preschool years,** *ages 3 through 5,* along with infancy and the toddler years, form a crucial part of the person's life. The preschool child is emerging as a social being. He/she participates more fully as a family member but begins to grow slowly out of the family, spending more time in association with **peers,** *children of the same age.* Physical growth is slowing, but body control and coordination are increasing. Many body activities are becoming routine. Emotional and intellectual growth is progressively apparent in the ability to form mental images; express self in anger; become acquainted with the environment; have some perception of social relationships and the status of self as an individual compared with others; identify with the play group and follow rules; control primitive (*id*) impulses, and begin to be self-critical with references to a standard set by others (*super ego formation*).

The parents, too, must learn to separate themselves from their growing child and revise decisions about how much free expression and initiative to permit the child while at the same time setting certain limits. The child's long step into the outside world is not always accomplished with ease for either the child or the parent. Thus gradually promoting more independence during the preschool years allows both the child and parents to be more comfortable about the separation that occurs when he/she goes to school.

Family Development and Relationships

The family unit, regardless of the specific form, is important to the preschooler, and in turn the preschooler affects relationships within the family by his/her behavior. The close relationship of the baby to the mother and father gradually expands to include other significant adults living in the home, siblings, and other relatives, and they will have some effect on the child's personality.

In one study of the effect of parenting styles on preschoolers, children were divided into three groups: (1) friendly, self-controlled, and self-reliant; (2) discontented and withdrawn; and (3) low in self-reliance and self-control. Parents of the first group were significantly more controlling, demanding, and loving than parents of either of the other groups. Parents of the discontented and withdrawn children were also controlling, but they were detached instead of warm and loving. Parents of the children who were low in self-reliance and self-esteem were warm but highly permissive. This study is representative of a number of other studies that indicate that children of relatively demanding but loving parents tend to be better adjusted, more independent, and more self-reliant (32, 38, 57). Other studies reveal that highly creative children have parents who are warm and loving and who expect more of them at an earlier age than do parents of less creative children (35). Parents who have a high need for achievement are more demanding that their children try new things and expect more of them at an earlier age than do parents with less need for achievement. These ambitious parents emphasize independence, show an interest in their children's activities, give emotional rewards for competence, and set high goals for them. In turn, their children have a high need to achieve (32, 38, 57).

Another study showed that the child's behavior affects parental reactions and is different toward each parent. When the child is more dependent in behavior, both parents interact more physically and verbally with the child and display more controlling behavior. In one study, the female child appeared to engage in specific tasks with father and in more personal interaction with mother. The father was more likely to help the child physically or become detached, whereas mother was more likely to encourage independence and to explain or question the child. More study needs to be done on the reciprocity of parent-child relationships and the effect of each on the other. For example, perhaps the parent who has been authoritarian and controlling over the child from birth on fosters dependent behavior in the child, which in turn stimulates more controlling behavior (32, 35).

Relationships with Parents

The preschooler's early emotional and physical closeness to the parents now leads to a different kind of relationship with them. This is the stage of the *family triangle, family romance,* or what Freud called the *Oedipal* or Electra† Complex* (35).

Various authors say that knowledge of the Oedipal or Electra conflict as it exists in general western culture, the manner in which it is resolved, and the significance of it in the preschool era are essential for understanding the development of the adolescent and adult in American culture. Others feel that this theory has been overpublicized. The intensity of this situation appears related to family attitudes and culture (35).

During this **Oedipal/Electra stage** or *phase of pregenital sexuality, positive, possessive, or love feelings are directed mainly toward the parent of the opposite sex while the parent of the same sex may receive competitive, aggressive, or hostile feelings.* The daughter becomes "Daddy's girl" and tries to imitate the mother's role; the father responds to her femininity. The son is "Mommy's boy" and imitates the father's role; the mother responds to his masculinity. The parent of the same sex may be told, "I hate you. Go away." The child may declare to the opposite-sex parent that he/she will marry the parent someday. Help parents recognize these feelings as developmentally normal. During this phase the child is establishing a basis for his/her own eventual mate relationship; the parents' positive handling of the Oedipal conflict is crucial.

✔ Help the parents feel comfortable with the sexuality of the child and with their own sexuality so that they are neither threatened by nor ignore or punish the child's remarks and behavior.

As the parent of the opposite sex continues to show love to his or her mate and the child, and as the parents desexualize the relationship with the child, the erotic aspects gradually disappear. The child can then get on with one of the major preschool tasks—identification. **Identification** *occurs first through imitation of the same-sex parent's overt behavior and finally through intrajection of attitudes, feelings, and values about sexual, moral, social, and occupational roles and behavior* (35).

In the one-parent or stepparent family (or in the abusive home), achieving identification may be more difficult. The little girl raised by a male may not fit in with other girls at school or be able to feel comfortable and relate to women later in life. The boy raised by a woman may relate to women but not to men.

✔ Explore with parents the importance of identification with the same-gender parent or adult, and ways to achieve this if the parent of the same gender as the child is not in the home. Divorced parents need to understand that to the child divorce signifies rejection and that the missing parent no longer loves the child. The child feels at blame, and there may be guilt about the separation or about the relief felt after the separation, if much discord preceded the divorce. Family discord may cause more distress than the absence of a parent, but the separation is still difficult. There are often practical problems, such as financial or lifestyle changes, as well as emotional trauma. Postdivorce, the child may manifest insomnia, grief and depression, digestive and elimination problems, irritability, anger, aggression, regressive behavior, fear, anxiety, and withdrawal. The child needs help in expressing feelings and in adapting to the change. The child needs loving interactions with an adult relative or friend who is of the same gender, and the mother or father should foster such a relationship. After divorce the child may have difficulty relating to or identifying with a stepparent. If possible, the child needs an ongoing involvement with the divorced parent who is no longer in the home. The child loves and needs both parents in most cases and needs to learn to live with and feel affection for and from the stepparent as well.

✔ These families benefit from: (1) your empathy; (2) your listening ear; (3) your exploration of their own and the child's feelings; (4) your suggestions of practical ways of helping the child spend time with both biological parents; (5) your discussion of ways to help the child mourn the loss he/she feels and adjust to the changed life situation; and (6) your counseling efforts and skills as the family works to resolve the crisis of separation, divorce, or remarriage.

✔ ***Gender or Sexual Identity.*** Help parents realize that gender is reinforced through name, clothing, color of clothing and room, behavior toward, and expectations of the child. The innumerable contacts between the child and significant adults contribute gender or sexual identification and should occur in this developmental period (32, 35, 38, 57). The sex of the child is a great determinant in personality development because each sex has different tasks and roles in every culture. Achieving a firm identity as a man

---

*Oedipus, a hero of Greek mythology, was the son of King Laius and Queen Jocasta. At the time of Oedipus' birth, the oracle prophesied that Oedipus would kill his father and marry his mother. To avoid the prophecy, Laius ordered the infant abandoned so that he would die. Through a series of uncontrollable events, the infant survived, and the prophecy came true.

†Electra was a legendary Greek woman who was obsessed by an intense love for her murdered father, plotted with her brother to kill her mother and mother's lover, whom she blamed for the father's death.

or woman is basic to emotional stability and ego development.

In the United States, most parents are less rigid about what clothing or colors are appropriate for boys and girls and are making an effort to teach both daughters and sons to talk about feelings, to do the same household tasks, and to engage in the same play activities. However, in some homes the daughter is reinforced for being cuddly, domestic, and emotional, and the son is reinforced for being physically aggressive or "tough." The 5-year-old son is not expected to set the table or help with dusting. Parents who have fixed ideas about gender-role behavior may not be responsive to your suggestions about the importance of both daughters and sons having the same play, learning, or social experiences or the appropriateness of pants as well as skirts for the daughters. Parental ideas frequently reflect their subcultural values and norms.

✔ Explain parental reactions to and expectations of the child. Help them clarify their feelings and behavior and convey their respect to the child, regardless of gender. The gender assigned to the child by significant adults may be physically realistic or unrealistic. The feelings and needs of the parents strongly influence their reactions to the child, so that gender assignment within the family can override biological factors. The parent can "make" little boys out of infant girls or vice versa by the way they name, handle, dress, play with, touch, or talk to the child. Attitudes about activity and passivity and feelings of mastery or being mastered go into development of male and female traits in most cultures.

The Oepidal or Electra phase brings the development of sexuality to the foreground. The child is interested in the appearance and function of his/her own body, in variations of clothing and hairstyles (the child at first assigns gender on this basis) and in the bodies of others, especially in their sex organs (35). Children at this age feel a sense of excitement in seeing and feeling their own and others' nude bodies and of exposing themselves to other children or adults.

✔ While some body exposure goes on in the average American home, help parents realize that the child needs to learn clothing norms for the culture. Unless the parents live in a nudist camp, there are limits to undressing in public. Help the parents realize that their nudity may stimulate considerable fantasy in the child during this stage and that sexual feelings aroused in the child may be difficult for child or parents to handle.

Now the girl learns that she is equal to or surpasses boys in size, intelligence, and physical capacities and that there are obvious differences in their genital organs. The so-called *penis envy* of Freudian theory is not so much envy but fascination with the difference. It becomes envy if the parents convey the attitude that masculinity is superior to femininity. Questions about the boy's penis can be answered along with the information that she will later have breasts and be able to bear children.

The child has many questions about conception and childbirth and usually develops or expands a personal theory: Babies come from a seed placed in the mother's mouth, from eating foods with seeds, from kissing, or from animals; babies are manufactured like household items; prenatally the baby sits on the mother's stomach, ingesting food as she eats; and babies come out of the anus or the navel.

✔ *Teaching Sexuality.* Teaching sexuality to the child is enmeshed in the acquisition of gender identity and positive feelings about the self. The basis for sex education begins prenatally with the parents' attitudes about the coming child. Parents and other child educators or caretakers, including nurses, continue daily thereafter to form attitudes in the child as well as impart factual knowledge in response to questions. You can assist parents in acquiring information to answer the child's questions.

Because of the child's consuming curiosity, he/she asks many questions: Will the man in the television come out? How do I tie my shoes? Why is that lady's tummy so big? What is lightning? These questions are originally asked with equal curiosity. The adult's response will determine into what special category the child places questions about sex.

If parent-child communication has been open—if the child feels free to ask questions about sex as well as other topics, and if the parent gives satisfactory and correct answers without embarrassment—the basis for a healthy sexual attitude exists.

✔ Although sex education must be tailored to the individual child's needs and interests as well as to the cultural, religious, and family values, the following suggestions are applicable to all children and can be shared with parents:

1. Recognize that education about the self as a sexual person is best given by example in family life through parents' showing respect and love for the self, mate, and the child.
2. Understand that the child who learns to trust others and to give as well as receive love has begun preparation for satisfactory adulthood, marriage, and parenthood.
3. Observe the child at play; listen carefully to statements of ideas, feelings, and questions and ask questions to understand better his/her needs.
4. Respond to the child's questions by giving informa-

tion honestly, in a relaxed, accepting manner, and on the child's level of understanding. Avoid isolated facts, myths, or animal analogies.

The question, "Where does baby come from?" could be answered, "Mommy carried you inside her body in a special place" rather than saying "The stork brought baby," "Baby was picked up at the hospital after a special order," or "God makes babies." Religious beliefs can be worked into the explanation while also acknowledging human realities.

5. Teach the child anatomical names rather than other words for body parts and processes. Parents may hesitate to do this because they do not want the child to blurt out *penis* or *vagina* in public. Parents can teach the child that certain topics, such as sexual and financial matters, are discussed in the home, just as certain activities, such as urinating, are done in private.
6. Grabbing the genitals and some masturbation are normal. Children explore their bodies, especially body parts not easily seen and which give pleasurable sensations when touched. Masturbation should be accepted if it occurs in the home. The child should be taught that this is not normal behavior in public.
7. Playing doctor or examining each other's body parts is normal for preschool children. Parents should not overreact. If children seem to be using each other in a sexual way, they should be instructed that this is not acceptable.
8. Realize that sex education continues throughout the early years. The child's changing self motivates the same or different questions again and again. Remain open to his/her ongoing questions. Explanation about reproduction may begin with a simple statement, for example: "A man and a woman are required to be baby's father and mother. Baby is made from the sperm in daddy's body and an egg in mother's body." A simple explanation of sperm and egg would be needed. Later, the child can be given more detail.

Influence of Nonfamily Members

🖊 Help parents realize that other people may be significant to the child, depending on frequency and duration of contact, warmth of the relationship, and how well the parents meet the child's needs (19, 35).

Other significant adults may include relatives, especially grandparents, aunts, uncles, cousins who are peers; the teacher at the day-care center or nursery school; the babysitter; or neighbors. Servants or the child's nurse–caretaker may provide positive or negative identification figures and should be chosen with care, especially if they live in the home. Relatives and friends also contribute to development of identity if contact is frequent.

Guests introduce the child to new facets of family life and parents' behavior, to different people with unfamiliar behavior, and to different ideas, religions, or occupations. Visits to others' homes aid socialization through comparison of the households, ability to separate from home, and interaction with people in new places.

Even domestic pets can be useful in meeting certain needs: loving and being loved; companionship; learning a sense of responsibility; and learning about sex in a natural way.

If the family utilizes day care, nursery school, or other early schooling for the child, the adults in the agency may exert a strong influence on the child. 🖊 Parents may ask you about each agency: the differences between them, their significance for the child, and the criteria for selection. Share the following information.

Day care *is a program to provide daily care away from home for any part of a 24-hour day, for compensation, or otherwise.* This program can be an important resource to many families: for example, when the single parent works and is the sole support of the family; when both parents work; when one parent is ill or a full-time student and the other parent works; or when the mother needs relief from child care for health or other urgent personal reasons.

Nursery school *is usually a half-day program that emphasizes an educational, socialization experience for the child to supplement home experiences.*

Early school experiences *may include a Montessori program, a compensatory program, or kindergarten,* which has now become the first step prior to school entry for most children in the United States. **Montessori programs** evolved from the Italian educator, Maria Montessori, who developed preschool education in Europe. They *emphasize: (1) self-discipline of the child; (2) intellectual development through training of the senses; (3) freedom for the child within a structure and schedule; and (4) meaningful individual cognitive experiences that are provided in a quiet, pleasant, educational environment.* **Compensatory programs,** which first began as Head Start and Follow Through Projects in the 1960s, *focus on making up for deprived conditions in the child's life, and include (1) giving physical care (good nutrition, dental care, immunizations); (2) fostering curiosity, exploring, creativity, and learning about the self and environment; (3) promoting emotional health through nurturing, positive self-concept, self-confidence, and self-discipline; and (4) teaching social skills and behaviors, how to interact with peers, teachers, and parents* (23, 32, 38, 57). **Kindergarten** *is a half- or whole-day educational program for the 5-*

year-old child that may be an extension of either a nursery school or a part of the elementary school system. In some parts of the country, kindergarten attendance is mandatory for entry into first grade because the cognitive learning that is begun is a foundation for the cognitive program of the first grade. The social behaviors that are learned also prepare the child to be better disciplined in the school setting and to interact appropriately with teacher and peers. The half-day program also helps the child and parents to separate from each other for a period of time if that has not been done through nursery school or day care.

Criteria Selection. Criteria for selection of the day-care center or nursery school may be discussed with parents as they seek assistance with child care and education. Some of the same criteria are useful in selecting a Montessori or compensatory program.

Criteria to observe for or ask about concern staff qualifications, approach to and care of the child, physical set-up, and experiences or curriculum. The day-care center should be:

1. Licensed by a state authority.
2. Located conveniently close to the home.
3. Provide a happy, comfortable, safe living and play space for the child.
4. Staffed with certified teachers and other workers.
5. Able to provide facilities for creative, dramatic, rough-and-tumble play; rest; meal service; bathroom; health services, and facilities for the child's clothing or other objects.
6. Able to provide supplies and equipment as required for the children.

The nursery school should be operated by a reputable person or organization and provide the aforementioned, except for a full noon meal. Usually only a midsession snack is served. In either center, the parent should observe the program to learn about the philosophy of the staff regarding childrearing, care, and discipline; administrative policies; the use of professional consultants for educational, social, or medical concerns; and the educational qualifications of the staff. They should note the warmth, emotional characteristics, and competence of the staff as they and children work and play together. Cost of the program, when services are available, and the parents' obligations to the agency are other aspects to consider.

In either agency, the child, under guidance of qualified staff, will get many experiences: socializing; investigating; imaginative experimenting; developing creative abilities; doing beginning problem solving; becoming more independent, secure, and self-confident in a variety of situations; handling emotions and broadening avenues of self-expression; learning basic hygiene; how to interact with others; and learning about the community in which he/she lives.

✓ You can help parents be aware of these resources, answer their questions, and give suggestions regarding criteria for selection. As a nurse, you may also assist with primary prevention and health consulting to teachers, children, and parents in such an agency. For example, public health workers in Hennepin County, Minnesota, designed a program to promote optimal health and safety of children in day-care settings through health education to staff, technical assistance support, nurse–child assessment, and evaluation of policies and procedures (55).

There are no accurate predictors of later academic success for preschool children. Some studies show that when infants and young children in a ghetto were given a planned educational experience aimed at preventing retardation and promoting parental interaction, environmental stimulation, and experiential opportunity, the experimental group showed superior cognitive abilities at 5.5 years compared to children in a control group raised in the usual way. Other studies showed that 3-year-old children who were given special educational opportunities showed better intellectual performance at the end of second grade than did children in a control group (32, 38, 57). Other authors say that pushing the child to develop reading and mathematics skills too early will create problems: fatigue, stress-related illnesses, disciplinary problems, and parental burnout (33).

✓ If parents use a day-care center, nursery school, or early school program, help them understand that they remain the most important people to the child and that their love and involvement with the child is crucial for later learning and adjustment to life. The care or enrichment of a preschool center or program where children attend a few hours daily cannot undo deprivation or abuse that is present in a family. Help the working mother realize that her working does not necessarily deprive the child. Many career women tend to do better than full-time homemakers. They do not see the child as an end in itself; they allow the child to develop autonomy and initiative in creative ways because they have a sense of self-fulfillment in their own lives.

✓ You can help the parents and child prepare for the separation if the child is to be enrolled in a nursery school or day-care center. Help the parents realize, too, that the child's emotional and social adjustment and overall learning depends on many factors. Because each child interprets entrance into the agency on the basis of his/her own past experience, each differs in adjustment. Being with a number of children can be an upsetting experience. The child needs adequate preparation to avoid feeling abandoned or rejected.

The mother needs to have confidence in the agency so that she can convey a feeling of pleasurable expectation to the child. The child should accompany the mother to see the building, observe the program, and meet the teachers and other children prior to enrollment. Ideally, the child should begin attending when both mother and child feel secure about the ensuing separation, and the mother should be encouraged to stay with the child the whole first day or for a shorter period of time for several days, until he/she feels secure without mother. If possible, the parent, rather than a neighbor or stranger, should take the child each day, assuring the child of the parent's return at the end of the day.

Relationships with Siblings

The discussion in Chapter 4 on the effect of the child's sex and ordinal position on family interaction is significant for understanding the preschooler.

Often the preschool child has **siblings**, *brothers or sisters*, either younger or older, so that family interaction is complex with many **dyads**, *groups of two people*. Siblings become increasingly important in directing and crystallizing the child's early development, partly because of their proximity but also because the parents change in their role with each additional child. Parents often are emotionally warmer after the firstborn, possibly because they feel more experienced and relaxed. In the following discussion you should realize that the relationships described could occur at other developmental eras in childhood, but in the preschool years, siblings begin to make a very definite impact (19, 35).

The sibling may be part of a multiple birth: twins, triplets, or more. Identical twins share traits, emotional bonds, and pain, and communicate with each other in their own language, in uncanny or mysterious ways, often when they are miles apart. Studies of identical twins who are reared separately in different environments can help to sort out the relative influence of heredity and environment. Twins seem to think about each other more than other siblings, so some of the ESP-like communication or experiences may be coincidence. Yet the extreme intimacy can be pathological; there may be jealousy of each other or a symbiotic interdependence that interferes with identity formation of each individual. For the parents, raising twins creates a delicate balance.

✔ You may teach the following suggestions: (1) By the way parents talk to, dress, and handle twins (or other multiple births), help the children realize they are individuals first and twins second. (2) Encourage each to develop separate interests, pursue different hobbies, subjects, or go to different schools to reduce competition and rivalry. (3) Talk to the twins about different kinds of relationships, their own special closeness, the rewards of developing separate friendships, and the importance of separate intimate relationships. (4) The magazine *Twins* (Overland Park, KS), The National Organization of Mothers of Twins Clubs (Albuquerque, New Mexico), and the 300 chapters of TWINLINE (Berkeley, California) can be helpful sources of information to parents (2). Refer also to Chapter 4 for more information on multiple births.

The Preschooler and the New Baby. The arrival of a new baby changes life: The preschooler is no longer the center of attention but is expected by the parents to delight in the baby. It is important for parents to prepare the young child (toddler or preschooler) for a new arrival. While a space of 3 to 4 years is ideal, such ideal spacing does not always occur.

✔ When pregnancy is apparent, there are some ways for parents to prepare the older child:

1. Share the anticipation in discussions and planning. Let the child feel fetal movements. Show the child a picture of when he/she was a newborn. Talk about what he/she needed as a baby and the necessary responsibilities. Read books that explain reproduction and birth on his or her level.
2. Include the child as much as possible in activities, such as shopping for furniture for the baby or decorating baby's room. The preschool child likes to feel important, and being a helper enhances this feeling.
3. Have the child visit mother and baby at the hospital, if rules permit, after delivery. Or the older child can talk to mother by phone.
4. Encourage relatives and friends to bring a small surprise gift for the older child when they visit and bring a gift for baby. Have them spend time with the older child also rather than concentrating only on baby.

Accepting the family's affection toward the baby is difficult for the firstborn, and jealousy is likely to occur if more attention is focused on the baby than on him/her. As a result, the preschooler may regress, overtly displaying a need to be babied. He/she may ask for the bottle, soil self, have enuresis, lie in the baby's crib, or demand extra attention. The child may harm the baby, directly or indirectly, through play or handling baby roughly. He/she may appear to love the baby excessively, more than is normal. The child may show hostility toward the mother in different ways: direct physical or verbal attacks, ignoring or rejecting her, or displacing anger onto the day-care, nursery, or Sunday school teacher.

✔ Teach parents that these outward behaviors and

the underlying feelings should be accepted: they are better handled with overt loving behavior than repressed through punishment. Jealousy can be handled by the parents in a variety of ways: Tell the child about the pregnancy but not too far in advance because a young child has a poor concept of time. Convey that the child is loved as much as before, provide a time for him/her only, and give as much attention as possible. In addition, avoid ridicule; emphasize pleasure in having the child share in loving the new arrival; and give increasing responsibility and status without overburdening him/her. Encourage the child to talk about the new situation or express hostility in play and involve him/her in preparing for the new baby. While the preschooler may have to give up a crib, getting him/her a new big bed can seem like a promotion rather than a loss. Reading stories about feelings of children with new siblings can help the child express personal feelings. Other effective advice you can give about ways to handle jealousy behavior are (1) do not leave the preschooler alone with the baby; (2) give him/her a pet or doll to care for as mother cares for the baby; (3) encourage the child to identify with the parents in helping to protect the baby since he/she is more grown up; and (4) avoid overemphasis of affection for the baby.

The Older Child and the Preschooler. The older sibling in the family who is given much attention for accomplishments may cause feelings of envy and frustration as the preschooler tries to engage in activity beyond his/her ability to also get attention. If the younger child can identify with the older sibling and take pride in the accomplishments while simultaneously getting recognition for his/her own self and abilities, the child will feel positive about self. If the younger child feels defeated and is not given realistic recognition, he/she may stop emulating the older sibling and regress instead. In turn, the older sibling can be helpful to the younger child if he/she does not feel deprived or is not reprimanded too much because of the preschooler.

Explore sibling relationships with parents and present suggestions for preventing conflicts. Often positive feelings exist between siblings. Quarrels are quickly forgotten if parents do not get overly involved. Because siblings have had a similar upbringing, they have considerable empathy for each other, similar values, similar superego development, and related perceptions about situations. Sibling values may be as important as the parents' values in the development of the child. Often recognition and other feelings of the sibling are of such importance to the child that he/she may conceal abiilty rather than move into an area in which the sibling has gained recognition, or he/she may engage in activity to keep the sibling from being unhappy. The children will learn to develop roles and regulate space among themselves to avoid conflicts, unless conflictual behavior is given undue attention or the children are manipulated against each other by the significant adults.

Developmental Tasks of the Family

While the preschool child and siblings are achieving their developmental tasks, the parents are struggling with childrearing and their own personal developmental tasks. A discussion of parental developmental tasks while raising a preschooler follows:

1. Encourage and accept the child's evolving skills rather than elevating the parent's self-esteem by pushing the child beyond his/her capacity. Satisfaction is found through reducing assistance with physical care and giving more guidance in other respects.
2. Supply adequate housing, facilities, space, equipment, and other materials needed for life, comfort, health, and recreation.
3. Plan for predicted and unexpected costs of family life such as medical care, insurance, education, babysitter fees, food, clothing, and recreation.
4. Maintain some personal privacy and an outlet for tension of family members while including the child as a participant in the family.
5. Share household and child-care responsibility with other family members, including the child.
6. Strengthen the partnership with the mate and express affection in ways that keep the relationship from becoming humdrum.
7. Learn to accept failures, mistakes, and blunders without piling up feelings of guilt, blame, and recrimination.
8. Nourish common interests and friendships to strengthen self-respect and self-confidence and to remain interesting to the spouse.
9. Maintain a mutually satisfactory sexual relationship and plan whether or not to have more children.
10. Create and maintain effective communication within the family.
11. Cultivate relationships with the extended family.
12. Tap resources and serve others outside the family to prevent preoccupation with self and family.
13. Face life's dilemmas and rework moral codes, spiritual values, and a philosophy of life (19).

Explore with parents the challenges as well as practical ways of meeting these tasks within the specific family unit.

Physical Growth and Development

Growth. Growth during the preschool years is relatively slow, but changes occur that transform the chubby toddler into a sturdy child who appears taller and thinner. Trunk and limb growth is apparent. Although development does not proceed at a uniform rate in all areas or for all children, development follows a logical, precise pattern or sequence (25, 40, 61). The preschool child grows about 2 to 2½ inches (5 to 6 cm) and gains less than 5 pounds (2.2 kg.) per year. The child appears tall and thin because he/she grows proportionately more in height than in weight. The average height of the 3-year-old is 37 inches (94 cm), of the 4-year-old is 41 inches (104 cm) (or double the birth length), and of the 5-year-old is 43 to 52 inches (110 to 130 cm). At 3 the child weighs about 33 pounds (15 kg); at 4 years, 38 pounds (17 kg); and at 5 years, about 40 to 50 pounds (18 to 23 kg).

Vital Signs. The *temperature* is 98 to 99°F (36.7 to 37.2°C). The *pulse* rate is normally 80 to 110 and the *respiratory rate* about 30 per minute. Blood pressure is about 90/60 mm. of mercury, systolic and diastolic.

Other Characteristics. *Vision* in the preschooler is farsighted; the 5-year-old has 20/40 to 20/30 vision, and is visually discriminative. By age 4, the cerebral cortex is fully connected to the cerebellum, permitting better control of fine muscle movements such as tying shoelaces, cutting with scissors, or holding a pencil or crayon. By the end of the preschool period the child is beginning to lose deciduous teeth (32, 38, 57, 61). *Physical characteristics* to assess in this child are listed in Table 9-1 (22, 32, 38, 40, 57, 61). *Because each child is unique, the normative listings indicate only where most children of a given age are in the development of various characteristics.* Characteristics are listed by age in all following tables for reasons of understanding sequence and giving comparison. Consideration of only the chronological age is misleading as a basis for assessment and care. The development of the whole and unique child and interrelationships among various aspects must be considered. Still, by using the norms for the child at a given age, you can assess how far the child deviates from the norm.

Developmental Assessment. The Denver Developmental Screening Test (DDST) is a test to evaluate gross motor, fine motor-adaptive, language, and personal–social behavior. It is used to determine whether the child is within normal range for various behaviors or is developmentally delayed. A study in Canada, in which public health nurses administered the DDST to over 2500 children, found the DDST to be predictive for some abilities but not predictive for problems and certain characteristics. The researchers concluded that the DDST may be relatively inefficient to use in a general community population of children (10).

However, Williams reports research with the DDST on over 6000 children in Manila, Philippine Islands. The DDST evaluation indicated developmental delays. Performance of children of college-educated mothers and fathers was significantly better than children of parents with less education. Another group of children who performed better came from a younger family with fewer children and greater spacing between children. Children performed better when the mother substitute–caregiver was older and when the child was an only child (62).

Southeast Asian children who had immigrated to the United States within a prior 2 years were found to be below the 50th percentile of normal for weight, height, and hematocrit. The longer the children were in the United States, the more their growth patterns paralleled U.S. norms, probably because of improved nutrition. Small size, weight-for-height, is related to genetics (15).

It is important to consider genetics, family factors, nutrition, and social environment when you care for children who are developmentally delayed. The DDST can be at least a general assessment tool which can also guide treatment and teaching.

Occasionally a child does not attain height within the norms for his/her age, although torso-leg proportions are normal, because the pituitary gland does not produce enough growth hormone (23, 40, 61). Growth hormone deficiency, which causes dwarfism in a preschool child, can now be treated with a synthetic growth hormone. The person still remains short in stature, but within a normal height range. The treatment is important because children who lag behind peers in growth are often teased, kept from participating in certain play activities, and may have difficulty finding clothes or play equipment such as a bicycle that is of correct size. The child may be regarded by others as retarded intellectually. He/she may feel inferior, suffer a negative self-concept, lack initiative, and become withdrawn, depressed, or antisocial in later childhood or adult years.

Nutritional Needs

The child needs the same Basic 4 food groups as the adult each day, but in smaller quantities. The slower growth rate and heightened interest in exploring the environment may lessen interest in eating. The preschool child needs 1 to 1½ pints of milk or equivalent milk servings per day, four or more servings of

TABLE 9–1. Assessment of Physical Characteristics: Motor Control

THREE YEARS	FOUR YEARS	FIVE YEARS
Occasional accident in toileting when busy at play; responds to routine times; tells when going to bathroom. Verbalizes difference between how male and female urinate. Needs help with back buttons and drying self. Nighttime control of bowel and bladder most of time.	Independent toilet habits; manages clothes without difficulty. Insists on having door shut for self but wants to be in bathroom with others. Asks many questions about defecation function.	Takes complete charge of self; does not tell when going to bathroom. Self-conscious about exposing self. Boys and girls to separate bathrooms. Voids 4 to 6 times during waking hours; occasional nighttime accident.
Runs more smoothly, turns sharp corners, suddenly stops.	Runs easily, with coordination. Skips clumsily. Hops on one leg. Legs, trunk, shoulder, arms move in unison. Aggressive physical activity.	Runs with skill, speed, agility, and plays games simultaneously. Increases strength and coordination in limbs.
Walks backward. Climbs stairs with alternate feet. Jumps from low step.	Heel–toe walk. Walks a plank. Climbs stairs without holding onto rail. Climbs and jumps without difficulty.	May still be knock-kneed. Jumps from 3 to 4 steps.
Tries to dance but inadequate balance, although sense of balance improving.	Enjoys motor stunts and gross gesturing.	Balances self on toes; dances with some rhythm. Balances on one foot about 10 seconds.
Pedals tricycle. Swings.	Enjoys new activities rather than repeating same ones.	Jumps rope. Roller skates. Hops and skips on alternate feet. Enjoys jungle-bar gym.
Sitting equilibrium maintained but combined awkwardly with reaching activity.	Sitting balance well maintained, leans forward with greater mobility and ease. Exaggerated use of arm extension and trunk twisting. Touches end of nose with forefinger on direction.	Maintains balance easily. Combines reaching and placing object in one continuous movement. Arm extension and trunk twisting coordinated. Tummy protrudes, but some adult curve to spine.
Undresses self; helps dress self. Undoes buttons on side or front of clothing. Goes to toilet alone if clothes simple. Washes hands, feeds self. May brush own teeth.	Dresses and undresses self except tying bows, closing zipper, putting on boots and snow suit. Does buttons. Distinguishes front. Brushes teeth alone.	Dresses self without assistance; ties shoelaces. Requires less supervision of personal duties. Washes self without wetting clothes.
Catches ball with arms fully extended 1 out of 2 to 3 times. More refined hand movement. Increasing coordination in vertical direction. Pours fluid from pitcher, occasional spills. Hits large pegs on board with hammer.	Greater flexion of elbow. Catches ball thrown at 5 feet 2 to 3 times. Throws ball overhand. Judges where a ball will land. Helps dust objects. Likes water play.	Uses hands more than arms in catching ball. Pours fluid from one container to another with few spills. Uses hammer to hit nail on head. Interest and competence in dusting. Likes water play.
Builds tower of 9 to 10 blocks, builds 3-block gate from model. Imitates a bridge.	Builds complicated structure extending vertically and laterally; builds 5-block gate from model. Notices missing parts or broken objects; requests parents to fix.	Builds things out of large boxes. Builds complicated 3-dimensional structure and may build several separate units. Able to disassemble and reassemble small object.
Copies circle or cross, begins to use scissors, strings large beads. Shows hand preference.	Copies a square. Uses scissors without difficulty. Enjoys finer manipulation of play materials.	Copies triangle or diamond from model. Folds paper diagonally. Definite hand preference.

TABLE 9–1. Continued

THREE YEARS	FOUR YEARS	FIVE YEARS
Trial-and-error method with puzzle.	Surveys puzzle before placing pieces. Matches simple geometric forms. Prefers symmetry. Poor space perception.	Does simple puzzles quickly and smoothly. Prints some letters correctly; prints first name.
Scribbles. Tries to draw a picture and name it.	Less scribbling. Form and meaning in drawing apparent to adults.	Draws clearly recognized life-like representatives; differentiates parts of drawing.

vegetables and fruits, two servings of 1½ to 2 ounces of meat or meat substitutes, and four servings of bread and cereals. A rule of thumb for the size of servings is 1 tablespoon for each year of age: 3 tablespoons of fruit or vegetables for a 3-year-old; 5 tablespoons for a 5-year-old. Protein requirements continue to be high—36 grams daily. Without adequate fruits and vegetables, vitamins A and C are likely to be lacking. Calcium and iron are needed for storage and are assured through eating the Basic 4 foods just described (47). (Refer to Appendix III.) Desserts should furnish protein, minerals, vitamins, as well as calories, and should be a natural part of the meal, not used as a reward for finishing the meal or omitted as punishment.

Children who are reared in vegetarian families may be shorter in height and weigh less, but by the end of the preschool era, the child's growth velocity has approached the norm (53).

A midmorning, midafternoon, and evening snack are necessary because of the child's high level of activity but should be wisely chosen: milk, juice, fruit wedges, vegetable strips, cereal without excess sugar, cheese cubes, peanut butter with crackers or bread, or plain cookies. Sweets (candy, raisins, sodas) should be offered only occasionally, not as a reward for behavior and not before a meal. This pattern will help prevent health problems now and later associated with overeating sweet foods, such as dental caries, malnutrition, or obesity, as well as associating only pleasure with food. Lifetime food habits are being formed (41). Weight gain between 2 and 3 years and 4 and 6 years for boys are the earliest times that are highly related to later obesity (51).

✔ Teach parents about eating patterns, for they differ in each developmental era. Eating assumes increasing social significance for the preschooler and continues to be an emotional as well as physiological experience. The child needs the right foods physically and a warm, happy atmosphere where he/she is included in mealtime conversation. The family mealtime promotes socialization and sexual identification in relation to meal preparation, behavior during mealtimes, language skills, and understanding of family rituals and situation. The training is positive or negative, depending on the parents' example. Such learning is missed if there are no family mealtimes. Table manners need not be rigidly emphasized; accidents will happen, and parental example is the best teacher.

The preschooler's eating habits are simple. There may be periods of overeating or not wanting to eat certain foods but these do not persist. The overall eating pattern from month to month is more pertinent to assess.

✔ The sense of taste is keen; color, flavor, form, and texture are important. Foods should be attractively served, mildly flavored, whole, plain, separated and distinctly identifiable in flavor and appearance rather than mixed as in creamed foods, casseroles, and stews, except for spaghetti and pizza; and preferably lukewarm rather than too hot or too cold, including drinks. The preschooler likes to eat one thing at a time. Of all food groups, vegetables are least liked, while fruits are a favorite. He/she prefers vegetables and fruits crisp, raw, and cut into finger-sized pieces. Strong-tasting vegetables, such as cabbage, onions, cauliflower, and broccoli, and those with tough strings, such as celery and green beans, are usually disliked. Meats should be easily chewed and cut into bite-sized pieces. New foods can be gradually introduced; if a food is refused once, offer it again after several days.

✔ If the child is eating insufficiently, the causes may include: (1) eating too much between meals; (2) unhappy mealtime atmosphere; (3) attention seeking; (4) example of parental eating habits; (5) excessive parental expectations; (6) unavailability of adequate variety and quantity; (7) tooth decay, which may cause nausea or toothache with chewing; (8) sibling rivalry; (9) overfatigue; (10) physical illness; or (11) emotional disturbance. Parents should consider, too, the difference in eating pattern of the 3-, 4-, and 5-year-old which can influence food intake. The 3-year-old either talks or eats, gets up from the table during meals but will return to eat more food, and rarely needs assistance to complete a meal. The 4-year-old normally combines talking and eating, rarely gets up from the table, and likes to serve self. The 5-year-old eats rapidly and is sociable during mealtime, so that family atmosphere is crucial (19, 35).

✔ Measures to increase food intake include letting the child help plan the menu, set the table, wash dishes, or prepare foods such as stirring instant puddings or gelatin desserts, beating cake or cookie mix, or kneading dough. Other aids are serving meals in courses in a quiet environment in which there are few distractions; avoiding coaxing, bribing, or threatening; providing a premeal rest period; giving small, attractive servings; providing comfortable chair and table; allowing sufficient time for eating; and avoiding between-meal nibbling. Making food an issue and forcing the child to eat create eating problems, and the child is likely to win the battle. The child's appetite will improve as his/her growth rate increases nearer school age.

✔ *Hypochromic anemia*, one of the most prevalent nutritional problems of young children, may be caused by inadequate intake of absorbable iron. Like other nutritional problems, hypochromic anemia is often associated with poor hygiene and chronic disease, but often it is a result of the slow transition from milk to solid foods. For reasons of convenience, economy, or ignorance, these children receive most of their calories from cow's milk—a very poor source of iron. Mothers of these children should be encouraged to gradually replace most of the milk with meats, eggs, and dark green, leafy vegetables, in addition to fruits and cereal products. In severe cases, iron supplements will be indicated (41).

Although vitamin—mineral supplements should not be a food substitute, many pediatricians recommend them, especially during these years when appetite fluctuates. Fluoride supplements should be continued if there is insufficient fluoride in the water.

✔ Share information about nutritional needs and eating patterns, as well as the psychological aspects of food and mealtime, with parents.

Exercise, Rest, and Sleep

✔ This is the period when the child has a seeming surplus of energy and is on the move, sometimes to the point of fatigue. Thus the adult must initiate rest periods alternated with activity. Share the following information with parents.

The 3-year-old does not always sleep at naptime but will rest or play quietly for 1 or 2 hours if undisturbed. The 4-year-old child resists naps but needs a quiet period. The 5-year-old is unlikely to nap if he/she gets adequate sleep at night.

The preschooler may still take a favorite toy to bed; he/she likes to postpone bedtime and is ritualistic about bedtime routines such as prayers, a story, or music. Sleeping time decreases from 10 to 12 hours for the younger preschooler to 9 to 11 hours for the older preschooler. Dreams and nightmares may awaken the 3- or 4-year-old, causing fear and a move into bed with parents or older siblings. The 5-year-old sleeps quietly through the night without having to get up to urinate and has fewer nightmares.

Dreams and nightmares occur during the light stages of sleep. During deep stages of sleep the child may sleepwalk or have night terrors. Often children do not awaken after they sleepwalk. In night terrors the child screams or cries, is confused, has tachycardia and tachypnea, dilated pupils, and sometimes facial contortions and diaphoresis.

✔ Help the parents understand that reassurance is needed with night terrors. Sleep problems usually subside spontaneously, but the child and parents may need therapy if the problem persists several times weekly or over a period of time.

Health Promotion and Health Protection

Immunization Schedules. These will be adjusted to the individual child; however, the 4-year-old should receive a DTP booster and a refeeding of oral polio virus vaccine (17, 50). Frequency of tuberculin testing depends on geographic region and personal environment.

✔ Help parents realize that the state law of requiring immunizations prior to school entry is indeed a beneficial one, since the organisms that cause childhood communicable diseases cannot be eliminated from the environment. The decrease in these diseases and their harmful effects has resulted only because of mass *inoculations of a disease antigen* (**active immunity**) or an *antibody* (**passive immunity**). The minimal reaction is far better than acquiring the disease.

✔ Before giving an immunization ask yourself the following questions:

1. Has the parent given consent? Members of some religious groups, such as Church of Christ, Scientist (Christian Scientist) do not believe in immunizations. (The school district may allow these children to attend without immunization, based on parents' rights regarding their children.)
2. Is the vaccination (immunization) indicated based on the child's age and previous immunization record?
3. Are there any contraindications, such as allergy to any of the constituents of the vaccine; presence of another infectious disease (febrile condition, dermatitis) or immune deficiency disease; presence of malignancy or immunosuppressive therapy; or administration of gamma globulin, plasma, or blood

transfusion in the previous 6 to 8 weeks that would have given passive antibodies?
4. Has the parent been informed of the method (route of administration) and benefits and risks involved in inoculation?
5. Has the parent informed you of any reactions or difficulties that occurred with or after previous immunizations? If the child has a minor reaction, remaining doses may be cut in half or thirds to decrease possibility of a systemic reaction. The child then returns an additional number of times to receive the full immunization series.
6. Has the parent been told that the antigens to the various diseases may be given separately but are usually combined for convenience of administration?
7. Has the vaccine been stored according to manufacturer's recommendations (usually refrigerated) and is there a date of expiration (40, 50, 61)?

Dental Care. Because caries frequently begin at this age and spread rapidly, dental care is equally important. Deciduous teeth guide in the permanent ones; they should be kept in good repair. Fluoride is important for preventing caries. If the child has teeth with deep grooves, a plastic coating can be applied to the teeth to prevent tooth decay and loss. If deciduous teeth are lost too early, permanent teeth grow in abnormally. Teeth should be brushed after eating, using a method recommended by the dentist, and intake of refined sugars limited to help prevent tooth decay.

✔ Before entering school the child is usually required to have a physical examination (including urinalysis) and a dental examination. Refer to Appendices I and II for a schedule of health screening measures for the preschool child.

The preschooler has more freedom, independence, initiative, and desire to imitate adults but still has an immature understanding of danger and illness. This combination is likely to get him/her into hazardous situations.

Safety Promotion and Injury Control. A major responsibility of caretaking adults is safety promotion and injury control; the child needs watchfulness and a safe play area. The adult serves as a bodyguard while slowly teaching caution and keeping the environment as safe as possible. Other siblings can also take some, but not total, responsibility for the preschooler. Protecting the firstborn is simple, since you can put dangerous objects away and there is likely to be more time and energy for supervision. When there are a number of children in a family, the activities of the older children may provide objects or situations that are dangerous to the younger ones.

✔ Preschoolers need clear-cut safety rules, explained simply, repeatedly, and consistently; and you can help parents establish these. As the child learns to protect self, he/she should be allowed to take added responsibility for personal safety and given appropriate verbal recognition and praise that reinforces safe behavior. Constant threats, frequent physical punishment, and incessant "don'ts" should be avoided, for the child will learn to ignore them, feel angry or resentful, and purposefully rebel or defy adults, thus failing to learn about real danger. Also if the parent voices fear constantly, natural curiosity and the will to learn will be dulled; the child may fear every new situation.

✔ Explore information in this section with parents so that they and you can utilize these safety suggestions.

1. Begin safety teaching early. Teaching done in the toddler years, for example, pays off later.
2. When you must forbid, use simple command words in a firm voice without anger to convey the impression that you expect the child to obey, for example, "stop," "no."
3. Phrase safety rules and their reasons in positive rather than negative terms when possible. For example, say: "Play in the yard, not the street, or you'll get hurt by cars"; "Sit quietly in the car to avoid hurt"; "Put tiny things (coins, beads) that you find in here (jar, bowl, box)."
4. Teach the child his/her full name, address, and telephone number (including zip code) and teach the child how to utilize the police or adults in service roles for help.
5. Teach the child not to give information over the phone about him/herself or the family.
6. Encourage the child to share any "secrets," emphasize that he/she does not have to be afraid to say anything.
7. Tell the child not to leave home alone or with a stranger. He/she should use a "buddy" system when going somewhere.
8. Never leave the child alone in public or in a car, unattended.
9. Teach the child escape techniques, for example, how to unlock home doors or car doors.
10. Never leave the child home alone. Make sure that the babysitter is reliable.
11. Never allow play in or near a busy driveway or garage. Forbid street play if other play areas are available. Teach children to look carefully for and get away from cars. Drivers must take all possible precautions. A fenced yard or playground is ideal, although not always available.
12. Teach the child how safely to cross the street.
13. Teach the child to refuse gifts or rides from strangers, to avoid walking or playing alone on a

deserted street, road, or similar area, and about the possibility of child molesters or abductors.
14. Keep matches in containers and out of reach.
15. Dispose of or store out of reach and in a locked cabinet as many poisons as possible: rat and roach killer, insecticides, weed killer, kerosene, cleaning agents, medicines. The child is less likely to pull these out of cabinets or swallow these than when he/she was a toddler, but brightly colored containers or pills, powders, or liquids raise curiosity and experimentation. Bright-colored pills can be mistaken for candy.
16. Observe your child closely while he/she plays near water. Cover wells and cisterns. Fence ponds or swimming pools.
17. Keep stairways and nighttime play areas well lit.
18. Equip upstairs windows with sturdy screens and guards. Have hand rails for stairways.
19. Store knives, saws, and other sharp objects or power tools out of reach.
20. Remove doors from abandoned appliances or cars and campaign for legislation for appropriate disposal of these as well as mandatory door removal.
21. Discourage playing with or in the area of appliances or power tools while they are in operation: a washing machine with a wringer, a lawn mower, a saw, or a clothes dryer.
22. Use safety glass in glass doors or shower stalls; place decals on sliding doors at child's eye level (and adult's eye level, too) to prevent walking or running through them.
23. Use adhesive strips in the bathtub.
24. Avoid scatter rugs, debris, or toys cluttered on the floor in areas of traffic.
25. Use seatbelts in the car that are appropriate for the weight of the child.

✔ If the child continually fails to listen and obey, ask the following questions: Is the child able to hear? Is he/she intellectually able to understand? Are demands too many and expectations too great? Are statements too lengthy or abstract? Is anger expressed with teaching and discipline to the point that it interferes emotionally with the child's perception and judgment?

Accidents. These are the most common cause of death. About one-third of the accidental deaths are caused by motor vehicles; the next most common causes are drowning, burns from fire or hot water, and poisonings (23). Running through sliding glass doors in homes, locking self in an abandoned refrigerator or freezer, and electric shocks from electrical equipment also frequently cause severe injury or death. Falls can cause minor bumps, bruises, and lacerations. Animal bites are common.

✔ **Minor head injury** is *any trauma to the head that does not alter normal cerebral functioning.* What appears a very minor head injury can result in a subdural or epidural hematoma—the preschooler bears very close monitoring. Parents or caretakers should be taught to check the preschooler every 2 hours in the first 24 hours after injury. If the preschooler cannot be awakened, is mentally confused, is unusually restless, disturbed, or agitated, starts vomiting, has a severe headache, has different sized pupils (unless previously that way), has weakness of arms or legs, has drainage from ears or nose, or has some sort of fit or convulsion, medical help must be sought (40, 53, 61).

✔ **Minor lacerations,** *cuts,* should be examined for dirt and foreign objects even after they have been cleaned with warm water and soap. The laceration should be covered with a loose bandage that will keep out dirt and protect the wound from additional trauma. The parent or caretaker should watch for signs of infection: redness, heat, swelling, and drainage. The child should have updated tetanus prophylaxis (29, 49, 61).

✔ **Burns** are *thermal injuries to the skin.* A **first-degree burn** usually *shows redness only;* a **second-degree burn** causes *blister formation,* sometimes with peeling and weeping. Scalds often produce this type of burn. A **third-degree burn** *chars the skin, causing a whitish appearance, and involves tissue under the skin.* It may cause anesthesia. Flame and hot metal often cause third-degree burns (29, 40, 49, 61).

For a first-degree burn the affected area should be plunged into cold water for a few minutes. Gentle washing with soap and water should be sufficient. A second-degree burn should have the same initial treatment. Blisters that form should be left intact, and the burned area should be covered with a nonadherent gauze and a bulky, dry, sterile dressing. Tetanus immunization should be up to date. A third-degree burn should be seen by the health-care worker and physician, along with any second-degree burn that covers an area greater than an adult's hand size, any facial burns, and any burn in which child abuse or neglect is suspected (29, 40, 49, 61).

✔ *Accidental ingestions and poisonings* occur under the age of 5 years, sometimes even when preventive measures as discussed in Chapter 8 are used. These ingestions can cause a great variety of symptoms and signs. The following guidelines should be taught to parents. The parent or caretaker should look for an empty container nearby if sudden unusual symptoms or abnormal odor to breath or clothes are observed. Try to determine what and how much was ingested and when. Call the poison control center for help. If there are no contraindications to vomiting (either from reading the side of the container or from getting directions at the poison control center), induce vomiting with syrup of ipecac. Mechanical stimulation of the posterior pharynx can be used to induce vomiting *except* with ingestion of corrosive agents, such as lye, gasoline, or kerosene. The child should be taken to the nearest clinic that is set up to deal with these problems (29, 40, 49, 61).

The *bite of any animal* will probably have few symptoms other than pain at the site and puncture wounds or small lacerations. Dog bites are most common, although the child may have contact with other animals that bite or scratch. Bites from other children can also occur.

✔ The chief concern is the possibility of rabies. It is essential to establish the vaccination status of the biting animal, if possible, for if the animal is properly vaccinated, there is little chance of acquiring and transmitting the disease to humans. Rabies prophylaxis will be determined by the physician. The wound should be washed with copious amounts of soap and water. After the soap is well removed, Zephiran Chloride or 40 to 70 percent alcohol or povidone—iodine solution should then be applied. Tetanus prophylaxis should be up to date (6, 40).

✔ *Lead poisoning*, especially in preschoolers, will produce **encephalopathy,** *or brain dysfunction.* The onset is insidious, with weakness, irritability, weight loss, and vomiting, followed by personality changes and developmental regression. Convulsions and coma are late signs. Often history will reveal pica involving cracking paint in old homes, lead toys, old yellow and orange crayons, artist's paints, leaded gasoline, or fruit tree sprays (4).

A recent study undertook to investigate the average daily dietary lead intake of a cross-sectional sample of American children from birth to 5 years. Daily lead intake should not exceed 100 mg. The study showed a daily average of 62 mg but a range from 15 mg to 234 mg. The higher levels may represent mouthing of objects and hands as well as the ingestion of some nonfood substances, in addition to the lead content in food (4).

✔ Prevention lies in keeping the preschooler in a lead-free environment as much as possible; someone should watch everything that goes in his/her mouth. You may call the housing inspector, with the family's permission, to test paint for lead. In many cities landlords are required to repaint the house interior when lead paint is found. Treatment for severe cases of lead poisoning involves hospitalization. General measures are to prevent re-exposure to lead and to give the preschooler a high-calcium, high-phosphorus diet (milk) and large doses of vitamin D to help in removing lead from the blood by depositing it in the bones (4).

Common Health Problems: Prevention and Treatment

✔ Teach parents that scheduled health maintenance visits to the doctor or nurse practitioner are important for early detection of problems.

✔ *Abuse.* An all-too-common health problem for the young child is *abuse, neglect,* or *maltreatment.* Garbarino et al. (24) describes behaviors of the psychologically abusing parents (see Chapters 7 and 8) toward the young child. Other family members or day-care teachers may abuse the child physically. Sexual abuse may also occur. Federation (21) described the feelings and treatment for the sexually abused child ages 3 to 5 years. Be aware, also, that when you encounter children with some of the previous accidental occurrences or health problems, the origin of the problems may be the beatings, burns, shakings, handling, or neglect received at the hands of the parents, stepparents, day-care teacher, or other adult caretaker.

✔ *Vision.* Vision is usually tested in the 4-year-old with an E chart, which is composed of capital Es with their legs pointing in various directions. You will point to the Es and ask the child to show you which direction each one is pointing. The child can use his/her fingers; verbalization is not necessary. First one eye and then the other should be tested. Visual fields can be tested much as with an adult. The parent or caretaker can hold the child, ensuring that his/her head remains straight forward. Using a small toy to place in the various visual fields is effective and can be made into a game. Vision can also be tested using Allen cards from the Denver eye screening test.

Colorblindedness is more likely found in boys than in girls. Thus, if a boy knows his colors, he can be asked to identify the basic colors in certain toys.

If an infant or toddler has had a "persistent deviating eye," he/she should have been referred to an ophthalmologist. **Strabismus** remains one of the most commonly seen abnormalities in preschool children. *Caused by the misalignment of each eye's optic axis, one or both of the child's eyes will turn in, out, up, or down.* **Double vision (diplopia)** next develops, followed by an *irreversible loss of vision in the suppressed eye* (**amblyopia**), if not treated early.

✔ Functional amblyopia can be remedied through the use of corrective lenses, contact lenses, prisms, and vision training. Patching of one eye is often employed. One test for detecting strabismus is to shine a penlight into the child's eyes. The light reflection should appear in the same position on each pupil if strabismus is not present (29, 40, 43, 49, 61).

Conjunctivitis is an *inflammation of the eyelid or*

conjunctiva, or both; it is caused by bacterial or viral infection or an allergic reaction. The allergic reaction is often associated with pollen irritation. The preschooler may experience mild irritation, excessive lacrimation, and redness but will have normal vision.

✔ Cool compresses may ease the irritation. If the conjunctivitis is purulent, refer the parents to a physician, because antimicrobial drops are necessary (29, 40, 43, 49, 61).

Hearing Loss. This should be suspected if the preschooler does not seem to hear as well as previously and has recurrent otitis media. Socialization and speech can become blocked if this occurs. Play techniques can be used with the preschooler to evaluate hearing. For example, earphones that will transmit various sounds can be placed on a child. He/she can be asked to put a peg in a pegboard every time a sound is heard. The result will be a variation of pure tone and audiometry (29, 40, 43, 49, 61).

✔ **Acute purulent otitis media** is usually a bacterial *infection of the middle ear with an accumulation of purulent fluid in the middle-ear cavity.* The preschooler will complain of earache, often have a fever, and have decreased hearing in the affected ear. Sometimes the tympanic membrane will perforate and the purulent fluid will flow into the external canal. A nurse with physical assessment skills can make this diagnosis with an otoscope. Antibiotic treatment should be prescribed (29, 40, 43, 45, 49, 61).

As in toddlerhood, susceptibility to *upper respiratory infections* remains high. Because the lymphatic tissue known as tonsils and adenoids is more abundant at this time than in later life, these structures are often involved in the infectious process. Formerly it was nearly standard procedure for children to have tonsillectomies and adenoidectomies. However, with the evolving belief that the lymphatic tissue would later help with body defenses, and realizing the risks involved, as well as the fact that children still had upper respiratory infections after these surgeries, the trend went away from these procedures. "Large" tonsils, recurrent colds and sore throats, recurrent streptococcal pharyngitis, parental pressure, school absence, and "chronic tonsillitis" *are not* valid reasons for tonsillectomy and adenoidectomy. Valid reasons for surgery would include persistent nasal or oral obstruction, recurrent peritonsillar abscess, suspected tonsillar tumor, recurrent cervical lymph gland infection, and, in some cases, recurrent ear problems (29, 40, 43, 49, 61).

Genitourinary Conditions. **Urinary tract infection** is a *bacterial infection of a part or all of the urinary tract, the collecting system of the kidneys and the bladder.* In preschoolers, this condition is 10 to 20 times more common in females than in males. The infection may be completely asymptomatic and may be picked up on a routine health screening visit, or the child may complain of urgency and frequency of urination, dysuria, and flank and suprapubic pain. The urine may be foul smelling or cloudy. The child may have an unexplained fever and be irritable or lethargic. After the appropriate urine studies, the preschooler will be placed on an appropriate antibiotic (29, 40, 43, 49, 61). Teach the preschool girl to wipe the perineum from front to back after urination and defecation to avoid bringing *E. coli* or other organisms toward the urethra.

Enuresis, *the involuntary passage of urine,* occurs nocturnally in about 10 to 15 percent of 5-year-olds. Usually the cause is unknown. Various theories have been speculated: psychological factors, small bladder capacity, slow neurological maturation, and deep sleep state. Boys are affected more frequently than girls and there is a familial tendency.

✔ The parents or caretakers of the preschooler should be counseled that if urine tests have ruled out infection, and if they can find no other contributing factors, this condition is usually self-limiting (5 percent of 10-year-olds and 1 percent of 15-year-olds still have the problem). Above all, the preschooler should not be ridiculed or punished for enuresis. The psychological problems can remain long after the enuresis is gone if the situation is improperly handled (29, 40, 43, 49, 61).

Nonspecific vulvovaginitis, *inflammation of the vulva and vagina, may involve discharge, pruritis, and erythema.* This type of vulvovaginitis, in which no specific organism is responsible, is usually due to poor hygiene. It may be aggravated by tight, nonporous undergarments.

✔ Tell the parents or caretakers to use the following measures to *prevent* this condition. If smegma is caked in the interlabial grooves, gently remove it. The child should wear loose, clean, cotton underpants. Bathe the perineum with warm water and a nonperfumed, nonmedicated soap twice daily and after defecation. Do not rub the perineum too dry; rather, blot. Educate the child about need for this hygiene and watch the preschooler practice. If the preschooler has vulvovaginitis, put her in a sitz bath at least once daily. Bubble bath in the bath water should not be used because it is irritating to mucous membrane and contributes to vulvitis. Use an acidifying solution of 2 tablespoons of white vinegar per quart of warm water. If the vulva is very swollen and tender, the caretaker may additionally apply cold compresses of tap water or Burow's (aluminum acetate) solution for 20 minutes four times a day (40, 42, 53, 61).

✔ *Other Health Problems.* Diarrhea can be a problem caused by several sources. *Giardia lambdia,* a protozoan parasite, and *Salmonella* are two causative organisms analyzed from stools of preschoolers, primarily in day-care centers. Proper handwashing after toileting, having separate tables for diapering and eating, and not allowing preschoolers in community wading pools are a few precautions.

✔ *Postural problems* may be developed at this age. You can find and help correct early deviations by observing the child anteriorly, laterally, posteriorly, and in a bending forward position.

Measles is a *highly contagious viral disease with serious complications and is best described by its rash, the 3 c's—coryza, cough, and conjunctivitis—and Koplik's spots which appear on the buccal mucosa 2 days before the rash begins.* Fever is persistent throughout the second or third day of the rash; the rash begins about the face and hairline and descends down the body.

✔ Prevention is possible by giving the live measles vaccine at 15 months of age along with mumps and rubella vaccine (MMR). Complications of the disease are pneumonia, otitis media, encephalitis, and tuberculosis (since tuberculin sensitivity is depressed during this period). If the child contracts measles, tell the parents to isolate the child from the time the diagnosis is made through the third day of the rash. Public health authorities should be notified immediately so control measures can be instituted. The immune status of the family and immediate contacts must be determined. Immune globulin should be given to those contacts not immunized. There is no specific therapy for the child with measles. Adequate fluid and nutritional intake is essential. A darkened room is traditional and may be more comfortable than a brightly lit one, but will not have any particular effect on the conjunctivitis. Antipyretic medicine can be given for fever, and if complications develop, specific antibiotic therapy is warranted (29, 40, 43, 49, 61).

Chronic health problems of the preschooler include glomerulonephritis (*an infection of the kidneys following infection elsewhere in the body*), leukemia, congenital heart defects, hemophilia, epilepsy, mental retardation, cerebral palsy, and emotional illness such as autism. For more information, consult a pediatric nursing book (28, 40, 61).

Reactions to Illness and Hospitalization. During this stage, when the child has heightened feelings of sexuality, fears of dependency and separation, fantasies, feelings of narcissism, and rivalry with parents, he/she is particularly vulnerable to fears about body damage. The child perceives and fears dental, medical, and surgical procedures as mutilating, intrusive, punishing, or abandonment. The resulting conflicts, fears, guilt, anger, or excessive concern about the body can persist and influence personality development into adulthood.

✔ Teach parents that many of these negative reactions can be averted by introducing the child to medical facilities and health workers when he/she is well. The best teaching is positive example. If the parent takes the child with him/her to the physician and dentist, and if the child observes courteous professionals, a procedure which does not hurt (or an explanation of why it will hurt), and a positive response from the parent, a great deal of teaching is accomplished. These visits can be reinforced with honest answers to the many questions the preschooler will have.

Hospitalization should be avoided if possible. Preparation for hospitalization is important to reduce the separation anxiety and grief and mourning response described in Chapter 8. Most families have had some experience with a hospital and can give some explanation to the child.

✔ Although children are forbidden in certain areas of a hospital, parents may arrange for a tour of the pediatric ward. The child should be told that special caring people work there and that if he/she is ever hospitalized, the parents will stay close by. The child can be further prepared through play, books, and appropriate films. Emphasize the importance of continued, ample contact with the child whenever either parent or child is hospitalized. Advise parents to (1) trust their intuition (they know the child best); (2) shop for a doctor and hospital; (3) prepare themselves so that they can prepare the child; (4) prepare the child a few days before hospitalization; and (5) be present at important times.

There are several books that will help ease the transition from home to hospital: *Elizabeth Gets Well*, by Dr. Alfons Weber; *Curious George Goes to the Hospital*, by H. A. Rey; *Wendy Well and Billy Better*, by John Walzenbach and Nancy Cline; and *What Happens When You Go to the Hospital*, by Arthur Shay.

✔ As a nurse, you will be in a position to offset the negative effects of hospitalization through planning individualized care, use of play or art therapy, and involvement in decision and policy making. The hospital needs to make the ward as homelike as possible through gay decor and furnishings, provision for toys, a playroom, and central dining area. The staff can wear pastel uniforms or smocks and provide for the child to remain in his/her own clothes, keep a favorite toy, eat uninterrupted by procedures, and follow normal living routines when possible. Flexible visiting hours are essential, since the presence of the mother can dramatically revive a child's interest in getting well and improve eating, sleeping, and general behavior. Because a mother feels concern, partial helplessness, and perhaps guilt when her child is hospitalized, she may have an impaired relationship with her child and consequently the entire family. Family affection, concern, and questions should never be considered an interference. Instead, the family should be seen as collaborators in care. Answer questions and ask questions related to parents' questions to clarify further and inform or reinforce their ideas. Ideally, if the parent wishes, he/she should be allowed to stay with the child during care, procedures, tests, or treatments. If not feasible, one nurse should consistently care for the child while involving the parent as much as possible.

✔ The parent needs to see the child receiving competent care, as well as to feel that he/she is important to the child and capable as a parent, even if staying with the child is not possible. Encourage the parent to talk about feelings of fear, anxiety, guilt, shame, or sadness that may be present and related to the child's illness or hospitalization or children left at home. Avoid a critical attitude, voice tone, or disapproving nonverbal behavior that conveys to the parent that he/she is not managing well as a parent. Help parents to talk about the unique aspects of their child's or family life so that care can be truly individualized. For example, the child may prefer to wear his shorts instead of pajamas in bed. If an Afro-American child with an intricate hairstyle that was just arranged before admission is admitted, do not automatically do a routine admission shampoo. Realize that the Oriental or American Indian child may not talk as freely, at least initially, as the average Caucasian child, but this response reflects family and cultural child-rearing practices and does not mean that the child is retarded or does not understand you.

✔ Obtain a developmental history from the mother on admission and use it to plan care to follow the child's usual living routine. Of great importance is the attitude of the staff caring for the child. The staff should be like the ideal parent: loving, honest, respectful, accepting, consistent. Cajoling, threatening, or rejection cannot help the child cope with problems. Acknowledge that children suffer great physical and emotional pain. Help the child get in touch with feelings and the pain. Do not tell him/her not to cry or that a procedure will not hurt when it will. Help the child displace aggression onto toys or staff rather than onto parents. Allow the child to be angry. Objective involvement is also important to avoid showing favoritism to only certain children.

Psychosocial Concepts

Cognitive-Intellectual Development

The child in Preoperational Stage is perceptually bound, unable to reason logically about concepts that are discrepant from visual cues. The child learns by being confronted with others' opinions and being actively involved with objects and processes (60). More important than the facts learned are the attitudes the child forms toward knowledge, learning, people, and the environment. Cognition and learning, at least partly a result of language learning and perceptual ability, can be studied through the child's handling of the physical environment and in connection with the concepts of number, causality, and time, abstractions highly developed in western civilization (54).

✔ By helping parents understand the cognitive development of their child, including concept formation, you will help them stimulate intellectual growth realistically, without expecting too much. **Concepts** *come about by giving precepts (events, things and experiences) a meaningful label; the name or label implies similarity to some other things having the same name and difference from things having a different name.* **Concept formation** *develops with perception progressing from diffuse to roughly differentiated and finally to sharply differentiated awareness of stable and coordinated objects.* The first concept is formed when a word comes to designate a crudely defined area of experience. As the late toddler and early preschooler acquire a number of words, each representing a loosely defined notion or thing, the global meaning becomes a simple concrete concept. As perceived characteristics of things and events become distinguished from each other, the child becomes aware of differences among words, objects, and experiences such as dog and cat, baby and doll, men and daddy, approval and disapproval. However, the preschooler cannot yet define attributes and cannot make explicit comparisons of the objects. The attributes are an absolute part of the object such as bark and dog; hence the child is said to *think concretely*. What he/she sees or hears can be named, which is different from conceptual or abstract thinking about the object (54).

Concrete concepts become true concepts when the late preschooler can compare, combine, and describe them and think and talk about their attributes. At this point, the child can deal with differences between concepts, such as "dogs bark, people talk," but not until after the ages 6 or 7 will he/she be able to deal with opposites and similarities together (54).

Some of the influences on concept development include the child's inability to distinguish between his/her own feelings and outside events; the ability to be impressed by the external, obvious features of a situation or thing rather than its essential features; his/her awareness of gaps in a situation; and emotional or contextual significance of words. The concreteness typical of a preschooler's concepts is found in the rambling, loosely jointed, circumstantial descriptions. Everything is equally important and must be included. One must listen closely to get the central theme, since young children learn things in bunches and not in a systematic, organized way. They can memorize and recite many things, but they cannot paraphrase or summarize their learning (35, 54).

Concepts of Relationships. These involve time, space, number, and causation, are more abstract than those based on the immediately observable properties of things and are greatly determined by culture (54).

Time Concept. For the preschooler, time is beginning to move; the past is measured in hours, and the future is a myth. At first, formal time concepts have nothing to do with personal time. Adults are seen as changeless while the child feels that he/she can mature in a hurry; thus the preschooler thinks he/she can grow up fast and marry his parent. Time concepts are further described in Table 9-2.

Spatial Concepts. These differ markedly in children and adults. There are five major stages in the development of spatial concepts. First, there is **action space,** *consisting of the location or regions to which the child moves.* Second, **body space** *refers to the child's own awareness of directions and distances in relation to his/her own body.* Third, there is **object space,** *where objects are located relative to each other, and without reference to the child's body.* The fourth and fifth stages, **map space** and **abstract space,** *are interrelated and depend on knowing directions of east, west, south, and north; allocating space in visual images to nations, regions, towns, rooms; and the ability to deal with maps, geographical or astronomical ideas, and three-dimensional space* that use symbolic (verbal or mathematical) relationships (54).

The preschool child has action space and moves along familiar locations and explores new terrain. He/she is beginning to orient self to body space and object space through play and exploration of his/her own body, up and down, front and back, sideways, next to, near and far, and later left and right. The child is not able until about age 6 to understand object space as a unified whole; he/she will first see a number of unrelated routes or spaces. He/she is generally aware of specific objects and habitual routes. The child does not see self and objects as part of a larger integrated space with multiple possibilities for movement. Map space and abstract space are not understood until later.

Quantitative Concepts. *Notions of quantity* are developed in the early preschool years, such as one and more than one, bigger and smaller. Understanding of the quantity or amount represented by a number is not related to the child's ability to count to 10, 20, or higher. Nor can he/she transfer numbers to notions of value of money, although he/she may imitate adults and play store, passing money back and forth. Ordinal numbers, indicating successions rather than totals, develop crudely in "me first" or "me last"; the concept of second or third will develop later. The preschooler cannot simultaneously take account of different dimensions, such as 1 quart equals 2 pints or equal volume in different-shaped containers (54). (See also Table 9-2).

Concepts of Causality. *The way of perceiving cause and effect* is magical. Things simply are. The child may be pleased or displeased with events but does not understand what brought them about. He/she does precausal thinking, confusing physical and mechanical causation or natural phenomena with psychological, moral, or sequential causes. He/she frequently says "n' then," indicating causal sequence. When the child asks "why?" he/she is probably looking for justification rather than causation. Most things are taken for granted; the child assumes that people, including self, or some motivated inanimate being are the causes of events. Perception of the environment is **animistic,** *endowing all things with the qualities of life Westerners reserve for human beings.* There is little notion of accident or coincidence. It takes some time to learn that there are impersonal forces at work in the world. Thinking is also **egocentric:** *Things and events are seen from a personal and narrow perspective and happening because of self* (54).

The late preschooler fluctuates between reality and fantasy and a materialistic and animistic view of the world; most adults never completely leave behind the magical thinking typical of the preschooler. The child plays with the idea of a tree growing out of the head, what holes feel like to the ground, and growing up starting as an adult. The adult finds no meaning in music, art, literature, love, and possibly even science and mathematics without fantasy or magic.

Preoperational Stage. The Preoperational Stage is divided into the Preconceptual and Intuitive Phases. During the Preconceptual Phase, from 2 to 4 years of age, the child gathers facts as they are encountered but can neither separate reality from fantasy nor classify or define events in a systematic manner. He/she is beginning to develop mental strategies from concept formation; concepts are constructed in a global way. He/she is capable of perceiving gross outward appearances but sees only one aspect of an object or situation at a time. For example, if you say, "Take the yellow pill," he/she will focus on either yellow or pill but cannot focus on both aspects at once. The child is unable to use time, space, equivalence, and class inclusion in concept formation. During the Intuitive Phase, the child gains increasing, but still limited, ability to develop concepts. He/she defines one property at a time, has difficulty stating the definition, but knows how to use the object. The child uses **transductive logic,** *going from general to specific in explanation,* rather than deductive or inductive logic. He/she begins to label, classify in ascending or descending order, do seriation, and note cause-effect relationships, even though true cause-effect understanding does not occur (42, 59).

The Preoperational stage is characterized by the following: egocentric thought; literal thinking with absence of reference system; intermingling of fantasy, intuition, and reality; **absolute thought,** *seeing all or nothing without shades of gray or any relativity;* **centering,** *focusing on a single aspect of an object,* causing distorted reasoning; lack of concept of **reversibility,** *for every action, there is one that cancels it;* static thinking; difficulty remembering what he/she started talking about so that when the sentence is finished he/she is talking about something else; and inability to state cause-effect relationships, categories, or abstractions, believing that events that occur together belong together (35, 42, 59).

In general, the preschooler has a consuming curiosity. Learning is vigorous, aggressive, and intrusive. The imagination creates many situations he/she wishes to explore. Judgment is overshadowed by curiosity and excitement. The preschooler has begun to develop such concepts as friend, aunt, uncle; accepting responsibility; independence; passage of time, spatial relationships; use of abstract words, numbers, colors; and the meaning of cold, tired, and hungry. Attention span is lengthening.

✔ The child's ability to grasp reality varies with individual intelligence and potential intelligence, the social milieu, and opportunities to explore the world, solve problems independently, ask questions, and get answers. (Table 9-2 summarizes major characteristics of mental development to help you in assessment [23, 25, 32, 38, 42, 54, 57, 59].)

An educational trend is underway to teach the preschooler more factual content, to provide some schooling from infancy on, as seen in the large number of preschoolers in the United States who are enrolled in preprimary-school programs. Impetus for this trend stems from the (1) Head Start program in the 1960s, (2) women's liberation campaigns for day-care centers, (3) the growing realization by the middle class that competition for school achievement and college entrance will continue to be intense, (4) awareness that most of the brain is developed by age 4, and (5) the theory that at least half of all human intelligence is developed by age 4, possibly even by 9 months. Another theory states that by age 5 the IQ is basically established, that attitudes toward learning and patterns of thinking will guide the child for the rest of his life (32, 38, 57). However, he/she needs informal learning opportunities, not facts.

✔ Parents can enhance the child's growth by realizing the importance of the following approaches. Share this information with them. Refer to the article by Pontious for ways to explain nursing procedures to a child (42).

✔ The single most critical factor in the child's learning is a loving caretaker, since that is whom the child imitates. How the mothering person speaks to, touches, and plays with the child governs the potential for socialization and cognitive development. A child's problem-solving abilities are shaped by the parents' method for handling problems and by opportunities for problem solving. In families where everyone gets a chance to speak out and jointly explore a problem, the child learns to express him/herself logically. Automatic obedience or acceptance of parental commands or decisions will interfere with reasoning (30). Important also are the opportunities provided for the child to learn, encouraging him/her to handle objects, explore, ask questions, and to play a variety of games. In the home the child learns how to learn or how not to learn. Teaching the child is more than telling him/her what to do. It involves demonstration, listening, talking about the situation in direct and understandable terms; and giving reasons. Cognitive development includes more than fluency with words, a good verbal memory, and information. It includes ability to use imagination, form mental pictures, engage in fantasy appropriately, along with art, music, and other creative activities. It includes expanding skills in logical thinking. Most important, it involves increasing integration of many kinds of brain functions. Much integrated learning comes from the child engaging in motor activity, play, language games, talking with adults and peers; paying attention to trivial as well as important aspects of the environment (30, 35).

Creative methods of teaching for preschoolers is seen in educational programs such as *Sesame Street* or *Mister Rogers' Neighborhood*. *Sesame Street,* presented as a lively, fast-moving, colorful program, emphasizes the alphabet, number concepts, similarities and differences, and positive body image. *Mister Rogers' Neighborhood* emphasizes positive body image, learning how things are done, and a personal one-to-one relationships between Mister Rogers and each child. It is difficult to assess the effect of these programs on the overall cognitive development of the child. Such programs appear to improve rote learning, although there is not much evidence that long-range concept formation is much different from what develops in children not exposed to these programs.

Because television is essentially a passive and solitary activity, more than occasional viewing may inter-

TABLE 9-2. Assessment of Mental Development

THREE YEARS	FOUR YEARS	FIVE YEARS
Knows he/she is a person separate from another. Knows own sex and some sex differences.	Senses self one among many.	Aware of cultural and other differences between people and the two sexes. Mature enough to fit into simple type of culture. Can tell full name and address. Remains calm if lost away from home.
Resists commands but distractible and responsive to suggestions. Can ask for help. Desire to please. Friendly. Sense of humor.	States alibis because more aware of attitude and opinions of others. Self-critical, appraises good and bad of self. Does not like to admit inabilities, excuses own behavior. Praises self; bosses or criticizes others. Likes recognition for achievement. Heeds others' thoughts and feelings; expresses own.	Dependable. Increasing independence. Can direct own behavior; but fatigue, excessive demands, fantasy, and guilt interfere with assuming self-responsibility. Admits when needs help. Moves from direct to internalized action, from counting what he/she can touch to counting in thought; uses more clues.
Uses language rather than physical activity to communicate.	Active use of language. Active learning. Likes to make rhymes, to hear stories with exaggeration and humor, dramatic songs. Knows nursery rhymes. Tells action implied in picture books.	Improves use of symbol system, concept formation. Repeats long sentences accurately. Can carry plot in story. Defines objects in terms of use. States relationship between two events.
Imaginative. Better able to organize thoughts. Can bargain with him/her. Sacrifices immediate pleasure for promise of future gain.	Highly imaginative yet literal, concrete thinking. Can organize his/her experience. Increasing reasoning power and critical thinking capacity. Makes crude comparisons.	Less imaginative. Asks details. Can be reasoned with logically. More accurate, relevant, practical, sensible than 4-year-old. Asks to have words defined. Seeks reality.
Understands simple directions; follows normal routines of family life, and does minor errands.	Concept of 1, 2, 3. Counts to 5. Does some home chores. Generalizes.	Begins to understand money. Does more home chores with increasing competence. Can determine which of two weights heavier. Idea in head precedes drawing on paper or physical activity. Interested in meaning of relatives.
Knows age. Meager comprehension of past and future. Knows mostly today.	Realizes birthday is one in a series and that birthday is measure of growth. Knows when next birthday is. Knows age. Birthday and holidays significant because aware of units of time. Loves parties related to holiday. Conception of time. Knows day of week.	Understands week as a unit of time. Knows day of week. Sense of time and duration increasing. Knows how old will be on next birthday. Knows month and year. Adults seen as changeless. Memory surprisingly accurate.
Has attention span of 10 to 15 minutes.	Has attention span of 20 minutes.	Has attention span of 30 minutes.

fere with the purposes that more traditional play activities offer (see section on Play Patterns pp. 277 to 280). Thus television viewing can negatively affect self-concept and social skills, as well as motor, cognitive, and emotional learning (32, 38, 57).

✔ Explore the use of television with parents. You can teach parents to see themselves as a parent educator rather than as "only a housewife" or "his pal, Dad." Parents can stimulate the intellectual development of their child by providing various practices: creating many and varied opportunities to learn about people and their environment; avoiding doing too much for the child; sharing activities with him/her; talking to him/her about situations the adult and child are in (shopping, cooking a meal, laundering); providing an interesting home; giving the child freedom to roam and follow natural curiosity within safe limits; giving daily individual attention to the child; obtaining information about child development and rearing from books, films, and other parents; experimenting with games and child-rearing practices and observing feedback from the child to determine which meet his/her needs; avoiding the push to learn academic subjects too early, causing undue frustration and a negative attitude about learning and school later. The child will sense which activities provide interest and challenges without excess difficulty. Let him/her develop his/her own learning style and see you and other adults as sources of information and ideas.

Communication Patterns

People have three types of communication at their disposal: (1) somatic or physical symptoms such as flushed skin color or increased respirations; (2) action such as play or movement; and (3) verbal expression. The preschool child uses all these.

Learning to use verbal expression—language—to communicate is an ongoing developmental process that is affected directly by the child's interaction with others. Language skills are enhanced, expanded, and refined as the child explores ideas with others and experiences a variety of social and educational environments. Language, cognition, and socialization are complex and interwoven. Verbal reasoning ability is dependent on the audible monologue of early toddler thinking, which then develops into inner speech and verbal thought (38, 57).

The child uses *language* for many reasons: to maintain social rapport, gain attention, get information, seek meaning about his/her experience, note how others' answers fit personal thoughts, play with words, and gain relief from anxiety. He/she asks why, what, when, where, how, repeatedly.

A child learns language from hearing it and using it. Words are at first empty shells until he/she has experiences to match. Parents should provide age-appropriate experiences so the child learns that words and actions go together. Equally important, parents should avoid saying one thing and doing another. Attaining trust in the utility and validity of verbal communication, learning that talking helps rather than hinders life, is crucial to transition from infancy to school years. If talking does not gain response from others or help the child solve problems and relate to those he/she needs, or if the world is too troublesome, the child is likely to find refuge in fantasy and neglect social, communicative meanings of language.

Directing his/her own life depends on language and an understanding of the meaning of words and logic with which they are used. When the child acquires language, he/she gradually becomes freed from tangible, concrete experiences and can internalize visual symbols, develop memory and recall, fragment the past, project the future, and differentiate fantasy from reality.

✔ Language is also learned from being read to and having printed material available. Share the following suggestions with parents for choosing books for the preschooler. The book should be durable, have large print that does not fill the entire page, and be colorfully illustrated. The concepts should be expressed concretely in simple sentences and should tell a tale that fits the child's fantasy conception of the world, such as a story with animals and objects who can talk and think like people. Or the story should tell about the situations he/she ordinarily faces, such as problems with playmates, discovery of the preschooler's world, nightmares, or the arrival of a new baby.

✔ Follow and share with the significant adults in the child's life these *effective ways of talking with the preschooler:*

1. Try to maintain mutual respect as you talk with the child.
2. Do not discourage talking, questions, or the make-believe in the child's language; verbal explorations are essential to learn language. Answers to questions should meet needs as well as give him/her an awareness of adult attitudes and feelings about the topics discussed.
3. Tell the truth to the best of your ability and on the child's level of understanding. Admit if the answer is unknown, and seek the answer with the child. A lie is eventually found out and causes a loss of trust in that adult as well as in others.
4. Do not make a promise unless you can keep it.
5. Respond to the relationship or feelings in the child's experience rather than the actual object or event. Talk about the child's feelings instead of

agreeing or disagreeing with what he/she says. Help the child understand what he/she feels rather than why he/she feels it.

6. Precede statements of advice and instruction with a statement of understanding of the child's feelings. When the child is feeling upset emotionally, he/she cannot listen to instructions, advice, consolation, or constructive criticism.
7. Do not give undue attention to slang or curse words and do not punish the child for using them. The child uses these words for shock value, and attention or punishment emphasizes the importance of the words. Remain relaxed and give the child a more difficult or different word to say. If he/she persists in using the unacceptable word, the adult may say, "I'm tired of hearing that word, say ———"; ask him/her not to say the word again since it may hurt others, or use distraction. Children learn unacceptable words as they learn all others, and parents would be wise to listen to their own vocabulary.
8. Sit down if possible when participating or talking with children. You are more approachable when at their physical level.
9. Seek to have a warm, friendly relationship without thrusting yourself on the child. How you feel about the child is more important than what you say or do.
10. Through attentive listening and interested facial expression, convey a tell-me-more-about-it attitude to encourage the child to communicate.
11. Regard some speech difficulties as normal. Ignore stuttering that does not persist. Often the child thinks faster than he/she can articulate speech.
12. Talk casually. Do not bombard the child with verbal information.

✔ Table 9-3 is a guide for assessing language skills of the preschooler. During assessment, keep in mind that how the child's parents and other family members speak and the language opportunities the child has influence considerably his/her language skills (25, 26, 32, 38, 57).

Play Patterns

Play is the work of the child. Play occupies most of the child's waking hours and serves to consolidate and enlarge his/her previous learning and promote adaptation. Play has elements of reality, and there is an earnestness about it.

The preschooler is intrusive in play, bombarding others by purposeful or accidental physical attack. He/she is into people's ears and minds by loud, assertive talking; into space by vigorous gross motor activities; into objects through exploration; and into the unknown by consuming curiosity (20).

The preschool years are the pregang stage in which the child progresses from solitary and parallel play to cooperating for a longer time in a larger group. He/she identifies somewhat with a play group; follows rules, is aware of the status of self compared with others; develops perception of social relationships; begins the capacity for self-criticism; and states traits and characteristics of others which he/she likes or dislikes. At first the child spends brief, incidental periods of separation from the parents. The time away from them increases in length and frequency, and eventually the orientation shifts from family to peer group (19, 35, 36).

A **peer** *is a person with approximately equal status, a companion, often of the same sex and age,* with whom one can share mutual concerns. The **peer group** *is a relatively informal association of equals who share common play experiences with emphasis on common rules and understanding the limits which the group places on the individual.* The preschool play group differs from later ones in that it is loosely organized; the activity of the group may be continuous but membership changes as the child joins or leaves the group at will, and the choice of playmates is relatively restricted in kind and number. This is the first introduction to a group which assesses him/her as a child from a child's point of view. The preschooler is learning about entering a new, different, very powerful world when he/she joins the group. Although social play is enjoyed, the child feels a need for solitary play at times.

The number and sex of siblings as well as the parent's handling of the child's play seems to influence behavior with the play group. If the family rejects the child, he/she may feel rejected by peers even when the child is not rejected, causing self-isolation, inability to form close friendships, and ultimately real rejection.

Purposes of Play. The natural mode of expression for the child is play. Purposes of play include the following:

1. Develop and improve muscular strength, coordination, and balance.
2. Work off excess physical energy.
3. Communicate with others, establish friendships, and develop concern for others.
4. Learn cooperation and sharing.
5. Express imagination, creativity, and initiative.
6. Imitate and learn about social activity and adult roles.
7. Test and deal with reality.
8. Explore, investigate, and manipulate features of the adult world.

9. Build self-esteem.
10. Feel a sense of power, make things happen, explore and experiment.
11. Provide for intellectual, sensory, and language development and dealing with concrete experiences in symbolic terms.
12. Assemble novel aspects of the environment.
13. Learn about self and how others see him/her.
14. Practice leader and follower roles.
15. Have fun, express joy, and feel the pleasure of mastery.
16. Work through a painful physical or emotional state by repetition in play so that it is more bearable and assimilated into the child's self-concept.

Play Materials. These should be simple, sturdy, durable, and free from unnecessary hazards. They need not be expensive. The child should have adequate space and equipment that is unstructured enough to allow for creativity and imagination to work unfettered. He/she will enjoy trips to parks and playgrounds. Often creative, stimulating toys can be made from ordinary household articles: plastic pot cleaners, empty thread spools, a bell, yarn, or empty boxes covered with washable adhesive paper. The child may like the box more than the toy.

There is increasing emphasis on high technology, interactive, and weaponry toys. These toys actually stifle imagination and discovery, and weaponry toys may cause fears, heighten aggressive fantasies, as well

TABLE 9–3. Assessment of Language Development

THREE YEARS	FOUR YEARS	FIVE YEARS
Vocabulary of at least 900 words. Uses language understandably; uses some sounds experimentally. Understands simple reasons. Uses some adjectives and adverbs.	Vocabulary of at least 1500 words. Uses language confidently. Concrete speech. Increasing attention span. Uses "I." Imitates and plays with words. Defines a few simple words. Talks in sentences. Uses plurals frequently. Comprehends prepositions.	Vocabulary of at least 2100 words. Uses language efficiently, correctly. No difficulty understanding others' spoken words. Meaningful sentences. Increasing skill with grammar.
Talks in simple sentences about things. Repeats sentence of six syllables. Uses plurals in speech. Collective monologue; does not appear to care whether another is listening. Some random, inappropriate answers. Sings simple songs.	Talks incessantly while doing other activities. Asks many questions. Demands detailed explanations with "why." Carries on long involved conversation. Exaggerates; boasts; tattles. May use profanity for attention. Frequently uses "everything." Tells family faults outside of home without restraint. Tells story combining reality and fantasy; appears to be lying. Likes to sing.	Talks constantly. No infantile articulation. Repeats sentences of 12 or more syllables. Asks searching questions, meaning of words, how things work. Can tell a long story accurately, but may keep adding to reality to make story more fantastic. Sings relatively well.
Knows first and family name. Names figures in a picture. Repeats three numbers. Likes to name things.	Calls people names. Names three objects he/she knows in succession. Counts to 5 without help. Repeats four numbers. Knows which line is longer. Names one or more colors.	Counts to 10 or further without help. Names four colors, usually red, green, blue, yellow.
Talks to self or imaginary playmate. Expresses own desires and limits frequently.	Talks with imaginary playmate of same sex and age. Seeks reassurance. Interested in things being funny. Likes puns.	Sense of social standards and limits seen in language use.

as cause injury and sometimes death. Young children need to direct their games, to be in control of their play and their fantasies. They use play to work out problems, to practice skills, and to act out roles in preparation for later real life experiences. If the toy is too limiting, it will be cast aside by the child, regardless of how much the parent enjoys it.

The play materials that are available will determine the play activities. Play materials are enjoyed for different reasons. For example, **physical activity,** *which facilitates development of motor skills,* is provided through play with balls, shovel, broom, ladder, swing, trapeze, slide, boxes, climbing apparatus, boards, sled, wagon, tricycle, bicycle with training wheels, wheelbarrow, and blocks. **Dramatic play,** *which is related to the ability to classify correctly objects, take another's perspective, and do problem solving,* is afforded through large building blocks, sandbox and sand toys, dolls, housekeeping toys, farm or other occupational toys, cars and other vehicles, and worn out adult clothes for dress-up. **Creative playthings,** *which promote constructive, nonsocial, cognitive, and emotional*

TABLE 9–4. Assessment of Play Characteristics

THREE YEARS	FOUR YEARS	FIVE YEARS
Enjoys active and sedentary play.	Increasing physical and social play.	More varied activity. More graceful in play.
Likes toys in orderly form. Puts away toys with supervision.	Puts away toys when reminded.	Puts away toys by self.
Fantasy not yielding too much to reality. Likes fairy tales.	Much imaginative and dramatic play. Has complex ideas but unable to carry out because of lack of skill and time.	More realistic in play. Less interested in fairy tales. More serious and ready to know reality. Restrained but creative.
Likes solitary and parallel play with increasing social play in shifting groups of 2 or 3.	Plays in groups of 2 or 3, often companions of own sex. Imaginary playmates. Projects feelings and deeds onto peers or imaginary playmates. May run away from home.	Plays in groups of 5 or 6. Friendships stronger and continue over longer time. Chooses friends of like interests. Spurred on in activity by rivalry.
Cooperates briefly. Willing to wait turn and share with suggestion.	Suggests and accepts turns but often bossy in directing others.	Generous with toys. Sympathetic, cooperative, but quarrels and threatens by word or gesture. Acts out feelings. Wants rules and to do things right; but beginning to realize peers cheat, so develops mild deceptions and fabrications.
Some dramatic play-house or family games. Frequently changes activity. Likes to arrange, combine, transfer, sort, and spread objects and toys.	Dramatic and creative play at a peak. Likes to dress up and help with household tasks. Does not sustain role in dramatic play; moves from one role to another incongruous role. No carry over in play from day to day. Silly in play.	Dramatic play about most life events, but more realistic. Play continues from day to day. Interested in finishing what started, even if it takes several days. More awareness of yesterday and tomorrow. Enjoys using tools and equipment of adults.
Able to listen longer to nursery rhymes. Dramatizes nursery rhymes and stories. Can match simple forms. Enjoys cutting, pasting, block building. Enjoys sand and water play. Enjoys dumping and hauling toys. Rides tricycle.	Concentration span longer. Sometimes so busy at play forgets to go to toilet. Re-enacts stories and trips. Enjoys simple puzzles with trial-and-error method. Poor space perception. Uses constructive and manipulative play material increasingly. Enjoys sand and water play.	Perceptive to order, form, and detail. Better eye-hand coordination. Rhythmic motion to music. Likes excursions. Interested in world outside immediate environment. Enjoys cutting out pictures, pasting, working on special projects. Likes to run and jump, play with bicycle, wagon, and sled.

development, include blank sheets of paper, crayons, finger or water paints, chalk, various art supplies, clay, plasticine, or other manipulative material, blunt scissors, paste, cartons, scraps of cloth, water-play equipment, and musical toys. **Quiet play,** *which promotes cognitive development and rest from physical exertion,* is achieved through books, puzzles, records, and table games (7, 35, 36).

✔ The role of the adult in child's play is to provide opportunity, equipment, and safety and to avoid interference of structuring of play. Allow the child to try things and enjoy personal activities. Assist only if he/she is in need of help. The child is not natural in play when he/she thinks adults are watching; avoid showing amusement or ridicule of play behavior or conversation. Allow playmates to work out their own differences. Distract, redirect, or substitute a different activity if the children cannot share and work out their problems. There are times to play with the child, but avoid overstimulation, teasing, hurry, talking about him/her as if he/she were not present or doing the activity for the child. Let him/her take the lead. Try to enter the child's world. If he/she wants you to attend the teddy bear's 100th birthday party, go. A book which is creatively illustrated and gives many ideas for play activity for and with the preschooler is *Learning Through Play* by Jean Marzolla and Janice Lloyd (36).

✔ Table 9-4 summarizes play characteristics as a further aid in assessment and teaching (5, 25, 26, 36).

✔ Share the above information with parents and explore their feelings about child's play and their role with the child.

Guidance and Discipline Needs

The child learns how to behave by imitating adults and by using the opportunities to develop self-control. If the adult tells the child, "Tell him I'm not home," when the child answers the door, the child may at first be astonished, then accept the lie, and eventually use this behavior too.

The child needs consistent, fair, and kind limits to feel secure, to know that the parents care for and love him/her enough to protect—a security he/she does not have when allowed to do anything, regardless of ability. Limits should be set in a way that preserves the self-respect of the child and parent and should not be applied angrily, violently, arbitrarily, or capriciously, but rather with the intent to educate and build character. Only when the child can predict the behavior of others can he/she accept the need to inhibit or change some of his/her behavior as well as work toward predictable and rational behavior. The parent should be an ally to the child as he/she struggles for control over inner impulses and convey to the child that he/she does not have to be afraid of impulses.

The preschooler needs discipline that is permissive with limits. However, *permissive discipline* needs to be distinguished from *overpermissive* discipline. **Permissive discipline** *accepts the childish behavior of the child as normal and recognizes that the child is a person with a right to have all kinds of feelings and wishes that may be expressed directly or symbolically.* It sets realistic limits but is not harsh or demanding of perfection. The adult should distinguish between the wish and act and set limits on the act, not on the wish. Feelings and wishes must be identified and expressed verbally or through other outlets; actions may have to be limited or redirected since destructive behavior cannot be tolerated.

Overpermissive discipline *permits undesirable behavior that can become harmful or destructive.* It causes the child to feel insecure and anxious; he/she perceives others' disapproval and feels that the parents do not care. Further, the child is unable to accomplish what he/she is ready to do because of lack of external or self-control; and he/she does not learn to like self. In turn, fantasies will increase, and the child will demand more privileges than should be granted. The vicious circle is uncomfortable for adult and child alike.

✔ Share the above information and explore with parents the importance of their guidance to the child. The following *techniques for guidance and limit setting* would be helpful to you personally in working with children and should be shared with parents when indicated:

1. Convey authority without anger or threat to avoid feelings of resentment, fear, or guilt.
2. Be positive, clear, and consistent; let the child know what is acceptable behavior.
3. Phrase specific limits on special actions when the occasion arises, maintaining some flexibility in rules.
4. Recognize the child's wish, and put it into words, "You *wish* you could have that but. . . . "; point out ways the wish can be partially fulfilled when possible.
5. Help the child express some resentment likely to arise when restrictions are imposed. "I realize you don't like the rules but. . . . "
6. Enforce discipline by adhering to the stated rules kindly but firmly. Do not argue about them nor initiate a battle of wills. Spanking is one way to discipline, but it may show the child an undesirable way of handling frustration. Spanking may interfere with superego development by relieving guilt too easily; the child feels he/she has paid for the misbehavior and is free to return to mischievous activity.

7. Positive suggestions rather than commands and "don'ts" help the child to learn how to get what he/she wants at the time and how to form happy relationships with others.
8. If the child has no choice about a situation, give direction that conveys what he/she has to do, for example, "It is time now to. . . ."
9. Convey that adults are present to help the child solve problems that cannot be solved alone.
10. Control the situation if the child has temporarily lost self-control; remove him/her from the stimulating event; stay with the child; talk quietly; use distraction if necessary; encourage thinking through the problem and finding a fair solution after he/she has become calm. Convey that you feel the child can regain self-control and handle the situation, and can rejoin the group or continue the former activity when he/she feels ready (35).

Emotional Development

If the child has developed reasonably well, if he/she has mastered earlier developmental tasks, the preschooler is a source of pleasure to adults. He/she is more a companion than someone to care for. The various behaviors discussed under development of physical, mental, language, play, body image, and moral-religious aspects contribute to his/her emotional status and development. The beginning motor self-control, high-energy level, use of language, ability to delay somewhat immediate gratification, ability to tolerate separation from mother, curiosity, strong imagination, and desire to move, all propel him/her to plan; attack problems; start tasks; consider alternatives; learn aggressively; direct behavior with some thought, logic and judgment; and appear more self-confident and relaxed. Tolerance of frustration is still limited but flares of temper and frustrations over failure pass quickly. As the child is learning to master things and handle independence and dependence, so is he/she increasing mastery of self and others, learning to get along with more people, children and adults. The preschooler attempts to behave like an adult in realistic activity and play and is beginning to learn social roles, moral responsibility, and cooperation, although he/she still grabs, hits, and quarrels for short bursts of time.

If the child has the opportunity to resolve the Oedipal triangle, to establish a sense of gender, and to identify with mature adults, if the attitude about self is sound and positive, if he/she has learned to trust and have some self-control, he/she is ready to take on the culture. The preschooler begins to decide what kind of person he/she is, and self-concept, ego strength, and superego will continue to mature. Self is still very important, but he/she does not feel omnipotent.

Developmental Crisis. The psychosexual crisis for this era is initiative versus guilt, and all the aforementioned behaviors are part of achieving initiative (20). **Initiative** *is enjoyment of energy displayed in action, assertiveness, learning, increasing dependability, and ability to plan.*

If the child does not achieve the developmental task of initiative, there is an overriding sense of guilt from the tension between the demands of the superego, or expectations, and actual performance.

Guilt *is a sense of defeatism, anger, feeling responsible for things which he/she is not really responsible for, feeling easily frightened from what he/she wants to do, feeling bad, shameful, and deserving of punishment.* A sense of guilt can develop from sibling rivalry, lack of opportunity to try things, restriction on or lack of guidance in response to fantasy, or when parents interfere with the child's activity. They stifle initiative by doing things for the child or by frequently asking, "Why didn't you do it better?" If the guilt feelings are too strong, the child is anxious and easily frightened, he/she cannot organize activity and cannot do what he/she is neuromuscularly, mentally, and socially ready to do. Such a child develops a rigid superego that exercises strong control over behavior but at the same time feels resentment and bitterness toward the restrictive adult. Excessive guilt and lack of initiative development may be shown in a variety of behaviors: poor motor coordination, stammering speech, fears, nightmares, eating and elimination problems, irritability, regressed behavior, inability to separate from mother without panic, fear of strangers, temper tantrums, or lack of interest in peers or childhood activities.

You can help parents understand that if the child is to develop a sense of initiative and a healthy personality, they and other significant adults must encourage use of imagination, creativity, activity, and plans. Punishment must be limited to those acts that are truly dangerous, morally wrong, socially unacceptable, or with a harmful or unfortunate consequence for self or others. Parents should encourage the child's efforts to cooperate and share in the decisions and responsibilities of family life. The child develops best when he/she is commended and recognized for accomplishments. Appropriate behavior should be reinforced so that it will continue. Affirming a child's emotional experience is as important as affirming his/her physical development. Parents should set aside a time each day, perhaps near bedtime, for the child to review emotional experiences. If there has been joy, pride, or anger, these can be recounted to the parents. In talking, the child conjures up the feelings once again and integrates these feelings with the event. This promotes emotional growth. The preschooler needs to learn what feelings of love, hate, joy, and antagonism are, how to cope with and express them in ways other than physically. He/she needs guidance toward mature behavior.

Self-Concept/Body-Image and Sexuality Development

Self-concept, including body image, is gradually developing in these years. Body boundaries and sense of self become more definite to the preschooler because of developing sexual curiosity and awareness of how he/she differs from others, increased motor skills with precision of movement and maturing sense of balance, improved spatial orientation, maturing cognitive and language abilities, ongoing play activities, and relationship identification with his/her parents.

The pleasurable feelings associated with touching the body and genitals and with masturbation heighten self-awareness, but also anxiety and anticipation of punishment. If the child is threatened or punished because of sexual curiosity, he/she may repress feelings about and awareness of the genitals or other body parts and develop a distorted body image. Of course, he/she must be taught that society does not condone handling of genitals in public. The preschooler needs to be able to stroke the body with affection; he/she needs adult caresses as well.

Learning about the body, where it begins and ends, what it looks like, and what it can do, is basic to the child's identity formation. Included in the growing self-awareness is discovery of feelings and learning names for them. The child is beginning to learn how he/she affects others and others' responses, and he/she is learning the rudiments of control over feelings and behavior. The concept of body is reflected in the way the child talks, draws pictures, and plays. The child with no frame of reference in relation to self has increased anxiety and misperception of self and others. Fantasies about self affect later behavior.

Parental and cultural attitudes about sex-appropriate behavior for boys and girls may heighten anxiety and body-image confusion, especially if the child's behavior and appearance do not match the expectations of others.

The artistic productions of the preschooler tell us about self-perceptions. The 3-year-old draws a man consisting of one circle, sometimes with an appendage, a crude representation of the face, and no differentiation of parts. The 4-year-old draws a man consisting of a circle for a face and head, facial features of two eyes and perhaps a mouth, two appendages, and occasionally wisps of hair or feet. Often the 4-year-old has not really formulated a mental representation of the lower part of the body. The 5-year-old draws an unmistakable person. There is a circle face with nose, mouth, eyes, and hair; there is a body with arms and legs. Articles of clothing, fingers, and feet may be added. The width of the person is usually about one-half the length (16, 25, 26). The child may think of the body as a house (35). For example, while eating, he/she may name the various bits as fantasy characters who will go down and play in his/her house. The child may create an elaborate play area for them. (You can take advantage of this fantasy if eating problems arise.)

When the 3-year-old is asked his/her gender, the child is likely to give his/her name; the 4-year-old can state gender, thus showing a differentiation of self. ✔ Discuss with the parents the concept of body image and how they can help the child's formulation of self. The child needs opportunities to learn the correct names and basic functions of body parts and to discover his/her body with joy and pride. Mirrors, photographs of the child, weighing, and measuring height enhance the formation of his/her mental picture. The child needs physical and mental activity to learn body mastery and self-protection, and to express feelings of helplessness, doubt, or pain when the body does not accomplish what he/she would like or during illness. The preschooler needs to manipulate the tools of his/her culture to learn the difference between self and machines, equipment, or tools. The child needs to be encouraged to "listen" to the body—the aches of stretched muscles, tummy rumblings, stubbed toes—and to understand what he/she feels. To deny, misinterpret, misname, or push aside physical or emotional activities and feelings promotes an unrealistic self-understanding and eventually a negative self-concept and unwhole body image. Specific nursing measures after illness or injury help the child reintegrate body image (8, 16, 40, 42, 49, 61).

Adaptive Mechanisms

Development proceeds toward increasing differentiation, articulation, and integration. **Differentiation** *involves a progressive separation of feeling, thinking, and acting and an increasing polarity between self and others.* Differentiation is seen in the child's ability to **articulate** or *talk about the perceived experience of the world and the experience of self as a being.* **Integration** is seen in the *development of structured controls and adaptive or defensive mechanisms* (32, 38, 57).

With increasing differentiation, articulation of language, perceptions, and experience, and integration of experience and adaptive mechanisms into self, the child is better able to talk about fears and other feelings. The infant demonstrates behaviorally and through crying that he/she fears sudden movements, loud noises, loss of support, flashing lights, pain, strange people, objects, or situations, and separation from familiar people. The toddler's fears of being alone, the draining bathtub, the vacuum cleaner, the dark, dogs or other animals, high places, insecure footing, and separation from familiar people are expressed behaviorally and vocally, although the adult may have difficulty determining which fear is being expressed because of imprecise language skills. The preschooler has gained both language and conceptual ability, greater experience, and a greater imagination. Now he/she can talk about and play out the fears of being alone, ghosts, the dark, strangers, dogs, tigers, spiders, bears, and snakes, closed places, thunderstorms, and separation from loved ones. These fears decline by age 5 but may persist until age 7 or 8.

✔ What the preschool child sees through the media or hears in stories (including traditional fairy tales) may produce great fear. The child has no way of knowing, unless explanations are given, that the big bad wolf will not eat him/her, or that the Indians attacking wagon trains will not attack his/her home next. Fears of ghosts, monsters, robbers, kidnappers, and other fantasized characters last through the preschool years, until age 7 or 8, especially if parents do not talk about them and help the child differentiate between reality and imagination. Help parents realize that to instill realistic fear is adaptive: Viewing and reading experiences that do not emphasize violence, bad people, or fearsome objects or animals, but rather gentle and calm experiences, are helpful for the child to gain a sense of self-control over fears.

✔ The child encounters a variety of frustrations as he/she engages in new activities, expects more of self, and others expect more of the child. Disappointments arise. The child must learn to cope with frustrations just as he/she learns to handle and overcome fears. Teach parents that they can help by: (1) showing concern and acceptance of the child's feelings; (2) helping the child talk about the feelings; (3) exploring with the child possible causes for the feelings; (4) helping the child realize that emotions have reasons and that they can discover causes for personal feelings; (5) emphasizing that the child is neither expected to be perfect nor should he/she expect that everything will always go as desired; and (6) helping the child make a decision about handling the frustrating situation, thus learning problem-solving strategies. How the parent handles frustrations and problems sets an example for the child.

During the preschool years, certain adaptive mechanisms are at a peak. They include introjection, primary and secondary identification, fantasy, and repression. These mechanisms may be used in other developmental eras to aid or hinder adjustment. Mechanisms previously discussed are also used in response to situations.

Introjection, *taking attitudes, information, and actions into the self through empathy and learning*, along with primary identification (imitation) are essential for secondary identification to occur. Through **secondary identification** *the child internalizes standards, moral codes, attitudes, and role behavior, including gender, as his/her own, and in his/her own unique way.*

Through **fantasy**, or *imagination*, the child handles tension and anxiety related to the problems of becoming socialized into the culture, family, and peer group. As the child mentally restructures reality to meet personal needs, he/she is gradually learning how to master the environment realistically. Because the child has difficulty distinguishing between wish and reality, parents need to be gently realistic when necessary without shattering fantasies when they are needed or cause no problem. Parents must realize that an active imagination is normal at this age and provides tension release.

The child has fantasies about many things, shown in fondness for fairy tales, as well as in the fears expressed. Some cultures allow magic, symbols, and fantasy to play a significant part in life; all cultures retain some. If the child is forced to distinguish reality too early or too quickly, if imaginings are not accepted, and if creativity is not encouraged, he/she is likely to lose the attributes which contribute to the creative adult—a personal and social loss to be avoided.

Repression occurs as the culture and parents continue to insist firmly on reality and following the rules. Excessive repression is related to guilt feelings, harsh punishment, or perceived strong disapproval and will later interfere with memories of this period as well as result in constricted creativity and restricted behavior. Some repression, such as that related to the Oedipal conflict is necessary to free the child's energies for new tasks to be learned.

✔ You can help parents understand the processes of differentiation, articulation, and integration as related to emotional development, ways to help the child learn coping skills, and the normality and importance of these adaptive mechanisms.

Moral-Religious Development

A great influence on the child during these early years is the parents' attitude toward moral codes, the human as creative being, spirituality, religion, nature, love of country, the economic system, and education. These convey to the child what is considered good and bad, worthy of respect or unworthy. With the developing superego and imitation of and identification with adults, the child is absorbing a great deal of others' attitudes and will retain many of them throughout life. He/she is also beginning to consider how his/her actions affect others.

✔ There are some general considerations you may find helpful pertaining to moral and religious education. The child cannot be kept spiritually neutral. He/she hears about morals and religion from other people and will raise detailed questions about the basic issues of life: Where did I come from? Why am I here? Why did the bird (or Grandpa) die? Why is it wrong to do . . . ? Why can't I play with Joey? How come Billy goes to church on Saturday and we go to church on Sunday? What is God? What is heaven? Mommy, who do you like best: Santa Claus, the Easter Bunny, the tooth fairy, or Jesus? These questions, often considered inappropriate from the adult viewpoint, should not be lightly brushed aside, for how they are answered is more important than the information given.

✔ Example is the chief teacher for the child; if adult actions do not match the words, he/she quickly notices and learns the action. For the child, the parent is like God, omnipotent. Parents would be wise to remember this and try to live up to the high ideals of the child while at the same time introducing him/her to the reality of the world, for example, that parents do make mistakes. Talking with the child about such a mistake and asking forgiveness (if the child was wronged) will help him/her understand the redeeming power of a moral code, religion, or an ideal philosophy.

✔ There are two major methods of religious education: indoctrination or letting the child follow the religion of his choice. Help parents realize that neither meets the real issues. The preschooler does not follow any religion because he/she understands it but because it encompasses daily life, offers concomitant pleasure, and is expected of him/her. The preschooler accepts the religion of the parents because to the child they are all-powerful. He/she is trusting and literal in the interpretation of religion. The first religious responses are social in nature; bowing the head and saying a simple prayer is imitated, but is like brushing teeth to the young preschooler. The child likes prayers before meals and bedtime, and the 3-year-old may repeat them like nursery rhymes. The 4-year-old elaborates on prayer forms, and the 5-year-old makes up prayers.

Interpretation of religious forms and practices, influenced by the child's mental capacity and experiential contact, is marked by mental processes normal for the age: (1) egocentricism; (2) **anthropomorphism,** *where the child relates God to human beings he/she knows;* (3) fantasy rather than causal or logical thinking; and (4) animism. The child thinks either God or human beings are responsible for all events. God pushes clouds when they move; wind is God blowing; thunder is God hammering; the sun is God lighting a match in the sky.

✔ Thus the child needs consistent, simple explanations matched with the daily practices and religious ceremonies, rituals, or pictures. Encourage parents to discuss religion and related practices with the child. The preschool child is old enough to go to Sunday school, vacation Bible school, or classes in religious education that are on an appropriate level for the child. Religious holidays raise questions, and the spirit of the holiday as well as ceremonies surrounding it should be explained. In America, where Christmas and Easter have become secularized and surrounded with the myth of Santa Claus and Easter Bunny, the child's fantasy and love of parties are likely to minimize the religious significance of the days. There is no harm to moral-religious development in telling the child about these myths so long as they are used to convey the religious spirit of the days rather than used as an end in themselves. The child thinks concretely, and such embodiments of ideas, as the material objects used in any religion, convey abstract meanings which words alone do not. When he/she expresses doubt about the myths, a more sophisticated explanation may be presented.

Conscience, or Superego, Development. This is related to moral-religious training, discipline, and other areas of learning. The **superego,** *that part of the psyche which is critical to the self and enforces moral standards,* forms as a result of identification with parents and an introjection of their standards and values, which at first are questioned (35). At this point, the child is in the Preconventional Period, Stage 2, of moral development (see Chapter 5, Table 5-1). The preschooler usually behaves even if there is no external authority standing around to avoid disapproval, although he/she will slip at times. The superego can be cruel, primitive, uncompromising. The child can be overobedient or resentful because parents do not live up to what the child's superego demands. The child is likely to overreact to punishment. This all-or-nothing quality of the superego is normally tempered later; a strict superego does not necessarily mean that the child has strict parents, but rather that he/she perceives them as strict. It is the result of the child's interpretation of events, teaching, admonitions, demands of the environment, discipline, punishment, and fears, guilt, and anxiety about fantasized and real deeds.

Superego development will continue through contact with teachers and other significant adults through the years. If the superego remains too strict, self-righteous, or intolerant of others, the person in adulthood will develop a reaction formation of moralistic behavior, so that prohibition rather than initiative will be a dominant pattern of behavior.

If the superego does not develop, if no or few social values are internalized, then the child will be increasingly regarded as mischievous or bad in his/her behavior. Eventually he/she may have no guilt feelings, no qualms about not following the rules. The child is then on the way to truancy, delinquency, or becoming a **sociopath,** *an adult person who is emotionally inadequate and unable to form mature relationships or follow social or ethical standards.*

✔ The child continues the moral development previously begun—learning a greater sense of responsibility, empathy, mercy, compassion, and fairness. The parents are the major teachers as they relate to the child fairly with compassion and gentleness. They teach also by being reliable and responsive. Further, they teach when they point out to the child the consequences of his/her behavior to others. If the child hurts physically or emotionally another child, the child needs to know that. Then the child learns an appropriate sense of guilt. That does *not* mean that the parent abuses the child or uses brute force to teach pain. Rather, a discussion and reasoning, but asserting authority (restraining and calming an angry, aggressive child), when necessary, are ways to positively influence the child's moral outlook. Withdrawal of love and physical punishment are not effective ways to teach moral behavior. In response to physical punishment, the child acts out even more physically or verbally from the consequent anger. Withdrawal of love results in a terrified, withdrawn, passive child who cannot respond to messages to be caring to others (47). If the child feels valued and values self, he/she will in turn treat other people, animals, the environment, and things as if they are valuable.

✔ Discuss with parents the importance of superego development and beginning moral development during this period. Share the preceding information.

Developmental Tasks

In summary, the developmental tasks for the preschooler are the following:

1. Settle into a healthful daily routine of adequately eating, exercising, and resting.
2. Master physical skills of large- and small-muscle coordination and movement.
3. Become a participating member in the family.
4. Conform to others' expectations.
5. Express emotions healthfully and for a wide variety of experiences.
6. Learn to communicate effectively with an increasing number of others.
7. Learn to use initiative tempered by a conscience.
8. Develop ability to handle potentially dangerous situations.
9. Lay foundations for understanding the meaning of life, self, the world, and ethical, religious, and philosophical ideas (19).

✔ Discuss with parents how these tasks may be achieved and encourage them to talk about their concerns or problems as they help the child mature in these skills.

When the preschool child becomes more realistic,

Table 9-5. Selected Nursing Diagnoses Related to the Preschooler[a]

PATTERN 1: EXCHANGING
Altered Nutrition: More than body requirements
Altered Nutrition: Less than body requirements
Altered Nutrition: Potential for more than body requirements
Potential for Infection
Potential for Injury
Potential for Poisoning
Potential Impaired Skin Integrity

PATTERN 2: COMMUNICATING
Impaired Verbal Communication

PATTERN 3: RELATING
Impaired Social Interaction

PATTERN 5: CHOOSING
Impaired Adjustment

PATTERN 6: MOVING
Sleep Pattern Disturbance
Feeding Self Care Deficit
Toileting Self Care Deficit
Altered Growth and Development

PATTERN 7: PERCEIVING
Body Image Disturbance
Self Esteem Disturbance
Sensory/Perceptual Alterations
Unilateral Neglect
Hopelessness

PATTERN 8: KNOWING
Knowledge Deficit

PATTERN 9: FEELING
Pain
Anxiety
Fear

[a] Other NANDA diagnoses are applicable to the ill preschooler.
Source: NANDA Approved Nursing Diagnostic Categories, *Nursing Diagnosis Newsletter,* 15, no. 1 (1988), 1–3.

relinquishes some fantasies, substitutes identity for rivalry with the parent of the same sex while seeking admiration of the parent of the opposite sex, and feels a sense of initiative rather than excessive guilt, he/she is ready to enter the period of latency.

✔ If maladaptive behavior persists, such as failure in language development, destructiveness, or excessive bedwetting, the parents and child need special guidance. You can obtain information on causes, associated behavior, and care for these and other special problems from a pediatric nursing book.

✔ NURSING APPLICATIONS

Your role with the preschooler and family has been discussed with each section throughout this chapter. Table 9-5 lists some *nursing diagnoses* that may apply to the preschooler based on assessments that would result from knowledge presented in this chapter. Interventions include your role modeling of caring behavior to the preschooler and family; child, parent, and family education, support and counseling; or direct care to meet the preschooler's physical, emotional, cognitive, social, or spiritual/moral needs.

References

1. Allport, Gordon, *The Individual and His Religion.* New York: Macmillan, 1961, pp. 28–36.
2. Anderson, Mary, The Mental Health Advantages of Twinship, *Perspectives in Psychiatric Care,* 23, no. 3 (1985), 114–116.
3. Baker, Susan, and Roberta Henry, *Parents' Guide to Nutrition: Healthy Eating from Birth through Adolescence.* Reading, MA:Addison-Wesley, 1986.
4. Bander, Laurie K., et al., Dietary Lead Intake of Preschool Children, *American Journal of Public Health,* 73, no. 7 (1983), 789.
5. Barnett, Lynn, Cognitive Correlates of Playful Behavior, *Journal of Physical Education and Recreation,* 50, no. 8 (1979), 40–43.
6. Bates, Barbara. *A Guide to Physical Examination* (3rd ed.). Philadelphia: J. B. Lippincott, 1983.
7. Bettelheim, Bruno, *A Good Enough Parent: A Book on Child-Rearing.* New York: Alfred A. Knopf, 1987.
8. Blaesing, Sandra, and Joyce Brockhaus, The Development of Body Image in the Child, *Nursing Clinics of North America,* 7 no. 4 (1972), 601–607.
9. Bonner, Alice, and Rosemary Dale, *Giardia Lamblia:* Day Care Diarrhea, *American Journal of Nursing,* 86, no. 9 (1986), 918–920.
10. Cadman, David, et al., The Usefulness of the Denver Developmental Screening Test to Predict Kindergarten Problems in a General Community Population, *American Journal of Public Health,* 74, no. 110 (1984), 1093–1097.
11. Chorba, T., et al., Control of a Non-Foodborne Outbreak of Salmonellosis: Day Care in Isolation, *American Journal of Public Health,* 77, no. 8 (1987), 979–981.
12. Corno, Donna, Some Age 5 Smoke Pot, Expert Says, *West County Citizen,* St. Louis, Mo., April 14, 1982, 1a. 12a.
13. Critchley, Deane. Therapeutic Group Work with Abused Preschool Children, *Perspectives in Psychiatric Care,* 20, no. 2 (1982), 79–85.
14. Day Care on the Job, *Newsweek* (September 2, 1985), 59–60.
15. Dewey, Kathryn, et al., Height and Weight of Southeast Asian Preschool Children in Northern California, *American Journal of Public Health,* 76, no. 7 (1986), 806–808.
16. DiLeo, J. H., *Young Children and Their Drawings.* Springfield, Ill.: Springer, 1971.
17. Doster, Sandra, et al., Measles and Rubella: Our Remaining Responsibilities, *American Journal of Nursing,* 83, no. 5 (1983), 490–491.
18. Dreskin, William, and Wendy Dreskin, *The Day Care Decision: What's Best for You and Your Child.* New York: M. Evans, 1983.
19. Duvall, Evelyn, and Brent Miller. *Marriage and Family Development* (6th ed.). New York: Harper & Row, 1984.
20. Erikson, Erik H., *Childhood and Society* (2nd ed.). New York: W. W. Norton, 1963.
21. Federation, Sharon, Sexual Abuse: Treatment Modalities for the Younger Child, *Journal of Psychosocial Nursing,* 24, no. 7 (1986), 21–24.
22. Frankenburg, William, and Josiah Dodds, The Denver Developmental Screening Test, *The Journal of Pediatrics,* 71, no. 2 (1967), 181–191.
23. Freiberg, Karen. *Human Development: A Life Span Approach* (3rd ed.). Monterey, Calif.: Wadsworth Health Sciences Division, 1983.
24. Garbarino, James, Edna Guttmann, and James Seeley, *The Psychologically Battered Child: Strategies for Identification, Assessment, and Intervention.* San Francisco: Jossey-Bass, 1987.
25. Gesell, Arnold, H. Halverson, H. Thompson, F. Ilg, B. Castner, L. Ames, and C. Amatruda, *The First Five Years of Life.* New York: Harper and Brothers, Publishers, 1940.
26. Gesell, Arnold, and Francis Ilg, *The Child from Five to Ten.* New York: Harper and Brothers, 1946.
27. *Health United States, 1982.* Washington, D. C. U.S. Government Printing Office 1982, Publication # PHS 83–1232.
28. Holmes, Janine, and Lana Magiera. *Maternity Nursing.* New York: Macmillan, 1987.
29. Hoole, Axalla, Robert Greenberg, and C. Glenn Pick-

ard, *Patient Care Guidelines for Nurse Practitioners* (3rd ed.). Boston: Little, Brown, 1988.
30. How Parents Determine Mental Skills, *St. Louis Post Dispatch*, August 6, 1986, 1, 5.
31. Immunizations Still Important for Children, *Health Scene*, Fall, 1987, 11.
32. Kaluger, George, and Meriem Kaluger, *Human Development: The Span of Life* (3rd ed.). St. Louis: Times Mirror/Mosby, 1984.
33. Krantz, Paul, Preschool Education: Too Much, Too Soon? *Better Homes and Gardens*, August, 1986, 22–23.
34. Lamb, Michael, *The Father's Role*. New York: John Wiley, 1986.
35. Lidz, Theodore, *The Person: His and Her Development Throughout the Life Cycle*, (2nd ed.). New York: Basic Books, 1983.
36. Marzolla, Jean, and Janice Lloyd, *Learning Through Play*. New York: Harper & Row, 1972.
37. Messer, Alfred, *The Individual in His Family, An Adaptational Study*. Springfield, Ill.: Charles C. Thomas, 1970.
38. Moshman, David, John Glover, and Roger Bruning, *Developmental Psychology*. Boston: Little, Brown, 1987.
39. Out of The Mouths of Babes, *Newsweek* (December 15, 1986), 84–86.
40. Pillitteri, Adele, *Child Health Nursing: Care of the Growing Family* (3rd ed.). Boston: Little, Brown, 1987.
41. Pipes, Peggy. *Nutrition in Infancy and Childhood* (3rd ed.). St. Louis: Times Mirror/Mosby, 1985.
42. Pontious, Sharon, Practical Piaget: Helping Children Understand, *American Journal of Nursing*, 82, no. 1 (1982), 114–117.
43. Potter, Diana, ed., *Assessment*, Springhouse, Pa.: Intermed Communications, 1982.
44. Pridham, Karen and Marc Hansoen, Helping Children Deal with Procedures in a Clinic Setting: A Developmental Approach, *Journal of Pediatric Nursing*, 2, no. 2 (1987), 13–21.
45. Sataloff, Robert, and Cynthia Colten, Otitis Media: A Common Childhood Infection, *American Journal of Nursing*, 81, no. 8 (1981), 1480–1483.
46. Schilder, Paul, *The Image and Appearance of the Human Body*. New York: International Universities Press, 1951.
47. Schulman, Michael, *Moral Development Training: Strategies for Parents, Teachers, and Clinicians*. Menlo Park, Calif.: Addison-Wesley, 1985.
48. Schuster, Clara Shaw, and Shirley Smith Ashburn, *The Process of Human Development: A Holistic Life-Span Approach* (2nd ed.). Boston: Little, Brown, 1986.
49. Scipien, G.M., Barnard, M.A., Howe, J., et al., *Comprehensive Pediatric Nursing* (3rd ed.). New York: McGraw-Hill, 1986.
50. Selekman, Janice, Immunization: What It's All About? *American Journal of Nursing*, 80, no. 8 (1980), 1440–1445.
51. Shapiro, Leona, et al., Obesity Prognosis: A Longitudinal Study of Children From Age 6 Months to 9 Years, *American Journal of Public Health*, 74, no. 9 (1984), 968–972.
52. Sherman, Jacques, Jr., and Sylvia Fields, *Guide to Patient Evaluation* (3rd ed.). Garden City, N.Y.: Medical Examination Publishing, 1978.
53. Shull, M. W., et al., Velocities of Growth in Vegetarian Preschool Children, *Pediatrics*, 60, no. 10 (1977), 410–417.
54. Stone, Joseph, and Joseph Church, *Childhood and Adolescence: Psychology of the Growing Person* (4th ed.). New York: Random House, 1979.
55. The Hennepin County Child Care Consultation Program, *American Journal of Public Health*, 76, no. 11 (1986), 1357–1358.
56. Troy, Petty, et al., Sibling Visiting in the NICU, *American Journal of Nursing*, 88, no. 1 (1988) 68–69.
57. Turner, Jeffrey, and Donald Helms, *Lifespan Development* (3rd ed.). New York: Holt, Rinehart and Winston, 1987.
58. U.S. Department of Health and Human Service, New Recommended Schedule for Active Immunization of Normal Infants and Children, *Morbidity and Mortality Weekly Report*. 35, no. 37 (September 19, 1986), 577–579.
59. Wadsworth, Barry, *Piaget's Theory of Cognitive and Affective Development* (3rd ed.). New York: David McKay, 1984.
60. Webb, Patricia, Piaget: Implications for Teaching, *Theory into Practice*, 19, no. 2 (1980), 93–97.
61. Whaley, Lucille, and Donna Wong, *Nursing Care of Infants and Children*. (3rd ed.). St. Louis: C. V. Mosby, 1987.
62. Williams, Phoebe, The Metro-Manila Developmental Screening Test: A Normative Study, *Nursing Research*, 33, no. 4 (1984), 208–212.

10

Assessment and Health Promotion for the Schoolchild

Study of this chapter will help you to

1. Discuss the family relationships of the schoolchild and the influence of peers and other adults on him/her.
2. Explore with the family their developmental tasks and ways to achieve them.
3. Compare and assess the physical changes and needs, including nutrition, rest, exercise, safety, and health protection, for the juvenile and preadolescent.
4. Assess intellectual, communication, play, emotional, self-concept, sexuality, and moral-religious development in the juvenile and preadolescent and influences on these areas of development.
5. Discuss the crisis of school entry and ways to help the child adapt to the experience of formal education, including latch key care.
6. Discuss the physical and emotional adaptive mechanisms of the schoolchild and how they contribute to his/her total development, including meeting the developmental crisis of industry versus inferiority.
7. Discuss the significance of peers and the chum relationship to the psychosocial development of the child.
8. Explore with parents their role in communication with and guidance of the child to foster healthy development in all spheres of personality.
9. Discuss influence of media on behavior.
10. State the developmental tasks of the schoolchild and discuss your role in helping him/her to achieve these.
11. Work effectively with the schoolchild in the nursing setting.

Key Terms

School-age years
Juvenile period
Preadolescence
Latch key child
Fluoride mottling
Preadolescent/prepuberty period
Accommodative esophoria
Scoliosis
Obesity
Otitis externa
Serous otitis media
Allergic rhinitis
Herpes simplex contact dermatitis
Tinea corporis
Tinea capitis
Warts
Pediculosis
Pediculosis humanus capitis
Diabetes mellitus
Mumps
Orchitis
Rabies
Concrete operations
    Classification
    Seriation
    Nesting
Multiplication
Reversibility
Transformation
Conservation
Decentering
Cognitive Conflict
School-phobic child
Gifted child
Gang
Chum stage
Chum
Altruism
Homosexuality
Competition
Morality of constraint
Compromise
Cooperation
Morality of cooperation
Collaboration
Industry
Inferiority
Sexuality education
Sex education
Ritualistic behavior
Undoing
Isolation
Regression
Malingering
Rationalization

As growth and development continue and the child leaves the confines of the home, he/she emerges into a world of new experiences and responsibilities. If previous developmental tasks have been met and the child has developed a healthy personality, he/she will continue to steadily acquire new knowledge and skills. If previous developmental tasks have not been met and the child's personality development is immature or warped, the child may experience difficulties mastering the developmental tasks of the school-age child. Peers, parents, and other adults may have a positive, maturing influence if the child is adequately prepared for leaving home, if individual needs are considered, and if he/she has some successful experiences.

The **school-age years** are divided into the juvenile and preadolescent periods. *About age 6, the* **juvenile period** *begins, marked by a need for peer associations.* **Preadolescence** *usually begins between 9 and 10 years of age and is marked by a new capacity to love, when the satisfaction and security of another person of the same sex is as important to the child as personal satisfaction and security. Preadolescence ends at about 12 years, with the onset of puberty. Preadolescence is also called prepubescence and is characterized by an increase in hormone production in both sexes,* which is preparatory to eventual physiological maturity. Psychological and social changes also occur as the child slowly moves away from the family. *This chapter discusses characteristics to assess and measure for you to use in relation to health care for the child and family.*

Family Development and Relationships

Relationships with Parents

Parents continue to be a vital part of the schoolchild's life. The schoolchild now channels energy, formerly expended in consuming curiosity and impulses, into intellectual pursuits, widens social horizons, and becomes familiar with the adult world. He/she has identified with the parent of the same sex, and through imitation continues to learn a social role. The family atmosphere has considerable impact on the child's emotional development and future response within the family when he/she becomes an adolescent. Research indicates that children can become positive in their behavior whether they are reared in authoritarian or permissive homes, if parents are consistent in their approach. The permissive child-rearing style does not necessarily produce a "spoiled brat"; the authoritarian style does not necessarily produce aggressive or inhibited children (74, 133, 160).

Parental support is needed, but the schoolchild pulls away from overt signs of parental affection. Yet during illness or when threatened by his/her new status, he/she turns to parents for affection and protection. Parents get frustrated with behavioral changes, antics, and infractions of household rules.

We have had the romantic notion of the "typical" American two-parent family with a male wage earner and a mother who stays home to care for two children. This stereotype represents about 1 of every 16 American families. It ignores (1) families of the millions of children whose mothers work outside home; (2) the millions of single-parent families which are more likely to be poor; (3) the millions of families that have at least one child with a physical, mental, or emotional handicap; (4) hundreds of thousands of children who do not have homes of their own; (5) millions of teen-age parents, themselves merely children, struggling to raise another generation.

However, not only poor, minority, or single-parent families need help. Many middle-class or upper-class families do not feel confident about raising their children. They may have all the help that professionals and housekeepers and nursemaids can give and may not be able to exercise effective control over what their children see on television or eat (34, 74).

Although the poor child frequently shares the helplessness of an unemployed parent, the higher-income child often feels the relentless pressure on the parent who is a high-powered corporate executive, lawyer, professor, or government official preoccupied with his/her own survival. Too often the demands of the workplace encroach on the needs and happiness of the family (34, 74).

In some families, abuse, neglect, or maltreatment may occur. Refer to Chapters 4, 6, and 7 for background information about precipitating factors, characteristics of abusing parents, and signs and symptoms of abuse. The research of Garbarino and colleagues shows that psychological abuse or maltreatment of the school child is demonstrated by the behavior described in Table 10-1 (41).

The **"latch key" child,** *the child who has the door key because no one is home when the child returns from school,* is seen increasingly since over 50 percent of women with children under 18 work. Children voice different feelings about the working mother and having no one home to meet them after school. Some like it. They enjoy the solitude, the privacy, the responsibility, the closeness of each other at day's end. Some hate it for the same reasons. Some tolerate it out of necessity, disliking the separation and lack of time together. Some are afraid for themselves and their mothers. Some are proud of mother and how they are managing together. Some become discipline problems. All appreciate the financial reasons, and sometimes the career and emotional reasons, that are usually the basis for mother working (53). Some girls say they want to work as a result. Some want to be homemakers when they grow up. More programs are being established to accommodate the child after school, such as YWCA Latch Key Programs and daycare centers that provide longer hours of care.

The child needs to be given time—physically, emotionally, mentally, and socially—to be a child, to learn about the world around him/her at an individual

Table 10–1. Parental Behavior Characteristic of Psychological Maltreatment

Rejecting	Communicates negative definitions of self to the child.
	Creates a sense of "bad-me" or negative self concept by consistently calling child negative names, such as stupid, dummy, monster.
	Belittles child's accomplishments regularly.
	Scapegoats child in the family system.
Isolating	Removes child from normal social relations with peers.
	Prohibits child from playing with or inviting children into the home.
	Withdraws child from school.
Terrorizing	Places child in double bind.
	Demands opposite or conflicting behavior or emotions simultaneously from the child.
	Forces child to choose one of the two parents.
	Changes rules of the house or of relationship with parents frequently.
	Criticizes constantly, so that child has no prospect of meeting expectations.
Ignoring	Fails to protect child from threats or intervene on behalf of the child.
	Does not protect child from assault from siblings or other family members.
	Does not respond to child's request for help or feedback.
Corrupting	Rewards child for stealing, substance abuse, assaulting other children, and sexual precocity.
	Goads child into attacking other children.
	Exposes child to pornography.
	Encourages drug use.
	Reinforces sexually aggressive behavior.
	Involves child sexually with adolescents or adults.

Source: Reference (41).

pace. Too often parents want to hurry the child into adulthood. The result will be a chronological adult who still acts and feels like a child. Television, films, advertisements, peers, and neighbors all exert pressure to wear adult clothes, to be sexually precocious, to manipulate parents into fewer limits and less guidance. Parents feel their child must be the "early maturer." The pressures and hurry, especially in the middle-class and lower-upper-class urban family, are contributing to a growing number of troubled children who are emotionally distressed or ill or who are antisocial. The child abuses self and others with alcohol, drugs, and sexual activity. He/she also may search for peace among various cults or even through suicide. If the child has to be *hurried* through childhood, if the child cannot be accepted for who he/she is, then feelings of being unloved, rejected, and inferior grow ever deeper and bigger.

✔ If we are committed to the family remaining the basic child-rearing institution—and we have not invented anything better for children than parents—our attitudes and policies must catch up with the fact that millions of American families need help at different times for various reasons to raise their children well. As a nurse, you care for the family as well as the individual. Help parents clarify and act on their values. As a school nurse, your assessment may be the key to a child receiving necessary care since many children do not have a family doctor. You can conduct many health promotion activities described throughout this chapter. You can counsel and teach parents as well as the children (12, 51, 114, 128, 129, 147, 148). Be aware of cultural beliefs and practices as you work with children and families. A family who has lived in this country for several generations may follow the same cultural patterns as the family who is a new immigrant (161). Finally, as a citizen, your vote on action to pass health-related legislation is important and may be as crucial to health promotion as immunizations (34).

Relationships with Siblings

Although parental influence is of primary importance, the child's relationship with siblings impacts on personality formation. The influence of siblings on the development of the school-age child depends on a number of factors, including the age and gender of the siblings, number of children in the family, proximity of their ages, and the type of parent-child interaction (131).

Relationships between the school-age child and siblings vary from jealousy, rivalry, and competition to protectiveness and deep affection. School-age children need privacy and personal space. Quarrels and conflicts erupt when this need is violated (136). Although sibling jealousy is less acute in school-age children than in preschool children, it still exists. An older child may be jealous of the attention given to younger siblings and may resent having to help with their care. The younger school-age child may feel jealous of the freedom given to older siblings. School-age children may feel the need to compete for parental attention and academic excellence. Parental comparisons of siblings' scholastic and artistic abilities or behavior should be avoided since they add to jealousy and resentment.

Adjustment outside the home is generally regarded as easier for the child with siblings than for the only child, who may develop a very close, intense relationship with the parents. The only child may cling to the notion of being the center of the family and may expect to be the center of attention in other groups as well. As a result, he/she may find the give and take of social living difficult (133). The differences in socialization between small and large families and for the only child is discussed in Chapter 4.

Family Development Tasks

⮕ Family activities with the school-age child revolve around expanding the child's world. You can assist families in meeting family development tasks, which include the following:

1. Take on parenting roles.
2. Adjust the marital system and the lifestyle to allow physical, emotional, and social space for the child(ren).
3. Keep lines of communication open among family members.
4. Work together to achieve common goals.
5. Plan a lifestyle within economic means.
6. Find creative ways to continue a mutually satisfactory married life, or satisfactory single parenthood.
7. Maintain close ties with relatives.
8. Realign relationships with the extended family to include parenting and grandparenting roles.
9. Expand family life into the community through various activities.
10. Validate the family philosophy of life. The philosophy is tested when the child brings home new ideas and talks about different lifestyles he/she encountered, forcing the family to reexamine patterns of living (33).

Relationships Outside the Family

With entry into school, the child's position within the family is altered. As the child's social environment widens, the influence of the family and the time spent with the family diminishes. Although the parents continue to be role models, teachers and other adults also begin to function as adult models and to influence the child (133). The child strives for independence and establishes meaningful relationships with teachers, peers, and other significant adults. These relationships provide the child with new ideas, attitudes, perspectives, and modes of behavior which may conflict with those of the family. Parents may feel a loss of control and may actually experience ambivalent feelings toward teachers as well as toward their child's peers. The child may verbalize less love and respect for parents and may resent limits imposed by the family. Through contacts with the peer group, the child learns that parents can make mistakes and he/she acquires a basis for judging parents as individuals (56, 95, 133).

The schoolchild has a growing sense of community that changes with increased mobility and independence and added responsibility. His/her understanding broadens to include a sense of boundaries, distance, and location, as well as spatial relationships of resources and organizations, demographic characteristics, and group identity (114, 133).

⮕ As a nurse, you are in a key position to listen to and explore with families their concerns related to being parents, to achieving the expected developmental tasks, and to adjusting to the growing and changing child as he/she interacts with parents, siblings, other relatives, and peers and other adults outside the home. At times you may validate their approach to a given situation. At other times you may help them clarify their values so they can, in turn, better guide the child. Such practical suggestions as how to plan more economically a nutritious meal or handle sibling rivalry can help a distraught parent feel and become more effective.

⮕ In the United States, nearly a million children live not in their own home but in facilities ranging from individual foster family and group homes to large institutions. Too many of these children are unnecessarily or prematurely removed from their homes before anyone has tried to work with or provide services to their families, who may be in poverty or unable to provide needed care but who love their children and are doing the best they can. If a poor rural family has no privy and no water, the answer is not to take away the children. Rather, your ability to maneuver the welfare system to provide a privy and a well may be the beginning of improved health for the entire family. Tens of thousands of children have been placed in inappropriate facilities for long periods of time, often away from their communities and even out of their states. They are shunted around frequently and denied a sense of permanence, loving attachments, the chance to trust, and to be continuously nurtured by caring adults. They languish in twilight, often neither returned home nor provided a permanent new family through adoption (34).

✔ Most parents try to do right by their children, but they may lack access, confidence, information, and power to deal alone with the people and institutions who could give help. Your ability to see beyond the obvious and to help the family use community resources effectively to meet basic needs is often the first step in promotion of both physical and emotional health. Your help may involve much effort over a period of time as you deal with a bureaucratic system and gain increasing empathy for the struggling family.

Physiological Concepts

Physical Changes

The child between 6 and 12 years old exhibits considerable change in physical appearance (114, 133, 136, 170).

Growth during this stage of development is hypertrophic (cells increase in size) instead of hyperplastic (cells increase in number). The growth rate is usually slow and steady, characterized by periods of accelerations in the spring and fall and by rapid growth during preadolescence (133).

Weight, Height, and Girth. These vary considerably among children and depend on genetic, environmental, and cultural influences. Afro-American children and Caucasian children from lower socioeconomic groups tend to be smaller in weight and height (132).

Changes in the height, weight, body mass index, triceps skinfold, and arm and estimated midarm muscle circumferences in lower socioeconomic Mexican-American children, 6 through 17 years of age, from Texas, were documented on the basis of surveys done in 1972 and 1983. With the exception of height in youths aged 14 to 17, all parameters showed gains at most ages, and in particular an increase in adipose tissue. These trends confirm the large proportion of relatively short but heavy children among Mexican-Americans (81).

The average schoolchild grows 2 to 2.5 inches (5 to 6 cm) per year to gain 1 to 2 feet (30 to 60 cm) in height by age 12. A weight gain of 4 to 7 pounds (2 to 3.5 kg) occurs per year. The average weight for a 6-year-old boy is 48 pounds (21.5 kg) and the average height is 46 inches (117 cm). By age 12 the average child weighs approximately 88 pounds (40 kg) and is over 59 inches tall (150 cm). During the *juvenile period*, girls and boys may differ little in size; their bodies are usually lean, with narrow hips and shoulders. There is a gradual decrease in the amount of baby fat with an increase in muscle mass and strength. Although the amount of muscle mass and adipose are influenced by muscle use, diet, and activity, males usually have more muscle cells while females have more adipose tissue. Muscle growth is occurring at a rapid rate. The muscles are changing in composition and becoming more firmly attached to the bones. Muscles may be immature in regard to function, causing children to be vulnerable to injury stemming from overuse, awkwardness, and inefficient movement. Muscle aches may accompany skeletal growth spurts as developing muscles attempt to keep pace with the enlarging skeletal structure. As the skeletal bones lengthen, they become harder. Ossification, the formation of bone, continues at a steady pace. The schoolchild loses the pot-bellied, sway-back appearance of early childhood. Abdominal muscles become stronger; the pelvis tips backwards, and posture becomes straighter (56, 133, 136, 162, 170).

Vital Signs. Vital signs of the schoolchild are affected by size, gender, and activity. Temperature, pulse, and respiration gradually approach adult norms with an average *temperature* of 98 to 98.6°F (36.7 to 37°C), *pulse* rate of 70 to 80 per minute, resting pulse rate of 60 to 76 per minute, and *respiratory* rate of 18 to 21 per minute. The average *systolic blood pressure* is 94 to 112 and average *diastolic blood pressure* is 56 to 60 millimeters of mercury. As respiratory tissues achieve adult maturity, *lung capacity* becomes proportional to body size. Between the ages of 5 and 10, the respiratory rate slows as the amount of air exchanged with each breath doubles. Breathing becomes deeper and slower. By the end of middle childhood, the lung weight will have increased almost ten times. The ribs shift from a horizontal position to a more oblique one; the chest broadens and flattens to allow for this increased lung size and capacity.

Cardiovascular System. The *heart* grows slowly during this age period; the left ventricle of the heart enlarges. After 7 years of age, the apex of the heart lies at the interspace of the fifth rib at the midclavicle line. Prior to this age, the apex is palpated at the fourth interspace just to the left of the midclavicle line. By the age of 9, the heart weighs six times its birth weight. By puberty, it weighs ten times its birth weight. Even though cardiac growth does occur, the heart remains small in relation to the rest of the body. Because the heart is smaller proportionately to the body size, the child may tire easily. Sustained physical activity is not desirable. The schoolchild should not be pushed to run, jog, or engage in excessively competitive sports such as football, hockey, or racquetball (114, 133, 136, 162).

Hemoglobin levels are higher for Caucasians than Afro-Americans for 10 to 15-year-olds. In all likelihood, racial differences in hemoglobin levels during childhood exist independent of nutritional values. Racial differences are consistent with that for infants, preschool children, teen-agers, pregnant women, and athletes, unrelated to nutritional variables (98).

Head. The growth of the *head* is nearly complete; head size measures about 21 inches (53 cm) in circumference. He/she loses the childish look as the face takes on features that will characterize him/her as an adult. Jaw bones grow longer and more prominent as the mandible extends forward, providing more chin and a place into which *permanent teeth* will be able to erupt. Girls lose teeth earlier than boys; deciduous or baby teeth are lost and replaced at a rate of four teeth per year until about the age of 11 or 12. The first permanent teeth are 6-year molars that erupt by age 7 and are the keystone for the permanent dental arch. Evaluation for braces should not be completed until all four 6-year molars have appeared. The second permanent molars erupt by age 14, and the third molars (wisdom teeth) come in as late as age 30. Some persons' wisdom teeth never erupt (Fig. 10–1). When the first permanent central incisors emerge, they appear too large for the mouth and face. Generally the teeth of males are larger than those of females (56, 114, 133, 162). The "toothless" appearance may produce embarrassment for the child. Children who live in areas with high fluoride content in the drinking water may demonstrate **fluoride mottling** (*brownish permanent discoloration*) of the teeth in late childhood and adolescence (19).

Digestive System. Secretion, digestion, absorption, and excretion of the digestive system become more efficient. Maturity of the gastrointestinal system is reflected in fewer stomach upsets, better maintenance of blood sugar levels, and an increased stomach capacity (162).

Urinary System. This becomes functionally mature during the school years. Between the ages of 5

Median Age of Eruption		Median Age When Shed		
6–9 months	—	6–7 years	—	Medial Incisor
7–10 months	—	7–8 years	—	Lateral Incisor
16–18 months	—	10–12 years	—	Cuspid
12–14 months	—	9–11 years	—	First Molar
20–28 months	—	9–11 years	—	Second Molar

THE PRIMARY TEETH

Median Age of Eruption		
6–7 years*	—	Medial Incisor
7–8 years*	—	Lateral Incisor
9–12 years*	—	Cuspid
10–12 years	—	First Premolar (Bicuspid)
11–12 years	—	Second Premolar (Bicuspid)
5½–7 years	—	First Molar
11–13 years*	—	Second Molar
16–21 years	—	Third Molar (Wisdom Tooth)

*Note: These specific teeth for the upper jaw erupt on the average of 1 year later than do the lower teeth.

THE PERMANENT LOWER TEETH

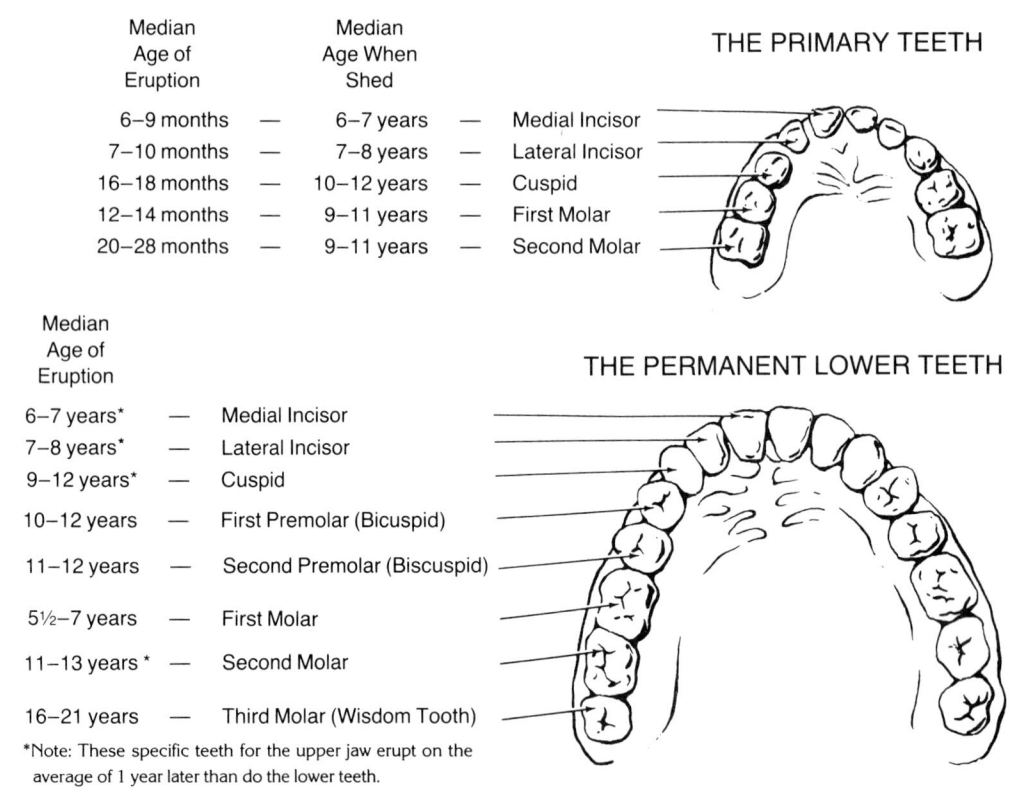

Figure 10–1 Normal Tooth Formation in the Child.

and 10, the kidneys double in size and the urine constituents and specific gravity become similar to an adult. However, 5 to 20 percent of school-age children have small amounts of albuminuria (133).

Vision. The shape of the eye changes during growth, and the normal farsightedness of the preschool child is gradually converted to 20/20 vision by age 8. By age 10, the eyes have acquired adult size and shape. Binocular vision is well developed in most children at 6 years of age; peripheral vision is fully developed. Girls tend to have poorer visual acuity than boys but their color discrimination is superior (56, 133). Large print is recommended for reading matter and regular vision testing should be part of the school health program.

Immune System. Lymphoid tissues reach the height of development by age 7, exceeding the amount found in adults. Enlargement of adenoidal and tonsillar lymphoid tissue is normal, as are sore throats, upper respiratory infections, and ear infections which are caused by the excessive tissue growth and increased vulnerability of the mucous membranes to congestion and inflammation. The frontal sinuses are developed about age 6. Thereafter, all sinuses are potential sites for infection. The immunoglobulins, IgG and IgA, reach adult levels by age 9 and the child's immunological system becomes functionally mature by preadolescence (114, 133).

Neuromuscular Development. By age 7, the brain has reached 90 percent of adult size. The growth rate of the brain is greatly slowed after age 7 but by age 12 the brain has virtually reached adult size. Myelinization is complete; memory has improved. The child can better listen and make associations with incoming stimuli. Neuromuscular changes are occurring along with skeletal development. Neuromuscular coordination is sufficient to permit the schoolchild to learn most skills he/she wishes (133).

The transformation of the "clumsy" 6-year-old into the coordinated 12-year-old is due in part to maturation of the *central nervous system* and improved transmission of nerve impulses. The 6-year-old moves constantly—hopping, running, roller skating. The child walks a chalk mark with balance. Hands are used as tools in manipulative skills of hammering, cutting, pasting, tying shoes, and fastening clothes. Large letters or figures are made as he/she awkwardly grasps a pencil or crayon (133, 170).

Children of 7 have a lower *activity level* and enjoy active and quiet games. The child sees small print without difficulty, reverses letters less frequently while printing, and prints sentences. The 8-year-old moves energetically but with grace and balance, even in more active sports. Increased myelinization improves the child's reaction time and coordination. Longer arms permit more skillful throwing. He/she grasps objects better and writes rather than prints because the hands are larger and he/she has better small-muscle coordination. The 9-year-old moves with less restlessness, is skillful in manual activities because of refined hand-eye coordination, and uses both hands independently. This child strives to improve coordination and to perfect physical skills, strength, and endurance. The preadolescent, aged 10 to 12, has energetic, active, restless movements with tension releases through finger drumming or foot tapping. Skillful manipulative movements nearly equal those of the adult, and physical changes preceding pubescence begin to appear (114, 133, 170).

Prepubertal Sexual Development. During the *preadolescent or prepuberty period*, both males and females develop preliminary characteristics of sexual maturity. This period is characterized by the growth of body hair, a spurt of physical growth, changes in body proportion, and the beginning of primary and secondary sex characteristics (56). They demonstrate some of the same physical changes, such as increased weight and height, vasomotor instability, increased perspiration, and active sebaceous glands. There is an increase in fat deposition approximately 1 year before the height spurt. These fat deposits last approximately 2 years or until skeletal growth and muscle mass increase. Females have more subcutaneous fat deposits, and the fat is lost at a slower rate, accounting for the fuller appearance of the female figure (56, 162, 170).

The girl's growth spurt begins as early as 8 years; the average is 10, and maximum height velocity is reached around 12 years. The boy's growth spurt begins around 12 years; maximum height velocity is reached about 14 years. The male grows approximately 4 inches (10 cm) per year for 2½ years and then begins a slower rate of growth. The female grows an average of 3 inches (7.5 cm) per year until menarche begins. For both males and females, the growth spurt begins in the hands and feet and progresses to the calves, forearms, hips, chest, and shoulders; the trunk is the last to grow appreciably (114, 166, 170).

As sebaceous glands of the face, back, and chest become active, acne (pimples) may develop. These skin blemishes are caused by collected sebaceous material being trapped under the skin in small skin pores. The preadolescent and later the adolescent are concerned with their appearance; these blemishes cause considerable embarrassment. The young person and the family may resort to use of numerous techniques, such as skin specialists, sun lamps, diets, makeup, lotions, and creams, to alleviate this problem. Basically, the skin should be kept clean. If the problem persists, a dermatologist should be seen. To prevent the youth's withdrawal from social contact, the parents and youth should be encouraged to seek medical attention as early as possible after acne occurs. Acne is further discussed in Chapter 11.

Vasomotor instability with rapid vasodilation causes excessive and uncontrollable blushing. This condition usually disappears when physical growth is completed.

Physical changes that occur in the female during prepuberty or preadolescence are:

1. Increase in transverse diameter of the pelvis.
2. Broadening of hips.
3. Tenderness in developing breast tissue and enlargement of areola diameter.
4. Axillary sweating.
5. Change in vaginal secretions from alkaline to acid pH.
6. Change in vaginal layer to thick, gray, mucoid lining.
7. Change in vaginal flora from mixed to Doederlein's lactic-acid producing bacilli.
8. Appearance of pubic hair from 8 to 14 years. Hair first appears on labia and then spreads to mons. Adult triangular distribution does not occur for approximately 2 years after initial appearance of pubic hair.*

Physical changes that occur in the male during this same period are:

1. Axillary sweating.
2. Increased testicular sensitivity to pressure.
3. Increase in testes size.
4. Changes in scrotum color.
5. Enlargement of breasts temporarily.
6. Increase in height and shoulder breadth.
7. Appearance of lightly pigmented hair at base of penis.
8. Increase in length and width of penis.†

✔ Teach parents about the physical and growth characteristics of the school-age child and the importance of nutrition, rest, immunizations, healthful activity, and regular medical and dental care. The rest of the chapter will refer to variables that influence physical health.

---

*These physical changes for females are listed in the approximate sequence of their occurrence (56, 95, 114, 133, 162, 166, 170).
† These physical changes for males are listed in the approximate sequence of their occurrence (56, 95, 114, 133, 162, 166, 170).

Modifications in Doing Physical Assessment with a School-age Child

✔ Information will be gained from the child, the parents or caretakers, or both when assessing the child.

A child may be better at drawing than at explaining what is wrong. For example, when asked to draw a big circle where it hurts, the child can normally identify the part if given a simple outline drawing of a child.

✔ The child over age 10 may wish to talk to the health-care worker without the parent present. Being alert to the child's chronological and developmental stage and his/her relationship with parents or caretakers will guide you in interviewing. Remember that the child is not there in isolation. Where the child lives (house or apartment, rural or urban area), how much personal space he/she has (own room, own bed), parents' marital situation, presence or absence of siblings, what is usually eaten, how much exercise and rest in 24 hours, who cares for the child after school if parents are working, and how he/she spends free time are all important in assessing the health status.

✔ When doing a review of systems, remember to use words the child understands. For example, instead of asking if the child has ever experienced any otitis problems, simplify as follows: Do your ears ever ache? Can you always hear when people talk to you?

✔ In assessing skin, remember that the school-age child is subject to allergic contact dermatitis, warts, herpes I, ringworm, and lice. When seeing any rash, a thorough history is in order to determine the diagnosis and necessary treatment.

A considerable number of children who appear normal in a vision screening test may suffer from accommodation and convergence difficulty. Close work becomes exhausting and almost overwhelming and may be the basis for poor achievement in school. One fairly common problem, **accommodative esophoria,** *where the eyes converge excessively in response to accommodation* can be corrected by the use of eyeglasses for near work (114, 119).

✔ Understanding that visual function is more than reading the 20/20 line on a Snellen chart will help you suggest a more comprehensive visual examination when a child is experiencing difficulty with school work.

Children and their parents do not always react predictably when there is a need for corrective lenses. Some children may feel self-conscious with their peers when wearing glasses. Parents may react as if the child's visual problem were a flaw and will deny, stating that they are sure the child will outgrow the problem, ignore the information, or even go from doctor to doctor in search of reassurance.

✔ If you are able to provide accurate information, using the principles of therapeutic communication, it will be exceedingly valuable to a child and family who are having difficulty adjusting to the need for therapy for a visual impairment. (This also holds true when therapy or a corrective device is needed on another body area.)

✔ When assessing a child's hearing and ears, remember that hearing should be fully developed by age 5. By age 7, most children should speak clearly enough to be understood by adults. If either of these factors seems deficient, a thorough investigation into congenital or inherited disorders and how this deficiency affects daily activities and communication is in order (119).

✔ In the young child, because the ear canal slants up, pull the auricle down, but not back as you would in an adult, when using the otoscope. Also, the ear canal is short in the young child, so take care not to insert the ear tip too far. The otoscope should be controlled so that if the young child moves suddenly, you can protect against the otoscope hitting the ear drum. The cone of light is more indistinct in a child than in an adult (119).

✔ Keep in mind the following as you continue assessment of the child's body systems: (1) if you think you hear fluid in the lungs, check the child's nose because sounds caused by nose fluid can be transmitted to the lungs; (2) a S_3 sound and sinus arrhythmia are fairly common in children's heart sounds; (3) a child's liver and spleen will usually enlarge more quickly than an adult's in response to disease; (4) the bladder is normally found much higher in a child than in an adult, and the kidneys can more often be palpated; (5) the genitalia should be inspected for congenital abnormalities that may have been overlooked and for irritation, inflammation, or swelling; (6) developmental guidelines must be used to assess the nervous system, specifically language development, motor and sensory functions, and cerebral function (8, 119).

✔ In the last 10 years musculoskeletal and posture problems, and especially scoliosis detection, have gained wide attention. **Scoliosis,** *lateral curvature of the spine,* is more common in girls than in boys and is of two types, functional and structural. Ask the child to bend over and touch the toes without bending the knees, and keeping the palms of the hands together. If the child has functional scoliosis, the external curve will disappear with this exercise; if it is structural, the curve will remain and sometimes become more pronounced. Early diagnosis is extremely important to arrest this problem (66, 114, 119). Refer the child and family to an orthopedic specialist. If scoliosis is not corrected early in life, it can result in mobility problems, obstructive pulmonary disease, and problems with body image later in life.

Nutritional Needs

Although caloric requirements per unit of body weight continue to decrease for the schoolchild, nutritional requirements remain relatively greater than the adult's. (See Appendix III.) The young schoolchild requires approximately 80 calories per kilogram daily or 35 calories per pound. By age 10 there is a decrease in the calories per kilogram for both boys (45 calories per kg) and girls (38 calories per kg). An individual child may require more or less calories than the RDA (Recommended Dietary Allowances), depending on size, activity, and growth rate (114, 116, 136, 172). Therefore, the total caloric range is from about 1600 to 2200 daily. Daily caloric needs can be approximated for the child by the formula 1000 calories the first year plus 100 calories for each additional year (116, 138, 166, 172).

Protein requirement for growth is 1 gram per pound or 36 to 40 grams of protein daily. Vitamin and mineral requirements are similar to those for the preschool child. Because of enlargement of ossification centers in the bone, vitamin D (400 units) and a large intake of calcium (800 to 1200 mg) are needed daily (116). Vitamin C needs are not met as easily as other nutritional requirements (116, 172). Many of the fruit-flavored juices supply significant amounts of ascorbic acid.

Water intake may be overlooked; the schoolchild needs 1.5 to 3 quarts daily, depending on the size of the child.

Nutritional needs for the schoolchild include one or more servings daily of the following foods (96, 114, 116, 172):

Meats and eggs (alternates: dry beans, dry peas, and lentils)	2 or more of a 2 or 3 ounce serving
Milk (whole, skim, or powdered)	2–4 cups
Fruits and vegetables (including a dark green or deep yellow vegetable for vitamin A and a fruit or vegetable that contains high vitamin C)	4 or more servings
Breads and cereals Fats and carbohydrates	4 or more servings to meet caloric needs

✔ Discuss with parents the importance of a balanced diet and foods that supply specific nutrients.

✔ Nutritional assessment is determined by a history of the child's food intake, looking at the general appearance and skin color and turgor; correlating height and weight; measuring subcutaneous tissue; checking for dental caries, allergies, and chronic illness; testing hemoglobin and hematocrit levels, and determining physical, cognitive, emotional, and social well-being (116, 172).

Eating Patterns

✔ It is important to discuss the child's eating needs and patterns with parents so that they can provide a diet with adequate caloric intake and nutrients. Parents should be encouraged to establish a consistent schedule for meals and to allow their school-age child to participate in the meal planning. The schoolchild of 6 or 7 is capable of learning about healthful eating and of helping plan and prepare meals. Such activities develop a healthy sense of industry and independence in the child if they are not overdone.

✔ Mealtime continues to cause dissension within most families. Parents are often upset by their child's terrible table manners. The young child stuffs food in with his/her hands, spills it, and incessantly chatters throughout breakfast, lunch, and supper. The time the family spends together eating can be much more pleasant if manners are not overemphasized. If discipline during meals is necessary, it should be kept to a minimum. When mealtime becomes a time of stress, digestive problems, poor eating habits, or a temporary aversion to food may occur. Making a fuss over eating certain foods may cause the child to reject them more strongly. Experience and time will improve eating patterns, as shown in Table 10–2 (43, 44, 133).

Food preferences and dislikes become strongly established during the school years. Food likes and dislikes are often carried over from the eating experiences of the toddler and preschooler. In addition, it is easy for the schoolchild, influenced by peers, TV commercials and other forms of advertisement, and the availability of "junk food," to avoid nutritious foods and to fill up on empty calories.

The child mimics family attitudes toward food and eating once he/she is a member of the family unit at mealtimes. Companionship and conversation at the child's level are essential for dining pleasure; the child wants to talk and participate in a group. He/she especially likes picnics and eating with peers. Because food and eating are such vital social and cultural concerns, the source of a nutritional problem may be as much a psychosocial problem as a physiological one.

Diet is also influenced by a child's activities. If the child has been active all day, he/she will be hungry and ready to eat. On the other hand, if the child has had limited activity or emotional frustrations during the

TABLE 10–2. Summary of Eating Patterns of Schoolchild

6 YEARS	7 YEARS	8 YEARS	9 YEARS	10 YEARS	11 YEARS	12 YEARS
Has large appetite. Likes between-meal and bedtime snacks. Is awkward at table. Likes to eat with fingers. Swings legs under table, often kicking people and things. Dawdles. Criticizes family members. Eats with better manners away from family.	Has extremes of appetite. Improves table manners. Is quieter at table. Is interested in table conversation. Leaves table with distraction.	Has large appetite. Enjoys trying new foods. Handles eating utensils skillfully. Has better table manners away from home.	Has controlled appetite. Eats approximately an adult meal. Acts more adult-like. Becomes absorbed in listening or talking.	Goes on eating sprees. Likes sweet foods. Criticizes parents' table manners. Has lapses in control of table manners at times. Enjoys cooking.	Has controlled appetite. Improves table manners when eating in a restaurant. Enjoys cooking.	Has large appetite. Enjoys most foods. Had adult-like table manners. Participates in table discussions in adult-like manner.

day, he/she may have no appetite. In addition, the schoolchild has more freedom to move without parental supervision and often has small amounts of money to spend on candy, soft drinks, and other treats. The schoolchild is eating on his/her own for the first time, eating school lunches or snacks at friends' homes; peers influence how he/she will apply what has been learned about diet. The child is frequently too busy to take time out to eat.

Share the following suggestions with parents to improve nutrition and meal-time:

1. Make food attractive and manageable.
2. See that food intake is sufficient.
3. Provide a rest period prior to meals.
4. Have a firm understanding with the child that play and television do not take precedence over eating properly.
5. Between-meal snacks are necessary and enjoyed and do not interfere with food intake at meals if eaten an hour or longer before mealtime. Milk, cheese, fresh fruits and vegetables, peanut butter, and fruit juices are desirable snacks for both general nutritional needs and dental health.
6. Breakfast is crucial for providing the child with sufficient calories to start the day. The child who attends school without breakfast frequently exhibits fatigue and poor attention (133).

Undernutrition in children can be manifested in underweight, fatigue, lassitude, restlessness, or irritability. Anorexia and digestive disturbances, such as diarrhea and constipation, signal improper utilization of nutrients. Poor muscular development may be evidenced by a child's posture—rounded shoulders, flat chest, and protuberant abdomen. Prolonged undernutrition may cause irregularities in dentition and may delay epiphyseal development and puberty (116, 133, 172).

Undernutrition and overnutrition may have the same causative factors: The child may be reflecting food habits of other family members, the parents and child may displace unrelated anxieties on food and mealtime, or eating may serve as a reward or punishment by both parents and child. *Overnutrition* and overweight are rarely caused by metabolic disturbances. **Obesity** is sometimes defined as an *individual who is 20 percent or more above ideal weight.* Obesity is the most frequent nutritional disorder of children in developed countries (121). In addition, childhood obesity can have serious social and emotional effects that may carry into adulthood (94). Prevention of childhood obesity through early nutrition education and established exercise habits is important. A weight gain in boys or girls between ages of 6 and 9 years is predictive of later obesity (139).

☛ Parents should be encouraged to promote food to their children as nourishment for their bodies, not as a reward or punishment. They should promote food as necessary and enjoyable. A healthy child's appetite corresponds to physiological needs and should be a valuable index in determining intake. Too often parents expect young children to eat as much as the parents do. The child should neither be forced to eat everything on his/her plate nor made to feel guilty if second portions of mother's special dish are not eaten.

☛ You can help parents learn about adequate nutrition for their child as well as what behavior to expect at each age. You can also aid teachers as they plan lessons on nutrition. For example, learning activities for the schoolchild could include visiting grocery stores, dairies, or farms as well as taking part in tasting parties and playing store. They could plan menus, cook various foods, and taste them. Such activities are unlimited.

Increasingly, dietary intake of excess sugar, food coloring, and other additives is being related to the child's behavior, especially hyperactivity. The whole family can benefit from natural foods, foods that have a minimum of preservatives or additives, and foods that are cooked properly (56, 85, 95, 141).

Rest and Exercise Needs

Rest. There is no rule of thumb for the amount of rest a child should have. Hours of sleep needed depend on variables such as age, health status, and the day's activities. Schoolchildren usually do not need a nap. They are not using up as much energy in growth as they were earlier. A 6-year-old usually requires about 11 hours of sleep nightly, but an 11-year-old may need only 9 hours (170). The schoolchild does not consciously fight sleep but may need firm discipline to go to bed at the prescribed hour. Sleep may be disturbed with dreams and nightmares, especially if he/she has considerable emotional stimulation before bedtime.

Exercise. Exercise is essential for muscular development, refinement of coordination and balance, gaining strength, and enhancing other body functions such as circulation, aeration, and waste elimination. The schoolchild should have a safe place to play and simple pieces of equipment. Because there are times when bad weather will keep a child from going outside, supplies should be available that will facilitate exercise indoors.

Parents should play actively with their children sometimes. Children benefit from their parents' knowledge of various activities and are encouraged by the attention. Exercise then becomes fun, not work. In America where the child can be constantly entertained by television, parents must sometimes encourage exercise.

↙ Review the child's rest and exercise needs with parents. At the same time, you may have an opportunity to discuss with parents how they are meeting their own needs for rest and exercise and how the parents and child can engage in activities that are mutually interesting and healthful.

Health Promotion and Injury Control

Immunizations. These should be given to the schoolchild, including immunization against measles, mumps, rubella, and polio if they have not been already. Diphtheria and tetanus toxoids combined with pertussis vaccine and OPV need to be given as indicated. Booster doses of DTP should be given by 6 years of age; pertussis vaccine is not necessary for children over this age. Girls should receive rubella vaccine before they enter puberty to prevent congenital defects in the baby should they be exposed to rubella during pregnancy. Boys should be immunized against mumps before the age of 12; mumps contracted during or after puberty can cause sterility. The need for tuberculin tests depends on the prevalence of tuberculosis and the risk of exposure (22, 114, 127, 136, 138, 164, 170). The influenza virus vaccine, pneumococcal vaccine, and hepatitis B vaccine are recommended for children in certain high-risk groups (3, 4, 162, 170).

In the United States, 20 million children under 13—almost 40 percent of all children—are not immunized against one or more preventable major childhood diseases. (In the developing world, 95 percent of the children are not immunized against common contagious diseases) (34).

↙ Emphasize to parents the importance of immunization and record keeping. Supply parents with information regarding free immunization programs and school requirements for immunization. Inform them of an appropriate immunization schedule. They should know, for example, that if 7-year-old Tommy steps on a rusty nail, he is protected from tetanus because of DTP immunization at age 5. Before a child receives an immunization, he/she should be told why and where it will be given. Such explanations will elicit cooperation and help the child to understand that neither the illness nor treatment is being imposed because he/she is bad.

Safety Promotion and Injury Control. These are of major concern for this age group as well as for younger children. Motor vehicle accidents and drowning are the leading causes of death for schoolchildren, while the rate of injuries from burns and poisonings are lowest in this age group (170, 173). Even though school-age children have developed more refined muscular coordination and control, their use of bicycles, skateboards, roller skates, and sports increases their risk for injury. They are susceptible to cuts, abrasions, fractures, strains, sprains, and bruises. The incidence of injury is significantly higher in school-age boys than girls, and the death rate of boys is twice that of girls (47, 170). Some of the injuries sustained during sporting activities may cause permanent disability due to damage to the epiphyseal cartilage or the neuromuscular system.

There is a group of children who appear to be *accident-prone.* They suffer more accidental injuries than the overall childhood population. Although the causative factors have not been completely determined, children who are overreactive, restless, impulsive, hostile, and immature are frequently found in this group (170).

↙ Parents should be encouraged to provide more supervision and attention to these children and to repeat, even to children who are not accident-prone, cautions as necessary. The child forgets when involved in play; conceptual thinking and judgment are not well developed so that the child does not foresee dangers.

↙ Accident prevention should be taught and enforced in school and at home. You need to promote safety by helping parents and children identify and avoid hazards. The school-age child has increasing cognitive maturity, including improved ability to remember past experiences and anticipate probable outcomes of his/her actions. This makes the child a good candidate for safety instructions (9, 170).

↙ Safety education should include information regarding the hazards of risk taking and improper use of equipment. Injury prevention should address motor vehicle injuries, drownings, burns, poisonings, falls, and sports-related injuries. The child should be taught the proper use of seatbelts in motor vehicles. Safe pedestrian behavior should be emphasized by teaching the child the proper way to cross streets, how to read traffic signals, and the dangers of street play. You should stress the safety and maintenance of two-wheeled vehicles (such as bicycles) and encourage the use of safety apparel where applicable (58). Water safety and survival skills should be taught with basic swimming skills at an early age. Families who go boating must teach related safety measures to their children.

↙ Meal preparation can be fun for the school-age child but the hazards of sharp knives, hot stoves, and hot liquids must be kept in mind. Supervise the use of matches or flammable chemicals, and teach the child the proper behavior if clothing becomes ignited. A family-designed fire escape plan should be initiated and practiced monthly.

✔ Most boys and girls love to climb trees; adults should teach them how to climb in the safest possible way. Explain the dangers involved in climbing electrical poles, water towers, and other dangerous structures. Instruct the child in the proper use of playground equipment and in the need to pick up toys from the floor to prevent falls.

✔ Instruct parents to keep potentially dangerous products in properly labeled receptacles. Educate the child regarding the dangers of taking nonprescription drugs and chemicals. Gun accidents are common during the school-age period (114). Parents who have a gun should keep it under lock and place the key in a child-proof location. Children of this age should be taught safety rules concerning guns.

✔ You can advise parents of the hazards associated with organized contact sports; stress the use of protective head, elbow, and knee gear. Instruct the child in the proper use of sporting equipment, especially the more hazardous devices—skis, trampolines, skateboards, mopeds, and all-terrain vehicles.

✔ You can reinforce any teaching that takes place in the home. Books, films, and creation of a mock situation can all supplement your verbal instruction. You and the parents will repeat the same cautions endlessly. Yet, caution and concern can be overdone. When a child is overly anxious about his/her welfare, tension can lead not only to accident-proneness but to being hurt worse when he/she does encounter danger. In the face of danger, panic prevents clear thinking and skillful action. In addition, overcaution stifles independence, initiative, and maturing. It is important to realize the necessity of shifting responsibility to the child with increasing age.

✔ Responsibility for the child's health rests with the parents, but you can emphasize to parents the importance of regular examinations at a clinic or from a family physician and dentist. Every child should have a thorough preschool examination, including visual and auditory screening, and posture and general health examination. Correction of health problems is essential, since they may be a cause for injuries, illness, or difficulties with school work or peers. Realize that in the United States 10 million children get basically no health care.

✔ As a nurse you have a responsiblity to strengthen the school health program in your community through direct services; teaching the board of education, teachers, parents, and students about the value and utilization of such a program, in spite of costs; and working for legislation to finance and implement programs that do more than first-aid care. A school health program should supervise not only the child's physical but also emotional, mental, and social health. Instruction in personal hygiene, disease prevention, nutrition, safety, family life, and group living are of interest to the schoolchild and should be under the direction of the school nurse.

✔ If there are chronically ill or disabled students in school, special preparation should be given to the teachers as well as the students and their parents. You can promote understanding of the child and his/her condition, of the child's need to use individual potential, and of a total rehabilitation program. Several references will be helpful (78, 114, 116, 133, 136, 139, 156, 166, 170).

Common Health Problems: Prevention and Treatment

Although the child should now remain basically healthy, health problems do exist.

✔ Inform parents of the need to treat both acute and chronic conditions. *Respiratory conditions* (colds, sore throats, and earaches) account for over 50 percent of the reported acute illnesses among children in this age group. *Infective and parasitic diseases* (scabies, impetigo, ringworm, and head lice) are of concern because of their health threat to the child and to others. *Diseases of the digestive tract* (stomachaches, peptic ulcers, colitis, diarrhea, and vomiting) may have a psychosocial as well as a physiological etiology (23). Visual and hearing impairment, sickle cell anemia, asthma, hyperactivity, epilepsy, migraine headaches, hypertension, diabetes mellitus, and obesity are *chronic health problems* which may affect the school-age child (114, 125, 177). Or the child may have been born with a congenital anomaly that can be only partially corrected or a disease such as hemophilia that needs continuing treatment. A considerable number of schoolchildren have risk factors which in adults are predictive of coronary heart disease: hypertension, increased serum cholesterol and triglycerides, and obesity. The elementary school population may also be the main reservoir of infectious hepatitis type A, for schoolchildren often have a mild undiagnosed disease that is spread person to person (52).

Because of the short urethra, girls are prone to *urinary infection;* this may be diagnosed by reddened genitals, a feeling of burning on urination, and an abnormal appearance and chemical analysis of the urine. Normal urinary output from 6 to 12 years is from 500 cubic centimeters to the adult output of 1500 cubic centimeters daily. Pinworms accompany urinary tract infections in about 50 percent of the cases (52).

The 7-year-old has fewer illnesses but may complain of *fatigue* or *muscular pain*. It is common to call these "growing pains"; however, this is not accurate since growing is not painful. Tension, overactivity or exertion, bruising, or injury may cause the leg pains. Pains in the knees with no exertional signs are also common in school-age children. Such pains usually occur late in the day or night and disappear in the morning (114).

✔ Children with persistent leg pains should be referred to a physician. The 8- and 9-year-olds are generally healthy but may complain of minor aches to get out of disagreeable tasks. Such behavior should not be reinforced by undue attention.

✔ *Visual impairments* that occur in the younger child may be undetected and untreated until the child attends school. Visual acuity may not develop normally. Table 10-3 lists signs and symptoms to assess when defective vision is present (52, 114, 136). It is essential that visual problems be corrected.

Otitis externa *is inflammation of the external auditory canal and auricle.* It can be caused by a variety of organisms and is most commonly called "swimmer's ear," although it can be caused by trauma from foreign objects. The condition usually causes pain in the ear and is aggravated by moving the auricle.

✔ Prevention is in the following measures: (1) Keep fingers and instruments out of ears; (2) keep the head out of water when bathing to avoid having the ear canals fill with dirty soap and water; and (3) use an acetic acid 2 percent solution immediately after swimming to restore the normal canal pH. Treatment lies in having any debris removed from the ear (by a healthcare worker), putting warm compresses to the ear, and applying as prescribed an antibiotic-steroid drop preparation (52).

Serous otitis media *is the accumulation of nonpurulent fluid in the middle ear,* caused by eustachian tube obstruction. With the use of an otoscope, clear or transparent yellowish or bluish fluid can be seen behind the tympanic membrane, sometimes with air bubbles. The schoolchild complains of fullness in the ear or a snapping sensation and often does not respond to usual verbal cues because of hearing loss.

✔ Although decongestants have frequently been used to treat this condition, there is no good evidence to show their usefulness in clearing more rapidly than it would on its own. However, the child should be followed for resolution because a chronic hearing loss may be a complication of longstanding serous otitis (52).

Allergic rhinitis *is an allergic reaction affecting the nasal mucosa* (and often the conjunctiva). The child has a clear, thin nasal discharge, is a mouth breather, and often has a broad midsection of nose with a horizontal crease along the lower portion because of "allergic salute," rubbing the nose upward and outward.

✔ Finding the offending antigen is the first step. If it is seasonal, the child should avoid exposure to heavy

TABLE 10-3 Signs and Symptoms Indicating Defective Vision in Schoolchildren

Behavior

Attempts to brush away blur; rubs eyes frequently; frowns, squints.

Stumbles frequently or trips over small objects.

Blinks more than usual; cries often or is irritable when doing close work.

Holds books or small playthings close to eyes.

Shuts or covers one eye, tilting or thrusting head forward when looking at objects.

Has difficulty in reading or in other schoolwork requiring close use of the eyes; omits words or confuses similar words.

Exhibits poor performance in activities requiring visual concentration within arm's length (reading, coloring, drawing, etc.). Unusually short attention span; persistent word reversals after second grade.

Disinterested in distant objects or fails to participate in games such as playing ball.

Engages in outdoor activity mostly (running, bicycling, etc.), avoiding activities requiring visual concentration within arm's length.

Sensitive to light.

Unable to distinguish colors.

Steps carefully over sidewalk cracks, or around light or dark sections of block linoleum floors.

Trips at curbs or stairs.

Poor eye-hand coordination for age, excessively hard-to-read handwriting, difficulty with tying shoelaces or buttoning-unbuttoning.

Appearance

Crossed eyes (iris of one eye turned in or out and not symmetrical with other eye.)

Red-rimmed, encrusted, or swollen eyelids.

Repeated styes.

Watery or red eyes.

Complaints

Cannot see blackboard from back of room.

Blurred or double vision following close eye work.

Dizziness, headaches, or nausea following close eye work.

Eyes itch, burn, or feel scratchy.

---

concentrations of ragweed, trees, or grass during the pollinating season. Using an air conditioner with a filter may be helpful. If the problem is perennial, a dust-free environment may be the goal. Damp cleaning the child's room as well as vacuuming should be carried out at least once a week. Bed pads, heavy rugs, stuffed animals, upholstered furniture, and feather pillows should be avoided since they hold dust. Pets need to be kept away from the bedroom and sometimes from the child completely. Tobacco smoke and chemical irritants may also cause problems. Use of an antihistimine can be effective if taken on a regular basis during symptomatic periods. If the above measures do not help, an allergist should be consulted (52). Other respiratory infections and allergies may occur. Consult a pediatric nursing text for more information.

Herpes simplex or **herpes type I** *is a vesicular eruption of the skin and mucous membranes above the umbilicus.* It usually appears in its primary and more severe forms in children. The most common signs and symptoms are soreness of the mouth from vesicular eruption of mucosa, inflammation and swelling of gums, usually enlarged submandibular lymph nodes, and a fever as high as 105°F. (Herpes type II will be discussed in Chapter 12).

✓ Because there is no specific cure, only general measures can be taken: (1) Maintain adequate fluid intake even though the mouth is too sore to tolerate carbonated or citrus fruits; give bland liquids through straws; (2) use saline solution as mouthwash; (3) take an antipyretic for fever; (4) apply topical anesthetic to lesions as necessary and helpful; (5) isolate the child from the newborn, people with open skin lesions, or persons on immunosuppressive therapy, as herpes I can become severe in these persons (52).

Contact dermatitis due to poison oak or poison ivy causes *itching vesicles, usually on the extremities.* Most cases come from contact directly or with the smoke of burning plants, from unwashed contaminated clothes, from dried uprooted plants that contain resin, or from a pet that has had contact with the plant.

✓ Prevention of disease development will be furthered by teaching the child to recognize the appearance of the plant, washing all clothes if contact is made, and washing the skin contact area immediately. The mainstay of therapy in a known case is soaking the affected area with saline or aluminum acetate solution or using cold compresses for 20 minutes four to six times daily. A drying lotion, such as calamine, after each soak or compress may be helpful. Sometimes a prescription medication is necessary to reduce itching and an injectable or oral steroid may be used in severe cases (52).

Tinea corporis, *ringworm of nonhairy skin, is a superficial infection involving the face, trunk or limbs, mostly the face and arms.* **Tinea capitis,** *ringworm of the head,* may also occur. The name *ringworm* is given because the lesions (usually one or two) start as red, small, scaling patches, then expand outward with the center clearing as they get larger. They are usually asymptomatic or mildly itchy. A topical antifungal agent applied daily for 1 or 2 weeks will usually clear the lesions (52).

Warts are *virus-caused intradermal papillomas* that usually appear in three distinct patterns: common, plantar, and venereal. (Venereal warts are usually a problem in later years.) *Common warts* usually appear on the hands and fingers but may appear on other skin areas or mucous membranes.

✓ The usual treatment is dichloroacetic acid that will eventually allow the lesion to dissolve. *Plantar warts* are usually on the feet. They have a central nodule with several punctate spots. Dichloroacetic acid may be applied after they are pared down with a scalpel (52).

Pediculosis *is an infestation of the head or body by pediculus humanis, or lice.* (**Phthirius pubis,** the *crab louse, affects the genital region* and is usually seen later than in childhood.) Both species are transmitted either by close personal contact or in shared clothing, combs, bedclothes, or upholstered seats in public places. *Head lice,* **Pediculus humanus capitis,** is usually diagnosed by seeing the nits or ova that are attached to the base of the hairs. The lice themselves are rarely seen. Neither are the lice often seen on the skin. Skin lesions appear from scratching the areas where the lice have been.

✓ Any contaminated clothing, hats, towels, bedclothing, and so on should be dry cleaned or washed in hot water and dried at a high temperature for as long as lice remain in the home. The infested head should be shampooed with gamma benzene hexachloride 1 percent shampoo. Combs and hairbrushes should be disinfected with hot water. In addition to thorough bathing, the body can be treated with the same medication used for the head in a 6 to 10 percent sulfur ointment base. Occasionally an oral antihistamine needs to be prescribed to relieve itching (52, 160). Everyone who lives in a lice-infested home should be inspected at least daily for 2 weeks. In addition, a complete change of clothes, scrubbing toilet seats, and vacuuming upholstered furniture and rugs should be done daily.

Diabetes mellitus is an *inherited disease with a metabolic component, which translates into elevated blood glucose, and a vascular component, which translates into problems with small blood vessels, especially in the eyes and kidneys.* Type I is called insulin-dependent diabetes mellitus (IDDM). It was previously called juvenile, brittle, or ketosis-prone. Type II is the other major category, generally referring to adult-onset diabetes.

✓ It is beyond the scope of this book to delve into type I, other than to say that a dip-stick urine test is a simple, effective method to screen children for this disorder. Symptoms include increase in urination, increase in thirst and hunger, along with weight loss and fatigue (52). Consult a pediatric nursing text for additional information (114, 170).

Mumps is a viral disease, characterized by acute

salivary gland swelling, especially the parotid. In addition to anterior ear pain, the child may have headache, lethargy, anorexia, and vomiting. Fever is usually present. The disease can be avoided with the live mumps virus vaccine. There is no specific treatment other than supportive: antipyretics for fever, rest, and plenty of fluids. Complications are meningoencephalitis, nerve deafness, usually unilateral, and **orchitis**, *inflammation of one or both testes,* also usually unilateral (impotence and sterility are extremely rare) (52).

Rabies, *an acute infectious disease characterized by involvement of the central nervous system, resulting in paralysis and finally death,* is fortunately not a common disease, but comes from a common problem: the biting of a human by a mammal (39). Refer to Chapter 9 for treatment.

✔ If a diagnosis of rabies is considered, it must be reported to the local health department and Center for Disease Control (CDC) in Atlanta. The CDC staff will act as consultants for the use of antirabies vaccine, as well as all other factors surrounding the case. The latest CDC recommendations are found in the *Morbidity and Mortality Weekly Report* (164). Prevention is in keeping the child away from unfamiliar animals, particularly ones that act agitated, in seeing that all pets are properly vaccinated, and in taking steps to get preexposure immunization for high-risk children—those living or visiting in countries where rabies is a constant threat (39).

Increasingly, the ill effects of *smoking and drug and alcohol abuse* are emerging as a regular health problem among adolescents. These habits are influenced by the habits of parents, sibilngs, and peers. In one study over 50 percent of the boys were given their first cigarette by parents. The boys did not enjoy smoking but felt a need to do it to show off; knowledge of the effects of cigarette smoking was not a deterrent (60, 155).

✔ In addition to the ill effects caused by actual smoking, children in families with cigarette smokers have an increased rate of respiratory conditions. These small children have an increased number of days per year when their activities are restricted due to illness (14). Teach parents that smoking may be interfering with the normal growth and development of schoolchildren, and that parental and other adult example is important. For example, in the West and Southwest United States, adult Hispanics have tended to smoke fewer cigarettes than nonHispanic Whites. One study showed that Hispanic children also smoked less than non-Hispanic White children. Interestingly, to date Hispanics have had fewer respiratory diseases associated with cigarette smoking—lung cancer, emphysema, and chronic obstructive pulmonary disease, presumably because of lower tobacco consumption (46).

✔ The school nurse and teacher can do considerable health teaching, giving students an introduction to positive health habits. Some programs emphasize that the body is a beautiful system, that no one should abuse the system by doing or using anything damaging, and to "just say no." The program should emphasize that people can be happy and active when they avoid the use of alcohol, drugs, or cigarettes to offset the preponderance of advertising that links youth, beauty, and excitement with these activities (13, 128, 129, 147, 155). Emphasize to adults that more effective than organized educational attempts is the influence of significant adults, those who take a personal interest in the child and who set an example: parents who neither smoke, drink, or use drugs nor give cigarettes, alcohol, or drugs to their children; the teacher who not only teaches content but also lives the teaching; parents and health care workers who have quit smoking; the athletic coach who is committed to no smoking; nurses and obstetricians who can help young women change habits; the nurse or pediatrician who counsels children and adolescents. Equally important, or more so, is the peer group; leaders of the peer group who have positive health habits should be used as models (10). Peer communication is also effective for initiating hygienic habits. You may have a role in working with the peer group.

Psychosocial Concepts

Cognitive-Intellectual Development

The schoolchild has a strong curiosity to learn, especially when motivation is strengthened by interested parents and opportunities for varied experiences in the home and school.

Learning, behavior, and personality are complex and are not easily explained by one theory. This section utilizes information from a number of theorists. Refer to Chapter 5 for a review of how the three major schools of theorists explain the development of learning, behavior, and personality.

The Pattern of Intellectual Development. This can be traced through the school years (43, 44, 105, 107, 108, 109, 165). In American culture the 6-year-old is supposed to be ready for formal education. The child in first grade is frequently still in the Preoperational Stage. Thinking is concrete and animistic; he/she is only beginning to understand semiabstract symbols. Thus the basis for formal study is lacking and depends on the direction and guidance of adult authority. The child still defines objects in terms of their use and effect upon self. He/she reads and knows numbers, but this ability depends on previous help. Learning occurs frequently through imitation and incidental suggestion. Because of centering, the child may not be able to consider parts and wholes in words at the same time. The child who cannot accurately do reversals may confuse *was* and *saw*. The child who cannot follow transformations may not be able to sound out words; individual sounds of *c*, *a*, and *p* may not be recognized as cap. There appears to be a high correlation between ability to converse and beginning reading achievement (168).

At about age 7, the child enters the stage of **Concrete Operations,** *which involves systematic reasoning about tangible or familiar situations and the ability to use logical thought to analyze relationships and structure the environment into meaningful categories.* The child must have interactions with concrete materials in order to build understanding that is basic for the next stage (108, 168). He/she uses visible props to form mental images and learn about many aspects of a concept or one aspect of a broad concept. For example, a car (broad concept) can be identified as a Ford or a Chevrolet (one aspect). This identification is based on instruction or experience and the use of memory. During this period, the child becomes less egocentric, less animistic, and better able to do cause-effect and logical reasoning. A number of mental strategies or operations are learned (165).

Operations characteristic of this stage include classification, seriation, nesting, multiplication, reversibility, transformation, conservation, and decentering (40, 105, 112, 165, 168).

1. **Classification** *involves sorting objects in groups according to specific and multiple attributes,* such as length, size, shape, color, class of animals, or trademark. School children can identify which kind of Ford is approaching on the highway.
2. **Seriation** *involves ordering objects according to decreasing or increasing measure,* such as height, weight or strength. The child knows A is longer than B, B longer than C, and A longer than C.
3. **Nesting** *involves understanding how a subconcept fits into a larger concept.* For example, a German Shepherd is one kind of dog; a lazyboy chair and a dining room chair are both chairs.
4. **Multiplication** *involves simultaneously classifying and seriating,* using two numbers together to come out with a greater amount.
5. **Reversibility** *involves returning to the starting point or performing opposite operations or actions with the same problem or situation.* The child can add and subtract, multiply and divide the same problems. A longer row of clips can be squeezed together to form a shorter row, and vice versa; the child realizes the number of clips has not changed.
6. **Transformation** *involves the ability to see the shift from a dynamic to static or constant state, to understand the process of change, to focus on the continuity and sequence, on the original and final states.* For example, the child realizes or anticipates how a shorter row of pennies was shifted to become a longer row or the gradual shift in level of fluid in a container as it is poured into another container, and the increasing level of fluid in the second container.
7. **Conservation** *involves understanding transformation conceptually and that a situation has not changed, to see the sameness of a situation or object in spite of a change in some aspect, and that mass or quantity are the same even if it changes shape or position.* For example, six paper clips moved from a 6-inch line to an 8-inch line remain six paper clips. Water, in boiled form is vapor, which can return to water, and freeze. It is still the same amount of water; nothing is lost in the process.
8. **Decentering** *involves coordination of two or more dimensions,* or the ability to focus on several characteristics simultaneously. For example, space and length dimensions can be considered; the youngest child would consider only one or the other. When twelve paperclips are spread from 6 inches to 12 inches, the child realizes the clips are spread, there are not more clips.

These operations increase in complexity as the child matures from an empirical to logical orientation. The child can look at a situation, analyze it, and come up with an answer without purposefully going through each step. For example, if two rows of coins have been spread out, the child does not have to count the coins. He/she realizes that nothing was added or subtracted to the rows, so each row still has the same number.

The child learns and can recall associations between sequences and groupings of events. At first he/she makes associations within a certain context or environment; later memory is used to transfer these associations to different contexts or environments. The child also rehearses; in the time between a learning experience and a memory test or application of learning he/she goes over mentally what has been learned (95, 165).

Thus by age 7 the child is more reflective and has a deeper understanding of meanings and feelings. He/she is interested in conclusions and logical endings. Now language is used freely, not only to establish rapport but to inquire and give a running commentary on the matters at hand. Attention span has lengthened enough that the child may work several hours alone on an interesting activity. He/she is more aware of the environment and the people in it. Although still interested in fairies, Superman, and magic, the child is beginning to have a scientific interest in causes and conditions. He/she is serious about such concepts as government and civilization and enjoys inventing with household odds and ends or using a chemistry or carpentry set. The child can seriate by length and understands area or mass (43, 56, 95).

The 8-year-old's thinking is less animistic and more aware of the impersonal forces of nature. The child does not grasp complex rules and instead improvises simple ones. He/she is intellectually expansive, inquiring about the past and future, the insides of earth and people, primitive people or people of other cultures, his/her own race and nationality. This is a favorable time to strengthen sensible attitudes against racial prejudice and reinforce natural tolerance and sympathy for others. The child begins to understand logical reasoning, conclusions, contexts, and implications. He/she is less self-centered in thinking and understands more than a personal perspective. He/she learns by experience as well as from others (43, 56, 95).

The 9-year-old is realistic, reasonable, self-motivated, and intellectually energetic and curious. The child has a growing capacity to put mind and energies to tasks on his/her own initiative and with minimal direction. The child is so busy and involved that he/she does not like to be interrupted and may work for 2 or 3 hours without anyone's reinforcement. The child likes to compete with self, so that he/she repeatedly tries an activity until the activity is mastered to satisfaction. At this age, the child is an excellent pupil and a perfector of skills. He/she likes to plan in advance. If a task is complicated, he/she asks to have successive steps explained. If unsuccessful in doing the task, he/she is realistic in self-appraisal. He/she likes to classify, identify, and make inventories or lists. The child is likely to know all the facts and figures about a baseball team, flags of different countries, or distinctions among different cars or airplanes. He/she can seriate by weight. The focus is on details. He/she does not like magic and believes in law (and that rules can be flexible) as much as luck or chance (43, 56, 95).

The 10-year-old's thinking is concrete and matter of fact. He/she likes to reason and to participate in elementary discussions about social problems. A reasonable amount of homework is accepted without resentment because learning is enjoyable. The child wants to measure up to a challenge, defined in the social norms of the group. He/she likes to memorize, identify facts, locate cities on a map, or list serially familiar items. There is still difficulty in seeing relationships, but he/she likes to think in terms of cause and effect. Attention span may be short and choppy. Frequently planned shifts in activity and a friendly classroom are helpful to intellectual activity. He/she ranges out into a wide sphere of interests and yet concentrates on each for the moment (43, 56, 95).

The 11-year-old has boundless curiosity but is not reflective. Thinking is concrete and specific. The child likes action in learning, to move about the classroom freely or try experiments. He/she concentrates well when working competitively with one group against another. The child prefers a certain amount of routine, wants school to be related to reality, and is better at rote memorization than at generalization. By now he/she can understand relational terms such as weight and size (43, 56, 95).

The child at 12 years likes to learn and consider all sides of a situation. He/she is more independent in doing homework, entering a self-chosen task with zeal and initiative. Motivation comes by an inner drive rather than by competition, but he/she likes group work. The child is better able to classify, arrange, and generalize, understands conservation of volume, and likes to discuss and debate. He/she is beginning abstract thinking. Verbal, formal reasoning is possible. Now the moral of a story is understood (43, 56, 95).

✔ Discuss the child's changing cognitive abilities with parents, as well as ways they can contribute to the cognitive achievement. If parents do not understand that certain cognitive behavior is age appropriate, their interactions with and guidance of the child may be less effective.

Cognitive development and an increasing understanding of implications and consequences, as well as of cause-effect relations, may be a factor in the changing fearfulness of the child. By age 7 or 8, most fears that are typical of preschoolers (darkness, spooks) have been resolved. The schoolchild is fearful of natural hazards, unsafe conditions, school problems, disease, bodily injury, separation, excess punishment, death, breaking the moral code, and hell. Ten- and 11-year-olds report fears of dangerous animals, people, machines, weapons, vehicles, natural hazards, war, the bomb, disease, separation from or death of loved ones, personal death, breaking the moral code, and hell. Some of these fears are realistic as the child increasingly moves out into the community alone, for example, fear of vehicles or dangerous people. Adults also express fears of dangerous animals and people, natural hazards, weapons, or war (91, 175).

✔ As a nurse, remember that the school-age child has great fear of bodily injury, disease, separation from loved ones, death, excess punishment (some diagnostic and treatment procedures seem like punishment), and doing wrong actions. Miller gives specific suggestions for nursing practice that help offset the child's fears (91).

Concept of Time. This evolves during the early school period (43, 44). The time sense of the 6-year-old is as much in the past as the present. The child likes to hear about his/her babyhood. The future concerns the child primarily in relation to significant holidays. Duration of an episode has little time meaning. Time is counted by the hours; minutes are disregarded.

The 7-year-old is interested in the present. Sense of time is practical, sequential, and detailed. The child likes a personal watch since he/she can read a clock, and knows the sequence of months, seasons, and years. Passage of time from one event to another and a specific time with a specific task are understood; thus he/she plans the day (43).

The 8-year-old is more responsible in relation to time and is extremely aware of punctuality. The 9-year-old can tell time without difficulty, plans the day, and generally tries to pack in more than possible. He/she likes to know how long a task will take when asked to do a task. The child is especially interested in ancient times (43).

The 10-year-old is less driven by time than the 9-year-old. He/she is interested in the present; the best time is now. The child is able to get places on time with his/her own initiative. The 11-year-old child feels the relentless passing of time and is more adept at handling time. He/she feels the difference between time dragging and flying by and defines time as a distance from one event to another (44).

The 12-year-old defines time as duration, a measurement, and plans ahead so he/she feels life is under personal control. He/she is well rooted in the present but is excited about what will happen in the future (44).

🖊 You can help parents understand that their school-age children do not have adult concepts of time. The mother who is distraught because her 6- or 7-year-old constantly dawdles in getting ready for school can be helped by understanding the child's concept of time. The mother must still be firm in direction but not expect the impossible. She can look forward to improvement in the 8-year-old.

🖊 Understanding maturing time concepts will also aid you as you explain the sequence of a procedure to the schoolchild in the doctor's office, school, clinic, or hospital.

Spatial Concepts. These concepts also change with more experience (43, 44). The 6-year-old is interested in specific places and in relationships between home, neighborhood, and an expanding community. He/she knows some streets and major points of interest. By the age of 7 the sense of space is becoming more realistic. The child wants some space of his/her own, such as a room or portion of it. The heavens and various objects in space and in the earth are of keen interest (43).

For the 8-year-old, personal space is expanding as the child goes more places alone. He/she knows the neighborhood well and likes maps, geography, trips. He/she understands the compass points and can distinguish right and left on others as well as on self (43).

Space for the 9-year-old includes the whole earth. He/she enjoys pen pals from different lands, geography, and history. For the 10-year-old, space is rather specific, where things are, such as buildings. The 11-year-old perceives space as nothingness that goes on forever, a distance between things. He/she is in good control of getting around in the personal space (43, 44).

The 12-year-old understands that space is abstract and has difficulty defining it. Space is nothing, air. He/she can now travel alone to more distant areas and understands how specific points relate to each other (44).

🖊 Encourage the parents to discuss spatial concepts with the child to facilitate abstract reasoning. Pontious (117) and Webb (168) give practical suggestions for using Piaget's concepts in care and teaching of children.

Entering School. School entry is a crisis for the child and family, for behavior must be adapted to meet new situations. The school experience has considerable influence on the child because he/she is in formative years and spends much time in school. School, society's institution to help the child develop the fullest intellectual potential and a sense of industry, should help the child learn to think critically, make judgments based on reason, accept criticism, develop social skills, cooperate with others, accept other adult authority, and to be a leader and follower. The course of instruction should be such that every child has a sense of successful accomplishment in some area. One must not think, however, that only school promotes these cognitive and social skills. The home and other groups, peer or organized clubs, are important in their own way for intellectual and social development and for promoting a sense of achievement and industry.

Regular attendance at school starts early for some children, perhaps at 2½ to 3 years in nursery school. But not all children are emotionally ready for school, even at age 6 or 7. If the child is unprepared for school, separation anxiety may be intense. The demands of a strange adult and the peer group may be overwhelming.

🖊 Various actions help to prepare the child for school, such as teaching the child his/her address and full name, independence in self-care, and basic safety rules. The preschool physical and dental examination and an orientation to the school and teacher promote a sense of anticipation and readiness. Parents should examine their attitudes about the child's entering school. Some parents seem eager to be rid of a portion of responsibility. Others are worried about the new influences and fear loss of control. Because the parents' attitudes so strongly affect the child, they should verbalize the positive aspects.

✔ The parent or classroom teacher (and the nurse in the health care setting) can stimulate the child's learning in the following ways:

1. Let each child's success be measured in terms of improved performance.
2. Structure for individuation, not for convergence. Avoid having all learning activities structured so that there is only one right answer.
3. Provide activities that are challenging, not overwhelming.
4. Arrange for individual activities to be accomplished in company of peers, when appropriate, since peer interaction provides encouragement and assistance.
5. Demonstrate problem solving and thinking behavior to serve as a model for the child (168).

There is increasing societal pressure to accelerate the child in the educational process. Piaget contends that optimal comprehension results from numerous experiences over a period of time. Studies of schoolchildren show that a child can quickly learn a specific and advanced task but often with limited retention and transfer. Further, apparent shifts from Concrete to Formal Operations may result from experiences unrelated to education. Direct verbal instruction and use of **cognitive conflict** (*getting the child to question perceptions*) can result in acquisition of conservation abilities, but transfer appears to be limited. Success at learning tasks of increasing complexity depends on levels and interactions of subskills already possessed by the learner. Rather than concentrating on learning of specific tasks, the home or classroom setting should encourage thinking in the child. A variety of experiences and teaching methods increase comprehension, learning, and transfer, which promote acceleration to the next cognitive level. Piecemeal acceleration often results in distorted or incomplete conceptual development that may hamper future thinking (95, 168).

The *teacher–pupil relationship* is important for it is somewhat similar to the parent–child relationship. Often, however, the classes are so large that the teacher is unable to give much individualized time and attention to each child or to become acquainted with his/her uniqueness. Although the teacher sometimes represents a greater authority figure than the parents, the emotional bond between parent and child is ordinarily stronger than between teacher and child, and the wise teacher does not act like a substitute parent. The child needs from the teacher a wholesome friendliness, consideration, fairness, sense of humor, and a philosophy that encourages his or her maturity. The teacher should be emotionally and physically healthy and have a thorough understanding of child development.

Problems of the family and child are brought into sharp focus when the child enters school. The teacher sees many difficulties: the loneliness of an only child; the pain of the child where there has been divorce or death in the family; the negative self-image of the child who is not as physically coordinated or intellectually sharp as his/her peers; the child with dyslexia or learning difficulties; the **school-phobic child** *who is fearful about or refuses to attend school*. Several theories have developed on the **school-phobic child,** one of which describes an overprotective mother, a sense of insecurity and uncertainty, and a sense that mother does not want the child to leave home and gain independence. Very little has been written about father's role, but he has been viewed by some as passive and by some as firm and controlling. School phobia or separation anxiety can be an indicator of underlying schizophrenia, or it can be nothing more than a normal child with a temporary conflict (99).

✔ School experiences are vivid in the child's memory. The child needs someone to listen to and talk about these experiences when he/she arrives home. This strengthens language skills, self-concept, and self-respect. If the child is put off or no one is there to listen, he/she will increasingly turn inward and may refuse to talk when the adult is ready. The parents taking a few minutes from supper preparation can be very important to the child.

✔ Help parents realize that the child's ability to learn and achieve in school is affected by factors other than intellectual ability. The educational level of the mother is one of the strongest predictors of a child's academic performance and measured intelligence at ages 4 and 7 (145). Failure to achieve may be the child's reaction to a hostile home environment, poor nutrition, physical illness, a troubled classroom, or a teacher's personal problem. Even the design of the school or physical attributes and appearance of the classroom may contribute to poor achievement. If the child cannot see or hear well, is uncomfortable or bothered by distractions and noise, feels unsafe, or has insufficient space, then attention, interest, and learning are reduced. Further, some classrooms are built to foster rigid teacher behavior; some children need more flexibility in the program (21, 146). Parents may project their inferiority feelings onto the child and he/she feels that it is useless to try. The child may be punishing self out of guilt about past misdeeds, real or imagined, or may be asking for attention. Or he/she may have been placed in the wrong learning group, either above or below personal abilities. Occasionally, these negative factors may cause a child to try harder, to sublimate and overcompensate, and to achieve well if ability is present.

✔ Too much pushing by parents for the child to be a success, perfect in physical skills, the most intellectual, or a hard worker can backfire. The pressure that is generated may be so intense that the child eventually does not succeed at anything. Perfectionistic, highly successful, career- or professional-focused parents are apt to push the child too much. If a parent cannot admit mistakes, he/she is unlikely to tolerate mistakes made by the child. And all of us—parents and children—*do* make mistakes. The child may become a perfectionist from parental example and behavior. Certain signs and symptoms are clues. The child manifests:

1. Extreme concern about appearance.
2. Avoiding tasks, play, or school because of fear of failure.
3. Dawdling or procrastinating on easy tasks to avoid harder ones; or working so slowly on projects that creativity is lost.
4. Jealousy and envy of the apparent success and perfection of others.
5. Wanting to do something for which the child has no ability or talent.
6. Low tolerance for mistakes; the person who wins the race may feel he was not successful because he did not set any records (29).

If these behaviors are present, teach the parents to work on relaxing themselves as well as the child and developing a sense of tolerance and humor. They can join the child in new activities—done for fun and without competition. They and the child can set realistic goals. They can praise the child's efforts, not focus on the outcome. You may be their counselor, or you may refer them to counseling (29).

School difficulty may arise from the misuse of IQ testing. IQ scores are not the same as intelligence; IQ scores tell what the child has learned at school. An IQ score can go up or down many points in 1 year. The child with a low IQ score may be placed in the class for slow learners; 1 year in such a group may damage the child for the rest of the school years, even if he/she is later placed with a brighter group. Teachers are likely to respond to this child differently, expecting little and offering little. Attention is usually directed to the child who scored high, which further improves the score. IQ scores can predict academic success generally, but they say nothing about a child's curiosity, motivation, inner thoughts, creativity, ability to get along with people, or ability to be a productive citizen. Group standardized aptitude, achievement, and vocational tests used in schools (and the business world) cost more than they are worth (56, 95). Certainly, children should not be separated into gifted or retarded classes only on the basis of IQ scores.

Standardized achievement tests should be given less weight in educational decisions; they do not screen even for mental retardation with any real-life validity. Of adults who scored below 79 on individually administered IQ tests (and who would have been labeled mentally retarded had they been in school), 84 percent had completed 8 or more years of school, 83 percent had a job, 80 percent were financially independent, and almost 100 percent could do their shopping or travel alone. The ability to handle school-related content declines after leaving school; ability to handle the real world increases (56, 95).

IQ test scores are affected by ethnic, racial, cultural, and language biases, the testing environment, and gender (56, 95). For example, many Afro-Americans score lower than Caucasians on IQ tests, but when the test is given by a Afro-American person they score higher than if it is given by a Caucasian, possibly because they turn hostile feelings inward when under the direction of Caucasians. Stress and low self-expectations also adversely affect scores. Afro-American children score lower than Caucasian children on tests involving abstraction but higher on rote-memory tests (56, 95, 114, 133). Male–female differences are also striking. In the early school years, boys and girls have equal scholastic standing although girls may be superior. Later, males surpass females on tests of speed and coordination of gross motor acts, spatial-quantitative problems, mechanical tasks, types of quantitative reasoning, and in the subjects of mathematics, science, social studies, and citizenship. Females surpass males in fine motor skills, perceptual skills, memory, numerical computations, verbal skills, and in the subjects of writing, music, reading, and literature. The test scores are the result of stereotyped social training and value systems. Girls are rewarded for acting "feminine"; they may drop behind to gain approval. Yet females are as capable as males in all avenues of educational attainment if society allows, expects, or demands it (56, 95, 114, 133).

The child from a minority group sometimes fares considerably worse in school than does the average child because of being handicapped with fewer verbal skills, the middle-class orientation of school programs and examinations, inadequately trained teachers and inferior school facilities in deprived areas, low motivation to achieve or compete, and the effect of the parents' and teacher's expectations on the child. Research shows that children tend to achieve what adults expect of them (56, 95, 113, 114, 133). Research also indicates that early childhood enrichment programs for disadvantaged children improve performance in the school years (140).

Research results show a low correlation between IQ scores, cognitive ability, and personality in the preschool years. However, teachers perceive students who show initiative or plunge into a new activity as the brightest and those who participate little or not at all as the least intelligent. Apparently the self-fulfilling prophecy occurs because of differential teacher expectations and differences in teacher interactions with various students: By the seventh grade a high correlation between personality characteristics and IQ scores exists (56, 74, 90, 95, 168).

A classroom with diversity in the children's intellectual ability, skills, and personality is helpful to the child; he/she learns about the real world. A low percentage of disabled, retarded, or maladjusted children in a classroom will not adversely affect the normal child. However, putting the exceptional child in a normal classroom does not make him/her feel normal; he/she still is perceived and perceives self as different. The exceptional child may need special classes to get the help needed; teachers cannot be expected to specialize in all areas of education, and large classrooms prevent teachers from spending the necessary time with the child who has learning disabilities (36, 56, 95, 137). Legislation has forced the special students to be "mainstreamed" back into the regular classrooms.

The **gifted child** *is characterized by superior educability and consumption of information and by ability to produce information, concepts, and new forms.* The child is adept at problem solving and problem finding. The gifted child is considered educationally exceptional, and the child's full intellectual, creative, and leadership potential may be neglected if: (1) parents are not attuned to the child's abilities and needs; (2) parents or teachers are threatened by the gifted child who grasps concepts more quickly than they; (3) parents do not value cognitive, creative, or leadership abilities; (4) the child is not given freedom to explore and be different; or (5) the school system does not have a program suited for his/her abilities (57, 90, 101, 134).

The articles by Miller and Schwartz detail the identification of and the emotional, social, and mental characteristics of gifted children and explain how the classroom teacher can help such children find their place in the world. Often the gifted child is misunderstood. Research indicates, however, that the gifted have higher self-esteem than others, and that gifted students are more popular with their peers than other children (90, 101, 134).

✔ You can encourage parents to respect the individual interests and talents of their child. If parents are not intimidated by the child's unusual interests and behavior, they will not fear deviations from neighborhood patterns and thereby not crush budding interests or creativity. That is perhaps the essence of raising a gifted child—to facilitate, provide opportunity, let alone, not hold back or insist that something be done a certain way. Likewise, the wise parent will be able to await the sprouting of interests that do not come quickly to the surface, even if the child is behind other children or group norms. It takes courage and patience to let the child develop at his/her own pace. You can be supportive to parents as they let the child assert his/her own initiative in a situation, even if the child is not at first successful. The impulse toward growth and development must first come from the individual's budding inclinations, not from a desire to conform to another's expectations.

Some parents believe the present public school system is inadequate to teach their children the needed skills. They are usually well-educated professionals and wish to teach their own children at home. References by Common and MacMullen and Richoux explore various facets of this movement (28, 126).

An issue of mounting emotional intensity in many communities is whether children who have auto immune deficiency syndrome (AIDS), regardless of cause, can attend school with other children. While not a common health problem, the child with AIDS has a unique problem in school, at home, or when hospitalized. Although no spread by casual contact has been reported, the dilemma of how to handle these children is overwhelming.

✔ Currently, these children are being treated with gamma globulin or with the drug AZT in a few selected hospital/clinic settings. School systems are handling the child in a variety of ways. In some systems, no one except a small panel knows which child, if any, has AIDS, which prevents the child from stigma but does not protect him/her from asserting self too much or getting into situations where an already low resistance might be compromised even further. Other school districts mandate that the child be taught at home. The lack of financial aid is a problem at all levels of living and treatment. Most of the children with AIDS do not have a family financial or insurance support system (62).

✔ Klug (62) has detailed information on the disease in the child from birth on and its effects and complications. She states that AIDS children can remain in school except when viral infections in others threaten the AIDS child's immune system and health. As a school nurse, you are in a key role to work with parents, teachers, school administrators, members of the school board, and the schoolchildren to help them understand the disease; to reduce fear, myths, and irrationality; to ensure health and welfare of all the people in the school building. Your communication and negotiation skills, as well as knowledge, place you in a special role to be listened to by others, to be an advocate for the child and family, to facilitate sensible decisions.

✔ In working with parents, you may describe parenting as analogous to growing a garden. The gardener is successful because he/she does not thrust impossible patterns on the plants, respects and even nurtures their peculiarities, tries to provide suitable conditions, protects them from serious threats to life, does not continually poke or probe to make plants sprout more quickly, does not seize the new sprouts to pull open the leaves, and does not trim them all to look alike. As with plants, so with children. *They* must do the growing and developing and only through their own motivation.

✔ You, the teachers, and administrators must work together for the health of the child. The teacher can pass his/her observations on to you. You can work with the child, parents, teachers, and administrators as a consultant or counselor. Treating difficulties early is likely to prevent major and long-term problems. You must help the parents understand that they are ultimately responsible for their child's behavior. Their understanding of growth and development through your teaching and their knowledge of the school and its functions through attending parent-teacher association meetings will help them in this demanding job. Parents with little education may need to learn the same subjects as their children are learning to be able to help their children. Special classes could be arranged.

✔ ***Intellectual Needs of the Hospitalized Child.*** You can help meet those needs. A hospital tour, if it can be prearranged, helps the child feel acclimated during illness when his/her energy reserve is low. Because the child is beginning logical thought, he/she needs simple information about the illness to decrease the fear of the unknown and promote cooperation in the treatment plan. He/she needs to handle and become familiar with the equipment used.

The child who must spend long periods in the hospital needs to learn about the outside world. Some hospitals take chronically ill children to the circus, athletic events, and restaurants. Teachers are also employed so that the child can continue with formal education.

Use of Nonschool Time

✔ Help parents realize the use of time by the child when he/she is not in school. One study (149) of over 200 children in grades 3, 6, 7, 9, and 11 gave interesting results, although results may have been influenced by the fact that these children lived in an affluent community in the East. However, the results are worth review, for they may help you talk with parents about their awareness of the child's activity and the importance of how the child uses time. In this study, children preferred activities with parents, such as going to museums or theaters or working on hobbies or projects, to watching television. These children spent little time on "learning-related" activities, such as model building, stamp collecting, visits to museums and art exhibits. In fact, they expressed a strong desire for "more interesting after school activities." Homework and reading received little time, from a daily weekday average of 45 minutes for third graders to 75 minutes for ninth graders. One-half as much time was spent on homework on weekends. Almost one-half of the students enjoyed reading "often," but most stated that they opposed more homework. Students at all grade levels were not involved in attending church and community events and in volunteering in community service activities. Yet they expressed a strong desire to participate in such programs at all ages.

If parents cannot initiate attendance at learning-related activities with their children, for whatever reasons, perhaps school and other education-related agencies should offer learning-related activities held at convenient, accessible locations throughout the community. A number of school districts have developed school—business partnerships, internship programs, and other work-related projects designed to help students better understand the realities of the world of work. In a midwest school district, one seventh grade science teacher has held, for over a decade, well-attended weekend family field trips to interesting places, related to classwork, for parents and seventh graders. The teacher feels the extra time and effort are well spent; the school system is supportive. Parents endeavor to get their children into his class, partly for the field trip experiences.

Parents, teachers, and school administrators may wish to examine "the seventh grade slump." Seventh graders watch more television than do all other groups, participate less in learning-related activities, and dislike school more than other groups. A reexamination of the seventh grade academic programs, extracurricular activities, and out-of-school opportunities for growth would be useful (149).

✔ At all grade levels studied, parents seem to spend little time with children. Children want more time with parents. Talk with parents to help them examine the role they now play in their children's lives, their various commitments, *their priorities*. This is difficult, when children come from homes with working mothers, or from one-parent homes. Nevertheless, this issue is worth raising. Perhaps other caring adults are available also to spend time with the children. Human interaction is an important need for children—in fact, for people of all ages (149).

Communication Pattern

Many factors influence the child's communication pattern, vocabulary, and diction. Some of these factors have been referred to in previous chapters. Influences include: (1) speech and verbal and nonverbal communication pattern of parent(s), siblings, other adults, such as teacher, and peers; (2) attitudes of others toward the child's efforts to speak and communicate; (3) general environmental stimulation; (4) opportunity to communicate with a variety of people in a variety of situations; (5) intellectual development; (6) ability to hear and articulate; (7) vocabulary skills; and (8) contact with television or other technology (56, 95, 153).

The 6-year-old has command of nearly every form of sentence structure. The child experiments less with language, using it more as a tool and less for the mere pleasure of talking than during the preschool period. Now language is used to share in others' experiences. He/she also swears and uses slang to test others' reactions. The child enjoys printing words in large letters (43, 44, 56, 95).

At 7, the child can print several sentences, while at 8 he/she is writing instead of printing. By 9, the child participates in family discussions, showing interest in family activities and indicating an individuality. Verbal fluency has improved; common objects are described in detail. Writing skill has improved; he/she usually writes with small, even letters. By 10, he/she can write for a relatively long time with speed. The preadolescent may seem less talkative, withdrawing when frustrated instead of voicing anger. Sharing feelings with a best friend is a healthy outlet (43, 44, 56, 95).

As the child shares ideas and feelings, he/she learns how someone else thinks and feels about similar matters. The child expresses self in a way that has meaning to others, at first to a chum and then to others. Thus he/she is validating vocabulary, ideas, and feelings. The child learns that a friend's family has similar life patterns, demands of the child, and frustrations. He/she learns about self in the process of learning more about another. The child recalls what has happened in the past, realizes how this has affected the present, and considers what effect present acts will have on future events. The child uses **syntaxic, or consensual, communication** *when he/she sees these cause-and-effect relationships in an objective, logical way and can validate them with others* (151).

✔ Convey love and caring, not rejection, when you talk with children. Love is communicated through nonverbal behavior, such as getting down to the child's eye level, as well as through words that value feelings and indicate respect. Children understand language directed at their feelings better than at their intellect and the overt action. Do not overreact to normal behavior. Avoid talking about touchy areas, if possible, or the child's babyhood. He/she is struggling to be grownup; any reminder of younger behavior creates anxiety about potential regression (74). The principles of communicating with the preschooler discussed in Chapter 9 are also applicable to the schoolchild.

Effects of Television on the Child

Television and movies have a powerful influence on a child's communication and behavior patterns. The average child will have viewed from 15,000 to 22,000 hours or more, of television by high school graduation; he/she will have spent fewer hours in formal classroom study (56, 95, 123, 149, 167).

If watching television is controlled by responsible parents, cognitive and social learning can be enhanced. Educational programs can model prosocial behaviors, present and reinforce techniques associated with various sports (93). For the person unable to attend church, the religious programs can be a substitute. Scenic programs have esthetic value. Geographical, science, historical or dramatic presentations are educational and/or relaxing. Television has the potential to educate, socialize, and teach content and communication skills. However, even viewing of ordinary programs has serious limitations, including the following:

1. Promotes passive rather than active learning.
2. Increases passivity from continual overstimulation.
3. Encourages low-level, nonconceptual thinking.
4. Takes time away or distracts from more creative and stimulating activity; reduces creativity of the child.
5. Encourages short attention span and hyperactivity through its use of snappy attention-getting techniques.
6. Causes lack of understanding or comprehension of what is seen because of fast pace of programming.
7. Causes loss of interest in less exciting but necessary classroom or home activities.
8. Creates a desire for the superficial rather than depth of information.
9. Creates uncertainty about what is real and unreal in life and family.

10. Promotes a desire for unhealthy products such as high-sugar or high-salt snacks, other products not normally used by the family, or toys or other products that may be unhealthy or dangerous.
11. Creates a confusion of values (26, 95, 130, 143, 144).

✔ Heavy television viewing is associated with lower school achievement. School teachers report that more children are entering school with decreased imaginative play and creativity and increased aimless running around, low frustration level, poor persistence and concentration span, and confusion about reality and fantasy. Rapid speech and constantly changing visuals on television prevent reflection. The child does not learn correct sentence structure, use of tenses, or the ability to express thought or feeling effectively. The result may be a child who is unable to enunciate or use correct grammar and who is vague in the sense of time and history, and cause-and-effect relationships. (24, 83, 95, 163, 174, 176).

Understanding television can involve active mental work for the young child, but often the child does not understand content, motives, or feelings; integrate events shown; or infer conditions not shown (95, 143). Those are the mental processes that are stimulated by adult and peer interactions and reading literature. Often television is used in the home to the extent that it stifles family interaction and bombards with noise, excitement, speed, and misdirected humor. The stereotypic, simplistic, and often romanticized view on family life shown by most programs is unrealistic and probably not attainable. False expectations about things and people are raised; most advertising is sexist, ageist, and racist, showing women as uninterested in or incapable of anything except putting on diapers and using detergents. Most advertisements are directed to middle-class young Caucasians.

Science fiction conveys that life in the future may be scary and difficult at best. The child may have nightmares. A steady diet of science fiction may influence the child's present and future value system (95, 163).

✔ Some television programming is frankly pornographic; the values depicted are lack of loyalty or commitment to relationships, the beautiful and young body, immediate gratification, and narcissism. Movies and daytime dramas depict "jumping into bed and from bed to bed." Consequences of such behavior and relationships are not shown (26). Often such programming is at prime viewing time. The child who has unsupervised television watching cannot miss programs about family life that teach unhealthy values (123).

✔ The violence in television programming is graphic, explicit, realistic, intensely involving, and affects both children and adults, but the children more so because they have less ego control. Children act out more directly what they see and hear. Many programs directly or indirectly teach violent behavior, showing specifically how to carry out violent acts. It is not unusual when a rape, hostage-taking, suicide, or homicide is described on the evening news on television to have, either locally or nationally, a number of such incidents repeated within a few days (123). The live and explicit portrayals of violence suggest that violence is normal and justified. Realistic or punitive consequences of violent behavior are not shown; the viewer gets the idea and forms an attitude over time that it is courageous to be violent, that violence is rewarded or socially acceptable, that the violent person is the hero with which to identify. Further, continual viewing of violence desensitizes the person to violence in general; it is no longer a noteworthy act in the home or society. Even worse, television violence shows inequality and domination; the most frequent victims are women, the old, and children. Research results on the effects of violence over a 15-year period in the United States have not shown a decrease in the television violence portrayed (26, 103, 133, 143, 144).

✔ Teach parents that, increasingly, research indicates that seeing violent, sexually seductive programs or pornographic material on television or on films has the following *long-term negative effects* on children:

1. Gives an unrealistic, irreverent view of life.
2. Teaches values of violence and materialism; teaches lack of respect for life and dignity of person; teaches justification of violence.
3. Presents sexual stimulation that the child cannot handle.
4. Confuses values.
5. Shows an unquestioning acceptance of dishonest, aggressive, violent, exploitative, or manipulative behavior toward others.
6. Presents sexual and racial stereotypes. The male is typically portrayed as more important, competent, authoritative, assertive, and aggressive than the female. The minority person may be shown as incompetent. The American Indian is often stereotyped as a violent killer.
7. Stimulates fear and anxiety.
8. Stimulates and causes acting out of or identification with aggressive and sexual impulses, anger, and hostile feelings.
9. Promotes excessive fears about war and the bomb, about walking in one's own neighborhood, about the "violent" world, about the police who only use force,. . . .

10. Increases aggressive behavior; in some children the behavioral changes may last 10 years.
11. Increases emotional problems (24, 26, 56, 69, 74, 75, 83, 93, 95, 130, 143, 144, 163, 167, 174).

✔ Children who have grown up in stable families, who feel secure and loved and who have a variety of interests and relationships, will not be adversely affected by the aggression, violence, and sex of television. They can separate fantasy from fact. Children growing up without positive identification models, who are already shaky in their self-concept and identity formation, are affected very negatively. Likewise, children from troubled or dysfunctional homes lack the supervision or guidance to help them handle and sort through what they see and hear (26).

✔ Discuss with parents the need to not only screen what their children are viewing but to work to reduce the trend to more violent and pornographic programming. Parents can be more vigilant about programs their children watch. Television programming can be improved. Networks and advertisers, of course, hope that parents will disregard research findings that make-believe violence makes for real violence in many settings. As long as violence on television is profitable, programming will contain violence. Parents can rebel: writing letters to stations, writing letters to advertisers, and refusing to buy the products advertised. This is a significant area of life that affects the child's and family's physical, emotional, cognitive, social, and spiritual health.

Not until the mid-1970s did such organizations as the American Medical Association, National Education Association, and Parent–Teacher Association unite in opposition against programming containing violent and sexual excesses. Now many parent, school, community, health care, and religious leaders are joining efforts to gain more educational and less destructive programming, including the National Coalition on Television Violence which is directed by a psychiatrist.

✔ In essence, interaction with parents and others, and real experiences, not passive observations, help the child learn to work through conflicts of development and to solve problems (111).

Play Patterns

Peer Groups. Peer groups, including the gang and the close chum, provide companionship with a widening circle of persons outside the home. Playing with peers teaches the child new roles, more independence, and the abilities to compete, compromise, and cooperate. He/she can test mastery in a world parallel to adult society, with rules, organizations, and purposes (10, 56, 114, 133, 170).

Play Activities. These change with the child's development. From 6 to 8 years he/she is interested chiefly in the present and in the immediate surroundings. Because he/she knows more about family life than any other kind of living, the child plays house or takes the role of various occupational groups with which there is contact: mailcarrier, nurse, storekeeper, teacher. Although the child is more interested in playing with peers than parents, the 6- or 7-year-old will occasionally enjoy having the parent as a "child" or "student." This allows the child to have imaginary control over the parent and also allows the parent to understand how the child is interpreting the parent or how the child perceives the teacher.

Both sexes enjoy some activities in common such as painting, cutting, pasting, reading, simple table games, television, digging, riding a bicycle, running games, skating, and swimming. Again, the parent can sometimes enjoy these activities with the child, especially if the parent has a special talent which the child wishes to learn. The child imitates the roles of his/her own sex and becomes increasingly realistic in play. By age 8, collections are a favorite pastime, and loosely formed, short-lived clubs with fluctuating rules are formed (62).

The schoolchild, usually about 8 or 9 years of age, enjoys computerized games which give a sense of control and power; of being a peer with, or even superior to, the adult; of challenge and inventiveness; an enjoyment of the complexity and expandability. The computer can be a tool for robot thinking or for development of thought; for passivity or releasing aggressive impulses or creativity; for play or for learning. Computer toys can help the schoolchild understand the nature of systems and control of information—skills needed in the adult world. However, let the child take the lead in when to move into computer games. There is no need to rush the child. He/she can pick up the skills and the enjoyment at any age. Further, some schoolchildren will prefer reading, painting, playing an instrument, doing crafts, or playing sports to working with computers. These skills, and what these activities teach, are as essential to the workplace as the ability to operate a computer (63).

From 9 to 12 years the child becomes more interested in active sports but continues to enjoy quieter activity. He/she wants to improve motor skills. Adult-organized games of softball, football, or soccer lose their fun when parents place excessive emphasis on winning. The hug from a teammate after hitting a home run means more than just winning. Further, adults taking over the games robs the child of independence (131, 162).

Now creative talents appear; the child may be interested in music, dance, or art. At about age 10, sex differences in play become pronounced. Each sex is developing through play the skills it will later need in society; this is manifested through the dramatizing of real-life situations. The child's interest in faraway places is enhanced through a foreign pen pal as well as through travel (44).

The Gang Stage. In preadolescence the gang becomes important. A **gang** *is a group whose membership is earned on the basis of skilled performance of some activity, frequently physical in nature. Its stability is expressed through formal symbols such as passwords or uniforms.* Gang codes take precedence over almost everything. They may range from agreement to protect a member who smoked in the boys' restroom at school to boycotting a school dance. Generally, gang codes are characterized by collective action against the mores of the adult world. In the gang, children discharge hostility and aggression against peers rather than adults and begin to work out their own social patterns without adult interference. Unfortunately, some gangs do turn their hostility against other youths or adults. When this occurs, the pattern is laid for delinquent behaviors (162). Gang formation is loosely structured at first, with a transient membership that cuts across all social classes. Early gangs may consist of both boys and girls in the same groups. Later, separate gangs for each sex occur (170).

The Chum Stage. The chum stage occurs around 9 or 10 years of age, and sometimes later, when affection moves from the peer group and gang to a **chum,** *a special friend of the same sex and age.* This is an important relationship, because it is the child's first love attachment outside the family, when someone becomes as important to him/her as self. Initially, a person of the same sex and age is easier than someone of the opposite sex to feel concern for and to understand. The friend becomes an extension of the child's own self. As he/she shares ideas and feeings, the child learns a great deal about self as well as about the chum. The child discovers that he/she is more similar to than different from others and learns to accept self for what he/she is. Self-acceptance of uniqueness increases acceptance of others, so that the child of this age is very sociable, generous, sympathetic, enjoys differences in people, and is liberal in ideas about the welfare of others. He/she learns that others can do things differently but that they are still all right as people. It is also through the chum relationship that the child learns the syntaxic mode of communication described earlier, for he/she learns to validate word meanings in talking with the chum. Thus ideas about the world become more realistic. Loyalty to the chum at this age may be greater than loyalty to the family (151). **Altruism,** *a concern for others in various situations,* as well as an ability to respond to others' happiness and distress, to develop intimate associations, including with individuals of the opposite gender, and a sensitivity and concern for all humanity, result from high-level chumship (150).

The chum stage has homosexual elements, but it is not an indication of homosexuality. It provides the foundation for later intimacy with an individual of the opposite sex as well as close friends of both sexes. If the child does not have a chum relationship, he/she has little capacity for adolescent heterosexuality or adult intimacy. Fixation at this level, according to Sullivan, results in **homosexuality,** *an inability to focus love on a member of the opposite sex* (151).

✔ Help parents understand the importance of the gang and chum stages.

Tools of Socialization

Competition, compromise, cooperation, and beginning collaboration are progressive tools the schoolchild uses in accomplishing satisfying relationships with peers. **Competition** *is comprised of all activities that are involved in getting to a goal first, of seeking affection or status above others.* When the child is competing, he/she has rigid standards about many situations, including praise and punishment. For example, regardless of the circumstance, the child feels that the same punishment should be given for the same wrongdoing. He/she cannot understand why a 3-year-old sibling and he/she should not be punished similarly for spilling milk on the kitchen floor. Similarly, the child thinks he/she should be praised for dressing self as is the 3-year-old. *The child accepts adult rules as compulsory and rigid; he/she experiences a* **morality of constraint** (106).

Compromise, *a give-and-take agreement,* is gradually learned from peers, teachers, and family. The child becomes less rigid in standards of behavior. **Cooperation,** *an exchange between equals by adjusting to the wishes of others,* results from the chum relationship with its syntaxic mode of communication. Through the **morality of cooperation** *the child begins to understand the social implications of acts.* He/she learns judgment through helping make and carry out rules. **Collaboration,** *deriving satisfaction from group accomplishment rather than personal success,* is a step forward from cooperation and enables experimentation with tasks and exploration of situations (74, 106, 151).

✔ If a child does not learn how to get along with others, future socialization will be inhibited. For example, if a person is fixated at the competition level and does not learn how to compromise or cooperate, he/she is hard on self and a hard person with whom to

TABLE 10-4. Assessment of Changing Behavioral Characteristics in the Schoolchild

6 YEARS	7 YEARS	8 YEARS
Self-centered. Body movement, temper outbursts release tension. Behavioral extremes; impulsive or dawdles, loving or antagonistic. Difficulty making decisions; needs reminders. Verbally aggressive but easily insulted. Intense concentration short time, then abruptly stops activity. Security of routines and rituals essential; periodic separation anxiety. Series of three commands followed, but response depending on mood. Self-control and initiative in activity encouraged when adult uses counting to give child time. ("I'll give you until the count of 10 to pick up those papers.") Praise and recognition needed.	Self-care managed. Quiet, less impulsive but assertive. Fewer mood swings. Self-absorbed without excluding others; may appear shy, sad, brooding. Attentive, sensitive listener. Companionable; likes to do tasks for others. Good and bad behavior in self and others noted. High standards for self but minor infractions of rules: tattles, alibis, takes small objects from others. Concern about own behavior; tries to win over others' approval. Angry over others' failure to follow rules.	Expansive personality but fluctuating behavior. Curious, robust, energetic. Rapid movements and response; impatient. Affectionate to parents. Hero worship of adult. Suggestions followed better than commands. Adult responsibilities and characteristics imitated; wants to be considered important by adults. Approval and reconciliation sought; feelings easily hurt. Sense of property; enjoys collections. Beginning sense of justice, but makes alibis for own transgressions. Demanding and critical of others. Gradually accepts inhibitions and limits.

9 YEARS	10 YEARS
More independent and self-controlled. Dependable, responsible. Adult trust and more freedom without adult supervision sought. Loyal to home and parents; seeks their help at times. More self rather than environmentally motivated; not dependent on but benefits from praise. More involved with peers. Own interests subordinated to group demands and adult authority. Critical of own and others' behavior. Concerned about fairness and willing to take own share of blame. More aware of society.	More adult-like and poised, especially girls. More self-directive, independent. Organized and rapid in work; budgets time and energy. Suggestions followed better than requests, but obedient. Family activities and care of younger siblings, especially below school age, enjoyed. Aware of individual differences among people, but does not like to be singled out in a group. Hero worship of adult. Loyal to group; chum important. Some idea of own assets and limits. Preoccupied with right and wrong. Better able to live by rules. Critical sense of justice; accepts immediate punishment for wrongdoing. Liberal ideas of social justice and welfare. Strong desire to help animals and people. Future career choices match parents' careers because of identification with parents. Sense of leadership.

11 YEARS	12 YEARS
Spontaneous, self-assertive, restless, curious, sociable. Short outbursts of anger and arguing. Mood swings. Challenges enjoyed. On best behavior away from home. Quarrelsome with siblings; rebellious to parents. Critical of parents, although affectionate with them. Chum and same-sex peers important; warm reconciliation follows quarrels. Secrets freely shared with chum; secret language with peers. Unaware of effect of self on others.	Considerable personality integration: Self-contained, self-competent, tactful, kind, reasonable, less self-centered. Outgoing, eager to please, enthusiastic. Sense of humor; improved communication skills. More companionable than at 11; mutual understanding between parents and child. Increasingly sensitive to feelings of others; wishes good things for family and friends, caught between the two. Others' approval sought. Childish lapses, but wishes to be treated like adult. Aware of assets and shortcomings.

TABLE 10-4. Continued

11 YEARS	12 YEARS
Strict superego; zeal for fairness. Future career choices fantasized on basis of possible fame. Modest with parents.	Tolerant of self and others. Peer group and chum important in shaping attitudes and interests. Ethical sense more realistic than idealistic. Decisions about ethical questions based on consequences. Less tempted to do wrong; basically truthful. Self-disciplined; accepts just discipline. Enthusiastic about community projects.

live. Eventually the person derives satisfaction only from competing but fails to enjoy the accomplishment, the end product. If a child is not relating well with peers, a group assertiveness training program can effectively increase social and assertive behavior through reinforcement procedures, relaxation techniques, guided imagery, and behavior contracts (72).

Guidance and Discipline

In guidance, parents should invite confidence of the child as a parent, not as a buddy or pal. The child will find pals among peers. In the adult he/she needs a parent! The atmosphere should be open and inviting for the child to talk with the parents, but the child's privacy should not be invaded. The parents should see the child as he/she is, not as an idealized extension of themselves.

✓ The schoolchild has a rather strict superego and also uses many rituals to maintain self-control. He/she prefers to initiate self-control rather than be given commands or overt discipline, and stability and routine in his/her life provide this opportunity. You can talk with parents about methods of guidance and the importance of not interfering with behavior too forcefully or too often. The child needs some alternatives from which to choose so that he/she can learn different ways of behaving and coping and be better able to express self later. If development has been normal during the preschool years, the child is now well on the way to absorbing and accepting the standards, codes, and attitudes of society. He/she needs ongoing guidance rather than an emphasis on disciplinary measures. Parents that are too controlled or punitive contribute to fearfulness in the child. If the parent is perceived as supportive and encouraging of autonomy, the child is less likely to be fearful. Research indicates that preadolescent girls perceive their mothers as more supportive but also more punitive than their fathers. Upper-middle-class parents are perceived by their daughters as less punitive and more autonomy granting than are lower-middle-class parents, and lower-class parents are perceived as even more punitive and less autonomy granting by their daughters (175). Boys who are less warmly treated by their parents are more responsive to social or peer influences than girls, which has implications for later antisocial behavior (74).

✓ For some parents, guiding a child can be a problem. They will ask, "When, what kind, and how much should you punish a child?" "How do you handle guilt or hostile feelings which often accompany discipline?" You are in a position to help parents learn the value of positive guidance techniques (10, 27, 48, 68, 74, 79, 133, 160, 162).

✓ When expressing anger to children, describe what you see, feel, and expect. Do not lower the child's self-esteem by humiliating him/her, especially in front of others. The child's dignity can be protected by using "I" messages: "I am angry. I am frustrated." Such statements are honest and are safer than "What's your problem? You are stupid!" If repeated frequently, the child may believe that he/she is stupid and carry that self-image for years. Although shouting is not recommended, the parent who shouts displeasure at the danger or inconvenience *only* is probably harming the child much less than the parent who quietly and continually verbalizes personal assaults against the child. Ideally, the limit should be set with firm conviction and should only deal with one incident at a time. More than one message can confuse the child.

✓ Our grandparents are reputed to have disciplined their children with authority and certainty. By contrast, some of today's parents seem afraid of their children. The child needs an understanding authority and a good example. He/she needs to know what constitutes unacceptable behavior and what substitute will be accepted. For instance, say, "Food is not for throwing; your baseball is." He/she will not obey rules if parents do not. Inconsistent discipline, or the "Do as I say, not as I do" approach, will lead to maladjustment, conflict, and aggression. The suggestions about guidance listed in Chapter 9 are applicable to the schoolchild as well.

Guidance at this age takes many other and less dramatic forms. A mother can turn the often harried "getting back to school clothes" experience into a pleasant lesson in guidance. She can accompany the child on a special shopping trip in which he/she examines different textures of material, learns about color coordination, understands what constitutes a good fit, and appreciates how much money must be spent for certain items. This principle can be carried into any parent—schoolchild guidance relationship, such as learning responsibility for some household task or earning, handling, and saving money.

Emotional Development

✔ The schoolchild consolidates earlier psychosocial development and simultaneously reaches out to a number of identification figures, expands interests, and associates with more people. Behavioral characteristics change from year to year. Table 10-4 (pp. 316–317) summarizes and compares basic behavior patterns, although individual children will show a considerable range of behavior. Cultural, health, and social conditions may also influence behavior (43, 44, 56, 95).

Developmental Crisis. The psychosexual crisis for this period is industry versus inferiority. **Industry** *is an interest in doing the work of the world, the child's feeling that he/she can learn and solve problems, the formation of responsible work habits and attitudes, and the mastery of age-appropriate tasks* (37). The child has greater body competence and applies self to skills and tasks which go beyond playful expression. The child gets tired of play, wants to participate in the real world, and seeks attention and recognition for efforts and concentrations on a task. He/she feels pride in doing something well whether a physical or cognitive task. A sense of industry involves self-confidence, perseverance, diligence, self-control, cooperation, and compromise rather than only competition. There is a sense of loyalty, relating self to something positive beyond the moment and outside the self. Parents, teachers, and nurses may see this industry at times as restlessness, irritability, rebellion toward authority, and lack of obedience.

The danger of this period is that the child may develop a sense of **inferiority,** *feeling inadequate, defeated, unable to learn or do tasks, lazy, unable to compete, compromise, or cooperate,* regardless of his/her actual competence (37). The child, and later the adult if this stage is not resolved, will not like to work or try new tasks; he/she will be moody, anxious, oversensitive to and isolated from others, excessively meek, and lacking in perseverance. Regressive behavior, excess fear of bodily injury or illness, or psychosomatic disorders may be observed. The child may try to prove self by various acting-out behavior such as lying or stealing. If the child feels excessively ashamed, self-doubting, guilty, and inferior from not having achieved the developmental tasks all along, emotional and behavioral problems may occur. Withdrawal, depression, speech difficulties, firesetting or other extreme antisocial behavior, or self-destructive or aggressive acts may be displayed. Sometimes opposite behavior may occur as the person tries to cope with feelings of being no good, inferior, or inadequate. Instead, the person might immerse self in tasks to prove personal worth and gain attention, become aggressive, bossy, and overcompetitive. He/she will want his/her own way regularly. There is no time for play or camaraderie. The child who is the "teacher's pet" because he/she is such a "good little worker" may well suffer a sense of inferiority. If work is all the child can do at home and school, he/she will miss out on a lot of friendships and opportunities in life, now and later, and eventually become the adult who is a slave to technology: He/she cannot stop working.

✔ Teach parents that they can contribute to a sense of industry and avoid inferiority feelings by not having unrealistic expectations of the child and by using the suggested guidance and discipline approaches. They can encourage peer activities as well as home responsibilities, help the child meet developmental crises, and give recognition to his/her accomplishments and unique talents. They must remember that part of the time their child may regress to jumping on the couch, drumming nervously on the table with fingernails, and insisting that keeping clean is only for parents. At other times they will marvel at the poised, contented child who is visiting so nicely with their guests.

Self-Concept, Body-Image, and Sexuality Development

Until the child goes to school, self-perception is derived primarily from the parents' attitudes and reactions toward him/her. The child who is loved for what he/she is, learns to love and accept self. If parental reactions have been rejecting, if he/she has been made to feel ugly, ashamed, or guilty about self or his/her behavior, the child enters school feeling bad, inadequate, or inferior. A positive self-concept is imperative for happiness and personality unity.

The child with a positive self-concept likes self and others; believes that what he/she thinks, says, and does makes a difference; believes he/she can be successful and can solve problems; has a realistic estimate of personal abilities and limitations, and expresses feelings of pleasure and enjoyment.

A negative self-image causes the child to feel defensive toward others and self and hinders adjustment to school and academic progress. Low self-concept children show more social withdrawal, academic difficulties, and inappropriate attention-seeking than high self-concept children (176).

At school the child compares self with and is compared by peers in appearance, motor, cognitive, language, and social skills. If he/she cannot perform as well as other children, peers will perceive the child negatively and eventually he/she will perceive self as incompetent or inferior because self-image is more dependent on peers than earlier. Schoolchildren are frequently cruel in their honesty as they make derogatory remarks about peers with limitations or disabilities.

Unattractive children may receive discriminatory treatment from parents, teachers, and babysitters because adults have learned the social value of beauty. Unattractive children are judged to be more antisocial and less honest than attractive children. Thus if an unattractive child expresses innocence, he/she is less likely to be believed. Attractive children are better liked by peers and adults and are judged to have a higher IQ and to be more likely to attend college. Because people tend to act as others expect them to, the prophecy is likely to become true (12). It is important for you to avoid this kind of reaction.

Cultural attitudes also affect self-concept. In studies with Afro-American and Caucasian children, both races of children indicated a distinct preference for dolls of their own color, but in the 1960s Afro-American children preferred white dolls instead of black dolls. The awakening of Black political consciousness in the 1960s was a forerunner of a more positive self-image in the Afro-American person (56, 95).

Self-concept and body image are also affected by gender and grade level of the child, father's education, history of illness, and type of illness, if any. Williams found that American and Filipino boys did not score significantly different in body image, whereas Filipino girls scored lower than American girls. Third-grade American children had a better understanding of the body than Filipino third graders, but fifth graders in both cultures did not score significantly different from each other. American and Filipino children whose fathers had a college education did not score significantly differently; however, Filipino children whose fathers had less education scored lower in body organ knowledge than American children whose fathers were not college educated. Regardless of these variables, ill Filipino children did not score significantly lower in body image and concept of illness than American children. More research is needed on the child's concept of self, body, and illness, both in this and other cultures (171).

Biracial children are increasing in number, and their special racial status affects racial identification, self-concept, self-esteem, and school adjustment. They must deal with overt racism affecting children of color, cope with outsiders who view their families as abnormal, sometimes cope with the loyalty issues and negative feelings from the extended family of each parent. Positive parental feelings about racial identification and positive extended family relationships are critical to sound emotional adjustment of the child and a positive self-concept. The child may have difficulty identifying with either parent because of racism, and these feelings and issues must be discussed (20).

✔ Parents, teachers, and health-care professionals can contribute to a positive self-esteem and competence in performance by emphasizing the child's positive, healthy characteristics and reinforcing the child's potential. You can be instrumental in fostering a healthy relationship.

✔ The perception and reaction of the teacher, nurse, and parent are extremely important. The parent and nurse should listen carefully to the child's own estimate of self, school progress, and relationship with peers. The teacher should be informed if the child questions his/her adequacy. The nurse can assess and help correct physical or emotional problems.

✔ The teacher (or nurse) can intervene when derogatory remarks are made among classmates. Teacher may move a child into another work or play group, appropriate for his/her ability, or explain to peers in simple language the importance of accepting another who is at a different developmental level. Meanwhile, teacher should encourage the child who has the difficulty. In turn, the nurse supports the teacher in such action. Thus the school experience may either reinforce or weaken the child's feeling about self as a unique, important person, with specific talents or abilities. If he/she is 1 of 30 children in a classroom and receives little attention from the teacher, self-concept may be threatened.

✔ The child's body image and self concept are very fluid. Schoolchildren are more aware of the internal body as well as differences externally. They can label major organs with increasing accuracy; heart, brain, and bones are most frequently mentioned, along with cardiovascular, gastrointestinal, and musculoskeletal systems. The younger child thinks that organs move about, and organ function, size, and position are poorly understood. Organs such as the stomach are frequently drawn in at the wrong place (this may reflect the influence of television ads). Children generally believe that they must have all body parts in order to remain alive and that the skin holds in body contents; consider the impact of injury or surgery on the child. This is an excellent age to teach about any of these inaccuracies (42, 118).

✔ The child is changing physically, emotionally, and socially. Physique is changing. Sexual identity is strengthening. He/she is learning how to get along with more people, peers and adults, and is developing academic skills. Table 10–5 shows how aspects of the child's view of self changes through the school years (10, 12, 27, 42, 43, 44, 118).

✔ *Self-concept, body image, and sexuality development are interrelated and are influenced by parental and societal expectations of and reactions to each sex.* You can assist parents in promoting a positive self-concept and body image. During latency boys and girls are similar in many ways. But differences are taught. Girls are reported to be less physically active, but they have greater verbal, perceptual, and cognitive skills than boys. Girls supposedly respond to stimuli—interpersonal and physical, including pain—more quickly and accurately than boys. They seem better at analyzing and anticipating environmental demands; thus their behavior conforms more to adult expectations, and they are better at staying out of trouble. Girls are encouraged to be dependent on and to rely on others' appraisals for self-esteem more than boys. Girls are not usually forced to develop internal controls and a sense of independent self in the way that boys are because of the difference in adult reactions to each sex. Innate physiological differences become magnified as they are reinforced by cultural norms and specific parental behaviors (7).

TABLE 10–5. Assessment of Changing Body-Image Development in the Schoolchild

6 YEARS	7 YEARS	8 YEARS
Is self-centered. Likes to be in control of self, situations, and possessions. Gains physical and motor skills. Knows right from left hand. Regresses occasionally to baby talk or earlier behavior. Plays at being someone else to clarify sense of self and others. Is interested in marriage and reproduction. Distinguishes organs of each sex but wonders about them. May indulge in sex play. Draws a man with hands, neck, clothing, and six identifiable parts. Distinguishes between attractive and ugly pictures of faces.	Is more modest and aware of self. Wants own place at table, in car, and own room or part of room. Has lower level physical activity than earlier. Does not like to be touched. Protects self by withdrawing from unpleasant situation. Dislikes physical combat. Engages less in sex play. Understands pregnancy generally; excited about new baby in family. Concerned he/she does not really belong to parents. Tells parts missing from picture of incomplete man.	Redefines sense of status with others. Subtle changes in physical proportion; movements smoother. Assumes many roles consecutively. Is ready for physical contact in play and to be taught self-defense mechanisms. Is more aware of differences between the sexes. Is curious about another's body. Asks questions about marriage and reproduction; strong interest in babies, especially for girls. Plays more with own sex.

9 YEARS	10 YEARS
Has well-developed eye–hand coordination. Enjoys displaying motor skills and strength. Cares completely for bodily needs. Has more interest in own body and its functions than in other sexual matters. Asks fewer questions about sexual matters if earlier questions answered satisfactorily. Is self-conscious about exposing body, including to younger siblings and opposite sex parents.	Is relatively content with and confident of self. Has perfected most basic small motor movements. Wants privacy for self but peeks at other sex. Asks same questions about sexual matters again. Investigates own sexual organs. Shows beginning prepubertal changes physically, especially girls.

11 YEARS	12 YEARS
States self is in heart, head, face, or body part most actively expressing him/her. Feels more self-conscious with physical changes occurring. Mimics adults, deepening self-understanding. Masturbates sometimes; erection occurs in boys. Discusses sexual matters with parents with reticence. Likes movies on reproduction.	Growth spurt; changes in appearance. Muscular control almost equal to that of adult. Identifies self as being in total body or brain. May feel like no part of body is his/hers alone but like someone else's because of close identity with group. Begins to accept and find self as unique person. Feels joy of life with more mature understanding.

Stereotypes are changing, however. Girls can cope with aggression and competition just as boys can. Title IX of the Education Amendments of 1972 prohibited persons from being excluded from educational programs and activities because of sex; females may now legally participate in school sports programs and qualify for competitive athletics against boys. (Postpubescent girls should not engage in heavy collision sports against boys, however, because of potential injury resulting from the girls' lesser muscle mass per unit of body weight [56, 95]).

Research shows that fears about the girl's harming her childbearing functions or her feminine appearance as a result of normal rigorous activity are unfounded. Traditionally, girls and women in rural areas have worked very hard physically with no ill effects. In addition, primarily the male hormones, not vigorous exercise, produce big bones, muscle mass, and a masculine appearance (56, 95). Early physical education activities teach general coordination, eye-hand coordination, and balance—basic movements that carry over into all movement and sports. Rigorous conditioning activities, such as gymnastics, are suggested for achieving high levels of physical fitness for prepubertal girls and will improve agility, appearance, endurance, strength, feelings of well-being, and self-concept.

Sexuality Education. **Sexuality education,** *learning about the self as a person who is a sexual being,* has begun by the school years. The child can learn that both sexes have similar feelings and behavior potential, which can instill attitudes about maleness and femaleness for adulthood. The traditional stereotypes of the aggressive, competitive, intelligent, clumsy, brave, and athletic male and the passive, demure, gentle, graceful, domestic, fearful, and emotional female must be discarded by parents, teachers, and other adults so that they will not be learned by the schoolchild. At this age both sexes are dependent and independent, active and passive, emotional and controlled, gentle and aggressive. Keeping such a range of behavior will contribute to a more flexible adult who can be expressive, spontaneous, and accepting of self and others.

✔ You will have to work through your own stereotypes to help the parents, child, and child's peers avoid sex typing.

Sex education, *factual information about anatomy, physiology, and birth control methods,* should begin now for both sexes. By 7 or 8, children usually know that both sexes are required for childbirth to occur, but they are not sure how.

✔ Almost all parents will experience at least some anxiety and embarrassment when they discuss sex with their children. Remember that these parents have come from a generation who were taught that the discussion of sex was at least partially taboo. Ideas about sexual behavior and what should be taught varies with socioeconomic level as well as age group.

✔ Following are some guidelines for parents, teachers, or yourself when handling this subject: (1) Know the facts. (2) Do not lecture or preach. (3) Do not skip anything because the youngster says, "I already know." Chances are the child has some twisted facts. (4) Answer all questions as honestly as possible. (5) Do not force too much at one sitting. (6) Aim the information at the child's immediate interest. (7) Do not pry into the child's feelings and fantasies. (8) Try to make the conversation as relaxed as possible.

✔ Many elementary schools are now introducing basic sex education at the fourth-grade level. Usually, parents are asked to preview the film or presentation and then give permission for their child to participate. Ideally, this procedure will stimulate a bond among parents, child, and teacher so that all focus on accurate and positive education. In planning a sex education program, realize that there are likely to be parents both in favor of and opposed to sex education classes. It is important to explore and clarify the attitudes of parents and teachers during the early planning phases.

Self-concept and sexuality can be traumatized by sexual advances from adults, sometimes family members. Burgess and other authors provide useful references for gaining additional information (16, 17, 50, 71, 76, 86, 157).

Burgess describes a study of school-age children who were sexually molested, feelings about the traumatic event, stages of resolution, defense mechanisms used by the children and parents, the issues, feelings of, and difficulties for the parents in the community who joined together to prosecute the offender (a busdriver), other community issues, and the therapists' role with the children and parents over a period of time (16). Swanson and Braggio discuss the dynamics of and consequent problems of father–daughter incest (152).

Adaptive Mechanisms

The schoolchild is losing the protective mantle of home and early childhood and needs order and consistency in life to help cope with doubts, fears, unacceptable impulses, and unfamiliar experiences. Commonly used adaptive mechanisms include ritualistic behavior, reaction formation, undoing, isolation, fantasy, identification, regressing, malingering, rationalization, projection, and sublimation (74).

Ritualistic behavior, *consistently repeating an act in a situation,* wards off imagined harm and anxiety and provides a feeling of control. Examples include stepping on cracks in the sidewalk while chanting certain words, always putting the left leg through trousers before the right, having a certain place for an object, or doing homework at a specific time.

Reaction formation, undoing, and isolation are related to obsessive, ritualistic behavior.

Reaction formation is used frequently in dealing with feelings of hostility. The child may unconsciously hate a younger brother because he infringes on the schoolchild's freedom. But such impulses are unacceptable to the strict superego. To counter such unwanted feelings, the child may become the classic example of a caring, loving sibling.

Undoing *is unconsciously removing an idea, feeling, or act by performing certain ritualistic behavior*. For example, the gang has certain chants and movements to follow before a member who broke a secret code can return. **Isolation** *is a mechanism of unconsciously separating emotion from an idea because the emotion would be unacceptable to the self*. The idea remains in the conscious, but its component feeling remains in the unconscious. A child uses isolation when he/she seems to talk very objectively about the puppy who has just been run over by a truck.

Fantasy compensates for feelings of inadequacy, inferiority, and lack of success encountered in school, the peer group, or home. Fantasy is necessary for eventual creativity and should not be discouraged if it is not used excessively to prevent realistic participation in the world. Fantasy saves the ego temporarily, but it also provides another way for the child to view self, thus helping him/her aspire to new heights of behavior.

Identification is seen in the hero worship of teacher, scoutmaster, neighbor, or family friend, someone whom the child respects and who has the qualities the child fantasizes as his/her own.

Regression, *returning to a less sophisticated pattern of behavior*, is a defense against anxiety and helps the child avoid potentially painful situations. For example, he/she may revert to using the language or behavior of a younger sibling if the child feels that the sibling is getting undue attention.

Malingering, *feigning illness to avoid unpleasant tasks*, is seen when the child stays home from school for a day or says he/she is unable to do a home task because he/she does not feel well.

Rationalization, *giving excuses when the child is unable to achieve wishes*, is frequently seen in relation to schoolwork. For example, after a low test grade, the response is, "Oh well, grades don't make any difference anyway."

Projection is seen as the child says about a teacher, "She doesn't like me," when really the teacher is disliked for having reprimanded him/her.

Sublimation is a major mechanism used during the school years. The child increasingly channels sexual and aggressive impulses into socially acceptable tasks at school and home. In the process, if all goes well, he/she develops the sense of industry.

Use of any and all of these mechanisms in various situations is normal, but overuse of any one can result in a constricted, immature personality. If constricted, the child will be unable to develop relationships outside the home, to succeed at home or school, or to balance work and play. Achieving a sense of identity and adult developmental tasks will be impaired.

✔ Help parents understand the adaptive mechanisms used by the child and how to help the child use healthy coping mechanisms.

The Child in Transition

American families are on the move. Moving from one part of the country to another, or even from one community and school system to another, brings a special set of tasks that should be acknowledged and worked through. Some families, because of the military or other career, or as part of an exchange program, may live in another country for a number of years, or move from country to country. This poses another kind of adjustment and set of tasks. Children who were born in a foreign country and then return with their parents to the United States undergo culture shock. They feel like citizens of another country and visitors in the land of which they are a citizen. Lykins describes the feelings of children of the "Third Culture" who have seen much of the world, know more than one language, who are cognizant of and accepting of various lifestyles, and who speak, dress, eat, and behave as if they were still in another land. He also describes family and employment dynamics. Educational considerations that must be made in school are also discussed. These students usually want to return to the country in which they had lived for some time, although they feel patriotism for the United States (77).

The school-age child is especially affected by a geographic move if he/she is just entering or is well settled into the chum stage. The child cannot understand why he/she cannot fit into the new group right away. Because routines are so important to the schoolchild, he/she is sometimes confused by the new and different ways of doing things. The parents will need to consult with the new school leaders about their child's adjustment.

✔ If a family can include the schoolchild in the decision about where to move, the transition will be easier. If not, then the following ideas can still be utilized. Share them with parents. Ideally, the whole family should make at least one advance trip to the new community. If possible, the new home and town should be explored and the child should visit the new school so that he/she can establish mentally where he/she is going. Writing to one of the new classmates before the actual move can enhance a feeling of friendship and belonging. If the child has a special interest, such as gymnastics or dancing, a contact with the new program can form another transitional step.

✔ When parents are packing, they are tempted to dispose of as many of the child's belongings as possible, especially if they seem babyish or worn. *Do not do this.* These items are part of the child, and they will help him/her feel comfortable and at home during adjustment to a new home and community.

✔ Sometimes parents in the new community are reticent about letting their children go to the new child's house. The new parents should make every attempt to introduce themselves to the new playmates' parents, assuring them that the environment will be safe for play. Or parents can have a get-acquainted party for the few children who are especially desired as playmates or chums.

✔ Just as the family initiated some ties before they moved, so should they keep some ties from the previous neighborhood. If possible, let the child play with old friends at times. If the move has been too far for frequent visits, then allow the child to call old friends occasionally. If possible, plan a trip back so that some old traditions can be reviewed and friends can be visited. The trip to the old neighborhood will cement in the child's mind that "home" is no longer there but in the new location.

✔ The parents must accept as natural some grieving for what is gone. Letting the child express his/her feelings, accepting these feelings, and continuing to work with the above suggestions will foster the adjustment.

✔ The nurse can foster the above through noticing the new child, watching his behavior, working with the teacher and peers, and contacting parents if necessary.

Moral—Religious Development

✔ You can assist parents in understanding the importance of their role in moral and spiritual religious development. If you care for a child over a period of time, you will also contribute to this development.

In the school years the child usually moves from the fairy tale stage of God being like a giant to the realistic or concrete state of God being like a human figure. For the Christian child, Jesus is an angelic boy growing into a perfect man.

The child is learning many particulars about his/her religion, such as Allah, God, Jesus, prayer, rites, ancestor worship, life after death, reincarnation, heaven, or hell, all of which are developed into a religious philosophy and used in interpretation of the world. These ideas are taught by family, friends, teachers, church, books, radio, and television.

The child of 6 can understand God as creator, expects prayers to be answered, and feels the forces of good and evil with the connotation of reward and punishment. The 6-year-old believes in a creative being, a father figure, responsible for many things such as thunder and lightning. The adult usually introjects the natural or scientific explanation. Somehow the child seems to hold this dual thinking without contradiction. The adult's ability to weave the supernatural with the natural will affect the child's later ability to do so.

The developing schoolchild has a great capacity for reverence and awe, continues to ask more appropriate questions about religious teaching and God, and can be taught through stories that emphasize moral traits. The child operates from a simple framework of ideas and will earnestly pray for recovery and protection from danger for self and others. The child believes that a Supreme Being loves him/her, gives the earth and a house, and is always near. He/she may say, however, "How does God take care of me when I can't see Him?" "Allah's here, but where?" "I don't know how to love God like I love you, Mommy, because I've never touched Him."

In prepuberty the child begins to comprehend disappointments more fully. He/she realizes that self-centered prayers are not always answered and that no magic is involved. The child can now accept totally the scientific explanation for thunder and lightning. He/she may drop religion at this point. Or, because of strong dependence on parents, the child may continue to accept the family preference. Yet the blind faith which previously existed is gradually replaced by reason.

The schoolchild can be in the conventional stage of moral development, according to Kohlberg (64). (See Chapter 5, Table 2). Beliefs about right and wrong have less to do with the child's actual behavior than with the likelihood of getting caught for transgression and the gains to be derived from the transgression. Other factors which influence moral development include the child's intelligence, ability to delay gratification, and sense of self-esteem. The child with a high sense of self-esteem and a favorable self-concept is less likely to engage in immoral behavior, possibly because he/she will feel more guilty with wrongdoing. Thus moral behavior may be more a matter of strength of will or ego strength than of strength of conscience or superego. Morality is not a fixed behavioral trait but rather a decision-making capacity. The child progresses from an initial premoral stage, in which he/she responds primarily to reward and punishment, through a rule-based highly conventional morality, and finally to the stage of self-accepted principles (64).

Table 10–6. Selected Nursing Diagnoses Related to the School Age Child[a]

PATTERN 1: EXCHANGING

Altered Nutrition: More than body requirements
Altered Nutrition: Less than body requirements
Altered Nutrition: Potential for more than body requirements
Potential for Infection
Potential for Injury
Potential for Trauma
Potential Impaired Skin Integrity

PATTERN 2: COMMUNICATING

Impaired Verbal Communication

PATTERN 3: RELATING

Impaired Social Interaction
Social Isolation

PATTERN 4: VALUING

Spiritual Distress

PATTERN 5: CHOOSING

Ineffective Individual Coping
Impaired Adjustment
Health Seeking Behaviors

PATTERN 6: MOVING

Impaired Physical Mobility
Fatigue
Sleep Pattern Disturbance
Diversional Activity Deficit
Bathing/Hygiene Self Care Deficit
Dressing/Grooming Self Care Deficit
Altered Growth and Development

PATTERN 7: PERCEIVING

Body Image Disturbance
Self Esteem Disturbance
Sensory/Perceptual Alterations
Hopelessness
Powerlessness

PATTERN 8: KNOWING

Knowledge Deficit

PATTERN 9: FEELING

Pain
Dysfunctional Grieving
Anticipatory Grieving
Anxiety
Fear

[a] Other NANDA diagnosis are applicable to the ill school age child.
Source: NANDA Approved Nursing Diagnostic Categories, *Nursing Diagnosis Newsletter*, 15, no. 1 (1988), 1–3.

Part of moral development is the ability to follow rules. Unlike the preschooler who initiates rules without understanding them, the 7-year-old or the 8-year-old begins to play in a genuinely social manner. Rules are mutually accepted by all players and are rigidly adhered to. Rules come from some external force, such as God, and are thought to be timeless. Not until the age of 11 or 12, when the Formal Operations level of cognition is reached, does the child understand the true nature of rules—that they exist to make the game possible and can be altered by mutual agreement (106).

A study of children ages 10 to 14 in seven cultures, including the United States, Europe, and Asia, revealed that this era is a crucial time for learning moral views and to obey rules. Almost all children in all cultures realized that laws and rules are norms that guide behavior and require obedience from all, and they realized that chaos would result without them (154). In five of the seven cultures, children accepted that rule breaking might be permissible for higher moral reasons. In six of the seven cultures, parents were seen as most able to make children follow rules. Only in Japan did the teacher rank higher than the parents. Police ranked at least fourth in all cultures except India. Thus affiliative, nurturant strategies rather than punitive ones were seen as most effective in inducing compliance and assuring the stability of systems (154).

Piaget also identified stages of moral development as he studied the child's pattern of reasoning to think about moral issues. These stages are:

1. Premoral—the child has no regard for rules.
2. Heteronomous—the child obeys rules because of fear of authority or powerful figures.
3. Autonomous—the child follows rules freely, expressing mutual rights and obligations. The person is increasingly able to distinguish between principles and rules, and, at more advanced stages the person applies principles to guide behavior in specific situations, instead of automatically following established rules (106).

Developmental Tasks

While the schoolchild continues working on past developmental tasks, he/she is confronted with a series of new ones:

1. Decreasing dependence on family and gaining some satisfaction from peers and other adults.
2. Increasing neuromuscular skills so that he/she can participate in games and work with others.
3. Learning basic adult concepts and knowledge to be able to reason and engage in tasks of everyday living.

4. Learning ways to communicate with others realistically.
5. Becoming a more active and cooperative family participant.
6. Giving and receiving affection among family and friends without immediately seeking something in return.
7. Learning socially acceptable ways of getting money and saving it for later satisfactions.
8. Learning how to handle strong feelings and impulses appropriately.
9. Adjusting the changing body image and self-concept to come to terms with the masculine or feminine social role.
10. Discovering healthy ways of becoming acceptable as a person.
11. Developing a positive attitude toward his/her own and other social, racial, economic, and religious groups (33).

↙ The accomplishment of these tasks gives the schoolchild a foundation for entering adolescence, an era filled with dramatic growth and changing attitudes. Your support, teaching, and guidance can assist the child in this progression.

↙ NURSING APPLICATIONS

Your role in caring for the school-age child and family has been described in each section of the chapter. Assessment, utilizing knowledge about this era that is presented in this chapter, is the basis for *nursing diagnosis*. Nursing diagnoses that may be applicable to the school child are listed in Table 10-6. Interventions may involve measures that promote health, such as immunization or control of hazards; teaching, support, counseling, or spiritual care with the child or family, or direct care measures to the ill child. Your understanding of the child developmentally will enable you to give holistic care—care that includes physiological, emotional, cognitive, social, and spiritual aspects of the person.

References

1. AIDS Against Itself. *Outlook, Washington University School of Medicine*, 23, no. 4 (Winter, 1986), 17–19.
2. All Terrain Vehicles Show Up in Nation's Injury Statistics, *The Nation's Health*, July, 1985, 9.
3. American Academy of Pediatrics, Committee on Infectious Diseases: Prevention of Hepatitis B Virus Infections, *Pediatrics*, 75, no. 2 (1985a), 362–364.
4. ———, Committee on Infectious Diseases: Recommendations for Using Pneumococcal Vaccine in Children, *Pediatrics*, 75, no.6 (1985b), 1153–1158.
5. Arons, Stephen, and Ethan Katsh, How TV Cops Flout the Law, *Saturday Review*, March 19, 1977, 11–18.
6. Baker, Susan, and Roberta Henry, *Parents' Guide to Nutrition: Healthy Eating from Birth through Adolescence*. Reading, MA: Addison-Wesley, 1987.
7. Bardwick, J., and E. Douvan, Ambivalence: The Socialization of Women, in *Readings on the Psychology of Women*, ed. J. Bardwick. New York: Harper & Row, 1972, 52–58.
8. Bates, Barbara, *A Guide to Physical Examination* (3rd ed.). Philadelphia: J. B. Lippincott, 1983.
9. Bergman, Abraham, Use of Education in Preventing Injuries, *Pediatric Clinics of North America*, 29, no. 2 (1982), 331–337.
10. Bettelheim, Bruno, *A Good Enough Parent: A Book on Child-Rearing*. New York: Alfred A. Knopf, 1987.
11. Black, Jeffrey, AIDS: Preschool and School Issues, *The Journal of School Health*, 56, no.3 (1986), 93–95.
12. Blaesing, Sandra, and Joyce Brockhaus, The Development of Body Image in the Child, *Nursing Clinics of North America*, 7, no. 4 (1972), 601–607.
13. Blust, La Delle, School Nurse Practitioner in a High School, *American Journal of Nursing*, 78, no. 9 (1978), 1532–1533.
14. Bonham, Gordon, and Ronald Wilson, Children's Health in Families with Cigarette Smokers, *American Journal of Public Health*, 71, no. 3 (1981), 290–293.
15. Boyce, W. Thomas, et al., Playground Equipment Injuries in Large, Urban School District, *American Journal of Public Health*, 74, no. 9 (1984), 984–986.
16. Burgess, Ann, and Lynda Holmstrom, Sexual Trauma of Children and Adults, *Nursing Clinics of North America*, 10, no. 3 (September, 1975), 551–563.
17. ———, Maureen McCausland, and Wendy Wolbert, Children's Drawings as Indicators of Sexual Trauma, *Perspectives in Psychiatric Care*, 19, no. 2 (1981), 50–58.
18. ———, Carol Hartman, Wendy Wolbert, et al. Child Molestation: Assessing Impact in Multiple Victims (Part I), *Archives of Psychiatric Nursing*, 1, no. 1 (1987), 33–39.
19. Butler, William, Vincent Segreto, and Edwin Collins, Prevalence of Dental Mottling in School-Aged Lifetime Residents of 16 Texas Communities, *American Journal of Public Health*, 75, (1985), 1408–1412.
20. Buttery, Thomas, Biracial Children: Racial Identification, Self-Esteem, and School Adjustment, *Kappa Delta Pi Record*, 23, no. 2 (Winter, 1987), 50–53.
21. Cacha, Francis, How Safe Are Students in School?, *Kappa Delta Pi Record*, 18, no. 3 (Spring, 1982), 72–73.
22. Carlstrom, Jane A., and Stella Nelson, Measles and Rubella: Old Problems in a New Generation, *Journal of Community Health Nursing*, 4, no. 2 (1987), 69–76.
23. Clemen-Stone, Susan, Diane Eigsti, and Sandra Mc-

Guire, *Comprehensive Family and Community Health Nursing* (2nd ed.). New York: McGraw-Hill, 1987.

24. Cohen, Dorothy, Is TV a Pied Piper? *Young Children*, 30, no. 1 (November, 1974), 4–14.
25. Coles, Robert, Children of Crisis: Vol. 5–*The Privileged Ones, The Well Off, and the Rich in America*. Boston: Little, Brown, 1978.
26. Comer, James, Television, Sex, and Violence, *Parents*, July, 1986, 160.
27. Comer, James, and Alvin Pouissant, *Black Child Care*. New York: Simon and Schuster, 1975.
28. Common, Ron, and Marilyn MacMullen, Home Schooling—A Growing Movement, *Kappa Delta Pi Record*, 23, no. 4 (Summer, 1987), 114–117.
29. Conroy, Mary, Is Perfectionism Killing Your Kid? *Better Homes and Gardens*, November, 1987, 79–80.
30. Coopersmith, Stanley, *The Antecedents of Self-Esteem*. San Francisco: W.H. Freeman, 1967.
31. DiClemente, L., Jim Zorn, and Lydia Temoshok, Adolescents and AIDS: A Survey of Knowledge, Attitudes, and Beliefs About AIDS in San Francisco, *American Journal of Public Health*, 76, no. 12 (1986), 1443–1445.
32. Diseker, Robert, et al., A Comparison of Height, Weight, and Triceps Skinfold Thickness of Children Ages 5–12 in Michigan (1978). Forsyth County, North Carolina (1978), and Hanes, Part I (1971–1974), *American Journal of Public Health*, 72, no. 7 (1982), 730–733.
33. Duvall, Evelyn, and Brent Miller, *Marriage and Family Development* (6th ed). New York: Harper & Row, 1984.
34. Edelman, Marian, Justice for Children Everywhere, *Today's Education* (February–March, 1979), 41–45.
35. Elkind, David, Why Children Need Time, *Parade* (January 10, 1982), 14–19.
36. Enright, Robert, and Sara Sutterfield, Treating the Regular Class Child in the Mainstreaming Process: Increasing Social Cognitive Development, *Psychology in the Schools*, 16, no. 1 (1979), 110–118.
37. Erikson, Erik, *Childhood and Society* (2nd ed.). New York: W. W. Norton, 1963.
38. Falkner, Frank, and J. M. Tanner, *Human Growth* (2nd ed.). New York: Plenum Press, 1986.
39. Fergusen, Cecilia, and Lena Roll, Human Rabies, *American Journal of Nursing*, 81, no. 6 (1981), 1175–1179.
40. Furth, H., and H. Wachs, *Thinking Goes to School: Piaget's Theory in Practice*. New York: Oxford University Press, 1975.
41. Garbarino, James, Edna Guttmann, and James Seeley, *The Psychologically Battered Child: Strategies for Identification, Assessment and Intervention*. San Francisco: Jossey-Bass, 1987.
42. Gelbert, Elizabeth, Children's Conceptions of the Content and Functions of The Human Body, *Genetic-Psychologic Monographs*, 65 (1962), 293–411.
43. Gesell, Arnold, and Francis Ilg, *The Child from Five to Ten*. New York: Harper and Brothers, 1946.
44. Gesell, Arnold, Frances Ilg, and Louise Ames, *Youth: The Years from Ten to Sixteen*. New York: Harper and Brothers, 1956.
45. Gordon, Leonard, and Donald Haynes, Smoking-Related Attitudes and Behaviors of Parents of Fourth-Grade Students, *The Journal of School Health*, 51, no. 6 (1981), 408–412.
46. Greenberg, Margaret, et al., Cigarette Use Among Hispanic and Non-Hispanic White School Children, Albuquerque, New Mexico, *American Journal of Public Health*, 77, no. 5 (1987), 621–622.
47. Greensher, J., Prevention of Childhood Injuries, *Pediatrics*, 74 (1984), 970–975.
48. Hammer, David, and Ronald Drabman, Child Discipline: What We Know and What We Can Recommend, *Pediatric Nursing*, 7, no. 3 (1981), 31–35.
49. *Health United States, 1982*. Washington, D.C. U.S. Government Printing Office 1982, Publication # PHS 83–1232.
50. Heindle, Mary Catherine, Symposium on Child Abuse and Neglect: Foreword, *The Nursing Clinics of North America*, 16, no. 1 (1981), 101–102.
51. Holt, Sandra, and Thelma Robinson, The School Nurse's Family Assessment Tool, *American Journal of Nursing*, 79, no. 5 (1979), 950–953.
52. Hoole, Axalla, Robert Greenberg, and C. Glenn Pickard, *Patient Care Guidelines for Nurse Practitioners* (2nd ed.). Boston: Little, Brown, 1982.
53. How Kids Rate Their Working Moms, *Women's Day* (June 16, 1987), 6–7.
54. Immunizations Still Important for Children, *Health Scene*, Fall, 1987, 11.
55. Jones, Franklin, Karl Garrison, and Raymond Morgan, *The Psychology of Human Development* (3d ed.). New York: Harper & Row, 1985.
56. Kaluger, George, and Meriem Kaluger, *Human Development: The Span of Life* (3rd ed.). St. Louis: Times Mirror/Mosby, 1984.
57. Karamessinis, Nicholas, Personality and Perceptions of the Gifted, *G/C/T*, 1, no. 1 (May–June, 1980), 11–13.
58. Karp, Stanley, A 10-point Program for Bicycle Safety, *Contemporary Pediatrics*, 4, no. 6 (1987), 16–21, 24, 26–27.
59. Katz, Lillian, Telling Children About Divorce, *Parents* (July, 1986), 152.
60. Kellam, Sheppard G., C. Hendricks Brown, and John P. Fleming, Social Adaptation to First Grade and Teenage Drug, Alcohol and Cigarette Use, *The Journal of School Health*, 52, no. 5 (1982), 301–306.
61. Kids Need More Time to be Kids, *Newsweek* (February 2, 1987), 56–68.
62. Klug, Ruth, Children with AIDS, *American Journal of Nursing*, 86, no. 10 (1986), 26–31.
63. Kohl, Herbert, Should I Buy My Child a Computer? *Graduate Woman*, 76, no. 6 (1982), 20–23.

64. Kohlberg, Lawrence, *Recent Research in Moral Development*. New York: Holt, Rinehart & Winston, 1971.
65. ———, Development of Moral Character and Moral Ideology, in M.L. Hoffman (ed.), *Review of Child Development Research*, Vol. 1., New York: Russell Sage, 1964, pp. 383–432.
66. Koltz, Charles, Reading Backs Is as Good as Reading Books, *Washington University Alumni News*, 34, no. 1 (1982), 1.
67. Kozinetz, Claudia, Two Noninvasive Methods to Measure Female Maturation, *The Journal of School Health*, 56, no. 10 (1986), 440–442.
68. Lamb, Michael, *The Father's Role*. New York: John Wiley, 1986.
69. Lambo, Alice, Children's Ability to Evaluate Television Commercial Messages for Sugared Products, *American Journal of Public Health*, 71, no. 9 (1981), 1060–1062.
70. Lamont, Anita, Bad Children Who Turn Out All Right, *St. Louis Globe-Democrat*, March 12–13, 1977, Sec. C., 1.
71. Leaman, Karen, Recognizing and Helping the Abused Child, *Nursing '79* 9, no. 2 (1979), 64–67.
72. Leone, Susan, and Jim Gumaer, Group Assertiveness Training of Shy Children, *School Counselor*, 27, no. 2 (1979), 134–141.
73. Levine, Carol, The DPT Dilemma, *Parents*, 62, no. 4 (1987), 228–231.
74. Lidz, Theodore, *The Person: His and Her Development Throughout the Life Cycle* (2nd ed). New York: Basic Books, 1983.
75. Liebert, Robert, and John Neale, TV Violence and Child Aggression, *Psychology Today*, 5, no. 1 (April, 1972), 38–40.
76. Lieske, Anna, Incest: An Overview, *Perspectives in Psychiatric Care*, 19, no. 2 (1982), 59–63.
77. Lykins, Robert, Children of the Third Culture, *Kappa Delta Pi Record*, (Winter, 1986), 39–43.
78. Lynds, Barbara, Suzanne Seyler, and Brenda Morgan, The Relationship Between Elevated Blood Pressure and Obesity in Black Children, *American Journal of Public Health*, 70, no. 2 (1980), 171–173.
79. Mackey, Wade, *Fathering Behaviors: The Dynamics of the Man-Child Bond*. New York: Plenum Press, 1985.
80. Maddocks, Gillian, Growing to Independence, *Nursing Mirror*, 152, no. 21 (1981), viii–xiv.
81. Malina, Robert, Anthony Zuvaleta, and Bertes Little, Body Size, Fatness, and Leanness of Mexican-American Children in Brownsville, Texas: Changes Between 1972 and 1983, *American Journal of Public Health*, 77, no. 5 (1987), 573–577.
82. Manning, M., Disappearing Childhood: 6 Going on 16, *Kappa Delta Pi Record*, (Fall, 1985), 14–18.
83. Markham, Lynda, and John Smith, Nickelodeon: An Alternative to Usual Television Fare? *Kappa Delta Pi Record*, 19, no. 4 (Summer, 1983), 125–128.
84. Marten, David, Cognitive Assessment of Diverse Populations, *Kappa Delta Pi Record* (Winter, 1986), 35–38.
85. Matthews, Patricia, Fast Food, *Nursing Times*, 82, no. 11 (1986), 47–49.
86. McKeil, Nancy Lynn, Child Abuse Can Be Prevented, *American Journal of Nursing*, 78, no. 9 (1978), 1478–1482.
87. Mead, Margaret, *Culture and Commitment—A Study of the Generation Gap*. Garden City, N.Y.: Doubleday, 1970.
88. Micozzi, Marc, Childhood Hypertension and Academic Standing in the Philippines, *American Journal of Public Health*, 70, no. 5 (1980), 530–532.
89. Miel, Alice, Making Room for the Future in the Curriculum, *Kappa Delta Pi Record*, Fall, 1984, 14–16.
90. Miller, Donald, Who is Gifted? A Quick Grasp of Concepts is One Clue, *Independent School*, 39, no. 4 (1980), 12–16.
91. Miller, Sally, Children's Fears: A Review of the Literature With Implications for Nursing Research and Practice, *Nursing Research*, 29, no. 4 (1979), 217–223.
92. Monmaney, Terence, Kids with AIDS, *Newsweek*, September, 1987, 51–59.
93. Moody, Kathryn, *Growing Up on Television*. New York: New York Quadrangle-The New York Times Company, 1980.
94. Morgan, Judith, Prevention of Childhood Obesity, *Comprehensive Pediatric Nursing*, 9 (1986), 33–38.
95. Moshman, David, John Glover, and Roger Bruning, *Developmental Psychology*, Boston: Little, Brown, 1987.
96. Natow, Annette, and Jo-Ann Heslin, *No-Nonsense Nutrition for Kids*. New York: McGraw-Hill, 1985.
97. New Recommended Schedule for Active Immunization of Normal Infants and Children, *Morbidity and Mortality Weekly Report*, 35, no.37, Washington, D.C.: U.S. Department of Health and Human Services, Public Health Service, (1980), 577–579.
98. Nicklas, Theresa, et al., Racial Contrasts in Hemoglobin Levels and Dietary Patterns Related to Hematopoiesis in Children: The Bogalusa Heart Study, *American Journal of Public Health*, 77, no. 10 (1987), 1320–1323.
99. Oakley, Mary, School Phobia, *Res Medica*, 3, no. 2 (1986), 11–14.
100. Oda, Dorothy, A Viewpoint on School Nursing, *American Journal of Nursing*, 81, no. 9 (1981), 1677–1678.
101. Oh, To Be Young and Gifted, *Newsweek*, February 23, 1987, 63–63.
102. Ornstean, Allan, A Difference Teachers Make: How Much, *The Educational Forum*, 49, no. 1 (Fall, 1984), 109–117.
103. Parke, R., and R. Slaby, The Development of Aggression, in *Handbook of Child Psychology, Vol. 4: Socialization, Personality, and Social Development*, E. Hetherton and P. Mussen (eds.). New York: Wiley, 1983.

104. Perry, Cheryl, Rebecca Mullis, and Marla Maile, Modifying the Eating Behavior of Young Children, *The Journal of School Health*, 55, no. 10 (1985), 399–402.
105. Piaget, Jean, *Judgment and Reasoning in the Child*. New York: Humanities Press, 1928.
106. ———, *The Moral Judgment of the Child*. New York: Harcourt, Brace, and Company, 1932.
107. ———, *The Growth of Logical Thinking from Childhood to Adolescence*. New York: Basic Books, 1958.
108. ———, *The Origins of Intelligence in Children*. New York: W. W. Norton, 1963.
109. ———, *The Child's Conception of Numbers*. New York: W. W. Norton, 1965.
110. ———, and B. Inhelder, *The Psychology of the Child*. New York: Basic Books, 1969.
111. ———, Introduction, in *Piaget in the Classroom*, M. Schwebel, (ed.) New York: Basic Books, 1973.
112. ———, and Barbel Inhelder, *Memory and Intelligence*. New York: Basic Books, 1973.
113. Piersel, W., G. Brody, and T. Kratochwill, A Further Examination of Motivational Influences on Disadvantaged Minority Group Children's Intelligence Test Performance, *Child Development*, 48 (1978), 142–145.
114. Pillitteri, Adele, *Child Health Nursing: Care of the Growing Family* (3rd ed.). Boston: Little, Brown, 1987.
115. Pink, William, Creating Effective Schools, *The Educational Forum*, 49, no. 1 (Fall, 1984), 91–107.
116. Pipes, Peggy, *Nutrition in Infancy and Childhood* (3rd ed.). St. Louis: Times Mirror/Mosby, 1985.
117. Pontious, Sharon, Practical Piaget: Helping Children Understand, *American Journal of Nursing*, 82, no. 1 (1982), 115–117.
118. Porter, Carol, Grade School Children's Perceptions of Their Internal Body Parts, *Nursing Research*, 23, no. 5 (September–October, 1974), 384–391.
119. Potter, Diana, (ed.) *Assesssment*, Springhouse, Pa.: Intermed Communications, 1982.
120. Price, James, AIDS, the School, and Policy Issues, *The Journal of School Health*, 56, no. 4 (1986), 137–141.
121. ———, and Linda Geronella, Childhood Obesity: A Review, *Health Values*, 5, no. 5 (1981), 192–198.
122. Pridham, Karen, and Marc Hansoen, Helping Children Deal with Procedures in a Clinic Setting: A Developmental Approach, *Journal of Pediatric Nursing*, 2, no. 2 (1987), 13–21.
123. R. Ratings: Most Violent Programming Shown as Children Watch, St. Louis Post Dispatch, September 11, 1986, Sec. C, pp. 17–18.
124. Reek, Jan van, Marie Drop, and Jan Joosten, The Influence of Peers and Parents on the Smoking Behavior of Schoolchildren, *Journal of School Health*, 57, no. 1 (1987), 30.
125. Richards, Warren, Allergy, Asthma, and School Problems, *Journal of School Health*, 56, no. 4 (1986), 151–152.
126. Richoux, Donna, A Look at Home Schooling, *Kappa Delta Pi Record*, 23, no. 4 (Summer, 1987), 118–121.
127. Robbins, Kenneth, David Brandling-Bennett, and Alan Hinman, Low Measles Incidence: Association with Enforcement of School Immunization Laws, *American Journal of Public Health*, 71, no. 3 (1981), 270–274.
128. Robinson, Thelma, School Nurse Practitioners on the Job, *American Journal of Nursing*, 81, no. 9 (1981), 1674–1676.
129. Rogers, Constance, Innovative School Nursing in Harlem: A Custom-Made Program, *American Journal of Nursing*, 77, no. 9 (1977), 1469–1471.
130. Rubenstein, E., Television and Behavior: Research Conclusions of the 1982 NIMH Report and Their Policy Implications, *American Psychologist*, 38 (1983), 820–825.
131. Schiamberg, Lawrence, *Human Development* (2nd ed.). New York: Macmillan, 1985.
132. Scholl, Theresa, Karp, Robert, Theophano, Janet, et al., Ethnic Differences in Growth and Nutritional Status: a Study of Poor Schoolchildren in Southern New Jersey, *Public Health Reports*, 102, no. 3 (1987), 278–283.
133. Schuster, Clara Shaw, and Shirley Smith Ashburn, *The Process of Human Development: A Holistic Life-Span Approach* (2nd ed.). Boston: Little, Brown, 1986.
134. Schwartz, Judith, Early Identification of Gifted, Talented, and Creative Children, *Kappa Delta Pi Record*, 20, no. 1 (Fall, 1983), 24–28.
135. Schwebel, Milton, and Jane Raph (eds.), *Piaget in the Classroom*. New York: Basic Books, 1973.
136. Scipien, G.M., Bernard, M.A., Howe, J., et al., *Comprehensive Pediatric Nursing* (3rd ed.). New York: McGraw-Hill, 1986.
137. Scott, Mary, The Real Issue of Mainstreaming: The Education of the Nonhandicapped, *Kappa Delta Pi Record*, 19, no. 1 (Fall, 1982), 17–20.
138. Selekman, Janice, Immunization: What's It All About? *American Journal of Nursing*, 80, no. 8 (1980), 1440–1445.
139. Shapiro, Leona, et al., Obesity Prognosis: A Longitudinal Study of Children From Age 6 Months to 9 Years, *American Journal of Public Health*, 74, no. 9 (1984), 968–972.
140. Shore, Milton, Norman Milgram, and Charlotte Malasky, The Effectiveness of an Enrichment Program for Disadvantaged Young Children, *American Journal of Orthopsychiatry*, 4, no. 3 (1971), 442–449.
141. Schultz, Cathleen, Sulfite Sensitivity, *American Journal of Nursing*, 86, no. 8 (1986), 914.
142. Silver, Henry K., C. Henry Kempe, Henry B. Bruyn,

Handbook of Pediatrics (12th ed.). Los Altos, Ca.: Lange Medical Publications, 1977.
143. Singer, D.C., A Time to Re-examine the Role of Television in Our Lives, *American Psychologist*, 38 (1983), 815–816.
144. Singer, J. L., and D. E. Singer, Implications of Childhood Television Viewing for Cognition, Imagination, and Emotion, in J. Bryant and D. Anderson (eds.), *Children's Understanding of Television: Research on Attention and Comprehension*. New York: Academic Press, 1983.
145. Smith, A., et al., Prediction of Development Outcome at Seven Years from Prenatal, Perinatal, and Postnatal Events, *Child Development*, 43 (July, 1972), 502ff.
146. Smith, Howard, Nonverbal Communication in Teaching, *Review of Educational Research*, 49, no. 4 (1979), 632–672.
147. Southall, Christine, Innovative School Nursing in Harlem: Family Life and Sex Education, *American Journal of Nursing*, 77, no. 9 (1977), 1473–1476.
148. Spratlen, Lois Price, Nurse-Role Dimensions of a School-Based Hypertension Screening, Education, and Follow-up Program, *The Journal of School Health*, 52, no. 3 (1982), 174–178.
149. Stedwitz, Ulreki, Carol Lariviere, and Vincent Rogers, What Do Kids Do When They're Not in School? *Kappa Delta Pi Record* (Winter, 1988), 44–47.
150. Strickland, Donna, Friendship Patterns and Altruistic Behavior in Preadolescent Males and Females, *Nursing Research*, 30. no. 4 (1981), 222, 228, 235.
151. Sullivan, Harry S., *The Interpersonal Theory of Psychiatry*. New York: W. W. Norton, 1953.
152. Swanson, Lisa, and Mary Kay Biaggio, Therapeutic Perspectives in Father—Daughter Incest, *American Journal of Psychiatry*, 142, no. 6 (1985), 667–674.
153. Tanner, J.M., *Foetus into Man: Physical Growth from Conception to Maturity*. London: Open Books, 1978.
154. Tapp, June, A Child's Garden of Law and Order, *Psychology Today*, 4, no. 7 (December, 1970), 29ff.
155. Tennant, Forest, and Jean La Cour, Children at High Risk for Addiction and Alcoholism: Identification and Intervention, *Pediatric Nursing*, 5, no. 1 (1980), 26–28.
156. Tesler, Mary, and Marilyn Savedra, Coping with Hospitalization: A Study of School-Age Children, *Pediatric Nursing*, 7, no. 2 (1981), 35–40.
157. Thomas, Joyce, and Carl Rogers, Sexual Abuse of Children: Case Finding and Clinical Assessment, *Nursing Clinics of North America*, 18, no. 1 (1981), 179–188.
158. Thompson, Sharen, Summertime and Ticks, *American Journal of Nursing*, 83, no. 5 (1983), 768–769.
159. Torney, Judith, and Patrick Brice, *Children's Concepts of Human Rights and Social Cognition*. Washington, D.C.: National Commission of UNESCO, 1979.
160. Tow, Patrick, and Warren McNab, Discipline: A Parenting Dilemma, *Health Education*, 16, no. 1 (1985), 45–47.
161. Tripp-Reimer, Toni, Retention of a Folk-Healing Practice (Matiasma) Among Four Generations of Urban Greek Immigrants, *Nursing Research*, 32, no. 2 (1983), 97–101.
162. Turner, Jeffrey, and Donald Helms, *Lifespan Development* (3rd ed.). New York: Holt, Rinehart and Winston, 1987.
163. U.S. Department of Health and Human Services, *Television and Behavior: Ten Years of Scientific Progress and Implications for the Eighties*. Washington, D.C.: 1982.
164. U.S. Department of Health and Human Service, New Recommended Schedule for Active Immunization of Normal Infants and Children, *Morbidity and Mortality Weekly Report*. 35, no. 37 (September 19, 1986), 577–579.
165. Wadsworth, Barry. *Piaget's Theory of Cognitive and Affective Development* (3rd ed.). New York: David McKay, 1984.
166. Waechter, E.H., J. Phillips, and B. Holaday, *Nursing Care of Children* (10th ed.). Philadelphia: Lippincott, 1985.
167. Warning from Washington: Violence in Television is Harmful to Children, *Time*, May 17, 1982, 77.
168. Webb, Patricia, Piaget: Implications for Teaching, *Theory Into Practice*, 19, no. 2 (1980), 93–97.
169. Welch, Lynne, Pediculosis at Summer Camp, *American Journal of Nursing*, 79, no. 6 (1979), 1073.
170. Whaley, Lucille, and Donna Wong, *Nursing Care of Infants and Children* (3rd ed.). St. Louis: C. V. Mosby, 1987.
171. Williams, Phoebe, A Comparison of Philippine and American Children's Concepts of Body Organs and Illness in Relation to Five Variables, *International Journal of Nursing Studies*, 15 (1978), 193–203.
172. Williams, Sue Rodwell, *Nutrition and Diet Therapy* (5th ed.). St. Louis: Times Mirror/Mosby, 1985.
173. Wintemute, Garen, Jess Kraus, Stephen Teret, et al., Drowning in Childhood and Adolescence: A Population-Based Study, *American Journal of Public Health*, 77, no. 7 (1987), 830–832.
174. Wolfe, Helen, Television—Reflector or Creator of Values? *Graduate Woman*, (May–June, 1979), 14–16.
175. Yanni, Mary, Perception of Parents' Behavior and Children's General Fearfulness, *Nursing Research*, 31, no. 2 (1982), 79–82.
176. Yeger, Trudi, and Solverga Miezitis, Self-Concept and Classroom Behavior of Preadolescent Pupils, *Journal of Classroom Interaction*, 15, no. 2 (1980), 31–37.
177. Yoos, Lorrie, Chronic Childhood Illnesses: Developmental Issues, *Pediatric Nursing*, 13, no. 1 (1987), 25–28.

11

Assessment and Health Promotion for the Adolescent and Youth

Study of this chapter will enable you to

1. Discuss the impact of the crisis of adolescence on family life and the influence of the family on the adolescent.
2. Explore with the family its developmental tasks and ways to achieve these, while giving positive guidance to the adolescent.
3. Correlate the physiological changes and needs, including nutrition, exercise, and rest, of early, middle, and late adolescence to those which occurred in preadolescence.
4. Discuss with parents the cognitive, self-concept, sexuality, emotional, and moral–religious development of the adolescent and ways in which the family can foster healthy progress of these.
5. Identify examples of adolescent peer-group dialect and use of leisure time in your region, and discuss how knowledge of these can be utilized in your health-promotion activities and teaching.
6. Explore the developmental crisis of identity formation with the adolescent and the parents, the significance of achieving this crisis for ongoing maturity, and how to counteract influences that interfere with identity formation.
7. Describe the developmental tasks of adolescence and how the adaptive mechanisms commonly used assist the adolescent in achieving these.
8. Assess and work effectively with an adolescent with instructor supervision.
9. Discuss the challenges of the transitional period to young adulthood and your role in assisting the late adolescent into young adulthood.
10. Discuss common health problems of the adolescent, factors which contribute to them, and your role in contributing to the adolescent's health.

How can I best describe my son? He is 13 years old but could pass for 16 physically and mentally. He has the physique of a football player and appears to grow taller each day. His general knowledge is superior because he watches television for at least 2 hours a day, scans the morning and evening papers, and listens to the radio periodically during the day. He is full of contradictions; for example, he talks about love but a hug or sign of affection from his mother will send him running to his room.

Historical and Cultural Perspectives

Adolescence has long been considered a critical period in human development, and the search for an understanding of the adolescent can be traced historically. Early writers, such as Rousseau, Francke, and Froebel, directed their interest toward the education of the adolescent as well as his/her characteristics. Then in the late nineteenth century, psychologists molded the Darwinian concepts into psychological terms and firmly established adolescence as an inevitable stage in human development. Before the twentieth century, however, most people thought of themselves as young adults after puberty.

Adolescence as a developmental era differs cross-culturally. In the United States, adolescence begins earlier than ever physiologically because of improved nutrition and health practices, and it is being ex-

Key Terms

Puberty
Spermatogenesis
Menstruation
Pubarche
Menarche
Adolescence
Preadolescence
Early adolescence
Middle adolescence
Late adolescence
Sperm production
Nocturnal emissions
Sex hormones
Androgens
Estrogens
Progesterones
Ovulation
Primary dysmenorrhea
Anorexia nervosa
Bulimia
Obesity
Peer group
Peer-group dialect
Identity
Identity formation
Personal/real identity
Ideal identity
Claimed identity
Identity diffusion
Sexuality
Masturbation
Ego
Frustration
Conversion
Teen walkaway
Teen runaway
Musculoskeletal chest pain
Strain/sprain
Minor ankle sprain
Hordoleum/stye
Epistaxis
Comedones
Tinea pedis/athlete's foot
Infectious mononucleosis
Hepatitis
Rocky Mountain spotted fever
Sexually transmitted diseases
Vaginitis
  Candidal
  Trichomonal
  Nonspecific
Chlamydia trachomatis
Phthirius pubis
Contraception
Abortion
Incest
Drug abuse
Drug
Drug dependence
Addiction
Tolerance
Cocaine
Crack/rock

Definitions

In the past, many people equated puberty and adolescence; they are now considered separate components. Puberty is preceded by prepuberty, discussed in Chapter 10.

Puberty *is the state of physical development between 10 and 14 years for females and 12 to 16 years for males when sexual reproduction first becomes possible with the onset of* **spermatogenesis** *(production of spermatozoa) and* **menstruation** *(onset of menses).* Common law usually fixes puberty at 12 years for females and 14 years for males. **Pubarche** *refers to the beginning development of certain secondary sex characteristics which precedes the actual onset of physiological puberty.* Some define puberty as a process involving a number of physical changes over a period of time that culminates in menstruation and spermatogenesis. The female may be unable to conceive for 1 to 2 years after **menarche,** *the first menstrual period,* and the male is usually sterile for a year or more after ejaculation first occurs. Some studies have shown, however, that some males become fertile at the onset of pubertal development (150, 177, 182).

Adolescence *is the period in life which begins with puberty and extends for 8 or 10 years, or longer, until the person is physically and psychologically mature, ready to assume adult responsibilities and be self-sufficient because of changes in intellect, attitudes, and interests* (92, 193). Exceptions occur; some people never become psychologically mature. This definition does not reflect the individuality of the adolescent. Generalizations should be avoided as much as possible to prevent unjustified expectations from the adolescent.

Keniston has further delineated this period between puberty and young adulthood by calling the period from 20 to 25 years *youth*. He feels that the affluent culture, especially in urban areas, has often created additional time before adult responsibilities must be assumed (84). For the purpose of this chapter, however, the adolescent period is divided into the subperiods of preadolescence, early, middle, and late adolescence. (The term *youth* will be used interchangeably with adolescence.) Although age ranges are assigned to each subperiod, they are approximate; each adolescent may vary as to when and how he/she proceeds through the various stages.

Preadolescence, *the stage of prepuberty,* is discussed in Chapter 10, since these children are a part of the school-age population in America.

Early adolescence *begins with puberty and lasts for several years* (11 or 12 to 13 or 14 for females and 12 or 14 to 16 for males). The growth spurt focuses attention on self and the task of becoming comfortable with body changes and appearance. The teen tries to separate from parents; the dependency–

tended longer developmentally because of social, economic, employment, industrial, and family changes. Adolescence may end in the teens for some people, but it generally ends in the mid-twenties for most (43, 84, 149, 182).

Adolescence is like old age in the United States: The roles are not well defined, and each population is considered something of a burden and unable to contribute much to society. Further, each developmental period has been extending in length of time as the people in these eras try to sort out their identities, changed status, and the meaning of life (83, 149, 182). Perhaps as a result of changes in population statistics, attitudes about each era will change, for all people who are capable of contributing will be needed as productive citizens. Certainly in some cultures even today, when puberty occurs, rites of passage signal adulthood.

independency struggle is shown by less involvement in family activities (and chores, if possible), being critical of the parents, and rebellion against parental and other adult discipline and authority. Conformity to and acceptance of peer group standards and peer friendships are gaining in importance. The peer group usually consists of the same-sexed friends; however, the adolescent has an increased interest in the opposite sex. Group activities with peers are popular (2, 149, 150).

Middle adolescence *begins when physical growth is completed and usually extends from age 13 or 14 to 16 for females and 14 or 16 to 18 or 20 for males.* The major tasks during this period are achievement of ego identity, attainment of greater independence, interest in the future and career planning, and establishment of heterosexual relationship. Peer group allegiance, at a peak in 15- to 16-year-olds, is manifested by clothing, food, and other fads, preferred music, and common jargon. Experimentation with adult-like behavior and risk taking is common in an attempt to prove self to peers. Sexual experimentation often begins now (or earlier) as a result of social exploration and physical maturation. Changes in cognitive functioning may first be evident in that the person moves to more abstract thinking, returning to more concrete operations during times of stress (2).

Some teens are expected to move into the tasks of young adulthood at this point. While they may be employed, or independent in other ways, developmentally the person is more likely to be in late adolescence.

Late adolescence *may occur from about 20 to 25 years of age.* The person has usually finished adolescent rebellion, formed his/her views, and established a stable sense of self. The youth is not fully committed to one occupation and questions relationships to existing social, vocational, and emotional roles and lifestyles. He/she may be a student or an apprentice (84). Lack of economic freedom may be a concern and prolong dependence on parents. The value system is being clarified; issues of philosophy, religion, life and death, and ethical decisions are being analyzed. The peer group has lost its primary importance, and the youth may take the final step in establishing independence from parents by moving away from home. More adult-like friendships begin between late adolescents and their parents as the earlier family turbulence subsides. At the same time there is more individual dating and fewer group activities with friends; often the first emotionally intimate relationship develops with a member of the opposite sex. At that point, the person is developmentally a young adult, having made the transition from adolescence. He/she is more realistically aware of strengths and limits in self and others (2, 79, 149).

Family Development and Relationships

Developmental Tasks

The overall family goal at this time is to allow the adolescent increasing freedom and responsibility to prepare him/her for young adulthood.

Although each family member has personal developmental tasks, the family unit as a whole also has developmental tasks. These include the following:

1. Provide facilities for individual differences and needs of family members.
2. Work out a system of financial responsibility with the family.
3. Establish a sharing of responsibilities.
4. Reestablish a mutually satisfying marriage relationship.
5. Strengthen communication within the family.
6. Rework relationships with relatives, friends, and associates.
7. Broaden horizons of the adolescent and parents.
8. Formulate a workable philosophy of life as a family (39).

✔ Discuss the developmental tasks and how to achieve them with the family. Generally speaking, the developmental tasks for a family at this time involve maintaining a grasp on these facets of life which continue to have meaning while striving for a deeper awareness and understanding of the present situation.

Family Relationships

During early adolescence, the teen remains involved in family activities and functions. Gradually family relationships change and the adolescent develops social ties and close relationships outside the family. The family's beliefs, lifestyles, values, and patterns of interaction influence the development of these relationships (149, 152).

It is during middle and late adolescence that the most severe changes occur in the parent–child relationship. The relationship must evolve from a dependency status to mutual affection, equality, and autonomy. This process of achieving independence usually creates family turmoil, conflict, and ambivalence as both parents and adolescent learn new roles. The emancipation process must be gradual. Parents should gradually increase the teen-ager's responsibilities and allow privileges formerly denied. The adolescent wants to make independent decisions and to have increased freedom of movement. At the same time, he/she wants financial support, food, and safe sanctuary. Parents must resist granting instant adult status when the child reaches teen years and instead remember that the adolescent needs to be independent yet dependent. Although he/she protests, the teen values parental restraints if the restraints are reasonable. The adolescent feels more self-confident in exploring the environment if reasonable limits are imposed. Parents should listen to their adolescent's view points concerning restrictions. Views may offer hints about the readiness for more independence and freedom (79, 133, 152, 193).

Most ambivalence and negative behavior in the adolescent stems from self-perceived external restrictions. Teen-agers may fight for grownup privileges that they never use—the actual battle is more important than the privilege. Disagreements and conflicts about sexual behavior, dress, drugs, school performance, homework, friendship, family car and telephone privileges, manners, chores and duties, money, and disrespectful behavior frequently disrupt family harmony (182, 193).

In addition to other conflicts, the youth must also work through feelings for the parent of the opposite sex and unravel the ambivalence toward the parent of the same sex. He/she reworks some of the gender identity and family triangle problems that remain from the preschool era. In an attempt to resolve this ambivalence, the adolescent may strive to be as different as possible from the parent of the same sex. Frequently, affection is turned to an adult outside the family—teacher, relative, family friend, neighbor, religious teacher, or someone in public life. "Crushes" of this nature are very common; they are usually brief and may occur once, twice, or on numerous occasions. Idolizing another adult person causes the adolescent to want to please that person; therefore, the adolescent's actions and language may change when the idolized person is present. Frequently, the adolescent identifies so completely with this person that he/she absorbs some of the person's adult characteristics into the personality. These relationships are not harmful to the adolescent unless the person who is chronologically an adult still feels confused and rebellious toward society and fosters immaturity. On the contrary, an adult outside the family will usually be more objective than the parent and can therefore help the adolescent grow toward psychological maturity. Parents are experiencing sexuality changes at the same time. They are facing midlife and menopause and are concerned with self-perceived decreased sexual attractiveness and potency.

During this period parents may feel that they are not as important to the adolescent as before. The adolescent complains that parents are old-fashioned and "out of it." He/she may appear hostile and resent parental authority and guidance. The teen seeks to find flaws in parental behavior and may try to build barriers between self and the parents to prove independence. The adolescent is critical, argumentative, and generally remote with both parents; a previously close and confiding relationship with the parents is lost. In their presence, the adolescent may ridicule parents. This rejection is not consistent; response to parents varies with mood changes. At times the relationship can be close and positive; the adolescent may actually support the parents in the presence of peers (152, 182).

In addition to dealing with a loss of authority, parents are faced with other stresses. They are forced to redefine past child–parent relations and rethink their own values. Parents may also be forced to evaluate their own career choices as their adolescent begins vocational pursuits. Competition between parents and the teen may exist; parents may actually admit to not liking the adolescent. They may be anxious to relinquish financial, physical, and emotional child-rearing responsibilities to increase their own freedom (133, 152, 182).

Stresses that frequently produce family discord grow out of conflicting value systems between the old and new generations. Parents are confused by the change from the firm, strict discipline which they experienced to the apparent lack of discipline or permissiveness. Even a balance between the two extremes serves as a threat to some parents. Many of today's parents lived as adolescents in a world restricted to a certain geographical area. The authority of their parents often went unquestioned; questions were not tolerated by the parents. Today's adolescents are a generation born with television, an instrument that has brought remote corners of the world into their homes and minds and has fostered the asking of questions instead of relying on authority.

✒ Parents need help to see that the adolescent is a product of his/her time, and the teen is reflecting what is happening socially.

Youngs' book is a practical reference for parents and professionals on teen-ager's behavior, factors that contribute to stress response, signs and symptoms that the youth and the family are having problems, and how to manage tense situations and teen-age behavioral problems (200).

Parental and adolescent response to the ambivalence and conflicts of this period varies. Parents may adhere to rules and the status quo to bolster their own security or cultural traditions rather than change for the offspring's benefit. Some parents cannot change as quickly as the child during puberty (79). Parents may overprotect. Others may be reluctant to admit that their child is establishing an independent lifestyle; they may dread facing the empty-nest stage (182). If the adolescent has come from a family who has provided past opportunities to learn responsibility, self-reliance, skills, and self-respect, they will make a smoother transition from childhood dependency to adulthood independence. If parents have been liberal, overly permissive, or uninterested, the adolescent will have more difficulty adjusting because the past lacked structure and a system of standards or values. He/she have no point of reference to determine if the behavior is suitable and decisions appropriate (79).

Fortunately some parents trust their offspring to live the basic values they taught, although at times behavior may appear differently. They realize that today's adolescent is growing up in a different historical era than when they were young, and they can accept the changes that result. They work at being communicative, flexible, yet supportive. They encourage but do not push or probe. They question the offspring to encourage thinking. They give reasons for rules and are firm when necessary. They accept that the adolescent may be as large as an adult but still behave childishly at times. The parents' behavior is adult-like, so that they are a model for their offspring. They feel enough self-confidence that they do not have to belittle the adolescent. They are not threatened by his/her sexuality, and they maintain a balance of closeness and distance so that the adolescent can rework gender identity. If the parent–child relationship has been close in the past, it can remain close now, in spite of superficial problems and responses.

Adolescence is not a period of conflict between parents and offspring in all cultures. For example, in Oriental and Indian cultures, some African groups, the Arabian countries, and certain European countries, behavior norms and role expectations provide the basis for a smoother transition from child to adult than is expected in the United States. Nontechnological societies have less adolescent–parent conflict because there is less choice in occupations and lifestyles and less variance between generational behavior (43).

✔ Discuss the above information with parents. Help them understand the interaction between parents and offspring. Encourage the parents to maintain open lines of communication. Adolescents must feel free to seek help from parents; they respond to honesty, fairness, and sincere interest. In essence, the adolescent must be understood and accepted as a person while being allowed as much independence as can be handled. The home should provide an accepting and emotionally stable environment for the adolescent, since the home situation affects later marital adjustments and the type of parent that he/she will become.

✔ *Abuse, Neglect, and Maltreatment.* These may occur with the adolescent, although health care professionals may not be alert to physical or psychological cues. The adolescent who is physically abused may be present in the emergency room with some of the same kinds of injuries that are seen in the younger child. (See Chapters 4, 6, and 7.) Sometimes bruises and lacerations are concealed from peers, teachers, and health care workers by cosmetics and clothes. Careful screening and astute communication skills are essential. You must establish a relationship and interview the adolescent alone. Then you are more likely to learn of physical, sexual, and psychological abuse (maltreatment) or neglect.

✔ Maltreatment of the adolescent is demonstrated by the behaviors described in Table 11-1.

Physiological Concepts

Influences on Physical Growth

The precise physiological cause for the physical changes characteristic of this period is unknown. It appears that the hypothalamus, probably in some way related to brain maturation, initiates the pubertal process through secretion of neurohumoral releasing factors. These neurohumors stimulate the anterior pituitary gland to release gonadotrophic hormones, somatotropic hormone (STH) or growth hormone (GH), thyroid-stimulating hormone (TSH), and adrenocorticotropic hormone (ACTH). The amygdala in the limbic system also apparently changes function and promotes hormonal production (150, 193).

Gonadotrophic hormones (follicle-stimulating hormone [FSH] and luteinizing hormone [LH]) stimulate the gonads to mature and produce sex hormones. FSH stimulates the ovaries in females to produce estrogen and the development of seminiferous tubules in males; LH stimulates the Leydig cells in the testes to produce testosterone. Growth and development of the adrenal cortex and stimulation of the secretion of androgens is promoted by ACTH. These androgens are responsible for producing secondary sex characteristics. Stimulation of deoxyribonucleic acid (DNA) synthesis and hyperplastic cell growth, particularly of the bones and cartilage, is produced by STH. Under the influence of TSH, thyroxin secretion is slightly increased during the pubertal period. Thyroxin levels increase to meet body metabolism needs (150, 193).

Both male and female hormones are produced in varying amounts in both sexes throughout life. During the prepubescent years, the adrenal cortex secretes a small amount of sex hormones. However, it is the sex hormone production that accompanies maturation of the ovaries and testes that is responsible for the physiological changes observed in puberty. Physiological changes in the male are produced by androgens while large amounts of estrogens produce the changes in the female. Both forms of gonadal hormones stimulate epiphyseal fusion by repression of the pituitary growth

Table 11-1 Parental Behavior Characteristics of Psychological Maltreatment

Rejecting	Refuses to acknowledge changing social roles and move to autonomy and independence.
	Treats adolescent like a young child.
	Subjects adolescent to verbal humiliation and excess criticism.
	Expels youth from family.
Isolating	Tries to prevent youth from participating in organized and informal activities outside the home.
	Prohibits adolescent from joining clubs or after-school activities.
	Withdraws youth from school to work or perform household tasks.
	Punishes youth for engaging in normal social activity such as dating.
Terrorizing	Threatens to expose youth to public humiliation, such as undressing youth, forcing encounter with police, or stay in jail.
	Threatens to reveal intensely embarrassing characteristics (real or fantasized) to peers or adults.
	Ridicules youth in public regularly.
Ignoring	Abdicates parental role.
	Shows no interest in youth as person or in activities. Refuses to discuss adolescent's activities, plans, interests.
	Concentrates on activities or relationships that displace adolescent from affections.
Corrupting	Involves youth in more intense or socially unacceptable forms of sexual, aggressive, or substance abuse behavior. Forces youth into prostitution.
	Rewards aggressive or scapegoating behavior to siblings, peers, or adults.
	Encourages trafficking in illicit drug use or alcohol use, or in sex rings.

hormone, thus slowing physical growth at the end of puberty (193).

Physical Characteristics

Growth. Adolescence is the second major period of accelerated growth (infancy was the first). The adolescent growth spurt occurs about 2 years earlier in the female than in the male. During the years of the growth spurt, females grow 2½ to 5 inches (6 to 12.5 cm) and gain 8 to 10 pounds (3.5 to 4.5 kg); males average 3 to 6 inches (7.5 to 15 cm) and gain 12 to 14 pounds (5.5 to 6.5 kg). In the initial phase of the growth spurt, the increase in height is due to lengthening of the legs; later, most of the increase is in the trunk length. The total process of change takes about 3 years in females and 4 years in males (34, 78, 79, 113, 150, 177).

Every system of the body is growing rapidly, but physiological changes occur unevenly within the person. Variation exists in age of onset of puberty and rapidity of growth between different groups of people as well. For example, Chinese show an earlier height spurt and menarche and advanced skeletal muturity than Europeans (79, 113).

Sexual Development. Four physical characteristics define puberty for most adolescents as they observe themselves and each other (44, 79, 150, 166, 182, 193).

Females
Height spurt: ages 8 to 17 years; peak age—12
Menarche: 10 to 16 years; average age—12.5
Breast development: 8 to 18 years
Pubic hair: 11 to 14 years

Males
Height spurt: 10 to 20 years; peak age—14
Penis development: 10 to 16 years
Testes development: 9 to 17 years
Pubic hair: 12 to 16 years

Menarche is the indicator of puberty and sexual maturity in the female. Ovulation usually occurs 12 to 24 months after menarche. The onset of menarche varies among population groups and is influenced by heredity, nutrition, health care, and other environmental factors. In the United States, the average age of onset is 12.6 to 12.9 years (152, 167). Research regarding the onset of menarche has revealed conflicting results. Some researchers have shown that in the United States menarche occurs at an average height of 158.8 centimenters and an average weight of 43 kilograms (159). Observations further established that body fat must make up 17 percent of the female's body weight before menarche occurs (46, 129). Other research has revealed no correlation between level of body fat and onset of menarche (50). Urban females have earlier menarche than rural females. Menarche onset varies among population groups: In the United

States, the average age of onset is 12.6 to 12.9 years; in Sweden, 12.9 years; in Italy, 12.5 years; in Africa, 13.4 to 14.1 years (79, 113, 133, 152, 177).

Secondary sex characteristics in the female begin to develop in prepuberty (see Chapter 10) and may take 2 to 8 years for completion. Breast enlargement and elevation occur; areola and papillae project to form a secondary mound. Axillary and pubic hair grows thicker, becomes darker, and spreads over the pubic area (113).

Spermatogenesis (**sperm production**) and seminal emissions mark puberty and sexual maturity in the male. The first ejaculate of seminal fluid occurs about 1 year after the penis has begun its adolescent growth, and **nocturnal emissions,** *loss of seminal fluid during sleep,* occur at about age 14 (133, 150, 152).

Secondary sex characteristics in the male also begin in prepuberty (see Chapter 10) and may take 2 to 5 years for completion. Body shape changes, growth of body hair, and muscle development may continue until 19 or 20, or even until the late twenties. North American males complete growth in stature by 18 or 19 years, with an additional ½ to 1 inch (1 to 2 cm) in height occurring during the twenties because of continued vertebral column growth (150, 159). The penis, scrotum, and testes enlarge; the scrotum reddens and scrotal skin changes texture. Hair grows at the axilla and base of the penis and spreads over the pubis. Body hair generally increases, especially facial hair. The voice deepens (133, 152, 193).

Sex hormones are biochemical agents that primarily *influence the structure and function of the sex organs and appearance of specific sexual characteristics.* **Androgens** *are hormones that produce male-type physical characteristics and behaviors.* **Estrogens** *are hormones that produce feminine characteristics.* **Progesterones** *are female hormones that prepare the uterus to accept a fetus and maintain the pregnancy.* All three sex hormones are in both sexes. Androgens are in greater amounts in males; the other two hormones are in greater amounts in females (113). More information about the function of sex hormones can be obtained in any physiology text.

The 28-day menstrual or reproductive cycle is controlled by an intricate feedback system involving (1) the hypothalamus, which audits the level of the hormones in the bloodstream; (2) the anterior lobe of the pituitary and its hormones, FSH and LH; (3) the ovaries and their hormones, estrogen and progesterone; and (4) the interplay between the ovarian hormones and FSH and LH (113).

At the onset of the cycle, when the estrogen level is lowest, the shedding of the endometrium (lining of the uterus) occurs. The hypothalamus, because of the low estrogen level, stimulates the pituitary gland to release FSH, which causes the maturation of one of the ova-containing ovarian or graafian follicles as well as increased production of estrogen. This is the time of the highest level of estrogen in the bloodstream. In response to estrogen, the endometrium begins to thicken to prepare to receive the zygote if fertilization occurs (113).

In response to the high level of estrogen, the anterior pituitary releases LH. The sudden increase of LH triggers **ovulation,** *release of the mature ovum,* from the follicle, which happens about 14 days after the onset of the cycle. The LH moves to the ruptured follicle, which causes the development of the glandular corpus luteum. This produces both estrogen and progesterone which, when acting together, cause the glands of the endometrium to prepare further for the nourishment of a possible zygote (113).

If fertilization of the ovum by a sperm cell does not occur, the ovum deteriorates. The pituitary stops production of both FSH and LH, and the corpus luteum becomes dormant and atrophies. The resulting drop in estrogen and progesterone levels stimulates the shedding of the endometrial lining. This consists of blood, mucus, and tissues, or the menstrual discharge. Menstruation lasts 3 to 5 days. The cycle then begins anew (113). **Primary dysmenorrhea,** *painful menstruation occurring without any evidence of abnormality in the pelvic organs,* may occur. The cause is unknown, but endocrine factors, natural pain processes, and psychological factors have all been considered. Various analgesics have been used for this condition through the years. More recently the nonsteroid, anti-inflammatory agents have been used with some success. Some women find that adherence to certain diet, such as decreased caffeine and sugar and increased protein intake, and exercise habits may decrease symptoms. Heat to the painful area may be palliative (69).

In the male, the hormonal system for reproductive behavior is much simpler because there is no cyclical pattern. The male gonads, the testes, serve to produce sperm continuously and to secrete androgens. The major androgen is testosterone (113).

Just as FSH promotes the development of the ovum in the female, FSH promotes the development of sperm in the male. A continuous level of sperm production takes place in the seminiferous tubules inside the testes. The secretion of LH (also called interstitial cell-stimulating hormone or ISCH) stimulates the Leydig cells lying in between these tubules to secrete the androgen (113).

Musculoskeletal System. Structural changes, growth in skeletal size, muscle mass, adipose tissue, and skin, are significant in adolescence. The skeletal system grows faster than the supporting muscles;

hands and feet grow out of proportion to the body; large muscles develop faster than small muscles. Poor posture and decreased coordination result. Males and females differ in skeletal growth patterns; males have greater length in arms and legs relative to trunk size, in part because of a prolonged prepubertal growth period in boys. (Males are also more clumsy than females.) Males also have a greater shoulder width, a difference which begins in prepuberty. Ossification of the skeletal system occurs later for boys than girls. In girls, estrogen influences ossification and early unity of the epiphyses with shafts of the long bones, resulting in shorter stature (133, 152, 193). Muscle growth continues in males during late adolescence because of androgen production. Muscle growth in females is proportionate to growth of other tissue. Adipose tissue distribution over thighs, buttocks, and breasts occurs predominately in females and is related to estrogen production (150).

Skin. Skin texture changes. Sebaceous glands become extremely active and increase in size. Eccrine sweat glands are fully developed, are especially responsive to emotional stimuli, and are more active in males. Apocrine sweat glands also begin to secrete in response to emotional stimuli (133, 152).

Cardiovascular System. The heart grows slowly at first compared to the rest of the body, resulting in inadequate oxygenation and fatigue. The heart continues to enlarge until age 17 or 18 (113, 150). Systolic blood pressure and pulse pressure increase; blood pressure averages 100–120/50–70. Pulse rate averages 60 to 68 beats per minute. Females have a slightly higher pulse rate, basal body temperature, and lower systolic pressure than males (133, 152). Hypertension is increasing in adolescents, both Caucasians and Afro-Americans, in males, the obese, and those with family history of hypertension. Higher systolic pressure is seen in urban dwellers; higher diastolic pressure was seen in those who smoked and lacked regular exercise. Routine hypertension screening should be done. Upper limits for normal blood pressure from 11 to 17 years is considered 130/90 (79, 113, 150, 175).

Respiratory System. The respiratory system also grows slowly relative to the rest of the body, contributing to inadequate oxygenation. Respiratory rate averages 16 to 20 per minute. Males have a greater shoulder width and chest size, resulting in greater respiratory volume, greater vital capacity, and increased respiration. The male's lung capacity matures later than that of the female, which is mature at about 17 or 18 years (193).

Blood Components. Red blood cell mass and hemoglobin concentration increase in both sexes because of increased hormone production. Hematocrit levels are higher in males; platelet count and sedimentation rate are increased in females, and white blood cell count is decreased in both sexes (193). Blood volume increases more rapidly in males. By late adolescence, males average 5000 ml and females 4200 ml of blood (150).

Gastrointestinal System. This system matures rapidly from 10 to 20 years. By age 21 all 32 *teeth* have usually appeared. *Stomach capacity* increases to about 1 quart (over 900 cubic centimeters), which correlates with increased appetite, as the stomach becomes longer and less tubular; increased gastric acidity occurs in order to facilitate digestion of the increased food intake. *Intestines* grow in length and circumference. Muscles in the stomach and intestinal wall become thicker and stronger. The *liver* attains adult size, location, and function (133, 150, 152).

Fluid and electrolyte balance changes reflect changes in body composition in terms of bones, muscle, and adipose tissue. Percentage of body water decreases, reaching adult levels. About 60 percent of the male's total body weight is fluid, compared to 50 percent in the female; the difference is caused by the greater percentage of muscle mass in the male. Exchangeable sodium and chloride decline; intracellular fluid and body potassium rise with the onset of puberty. Again, because of their greater muscle mass, males have a 15 percent higher potassium concentration (133, 152).

Renal System. Urinary bladder capacity increases; the adolescent voids up to 1½ quarts (1500 cubic centimeters) daily (133, 152, 160). Renal function is like that of the adult.

Special Sense Organs. The eyeball lengthens, increasing the incidence of myopia in early adolescence. Auditory acuity peaks at 13, and from that age on, hearing acuity gradually decreases. Sensitivity to odors develops at puberty; the female's increased sensitivity to musk-like fragrances may be related to estrogen levels (72, 193).

Unique Differences. Racial differences in physical development occur, although adult statures are about the same. For example, Afro-American boys and girls attain a greater proportion of their adult stature earlier. Skeletal mass is greater in the Black person; using Caucasian norms means that bone loss could go undetected. Normal values for hemoglobin concentration is 1 gram less. Thus a low hemoglobin reading for Afro-Americans has a different nutritional implication; the person may not be iron deficient (50). Continued research is necessary to determine other differences that may exist.

✔ Because of the changing body, the adolescent needs information about the normality of anatomical and physiological changes in addition to sex education. Adults should be cautioned not to pass on superstitions and taboos, for example, that girls must rest and not participate in social or sport activities or that they should not take showers during menstruation. The adolescent male needs to be told that the release of spermatic fluid through nocturnal emissions is *not* the result of disease or punishment for masturbation or sexual daydreaming.

✔ If the parents are knowledgeable about pubertal growth changes, they can predict coming physical changes based on how the teen presently looks, which can be reassuring to the child whose onset of puberty is delayed. This may be more difficult in one-parent families, since the man or woman is less equipped to understand and help the opposite-sexed child.

✔ You can be very helpful in teaching not only the adolescent but also helping parents understand what they should teach their children. They both need realistic information about these subjects and an opportunity for discussion. Additional information can be obtained from the local library or health association, doctor, religious leader, counselor, or personal product companies. Having this knowledge can eliminate much fear and guilt and will help the adolescent understand his/her normal development.

Physical Assessment of the Adolescent

✔ Regular physical examinations should be encouraged. See Appendix II for a suggested schedule. Useful references to help you formulate a health history are Bates (11), Hoole (69), and Sherman (155).

✔ The examination is conducted much as for the adult. However, it is crucial that the examiner knows and understands the special emotional needs, developmental changes, age and maturation level of the person, and physiological differences specific to adolescence.

✔ Honest and genuine interest in the adolescent and not "speaking down" as though the young person is a child are essential. Confidentiality and trust are key issues. Be sure to express honestly to the teen what part of the interview and examination can be kept in strict confidence and what may need to be shared. Specific age of the person and the nature of the findings will determine these factors. Above all, do not say, "This is completely confidential, " only to later say, "I believe we better share that."

Physical complaints, as well as emotional symptoms, may relate to underlying problems of drug abuse, alcoholism, sexual uncertainties and stress, pregnancy or fear of pregnancy, fear of or actual sexually transmitted disease, depression, family or peer adjustment problems, school problems, or concerns about future plans.

✔ Because the adolescent may be extremely shy about his/her body, every effort must be made to protect privacy within the confines of the situation. With the advent of the female nurse practitioner and physician's assistant conducting examinations on male patients, the traditional "embarrassment roles" are switched. Much has been written on the conduct of the male examiner with the female patient, but not on the reverse. The younger the adolescent male in terms of sexuality development, the more concern he has about a female examiner seeing and touching his body parts that are considered private (111). The female examiner ought to provide proper draping and emphasize the touching as little as possible. She may make the preliminary statement, "It is important that I palpate your scrotum to detect. . . . I know this is a tender area and I will proceed as quickly as possible while being thorough in my exam."

The blood pressure ought to be at adult levels. The athlete in training may have a slower pulse rate than his/her peers.

Pallor, especially in girls, should be a clue to check hemoglobin levels.

The teen will need frequent dental visits as most will have caries. Many young adolescents whose parents have insurance for the service or have sufficient fund will have orthodontic work in progress (133, 152).

Because myopia seems to increase during these years, increased reading and study encourages eye strain. Many teens are now being fitted with contact lenses (155).

✔ Although breast neoplasms are not common to this age group, females should be taught breast self-examination. Also, the girl should not be surprised if there is some asymmetrical development. Some increase in breast tissue can also be expected in adolescent males. Excessive growth should be referred for evaluation. Both male and female breasts should be examined (155).

✔ The heart should be found at the fifth left intercostal space, as in the adult, and most functional murmurs should be outgrown (155). Serum cholesterol and triglyceride levels should be obtained if there is a family history of cardiovascular disease, and preventive dietary and exercise regimens should be discussed (193).

Striae may be found on the abdomen of females because of the rapid weight gain and loss experienced by fad diets followed by return to overeating (155).

✔ The examiner should be acutely aware not only of the pattern of sexual development of both males and females, but of the concerns and questions that may be voiced. The presence of the testes in the scrotum is of primary importance because undescended testicles at this age can mean sterility (155).

✔ Pap smears and pelvic examinations are done when the adolescent becomes sexually active. This test, done the first time with explanation and as much gentleness as possible, can set a positive tone for future exams (155).

✔ Some have suggested that urine cultures be taken periodically on females between the ages of 15 to 18 because of the number of asymptomatic urinary infections (155).

✔ Scoliosis is common in teen-agers, so a close look for asymmetry of the musculoskeletal system is essential and any severe, persistent pain in the long bone area should also be referred (155).

Nutritional Needs

✔ Teach parents and the teens the following information about normal nutrition. Refer also to Table 11-2 and Appendix III. During this time of accelerated physical and emotional development the body's metabolic rate increases; accordingly, nutritional needs increase. The peak requirements occur in the year of maximum growth. This takes place between the tenth and twelfth years in girls and about 2 years later in boys. The calorie and protein requirements during this year are higher than at almost any other time of life. The adolescent female's requirements are equalled or surpassed only during pregnancy and lactation. Even after the obvious period of accelerated growth has ended, nutritional intake must be adequate for muscle development and bone mineralization, which continues (110, 134). The adolescent's nutritional status encompasses the life span; it begins with the nutritional experience of childhood and determines the nutritional potential of adulthood.

Both males and females have an increased appetite; they are constantly hungry. A fast-growing boy may never feel filled up. His stomach capacity may be too small to accommodate the amount of food he requires to meet growth needs unless he eats at frequent intervals. Adolescent females between 11 and 14 years of age may need 2200 kilocalories per day; males of the same age need 2700 kilocalories. Females between 15 and 18 years of age need 2100 kilocalories and males need 2800 kilocalories (133). However, stage of sexual maturation, rate of physical growth, and amount of physical and social activity should be considered before determining exact caloric needs. In addition, the nutritional needs differ for the pregnant and nonpregnant adolescent.

Protein needs increase to between 45 to 56 grams daily; approximately 15 percent of the total caloric intake should be derived from protein consumed in adequate quantities; protein helps to maintain a positive nitrogen balance within the body during the metabolic process (133, 134, 152). Protein may be obtained from milk, cheese, eggs, meat, legumes, nuts, and whole grains. There is an additional need for iron during adolescence because of the increased muscle and soft tissue growth and the rapid growth demands of an expanding red cell mass. Girls may be especially susceptible to iron deficiency at menarche (110, 134, 196).

Calcium is needed for bone growth and continued teeth formation; intake should be increased to 1200 milligrams daily. If the adolescent drinks a quart of milk daily, this dietary requirement can be easily met (110, 134).

The nutritional needs differ for the pregnant and nonpregnant adolescent. Table 11-2 shows the daily recommended number of servings for each food group.

✔ *Underweight and overweight* are probably the two most common but overlooked symptoms of malnutrition. Assess the adolescent; teach the adolescent and parents as indicated to foster health.

✔ *Underweight.* This can be caused by an inadequate intake of calories or poor utilization of the energy. It is often accompanied by fatigue, irritability, anorexia, and digestive disturbances such as constipation or diarrhea. Poor muscular development evidenced by posture and hypochromic anemia may also be observed. In children and adolescents, growth and development may be delayed. Even with the recommended dietary intakes, malabsorption of protein, fat,

TABLE 11–2. Recommended Minimum Daily Serving of Basic Four Food Groups

FOOD GROUP	NONPREGNANT TEEN-AGER	PREGNANT TEEN-AGER
Dairy products	4 servings	4 servings
Meat and meat alternatives	2 servings	3 servings
Fruit, vegetables, or juices	4 servings	5 servings
Breads and cereals	4 servings	4 servings

Note: The following amounts equal one serving:
- Dairy products: 1 cup milk, 1 oz hard cheese, 1¼ cups cottage cheese, ⅓ cup dry milk, 1¾ cup ice cream.
- Meat and meat alternatives: 2 eggs, 2 oz lean meat, 1 cup beans or split peas, 4 tablespoons peanut butter, 2 oz chedder cheese, ½ cup cottage cheese.
- Fruits, vegetables, or juices: ½ cup or 1 medium fresh fruit or vegetable.
- Breads and cereals: 1 slice of bread, ½ cup cooked cereal, ¾ cup ready-to-eat cereal, ½ to ¾ cup cooked macaroni, spaghetti, rice, or grits.

or carbohydrate can result in undernutrition. Underweight may be a symptom of an undiagnosed disease (133, 150, 152). The most severe form of underweight is seen in anorexia nervosa and bulimia. You may be the first person to assess these conditions in the adolescent.

Anorexia nervosa *is a syndrome*, occurring usually in females between the ages of 12 to 18 although onset may occur in the twenties and thirties, *in which the person voluntarily refuses to eat, presumably because of lack of hunger.*

Symptoms and signs of anorexia nervosa include the following:

1. Refusal to eat or only eats small amounts, yet guilt about eating.
2. Denial of hunger (hunger becomes a battle of wills), yet a preoccupation with food.
3. Intense fear of becoming obese, even when underweight; refusal to maintain body weight.
4. Large weight loss with no physical illness evident.
5. Abuse of laxatives and/or diuretics.
6. Distorted body image.
7. Vital sign changes: bradycardia, hypotension, hypothermia.
8. Interruption of normal reproductive system processes in females, at least three consecutive menses when otherwise expected to occur.
9. Malnutrition, adversely affecting (a) the skeleton-causing decalcification, decreased bone mass and osteoporosis; (b) muscular development; and (c) cardiac and liver function, arrhythmia and decreased body metabolic functions from liver involvement may occur.
10. Skin dry, pale, yellow-tinged; lanugo present.
11. Enlargement of brain ventricles, with shrinkage of brain tissue surrounding them (9, 17, 21, 23, 24, 32, 40, 200).

Males may also suffer from this disease, but may be even more reticent than women to reveal symptoms or seek treatment (40).

Bulimia may be associated with anorexia nervosa and *is a syndrome characterized by voluntary restriction of food intake followed by extreme overeating and self-induced vomiting and laxative abuse.*

Symptoms and signs for bulimia include:

1. Binge eating—consuming excessively large amount of food—followed by self-induced vomiting or laxative and/or diuretic abuse—at least twice weekly.
2. A feeling of lack of control over the eating behavior during eating binges.
3. Preoccupation with food and guilt about eating.
4. Weight fluctuations, fluid and electrolyte imbalance due to binges, fasts, and vomiting/laxatives.
5. The use of crash diets to control weight.
6. Orthostatic hypotension, due to fluid depletion.
7. Scars on dorsum of hand from induced vomiting.
8. Loss of tooth enamel in vomiters.
9. Chest pain from esophageal reflux/spasm.
10. Parotid gland enlargement in vomiters.
11. Increased peristalsis, rectal bleeding, constipation if laxative abuser (21, 40).

In the adolescent, anorexia nervosa is more common (21, 138). Impaired psychological functioning, disturbed body image, confused or inaccurate perceptions about body functions, and a sense of incompetence and helplessness are present in all anorectic and bulimic clients (17, 21). There are several theories about causation and dynamics of anorexia nervosa (21, 23, 24, 110, 134, 138).

↙ The person is usually treated on an outpatient basis; however, hospitalization, with nutritional support and intense psychotherapy, is recommended when loss of 25 percent or more of body weight leaves the person physically, emotionally, and socially compromised to the point of being in a life-threatening situation. The anorexic person should be hospitalized if there is low serum electrolyte or fluid level; depression with suicidal thoughts or attempts; substantial disorganization of the family, or failure of outpatient treatment. These criteria also apply to the bulimic; the additional criterion is spontaneous vomiting after binges. Hospitalization may also be helpful in diffusing parent-adolescent tensions and the resultant power struggle and in preventing suicide (9, 21, 23, 24, 40, 138).

↙ The goals of treatment for the anorectic and bulimic client are to maintain normal weight, treat the hypokalemia and metabolic alkalosis, change attitudes toward food, and develop more effective coping skills to overcome the underlying conflicts. The nursing approach is holistic: You will work with the interdisciplinary team and the psychological, physiological, family, spiritual, and sociocultural dimensions of the person to promote adaptive behavior. Treatment involves any of the following methods: behavior modification, insight-oriented, supportive, group, or family therapy. For further information refer to articles at the end of the chapter (9, 21, 23, 24, 40, 138).

↙ The family as well as the adolescent needs therapy. Goals of family therapy include reducing pathogenic conflict and anxiety within the family relationships, becoming more aware of and better meeting each other's emotional needs, promoting more appropriate role behavior for each gender and generation, and strengthening the capacity of the adolescent and family as a whole to cope with various problems (21, 88).

↙ *Overweight.* This is rarely the result of an endocrine, metabolic, or neurological disturbance. Teach adolescents and parents the following information. Genetic predisposition to obesity may exist, as shown by studies that correlate parental weight more closely with the weight of their natural children than with those of adopted children (110). *Most often weight status is a result of lifelong food and activity habits.* Children grow up associating food with much more than nourishment for their bodies. Food means celebration, consolation, reward, or punishment. People give and receive food as symbols of their love. Food and drink are chief forms of entertainment both at home and "on the town." We have learned to expect to be offered at least a beverage when we visit friends. This misuse of food, accompanied by a decrease in physical activity levels during the twentieth century, has led to a steady increase in the prevalence of obesity. Energy input is greater than energy output.

Various theories are proposed regarding the deposition of fat in the body. Apparently, obese persons have either more fat cells (hyperplastic obesity) or the fat cells are bigger than those of normal-weight persons (hypertrophic obesity). Hyperplastic obesity is usually associated with early onset obesity, and hypertrophic obesity is usually associated with adult-onset obesity. Critical times for development of proliferation of fat cells may be the last prenatal trimester, the first 3 years of life, and adolescence. Afro-American infants tend to be fatter than Caucasian infants, but this reverses later in childhood. Socioeconomic class may also affect weight. Males living in poverty are thin as children and grow to be thin adults. By contrast, females living in poverty are thin children who become fat women. Affluence results in overweight children who become slim adults (91, 110, 134, 196). Childhood obesity does not always lead to adult obesity. Early-onset obesity may be caused by a metabolic genetic defect that is compounded by excess calorie intake, with later-onset obesity caused by excess caloric intake. Onset of obesity in later life may have a situational basis; crises trigger fat cell hypertrophy or upset in appetite-control mechanisms (110, 134, 196).

According to most research, **obesity** *exists if more than 20 percent of the male's body weight and 30 percent of the female's body weight is adipose tissue.* (Normal values of adipose tissue are 12 to 18 percent for men and 18 to 24 percent for women.) Another means of determining the degree of obesity is to measure skinfold thickness at about midpoint of the upper arm with a skinfold caliper. Skinfold thickness exceeding 15 millimeters in males and 25 millimeters in females indicates obesity (111, 196).

✔ It has been estimated that 10 to 30 percent of adolescents are obese and approximately 80 percent of these teens will remain obese as adults (193). As with most abnormal states of health, prevention of obesity is better than treatment. A pound of body fat contains approximately 3500 calories. An intake in excess of need of even 100 calories a day will add up to 3000 calories a month, or almost 1 pound of body weight. With the obese adolescent, food intake and activity habits should be assessed with weight loss and/or control in mind. Numerous approaches exist for the treatment of obesity; few of these methods are successful with the adolescent. The approaches can be classified into seven categories: drugs, caloric restriction, mechanical methods, exercise, therapeutic starvation, surgery, and behavior modification (110).

✔ Both prescription and over-the-counter appetite depressants are available. Many of these contain caffeine which can cause an elevated heart rate and blood pressure. Like other drugs, these appetite depressants can be addictive and have other side effects that might produce health problems. Thyroid hormone is beneficial only to persons who are in a hypometabolic state. Because thyroid hormone medication can inhibit thyroxin production in metabolically normal persons, it can be detrimental to their efforts at weight reduction. Thyroid hormones can also have adverse effects on the cardiovascular system. Similarly, the use of diuretics by a person who needs to lose fat is misleading as well as dangerous. The person loses necessary fluid and electrolytes instead (193, 196).

✔ Dietary manipulation has ranged from total fasting (therapeutic starvation) to changing the foods allowed, the amount, frequency of eating episodes, and the speed at which food is eaten. Caloric restriction does not work well with adolescents. Teens want rapid, easy results. Eating also is an important part of the adolescent socialization pattern. Thus limiting caloric intake or restricting foods eaten may alter their social interaction.

Mechanical methods, often advertised in popular magazines, include sauna suits, special exercise outfits, mechanical spot reducers, and steam baths. Because overweight is a problem of energy input and output, these methods have no long-term benefit.

Surgery is a drastic approach to weight reduction. Intestinal bypass and similar surgical procedures prevent the absorption of glucose for energy as well as many vitamins, minerals, and electrolytes. Severe complications can result from this surgery even years after an apparent uneventful recovery (108, 193). Gastric partitioning decreases the size of the stomach and slows the stomach's emptying ability; individuals feel full and curtail their food intake. Although neither type of surgery does anything to alter the cause—eating habits—these procedures are sometimes indicated in cases of life-threatening obesity when all other attempts have failed.

Because obese people tend to gauge their eating

according to external environmental cues, rather than hunger, programs using behavior modification on eating habits have been used with some success (110, 134). By learning to change problem behaviors associated with eating or exercise, they can change habits and maintain their subsequent weight loss. Through daily school physical education classes, exercise programs should be designed.

✔ An eating pattern assessment is described by White and Schroeder, as are areas for psychological, physiological, and sociocultural assessment (194). Based on assessment, the following suggestions, if followed, can help most obese adolescents lose weight:

1. Consciously ask self before eating, "Am I really hungry?"
2. Eat only at mealtimes and at the table; avoid snacks. To lose 1 pound weekly, dietary intake must be reduced by 500 calories daily.
3. Count the mouthfuls, cut food into small pieces, and eat slowly to eat less. Set down eating utensils between each bite of food.
4. Keep a food diary, with the goal of reinforcing the adherence to the Basic 4 and avoidance of empty calories (91, 124).
5. Engage in planned, regular exercise, such as bicycle riding, walking the pet dog, gardening, yard work, calisthenics, or swimming.
6. Maintain proper posture and an overall attractive appearance.

✔ Families should be given the following suggestions to help the adolescent achieve weight loss:

1. Limit purchases and cooking and baking of carbohydrate foods or snacks.
2. Remove tempting snacks from the home such as candy and cookies.
3. Ban eating in front of the television or reading while eating.
4. Make dining at the table a pleasant time.
5. Avoid using food as reward or punishment.
6. Serve food in individual portions on the plate, rather than in bowls on the table, to avoid second helpings, and serve food on smaller plates.
7. Praise even a small weight loss; avoid nagging (91, 119).
8. Participate in physical activity with the adolescent when possible.

✔ Further, you can reinforce the permanence of new food habits and achievement of weight loss through your continued guidance and realistic praise. The key to successful treatment may be in improving the adolescent's self-image. If emotional problems exist, you will need to counsel the adolescent or refer him/her to an appropriate source. Regardless of the methods of treatment used, parental understanding and cooperation are needed, and you are one member of the health team with whom both parents and the adolescent can discuss their concerns. Your listening, discussing, teaching, and referral when necessary can help the adolescent prevent or overcome the health hazard of obesity. You can also work with the school system to establish daily physical exercise programs that stimulate the teen to remain physically active. Cecere describes a program which uses a multidisciplinary approach of dietary instruction, checking of weight, low-calorie refreshments, behavior modification techniques, exercise, and individual support (22).

Obesity presents physical health hazards as well as problems with social and emotional adjustment. The obese adolescent is frequently rejected by the peer group and harassed by his/her parents. Many overweight teen-agers withdraw from social interactions and develop feelings of inadequacy and inferiority. Such physical health problems as abnormal menstrual cycles, orthopedic difficulties, kidney stones, and gallbladder disease develop. If obesity persists into adulthood, the incidence of diabetes mellitus, cardiovascular diseases, and other illnesses increases.

✔ Therefore, preventing adolescent obesity through education of the child and the parents and treating it when it occurs can eliminate future health problems. More information on types, effects of, and treatment of obesity can be found in various references (3, 10, 110, 133, 134, 142, 150, 193, 196).

Adolescent Pregnancy. Adolescent pregnancy, discussed later in the chapter, presents another health problem related to nutrition as well as to other physical, social, and emotional factors. Clearly, many teen-agers lack the physiological maturity needed to withstand the stresses of pregnancy. The adolescent's nutritional intake may be only barely sufficient to support her own development—not adequate to satisfy two nutritional requirements (68, 107, 133, 134, 152, 196).

Exercise and Rest Needs

✔ Both exercise and rest must be balanced. Teach adolescents and parents the following information.

Planned Exercise Sessions. These are seldom followed, but adolescents do participate in physical activities that are socially determined.

Teen-age boys are concerned with activities that require physical abilities and demonstrate their manliness. This age group probably spends more time and energy practicing and participating in sport-related activities than any other age group. Many boys attempt to participate in sports like basketball, football, baseball, hockey, and soccer, or work on cars or machines. There is growing acceptance, however, of the male who wants to cook, garden, or do other activities which traditionally were not so popular or acceptable.

Adolescent girls, on the other hand, were expected to develop the traditional interests in social functions and domestic skills such as cooking, cleaning, and serving. This, too, is changing. The teen-age female in the United States may be on the football or rugby team. While most girls are involved in swimming, gymnastics, jogging, ice skating, dancing, and horseback or bike riding, those who try out for and succeed on boys' teams are challenging long-accepted ideas about femininity, masculinity, strength and endurance of each gender, and competition. There is no physiological reason why girls should not play aggressive sports; the uterus is well protected and a blow to the breast does not result in long-term harm. In fact, the male reproductive organs are actually more vulnerable to injury than the female reproductive organs. The key is that we have not wanted to raise girls to be aggressive. While aggressive behavior in females is specific to the competitive sports, female athletes describe themselves as acting in the socially expected way in nonathletic situations (60).

✔ Help parents and teens realize that competitive activities prepare young people to develop a process of self-appraisal that will last them throughout their lives. Learning to win and to lose can also be important in developing self-respect and concern for others. Physical activities provide a way for adolescents to enjoy the stimulation of conflict in a socially acceptable manner. Participation in sports training programs in junior and senior high schools can also help decrease the gap between biological and psychosocial maturation (69, 150, 152, 193) while providing exercise. Some form of physical activity should be encouraged to promote physical development, prevent overweight, formulate a realistic body image, and promote peer acceptance. Being an observer on the sidelines will not fulfill these needs.

As women join the labor force in growing numbers, the importance of the sports experience increases, since the working woman, like the working man, is involved in a structure in which rules are modeled on competitive sports teams. The worker has to be able to play the game: follow rules, get along with all kinds of people, and not disparage colleagues or talk back to the boss (60). In nursing, these attributes are increasingly important for the successful professional in the health-care system. The emphasis in nursing education on the individual nurse and individual patient has often caused real frustration and conflict for the individual nurse in the work setting. A sense of the competition and teamwork that exists in the real world is as essential in nursing as in other occupations and professions. Perhaps in the future the professional nurse, who has participated in competitive team sports as a child and adolescent, will adjust better to system demands while maintaining quality of practice.

Rest and Sleep. More rest and sleep are needed now than earlier, at a time when the adolescent is busy with an active social life. The teen is expending large amounts of energy and functioning with an inadequate oxygen supply; both of these contribute to fatigue and need for additional rest. In addition, protein synthesis occurs more readily during sleep. Because of the growth spurt during adolescence, protein synthesis needs are increased (193). Increased rest may also be needed to prevent illness.

✔ Limit setting may be necessary to ensure adequate opportunities for rest. Rest is not necessarily sleep. A period of time spent with some quiet activity is also beneficial. Every afternoon should not be filled with extracurricular activities or home responsibilities, and when there is school the next morning, the adolescent should be in bed at a reasonable hour.

Psychosocial Concepts

Cognitive Development

Formal Operations Stage. Tests of mental ability indicate that adolescence is the time when the mind has great ability to acquire and utilize knowledge. One of the adolescent's developmental tasks is to develop a workable philosophy of life, a task requiring time-consuming abstract and analytical thinking.

The adolescent uses available information to entertain theories and look for supporting facts, consider alternate solutions to problems, project his/her thinking into the future, and try to categorize thoughts into usable forms. He/she is capable of highly imaginative thinking, which, if not stifled, can evolve into significant contributions in many fields—science, art, music. The adolescent's theories at this point may be oversimplified and lack originality, but he/she is setting up the structure for adult thinking patterns, typical of the Period of Formal Operations. The adolescent can solve hypothetical, mental, and verbal problems, use scientific reasoning, deal with the past, present, and future, and understand causality. The Formal Operations Period differs from Concrete Operations in that a much larger range of symbolic processes and logic is used (131, 186).

Keniston describes cognitive development of

youth or late adolescence as proceeding through a complex transition of dualism, such as a simple understanding of right and wrong and either–or of an issue, to an awareness of multiplicity, a realization of relativism, and a more existential sense of truth. Keniston believes that an aspect of this stage of cognitive development is to think about thinking: the ability to achieve a new level of consciousness, an awareness of consciousness, and a decrease in self-consciousness which permits intellectual tricks, phenomenological games, and a higher level of creativity. This stage involves being very aware of inner processes, focusing on states of consciousness as something to be controlled and altered, and thinking about the ideal self and society (83, 84).

The abstract level of thinking described by Keniston can be considered a part of the Period of Formal Operations. Even though there are no overall differences between female and male adolescents' intelligence, females have shown greater verbal skills, while males have shown more facility with quantitative and spatial problems. These differences are apparently the result of interest, social expectations, and training rather than different innate mental abilities (79, 113).

✔ Parents sometimes underestimate the cognitive abilities of the adolescent. Help them to work with the adolescent from an intellectual and creative perspective. Parents can learn from adolescents, just as adolescents learn from parents. Help the adolescent learn how to use cognitive skills in a way that will not antagonize parents.

The adolescent does not always develop intellectual potential by staying in school. School drop-out occurs for a variety of reasons and has unfortunate consequences. Sherraden's article describes school drop-out in more detail (156).

Peer Group Influences

The **peer group,** *friends of the same age,* influences the adolescent to a greater extent than parents, mass media, teachers, popular heroes, religious leaders, or other adults. This finding contradicts a survey 20 years ago that showed parents and teachers to have greater influence than peers (113).

Because peer groups are so important, the adolescent has intense loyalty to them. Social relationships take precedence over family and counteract feelings of emptiness, isolation, and loneliness. Significance is attached to activities deemed important by peers. Peers serve as models or instructors for skills yet to be acquired. Some peers are likely to be near the same cognitive level as the learner; their explanations may be more understandable. When student peers of varying cognitive levels discuss problems, less advanced students may gain insights and correct inaccuracies in thinking. The more advanced students also profit; they must think through their own reasoning to explain a concept (189).

Peer groups provide a sense of acceptance, prestige, belonging, approval, and opportunities for learning how to behave. Adolescents feel they have to have immediate, useful function; the real business of life is ahead of them. The peer group provides a sense of immediacy concentrating on the here-and-now, what happened last night, who's doing what today, what homework is due tomorrow. Thus, the adolescent is given reason for *being* today, a sense of *importance* right now, and not just dreams or fears about what he/she might become in some vague future time (39, 92). In addition, relationships with peers provide learning for later adult roles.

The peer group helps the adolescent define personal identity as he/she adapts to a changing body image, more mature relationships with others, and heightened sexual feelings. The peer group has well-defined types of behavior for masculinity and femininity, although adults may not recognize the distinctions. As the adolescent tries a variety of acceptable behaviors within the safety of the group, he/she incorporates new ideas into the body image and self-concept. The adolescent who is rejected by peers may be adversely affected, since he/she does not learn the high degree of social skill and ability to form relationship that are necessary for the adult culture.

✔ Peer group relations are beneficial, but they can also direct the adolescent into antisocial behavior because of pressure to conform and the need to gain approval. The adolescent may participate in drug and alcohol abuse, sexual intercourse, or various delinquent acts not because he/she wants to or enjoys them, but rather to prove self, to vent aggression, or to gain superiority over younger or fringe members of the group. He/she may even gain pleasure from sadistic activities toward others (150). Parents have reason to be concerned about their adolescent's peers and to guide their child into wholesome activities and groups that will reinforce the values they have taught. Help parents and teachers understand peer groups and work through crises related to peer relations.

Peer-Group Dialect. This is a communication pattern seen in the adolescent period. Slang, or jargon, is one of the trademarks of adolescence and may be considered a **peer-group dialect.** *It is a highly informal language which consists of coined terminology and of new or extended interpretations attached to traditional terms.*

Slang is used for various reasons. It provides a sense of belonging to the peer group and a small, compact vocabulary for a teen-ager who does not want to waste energy on words. Slang also excludes authority figures and other outsiders and permits expression of hostility, anger, and rebellion. Unknowing adults do not understand the digs given with well-timed pieces of slang. Other adults sense the flippancy of underlying feelings, but to their chagrin, can do little other than try to understand. By the time they learn the meanings of the current terms, new meanings have evolved.

✔ You can help parents understand the purposes of teen-age dialect and the importance of not trying to imitate or retaliate verbally. In addition, encourage parents to enter into discussion with their teen-ager to understand more fully him/her as well as the teen-age dialect.

Use of Leisure Time. Leisure time with the peer group is important for normal social development and adjustment. The adolescent spends more time away from home, either in school, other activities, or with peers, as he/she successfully achieves greater independence. School is a social center, even though abstract learning is a burden to some students. In school, students seek recognition from others and determine their status within the group, depending on success in scholastic, athletic, or other organizations and activities.

Dating Pattern. Dating is one use of leisure time and is influenced greatly by the peer group but also varies according to the culture and social class, as well as religious and family beliefs. Dating prepares the adolescent for intimate bonds with others, marriage, and family life. The adolescent learns social skills in dealing with the opposite sex, in what situations and with whom he/she feels least and most comfortable, and what is expected sexually.

In America dating may begin as early as age 10 or 11, especially with pressures from peers and family to attract the opposite sex. Generally, however, girls in junior high school are more mature than boys. Girls may seek male companionship, but boys frequently prefer activities with other males. Many fellows at this age are women haters. About age 15, boys begin to catch up with girls in physical and emotional maturity, and their interests become better correlated. Social pursuits take on more meaning for boys.

Not all American adolescents assume this dating pattern. Some begin early to date one person and continue that pattern until marriage. Others do not date until young adulthood. A few will prefer homosexual relationships. Isolated homosexual encounters are not unusual, especially among males, and do not mean the person will remain a homosexual. The dynamics behind homosexuality are more complex. Because the person is usually a young adult when homosexuality is declared the chosen sexual pattern, the topic is discussed in greater detail in Chapter 12. However, the adolescent may have always felt more comfortable with or more cared for by the same-sexed person.

When dating begins, the emphasis is first on commonly shared activities. Later the emphasis includes a sharing, close relationship. Similarly, dating may start with groups of couples, move to double dates, and finally single couples. With each step, the adolescent learns more about and feels more comfortable with the opposite sex. He/she also learns personal acceptability to others. Going steady has become popular because it provides a readily available partner for social activities, but it can be detrimental if it stops the adolescent from searching for the qualities he/she wants in a future mate or involves sexual experimentation that he/she is unprepared to handle.

✔ As you work with adolescents, you should assess the stage of peer-group development and dating patterns. A few years will make a considerable difference in attitudes toward the opposite sex. You must be able to build your teaching on current interests and attitudes. The same age groups in different localities may also be in different stages. Adolescents from another culture may sharply contrast in pattern with American adolescents. For example, in Egypt the male is not supposed to have any intimate physical contact with the female until marriage. In America certain physical contact is expected.

Leisure Activities. Sports; dancing; hobbies; reading; listening to the radio or stereo; talking on the telephone; daydreaming; experimenting with hairstyles, cosmetics, or new clothes; or just loafing, have been teen-agers' favorite activities for decades. Motorcycle riding, driving and working on cars, watching television, and playing video games are also popular. Political activism draws some youth; various causes rise and then fade in interest as the youth matures. "Everybody's doing it" is seemingly a strong influence on the adolescent's interests and activities.

Socioeconomic and educational levels determine to some extent how youth use free time. Upper-class youths may travel extensively, go boating, attend cultural events or debutante parties. Middle-class emphasis is on participation in activities. During adolescence these youths are involved in church- or school-related functions, such as sports, theater, and musical organizations. Lower-class youths may spend more time in unstructured ways, such as standing on the corner, talking to peers, or finding ways to earn extra money. In many homes, however, the absence of money does not mean the absence of healthy leisure activity. Smoking and using alcohol and drugs cannot be attributed primarily to lower-class youths, for a great deal of money is required to supply some of these habits. Shoplifting, for example, is sometimes done for "kicks."

Many parents consider a party in the home for a group of teenagers a safe use of leisure time. This is undoubtedly true if parents and other adults are on the premises and can give guidance as needed; and if the parents are not themselves supplying the teens with alcohol and drugs.

✔ Known to most teens, but not to most parents, is the phenomenon of the "Kegger." Usually hosted when parents are out of town, teenagers chip in for beer for an "open" party (any number of people may attend). When behavior becomes boisterous, police are often called by the neighbors, but they find the situation difficult to handle because there is no responsible authority figure on the premises. The police in one community give the following guidelines to help parents and teens *host and attend* parties. You may wish to share these suggestions with parents.

1. Parents should set the ground rules before the party to express feelings and concerns about the party, ask who will attend and whether adults will be present, and learn what is expected of their adolescent. The address and phone number of the host should be known by the parents of the teens who are attending.
2. Notify neighbors that you will be hosting a party, and encourage your teen to call or send a note to close neighbors notifying them of the party and asking them to let the family know if there is too much noise.
3. Notify the police when planning a large party. They can protect you, your guests, and your neighbors. Discuss with the police an agreeable plan for guest parking.
4. Plan to have plenty of food and nonalcoholic beverages on hand.
5. Plan activities with your teen-ager prior to the party so that the party can end before guests become bored (about 3 or 4 hours is suggested as sufficient party time).
6. Limit party attendance and times. Either send out invitations or have the teen-ager personally invite guests beforehand. Discourage crashers; ask them to leave. Open house parties are difficult for parents and teen-agers to control. Set time limits for the party that enable guests to be home at a reasonable time, definitely before a legal curfew. Suggested closing hours are grades 7 and 8, 10:30 PM; grades 9 and 10, 11:30 PM; grades 11 and 12, 12:00 PM. Check curfew times for your locale. Transportation home for each teen who attends should be planned in advance by parents and the adolescent.
7. A parent should be at home during the entire time of the party. The parent's presence helps keep the party running smoothly; it also gives the parent an opportunity to meet the teen-ager's friends. Invite other adults to help supervise.
8. Decide what part of the house will be used for the party. Pick out where your guests will be most comfortable and you can maintain adequate supervision. Avoid having the bedroom area as part of the party area.
9. Do not offer alcohol to guests under the age of 21 or allow guests to use drugs in your home. This sounds prudish in this permissive era. However, you may be brought to court on criminal charges or have to pay monetary damages in a civil lawsuit if you furnish alcohol or drugs to minors. Be alert to the signs of alcohol or drug use.
10. Do not allow any guest who leaves the party to return. This will discourage teen-agers from leaving the party to drink or to use drugs elsewhere and then return to the party.
11. Guests who try to bring in alcohol or drugs or who otherwise refuse to cooperate with your expectations should be asked to leave. Notify the parents of any teen-ager who arrives at the party drunk or under the influence of any drug to ensure his/her safe transportation home. Do not let anyone drive under the influence of alcohol or drugs.
12. Teen-agers frequently party at homes when parents are away. Typically, the greatest problems occur when parents are not at home. Tell your neighbors when you are going to be out of town.
13. Many parties occur spontaneously. Parents and teens should understand before that these guidelines are in effect at all parties. If, despite your precautions, things get out of hand, do not hesitate to call the local police department for help (56).
14. Emphasize to parents the importance of their being role models through minimal drinking of alcoholic beverages or use of drugs.

In some states, there is legal parental responsibility in the home. A parent commits the crime of endangering the welfare of a child less than 17 years of age if he/she recklessly fails to exercise reasonable diligence in the care or control of a child to prevent him/her from behavior, environment, or associations that are injurious to the welfare of the child or to the welfare of others. In some states, a person commits the crime of unlawful transactions with a child if he/she knowingly permits a minor child to enter or remain in a place where illegal activities in controlled substances are maintained or conducted. Parents have responsibility (possibly in all states) if a minor is killed or injured after leaving their home where an illegal substance was consumed. Juvenile officers identify an adult doing an act "knowingly and recklessly" where a minor is involved as a criterion for possible prosecution. In the opinion of attorneys and judges, parents could be subject to suit for damages for careless or imprudent behavior (56).

The teen-ager may also feel more secure when the parent is actively interested in knowing where he/she will be and what he/she will be doing even though rebellion may ensue. Parents should be awake or have the teen awaken them when arriving home from a party. This is a good sharing time. Peers are important, but if peer activity and values are in opposition to what has been learned as acceptable, the adolescent feels conflict. Parental limits can reduce feelings of conflict and give an excuse to avoid an activity he/she does not want to engage in. Parental limits appropriate to the situation and not unduly constraining develop ego strength within the adolescent.

✔ Explore with parents the adolescent's need for constructive use of leisure time and the importance of participation in peer activities.

For some teen-agers, there is little leisure time. They may have considerable home responsibility, such as occurs in rural communities, or work to earn money to help support the family. Other youths are active in volunteer work. Ideally, the adolescent has some free time for personal pursuits, to stand around with friends, and to sit and daydream.

Emotional Development

Emotional Characteristics. Emotional characteristics of the personality cannot be separated from family, physical, intellectual, and social development. Emotionally, the adolescent is characterized by mood swings and extremes of behavior. Table 11–3 lists typical contradictions (53, 79, 92, 113, 150). Emotional development requires an interweaving and organization of opposing tendencies into a sense of unity and continuity. This process occurs during adolescence in a complex and truly impressive way to move the person toward psychological maturity (53).

✔ Share this information with parents and the adolescent. Through using principles of communication and crisis intervention, and through your use of self as a role model, you will be able to help the adolescent work through identity diffusion and achieve a sense of ego identity and an appropriate sense of independence.

We regularly hear of the rebellious, emotionally labile, egocentric adolescent, but do not stereotype all

TABLE 11-3. Contrasting Emotional Responses of Adolescents

INDEPENDENT BEHAVIORS	DEPENDENT BEHAVIORS
• Happy, easy-going, loving, gregarious, self-confident, sense of humor.	• Sad, irritable, angry, unloving, withdrawn, fearful, worried.
• Energetic, self-assertive, independent.	• Apathetic, passive, dependent.
• Questioning, critical or cynical of others.	• Strong allegiance to or idolizing others.
• Exhibitionistic or at ease with self.	• Excessively modest or self-conscious.
• Interested in logical or intellectual pursuits.	• Daydreaming, fantasizing.
• Cooperative, seeking responsibility,	• Rebellious, evading work, dawdling, ritualistic behavior, drop out from society.
• Impatient to be involved or finish project.	• Unaccepting of new ideas.
• Suggestible to outside influences, including ideologies.	• Apprehensive about adult responsibilities.
• Desirous for adult privileges.	

adolescents into that mold. Some, perhaps more than we know of, can delay gratification, behave as adults, and have positive relationships with family and authority figures (32).

Developmental Crisis. The psychosexual crisis of adolescence is identity formation versus identity diffusion: "Who am I?" "How do I feel?" "Where am I going?" "What meaning is there in life?" **Identity** *means that an individual feels he/she is a specific unique person;* he/she has emerged as an adult. **Identity formation** *results through synthesis of biopsychosocial characteristics from a number of sources, for example, earlier gender identity, parents, friends, social class, ethnic, religious, and occupational groups* (41, 42).

There are a number of influences that can interfere with identity formation:

1. Telescoping of generations, with many adult privileges granted early so that the differences between adult and child are obscured and there is no ideal to aspire to.
2. Contradictory American value system of individualism versus conformity in which both are highly valued and youth feel that adults advocate individualism but then conform.
3. Nuclear family structure; the adolescent perceives most adults as parent figures and has primarily parents as targets for conflicts and aggressions.
4. Middle-class cultural emphasis in childrearing,

with inconsistencies between proclaimed and actual parental concern.
5. Emphasis on sexual matters and encouragement to experiment without frank talking about sexuality with parents.
6. Diminishing hold of Judeo-Christian traditions and ethics in all society, so that the adolescent sees that failure to live by the rules is not necessarily followed by unpleasant consequences.
7. Increasing emphasis on education for socioeconomic gain, which prolongs dependency on parents when the youth is physically mature.
8. Lack of specific sex-defined responsibilities. (Blurring of the traditional male–female tasks has its positive and negative counterparts. Although eventually allowing more individual freedom, it can be very confusing to the adolescent who must decide how to act as a male or female.)
9. Rapid changes in the adolescent subculture and all society with emphasis on conforming to peers.
10. Diverse definitions of adulthood: After 12, the adolescent pays adult airline fares; after 16, he/she can drive; after 18, he/she can vote (41, 42, 43, 79, 92, 113).

Identity formation *implies an internal stability, sameness, or continuity, which resists extreme change and preserves itself from oblivion in the face of stress or contradictions.* It implies emerging from this era with a sense of wholeness, knowing the self as a unique person, feeling responsibility, loyalty, and commitment to a value system. There are three types of identity which are closely interwoven: (1) **personal,** or **real identity**-*what the person believes self to be;* (2) **ideal identity**—*what he/she would like to be;* and (3) **claimed identity**—*what he/she wants others to think he/she is.*

✔ Identity formation is enhanced by having support not only from parents but also from another adult who has a stable identity and who upholds sociocultural and moral standards of behavior (41). If the adolescent has successfully coped with the previous developmental crisis and feels comfortable with personal identity, he/she will be able to appreciate the parents on a fairly realistic basis, seeing and accepting both their strengths and shortcomings. The values, beliefs, and guidelines they have given him/her are internalized. The adolescent needs parents less for direction and support; he/she must now decide what is acceptable and unacceptable behavior.

Identity diffusion *results if the adolescent fails to achieve a sense of identity.* He/she feels self-conscious and has doubts and confusion about self as a human being and his/her roles in life. With identity diffusion, he/she feels impotent, insecure, disillusioned, and alienated. The adolescent feels that he/she is losing grip with reality. He/she is impatient but unable to initiate action. The teen-ager vacillates in decision making; he/she cannot delay gratification and appears brazen or arrogant. Behavior at work, with peers, and in sexual contacts is distorted. The adolescent is apprehensive about and avoids adult behavior, fearing loss of uniqueness by entering adulthood. The real danger of identity diffusion looms when a youth finds a negative solution to the quest for identity. He/she gives up, feels defeated, and pursues antisocial behavior, since "it's better to be bad than nobody at all." Identity diffusion is more likely to occur if the teenager has close contact with an adult who is still confused about personal identity and who is in rebellion against society (43, 44).

✔ Assist parents to work with the adolescent who feels identity diffusion. Most adolescents reach physical maturity before they achieve ego identity or the emotional maturity expected as a sign of having completed the adolescent era. One study showed that individuals between 17 and 20 report significantly more ego diffusion than those between 21 and 24. Females report less ego diffusion in all age groups than males (42).

✔ References by Norris and Kunes-Carroll (121) and by Oldaker (122) describe nursing diagnoses pertinent to the adolescent who is having difficulty with identity formation.

Self-Concept and Body-Image Development

Development of self-concept and body image is closely akin to cognitive organization of experiences and identity formation. The adolescent cannot be looked at only in the context of the present; earlier experiences have an impact which continues to affect him/her. The earlier experiences that were helpful enabled the adolescent to feel good about the body and self. If the youngster enters adolescence feeling negative about self or the body, this will be a difficult period.

Other factors influence the adolescent's self-concept, including age of maturation, degree of attractiveness, name or nickname, size and physique appropriate to gender, degree of identification with the same-sexed parent, level of aspiration and ability to reach ideals, and peer relationships (34).

The rapid growth of the adolescent period is an important factor in body-image revision. Girls and boys are sometimes said to be "all legs." They are often clumsy and awkward. Because the growth changes cannot be denied, the adolescent is forced to alter the mental picture of self in order to function. More important than the growth changes themselves is the meaning given to them. The mother who says, "That's all right, Tom, we all have our clumsy moments," is providing the understanding that a comment such as "Can't you ever walk through the room without knocking something down?" denies. The adolescent needs this understanding because he/she fears rejection and is oversensitive to the opinions of others. Physical changes in height, weight, and body build cause a change in self-perception, as well as in how the adolescent uses his/her body. To some male adolescents, the last chance to get taller is very significant.

The body is part of one's inner and outer world. Many of the experiences of the inner world are based on stimuli from the external world, especially from the body surface. Therefore, the adolescent focuses attention on body surface. He/she spends a great deal of time in front of mirrors and for body hygiene, grooming, and clothing. These are normal ways for the early adolescent to integrate a changing body image. If the teen does not seem to care about appearance, he/she may have already decided: "I'm so ugly, so what's the use?"

Growth and changes draw the adolescent's attention to the body part that is changing, and he/she becomes more sensitive to it. This can cause a distorted self-view. He/she may overemphasize a defect and underevaluate self as a person. The body acts as a source of acceptance or rejection by others. If the adolescent does not get much acceptance for self and his/her body, he/she may try to compensate for real or imagined defects through sports, vocational or academic success, a religious commitment, or a date or group of friends that enhances prestige. The adolescent is idealistic and may not be able to achieve an ideal body. Thus he/she may discredit self by seeing the body and self as defective, inferior, or incapable.

If the adolescent does have a disability or defect, peers and adults may react with fear, pity, repulsion, or curiosity. The adolescent may retain and later reflect these impressions since a person tends to perceive self as others perceive him/her. If the adolescent develops a negative self-image, then motivation, behavior, and eventual lifestyle may also be inharmonious and out of step with social expectations.

By late adolescence self-image is complete, self-esteem should be high, and self-concept should have stabilized. The person feels autonomous, but no longer believes he/she is so unique that no one has ever experienced what he/she is currently experiencing. The late adolescent no longer believes everyone is watching or being critical of his/her physical or personality characteristics. Egocentricity has declined. Interactions with the opposite sex are more comfortable, although awareness of gender is keen.

✔ Your understanding of the importance of the value the adolescent places on self can help you work with the adolescent, parents, teachers, and community leaders.

Your goal is to avoid building a false self-image in the adolescent; rather, help him/her evaluate strengths and weaknesses, accept the weaknesses, and build on the strengths. You will have to listen carefully to the adolescent's statements about self. You will have to sense when you might effectively speak and work with him/her and when silence is best. Share an understanding of influencing factors on body-image and self-concept development with parents, teachers, and other adults so that they can positively influence adolescents.

✔ You may wish to use a therapeutic group, such as reality therapy or rational thinking group described by Cangelosi et al., using cognitive restructuring exercises to help adolescents think more positively about themselves and reduce anxiety (20). Small group sessions outside the regular classroom have also been found effective in enhancing self-concepts of junior high students. Group sessions can focus on personal and social awareness and how to cope with age-related problems.

Sexuality Development

Sexuality *encompasses not only the individual's physical characteristics and the act of sexual intercourse but also the following: (1) search for identity as a whole person, including a sexual person; (2) role behavior of men and women; (3) attitudes, behaviors, and feelings toward self, each gender, and sexual behavior; (4) relationships, affection, and caring between people; (5) the need to touch and be touched; and (6) recognition and acceptance of self and others as sexual beings* (168). One of the greatest concerns to the adolescent is sexual feelings and activities. Because of hormonal and physiological changes and environmental stimuli, the adolescent is almost constantly preoccupied with feelings of developing sexuality.

Sexual desire is under the domination of the cerebral cortex. Differences in sexual desire exist in young males and females, and desire is influenced by cultural and family expectations for sexual performance. The female experiences a more generalized pleasurable response to erotic stimulation but does not necessarily desire coitus. The male experiences a stronger desire for coitus because of a localized genital sensation in response to erotic stimulation, which is accompanied by production of spermatozoa and secretions from accessory glands that build up pressure and excite the ejaculatory response. The male is stimulated to seek relief by ejaculation (133, 152).

Menarche is experienced by the girl as an affectively charged event related to her emerging identity as an adult woman with reproductive ability. Menarche may be perceived as frightening and shameful by some girls; previous factual sex education does not necessarily offset such feelings. Often information in classes is not assimilated because of high anxiety in the girl during the class. The girl is likely to turn to her mother for instruction at the time of menarche, even if the two of them are not close emotionally.

Family and cultural traditions are needed to mark the menarche as a transition from childhood to adulthood. Menarche is anticipated as an important event, but in the United States no formal customs mark it, and no obvious change in the girl's social status occurs. The girl may get little help from mother, other female adults, or peers in working through feelings related to menarche. Often menses is perceived as an excretory function, and advertisements treat it as a disease (179).

Nocturnal emissions are often a great concern for the boys.

Both sexes are concerned about development and appearance of secondary sex characteristics, their overall appearance, their awkwardness, and their sex appeal, or lack of it, to the opposite sex (133, 152).

The most common form of sexual outlet for both sexes, but especially males, is **masturbation**, *manipulation of the genitals for sexual stimulation*. Public education about the normality of masturbation is reducing guilt about the practice and fears of mental illness (92).

Intercourse is an increasing sexual activity among adolescents. Premarital sexual activity is often used as a means to get close, sometimes with strangers, and may result in feelings of guilt, remorse, anxiety, and self-recrimination. The feelings associated with the superficial act may be damaging to the adolescent's self-concept, and possibly to later success in a marital relationship. Half the adolescent males and females reported that the initial coitus was not pleasurable (150). In spite of overt sophistication and widespread availability of information on birth control devices, pregnancy or fear of pregnancy is the deciding factor in close to half of all high school marriages. The number of pregnant teenage females who are not marrying is significantly increasing, which has implications for the future care and well-being of the baby as well as implications for future intimate relations of the teen-age girl. If teen-agers do marry, the marriage is considerably more likely to end in separation and divorce than is true for the general population, which also has a high divorce rate, because of the unstable sense of self (45).

✔ You can teach parents and adolescents of both sexes that they and other people are not like disposable plastic cartons and that an intimate and important experience is cheapened and coarsened when it is removed from love. Some youths argue that sex can be pleasurable if one hardly knows or even loathes one's partner, but most youths are likely to get emotionally involved in the sexual act and their feelings will be bruised when the act leads nowhere (113). A wide variety of sexual experiences prior to marriage may cause the person to feel bored with a single partner later.

Americans have to relearn the satisfactions of self-denial and anticipation. The adolescent will not be harmed by knowing about the body and sexuality and yet not engaging in intercourse. A certain amount of tension can be endured; in fact, it can be useful to become mature and creative. The values of self-discipline and self-denial with anticipation must be taught before adolescence begins, however (113).

Other countries are also having their problems with teen-age sexuality. In the third-world country of Kenya, East Africa, adolescent sexual development has for years been controlled by tribal customs. Recently, however, Western permissiveness has crept in, especially among the teen-agers in the larger cities. Pregnancy among girls from 14 to 18, with a rash of self-induced abortions, has caused leaders to insist on some sex education for their youth. Small pilot programs, sponsored jointly by government and church groups in connection with African educators, are just now making some impact at the secondary education level (202).

Adaptive Mechanisms

The **ego** is the *sum total of those mental processes that maintain psychic cohesion and reality contact; it is the mediator between the inner impulses and outer world.* It is that part of the personality which becomes integrated and strengthened in adolescence and has the following functions:

1. Associating concepts or situations which belong together but which are historically remote or spatially separated.
2. Developing a realization that one's way of mastering experience is a variant of the group's way and is acceptable.
3. Subsuming contradictory values and attitudes.
4. Maintaining a sense of unity and centrality of self.
5. Testing perceptions and selecting memories.
6. Reasoning, judging, and planning.
7. Mediating among impulses, wishes, and actions, and integrating feelings.
8. Choosing meaningful stimuli and useful conditions.
9. Maintaining reality (92).

When a strong ego exists, the person can do all these tasks. He/she has entered adulthood psychologically. Adolescence provides the experiences necessary for such maturity.

Ego changes occur in the adolescent because of broadening social involvement, deepening intellectual pursuits, close peer activity, rapid physical growth and social role changes, all of which cause frustrations at times. **Frustration** *is the feeling of helplessness and anxiety which results when one is prevented from getting what one wants.* Adaptive mechanisms leading to resolution of frustration and reconciling personal impulses with social expectations are beneficial, because they permit the self to settle dissonant drives and to cope with strong feelings. All adaptive mechanisms permit one to develop a self, an identity, and to defend the self-image against attack. These mechanisms are harmful only when one pattern is used to the exclusion of others for handling many diverse situations or when several mechanisms are used persistently to cope with a single situation. Such behavior is defensive rather than adaptive, distorts reality, and indicates emotional disturbance.

The Adaptive Mechanisms used in adolescence are the same ones used (and defined) in previous developmental eras, although they now may be used in a different way.

Compensation, a form of compromise, *sublimation*, and *identification* are particularly useful because they often improve interaction with others. They are woven into the personality to make permanent character changes, and they help the person reach appropriate goals.

✓ Teach parents that adaptive abilities of the adolescent are strongly influenced by inner resources built up through the years of parental love, esteem, and guidance. The parents' use of adaptive mechanisms and general mental health will influence the offspring. Are the parents living a double standard? Has the teen-ager seen the parents enjoy a job well done or is financial reward the key issue? Do the parents covertly wish the teen-ager to act out what they could never do?

Even with mature parents, the adolescent will at times find personal adaptive abilities taxed. But the chances for channeling action-oriented energy and idealism through acceptable adaptive behavior are much greater if parents set a positive example.

Other factors influence ability to adapt to stress and the adaptive mechanisms that will be used. In one study, adolescents from upper and middle socioeconomic levels reported that the life events that were most stressful to them agreed with what adults consider the most stressful life change. In a study of Mendez et al. (106), upper-class adolescents included "quitting school" and "parent losing a job" as more stressful than individuals of other ages and social classes; the importance of education and occupation are related to socioeconomic class. Middle-class adolescents viewed drug and alcohol abuse and hassling with parents as more stressful, which is reflective of middle-class moral values. Middle-class adolescents revealed more reliance on physical appearance than upper-class subjects; the advantages of family status and more money for clothing and entertaining may make the upper-class adolescent less dependent on appearance for social acceptance. Items written in as stressful life events for both classes were "wrecking the car," "not getting selected for an activity," "brother getting someone pregnant," and "sister getting pregnant." Age in this sample was not a significant variable in scaling the events, but the number of events experienced increased with age. Girls perceive more events to be more stressful than boys (106).

Moral–Religious Development

Refer to Kohlberg's Theory of Moral Development given in Table 5–1. According to Kohlberg, the adolescent is likely to be in the conventional level most of the time. However, the adolescent may at times show behavior appropriate to the second stage of the Preconventional Level or the first stage of the Post-Conventional Level (87). Munhall found that the average normal reasoning for baccalaureate nursing students was at the Conventional Level (114).

The early adolescent is described by one author as being in the Conformist Stage; structure and order of society takes on meaning for the person and rules are followed because they exist (analogous to Kohlberg's Conventional Level). The late adolescent is in the Conscientious Stage, where the person develops a set of principles for self that is used to guide personal ideals, actions, and achievements. Rational thought becomes important to personal growth (analogous to Kohlberg's Post-Conventional Level, Stage One) (79, 113). The young adolescent must examine parental moral and religious verbal standards against practice and decide if they are worth incorporating into his/her own life. He/she may appear to discard standards of behavior previously accepted, although basic parental standards are likely to be maintained. In addition, he/she must compare the religious versus the scientific views. While moral–religious views of sensitivity, caring, and commitment may be prevalent in family teaching, the adolescent in the United States is also a part of the scientific, technological, industrial society which emphasizes achievement, fragmentation, and regimentation. Often youth will identify with one of the two philosophies (43). These two views can be satisfactorily combined, but only with sufficient time and experience, which the adolescent has not had (6, 113).

If the adolescent matures in religious belief, he/she must comprehend abstractions. Often when he/she is capable of the first religious insights, the negativism tied with rebellion to authority prevents this experience.

Probably by age 16 the youth will make a decision. He/she may accept or reject the family religion. If the parents represent two faiths, the teen may choose one or the other, or neither. He/she may be influenced by a friend or someone who is admired. He/she may have a religious awakening experience in the form of a definite crisis called, by some, **conversion,** or **getting saved.** *This connotes an emotional as well as mental decision to conform to some religious pattern.* Or the form may be a definite but not dramatic decision at a confirmation or first communion. Another form is the gradual awakening, one which is not completely accomplished in adolescence.

🡒 Help parents and adolescents realize that the adolescent who does find strength in the supernatural, who can rely on a power greater than self, can find much consolation in this turbulent period of awkward physical and emotional growth. If he/she can pray for help, ask forgiveness, and believe he/she receives both, a more positive self-image develops. In this period of clique and group dominance, the church is a place to meet friends, to share recreation and fellowship, to sense a belonging difficult to find in some large high schools.

Adolescents whose faith is mixed with some God-fearing are probably less likely to experiment in behavior which they have been taught will bring them harm. Adolescents who have been taught that they are part of a divine plan and who have been given a specific moral code may better answer the essential questions, "Who am I?" "Where am I going?" "What meaning is there in life?" However, adolescents who have been raised very strictly may instead develop a reaction formation pattern of adjustment—rebelling and pursuing the previously forbidden activities.

🡒 The following methods of moral development have been most widely used: setting an example, persuading, limiting choices, dramatizing, establishing rules and regulations, teaching religious or cultural dogma, and appealing to conscience. Advice, approval, commands, lessons, sermons, warnings, criticisms, and interrogation have produced few results in the field of ethical development. Recent experiments show that a Socratic approach, which promotes moral development and clarifies values, produces fruitful results that have not been achieved by simply handing down rules of conduct. You can be instrumental in working with parents and teachers to use the Socratic approach as well as other value clarification exercises (87).

Late Adolescence: Transition Period to Young Adulthood

In some cultures, parents select schooling, occupation, and the marriage partner for their offspring. In the United States the youth is usually free to make some or all of these decisions.

By the time the youth is a junior or senior in high school, he/she should be thinking about the future: whether to pursue a mechanical or academic job; to attend some form of higher education; to live at home or elsewhere; to travel; to marry soon, later, or not at all; to have children soon, later, or not at all. Answers to these questions will influence the adolescent's transition into young adulthood.

Those who seem not to be making the transition into young adulthood—who continue to rebel against society, who wander from job to job or from college to college, who rely heavily on drugs and alcohol or sexual exploitation for emotional "highs," who cannot seem to make decisions about the future—may be the children of affluent parents and may not have had to become independent. The parents continue to dole out money and demands. The money is taken; the demands are ignored.

Establishing a Separate Residence. This is one marker of reaching young adulthood. The late adolescent often spends less time at home and prepares for separation from parents. If there is intense intrafamily conflict, if the adolescent feels unwanted, or if the adolescent is still struggling with dependence or parents or identity diffusion, a different mode of separation may occur.

In an effort to find self and think about the future, the adolescent may become either a walkaway or a runaway. The **teen walkaway** *leaves home before finishing high school or before reaching legal age; however, parents generally know where the child is and are resigned to the child's new living arrangements.* The **teen runaway** *leaves home without overt notice and his/her whereabouts are unknown to parents, friends, or police* (109). Some walkaways may continue high school or get some type of job while living with relatives, friends, or a boyfriend or girlfriend. The problem with the walkaway is that the adolescent can better achieve developmental tasks in a stable family situation, where parents continue to give support and assist him/her as necessary while treating the offspring in an adult manner. If the newly found living situation is unstable or emotionally unsupportive, or if the adolescent has no means of financial support, he/she may be forced into prostitution or juvenile offenses (18, 34, 92, 109).

🡒 You may have an opportunity to discuss residence situations with the adolescent. If you can get to the person before he/she walks or runs away, help him/her consider intolerability of parental demands and the family situation. Discuss alternative ways of handling the problem. You may contact a high school counselor or potential employer. While either walkaway or runaway is to be avoided if possible, the teen should be encouraged to report incest or abuse so that the teen's parents and other siblings can receive proper therapy and an appropriate, healthy living situation can be found for the teen.

✔ Health care is a problem for adolescent runaways. Refer to the article by Manov and Lowther which describes general health problems and sex-related health concerns, such as pregnancy, sexually transmitted diseases, prostitution, alcohol abuse, and child abuse and incest. The following intervention strategies are described: (1) clarification of the health worker's attitudes and values; (2) establishment of trust; (3) use of effective interviewing skills; (4) ability to provide maximum medical treatment and information when the client presents self for care; and (5) establishment of foundations for future interactions and care (97).

Career Selection. This has often been haphazard. High school counselors often do more record keeping than realistic guiding toward career choices. Youth are influenced by parental wishes or friend's choices. In addition, jobs or college study programs which were once for males or females are now open to both. A woman may now comfortably major in mathematics, architecture, or medicine. A man may study home economics or nursing. A female may be a lineman for the telephone company, and a male may be an operator.

✔ While these changes are positive, understand that the selection is more vast and thus more confusing to adolescents. You can guide them to testing centers where their skills and interests are measured and jobs are recommended. You may direct them to members of various professions who can tell them about their jobs. You will also need to be aware of the national adolescent mood. Group biases and fads should not dictate career choices that do not coincide with the person's skills.

Occupation represents much more than a set of skills and functions; it is a way of life. Occupation provides and determines much of the physical and social environment in which a person lives, his/her status within the community, and a pattern for living. Occupational choice is usually a function or a reflection of the entire personality, but then the occupation, in turn, plays a part in shaping the personality by providing associates, roles, goals, ideals, mores, lifestyle, and perhaps even a spouse.

For many youth, the college years are a time to consider various careers, to decide what type of people he/she wishes to associate with and imitate, and to measure self against others with similar aspirations.

Although college attendance and pursuit of a profession are still the ideal of many, a growing emphasis and opportunity exists for vocational and technical training. Many will enter jobs right out of high school.
✔ You can be a key person in helping adolescents clarify values and attitudes related to occupational selection and in talking with parents about their concerns.

Moral–Religious Development. This may take on a special significance if the adolescent period is extended into the twenties because of college education or military duty. Instead of settling into the tasks coexistent with marriage, job, and family, the adolescent has a period in which a great deal of thinking can be accomplished. He/she has passed the physically awkward stage, so that time and energy formerly spent in making the transition into physical adulthood can be turned toward philosophy.

The mid-twenties is the least religious period in life. In one study 56 percent of college youth rejected their childhood church. Why? Perhaps it is part of their break from dependence to independence. They also are secure in pursuing their ambitions; they are not yet aware that their goals may not be met. They do not yet have children whom they want to educate to a religion; and they have not developed a perspective about the importance of their own upbringing. Yet these late adolescents are often altruistic: They wish to help others, defend a cause, and do not hesitate to devote many hours of the day to their goals (6).

Veterans, especially combat returnees or prisoners of war, are in a difficult position. The protective childhood religion of fantasy, left in some, is forcibly removed as they experience violence, torture, hatred—the worst of human nature. If they salvage a religious experience, it is one of maturity.
✔ Explore moral–religious development with adolescents and parents. Your own behavior may be the best teacher.

Developmental Tasks

The following developmental tasks should be met by the end of adolescence:

1. Accepting the changing body size, shape, and function and understanding the meaning of physical maturity.
2. Learning to handle the body in a variety of physical skills and to maintain good health.
3. Achieving a satisfying and socially accepted feminine or masculine role, recognizing how these roles have similarities and distinctions.

4. Finding the self as a member of one or more peer groups and developing skills in relating to a variety of people, including those of the opposite sex.
5. Achieving independence from parents and other adults while maintaining an affectionate relationship with them.
6. Selecting an occupation in line with interests and abilities (although the choice of occupation may later change) and preparing for economic independence.
7. Preparing to settle down, frequently for marriage and family life, or for a close relationship with another, by developing a responsible attitude, acquiring needed knowledge, making appropriate decisions, and forming a relationship based on love rather than infatuation.
8. Developing the intellectual and work skills and social sensitivities of a competent citizen.
9. Desiring and achieving socially responsible behavior in the cultural setting.
10. Developing a workable philosophy, a mature set of values, and worthy ideals and assuming standards of morality (39, 61).

✔ Until these tasks are accomplished, the person remains immature, an adolescent regardless of chronological age. How you interact with, or teach other adults to interact with, the adolescent will contribute to the adolescent's maturity.

✔ ADOLESCENT HEALTH PROBLEMS AND NURSING APLICATIONS

Scope of the Nursing Role

Your role in caring for the adolescent may be many faceted. Astute assessment is needed; knowledge from this chapter and communication principles described in Chapter 17 may be useful in gaining information from a patient/client or family who may be hesitant to disclose about self. *Nursing diagnoses* that may be applicable to the adolescent are listed in Table 11–4. Interventions that may involve direct care to the ill adolescent or involve various health promotion measures are described in the previous or following sections.

A mature or maturing body and an immature emotional state make the adolescent a source of misunderstanding, fear, and laughter. Mood swings, rebellious behavior, and adherence to colorful fads baffle many adults, who then cannot look beyond the superficial behavior to identify health needs. Yet, health care needs of todays adolescents are great.

Health care needs of today's adolescents are staggering. Millions of teen-agers in the United States between the ages of 13 and 19 years are sexually active. Many adolescent girls between ages 13 and 19 years

TABLE 11–4. Selected Nursing Diagnosis Related to the Adolescent[a]

PATTERN 1: EXCHANGING

Altered Nutrition: More than body requirements
Altered Nutrition: Less than body requirments
Altered Nutrition: Potential for more than body requirements
Potential for Infection
Potential for Injury
Potential for Trauma
Potential Impaired Skin Integrity

PATTERN 2: COMMUNICATING

Impaired Verbal Communication

PATTERN 3: RELATING

Impaired Social Interaction
Social Isolation
Altered Sexuality Patterns

PATTERN 3: VALUING

Spiritual Distress

PATTERN 5: CHOOSING

Ineffective Individual Coping
Impaired Adjustment
Defensive Coping
Ineffective Denial
Decisional Conflict
Health Seeking Behaviors

PATTERN 6: MOVING

Fatigue
Potential Activity Intolerance
Sleep Pattern Disturbance
Diversional Activity
Altered Health Maintenance
Altered Growth and Development

PATTERN 7: PERCEIVING

Body Image Disturbance
Self Esteem Disturbance
Chronic Low Self Esteem
Situational Low Self Esteem
Personal Identity Disturbance
Sensory/Perceptual Alterations
Hopelessness
Powerlessness

PATTERN 8: KNOWING

Knowledge Deficit

PATTERN 9: FEELING

Pain
Dysfunctional Grieving
Anticipatory Grieving
Post-Trauma Response
Anxiety
Fear

[a]Other NANDA diagnoses are applicable to the ill adolescent.
Source: NANDA Approved Nursing Diagnostic Categories, *Nursing Diagnosis Newsletter*, 15, no. 1 (1988), 1–3.

become pregnant each year. A number of adolescents will run away from home. A significant number of youths will die from motor vehicle and other accidents and from homicide and suicide (200). Other health problems abound, including sexually transmitted diseases, substance abuse, chronic illness, and obesity and nutritional deficiency (2) (the latter two previously discussed). While the scope of this book does not allow discussion of needs assessment and intervention for adolescents with physical disabilities, you may wish to consult several references for information. Hadahl describes how a college health program can assist the adolescent with physical disabilities (63).

Immunizations

Immunizations are a part of health protection to the adolescent, although they may be overlooked by that time of life. You should take a careful health history. If the immunizations discussed in relation to other age groups have not been received, they should be given as indicated. If the adolescent has been routinely immunized, combined tetanus and diphtheria toxoids (adult-type Td) should be given about 14 to 16 years of age and every 10 years thereafter. This preparation contains less diphtheria antigen than the DTP preparations given to children.

The oral form of polio virus (OPV) is recommended for all children younger that 18 years of age unless contraindicated. Influenza virus vaccine, pneumococcal polysaccharide vaccine, and hepatitis B vaccine should be given to adolescents in selected high-risk groups. For clean wounds, no tetanus booster is needed by a fully immunized person unless more than 10 years have elapsed since the last dose. For dirty or contaminated wounds, a booster dose can be given if more than 5 years have elapsed since the last dose. Pertussis vaccine should not be given to anyone over 6 years of age. Periodic testing for tuberculosis should be included in all adolescent immunization programs (133, 153, 193).

Your actions and teaching in relation to immunizations are important for the teen-ager's health now and in the adult years.

Safety Promotion and Accident Prevention

Accidents, homicide, and suicide are responsible for about 75 percent of all deaths between the ages of 15 and 24 (4). Motor vehicle accidents account for nearly half of the deaths of adolescents between the ages of 16 and 19 (126, 193). One of the biggest adolescent–parent hurdles comes with learning to drive. The adolescent needs to learn this skill; yet the arguments between parents and their children concerning how to drive, what vehicle to drive, where to go or not to go often keep parents in a state of anxiety and children in a state of rebellion.

Head and spinal cord injuries, skeletal injuries, abrasions, and burns may all result from an accident involving a car, motorcycle, motor scooter, moped, all-terrain vehicle, snowmobile, or minibike. Sports-related accidents are also common, such as drowning, football, hockey, gymnastic and soccer injuries, and firearm mishaps. Contusions, dislocations, sprains, strains, overuse syndromes, and stress fractures occur frequently (176). In the adolescent the epiphyses of the skeletal system have not yet closed and the extremities are poorly protected by stabilizing musculature. These two physical factors, combined with poor coordination and imperfect sport skills, probably account for the numerous injuries (12, 133, 152, 193, 197).

Homicide is the second leading cause of death in the 15- to 24-year-old group, and the leading cause of death among non-Caucasian youths in this age group. Handguns are the most frequently used weapons (4, 133, 152).

Suicide, the third leading cause of death, is discussed on pages 358 to 359.

Safety Education. Safety courses should be required for every adolescent, including driver education, knowledge of safety programs in the community, instruction in water safety, routine safety practices, and emergency care measures. Many accidents and deaths could be avoided if the adolescent were better equipped to handle the new freedom. As an informed citizen in the community or in relation to your job, you can initiate and teach in such programs with the school, church, clinic, industry, Red Cross, or other civic organizations. If you do not teach, you can insist on qualified and objective instruction. Parents and youths should be informed on the dangers, as well as exercise and prestige value, involved with certain sports and privileges. A teen-age safety checklist can be obtained from the National Society for Crippled Children and Adults, 2023 W. Ogden Ave., Chicago, IL, 60612, to help the adolescent be aware of how to improve safety behavior.

Because of the sports activities that adolescents are involved in, they may sometimes experience musculoskeletal chest pain, minor strains or sprains to a joint, and minor ankle strain. You should know how to advise for these conditions.

Musculoskeletal chest pain *arises from the bony structures of the rib cage and upper-limb girdle, along with the related skeletal muscles.* Age does not automatically rule out heart-related problems. Although musculoskeletal pain is usually aggravated by activity that involves movement or pressure on the chest cage rather than by general exertion (such as stair climbing), a thorough lung and cardiac examination is merited. Putting heat to the area (unless it is a fresh injury), resting the area, and taking an antipyretic can be recommended (69).

Minor strains and sprains *to a joint involve a mild trauma that results in minimal stretching of involved ligaments and contusion of the surrounding tissues.* The treatment is immobilization of the affected joint and use of an ice pack for 24 to 36 hours. Local heat can then be used if needed. Aspirin, if tolerated, can be used for its analgesic and anti-inflammatory effects (69).

A **minor ankle sprain** involving *a stretching of the ligament without tearing* can be treated the same as minor strains and sprains with the addition of an Ace bandage and possibly keeping weight off the ankle longer than 24 to 36 hours through the use of crutches (69).

Common Health Problems: Prevention and Treatment

As you care for the adolescent, refer to Appendices I and II for a schedule of health screening measures. For information on how to conduct physical assessments with the adolescent, refer to Bates (11).

In addition to the hazards of accidents, health problems other than obesity and teen-age pregnancy, already discussed, are also apparent among adolescents. These conditions are styes (hordeolum), nosebleed (epistaxis), acne vulgaris, athlete's foot (tinea pedis), infectious mononucleosis, hepatitis, and Rocky Mountain spotted fever.

Localized Conditions. The following conditions have primarily localized affects.

A **hordeolum** or **stye** is a *localized infection of a sebaceous gland on the margin of the eyelid.* It sometimes causes painful reddened swelling in the area as well as purulent drainage. It can usually be cleared with an antibiotic drop and hot compresses applied every 30 minutes for several hours (69).

Epistaxis or **nosebleed** is a *spontaneous bleeding from the nose* caused by the rupture of a blood vessel in the area. Often a precursor is drying and cracking of the nasal mucosa. Prevention involves not picking at the nose, keeping the humidity sufficient (especially in the sleeping area in the winter), and rubbing a small amount of petrolatum over the nasal septum. If epistaxis does occur, the adolescent should sit with head slightly forward and pinch his/her nostrils with thumb and forefinger, applying continuous pressure for at least 15 minutes. Cold compresses may also help. Bleeding that cannot be controlled with these measures may need further investigation (69).

Acne is a major adolescent problem. Because of increased activity of the sebaceous glands, **comedones** (*blackheads and whiteheads*), *pimples, and cysts form on the face, chest, or back or on all three areas.* If not handled correctly, these can leave physical as well as psychological scars. There may be no way to avoid acne, but in general teens can follow these guidelines: (1) avoid picking at the lesions; (2) do not use greasy cosmetics and creams; (3) expect better and worse periods (stress and menses can bring about a rise in sebaceous gland activity); (4) eat a normal balanced diet. There is no firm evidence that colas and chocolate should be completely avoided. For a minor case of acne, washing the face and other affected areas three or four times daily to remove the oil film may be sufficient. For moderate cases, such special cleansers as Fostex and drying lotions as Desquam-X can be applied. For more severe cases the above measures plus the antibiotic tetracycline may be prescribed. Recently a synthetic isomer of a naturally occurring derivative of vitamin A (13-*cis*-RA) has been used with initial success to treat severe formerly "treatment-resistant" acne (69). Psychological support should be ongoing.

Dental caries are prevalent in the second decade of life and many adolescents have corrective braces in place for several years. If good daily habits of dental care have not been established, damage to the teeth and gingivae may result. Because the need for visits to the dental office for routine cleaning and examination varies widely from person to person, the frequency of the visits should be prescribed by the dentist. You may be instrumental in getting parents and adolescents to schedule a visit with the dentist as well as to maintain oral hygiene.

Tinea pedis or *athlete's foot* is a *fungal infection which affects the feet, especially the toe webs, causing intense itching, cracking, and peeling.* Treatment consists of soaking the feet in a tap water or aluminum acetate solution two times a day followed by a thorough drying (especially between the toes), and application of an antifungal agent and the wearing of absorbent cotton socks which should be changed after each soak (69).

Systemic Conditions. The following conditions have a systemic, and often prolonged, consequences. **Infectious mononucleosis,** *caused by the Epstein-Barr virus, is evidenced by a fever, sore throat, enlarged lymph nodes, general malaise, often an enlarged spleen, and sometimes jaundice.* Because it mimics other upper respiratory infections, a special laboratory test is done to determine the diagnosis. Treatment is symptomatic: rest, increased fluids, and an antipyretic for fever (69). The adolescent should be encouraged to remain under a physician's care during time of illness.

Hepatitis is a *viral disease with three recognized forms: hepatitis A, hepatitis B, and hepatitis non-A/non-*

B. All types present with similar findings, although B is usually the most severe. The average clinical course runs 12 weeks and consists of a prodromal stage of 2 to 20 days, followed by a jaundice phase of 2 to 8 weeks, and a recovery phase of 2 to 24 weeks. Hepatitis A, formerly called infectious hepatitis, is transmitted via fecal contamination of food and water with subsequent close person-to-person contact. It accounts for about 25 percent of the hepatitis cases. Hepatitis B, known previously as serum hepatitis, is associated with complications such as gastrointestinal bleeding, clotting abnormalities, cirrhosis of the liver, chronic hepatitis, and primary hepatocellular cancer. It is transferred primarily by the parenteral route, although person-to-person contact is possible. This type accounts for about 50 percent of the hepatitis cases. A vaccine is now available for high-risk individuals who might be working in hemodialysis units, laboratories, or other health care areas. Non-A/non-B hepatitis or hepatitis C, which affects 25 percent of hepatitis cases, is diagnosed by deduction. A person who has hepatitis symptoms, a history of transfusion, but no serologic evidence of hepatitis would be put into this category (45, 69, 98).

Prevention lies in staying in good physical condition, taking precautions if there is anyone around with hepatitis, and following the type-specific immunization regimens which can be learned from the Centers For Disease Control in Atlanta (69). The most recent guidelines are found in *Morbidity and Mortality Weekly Report*, September 4, 1981, vol. 30, no. 34, pp. 423–428, 433–435, and in the June 25, 1982, issue, vol. 31, no. 24, pp. 317–328 (51). Treatment is symptomatic (69).

Rocky Mountain spotted fever is an *acute febrile illness caused by Rickettsia rickettsii*. It is passed to the human by the bite of an infected tick or by contamination by an infected tick through skin abrasions. Symptoms start 2 days to 2 weeks after contamination. It is most common in the southeastern United States and can cause death if left untreated. The main symptoms are severe headache, pain in the back and leg muscles, fever that may reach 103° or 104°F, followed by a discrete rash that usually begins on the wrists, ankles, palms, or soles, and then may disappear within 24 hours. Laboratory studies are necessary. Treatment is in the form of tetracycline. Prevention is in the form of awareness. Ticks are most often encountered along edges of paths in woodland areas. They are also found on pets. Anyone who is exposed to ticks should be able to identify and know how to remove them (69).

Neoplasms both benign and malignant, are the fourth leading cause of death (133, 152, 193). Females exposed to diethylstilbestrol (DES) in utero should be watched closely for adenocarcinoma of the vagina. Males exposed to DES in utero have an increase in urinary tract abnormalities and a higher incidence of infertility (193). Dysplasia of the cervix, a precursor of cervical carcinoma, is a sexually transmitted disease that is occurring with increased frequency in adolescent females (161). Sexually active females should receive annual Papanicolaou (Pap) smears. Testicular cancer, Hodgkin's disease, and certain bone cancers are not uncommon in this age group.

Cardiovascular disease is the fifth leading cause of death. Although essential hypertension is consistently higher in Afro-American adults than in Caucasian adults, the same does not hold true for adolescents. According to one study, blood pressure levels in Caucasian youths equalled or exceeded that of Afro-American youths (131, 175).

Other Conditions. Allergic dermatitis, cysts, and keloid formation of the earlobes are also seen with more frequency since ear piercing has become popular. Inner ear damage from exposure to rock music is increasing and can be assessed by pure tone audiometry. The adolescent is also subject to postural defects, fatigue, anemia, and respiratory problems. Discuss prevention of these problems with adolescents.

Suicide. Suicide now ranks as the third most frequent cause of death in adolescence (59, 133, 152, 193). Suicide in adolescents is frequently reported as an accidental death. Motor vehicle accidents, drug and alcohol overdose, firearm accidents, and even homicides can be disguised suicides (59, 82). Psychological, social, and physiological stressors are the apparent causes for the rising number of suicides. Television dramatizations on the nightly news or in movies of teen-age suicides appear to contribute to an increased wave of teen-age suicide attempts and successes (172).

Adolescents who attempt suicide often come from families who have nonproductive communication patterns, inconsistent positive reinforcement behaviors, and a high level of conflict or child abuse. Suicides occur in rich and poor, urban and rural families. Adolescent suicides occur most frequently in 15- to 25-years old Caucasian males; Afro-American male incidence is lower. Females are now using forms of suicide usually associated with males and account for 40 percent of all successful suicides (163, 172). The males, however, are more successful, more violent, and less likely to give warning prior to the suicidal act (172).

Frequently, physical fatigue contributes to emotional stress which precipitates a suicide attempt (36, 163). Most adolescents have short bouts with suicidal preoccupations in the presence of these stresses. Sometimes even a small disappointment or frustration can

11 Assessment and Health Promotion for the Adolescent and Youth 359

lead to an impulsive suicidal attempt. Often the impulsive acts are committed to force parents to pay attention to the adolescent's pleas for help, and get needs met. Because the adolescent often feels great ambivalence toward parents, he/she rejects parents and yet solicits love, sometimes by attempting suicide. In reality the parents may be giving all the love they can. In other situations, the adolescent may be experiencing: (1) an intense sense of loss, external or internal, real or imagined, that is felt to be permanent; or (2) anger at parents, teachers, or another significant person, whereby hurting self is a way to get even and make the other sorry for not treating the person right. Death is not seen as irreversible. If there is a history of family suicide, the adolescent may attempt reunion with the deceased, often on the anniversary of the suicide. Other reasons for suicide are discussed in references at the end of the chapter (7, 36, 59, 82, 130, 200).

Signs of suicide are often subtle to detect; but a composite of behaviors should be a clue that the teen is experiencing severe stress. Table 11-5 lists behaviors associated with or indicators of suicide attempts (7, 59, 130, 163, 200). Do not be afraid to ask if the youth has thought of suicide. The stressed person welcomes this query and the fact that you are taking the statements and behavior seriously.

The suicidal adolescent may be a loner at school and feel unable to meet scholastic expectations of parents. School performance often drops; there may be frequent absences. If peers state that a friend is suicidal, investigate their concerns. No threat should be ignored. Depression is found in two-thirds of suicidal adolescents; depression may be masked by restlessness, aggression, acting out, excessive smoking, social withdrawal, impulsiveness, mood swings, poor concentration, somatic complaints, loses energy, and change in daily habits. The adolescent feels bored, apathetic, loses interest in usually pleasurable activities, has a negative self-image, and feels unloved, guilty, hopeless, and frequently, physically fatigued (7, 59, 200).

Rarely does the adolescent plan a suicide because he/she really wants to die. At times, however, when death is desired, the adolescent is engaging in self-destructive behavior as a punishment for guilt over actions or thoughts that he/she has committed or experienced.

Screen for emotionally distressed adolescents and be available to listen to and ask about their problems. Take a careful history to identify the underlying stresses. Refer to several references for guidelines in assessing family and school indicators, personality traits, and danger signs (59, 82, 200). If you feel unable to handle the situation, discuss it with the teen and refer him/her to a guidance counselor, school psychologist, or private or school physician. Frequently, the adolescent will turn to an adult with whom he/she has had a personal relationship or sees as an advocate for youth. This relationship may help the adolescent through the present crisis. As a nurse, you can accept, support, inform, and serve as an advocate for youth, working with parents and adolescents (82, 193).

Follow-up care with the family and adolescent after suicidal gestures is important. At least 10 to 15 percent of those who attempt suicide ultimately do commit suicide. At least 25 percent of those who commit suicide have made previous attempts (171).

If the adolescent makes a suicide attempt, crisis intervention is essential after the necessary medical and physical care is given. The goals, once life is assured, are to help the person work through feelings that led to and resulted from the suicide attempt, feel hope, identify the problem, see alternative ways of handling it, and mobilize supportive others to continue caring contact with the client. The family also needs your support and help in working through their feelings of anxiety, shame, guilt, and anger. Several references describe effective intervention for the suicidal person and **postvention,** *care of the surviving family, friends, and peers of a successful suicide victim* (82, 115).

Alcoholism and Abuse. Alcohol intake among adolescents also greatly increased in recent years. Ten to 20 percent of adolescents are problem drinkers (169). Frequent, heavy drinking patterns often begin in the eighth grade and peak between the ages of 18 and 22 years (123). Over a million Americans from the ages of 10 to 19 are addicted to liquor (66, 79, 113). Most states restrict the purchase and consumption of alcohol to people over 18 or 21 years of age, but this does little to prevent the underage drinker from acquiring alcohol when desired.

Drinking habits between male and female adolescents differ considerably. Males who occasionally drink tend to drink beer and whiskey, and they drink away from home. Most of the females who occasionally drink prefer drinking wine at home under parental supervision.

Adolescents drink because drinking is a widespread social custom in this country and drinking makes them feel more mature. The adolescent's drinking behavior is more closely related to the drinking behavior of the parents than to peer group pressure. The adolescents who drink regularly generally start drinking at an unusually early age, and they use alcohol specifically for its mind-altering effects to participate in some activity that they would otherwise consider difficult or as a defense against depression, anxiety, fear, and anger. They become tolerant to the

TABLE 11-5. Some Signs That Indicate Risk for Suicide Attempt

- Radical personality changes such as persistent sadness, loss of interest in usual activities, feelings of guilt, worthlessness, helplessness, failure.
- Withdrawal from family, friends, school, and regular activities.
- Experiencing major disappointment, loss, or humiliation.
- Falling grades or a decline in the quality of schoolwork; inability to compete.
- Noticeable changes in eating or sleeping habits or energy level; neglect of personal appearance.
- Physical symptoms often related to emotional disturbances, such as stomachache, headache, or fatigue.
- Difficulty in concentrating.
- Give verbal hints of despair, death; statements such as, "I won't be a problem for you much longer," and "Nothing matters."
- Put affairs in order—give away favorite possessions, throw things out, clean up his/her room.
- Suddenly become cheerful after prolonged depression—the final decision has been made, which is in itself a form of relief.
- Suicide attempts, even those that are meant to fail.

drug and use of sedatives with alcohol is common. By the time they reach late adolescence, they may well be alcoholics (66, 193). [Usually the person is also abusing illicit drugs as well (38, 76)]. There are several programs in the United States for the rehabilitation of youthful alcoholics, such as Alateen.

The use of alcohol by adolescents has compounded the problem of motor vehicle injuries in youth. Overindulgence in alcohol impairs the ability of these inexperienced drivers and encourages risk taking while the adolescent is behind the wheel of the vehicle (16). Alcohol may also be involved in suicide attempts and drug-related deaths.

Medical hazards of alcohol abuse are numerous. All body systems may eventually become involved because of the toxic effects of alcohol, including conditions of (24, 33, 115, 200):

1. Gastritis (nausea, vomiting, headache, gastric pain, may vomit blood or ropy, thick mucus)
2. Pancreatitis (severe abdominal pain, nausea, vomiting)
3. Hepatitis (fever, jaundice, abdominal edema, ankle and foot edema, tenderness in area of liver)
4. Gastric and duodenal ulcers (vomiting of blood, severe pain, indurated abdomen; obstruction and perforation of stomach or intestine may occur)
5. Impotency (inability to maintain or sustain erection)
6. Neuritis (tingling, burning, itching, numbness, weakness, and finally paralysis of limbs if untreated)
7. Fatty liver (enlarged liver on palpation, symptoms of hepatitis may persist)
8. Cirrhosis (weight loss, chronic nausea, vomiting, weakness; impotency; abdominal pain; bloated, indurated abdomen; hemorrhage; seventh leading cause of death)
9. Esophageal varices (varicose veins of the esophagus, internal hemorrhage may cause death)
10. Degeneration of cerebellum (permanent loss of motor coordination, unsteady walk, tremors)
11. Esophageal cancer (difficulty swallowing, sense of blockage behind sternum)
12. Delirium tremens (withdrawal from alcohol causes tremors, sweating, nausea, insomnia, confusion, delusions, hallucinations and convulsions; may be fatal 10 percent of the time)
13. Birth defects (fetal alcohol syndrome; infant is underweight, has small brain and head size, may have cleft palate and congenital heart defect; slow growth in childhood; slower mental development)

Various other health problems, or injuries, or death may result from alcohol abuse, including (1) automobile accidents, (2) suicide (over 60 percent of fatal accidents and suicides involve alcohol); (3) fire deaths (50 percent); (4) choking on foods (25 percent of these deaths); (5) freezing to death (20 percent of these deaths); (6) drowning (20 percent of these deaths); (7) accidental asphyxiations (20 percent); and (8) falls (20 percent of all falls) (5, 33).

Social problems, which may in turn cause physical and emotional health problems, and death, that arise from alcohol abuse include child and spouse abuse and homicide (70 percent of all violent crimes involve alcohol) (5, 33).

Avoid lecturing to adolescents concerning the hazards of drinking and driving and medical effects of drinking. Help the person to clarify values about healthful activities and see the detrimental effects of drinking—physically, emotionally, mentally, and socially. Point out people who have suffered the ill effects of excessive alcohol intake. Teach adolescents how to identify hazards and to act responsibly to avoid injury to themselves and others.

Care of the alcoholic person and family is complex; specific measures vary with the stage of alcoholism and manifestations of the disease. For additional information on the needs of and nursing care for alcoholism, refer to references at the end of the chapter (16, 33, 59, 67, 94, 146, 169, 193, 200).

Conditions Associated with Sexual Activity

Sexual decision making and premarital coitus were controlled in the past by family, social, and religious rules and restrictions. Today sexual activity is almost completely regarded as an individual responsibility. Because of the emotional and social characteristics of adolescents, the individual may neither have the readiness or desire to engage in sexual activity nor the decision-making skills *and* ego strength to behave counter to the peer group and abstain. Educationwise, there is not much to help the adolescent develop the necessary decision-making or value-clarification skills or the emotional strengths to be autonomous from the group, or to avoid what is perceived as expected behavior. Add to that the stimulating influence of mass media, and the adolescent may feel caught.

The areas related to the adolescent's sexual activity which influence health are those involving sexually transmitted diseases and the use of contraceptives, pregnancy, and abortion.

Sexually transmitted diseases (STD), *are infections grouped together because they spread by transfer of infectious organisms from person to person during sexual contact.* STD is currently replacing the term *venereal disease* (VD), defined as *a condition of the genital organs usually acquired through sexual intercourse.* The very words *venereal disease* produce responses of fear, shame, guilt, anger, and disgust in most individuals. These feelings may impede a person from seeking medical help or telling who his/her contacts were, even though the person may know rationally that treatment is needed for self and the contacts. The term *sexually transmitted disease* is broader in scope; it covers diseases not included in the traditional definition.

Sexually transmitted diseases are a public health epidemic and a major problem because of high communicability. Reports of new cases probably represent about 30 percent of those affected (168). Enormous human suffering, the cost of hundreds of millions of dollars, and the tremendous demands on health-care facilities all result. The problem is rooted in ignorance, apathy, and neglect. Women and children bear an inordinate share of the problem through sterility, ectopic pregnancy, fetal and infant deaths, birth defects, and mental retardation. Cancer of the cervix may be linked to the sexually transmitted herpes II virus (55, 70, 173). Some of the specific reasons for the increase in recent years include changing sexual patterns, changing attitudes and cultural mores regarding sexual behavior, lack of understanding about STD, the feeling of "it can't happen to me," breakdown of the family unit, increased mobility within the population, and the widespread use of contraceptives (45, 200). Adolescents have many reasons for wanting to be sexually active, including to (1) enhance self-esteem; (2) have someone care about them; (3) experiment; (4) be accepted by peers; (5) feel grown-up; (6) be close and touched by another; (7) feel pleasure or have fun; (8) seek revenge; (9) determine normality; (10) love and be loved; and (11) gain control over another (168).

The four most common sexually transmitted diseases are herpes genitalis, syphilis, gonorrhea, and autoimmune deficiency syndrome (AIDS). The increasing incidence of syphilis is not as well known as the increasing incidence of AIDS. (165). The disease AIDS is discussed primarily in Chapter 12, although reference is made to AIDS in Chapter 10 and later in this chapter. Table 11-6 compares the causes, common symptoms, prognosis, and treatment to assist you as you assess and care for clients (13, 54, 55, 69, 70, 100, 168, 185, 200). Other sexually transmitted diseases are discussed in the following pages to assist you in nursing care.

Other Sexually Transmitted Diseases. Vaginitis can be grouped into four categories—candidal, trichomonal, nonspecific, and chlamydial—which may or may not be related to sexual activity (69).

Candidal vaginitis is an *inflammatory process caused by a common skin fungus, Candida albicans.* This condition may accompany diabetes mellitus or be related to the use of antibiotics, birth control pills, bath oils, lack of moisture-absorbing underpants, or sexual intercourse. The most common sign is a copious, cheesy vaginal discharge, accompanied by an intense vulval inflammation, and itching or burning. In addition to the application of cool compresses, a vaginal cream is prescribed and used one or two times daily for 2 to 7 days (69).

Trichomonal vaginitis *is an inflammatory process caused by the common flagellate parasite Trichomonas vaginalis.* The most common sign is frothy, bubbly, greenish-yellow, foul-smelling vaginal discharge with minimal vulval inflammation but some itching. The nonpregnant female is treated with oral medication; if pregnant, she is treated with a vaginal cream (69).

Nonspecific vaginitis is an *inflammation caused by*

TABLE 11–6. Comparison of Gonorrhea, Syphilis, and Herpes Genitalis

	GONORRHEA	SYPHILIS	HERPES GENITALIS (HERPES II) (HSV-2 INFECTION)
Cause	*Neisseria gonorrhoeae*	*Treponema pallidum*	Herpes simplex virus, type II
Incubation period	3 to 9 days.	10 to 90 days; average 3 weeks.	Several days to 3 weeks.
Symptoms	Male: Asymptomatic at times, including when organism lodged rectally. Urethritis: thin, watery, white urethral discharge, becoming purulent. Dysuria. Female Asymptomatic in 60 to 90 percent of cases, including when organism lodged rectally. Dysuria and vaginal discharge common symptoms. Trichomoniasis vaginalis present in 50 percent of cases. Both sexes: Gonococcemia, systemic gonorrhea, with skin lesions, malaise, fever, tachycardia.	Male and female: Stage One (Primary): Chancre: solitary, indurated, painless, ulceration on genitalia 10 to 28 days after sexual contact. Lesion occasionally on mouth, nipples, anus. Lesion healing within 4 to 6 weeks. Treponemes multiplying rapidly. Stage Two (Secondary): Rash covering skin, mouth, and genitalia (red-copper color on white skin, gray-blue on black skin. Red rash on palms and soles). Hair loss. Eyes and ears inflamed. Lymphadenitis, low-grade fever; sore throat. Pain from bone involvement. Albuminuria. Liver and spleen enlarged, jaundice, nausea. Blood test positive after 5 weeks. Stage Three (Latent): Symptoms gone in 2 to 6 weeks. Symptoms possibly absent from a few months to a lifetime. Blood test positive. The person is noninfectious, but possible for syphilitic pregnant woman to give birth to congenitally syphilitic child. Stage Four (Tertiary): Complications after 3 to 30 years in 30 percent of untreated cases.	Male and female: Beginning Infectious Stage: After intercourse with infected partner, itchy, tingling, numb, when virus beneath skin. Active Infectious Symptomatic Stage: Blister-like sores that ulcerate appear on skin, mucous membranes, vagina, cervix, penis, anal area. Fever. Headache. Muscle aches. General malaise. Vaginal discharge. Enlarged lymph glands. Dyspareunia (painful intercourse). Lesions heal 5 to 7 days but are sites for secondary infection. Symptoms last several weeks. Infectious Dormant Stage: Lesions heal; no symptoms. Blisters within vagina or urethra may go undetected. May be transmitted sexually at this time. Recurring Symptomatic Stage: Most people have recurrence of repeated painful attacks because virus remains dormant near base of spine between attacks. Duration of time between attacks varies; may be precipitated by emotional stress, ovulation, onset of menses, poor diet, excess sun or wind, lack of sleep, friction from clothes.

TABLE 11-6. Continued

	GONORRHEA	SYPHILIS	HERPES GENITALIS (HERPES II) (HSV-2 INFECTION)
		Symptoms affecting heart, blood vessels, brain, spinal cord, eyes, skin, and bones. Blood test positive. *Note:* Symptoms from all stages may be present at once.	
Prognosis	Male: Usually treated successfully. Female: Sterility. Both sexes: Arthritis, endocarditis. No immunity to future infections. Reinfection common.	Can be treated successfully. No immunity. Transmitted to fetus via placenta unless mother treated before 16 weeks' gestation. Untreated: Aortic aneurysm, heart failure. Complete or partial paralysis or crippling. Personality changes. Blindness. Gumma, lesions of granulation tissue, causing tissue breakdown and impaired circulation. Pain from bone involvement. Convulsions. Death: Congenital syphilis or death for fetus	Incurable; one-half to 1 million new cases annually with several million recurrence. Complications: Herpes keratitis, eye infection, results from rubbing eye after touching herpes sore. Repeated attacks and blindness may occur. Females: Five times more likely to develop cervical cancer. Pregnant women: Pregnancy often ends in abortion, stillbirth, prematurity, neonatal infection, or death. Fetal infection may occur in utero. Infant: Virus transmitted through placenta or by direct contact at birth. Fifty percent chance of being born with disease unless delivered by cesarean section; 75 percent of infected neonates are blind or have brain damage. Death may occur.
Treatment	Aqueous penicillin. Some drug-resistant strains of organisms developing.	Benzathine P.G. or Procaine Penicillin.	Aseptic technic used in care of patient. Cleanse lesions with soap and water. Use drying medications. Experimental drugs reported to reduce symptoms. Antibiotics for secondary infection. Refer to psychological counseling. Prevent further spread by avoiding any contact with genitals and sexual intercourse while lesions are present unless male wears condom.

more than one bacteria but especially *Hemophilus vaginalis.* The most common sign is a small amount of yellowish-white vaginal discharge that has a "fishy" smell. Itching is usually not intense. Treatment consists of an initial douche followed by vaginal cream applied two times a day for 7 days *or* oral medication. If the oral medication is used, the sexual partner should have identical treatment (69).

Chlamydia trachomatis *is a vaginal infection caused by an intracellular parasite, C. trachomatis, which often causes no symptoms in the woman but is transmitted to sexual partners or the infant at birth.* The woman may have vaginal discharge or pelvic inflammatory disease. Antibiotic treatment (tetracycline, erythromycin) is effective. The infected male may develop urethritis or epididymitis. He may complain of painful urination and frequency. A discharge may be milky and purulent but does not culture out as gonorrhea. This condition is treated with an oral antibiotic. Usually there are no complications. The infected infant may develop conjunctivitis or pneumonia (101). Chlamydia was estimated to effect 4 million Americans in 1987, at a treatment cost of over 1 billion dollars, making it the *most common* sexually transmitted disease in the United States.

Genital warts *are caused by the human papilloma virus and are seen on the foreskin and penis in males (especially in uncircumcised males) and on the perineum and vaginal mucosa in females.* They can appear from 1 to 3 months after contact. Unless a large number of warts are present, they can be treated by repeated topical application of a medication followed in 3 to 5 hours by a sitz bath. This is repeated at weekly intervals until warts are gone (69).

Phthirius pubis, *pubic lice, or "crabs"* should be treated with gamma benzene hexachloride cream or lotion. The application should be repeated in 7 to 10 days. Sexual contacts should be treated simultaneously, and any family and close contacts should be examined carefully, but treated only if infested. Sometimes oral antihistamines are prescribed to relieve intense itching (69).

Contraceptive Practices. **Contraception,** or **birth control,** *is the use of various devices, chemicals, or abortion to prevent or terminate pregnancy.* The adolescent may choose contraception to avoid pregnancy while continuing sexual activity. Contraceptive practices are summarized in Table 11–7 and additional information may be obtained from various references at the end of this chapter (35, 45, 58, 68, 69, 86, 113, 132, 141, 179, 190). While contraceptives may prevent pregnancy (and sexually transmitted diseases when the contraceptive device is the condom), they have unwanted side effects or disadvantages. The only way to avoid both pregnancy and the unwanted side effects is sexual abstinence. Your approach and the structure of the health-care environment are critical to the teen-age female adhering to instructions about contraceptive practices or abstinence (117).

About one-half of the teens in the United States have sexual intercourse by age 18; education and contraceptive services have not kept abreast of the changing sexual mores. Some youth, however, do not use contraceptives because of misconceptions or ignorance about them, inability to secure appropriate contraceptives, inability to plan ahead for their actions, a belief that this marks them as promiscuous, or rebelliousness. Males are less likely to recognize risk of pregnancy as a result of sexual activity, have less information about contraceptives, and are less supportive of contraceptive use than females. The attitude of the male may indeed influence the female toward sexual activity without contraceptive use, even though she realizes the hazards and wishes to avoid them (45).

Adolescent Pregnancy. Adolescent pregnancy is at epidemic proportions. The United States exceeds other nations in incidence: 10 percent of teen-age girls between 15 and 19 become pregnant. Twenty percent of babies born are to females under 19; 10 percent of babies in the United States are born to girls under 16 years; and 70 to 85 percent of the pregnancies are unplanned. Afro-American teen pregnancy rates are higher, although 8 percent of Caucasians in the 15 to 19 age group become pregnant. One-third of all births to teen-age mothers are out of wedlock (184).

Teen-age girls in the United States do not engage in sex earlier or more frequently than girls in the other countries. Researchers conclude that the main difference between incidence in the United States and Sweden, France, the Netherlands, England, Wales, and Canada is American attitudes toward sex. The media constantly offers messages that suggest sex. Almost nothing that teen-agers see or hear about sex informs them about contraceptives or the importance of avoiding pregnancy (184).

The other countries studied appear to be more tolerant of teen-age sexual activity than the United States, and more open about sex in general. The lowest pregnancy rates exist in countries with the most liberal attitudes toward sex.

Studies show that teen-agers in the other countries studied are not too immature to use contraceptives effectively, and that they do not get pregnant just to become eligible for welfare benefits. Further, teen-age pregnancy in the United States cannot be ascribed to high teen-age unemployment, since unemployment among the young is a serious problem in all the countries studied (183).

Various factors influence whether the adolescent becomes pregnant. While some pregnancies may be accidental, four other themes may underlie the mask of "accident" (68, 80, 200):

1. Self-destruction or self-hate.
2. Rebellion, anger, hate, reverse aggressiveness toward parents and authority.
3. Lack of responsibility for self and personal behavior, related to identity diffusion or confusion.
4. Plea for attention and help, either from parents, the boy involved, or others.

Pregnancy may also be the result of the teen's need to be close to someone, to relieve loneliness, to punish herself for earlier sexual activity for which she feels

TABLE 11-7. Contraceptive Measures: Effectiveness and Disadvantages

NAME	DESCRIPTION	EFFECTIVENESS	DISADVANTAGES
Oral contraceptives	Pills used to suppress chemically ovulation. New low dose pill available, with one-tenth amount of hormones, thus fewer side effects.	Highly effective, 2 pregnancies in 100.	Fewer serious effects than previously seen. Screen for nausea, edema, depression, anemia, blood clots, myocardial infarction, and liver cancer. Smokers have increased triglycerides, total cholesterol, and lipoproteins and greater cardiovascular disease risk.
Intrauterine device (I.U.D.) (Progestasert)	Metal coil inserted in uterus, preventing implantation of fertilized ovum.	Very effective, 5 pregnancies in 100.	Cramping and bleeding between periods, heavy periods, anemia, perforation of uterus, and pelvic infection.
Spermicidal chemicals	Chemical substances inserted in vagina before intercourse.	Less effective, 5 to 24 pregnancies in 100. Effective if used with diaphragm.	Irritation of penis or vagina.
Billings ovulation method	Changes in cervical discharge show presence of ovulation.	Very effective when followed and abstinence maintained during fertile time.	Accurate observation by the woman is necessary.
Diaphragm	Small occlusive device inserted over cervix before intercourse.	Very effective when properly placed and checked often.	Irritation of cervix. Esthetic objections.
Condom	Occlusive device placed over penis before ejaculation.	Effective when properly used. 9–10 pregnancies in 100.	Esthetic objections. Possibly impaired sensation in male.
Rhythm	Abstinence of intercourse before and during ovulation, increased body temperature during fertile days.	Less effective, 5 to 24 pregnancies in 100.	Pregnancy unless menstrual periods are regular, ovulation is closely observed, and abstinence adhered to.
Sponge	Two-inch circular sponge of soft polyurethane saturated with spermicide. Sponge inserted vaginally, removed by string loop.	If left in 6 hours after intercourse, 88 to 90% effective.	Not well tested; concern about TDA in sponge being a possible carcinogen to liver and breasts. Not to be used during menses or may cause toxic shock syndrome.
Prostaglandins	Chemicals which regulate intracellular metabolism administered parenterally or orally for contraception or to induce abortions.	Effectiveness uncertain.	Nausea, vomiting, diarrhea, and pelvic pain.
Luteinizing hormone-releasing hormone (LHRH)	Daily injection of hormone decreases sperm; substance inhibits pituitary gland's release of hormone that controls ovulation and spermatogenesis.	In women, 98 percent effective. Useful in men and women.	Experimental. Data on men still limited.
Injections	150-mg injection of a progestogen, Depo-Provera (DMPA), or medroxy progesterone acetate. 200-mg injection of Norigest (NET-EN), a progestogen.	Injections 98 percent effective for 3 months.	Licensed for use in 84 countries. Not approved by FDA in United States. Experimental.

TABLE 11–7. Contraceptive Measures—Continued

NAME	DESCRIPTION	EFFECTIVENESS	DISADVANTAGES
Implants	Levo-norgestrel (progestin) inserted via silicone rubber, matchstick-size tubes into woman's arm.	Implants last 5 yr: Continual release of synthetic hormone inhibits ovulation, thickens cervical mucus, and impedes sperm passage. Removed if woman desires pregnancy.	Experimental in Europe and Asia. Not FDA approved in United States.
Hysterectomy	Surgical removal of uterus. Usually done for pathological condition of uterus rather than for sterilization only.	Completely effective. Ovum and hormonal production unchanged; menstruation ceases.	Mortality rate higher than after tubal ligation. Possible postoperative complications. Irreversible procedure.
Tubal ligation	Surgical interference with tubal continuity and transport of an ovum.	Effectiveness depending on type of procedure done, 0.5 to 3 pregnancies in 100. Ovum maturation, menstruation, and hormonal production unchanged.	Occasional recanalization (Fallopian tube ends regrowing together) causing fertility. Adhesions, infection, or swelling of tubes postoperatively.
Vasectomy	Surgical severing of the vas deferens (sperm duct) from each testicle.	Effectiveness depending on type of procedure done; failure rate low. Less expensive and time consuming and easier to obtain than female sterilization. No risk to life. No effect on hormone production of testes or sexual functioning.	Bleeding, infection, and pain postoperatively in 2 to 4 percent. Occasional recanalization of severed ends of vas deferens causing fertility. Uncertain reversibility.

Note: A combination of contraceptive practices may be used by the couple.

ashamed and guilty, to prove herself a woman, to break a symbiotic tie between herself and her mother, or to fulfill mother's prophecy if mother has indicated she expects such behavior (80).

The early adolescent is not physically, socially, emotionally, educationally, or economically ready for pregnancy or parenthood. The late adolescent is physically mature but may not be ready for pregnancy emotionally, socially, or economically. These latter factors override the biological advantages of early pregnancy and may account, in part, for the lack of health care that is sought during pregnancy (112). In turn, health providers often do not understand the needs underlying the adolescents' behavior, and thereby fail to provide the necessary services.

Neonatal risks associated with teen-age maternity are not uniform, but are high. The risks vary by age of the adolescent mother, amount of prenatal care, and racial identification. In the United States, socioeconomically advantaged teen-agers, with healthy and unimpaired physical growth and development, rarely bear children. Disadvantaged Americans, on the other hand, often initiate childbearing by their late teens and currently account for the majority of teen-age births. Teen-agers at highest risk of adverse pregnancy outcomes, specifically those under 17-years-old, are more likely to be Afro-American, live in rural areas (especially if White), and receive inadequate prenatal care (especially if White) than older first time mothers. Risks are highest for 11- to 14-year-old teens. However, sexual activity is still atypical in the United States at such early ages; very peculiar social circumstances (extreme isolation from the social and economic mainstream, or even such possibilities as rape or incest) may account for these pregnancies and births and the negative outcomes. Early fertility implies early menarche, which is associated with short stature, a risk factor for poor neonatal outcome. The excessive rates of short gestation, low-birth-weight, and neonatal mortality may result from a variety of physiological consequences of environmental disadvantage, not primarily from inherent and intractable biological developmental limits (52).

The late adolescent male is more likely to be involved in the pregnancy and supportive to the girl than his younger counterpart. Urban teen-age Afro-American fathers are more involved with their children and the children's mothers than stereotypes suggest (90, 163). The more mature the adolescent girl and boy when they become parents, the more likely they will manifest positive parenting characteristics described in Chapter 7. The younger the adolescent, the more likely that negative parenting behaviors will occur, with one possible exception. During middle adolescence, Caucasian mothers who are poor are more likely to exhibit picking, poking, and pinching behaviors toward the infant. Often the adolescent parent expects behavior beyond the developmental ability of the baby, which creates intense frustration and anger that results in child abuse or neglect. You may be able to assess these behaviors and intervene with support, teaching, and counseling. Agencies that have adolescent pregnancy programs should provide teen fathers, as well as mothers, with parenting classes and child development information (160).

A major problem in adolescent parenting is that many teen-age females who become mothers have themselves come from single-parent homes or homes where active participation by father is lacking. Further, the teen-age father often gives no real support. The maternal grandmother is the one who is expected to raise the child; if she cannot, then the adolescent single parent is likely to lack the emotional maturity or knowledge to demonstrate positive parenting characteristics (133, 152). If the teen-age couple marries, divorce is often within the first year or two, so that the baby is in a single-parent home. Smith's article discusses the nurse's meeting psychosocial needs of the teen-age mother and father (160).

Abortion. Abortion is a *method of terminating a pregnancy through expulsion or extraction of the fetus,* usually for economic, emotional, or social reasons. One-fourth of the pregnancies in the world end in abortion, and in the United States, many are done on teen-agers (68, 150). Poor women who economically cannot take care of another child often resort to this drastic form of birth control when they feel they cannot possibly meet the demands of parenting. While abortion carries possible risks to the physical and psychological health of the female, the legal abortion is statistically safer physically than giving birth (25). However, more widespread use of abstinence or contraception would reduce the need for abortion. You may be involved in helping the female who is pregnant, the parents, and even the father of the baby to determine their values and feelings about remaining pregnant versus having an abortion. The persons involved should decide; it is not appropriate for you to give advice. Rather give full information, be nonjudgmental of the people, and listen. The people involved will be capable of arriving at a decision. Refer to Neidhardt's article about feelings of the woman and the nurse, issues and concerns when the woman seeks abortion in the second trimester of pregnancy (118).

Incest. A universal taboo in all cultures is **incest**, *sexual intercourse between persons in the family too closely related to marry legally.* Incest has been present at epidemic levels for some time but is now being admitted more freely by the victims as they speak of the resultant emotional and physical pain. (The female may be in her thirties, forties, or fifties before she can talk about incest that occurred in early childhood.) In your assessment, be aware that the adolescent, either male or female, but especially the female, is at risk for incest or for youth prostitution (18).

In the home where incest occurs, often the daughter is seduced by the father, who is dominant, by physical force or intimidation. The mother is often physically ill or disabled, absent from the home for various reasons, or overwhelmed by responsibilities of child care. The oldest daughter is given the mother's role (64). The incestuous behavior may have begun as early as preschool age, sometimes through subtle coercion, enticement of cookies, special favors, or just overt approval. Incest may also occur with stepbrother, grandfather, uncle, or other males who usually live in the home. The girl, from the first encounter, is afraid to tell anyone what is happening, either because of fear of violence or because of other intimidation or enticement. Incest between mother and son, the child and parent of the same gender, or siblings may also occur. Of all the entanglements, incest between siblings appears to be least harmful psychologically. The child will tell you if you pick up the initial verbal cues or if you ask if she has been the victim of such activity. Suspect incest when there are suicide attempts, drug abuse problems, attempts at running away from home, or sexual behavior outside the home (18, 64).

The victim of incest needs your acceptance and understanding and to talk through feelings related to the experience; this exploring takes time and often many sessions. The person committing incest needs psychiatric counseling; however, this person is often no longer available, is unapproachable for referral, or may refuse counseling. In addition to counseling the adolescent (or younger) girl, the mother should be counseled. Strengthening and supporting the mother in her role as woman of the house can indirectly benefit the daughter, in that father may look less to the daughter for a sexual relationship. The best approach is family therapy, since the emotional dynamics behind the incest are complex, value and role shifts in all family members are essential, and the incest has usually occurred for a long period of time (64).

The youth may be the victim of rape and other sexual abuse as well. Burgess describes three types of sex rings: child sex initiation rings, youth prostitution rings, and syndicated pornography and prostitution rings (18).

As you work with sexual assault victims, be aware of various types of assault and entanglements that exist so that you can better detect verbal and nonverbal cues, give immediate assistance, and refer the person (and parents) to receive the necessary medical and legal assistance. References at the end of the chapter will be helpful (18, 19, 57, 64, 115, 140).

Drug-Abuse Problems

Drug abuse is an epidemic adolescent health problem that is not new. The history of drug abuse is long throughout the world. The problem continues to intensify in America, a drug-conscious nation. It is an epidemic with serious consequences for future generations. A major problem is the increasing number of infants born with addiction to one or several drugs (1, 26, 33, 85, 174). Every age group takes a certain amount of medication at one time or another. Usually these drugs are taken for therapeutic reasons. However, reports show that schoolchildren, adolescents, and young adults are increasingly using drugs that cause dependence and toxicity (174).

Drug abuse *is the use of any drug in excess or for the feeling it arouses. A* **drug** *is a substance that has an effect on the body or mind.* Excessive use of certain drugs causes **drug dependence,** *a physical need or psychological desire for continuous or repeated use of the drug.* **Addiction** *is present when physical withdrawal symptoms result if the person does not repeatedly receive a drug and can involve* **tolerance,** *having to take increasingly larger doses to get the same effect.*

Reasons for drug abuse are many: curiosity; peer pressure; need to overcome feelings of insecurity and aloneness, and to be a part of the group; need for acceptance; easy availability; imitation of family; rebellion, escape, or exhilaration; need for a crutch; unhappy home life; sense of alienation or identity problem; or an attempt at maturity or sophistication. Gradually, the drug subculture replaces interest in family, school, church, hobbies, or other organizational activity. The beliefs and attitudes of the drug subculture are learned from experienced drug users and are fortified by certain rock-and-roll songs and stars (1, 33, 162, 174, 200).

Drug dependence is epidemic among the wealthy as well as among the middle class and poor. Children of wealthy parents may develop such traits as poor impulse control, poor frustration tolerance, depression, and poor coping ability. As a result, drugs may be used to cope. Predictably, these traits make children from wealthy homes a difficult population to treat. When drug abuse is the presenting problem, the financial ability to buy drugs of high quality, subcultural accceptance of their use, and at least a relative immunity from legal consequences do not motivate behavior change (188).

Ingestion of alcohol and illicit drugs depresses the cerebral cortex, a still immature reasoning and intellectual center in the teens, and releases inhibitions in the limbic system, the center of love, pleasure, anger, pain, and other emotions. The limbic system seeks instant and constant gratification or stimulation and contributes to the adolescent's sense of boredom. Thus, some adolescents go to extremes in seeking television, alcohol, hard drugs, hard rock, and aggressive video games. There is a loosening of social controls and increase in aggressive and sexual behavior when the limbic system is stimulated (33). Table 11–8 describes the primary or general signs of drug abuse (1, 65, 71, 147, 200).

Therapy is usually entered into as a result of family pressure—often in the form of threatened financial loss such as the withdrawal of allowance or inheritance—or a crisis event such as attempted suicide or arrest. The behavior and illness of the young drug abuser controls the entire family, causing family illness. Parents must regain control of their home, forcing the youth to face the illness by seeking treatment. Love and care in a family is essential, but that alone will not cure the drug abuse problem or the craziness that results in a family where a member is a drug abuser, nor will parental strictness solve the problems. Professional treatment should be obtained in a center that treats the whole person and family, using an interdisciplinary team approach, and that provides after discharge care to the person and family. Intensive treatment over time to the entire family system creates the attitude change that is essential for remaining healthy and functional and for ongoing maturity. A combination of drug detoxification, methadone maintenance, and emotional, cognitive, didactic, and experiential therapies is helpful to reduce symptoms and work through underlying character and interactional pathology (188). Adolescent treatment centers typically prohibit use of stereo and rock music, television, video games, drugs, cigarettes, alcohol, and even rock-star T-shirts. Instead, the teens participate in a structured schedule that involves nutritious foods, jogging and other exercise, group discussions, individual therapy, reading, art and music therapy, school work, responsibility to follow rules, goal setting, and a milieu that builds a spiritual foundation similar to the 12 steps of Alcoholics Anonymous (33, 47, 143, 200).

If upon discharge the youth returns to his/her drug-using friends, there will be a return to drug abuse and all the consequences. It is not easy for the youth to give up drugs or to overcome the drug abuse reputation at school, among peers, or elsewhere. It may be very difficult to work into a new group of friends, unless during the treatment program the youth and family were helped to establish new interests, new hobbies,

TABLE 11—8. General Signs and Symptoms of Drug Abuse

Primary and general signs of drug abuse in the young person include:

- Decrease in quality of school work without a valid reason. Reasons given may be boredom, not caring about school, not liking the teachers.
- Personality changes, behaving in unexpected ways; becoming more irritable, less attentive, less affectionate, secretive, unpredictable, uncooperative, apathetic, depressed, withdrawn, hostile, sullen, easily provoked, oversensitive.
- Less responsible behavior, not doing chores or school homework, school tardiness or absenteeism, forgetful of family occasions such as birthdays.
- Change in activity, antisocial pattern, no longer participating in family activities, school or church functions, sports, prior hobbies, or organizational activities.
- Change in friends, new friends who are unkempt in appearance or sarcastic in their attitude; the youth is secretive or protective about these friends, not giving any information.
- Change in appearance or dress, in vocabulary, music tastes to match that of new friends, imitating acid rock and roll stars.
- More difficult to communicate with, refuses to discuss friends, activities, drug issues; insists it is all right to experiment with drugs; defends rights of youth, insists adults hassle youth; prefers to talk about bad habits of adults.
- Irrational behavior, frequent explosive episodes, driving recklessly, unexpectedly stupid behavior.
- Loss of money, credit cards, checks, jewelry, household silver, coins, in the home that cannot be accounted for.
- Addition of drugs, clothes, money, albums, tapes, or stereo equipment that are suddenly found in the home.
- Presence of whisky bottles, marijuana seeds or plants, hemostats, rolling papers, drug buttons, and marijuana lead buttons. There may also be unusual belt buckles, pins, bumper stickers, or t-shirts, and the *High Times* magazine in the car, truck, or home.
- Preoccupation with the occult, various pseudo-religious cults, satanism, or witchcraft; and evidence of tattoo writing of 666, drawing of pentagrams on self or elsewhere, or misrepresentation of religious objects.
- Signs of physical change or deterioration; including pale face; dilated pupils; red eyes; chewing heavily scented gum; using heavy perfumes; using eye wash or drops to remove the red; heightened sensitivity to touch, smell or taste; weight loss, even with increased appetite (marijuana smoking causes the "munchies"—extra snacking).
- Signs of mental change or deterioration, including disordered thinking or illogical patterns, decreased ability to remember or in rapid thought processes and responses, severe lack of motivation.

new social ties and friendships, and new organizational connections. Remaining drug free may mean giving up the prior boyfriend or girlfriend, certain favorite clothes or possessions, certain words in the vocabulary, certain mannerisms or aspects of appearance. The change in attitudes, self-concept, and body image must be total enough so the person feels like a new person and is strong enough in that identity that the new self is maintained in the face of inevitable peer, school, family, and other stressors. The ability to give up aspects of the old self and maintain the new identity begins in the treatment center, but can only be accomplished with love, support, and encouragement (not nagging) from family and other loved ones. *The person must feel that he/she is gaining more than what is being lost in order to maintain the changes begun in treatment and to move forward in maturity* (33). Support groups in the school, church, and community for the teens who do not want to use alcohol or drugs are essential to prevent the loneliness and ostracism some teens feel when they go against peers (33).

The following case study illustrates how the normally developing person can become hooked into a drug abuse lifestyle, as well as the complexity of the problem for the person and family.

CASE STUDY

Jess, 17, was taken for treatment to an adolescent chemical abuse unit. "My parents, when they put me in (the hospital) thought I was just drinking and using pot. When they got my toxscreen back, my mom almost fainted."

The drug-screening analysis showed that marijuana, Valium, Demerol, Dilaudid, and Codeine all had been ingested within a week. All I did was live to get high—and, I guess you could say, get high to live," he said.

"I used to work at the home of a doctor who had a medicine cabinet full of everything anybody could dream of. He had a bunch of narcotics and stuff, and I thought I was in heaven. But I could go out right now and get drugs in about 15 minutes if I wanted. People, they're waiting for you to buy it. Around 10, I started drinking a little bit—just tasting it, and getting that warm feeling. The first time I got high, I was 12 and I loved it. There wasn't no stopping me then. I got high all I could. I used to wake up and think, 'How can I get high today?'"

His friends put pressure on him to try other drugs. "I told myself I'd never do any pills, never drop any acid, but those promises went by the wayside." He first took Quaaludes in the ninth grade, and dropped acid that year at a concert. Soon he was drinking a lot and taking speed, and Valium and other depressants.

"If I drank any beer, I'd want another one. If I got drunk, I'd want to get high; if I got high, I'd want to get pills. When I started out I thought it was just cool, and that feeling was great. Instead of dealing with normal, everyday problems, I'd run off and get high. It got so I was picking fights just so I could stomp out of the house and get high."

He became a connoisseur. "I didn't buy dope at school. Theres no good dope at school."

He also became more difficult to handle at home and at school.

"That period of time, I started fighting a lot with my parents. My grades dropped. I got into fist fights at school. I was real rebellious. I usually was high during class."

"I think it was real obvious to my teachers, because of the way I dressed and the way I acted in class. All the guys I hung around with had real long hair, moccasin boots, heavy metal T-shirts and leather pants."

"I was pretty much an A student, and they (grades) dropped to low Cs and Ds. I was really withdrawing into myself."

"I wasn't myself when I was stoned. For years, I didn't even know how to feel (emotions). I've left home a few times."

"One time I was on LSD and I took a razor blade and cut my leg up. I still have the scars from that. I blanked out a lot. I'd come home beaten-up looking, and didn't know why."

Jess spent 8 weeks in treatment and now says he's been straight for over a year.

"It's a dependency," he said. "There's no way to eliminate it. You just try to control it. If I smoked a joint today, or took a drink, I'd be right back."

Jess agrees with other former addicts: part of the problem is the naiveté of the parents.

"My parents, when I started getting in trouble, weren't going to admit it." Advice for parents who uncover a drug problem is simple: "Get some help. Not just for your kids, but for the parents and siblings also, because the whole family gets crazy. It's a family disease."

"I'll have to be on the lookout for the rest of my life to avoid falling back into drug use. I've learned just to be myself, and people will like me—and I never would have believed that before."

Table 11-9 will assist you in assessing the **specific signs** (*objective evidence*) and *symptoms* (*subjective evidence*) **resulting from drugs commonly abused.** Often the youth is taking a mixture of these drugs, since use of any of these is likely to increase use of other drugs. Assessment becomes more complex. At times neither the person nor friends know for sure what drugs have been used. Various references at the end of this chapter give information on drug abuse (1, 33, 38, 45, 65, 71, 74, 76, 99, 113, 128, 143, 145, 147, 157, 162, 185, 192, 200, 201).

Because the use of cocaine (or crack) is a serious health and social problem, a discussion in addition to the information under the stimulant abuser in Table 11–9 is presented in the following pages.

Cocaine is an alkaloid extracted from the leaves of the coca bush, which grows mainly on the eastern slope of the Andes mountain in Peru and Bolivia. It is sold on the streets as a hydrochloride salt; it is a fine, white crystalline powder known as "coke, " "snow, " "flake, " "blow." Freebase cocaine resembles rock candy chunks. Street cocaine is diluted with cornstarch, talcum powder, sugar, amphetamines, and quinine. Its purity is usually 5 to 50 percent; it may be 80 percent. Cocaine is taken by (1) snorting (inhaled through a straw or a rolled up dollar bill or a coke spoon), (2) freebasing (smoked in a small water pipe filled with rum instead of water), or (3) mainlining (taken intravenously) (1, 27, 28, 85, 162).

Cocaine is addicting because of the sense of stimulation (rush) that comes from activation of nerve cells in the brain that release dopamine. The sense of pleasure or good feeling is so great that the person develops a stronger compulsion for cocaine each time he/she uses it, so that addiction results. Chronic cocaine use blocks the ability of the brain cells to release dopamine without increasing amounts of cocaine. The person feels terrible without the drug. Finally, there is the "kindling effect, " a small amount of cocaine can trigger unexpectedly severe dopamine reactions, resulting in seizures or bursts of psychotic behavior (1, 27, 28, 85, 162).

Physical changes that occur from cocaine use are:

1. Cardiovascular: tachycardia, arrhythmias.
2. Respiratory: nasal stuffiness, tachypnea, shortness of breath.
3. Musculoskeletal: twitching, tremors, weight loss.
4. Gastrointestinal: nausea, constipation.
5. Genitourinary: difficult urination, impotency.
6. Dermatological: pallor, cold sweats.
7. Ophthalmological: dilated pupils, blurred vision.
8. Central nervous system: fever, insomnia, fatigue, headache, seizures (1, 27, 28, 85, 162).

Medical hazards that result from cocaine use include:

1. Nasal septum and mucous membrane destruction from inhalation.
2. Bronchitis, with infection, hemorrhage, and blocking of the respiratory tract from inhalation of foreign particles.

3. Respiratory failure from vasoconstriction of blood vessels in the lung, cyanosis, shortness of breath, dyspnea, pulmonary edema, respiratory collapse, and death.
4. Cardiac arrhythmias, tachycardia, myocardial infarction, cardiac arrest, sudden death.
5. Seizures from freebasing and mainlining, which cause strong, explosive stimulation; convulsions may result in death.
6. Phlebitis from repeated injections in the veins; resulting thrombus can cause an embolus, causing myocardial infarction, pulmonary embolus, renal embolus, or cerebralvascular accident.
7. Endocarditis from mainlining with bacterial-contaminated needles, causing infection of heart values; fatality 50 percent.
8. Hepatitis from mainlining with blood-contaminated needles, causing tender, enlarged liver, jaundice; repeated attacks can be fatal.
9. Brain abscess from mainlining with bacterial-contaminated needles, causing fever, convulsions, paralysis, and possible death.
10. Acquired Immune Deficiency Syndrome from mainlining with blood-contaminated needles; 75 percent of all intravenous addicts have been exposed to the virus, 5 to 10 percent or more, will develop the fatal disease (1, 27, 28, 85, 162).

Crack or **rock** *is an extremely potent, highly addictive, inhalant form of cocaine.* It is beige or slightly brown, white or yellowish white, and it is sold in pellet-sized chips called "rocks," or in small plastic vials, in an envelope, or in foil wrap. It can be smoked using a glass pipe or a tin can; the user inhales the vapor from the heated crack. It may be mixed with marijuana or tobacco, or it may be mixed with PCP (angel dust), which is called "space blasting," or with other drugs. Some users smoke in a "base house," "crack house," or "rock house" where the person pays a fee to use the house, pipes, and torches. Or the business executive may use crack in his/her suburban or urban home (28, 30, 162).

The frightening aspect about crack is that the person may become addicted the first time of use, or in a matter of weeks. The addiction is as powerful as heroin addiction. The intense high feeling is produced in 4 to 6 seconds and lasts 5 to 7 minutes. The high is followed by an intensely uncomfortable low feeling, so that the person will do anything to get more crack. The person may become violent toward friends or family; the person may become paranoid or psychotic, or the person may commit suicide. Death may occur in the user because of heart or respiratory failure. The first dose only costs $10.00; but a binge that lasts 1 or 3 days, and is repeated weekly, may cost hundreds or thousands of dollars. Crack becomes the most, the only, important thing in life, so that all other aspects of life suffer: family relations, friendship, jobs, social status, ability to think or behave rationally, personal hygiene or self-care, activities of daily living. If the user is a pregnant woman, there is risk of miscarriage, stillbirth, an addicted baby, impaired physical and mental development in the child, the risk of respiratory failure or strokes in the baby (28, 30, 162).

Your Role in Health Promotion

The adolescent is between childhood and adulthood. Allow him/her to handle as much personal health care and business as possible, yet be aware of the psychosocial and physical problems with which he/she cannot cope without help. Watch for hidden fears which may be expressed in unconventional language. For example, the high-school junior may state concern about her figure. Underlying this statement may be a fear that she will not adequately develop secondary sex characteristics. She may feel she is not physiologically normal, not sexually attractive, and will not be able to have children. With adequate assessment, you may discover that she is simply physically slow in developing. Explaining that not all adolescents develop at the same rate and that she is normal may rid her mind of great anxiety.

Today's adolescent, because of improved communications, knows more about life than did former generations. He/she is bombarded with information but does not have the maturity to handle it. Do not assume that because of apparent sophistication he/she understands the basis of health promotion. The adolescent may be able to discuss foreign policy but thinks that syphilis is caught from toilet seats.

Some teen-agers, especially those with understanding and helpful families, go through adolescence with relative ease; it is a busy, happy period. But the increases in teen-age suicide and in escape activities, such as drugs and alcohol, speak for those who do not have this experience. Adolescents are looking for adults who can be admired, trusted, and leveled with, and who genuinely care. Parents are still important as figures to identify with, but the teen-agers now look more outside the home—to teachers, community, and national leaders. They idealize such people and if the leaders are found to be liars or thieves, their idealism turns to bitterness. As a nurse, you will be one of the community leaders with the opportunity, through living and teaching health promotion, to influence these impressionable minds.

TABLE 11-9. Symptoms of Common Forms of Drug Abuse

TYPE	SIGNS AND SYMPTOMS
The inhalant abuser: • Squeezes airplane glue into paper bag, holds nose, inhales fumes. May sniff gasoline, lighter fluid, or refrigerants.	1. Odor of substance on person's clothes, breath, in plastic or paper bags. 2. Secretions of nose or eyes. 3. Euphoria. 4. Disordered perception, diplopia, tinnitus. 5. Muscular weakness, staggers as if drunk. 6. Drowsy, sleepy after 35 to 45 minutes, or unconscious. 7. Severe anemia if persistent use. 8. Hallucinations, violent behavior. 9. Dependence emotionally, not physically. 10. Kidney, liver, and brain damage or death from excess inhalation.
The depressant abuser: • Uses barbiturates, sedative-hypnotics, and tranquilizers, which depress central nervous system.	1. Varied onset and duration of effects according to preparation used and route of administration. 2. Symptoms of alcohol intoxication with no odor of alcohol on breath. 3. Sleepy, drowsy, irritable. 4. Interest in usual activities diminished; poor hygiene; depression; talks slowly. 5. Behavior changes suddenly; impaired judgment. 6. Pulse rate and blood pressure lowered. 7. Respirations slow and shallow. 8. Confusion and disorganized behavior. 9. Drug ingested, one after another, without user's awareness of action. 10. Tolerance possible. 11. Dependence and physical addiction, with consequent withdrawal symptoms. 12. Liver, brain, and kidney damage from long-term use. 13. Coma, death from overdosage.
The stimulant abuser: • Uses caffeine orally, amphetamines orally or intravenously, cocaine by snorting or intravenously, or other drugs which stimulate the central nervous system.	1. Needles and syringes present, usually concealed; scars on body. 2. Euphoria, increased alertness, energetic, talkative, decreased sense of fatigue. 3. Insomnia, anorexia. 4. Pupils dilated. 5. Pulse rate increased. 6. Mouth and nose dry, halitosis. 7. Speech slurred. 8. Agitated, excessive activity, irritable, suspicious. 9. Disoriented, confused, hallucinates, psychotic. 10. Dependence psychologically. 11. Injuries occurring from activity while under drug effects, or death from large doses. 12. Caffeine may cause symptoms described in signs 2 through 8; may be chronic caffeinism. 13. Cocaine causes nasal congestion and hole in nasal septum when snorted (snuffed).
The narcotic abuser: • Uses drugs from the opiate plant (heroin or morphine) which relieve pain and induce euphoria and sleep.	1. Traces of white powder around nostrils from inhaling heroin. "Persian Brown," dark red-brown granular powder from Iran, is more potent, may be smoked or snorted. 2. Scars on the body from injecting narcotic into vein or under skin. 3. Needles and syringes left in hidden places at home or school.

TABLE 11–9. Continued

TYPE	SIGNS AND SYMPTOMS
	4. Flushed skin, tingling sensations. May become pale, clammy, and increasingly cyanotic. 5. Euphoria. 6. Lethargic, drowsy, nodding, reduced physical activity. Slow respirations. 7. Pupils constricted and unresponsive to light, reduced visual acuity. 8. Concentration impaired, apathy. 9. Vomiting, constipation, urinary retention. 10. Pulmonary complications from snorting powder. 11. Physical deterioration from poor health practices. 12. Tolerance. 13. Dependence physically and psychologically. 14. Death from overdosage; 10 percent of addicts die in 10 to 12 months; death six times rate for general population, adjusted for age.
The marijuana abuser: • Uses marijuana (cannabis), Indian hemp, which produces varying grades of hallucinogenic material: hashish, pure cannabis resin, the most powerful grade from leaves and flowering tops of female plants; ganja less potent preparation of flowering tops and stems of female plant and resin attached to these; Bhang, least potent preparation of fried mature leaves and flowering tops of male and female plants. • THC in fat part of cell prevents nutrients from crossing cell membrane; RNA production and new cell growth reduced, *all* cell function interfered with.	1. Nervous system: • Stored in fat portion of cells; remains in brain 6 weeks after cessation of smoking. • Speech comprehension, ability to express ideas, and ability to understand relationships are impaired because of damage to the cerebral cortex. • Memory and ability to concentrate or focus is impaired because of effects on cells in the hypocampus and cerebrum. • Emotional swings, depression, pessimism, irritability, low frustration tolerance, and temper outbursts occur because of cell damage in the limbic system. The person does not learn adaptive skills or how to cope with stressors. • Lack of motivation, fatigue, moodiness, depression, inability to cope, loss of interest in vigorous activity or all previously enjoyed activities occur because of THC effects on various parts of the brain. The person fails to continue in emotional development. • Insomnia occurs because of damage to cells in the hypothalamus. • Vision blurred and irregular visual perception occur because of damage to cells in the occipital areas. • Body coordination, maintenance of posture and balance, ability to perform sports or drive a car are impaired because of damage to cells in the cerebellum. 2. Respiratory System: • Upper respiratory infections are common because of destruction to mucosal cells from the smoke (more destructive than tobacco smoke). • Sinusitis, inflammation of the lining of one or more of the sinuses, occurs from nasal infection. • Bronchitis, with low-grade fever, chest pain, a chronic cough and yellow-green sputum, is common because of inflammation to the bronchial tree caused by smoke inhalation. • Lung cancer is more likely to occur because of the numerous chemicals in marijuana. Smoking 3 to 5 joints a week is equivalent to smoking 16 cigarettes daily for 7 days a week. • Emphysema and chronic obstructive pulmonary diseases occur from long-time smoking and deep inhalation; lung function is permanently damaged.

TABLE 11–9. Symptoms of Common Form of Drug Abuse—Continued

TYPE	SIGNS AND SYMPTOMS
The marijuana abuser (continued):	3. Cardiovascular system: • Cardiac arrhythmias and tachycardia are related to the dose of THC absorbed (one joint immediately raises heart rate by as much as 50 percent). • Hypertension, which may contribute to aneurysm formation or cardiovascular accident, is common. • Myocardial infarction can occur. 4. Congested conjunctiva is associated with hypertension. 5. Reproductive system: • Infertility in males occurs from moderate to heavy use because production of testosterone is reduced, and a low sperm production or production of abnormal sperm occurs. • Impotence, inability to ejaculate sperm, results. • Gynecomastia, enlarged breast formation, occurs in puberty when secondary sex characteristics are being developed. Lower testosterone causes fat deposits around the breast tissue. • Hirsutism occurs in females, with increased androgen production resulting in male secondary sex characteristics (increased hair growth on face and arms, deeper voice), irregular menstrual cycles, serious acne, and lack of development of female secondary sexual characteristics. • Infertility in the female because of damage to the ova and menstrual cycle irregularity occur. • Pregnancy, if present when marijuana is smoked, endangers the embryo and fetus, increasing chance of congenital defects and fetal mortality because THC crosses the placental barrier. • Lactation, if breast-feeding while smoking marijuana, endangers baby's health because THC transfers through breast milk. 6. Marijuana combined with PCP causes psychosis; if taken with other substances; effect of each drug multiplied.
The psychedelic drug abuser: • Uses lysergic acid from ergot, which can be converted to LSD or lysergic acid diethylamide tartrate (LSD 25), a potent hallucinogen which is chemically synthesized and alters mood, perception, and thinking.	1. Euphoria, impaired judgment, anxiety, hyperactive, suspicious. 2. Pupils dilated. 3. Hallucinations, illusions, trancelike state. 4. Senses of sight, hearing, touch, body image, and time distorted. 5. Depression, confusion, disorientation. 6. Fear, excitement, terror. 7. Flashback effects re-experienced without further use of drug. 8. Chromosome changes possible.

Note: Besides LSD and marijuana, a number of other hallucinogens exist naturally, such as psilocybin (mushroom), peyote and mescaline (peyote cactus), and chemically, such as DMT and DOM (STP). Their effects are similar to the above.

Counseling the Adolescent for Health Promotion

Help the person clarify values, beliefs, and attitudes that are important and be more analytic in thinking, as first steps in bringing behavior into congruence and to reduce a sense of conflict. Tauer describes value clarification exercises (168).

Teach the adolescent effective decision-making skills, so that the person learns how to develop a plan of action toward some goal. The decision-making model involves: (1) defining the problem; (2) gathering and processing information; (3) identifying possible solutions and alternatives of action; (4) making a decision about action; (5) trying out the decision; (6) evaluating whether the decision, actions, and consequences were effective or desirable; (7) rethinking other alternate solutions with new information; and (8) acting on these new decisions. Having the adolescent write out answers when settling goals, thinking of possible solutions, and analyzing consequences can help make an abstract process more concrete and more useful to the person who needs signs of structure (168).

McCreary-Jahasz and Kavanaugh show a model for sexual decision making which you can use to help the person clarify values, make decisions, and understand consequences related to sexual behavior (102).

Promote warm, accepting, supportive, nonjudgmental feelings and honest feedback as the adolescent struggles with decisions. Help him/her make effective choices by fostering a sense of self-importance (he/she is a valuable and valued individual). Helping the person look ahead to the future in terms of values, goals, and consequences of behavior can strengthen a sense of what is significant in life and a resolve to live so the values and goals are fulfilled and positive consequences are achieved.

Both individual and group counseling are useful. In the group setting, the adolescent may be asked to bring a close friend or parent to share the experience. Some concerns and conflicts, however, are best worked through with the individual. Group sessions are effective for the following reasons (20, 168):

1. The person realizes concerns, feelings, and sense of confusion are not unique to him or her.
2. Experiences and successful solutions to problems can be shared with others who are at different points of development.
3. Ideas and roles can be tried out in the group before being tried in real life.
4. Values can be clarified and decisions made with support and feedback from others.

Tauer describes a number of group exercises that can be used (168). Additional information on counseling methods is also available (97, 115).

Education About Sexuality

Personal Attitudes First examine personal attitudes toward yourself as a sexual being, the sexuality of others, family, love, and changing mores regarding sexual intercourse before you do any sex education through formal or informal teaching, counseling, or discussion. How objective are you? Can you talk calmly about biological reproduction and use the proper anatomical terms? Can you relate biological information to the scope of family life? Can you emotionally accept that masturbation, homosexuality, intimacy between unmarried persons, unwed pregnancy, sexually transmitted diseases, and unusual sexual practices exist? Can you listen to others talk about these subjects? If you cannot, let some other nurse do sex education. Realize that no one can do all areas of nursing intervention. Your astute assessment, case finding, and ability to refer the adolescent elsewhere are still major contributions toward helping him/her stay healthy. The rapport necessary to work with the adolescent in any area is highly sensitive, and if he/she has no rapport with the family, your attitudes are crucial.

Promoting Education. You can promote education about sexuality, family, pregnancy, contraceptives, and sexually transmitted diseases through your own intervention and by working with parents and school officials so that objective, accurate information can be given in the schools. Most adults favor sex education in school as well as on television, as a way to reduce the problem of teen-age pregnancy (135).

Teen-agers need the opportunity to identify what they consider important problems, a chance to discuss their feelings, attitudes, and ideas as well as to obtain factual information and guidance with effective solutions. The sex act should be discussed as part of a relationship between individuals requiring a deep sense of love, trust, and intimacy and not just as a means of biological gratification. Sexual behavior is not solely a physical phenomenon but one of great psychosocial significance. The consequences of sexual activity must be explored honestly. More progressive schools include this in the curriculum, and the teacher or school nurse must be comfortable, knowledgeable, and able to promote discussion. Studies show that 15- and 16-year-olds that have participated in sex education are less likely to engage in sexual behavior. Sex education courses given outside the home supplement the influence of parental guidance and teaching (48).

Such sex education and related discussions can also be offered through church youth groups, the Red Cross, local YMCA or YWCA, or other public organizations. Again, you can initiate and participate in such programs.

Perhaps most important, you can encourage the teen-ager and family to talk together and teach the parents how and what to teach, where to get information, and the significance of formal sex education beginning in the home. References at the end of the chapter can be helpful in sexuality counseling (8, 90, 92, 102, 104, 113, 127, 168).

Care and Counseling. You may work directly with a pregnant teen-ager or one with sexually transmitted disease as a school or clinic nurse or in your primary-care practice. That person needs your acceptance, support, and confidentiality as you do careful interviewing to learn his/her history of sexual activity, symptoms, and contacts. Effective interviewing, communication, and crisis intervention discussed by Murray and Huelskoetter are essential to reduce unwanted consequences of sexual activity (115). Because of the stigma and legal problems associated with unwed pregnancy, abortion, and sexually transmitted diseases, fear of reprisals, and the quixotic personality of the adolescent, your behavior at the first meeting is crucial. You may not get another chance for thorough assessment or beginning intervention.

Basically, the teen with sexually transmitted disease wants your help and comfort; he/she is a troubled person. Information is needed about the type of disease, symptoms, the contagious nature, consequences of untreated disease, and where to get treatment. In all of these diseases, both male and female partners (along with any other person who has had sexual contact with these partners) should be treated by medication and use of hygiene measures as well as by counseling and teaching. You are in a key position to determine signs and symptoms and help to make a differential diagnosis. Refer to references at the end of the chapter that were cited earlier. You can also teach about the importance of continued body hygiene, avoiding unprescribed douching or other self-medication, the danger of continued reinfection from sexual intercourse, and the long-term damage to genital tissue from any sexually transmitted disease or repeated abortions. Remind your clients that the *symptoms* of the disease may go away, but the *disease* may not. Hence, a complete round of treatment is essential. Further, there are two reliable ways to prevent infection or reinfection: abstinence or the male's use of a condom. One sexual contact is all that is necessary to acquire sexually transmitted diseases.

The girl wants to confirm whether pregnancy exists and talk about personal feelings, family reactions, and what to do next. Explain what services are available and answer her questions about the consequences of remaining pregnant, keeping or placing the baby for adoption, or terminating pregnancy.

Comprehensive maternity services for pregnant adolescents can reduce maternal and neonatal complications, including prematurity, low birth weight, congenital defects, and infant death, so often found in this age group. One model for such services, the teen clinic in the family-centered program of Salvation Army's Booth Maternity Center in Philadelphia, is described by Daniels and Manning (32). Various references at the end of this chapter will be helpful (2, 25, 32, 42, 63, 68, 75, 80, 106, 107, 127, 133, 134, 152, 170, 196, 200).

An adolescent girl may want to know about methods of abortion and services available. Reputable abortion clinics will do counseling prior to the abortion so that the girl does not regret her decision, but you can begin counseling. The questions you raise and guidance you give can help her make necessary decisions. Various references at the end of this chapter cover more deeply your role in teaching, counseling, or working with someone who is considering abortion (2, 20, 115).

Many states now have the law that a minor can be treated for sexually transmitted diseases and other conditions without parental consent. Although this prevents parents from being with their child in a serious situation, the law does enable minors to receive treatment without fear of parental retribution or without having to wait until parents feel ready. Encourage the adolescent to confide in the parents if at all possible and to seek their support. In turn, encourage the parents to be supportive.

Consent and confidentiality are key concerns in all areas of health care of the adolescent: emergency care and treatment for drug abuse, alcoholism, sexually transmitted disease, pregnancy, and other problems. The publication *Family Planning/Population Reporter*, obtained from The Center for Family Planning Program Development, 1666 K Street, N.W., Washington, D.C. 20006, is a useful reference on recent state legislation, court action, and federal local policies dealing with legal age and treating of minors.

Present Health Care System. Reforming the present health-care system seems essential, since present public health services are frequently incapable of kindly or completely handling the problems resulting from adolescents' sexual activity, either because of policy, philosophy, understaffing, or underfinancing. You can participate in change by working through your professional organization and as an informed citizen. You can promote a deeper awareness of the adolescent as an individual with unique needs and work to extend education and counseling services, including peer-group counseling and teen-age advisory boards. Further, you can help establish community services to work with the adolescent/youth in a health-care crisis. The disabled adolescent also requires special care and teaching needs.

Working with the Drug Abuser and Alcoholic

Personal Feelings. You must work through your feelings about drug use and abuse to assess the person accurately or intervene objectively. Why does a drug problem exist? Do you feel drugs are the answer to problems? How frequently do you use drugs? Do you use amphetamines or barbituates? Have you ever tried marijuana, LSD, or heroin? What are the multiple influences causing persons to seek answers through using illegal drugs? What are the moral, spiritual, emotional, and physical implications of excessive drug use, whether the drugs are illegal or prescribed? What treatment do drug abusers deserve? How does the alcoholic differ from the drug abuser? Until you can face these questions, you will not be able to help the adolescent drug abuser or alcoholic.

Knowledge. Knowledge about drugs—current ones available on the street, their symptoms and long-term effects, legislation related to each—is necessary for assessment, realistic teaching, and counseling. Also, learn about the effects of alcohol. Know local community agencies which do emergency or follow-up care and rehabilitation with drug abusers and alcoholics.

Help teen-agers understand that problems of drug abuse and alcoholism may be avoided in several ways. They must get accurate information and make decisions based on knowledge rather than on emotion, have the courage to say "no, " and know and respect the laws. They must also participate in worthwhile, satisfying activities, have a constructive relationship with parents, and recognize that the normal, healthy person does not need regular medication except when prescribed by a doctor. Also, help youths realize the unanticipated consequences of drug and alcohol abuse. These include loss of friends; alienation from family; loss of scholastic, social, or career opportunities; economic difficulties; criminal activities; legal penalties; poor health; and loss of identity rather than finding the self.

Every person with whom you work is a potential drug abuser or addict, and all drugs and chemical substances have a potential for harm from allergy, side effects, toxicity, or overdosage. Different drugs taken simultaneously may have an unpredictable or increased effect. In addition, taking unprescribed drugs may mask signs and symptoms of serious disease, thus postponing necessary diagnosis and treatment. Hence a major responsibility on your part is to teach others how to take drugs safely, the importance of taking only prescribed drugs as directed, and the hazards of drugs. Adolescents may not realize that drugs obtained illegally have an unknown purity and strength and are frequently produced under unsanitary conditions. They may not realize that when injections are given without sterile technique, infectious hepatitis, tetanus, or vein damage may result. Help parents realize the impact their behavior and attitudes regarding drug and alcohol use have on their children.

Accepting Attitude. An accepting attitude toward the drug abuser and alcoholic as a person is essential while at the same time you help him/her become motivated and able to cope with stresses without relying on drugs or alcohol. You will need to use effective communication and assessment, but since these problems are complex, you need to work with others. The treatment team should consist of other health-care professionals, representatives from law enforcement and religious agencies, and self-help groups, established in various cities by previous drug or alcohol abusers who have been rehabilitated and now seek to rehabilitate others.

Various references at the end of this chapter, which were cited earlier, provide more detailed information to aid you in your care.

Members of society impose heavy responsibilities on the young adult. With your intervention, some adolescents who could not otherwise meet these forthcoming demands will exert a positive force in society.

References

1. Acee, Anna, and Dorothy Smith, Crack, *American Journal of Nursing*, 87, no. 5 (1987), 614–617.
2. Adams, Barbara, Adolescent Health Care: Needs, Priorities, and Services, *Nursing Clinics of North America*, 18, no. 2 (1983), 237–248.
3. Adeyanju, Matthew, William Creswell, Donald Stone, et al., A Three-year Study of Obesity and Its Relationship to High Blood Pressure in Adolescents, *Journal of School Health*, 57, no. 3 (1987), 109–113.
4. Advance Report of Final Mortality Statistics, 1983, National Center of Health Statistics, DHHS P#85-1120, *Monthly Vital Statistics Report*, 34, no. 6 (September 26, 1985), 18–20.
5. Alcohol-Related Deaths May Be More Common Than Thought, *The Nation's Health*, September, 1987, 3.
6. Allport, Gordon, *The Individual and His Religion*. New York: Macmillan, 1961.
7. Amanat, Ebrahim, Adolescent Depression, Covert Anger, and Suicide, *Res Medica*, 3, no. 2 (1986), 5–10.
8. Amonker, R. G., What Do Teens Know About the Facts of Life?, *Journal of School Health*, 50, no. 9 (1980), 527–530.
9. Anorexia May Have Effect on Brain, Bones, Studies Show *Health Scene*, Fall, 1987, 3.
10. Baker, Susan, and Roberta Henry, *Parents' Guide to Nutrition: Healthy Eating from Birth through Adolescence*. Reading, MA: Addison-Wesley, 1986.

11. Bates, Barbara, *A Guide to Physical Examination* (3rd ed.). Philadelphia: J. B. Lippincott, 1983.
12. Berzonsky, M. D., Formal Reasoning in Adolescence: An Alternate View, *Adolescence*, 13, no 50 (1978), 279–290.
13. Bettoli, Elena, Herpes: Facts and Fallacies, *American Journal of Nursing*, 82, no. 6 (1982), 924–929.
14. Bonaguro, John, and Ellen Bonaguro, Self-Concept, Stress Symptomatology, and Tobacco Use, *Journal of School Health*, 57, no. 2 (1987), 56–58.
15. Brodsley, Laurel, Avoiding a Crisis: The Assessment, *American Journal of Nursing*, 82, no. 12 (1982), 1865–1871.
16. Brown, R.C., J.M. Sanders, and S.K. Schonberg, Driving Safety and Adolescent Behavior *Pediatrics* 77 (1986), 603–607.
17. Bruch, Hilde, *Eating Disorders: Obesity, Anorexia, and The Person Within*. New York: Basic Books, 1978.
18. Burgess, Ann, and H. Jean Birnbaum, Youth Prostitution, *American Journal of Nursing*, 82, no. 5 (1982), 832–834.
19. ———, and L. Holmstrom, The Rape Victim in the Emergency Ward, *American Journal of Nursing*, 73, no. 10 (1973), 1741–1745.
20. Cangelosi, Andrew, Charles Gressard, and Robert Mines, The Effects of a Rational Thinking Group on Self-Concept in the Adolescent, *The School Counselor*, 27, no. 5 (1980), 357–361.
21. Carino, Constance, and Patricia Chmelko, Disorders of Eating in Adolescence: Anorexia Nervosa and Bulimia, *Nursing Clinics of North America*, 18, no. 2 (1983), 343–352.
22. Cecere, M. Carolyn, PIP (Positive Image Program): A Group Approach for Obese Adolescents, *Nursing Clinics of North America*, 18, no. 2 (1983), 249–256.
23. Ciseaux, Anne, Anorexia Nervosa: A View from the Mirror, *American Journal of Nursing*, 80, no. 8 (1980), 1468–1470.
24. Claggert, Marilyn, Anorexia Nervosa: A Behavioral Approach, *American Journal of Nursing*, 80, no. 7 (1980), 1471–1472.
25. Clark, Bernadine, Improving Adolescent Parenting Through Participant Modeling and Self-Evaluation, *Nursing Clinics of North America*, 18, no. 2 (1983), 303–310.
26. Cocaine Babies: Hooked at Birth, *Newsweek* (July 28, 1986), 56–57.
27. Cocaine: Effects of Epidemic Now Hitting Home in U.S., *The Nations Health* (October–November, 1985), 1, 5.
28. Cocaine, Glamorous Status Symbol of the "Jet Set," Is Fast Becoming Many Students' Drug of Choice, *Chronicle of Higher Education*, 31, no. 11 (November 12, 1985), 33–35.
29. Cohn, Lucile, The Hidden Diagnoses, *American Journal of Nursing*, 82, no. 12 (1982), 1862–1864.
30. Crack and Crime, *Newsweek* (June 16, 1986), 16–22.
31. Craft, Martha, Health Care Preferences of Rural Adolescents: Types of Service and Companion Choices, *Journal of Pediatric Nursing*, 2, no. 1 (1987), 3–12.
32. Daniels, Mary, and Dianne Manning, A Clinic for Pregnant Teens, *American Journal of Nursing*, 83, no. 1 (1983), 68–71.
33. Davis, Anne, Teenagers and Drink Risky Duo, *Adolescent Program Newsletter*. Memphis, Tenn.: Charter Lakeside Hospital, Fall, 1987, 1.
34. Dempsey, Mary, The Development of Body Image in the Adolescent, *The Nursing Clinics of North America*, 7, no. 4 (1972), 609–615.
35. Dickerson, Janet, Oral Contraceptives: Another Look, *American Journal of Nursing*, 83, no. 10 (1983), 1392–1398.
36. Diekstra, R.F, and K. Hawton (eds.), *Suicide in Adolescence*. Boston: Martinus Nighoff, 1987.
37. Does Your College Bound Teenager Need a Measles Shot, *American Journal of Nursing*, 87, no. 6 (1987), 766–768.
38. Donovan, John, and Richard Jesser, Problem Drinking and the Dimension of Involvement with Drugs: A Gultman Scalogram Analysis of Adolescent Drug Use, *American Journal of Public Health*, 73, no. 5 (1983), 543–552.
39. Duvall, Evelyn, and Brent Miller, *Marriage and Family Development* (6th ed.). New York: Harper & Row, 1984.
40. Eating Disorders—Not for Women Only, *Health Scene*, Fall, 1987, 10.
41. Erikson, Erik H., *Childhood and Society* (2nd ed.). New York: W. W. Norton, 1963.
42. ———, *Identity: Youth and Crisis*. New York: W. W. Norton, 1968.
43. ———, Memorandum on Youth, in *Human Life Cycle*, ed. William Sze. New York: Jason Aronson, 1975, pp. 351–359.
44. Falkner, Frank, and J.M. Tanner (eds.), *Human Growth* (2nd ed.). New York: Plenum Press, 1986.
45. Freeman, Ellen, et al., Adolescent Contraceptive Use: Comparisons of Male and Female Attitudes and Information, *American Journal of Public Health*, 70, no. 8 (1980), 790–797.
46. Frisch, R.E., and J.W. McArthur, Menstrual Cycles: Fatness as a Determinant of Minimum Weight for Height Necessary for their Maintenance or Onset, *Science*, 186 (1974), 949–951.
47. Fultz, J., et al., When a Narcotic Addict is Hospitalized, *American Journal of Nursing*, 80, no. 3 (1980), 478–481.
48. Furstenberg, Frank, Kristin Moore, and James Peterson, Sex Education and Sexual Experience Among Ado-

lescents, *American Journal of Public Health*, 75, no. 11 (1985), 1331–1332.
49. Garbarino, James, Edna Guttman, and James Seeley, *The Psychologically Battered Child: Strategies for Identification, Assessment, and Intervention.* San Francisco: Jossey-Bass, 1987.
50. Garn S.M., and Diane Clark, Problems in the Nutritional Assessment of Black Individuals, *American Journal of Public Health*, 66. no. 3 (March, 1976), 262–267.
51. General Recommendations on Immunizations, *Morbidity and Mortality Weekly Report*, 31, no. 24 (1982), 317–328.
52. Geronimus, Arlene, The Effects of Race, Residence, and Prenatal Care on the Relationship of Maternal Age to Neonatal Mortality, *American Journal of Public Health*, 76, no. 12 (1986), 1416–1421.
53. Gesell, Arnold, Frances Ilg, and Louise Ames, *Youth: The Years from Ten to Sixteen.* New York: Harper and Brothers, 1956.
54. Gonococcal Vaccines Pass Early Trials, *Medical News* (June 7, 1980) 3, 20.
55. Grossman, J. H., et al., Management of Genital Herpes Simplex and Virus Infection During Pregnancy, *OB-Gyn*, 58, no. 7 (1981), 1–4.
56. Guidelines for Teenage Parties, *Olivette Advisory* (Olivette, Mo.), 6, no. 4 (January, 1983), n.p.
57. Guio, M. V., et al., Child Victimization, Pornography, and Prostitution, *Crime and Justice*, 3 (1980), 65–81.
58. Hall, Peter, and Susan Holch, Injectable Contraceptive, *World Health* (May, 1982), 2–4.
59. Hatton, Corrine, and Sharon Valente, *Suicide: Assessment and Intervention.* Norwalk, CT.: Appleton-Century-Crofts, 1984.
60. Hammer, Signe, My Daughter, The Football Star, *Parade* (August 5, 1979), 6–7.
61. Havighurst, R., *Developmental Tasks and Education* (3rd ed.), New York: David McKay, 1972.
62. *Health United States, 1982.* Washington, D.C. U.S. Government Printing Office 1982, Publication # PHS 83–1232.
63. Hedahl, Kathleen, Assisting the Adolescent with Physical Disabilities Through a College Health Program, *Nursing Clinics of North America*, 15, no. 2 (1983), 357–374.
64. Herman, J., and L. Hirschman, Families at Risk for Father-Daughter Incest, *American Journal of Psychiatry*, 138 (July, 1981), 967–970.
65. Hickey, Susan, Short-Term Marijuana Effects of National Concern, Says IOM, *The Nation's Health*, 12, no. 4 (1982), 10.
66. Higher Education's Drinking Problem, *Chronicle of Higher Education*, 24, no. 21 (July 21, 1982), 1, 6–7.
67. Higher Education's Drinking Problem, *Chronicle of Higher Education*, 24, no. 21 (1982), 1, 6–7.
68. Holmes, Janine, and Lana Magiera, *Maternity Nursing.* New York: Macmillian, 1987.
69. Hoole, Axalla J., Robert A. Greenberg, and A. Glenn Pickard, Jr., *Patient Care Guidelines for Nurse Practitioners* (3rd ed.). Boston: Little, Brown, 1988.
70. How to Cope with Herpes, Palo Alto, Calif.: American Social Health Association, 1980.
71. How Safe Is Pot? *Newsweek* January 7, 1980), 44–45.
72. Howe, Jeanne, *Nursing Care of Adolescents.* New York: McGraw-Hill, 1980.
73. Hulka, B. D., et al., Protection Against Endometrial Carcinoma by Combination Product Oral Contraceptives, *Journal American Medical Association*, 247 (January 22–29, 1982), 475–477.
74. Janowsky, D. S., et al., Interpersonal Effects of Marijuana, *Archives of General Psychiatry*, 36, no. 7 (1979), 781–785.
75. Jekel, James, and Janet Forbush, Service Needs of Adolescent Parents, *The Journal of School Health*, (November, 1979), 527–530.
76. Jessor, Richard, James Chase, and John Donevan, Psychosocial Correlates of Marijuana Use and Problem Drinking in a National Sample of Adolescents, *American Journal of Public Health*, 70, no. 6 (1980), 604–613.
77. Joe, George, and D. Simpson, Mortality Rates Among Opioid Addicts in a Longitudinal Study, *American Journal of Public Health*, 77, no. 3 (1987), 347–348.
78. Jones, Franklin, Karl Garrison, and Raymond Morgan, *The Psychology of Human Development* (2nd ed.). New York: Harper & Row, 1985.
79. Kaluger, George, and Meriem Kaluger, *Human Development: The Span of Life* (3rd ed.). St. Louis: Times Mirror/Mosby, 1984.
80. Kandell, Netta, The Unwed Adolescent Pregnancy: An Accident? *American Journal of Nursing*, 79, no. 12 (1979), 2112–2114.
81. Karp, Stanley, A 10-Point Program for Bicycle Safety, *Contemporary Pediatrics*, 4, no. 6 (1987), 16–21, 24, 26–27.
82. Keidel, Gladys, Adolescent Suicide, *Nursing Clinics of North America*, 18, no. 2 (1983), 323–332.
83. Keniston, Kenneth, Youth: A New Stage of Life, *The American Scholar*, 39 (1970), 631–654.
84. ———, Youth as a Stage of Life, in *Human Life Cycle*, ed. William Sze. New York: Jason Aronson, 1975, 332–349.
85. Kids and Cocaine, *Newsweek* (March 17, 1986), 58–65.
86. Klaus, Hannah, The Ovulation Method, *St. Louis University Magazine*, 47, no. 3 (Spring, 1974), 12–14.
87. Kohlberg, L., Moral Stages and Moralization: The Cognitive Development Approach, in *Moral Development and Behavior*, ed. T. Lickera. New York: Holt, Rineholt, & Winston, 1976.
88. Kornguth, Mary, Nursing Management When Your

Patient Has a Weight Problem, *American Journal of Nursing*, 81, no. 3 (1981), 553–554.
89. Krohn, Marvin, Michele Naughton. William Skinner, et al., Social Disaffection, Friendship Patterns and Adolescent Cigarette Use: The Muscatine Study, *The Journal of School Health*, 56, no. 4 (1986), 146–150.
90. Lamb, Michael, *The Father's Role*. New York: John Wiley, 1986.
91. Langford, Rae, Teenagers and Obesity, *American Journal of Nursing*, 81, no. 3 (1981), 556–559.
92. Lidz, Theodore, *The Person—His and Her Development Throughout the Life Cycle* (2nd ed.) New York: Basic Books, 1983.
93. Loucks, Arlene, Chlamydia: An Unheralded Epidemic, *American Journal of Nursing*, 87, no 7 (1987), 920–922.
94. Magilvy, Joan, Marty McMahon, Marty Bachman, et al., The Health of Teenagers: A Focused Ethnographic Study, *Public Health Nursing*, 4, no. 1 (1987), 35–42.
95. Majzisik, Cathy, and Edward Martin, Gastric Partitioning: The Latest Surgical Means to Control Morbid Obesity, *American Journal of Nursing*, 81, no. 3 (1981), 569–572.
96. Manning, M., Disappearing Childhood: 6 Going on 16, *Kappa Delta Pi Record*, Fall, 1985, 14–18.
97. Manov, Ariana, and Laura Lowther, A Health Care Approach for Hard-to-Reach Adolescent Runaways, *Nursing Clinics of North America*, 18, no. 2 (1983), 333–341.
98. Mar, Dexter, New Hepatitis B Vaccine: A Breakthrough in Hepatitis Prevention, *American Journal of Nursing*, 82, no. 2 (1982), 307–309.
99. Marijuana Smoking on Rise Among Youth, *The Nation's Health*, 10, no. 5 (1980), 1 ff.
100. McCaul, Kevin, et al., Predicting Adolescent Smoking, *The Journal of School Health*, 52, no. 8 (1982), 342–347.
101. McCormack, W. M., et al., Fifteen Month Follow-Up Study of Women Infected with Chlamydia Trachomatis, *New England Journal of Medicine*, 300 (January 18, 1979), 123–125.
102. McCreary-Jahasz, Anne, and Jack Kavanaugh, Factors Which Influence Sexual Decisions, *Journal of Sex Education and Therapy*, 4, no. 2 (1978), 35–39.
103. McKenry, Carol Tishler, and Karen L. Christman, Adolescent Suicide and the Classroom Teacher, *Education Digest*, 46, no. 1 (1980), 42–45.
104. McMullan, James, Enhancing Self-Concept of Junior High Students, *Humanist Education*, 18, no. 4 (1980), 169–175.
105. McNar, W. L., The 'Other' Venereal Diseases: Herpes Simplex, Trichimoniasis, and Candidiasis, *Journal of School Health*, 49, no. 2 (1979), 79–83.
106. Mendez, Lois, et al., Factors Influencing Adolescents: Perceptions of Life Change Events, *Nursing Research*, 29, no. 6 (1980), 384–388.
107. Mercer, Ramona, Assessing and Counseling Teenage Mothers During the Perinatal Period, *Nursing Clinics of North America*, 18, no. 2 (1983), 293–301.
108. Miller, Barbara K., Jejunoileal Bypass: A Drastic Weight Control Measure, *American Journal of Nursing*, 81, no. 3 (1981), 564–568.
109. Mindruin, Beverly, Teen Walk-Aways, *St. Louis Globe Democrat*, January 13, 1978, Sec, B, pp. 1–2.
110. Mitchell, Helen, et al., *Nutrition in Health and Disease* (17th ed.). Philadelphia: J. B. Lippincott, 1982.
111. Mitchell, Judith, Adolescents Concern About Physical Examination by a Female, *Nursing Research*, 29, no. 3 (1980), 165–169.
112. Morris, Naomi, The Biological Advantages and Social Disadvantages of Teenage Pregnancy, *American Journal of Public Health*, 71, no. 8 (1981), 796.
113. Moshman, David, John Glover, and Roger Bruning, *Development Psychology*. Boston: Little, Brown, 1987.
114. Munhall, Patricia, Moral Reasoning Levels of Nursing Students and Faculty in a Baccalaureate Nursing Program, *Image*, 12, no. 3 (1980), 57–61.
115. Murray, Ruth, and M. Marilyn Huelskoetter, *Psychiatric/Mental Health Nursing: Giving Emotional Care*. Englewood Cliffs, N.J.: Prentice-Hall, 1983.
116. Narcotics Identification Chart, *Perspectives of Psychiatric Care*, 9, no. 5 (1971), 212.
117. Nathanson, Constance, and Marshall Becker, The Influence of Client-Provider Relationships on Teenage Women's Subsequent Use of Contraception, *American Journal of Public Health*, 75, no. 1 (1985), 33–38.
118. Neidhardt, Anne, Why Me? Second Trimester Abortion, *American Journal of Nursing*, 86, no. 10 (1986), 1133–1134.
119. New Look at Marijuana, *Newsweek* (January 7, 1980), 41–46.
120. Nkowane, Benjamin, et al., Measles Outbreak in a Vaccinated School Population: Epidemiology, Chains of Transmission, and the Role of Vaccine Failures, *American Journal of Public Health*, 77, no. 4 (1987), 434–438.
121. Norris, Jean, and Mary Kunes-Carroll, Self-Esteem Disturbance, *Nursing Clinics of North America*, 20, no. 4 (1985), 745–761.
122. Oldaker, Syble, Identity Confusion: Nursing Diagnoses for Adolescents, *Nursing Clinics of North America*, 20, no. 4 (1985), 763–773.
123. O'Malley, P.M., J.G. Bachman, and L.D. Johnston, Period, Age, and Cohort Effects on Substance Abuse Among American Youth, 1976–1982, *American Journal of Public Health*, 74 (1984), 882–888.
124. Overeaters Anonymous: A Self-Help Group, *American Journal of Nursing*, 81, no. 3 (1981), 560–563.
125. Pallikkathayil, Leonie, and Sandra Tweed, Substance Abuse: Alcohol and Drugs During Adolescence, *Nursing Clinics of North America*, 18, no. 2 (1983), 313–321.

126. Paxman, J.M., and R.J. Zuckerman, *Laws and Policies Affecting Adolescent Health*. Geneva: World Health Organization, 1987.
127. Peach, Ellen Hammerlund, Counseling Sexually Active Very Young Adolescent Girls, *The American Journal of Maternal-Child Nursing*, 5, no. 3 (1980). 191–195.
128. Persian Brown—Potent New Heroin, *Health Care Horizons*, 3, no. 19 (August 17, 1980), 4.
129. Petersen, Anne, Those Gangly Years, *Psychology Today*, 21, no. 9 (1987), 28–35.
130. Pfeffer, Cynthia, *The Suicidal Child*. New York: The Guilford Press, 1986.
131. Piaget, Jean, *The Growth of Logical Thinking from Childhood to Adolescence*. New York: Basic Books, 1961.
132. Pill Benefits Outweigh Risks in Young Women, Says Report, *The Nation's Health*, 11, no. 2 (1981), 4.
133. Pillitteri, Adele, *Child Health Nursing: Care of the Growing Family* (3rd ed.). Boston: Little, Brown, 1981.
134. Pipes, Peggy, *Nutrition in Infancy and Childhood* (3rd ed.). St. Louis: Times Mirror/Mosby, 1985.
135. Poll: Most Adults Favor Sex Education in School, *Health Link* (March, 1987), 45.
136. Pridham, Karen, Freddi Adelson, and Marc Hansen, Helping Children Deal with Procedures in a Clinic Setting: A Developmental Approach, *Journal of Pediatric Nursing*, 2, no. 2 (1987), 13–21.
137. Reid, Wornie, Racial Differences in Blood Pressure Levels of Adolescents, *American Journal of Public Health*, 71, no. 10 (1981), 1165–1167.
138. Richardson, Thomas, Anorexia Nervosa: An Overview, *American Journal of Nursing*, 80, no. 7 (1980), 1470–1471.
139. Robinson, Dick, The Suicide Factor, *Health*, 14, no. 3 (1982), 33–34.
140. Rossman, Parker, *Sexual Experience Between Men and Boys*. New York: Association Press, 1976.
141. Rothman, Kenneth, Spermicide Use and Down's Syndrome, *American Journal of Public Health*, 72, no. 4 (1982), 399–401.
142. Roy, C.C., and N. Galeano, Childhood Antecedents of Adult Degenerative Disease, *Pediatric Clinics of North America*, 35 (1985), 517.
143. Russaw, Ethel, Nursing in a Narcotic-Detoxification Unit, *American Journal of Nursing*, 70, no. 8 (1970), 1720–1723.
144. Sachs, Barbara, Reproductive Decisions in Adolescence, 18, no. 2 (1986), 69–72.
145. Samkoff, Judith, and Susan Baker, Recent Trends in Fatal Poisoning By Opiates in the United States, *American Journal of Public Health*, 72, no. 11 (1982), 1251–1256.
146. Scales, Peter, Promoting Adolescent Health: The Need to Model Positive Skills and Challenge Assumptions, *Health Education*, 17, no. 1 (1986), 27–30.
147. Schaffner, Amy, and Dawn Dieterich, Streetwise Narcotic Safety: Precautions in Home Care, *American Journal of Nursing*, 86, no. 6 (1986), 707–708.
148. Scherwets, Priscilla, An Alcohol Treatment Team, *American Journal of Nursing*, 82, no. 12 (1982), 1878–1879.
149. Schiamberg, Lawrence, *Human Development* (2nd ed.). New York: Macmillan, 1985.
150. Schuster, Clara Shaw, and Shirley Smith Ashburn, *The Process of Human Development: A Holistic Life-Span Approach* (2nd ed.). Boston: Little, Brown 1986.
151. Schwart, R.H., et al., Drinking Patterns and Social Consequences: A Study of Middle-class Adolescents in Two Private Pediatric Practices, *Pediatrics*, 77 (1986), 139–143.
152. Scipien, G.M., M.U. Barnard, M.A. Chard, et al., *Comprehensive Pediatric Nursing* (3rd ed.). New York: McGraw-Hill, 1986.
153. Selekman, Janice, Immunization: What's It All About? *American Journal of Nursing*, 80, no. 8 (1980), 1440–1445.
154. Sexually Transmitted Illness is on Increase, Warns WHO, *The Nation's Health*, 10, no. 2 (1980), 11.
155. Sherman, Jacque, and Sylvia Fields, *Guide to Patient Evaluation* (3rd ed.). Garden City, N.Y.: Medical Examination Publishing Co., 1977.
156. Sherraden, Michael, School Dropouts in Perspective, *The Education Forum*, 51, no. 1 (1986), 15–31.
157. Short-Term Marijuana Effects of National Concern, Says IOM, *The Nation's Health*, 12, no. 4 (1982), 10.
158. Showers, Jacy, and Charles Johnson, Child Development, Child Health and Child Rearing Knowledge Among Urban Adolescents: Are They Adequately Prepared for the Challenges of Parenthood? *Health Education*, 16, no. 5 (1985), 37–41.
159. Smith, D.W., E.L. Bierman, and N.M. Robinson (eds.), *The Biologic Ages of Man: From Conception Through Old Age* (2nd ed.). Philadelphia: W. B. Saunders, 1978.
160. Smith, Diann, Meeting the Psychosocial Needs of Teenage Mothers and Fathers, *Nursing Clinics of North America*, 19, no. 2 (1984), 369–379.
161. Spitzer, Mark, and Burton Krumholz, Pap Screening for Teenagers: A Lifesaving Precaution, *Contemporary Pediatrics*, 4, no. 5 (1987), 41–49.
162. Staus, Hal, From Crack to Ecstasy, *American Health* (June, 1987), 50–53.
163. Study Shows that TV Suicide Dramas May Contribute to Teen Suicide, *Journal of Child Adolescent Psychotherapy*, 4, no. 2 (1987), 139–140.
164. Study: Teenage Fathers Are Involved with Babies Too, *The Nation's Health* (September, 1986), 11.

165. Syphilis Shows Major Increase, *The Nation's Health* (December, 1987), 3.
166. Tanner, J.M., *Foetus into Man: Physical Growth from Conception to Maturity*. London: Open Books, 1978.
167. Tanner, J.M. Growth and Maturation During Adolescence, *Nutrition Review*, 39 (1981), 43–55.
168. Tauer, Kathleen, Promoting Effective Decision-Making in Sexually Active Adolescents, *Nursing Clinics of North America*, 18, no. 2 (1983), 275–292.
169. Teen Alcoholism Prevalent, Often Not Diagnosed, *Child and Adolescent Psychotherapy*, 4, no. 1 (1987), 53.
170. Teenage Pregnancy: A Social Phenomenon Becomes a Social Problem, *Health and Medicine*, 1, no. 3 (1982), 13–22.
171. The Adolescent in Despair, *Emergency Medicine*, 17, no. (1985), 51–66.
172. The Copycat Suicides, *Newsweek* (March 23, 1987), 28–30.
173. The Misery of Herpes II, *Newsweek* (November 10, 1980), 105.
174. The Plague Among Us, *Newsweek* (June 16, 1986), 16.
175. Thomas, Sandra, and Maureen Groer, Relationships of Demographic, Life-Style, and Stress Variables to Blood Pressure in Adolescents, *Nursing Research*, 35, no. 3 (1986), 169–172.
176. Thompson, Carol, and Sally Dawley Stroud, The Motorized Tricycle: An Accident Waiting to Happen, *Journal of Pediatric Nursing*, 2, no. 2 (1987), 120–125.
177. Thornburg, Hershel, *Development in Adolescence* (2nd ed.). Monterey, Calif.: Brooks/Cole, Publishing, 1982.
178. Thorne, Barbara, A Nurse Helps Prevent Sports Injuries, *The American Journal of Maternal-Child Nursing*, 7 no. 4 (1982), 236–239.
179. Timby, Barbara, Ovulation Method of Birth Control, *American Journal of Nursing*, 76, no. 6 (June, 1976), 928–929.
180. Tow, Patrick, and Warren Mc Nab, Discipline: A Parenting Dilemma, *Health Education*, 16, no. 1 (1985), 45–47.
181. Trinkoff, Alison, and Susan Baker, Poisoning Hospitalizations and Deaths From Solids and Liquids Among Children and Teenagers, *American Journal of Public Health*, 76, no. 6 (1986), 657–660.
182. Turner, Jeffrey, and Donald Helms, *Lifespan Development* (3rd ed.). New York: Holt, Rinehart and Winston, 1987.
183. U.S. Far Exceeds Other Nations in Teen Pregnancy, *Health Link* (March, 1987), 45–46.
184. U.S. Department of Health and Human Service, New Recommended Schedule for Active Immunization of Normal Infants and Children, *Morbidity and Mortality Weekly Report*. 35, no. 37 (September 19. 1986), 577–579.
185. Vourakis, Christine, and Gerald Bennett, Angel Dust: Not Heaven Sent, *American Journal of Nursing*, 79, no. 4 (1979); 649–653.
186. Wadsworth, Barry, *Piaget's Theory of Cognitive and Affective Development* (3rd ed.). New York: David McKay, 1984.
187. Waechter, E.H., J. Phillips, and B. Holaday, *Nursing Care of Children* (10th ed.). Philadelphia: Lippincott, 1985.
188. Walker, Lynna, Coping with Drug Abuse by Children of the Wealthy: A New High-Risk Group, *Perspectives of Psychiatric Care*, 20, no. 2 (1982), 66–68.
189. Webb, Patricia, Piaget: Implications for Teaching, *Theory Into Practice*, 19, no. 2 (1980), 93–97.
190. Webber, Larry, et al., The Interaction of Cigarette Smoking, Oral Contraceptive Use, and Cardiovascular Risk Factor Variables, in Children: The Bogalusa Heart Study, *American Journal of Public Health*, 72, no. 3 (1982), 266–274.
191. Weist, Jean, Marlene Lindeman, and Marian Newton, Hospital Dialogues, *American Journal of Nursing*, 82, no. 12 (1982), 1874–1882.
192. Wetli, C. V., and R. K. Wright, Death Caused by Recreational Cocaine Use, *Journal of American Medical Association*, 241 (June 8, 1979), 2519–2522.
193. Whaley, L., and D. Wong. *Nursing Care of Infants and Children* (2nd ed.). St. Louis: C. V. Mosby, 1987.
194. White, Jane and Mary Ann Shroeder, Nursing Assessment When Your Patient Has a Weight Problem, *American Journal of Nursing*, 81, no. 3 (1981), 550–553.
195. Wilbur, Robert, Medicine for Addicts: Drugs That Fight Coke, *American Health*, June, 1987, 44–49.
196. Williams, Sue Rodwell, *Nutrition and Diet Therapy* (5th ed.). St. Louis: Times Mirror/ Mosby, 1985.
197. Wintemute, Garen, Jess Kraus, Stephen Teret, et al., Drowning in Childhood and Adolescence: A Population-Based Study, *American Journal of Public Health*, 77, no. 7 (1987), 830–832.
198. Yeager, A.S., et al., Need for Measles Revaccination in Adolescents: Correlation with Birth Date prior to 1972, *Journal of Pediatrics*, 102, no. 2 (1983), 191–195.
199. Yoos, Lorrie, Chronic Childhood Illnesses: Developmental Issues, *Pediatric Nursing*, 13, no. 1 (1987), 25–28.
200. Youngs, Bettie, *A Parent's Survival Guide: Helping Your Teenager Deal with Stress*. Los Angeles: Jeremy P. Tarcher, 1986.
201. Yowell, Sharon, and C. Brose, Working with Drug Abuse Patients in the ER, *American Journal of Nursing*, 77, no. 1 (1977), 82–85.

Personal Interview

202. Leonard, Juanita, coordinator of sex education program in Kenya, 1983.

PART IV

The Developing Person and Family: Young Adulthood Through Death

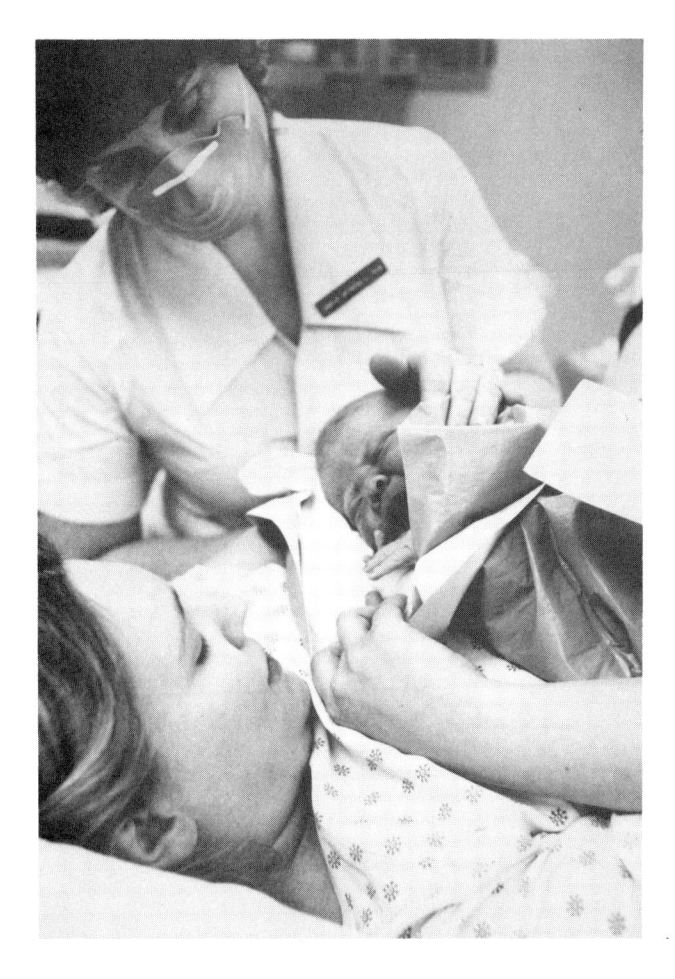

12

Assessment and Health Promotion for the Young Adult

Study of this chapter will enable you to

1. Discuss young adulthood as a developmental crisis and how and why the present young adult generation differs from earlier generations.
2. Explore with middle-aged and older adults their feelings about and ways to be helpful to young adults.
3. List the developmental tasks of the young adult's family, and describe your role in helping families to meet these tasks.
4. Assess the physical characteristics of a young adult.
5. Explain facts from sex behavior research when asked for information about sexuality.
6. Teach nutritional requirements to the young adult male and female, including the pregnant and lactating female.
7. Identify various body rhythms and give examples of body rhythms that maintain adaptation.
8. Describe factors that influence biological rhythms, illness, and dyssynchrony that may result.
9. Discuss nursing measures to assist the person's maintenance of normal biological rhythms during illness.
10. Compare the stages of the sleep cycle, effects of deprivation of the different stages of sleep, and sleep disturbances that occur.
11. Discuss with the young adult his/her need for rest, sleep, exercise, and leisure.
12. Assess emotional characteristics, self-concept and body image, and adaptive mechanisms of a young adult, and determine nursing implications.
13. Explore the meaning of intimacy versus isolation.
14. Contrast the lifestyle options of the young adult and the influence of these on health status and your plans for his/her care.
15. Discuss how cognitive characteristics, social concerns, and moral–religious–philosophical development influence the total behavior and well-being of the young adult.
16. State the developmental tasks of the young adult, and describe your role in helping him/her achieve these.
17. Assess a young adult who has one of the health problems described in this chapter, write a care plan, and work effectively with him/her to enhance health status.

When does young adulthood begin in the United States? The person must be 18 to vote, 30 to be a senator, 35 to be the president. The woman may have her first child at 15 or at 35, or she may have none. Even with these variations the generally accepted age for young adulthood in America is 25 to 45 years.

Childhood and adolescence are the periods for growing up; adulthood is the time for settling down. The changes in young adulthood relate more to sociocultural forces and expectations and to value and cognitive changes than to physical development. The young adult generally has more contact with people of different ages than previously. This experience tends to influence the young adult toward a more conservative, traditional viewpoint (97, 266, 354).

The young adult is expected to enter new roles of responsibility at work, at home, and in society and to develop values, attitudes, and interests in keeping with these roles. The young adult may have difficulty simultaneously handling work, school, marriage, home, and

Key Terms

Average weight	Intimacy
Desirable weights	Isolation/self-absorption
Sexuality	Body image
Gender identity	Singlehood
Gender role	Announcement phase
Absolutistic position	Moratorium period
Hedonistic view	Focusing period
Relativistic position	Amniocentesis
Premenstrual syndrome	Infertility
Mittelschmerz	Surrogate parent
Human sexual response	Hepatitis B
cycle	Influenza
Vasocongestion	Dental caries
Myotonia	Periodontal disease
Four phases of the cycle	Mitral Valve Prolapse
Excitement phase	Syndrome
Plateau phase	Iron deficiency anemia
Orgasm	Atopic dermatitis
Resolution phase	Folliculitis
Biological rhythms	Furuncles
Exogenous rhythms	Carbuncles
Endogenous rhythms	Urticaria
Circadian rhythm	Simple diarrhea
Chronopharmacology	Lactose intolerance
Sleep	Anxiety
Electroencephalogram	Tension headaches
Alpha rhythm	Migraine headaches
Delta rhythm	Aura
Sleep spindles	Functional bowel disease
K-complexes	Pediculosis
NREM sleep	Scabies
REM sleep	Cystitis
NREM Stage I sleep	Acute pyelonephritis
NREM Stage II sleep	Acquired Immune Deficiency Syndrome
NREM Stage III sleep	
NREM Stage IV sleep	Biofeedback training
Insomnia	Stress reactions
Burnout	Homosexuals
Substance abuse	Lesbian
Leisure	Gay
Physical fitness	Transsexuals
Vascularization	Cohabitation
Life Structure	Divorce
Homogamy	

childrearing. He/she may work at primarily one of these at a time, neglecting the others, which then adds to the difficulties (124, 354).

During the twenties, the tasks include finding an occupation, staying in one place, and establishing a new family, which involves focusing affections on one person with whom daily details of life are shared and assuming responsibility for offspring whose care is a continuous operation.

The definition, expectations, and stresses of young adulthood are influenced by socioeconomic status, urban or rural residence, ethnic and educational background, various life events, and the historical era. This generation of young adults is unique. They were born in the forties, fifties, and sixties, have experienced economic growth and related abundance of material goods and technology, rapid social changes, and sophisticated medical care. They have never known a world without the threat of nuclear war, pollution, overpopulation, and threatened loss of natural resources. Instant media coverage of events has made the world a small and familiar place and has focused attention on outer space. Changes in the role of women, the decreasing birth rate, and increasing longevity are modifying the timing of developmental milestones in many people (289). Small wonder that the older generations feel a distance between themselves and young adults.

Further, the person who is 25 or 30 (the young-young adult) works at developmental tasks differently from the person who is 35, 40, or 45 (the old-young adult).

Family Development and Relationships

The major family goal is the reorganization of the family into a continuing unity while releasing maturing young people into lives of their own. Most families actively prepare their children to leave home.

Family Relationships

In America the young adult is expected to be independent from the parents' home and care, although if the person has an extended education, he/she may choose to remain living with the parents in order to save expenses. Sometimes the young adult does not leave the parents' home as quickly as parents would like. With the increasing number of separations and divorces, the tight job market, and increasing apartment rental rates the young adult child may move back home, sometimes with children. Emancipation from parents may not occur for years. Parents may resent the intrusion. As one mother said, "My son is 27, and I don't think he's ever going to leave home. I'm tired of being his cook, his cleaning maid, his laundress, his therapist, and his bank." If the young adult does live at home, he/she should expect, and be expected, to assume a share of the home responsibilities and to adjust lifestyle to that of the parents, to whom the home belongs. Sometimes the adult offspring can be a real help to the parents. Eventually the parents may have to ask the adult offspring to move out so that

12 Assessment and Health Promotion for the Young Adult

both parents and offspring can resume achieving their developmental tasks (97, 119, 308).

Some parents delay this emancipation process because of their own needs to hold onto their offspring. They may have a strong desire to be needed by or wish to continue living vicariously through their children. However, families have much less control over the lifestyle, vocational choice, and friends or eventual mate of their offspring than they did in earlier generations. For emancipation to occur, the parents must trust their offspring while the offspring feels the parents' concern, support, and confidence in his/her ability to work things through.

↳ You can help parents understand that while they are releasing their own children, new members are being drawn into the family circle through their offspring's marriage or close relationships. That the young adult is ready to leave home indicates the parents have done their job.

In a family with several children, the parents may anticipate having the older children leave. The parents then have less responsibility and the remaining children get the benefit of a less crowded home and more parental attention. At the same time, the emancipated offspring can still use home as a place to return during times of stress (354).

Often family expenses are at a peak during this period, as parents pay for education, weddings, or finance their offspring while they get established in their own home or profession. Young adults will earn what they can, but they may not be able to be financially independent even if they are no longer living at home. Both parents may work to meet financial obligations. As young adult offspring establish families, parents should take the complementary roles of letting go and standing by with encouragement, reassurance, and appreciation.

Often the main source of conflict between the parents and young adult offspring is the difference in philosophy and lifestyle between the two generations. The parents who sacrificed for their children to have a nice home, material things, education, leisure activities, and travel may now be criticized for how they look, act, and believe. In fact, the young adult may insist that he/she will *never* live like the parents.

↳ Help the parents resolve within themselves that their grown children will not be carbon copies of them. However, the parents can secretly take solace in knowing that usually the basic values they instilled within their children will remain their basic guidelines, although outward behavior may seem different. This becomes even truer as the young adult becomes middle-aged. Help the parents to realize the importance of their acceptance and understanding of their offspring and of not deliberately provoking arguments over ideologies.

↳ The parents need help in providing a secure home base, both as a model for the young adult and to reduce feelings of threat in the younger children. While the parents are withstanding the criticism of their grown children, they must remain cognizant that younger children in the home will be feeling conflict, too. The parents are still identification models to them, but young children and adolescents value highly the attitudes and judgments of young adult siblings, who, in turn, can have a definite influence on younger children. The parents can help the younger children realize that there are many ways to live and that they will encourage each to find his/her own way when the time comes.

Gradually the parents themselves must shift from a household with children to a husband–wife pair again as the last young adult establishes a home. Family structure, roles, and responsibilities change, and use of space and other resources change.

↳ Use the above knowledge to teach and counsel families as they work through concerns about family relationships.

Family Developmental Tasks

↳ In summary, the following tasks must be accomplished by the family of the young adult. Your listening, teaching, and counseling may assist the family to meet these tasks.

1. Rearrange the home physically and reallocating resources (space, material objects) to meet the needs of remaining members.
2. Meet the expenses of releasing the offspring and redistribute the budget.
3. Redistribute the responsibilities among grown and growing children and finally between the husband and wife or between the adult members living in the household on the basis of interests, ability, and availability.
4. Maintain communication within the family to contribute to harmony and happiness while remaining available to young adult and other offspring.
5. Enjoy companionship and sexual intimacy as a husband–wife team while incorporating changes.
6. Widen the family circle to include the close friends or spouses of the offspring as well as the entire family of in-laws.
7. Reconcile conflicting loyalties and philosophies of life (97).

Physiological Concepts

While body and mind changes continue through life, most physical and mental structures have completed growth when the person reaches young adulthood.

Changes that occur during adult life are different from those in childhood; they are slower and smaller in increment.

Physical Appearance and Characteristics

Weight and Height. Norms denote a set standard of development or the average achievement of a group. However, an average adult person has never really been described. Each person is an individual, and normal values cover a wide range in healthy individuals. Height and weight depend on many factors: heredity, sex, socioeconomic class, geographic area, food habits and preferences, level of activity, and emotional and physical environments. Weight loss or gain is unpredictable in this age group, and norms for height and weight are difficult to determine. Most height and weight tables do not consider the individual and specific influencing factors. Tables usually record either average weight for a given height and age or ideal or desirable weight for a specific height. The **average weight** *is a mathematical norm, found by adding the weights of many people and dividing by the number in the sample.* **Desirable weights** are usually 15 to 25 pounds (6.8 to 11.3 kilograms) below average weights for both sexes and are associated with the lowest mortality rates for a given group (354, 445).

Height and weight tables are frequently prepared by insurance companies; their standards do not represent the total population but represent only people who buy insurance. In an example of tables based on insurance statistics, 25-year-old females in shoes with 1-inch heels ranged in height from 4 feet, 10 inches to 6 feet (147 to 183 centimeters); males of the same age ranged from 5 feet, 2 inches to 6 feet, 4 inches (137.5 to 193 centimeters), and there is an increasing number of males over 6 feet, 4 inches in height. The weights associated with these heights did consider body frame: the clothed weight for females varied from 102 to 179 pounds (46.4 to 81.5 kilograms) and for males the range was from 128 to 207 pounds (58.3 to 94 kilograms). According to a table reflecting mean heights and weights, a female between the ages of 23 and 50 years of age should weigh 120 pounds (55 kilograms) and average 5 feet, 4 inches (163 centimeters) in height. A male of the same age should weigh 154 pounds (70 kilograms) and average 5 feet 10 inches (178 centimeters) in height (445).

Musculoskeletal System. Skeletal growth for the young adult is completed by age 25 when the epiphyseal line calcifies and fuses with the mainshaft of the long bones. The vertebral column continues to grow until the individual reaches the age of 30; 3 to 5 millimeters may be added to an individual's height. Smaller leg bones, the sternum, pelvic bones, and vertebrae attain adult distribution of the red marrow by about 25 years of age. By the early forties, the bones will have lost some mass and density. The process begins earlier in women. With increasing age, the cartilage in all joints has a more limited ability to regenerate itself. Normally, posture is erect (124, 354).

Body systems are functioning at their peak efficiency, and the individual has reached optimal physiological and motor functions and stamina. Peak muscle strength is attained, and maximum physical potential occurs between the ages of 19 and 30. It is during young-young adulthood that most athletes accomplish their greatest achievements. After this peak period, there is a 10 percent loss of strength between the ages of 30 and 60; this loss usually occurs in the back and leg muscles. However, a person can maintain peak performance through the thirties and much of the forties with regular exercise and dietary moderation (190, 414).

Skin. The skin of the young adult is smooth and skin turgor is taut. Acne usually disappears because sex hormones have less influence on secretion of oils from sebaceous glands of the skin (124). The skin of the Afro-American may manifest some conditions that are not seen or are manifested differently in Caucasians, such as hypopigmentation, keloids, pigmentary disorders, pseudofolliculitis (razor bumps), and alopecia. Refer to the article on Afro-American skin problems for a pictorial and descriptive summary (396). In late-young adulthood, the skin begins to lose moisture, becoming more dry and wrinkled. Smile lines and lines at the corners of the eyes are usually noticeable (354).

Cardiovascular System. **Heart** and **circulatory** changes occur gradually with age, depending on exercise and diet patterns. During young adulthood, the total *blood volume* is 70 to 85 millimeters per kilogram of body weight. Maximum *cardiac output* is achieved and peaks between 20 and 30 years of age. The male's heart weighs an average of 10 ounces and the female's an average of 8 ounces. Heart rate averages 72 beats per minute; the *blood pressure* gradually increases, reaching 100 to 120 millimeters of mercury systolic and 60 to 80 millimeters of mercury diastolic. Heart and blood vessels are fully mature and cholesterol levels increase (190, 354, 414). Arteries become less elastic. Hemorrhoids and other varicose veins may become health problems, especially in the childbearing woman.

Respiratory System. Since birth, the lungs have increased in weight 20 times. Breathing becomes slower and deeper, 12 to 20 breaths per minute. The maximum breathing capacity decreases between ages 20 and 40. Breathing rate and capacity will differ according to the size of the individual (414).

Gastrointestinal System. The digestive organs function smoothly during this period of life. The amount of ptyalin decreases after 20 years of age, and digestive juices decrease after 30 years of age. *Dental maturity* is achieved in the early twenties with emergence of the last four molars (wisdom teeth) (124). Some people need to have their wisdom teeth removed because they become impacted and cause pain.

Neurological System.. The brain continues to grow into adolescence and young adulthood; the brain reaches maximum weight during adulthood. Mature patterns of brain wave activity occur after the age of 20, maturation continues to age 30 (414).

Visual and auditory sensory perceptions should be at peak. Gradually during young adulthood the lens of the eyes lose elasticity and begin to have difficulty changing shape and focusing on close objects. Women in this age group can detect high auditory tones better than men (414). Some young adults wear corrective glasses, contact lenses, or hearing aids. Assess for these when you are giving emergency care, especially if the person is unconscious, so that they are not lost or the person does not suffer eye or ear injury. Information on how to remove contact lenses from another person's eyes can be obtained from your local optometry association or optometrist.

Endocrine System. Adrenal secretion of cortisol (hydrocortisone) decreases about 30 percent over the entire adult life span. Because plasma cortisol levels remain constant, the person maintains good response to stress in young adulthood. A decrease in **basal metabolic rate** (body's consumption of oxygen) occurs gradually, which is related to decrease in the mass of muscle tissue (primarily large oxygen-consuming tissue). Gradual decrease in thyroid hormone is an adjustment to the progressively slower rate at which it is broken down and removed from the blood. The blood level of thyroxine (T4) falls about 15 percent over the adult life span. The blood level of triiodothyronine (T3), the active thyroid hormone, declines only when the person is ill and not eating (124).

↳ Use the above knowledge in assessment or in health teaching with young adults.

Sexuality

Sexual Maturity. Sexual maturity for men is usually reached in the late teens, but their sexual drive remains high through young adulthood. In healthy women, menstruation is well established and regular by this time. Female organs are fully matured; the uterus reaches maximum weight by the age of 30. The woman is well equipped for childbearing; optimal period for reproduction is between 20 and 30 years of age; many of the dangers associated with adolescent pregnancy or pregnancy in the late thirties or early forties are not present. The Leydig cells, source of male hormones, decline in number after the age of 25 (124, 354).

Sexuality *may be defined as a deep, pervasive aspect of the total person, the sum total of one's feelings and behavior as a male or female, the expression of which goes beyond genital response.* Sexuality includes **gender identity,** *the sense of self as male, female, bisexual (feeling comfortable with both sexes), homosexual, or ambivalent (transsexual).* Gender identity also includes **gender role,** *what the person does overtly to indicate to self and others maleness, femaleness, bisexuality, or ambivalence* (416). Throughout the life cycle physiological, emotional, social, and cultural forces condition sexuality. Today's society offers many choices in sexual behavior patterns.

You will encounter three basic values taken by young adults toward sexuality: absolutist, hedonistic, and relativistic. The **absolutistic position** *states that sexuality exists for the purpose of reproduction. The* **hedonistic view** *has pleasure and pursuit as its central value and is interested in ultimate fulfillment of human sexual potentials. The* **relativistic position** *is based on research and has become the basis for the new morality which says that acts should be judged on the basis of their effects.* You will have your private set of values, but you must recognize that others' values may be as valid as yours (13).

During adulthood a number of sexual patterns may exist, ranging from heterosexuality, bisexuality, and homosexuality, to masturbation and abstinence. Few people are totally homosexual or heterosexual; most people feel attracted or sexually responsive at some time to both sexes. Within each of these patterns the person may achieve a full and satisfactory life or be plagued with lack of interest, impotence, or guilt. Young adulthood is the time to reap the rewards or disasters of past sex education. Changes in sexual interest and behavior occur through the life cycle and can be a cause of conflict, unless the partners involved can talk about their feelings, needs, and desires. Many misunderstandings arise because of basic difference between the male and female in sexual response. The more each can learn about the other partner, the greater the chance of working out a compatible relationship for successful courtship, marriage, and intimacy. The person cannot assume that the partner knows his/her wishes or vice versa. Each must declare his/her needs.

▱ **Sexuality Education.** Often the popular literature available for reading promotes misinformation, and you should be prepared to give accurate information. Because people feel freer now to discuss sexual matters, you may be questioned frequently by the person recuperating from an illness, by the man or wife after delivery, or by the healthy young adult who feels dissatisfied with personal knowledge or sexual pattern. Various references provide in-depth information on this subject (26, 70, 122, 124, 173, 193, 199, 229, 240, 251, 253, 338, 344, 359, 407, 430, 452). An organization which offers workshops and publications is AASECT (American Assocation of Sex Educators, Counselors, and Therapists).

▱ The following are facts, based on current research, that you can teach young adults:

1. Sexual mores and norms vary among ethnic groups, socioeconomic classes, and even from couple to couple. Sexual activity that is mutually satisfying to the couple and not harmful to themselves and others is acceptable.
2. Sexual activity varies considerably among people in relation to sex drive, frequency of orgasm, or need for rest following intercourse.
3. The more sexually active person maintains the sex drive longer into later years.
4. The human sexual drive has no greater impact on the total person than any other biological function. Sex is not the prevailing instinct in the human, and physical or mental disease does not result from unmet sexual needs.
5. Erotic dreams that culminate in orgasms occur in 85 percent of all men at any age and commonly in women, increasing in older women.
6. The woman is not inherently passive and the male aggressive. Maximum gratification requires each partner to be both passive and aggressive in participating mutually and cooperatively in sexual intercourse.
7. Women have as strong a sex desire as men, sometimes stronger.
8. Women have greater orgastic capacity than men with regard to duration and frequency of orgasm. The female can have several orgasms within a brief period of time.
9. Female orgasm is normally initiated by clitoral stimulation, but it is a total body response rather than clitoral or vaginal in nature.
10. The woman may need stimulation to the clitoris, other than received during intercourse, to achieve orgasm. Some studies show that a large percentage of women regularly do not have orgasm in sexual intercourse. Overall sexual response is enhanced for the woman when there is warm, loving behavior from the partner before, during, and after intercourse, when foreplay between partners increases arousal, and when she has worked through strict parental admonitions against touching self, enjoying her body, masturbation, or sexual intercourse.
11. Simultaneous orgasm of both partners may be desired but is an unrealistic goal and occurs only under the most ideal circumstances. It does not determine sexual achievement or satisfaction.
12. No physiological reason exists for abstinence during menses since menstrual flow is from the uterus, no tissue damage occurs to the vagina, and the woman's sex drive is not necessarily diminished.
13. No relationship exists between penis size and ability of the man to satisfy the woman, and little correlation exists between penile and body size and sexual potency. However, the woman's reaction to penis size or feelings with penile penetration do affect the man's ability for orgasm and satisfaction.
14. No single most accepted position for sexual activity exists. Any position is correct, normal, healthy, and proper if it satisfies both partners.
15. Achievement of satisfactory sex response is the result of interaction of many physical, emotional, and cultural influences and of the total relationship between the man and woman (20, 70, 171, 253, 359, 430, 452).
16. Making love and having sex are not necessarily the same, although ideally they occur together.

▱ Additionally, you may wish to share the following information. In the normal male, spermatozoa are produced in optimal numbers and motility when ejaculation occurs two or three times weekly. A decreased or increased frequency of ejaculation is associated with decreased number of sperm (452).

▱ Menstruation is a part of sexuality in women. Discomforts and disabilities associated with menstruation may be caused by social, cultural, and emotional factors and hard physical labor, not just by changing hormone levels. Many women learn to react to menstruation as "the curse" and treat it as an illness with medication and bed rest. Different sociocultural backgrounds teach women different responses. Women who strongly identify with traditional sexual roles are more likely to experience menstruation as a disabling illness. Periods of emotional stress, either happy or upsetting, can cause irregular menses (224, 354).

Premenstrual Phenomena. Two periodic cyclic occurrences may occur in the menstrual history: mittelschmerz and premenstrual syndrome.

Mittleschmerz (the German word for middle pain) *is a sharp, brief pain associated with ovulation.* Because a slight fever may accompany this pain, it may be confused with appendicitis until a white blood count is done. Using *mittelschmerz* as a guide for the practice of rhythm is unreliable; pain might be related to flatulence (354).

The **premenstrual syndrome** (**PMS**) *is a group of signs and symptoms occurring about a week premenses and associated with fluid retention:* mild cerebral edema and edema of fingers, feet, thighs, legs, hips, breasts, abdomen, and around the eyes. The following chart shows symptoms and signs, physiologically, as well as emotional reactions that are reported by some women.

Physiological Symptoms and Signs	*Psychological Reactions*
Appetite change, craving salty or sweet foods	Apprehension/anxiety
Acne/hives	Confusion
Abdominal distention	Sadness/depression
Alcohol tolerance lower	Forgetfulness
Breast tenderness	Frequent crying
Clumsiness	Indecisiveness
Constipation	Irritability
Diarrhea	Restlessness
Dizziness	Suspicious
Edema	Tense
Fatigue, need for sleep increases	Withdrawn
Headache/backache	
Menstrual cramps	
Nausea	
Prone to infection	
Sex drive changes	
Thirst	
Weight gain	

✔ Not all these signs and symptoms appear together; they are variable in degree, and they decrease after menses begins (37, 136, 157, 162, 195, 258, 291, 314, 319, 382, 431). Be empathic to the woman who describes these symptoms or feelings. Help the spouse and other family members recognize their significance, the importance of medical treatment, and that their caring and reduced stress may contribute to a decrease in symptomatology.

Estimates are that fewer than 10 percent of women have severe symptoms or disability resulting from mittelschmerz, PMS, or menstruation. (Recent media publicity would lead one to think that all women are incompetent or commit crimes or suicide during this time of the menstrual cycle.) The etiology for either condition is uncertain; there may be several causes. Theories that have been proposed include too little estrogen or too little progesterone. More recent studies show that PMS symptoms may appear because of how neurochemicals and hormones interact with estrogen and progesterone, and these interactions are affected by nutrition and stress. Other factors may be emotional conflicts related to femininity, or other emotional stress (38, 61, 195, 258, 291). Woods found that negative attitudes toward menstruation and a stressful social milieu increases PMS symptoms (451). Regardless of cause, symptoms are not evidence of biological or emotional inferiority. For the majority of women, the menstrual cycle is an ongoing but insignificant part of their lives—one that causes little discomfort (162, 453).

A study by May (258) showed that while some women felt depression as part of PMS, others were at their happiest mood. Sometimes women did not remember feelings, mood, or symptoms during the postmenstrual cycle. May's impression was that there are two common areas of anxiety about menstruation which could be associated with a motivated ignoring of that process and its emotional correlates. The first involves experiencing menstruation as a sign of helplessness, of being controlled by bodily processes in a way that insults one's cherished sense of strength and free will. The second area of anxious response stems from the tendency, rooted in centuries of tradition, to think of menstruation as both dirty and dangerous. This study suggested that these underlying emotional or symbolic relationships, the complex interaction of physiological or psychological events, were involved in menstrual mood.

Golub (136) and Jensen (188) found no consistent relationship between premenstrual mood and cognitive function. The magnitude of the premenstrual mood change was not great enough to affect intellectual functioning.

✔ Treatment for PMS may be symptomatic, with progesterone, diuretics, antidepressants, or other drugs. Some of the time these drugs are not necessary. Dietary measures may also be suggested.

✔ Teach women that the following measures can offset symptoms (151, 162, 314, 319, 335, 382);

1. Consume less caffeine, sugar, alcohol, and salt, especially during the premenstrual period.
2. Eat four to six small meals a day rather than two or three meals, to minimize the risk of hypoglycemia that accompanies PMS.
3. Snack on complex carbohydrates, such as fresh fruits, vegetable sticks, whole wheat crackers, which provide energy without excessive sugar.
4. Drink six to eight glasses of water; it will help prevent fluid retention by flushing excess salt from the body.
5. Limit fat intake, especially in red meats, which

build hormones that cause breast tenderness and fluid retention. Choose dairy products low in fat.
6. Eat more whole grains, nuts, and raw greens, which are high in Vitamin B, magnesium, and potassium, and add Vitamin B₆ and calcium to reduce symptoms.
7. Develop a variety of interests, including maintaining exercise routines, so that focus is not on self and body symptoms during this period.
8. Get extra rest and use relaxation techniques, meditation, and massage. Treat yourself to a relaxing and creative activity.
9. Discuss your feelings with family and friends so that they can be more understanding of your behavior.
10. Join a self-help group to gain other ideas on how to more effectively cope with symptoms.

Brown gives a thorough review of different treatment approaches to primary dysmenorrhea (41). Speroff describes treatment for PMS (382). Treatment is also referred to in Chapter 11.

Ovulation. Share the following information about ovulation, especially to couples who desire natural family planning (199, 251, 407). Ovulation normally occurs in every menstrual cycle but not necessarily midcycle. The ovum is capable of being fertilized for 24 hours postovulation.

The mucous cycle by which to predict ovulation is as follows. It begins with menstruation. The period is usually followed by a few "dry days," variable in number, when no mucus is seen or felt. As the ovum begins to ripen, some mucus is felt at the vaginal opening and can be seen if the woman wipes the vaginal area with toilet tissue. This mucus is generally yellow or white, but definitely opaque and sticky. When the blood estrogen level (derived from the ripening ovum) reaches a critical point, the glands of the cervix respond with a different mucus. This fertile mucus starts out cloudy and is not sticky and becomes very clear, like raw egg white. After ovulation, progesterone causes the abrupt cessation of the clear, slippery, fertile mucus and produces its own mucus, which is sticky, much less preponderant, and sometimes not present at the vagina. Progesterone prepares the uterine lining for the reception of the egg if the egg has been fertilized. Usually the egg is ovulated within 24 hours of the peak of wetness, but this interval may be as long as 48 hours. Although the sticky mucus does not allow a sperm to live very long, the sperm could possibly survive long enough to reach a freshly ovulated egg through a lingering fertile mucous channel. If this method is to be used to avoid pregnancy, there should be abstinence from intercourse from the beginning of the slippery fertile mucus until the height of wetness ("peak day," when there may be so much wetness that mucus is not seen but moisture is noted on the underclothing), *plus a full 72 hours* to assure that the ovum will not be impregnated.

Because the lifetime of the sperm depends on the presence of the fertile mucus, all genital contact between the partners must be avoided. The first drop of semen (the one which escapes before ejaculation) has the highest concentration of sperm. A woman can conceive even if only one drop of semen touches her external genital organ; sperm are powerful, and the mucus is equally potent.

✔ Teach that spotting or bleeding may occur between menses, which may be associated with ovulation, a cervical polyp, postintercourse in the presence of cervicitis, or carcinoma. Any abnormal pattern of bleeding should be investigated by a gynecologist.

✔ ***Human Sexual Response.*** The human sexual response cycle involves physiological reactions, psychological components, and psychosocial influences or behavior. You may be asked to discuss the following information.

The two main physiologic reactions of the cycle are **vasocongestion,** *engorged blood vessels,* and **myotonia,** *increased muscular tension.*

The **four phases of the cycle** *are excitement, plateau, orgasm, and resolution;* the phases vary with each person and from time to time. The **excitement phase** develops from any source of bodily or psychic stimuli, and if adequate stimulation occurs, the intensity of excitement increases rapidly. This phase may be interrupted, prolonged, or ended by distracting stimuli. The **plateau phase** is a consolidation period that follows excitement, during which sexual tension intensifies. **Orgasm** is the climax of sexual tension increase which lasts for a few seconds, during which vasocongestion and myotonia are released through forceful muscle contractions. The **resolution phase** returns the body to the pre-excitement physiology. The woman may begin another cycle immediately if stimulated, but the man is unable to be restimulated for about 30 minutes (253).

Physiological requisites for the human sexual response include (1) an intact circulatory system to provide for vasocongestive responses and (2) an intact central and peripheral nervous system to provide for sensory appreciation and muscular innervation and to support vasocongestive changes (452). For a detailed account of changes that occur in both the genital system organs and other body systems during the four phases of the human sexual response, see references 20, 67, 171, 253, and 452 at the end of this chapter.

✔ You may be asked subtly or directly about *sexual*

activity during pregnancy. Be prepared to share the following information.

Intercourse can continue during pregnancy, although either partner may prefer other intimate behaviors: the woman because of comfort and fear that her appearance may be displeasing to the man and the man because of concern about discomfort to the woman or fetal distress, or because he finds her body less attractive as pregnancy progresses. While infection from intercourse is a possibility during pregnancy, this problem also applies to the nonpregnant state (67). Genital cleanliness is always an important measure in preventing infection. Concern for the partner's well-being is also an important concern. Signs of infection should always be reported early to a physician so that treatment can be given.

Sexual response during and after pregnancy varies slightly from the usual pattern. During orgasm, spasm of the third-trimester uterus may occur for as long as a minute. Fetal heart tones are slowed during this period, but normally no evidence of prolonged fetal distress occurs. Vasocongestion is also increased during sexual activity in genital organs and the breasts. During the resolution phase the vasocongested pelvis is often not completely relieved; as a result, the woman has a continual feeling of sexual stimulation. Residual pelvic vasocongestion and pressure in the pelvis from the second- and third-trimester uterus cause a high level of sexual tension (253).

✔ Teach couples that coital activity is prohibited if there is any threat to fetal viability throughout the pregnancy and during the postpartal period if there is concern about episiotomy breakdown or endometriosis. If there is potential aggravation by the physical nature of coitus with penile penetration, then only that form of sexual activity should be avoided. If the problem is one of potential uterine contractility, then abstinence from all orgasmic sexual activity, including masturbation by the female, should be recommended. If prostaglandins in semen contribute to the problem, the male should wear a condom during intercourse. If the problem is a combination of the above, then all sexual activity with the female is contraindicated; however, sexual activity directed at the male may continue (67).

✔ Couples should always receive specific instruction about continuing sexual intercourse during the last month of pregnancy, depending on the condition of the woman.

✔ Teach couples that such orogenital sexual activity as blowing air into the vagina should be avoided during pregnancy and for at least 6 weeks postpartum. Inflation of air into the vagina may cause air embolism; death has occurred in minutes after air is blown into the vagina. (Air embolism is also the reason that douching is avoided during pregnancy and postdelivery) (67). By the fourth or fifth week postpartum, sexual tensions are similar to nonpregnant levels, but physiologically the woman has not returned to the nonpregnant state. By the third postpartum month, physiological status has returned to prepregnancy levels (253).

✔ *Sexual Dysfunctions.* Sexual dysfunctions affect both the male and female for various reasons. Several references provide additional information on sexual dysfunctions (173, 229, 240, 253, 281, 430, 450, 452). Your education and referral can assist couples in obtaining effective diagnosis and treatment.

Female Circumcision. Such procedures may be appalling to you, but it is a widespread culturally and religiously based practice in some parts of the world, such as some countries in the Middle East, Africa, Indonesia, and Malay. The circumcision may occur the eighth day after birth, the tenth day after birth, at age 3 or 4 years, or at 8 or 10 years as part of prepuberty rites to womanhood. You may care for circumcised women, especially in maternity and gynecological services, who have migrated to this country. There are several types of circumcisions, classified on the basis of severity. All types of this practice are likely to be followed by a variety of complications. Initially, there is shock, hemorrhage, sepsis, and lacerations to surrounding tissue. Shortly thereafter retention of urine and tetanus may occur. Dysmenorrhea, urinary tract infections, pelvic inflammatory disease, and infertility are common. After marriage, painful intercourse, forceful cutting of the circumcision scar, perineal lacerations, infections, hemorrhage, frigidity, and severe anxiety occur. During childbirth, the scar tissue must be cut during the second stage of labor, or mother and baby may die because of obstruction to delivery, sepsis, or hemorrhage (364).

In most countries where female circumcision occurs, it is a way to control women sexually, economically, and religiously and to control the heritage line and inheritance. The tradition is practiced among Christians, Muslims, and Jews in some parts of Africa (364).

Some nurses in Kenya report their efforts to stop this practice. They report that Western approaches will not work in eliminating this problem because the practice is so traditional. It is accepted by women because in countries where it is practiced, the uncircumcised woman would not be considered for marriage. These nurses report that, as the population becomes generally better educated, traditional practices, including circumcision, decline. Thus, the nurses are heavily committed to promoting general and health education, so that a better educated population will pass legislation prohibiting the practice.

▸ When you care for women from the non-Western part of the world, assess for circumcision and its effects; be nonjudgmental to the woman. Focus on care that will prevent further complications. Help her gain understanding why this practice may be harmful to her daughter(s). Since the male is the decision maker in these cultures, you will have to establish a working relationship with him if any changes are to be made for the female children. Be aware that female circumcision may be being practiced in this country, outside of the traditional health-care system. You may encounter the woman postcircumcision in the emergency room, the maternity service, the clinic, or the home. Work through your own feelings with a supervisor or counselor. This woman needs a sensitive caretaker. Refer to the article by Shaw for greater detail in the maternity care needed by circumcised women (364).

▸ *Personal Attitudes.* To incorporate human sexuality into nursing practice, you must accept your own sexuality and understand sexuality as a significant aspect of development. Then you can acknowledge the concerns of the patients/clients, recognize your strengths and limits in working with people who have sexual concerns, help these people cope with threats to sexuality, and counsel, inform, or refer as indicated.

▸ Supporting, caring, and nurturing are nursing behaviors. But at times you will have other feelings and may feel guilty about being sexually attracted to (or repulsed by) a patient/client. These are honest feelings to be acknowledged. After all, every thought and behavior will not result in intimacy or rejection. Feeling positively toward someone can help you give effective care. If you have negative feelings about someone, you can deal with these feelings if you can recognize the possible reasons for your feelings. If necessary, someone else can be assigned to the person. Actually, when you begin to understand another person, most likely you will find that person interesting, even if that person might not be an individual you would choose for a friend. When someone is perceived as unique and interesting, it becomes easier to give effective care and form a relationship.

▸ If a patient expresses sexual behavior by brushing against you, trying to feel breasts or hips or referring to sexual topics in conversation, it may be best to ignore the behavior unless it persists. Recognize the behavior as an energy outlet or as a way to validate himself or herself as a person. If the patient is observed masturbating, do not make a joke of this discovery. Realize that this is an acceptable sexual release and provide privacy (452). However, if a patient becomes obnoxious either in words or actions, you will have to tell him/her what behavior is appropriate in the particular situation.

▸ *Sexual History.* If you feel comfortable, and if there is sufficient rapport between you and the client, take a sexual history, especially with patients/clients who have conditions that interfere with sexual activity. Follow these guidelines when you are taking a sexual history:

1. Ensure privacy and establish confidentiality of statements.
2. Progress from topics that are easy to discuss to those that are more difficult to discuss.
3. Ask the person about how he or she acquired sexual information before asking about sexual experience.
4. Precede questions by informational statements about the generality of the experience, when appropriate, to reassure the person and reduce anxiety, shame, and evasiveness.
5. Observe nonverbal behavior while you listen to the person's statements.
6. Do not ask questions just to satisfy your curiosity.

▸ Topics to include in the sexual history are:

1. How sex education was obtained.
2. Accuracy of sex education.
3. Menstrual history if female or nocturnal emission history if male.
4. Past and present ideas on self as a sexual being, including ideas on body image, masturbation, coitus, childbirth, parenting.
5. Attitudes of marital versus nonmarital sexual experiences.
6. Sexual dreams and fantasies.
7. Ability to communicate sexual needs and desires.
8. Partner's (if one exists) sexual values and behavior.

▸ If necessary, use several interviews to obtain information, and be sure to include any specific questions or concerns that the person voices. Respect the person's desire not to talk about sexual matters and moral, religious, or aesthetic convictions. Know the terminology and have a nonjudgmental attitude when the person talks about sexuality concerns. Your matter-of-fact attitude helps the adult to feel less embarrassed. Be aware of how illness and drugs can affect sexual function. Do not assume that chronic or disabling disease or mutilating surgery ends the person's sexual life.

▸ Give accurate information and counseling when the person or family asks questions or indicates concerns. You may wish to prepare instructional units (244) for a specific teaching plan to share with patients with various conditions, especially chronic diseases, and with their families to help them better understand how to meet sexual needs (240, 430). Give gentle encouragement related to pursuit of sexual activity rather than personal advice or judgment. Know community resources for consultation or referral when necessary.

References at the end of the chapter will also be helpful on how to work with rape victims (26, 48, 184, 278, 383, 440).

Nutrition

As the nutrition of childhood set the stage for the health of the young adult, so now the stage is being set for health in middle and old age. Growth is essentially finished by young adulthood. Activity level may stabilize or diminish. Caloric intake should be based on occupation, amount of physical activity or mental effort, emotional state, age, body size, climate, individual metabolism, and presence of disease. (A calorie or kilocalorie is a unit of measure of the amount of energy required to raise 1 kg of water 1 degree Centigrade.) Women have a 5 to 10 percent lower metabolism than men of comparable height and weight; thus, in the healthy, nonpregnant state, women need lower caloric intake. The greater the body surface, the higher the basal metabolism rate. However, the obese person requires fewer calories for size because adipose tissue consumes less oxygen than muscles; thus, less energy is expended comparatively. Table 12–1 shows calorie expenditure for activity (445):

✔ *Nutrition Assessment.* Incorporate nutritional status into nursing assessment and the health history. Ask questions related to the following list to guide your assessment with the person/family (312, 445):

1. Knowledge of nutrients, food groups, balanced diet, and their relationship to health.
2. Knowledge of nutrient requirements at present level of growth and development and whether nutrient needs are being met.
3. Associations with food and how they influence food and eating patterns.
4. What increases or decreases appetite.
5. Cultural background, including religious beliefs, ethnic patterns, and geographic area, and how these beliefs influence food intake and likes and dislikes.
6. Relationship of lifestyle and activity to food intake.
7. Income level and food buying power; influence of income on dietary habits.
8. Knowledge of alternatives to high-cost foods.
9. Usual daily pattern of intake: times of day, types, amounts.
10. Which is main meal of day.
11. Eating environment.
12. Special diet requirements.
13. Food allergies.
14. Relationship of eating patterns of family or significant others to individual's habits and patterns.
15. Medications and methods used to aid digestion and nutrition intake; influence of other medications on nutritional intake.
16. Condition of teeth and chewing ability.
17. Use, condition, and fit of dentures.
18. Types of food individual has difficulty chewing or swallowing.
19. Condition of oral cavity and structures.
20. Disabilities that interfere with nutritional intake.
21. Assistance or special devices needed for feeding.

Owen, Lanna, and Owen provide in-depth information on nutritional assessment (299). Schweiger, Lang, and Schweiger give a descriptive and pictorial assessment guide for the oral cavity, which can be included in a nutritional assessment as well as at other

TABLE 12–1. Kilocalorie/Hour Energy Expenditure for Activity

	TYPE OF ACTIVITY				
	Sedentary: Sitting, working on leisurely activity with little arm movement	**Light:** House or office work, sitting and standing, some arm movement	**Moderate:** Housecleaning, gardening, laundry, carpentry, walking moderately fast, vigorous arm movement with sitting activity	**Vigorous:** Heavy housecleaning, walking fast, golfing, bowling	**Strenuous:** Swimming, athletic games, running, dancing, skiing.
Males	100	160	240	350	Over 350
Females	80	110	170	250	Over 350

TABLE 12–2. Recommended Number of Servings from Each Food Group

FOOD GROUP	YOUNG ADULT	PREGNANT WOMAN	LACTATING WOMAN
Milk and Milk Products	2 or more cups	3 or 4 cups	4 or more cups
Meat, Fish, or Protein Equivalent	2 (2 to 3 oz) servings	3 (2 to 3 oz) servings	3 to 4 (2 to 3 oz) servings
Fruits and Vegetables (including a high vitamin C source)	4 (½ cup) servings	4 to 5 (½ cup) servings	4 to 5 (½ cup) servings
Grain, Bread, and Cereals	4 servings	4 or more servings	4 or more servings

times of nursing care (355). Other references also give guidelines for oral assessment (268).

Normal Nutrition. Table 12–2 lists the recommended daily number of servings for each food group for young adults and pregnant and lactating women (183, 416, 445). Appendix III shows the requirements for vitamins and minerals, comparing adults to children (183, 192, 416, 445). Appendix IV lists the functions and sources of the various nutrients (86, 192, 416, 445). Refer to these nutrition references (74, 124, 163, 173, 183, 192, 299, 312, 326, 354, 387, 445) and to *Mosby's Medical and Nursing Dictionary* (416) for additional information.

Theoretically, a man between the ages of 25 and 45, living in the United States, under the usual environmental stresses, and who weighs 154 pounds (40 kg) and is 69 inches (172 cm) tall will consume approximately 2700 *calories* daily to maintain nutritional status and weight; 56 grams of his food should be *protein*.

A woman between the ages of 25 and 45, living in the United States, under the usual environmental stresses, and who weighs 128 pounds (58.2 kg) and is 65 inches (162 cm) tall will consume approximately 2000 *calories* daily to maintain nutritional status and weight; 45 to 65 grams of her food should be *protein*. That same woman when *pregnant* should increase her calories by at least 300 daily and her protein by 30 grams. Weight gain during pregnancy should be 22 to 27 pounds. Rigid calorie restriction may be dangerous (397). When *lactating*, her calorie intake should increase by 500, her protein intake by 30 grams, and calcium intake should be 1200 mg for optimal health. Refer to Chapter 6 for additional information.

Nutrition-Disease Relationships. Although overt clinical symptoms of *vitamin or mineral deficiencies* are seldom observed in most Americans, you will see individuals and families in whom you suspect inadequate nutrition. Pallor; listlessness; brittle, dull nails and hair; dental caries; complaints of constipation and poor resistance to common infections; and over- or underweight suggest a need for a complete diet history (445).

Laboratory evaluations of blood and urine supply meaningful information for a nutritional assessment. Hemoglobin, hematocrit, serum proteins and lipids (including cholesterol), glucose, sodium, and potassium levels are all important diagnostic tools.

One glaring deficiency you may find, however, is the lack of iron in women. Approximately one-third of all women between the ages of 10 and 55 are anemic and receive only one-third of their daily iron requirement. The male can suffice with 10 milligrams of iron daily, but the female needs 18 milligrams (283, 445).

Your assistance will be sought when dietary problems occur during early pregnancy, usually from the transitory nausea and vomiting, commonly called *morning sickness*. Physiological and psychological factors contribute to this condition. Small frequent meals of fairly dry, easily digested energy foods, such as carbohydrates, are usually tolerated. Separating intake of liquids and solids and drinking flavored or carbonated beverages instead of plain water may also help. Constipation resulting from pressure of the expanding uterus on the lower portion of the intestine occurs in later pregnancy. Increased fluid intake and use of dried fruits, fresh fruits and juices, and whole-grain cereals should induce regularity of elimination. Laxatives should be avoided unless prescribed by a physician.

Americans have a vast array of food from which to pick, yet malnutrition may result from being overfed but undernourished. Additionally, *six of the ten leading causes of death in the United States are connected to eating habits.* These are heart disease, cancer, stroke and hypertension, diabetes, arteriosclerosis, and cirrhosis of the liver. Formerly thought of as middle-aged diseases, some of these diseases are taking the lives of young adults.

Essentially, Americans have shifted from a diet of fruits, vegetables, and grains to one based on fats and sugar. The result is a big drop in vitamin and mineral intake. Americans have also moved from brown to white, that is, white bread, sugar, and rice instead of their brown counterparts. Television is advertising heavily in the sugar, fat, and salt areas. Young adult working wives, as well as singles, are not spending time in the kitchen. Instead, they are paying the higher prices for the instant, less nutritious foods. In fact, some young adults have grown up on the junk food they have seen advertised on television and on the ever growing "instant" dinners prepared by their parents or bought at the fast-food restaurants.

✔ Because of the claim that saturated fat and cholesterol are related to cardiovascular disease, some manufacturers have responded with low-cholesterol and polyunsaturated products. (Contrasting research shows that some African tribes consume enormous amounts of animal fats but rarely show signs of coronary disease [246], but the African tribal lifestyle differs drastically from that of the American lifestyle.) In American society you can be helpful in recommending that young adults steer away from too much sugar, an abundance of animal products and red meats, and a steady diet of foods in which there are additives and preservatives (especially nitrates and nitrites) (445).

✔ Other diseases thought to be related to diet are diverticular disease of the colon and colon cancer, appendicitis, hiatus hernia, hemorrhoids, and varicose veins, again diseases affecting young adults. One theory relates these diseases to lack of fiber in the diet. Fiber (found mainly in plant foods) increases stool weight and transit time. Pressure is thus relieved all along the gastrointestinal tract, so that these problems are not so likely to arise. Possibly potential carcinogens formed in the gastrointestinal tract do not have a chance to develop to the harmful level (124, 354, 445). You can suggest an increase in fiber through eating bran or other foods (whole wheat bread, whole grain cereals, raw fruits or vegetables) so that young adults can cut down on disease proneness as well as improve their elimination pattern.

Obesity. This is a persistent problem, is usually related to restricted activity, psychological and body-image problems, worry, diabetes, hypertension, cardiovascular disease, pain, and premature mortality (386). However, overweight people in Laffrey's study perceived themselves to be as healthy as their normal weight peers (212). Often the active adolescent becomes the sedentary young adult but does not lower caloric intake. Thus more calories are eaten than are needed for energy. In an attempt to lose weight, the young adult may try a variety of approaches.

✔ You can help dieters by insisting that any special diet must be analyzed for its nutritional value and overall effect on the body (312). Additionally, you might suggest a group approach and behavior modification techniques. Many people can lose weight, but they gain it back as soon as they abandon their diets. Often an increase in exercise is recommended, rather than a continual decrease in calories, for the following reasons:

1. Appetite is decreased following exercise because of lowered blood supply to the gastrointestinal tract.
2. Exercise may decrease tension and stress, resulting in less frequent eating for nonnutritive purposes.
3. Adequate energy or caloric intake is necessary for efficient utilization of protein for growth and tissue maintenance.
4. Basal metabolism decreases after a period of caloric restriction.
5. Caloric restriction combined with mild exercise can result in greater fat loss and reduced loss of lean body mass than caloric restriction alone.
6. Nutritional adequacy of diets low in energy value (less than 1800 to 2000 kcal) is questioned since many of the essential nutrients, especially minerals, are found in relatively low concentrations in foods.

Generally, a low potency vitamin–mineral supplement is recommended for persons on caloric-restricted diets (163). Refer also to the article by Mahan (244) for a summary of treatments for the obese person.

Vegetarianism. In contrast to the obese person, the vegetarian is seldom obese. Vegetarianism has grown popular with young adults over the last decade, but it is not new. Certain religious groups, for example, the Seventh-Day Adventists, have been effectively practicing a form of vegetarianism for years. In addition to religious reasons, people are vegetarians for moral reasons—they are opposed to killing animals for food; for economic reasons—they cannot afford animal protein; and for health reasons—they may believe that a significant amount of animal food is detrimental or that a large amount of plant food is beneficial. Young adults probably fall mainly into the last category.

People who consider themselves vegetarians range from those who eat limited amounts of meat, milk products, or fish and animal products to vegetarians who eat only vegetables, fruits, legumes, nuts, and grains. Ovovegetarians consume eggs and lacto-vegetarians consume milk products in addition to plant foods.

Depending upon the extent of the vegetarian's dietary restrictions, certain precautions must be taken to maintain an adequate intake of required nutrients (445). If animal proteins, eggs, or milk are inadequate in the diet, the person may need supplementary calcium, iron, and Vitamins B_2 and B_{12}. Soy milk fortified with Vitamin D can supply that vitamin. Iron supplements may be needed even if enriched grain products are used. If caloric and protein intake is minimal, serum albumin and total serum protein may be low (445).

Eight amino acids are essential nutrients that must be obtained daily in the diet: isoleucene, tryptophane, theonine, leucine, lysine, methionine, valene, and phenylalanine. Cystine and tyrosine are quasi-essential. In addition, infants must have arginine and histidine. The bioavailability of protein depends on proper balance of essential amino acids. Dietary deficiency of any substance may enhance our vulnerability to herpes, anxiety, overeating, high blood pressure, as well as insomnia, and other disorders. There is increasing evidence that specific amino acids play important roles in central nervous system function and, therefore, behavior. Some medical disorders, such as a few of the many types of schizophrenia, may be helped through dietary manipulations of amino acids (306, 416, 445).

A wide variety of legumes, grain, nuts, seeds, vegetables, milk, and eggs can supply adequate amounts of required nutrients. Although the proteins in these foods are considered incomplete (in contrast to the complete proteins—meat, fish, poultry, and dairy products—which contain all essential amino acids) certain proteins complement each other when eaten together (216, 306). For example, peanut butter or chili beans (high in lysine but low in methionine) can be served with whole wheat bread or corn bread (low in lysine but high in methionine). Other complementary combinations are:

- beans—wheat in baked beans/brown bread
- lentil—rice in soup
- beans—rice in casserole
- peas—rye in split pea soup and rye bread

Further, amino acids in milk products and eggs complement plant proteins. Such combinations are:

- cereals—milk in breakfast cereal with milk
- pasta—cheese in macaroni and cheese; pizza
- bread—cheese in cheese sandwich
- rice—milk in rice cooked in milk instead of water
- bread—egg in poached egg on toast
- peanuts—milk in peanut butter sandwich and yogurt (306).

Pure vegetarians who consume no milk and no eggs will need Vitamin B_{12} supplements. A helpful guide in complementing proteins can be found in *Diet for a Small Planet* (216) and other references (306, 445).

✔ **Nutrition Education.** You may be able to advise young adults about nutrition in a variety of settings. Even though this is a "I'll-do-it-my-way culture," you will find that young adults will question you about various diets, the value of vitamin supplements, and the value of certain foods. Keep in mind the Basic 4 as you suggest a diet pattern and adjust your information to the vegetarians or those who have allergies or specific ethnic or cultural preferences. These suggestions, if followed, will contribute to nutritional health:

1. Increase consumption of fruits, vegetables, and whole grains.
2. Decrease consumption of foods or beverages high in refined sugars. Instead, drink more water and fruit juices.
3. Do not add salt to foods during cooking or at the table and avoid snack foods with visible salt or foods prepared in brine. Instead use herbs, spices, and lemon for seasoning.
4. Decrease consumption of foods high in total fat and animal fat, and partially replace saturated fats (beef, pork, butter, fatty meats) whether obtained from animal or vegetable sources, with polyunsaturated fats (fish, poultry, veal, lean meats, margarine, vegetable sources).
5. Substitute low-fat and nonfat milk for whole milk, and low-fat dairy products for high-fat products, except for young children.
6. Reduce use of luncheon or variety meats (sausage, salami).
7. Use skim or low-fat milk and cheeses instead of whole milk and cream.
8. Avoid deep fat frying; use baking, boiling, broiling, roasting, or stewing, which help remove fat.
9. Avoid excessive intake of any nutrient or food since excess consumption of, and in turn deficiency of, any substance can contribute to disease (173, 312, 326, 445).
10. Avoid more than a minimal intake of alcohol.

Owen, Lanna, and Owen also give in-depth guidelines for teaching and counseling people about diet and nutrition supplements (299).

✔ Suggest that young adults take vitamins and mineral supplements only with a practitioner's sanction and after a complete blood and urine analysis has been done. Suggest that exercise is as important as food intake when considering the number of calories needed. Suggest exercise not only to burn off calories but to maintain muscle tone, elimination, circulation, to regulate sleep, and to release tension.

✔ Keep in mind the young adult who may need suggestions on economical but nutritious foods. Using powdered skim milk, less expensive cuts of meat, and home cooked cereals does not sacrifice nutrition, but it does save money.

✔ Teach about the need for fiber in the diet which can prevent constipation, and helps reduce the incidence of cancer of the colon, diverticulosis, appendicitis, gallstones, and heart disease. However, having only one source of fiber, such as bran, while excluding the fiber from vegetables and fruits, can produce problems. Some fibers will contribute to constipation if they are not diluted with substantial amounts of water (112, 124, 445).

✔ Teach about the adverse effects of caffeine. Effects of caffeine can be detrimental to health. Hallal (147) and other authors describe sources and effects of caffeine. Warn also that the herbal teas may contain strong drugs which can cause severe problems. Those containing catnip, juniper, hydrangea, jimson weed, lobelia, nutmeg, and wormwood can be toxic to the central nervous system and can cause severe reactions, including hallucinations. People with allergies should stay away from teas like camomile, goldenrod, marigold, and yarrow. Also, be aware that some herbal teas have as much as twice the caffeine as a regular cup of coffee (112).

✔ Hospitalized young adults may be suffering from nutritional deficiencies resulting from a specific diet. Also be aware that hospital-induced malnutrition exists. Patients whose meals are withheld because they are undergoing various diagnostic tests or treatments, especially over a long period of time, are candidates for this problem.

Biological Rhythms

Rhythms occur throughout the life cycle of each individual. From the time of birth, different body structures and functions develop rhythmicity at different rates. By the time the individual reaches young adulthood, biological rhythms are established. **Biological rhythms** are *self-sustaining, repetitive, rhythmic patterns found in plants, animals, and man*. The rhythms are found throughout our external and internal environment and can be exogenous or endogenous.

Exogenous rhythms *depend on the rhythm of external environmental events*, such as seasonal variations, lunar revolution, or night-and-day cycle, which function as time givers. These events help to synchronize internal rhythms with external environmental stimuli and establish an internal time pattern or biological clock.

Endogenous rhythms arise *within the organism,* such as sleep–wake and sleep–dream cycles. Endogenous and exogenous rhythms are usually synchronized. Many internal rhythms do not readily alter their repetitive patterns, however, even when the external stimuli are removed. For instance, when a person shifts to sleeping by day and waking at night, as frequently happens with nurses, a transient or temporary desynchronization occurs. Body temperature and adrenal hormone levels are usually low during the sleep cycle. With the shift in sleep and walking, the person is awake and making demands on the body during the usual sleep period. Three weeks may be needed before internal rhythms adapt to shift. A similar period of desynchronization occurs when a person makes a flight crossing time zones (18, 283).

Within any 24-hour period, physiological and psychological functions reach maximum and minimum limits. When a physiological function approaches a high or low limit, the body's feedback mechanisms attempt to counterregulate the action. *This form of endogenous rhythm that reoccurs in a cyclic pattern within a 20- to 28-hour period is a* **circadian rhythm**. Body temperature, blood pressure, urine production, and hormone, blood sugar, hemoglobin, and amino acid levels demonstrate this rhythmic pattern. Similar variations or rhythms in the levels of alertness, fatigue, tenseness, and irritability can also be demonstrated.

In humans mental efficiency and performance appear to be related to the rhythms of body temperature and catecholamine excretion in the adult. The body temperature rises and drops by approximately 2 degrees over each 24-hour period. The body temperature begins to decline about 10 P.M., is lowest on awaking, gradually rises during the morning, levels off in the afternoon, and then drops again in the evening. The level of adrenocortical hormone secretion appears correlated with body temperature rhythms and the individual's state of alertness and wakefulness. The level of adrenocortical hormones rises early in the morning, peaks around the time we typically awaken, and then drops to a low point by late evening (110, 167, 441). Usually the best mental and physical performances coincide with peak temperature and the least desirable performances tend to coincide with intervals of lowest body temperature. In addition, studies have shown that the lowest excretory rates of epinephrine in day-active people correlate with the time of maximum fatigue and poorest performance (399, 441).

Studies have also shown that the daytime performance on verbal and spatial matching tasks does not remain constant but fluctuates cyclically within a 90- to 100-minute period. When performance improves in one task, the individual's skill decreases in another (117). Researchers have theorized that many disasters were the result of failure to consider human biology. For example, at the nuclear accident at Three Mile Island, the three young men in the control area worked on a shift system called slow rotation—days for a week, evenings for a week, and late nights for a week. Such a rotation causes a desynchronization of circadian rhythms that alters performance levels. The President's investigating commission stated that during the first 2 hours of the accident the operators ignored and failed to recognize the significance of several items that should have warned them that they had an open valve and an accident related to loss of coolant (67).

Circadian Rhythms in Illness. There is an interrelationship between circadian rhythms and mental or physical illness. The pattern of living taught by the culture also affects body rhythms. A few examples of how circadian rhythms influence the health of young adults are presented next. (For more extensive discussion, refer to references (46, 47, 49, 50, 57, 110, 189, 273, 320, 341, 425, 441).

Diagnostic cues are influenced by biological rhythms. Observing the integration of the body's rhythms (or lack of such integration) can be used to determine the person's health status. Diagnosis and treatment of some illnesses can be determined from the study of circadian rhythms or biological time. In some instances, the illness alters the pattern of circadian rhythm. Other illnesses show exaggerated or decreased symptoms at a particular biological time. Blood pressure and temperature values, laboratory findings, and biopsy specimens for cell study differ according to the biological time of day. For instance, growth hormone levels in the blood are highest during the night hours; therefore routine blood values taken at 8 A.M. will not give a total picture. The percentage of red blood cells drops about 4½ percent late at night; a decrease in red blood cells of 5 percent prompts blood transfusions in some hospitals. Ambiguous laboratory findings, the need for repeated medical tests, and the potential for unnecessary medical therapies can be avoided if the person's normal biological rhythms are considered first.

Rhythmic time cycles appear to influence many aspects of human life. Births and deaths occur more frequently at night and during the early morning. Persons with ulcers and allergies suffer more in the spring; allergic responses, including asthmatic attacks, occur more frequently at night and in the early morning hours. There are certain yearly peaks in the number of suicides, psychotic episodes, and accidents. Eventually knowledge about circadian rhythms and biological time may serve as a major tool in preventive health programs.

Depression may be directly related to biological rhythms of depressed people. Altered biochemical rhythms, diurnal (daytime) mood swings, and altered sleep cycles have been noted. Researchers have hypothesized that abnormalities of sleep patterns in some types of depression are due to abnormal internal phase relationships of circadian rhythms. The circadian rhythm of REM sleep may occur abnormally early (225, 441). Depressed persons usually experience insomnia or periods of predawn wakefulness. Their sleep cycles are shortened and fragmented and they are easily disturbed by environmental changes. Successful treatment frequently comes in the form of antidepressant drugs that slow biological clocks (that is, lithium carbonate) or speed biological clocks (that is, imipramine) (320, 421).

Various mental functions and the emotion, behaviors, and autonomic responses associated with them depend on certain chemicals secreted at the synapses of the neurons in specific pathways of the brain. Several brain neurotransmitters (norepinephrine, dopamine, serotonin, and acetylcholine) undergo cyclic changes in amount of chemical present. These fluctuations are thought to be related to factors concerned with periodicity and emotion (225, 274, 399, 441).

Cells in almost every tissue of our body divide or reproduce in a circadian rhythm. Normal cells show intervals of accelerated reproductive activity. In human beings, for example, skin and liver cells are more active at night. Cancer cells do not reproduce at the same rate as normal cells; abnormal mitosis (cell-reproduction) rhythms and, in many instances, a complete lack of circadian rhythms have been reported.

Research suggests that people who are desynchronized or constantly consuming foods and drugs that change the phase of their circadian rhythms may be a high risk group for cancer (32, 320, 441). Health teaching should include the need to decrease the intake of coffee, tea, and certain barbiturates that may be carcinogens.

Adrenal hormone production in man is cyclic. The blood and urine concentrations of adrenocorticosteroid hormones in persons on schedules of diurnal activity and nocturnal sleep drop at night and rise to highest levels in early morning. The course of the adrenal cycle may also be followed by measuring the eosinophil (white blood cell) level; eosinophils decrease as the blood level of adrenal hormones increases.

Light is probably the synchronizer of the adrenocorticosteroid rhythm. This factor has implications for people who are night workers or who have varying degrees of blindness. Because adrenal hormones control other circadian rhythms within the body, knowledge of their cycle is important in the study and treatment of numerous conditions.

Low blood levels of adrenal hormones affect the nervous system and cause a person to be more sensitive to sounds, tastes, and smell. Sensory acuity reaches its maximum at the time of lowest steroid levels. A sudden drop in acuity occurs in the early morning as steroid levels begin to rise. A person is therefore better able to detect taste, smell, or sound at the end of the day. Daily fatigue from lack of sleep and neurologically related symptoms associated with adrenal insufficiency (Addison's disease) may be related to low levels of adrenal hormones.

Adrenal rhythm is also important in handling certain allergies. Sensitivity to histamine follows a circadian rhythm: it peaks about the time of evening or night when adrenocorticosteroids are reaching their lowest levels. Nasal congestion from hayfever, skin reactions from drug sensitivity, and breathing crises in asthma patients occur more frequently during the evening or night. Suggest to individuals with hayfever and asthma that they do their gardening and weeding in the morning when their adrenocorticosteroid levels are at their highest.

Nursing Assessment and Intervention. Nursing care should be planned with biological rhythms in mind. Because our cyclic functioning is synchronized with environmental stimuli, physiological disequilibrium occurs whenever we are confronted with environmental or schedule changes. Transient desynchronization may occur whenever a person is exposed to the hospital or nursing home stimuli. New noise levels; lighting patterns; schedules for eating, sleeping, and personal hygiene; and unfamiliar persons intruding on the person's privacy may all contribute to this desynchronization. Disturbed mental and physical well-being and increased subjective fatigue reflect the conflict between the internal time pattern and external events. Several days are usually required before the person adapts to the environment and thereby regains synchronization—normal biological rhythms.

✔ You can control some external factors, such as meals, baths, and various tests, make them more nearly similar to the patient's normal (outside) routine, and lessen the stress to which the patient is subjected. Obtaining and using a nursing history is one method of lessening this stress.

✔ Your *nursing history* should be directed at getting information about the patient's pre-illness or prehospital patterns for sleep, rest, food and fluid intake, elimination, and personal hygiene. Questions such as, Do you consider yourself a "day" person or a "night" person? Do you feel cheerful when you first wake up? What time of day do you feel most alert? What hours do you prefer to work? Why do you prefer these hours? How do you feel when something causes you to change your routine?, will provide you information about the patient's daily patterns (3, 185, 311). Once this information has been obtained, nursing actions can be initiated that support these established patterns and possibly prevent total disruption of body rhythms during hospitalization.

✔ After the patient has been hospitalized for a few days, certain objective data are available that will assist you in determining a rough estimate of the person's circadian patterns. The routine graphic record supplies information about the patient's vital signs. Using this source, you might be able to identify peaks and lows in blood pressure, pulse, or temperature curves. Also, an intake and output record that shows both the time and the amount voided will aid in determining the patient's daily urinary–excretory pattern. In addition to the postadmission nursing history, a daily log of sleep and waking hours, meal times, hunger periods, voiding and defecation patterns, diurnal moods, and other circadian rhythms recorded for 28 days prior to hospitalization can help determine the person's cyclic patterns. Diagnostic tests and certain forms of medical and nursing therapy can then be appropriately prescribed by using the person's own baseline rhythms measurements. Determination of each patient's rhythms before, during, and after hospitalization or illness will eventually be possible when more simplified, economic, and accurate measurement devices are available.

✔ The patient's/client's *medication schedule* can also reflect your understanding of biological rhythms. Drug effectiveness can be altered by the time of day that the particular drug is administered. Aspirin administered at 7 A.M. will remain 22 hours in the body; aspirin admitted at 7 P.M. will last 17 hours. Some antihistamines last only 6 to 8 hours if taken at night but are effective 15 to 17 hours when taken at 7 A.M. Digitalis (a cardiac glycoside) is several times more effective when administered in the early morning than when administered at other times. The dosage of analgesics needed to relieve pain during the evening or dark hours is more than that needed during the daytime. Sensitivity to pain increases in the evening (320, 415, 441).

✔ One area of **chronopharmacology** (*study of cellular rhythms in relationship to drug therapy*) that has been researched extensively is the relationship of adrenocortical function and corticosteroid drug administration. The secretion of corticosteroids by the adrenal cortex has a 24-hour rhythm, with the highest corticosteroid values expected after the usual time of awakening. When corticosteroids are administered either daily or on alternate days, adrenal suppression and possibly growth disturbance can be minimized by timing to the circadian crest in adrenocortical function. Morning doses of prednisolone (a glucocorticoid) are less likely to cause alterations in the rhythmic pattern of urinary excretion than twice-daily divided doses or a single dose in the late evening (320, 377).

✔ Circadian rhythms are also important factors in determining drug toxicity. A distinct 24-hour rhythm of vulnerability or resistance to drugs has been identified. Before setting a drug's toxic level, both the person's biological clock and the drug dosage must be considered. At present, problems exist in determining toxicity levels. Federal research guidelines do not consider the circadian rhythms of the animals being tested. Noctural animals are tested in the daytime; animals are tested before they have had time to adjust to a new laboratory environment; animals are tested in light and dark cycles that are not regulated; and animals whose feeding schedules are not fixed and recorded are tested. All these factors can cause altered rhythms in animals and altered vulnerability or resistance to the drug being tested (167, 320).

✔ Without the aid of suitable measurement devices, it is impossible to determine a person's biological clock. Drug administration is therefore usually based on other factors. Most medications are given before or after meals, at bedtime, or at the convenience of the nursing personnel and patients. In the future, as knowledge of the internal clock increases, you, the nurse, will find yourself altering drug administration times to suit the person's biological time. Perhaps you will be in charge of a master computer that, after analyzing information about each person's biological clock, will send the appropriate medication dose at the appropriate time.

✔ *Vital signs routine* should be based on circadian rhythm patterns rather than tradition or convenience of the agency staff. A person's internal and skin temperature each shows a systematic rise and fall over a 24-hour period, a cycle difficult to alter in normal adults. Body temperature usually peaks between 4 P.M. and 6 P.M. and reaches its lowest point around 4 A.M. in people who are active by day and sleep by night. When the internal temperature is normally peaking, other body functions, such as pulse rate, blood pressure, and cardiac output (volume of blood pumped by the heart), are also changing. Pulse rate is high when the temperature is highest and drops during the night. The human heart rate will vary as much as 20 or 30 beats per minute in 24 hours. Blood pressure shows a marked fall during the first hour of sleep, followed by a gradual rise during the remaining time, with a peak between 5 and 7 P.M. Cardiac output reaches minimum levels between 2 and 4 A.M., the period of lowest temperature findings (118, 167, 341, 425, 441).

✔ *Work Schedules.* These should be developed with biological rhythms in mind. You can also establish your own circadian patterns to help you to gain insight into physical feelings and behaviors. You can use this information to plan your days to advantage. You might choose to cope with the most difficult patient assignment during the time of peak mental and physical performance, for example.

Nurses as well as many industrial and law-enforcement personnel are frequently required to change shifts every week or month. Night and rotating shift workers are at an excessive risk for accidents and injuries on the job because of disrupted circadian rhythms. Sleep cycles are interrupted. There is difficulty in falling asleep, a shorter duration of sleep, poorer quality of sleep, and persistent fatigue. Alertness and other physiological processes suffer. Eating habits are disrupted; diets are poorer. Digestion is interfered with. Constipation, gastric and peptic ulcers, and gastritis are more common. Social activities and interactions, essential to physical and mental health, are interrupted. Family life and relationships are interfered with; shift workers have difficulty fulfilling family and parental roles. Rotating shift assignments are thus relevant to worker's health and quality of work performance (49, 78, 189, 273, 276, 360, 448). Altering the sleep–wake sequence requires time for the person to make adjustments and regain synchrony.

If shift rotation cannot be eliminated, then individuals should be required to rotate no more frequently than once a month. Consistently working at night allows a person to acquire a new sleep–wake rhythm. Therefore night work should be made more attractive to persons who can adapt to the shift and are willing to remain on it permanently. Those who cannot adapt should be exempt from rotation.

✔ Health teaching of any rotating-shift worker concerning the possible consequences of such a routine should not be overlooked. Night workers on medications should be made aware that the effects of medications may vary somewhat from those they usually experience when working days. The susceptibility to various degrees of drug metabolism occurs throughout the day but even more when a person is experiencing jet lag or the early phase of shift rotation. Individuals with chronic illness, such as diabetes, epilepsy, hypertension and cardiac problems, must consider these factors when they plan their medication regimen.

Rest and Sleep

✔ *Sleep is a complex biological rhythm, intricately related to rest and other biological rhythms.* Help clients realize that factors such as emotional and physical status, occupation, and amount of physical activity determine the need for rest and sleep. For example, workers who alternate between day and night shifts frequently feel more exhausted and may need more sleep than people who keep regular hours. Surgery, illness, pregnancy, and the postpartum state all require that the individual receive more sleep. Mothers of infants, toddlers, and preschoolers may need daytime naps.

Some young people find themselves caught in a whirlwind of activities. Jobs, social activities, family responsibilities, and educational pursuits occupy their every minute. The young adult can adjust to this pace and maintain it for a length of time without damaging physical or mental health. The person may think he/she is immune to the laws of nature and can go long

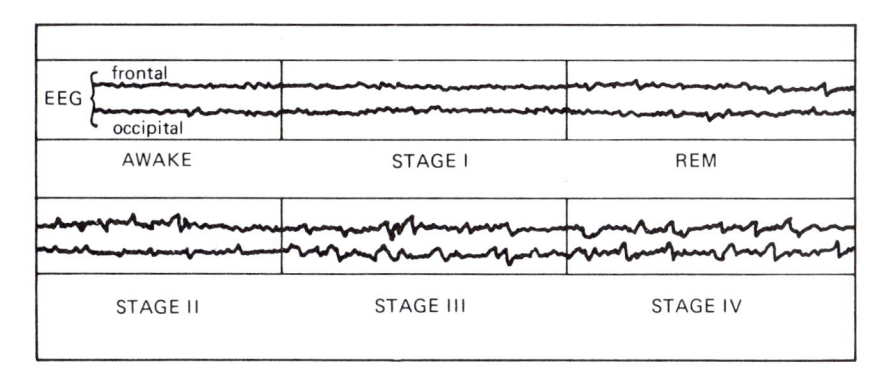

Figure 12-1 Electroencephalogram Changes during Sleep.

periods without sleep. If the person finds that he/she is not functioning well on a certain amount of sleep, the schedule should be adjusted to allow for more hours of rest. He/she needs also to be cognizant of the biological rhythms for rest and activity. Setting aside certain periods for quiet activities, such as reading, sewing, watching television, or various hobbies, is restful but not as beneficial as sleep.

Each person has his/her own sleep needs and cycle, and research is helping us better understand the different stages of sleep and the importance of sleep to wellbeing. The tradition that young adults should have 7 to 8 hours of sleep seems valid, although some get along fine with less (354). When left to the body's natural pace, the person is likely to sleep every 25 hours.

Normal Sleep Pattern. When the waking center, the reticular formation in the midbrain, fails to function or functions less efficiently, sleep ensues. **Electroencephalograms** (**EEG**), *recordings of brainwave activity*, vary with the awake and asleep states and at different intrasleep cycles (Fig. 12–1). When a person is wide awake and alert, the EEG recordings show rapid, irregular waves. High frequency beta and alpha waves predominate. As he/she begins to rest, the wave pattern changes to an **alpha rhythm,** *a regular pattern of low voltage, with frequencies of 8 to 12 cycles per second*. During sleep a **delta rhythm** occurs, *a slow pattern of high voltage and 1 to 2 cycles per second*. At certain stages of sleep, **sleep spindles,** *sudden short bursts of sharply pointed alpha waves of 14 to 16 cycles per second*, and **K-complexes,** *jagged tightly peaked waves, occur* (33, 155, 235, 379).

Sleep is divided into **NREM** (*nonrapid eye movement*) and **REM** (*rapid eye movement*) stages. NREM sleep is divided into 4 stages—light to deep. REM sleep follows the deepest NREM sleep as the person ascends to Stage II sleep, and occurs prior to repeated descent through Stages II, III, and IV. In **NREM Stage I sleep,** *the person makes a transition from wakefulness to sleep* in about a 5-minute period. The alpha rhythm is present, but the waves are more uneven and smaller than in later stages. The person is drowsy, relaxed, has fleeting thoughts, is somewhat aware of the environment, can be easily awakened, and may think he/she has been awake. The pulse rate is decreased. **NREM Stage II sleep** *is the beginning of deeper sleep* and fills 40 to 45 percent of total sleep time. The person is more relaxed than in the prior stage but can be easily awakened. Sleep spindles and K-complexes appear in the brain waves at intervals. **NREM Stage III sleep** *is a period of progressively deeper sleep* and begins 30 to 45 minutes after sleep onset. EEG waves become more regular; delta waves appear; sleep spindles are present; muscles are more relaxed; vital signs and metabolic activity are lowered to basal rates; and the person is difficult to awaken. **NREM Stage IV sleep** *is very deep sleep, occurs about 40 minutes after Stage I, and rests and restores the body physically*. This stage is as of great importance as REM sleep. Delta waves are the dominant EEG pattern. The person is very relaxed, seldom moves, is difficult to arouse, and responds slowly if awakened. Physiological measures are below normal. Sleep walking and enuresis may occur during this stage. After strenuous physical exercise, this stage is greatly needed (33, 53, 155, 379, 429).

REM (**rapid eye movement**) *sleep is called active or paradoxical sleep and is the stage of rapid eye movements and dreaming prior to descending to the deeper sleep of Stages II, III, and IV*. This stage is of great importance. In REM sleep, the EEG readings are active and similar to Stage I sleep, but various physiological differences from other sleep stages are present. These differences, in addition to rapid, side-to-side eye movements are:

1. Muscular relaxation and absent tendon reflexes, with occasional twitching, so that the body is in immobility-like paralysis.
2. Respiratory rate increased 7 to 20 percent, alternating between rapid and slow with brief apneic periods.

3. Pulse rate irregular and increased 5 percent.
4. Blood pressure fluctuations up to 30 mm of Hg.
5. High oxygen consumption by the brain.
6. Increased production of 17 hydroxycorticoid steroids, posterior pituitary hormones, and catecholamines.
7. Increased gastric secretions.
8. Penile erections occur in men of all ages.

REM sleep occurs in 70- to 90-minute cycles that increase as the night progresses. It rests and restores mentally and is important for learning and psychological functioning. It allows for review of the day's events, categorizing and integrating of information into the brain's storage systems, and problem solving. During psychological stress this stage is vital (155, 379, 429).

In a 7- or 8-hour period, the person will have 60- to 90-minute cycles of sleep descending from Stage I to IV and back to REM sleep. After 10 to 15 minutes of REM sleep, the person again descends to Stage IV. The person may ascend to REM sleep three or five times a night, but each time he spends a longer period of time in it. In the first third of the night, he/she spends more time in Stage IV sleep, in the last third of the night more time is spent in REM sleep. Dreams in the early REM stages are shorter, are less interesting, and contain aspects of the preceding day's activities. As the night progresses, the dreams become longer, more vivid and exciting, and less concerned with daily life. Stages III and IV together comprise about 20 percent of sleep time until old age, when deep sleep almost disappears (429).

✔ *Variations in Sleep Patterns.* The percentage of time a person spends in sleep differs with age and with body temperature at the time of falling asleep. If the person's body temperature is at its high point in the biological rhythm, he/she will sleep two times longer than if the temperature is at a low point in the biological rhythm (3, 435). REM sleep remains constant throughout adult life, comprising about 25 percent of sleep, in contrast to 50 percent of sleep for babies. But the percentage of time spent in Stage IV sleep decreases 15 to 30 percent with age, so that the aged person sleeps less time and awakens more frequently. Elderly women's sleep patterns change about 10 years later than men's patterns. The aged person's adjustment to sleep seems dependent on arteriosclerotic changes, so that the alert aged person sleeps about the same as the young adult. The aged with cerebral arteriosclerotic changes sleep 20 percent less than the young adult (3, 155).

REM sleep is related to the onset of certain diseases. Convulsions are more likely to occur in the epileptic just prior to awakening, which is during REM sleep. Because the pulse is irregular during REM sleep, myocardial infarctions and arrhythmias are more likely to occur. Gastric secretion is increased during the REM stage. The person with a peptic ulcer has more pain at these times (155).

✔ Sedatives, antidepressants, and amphetamines significantly decrease REM sleep. If the person continually takes a sedative, there is a gradual return to the usual amount of REM sleep. But when the drug is withdrawn, REM sleep is markedly withdrawn, causing insomnia and nightmares, irritability, fatigue, and sensitivity to pain, all of which persist up to 5 weeks. Thus sedatives should be given sparingly, including to the young adult, although different sedatives cause different effects, and effects differ from person to person. You should learn from the person if he/she is regularly on sedatives. If the person is, he/she will need to continue them to avoid withdrawal symptoms while receiving health care. More information about the effects of various drugs on the sleep cycle can be obtained from current research (155, 372, 379, 429).

✔ If REM deprivation and the rebound of more REM sleep later occur because of administration of sedatives, the patient with any health problem, but especially cardiovascular disease, should have sedative administration stopped prior to discharge. At home the person will not have the close observation needed during the prolonged periods of REM sleep when myocardial infarction is more likely to occur. Further, in contrast to popular belief, alcoholic beverages should not be used to promote sleep. Alcohol speeds the onset of sleep but interferes with REM sleep, which may contribute to hangover feelings (155).

Sleep Deprivation. This should be avoided by the young adult. The person may feel rested if he/she awakens after 4 or 5 hours of sleep, but there has been insufficient time for REM sleep. If the person is awakened frequently, the sleep cycle must be started all over again. Generally with sleep deprivation the person appears anxious, insecure, suspicious, introspective, and unable to respond to support from others. In deprivation of REM sleep, changes in personality and performance occur. These changes are withdrawal, depression, and apathy alternating with irritability and aggression; lack of alertness; fatigue; feeling of pressure around the head; momentary illusions; and difficulty concentrating on a task although reaction time for performance is not necessarily slowed down. The person does less work overall, makes more errors, and uses poor judgment. Prolonged deprivation of REM sleep may cause confusion, disorientation, and hallucinations. In deprivation of Stage IV sleep the person becomes physically uncomfortable, withdrawn, depressed, less aggressive, and hypochondriacal, showing concern over vague physical complaints and changes in bodily feelings.

When the person decides to recover lost sleep by sleeping longer hours, he/she will spend more time in REM sleep. The need to dream (which occurs during REM sleep) seems apparent. Wish fulfillment finds expression in dreams, and potentially harmful thoughts, feelings, and impulses are released so that they do not interfere with the waking personality.

After 48 hours of sleep loss, the body produces a stress chemical related structurally to LSD-25, which may account for behavioral changes. After 4 days of sleep deprivation, the body does not produce adenosine triphosphate (ATP), the catalyst for energy release, which may be a factor in fatigue. With total sleep deprivation, confusion, hallucinations, and psychosis occur (34, 155, 435).

✔ Thus the patient, who needs all stages of sleep for physical and psychological restoration, *should not be awakened during the night if at all possible*. Observe the person before awakening by studying eye movements under the lids. If he/she is in REM sleep, wait a few minutes for it to end before awakening the person, since this is a short and important stage. Sleep should have priority over taking vital signs, especially since the vital sign measurement is affected by the stage of sleep and therefore cannot be compared accurately to daytime measurements. Steroids are released during REM sleep; disturbance of REM sleep causes steroid release to be out of synchrony with other biological rhythms, which affects all areas of function in the person (155).

Young adults sometimes try to reduce their total normal sleeping time. One young man in college would allow himself no more than 2 hours of sleep at one time during exam week. Another student slept 4 hours a night on week nights but 12 on weekends. A reduced period of sleep is *not* a miniature of a full night's sleep; the person remains mostly in Stage IV and has little REM sleep. When REM sleep is lost, he/she will be less able to carry out various roles and responsibilities optimally and will suffer the discomforts described above.

Being frequently awakened during the night, such as happens to young parents with young children, produces the same effects as sleeping fewer hours, even if the total length of time asleep is the usual amount. Blocks of uninterrupted sleep are a definite physical and psychological need.

✔ Help parents work out a system that responds to baby's need but also allows each parent to get as much uninterrupted sleep as possible. Use the above information on sleep stages and effects of sleep interruption and deprivation to teach the young adults.

Sleep Disturbances

About 50 million people in the United States do not get normal sleep daily. They either sleep too much or not enough, suffer night terrors, or stop breathing for a minute or two during sleep. The cost of sleep disorders is enormous; some people pay a great deal for pills and potions to maintain normal sleep (372).

✔ **Insomnia**, *inability to sleep*, is sometimes a complaint of young adults. You should be alert to this growing problem. Young adults take self-hypnosis courses and buy records, water beds, and noise-blocking machines in a desperate search for sleep.

Insomnia means different things to different people, depending upon their value of sleep. Insomnia may be divided into three types: initial, intermittent, and terminal, depending on whether the person has difficulty falling asleep initially, awakens frequently during the night, or awakens early in the morning and cannot return to sleep. The initial type is the most common (435). Causes of insomnia are various physical conditions, disturbed body rhythm, use of stimulants, anxiety or other strong emotions, and environmental conditions. Some people simply do not need much sleep. Psychological causes are the most common (91, 155).

✔ You can help the insomniac by being an interested, calm listener and by suggesting that the following measures be tried:

1. Maintain a regular schedule of prebedtime relaxation, sleep, and wakefulness to keep biorhythms in synchrony.
2. Avoid strenuous activity in the evening before retiring; instead, rely on soothing but enjoyable stimuli, such as a backrub for muscular and emotional relaxation, quiet music, warm bath, progressive relaxation to loosen tight muscles, or a nonstimulating book or hobby.
3. Try a glass of warm milk, which contains l-tryptophane, a chemical that increases brain serotonin and induces sleep.
4. Improve the sleeping environment: make the bedroom dark, quiet, and comfortable as possible so it is associated only with pleasurable feelings.
5. Purposefully relax after going to bed. Stretch out, get comfortable, let the body become heavy and warm.
6. Use pleasant imagery; let the mind "float."
7. Suggest that the person sleep on the back on a firm mattress. If the person sleeps on the side, a small pillow should be tucked between the waist and the mattress to provide proper support. Sleeping on the abdomen is not recommended because the head is turned sharply to one side all night, affecting

neck joints as well as the lower back. In addition, pressure on one side of the face can irritate the jaw. Sleeping with one arm under the pillow stresses the jaw and may interfere with circulation or pinch a nerve in the wrist.

8. If not asleep in 20 minutes, get out of bed, go to another room. Stay calm. Do something boring or relaxing until you are sleepy (99, 155, 429).

✔ Tranquilizers and sedatives are a last resort. For the ill person, first try a monotonous, rhythmic stimulus, such as the backrub, quiet music, a dim light, a wrinkle-free bed, or reading a dull book which are conducive to sleep if they do not irritate the person, since the cerebral cortex has nothing for which to stay alert. In effect, with monotony or boredom, the cerebral cortex does not respond to the reticular formation.

✔ Assess the ill person's sleep pattern and help him/her adhere to the normal pattern. The hospital routine of "pass the pills at 9:00 and be asleep by 9:30" fits very few individuals.

✔ If the person does complain of sleep problems, they should be explored with the goal of eventual correction. Refer the person to a sleep research center so that, through electronic monitoring of the sleep cycle and close surveillance, the problem can be identified and treated.

Work

While the following discussion focuses on work outside of the home, implying paid employment, we do not demean or overlook the young adult woman or man who chooses to stay at home and rear a family. *Homemaking and childrearing are essential and important work;* each is fatiguing and stressful in its own way. In fact, Freedman (123) and other references say that staying at home can be hazardous to health and discuss the many noise and air pollutants or chemical toxins that come from appliances, building materials, cleaning products, and combinations of materials or supplies used in a home.

Burnout. **Burnout,** *the feeling of worthlessness, of not being appreciated, a sense of hopelessness, or loss of creativity,* is discussed primarily in relation to a job. The person who continually stays at home, with or without child care, can also suffer burnout. Some people propose that the homemaker's or mother's work should be assigned monetary worth, since our society equates one's worth with earning power. Certainly the wife, husband, homemaker, mother, and father roles are each work and worthy, and the worth of each has yet to be calculated. Yet a look at history and all cultures tells us that we cannot survive without these roles, regardless of how they are acted out.

The choice of vocation, occupation, or profession depends to a great extent on the person's self-concept, personality, and opportunities and not only on abilities and interests. The young adult provides a livelihood for self and dependents through a chosen job or profession. This work can create feelings of happiness, pleasure, and fulfillment or feelings of being frustrated, blocked, and dehumanized (124, 354). Job satisfaction increases with the level of job skill, variety of work, and opportunity for decision making. Job dissatisfaction increases with automation, lack of attention to the individual worker, and controlled decisions. Income and comfort factors, although important, do not play as big a role as challenge factors in job satisfaction.

Stress response to the unrewarding, demanding work situation may become so great that the person undergoes physiological and psychological changes in response to work. There is inadequate emotional and physical energy for tasks, responsibilities, and roles. This stress response has been popularly called **burnout.** The physical and emotional exhaustion is accompanied by a sense of frustration and loss of control, a sense of tedium and apathy about first the job and then other aspects of life, anger about what is perceived as excessive work demands, guilt about not doing a good job or neglecting the family, depression, a number of somatic complaints, reduced productivity, disillusionment about the job, increased absenteeism, job turnover, low self-esteem, and poor morale. While at first these feelings are related to the job, later they are also directed toward the family, home, friends, and other interests (116, 125, 281).

✔ Professional health workers, including nurses, may suffer from burnout, especially if the nurse works in a high-stress area, such as critical care, emergency, high-risk nursery, or a regularly understaffed unit, or does frequent shift rotation that causes dyssynchrony of circadian rhythms and the consequences described on page 402. Because of the physiological and emotional toll of the workplace, especially if there are rotating shifts, women shift workers have higher use of sleeping pills, tranquilizers, and alcohol. Men have a higher use of digestive aids and alcohol (138, 176, 214). It is important to assess yourself in relation to work satisfaction and response to the stresses at work. Several references will assist in job self-assessment, including Chapter 24 of *Psychiatric/Mental Nursing: Giving Emotional Care* (281), and the references by Brocher (35), Buechler (44), Jacobson (186), Kramer (204), McConnell (261), Pines (310), Scully (357), and Swogger (395). Ways to overcome burnout are described by Freudenberger (125), Kramer, (204, 205), Murray and

Huelskoetter (281), Potter (313), Rich and Rich (321), Schmalenberg (353), Scully (358), Swogger (395), and Veninga (423).

Kramer and her colleagues investigated the process of new graduate nurses' socialization into the first work experience and termed the reaction *reality shock* (204, 205, 353). The new graduate often suffers from the discovery that values learned in nursing school conflict with those in the work setting. They proposed strategies to help the nurse become bicultural: (1) adjust at work while maintaining some of the ideals learned in school; (2) maintain the personal/professional identity in the work subculture while reacting appropriately on the job; and (3) initiate new ideas and values into the work subculture. These strategies and the renewed sense of hope and growth help prevent burnout (204, 353).

Each of us needs to realize that every job has stresses and that stress can be viewed as a challenge. We all need to realize, too, that every job, no matter how exciting it appears, has boredom and repetitive, routine, and noncreative aspects; it is unlikely that those aspects can be eliminated entirely. Thus, each of us needs to be continually mindful of the satisfaction obtained from all pursuits of life; healthy ways to expand interests, hobbies, or social contacts; and ways to make the job more satisfying or interesting, if possible. Further, developing a sense of humor and a philosophical, spiritual outlook can give a balance to life that results in positive feelings about self, work, and others.

Work Options and Attitudes. There are many work options and attitudes. There is the young adult "workaholic" executive who puts in 70 to 80 hours weekly at the job, thinks about the job most of the remaining hours, feels guilty when not working, and channels much anger and aggression through work. There is the factory worker who, while feeding a certain part into the assembly line, is planning what he/she will do the minute he/she leaves the factory. To this person work is only a means of livelihood. There is the blue-collar worker who has more stress than the executive. There is the young adult who, after several years, has lost interest in the job and is trying to decide whether to "stick it out" 35 more years to retirement or risk going into another field that appears challenging. There are also completely opposite attitudes about the same kind of work. For example, one young adult will choose to be a police officer or fire department employee because he/she cares more about adventure and challenge than money. Another will say, "Why should I put my life on the line when the public does not think enough of me to pay decent wages?"

In addition to agricultural, skilled and semi-skilled workers, blue-collar and white-collar workers, managerial or executive personnel, and professionals, a new classification exists—the knowledge worker. Because of expanding technology, rapid change, the burgeoning size of industries and mega-industries, and the knowledge explosion, some people are hired to do job planning, create, innovate, and make decisions within the organization. The ultimate goal of the knowledge worker is cost containment for the company, improved efficiency of the worker, a more marketable product, and a more willing buyer. As a knowledge worker, your task will be less well defined. For example, you might be helping the health-care agency develop long-range plans and goals; you might be a consultant, or you might be observing other nurses at work to determine a more effective way to deliver nursing care and avoid nonnursing tasks. You will have to cope with unanticipated changes, predict changes, and collaborate with others.

You may find the worker—all the way from the executive level to the delivery person—a victim of **substance abuse,** *ingesting excessive alcohol or drugs, or engaged in pushing illicit drugs* on the job. Substance abuse is a response to stress, often job related. Pushing drugs may be a way to earn extra money at work as well as a way to pay for personal drug use. The implications of substance abuse are grave, including job errors, accidents to self or others, poor job performance, a product that does not meet standard results, and increased insurance and worker's compensation benefits to employees, all of which increases the cost of the product to the consumer. In addition, the lives of family, friends, and co-workers are affected. Work with the personnel director, safety director, employee assistance programs, administrative personnel as well as the affected individual (and family, if possible) to help the person get the necessary medical treatment. A recovered employee saves the company money. The employee keeps a job, and it is more expensive to hire and train a new worker in many situations (95, 384).

More and more young adult women are entering the work force. Sometimes the move is a necessity: if she is single, divorced, and with children, or her husband has only seasonal work or a low-paying job. Many women are working to maintain occupational skills, self-esteem, and independence. If a woman is trying to work in addition to carrying on the traditional wife–mother–housekeeper roles, she will likely feel conflict. Finding day-care facilities for young children can be a problem. If the family can learn to work together on various home roles, the working wife–mother can be a real asset to the family because she will bring home her attitude of self-confidence and satisfaction. Also, the children will probably be more adaptive as they mature if they learn various household responsibilities and see their mother and father in a variety of roles instead of those stereotyped by traditional society. (Mom sews, cooks, cleans; Dad mows the lawn, paints the house, repairs the car). Further, the children will learn that it is essential to become well prepared for adult work roles. The woman, as well as the rest of the family, needs some time free from responsibility (19, 186, 215).

Balancing work and family life responsibilities is often stressful for the woman who is a single parent or who is a member of a two-career family. There is never enough time and too much to do. Employers are beginning to confront these dilemmas. Some employers, to attract and keep competent workers, are offering flexible work schedules, job sharing, on-the-site day care, and paternity leaves as well as extended maternity leaves. These suggestions can be shared with the parent who has the greatest responsibility for balancing home and work:

1. Identify priorities. Discuss with the spouse, or the children if they are old enough, what tasks must be done, what can be delegated (either on the job or to a service company in the home), and who can take on which responsibilities to even the load.
2. Allocate tasks. Design a system for assigning tasks, based on skill, age, availability, and fairness. Rotate tasks, if possible, or assign tasks that are especially requested.
3. Use a support network. Family, friends, neighbors, and child care providers can be asked for assistance on a regular basis or for help in emergencies.
4. Assess progress. Plan frequent review sessions to discuss effectiveness of the plan and problem areas to avoid resentments or rebellions, or someone taking advantage (260).

Differences between male and female personalities and behavior in young adulthood are related to occupation and whether the woman is solely a homemaker and mother. The young adult who is employed develops characteristics appropriate to achievement in the outside world: confidence, assurance, dependability, and is controlled, goal-oriented, self-satisfied. These gains may be accompanied by certain costs: detachment, compulsiveness, being less relaxed, being less responsive to humor, being less sensitive esthetically, and being less interesting as a person. The woman who is a homemaker–mother shows a deeper understanding of relationships, feels more secure, shows more warmth, nurturance, tenderness, and giving, and yet is inclined to guilt feelings and worry (19). Often the profession or career demands a combination of seemingly opposite characteristics—competitiveness and nurturance.

Fellow employees need to be aware that women often look differently at the same work situation and respond to different rewards in the workplace than men, that they bring a perspective and judgment level that is not based solely on competition and aggressiveness. Further, equipment or protective clothing that fits men may well be hazardous to women because of size, weight, muscle stretching involved, or poor fit. The employer can benefit from the qualities and expertise women bring to the work force. In turn, women need to utilize the skills learned in the homemaking role as well as skills based on mathematics, technology, and information–computer systems (19, 93, 259, 277). Technological change will increasingly compete with a rising demand for human services, especially in health, law, and recreation. Technology can help free people for service work. However, in a technological age, skills related to caring for or serving others are often neglected. Colleges are already preparing for computer-addicted students with few human relation skills (385), since human relation skills will be as essential in the future as technological skills.

Regardless of the various attitudes about work, it remains a central part of the adult self-concept in most Americans, and a close relationship exists between occupational and family satisfaction. If the person is dissatisfied in one, either work or family life, he/she will try to compensate in the other (124, 354).

✔ Because you are a nurse and view the person holistically, you may be asked for assistance by the manager, executive level employees, or the employers. They may find it difficult to understand the young adult worker who acts differently than the middle-aged or older worker; the behavior of the young adult who has newly achieved an executive position may be poorly understood by employees who are middle-aged and near retirement. Help them understand that each generation of worker has a different value system and responds to different values, as well as to different motivational stimuli (156, 277, 354).

✔ Because you are a nurse, others will seek you out as someone who can assist with safety and health problems, listen to and counsel about job problems, help another make decisions pertinent to occupation, and assist in resolving conflicts related to the work setting or homemaker–career woman–mother roles. You may also become an advocate for the woman who is undergoing sexual harrassment on the job. Increasingly women workers are gaining the courage to talk publicly about and to seek legal aid for sexual harrassment in factories, mines, offices, migrant farm fields, and health-care facilities.

One report describes how harassment can range from a passing caress to threats of or actual rape (285). Yet women or men who are harassed on the job may not complain, whether it is from the hug that the supervisor gives everyone daily—wanted or not—to actual body contact, because of fear of lack of confidentiality, fear of greater or more subtle harassment or retaliation, and fear of poor evaluations, loss of pay raises or actual job loss (393).

▶ You will need to resolve your own job-related conflicts before you can help others. By using the above information and insights you gain from being a professional who works with and learns from many other people, you are indeed in a key position to assist the worker—whether you work in an occupational health setting, a clinic, the emergency room, or in a psychiatric–mental health, obstetric, medical, or surgical unit. Refer also to Puetz on the role of the occupational health nurse in promoting employee mental health (316).

Leisure

Many young American adults are in pursuit of leisure—and rightly so. As job hours per week are being cut (especially in automated jobs), the time for leisure increases. Additionally, the work ethic is decreasing (300).

Leisure *is freedom from obligations and formal duties of paid work and opportunity to pursue, at one's own pace, mental nourishment, enlivenment, pleasure, and relief from fatigue of work* (300). Leisure may be as active as backpacking up a mountain or as quiet as fishing alone in a huge lake. Some people never know leisure, and others manage a certain leisure even as they work. Various factors influence the use of leisure time: gender; amount of family, home, work, or community responsibilities; mental status; income and socioeconomic class; and past interests.

Some people have never learned to pursue a hobby or an activity just for the "fun of it." Others have learned hobbies or have pursued recreational interests but use the same competitive spirit in the hobby or recreation as in work. Others pursue hobbies as the "current thing to do" but feel no real sense of pleasure.

Leisure gadgetry have invaded the marketplace. Electronic games have replaced household appliances as America's favorite gadgets. Technology affects leisure through changes in both products and values. As technology dictates specialized work, the games increasingly create specialized players and skills. The electronic games that reward aggressive and competitive behavior teach values and behavior that will be carried over to other leisure activities and the work force. The result may be contradictory to the meaning of leisure (385).

The real answer to the work–leisure dilemma is that the worker and the player are one. The unhappy worker will not automatically become the happy player. Challenging work makes leisure a time of refreshment. Successful leisure prepares the worker for more challenge.

Maintaining friendships is a healthy use of leisure time. It takes time, self-disclosure, and sharing of interests to form friendships. Gradually, a sense of reliability and confidentiality grows as a core to the friendship. Some conflict may surface and is natural as intimacy deepens. Getting closer to friends, rather than making more friends, is the way to reduce loneliness. Avoid developing all the friendships at the workplace. In today's competitive world, people at work may not be able to be close. It is wiser to start out being more formal and distant until the trusting relationship evolves. In a world where women juggle career, love, and family, time may limit the size of the friendship circle. Several close friends should be made. Successful friendship combines the freedom to depend on one another with the freedom to be independent. If free time is too limited, fewer friendships can be formed, as you will have little to give to anybody emotionally.

▶ Help the patient/client realize the importance of leisure as a part of balanced living. The young adult needs to develop a variety of interests as preparation for the years ahead.

Physical Fitness—Exercise

Physical fitness *is a combination of strength, endurance, flexibility, balance, speed, agility, and power* and reflects ability to work for a sustained period with vigor and pleasure, without undue fatigue, with energy left for enjoying hobbies and recreational activities and for meeting emergencies. Fitness relates to how the person looks and feels physically and mentally. Basic to fitness are regular physical exercise, proper nutrition, adequate rest and relaxation, conscientious health practices, and good medical and dental care (86).

Jogging makes joints in good condition stronger. Jogging as a form of exercise may aggravate old injuries of the back, hips, knees, and ankles, since jogging puts as much as five times normal body weight on lower joints and extremities. Jogging may cause abnormal wear on joints and muscles. The person who jogs needs to also engage in exercise for the upper extremities and other muscles. Weight lifting can strengthen. Swimming is probably the best overall activity because it increases strength and endurance, stimulates heart and blood vessels, lungs, and many muscle groups without putting excess stress on the person because of less gravity pull in the water. Further, swimming keeps joints supple, aids weight loss or weight control, reduces hypertension. Perhaps more important, it is an enjoyable activity, either alone or with others (408).

Regular physical fitness has been viewed as a natural tranquilizer, for it reduces anxiety and muscular tension. Some studies show that regular physical exercise improves a number of personality characteristics, correlating with composure, extraversion, self-confidence, assertiveness, persistence, adventuresomeness, and superego strength (86, 414).

Exercise periods are frequently not planned by young adults. Some will get abundant exercises in their jobs, but many will not. Those who do not can check with the local Y.M.C.A. or Y.W.C.A. organizations, community recreation departments, continuing education departments of 2-year colleges, or commercial gymnasiums and health salons for exercise programs appropriate to their lifestyles and physical conditions.

One of the 1990 Health Objectives established by the U.S. Department of Health and Human Services is for 60 percent of adults 18 to 65 years of age to be participating regularly in vigorous physical exercise. No valid or practical measurement system is available that will allow assessment of leisure time physical activity participation of large populations. Consequently, it is difficult to assess progress toward the 1990 goal; an accurate baseline from which to measure potential progress does not exist. A diary technique for measuring aggregate population physical activity participation was utilized by Brooks in a study of adults through the Institute for Social Research in 1981 to arrive at a possible baseline. In her study, Brooks developed an activity index based on intensity of the activity and time of participation, so that an index energy expenditure can be calculated. She explains her formula, and lists the following activities under the intensity of light, moderate, or heavy, as shown below. American adults are quite sedentary. Over a period of 1 week, 31 percent undertake no leisure time physical activity; 14 percent expend more than 1600 kcal/week in leisure time physical activity. Only 10 percent meet the DHHS physical activity requirements (38).

Light Intensity Activities:
Bowling   Gardening indoors
Fishing   Pet care
Boating/sailing   Swinging, feeding birds
Horseback riding

Moderate Intensity Activities:
Golfing   Bicycling
Frisbee/catch   Swimming
Exercises/yoga   Carpentry
Hunting   Gardening outdoors
Walking   Grounds improvement
Hiking   Social dancing

Heavy Intensity Activities:
Team sports   Lessons in body
Racquet ball   movements
Skating/skiing   Aerobic dance
Jogging

Gender Differences. Women and men sometimes share the same physical exercise activities; sometimes interests and energy levels are different and partners may engage in exercise activities separately. Women may have as much endurance as men, especially with training, but there are some physiological differences that account for differences in performance in physical exercise activities or athletic events.

Males have greater upper-body strength due primarily to their longer arms, broader shoulders, and higher muscle fiber counts. Muscle can be conditioned by exercise, but muscle fiber count cannot be increased. Whether males exercise or not, their muscle fibers gain bulk from the hormone testosterone. In males, the heart and lungs, which are an average of 10 percent larger than in females, provide more powerful and efficient circulation. The delivery of oxygen to men's muscles, a factor crucial to speed, is further enhanced by the higher concentration of hemoglobin in the blood. Finally, the longer limbs provide them with greater leverage and extension.

The aspects of female physiology that result in women's athletic advantages are not as self-evident as in males. In females, bodies contain an average of 9 percent more adipose than in the male body. This adipose is deposited not only on the thighs, buttocks, and breasts, but in a subcutaneous layer that covers the entire body. It is this adipose that makes the female more buoyant and better insulated against cold, both of which are advantages in long-distance swimming. (The record for swimming the English Channel—7 hours and 40 minutes—is held by a woman, Penny Dean.) Body adipose tissue may also be one of the reasons few female runners report the pain and weakness that most male runners encounter. The body is conditioned to call on stored fats once its supply of glycogen, which fuels the muscles, has been exhausted. Since women have greater reserves of body fat, they are able to compete in athletics longer. Females perspire less and less quickly than males. Perspiring is the body's way of avoiding overheating. Yet, women may tolerate heat better than men. Not only can body temperature rise in females several degrees higher before she begins to sweat, but women sweat more efficiently due to the even distribution of their sweat glands. In women, **vascularization**, *capacity for bringing blood to the surface for cooling*, is also more efficient. The female has certain structural advantages for all types of running and swimming events. In swimming, narrower shoulders offer less resistance through water. Even at identical heights (and ideal weights), female bodies are lighter than male, leaving them with less weight to carry while running (449).

Foot Care. Foot care is not considered often enough in an exercise program. The feet, during walking, will meet the surface at 1½ to 2 times the body weight, and up to 3 times when running. Proper shoe fit which includes heel height, stability, and cushion; wedge support; and forefoot cushion must all be considered. Also, proper fitting and absorbent socks are important, along with proper washing and careful drying of feet after exercise (94).

After the person has had a thorough physical examination and has been cleared by a physician, three sessions weekly of 30 minutes are recommended for developing muscle tone and strength and increasing cardiovascular efficiency. Teach that very fast walking that increases heartbeat to between 70 to 85 percent of maximum heart rate is considered the best exercise of all; people who cannot jog or run can usually walk 20 to 30 minutes on alternate days. Maximum heart rate (MHR) is calculated by subtracting your age from 220. During exercise the pulse should be 80 percent of that level. (For example, the 40-year-old should have a pulse of 144 during exercise [86].) Activities which are good physical exercise include calisthenics, jogging, swimming, jumping rope, and games like tennis if they are played regularly (86, 312, 354, 414). Dee's book, *A Fitness Program for Adults*, is a helpful reference for specific warm-up conditioning, circulatory, and cool-down exercises (86). A health self-appraisal questionnaire and program (306, 311) can help the person determine the present state of health and fitness and implications for the years ahead.

Psychosocial Concepts

Cognitive Development

Different learning abilities are required in different life stages. Youth is the time for acquisition; young adulthood is the time for achievement; middle age is the time for responsibility; and old age is the time for reintegration (347).

Theories About Cognitive Development. Cognitive theories are described here; refer also to Chapter 5. Erikson theorized that the basis for adult cognitive performance is laid during the school years when the child accomplishes the task of industry, learns how to learn and win recognition by producing and achieving, and learns to enjoy learning. The child learns an attitude that lasts into adulthood: how much effort a task takes and how long and hard he/she should work for what is desired or expected (104). The sense of industry is useful in adult life, both in coping with new experiences and in functioning as a worker, family member, citizen, and lifelong learner.

Current researchers and theorists propose that learning continues throughout the adult years. The longitudinal study conducted by Vaillant indicates that the brain continues to change in structure and complexity until age 40 or 50 years (419, 420). The brain shows increasing myelinization until middle age, which permits more integrated modes of social response and stable or increasing intellectual functions (307).

Heath describes how becoming mature in young adulthood involves intellectual growth, becoming more knowledgeable about self, forming values, and developing increasing depth in analytic and synthetic thinking, logical reasoning, and imagination. Further, developing social and interpersonal skills, and personal friendships may have a powerfully maturing effect on intellectual skills (156).

Influences on Learning. Influences differ somewhat from childhood to adulthood, and include (1) level of knowledge in society generally, (2) personal perceptions and previously learned associations, (3) level of education, (4) available life opportunities, (5) interests, (6) participation by the person in the learning activity, (7) the learning environment, and (8) life experiences.

Formal Operations Stage. The young adult remains in Formal Operations, according to Piaget. The adult is creative in thought. He/she begins at the abstract level and compares the idea mentally or verbally with previous memories, knowledge, or experience. The person combines or integrates a number of steps of a task mentally instead of thinking about or doing each step as a separate unit. He/she considers the multiplicity and relativism of issues and alternatives to a situation, synthesizing and integrating ideas or information into the memory, beliefs, or solutions so that the end result is a unique product. Adult thought is different from adolescent thought in that the adult can differentiate among many perspectives, and the adult is objective, realistic, and less egocentric. Thinking and learning are problem centered, not just subject centered. Reality is considered only a part of all that is possible. The person can imagine and reason about events that are not occurring in reality, but which are possible, or in which he/she does not even believe. Hypotheses are generated; conjectures are deduced from hypotheses, and observations are conducted to disconfirm the expectations. The thought system works independent of its context and can be applied to diverse data. The person can evaluate the validity of a train of reasoning independent of its factual content. A concrete proposition can be replaced by an arbitrary sign of symbolic logic, such as *p* or *q*. Probability, proportionality, and combining of thought systems occur (206, 426, 433).

Arlin cites Gruber as proposing that some people continue to develop cognitively beyond the Formal Operations proposed by Piaget into a *fifth stage* of cognitive development that progresses through adulthood. The Stage of Formal Operations describes strategies used in problem solving. The *problem-finding stage* goes beyond the problem-solving stage and is characterized by creative thought in the form of discovered problems, the formation of generic problems, the raising of general questions from ill-defined problems, and the development of significant scientific thought (17).

The person may use different thinking for scientific operations, business transactions, artistic activities, and intimate interpersonal interactions. Thus mature thinkers can accept and live with contradictions and conflicts and engage in a number of activities (354). However, at times the adult will of necessity do thinking typical of Concrete Operations. At times the adult may regress to the Preoperational Stage (some never get beyond this period), as shown by superstitious, egocentric, or illogical thinking. The adult may not have the ability to perform formal operations.

A further distinction in types of adult thinking separates the *managers*, those who have a better developed right brain and who synthesize data to see the overall picture, from the *planners*, those who have a better developed left brain and who analyze sequentially and look closely to the minute details. Women tend to have a better integrated brain and usually combine both manager and planner thinking (146, 228).

The young adult continues to learn both formally and informally. Learning may be pursued in "on-the-job training," job-sponsored orientation courses, trade schools, college studies, or continuing education courses. Environmental stimulation is important in continued learning. Increasingly young adults are changing their minds about their life work and will change directions after several years of study or work in the original field. Formal operations or abstract thinking appears linked to the content areas in which the person has extensive training. Berzonsky, cited in Webb (433), proposed that after Concrete Operations, a person may acquire abstract thinking in behavioral, symbolic, semantic, or figural content areas, depending on experience.

Gender Differences. Gender differences in cognitive ability have also been descibed on the basis of different functions in each cerebral hemisphere, although brain structure is the same in males and females. The left hemisphere is dominant in 97 percent of people for language, logical reasoning, and mathematical calculation. The right hemisphere is nonverbal and mute: It knows but cannot tell what it knows without processing the knowledge through the left hemisphere. The right hemisphere processes spatial and visual abstractions, recognition of faces, body image, music, art forms, and intuitive, preconscious, and fantasy processes. At birth, asymmetry in the left hemisphere is more marked in the male. Female infants have a somewhat larger area of visual cortex in the right hemisphere than male infants, which implies an anatomical advantage for nonverbal ideation. The female's brain matures earlier; thus, the two hemispheres are more integrated in the female as indicated by less impairment of intellectual function in women who have suffered either right or left hemisphere damage. Males are more vulnerable to brain damage. On tests women use verbal strategies to solve spatial problems because of the greater interplay between the two hemispheres. In adulthood, women are better able to coordinate activities of both hemispheres, thus they can think intuitively and globally. Men are better at activities where the two hemispheres do not compete such as problem solving or determining spatial relationships (19, 224, 277, 307).

A summary comparison of cognitive, as well as other characteristics, of males and females is found in Appendix V. The comparison is based on a variety of research. Consider that differences between men and women may be due to test methodology, definition of terms, or sex stereotypes, not gender.

Nonconformity to sex-role stereotypes is positively related to IQ. The more assertive and active female has greater intellectual ability and more interests. The less aggressive male focuses less on developing physique and develops intellectual ability and interests to a greater extent (19).

Cognitive abilities have often been related to personality traits and interpersonal orientation. Sex-role socialization has been related to cognitive style. Some researchers believe the level of information processing a person attains exerts a profound influence on personality as well as ability to integrate and differentiate in problem solving (229).

Claims about sex differences in other cognitive abilities, such as creativity, analytic ability, and reasoning, also appear to be the result of differences in verbal, quantitative, or visual-spatial abilities (229).

Both female and male young adults who are in formal education are causing shifts in the educational system. They are more vocal, persuasive, and determined about what they consider pertinent. They are stimulating diversity and quality in the higher-education patterns. The young adult wants to learn more about something or learn to do something better and wants a voice in planning education. The nontraditional education offered by some colleges is more an attitude than a system; the students' needs are first, and the institution's convenience second. Competent performance and concern for the learner of any age rather than just obtaining degrees are being emphasized in adult education, including noncollegiate programs. Full educational opportunity through life is the goal of many young adults, enabling each to meet potential personally and as a citizen. The young adult is concerned about the most important principles or concepts to be learned to provide the balance between the timely and timeless in this modern world.

The confident young adult takes pride in being mentally astute, creative, progressive, and alert to events. He/she normally has the mental capacity to make social and occupational contributions, is self-directive and curious, and likes to match wits with others in productive dialogue.

✔ *Teaching the Adult.* Information on cognitive development and the principles of learning described in Chapter 17 should be considered whenever you are teaching adults. Avoid canned audiovisual presentations. Emphasize a sharing of ideas and experiences, role play, and practical application of information. In some cases, you will be helping the person to unlearn old habits, attitudes, or information to acquire new habits and attitudes.

✔ If you teach illiterate young adults, you will have to compensate for their inability to read and write. Slow, precise speech and gestures and the use of pictures and audiovisual aids will be more crucial than with literate adults. Demonstration and *return demonstration* will assure learning. Do not underestimate the importance of your behavior and personality as a motivating force, especially if some members of the person's family do not consider learning important.

Emotional Development

Young adulthood is a time when there is increased clarity and consistency of personality, a stabilization of self and identity, established preferences of interests and activities, increased coping ability, less defensiveness, decrease in youthful illusions, fantasy, and impulsiveness, more responsiveness to and responsibility for self and others, more giving than taking, and more appreciation of surroundings, and it is a time to develop expanded resources for happiness. There are restrictions and continuities not previously experienced, some sacrifice of freedom and spontaneity, and less opportunity for variety, novelty, and impulsive adventure. However, there is more challenge to develop empathy, a depth of feeling and understanding, to learn in detail how systems work, and to reevaluate self and the world. If behavior is not too heavily bound by defenses against anxiety, it becomes more varied as experience accumulates (346).

Certainly adult experiences, lifestyle, and geographical changes can contribute to personality development and change. Yet Nassi found that the psychosocial and political development of the adolescent maintains a pattern or direction into young adulthood, as shown in a study of youth activists in the 1960s (286). In a longitudinal study of psychosocial development, it was found that most behavior and personality characteristics of the school-age child between 6 and 10 years were good predictors of early adult behavior and personality. However, various life experiences modify behavior and personality in adulthood. A major modifying variable is gender. Degrees of childhood passivity and dependency remained continuous for women but not for men (277). The longitudinal study by Maas and Kuyper also shows the influence of childhood experiences on adult personality and the continuity of adult personality characteristics over the years (239).

Theories of Emotional Development. Various stage theorists (Second Force) referred to in Chapter 5 also have research findings on which to base their beliefs about adult personality development. The findings of Vaillant, Gould, Sheehy, Levinson, Sullivan and Erikson will be discussed in the following pages.

From his longitudinal study of adult men, Vaillant proposes that development continues through adulthood in a number of ways: emotionally, mentally, socially in relationships, and in career. Simultaneously, the developing and successful adult also demonstrates what Freud calls the psychopathology of everyday life. All have special adaptational problems and mechanisms. Vaillant believes that emotional health and development are evolutionary, not static. Isolated traumatic events rarely mold individual lives, but rather development comes from continued interaction between choice of adaptive mechanisms and sustained relationships with others. Poor adaptation, which lowers the threshold for perceiving or handling stress, leads to anxiety, depression, and physical illness. Vaillant's study identifies mature defenses—altruism, humor, suppression or minimization of discomforts, anticipation, sublimation—that promote adaptation. Successful adapters have had good relationships with parents, are energetic and alert, feel good about themselves, love their work, have very close relationships with wives and friends, and sublimate aggression into enthusiastic pursuits of projects, work, or competitive sports (419, 420). His findings seem applicable to adult women as well.

Gould describes life stages and key issues or tasks in late adolescence and young adulthood. Gould believes there is an increasing need throughout adulthood to win permission from the self to continue development. The direction of change through adulthood is becoming more tolerant of self and more appreciative of the surrounding world. While Gould does not list specific assumptions about adult development, he sees adulthood as a time of thoughtful confrontation with the self—letting go of an idealized image, the desire to be perfect, and acknowledging the realistic image of self and personal feelings. Conflicts between past and present beliefs are resolved. Through constant examination and reformulation of beliefs embedded in feelings, the person can substitute a conception of adulthood for childhood legacy and fantasies. While children mark the passing years by their changing bodies, adults change their minds, deepen their insights about self, and mature emotionally (140).

Sheehy believes that development occurs throughout adulthood and is influenced by external events or crises, the historical period, membership in the culture, and social roles, as well as by the internal realism of the person—the values, goals, and aspirations. Sheehy ties developmental stages in late adolescence and young adulthood to Erikson's development stages (365, 366).

Levinson, like Vaillant, studied only men in formulating a concept of adult developmental stages. However, he believes the stages are age linked and universal; thus they should be applicable to women. In each period, biological, psychodynamic, cultural, social, and other timetables operate in only partial synchronization, which makes for developmental difficulties (223). The organizing concept of **life structure** *refers to a pattern of the person's life at a specific time* and is used to focus on the boundary between the individual and society. In its external aspects, life structure refers to roles, memberships, interests, conditions or style of living, and long-term goals. In the internal aspects, life structure includes the personal meanings of external patterns, inner identities, core values, fantasies, and psychodynamic qualities that shape the person (223).

Sullivan believes young adulthood is normally the time when the sexuality of human development is powerful, and there is a need to find adequate and satisfying expression (391). Now is the time of expanding experiences with people. If for some reason the person is thwarted in expression or sublimation of sexual feelings, perhaps because of illness or injury which causes a felt or imagined change in body, sexual concerns may become paramount.

Developmental Crisis. According to Erikson, the psychosexual crisis is intimacy versus self-isolation.

Intimacy *is reaching out and using the self to form a commitment to and an intense, lasting relationship with another person, or even a cause, an institution, or creative effort* (104). In an intimate experience there is mutual trust, sharing of feelings, responsibility to and cooperation with each other. The physical satisfaction and psychological security of another are more important than one's own. The person is involved with people, work, hobbies, and community issues. He/she has poise and ease in the lifestyle because identity is firm. There is a steady conviction of who he/she is, a unity of personality which will improve through life. Intimacy is a situation involving two people which permits acceptance of all aspects of the other and a collaboration in which the person adjusts behavior to the other's behavior and needs in pursuit of mutual satisfaction (391).

A person's mental health is dependent on the ability to enter into a relationship and experience self-disclosure; in so doing, the support and maintenance of the relationship alleviates feelings of loneliness. Mahon found that women self-disclose more easily than men. Highly self-disclosing people are less lonely. Interpersonal dependency, an element of the normal adult personality, encompasses attachment and dependency. Anxious or insecure attachment develops when a natural desire for a close relationship with another is accompanied by apprehension that the relationship will end. If anxiety is transferred to the other person, the response may be a withdrawal from the relationship, contributing to feelings of loneliness. If a healthy balance between dependence and independence exists, social relationships and intimacy are maintained more easily and the risk of experiencing loneliness and isolation decreases (244).

Although intimacy includes orgasm, it means far more than the physical or genital contact so often described in how-to sex manuals. With the intimate person the young adult is able to regulate cycles of work, recreation, and procreation (if chosen), and to work toward satisfactory stages of development for all offspring and ongoing development and self and the partner. Intimacy is a paradox. While the person shares his/her identity with another for mutual satisfaction or support (via self-abandon in orgasm or in another shared emotional experience), he/she does not fear loss of personal identity. Each does not absorb the other's personality.

Many in late adolescence or early young adulthood do fear a loss of personal identity in an intimate relationship. You can explore intimacy issues with the young adults. In an increasingly complex society the search for self-definition is a difficult one. Identity is not always solidly possessed by the time one is 20 or even 25. Achieving a true sense of intimacy seems very illusive to many of this generation. The media encourages self-seeking sexual gratification. Movies, novels, plays, and pornographic books glorify sex for kicks, and peer groups may pressure each other into sexual activity before they are ready for it. Many are puzzled, hurt, or dismayed when they find such sexual encounters to be very disappointing. It is easy to *say* that understanding or insight into one's own sexuality is possible only when the self is fully defined. It is much more difficult to *act* on this principle. To come to the realization that sex is not a synonym for sexual intercourse may be a long and painful road.

Love. Love is the feeling accompanying intimacy (104, 391). The young adult often has difficulty determining what love is. A classic description of love stated by the Apostle Paul in I Corinthians 13: 4–7 has been the basis for many statements on love by poets, novelists, humanists, philosophers, psychiatrists, theologians, and common people.

> Love is patient and kind; love is not jealous or boastful; it is not arrogant or rude. Love does not insist on its own way; it is not irritable or resentful; it does not rejoice at wrong, but rejoices in the right. Love bears all things, believes all things, hopes all things, endures all things.

One of the most important things the person can learn within the family as a child and adolescent is to love. By the time the person reaches the midtwenties, the person should be experienced in the emotion of love. If there was a deprivation or distortion of love in the home when he/she was young, the adult will find it difficult to achieve mature love in an intimate relationship. By this time, the person should realize that one does not *fall* in love; one *learns* to love; one *grows* into love.

As a nurse, you will have many opportunities for discussions, individual and group counseling, and education on marriage, establishing a home, the relationship between spouses, and the relationship between parents and children.. When you help people sort through feelings about life and love, you are indirectly making a contribution to the health and stability of them and their offspring.

Marriage. The socially accepted way for two people in love to be intimate is in marriage, a social contract or institution implying binding rules and responsibilities that cannot be ignored without some penalty. Marriage is endorsed in some form by all cultures in all periods of history because it formalizes and symbolizes the importance of family. Social stability depends on family stability. Marriage is more than getting a piece of paper.

There are norms in every society to prevent people from entering lightly into the wedded state, for example, age limits, financial and property settlements, ceremony, witnesses, and public registration and announcement. One of the major functions of marriage is to control and limit sexuality and provide the framework for a long-term relationship between a man and a woman. Marriage gives rights in four areas: sexuality, birth and rearing of children, domestic and economic services, and property.

Most young people recognize that marriage is a decisive commitment. It marks the start of a new way of living and the achievement of a different status in life. A bride and groom have reason to experience anxiety. Marriage is both a special commitment and a voluntary choice made by them, and the consequences must be accepted in advance. But the potential sources of disturbance and danger are overshadowed by the recognition of marriage as a new source of strength and support in which the well-being of each is bound up with the fate of the other.

The pattern and sequence of a person's life history influence whom, when, and why he/she marries. Apparently, many people do not really know the person they are marrying and do not realize how greatly the partner's personality will influence their own. The problems of marital adjustment and family living have their roots and basis in the choice of the partner (226).

Mates often choose each other on the basis of unconscious needs, which strive to be met through a mate whose personality complements rather than replicates one's own, or out of fear, loneliness or on the basis of physical attraction. The person chooses someone for an intimate relationship whose lifestyle and personality pattern strengthen and encourage personal development.

Although the person tends to marry an individual who lives and works nearby and has similar social, religious, and racial backgrounds, in America an increasing number of mixed marriages are occurring, an outgrowth of more liberal social attitudes. A number of factors influence the success of the marriage that crosses religious, ethnic, socioeconomic, or racial boundaries:

1. Motive for marriage.
2. Desire, commitment, and effort to bridge the gulf between them and their families.
3. Ability and maturity of the two poeple to live with and resolve their differences and problems.
4. Reaction of the parental familes, who may secretly or openly support **homogamy** (*marriage between a couple with similar or identical backgrounds*).

In America every married couple belongs to three families: to each other, to his family, and to her family. If the young adults are to establish a strong family unit of their own and avoid in-law interference, their loyalties must be to their *own* family before his or hers. The following guidelines may be helpful.

1. In-laws should not take priority over the spouse and home of the couple. If friends of either husband or wife are offensive to the partner, be prepared to minimize this friendship. Husband and wife together build new friendships.
2. Be faithful to the spouse. If one person engages in an extramarital affair, it is possible to repair the brokenness but a feeling of mistrust may remain and is difficult to overcome.
3. Be mindful of sensitive areas, those which are sources of irritation in each other's life. Each needs to *work* at coping with the other's idiosyncrasies or habits and try to meet the other's preferences to keep love in the relationship.
4. Manage money and material possessions or they will manage the couple. Money and things are important, but the focus in a relationship should be on the person.
5. Maintain a spirit of courtship, spontaneity, and freshness to keep love in a marriage.

Marriage is coming to be recognized as a close and loving partnership between two people rather than only a social institution in which the husband is the undisputed head of the house and the wife a child bearer. The current concept of companionship suggests intimacy and affection in a free and equal relationship. This concept imposes high standards. The success of the marriage depends ultimately on the two discovering and being able to fulfill mutual physical and psychological needs.

Whether the young couple is going through the regular channels of engagement and marriage or through less traditional ways of living together, the following tasks must be accomplished if the couple will remain a viable, intimate unit:

1. Establishing themselves as a collaborative pair in their own eyes and in the eyes of mutual friends and both families.
2. Working through intimate systems of communication that allow for exchange of confidences and feelings and an increased degree of empathy and ability to predict each other's responses.
3. Planning ahead for a stable relationship and arriving at a consensus about how their life should be lived.
4. Giving each other positive reinforcement to release love rather than focus on problems.

✔ You may ask certain questions to ascertain readiness for marriage in the young adult or self. Can you take responsibility for your own behavior? Are you emotionally weaned from your parents? Have both of you thought about what lies ahead: the disagreements as well as the agreements, days of sickness as well as health, periods of depression as well as happiness, financial difficulties? Have you considered whether or not to have children? Have you had any education about childrearing to know what it entails? Do you understand female and male sexuality—the differences as well as the similarities? What do you each want out of marriage? What can you each give to marriage? Do you have mutual agreement on boundaries: Does it include group sex, nonmarital play, or complete monogamy? You can explore these and other questions in premarital counseling or courses in family living.

Isolation, or **self-absorption,** *is the inability to be intimate, spontaneous, or close with another (104), thus becoming withdrawn, lonely, conceited, and behaving in a stereotyped manner.* The isolated person often experiences a long succession of unsuccessful relationships, overextending self without any real interest or feeling, and then being unable to sustain close friendships. No real exchange of fellowship occurs, which is why encounter groups appeal to the isolated person. The forced fellowship and explorative closeness temporarily remove the sting of alienation.

The isolated person lives a facade, making pretentious claims. He/she may be naively child-like, easily disillusioned and embittered, and avoid the issues of life when possible. The person is distrustful, pessimistic, ruthless, and vacillating in behavior. Because he/she cannot see beyond personal needs and desires, he/she is progressively more alone. The person may establish a pattern of pseudo-intimate relationships in which he/she is initially friendly, but then sabotages the relationship as it grows closer to avoid true intimacy. For example, the person may have a history of numerous dating partners or broken engagements but can never get to the intense stage of preparation for or settling into marriage. If he/she does marry, the partner is likely to find personal emotional needs unmet while giving considerably of the self to the isolated, self-absorbed person (104, 226).

✔ You may counsel the self-absorbed person and help him/her achieve the tasks of intimacy. You can also be a role model of commitment to serving others. Use principles of communication and relationship described by Murray and Huelskoetter (281).

Moral–Religious Development

The young adult may be either in the Conventional or Postconventional Level of moral development (see Chapter 5). In the Postconventional Level he/she follows the principles defined as appropriate for life.

There are two stages in this level. In both stages the person has passed beyond living a certain way just because the majority of people do. Yet, in Stage 1 of this level the person adheres to the legal viewpoint of society. The person believes, however, that laws can be changed as people's needs change and he/she is able to transcend the thinking of a specific social order and develop universal principles about justice, equality, and human rights. In Stage 2 the person still operates as in Stage 1 but is able to incorporate injustice, pain, and death as an integral part of existence (199).

Kohlberg espouses that the reason for the behavior indicates the level of moral development, and that for a person to be at any level, the reasons for behavior should be consistent to the stage 50 percent of the time (199). Therefore, it would appear difficult for the average young adult, concerned about family, achieving in a career, paying the bills, and so on to be in the Postconventional Level (194). While the person may follow principles some of the time, conflicting situations and demands arise. To be consistently in the Postconventional Level takes considerable ego strength, a firm emotional and spiritual identity, and a willingness to stand up to societal forces. It may take years of maturing before the adult can be that courageous and consistent in Western society. For example, how does the young adult handle the dishonesty seen on the job? How does the mother handle the child viewing violence on television or demanding that clothes be the same designer outfits the other children are wearing? How does the couple react when a friend brags that he is having extramarital sexual experiences?

Probably only a few adults ever get to the second stage: 5 to 10 percent may reach Stage 1 of the Postconventional Level; 20 to 25 percent stay in the Conventional level, and the rest stay locked into the Preconventional described in Chapters 5 and 11 (199).

Today's young adults have grown up with the influence of science and technology. As early as World War II some prophesied that the children born then would be postreligious, disinterested in other worlds, and concerned only in the secular existence of the present.

While some young adults fit this description and others are rejecting the institutional church, there remains in many a desire and ability to apply religious and moral principles in this world.

In young adulthood there is a humanizing of values and a trend toward relativism as conflicts are encountered. The person increasingly discovers the meaning of values and their relation to achievement of social purposes, and he/she brings both personal experiences and motives to affirm and promote a value system. The person's values, whatever they are, become increasingly his/her own and a part of a unified philosophy of life. At the same time, there is expanding empathy for others and their value systems (156).

The religious awakening often experienced during adolescence, which might have receded with seeking of success, may now take on a more mature aspect, as the young adult becomes firmly established in another life stage. If the person has children, he/she must rear them with some underlying philosophy. Their religious–moral questions must be answered. The young adult's religious teaching, perhaps previously rejected, may now be accepted as "not so bad after all." Or the young adult may build a new version of it.

Several qualities contribute to a religiously mature sentiment or disposition. The disposition is:

1. *Individualized and integrated.* The person translates the abstract knowledge into practical action. It helps him/her reach goals and attain harmony in various aspects of living.
2. *Consistent.* It produces basic standards of morality and conduct.
3. *Comprehensive, dynamic, and flexible.* It never stops searching for new attitudes and ideas. The person can hold ideas tentatively until confirmed or until evidence produces a more valid belief.

Because new and different ideas are always available, the mature disposition can continue for a lifetime. The person realizes that there is always more to learn (13).

One of the dilemmas for the interfaith or interculture couple is what values and religion, if any, to follow in the home, and to teach the children; how to celebrate holidays; what rituals and traditions to follow (e.g., Hanukkah or Christmas). Even when the couple makes a choice, there may be conflicts with relatives. Grandparents often have difficulty accepting that their child married someone of another faith or culture. Such marriages can work, and the children can have a firm moral and spiritual development. It is important for both spouses and families to discuss their feelings openly from the beginning. The couple should learn as much as possible about each other's religion/culture and talk to their families and friends about their experiences. It is critical that each family group remain open and accepting of the other. In turn, the children can learn deeper dimensions of spirituality, moral values, and their cultural background.

Although religious development and moral development follow sequential steps and are often thought of simultaneously, there is no significant link between specific religious affiliation or education and moral development. Moral development is linked positively with empathy, the capacity to understand another's viewpoint, and the ability to act reciprocally with another while maintaining personal values and principles. Being with people who are at a higher moral level stimulates the person to ask questions, consider his/her actions, and move to a higher moral level (199).

Adaptive Mechanisms

When the young adult is physically and emotionally healthy, total functioning is smooth (226, 293). Adaptation to the environment, satisfaction of needs, and social interaction proceed relatively effortlessly, and with minimal discomfort. The young adult behaves as though he/she is in control of impulses and drives and in harmony with superego ideals and demands. He/she can tolerate frustration of needs and is capable of making choices that seem best for total equilibrium (293). The person is emotionally mature for this life stage.

Emotional maturity is not exclusively related to physical health. Under stress, the healthiest people might momentarily have irrational impulses. The extremely ill have periods of lucidity. Emotional health and maturity have an infinite gradation of behavior on a continuum rather than a rigid division between healthy and ill. Concepts of maturity are generated by culture. What is normal in one society may be abnormal in another.

In coping with stress in the environment, the young adult uses any of the previously discussed adaptive mechanisms. Use of these mechanisms, such as *denial* or *regression*, becomes abnormal or maladaptive only when the person uses the same mechanism of behavior too frequently, in too many situations, or for too long a duration.

Self-Concept and Body-Image Development

Self-concept and body image, defined in Chapters 5 and 7 and discussed in each developmental era, are now redefined and expanded to fit the young adult perspective.

The person's perception of self physically, emotionally, and socially, based on reactions of others that have been internalized, self-expectations, perceived abilities, attitudes, habits, knowledge, and other characteristics, affect how that person will handle situations and relate to others. How the person behaves depends on whether he/she feels positively or negatively about self, whether the person feels that others view him/her positively or negatively, and how he/she feels others expect the person to behave in this situation. Additionally, the person discloses different aspects of self to various people and in various situations, depending on needs, what is considered socially acceptable, reactions of others, and past experience with self-disclosure (72).

Body image, *a part of self-concept, is a mental picture of the body's appearance integrated into the parieto-temporal area of the cortext. Body image includes the surface, internal, and postural picture of the body and values, attitudes, emotions, and personality reactions of the person in relation to the body as an object in space, separate from others.* This image is flexible, subject to constant revision, and may not be reflective of actual body structure. Body image shifts back and forth, at different times of the day, and at different times in the life cycle (280, 352).

Under normal conditions, the body is the focus of an individual's identity, and its limits more or less clearly define a boundary which separates the person from the environment. One's body has spatial and time sense and yields experiences which cannot be shared directly with others. A person's body is the primary channel of contact with the world, and it is a nucleus around which values are synthesized. Any disturbance to the body influences total self-concept (114, 280).

Contributing Influences

Many factors contribute to the body image:

1. Parental and social reaction to the person's body.
2. The person's interpretation of others' reactions to him/her.
3. The anatomical appearance and physiological function of the body, including sex, age, kinesthetic and other sensorimotor stimuli, and illness or deformity.
4. Attitudes and emotions toward and familiarity with the body.
5. Internal drives, dependency needs, motivational state, and ideals to which the person aspires.
6. Identification with the bodies of others who were considered ideal. A little bit of each person significant to the person is incorporated into the self-concept and personality.
7. Perception of space and objects immediately surrounding the body, such as a chair or car, the sense of body boundaries.
8. Objects attached to the body, such as clothing, a wig, false eyelashes, a prosthesis, jewelry, makeup, or perfume.
9. The activities which the body performs in various roles, occupations, or recreations (280).

The kinesthetic receptors in the muscles, tendons, and joints and the labyrinth receptors in the inner ear inform the person about his/her position in space. By means of perceptual alterations in position, the postural image of the body constantly changes. Every new posture and movement is incorporated by the cortex into a **schema** (*image*) in relation to or association with previously made schemata. Thus the image of the body changes with changing movements—walking, sitting, gestures, changes in appearance, changes in the pace of walking (113, 114, 352).

Self-produced movement aids visual accuracy. When a person's body parts are moved passively instead of actively, for example, sitting in a wheelchair instead of walking, perceptual accuracy regarding space and the self as an object in space is hindered. Athletes, ballet dancers, and other agile people are more accurate than most in estimating the dimensions of the body parts that are involved in movement (114). Adults fitted with distortion glasses adapt to the perceived distortion if they are permitted to walk around in the environment wearing the glasses. If they are moved passively in a wheelchair, little or no adaptation takes place. Thus activity appears to enhance sensory information in a way that passive movements do not. If a person undergoes bodily changes, he/she must actively explore and move the involved part to reintegrate it (113, 114, 352, 411).

✔ *Self-Knowledge.* How do you visualize your body as you walk, run, stand, sit, or gesture? How do you feel about yourself as you go through various motions? What emotions are expressed by your movements? How do you think others visualize you at that time? Movement of the body parts, gestures, and appearance communicate a message to the observer, for example, the patient or family member, which may or may not be intended. The message you convey about yourself to another may aid or hinder the establishment of a therapeutic relationship. You need to be realistically aware of the posture and movement of your body and what these may be conveying to another.

Self-knowledge is not necessarily the same as knowledge gained about the self from others. Each person sees self differently from how others see him/her although the most mature person is able to view self as others do. New attributes or ideas are integrated into the old ones, but all ideas received are not necessarily integrated. Before any perception about the self can affect or be integrated into one's self-concept, the perceptions must be considered good or necessary to the self. If the person feels that he/she is competent, a statement about incompetence will not be integrated into the self-image unless he/she is repeatedly told about being incompetent. However, if the person has a negative self-image, it will also take many statements of his/her worth before they can be accepted and integrated into the self-concept.

A person has definite ideas and feelings about his/her own body, what is satisfying and what is frustrating. The person discovers that he/she has certain abilities and disabilities, likes and dislikes. He/she thinks of self as shy or outgoing, irritable or calm, and learns something of how he/she affects others. What the person thinks of self has remarkable power in influencing behavior and the interpretation of other's behavior, the choice of associates, and goals pursued.

Feelings about certain self-attributes vary according to the importance placed on them and how central or close they are to the essence of self. Events such as illness or injury involving the face and torso are usually more threatening than those involving the limbs, since the face and the torso are first integrated into the young child's self-perception. The extremities are seen as part of the self later and are therefore usually less highly valued in comparison (114, 352, 411).

One's feelings about one's characteristics also depend on whether a characteristic or body part is viewed as a functional tool for living or as a central personal attribute. For example, teeth can be viewed as a tool for eating or as central to the face, smile, youth, and personality. Dentures can be accepted and integrated as part of the body image more easily if they are viewed as a tool rather than if they are thought of as a sign of decline and old age. The person's work may also be viewed as a tool, function, or way to earn a living and help others, or as central to the self. For example, is your image that of a woman or man who works as a nurse and does other things as well, or is your whole image primarily that of being a nurse? Age and sex are also characteristics that differ in degree of centrality or importance to the person (114, 352, 411).

Also involved in self-concept and body image are the body parts which are supposed to be strategically important in the character of the ethnic group or race, for example, the German backbone, the Jewish nose, or the dark skin of the Black person. The body part with special significance, which would also include the afflicted limb in a disabled person, is felt to be heavier, larger, or more conspicuous, and seems to the bearer of it to be the focus of others' attention, although it may not be.

The location and history of family residence, religion, socioeconomic background, and even attempts at climbing to another social class level are integrated into the adult self-concept but not the body image (114, 352, 411).

Body image in the adult is a social creation. Normality is judged by appearance, and ways of using the body are prescribed by society. Approval and acceptance are given for normal appearance and proper behavior. Self-concept continually influences and enlarges the person's world, mastery of and interaction with it, and ability to respond to the many experiences it offers. This integration, largely unconscious, is constantly evolving and can be identified in the person's values, attitudes, and feelings about self. The experiences with the body are interpreted in terms of feelings, earlier views of the self, and group or cultural norms (63, 211, 352, 367).

In the adult there is a close interdependence between body image and personality, self-concept, and identity. A mature body image and mature behavior are built on having coped with the changing demands of each previous developmental crisis, particularly as these crises relate to dominant body parts—the mouth, limbs, and genitalia. If each of these body zones and their functioning are not integrated, in turn, into the total body image, the adult person's body image will remain immature in some respects. The immature body image may interfere with securing adult satisfactions and may be evidenced by personality disturbance. The young adult who can accept the body without undue preoccupation with its function or control of these functions is free for other experiences (114, 211, 352, 382).

✔ You need to remember and utilize information about self-concepts and body image, for as a nurse your feedback to others is important. If you are to help another elevate self-esteem or feel positively about his/her body, you will need to give repeated positive reinforcement. Saying something positive or recognizing abilities once or twice will not be enough. The self-concept, whether wholesome or not, is difficult to change since the person perceives others' comments and behavior in relation to an already established image to avoid conflict and anxiety within self. The person with a sense of trust, self-confidence, or positive self-concept is less threatened by others' ideas, remarks, or behavior. He/she is more flexible, able to change, and admit new attributes to self.

Stereotyped Ideas About Correlation Between Personality and Body Type. Certain characteristics are attributed to a person on the basis of how he/she looks. You should be aware of how a client might perceive you on the basis of your shape. The stereotypes are numerous: The skinny are pinched and mean; the fat are gluttonous, unattractive, insensitive, or very jolly; the broad, overweight person is calm and passive; the thin, narrow person is active, excitable, tense, or reacts quickly. Reactions to body build are important to the individual, both in terms of how the person is treated by others and in terms of what others expect of him/her.

In one study to determine social stereotypes about physique and temperament, all subjects were shown silhouettes of Sheldon's three body types and one silhouette of an average physique. All four silhouettes were the same height. The endomorph silhouette was rated fatter, older, shorter, lazier, less strong and good looking, more talkative, warm-hearted, sympathetic, old-fashioned, good-natured, dependent, and trusting. The mesomorph silhouette was rated stronger, better looking, more attractive, adventuresome, younger, taller, more mature in behavior, and more self-reliant. The ectomorph silhouette was rated thinner, younger, taller, more suspicious of others, more tense and nervous, less masculine, more stubborn, pessimistic, and quieter (367).

These stereotypes of behavior and personality rated by persons who had no formal knowledge of body image and equally paired from the three socioeconomic classes were the same as had been described by Sheldon and other researchers. The results show that people generally believe that different temperaments go with different body physiques (367).

✔ Certainly this research has implications for you. Individualized care can hardly be given if you see only the physique of the person and label him/her accordingly. On the other hand, the patient/client and family may be reacting to you on the basis of how they expect someone with your specific physique to behave.

In America there is much emphasis on the ideal adult figure. In one study on degree of satisfaction reported by people about aspects of the body, large women wanted to be smaller but not as small as small women. Small women wanted to be larger, but not as large as large women. Small size was desirable for all body parts except the breasts. The small range of variation for the ideal size of the different body parts as stated by the women in the study indicates that cultural stereotype of the ideal female figure sets limits for acceptable size that are narrower than those produced by nature and eating habits. Few women have the physical dimensions that were identified as ideal, and none rated positively all their body parts (352). In another study the large, thin women rated their bodies as best liked by the self, while the broad-hipped, big-breasted women rated themselves as most potent (211).

Women's status and security are in some cases highly conditioned by their perceived and demonstrated attractiveness to males, irrespective of skills, interests, and values. Because most women do not attain the ideal proportions, they may not feel beautiful. The internalized ideal is indirectly responsible for much insecurity among women (114).

Men rate large size and height as desirable. The mesomorphs, large muscular men, rated their bodies as best liked by the self and as more active than the ectomorph or endomorph. Tall height symbolizes dominion, self-confidence, leadership, and power (211).

Women have a more clearly defined and stable body concept than men. Girls seem to have an earlier realistic appreciation than boys of the smallness of their own bodies in relation to adults, of a sexual definition of self, and a more realistic concept of the body thereafter. The difference between male and female body images seems related partly to different anatomical structure and body functions but also to the contrasts between males and females in their upbringing, style of life, and role in culture (133).

Presumably, persons having a well-integrated body image react to people and situations differently from those with a poorly integrated body image. The person with a firm ego boundary or body image is more likely to be an independent person, with definite goals and forceful, striving ways of approaching tasks. He/she will be an influential member of the group. Under stress, these persons are more likely to develop diseases of the periphery of the body—skin and muscles. Persons with a poorly integrated body image or poorly defined body boundaries are more likely to be passive, less achievement minded, less goal striving. These persons are less influential in a group and more susceptible to the influence of others and external pressure. Under stress, the maximum physiological response occurs internally, taking the form, for example, of heart disease or gastrointestinal disease (113).

Stereotyped Ideas Affecting Self-Concept in Women and Men. In America, the woman is stereotyped to be an underachiever in education and occupation. Dependent, passive, and subordinate are terms frequently associated with women; the woman may also cry and show weakness. Yet, most people recognize the quiet strength in many women. The woman is thought to be cooperative and creative (as long as she is doing handicrafts). If she is academically or occupationally successful, she is said to be aggressive or unfeminine.

The man is stereotyped to be aggressive and competitive, even in a service role. Weakness is not accepted. If the man is gentle and passive, he is labeled a "sissy" or effeminate (19, 124, 177, 229).

The classic studies by Margaret Mead show that the personality traits that we have traditionally called masculine and feminine in the United States are an artifact of culture, not biology (267). In her study of three different groups of people, she found that in the first group, men and women were equally cooperative, unaggressive, and responsive to the needs and demands of others. Sex drive was not a driving force for men or women. In the second group both men and women were equally ruthless, aggressive, violent, sexually active, and with maternal cherishing aspects of personality at a minimum. In the third group the ideal is the reversal of American culture, with the woman the dominant, impersonal, and managing partner and the man the less responsible and emotionally dependent person (267). Knowledge of these studies should help men and women feel freer to explore and incorporate a wide range of behaviors into the self-concept. The women's liberation movement and new occupational trends appear to be giving some impetus to this area.

✔ Consciousness-raising groups for women also can help work through anger related to social reactions and differential treatment of men and women. Such groups can reaffirm a positive self-concept in the woman, as well as teach ways to cope with sexism (229, 281). You can initiate and lead such groups.

✔ *In Illness, Body-Image Changes Occur.* A wide variety of messages about the body are constantly fed into the self-image for rejection, acceptance with integration, or revision. You will see disturbances in the person's body image following loss of a body function, structure, or quality—teeth, hair, vision, hearing, breast, internal organs, or youth—which necessitate adjustment of the person's body image. Because the body image provides a base for identity, almost any change in body structure or function is experienced as a threat, especially in America where wholeness, beauty, and health are highly valued.

✔ A threat to body image is related to the person's pattern of adaptation. Some behavior patterns may depend heavily on certain organs of the body. If these organs become diseased or have to be removed, the threat is greater than if an organ unimportant to the person is affected. The degree to which this loss of bodily control creates loss of customary control of self, physical environment, time, and contacts with others is very closely related to the degree of threat felt. To understand the nature of the threat, you must assess the pattern of adaptation, the value of this pattern for the person, and the usual coping mechanisms. The person with limited adaptive abilities, who easily feels helpless and powerless, will experience greater threat with a change in body structure or function.

✔ Any adaptation to alterations in body size, function, or structure then depends on the nature and meaning of the threat to the person, previous coping pattern, response from others, and the help you provide in helping him/her undergo change. The phases of crisis discussed in *Nursing Concepts for Health Promotion*, Chapter 8, are a normal sequence of behavior in response to body image changes (282).

✔ *Assessment of the Adult Undergoing Body Changes.* Assessment during illness, injury, or disability, which necessitate eventual changes in self-image, is often difficult because of the abstractness of self-image. But if you listen closely to the person, validate statements for less obvious meanings, and explore feelings with him/her you can gain considerable information for worthwhile intervention. Direct or probing questions about the following items *do not* obtain any information, but through open-ended questions you should gradually be able to obtain information about the following aspects which relate to body image. Assessment could include determining the person's response to the following:

1. Feelings about the self before and since the condition occurred.
2. Values about personal hygiene.
3. Values on beauty, self-control, wholeness, activity.
4. Value of others' reactions.
5. Meaning of the body part affected.
6. Meaning of hospitalization, treatment, and care.
7. Awareness of extent of condition.
8. Effect of condition on person, roles, daily activities, family, and use of leisure time.
9. Perception of others' reaction to person with this condition.
10. Problems in adjusting to condition.
11. Mechanisms used in adapting to condition and its implication (280).

✔ Observation of the patient/client must be combined with purposeful conversation. Observe movements, posture, gestures, and expressions as he/she answers your questions or talks about self to validate the consistency between what is said and what is meant.

✔ *Nursing Intervention.* Measures to help someone with a threat to or change of body image involves assisting the person reintegrate the self-view and self-esteem in relation to his/her condition. You can help the person in the following ways (280, 281):

1. Encourage talking about feelings in relation to the changed body function or structure. Talking about feelings is the first step to reintegration of body image.
2. Assist, without pressure, to become reacquainted with self by looking at the dressing or wound, feeling the cast, bandage, or injured part, or looking at self in the mirror. The patient who wants to "show the scar" should be allowed to do so. Reaction from you and the family can make a difference in how the person accepts the changed body.
3. Provide opportunity for gaining information about the body, the intact as well as changed parts, strengths and limits.
4. Provide opportunity to learn mastery of the body, to resume activities of daily care and living routines as indicated, to move about, become involved with others, resume roles, and handle equipment.
5. Give recognition for what the person can do. Avoid criticism, derogation, or a nonverbal reaction of disgust or shame.
6. Help him/her see self as a whole person in spite of losses or changes.
7. Encourage talking about unresolved experiences, distortions, or fears in relation to body image.

✔ You will be encountering many young adults with body-image distortions or changes as a result of accidental or war injuries, disease, weight gain or loss, pregnancy, or identity problems. You can make a significant contribution to the health of this person for the remainder of life by giving assistance through physical care, listening, counseling, teaching, and working with the people important to his/her life.

✔ Be aware that health-care professionals and certain treatment practices contribute to a negative self-concept and sexual stereotypes, and often the health-care system treats the patient (well or ill) as an unthinking, incompetent object. Broverman's study of 79 psychologists, psychiatrists, and social workers, 46 male and 33 female, revealed that these professionals held the same stereotypes about male and female behavior as the general public (39). While there may be some attitudinal change since the Broverman study, many men and women still hold traditional stereotyped beliefs about sex-related behavior.

✔ You will encounter health professionals in every field who are influenced by a sexist orientation when working with you and patients/clients. By your behavior, use of problem solving, verbal facility, and nonverbal messages you can work to change sexist attitudes. Your efforts are important for your own positive self-concept and for unbiased care of each person—thus promoting a positive self-concept.

Lifestyle Options

The increased pace of life in America has brought people an unparalleled degree of social alienation at all levels of society. Choosing a lifestyle very different from one's child-rearing experiences is an attempt to ward off alienation and organize one's life around meaning. The young adult has many options. He/she may decide to base the style of living around age (the youth cult); work (the company man or woman executive); leisure (the surf bum); drugs; or marriage and family.

Singlehood, *remaining unmarried and following a specific lifestyle,* is not new. Maiden aunts and single school teachers are traditional, as are those whose religion calls for singlehood. But remaining unmarried is increasingly an option, either as an end in itself or as a newly prolonged phase of postadolescence. The unequal numbers of men and women in the United

States contribute to this trend. There are also more working women who are independent and unlikely to tolerate an unequal relationship. Further, some men are wanting less responsibility, and are making less commitment to marriage.

The single person may be in emotional isolation, unable to establish a close relationship, alienated from self and others, or may feel depressed about the life situation. However, not all singles fit this description. The single person can accomplish the task of intimacy through emotional investment of self in others. Many are extroverts, have several very close friends with whom they share activities, have a meaningful career, and have a harmonious rather than conflictual relationship with parents. If they marry, they want to feel that they have chosen the right partner and have spent time living just for themselves so that they do not resent the responsibilities of marriage.

Many prefer to remain single as they pursue prolonged education and strive to become established in their occupational field. Others find that being free of relationships and to sample a variety of lifestyles and travel as they please before settling down to raise a family is an important part of establishing a comfortable identity. They avoid living out their lives in the same manner and location as their parents, and may live in apartment complexes for singles only, following a lifestyle that is supposed to convey freedom. For whatever reasons, the number of single people in this country is on the rise, especially in the 20 to 34 age group.

Trends suggest that young people are marrying later than they did in the 1960s. There still exists a great deal of cultural and family pressure for this age group to marry by the midtwenties. America so values family life that unmarried adults have been treated as immature and incomplete, or even as failures and willful renegades who cannot or will not take up a respectable and responsible family role. Single adults have had to take reduced credit ratings and higher insurance rates just because they are single. Pressure from "embarrassed" families and friends leads many of these individuals to marry prematurely lest they be lifetime misfits.

✒ The single person may need help in understanding that lifestyle choice is not irresponsible, that he/she can make significant contributions as a citizen, and that marriage and parenthood are only one way to demonstrate emotional maturity. If the person is single because of isolation and self-absorption, psychiatric counseling may be needed, not for singlehood, but because of feelings about self and others. Several books listed in the references give suggestions for managing alone (25, 70, 93, 96, 149, 333, 387). Haber describes family therapy with single young adults (145). For additional information on singlehood, refer to Chapter 4.

Family Planning: The Expectancy Phase and Parenthood

Parenthood is an option for either the couple or single person. It was not until the early 1960s that people felt in control of family planning. Birth control methods were often not successful either aesthetically or mechanically. But today oral contraceptives for the female and more skilled vasectomy procedures for the male make it possible for couples to say "We don't want children now." "We don't want children ever." "We want to try to have two children spaced 3 years apart."

✒ Information presented in Chapter 11, Table 11–4, that summarizes contraceptives, and various references at the end of this chapter will help you teach about all aspects of family planning. Chapter 4 presents information that will also be useful for understanding the family you are working with.

✒ You may be in a position to use Decision Theory with a couple who have many questions about having a family. In this method, the couple writes their separate values in a hierarchy of importance and then examines the costs and benefits associated with their decision to have or not to have children. This approach is a variation of the old decision-making method of listing all the reasons *for* on one side and all the reasons *against* on the other side to get an accurate view of the components involved in the decision.

Reasons for Childbearing. The couple may have a child for a variety of reasons: (1) extension of self; (2) to offset loneliness; (3) sense of pride or joy; (4) psychological fulfillment of having a child; (5) having someone to love self; (6) attempt to hold a marriage together; (7) feeling of power, generated by ability to create life; (8) representation of wealth; (9) to secure replacements for the work force; (10) to have an heir for family name and wealth; and (11) religious convictions (409). Whether the couple chooses to have only one child or more children is related to more than fertility and religious background. Lifestyles, finances, career, available support systems, and emotional maturity are factors. The woman who has had the opportunity to pursue career and social activities may be more ready emotionally to settle down, commit self to the rsponsibilities of child care and parenting, in contrast to the female in the teens, twenties, or even early thirties (294, 442). End of chapter references give several perspectives on this decision (1, 2, 294, 371, 374, 401, 403).

📐 **Developmental Tasks for the Couple During the Expectancy Stage.** You are in a position to assist the couple in understanding the changes that childbearing will create and the following developmental tasks for this stage of family life:

1. Rearrange the home to provide space, facilities, and supplies for the expected baby.
2. Rework the budget and determine how to obtain and spend income to accommodate changing needs and maintain the family unit financially.
3. Evaluate the changing roles, division of labor, how responsiblities of child care will be divided, who has the final authority, and whether the woman should continue working outside the home if she has a career/profession.
4. Adapt patterns of sexual relationships to the pregnancy.
5. Rework the communication system between the couple; explore feelings about the pregnancy and ideas about childrearing, and work to resolve the differences.
6. Acquire knowledge about pregnancy, childbirth, and parenthood.
7. Rework the communication system and relationships with family, friends, and community activities, based on the reality of the pregnancy and their reactions.
8. Utilize family and community resources as needed.
9. Examine and expand the philosophy of life to include responsibilities of child bearing and rearing (97).

Developmental tasks that must be mastered during pregnancy and the intrapartum period to ensure readiness for the maternal role, according to Clark, are:

1. *Pregnancy validation,* accepting the reality of the pregnancy, working through feelings of ambivalence.
2. *Fetal embodiment,* incorporating the fetus and enlarging body into the body image.
3. *Fetal distinction,* seeing the fetus as a separate entity, fantasizing what the baby will be like.
4. *Role transition,* after birth, an increasing readiness to take on the task of parenthood (173).

A number of authors have researched transition to parenthood, feelings, symptoms, body-image changes, and needs for social support during pregnancy. Refer to references at the end of the chapter for more information (40, 42, 75, 76, 108, 109, 173, 245, 272, 410, 424, 427).

Father's Response. Some research indicates that attachment of the father to baby begins during pregnancy, rather than after birth, and that a strong marital relationship and vicariously experienced physical symptoms resembling pregnancy strengthen attachment (Couvade Syndrome) (64, 108, 109, 237).

Studies indicate a characteristic pattern of development of subjective emotional involvement in pregnancy among first-time expectant fathers. Three phases occur: an announcement phase, a moratorium, and a focusing period (257).

The **announcement phase** is *when pregnancy is suspected and confirmed.* If the man desired the pregnancy, he shows desire and excitement. If he did not want the pregnancy, he shows pain and shock (257).

During the **moratorium period,** *the man suppresses thoughts about the pregnancy.* This period can last from a few days to months and usually ends when the pregnancy is obvious. This period is characterized by emotional distance, a feeling the pregnancy is not real, concentration on himself and other life concerns, and sometimes leaving home. The man's emotional distance allows him to work through ambivalence and jealousy of the woman's ability to bear a child, but his distance causes her to feel unloved, rejected, angry, and uncared for. Marital tension exists. Pregnancy often emphasizes the disparity in the couple's life pace and focus. Gradually the man faces the financial and lifestyle implications of the pregnancy. If the man feels financially insecure, unstable with his partner, or wishes to extend the childless period, he resents pregnancy and spends a longer time in the moratorium stage. Most men eventually come around to being enthusiastic about the pregnancy and baby when he feels baby move or hears the heartbeat. If he does not become enthusiastic and supportive, the couple may then be at risk for marital and parenting problems (257).

The **focusing period** occurs *when the man perceives the pregnancy as real and important in his life.* This begins about 25 to 30 weeks' gestation and extends until labor onset. The man redefines himself as father; he begins to feel more in tune with and is more helpful to his wife. He begins to read or talk about parenting and child development, notices other children, and is willing to participate in childbirth classes and purchasing baby supplies. He constructs a mental image of baby, sometimes different from the woman's mental image of the baby. The circle of friends may change to those who have children. He may feel fear about the coming labor and birth and feel responsible for a successful birth (257). The man who participates in pregnancy and birth experiences greater closeness with the infant and spouse and heightened self-esteem and esteem for the spouse. The man's readiness for pregnancy may significantly influence emergence of father involvement. The man's unconscious feelings and his earliest memories of childhood play an important role in his emotional reaction and adjustment to pregnancy and childbirth (211, 237, 402, 410).

Certainly one would expect that an even stronger attachment would occur in the woman as she physically experiences the fetus as well as physical symptoms related to pregnancy, and that her feelings for the child are stronger if she has a loving, supportive partner.

✔ *Nursing Roles.* An important decision for the expectant parents is whether to attend childbirth education classes. Encourage the pregnant woman and her partner to attend childbirth education classes during pregnancy that are taught by ASPO (American Society for Prophylaxis in Obstetrics) certified childbirth educators. Insist that they be allowed to use the techniques and practical suggestions they learned during the labor and delivery process. The woman who is well supported during pregnancy experiences fewer complications during labor and delivery. The woman who has had childbirth education during pregnancy and can practice Lamaze techniques during labor uses less medication and is more likely to choose rooming-in with the baby (275).

✔ Your support, acceptance, flexibility, helping the couple to use what they learned and practiced in prenatal classes, letting them assume responsibility for decisions when possible, and assistance to mother and teaching during the postpartum period are crucial to family-centered care. To clarify your patterns of caring for patients/clients, refer to Cronenwett and Brickman for a discussion of four models that professionals use in maintaining parent and infant health (76).

✔ Refer to an obstetric nursing book for specific information on prenatal care, the labor and delivery process, and postpartal care—for both the normal and high-risk pregnancy and delivery. Refer also to the "Symposium on Maternal and Newborn Nursing," *Nursing Clinics of North America,* March, 1982. Helpful references are also found at the end of Chapter 7 and at the end of this chapter (40, 72, 87, 272, 323, 389, 410).

✔ Be aware that in contrast to the societal romanticized view of pregnancy and care of the pregnant woman, the pregnant woman may be a victim of battering. Helton's article is an informative reference on assessment, how to assist the woman in the decision to leave the partner, and resources for help (159). Sonkin et al. described assessment of and intervention with the male batterer (378). Refer also to pages 437 to 440 in this chapter for general information on spouse abuse and the male batterer.

Other Approaches to Parenthood. *Some couples delay childbearing* until they are in their thirties or early forties. The woman may wish to pursue her education, a career, or a profession; the couple may choose to travel, start a business, become financially established, or have a variety of experiences before they settle down with one or two children. With genetic counseling, the surgical ability to undo vasectomy and tubal ligation, improved prenatal and neonatal care, and reduced risk of maternal or neonatal complications, pregnancy is safe for the mother in her thirties and even early forties (87, 218). Because of concern about congenital abnormalities, **amniocentesis,** *a procedure in which a small amount of amniotic fluid is removed for analysis*, can be done in the early prenatal period. This allows the couple to begin the adjustment if the child has an abnormality—or to terminate the pregnancy if the abnormality is severe (84). Many of the risks of late parenthood may be related to preexisting disease, if any, rather than to late conception. Of equal concern are the emotional and social implications, especially after birth when the couple's life revolves around baby rather than work or earlier interests (331).

Maternal age does not affect maternal role behaviors, and the sense of challenge, role strain, and self-image in the mother role is similar during the first year for the childbearing women of all ages. Mercer's study of the process of maternal role attainment in three age groups (15 to 19 years, 20 to 29 years, and 30 to 42 years) over the first year of motherhood found that love for the baby, gratification in the maternal role, observed maternal behavior, and self-reported ways of handling irritating child behaviors remained the same over the year (272).

The single person may desire to be a parent. The single woman may, through pregnancy or adoption, choose to have a child(ren). More is being written about the single woman who decides to become a mother and remain single. Some of these are well-educated, professional women in the late thirties or forties, who believe they have no chance of becoming married, for various societal reasons, but who wish to have the experience of motherhood (371). The number of both Afro-American and Caucasian single women who are choosing to be mothers and heads of the family is increasing. A few single men have also decided to adopt a child in order to be a parent. The decision to parent without a father or mother figure for the child should be carefully considered, for the child needs both female and male caregivers and the characteristics, responses, and relationships that each can give. The woman may choose to remain single but maintain a relationship with the biological father or with a man who can act as father to the child. The man may have a close relationship with a woman who can assist in mothering, or he may decide to nurture alone.

✔ You are in a key position to help the person as he/she thinks through why there is a wish to have a child and remain single. Who the support system will be, who can act in the father or mother role to the child, the consequences of a single mother or father to the child during school years or adolescence, and the social, familial, and economic consequences of single parenthood should be discussed. Poverty is more common among single mothers, and fewer single mothers finish high school (298). Implications related to the cultural and religious background of the person must also be considered.

Family planning is sometimes made difficult by **infertility,** *inability to achieve pregnancy after 1 year of regular, unprotected intercourse or the inability to carry a pregnancy to a term, live birth,* which is a health problem for 15 percent of childbearing age. Both partners should be given diagnostic tests together, since 50 percent of infertility factors are seen in women and 30 to 40 percent are seen in men. Infertility can create great psychological problems for the woman and man, between the couple, and between families of each partner. The problem becomes compounded by the increasing difficulty in adopting a local healthy baby in most communities, since 90 percent of single mothers retain their babies. Artificial insemination and a surrogate mother are alternatives that may not always be acceptable to the couple. Menning describes the emotional reactions in detail (271).

Sandelowski (342) found in her study that feelings of ambiguity or uncertainty about identity, life pursuits and control, and the infertility diagnostic procedures, cause, and cure were the most prevalent feelings. Even when pregnancy was achieved, ambiguity and a sense of unrealness about the pregnancy and its outcome was still the most prevalent feeling.

✔ The articles by Friedman (126), Menning (271), and Wood (450) describe causes of infertility and diagnostic and treatment procedures for the female and male. You may also refer your patient/client to local infertility clinics or the American Fertility Society, 1688 13th Avenue South, Birmingham, AL 35256. Another organization, Resolve, formed by people with infertility problems, gives counsel and support to people in 26 metropolitan areas. You may obtain more information by writing Resolve, Department P, Box 474, Belmont, MA 02178.

✔ The couple who cannot biologically have a child may consider a **surrogate parent,** *where a woman for a fee will conceive through insemination, carry, and deliver a child for the woman who cannot conceive.* Many ethical concerns arise with this practice: the meaning of family, psychological effects on the surrogate and contracting parents, relationship between fetus and pregnant woman, the possibility that the child who is born may not meet the desires of the contracting parents, care of the deformed child, and effect on the child when he/she finds out about the surrogate parent. Does the couple have a right to children by any means? What are the cultural, moral, and religious implications? Further, legal aspects are also tenuous. As of now, there are no answers, just many questions. You can help a couple considering the surrogate parent method work through the above issues and questions, related to their religious, cultural, and family values and beliefs, and their personal philosophies, values, and beliefs.

Developmental Tasks

The specific developmental tasks of the youth as he/she is making the transition from adolescence into young adulthood are discussed in Chapter 11 and can be summarized as choosing a vocation, getting appropriate education, establishing a residence, and formulating ideas about selection of a mate or someone with whom to have a close relationship.

For the young adult in general, the following tasks must be achieved, regardless of the station in life:

1. Accepting self and stabilizing self-concept and body image.
2. Establishing independence from parental home and financial aid.
3. Becoming established in a vocation or profession that provides personal satisfaction, economic independence, and a feeling of making a worthwhile contribution to society.
4. Learning to appraise and express love responsibly through more than sexual contacts.
5. Establishing an intimate bond with another, either through marriage or with a close friend.
6. Establishing and maintaining a home and managing a time schedule and life stresses.
7. Finding a congenial social and friendship group.
8. Deciding whether or not to have a family and carry out tasks of parenting.
9. Formulating a meaningful philosophy of life and reassessing priorities and values.
10. Becoming involved as a citizen in the community (97).

McCoy, using the stages of development proposed by the life-stage theorists discussed earlier, formulated similar developmental tasks for each stage (262). These are depicted in Table 12–3.

✔ You can assist young adults in meeting these developmental tasks through use of therapeutic communication principles, counseling, teaching, and crisis intervention. An in-depth source of information to help you understand and work with the marital and young

TABLE 12-3. Developmental Tasks and Outcomes for the Stages of Young Adulthood

DEVELOPMENTAL STAGES	DEVELOPMENTAL TASKS	OUTCOMES SOUGHT
Becoming adults, 23–28 years old	1. Select mate. 2. Settle in work, begin career ladder. 3. Parent. 4. Become involved in community. 5. Consume wisely. 6. Homeown. 7. Socially interact. 8. Achieve autonomy. 9. Problem solve. 10. Manage stress accompanying change.	1. Successful marriage. 2. Career satisfaction and advancement. 3. Effective parents; healthy offspring. 4. Informed, participating citizen. 5. Sound consumer behavior. 6. Satisfying home environment. 7. Social skills. 8. Fulfilled single state, autonomy. 9. Successful problem solving. 10. Successful stress management, personal growth.
Catch-30, 29–34 years old	1. Search for personal values. 2. Reappraise relationships. 3. Progress in career. 4. Accept growing children. 5. Put down roots, achieve "permanent" home. 6. Problem solve. 7. Manage stress accompanying change.	1. Examined and owned values. 2. Authentic personal relationships. 3. Career satisfaction, economic reward, a sense of competence and achievement. 4. Growth producing parent–child relationship. 5. Sound consumer behavior. 6. Successful problem solving. 7. Successful stress management, personal growth.
Midlife re-examination, 35–43 years old	1. Search for meaning. 2. Reassess marriage. 3. Reexamine work. 4. Relate to teen-age children. 5. Relate to aging parents. 6. Reassess personal priorities and values. 7. Adjust to single life. 8. Problem solve. 9. Manage stress accompanying change.	1. Coping with existential anxiety. 2. Satisfying marriages. 3. Appropriate career decisions. 4. Improved parent–child relations. 5. Improved child–parent relations. 6. Autonomous behavior. 7. Fulfilled single state. 8. Successful problem solving. 9. Successful stress management, personal growth.

adult family and with families across generations is the text by Kramer (203).

COMMON HEALTH PROBLEMS AND NURSING APPLICATIONS

Nursing Applications

Your role in caring for the young adult may be many faceted. Assessment based on knowledge presented throughout this chapter is the basis for formulating *nursing diagnoses*. Nursing diagnoses that may be applicable to the young adult are listed in Table 12–4. Health promotion interventions to assist the young adult and the family to meet physical, cognitive, emotional, social, and spiritual needs are described in the following, as well as in the previous, sections.

Immunizations. The young adult may need immunizations, depending on his/her history. Five to 20 percent of young adults remain susceptible to measles, rubella, or both. The American College Health Association recommends that colleges and universities require student documentation of immunity to preventable diseases as a prerequisite to registration (418). Adults should be vaccinated against influenza; hepatitis B; rubella (German measles); regular measles; and receive a tetanus booster every 10 years.

Common Physical Health Problems

Health problems and risks, preventive behavior and response to illness are influenced by gender as well as lifestyle. Refer to references at the end of the chapter for specific information on gender-related health issues (11, 57, 69, 120, 186, 221, 297, 436, 437).

Influenza. Influenza is an *acute, contagious, viral illness*, often associated with epidemics. The viruses causing influenza mutate, but a yearly updated vaccine is available. Influenza is characterized by fever, general malaise, muscle aching, and respiratory symptoms. Treatment consists of rest, an antipyretic, increased fluid intake, and a mild cough suppressant, if a nonproductive cough is persistent (175, 235).

Your primary responsibility lies in teaching preventive measures. Prevention is directed at supporting the

TABLE 12–4. Selected Nursing Diagnoses Related to the Young Adult[a]

PATTERN 1: EXCHANGING Altered Nutrition: More than body requirements Altered Nutrition: Less than body requirements Altered Nutrition: Potential for more than body requirements Potential for Infection Potential for Injury Potential for Impaired Skin Integrity PATTERN 2: COMMUNICATING Impaired Verbal Communication PATTERN 3: RELATING Impaired Social Interaction Social Isolation Altered Role Performance Altered Parenting Potential Altered Parenting Altered Family Processes Parental Role Conflict Altered Sexuality Patterns PATTERN 4: VALUING Spiritual Distress PATTERN 5: CHOOSING Ineffective Individual Coping Impaired Adjustment Defensive Coping Ineffective Denial Ineffective Family Coping: Disabling Ineffective Family Coping: Compromised Family Coping: Potential for Growth	Decisional Conflict Health Seeking Behaviors PATTERN 6: MOVING Fatigue Potential Activity Intolerance Sleep Pattern Disturbance Diversional Activity Deficit Impaired Home Maintenance Management Altered Health Maintenance PATTERN 7: PERCEIVING Body Image Disturbance Self Esteem Disturbance Chronic Low Self Esteem Situational Low Self Esteem Personal Identity Disturbance Sensory/Perceptual Alterations Hopelessness Powerlessness PATTERN 8: KNOWING Knowledge Deficit PATTERN 9: FEELING Pain Chronic Pain Dysfunctional Grieving Anticipatory Grieving Potential for Violence: Self-directed or directed at others Post-Trauma Response Rape-Trauma Syndrome Anxiety Fear

[a]Other NANDA diagnoses are applicable to the ill young adult.
Source: NANDA Approved Nursing Diagnostic Categories, *Nursing Diagnosis Newsletter*, 15, no. 1 (1988), 1–3.

body's defenses and reducing the person's susceptibility: avoiding unnecessary chills, air contaminants, and excesses in alcohol or smoking; observing basic health practices (adequate rest, sleep, exercise, liquids, and nutritious diet); and obtaining influenza immunizations as indicated. The young adult should also be encouraged to seek medical treatment when necessary and cautioned that chronic respiratory problems can develop later in life if precautions are not taken now.

Hepatitis. Hepatitis B, *a type of inflammation of the liver*, is said to be on the rise. The disease, which causes 80 percent of the world's primary liver cancer as well as high incidence of cirrhosis, is often undetected. The disease itself can cause death. Some people never develop the main symptom, jaundice. About 10 percent become carriers of the disease who in turn infect others. The Centers for Disease Control urge that anyone at risk for the disease get vaccinated. People at high risk include health care workers, male homosexuals, persons with multiple sex partners, intravenous drug users, institutionalized mentally ill persons, prisoners, and kidney dialysis patients (56, 302).

Accidents. Accidents are a leading cause of death for young adult males, and the second leading cause of death for young adult females, with motor vehicle accidents producing the most deaths in both sexes. Among the young male population, industrial accidents and drownings also rank high as major causes of accidental death. Other injuries typical in young adulthood are fractures, dislocations, lacerations, abrasions, and contusions (60, 328). These injuries require restriction of activity, which also presents the young adult with social and economic problems.

✔ Because accidents and their resultant injuries are serious health hazards for the young adult, safety education should be a prime concern for you in all occupational settings. You should initiate and actively participate in safety programs in various settings: employment, school, or recreation. Young adults should be reminded of the safety rules involved in swimming and other sports and encouraged to drive defensively. The groundwork in safety education should be established when the individual is young. Old habits and patterns are difficult to change.

✔ **Dental Problems.** Not so commonly considered health problems for the young adult are **dental caries** (*decay*) and **periodontal disease,** *characterized by spongy, bleeding, hypertrophied gums, later receding of gums and bone, and eventual loss of teeth.* Twice yearly visits to the dentist for regular care increase the likelihood of avoiding dentures or health problems of the mouth in later life. Proper diet and tooth and mouth care should be taught to the young adult (98, 354, 445).

✔ *Malignancies.* **Cancer of the mouth** begins to appear in the young adult age group. Oral cancer has a poorer survival rate than cancer of the breast, colon, rectum, or prostate; therefore, early detection is essential. The nurse should examine the mucous membranes of the mouth as part of the physical assessment and report and record any abnormalities (268, 355).

✔ Periodic pelvic examinations and cytologic smears are essential in all women who are sexually active or over the age of 20. Cancer is the leading cause of death in females between 25 and 44 years of age. The risk of cancer of the reproductive organs of females increases with age (62, 178, 235, 379). Afro-American women are more likely than Caucasian women to suffer **cancer of the cervix.** Pelvic examinations are also indicated for females with physical symptoms such as excessive menstrual flow, watery discharge, or bleeding between periods. The history of the person is especially significant if her mother took diethystilbestrol (DES). It is estimated that between 1941 and 1971 2 to 4 million women received the drug during pregnancy, particularly in the North and Midwest. The majority of daughters will develop an abnormal glandular cell growth called vaginal adenosis, a possible precursor to cancer. They may also have difficulty becoming pregnant and retaining the pregnancy (220, 235, 265).

Breast cancer is rare under the age of 25, but the risk increases steadily after the age of 30. All young women should be taught and encouraged to do self-breast examinations, since most breast cancers are first found by the individual woman. In addition, examination by a physician or nurse practitioner should be done annually. Many women are hesitant to do self-breast examinations: fear, lack of knowledge, modesty, health orientation, education level, and age contribute to this reluctance (121, 142, 235). Women are likely to practice self-examination of the breasts if they have a positive self-concept, if they are aware of the benefits, and if barriers are minimized (339). Women who perform other preventive health measures are more likely to do self-breast examination. Also, media coverage of someone who has successfully recovered from a mastectomy increases self-examination.

✔ You should teach the following information concerning self-breast examination. Examination should include systematic inspection and palpation. The woman should sit in front of a well-lit mirror and with arms hanging, inspect each breast for asymmetry or irregularities. The woman should then raise her hands above her head and observe for retraction or distortion of the nipple, which is common in breast carcinoma. Then with hands on her hips, the woman should forcefully contract the pectoral muscles; through this maneuver a lesion adherent to the pectoral muscles can be seen to move. Finally, the woman should bend forward with her hands up to determine if there is fixation of the breast to the chest wall. While lying in a supine position, keeping under her head the hand closest to the breast being examined, the woman should palpate each breast. Using the palm of her free hand in a circular motion, she should feel all tissue systematically to determine the presence of either a fixed or movable nodule. After both breasts are examined, she should repeat the palpation process standing up. The examination should be done monthly, at a specific time of the month, so that the woman is familiar enough with her breasts to detect any abnormalities.

✔ During young adulthood the male should be taught to regularly examine his scrotum and penis, since **cancer of the testes** may occur and may be detected by palpating unusual nodules. Teach the following information concerning the examination. The examination should be done immediately following a shower or warm bath, when both the scrotum and the examiner's hands are warm. The scrotum should be held in the palms of the hand and palpated with the thumb and fingers of both hands. Each testicle should be examined individually. Locate the epididymis (found on top of and extending down behind the testicle); it should be soft and slightly tender. The spermatic cord should be examined next; it ascends from the epididymus and has a firm, smooth, tubular structure (131, 235). It is important to become familiar with the consistency of normal testicular structures so that changes can be detected. In later young adullthood an annual rectal examination is helpful to detect prostatic enlargement and possible cancer of the prostate gland, although prostatic cancer is more common in later adulthood. In addition, proctosigmoidoscopy (examination of the rectum and lower colon with a lighted instrument) should be done on both men and women as part of the annual or biennial physical examination in an attempt to detect early rectal cancer. This examination is done less frequently on people with low cancer risk level (168, 235). See Appendix II for recommended physical examination procedures to be done for this age group.

↙ Teach clients the danger signs of cancer. Often it seems that the public is oblivious to health hazards in spite of information presented in the media. For example, **skin cancer** is increasing in incidence, due primarily to overexposure to sunlight. In the early stages, skin cancer can usually be cured. Teach protection through use of a sunscreen or covering skin when exposed to sunlight for an excessive time, especially from 11 AM to 2 PM. Teach also signs that should be considered suspicious and reported to a physician:

1. Changes in a dark-colored mole or spot.
2. Pink or flesh-colored nodule that slowly grows larger.
3. Open or crusted sore that does not heal.
4. Red, rough patch or bump that persists.
5. Mole that grows, changes, hurts, bleeds, or itches.
6. Mole that is larger in size than a pencil eraser, has irregular borders or variegated colors with shadings of red-white or blue-black.
7. Elevation or bulge in a mole that was flat.
8. Mole on the bottom of the feet or in an area of repeated trauma.

↙ Daily habits may contribute to risk for cancer in other ways. For example, risks for lung and hematopoietic cancers appear to be increased in adulthood after childhood exposure to parental smoking (343). Consuming two or more cups of caffeinated coffee a day may be associated with increased risk of colon or bladder cancer (235). Realize that some cultural groups are more prone to cancer. For example, Sievers found that environmental and cultural factors (e.g., diet, lifestyle stress, exposure to pollutants) contribute significantly to increased incidence of cancer. American Indians, in comparison to Caucasians, have lower rates for cancer of the lung, breast, and colon and higher rates for gallbladder, kidney, and cervical cancer, possibly related to genetics, diet, or lifestyle (370). American Indians have a higher rate of alcoholism than Caucasians. Although Oriental populations have a low rate of breast and colon cancer, those who have migrated to Western countries experience higher frequency of carcinoma of each anatomic site than prevails in their adopted country. Tell women that incidence of breast cancer or fibrocystic disease is higher in those who consume increased amounts of caffeine (249).

Cardiovascular Conditions. **Hypertension** is another significant health problem for both males and females in later young adulthood. The Afro-American person is more likely than the Caucasian to have hypertension (235, 318). Any person under 40 whose *blood pressure is 140/90 or higher* is considered hypertensive and should be followed closely (143, 233, 412). If untreated, hypertension reduces the life span.

↙ You can take an active role in the detection, prevention, and treatment of this condition. As with the adolescent, a reduction in weight and a decreased intake of calories, salt, and saturated fats will help alleviate the problem. In addition, a change in the young person's lifestyle, such as increasing physical activity, increasing periods of relaxation, and decreasing or stopping smoking, may also be therapeutic.

↙ **Mitral Valve Prolapse Syndrome** is a relatively benign but extremely frightening condition that is being diagnosed more frequently in young adult females, especially those who are tall and lanky because the heart has to pump harder to maintain normal flow of blood throughout the tall body. The individual experiences chest pain, arrhythmias and palpitations and may be unable to meet social, economic, and family expectations (16, 55, 85, 141, 417). Onset is often after the first pregnancy. The syndrome may be misdiagnosed as an acute anxiety reaction because of the similarity to those symptoms. A thorough physical examination is necessary. The condition can be controlled through medication and adequate rest.

Iron deficiency anemia *is defined as a blood hemoglobin level of 10 g/100 ml, compared to the normal 12 to 16 g/100 ml.* Menstruation is the most common cause of iron deficiency in women. The average woman loses 0.5 mg of iron daily during menses. An inadequate absorption of iron, frequently related to a diet that is low in iron, may also cause this form of anemia (235). Often there are no signs and symptoms.

↙ This condition is picked up on a screening examination. However, fatigue, irritability, lack of initiative, depression, weakness, dizziness, and headache, muscle aches, pallor of skin and conjunctivae, fissures of lips, and brittle nails may be part of the clinical picture. Treatment is straightforward: an iron preparation taken orally several times a day for about 3 months. The person should introduce more iron-rich foods in the diet to avoid a future relapse (175).

↙ *Skin Conditions.* *Atopic dermatitis*, already discussed in the chapter on infancy, often takes on a different appearance in adulthood. Dry, thickened skin, which accentuates normal lines and folds and often causes hyperpigmentation, is commonly located on the flexor areas of extremities, eyelids, dorsi of hands and feet, and back of neck. Prevention includes keeping the skin dry in humid conditions, using mild nondrying soap, applying agents that seal water into the skin, and, during acute phases, frequently applying a small amount of hydrocortisone cream to the affected area (175).

↙ Sometimes young adults are prone to **folliculitis**, *a*

localized infection of a hair follicle; to **furuncles** (**boils**), *a follicular infection which becomes large and deep and has one draining point;* and to **carbuncles,** *a large group of furuncles with several drainage points.* These are infected with the opportunistic *Staphylococcus aureus.* Folliculitis usually abates with the washing of the area followed by application of hot compresses several times a day for 15 to 20 minutes. Furuncles and carbuncles need the same treatment, but additionally may need to be incised and drained and packed with a sterile gauze until healing takes place (175).

📍 **Urticaria** (**hives**) *is an allergic reaction,* usually to drugs, foods, inhalants, or insect bites. Sometimes no cause is found. The person often first has itching, which is followed by red, raised welts forming usually on the trunk or extremities. The lesions or welts usually fade in less than 12 hours and sometimes in less than an hour. There are no accompanying respiratory complications. An intense reaction may require an injection of epinephrine followed by an oral antihistamine. Soaking in a tub of cool water or using an oatmeal bath may relieve the itching. A careful search for the offending agent is important (175).

📍 *Gastrointestinal Disorders.* **Simple diarrhea,** consisting of *frequent, loose, watery stools that are not greasy, bloody, or purulent,* usually originates because of an acute viral infection, a psychological disturbance related to stress, dietary changes, and sometimes laxatives. Treatment consists of a clear liquid diet of tea, carbonated beverages, and clear soups along with symptomatic management with an over-the-counter preparation, such as kaolin and pectin or a prescription medication such as paregoric (175).

Lactose intolerance or **milk malabsorption syndrome** may first become apparent in young adulthood. In a *large percentage of ethnic people of dark skins, the lactose (milk in sugar) is not hydrolyzed because they lack sufficient amounts of the enzyme lactose.* Ingesting milk or milk products can cause severe discomfort. The syndrome is more fully described in Chapter 1. Englert and Guillon (103) also describe the syndrome in detail.

📍 The person may obtain relief by using LactAid (Sugar Lo Company, Pleasantville, NJ), which is a concentrated form of this enzyme. Ten drops added to a quart of milk, and refrigeration for 1 day following, will reduce lactose by 90 percent. Lactobacillus milk also marketed for this condition is less likely to cause symptoms. A lactose-free diet is the best treatment. The person should avoid all milk and milk products and check labels for whey or other lactose ingredients in foods that would not normally be considered as milk foods or products. For example, other foods to avoid include:

1. Cream of rice; instant cream of wheat.
2. Breads, rolls, biscuits, crackers, muffins, and pancakes.
3. Packaged bread crumbs, breading, or croutons.
4. Fruits dried or frozen or canned with lactose.
5. Fruits or vegetables prepared with cheese, milk, milk products, butter, or margarine.
6. Creamed or breaded meats, fish, poultry.
7. Lunchmeats that have milk products, frankfurters, sweetbreads, canned soup (103, 174, 305, 332).

Lifestyle and Physical Illness

Life is rooted in and organized around a person's changing culture and society, whether the changes are dramatic or subtle. Coping with extreme change taxes the person physically and psychologically and may be responsible for physical disease. Research shows relationships between physical adaptation and illness and sociocultural experiences. Death rates from cancer, diabetes, tuberculosis, heart disease, and multiple sclerosis for urban populations are inversely proportional to income, implying that stresses of poverty may be a cause of disease (77, 175, 281).

The adult is most likely to fall ill when he/she is experiencing the "giving up—given up complex": feelings of lowered self-esteem, discouragement, despair, humiliation, depression, powerlessness to change or cope with a situation, imagined helplessness, loss of gratifying roles, sense of uncertain future, and memories of earlier periods of giving up. Apparently such feelings modify the capacity of the organism to cope with concurrent pathogenic factors. Biologically, the central nervous system fails in its task of processing the emergency defense system, so that the person has a higher statistical tendency toward illness or death. Conversely, contentment, happiness, faith, confidence, and success are associated with health (21, 77, 181, 280).

Anxiety is a combination of *fearfulness, nervousness, apprehension, and restlessness* that is often associated with a family or personal crisis, and sometimes with a physical or mental illness. The symptoms may be loss of appetite (or increased appetite), lack of sleeping ability, increased perspiration, a "thumping of the heart," headaches, weakness, or fatigue. Occasionally trembling hands and tightly drawn facial muscles are noticeable.

📍 More information on how to assess anxiety is available in other texts. Supportive therapy and crisis intervention are the best treatment. The young adult may need short-term treatment with an antianxiety medication, but this should only be an adjunct to understanding, counseling, and eliminating the cause of anxiety (281, 282).

↙ **Tension headaches** are often associated with periods of stress and are usually described as a *band-like pressure across the forehead and around the back of the skull*. The pain is usually described as dull and aching with an accompanying feeling of tightness. It may last for long periods. The examiner may find the muscles in the posterior neck, as well as the scalp, to be sore because these headaches are essentially a *musculoskeletal phenomenon*. Relief usually comes with reassurance, mild analgesics, massage, or manipulation, and elimination of some of the tension (175).

Migraine headaches are thought to be *vascular in origin. Arterial spasm followed by dilatation is thought to cause the pain, which is usually of a throbbing, unilateral nature*. Often the headaches are preceded by an **aura,** an *inherent warning*, usually visual, during which surroundings may look different than usual, followed by some neurological signs such as tingling and weakness of the extremities. The headache may last 1 hour to several days and is sometimes associated with nausea and vomiting. Often a family history of similar episodes is found.

↙ Several prescription medications are used to try to avert an impending migraine. Caffeine is also thought to help prevent the onset. Once the headache is established, however, relief usually comes only with rest in a dark room and a strong analgesic such as Demerol or codeine. Various alternate methods used with some success are nutrition, chiropractic, and biofeedback. Sometimes readjustment of the temporomandibular joint will cause migraines to disappear (175).

Functional bowel disease or **irritable colon syndrome** is characterized by *four to six small, loose, watery bowel movements daily along with lower abdominal discomfort and a sensation of the need for further defecation*. It is often associated with tense and anxious young adults. Prevention of recurrence is in the form of stress reduction and reassurance of the nature of the problem. Antidiarrheal agents are not indicated. A mild tranquilizer may be used temporarily (175).

Lifestyle influences illness in yet another way. Multiple living arrangements, sexual experimentation, and mobility from group to group are responsible for a number of conditions. These include the present epidemics of sexually transmitted diseases and insect infestation, such as *body and pubic lice* (**pediculosis**), bedbugs, or ticks; airborne diseases, such as respiratory infections; and skin infections, such as staphylococcal or fungal infections. Other conditions are hepatitis from fecal contamination of food and water or use of unsterile equipment in drug abuse; gastrointestinal disorders from unhygienic food preparation; and malnutrition from lack of proper food intake.

Scabies is caused by a *mite* which initially burrows into the skin, *causing a papule or vesicle to form*. After several days, sensitivity to the mite causes *severe pruritis and punctate excoriation*. Scratching can cause additional *skin damage and change*. This condition is found most frequently in association with poor personal hygiene and crowded living conditions. Because it requires only close personal contact for transfer, prevention may be difficult.

↙ On diagnosis, not only should the initially symptomatic person be treated, but also symptomatic members of the household and sexual contacts. All underclothing, pajamas, and sheets should be washed in boiling water. Treatment is with gamma benzene hexachloride, a cream or lotion applied from the neck down and removed after 24 hours. Several applications may be necessary. An antipruritic may also be precribed (175).

Cystitis is frequently seen in the young adult female, especially at the onset of sexual activity. *Inflammation of the bladder* is characterized by dysuria and frequency. The offending organism is often Escherichia coli.

↙ A clean catch urinalysis and a urine culture will identify the organism. In addition to appropriate antibiotic treatment, another medication is sometimes given for bladder analgesic effect. A minimum of eight 8-ounce glasses of water should be consumed daily both as prevention and treatment (175).

↙ **Acute pyelonephritis** is basically the same disease as cystitis except more serious because it involves more of the urinary system. *The kidneys and the collecting system are inflamed*. Again, a urinalysis and urine culture can help determine the diagnosis. The person, in addition to dysuria and frequency, may have flank pain, chills, nausea and vomiting, and a temperature of 101° F or more. Appropriate antibiotic therapy is initated plus a medication for nausea and vomiting, if appropriate. Both cystitis and pyelonephritis can become chronic and result in damage to the urinary system, so appropriate diagnosis and antibiotic treatment (based on sensitivity tests) are essential (175).

Acquired Immune Deficiency Syndrome (**AIDS**) is the label for a group of *health-related problems resulting from severe loss of the body's natural immunity to disease*. At this time, AIDS is a fatal disease. There are currently experimental attempts to slow the progress of the disease, and there are attempts to develop a vaccine.

AIDS is caused by a virus known as human immunodeficiency virus or HIV. If an individual is infected with this virus, a condition may result which destroys the body's natural defenses against disease. It was first reported in the United States in 1981 but more likely occurred in 1977. Dramatic and swift action was taken by the Public Health Service to isolate the causative virus, screen the nation's blood supply, and educate the public as to its spread. The AIDS virus infects and destroys white blood cells known as T-helper cells. These particular cells regulate the body's immune system and if destroyed, there is no longer a capability to fight disease. In addition, the HIV virus can infect the cells of the central nervous system (51).

Infection with the AIDS virus does not always lead to AIDS, but if the person tests positive for HIV he or she can transmit the virus to another human being.

Transmission of the blood-borne virus occurs through the following ways:

1. Sexual intercourse with an infected person, male or female.
2. Contact with contaminated blood equipment such as sharing equipment for IV drug abuse.
3. A mother may give HIV to her unborn fetus during pregnancy or transmit the virus during birth or while breast-feeding.

The virus has been isolated in semen, vaginal secretions, blood, saliva, and tears. Even though the virus has been found in saliva and tears, there are no known documented cases of transmission other than by the ways just listed (51).

In an individual over 4 months of age, the AIDS antibody test can determine whether or not a person has been exposed to the AIDS virus. This does not mean that the person will necessarily develop AIDS. Unfortunately, the antibodies are not protective to the person like the antibodies to other disease organisms. It is not yet understood why this is so but research is seeking an answer. It is also suggested that large amounts of virus are required to cause the infection and possibly co-factors are necessary for invasion to occur. The co-factors that have been suggested are an already decreased immune system, alcohol use, recreational drugs, poor nutrition, inadequate rest or exercise, severe stress, and other infections (51).

Public education is the only way of dealing with this public health menace. It is estimated that 1 to 1½ million Americans have been infected with the AIDS virus. Of this group, approximately 10,000 people are known to have the disease, leaving the remainder capable of transmitting the virus for several years. The incubation period of the virus varies from months to as many as ten years (51).

✔ The prevention of AIDS is dependent on behavior which reduces or eliminates the possibility of contracting or transmitting the disease. The Public Health Service recommends these behaviors (24, 51, 58, 82):

1. Do not have sexual intercourse with multiple persons, or with persons who had multiple partners (including prostitutes). The more partners you have, the greater your risk.
2. Avoid sexual intercourse with persons with AIDS, with people at risk for AIDS, or persons who have had a positive result on the AIDS antibody test. However, if you do have sexual intercourse with a person you think may be infected, protect yourself by taking precautions to prevent contact with that person's body fluids. ("Body fluids" include blood, semen, urine, feces, saliva, and vaginal secretions.) *Use of a condom* will reduce the chances of spreading the virus. The intact correctly applied rubber condom is effective against transmission of sexually transmitted diseases. Dirubbo specifies types and their use; directions are given for teaching patients/clients so that the condom will be correctly used (89). Avoid practices such as anal intercourse that may injure body tissues and make it easier for the virus to enter the bloodstream. Oral–genital contact should also be avoided, as should open-mouthed, intimate kissing.
3. Do not use intravenous drugs. If you do, do not share needles or syringes.
4. Consult your doctor for counseling if you believe that you may be at increased risk for infection by the AIDS virus. Consider taking the AIDS antibody test, which will enable you to know your status and take appropriate action.

Persons in the following groups are at increased risk for infection from the AIDS virus (24, 51, 82):

1. Homosexual and bisexual men (or men who have had sexual intercourse with another man since 1977).
2. People who inject illegal intravenous drugs or who have done so in the past.
3. Persons with symptoms of AIDS or AIDS-related illnesses.
4. Persons from Haiti and Central African countries, where heterosexual transmission is thought to be more common than in the United States.
5. Male or female prostitutes and their sex partners.
6. Sexual partners of persons infected with the AIDS virus at increased risk of infection.
7. Persons with hemophilia who have received clotting factor products.
8. Infants of high-risk or infected mothers.

✔ Kuhls et al. (208) found that if hospital infection control practices are followed when health care workers care for patients with AIDS, or work with their biological specimens, there is low risk of occupationally acquiring the opportunistic infections associated with AIDS: (1) Human Immunodeficiency Virus (HIV) through serum conversion, (2) cytomegalovirus (CMV), (3) Hepatitis B Virus (HBV), or Herpes Simplex Virus Type 2 (HSV-2). Seroconversion to HIV is most likely to follow a contaminated needlestick injury. Health care professionals who use rubber gloves are effectively protected against transmission of AIDS when they are correctly fitted and worn and are intact (89).

✓ In adults, the ten warning symptoms are as follows:

1. Swollen glands, especially in neck, armpits, or groin.
2. Blotches or rashes, usually pink to purple, which grow in size, are harder than surrounding areas, and may appear under skin, in the mouth, nose, rectum, and among other body sites.
3. More than 10 pounds weight loss of unexpected nature within 2 months.
4. Fever persisting for more than a week and night sweats.
5. A cough which is persistent and dry.
6. Diarrhea.
7. Malaise and persistent fatigue.
8. Thrush or white coating on the tongue.
9. Easy bruising.
10. Blurred vision or persistent headaches.

These symptoms may indicate early stages of various diseases which may lead to death, such as Kaposi's sarcoma and *Pneumocystis carinii* pneumonia (24, 82).

✓ As a nurse, you may care for the person with AIDS either in the hospital or the home. Schietinger describes home care of the AIDS patient, as well as the disease process and complications (351). A toll-free hotline has been set up by the Public Health Service to answer questions about AIDS as information is revealed, and a publication spelling out developments in the disease has being issued.

Refer also to Chapter 11 for information on other **sexually transmitted diseases** that can also be contacted by the adult.

Cultural Differences. Another lifestyle that involves geographic mobility, transient and inadequate housing, hard work, poor nutrition, and inadequate immunizations or other health promotion measures is that of the **migrant farm worker**. The migrant worker has unique and numerous health care needs: because of the following: (1) the opportunity for prevention of certain illnesses is nonexistent; (2) prenatal and maternal care is lacking; (3) chronic health problems are numerous; (4) economic resources are scant; and (5) contacts with the health-care system are sporadic and temporary. Specific ways to work with Mexican-American seasonal workers and their families are described by O'Brien. (Migrant workers from other cultural backgrounds would have some of the same needs as those described by O'Brien [292]). Refer also to Chapter 1.

✓ Be attuned to cultural differences, including language difficulties, definitions of health and illness, food preferences, lines of authority, health practices, job-related diseases, and general lifestyle of your clients.

Health problems in women and the related issues of sex-stereotyped treatment are experienced especially by women from minority groups, be they Afro-American, Hispanic, Asian-Pacific, or American Indian. Painter describes the socioeconomic and health disadvantages of Afro-American women in America, related to the historical roots of slavery and complex problems or racism and sexism. The attempts that Afro-American women (and men) have made to adapt to their plight have produced relationships within the family that, in many cases, do not conform to the gender roles and values prevalent in the dominant Caucasian society. Afro-American women deserve praise for their resourcefulness and ability in maintaining the family unit against overwhelming odds. Although the infant mortality rate for Afro-American babies is 1½ times that of Caucasian babies in the United States, Afro-American families have tried to give the best possible care to their children, within often unresponsive social and health-care systems (301).

The American Indian has an infant mortality rate as high as that for Afro-American children and the deficiency of medical care facilities for nonreservation rural Indians as well as reservation Indians is great (318).

In contrast in the United States, women who are in higher socioeconomic levels, who are high achievers, and who have professional or executive positions have been found to have a 29 percent better life expectancy than other women. The same trend is true for men who are in the higher socioeconomic levels, who are achievers, and who have professional or executive positions (318). Thus it appears that many health and related social and economic issues are not just women's issues, but they are equally relevant to men (206).

✓ You can use this information for health promotion. Illness can be prevented through counseling susceptible persons not to make too many life changes in too short a time, since the more rapid the pace, the more disorganized the individual becomes. Listen to what the person says, whether he/she is well or ill, and note the degree of change occurring in his/her life. If unavoidably rapid change and a high degree of stress are occurring, a detailed, frequent follow-up program that uses the principles of crisis intervention may prevent the onset of illness or complications of an already present condition.

✓ Explore ways, being non-judgmental, to improve hygienic conditions for young adults. Sincere interest, factual information, and willingness to give care without preaching are essential to health promotion for young adults.

Biofeedback. The young adult is likely to be interested in and benefit from **biofeedback training,** *learning to control body functions once thought to be involuntary,* such as heartbeat, blood pressure, breathing, and muscle contractions. People are being taught to use their brains to cope with physical problems, to prevent symptoms or disease states, or reduce symptom severity by learning what their organs are doing within predetermined limits and by controlling organ function. Learning biofeedback is much like learning other skills of muscular coordination and physical activity. Involved in this is controlled production of alpha waves, the brain waves typical of relaxation and reverie, the fringe of consciousness. Mental functions such as perception, memory, learning, creativity, and control of sleep are also affected by control over alpha output and can help the young adult feel more alive and healthy and able to function closer to his/her optimum potential (6, 81, 217, 348). Biofeedback has been used to treat a variety of conditions. Putt describes assessment prior to and implementation of a biofeedback service operated by nurses (317).

Meditation has also become a popular method to relax and to produce physiological changes that are healthful, such as lower metabolism, pulse, respirations, and blood pressure. You may teach meditation techniques to clients. Acupressure and yoga are other self-care measures.

Emotional Health Problems

Stress reactions, *physiological and psychological changes resulting in unusual or disturbed adaptive behavior patterns,* result when the young adult is unable to cope with the newly acquired tasks and responsibilities. Mate selection, marriage, childrearing, college, job demands, social expectations, and independent decision making are all stressors that carry threats of insecurity and possibly some degree of failure. Some of these stress reactions take the form of physical illnesses just described. Others take the form of self-destructive behavior, such as suicide, alcoholism, drug abuse and addiction, and excessive smoking. Other stress reactions include abuse of spouse.

Self-destructive behavior, in the form of death by suicide, is increasing in spite of the many religious, cultural, and moral taboos. Thousands of people take their own lives or attempt suicide yearly. Other behaviors are also self-destructive in nature.

Suicide. Suicide is the fourth leading overall cause for death among young adults in the United States (415). Although medicine has decreased the threat of many physical illnesses, the present-day lifestyle has increased the physical, mental, and emotional stress on individuals. Suicide statistics might actually prove to be higher if all accidental deaths were investigated more closely for clues of suicidal intent. Many people deliberately conceal their suicide under the guise of an accident: driving their car off the road, combining alcohol and barbiturates, or discharging a gun while cleaning (134, 303, 329).

Women make the majority of unsuccessful suicide attempts while men complete suicide more frequently. Both physiological and psychological factors influence the choice of method for suicide. Women tend to use less lethal methods, such as aspirin or barbiturate overdose, poisoning, or cutting the wrists. Men usually use the more lethal methods: gunshot wounds of the head or hanging. Women may see attempted suicide as a means of expressing aggression or manipulating relationships or events in the environment; therefore, they select the less lethal methods. Degree of physical strength and the subconscious fear of disfigurement may also influence the females' choice of methods (148). Most of the time the person does not really desire death but rather a way out of an apparently hopeless or intolerable situation.

Statistics indicate that suicide occurs less frequently among married persons. Suicide is higher among single (especially males) and widowed individuals and highest among the divorced. Apparently, the married person does not suffer from the social isolation and total lack of someone with whom to communicate as do the single, divorced, or widowed individuals. But the suicide rate in married persons under 24 years of age is higher than for single persons. Perhaps these people sought marriage as an attempt to escape from their unmanageable situations. When marriage does not immediately solve their problems or creates new stresses, they end their lives (148, 373).

Occupation is also an important factor in suicide rates. Professional groups such as dentists, psychiatrists, and physicians are considered high-risk groups, although the underlying causes for this are undetermined. The required strenuous educational courses or the stressful demands and responsibilities of their positions may be factors.

✔ Consider three factors when planning primary prevention of suicide among young adults. Educate the public about emotional needs of the person and early signs of suicide so that high-risk persons can be more easily identified by family and friends. See Chapter 8 in *Nursing Concepts for Health Promotion* (282). To compensate for the effects of separating from home and encountering a variety of stressors, a close and significant relationship between high-risk persons and a caring person should be established. The person needs opportunity to talk through frustration, anger, and despair and formulate life plans.

Finally, encourage young adults to participate in group and extracurricular activities that prevent social isolation.

✔ Nursing responsibility for the suicidal person extends to the industrial setting, clinic, general or psychiatric hospital, and the general community. You are in contact with and in the position to identify persons who may be potential candidates for suicide: unwed mothers, divorcees, widows and widowers, alcoholics, the terminally ill, and depressed people. Watch for signs of depression. If the person speaks of overwhelming sadness, worthlessness, hopelessness, or emptiness and complains of sleep and gastrointestinal disturbances, lack of energy, or chronic illness, he/she is in a depressed state. Decreased muscle tone with slumped shoulders, slowed gait, drooped facies, and decreased interest in work, personal appearance, religion, family and friends, or special events are also signs of depression. The person prefers being alone and is self-preoccupied. He/she is unable to carry out ordinary tasks or make simple decisions. Once identified, these signs of depression must be communicated to others: friends, relatives, a physician, or other persons concerned with the potentially suicidal person.

✔ The person is more prone to attempt suicide *when the depression is lifting* and energy is greater. Listen closely to the person who speaks of being alienated, in an impossible situation, or of the future looking bleak and unchangeable, even after saying the situation is improving. He/she is a high-risk suicidal candidate, as is the person who talks of suicide, who has made an attempt, who is in crisis, or who is an alcoholic or drug abuser (148).

✔ Your responsibility in individual suicide prevention varies according to the setting, the source, and extent of distress. You will need to protect the person against self-destructive behavior by reducing environmental hazards; but emotional support is of greater importance while the person works through problems. The principles of crisis intervention, therapeutic communication, and nurse–client relationship are discussed in *Nursing Concepts for Health Promotion* (282) and psychiatric nursing texts (281). Show the person verbally and nonverbally that someone—you—understands, respects, and cares about him/her.

✔ You must know your own feelings about suicide and other self-destructive behavior. If you have more than transient depression, you cannot help another. You must see yourself and each person as an individual who possesses dignity and worth. Acceptance, understanding, and respect must be shown each person. Above all, you must be available and willing to listen. You can always listen long enough to assess and refer, even if you can't work with the situation (281).

Alcoholism. Alcoholism, a complex disease, is also a form of self-destructive behavior. One suicide in every five is an alcoholic (148). In addition, many alcoholics literally drink themselves to death, or die as a result of physical debilitation or injuries sustained while under the influence of alcohol.

In the United States there is much ambivalence about drinking. Some states prohibit the purchase and consumption of alcohol until the age of 21; other states have lowered the age to 18. Drinking frequently starts during preadolescence or early adolescence, is introduced by the parents, and follows the pattern of the person's parents. Thus, with drinking behavior and expectancies poorly defined during the young years, lack of cultural norms for alcohol consumption, and individual biochemical predispositions, the stage is set for alcoholism in later life.

Alcoholism may occur during any life period. Male alcoholics outnumber female alcoholics; however, identification of female alcoholics is increasing yearly. The alcoholic's life span is shortened about 12 years, and most alcoholics show physical and cognitive complications because of their prolonged drinking. In addition, millions of dollars are lost yearly in business as a result of absenteeism, lowered work efficiency, and accidents (65).

Alcoholism is a disease with physiological, psychological, and sociological aspects. Excessive drinking causes physiological addiction and psychological dependence. Not drinking causes mild to severe withdrawal symptoms. Alcohol is used to relieve worry and guilt and it falsely leads to an increased sense of adequacy and sociability (65). In turn, the person becomes more anxious and guilty when learning of his/her behavior while drinking. He/she drinks again to forget and deny. The vicious cycle becomes worse; behavior, performance, and health deteriorate until he/she is forced to seek help or else dies. References at the end of this chapter give more information on the etiology, psychodynamics, symptoms, and treatment of alcoholism (4, 9, 10, 23, 101, 115, 191, 281, 405).

✔ The same stress-producing situations which lead to suicide may also promote alcoholism in the young adult. Early case finding and early treatment are important in alcoholism. You can be active in both.

✔ Acceptance of the alcoholic as a sick person and support for those close to him/her are as important as the technical care you give during or after detoxification. You might write for the self-administered test for alcoholism that is available through National Council for Alcoholism or Alcoholics Anonymous. A certain score indicates alcoholic tendencies.

Drug Abuse and Addiction. These are another form of self-destructive behavior. Drug use and the

TABLE 12–5. Signs/Symptoms of Drug Abuse in the Young Adult

- Late to work frequently; late in producing assignments.
- Absenteeism increases; abusers miss twice as much work as nonabusing employees.
- Increased productivity in work for a short period; cocaine will cause some people to perform better than normal or more creatively for a short time; overachievement can be used to compensate for or cover up initial stages of abuse.
- Falling productivity, poorer quality work, disorganized thinking and work outcome, missing deadlines.
- Forgetfulness, failure to follow instructions properly, to carry out usual steps of a procedure.
- Personality change, increasing irritability, depression, suspicion.
- Chronic runny nose from cocaine inhalation, or sniffing glue or other chemicals, that causes irritation of the nasal mucous membrane; complains of a cold regularly.
- Nodding or sleeping on the job.
- Accident proneness, clumsy at work, poor gross or fine motor coordination on the job, reports of accidents in the auto or at home.
- Clandestine meetings and discussions with other employees; users become dealers for fellow employees and withdraw from supervisory staff.

---

nurse's responsibility are discussed in Chapter 11. The same information is applicable to the young adult. Drug abuse is increasing in the young adult, including all levels of workers.

As with alcoholism, male addicts are more numerous than female. Symptoms of drug addiction differ with the type of drug, amount used, and personality of the user (see Table 11–6). Symptoms may also differ for the young adult at work. Table 12–5 summarizes signs and symptoms seen in the worker who is abusing drugs—sometimes in the workplace.

✔ Treatment for drug abuse and addiction involves helping the person work through emotional problems, seeing that he/she has proper medical and nutritional regimens, helping him/her return to a community where the dangers of becoming addicted again are not too great, and helping him or her get involved in worthwhile work or activities.

Excessive Smoking. This is also considered suicidal behavior because nicotine causes many harmful physiological effects and is habit forming. Many people, even some with serious respiratory and vascular disorders, continue to smoke heavily despite the warnings from their physicians and reports from the Surgeon General's office regarding the harmful effects of smoking. Various reasons are given for smoking: Smoking is relaxing; it prevents nervousness and overeating; and it gives the person something to do with his/her hands in social gatherings. All these reasons may stem from internal tensions and may well be the young person's way of dealing with stress. If the pattern of excessive smoking is not altered during the stage of young adulthood, it may be impossible for changes to be made later in life. Excessive smoking is taking a heavy toll of cardiac deaths among younger women. Women are now catching up to men in the incidence of sudden death from heart attack and lung cancer, attributable chiefly to the burgeoning use of cigarettes among females (30, 80, 169, 206, 264, 296, 340). More women than men now smoke cigarettes. Other health problems are also attributed to smoking if the woman smokes more than ten cigarettes a day during pregnancy: periodontal disease; abnormal sperm and chromosome damage; carcinoma in situ of the cervix; chronic respiratory disease; increased spontaneous abortions, bleeding, fetal and neonatal deaths, and low-birth weight and premature births (106, 153, 269, 270, 363). All cigarette smokers appear to have a shortened life expectancy, whatever the direct cause of death. Further, offspring of the person who smokes are subject to more respiratory infections and allergies (392). Even less well known, but equally dangerous, is that chemicals found in cigarette smoke are also commonplace in many work environments. Thus, the person who smokes may suffer double jeopardy. Blackwood describes these chemicals, their effects, and ways to reduce exposure (30).

✔ Work with the young adult to reduce or stop cigarette smoking. To achieve this goal, you will have to do more than give information about morbidity and mortality rates. Explore his/her ideas of health and personal vulnerability to adverse effects from smoking. The social dynamics of smoking must also be considered. Smoking may mean being an adult, or a way to get peer approval or identify with the in-group, and exchanging cigarettes is a gesture of solidarity. It is important not to ridicule the smoker or interpret his/her behavior and smoking norms. Rather, deglamourize gestures of smoking, and hold up as models of adulthood those individuals who do not smoke. Further, realize that to give up smoking represents a loss. Help the person who is trying to stop smoking to acknowledge feelings of loss and grief related to giving up a part of self and social lifestyles. Instead of emphasizing that the person is "giving up" smoking, help the person verbalize feelings and then identify what is being gained by a smoking cessation program. Encourage the person to find a substitute other than eating to overcome the sense of emptiness. Help the person find ways of rewarding self for not smoking. Further, you can give the person positive feedback for not smoking. Give the person time to change habits. If the person has smoked for many years, it is not easy to stop (23, 99, 264, 269, 270, 322).

Battered or Abused Women. Battering is a social and emotional health problem of all socioeconomic levels which has gained increasing public attention. Wife beating has always been a problem: Woman was the man's property and beating was accepted behavior in some cultures. Traditionally, the woman was too ashamed or too helpless to admit the problem or seek help. Further, no help existed. Perhaps acknowledgement of and efforts to overcome child abuse and the women's liberation movement together helped to initiate change. Efforts are being made in some cities to make the police and legal system more aware of the *battered woman syndrome,* a symptom complex of violence in which a woman has received deliberate and severe injury more than three times from the husband or a man with whom she has a close relationship. Further, attempts have been made to make the police and legal system more protective to the woman who has been treated violently and more punitive to the violent man. Emergency shelters for battered women and their children are increasingly being established in urban areas so that the woman who seeks help does not have to return home or be at home when the man who was released shortly after arrest returns home even more violent than before. Crisis telephone lines have been established and publicized by the media, and hundreds of women have memorized these numbers. In some communities rap sessions and referrals are available for battered women. Assistance to women seeking divorce is inadequate in most cities because of the cost and bureaucratic red tape (92, 161, 227).

✔ You can work with other health and legal professionals to identify and overcome the problem of abused women. *Assessment of a family and woman* suffering adult abuse often reveals the following typical characteristics (92, 127, 145, 159, 161, 227, 236, 304, 349, 378):

1. The family and the woman are isolated socially or physically from neighbors, relatives, and friends.
2. The woman feels increasing helplessness, guilt, isolation, and low self-esteem. She feels trapped and has been forced to be dependent on the man.
3. The woman may range in age from 17 to 76, may suffer violent injury for months or years.
4. The woman's educational and occupational status is often higher than the man's.
5. Most beatings begin early in marriage and increase in frequency and intensity over the decades.
6. Most violence occurs in the evening, on weekends, and in the kitchen.
7. Generally there are no witnesses.
8. The woman is frequently unable to leave the home because of lack of money, transportation, a place to go, support people, or support agencies in the community. Further, she has learned helplessness behaviors and feels unable to try to escape.
9. The injuries from abuse may not be visible, but if abuse is present, the woman usually talks about the problem freely when asked directly if abuse is occurring.
10. With increasing incidence of abuse and the physical and emotional consequences of abuse, the woman becomes more passive, less flexible, less able to think logically, more apathetic, depressed, and possibly suicidal.
11. Eventually the frustration, stress, and anger may be externalized into physical behavior that is more than protective of the self or the child(ren); she may in turn become violent to the point of killing the battering partner.

✔ The *typical adult and parental behavior of the male batterer,* in order of incidence, according to the research by Sonkin et al., is as follows (378):

1. Has battered a previous partner.
2. Is employed, frequently under stress at work.
3. Has children who have viewed the domestic violence and his battering behavior.
4. Was under the influence of alcohol or drugs at the last battering incident.
5. Uses physical punishment on his children.
6. Has been violent with others not in their family, outside the home.
7. Has been violent both when and when not under the influence of drugs and alcohol.
8. Has a family history of suicide (attempted and completed).
9. Has been violent only when under the influence of alcohol and drugs.
10. Has been violent only when not under the influence of alcohol or drugs.
11. Lack of close friends or someone to talk with.

✔ **Psychological violence by the male against female** can be categorized as follows (378):

1. Explicit threats.
2. Extreme controlling type of behavior, taking her everywhere; saying when she must come home; knowing her whereabouts, companions, and life activities.
3. Pathological jealousy; continually questioning her about her behavior; making accusations without cause; highly suspicious.
4. Mental degradation; calling her names or telling her she is incompetent, stupid, and no good.
5. Isolating behavior. Because of his jealousy, suspicion, and dependence, he controls the woman's

behaviors so that she in turn becomes extremely isolated and dependent on him.

The male who batters the female partner has the following typical childhood history, in order of incidence, according to research by Sonkin et al (378):

1. Received physical punishment as a child.
2. Saw his mother abused or treated violently by the father.
3. Attacked one of the parents.
4. Physically abused as a child.
5. Sexually abused as a child.

The male batterer comes from all walks of life and cultures. Personality characteristics of the male batterer that are typical include:

1. Denying of or minimizing the violent behavior and its effects. The batterer may actually lose memory of the event because of his rage.
2. Blaming the behavior of the woman on others as the cause of the violent scenes.
3. Periodic uncontrollable anger and rage, which is externalized into physical and verbal behavior.
4. Dependency on the partner as sole source of love, support, intimacy, and problem solving, resultant from the controlling and isolating behavior that entwined him as well as the partner and children.
5. Sense of alienation from others and society, he considers himself a loner and therefore his "own boss"—means he can do whatever he wants in his home.
6. Jealousy of and suspiciousness of his partner, children, and finally everyone else.
7. Low self-esteem; lack of confidence in his ability to keep his partner, lack of skill or ability to ask for what is wanted in a nonthreatening way.

Some stresses predispose to family violence and male battering of the woman and children. These stresses are listed in Table 12–6.

Another form of battering that may effect either the male or female, but more commonly the female, is **incest,** one form of sexual abuse, although adult family members may convey that incestual behavior is normal. Woman victims of incest outnumber men ten to one.

✔ Symptoms and problems in adulthood resulting from childhood *sexual abuse and incest* are:

1. Chronic depression, hopelessness related to shame and guilt.
2. Drug and alcohol abuse.
3. Various physical complaints, including symptoms of panic attacks, headaches, hysterical seizures.
4. Problems with trusting or intimate relationships with the opposite gender.
5. Character disorders such as borderline or narcissistic states.
6. Multiple personality disorders.
7. Sexual dysfunction, gynecological problems.

Kuhn describes group therapy as an effective form of treatment for these victims (209).

✔ Because you are a nurse, you are in a position to (1) encourage the battered woman to share her secret with you, a social worker, confidante, or religious leader; (2) help her secure help from social service agencies, legal aid societies, counselors, health centers, and the welfare office; and (3) encourage separation from her husband if her life is in danger (227). Work with the individual woman to the extent possible for her to talk through her feelings of shame, guilt, embarrassment, anger, and fear. Help her gain courage to make decisions, including decisions on how to protect herself and her children, how to leave her husband, and where to go. Work with the children if possible. Finley's research shows that children of battered women (ages 2 to 12) have deep feelings of fear about safety and abandonment, anger, confusion, social isolation, and aggression. Themes in the children's play reveal conflicts about overpowering adults, identification with the same-sexed parent, and that children are learning abnormal behavior and roles that could in all likelihood be carried into their adult relationships and lifestyle (277). You can also work with others to establish emergency centers or crisis phone lines for the woman and to exert pressure to reform the current legal and judicial system to be more equitable to women.

✔ The problem of spouse abuse, like child abuse discussed in Chapter 6 and violent television programming discussed in Chapter 10, is part of overall soci-

TABLE 12–6. Stresses That Predispose to Family Violence

- Financial pressures, low pay, high cost of living.
- Family separation, loss of family support.
- Geographic mobility, loss of friends, social supports, and familiarity.
- Isolation and communication barriers.
- Cultural differences, living in a strange environment or with unfamiliar customs, creating higher mutual dependence.
- Lack of family support.
- Living abroad, such as in military families.
- Inability to separate administrative or work roles from home life, behavior that is functional at work may not be at home.
- Lack of privacy at work or at home.
- Job pressures or competitiveness; lack of support from supervisor.

etal violence. Each nurse, as a citizen and health-care worker, must work in whatever way possible to decrease violence, its causes and effects. Refer to Friedman (127), Hendrix (161), Lieberknecht (227), Lyer (236), Parker (304), Roberts (324) and Sonkin (378) for additional information. Check also with the legal services of your area for information.

✓ Many communities now also have shelters or homes for abused women which are sponsored by Salvation Army, Women's Self-Help Centers, or family service agencies. These homes provide peer discussion and support, help the woman work through her feelings in a positive way and build self-esteem, and give education about how to cope with the situation and to find an alternative lifestyle. Some communities have organizations that also work with the abusing man in an effort to help him recognize anger and frustration feelings in self, realize it is not acceptable to vent feelings through violent behavior to the spouse, and learn alternate coping and behavior patterns.

Variations in Sexual Behavior

The identity crisis which occurs during adolescence may not be completely resolved by the time the person enters young adulthood chronologically. Identity confusion may lead to confusion over sexual identity. This may precipitate homosexual and heterosexual experimentation and arouse homosexual fears and curiosity.

Homosexuality. **Homosexuals** *are people who are regularly aroused by and who engage in sexual activity with members of their own sex.* There are many theories which attempt to explain the causes of homosexual behavior. Bullough and Bullough provide interesting insights into the historical development of thought about homosexuality (45). Homosexuality was accepted by many ancient cultures. Freud believed that bisexuality is inherent in all people. In contrast, members of some religious groups believe homosexuality is a sin. A review of several theories follows to help you understand beliefs and attitudes that are held, as well as to help you realize that there may be more than one way to explain any lifestyle option.

Some believe that if the first pleasurable sexual experience is homosexual, homosexual preference will remain since the initial experience is predominant in memory (20, 45). However, *homosexual experiences are a part of normal growth and development in childhood and early adolescence* (122). Most people can report having had a close emotional attachment, with or without sexual contact, to a peer or adult that involved sexual feelings (20, 248). Sullivan theorized that the normal homosexual period in life is the chum stage in preadolescence (see Chapter 10), when the person first cares for someone as much as he/she cares for self (391). While the chum stage involves a very close emotional experience, it may include some fondling or exploration between the two chums. Sullivan believed that if the person did not have a chum in preadolescence or adolescence, he/she would enter young adulthood still seeking a chum in the same sex. However, at this point the societal expectation is heterosexuality, and the person's behavior is interpreted in a sexual rather than emotional way. The person is labeled homosexual. If the person is rejected by, or is uncomfortable with, persons of the opposite gender, he/she may receive the greatest acceptance (friendship) from others of the same gender. That reinforces the homosexual preference. The person feels more comfortable being close to or intimate with someone of the same gender (391). Perhaps the most publicized is the theory of pathogenic parenting; this is often related in the history of the homosexual. According to this theory, the male child grows up in the home environment with a close, protective, overpossessive, seductive, and overcontrolling mother and with a father who is detached, disinterested, competitively hostile, or absent. The female child is confronted by a mother who is possessive, controlling, and dominating or rejecting, critical, and defeminizing. The girl's father may be one of two types: He may be detached, rejecting, not affectionate, or overpossessive, seductive, and overtly encourages the girl to be a tomboy (20, 248). Recent research also suggests that homosexuality is linked to a biological cause (20, 248). There are both heterosexual and homosexual people who have been reared in such an environment. Prenatal hormone levels are being investigated for their possible relationship to later sexual development. Perhaps a combination of both hormonal and environmental factors exists in some homosexuals (132, 248).

Research by Masters and Johnson showed that the sexual response in homosexuals is the same as that of heterosexuals (254). Family interactions of homosexual partners and heterosexual partners without children are similar (20).

Bell, Weinberg, and Hammersmith, in their studies, found that homosexual men and women can be categorized as:

1. Close coupled—involved in a quasi-marriage, affectionate with a same-sexed partner.
2. Open coupled—involved in marital relationships, interest in sexual contacts other than with the partner, and feelings of regret about the homosexuality.
3. Functional—single individuals with a high number of partners and level of sexual activity and low regret about homosexuality.
4. Dysfunctional—single individuals with a high number of partners, many sexual problems, and much regret about their homosexuality.

5. Asexual—single, uncoupled individuals, with low interest in sexual activity, few partners, and significant regret about their homosexuality (20).

People who prefer homosexuality as a lifestyle are no longer considered emotionally ill. Homosexual behavior is not considered a pathological sexual deviation in the *DSM III-R* (15). It is important to diminish the forces of interpersonal alienation, to realize that people who identify themselves as homosexual evidence a complexity and diversity of lifestyles, interests, problems, and relationships comparable to heterosexuals; and to enable people to become increasingly reconciled to themselves, as well as to others; there is also a wide spectrum of emotional experience on the homo–heterosexual continuum. Contrary to the stereotype, sexual intercourse is not the predominant concern; meaningful relationships are the key (20, 248).

There is a wide variation among both male and female homosexuals in their emotional and social adjustment, just as there is among heterosexuals. Some people will be homosexual only under extreme conditions such as imprisonment. Some have their total life adjustment dominated by homosexuality and live in a homosexual subculture. For some, sexual behavior is only an aspect of their total life experience; they may remain discrete and secretive about their homosexuality. Others will also seek out heterosexual activity, marry, and have families. (See *The Bisexual Spouse*, by Ivan Hill ed., Barlina Books, McLean, Va, 1988.) Although homosexuality is now less taboo in American society than formerly, stigma and resulting guilt still exist. Homosexual activity is becoming better publicized and understood (144).

The **female homosexual** (*lesbian*) has not been studied as much as the **male homosexual** (*gay*). It is still more socially acceptable for two women to live together in one dwelling than for two men. There may also be less societal fear of gay women than of gay men. As a result, little is known about their feelings, reactions, lifestyles, or health problems. One study was reported that found no syphilis, gonorrhea, herpes, or chlamydial infections in a group of 148 lesbians. There was a longer than usual interval since the last Pap smear and a higher than normal prevalence of cervical dysplasia when the group was compared with a group of heterosexual women (328). It is thought that, compared with both gay men and heterosexual men and women, lesbians have the lowest incidence of sexually transmitted diseases, but little else is known about their health (444). A concern is that lesbians are not receiving preventive care, such as routine Pap smears, because of their tendency to avoid the unpleasantness of the experience (327).

The occurrence of sexually transmitted diseases, such as pediculosis, gonorrhea, syphilis, urethritis, anorectal warts and infection, herpes genitalis, autoimmune deficiency disease, intestinal infections, shigelosis, and hepatitis, has been publicized. Further, these diseases are more common in homosexual men, who often report many contacts, than in women. The rapidly increasing incidence of AIDS has caused some homosexuals to change their sexual practices, to limit number of sexual partners, or to increase use of condoms (250). Heterosexual partners also get these diseases through sexual intercourse. All homosexuals do not get these diseases (83). Refer to Chapter 11; sexually transmitted diseases do not occur only in adolescence but are likely to first occur in those years. Refer also to the section on health problems in this chapter.

✔ It is essential that you do not convey a judgmental attitude toward the homosexual person. This person needs your respect and acceptance as a human being who is more than a bundle of sexual activity. This person may be a business executive, minister, inventor, delivery person, artist, homemaker, or parent. The person may be contributing as much to society's betterment as any heterosexual person. If this person indicates a desire to change to a heterosexual identity, or to relate more comfortably to people of both sexes, refer the person to a counselor who can help the person grow in ability to relate or acquire a new identity without labeling, moralizing, rejecting, or becoming impatient as the person works through emotional and spiritual pain.

✔ Parents of homosexual offspring are often not considered, but they may also need help in coping with the child's homosexuality. Parents of the gay or lesbian offspring may feel too embarrassed to talk about their feelings; some feel that they have lost a child; some grieve at the prospect of not having a grandchild; some fear meeting a same-sexed lover. Acceptance of the fact that their child is a homosexual may be a long time in coming, but most parents eventually do (295). Listen to their feelings and concerns; help them focus on a wholesome relationship; caution against punitive behavior toward the offspring, and refer them to a counselor to work through spiritual and emotional conflicts related to the situation (345). You can refer parents to the Parents of Gays organization. A list of local chapters is available by writing 201 W. 13th Street, New York, NY 10011, or Box 24528, Los Angeles, CA 90024. You can also refer parents to the Federation of Parents and Friends of Lesbians and Gays, Inc. (Parent's FLAG) P.O. Box 20308, Denver, CO 80220. This organization has a booklet entitled *About Our Children*, published in several languages simultaneously. The organization also sponsors a newsletter, national projects, and regional meetings.

Transsexuality. **Transsexuals** *are people who lack harmony between their anatomical sex and their* *psychological sex.* A disorder of gender identity occurs. Hormone therapy and surgery are being used for people with this problem. Both therapies are directed at making the anatomical sex compatible with the psychological sex (22).

✔ To care for persons with sexual-identity confusion, you must first determine your own feelings toward yourself as a sexual person and then your feelings toward them. These people need someone to listen to their fears and insecurities and a consistent, accepting approach. You may not be able to work with these people, but you can make appropriate referrals. If problems of gender identity are assessed in a child, you should encourage early treatment. Without intervention, the majority of people will become more deeply frustrated by their lack of gender identity.

Sexual Experimentation Outside Marriage

Sexual activity outside marriage may include homosexuality, group sexual experiences, premarital intercourse, cohabitation, or infidelity.

The moral, emotional, and psychological aspects of premarital sexual behavior have been widely discussed. Sexual intimacy without a sense of commitment and love, responsibility, and care for the other means using another to meet one's needs, taking the other as an object rather than as a person. Such activity and attitudes can be poor preparation for marriage and establishing a lasting relationship and personal maturity. Compatibility between two people is in the head, not the pelvis. The rationalization of finding a compatible partner through premarital sexual intimacy is unfounded.

Yet, **cohabitation,** *two persons of the opposite sex living together without being married*, is not unusual. Sometimes the arrangement of the young adult man and woman living together is asexual. They are friends and for economic, companionship, or convenience reasons wish to share an apartment. Sometimes the person may have had no siblings or no siblings of the opposite gender, and the person wants the experience of living with someone of the opposite gender who would be like a sibling. In such a situation, both work to keep the relationship asexual (128).

Young adults sometimes live together in an effort to avoid some of the problems they saw in their parents' marriage or to test the degree of the partner's commitment before actually becoming married. Those goals may be achieved for some, but the danger is that one partner may take the commitment very seriously and the other may use the situation only as a convenient living arrangement. The uncaring person may suddenly decide to leave, an easy process since no legal ties are involved, and the other person is left with much the same hurt as a married person going through a divorce.

American society probably expects too much of marriage. The partners in the ideal marriage are supposed to stay passionately and exclusively in love with each other for the rest of their lives. Yet infidelity is a growing problem in an increasingly liberal society.

Various factors contribute to infidelity: the need to prove masculinity or femininity; difficulty in maintaining a steady and continuing relationship; feelings of insecurity, rejection, or jealousy; and a sense of loss when heightened passions of the initial stages of love do not remain constant. Believing that one can love two people simultaneously, getting great satisfaction from doing something forbidden and secretly, or wishing to recapture one's youth may also be involved.

Staying married to one person and living with the frustrations, conflicts, and boredom that any close and lengthy relationship imposes requires constant work by both parties. Couples are unrealistic when they think that marriage will suddenly shield them from further attraction to members of the opposite sex. The mature couple will expect to feel physically attracted to others at times and will have to resolve the feelings within themselves, through discussion with and understanding from their partner or with the help of a counselor.

American society offers no alternate to the family unit. Although society as a whole is in a state of flux, the family unit seems fundamental. The strains which infidelity places on it are damaging for most people.

Social Health Problems

Divorce. **Divorce** *is the termination of marriage, preceded by a period of emotional distress in the marriage, separation, and legal procedures.* Divorce is a crisis for those involved and can affect society in general as well as the emotional health of the persons involved (164).

Some young people enter marriage to escape the problems of young adulthood. Marriage provides them with a ready-made role, and it supposedly solves the problem of isolation. However, if marriage takes place before the individual has developed a strong sense of identity and independence, intimacy cannot be achieved.

Most divorces occur in the first 3 to 5 years of married life and involve persons under 29 years of age. These couples are frequently from lower economic groups and have married at an early age. They tend to have less education and money and fewer personal resources than couples from higher economic groups (97).

Marriage often breaks down because of the partners' inability to satisfy deep mutual needs in a close demanding relationship. One of the partners may be overly dependent and seek in the other a mother or father. Dependent behavior may at first meet the needs of the more independent partner. But as the dependent person matures, the relationship is changed. If the stronger partner neither understands nor allows this change, divorce may follow.

Emotional deprivation in childhood is also a poor foundation for marriage. The deprived person grows up without sufficient experience of feeling acknowledged, wanted, appreciated, or loved. He/she has low self-esteem and is too sensitively tuned to rejection and not adequately responsive to acceptance and approval. He/she can easily misinterpret the partner's behavior, feel exploited, and have difficulty accepting any form of appreciation and love. The person from a home where the parents' marital relationship was one of detachment, disharmony, or conflict, or where abuse or divorce occurred, is poorly prepared for marriage. He/she has no healthy or loving marital model to follow. The person may try to model the marriage after another's happy marriage; however, the person learns most thoroughly that which is lived during childhood.

The divorce rate reflects the ease in which a divorce can be obtained. The lack of commitment to people and relationships when the going gets tough, seen as well in other areas of life, and the dichotomy between the romanticized ideal of marriage and the fact that much of married life has a routine and sameness about it contributes to separation and divorce. Further, our youth are not educated for family life in any formal sense, and what they learn in the home may be poor preparation for marriage and good preparation for the divorce court.

When marriage fails and bonds are broken, aloneness, anger, mistrust, hostility, guilt, shame, a sense of betrayal, fear, disappointment, loss of identity, anxiety, and depression, alone or in combination, can appear both in the divorcee and the one initiating the divorce. Eventually there may be a feeling of relief. There has to be an interval of adjustment to the physical and emotional loss. Often the second marriage is a rebound affair: A partner is selected as soon as possible to help assuage the feelings from the divorce and relieve the loneliness. Second and subsequent remarriages can be successful, but they carry a higher risk of instability and are more likely to end in divorce because of (1) the person's lack of ability to form a mutually satisfactory new relationship; (2) the past experiences, vulnerability, guilt, and insecurity that cannot be easily removed; (3) the hassles of her kids, his kids, and our kids; (4) child and wife support; and (5) interference from the ex-spouse (242, 380). Psychological effects of divorce vary because of the following factors: (1) family psychodynamics prior to divorce; (2) nature of the marital breakup; (3) relationship between the ex-spouses after the divorce; (4) developmental age and coping skills of the children, if any, during the time of marital disharmony and divorce; (5) coping skills of each ex-spouse (380). If the offspring are adolescents, expression and control of aggressive and sexual impulses, dependency—independency issues, deidealization of the parents, peer acceptance and social approval, and premature responsibilities of adulthood may intensify.

If the person embarks on a second marriage with an understanding of how he/she has matured and of the reasons the first marriage failed, the second marriage may be satisfactory. If the mistakes of the first marriage are repeated in finding a partner, the second marriage is also likely to fail. The person may meander from one relationship to another, hoping for satisfaction, but always finding frustration and disappointment, because he/she carries within self the seeds of failure. Ideally, the second marriage should be entered into with time (at least 1 year) and thought. The success of the second marriage depends on finding another person with whom common needs can be met and whose personality development matches that of the divorcee (162).

Recently more emphasis has been given to helping people through the emotions involved in divorce. Divorce has been likened to death, except that contact is often maintained, especially if small children are involved (164).

✔ Books with such titles as *Creative Divorce* have appeared on the market, and in some cities group work specifically designed to foster emotional health during this time is available. Refer to Duffy to understand better the needs of the woman who heads the household and ways to assist her (96).

Hewlett (165) discusses how laws intended to make life better for women and divorce fairer ended up hurting women. Consequences of divorce are worse in the 1980s than ever. The standard of living after divorce falls by 73 percent for the woman; it raises by 42 percent for the man. Many divorced women have had difficulty with custody rights and with obtaining child support.

✔ A support group for the divorced woman is Displaced Homemakers Network, which has chapters around the country. The national office can be contacted at 1010 Vermont Avenue NW, Washington, D.C. 20005.

Divorce has an impact on the children involved. Children do not like change. The controversy exists between (1) maintaining marriage at all costs for the sake of the children and (2) admitting that a conflict-filled home is damaging to the child. The child's loyalties are stretched in an unhappy home, since the child is often forced to ally self with one or the other parent. The child feels much turmoil and conflict, often for many years.

✔ The ideal situation is for the departing parent to be pictured in the best possible light by the one with whom the child remains and for unimpeded contact to be maintained. The child should be given honest information at whatever level he/she can understand. The child must know that he/she did not cause the divorce. Delinquency, lack of gender identification, and eventually inability to form a lasting relationship may result in the child unless he/she is handled with care. Tickfer discusses ways for the nurse to help children of divorce (406). A helpful book is *Caring About Kids When Parents Divorce* (52). Other pertinent references are 70, 93, 164, 333 and 380.

The divorce rate has increased in America, but that is not necessarily a symptom of decay of the institutions of marriage and family. Most couples who marry plan to stay married, and those who seek divorce usually also seek remarriage. The rate does reflect a departure from the prison-like life of some past marriages when the partners remained locked together in misery by conventions of respectability or religion.

Abortion. Because of changing legislation and changing social attitudes toward women's rights, sexual mores, and human life, many young adult women, married and unmarried and of all socioeconomic classes, are resorting to abortions to terminate unwanted pregnancies. While abortion can be the treatment of choice at times, it is no panacea and should not be considered lightly. Even legal abortions may occasionally induce physical complications such as hemorrhage or later cervical incompetency. Emotional anguish, guilt, unhappiness, or self-directed anger sometimes follow the decision to have an abortion. The mature young adult must consider the implications of sexual activity.

✔ As a nurse you may experience considerable emotional turmoil unless you think through the abortion issue. Women or men seeking your counsel on this issue need to hear both positive and negative considerations in a professional presentation. If you feel incapable of this counsel, refer the person to someone who can counsel.

✔ As a nurse, realize that the health state of the young adult and type of health care sought is influenced by the person's background, knowledge, experience, philosophy, and lifestyle. Young adults with health problems might more readily seek care and information if they could find programs compatible with their expectations and lifestyles. You can initiate programs that are specifically aimed at young adults since they seem to accept the treatment plan more readily when they understand the rationale and expected effects. Keep the previously discussed health problems and unmet physiological needs in mind as you talk with young adults and plan and give care. Young adulthood ends in the forties when the person should have a stable position in society and the knowledge of what he/she can make out of life. Your efforts at teaching and counseling can enhance the young adult's awareness of health promotion and establish a program to make that position more stable.

Continuing Adjustments. One couple invited others to a celebration of their twenty-fifth wedding anniversary with the following words (455):

> We continue to adjust to each other, an adjustment that started 25 years ago, and will never stop because we each continue to give and change. We will always be different.
>
> Don't mistake it for a solid marriage. There is no such thing. Marriage is more like an airplane than a rock. You have to commit the thing to flight, and then it creaks and groans, and keeping it airborne depends entirely on attitude. Working at it, though, we can fly forever. Only the two of us know how hard it has been or how worthwhile.
>
> Celebrate with us. . . .

References

1. A Mother's Choice, *Newsweek* (March 31, 1986), 46–51.
2. A Revolution: How Parents Are Trying to Improve, *St. Louis Post-Dispatch*, August 13, 1986, 1, 10.
3. Abe, Kazuhiko, and Tukashi Suzuki, Age Trends of Early Awakening and Feeling Worse in the Morning Than in the Evening in Apparently Normal People, *Journal of Nervous & Mental Disease*, 173, no. 8 (1983), 495–498.
4. Abel, Ernest, and Phillips Zeidenberg, Age, Alcohol and Violent Death: A Postmortem Study, *Journal of Studies in Alcohol*, 46, no. 3 (1985), 228–231.
5. Abraham, Ivo, and Heidi vanKoss Krowchuk, Unemployment and Health: Health Promotion for the Jobless Male, *Nursing Clinics of North America*, 21, no. 1 (1986), 39–50.
6. Abramowitz, Stephen, and Noa Bell, Biofeedback, Self-Control, and Tension Headache, *Journal of Psychosomatic Research*, 29, no. 1 (1985), 95–99.
7. Abrams, D.I., Routine Care and Psychosocial Support of the Patient with Acquired Immunodeficiency Syndrome, *Medical Clinics of North America*, 70, no. 3 (1986), 707–720.
8. Adams, G., and R. Haselow, Oral and Pharyngeal

Cancer: Early Diagnosis for Optimal Treatment, *Hospital Medicine*, 19 (February 1983), 173.
9. Aitken, P.P., An Observational Study of Young Adults' Drinking Groups, *Alcohol & Alcoholism*, 20, no. 4 (1985), 445–457.
10. Allan, Carole, and D.J. Cooke, Stressful Life Events and Alcohol Misuse in Women: A Critical Review, *Journal of Studies in Alcohol*, 46, no. 2 (1985), 147–152.
11. Allen, David, and Marianne Wheatley, Nursing and Men's Health: Some Critical Considerations, *Nursing Clinics of North America*, 21, no. 1 (1986), 3–13.
12. Allen, Janice. Emergency Admissions and Lunar Cycles, *Journal of Emergency Nursing*, 12, no. 2 (1986), 85–88.
13. Allport, Gordon. *The Individual and His Religion*. New York: Macmillan, 1961.
14. *American Cancer Society: Cancer Facts and Figures*. New York: American Cancer Society, 1984.
15. American Psychiatric Association. *Diagnostic and Statistical Manual of Mental Disorders III-R*. Washington, D.C.: American Psychiatric Association, 1987.
16. Anderson, U.K., Mitral Valve Prolapse: A Diagnosis for Primary Nursing Intervention, *Journal of Cardiovascular Nursing*, 1, no. 3 (1987), 41–51.
17. Arlin, P., Cognitive Development in Adulthood: A Fifth Stage? *Developmental Psychology*, 11, no. 5 (1975), 602–606.
18. Arms, Karen, and Pamela Camp, *Biology* (3rd ed.). Philadelphia: Saunders College Publishing, 1987.
19. Basow, S., *Sex Role Stereotypes: Traditions and Alternatives*. Monterey, Calif.: Brooks/Cole, 1980.
20. Bell, Alan, Martin Weinberg, and Sue Hammersmith, *Sexual Preference: Its Development in Men and Women*. Bloomington, Ind.: Indiana University Press, 1981.
21. Bell, J.B., Stressful Life Events and Coping Methods in Mental Health and Wellness Behaviors, *Nursing Research*, 26 (1981), 236–241.
22. Benjamin, Harry, and Charles Ihlenfeld, Transsexualism, *American Journal of Nursing*, 73, no. 3 (1973), 457–461.
23. Bennett, Gerald, Christine Vourakis, and Donna Woolf (eds.), *Substance Abuse: Pharmacologic, Developmental, and Clinical Perspectives*. New York: John Wiley, 1983.
24. Bennett, Jo Anne. What We Know About AIDS, *American Journal of Nursing*, 86, no. 9 (1986), 1016–1021.
25. Benson, Herbert, *Relaxation Response*. New York: William Morrow, 1975.
26. Bernhard, Linda, and Alice Dan, Redefining Sexuality From Women's Own Experiences, *Nursing Clinics of North America*, 21, no. 1 (1986), 125–136.
27. Bettelheim, Bruno, *A Good Enough Parent: A Book on Child-Rearing*. New York: Alfred A. Knopf, 1987.
28. Birth Control Update, *City of St. Louis Weekly Health Letter*, June 6, 1986, 1–2.
29. Bissell, LeClair, and Robert W. Jones, The Alcoholic Nurse, *Nursing Outlook*, 29, no. 2 (1981), 96–101.
30. Blackwood, Mary. Cigarette Smoking and the Workplace: A Deadly Duo, *Occupational Health Nursing*, 30, no. 5 (1982), 26–28.
31. Blank, Mike, Addictive Attitudes—Mythology Which Surrounds the Drug Problem, *Nursing Times*, 81, no. 48 (1985), 64.
32. Boilleul, Francois, et al., Interindividual Differences in the Circadian Hematologic Time Structure of Cancer Patients, *Chronobiology International*, 3, no. 1 (1986), 47–54.
33. Bouton, Jeanette, Falling Asleep, *Nursing Times*, 82, no. 50 (1986), 36–37.
34. Brewer, M.J., To Sleep or Not to Sleep: The Consequences of Sleep Deprivation, *Critical Care Nurse*, 5, no. 6 (1985), 35–41.
35. Brocher, Tobias, Understanding Variables in Occupational Stress, *Occupational Health and Safety*, 48, no. 2 (1979), 26–31.
36. Brodsley, Laurel, Avoiding a Crisis! The Assessment, *American Journal of Nursing*, 83, no. 12 (1983), 1865–1871.
37. Brookes, J. A Study of the Pre-menstrual Syndrome, *Health Visitor*, 56 (1983), 416–417.
38. Brooks, Christine, Leisure Time Physical Activity Assessment of American Adults Through an Analysis of Time Diaries Collected in 1981, *American Journal of Public Health*, 77, no. 4 (1987), 455–460.
39. Broverman, I., Sex-Role Stereotypes and Clinical Judgments of Mental Health Professionals, *Journal of Consulting and Clinical Psychology*, 34, no. 1 (1970), 1–7.
40. Brown, Betty, Consensus About the Marital Relationship During Transition to Parenthood, *Nursing Research*, 33, no. 4 (1984), 223–228.
41. Brown, Marie, Primary Dysmenorrhea, *Nursing Clinics of North America*, 17, no. 1 (1982), 145–153.
42. Brown, Marie, Social Support During Pregnancy: A Undimensional or Multidimensional Construct? *Nursing Research*, 35, no. 1 (1986), 4–9.
43. Bryant, Gay, *The Working Woman Report: Succeeding in Business in the 80's*. New York: Simon and Schuster, 1984.
44. Buechler, Anna, Help for the Burned Out Nurse?, *Nursing Outlook*, 33, no. 4 (1985), 181–182.
45. Bullough, Bonnie, and Vern Bullough, The History and Present Status of the Medical Model as an Explanation for Homosexuality, *Health Values: Achieving High Level Wellness*, 3, no. 5 (1979), 256–259.
46. Bunning, Erwin, *The Physiological Clock* (3rd ed.). New York: Springer-Verlag, 1973.
47. Burgener, S., Circadian Rhythms: Implications for Evaluation of the Critically Ill Patient, *Critical Care Nurse*, 5, no. 5 (1985), 43–48.
48. Burgess, Ann, and Lynda Holmstrom, *Rape: Crisis and Recovery*. Bowie, Md.: Robert J. Brady, 1979.
49. Burke, G., The Effects of Shift Rotation on the Quality of Nursing Care and the Well-Being of Nurses, *Nursing Management*, 17, no. 12 (1986), 42.

50. Campbell, I.T., et al., Are Circadian Rhythms Important in Intensive Care?, *Intensive Care Nursing*, 1, no. 3 (1986), 144–150.
51. Cantril-Kersey, C., and P. McCarthy-Kitzpoksi, AIDS: Meeting the Challenge, *Current Concepts in Nursing*, 1, no. 2 (1987), 2.
52. Caring About Kids When Parents Divorce, Washington, D.C., U.S. Department of Health and Human Services, 1981.
53. Carmen, George, Linda Mealey, Susan Thompson, et al., Patterns in the Distribution of REM Sleep in Normal Human Sleep, *Sleep*, 7, no. 4 (1984), 347–355.
54. Carmichael, Carrie, *Non-Sexist Childrearing*. Boston: Beacon Press, 1977.
55. Cash, J.T., et al., Not Life Threatening: Mitral Valve Prolapse Syndrome, *Focus on Critical Care*, 12, no. 6 (1986), 54–57.
56. CDC, Others Call for an Increased Effort for Hepatitis B Vaccination, *The Nation's Health*, January, 1985, 1, 9.
57. Censullo, M., et al., Rhythmic Patterning in Mother–Newborn Interaction, *Nursing Research*, 34, no. 6 (1985), 342–346.
58. Centers for Disease Control, Update: Acquired Immunodeficiency Syndrome—United States, *Morbidity and Mortality Weekly Report*, 35, (1986), 757–766.
59. Childbirth Sitting Up, *Newsweek* (March 2, 1982), 79.
60. Chlamydia, *Health Line* (March–April, 1986), 10.
61. Clare, A.W., Pre-menstrual Syndrome: Single or Multiple Causes?, *Canadian Journal of Psychiatry*, 30 (1985), 474–480.
62. Clemen-Stone, Susan, Diane Eigsti, and Sandra Mc Guire, *Comprehensive Family and Community Health Nursing* (2nd ed.). New York: McGraw-Hill, 1987.
63. Cleveland, S., and R. Morton, Group Behavior and Body Image, *Human Relations*, 15, no. 1 (1962), 77–85.
64. Clinton, Jacqueline, Expectant Fathers at Risk for Couvade, *Nursing Research*, 35, no. 5 (1986), 290–294.
65. Cohn, Lucille, The Hidden Diagnosis, *American Journal of Nursing*, 82, no. 12 (1982), 1862–1864.
66. Cohn, Robert, Walking Called Best Exercise for All, *St. Louis Post-Dispatch*, February 15, 1979, Sec. B, p. 1.
67. Cohn, Sarah, Sexuality in Pregnancy: A Review of the Literature, *Nursing Clinics of North America*, 17, no. 1 (1982), 91–98.
68. Colarusso, Calvin, and Robert Nemeroff, *Adult Development*. New York: Plenum Press, 1981.
69. Collier, Phyllis. Health Behaviors of Women, *Nursing Clinics of North America*, 17, no. 1 (1982), 121–126.
70. Collins, Emily. *The Whole Single Person's Catalogue*. New York: Peebles Press, 1979.
71. Collins, Ruth, Why Do Women Work? Because The Economy Needs Them—That's Why!, *Graduate Women*, 73, no. 5 (1979), 12–13.
72. Coopersmith, Stanley, *Antecedents of Self-Esteem*. San Francisco: W. H. Freeman, 1967.
73. Cranley, Mecca, K. Hedahl, and S. Pegg, Women's Perceptions of Vaginal and Cesarean Deliveries, *Nursing Research*, 32, no. 1 (1983), 10–15.
74. Crocker, Kathleen, Frances Gerber, and Jeffrey Sheerer, Metabolism of Carbohydrate, Protein, and Fat, *Nursing Clinics of North America*, 18, no. 1 (1983), 3–27.
75. Cronenwett, Linda, Parental Network Structure and Perceived Support After Birth of First Child, *Nursing Research*, 34, no. 6 (1985), 347–352.
76. Cronenwett, Linda, and Philip Brickman, Models of Helping and Coping in Childbirth, *Nursing Research*, 32, no. 2 (1983), 84–88.
77. Custer, Marcia, Stress, Life Events, and the Epidemiology of Wellness, *Journal of Community Health Nursing*, 2, no. 4 (1985), 215–222.
78. Czeisler, Charles, Martin Moore-Ede, and Richard Coleman, Rotating Shift Work Schedules that Disrupt Sleep Are Improved by Applying Circadian Principles, *Science*, 217, no. 30 (1982), 460–463.
79. Czeisler, Charles, et al., Bright Light Resets the Human Circadian Pacemaker Independent of the Timing of the Sleep–Wake Cycle, *Science*, 233, no. 4764 (1986), 667–670.
80. Dalton, Jo Ann, and Ingrid Swenson, Nurses: The Professionals Who Can't Quit, *American Journal of Nursing*, 83, no. 8 (1983), 1149–1151.
81. Daly, Edward, Jay Zimmerman, Patsy Donn, et al., Psychophysiological Treatment of Migraine and Tension Headaches: A 12-month Followup, *Rehabilitation Psychology*, 30, no. 1 (1985), 3–10.
82. Darrow, William, Risk Factors for Human Immunodeficiency Virus (HIV) Infections in Homosexual Men, *American Journal of Public Health*, 77, no. 4 (1987) 479–483.
83. Darrow, William, et al., The Gay Report on Sexually Transmitted Diseases, *American Journal of Public Health*, 71, no. 9 (1981), 1004–1011.
84. Davies, Barbara, and Terence Doran, Factors in a Woman's Decision to Undergo Genetic Amniocentesis for Advanced Maternal Age, *Nursing Research*, 31, no. 1 (1982), 56–59.
85. Dean, G.A., Mitral Valve Prolapse, *Hospital Practice*, 20, no. 9 (1985), 75–82.
86. Dee, David. *A Fitness Program for Adults*. New York: Delair, 1980.
87. DeVore, Nancy, Parenthood Postponed, *American Journal of Nursing*, 83, no. 8 (1983), 1160–1163.
88. Dickerson, Janet, The Pill: A Closer Look, *American Journal of Nursing*, 83, no. 10 (1983), 1392–1398.
89. Dirubbo, Nancy, The Condom Barrier, *American Journal of Nursing*, 87, no. 10 (1987), 1306–1309.
90. Doohor, Mary, Lamaze Method of Childbirth, *Nursing Research*, 29, no. 4 (1980), 220–224.
91. Douglas, J., Coping with Sleeping Problems, *Health Visitor*, 60, no. 2 (1987), 52–53.

92. Drake, Virginia Koch, Battered Women: A Health Care Problem in Disguise, *Image*, 14, no. 2 (1982), 40–47.
93. Dressen, Sheila, The Young Adult Adjusting to Single Parenting, *American Journal of Nursing*, 76, no. 8 (August 1976), 1286–1289.
94. Drimmer, Ami, If the Shoe Fits, Wear It, *St. Louis Manager*, March, 1986, 24–26.
95. Drugs on the Job: The Quiet Problem, *Newsweek* (September 15, 1980), 83–84.
96. Duffy, Mary, When a Woman Heads a Household, *Nursing Outlook*, 30, no. 5 (1982), 468–473.
97. Duvall, Evelyn, and Brent Miller, *Marriage and Family Development* (6th ed.). New York: Harper & Row, 1984.
98. Dyer, Elaine, M. Monson, and M. Cope, Dental Health in Adults, *American Journal of Nursing*, 76, no. 7 (July 1976), 1156–1158.
99. Eckert, Penelope, Beyond the Statistics of Adolescent Smoking, *American Journal of Public Health*, 73, no. 4 (1983), 439–441.
100. Edmunds, Leland (ed.), *Cell Cycle Clocks*. New York: Marcel Dekker, 1984.
101. Eells, Mary Ann, Interventions with Alcoholics and Their Families, *Nursing Clinics of North America*, 21, no. 3 (1986), 493–504.
102. Engel, George, A Life Setting Conducive to Illness: The Giving-Up—Given-Up Complex, *Annals of Internal Medicine*, 69, no. 8 (1968), 293–300.
103. Englert, Deana, and Joyce Guillon, For Want of Lactose, *American Journal of Nursing*, 86, no. 8 (1986), 902–906.
104. Erikson, Erik. *Childhood and Society* (2nd ed.). New York: W. W. Norton, 1963.
105. Estes, Nada, K. Smith-DiJulio, and M. Heineman, *Nursing Diagnosis of the Alcoholic Person*. St. Louis: C. V. Mosby, 1980.
106. Evans, H., and J. Fletcher, Sperm Abnormalities and Cigarette Smoking, *Lancet* (March 21, 1981), 627–629.
107. Fagin, Claire, Stress: Implications for Nursing Research, *Image: The Journal of Nursing Scholarship*, 19, no. 1 (1987), 38–41.
108. Fawcett, Jacqueline, and Ruth York, Spouses' Physical and Psychological Symptoms During Pregnancy and the Post-partum, *Nursing Research*, 35, no, 3 (1986), 144–148.
109. Fawcett, Jacqueline, et al., Spouses' Body Image Changes During and After Pregnancy: A Replication and Extension, *Nursing Research*, 35, no. 4 (1986), 220–223.
110. Felton, Gerry, Human Biologic Rhythms, *Annual Review of Nursing Research*, 5 (1987), 45–77.
111. Finley, Britt, Primary and Secondary Prevention of Substance Abuse in Nurses, *Occupational Health Nursing*, 30, no. 11 (1982), 14–17.
112. Fiscella, Michael, *Your Health Newsletter*, January, 1983, 1.
113. Fisher, S., Sex Differences in Body Perception, *Psychological Monographs*, 78, no. 14 (1964), 1–22.
114. ———, and S. Cleveland, *Body Image and Personality*. New York: Dover Publications, 1968.
115. Fisk, N.B., Alcoholism: Ineffective Family Coping, *American Journal of Nursing*, 86, no. 5 (1986), 586–587.
116. Fletcher, B., et al., Exploding the Myth of Executive Stress, *Personnel Management*, 11, no. 5 (1979), 30–34.
117. Folkard, Simon, et al., Independence of the Circadian Rhythm in Alertness from the Sleep/Wake Cycle, *Nature*, 313, no. 6004 (1985), 678–679.
118. Follett, B.K., and D.E. Follett, *Biological Clocks in Seasonal Reproductive Cycles*. New York: John Wiley, 1981.
119. Foote, Audrey, The Kids Who Won't Leave Home, *The Atlantic*, 243, no. 3 (1978), 118–121.
120. Forrester, David, Myths of Masculinity: Impact Upon Men's Health, *Nursing Clinics of North America*, 21, no. 1 (1986), 15–24.
121. Foster, R.S., and M.C. Costanza, Breast Self-Examination Practices and Breast Cancer Survival, *Cancer*, 53 (February 15, 1984), 999.
122. Frank, Deborah, Elizabeth Downard, and Alan Lang, Androgyny, Sexual Satisfaction, and Women, *Journal of Psychosocial Nursing*, 24, no. 7 (1986), 11–15.
123. Freedman, Tracy, Warning: Staying at Home Can Be Dangerous to Your Health, *Common Cause*, June, 1982, 13–17.
124. Freiberg, Karen, *Human Development: A Life-Span Approach* (2nd ed.). Monterey, Calif.: Wadsworth Health Sciences Division, 1983.
125. Freudenberger, H., *Burn-out: High Cost of High Achievement*. New York: Doubleday & Co., 1980.
126. Friedman, Barbara, Infertility Workup, *American Journal of Nursing*, 81, no. 11 (1981), 2040–2046.
127. Friedman, Kathleen, The Image of Battered Women, *American Journal of Public Health*, 67, no. 8 (1977), 723.
128. Friends of the Opposite Sex, *Universitas—St. Louis University*, Spring, 1987, 12–13.
129. Fultz, J., et al., When a Narcotic Addict Is Hospitalized, *American Journal of Nursing*, 80, no. 3 (1980), 478–481.
130. Galland, Leo, Herbert Benson, and Patricia Carrington, How to Help Patients Learn to Relax, *Patient Care*, 14, no. 20 (1980), 139ff.
131. Gault, Patricia, Taking Your Part in the Fight Against Testicular Cancer, *Nursing '81*, 11, no. 5 (1981), 47–50.
132. Gays and Lesbians on Campus, *Newsweek* (April 5, 1982), 75–77.
133. Geary, Geraldine, Is She A Battered Woman? A Guide for Emergency Response, *American Journal of Nursing*, 84, no. 6 (1984), 725–727.
134. Giovacchini, Peter, *The Urge to Die: Why Young People Commit Suicide*. New York: Macmillan, 1981.

135. Goleman, Daniel, Leaving Home: Is There a Right Time to Go?, *Psychology Today*, August, 1980, 52–61.
136. Golub, S., The Effect of Pre-Menstrual Anxiety and Depression on Cognitive Function, *Journal of Personality and Social Psychology*, 34, no. 7 (1976), 99–104.
137. Good Health: Rate Yourself, *Graduate Women*, 77, no. 1 (1983), 21.
138. Gordon, Nancy, et al., The Prevalence and Health Impact of Shiftwork, *American Journal of Public Health*, 76, no. 10 (1986), 1225–1228.
139. Gorline, Lynne, and Cheryl Stegbauer, What Every Nurse Should Know About Vaginitis, *American Journal of Nursing*, 82, no. 12 (1982), 1851–1855.
140. Gould, Roger, Adult Life Stages: Growth Toward Self-Tolerance, *Psychology Today*, 8, no. 7 (February, 1975), 74–78.
141. Grass, Susan, and Sharon Utz, Mitral Valve Prolapse: A Review of the Scientific and Medical Literature, *Heart & Lung*, 15, no. 5 (1986), 507–512.
142. Grey, Alison, What Every Woman Should Know, *Nursing Times*, 77, no. 34 (1981), 1469–1470.
143. Grim, Carlene Minks, Nursing Assessment of the Patient with High Blood Pressure, *Nursing Clinics of North America*, 16, no. 2 (1981), 349–363.
144. Growing Up Gay, *Newsweek* (January 13, 1986), 50–52.
145. Haber, Judith, Family Therapy with Single, Young Adults, *Perspectives in Psychiatric Care*, 19, nos. 5–6 (1981), 174–179.
146. Hall, Lynne, Effect of Teaching Primiparas' Perceptions of their Newborns, *Nursing Research*, 29, no. 5 (1980), 317–321.
147. Hallal, Janice, Caffeine, *American Journal of Nursing*, 86, no. 4 (1986), 423–425.
148. Hatton, Corrine, and Sharon Valente, *Suicide: Assessment and Intervention*. Norwalk, CT.: Appleton-Century-Crofts, 1984.
149. Hans, Bruno, *Breathe Away Your Tensions*. New York: Random House, 1973.
150. Hansen, Shirley, Single Custodial Fathers and the Parent-Child Relationship, *Nursing Research*, 30, no. 4 (1981), 202–204.
151. Harrison, Michelle, *Self Help for Premenstrual Syndrome*. Cambridge, Mass.: Matrix Press, 1982.
152. Hart, Kathleen, and Thomas Ollendick, Prevalence of Bulimia in Working and University Women, *American Journal of Psychiatry*, 142, no. 7 (1985), 851–854.
153. Hartz, Arthur, Sheryl Kelber, Harold Borkowf, et al., The Association of Smoking with Clinical Indicators of Altered Sex Steroids—A Study of 50,145 Women, *Public Health Reports*, 102, no. 3 (1987), 254–259.
154. Hausl, P., Treating Psychophysiologic Insomnia With Biofeedback, *Archives of General Psychiatry*, 38, no. 7 (1981), 752–758.
155. Hayter, Jean, The Rhythm of Sleep, *American Journal of Nursing*, 80, no. 3 (1980), 457–461.
156. Heath, D., Model of the Maturing Person, in *Growing Up in College*, ed. D. Heath. San Francisco: Jossey-Bass, 1968, 4–17.
157. ———, Academic Predictors of Adult Maturity and Competence, *Journal of Higher Education*, 48, no. 6 (1979), 613–632.
158. Heinrick, Kathleen, Effective Responses to Sexual Harassment, *Nursing Outlook*, 35, no. 2 (1987), 70–72.
159. Helton, Anne, et al., Battered and Pregnant: A Prevalence Study, *American Journal of Public Health*, 77, no. 10 (1987), 1337–1339.
160. Henderson, M.M., Pap Smears: Current Recommendations on Their Frequency, *Consultant*, 22 (January 1982), 77.
161. Hendrix, Melva, Gretchen La Godna, and Cynthia Bohen, The Battered Wife, *American Journal of Nursing*, 78, no. 4 (1978), 650–656.
162. Henig, Robin, Severe Menstrual Distress: A New Approach, *St. Louis Post-Dispatch*, March 7, 1982, Sec. 1, 3.
163. Henley, E. C., and Saraj Bohl, Nutrition Across the Woman's Life Cycle, *Nursing Clinics of North America*, 12, no. 1 (1982), 99–110.
164. Herman, Sonya, Divorce: A Grief Process, *Perspectives in Psychiatric Care*, 12, no. 3 (1974), 108–112.
165. Hewlett, Sylvia, *A Lesser Life: The Myth of Women's Liberation*. New York: Warner Books, 1987.
166. Hilgers, T., et al., Natural Family Planning III. Intermenstrual Symptoms and Estimated Time of Ovulation, *Obstetrics and Gynecology*, 58, no. 7 (1981), 152–155.
167. Hilts, Philip, The Clock Within, *Science '80*, 1, no. 8 (1980), 61–67.
168. Hocutt, John, et al., Flexible Fiberoptic Sigmoidscope, *American Family Physician*, 26, no. 5 (1982), 133–141.
169. Hodgkinson, Peter, Slow Motion Suicide, *Nursing Mirror*, 154, no. 1 (1982), 30–32.
170. Hoff, Lee Ann, and Marcia Resing, Was This Suicide Preventable?, *American Journal of Nursing*, 82, no. 7 (1982), 1106–1111.
171. Hogan, R. *Human Sexuality: A Nursing Perspective* (2nd ed.). Norwalk, CT: Appleton-Century-Crofts, 1985.
172. Holder, Gaye, Starting Over: The Remarriage Game, *St. Louis*, March, 1982, 89ff.
173. Holmes, Janine, and Lana Magiera, *Maternity Nursing*. New York: Macmillan, 1987.
174. Hongladorom, Gail, and Millie Russell, An Ethnic Difference—Lactose Intolerance, *Nursing Outlook*, 24, no. 12 (1976), 764–765.
175. Hoole, Axalla, Robert Greenberg, and C. Glenn Pickard, *Patient Care Guidelines for Nurse Practitioners* (3rd ed.). Boston: Little, Brown, 1988.
176. Hoskins, Carol, Chronobiology and Health, *Nursing Outlook*, 29, no. 10 (1981), 572–576.
177. Howard, Suzanne, Why Are So Many Women Underachievers?, *AAUW Journal* (May 1976), 12.

178. Howe, H.L., and Helen Bzduch, Recency of Pap Smear Screening: A Multivariate Model, *Public Health Reports*, 102, no. 2 (1987), 295–301.
179. Howe, Holly, Social Factors Associated with Breast Self-Examination Among High Risk Women, *American Journal of Public Health*, 71, no. 3 (1981), 251–254.
180. Hrobsky, Diane, Transition to Parenthood: A Balancing of Needs, *Nursing Clinics of North America*, 12, no. 3 (September, 1977), 457–468.
181. Hyman, R.B., and P. Woag, Stressful Life Events and Illness Onset: A Review of Crucial Variables, *Research in Nursing and Health*, 5 (1982), 155–163.
182. Infertility: Babies by Contract, *Newsweek* (November 4, 1985), 74–77.
183. Interim Diet Guides Recommended by NRC, *The Nation's Health*, 12, no. 8 (1982), 9.
184. Ipema, Donna, Rape: The Crisis of Recovery, *Nursing Research*, 28, no. 5 (1979), 272–275.
185. Irlenbusch, U., et al., Essay in the Classification of Morning and Evening Types of Activity in Light of the Daily Course of Autonomically Influenced Body Functions, *Chronobiologia*, 12, no. 4 (1985), 339–349.
186. Jacobson, Sherol, Psychosocial Stresses of Working Women, *Nursing Clinics of North America*, 17, no. 1 (1982), 137–144.
187. Jannson, Peg, Early Postpartum Discharge, *American Journal of Nursing*, 85, no. 5 (1985), 547–550.
188. Jensen, BK., Menstrual Cycle Effects on Task Performance Examined in the Context of Stress Research, *Acta Psychologica*, 50, (1981), 159–178.
189. Johnson, Laverne, et al. (eds.), *Biological Rhythms, Sleep and Shift Work*. New York: S.P. Medical & Scientific Books, 1981.
190. Kaluger, George, and Meriem Kaluger, *Human Development: The Span of LIfe* (3rd ed.). St. Louis: Times Mirror/Mosby, 1984.
191. Kaplan, Howard, Substance Abuse Patterns and Their Relationships to Family Attitudes and Values, *Health Values*, 11, no. 2 (1987), 40–46.
192. Kennedy-Caldwell, Christine, and Mary Hansen, Metabolism of Vitamins and Trace Minerals, *Nursing Clinics of North America*, 18, no. 1 (1983), 29–45.
193. Kenny, Richard, *Physiology of Aging: A Synopsis*. Chicago: Year Book, 1982.
194. Ketefian, Shake, Moral Reasoning and Moral Behavior Among Selected Groups of Practicing Nurses, *Nursing Research*, 30, no. 3 (1981), 171–175.
195. Kinch, R.A., & E. G. Robinson, Symposium: Premenstrual Syndrome—Current Knowledge and New Directions, *Canadian Journal of Psychiatry*, 30, no. 7 1985, 467–468.
196. King, Louise, The Dual-Career Couple Faces Corporate Relocation, *St. Louis Post-Dispatch*, August, 1986, 12–13, 33.
197. Klaus, Hanna, The Ovulation Method, *St. Louis University Magazine*, 47, no. 3 (1974), 4–6.
198. Klug, Ruth, Children with AIDS, *American Journal of Nursing*, 86, no. 10 (1986), 26–31.
199. Kohlberg, Lawrence, *Recent Research in Moral Development*. New York: Holt, Rinehart & Winston, 1971.
200. Kopf, R. M. Salamon, and P. Charytan, The Preventive Health History Forum: A Questionnaire for Use with Older Patient Populations, *Journal of Gerontological Nursing*, 8, no. 9 (1982), 519–523.
201. Kopp, Claire (ed.), *Becoming Female: Perspectives on Development*. New York: Plenum Press, 1979.
202. Kovalesky, Andrea, Usually Benign, But Always Frightening—That's Mitral Valve Prolapse, *Nursing '81*, 11, no. 4 (1981), 58–61.
203. Kramer, Jeannette, *Family Interfaces: Transgenerational Patterns*. New York: Brunner/Mazel, 1985.
204. Kramer, Marlene, *Reality Shock: Why Nurses Leave Nursing*. St. Louis: C. V. Mosby, 1974.
205. Kramer, Marlene, and C. Schmalenberg, Bicultural Training and New Graduate Role Transformation: Part I, *Nursing Digest*, 5 (Winter, 1978), 1–47.
206. Kreps, Juanita, Stop Calling Them Women's Issues, *Graduate Women*, 75, no. 6 (1981), 36.
207. Kristiansen, Connie, Smoking, Health Behavior, and Value Priorities, *Addictive Behaviors*, 10, no. 1 (1985), 41–44.
208. Kuhls, Thomas, et al., Occupational Risk of HIV, HBV, and HSV-2 Infections in Health Care Personnel Caring for AIDS Patients, *American Journal of Public Health*, 77, no. 10 (1987), 1306–1309.
209. Kuhn, Lawrence, The Aftermath of Childhood Incest and Sexual Abuse, *Res Medica*, 3, no. 2 (Fall, 1986), 15–18.
210. Kurose, Kasi, et al., A Standard Care Plan for Alcoholism, *American Journal of Nursing*, 81, no. 5 (1981), 1001–1006.
211. Kurtz, R., Your Body Image: What It Tells About You, *Science Digest* (1969), 52–55.
212. Laffrey, Shirley, Normal and Underweight Adults: Perceived Weight and Health Behavior Characteristics, *Nursing Research*, 35, no. 3 (1988), 173–177.
213. Lamb, Michael, *The Father's Role*. New York: John Wiley, 1986.
214. Lanberg, Lynn, Your Body Clock and What Makes It Tick, *Better Homes and Gardens*, August, 1987, 57.
215. Lancaster, Jeannette, Coping Mechanisms for the Working Mother, *American Journal of Nursing*, 75, no. 8 (August, 1975), 1322–1323.
216. Lappe, Frances, *Diet for a Small Planet*. New York: Ballantine Books, 1971.
217. Large, Robert, Prediction of Treatment Response in Pain Patients: The Illness Self-Concept Repertory Grid and EMG Feedback, *Pain*, 21, no. 3 (1985), 279–287.
218. Later Childbearing May Not Be So Risky, *The Nation's Health*, 12, no. 7 (1982), 5.
219. Lazieh, Marie, The Breast Feeding Worker—Risk or

Benefit, *Occupational Health Nursing*, 30, no. 11 (1982), 34–37.

220. Lehmann, A., DES: A Living Legacy—What Can Nurse Do About It? *Canadian Nursing*, 79 (December 1983), 34.

221. Leslie, Linda, Changing Factors and Changing Needs in Women's Health Care, *Nursing Clinics of North America*, 21, no. 1 (1986), 111–123.

222. Levinson, Daniel, *The Seasons of a Man's Life*. New York: Ballantine Books, 1978.

223. ———, et al., Periods in the Adult Development of Men: Ages 18 to 45, *The Counseling Psychologist*, 6, no. 1 (1976), 21–25.

224. Levinthal, Charles, *The Physiological Approach to Psychology*. Englewood Cliffs, N.J.: Prentice-Hall, 1979.

225. Levy, David, Optimism and Pessimism: Relationships to Circadian Rhythms, *Psychological Reports*, 57, no. 3 (1985), 1123–1126.

226. Lidz, Theodore, *The Person: His and Her Development Throughout the Life Cycle* (2nd ed). New York: Basic Books, 1983.

227. Lieberknecht, Kay, Helping the Battered Wife, *American Journal of Nursing*, 78, no. 4 (1978), 654–656.

228. Lipman-Blumen, Jean, and Harold Leavitt, Vicarious and Direct Achievement Patterns in Adulthood, *The Counseling Psychologist*, 6, no. 1 (1976), 17–22.

229. Lips, H., and N. Colwill, *The Psychology of Sex Differences*. Englewood Cliffs, N.J.: Prentice-Hall, 1978.

230. Long, Huey, Kay McCrary, and Spencer Ackerman, Adult Cognition: Piagetian Based Research Findings, *Adult Education*, 30, no. 1 (1979), 3–18.

231. Loucks, Arlene, Chlamydia: An Unheralded Epidemic, *American Journal of Nursing*, 87, no. 7 (1987), 920–922.

232. Lowman, Kay, *Of Cradles and Careers: Guide to Reshaping Your Job to Include a Baby In Your Life*. Franklin Park, Il.: La Leche League International, 1984.

233. Lowther, Nola, and Vicki Davis Carter, How to Increase Compliance in Hypertension, *American Journal of Nursing*, 81, no. 5 (1981), 963.

234. Lubic, Ruth, The Rise of the Birth Center Alternative, *The Nation's Health*, 12, no. 1 (1982), 7.

235. Luckmann, Joan, and Karen Sorensen, *Medical—Surgical Nursing: A Psychophysiologic Approach* (3rd ed.). Philadelphia: W.B. Saunders, 1987.

236. Lyer, Patricia W., The Battered Wife, *Nursing '80*, 10, no. 7 (1980), 52–55.

237. Lynn, David, *The Father: His Role in Child Development*. Monterey, Calif.: Brooks/Cole, 1974.

238. Lyon, Joseph, et al., Smoking and Carcinoma in Situ of the Uterine Cervix, *American Journal of Public Health*, 73, no. 5 (1983), 558–562.

239. Maas, Henry, and Joseph Kuyper, *From Thirty to Seventy*. San Francisco: Jossey-Bass, 1974.

240. MacRae, Isabel, and Gloria Henderson, Sexuality and Irreversible Health Limitations, *Nursing Clinics of North America*, 10, no. 3 (1975), 587–597.

241. Maccoby, E., and C. Jacklin, *The Psychology of Sex Differences*. Stanford, Calif.: Stanford University Press, 1974.

242. Maddox, Brenda, *The Half-Parent: Living With Other People's Children*. New York: M. Evans and Company, 1975.

243. ———, Homosexual Parents, *Psychology Today*, 16, no. 2 (1982), 62–69.

244. Mahon, Noreen, The Relationship of Self-Disclosure, Interpersonal Dependency, and Life Changes to Loneliness in Young Adults, *Nursing Research*, 31, no. 6 (1982), 343–347.

245. Majewski, Janice, Conflicts, Satisfactions, and Attitudes During Transition to the Maternal Role, *Nursing Research*, 35, no. 1 (1986), 10–14.

246. Mann, G., et al., Atherosclerosis in the Masai, *American Journal of Epidemiology*, 95 (January, 1972), 26–37.

247. Marks, Vida, Health Teaching for Recovering Alcoholic Patients, *American Journal of Nursing*, 80, no. 11 (1980), 2058–2061.

248. Marmor, Judd (ed.), *Homosexual Behavior: A Modern Reappraisal*. New York, Basic Books, 1980.

249. Marshall, James, Saxon Graham, and Mya Swanson, Caffeine Consumption and Benign Breast Disease: A Case-Control Comparison, *American Journal of Public Health*, 72, no. 6 (1982), 610–613.

250. Martin, John, The Impact of AIDS on Gay Male Sexual Patterns in New York City, *American Journal of Public Health*, 77, no. 5 (1987), 578–581.

251. Martin, Mary, Natural Family Planning and Instructor Training, *Nursing and Health Care*, 2, no. 12 (1981), 554ff.

252. Marut, Joanne, and Ramona Mercer, Comparison of Primiparas' Perceptions of Vaginal and Cesarean Births, *Nursing Research*, 28, no. 5 (1979), 260–266.

253. Masters, W., and V. Johnson, *The Human Sexual Response*. Boston: Little, Brown, 1966.

254. Masters, William, and Virginia Johnson, *Homosexuality in Perspective*. Boston: Little, Brown, 1979.

255. Mathewson, Merrily, Prolapsed Mitral Valve Syndrome, *American Journal of Nursing*, 80, no. 8 (1980), 1431–1432.

256. Maugh, Thomas, Fighting the Plague: 27 New Drugs to Stop a Killer, *American Health* (June, 1987), 73 ff.

257. May, Katharyn, Three Phases of Father Involvement in Pregnancy, *Nursing Research*, 31, no. 8 (1982), 337–342.

258. May, R.R., Mood Shifts and the Menstrual Cycle, *Journal of Psychosomatic Research*, 20 (1985), 125–130.

259. Mayhew, Deborah, Tomorrow's Technology: An Owner's Manual, *Graduate Women*, 76, no. 6 (1982), 14–16.

260. McBride, Angela, Orchestrating a Career, *Nursing Outlook*, 33, no. 5 (1985), 244–247.

261. McConnell, E., How Close Are You to Burn-out?, *RN*, 44, no. 5 (1981), 29–33.
262. McCoy, Vivian, Adult Life Cycle Tasks/Adult Continuing Education Program Response, *Life Long Learning: The Adult Years* (October, 1977), 16.
263. McKay, Susan, Second Stage Labor—Has Tradition Replaced Safety?, *American Journal of Nursing*, 81, no. 5 (1981), 1016–1019.
264. McKool, K., Facilitating Smoking Cessation, *Journal of Cardiovascular Nursing*, 1, no. 4 (1987), 28–40.
265. McTaggart, Lynne, DES—The Pregnancy Vitamin That Was A Time Bomb, *Parade*, September 9, 1979, 22–24.
266. Mead, G. H., *Mind, Self, and Society*. Chicago: University of Chicago Press, 1962.
267. Mead, Margaret, *Sex and Temperament in Three Primitive Societies*. New York: William Morrow, 1935.
268. Meissner, Judith, A Simple Guide for Assessing Oral Health, *Nursing '80*, 10, no. 4 (1980), 84–85.
269. Menhies, Janet, Smoking: The Physiological Effects, *American Journal of Nursing*, 83, no. 8 (1983), 1143–1146.
270. ———, Smoking: One Way to Stop, *American Journal of Nursing*, 83, no. 8 (1983), 1147–1148.
271. Menning, Barbara, The Psychosocial Impact of Infertility, *Nursing Clinics of North America*, 17, no. 1 (1982) 155–163.
272. Mercer, Ramona, The Process of Maternal Role Attachment Over the First Year, *Nursing Research*, 34, no. 4 (1985), 198–203.
273. Minors, D.S., et al., Circadian Rhythms in Deep Body Temperature, Urinary Excretion and Alertness in Nurses on Night Work, *Ergonomics*, 28, no. 11 (1985), 1523–1550.
274. Monk, Timothy, Diurnal Variation in Mood and Performance in Time-Isolated Environment, *Chronobiology*, 2, no. 3 (1985), 185–193.
275. Moore, Dianne, Prepared Childbirth and Marital Satisfaction During the Antepartum and Postpartum Periods, *Nursing Research*, 32, no. 2 (1983), 73–79.
276. Moore-Ede, Martin, Physiology of the Circadian Timing System: Predictive Versus Reactive Homeostasis, *American Journal of Physiology*, 19, no. 5 (1986), R737–752.
277. Moshman, David, John Glover, and Roger Bruning, *Developmental Psychology*. Boston: Little, Brown, 1987.
278. Moynihan, Barbara, and Joan Duncan, The Role of the Nurse in the Care of Sexual Assault Victims, *Nursing Clinics of North America*, 16, no. 1 (1981), 95–100.
279. Murray, Barbara, and Linda Wilcox, Testicular Self Examination, *American Journal of Nursing*, 78, no. 12 (1979), 2074–2075.
280. Murray, Ruth, Body Image Development in Adulthood, *Nursing Clinics of North America*, 7, no. 4 (1972), 617–621.

281. ———, and M. Marilyn Huelskoetter, *Psychiatric/Mental Health Nursing: Giving Emotional Care* (2nd ed). Englewood Cliffs, N.J.: Prentice-Hall, 1987.
282. ———, and Judith Zentner, *Nursing Concepts for Health Promotion* (3rd ed.). Englewood Cliffs, N.J.: Prentice-Hall, 1985.
283. Myers, L., et al., Prevalence of Anemia and Iron Deficiency Anemia in Black and White Women in the United States Estimated by Two Methods, *American Journal of Public Health*, 73, no. 9 (1983), 1042–1047.
284. Mystery of Sleep, *Newsweek* (July 13, 1981), 48–55.
285. Myths About Sexual Harassment, *Graduate Women*, 73, no. 3 (1979), 6–7.
286. Nassi, Alberta, Survivors of the Sixties: Comparative Psychosocial and Political Development of Former Berkeley Student Activists, *American Psychologist*, 36, no. 7 (1981), 753–761.
287. Neff, James, Evaluating the Stress-Buffering Role of Alcohol Consumption: Variation by Type of Event and Type of Symptom, *Alcohol & Alcoholism*, 20, no. 4 (1985), 391–401.
288. Neugarten, Bernice, Adaptation and the Life Cycle, *The Counseling Psychologist*, 6, no. 1 (1976), 16–20.
289. ———, and N. Datan, Sociological Perspectives on the Life Cycle, in *Life-Span Developmental Psychology: Personality and Socialization*, eds. P. Baltes and K. Schail. New York: Academic Press, 1973, 53–59.
290. A New Kind of Life With Father, *Newsweek* (November 30, 1981), 93–96.
291. O'Brien, M.M.S., Premenstrual Syndrome: A Review of the Present Status of Therapy, *British Journal of Obstetrics and Gynecology*, 86, (1982), 104–150.
292. O'Brien, Mary Elizabeth, Reaching the Migrant Worker, *American Journal of Nursing*, 83, no. 6 (1983), 895–897.
293. Oelbaum, Cynthia, Hallmarks of Adult Wellness, *American Journal of Nursing*, 74, no. 9 (September, 1974), 1623–1625.
294. Older Mothers: Risks, Realities, and Rewards, *St. Louis Post-Dispatch*, July 8, 1987, Sec. D, pp. 1, 2.
295. One Family's Struggle, *Newsweek* (January 13, 1985), 55–58.
296. Orlandi, M.A., Gender Difference in Smoking Cessation, *Women Health*, 11, no. 314 (1986), 237–251.
297. Ossler, Charlene, Men's Work Environments and Health Risks, *Nursing Clinics of North America*, 21, no. 1 (1986), 25–36.
298. Out of Wedlock Births Doubled, *The Nation's Health*, 10, no. 11 (1980), 7.
299. Owen, Anita, Gemma Lanna, and George Owen, Counseling Patients About Diet and Nutrition Supplements, *Nursing Clinics of North America*, 14, no. 2 (1979), 247–267.
300. Pagano, Helen, Changing Urban Work Ethic, *Adult Leadership*, 23, no. 4 (October, 1974), 100–104.

301. Painter, Deann, The Black Woman in American History, in *Women's Lives: Perspectives in Progress and Change*, eds. Virginia Lussier and Joyce Walstedt. Boston: Little, Brown, 1979.
302. Panel Recommends Hepatitis B Vaccine for Health Workers, Some Heterosexuals, *The Nation's Health* (July, 1985), 12.
303. Papa, Lorraine, Response to Life Events as Predictors of Suicidal Behavior, *Nursing Research*, 29, no. 6 (1980), 362–369.
304. Parker, Barbara, and Dale Schumacher, The Battered Wife Syndrome and Violence in the Nuclear Family of Origin: A Controlled Pilot Study, *American Journal of Public Health*, 67, no. 8 (1977), 760–761.
305. Payne, D., et al., Effectiveness of Milk Products in Dietary Management of Lactose Malabsorption, *American Journal of Clinical Nutrition*, 34 (1981), 2711–2715.
306. Pender, Nola, *Health Promotion in Nursing Practice* (2nd ed.). E. Norwalk, CT: Appleton and Lange, 1987.
307. Peterson, B., Biopsychological Processes in the Development of Sex-Related Differences, in *The Psychology of Sex Differences and Sex Roles*, ed. J. Parsons. Washington, D.C.: Hemisphere Publishing, 1980, 31–55.
308. Peterson, Norma, Is The Rebellion Over?, *Parade*, January 31, 1982, 10–11.
309. Pillitteri, Adele, *Child Health Nursing: Care of the Growing Family* (3rd ed.). Boston: Little, Brown, 1987.
310. Pines, A., and E. Aronson. *Burn-out: From Tedium to Personal Growth*. New York: Macmillan, 1981.
311. Pinnell, Norma, and Mary deMeneses, *Nursing Process: Theory, Application, and Related Processes*. Norwalk, Conn.: Appleton-Century-Crofts, 1986.
312. Pike, Ruth, and Myrtle Brown, *Nutrition: An Integrated Approach* (2nd. ed.). New York: John Wiley, 1975.
313. Potter, B., Avoiding Burn-out: Joint Employer-Employee Responsibility, *Hospital Progress*, 62, no. 6 (1981), 50–55.
314. Premenstrual Syndrome: An Ancient Woe Deserving of Modern Scrutiny, *Journal of American Medical Association*, 245, no. 14 (April 10, 1981), 1393–1396.
315. Primrose, R.B., Taking the Tension Out of Pelvic Exams, *American Journal of Nursing*, 84, no. 1 (1984), 72.
316. Puetz, Belinda, Occupational Health Nursing, Employee Mental Health, *Occupational Health Nursing*, 28, no. 9 (1980), 7–11.
317. Putt, Arlene, A Biofeedback Service by Nurses, *American Journal of Nursing*, 79, no. 1 (1979), 88–89.
318. Ramey, Estelle, Women's Health in the 1980's, *Graduate Women*, 77, no. 1 (1983), 13–16.
319. Reid, Robert, Premenstrual Syndrome, *American Journal of Obstetrics and Gynecology*, 134, no. 9 (1981), 85–104.
320. Reinberg, Alain, *Biological Rhythms and Medicine: Cellular, Metabolic, Physiopathic, and Pharmacologic Aspects*. New York: Springer-Verlag, 1983.
321. Rich, Victoria, and Alexander Rich, Personality Hardiness and Burnout in Female Staff Nurses, *Image*, 19, no. 2 (1987), 63–66.
322. Richard, Elaine, and Ann Shepard, Giving Up Smoking: A Lesson in Loss Theory, *American Journal of Nursing*, 81, no. 4 (1981), 755–757.
323. Rising, Sharon, The Fourth Stage of Labor: Family Reintegration, *American Journal of Nursing*, 74, no. 5 (1974), 870.
324. Roberts, Albert, *Battered Women and Their Families: Intervention Strategies and Treatment Programs*. New York: Springer, 1984.
325. Roberts, Florence, Model for Parent Education, *Image*, 13, no. 10 (1981), 86–89.
326. Roberts, H.J., Perspective on Vitamin E as Therapy, *Journal of American Medical Association*, 246 (July 10, 1981), 129–131.
327. Roberts, Susan, Gay Health Issues, in Linda Jarvis (ed.), *Community Health Nursing: Keeping the Public Healthy*. Philadelphia: F. A. Davis, 1985, 679–693.
328. Robertson, L.S., Motor Vehicle Injuries, *Public Health Review*, 100, no. 6 (1985), 580–581.
329. Robinson, Dick, The Suicide Factor, *Health*, 14, no. 3 (1982), 33–34.
330. Rogers, Carl, *Client-Centered Therapy*. Boston: Houghton-Mifflin, 1951.
331. Roghmann, Klaus, and Richard Doherty, Reassurance Through Prenatal Diagnosis and Willingness to Bear Children After Age 35, *American Journal of Public Health*, 73, no. 7 (1983), 760–762.
332. Rosenberg, Frances, Lactose Intolerance, *American Journal of Nursing*, 77, no. 5 (1977), 823–824.
333. Rosenthal, Kristine, and Harry Keshet, *Fathers Without Partners*. Totowa, NJ: Rowman and Littlefield, 1981.
334. Rosenthal, L., et al., Periodic Movements During Sleep, Sleep Fragmentation, and Sleep-Wake Complaints, *Sleep*, 7, no. 4 (1984), 326–330.
335. Rossignol, Annette, Caffeine—Containing Beverages and Premenstrual Syndrome in Young Women, *American Journal of Public Health*, 75, no. 11 (1985), 1335–1337.
336. Rowan, Christopher, *Understanding Aids: A Self-Defense Manual*. Halifax, England: Ryburn Publishing, 1987.
337. Roznoy, Melinda, The Young Adult: Taking a Sexual History, *American Journal of Nursing*, 76, no. 8 (1976), 1279–1282.
338. Rubin, Reva, Maternal Tasks in Pregnancy, *Maternal-Child Nursing Journal*, 4, no. 3 (Fall, 1975), 143–153.
339. Rutledge, Dana, Factors Related to Women's Practice of Breast Self-Examination, *Nursing Research*, 36, no. 2 (1987), 117–121.
340. Sadava, Stan, and Heidi Weithe, Maintenance and

Attributions about Smoking Among Smokers, Non-smokers, and Ex-smokers, *International Journal of Addictions*, 20, no. 10 (1985), 1533–1544.
341. Samples, J.F., et al., Circadian Rhythms: Basis for Screening for Fever, *Nursing Research*, 34, no. 6 (1985), 377–379.
342. Sandelowski, Margarete, The Color Gray: Ambiguity and Infertility, *Image*, 19, no. 2 (1987), 70–74.
343. Sandler, Dale, et al., Cancer Risk in Adulthood from Early Life Exposure to Parents' Smoking, *American Journal of Public Health*, 75, no. 5 (1985), 487–492.
344. Santopietro, Mary, Effectiveness of a Self-Instructional Module in Human Sexuality Counseling, *Nursing Research*, 29, no. 1 (1980), 14–19.
345. Satchell, Michael, How to Cope If Your Child Is Gay, *Parade* (June 4, 1978), 6–7.
346. Saul, I. J., *Emotional Maturity* (2nd ed.). Philadelphia: J. B. Lippincott, 1962.
347. Schaie, K., and J. Parr, Intelligence, in *The Modern American College: Responding to the New Realities of Diverse Students and a Changing Society*, eds. A. Chickering and Associates. San Francisco: Jossey-Bass, 1981.
348. Scandrett, S.L., et al., A Comparative Study of Biofeedback and Progressive Relaxation in Anxious Patients, *Issues in Mental Health Nursing*, 8, no. 3 (1986), 255–271.
349. Schechter, Susan, *Women and Male Violence: The Visions and Struggles of the Battered Women's Movement*. Boston: South End Press, 1982.
350. Scherwerts, Priscilla, The Alcohol Treatment Team, *American Journal of Nursing*, 82, no. 12 (1982), 1878–1879.
351. Schietinger, Helen, A Home Care Plan for AIDS, *American Journal of Nursing*, 86, no. 9 (1986), 1021–1028.
352. Schilder, P., *The Image and Appearance of the Human Body*. New York: International University Press, 1951.
353. Schmalenburg, C., and Marlene Kramer, *Coping With Reality Shock: Voices of Experience*. Wakefield, Mass.: Nursing Resources, 1979.
354. Schuster, C., and S. Ashburn, *The Process of Human Development* (2nd ed.). Boston: Little, Brown, 1986.
355. Schweiger, Joyce, John Lang, and James Schweiger, Oral Assessment: How To Do It, *American Journal of Nursing*, 80, no. 4 (1980), 654–657.
356. Scott, Patricia, What's Happening to the Dual-Career Family? *Nursing Economics*, 2, no. 5 (1984), 351–355.
357. Scully, R., Stress in the Nurse, *American Journal of Nursing*, 80, no. 5 (1980), 912–917.
358. Scully, R., Staff Support Groups: Helping Nurses Help Themselves, *Journal of Nursing Administration*, 11, no. 1 (1981), 48–51.
359. Sedgwick, Rae, Myths in Human Sexuality, *Nursing Clinics of North America*, 10, no. 3 (September, 1975), 539–550.
360. Sehloff, J.A., Night Shift: Problems and Coping Strategies, *Medical Laboratory Observer*, 18, no. 8 (1986), 63–66.
361. Seidell, Jacob, et al., The Relation Between Overweight and Subjective Health According to Age, Social Class, Slimming Behavior, and Smoking Habits in Dutch Adults, *American Journal of Public Health*, 76, no. 12 (1986), 1410–1415.
362. Selekman, Janice, Immunization; What's It All About? *American Journal of Nursing*, 80, no. 8 (1980), 1440–1445.
363. Seligman, J., et al., Women Smokers: The Risk Factor, *Newsweek*, 106, no. 22 (1985), 76–78.
364. Shaw, Evelyn, Female Circumcision, *American Journal of Nursing*, 85, no. 6 (1985), 684–687.
365. Sheehy, Gail, *Passages: Predictable Crises of Adult Life*. New York: Bantam Books, 1976.
366. ———, Introducing the Postponing Generation: The Truth About Today's Young Men, *Esquire Magazine* (October, 1979), 264–272.
367. Sheldon, W. H., S. S. Stevens, and W. B. Tucker, *The Varieties of Human Physique*. New York: Harper and Brothers, 1940.
368. Siegelman, M., Parental Background of Male Homosexuals and Heterosexuals, *Archives of Sexual Behavior*, 3 (1974), 3–18.
369. Siegelman, M., Parental Backgrounds of Homosexual and Heterosexual Men: A Cross-National Replication, *Archives of Sexual Behavior*, 10 (1981), 505–573.
370. Sievers, Maurice, and Jeffrey Fisher, Cancer in North American Indians, *American Journal of Public Health*, 73, no. 5 (1983), 485–486.
371. Single Mothers' Perceptions of the Newborns, *American Journal of Nursing*, 55, no. 12 (1985), 1397.
372. Sleep: A Mystery Unfolding, *TEMPO*, 10, no. 1 (1982), 1–4.
373. Smith, Jack, James Mercy, and Judith Conn, Marital Status and the Risk of Suicide, *American Journal of Public Health*, 78, no. 1 (1988), 78–80.
374. Smith, Sara, Big Families Can Be Happy, Too, *Newsweek* (January 14, 1985), 12–13.
375. Smoking Dangers for Females, *The Nation's Health*, 10, no. 2 (1980), 15–16.
376. Smoking is Linked to Gum Disease, *The Nation's Health*, 14, no. 6 (1983), 6.
377. Smolensky, M.H., and A. Reinberg, The Chronotherapy of Corticosteroids: Practical Application of Chronobiologic Findings to Nursing, *Nursing Clinics of North America*, 11, no. 4 (1976), 609–619.
378. Sonkin, Daniel, Del Martin, and Levone Walker, *The Male Batterer: A Treatment Approach*, New York: Springer, 1985.
379. Sorensen, Karen, and Joan Luckman, *Basic Nursing: A Psychophysiologic Approach* (2nd ed.). Philadelphia: W. B. Saunders, 1986.
380. Sorosky, A. D., The Psychological Effects of Divorce on Adolescents, *Adolescence*, 12 (1977), 123–136.

381. Spencer, Jim, Why Nurses Smoke, *Nursing Mirror*, 154, no. 1 (1982), 26–29.
382. Speroff, Leon, PMS—Looking for New Answers to an Old Problem, *Contemporary OB-Gyn*, 22, no. 2 (1983), 102–129.
383. Sredl, Darlene, Catherine Klenky, and Maria Rojkind, Offering The Rape Victim Real Help, *Nursing '79*, 9, no. 7 (1979), 38–43.
384. Stamell, Marcia, and Jane Doe, The Plight of Executive Junkies, *PD, St. Louis Post-Dispatch*, December 19, 1982, pp. 14–16.
385. Stearns, Peter, Machines, People, and the Future, *Graduate Women*, 76, no. 6 (1982), 17–19.
386. Stewart, Anita, and Robert Brook, Effects of Being Overweight, *American Journal of Public Health*, 73, no. 2 (1983), 171–178.
387. Stoppard, Miriam, *Being a Well Woman: How to Achieve and Maintain Personal Fitness, Health, and Happiness*. New York: Holt, Rinehart & Winston, 1982.
388. Stranik, Mary Kay, and Betty Lou Lea Hogberg, Transition into Parenthood, *American Journal of Nursing*, 79, no. 1 (1979), 90–93.
389. Strickland, Ora, The Occurrence of Symptoms in Expectant Fathers, *Nursing Research*, 36, no. 3 (1987), 184–189.
390. Strickland, S., Critical Health Issues in the Workplace . . . Alcohol and Substance Abuse, *American Association of Occupational Health Nursing*, 34, no. 9 (1986), 443–444.
391. Sullivan, H. S., *The Interpersonal Theory of Psychiatry*. New York: W. W. Norton, 1953.
392. Surgeon General Warns of Smoking Risk to Women, *American Journal of Nursing*, 80, no. 5 (1980), 847–848.
393. Survey: Women Face Harassment, *Higher Education and National Affairs*, 34, no. 5 (1985), 5.
394. Swartz, M.H., and S. Dock, Mitral Valve Prolapse Syndrome, *Hospital Medicine*, 18 (December 1982), 49.
395. Swogger, G., Jr., Toward Understanding Stress: A Map of the Territory, *Journal of School Health*, 51, no. 1 (1981), 29–33.
396. Sykes, Julie A., Paul Kelly, and John A. Kennedy, Jr., Black Skin Problems, *American Journal of Nursing*, 79, no. 6 (1979), 1092–1094.
397. Taffel, Selma, and Kenneth Keppel, Advice About Weight Gain During Pregnancy and Actual Weight Gain, *American Journal of Public Health*, 76, no. 12 (1986), 1396–1399.
398. Taking Drugs on the Job, *Newsweek* (August 22, 1983), 52–57.
399. Testu, Francois, Diurnal Variations of Performance and Information Processing, *Chronobiologia*, 13, no. 4 (1986), 319–326.
400. The Panic Over AIDS, *Newsweek* (July 4, 1983), 20–21.
401. The Parental Leave Debate: How Much is Enough? *Newsweek* (February 17, 1986), 64.
402. The Real Mr. Moms, *Newsweek* (March 31, 1986), 52–53.
403. *The Unseen Crisis: Blacks and Alcohol*. Washington, D.C.: U.S. Department of Health, Education, and Welfare, 1978.
404. Three's A Crowd, *Newsweek* (September 1, 1986), 68–76.
405. Throwe, A.N., Families and Alcohol, *Critical Care Quarterly*, 8, no. 4 (1986), 79–88.
406. Tickfer, Milldred, Nurses Teach Children of Divorce, *Free Association*, 10, no. 1 (1983), 1ff.
407. Timby, Barbara, Ovulation Method of Birth Control, *American Journal of Nursing*, 76, no. 6 (June, 1976), 928–929.
408. Tips for Joggers, *Health Scenes*, Fall, 1987, 12.
409. Tishler, Carl, The Psychological Aspects of Genetic Counseling, *American Journal of Nursing*, 81, no. 4 (1981), 733–734.
410. Tomlinson, Patricia, Spousal Differences in Marital Satisfaction During Transition to Parenthood, *Nursing Research*, 36, no. 4 (1987), 239–242.
411. Traub, A., and J. Orbach, Psychophysical Studies of Body Image, *Archives of General Psychiatry*, 11, no. 7 (July, 1964), 53–66.
412. Tu, Edward Jow-Ching, Multiple Cause-of-Death Analysis of Hypertension-Related Mortality in New York State, *Public Health Reports*, 102, no. 3 (1987), 329–334.
413. Turek, Fred, Circadian Principles and Design of Rotating Work Shift Schedules, *American Journal of Physiology*, 20, no. 3 (1986), R636–637.
414. Turner, Jeffrey, and Donald Helms, *Lifespan Development* (3rd ed.). New York: Holt, Rinehart and Winston, 1987.
415. U.S. Bureau of the Census, *Statistical Abstract of the United States: 1981* (102nd ed.). Washington, D.C.: U.S. Government Printing Office, 1981.
416. Urdung, Laurence, ed., *Mosby's Medical and Nursing Dictionary*. St. Louis: C. V. Mosby, 1983.
417. Utz, Sharon, et al., Mitral Valve Prolapse: Self-Care Needs, Nursing Diagnoses, and Interventions, *Heart and Lung*, 16, no. 1 (1987), 77–83.
418. Vaccines for Adult Diseases, *Newsweek* (October 12, 1987), 92–93.
419. Vaillant, George, How the Best and the Brightest Came of Age, *Psychology Today*, 11, no. 9 (1977), 34ff.
420. ———, The Normal Boy in Later Life: How Adaptation Fosters Growth, *Harvard Magazine*, 55, no. 6 (1977), 234–239.
421. Vander Kolk, Bessel, Uses of Lithium in Patients without Major Affective Illness, *Hospital & Community Psychiatry*, 37, no. 7 (1986), 675, 684.
422. Vander Waerdt, Lois, Sexual Harassment in the Work-

place: Defusing the Time Bomb, *St. Louis Manager* (February, 1987), 15.
423. Veninga, R., Administrator Burn-out—Causes and Cures, *Hospital Progress*, 60, no. 2 (1979), 45–52.
424. Ventura, Jacqueline, Parent Coping, A Replication, *Nursing Research*, 35, no. 2 (1986), 77–80.
425. Vitiello, Michael, et al., Circadian Temperature Rhythms in Young Adult and Aged Men, *Neurobiology of Aging*, 7 (1986), 97–99.
426. Wadsworth, Barry, *Piaget's Theory of Cognitive and Affective Development* (3rd ed.). New York: David McKay, 1984.
427. Walker, Lorraine, Helen Cran, and Earl Thompson, Maternal Role Attainment and Identity in the Postpartum Period: Stability and Change, *Nursing Research*, 35, no. 2 (1986), 68–71.
428. Wallace, Robert, and Herbert Benson, The Physiology of Meditation, in *Altered States of Awareness*. San Francisco: W. H. Freeman, 1972, 125–131.
429. Walsleben, Joyce, Sleep Disorders, *American Journal of Nursing*, 82, no. 6 (1982), 936–939.
430. Watts, Rosalyn, Dimensions of Sexual Health, *American Journal of Nursing*, 79, no. 9 (1979), 1568–1572.
431. Watts, S., L. Dennerstein, & D. Horne, The Premenstrual Syndrome, *Journal of Affective Disorders*, 2 (1980), 257–266.
432. Weaver, Ruth, and Mecca Cranley, An Exploration of Paternal-Fetal Attachment Behavior, *Nursing Research*, 32, no. 2 (1983), 68–72.
433. Webb, Patricia, Piaget: Implications for Teaching, *Theory Into Practice*, 19, no. 2 (1980), 93–97.
434. Webb, W. B., *Sleep: The Gentle Tyrant*. Englewood Cliffs, N.J.: Prentice-Hall, 1975.
435. Webb, Wilse, A Further Analysis of Age and Sleep Deprivation Effects, *Psychophysiology*, 22, no. 2 (1985), 156–161.
436. Webster, Denise, Changing Definitions, Changing Times, *Nursing Clinics of North America*, 21, no. 1 (1986), 87–97.
437. Webster, Denise, and Ginna Ipema, Women and Mental Health: A Model for Practice, *Nursing Clinics of North America*, 21, no. 1 (1986), 127–150.
438. Weil, Susan, The Unspoken Needs of Families During High Risk Pregnancies, *American Journal of Nursing*, 81, no. 11 (1981), 2047–2049.
439. Weinberger, Morris, et al., Health Beliefs and Smoking Behavior, *American Journal of Public Health*, 71, no. 11 (1981), 1253–1255.
440. Welch, Mary, Rape and the Trauma of Inadequate Care, *Nursing Digest*, 5, no. 1 (1977), 50–52.
441. Weston, Lee, *Body Rhythms: The Circadian Rhythms within You*. New York: Harcourt Brace Jovanovich, 1979.
442. When Childbearing is Postponed, *Medical Aspects of Human Sexuality*, 19, no. 8 (1986), 108–110.
443. Whitbourne, Susan Krauss, *The Aging Body: Physiological Changes and Psychological Consequences*. New York: Springer-Verlag, 1985.
444. Williams, D.C., Hepatitis and Other Sexually Transmitted Diseases in Gay Men and Lesbians, *Sexually Transmitted Diseases*, 8, no. 4 (1981), 330–332.
445. Williams, Sue Rodwell, *Nutrition and Diet Therapy* (5th ed.). St. Louis: Times Mirror/Mosby, 1985.
446. Windom, Robert, Adult Immunization Should Be Routine, Too, *Public Health Reports*, 102, no. 3 (1987), 245–246.
447. Wiver, Rutger, Use of Light to Treat Jet Lag: Differential Effects of Normal and Bright Artificial Light on Human Circadian Rhythms, *Annals of the New York Academy of Sciences*, 453 (1985), 282–304.
448. Wojtczak-Jaroszowa, J., and D. Jarvsz, Time-Related Distribution of Occupational Accidents, *Journal of Safety Research*, 18, no. 1 (1987), 33–41.
449. Women and Athletic Endurance, *Graduate Woman*, 79, no. 4 (1985), 5.
450. Wood, Robin, and Karla Rose, Penile Implants for Impotence, *American Journal of Nursing*, 78, no. 2 (1978), 234–238.
451. Woods, Nancy, Relationship of Socialization and Stress to Premenstrual Symptoms, Disability and Menstrual Attitudes, *Nursing Research*, 34, no. 3, (1985), 145–149.
452. Woods, Nancy, and Anne Mandetta, Human Sexual Response Patterns, *Nursing Clinics of North America*, 10, no. 3 (September 1975), 529–538.
453. Woods, Nancy, Ada Most, and Gretchen Dery, Prevalence of Perimenstrual Symptoms, *American Journal of Public Health*, 72, no. 11 (1982), 1257–1263.
454. Worick, Wayne, and Warren Shaller, *Alcohol, Tobacco, and Drugs: Their Use and Abuse*. Englewood Cliffs, N.J.: Prentice-Hall, 1977.
455. Heuermann, Penni and Jake. Personal Correspondence—Twenty-fifth Wedding Anniversary Invitation, August, 1988, Des Moines, Ia.

13

Assessment and Health Promotion for the Middle-Aged Person

Study of this chapter will enable you to

1. Explore with a middle-aged person ideas about his/her generation, lifestyle, and the conflict between the generations.
2. Discuss the family relationships and sexuality development of the middle-ager, conflicts which must be resolved, and your role in helping the family work through concerns and conflicts.
3. List the developmental tasks for the middle-aged family, and give examples of how these can be accomplished.
4. Discuss the emotional, social, economic, and lifestyle changes usually encountered by the widow(er).
5. Describe the hormonal changes of middle age and the resultant changes in appearance and body image, physiologically and emotionally.
6. Discuss the nutritional, rest, leisure, work, and exercise needs of the middle-ager, factors which interfere with meeting those needs, and your role in helping him/her meet these needs.
7. Describe how the middle-ager's cognitive skills and emotional and moral development will influence your nursing care plan.
8. State the developmental crisis of this era and its significance to social welfare.
9. Contrast the behavior of generativity, or maturity, and self-absorption, or stagnation, and related adaptive mechanisms.
10. Describe the developmental tasks for this person and your role in helping him/her accomplish these tasks.
11. Explore with a middle-ager ways to avoid injury and health problems.
12. Assess the body image, physical, mental, and emotional characteristics and family relationships of a middle-aged person.
13. Plan and give effective care to a middle-aged person by using scientific principles and considering special needs and reaction to illness and hospitalization.

Key Terms

Middle age	Gout/hyperuricemia
Generation gap	Diabetes type II
Social mobility	Acute bacterial prostatitis
Widow(er)hood	Chronic prostatitis
Filial responsibility	Lumbosacral strain
Menopause	Foot balance
Perimenopausal years	Callus
Climacteric	Sexual dysfunction
Presbyopia	Generativity
Sleep apnea	Mentor
Sinusitis	Stagnation/Self-absorption
Hiatal hernia	Maturity
Duodenal peptic ulcer	Adult socialization
Angina pectoris	Midlife crisis
Essential hypertension	Midlife transition
Secondary hypertension	

The next generation complains about what we are and do. They say they'll do better. They should! They're standing on our shoulders.

Middle age is a modern invention attributed to improved nutrition, control of communicable disease, discovery and control of familial disease, and other medical advances. Life has been stretched out in the middle; what used to be old age is now middle age.

Further, as the work structure and roles and technological development become more complex, as family life and child-rearing patterns change toward smaller families and a longer postparental period, the periods of childhood and youth are lengthened. Life is divided into more stages with more precise time periods and special developmental tasks for each age group. Thus in the past two decades, middle age has become a distinct life period. New concepts of adulthood involve a change in definitions of sex as well as age roles. Midlife development implies growth of the personality to encompass some characteristics that had stereotypically in the past been assigned to the opposite sex. Thus biology diminishes its influence on much of what had been held to be immutably biological characteristics. Individuals may also work out more flexible adaptations (90). Middle adulthood is a time of widening social interest in which the family becomes increasingly oriented to its responsibility to the greater society. Parental attention is directed toward assisting integration of offspring's wishes with social requirements.

Defining middle age is a nebulous task. Chronologically, **middle age** *covers the years of approximately 45 to 65, but each person will also consider the physiological age condition of the body, and psychological age—how old he/she acts and feels*. Point of view alters definition: A child may think age 45 is old; the 45-year-old may consider himself/herself young. A representative sample of U.S. citizens in the mid-1960s placed early middle age between 40 and 55 and late middle age between 56 and 64. Many people today consider themselves young until nearly age 50 and middle-aged until around 70 years, or even beyond. Age assignment varies according to social class; the poorer person perceives the prime or midpoint of life to vary from the midtwenties to midthirties (76).

Over 40 million Americans, one-fourth the population, are considered middle-aged. They earn most of the money, pay the bills and most of the taxes, and make many of the decisions. Thus the power in government, politics, education, religion, science, business, industry, and communication is often wielded not by the young or the old, but by the middle-aged.

Middle age is a time of relatively good physical and mental health, new personal freedom, and maximum command of self and influence over the social environment. At work the person has increasing ability to make decisions, hold high status jobs, and earn a maximum income. The person has expanding family networks and social roles, and married life for postparental couples can be as harmonious and satisfying as the early married years.

In his book, *Time Flies*, Bill Cosby has popularized becoming middle-aged. Some of the toils and deficits may be exaggerated, but the book conveys a middle-ager's attitude—the ability to see his/her strengths and limits and to accept, with a sense of humor, those normal changes that are part of development (24).

Family Development and Interaction

Relationship with Children

Mead (75) and Petersen (95) wrote about the **generation gap**, *the conflict between parents and adolescents* which has always existed to some degree (66). The experience of elders, and therefore their values and expectations, differs from that of their offspring. However, Carlson and Kaplan say the term *generation gap*, which was coined in the 1960s, is inaccurate. The generations are not really in conflict with each other but rather each generation is concerned about the other, although for different reasons. In fact, the younger and older generations can successfully combine efforts to work for legislation, policy changes, or social justice (17, 58).

The middle-ager was born sometime between the end of World War I and the occurrence of World War II. He/she learned that interdependence of nations, economic security, and material possessions may be lost for reasons beyond personal control. Values and behavior have been influenced by growing up with inadequate material resources after the Great Depression and during World War II and by rapid social and technological changes.

The nuclear family, prominent in America, in which each generation must learn new ways of living and which excludes grandparents from the family circle, causes children, in turn, to seek this arrangement and discount learning from elders. The offspring cannot be fully prepared for the future. Youth must develop new patterns of behavior on their own experience and learn from peers. Youth's present affluence, emphasis on age differences, independence, and insistence on a unique lifestyle add to the conflict. Youth's seeking of control over self and cultural institutions and incorporating into the self some of the behavior of the opposite sex or counterculture may enrage and confuse middle-agers. Negative reactions of offspring reawaken in parents personal conflicts engendered by the remembrances of personal early commitments to ideals which became compromised over the years to fit narrower concerns. The addition of innate parental feelings of affection, admiration, and compassion for youth to the negative feelings produces an ambivalence (56, 74, 105).

Social mobility, *where the child moves away from the social position, educational level, class, occupation, or* *ethnicity of parents,* causes offspring overtly to forsake parental teaching and seek new models of behavior. The mass media help to set standards and expectations about behavior which may be counter to parental teaching or wishes. Rapid social changes and awareness that much about the future is unknown threaten established faiths and stimulate attraction to new ideologies and exceptional behavior.

✔ As a nurse you may discuss with middle-agers what they as adults have to offer their children. They are the only generation to ever know, experience, and incorporate such rapid changes. They can give their offspring imaginative, innovative, and dedicated adult care, a safe and flexible environment in which children can be given support, feel secure, grow, and discover themselves and the world. Reaffirm that it is up to the parents to teach *not what* to learn but *how to learn, not what to be* commited to but the *value of commitment.* Tell parents that research shows the continuity of values from generation to generation within a family. Typically, the values of young adults are more similar to their parents' values than to those of other adults or peers (60). Help youth ask questions adults do not think of, but yet trust their parents enough to work on the answers together. The middle-aged parent can be taught to listen and exchange information and ideas honestly and with a sense of humor. The parent can accept youth's rejection of the faulty areas of society while supporting the values, principles, and institutions he/she knows to be sound and necessary. As parent and offspring learn together to cope with the future, the parent will be able to assist youth to reach responsible, independent adulthood without a false maturity or alienation. The adult cannot abdicate the role of parent. If the parent works to maintain open communication, the generation gap may be minimal. Your work with families can promote greater harmony.

The effect of divorced children on middle-aged parents cannot be overlooked. The parents may feel that their effort and help in getting the child "out of the nest" through marriage or helping the couple set up a home were to no avail. This feeling may be especially strong if the divorced family member decides to live at home again.

If younger children are still at home, their needs may be temporarily neglected because the emphasis is on the divorce crisis. Furthermore, the younger children may have to give back a room to the divorced brother or sister. The parents, in an attempt to make the divorced family member feel comfortable, may negate their own new patterns of freedom. Additionally, they may question their child-rearing ability and be too embarrassed, guilt ridden, or depressed to talk about the situation with others. If the divorced son or daughter is in a financial crisis, the parents' money may also go to help him or her instead of as originally planned. If the divorcing couple has children, an additional strain will be added to the middle-aged grandparents who wonder what their future relationship with their grandchildren will be. There may be strained relations between the in-laws. Recent cordiality and affection may turn to anger and criticism.

The divorce may not have a completely negative effect on the middle-aged parents. If the parents have a healthy self-esteem and an ability to proceed cautiously, they may help their offspring to gain the essential maturity that he or she was previously lacking. However, the crisis of divorce is still keenly felt.

Young adults may return home to live with parents for reasons other than separation or divorce. This may cause stress, since most middle-aged parents look forward to having children leave the home—the so-called "empty nest" (85). The middle-ager wants space, time, and financial resources to pursue personal, organizational, and civic goals rather than to continue child-care responsibilities. Prolonged dependence of young adult offspring may also create conflict with grandparents and other children who are still at home.

The sense of responsibility and loss of independence is heightened if the young adult offspring brings grandchildren with him/her. The middle-aged woman, especially, may resent the demands and constraints placed on her by having young children, including grandchildren, in the home full-time. The middle-ager is not necessarily happy about being a grandparent since that may indicate old age. If there are grandchildren, the relationship to the grandchild is informal and playful; the child is a source of fun, leisure activity, and self-indulgence. Emphasis is on mutual satisfaction, authority lines are irrelevant, and the child is seen as a unit of consumption (85). Such a relationship is less likely if the grandchild lives in the home with the middle-ager. Further, having extra children and grandchildren in the home interferes with the relationship with the spouse. Normal developmental tasks cannot be met. The return of children into the home and the resultant demands may also serve to prevent the middle-aged woman from attempting to pursue new career goals, either because of a defensive withdrawal from an anxiety-producing new situation or because her conflict about roles prevents her from finding reasonable creative solutions to meet her own needs (60).

✔ Increasingly you will be caring for middle-aged parents who are being threatened emotionally or who are having social or financial problems because of their children's separation or divorce. Use the principles of communication and crisis intervention described in Chapters 3 and 8 of *Nursing Concepts for Health Promotion* (82). Help the middle-aged couple regain a sense of self-esteem, a sense of confidence in setting limits so that they can pursue their own life goals, and a method of working through decisions and problems with the young adult offspring.

Relationship with Spouse

Equally important as rearing the children and establishing wholesome affectional ties with them, and later the grandchildren, is the middle-ager's relationship with the spouse.

A *happy marriage* has security and stability, although there are also struggles. The couple knows each other well; they no longer have to pretend to each other. Children can be a source of pleasure rather than concern, since conflicts that arose between partners about rearing or disciplining children vanish when the children leave home. Each knows that his or her way of life and well-being depend on the other. Each has become accustomed to the way of the other. There is increased shared activity. Because the middle-ager is likely to have roots firmly implanted in the community of choice, he/she is able to cultivate warm friendships with members of the generation as well as with parents, the family of the spouse, and families of married children. Marriage can be secure economically, for the median income is likely to be above the national average. The middle-aged generally have more money in savings accounts and proportionately less debt than other age groups. Economic influence begins to wane as retirement nears, but the middle-aged working wife helps to offset this. Nationally, many working women are over 45 (25, 37, 56).

Although there is much discussion in the literature about the crisis of menopause and the "empty nest," menopause and middle age may bring both men and women an enriched sense of self and enhanced capacity to cope with life. It is a crisis in that behavioral changes are necessary but not a crisis in the negative sense of incapacitation.

In a study of 54 middle- and lower-middle-class men and women whose youngest child was about to leave home, Lowenthal and Chiriboga found that the parents anticipated the departure with relief (70). The years before retirement were anticipated as promising, for responsibility for the children was over; adult-like, peer relationships were sought with the children; job security was stable; and both partners felt more relaxed. In this study the men were more likely than the women to be dissatisfied with their work, perhaps as a kind of preparation for retirement or because they had longer experience in out-of-the-home work than women. The men spoke positively of their wives, describing them as warm, understanding, and competent homemakers. Women were twice as likely to speak of their husbands in negative terms, criticizing particularly the man's poor responsiveness to them. In a comparison of the views of both sexes, women were found to have a somewhat more negative outlook than men and to be more critical of themselves, their spouses, and their lives. These differences may be the result of the men giving traditional responses and the women feeling freer to state complex, negative, or ambivalent feelings (70).

Negative, critical feelings can gradually erode what was apparently a happy relationship (70). At some point the husband and wife may feel they are each living with a stranger, although the potential still exists for a harmonious marriage. With everything seeming to go well for them, the middle-aged couple may now feel that the zest has gone out of their love life. The wife and husband may have drifted apart instead of growing closer together with the years. The wife feels neglected; the husband feels nagged; and both feel bored with each other. Why has their relationship changed so suddenly? It has not! It only seems that way. Their relationship is changing because they are changing. Marital crisis may result from feelings of disappointment with self, feeling depleted emotionally because of lack of communication with the spouse, seeking rebirth or changing directions, or seeking escape from reality and superego pressures (70).

Disenchantment in any or all areas of life, with lack of enthusiasm for self and each other as well as for their physical relationship, may threaten the marriage of the middle years. Husband and wife are no longer distracted by daily activities of raising a family and children are no longer present to act as buffers. There is increasing awareness of aging parents, aging friends, and signs of their own aging. Each becomes preoccupied with the self, anxious about losing youthfulness, vitality, sex appeal, and the partner's love. Each needs the other but may hesitate to reach out and demonstrate affection or intimacy. The end result may be for one or the other to reach outside the marriage to prove youthfulness, masculinity, or femininity. Often the woman and man may overlook that they still do really love each other. They simply have to get reacquainted.

It may be difficult for the middle-aged man and woman to "tune in" to each other because both are encountering problems peculiar to their own gender. The woman may equate ability to bear children with capacity to enjoy sexual relationships, although they have nothing to do with each other. While the woman needs the man's support to reinforce her femininity, he too is undergoing a crisis; he feels that he is losing his vigor, virility, and self-esteem, which are products of primarily psychological reactions rather than physiological inabilities. In the fifties, there may be a reduction of male potency triggered by fears of incompetence and feelings of inability to satisfy his wife, who may be sexually more active after menopause. He may equate success on the job with success as a husband, feel that he is losing both, and covet his son's potency and youth.

Society and health-care professionals have until recently ignored the sexual needs or problems of the married middle-ager. But the middle-ager is an active sexual being. Physical changes in appearance and energy and the multiple stress of daily living may result in an increased desire for physical intimacy and the need for reassurance of continuing sexual attractiveness and competency. Intercourse is not valued for procreation but for body contact, to express love and trust, and to reaffirm an integral part of the self-concept. The person may fear loss of potency and rejection by the partner, but talking with the spouse about feelings and preferences related to sexual activity can promote increased closeness (28).

Men and women differ in their sexual behavior: Males reach their peak in their late teens and early twenties. Females peak in desire in the late thirties or forties and maintain that level of desire and activity past the menopause into middle age. The enjoyment of sexual relations in younger years, rather than the frequency, is a key factor for maintenance of desire and activity in the female, while frequency of relations, as well as enjoyment, are important factors for males (28, 33).

The man who feels frustration in his marriage or that his wife is nagging or unattractive may pursue a younger woman to feel youthful, masculine, and admired. Relationships with work colleagues may set the stage for the extramarital affair. This tendency is increased when the younger woman finds the company of an older man more interesting than that of the men in her own age group. Although divorce occurs during these years, the extramarital affair does not necessarily lead to the divorce courts. Divorce is major surgery, and the man may be reluctant to cut that much out of his life. Besides, he may find, having aroused the ardor of the younger woman, that he is no match for her physical demands. With increased consciousness of his age, he may return to his wife, particularly if she has in the meantime assessed her own situation and tried to change her behavior (5, 43, 51, 56). Midlife crisis will be further discussed in another section.

The woman may overcompensate for her felt loss of femininity by getting her face lifted, dressing more youthfully, acting like a teenager, and being flirtatious with her daughter's suitors.

Such vicious circles of behavior by either the man or the woman may be broken either by self-insight or with the help of friends, a religious leader, professional marriage counselor, or psychiatrist. You, as a nurse, may also be sought as counselor. In the community mental health setting you will increasingly work with troubled families.

Helping the couple regain closeness and happiness is worth the effort, for the mature years can be regarded as the payoff on an investment of many years together, many problems shared, and countless expressions of love exchanged. Each knows that his or her way of life and well-being depend on the other, so that there is a willingness to change outlook, habits, and lovemaking, if necessary, to enhance their marriage. You can promote such changes.

You may teach or counsel the middle-ager who is having difficulty in relating to his/her spouse. Share the above information as well as information in this chapter. Help the person determine, and then live out, the values of continuing to love, being patient with, and forgiving when the spouse has been unfaithful. Facilitate a desire to change behavior so that two people can grow together rather than apart. Work with the couple or refer them to counseling.

The following guidelines to couples may help them reduce stress in the marriage:

1. Talk daily to each other about feelings so that small problems are solved continually, rather than allowing emotional tensions to accumulate, creating a breaking-point scene.
2. Explore with each other feelings and ideas about possible, even if unlikely, life events that may occur—"what if" conversations. Such anticipatory worry helps the couple expand the repertoire of ideas and behavior so that if unexpected events occur, each will have more adaptive resources.
3. Vary schedules and chores, family goals or expectations, roles and rules, or make other periodic changes, just to stay comfortable with change and to be prepared to adapt if a crisis requiring flexibility occurs.
4. Utilize each other as a resource. Talk to each other about individual problems, validate solutions, or ask each other about options for dealing with problems. Each must be willing to disclose about self to the other and be willing to be supportive and helpful to the other.
5. Maintain contact with others, including the extended family, who can help during a crisis. Sometimes the family does not exist or cannot be supportive; seek other resources, such as a church or other support group.
6. In times of high stress or crisis, each should express the feelings of anger, grief, or helplessness to each other and to others who are caring. Expressing feelings about the circumstance, not about the spouse, allows conflict to surface and be handled.

7. Keep active with each other and with others, which prevents feelings of either stagnation during routine times or helplessness during stressful times.

Refer also to the section on midlife crisis later in the chapter for ideas on how to assist the couple.

Widow(er)hood, *the status change that results from death of husband (or wife),* is a crisis in any life era, but it is more likely to first occur in middle age. The woman who is about to become a widow usually appreciates being able to participate in her husband's care but must feel that her husband will not suffer lack of care or support if she takes a few hours for her own rest. She needs someone to listen as she expresses feelings of anger, sadness, and guilt; the nurses may be better able to listen, support, and encourage than family or friends. The nurse can gently test her reactions to determine if she is ready for the shock of death by offering to call a clergyman or by asking if family members need to be prepared for deterioration of the husband's condition. If the woman appears brave and strong, allow her to keep her veneer of courage if that is holding her together. Realize the wife may feel much ambivalence; not wanting the husband to suffer pain and yet wanting him to be alert so that she can talk with him; or praying that death relieve his suffering and yet hoping for his survival. After death she may linger on the nursing unit—a place of support—rather than leaving for home—a very empty place.

The person's reaction to death of a spouse depends upon personality and emotional make-up, the relationship between the couple; how long they have been married; how long the mate has been ill; and religious, cultural, and ethnic background.

The loss of a spouse may mean many things: loss of a sexual partner and lover, friend, companion, caretaker, an audience for unguarded spontaneous conversation, accountant, plumber, gardener, depending on the roles performed by the mate. Managing finances is often a major problem, especially for the widow. Secondary losses involve reduced income, which frequently means moving to a new residence and strange environment, change in lifestyle and social involvements, return to the work force, and giving up any number of things previously taken for granted (98). Widowhood is a threat to self-concept and sense of wholeness; now the person is seen as "only one." Often the woman's identity is so tied to that of her husband that she feels completely lost, alone, indecisive, and as a nonperson after his death. If she had no one else close to talk to or receive help from, she may feel that she will lose her mind or become suicidal. The widow(er) misses having someone with whom he/she can share happy occasions as well as sad news and problems. He/she can dial a crisis line to talk about a problem; it may be more difficult to tell about a source of happiness. The pet or houseplant is a poor substitute for a person. The emotional burden is increased if the woman still has children in the home to raise by herself. She has a hard time helping them work through their grief when she is in mourning. Friendship patterns and relations with in-laws also often change. The widow is a threat to women with husbands; they perceive her as competition and she is a reminder of what they might experience. With friends, the widow is the odd person in number, so that social engagements become stressful and are a constant reminder of the lost partner. The widow also becomes aware that she is regarded as a sexual object to men who may offer her their sexual services at a time when she has decreased sexual desires but a great need for companionship and closeness.

Although the widower is more accepted socially, he too will have painful gaps in his life. If the wife concentrated on keeping an orderly house, cooking regular and nutritious meals, and keeping his wardrobe in order, he may suddenly realize that what he had taken for granted is gone. Even more significant is the loss if his wife were a "sounding board" or confidante in business matters and if she were actively involved in raising children still in the home.

The bereavement of widowhood affects physical health; somatic complaints related to anxiety are not unusual. The widow(er) may experience symptoms similar to those of the deceased spouse.

One study showed that mortality rates, based on person-years at risk, were about the same for widowed as for married women but significantly higher for widowed than married men. Mortality rates among widowed males who remarried were very much lower than among those who did not remarry, but no significant difference was observable among widowed women who did or did not remarry (48).

↙ Your contact with the widow(er) can help to resolve the crisis. Encourage the bereaved to talk about feelings as you provide a supportive relationship (or help the widow[er] to find one). Death of husband in middle age is more common than that of wife; you will encounter more widows. Building up the widow's confidence and self-esteem, especially if she had lived a protected life, is essential. Encourage her to try new experiences, expand interests, join community groups, do volunteer work, seek new friends, and to become a person in her own right (98). Now is a good time to pursue activities formerly not engaged in because the mate did not enjoy them. Encourage a medical checkup and healthful practices in response to physical complaints, and help her recognize the somatic aspects of grief and mourning (30, 68, 82, 94). You may want to offer group crisis intervention through the local Red Cross, a church, or school (77, 108). Several books and articles can be useful to the widow(er) (37, 40, 44, 66, 104).

✔ There are national organizations to which you can refer that help widow(ers). Naim was founded by a couple in cooperation with a priest in Chicago. The chapters have well-planned monthly meetings covering educational, spiritual, legal, and social needs of the widowed. Information can be obtained from Father Corcoran, Naim, St. Patrick's Roman Catholic Church, in Chicago (13).

✔ Parents Without Partners, Inc. is an international nonprofit, nonsectarian, educational, and social organization which is devoted to the welfare and interest of one-parent families and their children. Monthly meetings help the widow(er) get practical assistance and information as well as work through mourning (13).

✔ THEOS (They Help Each Other Spiritually) is a national, nonsectarian organization designed primarily to help recently bereaved persons and the young and middle-aged who need to resolve the grief related to the death of a loved one. Monthly meetings deal with various problem areas: reorganizing life, working through grief and loneliness, coping with the feeling of being a fifth wheel, raising children alone, finances, dating and remarriage, expression of bitterness, anger and fear, and integrating loss and grief into belief in God and spiritual life (13).

✔ Another organization that is an informational resource to help the woman adapt and plan for the future is Older Women's League. The address is 730 11th Street N.W., Suite 300, Washington, D.C. The middle-aged woman can get information related to life insurance and Medicare, as well as in response to other questions. Such information can help plan for later maturity.

✔ Many of the problems that confront the widow(er) will also confront the divorced person. Your intervention principles will be similar although the words will be different.

Relationship with Aging Parents and Relatives

The middle-ager is in the middle in many ways—including in the middle of two demanding generations. Although child-care responsibilities may be decreasing, there may still be considerable care of or involvement with offspring at the same time that there is increasing care of, involvement with, and responsibility for aging parents, aunts, uncles, or grandparents.

Responsibility for Elderly Relatives. Three cultural trends affect the dilemma of caring for older dependent relatives:

1. Long-term societal emphasis on personal independence and social mobility of middle-aged and young adults, which creates physical separateness of generational households and new kinship patterns of intimacy at a distance.
2. Focusing on the dynamics of the marriage bond and socialization of young children, the emphasis on affection, compatibility, and personal growth of each person in the nuclear family as the most important aspects of family life.
3. Longer life spans of older people and the problem of caring for the older generation when they become dependent (53).

Filial responsibility *is an attitude of personal responsibility towards the parents that emphasizes duty, protection, care, and financial support,* which are indicators of the family's traditional protective function. Middle-class Caucasian culture in the United States believes that good relationships between the aged and their adult children are dependent on the autonomy of the parents. They believe that a satisfactory role reversal between generations is not possible since the mores of society do not sanction it and both children and parents resent it. However, older persons expect children to assume responsibilities when they can no longer maintain their independence. Families do in fact continue to provide nurturance, information, assistance in decision making, immediate response to crisis, a buffer against bureaucracies, help in searching out services, and facilitation for continuity of individual–bureaucracy relations. In many ethnic or racial cultures, there has evolved a structure and style for the younger generation(s), through an extended family system, to provide support, assistance, protection, and mobility (46).

For the Afro-American, an extended family serves as a mechanism for meeting physical, emotional, and economic needs. However, most aged Afro-Americans do not live in extended families. Influences such as Black power, economic and social mobility, and self-fulfillment may have weakened the perceived filial obligations of younger Afro-Americans more than those of their Caucasian counterparts. These influences may be eroding parental care in other subcultures, or ethnic and racial groups, as well. Adult offspring may be anxious about their competence in taking care of elderly persons. The average American family does not have the structure, organization, or economic resources necessary to care for older persons over long periods of time. Members of other racial groups in general have fewer resources and opportunities than Caucasians. Some of the differences in adult children's support of filial responsibility may stem from the greater worries and fears they have with regard to being able to provide support for their parents (46). Yet, many families have four or five generations; the young middle-ager may have parents, grandparents, and great-grandparents. Further, elderly siblings, aunts, uncles, or cousins may also be living and need and expect help from the middle-ager. The person who is in the forties, fifties, or early sixties may be seen as possessing energy, free time, and money. Older relatives become more demanding just when the middle-ager feels he/she deserves time for self, a vacation, and an opportunity to pursue additional education or a social cause. The additional stress occurs when the older relatives want their needs met *right now;* they can create considerable guilt in the middle-agers.

Certainly the older and middle-aged generations can give a great deal to each other. the older generation(s) can share insights and wisdom about life. Sometimes they can give assistance financially or with various tasks. The older generation(s) can be a source of joy, pride, and inspiration. However, if they live long enough, the middle-ager will face someone who is increasingly dependent and in need of help. Sometimes the middle-ager realizes the dependence and need for help before the elderly person is ready to admit the need and that can become a source of frustration and stress.

Caregiver Role. Care of parent is a normative but stressful experience, although most people willingly help the parent and derive satisfaction from doing so. Meeting parent's dependency needs may have many effects:

1. Financial hardship.
2. Physical symptoms such as sleeplessness and decline in physical health, especially in the main caregiver.
3. Emotional changes and symptoms in the caregiver and other family member, including frustration, anxiety, helplessness, depression, and lowered morale.
4. Emotional exhaustion related to restrictions on time and freedom.
5. A sense of isolation from social activities.
6. Conflict because of competing demands, with diversion from care of other family members.
7. Difficulty in setting priorities.
8. Reduced family privacy.
9. Inability to project future plans.
10. Interference with lifestyle and social and recreational activities. Thus, the whole family and its relationships are affected (10).

The dilemma of care for the elderly inevitably has an emotional impact on their grown children. The *caregiver role* is a major one, especially for the woman. The middle-aged woman who is the older daughter is most likely to do the caregiving. Caregiving appears to be a woman's career. Care of the dependent parent is only one phase of the woman's caregiving career. The woman often is caring for children in the home simultaneously with caring for aged parents, grandparents, other aged family members, parents-in-law, and finally the husband in old age. Interestingly, women who work provide as much caregiving as women who do not work outside the home. Some may reduce the working hours; others quit their jobs, especially if the aged parent lives with them. Parent care makes the woman feel tied down and competes for time with the husband. Relations between husband and wife are affected because of financial or other help one person may give to the elderly parent(s), especially when done without consulting the other spouse. The needs of elderly parents may cause discord among their sons and daughters by recalling childhood rivalries and jealousies. A common phenomenon is when the middle-ager resents those siblings who will not help care for the elderly parent(s) or other relatives. Further, if the middle-ager feels he/she was not well cared for by the parents as a child, there may be continued resentment, anger, or hate that inhibits a nurturing attitude or even minimal assistance.

The meaning of caring for the dependent parent is different than for caring for the dependent child. The child's future holds promise for reducing dependency needs; the older parent will have increasing dependency needs. Parent care also stimulates anticipation of the final separation from the parent and of one's potential dependence on one's child. The way filial care is negotiated depends on the past and has implications for the future when the adult child is old.

Sometimes the adult child continues to care for the parent beyond physical and psychological means to do so, rather than to use formal support systems. Various dynamics are at work: (1) symbiotic ties, (2) gratification of being the burden bearer, (3) a fruitless search for parental approval that has never been received, and (4) expiation of guilt for having been a favorite child. Thus successful resolution of the filial crisis may be acceptance of what cannot be done as well as of what can and should be done. For the elderly, successful adaptation to dependence includes accepting what adult children cannot do (10).

The popular trend of expecting the middle-aged family to care for the dependent aged in their home assumes an emotional closeness and family cohesion that may not exist. The caregiving may instead contribute to a deterioration of relationships even though a commitment to caring for family members is a value. Closeness may not be a basis for caregiving.

Nor can we assume that satisfactory family relationships in early and middle adulthood will persist without change into late adulthood. There appears to be a periodic rebalancing in family ties throughout life. Bonds may either loosen or grow closer with the conflicts and demands inherent in the caregiving role (53).

A kind of psychological distancing between parents and caregiving children may occur. The adult children may feel little affection for the parent, feeling rather a kind of grief, and may hesitate to cancel the caregiving burden out of a sense of respect and loyalty to the parent. The adult child, often a married daughter, does not feel enough gratification from the caregiving to offset the sense of burden, yet the cultural expectation of closeness and love for family members leads her to feel guilt or despair. The person may question whether she can care for the parent if she does not feel love and may be concerned about the cost of caregiving to personal emotional stability.

Adult offspring with disrupted marriages (divorce, widow(er)hood, or remarried) give significantly less help, perceive fewer parental needs, feel less filial obligations, and feel more limited in helping due to job responsibilities (18).

Future parallel situations may be drawn between the older parent or relative and the middle-ager. Some of the impatience, aggravation, and desire to see less of the older person comes from the middle-ager's dawning realization that the older person is a picture of what the middle-ager may well become. The person who is in the prime of life may fear greatly the physical disabilities, illness, personality eccentricities, intellectual impairments, or social changes that old age brings.

Research findings document the strength of intergenerational ties, the continuity of responsible filial behavior, the frequency of contact between generations, the predominance of families rather than professionals in providing health and social services, the strenuous family efforts to avoid institutional placement of the old, and the central role played by families in caring for noninstitutionalized impaired elderly (9).

One of the most difficult decisions when parents become aged and dependent is the housing arrangement. The older daughter is more likely to be the one to take the dependent parent into her home—a phenomenon called the "refilling of the empty nest" (10). When the parent(s) cannot manage living alone, the middle-ager may not have the room to take the parent(s) into his/her home. Even if there is adequate space, if all members of the household are working, finding someone to stay during the day may be difficult and cost prohibitive. Most communities do not have adequate, or any, day-care facilities. Placing the parent(s) in an institution may be the only answer. Refer to Chapter 14 for more information on what to consider in that event.

✔ Considerable research has been done on the middle-ager's caregiving role to parents, the tasks faced by and effect on the caregiver and the middle-ager's family relations, physical and emotional health, and lifestyle. For additional information see references 9, 10, 11, 16, 19, 39, 53, 54, 99, 105, 118, 121 at the end of the chapter.

✔ *Nursing Role.* You are in a key position to help the middle-ager work through the conflicts, feelings of frustration, guilt, and anger about the increased responsibility, and past conflicts or old hurts from parents or siblings. The middle-ager who verbally expresses great irritation will typically also love the older relative very much. Assist the middle-ager to gain a sense of satisfaction from the help he/she gives as well as a greater understanding of the person being helped. The generation gap and negative feelings that exist between the middle-ager and elderly person can be overcome with love, realistic expectations, a sense of forgiveness, and the realization that sometimes it is all right to say "No" to the demands of the elderly. Refer also to Chapter 14 for specific information you can share about physiological, emotional, cognitive, and social needs, changes, and characteristics of the elderly person. Refer to a counselor or spiritual leader if necessary. Counseling can promote a resolution of feelings that in turn fosters a more harmonious relationship between the middle-ager and parents.

✔ One way to help the adult child to continue the caregiving role, set aside guilt, and gain more positive feedback is to offer a *relabeled perspective*. The cultural mandate of affection for aging parents is of recent origin. Historically, aged parents have been cared for on the basis of obligation. Being a good child means not feeling great affection but rather showing concern for the well-being of the parent and giving care to the limits of one's ability. Helping the adult child internalize this perspective helps him/her to begin to cope with the stresses without being overwhelmed. Thus the parent cared for in the adult child's home has the advantage of a home environment. Further, outside resources can be used to support the adult child in the caregiving role. Often a little help will enable the person to make changes and utilize inner resources in a distressing situation. Having the caregiver keep a daily list of helping behaviors as well as of negative behaviors (not feelings) is a way of assisting the caregiver to see the role and behavior in a positive light and to gain reinforcement from the caregiving since almost always the helping far outnumber the negative behaviors. Such a log can provide a base for talking with the adult child about the interaction with the parent and ways to resolve feelings and improve the interaction (53).

✔ While some adult children will be helped through this relabeling process, some ethnic or racial groups would not respond to this technique. For example, Afro-Americans have maintained a kind of behavioral closeness between generations that would produce a different pattern of attitudes and less social and emotional distance between middle generation adults and their parents.

Death of Parents in Adulthood

A critical time for the adult is when both parents have died, regardless of whether the relationship between parent(s) and offspring was harmonious or conflictual. The first death of a parent signals finiteness and mortality of the self as well as of the other parent and other loved ones. Memories of childhood experiences are recalled. The person may wish deeply, even though simultaneously realizing it is impossible, to be able to relive some of those childhood days with the parent, to undo naughty behavior, to be a good child just once more, to sit on the parent's lap and be cuddled one more time, to return to the relatively carefree days, to relive holidays. Further, more recent memories are recalled, the joys that were shared, the disharmonious times that are normal in any relationship but that are likely to engender guilt. There may be deep yearning to hold the parent one more time. Mourning may be done not only for the parent but previously lost loved ones, and some mourning is in anticipation of future losses of the other parent, other beloved relatives and friends, and self. When the other parent dies, the adult is now an orphan. Now he/she is no longer anyone's "little boy" or "little girl." The person may now feel forlorn and alone, especially if there are few other relatives or friends. Sometimes there are no other living relatives and no sons, so that the adult offspring represents the last of the family line. The person may question: Who and what will be remembered? By whom? This is a time of spiritual and philosophical searching, whether or not the adult child is alone, has siblings, or has other relatives.

If there was conflict between the adult offspring and parents to the point of one-sided or mutual hate and unforgiveness, grief feelings may be denied or repressed, or may be especially guilt laden. Consequently, the mourning process is delayed and not resolved as effectively. There is a yearning that life experiences with the parent(s) could have been better or different, a wish that harsh feelings could have been smoothed, a sadness over what was never present more so than a sadness over what has been lost. The adult survivor may fear that he/she in turn may have similarly parented children, if any, and anxiety may arise about how the third or current child generation will feel when this parent dies. Will the scene and feelings be replayed? Can that be prevented? Certainly this can be a time for the adult to take stock, undo past wrongs with his/her children (and others), resolve old conflicts, and become motivated to move ahead into more harmonious relations with family members and others.

✔ Throughout the period of parental loss, you may be a key person in helping the adult survivor or adult orphan relive, express, and sort out feelings; accept that any close relationship will not always go smoothly; and finally achieve a balance between happy, sad, and angry memories and feelings in regard to the parent(s). Finally, through such counseling the person can mature to better accept and like self and other significant persons, and to change behavior patterns so that future relationships are less thorny.

Little is written specifically about bereavement experienced when the adult's parents die. One useful book is *The Orphaned Adult: Confronting the Death of a Parent,* by Marc Angel (2).

Developmental Tasks

In summary, the following developmental tasks must be accomplished for the middle-aged family to survive and achieve happiness, harmony, and maturity:

1. Maintain a pleasant and comfortable home.
2. Assure security for later years, financially and emotionally.
3. Share household and other responsibilities, based on changing roles, interests, and abilities.
4. Maintain emotional and sexual intimacy as a couple or regain emotional stability if death or divorce occurs.
5. Maintain contact with grown children and their families.
6. Decrease attention on child care tasks and adapt to departure of the child(ren).
7. Meet the needs of elderly parent(s) in such a way as to make life satisfactory for both the parent(s) and middle-aged generations.
8. Participate in community life beyond the family, recommitting energy once taken by child care.
9. Use competencies built in earlier stages to expand or deepen interests and social or community involvement (29).

McCoy has formulated developmental tasks and their outcomes for the stages of middle age, as shown in Table 13–1 (74).

Table 13–1. Middle Age Developmental Tasks and Their Outcomes

DEVELOPMENTAL STAGES	DEVELOPMENTAL TASKS	OUTCOMES SOUGHT
Restabilization, 44–55 years old	Adjust to realities of work.	Job adjustment.
	Launch children.	Letting go of parental authority.
	Adjust to empty nest.	Exploring new sources of satisfaction.
	Become more deeply involved in social life.	Effective social relations.
	Participate actively in community concerns.	Effective citizenship.
	Handle increased demands of older parents.	Better personal and social adjustment of elderly.
	Manage leisure time.	Creative use of leisure.
	Manage budget to support college-age children and ailing parents.	Sound consumer behavior.
	Adjust to single state.	Fulfilled single state.
	Problem solve.	Successful problem solving.
	Manage stress accompanying change.	Successful stress management, personal growth.
Preparation for Retirement, 56–64 years old	Adjust to health problems.	Healthier individuals.
	Deepen personal relations.	Effective social skills.
	Prepare for retirement.	Wise retirement planning.
	Expand avocational interests.	Satisfaction of esthetic urge; broadening of knowledge; enjoyment of travel.
	Finance new leisure.	Sound consumer behavior.
	Adjust to eventual loss of mate.	Adjustment to loss, fulfilled single state.
	Use problem solving.	Successful problem solving.
	Manage stress accompanying change.	Successful stress management, personal growth.

✔ As a nurse you will have the opportunity and responsibility to help the middle-age couple meet their developmental tasks.

Physiological Concepts

The growth cycle continues with physical changes in the middle years, and different body parts age at a different rate. One day the person may suddenly become aware of being "old" or middle-aged. Not all people decline alike. How quickly they decline depends partly on the stresses and strains they have undergone. If the person has always been active, he/she will continue with little slowdown. People from lower socioeconomic groups often show signs of aging earlier than people from more affluent socioeconomic groups because of their years of hard physical labor, poorer nutritional status, and lack of money for beauty aids to cover the signs of aging (56).

Now the person looks in the mirror and sees changes which others may have noticed some time ago. Gray, thinning hair, wrinkles, coarsening features, decreased muscular tone, weight gain, varicosities, and capillary breakage may be the first signs of impending age.

✔ Because a number of your patients/clients will be middle-aged, you are in a key position to help them understand the physiological changes that occur in middle age, work through feelings about these changes, reintegrate the body image, and find specific ways to remain as healthy as possible. Use the following information to assist you in listening, teaching, reaffirming a positive self-concept, and counseling.

Hormonal Changes

Female Climacteric. This is the era of life known as the *menopause* for the woman or the *climacteric* for either sex. The terms are often used interchangeably. The **menopause** *is the permanent cessation of menstruation preceded by a gradually decreasing menstrual flow.* The term **perimenopausal years** *denotes a time of gradual diminution of ovarian function and a gradual change in endocrine status* (90). The **climacteric** *is the period in life when important physiological changes occur, with the cessation of the woman's reproductive ability, and the period of lessening sexual activity in the male* (90). Basic to the changing physiology of the middle years is the declining hormonal production (45). Contrary to myth, depression or other symptomatology are neither inevitable nor clearly related to the perimenopausal or climacteric years (90). The worst part about the menopause or climacteric may be not knowing what to expect, since there is still a dearth of research and scientific knowledge about this normal period of life. Myths abound (63).

Menopause has historically been regarded as a negative experience. Yet not all the research findings in the literature are wholly negative. Attitudes toward menopause have been found to improve as women move from pre- to postmenopause and perception of health has been observed to become more positive as menopause proceeds (31).

Traditional homemakers in the United States have been observed to experience greater difficulty with menopause. In societies where women rise in status after menopause or generally enjoy high status regardless of reproductive stage, a menopausal syndrome is nonexistent. A woman's perception of her menopause experience is largely her perception of the physical, social, and psychological changes she undergoes (31).

In a study of the impact of menopausal stage, current life change, and attitude toward traditional women's roles on perceived health status in women 40 to 55 years of age, well women perceived few current life changes. Apparently negative life changes have a greater impact on one's health perception than positive life changes, in contrast to mainstream opinion that all life changes tax individuals' coping ability. However, the perception of the stressfulness of a life event could be biased by assessment of its positive or negative value. Attitude toward women's roles may be associated with perceived health status among midlife women (31).

Male Climacteric. This comes in the fifties or early sixties, although the symptoms may not be as pronounced as in the female climacteric. A man's "change of life" is passed almost imperceptibly, but he usually notices it when he makes comparisons with past feelings and performance. A few men may even complain of hot flashes, sweating, chills, dizziness, headaches, and heart palpitations. Unlike women, however, men do not lose their reproductive abilities, although the likelihood diminishes as age advances. The output of sex hormones of the gonads does not stop; it is merely reduced. The testes become less firm and smaller; cells in the tubules degenerate; and sperm production decreases. Because of decreased testosterone production, the man may need a longer time to achieve erection and may experience premature or less forceful ejaculation. Testosterone level is likely to be lower in the middle-aged male who has high stress, lowered self-esteem, and depression. Testosterone therapy should be cautious because administration may increase prostatic hypertrophy and cancer development (45, 73, 88).

In about 20 percent of the males, hypertrophy of the prostate begins naturally late in middle age so that gradually the enlarging prostate around the urethra causes the embarrassment of frequent urination, dribbling, and nocturia. In addition, urine stasis may predispose the man to urinary infections.

Menopause. The average age for menopause onset is 50; the usual range is between 45 and 55 years, although it may occur as early as age 35. In the woman the process of aging causes changed secretion of the follicle-stimulating hormone (FSH), which brings about progressive and irreversible changes in the ovaries, leading to the menopause and loss of childbearing ability. The primordial follicles, which contain the ovum and grow into vesicular follicles with each menstrual cycle, become depleted, and their ability to mature declines. Finally, ovulation ceases, since all ova are either degenerated or have ovulated. Thus the cyclic production of progesterone and estrogen fails to occur and levels rapidly fall below the amount necessary to induce endometrial bleeding. The menstrual cycle becomes irregular; periods of heavy bleeding alternate with amenorrhea for 1 or 2 years, eventually ceasing altogether (45).

The pituitary continues to produce FSH and luteinizing hormone (LH), but the aging ovary is incapable of responding to its stimulation. With the pituitary no longer under the normal cyclic or feedback influence of ovarian hormones, it becomes more active, producing excessive gonadotropins, especially FSH. A disturbed endocrine balance influences some of the symptoms of menopause. While the ovaries are producing less estrogen and progesterone, the adrenals may continue to produce some hormones, thus helping to maintain younger feminine characteristics for some time (45).

During the perimenopausal period (about 5 years) some discomforts may occur in a small percentage of women: Vasomotor changes cause hot flashes associated with chilly sensations, dizziness, headaches, perspiration, palpitations, water retention, nausea, muscle cramps, fatigability, insomnia, paresthesia of fingers and toes. Many symptoms including irritability, depression, emotional lability, and palpitations are frequently attributed to menopause. But in a study of 1630 men and women, only sweating and hot flushing were found to be consistently related to menopause. Difficulties experienced during menopause may be associated with concurrent life change or recent loss, or marital, psychological, or social stress (31). The etiology of the symptoms appears to be more complex than simple estrogen deficit. Psychological factors, such as anger, anxiety, and excitement, are considered as important in precipitating hot flashes in susceptible women as conditions giving rise to excess heat production or retention, such as a warm environment, muscular work, or hot food. However, the symptoms may arise without any clear psychological or heat-stimulating mechanism (90).

Related Changes. The hormonal decline brings additional changes. The skin, subcutaneous tissue, and mucous membranes become dry and begin to atrophy. The loss of skin turgor and muscle tone results in wrinkles, pouches under the eyes, sagging jowls, and loss of muscle tone, including of the pelvic floor. The loss of tone of the bladder mucosa and sphincter and urethral tissue and supporting structures results in frequent, urgent urination, stress incontinence, and embarrassment, which may limit social activities. The uterus, ovaries, external genitalia, and breast tissue begin to atrophy. Atrophy, loss of elasticity of the vaginal mucosa, and less vaginal lubrication during sexual arousal may interfere with the pleasure of the sexual experience and cause dysuria after intercourse. Regular sexual intercourse helps to maintain an adequate vaginal outlet and to prevent shrinkage of the vaginal mucosa (45, 73). If the couple experiences difficulty with sexual response, and if the sexual problems result from changes in lubrication, use of estrogen vaginal cream can be effective in maintaining lubrication and distensibility and preventing vaginitis, dyspareunia, and burning on urination. Because estrogen is absorbed via the vaginal mucosa, the same concerns that apply to treatment with oral estrogens may be relevant to this treatment.

Estrogen Treatment. Administration of estrogen will reverse the vasomotor symptoms and a gradually decreasing dose avoids severe symptoms, but such treatment also prolongs the symptoms and may be of little assistance in treating emotional symptoms except as a placebo (45).

Some middle-aged women whose vaginal smears show changes in vaginal cells—decreased number, small and round instead of large and quadrilateral, blue instead of pink, thinning, drying, inflamed, and scant in acid secretion—are described as *estrogen-dependent*, or *estrogen-sensitive*. Such a woman's mental and physical well-being has previously depended on a high level of estrogen, as manifested by the following signs: She had optimum feeling of well-being during pregnancy when estrogen level was high, depression several weeks after delivery when the estrogen level fell to normal, and great improvement of vasomotor and psychic symptoms associated with estrogen administration when approaching menopause. If a trial dose of estrogen shows improvement physically and emotionally, this woman is a candidate for long-term low-dose estrogen treatment to improve the metabolic state, postpone and reduce osteoporosis, and promote a feeling of well-being (12, 45). Studies also indicate that women have reduced heart disease because of this natural supply of estrogen. Prolonged estrogen therapy (5 to 10 years) predisposes to cancer of the breast and endometrium, hypertension, myocardial infarction, and cerebrovascular accident. Thus women should take estrogen in the lowest possible doses and be carefully monitored. Breast carcinoma is the principal cause of death from cancer in women, with the highest mortality rate occurring between ages 55 and 74 (45, 111). Long-term studies have shown that the rise in incidence of endometrial cancer from the mid-1960s through mid-1970s was related to increased use of replacement estrogen treatment. With more careful estrogen prescription there has been an associated decline in incidence rates of endometrial cancer in the United States (4, 49, 92).

✓ Reinforce in the middle-aged woman that hormonal changes are normal, that they can be adapted to and lived with. Emphasize that estrogen products, whether facial and skin products or vaginal creams, should be purchased with medical guidance; likewise, replacement therapy is done only when deemed by the physician to be essential.

✓ All women receiving estrogen replacement therapy because ovaries were surgically removed or to relieve menopausal symptoms should be seen every 6 months for a Papanicolaou test, breast examination, and blood pressure reading. All menopausal women should be taught that any abnormal bleeding (if in estrogen–progestagen therapy) or spotting 12 months after cessation of menses indicates an increased risk of carcinoma and should be reported immediately to a physician.

Metabolic Changes

Metabolic changes include decalcification of the bones, producing decreased bone density and a gradual osteoporosis. With the bone porosity and gradually shrinking intervertebral discs, the woman will eventually be an inch or 2 shorter and the "dowager's hump" will form in the cervical upper thoracic area (56). By age 55, a woman runs 10 times the risk of bone fractures as the 55-year-old man. Most vulnerable to fractures are forearms, hips, and spinal vertebrae.

Some of the changes in the woman result because the level of androgen in the body remains constant while the estrogen is decreasing. Thus the woman is dismayed to find a small amount of hair growth, especially on the chin. She also experiences a loss of weight in the face and limbs at a time when diminishing muscle tone and additional adipose deposits make her look and feel larger in the middle. The coarseness of skin and sharpness of contours are the result of loss of some subcutaneous tissue (45).

↳ Teaching should encompass safety as well as nutritional measures to prevent fractures. A confirmed diagnosis of postmenopausal osteoporosis and a demonstration of calcium malabsorption or intestinal lactose deficiency require the following diet supplementation: 1 to 2.0 grams daily of elementary calcium alone or with 50,000 U of vitamin D or with less than 60 mg daily of sodium fluoride may decrease the annual rate of cortical bone loss (71, 96). Ideally nutrition and exercise are utilized before the midlife years to prevent or reduce osteoporotic effects.

Other Changes

Cell atrophy and changes in cell regulation and repair cause the number of cells to be reduced gradually after about 30 years. The body starts to shrink minutely. A gradual loss in efficiency of nerve conduction and muscle function contribute to gradual muscle atrophy and impaired sensation to heat and cold.

There are also changes in the *special senses* such as dimming of vision. **Presbyopia,** *a decreasing elasticity of the lens and decreasing power of accommodation,* occurs in middle age, so that the person reads the morning paper at arm's length. The pupil takes in half as much light at 50 as at 20 years. Pupils react more slowly in late middle age. Glasses are often needed, but self-consciousness can delay getting the needed visual aid. Some degree of hearing is also gradually lost, especially for high-pitched sounds. Auditory reaction time slows; sound discrimination decreases. Other sensory acuity remains intact (25, 56, 100).

The *decreasing elasticity of blood vessels,* particularly in the coronary arteries, causes the middle-aged person to be more susceptible to hypertension and cardiovascular disease. The woman becomes as prone to coronary disease as the man after the menopause; thus estrogen appears to be a protective agent. There is a rise in serum cholesterol after the menopause, but administration of estrogen alters the serum cholesterol, alphalipoproteins, and cholesterol-phospholipid ratio to retard the process of atherosclerosis. Cardiac output and glomerular filtration rate gradually decrease (100).

Tooth decay is not caused by aging but chiefly by circulatory changes, poor dietary habits, poor mouth hygiene, or poor dental care over the years. Hence the middle-ager may have dentures or a partial plate or be in need of dental care either for dental caries or periodontal disease.

↳ You are in a key position to help the middle-ager work through feelings about the meaning of mid-life changes and ways to offset their effects.

Emotional Changes Related to Physical Changes

Depression, irritability, and a change in sexual desire may occur in response to physical changes and their meaning. Some women fear loss of sexual identity. Severe symptoms occur in fewer than 10 percent of women, so these symptoms may be minor and little noticed. Earlier personality patterns and attitudes are more responsible for the symptomatology than the cessation of glandular activity (45, 66, 93, 100). Women who had previous low self-esteem and life satisfaction are more likely to have difficulties with menopause. Reactions to menopause are consistent with reactions to other life changes, including other reproductive turning points such as puberty. Women with high motherliness scores and heavy investment in childbearing react more severely to the menopause (93, 100).

Reactions to menopause vary across social classes and consequent availability of alternate roles. Middle- and upper-class women appear to find the cessation of childbearing more liberating than lower-class women, perhaps because more alternatives are open to them. In the relatively advantaged social classes younger women anticipating menopause express the most concern. Postmenopausal women generally take a more positive view than premenopausal women, agreeing that the menopause creates no major discontinuity in life and, except for the underlying biological changes, women have a relative degree of control over their symptoms and need not inevitably have difficulties. In general, menopausal status is not associated consistently with measurable anxiety in any group (90).

A study of 100 normal women, aged 43 to 53 years, from working- and middle-class backgrounds, who were in good physical health, married, and had at least one child showed that these women saw the menopause as a normal life event rather than as a threat to feminine identity. They minimized the significance of the menopause and regarded it as unlikely to cause much anxiety or stress. Some felt health improved after menopause, and 65 percent felt there was no effect on sex life. Any changes in sexual activity during the climacterium was seen as a function of the woman's (or couple's) attitudes. Half reported sexual relations as more enjoyable because menstruation and fear of pregnancy were removed. Few reported having symptoms sufficient to seek medical treatment, although 75 percent reported minor discomforts. A majority felt change in health or emotional status during the menopause reflected individual differences in coping with stress or idiosyncrative factors. Only 4 of the 100 regarded the menopause as a major source of worry. Women who had difficulties with the menarche, menses, or pregnancy were more likely to have menopausal problems. More than half indicated that the death of the husband was the greatest concern; other concerns were fear of cancer and the implications of getting older (27, 85).

In another study, 80 percent attributed little or no change in their lives because of the menopause. Most felt the woman had control over the symptoms and need not have symptomatic difficulties (85).

Cross-cultural studies of the male climacteric have not been done. A construction worker who gauges his age by physical strength may feel middle-aged or old before he reaches 40 or 45. The factory worker may not have as many frustrations of unattainable goals as a white-collar worker and thus may be less likely to undergo a midlife crisis. Another manual laborer who feels oppressed by his foreman and stifled by his job may fear the day when physical powers decline and he may lose his only source of security—his job. The Afro-American man apparently experiences a midlife crisis much like that of the Caucasian man. Bachelors and widowers who may be lonely and lack the warmth of family ties frequently suffer at least temporary loss of libido in the middle years and symptoms of midlife crisis related to fears of mortality and the meaninglessness of their life. Some men may experience again a long-dormant homosexual interest (51).

✔ Refer to Chapter 12, pages 418 to 422, for ways to help the person work through self-concept and body image changes and for ways to enhance self-concept.

Nutritional Needs

Basal metabolism rate gradually decreases. For each decade after 25 years, there should be a reduction in caloric intake by approximately 7.5 percent (96). The reduced basal energy requirements, caused by losses in functioning protoplasm and the frequently reduced physical activity, combine to create less demand for calories.

✔ Teach that intake of carbohydrate and fat foods should be reduced, especially the foods with "empty" calories: rich desserts, candies, fatty foods, gravies, sauces, alcoholic and cola beverages. Overweight should be avoided since it is a factor in diabetes, cardiovascular, and hypertensive disease, and in problems with mobility such as arthritis.

✔ Dietary intake will be imbalanced nutritionally if meals are not wisely planned. For the healthy person, diet should contain the Basic 4 food groups with emphasis on protein, minerals, vitamins, and low-cholesterol and low-calorie foods. Refer to Table 12–2 for a recommended daily servings. Plenty of fluids, especially water and juices, along with an adequate diet, will maintain weight control and vigor and help prevent "heartburn," constipation, and other minor discomforts caused by physiological changes. Equally important, the person should chew food well, eat smaller portions, eat in a pleasant and unhurried atmosphere, and avoid eating when overtired.

There is no evidence that commercial vitamin–mineral preparations are necessary unless they are prescribed by a doctor because of clinical signs of deficiency and insufficient diet (96). Conflicting information may appear in the media about increasing need for calcium in midlife. The exact level of calcium needed by the postmenopausal woman is still unknown, although research is continuing in this field. However, adequate calcium intake—1000 mg per day—is necessary. After menopause, bone loss may not be calcium related, but an adequate calcium intake may reduce the amount of estrogen the woman needs to prevent bone loss (91).

✔ Considerable information is available to the public concerning healthful nutrition. Yet the American diet remains overloaded with sugar-filled and fatty foods. Only as values change will diet change. Health teaching must begin with understanding cultural concepts and values before a significant trend toward wise eating habits can begin. Self-help groups such as Weight Watchers or TOPS (Take Off Pounds Sensibly) are effective for many people. It is possible to change habits of overeating and to lose weight in middle age.

Need for Rest and Exercise

Middle age need not be a time when a person's body fails, but it is a period which requires better maintenance than was necessary in the earlier years.

Exercise. One of the most stable characteristics is *activity level*. Although there is a general and gradual decline in quickness and level of activity during the latter part of life, people who were most active among their age group during adolescence and young adulthood tend to be the most active among their age group during middle and old age. It is almost as though each person has a physical and mental "clock" that runs at a fast or slow rate throughout life. The rate at which an individual's clock runs is reflected as well in various cognitive and personality characteristics (60).

The physical strength of the man peaks around 21 and gradually diminishes to the late sixties, when degenerative diseases begin to increase. The arduous training program of the astronauts, a number of whom have been over age 40, has shown that a man can double his normal physical competence at ages much beyond 21.

There is frequently a postmenopausal rise in energy and activity (90), possibly for several reasons.

Less time and energy goes into childrearing. The children leaving home allows time for self and pursuits in creative, social, or community projects. The person may feel more self-confident and satisfied with life achievements and less competitive. Less physical and psychic energy may be used in various internal conflicts or in worrying unnecessarily about the details in life. New self-awareness and flexibility can increase psychic and physical energy and a feeling of well-being. This new energy permits a developmental impetus and opportunities for personal growth.

The middle-ager invests considerable energy in occupational, home, and organizational activity as well as leisure-time pursuits. He/she often has fine physical health. Although chronic disease is more prevalent than in the young, there is ordinarily good resistance to communicable diseases, superior emotional stamina, and a willingness to work despite minor illnesses. The person brings economy of effort, singleness of purpose, and perseverance to various roles.

✔ Teach that while physical changes do occur, adopting sedentary habits will not maintain health. Balanced with rest and sleep must be physical activity to keep the body posture and functioning at its optimum. Capacity for intense and sustained effort diminishes, especially if engaged in irregularly, but judicious exercise may modify and retard the aging process (90). Exercise stimulates circulation to all body parts, thereby improving body functions; physical agility, muscle tone, and stamina are maintained. In addition, vigorous exertion is an excellent outlet for emotional tensions as well as an ally in fighting the characteristic weight gain. Walking briskly with both arms swinging, bicycle riding, and a variety of sports are recommended.

✔ Teach about the value of exercise. The type of exercise does not matter as long as the person *likes* it, engages in it *regularly*, and it is *suitable* for personal strength and physical condition. There are certain precautions which the middle-ager should take: (1) gradually increase the exercise until it is moderate in strenuousness, (2) exercise consistently, and (3) avoid overexertion. Ten minutes after strenuous exercise, the heart should be beating normally again, respirations should be normal, and there should be no sense of fatigue. If the person is overweight, has a personal or family history of cardiovascular disease, or has led a sedentary life, new exericse routines should not be started until after a thorough physical checkup. Using exercise as an overcompensation to prove youthfulness, health status, or prevent old age is pointless. The person may benefit from enrolling in an exercise program that is directed by a health professional.

Sleep. Most middle-agers sleep without difficulty; the 7 to 8 hours of sleep is considered a normal pattern. Refer to Chapter 12 for more information on normal sleep patterns. However, one kind of sleep disturbance—sleep apnea—in middle age is becoming better researched.

Sleep apnea, *more than five episodes of cessation of air flow for at least 10 seconds each hour of sleep*, is a problem that is being increasingly recognized. This syndrome is found primarily in men over 50 and postmenopausal women. Thirty-five to 40 percent of the elderly suffer sleep apnea. Often it is first detected because the person snores loudly or does daytime dozing. Sleep apnea can be life threatening. There are three types:

1. Obstructive—respiratory effort continues despite pharyngeal obstruction to air flow.
2. Central—no respiratory effort with air flow.
3. Mixed—episodes of no respiratory effort initially is followed by respiratory effort and then air flow.

The person may have the following symptoms: (1) excessive daytime sleepiness, (2) frequent nocturnal awakening, (3) insomnia, (4) loud snoring, (5) morning headaches, (6) intellectual deterioration, (7) irritability and personality changes, (8) impotence, (9) hypertension, and (10) arrhythmias. Weaver and Millman give a detailed description of the signs and symptoms, associated physical conditions in pathology, diagnostic measures, and treatment (117).

Injury Control and Common Health Problems and Related Nursing Responsibilities

Injury and Accidents. The gradually changing physical characteristics, as well as preoccupation with responsibilities, may contribute to the middle-aged person's having accidents.

Fractures and dislocations are the leading cause of injuries for both sexes, with more males affected than females, probably because of occupational differences. Because of the middle-agers' changing physical abilities, motor-vehicle accidents are the most common cause of accidental deaths in the later years, especially for men. Occupation-related accidents rank second, and falls in the home rank third as causes of death. However, women suffer less than one-third as frequently as men from fatal falls during the middle years (56).

The middle-ager is a person at work in an industry, office, school, home, or out-of-doors. Accidents that disable for 1 week or more sharply increase for the worker after age 45 (29). Because of their interest in accident-protection legislation, industries and other occupational settings are increasingly health- and safety-conscious. Efforts must continue in this direction.

✔ As a nurse, you can teach about safety related to

remodeling a home, maintaining a yard, or establishing a work center. Handrails for stairways; a handgrip at the bathtub; conveniently located electrical outlets; indirect, nonglare, and thorough lighting; and tools, equipment, and home or yard machines kept in proper working condition are all ways to avoid an accident, especially in later middle age. Sensible middle-aged people plan for the gradual failing of their physical abilities by making the home as safe, convenient, and comfortable as possible as they rethink homemaking functions for the coming decades. Further, you can be instrumental in initiating or strengthening a safety program in an occupational or school setting.

Illness Prevention. Middle age is not automatically a period of physical or psychological hazard or disease. There is no single disease or mental condition that is necessarily related to the passage of time, according to an American Medical Association Subcommittee on Aging, although the middle-aged person should be carefully assessed for signs of illness (25). Major health problems of this era are cardiovascular disease, cancer, pulmonary disease, diabetes, obesity, alcoholism, anxiety, depression, and glaucoma.

✔ You can help the person maintain energy and improve health by teaching the information presented in this chapter. The person can learn to moderate eating, drinking, or smoking habits and to use only medically prescribed drugs. Many measures promote health: regular physical examinations (see Appendix II), pursuit of leisure activity, use of relaxation techniques, working through the emotional and family concerns related to middle age, affirming the worth of self as a middle-ager, preparing for the later years, and confronting developmental tasks. The person also needs to prepare for possible accidents or illness.

✔ Teach that the mounting statistical, experimental, and autopsy findings point to excessive cigarette smoking as an etiological factor in breast and lung cancer, cardiovascular disease, chronic obstructive pulmonary disease, and peptic ulcer. For the person who feels trapped, depressed, frustrated, or isolated, easily accessible escapes are alcoholism, drugs, or excess food intake. Assist the person in finding other ways to cope with stressors (81).

✔ The medicine cabinet may look like a pharmaceutical display if the self-absorbed person retreats into hypochondriasis. Old injuries may start to be bothersome, and new injuries do not heal as quickly. Illness or accident proneness can also be a means of resolving serious difficulties or of escaping responsibilities. If understanding and help from others are negligible or nonexistent, and the possibility of recouping losses or rearranging one's life seems unlikely, then the brief care and attention given during illness or after injury may not offer sufficient gratification. Suicidal thoughts and attempted or actual suicide are a call for help or an escape from problems (81). The prop of ill health should not be removed without study and caution, for removing one syndrome may only result in discharge of emotional tension through another physical or emotional syndrome. Thus nursing intervention and medical treatment must be directed toward both physical and emotional factors.

✔ Because nursing care is holistic, you can meet emotional and spiritual needs of the person while giving physical care and doing health teaching related to common health problems discussed in the following pages.

Common Health Problems. A variety of health problems may occur, although many middle-agers remain healthy. Refer to a medical-surgical nursing text for more information on the following diseases. *Respiratory conditions* are a frequent cause for days absent from work. Generally, middle-aged women have more disability days from work because of respiratory and other acute disorders; men have more disability days from injuries.

Sinusitis is an *inflammation of the mucous membrane lining of the paranasal sinuses*. It may be caused by bacteria, viruses, allergic or vasomotor problems, or irritants such as smoke. *Normal sinus drainage is prohibited*. In nonbacterial sinusitis, the nasal discharge is usually clear and no fever or only a low-grade fever exists.

✔ Usually an oral antihistamine or decongestant, or both, provides sufficient symptomatic relief. In bacterial sinusitis there is usually mucopurulent nasal discharge, sometimes cellulitis in the involved sinus, and usually a temperature of 101°F or higher. A topical decongestant, an oral decongestant, an antipyretic, and an appropriate antibiotic are suggested treatment (50).

Hiatal hernia with esophagitis is the *herniation of the stomach through the diaphragm with reflux of acid into the esophagus*. The person often has substernal pain and fears a myocardial infarction or other heart problems. It is important to rule out such possibilities. The pain with hiatal hernia is usually worse when bending over or lying down, particularly after meals. There may be nausea and vomiting.

✔ Recommendations and treatment usually involve maintaining ideal weight; avoiding tight clothing around the abdomen and chest; eating frequently in small amounts, and no closer than 2 hours before bedtime; elevating the head of the bed; and taking an antacid (50).

A condition with somewhat related symptoms is uncomplicated **duodenal peptic ulcer,** which is *ulcera-*

tion of the duodenal mucosa. Pain results, but no bleeding and no obstruction are found. The cause is unknown but can be related to stress, personality traits, certain drugs, and diseases. The person experiences pain in the epigastrium or right upper quadrant usually 1 to 2 hours after meals, has pain relief with foods and antacids, and sometimes has nausea, vomiting, and belching.

✔ Treatment is in the form of small, frequent feedings, and avoiding caffeine, strong spices, alcohol. Antacids or cimetadine may be prescribed. The person should be followed closely and have medication tapered to none with progressive relief (50).

Another problem manifesting itself with pain in the substernal region, but occasionally in the epigastrium, neck, back, or arms, is **angina pectoris,** a condition caused by an *imbalance between the oxygen needed in the myocardium and the oxygen supplied.* Classically in this condition pain is evident with an increase in the heart's workload and is relieved, usually in 3 to 5 minutes, with rest. A differential diagnosis should be carefully made to rule out myocardial infarction or preinfarction, ulcer, musculoskeletal pain, esophagitis, or pulmonary, psychogenic, and nerve root problems.

✔ Many people mistake angina for indigestion and ingest large amounts of antacids, when the person should be receiving prompt treatment. If angina is diagnosed and is stable, that is, recurs with approximately the same amount of exertion and is relieved with the same amount of rest each time, treatment measures can be directed toward relieving the heart's workload or improving cardiac performance. Sublingual, short-acting nitroglycerine is the mainstay of specific therapy, although some people are now taking longer-acting nitrates (50).

Uncomplicated **essential hypertension** is one condition that may add to an angina pectoris problem unless the hypertension is controlled. This condition is defined as *a persistent elevation of arterial blood pressure greater than 150/100 mm Hg, but not over 200/210.* Persistent is defined as present on at least three weekly chronological readings. Diagnostic studies must not find a *specific etiology.* If one is found, it is called **secondary hypertension.** Usually the person with essential hypertension is asymptomatic and the condition is discovered on routine screening. However, the person may have headaches, typically in the occipital region. These usually begin early in the morning and become less severe as activity increases. Sometimes a person experiences an unsteadiness and says, "I feel swimmyheaded." Signs are few: sometimes a narrowing or kinking of the optic fundi and minimal left ventricle hypertrophy are found. Laboratory studies are usually normal.

✔ The diagnosed person should follow a diet with not more than 2 grams of sodium daily and should take in calories to either maintain or reduce to within 10 pounds of normal weight. The person should participate in moderate exercise. Sometimes these measures are sufficient. Biofeedback and relaxation techniques have also helped to reduce the blood pressure. If medication is deemed necessary, it is prescribed in a stepped approach, starting with the lowest helpful dose of one drug and only slowly adding dosage and an additional medication, if necessary. The hypertensive person needs to be carefully monitored, not only for blood pressure readings but for side effects of drugs (50).

Prevention or adequate treatment of angina pectoris and hypertension can prevent more serious heart damage and disease. The mortality rate in middle-aged White men is double that of White women, with coronary disease being responsible for most of the differential. Mortality rate differs less between non-White males and females (50).

Hyperthyroidism may present symptoms similar to cardiac disease, even myocardial infarction. The person over 50 may have hyperthyroidism but have few of the usual signs and symptoms, so that the disease is misdiagnosed. Martyn gives in-depth information to assist you in assessment and intervention (72).

Gout and **hyperuricemia** can be side effects of a blood pressure medication, thiazide, or they can be the result of an *inborn error of metabolism causing acute inflammatory arthritis and uric acid deposits that appear as kidney stones or tophi* (deposits near joints, in the ear, or in bone). The person with acute gout usually presents with a red, hot, tender joint surrounded by inflammatory tissue. Classically the big toe is involved, but the joints of the feet, ankles, wrists, and hands may also be affected. Laboratory studies usually confirm the diagnosis with a uric acid level greater than 7.0 mg per deciliter and a white blood cell count over 10,000 per cubic millimeter.

✔ Several drugs are available for treating the acute and chronic conditions. Rest, elevation, and application of cold compresses to the affected joint may be beneficial. Chronic gout may be evidenced only by a serum uric acid level over 7.5 mg per deciliter and by an increase in tophi. Chronic gout is treated with different drugs than acute gout.

Diabetes Type II is *noninsulin dependent (IDDM).* It was previously referred to as adult or maturity onset, stable, and ketosis resultant. In this category there are two subtypes: obese and nonobese. Many Type II diabetics respond to diet alone, although some of the nonobese subtypes may require insulin.

✔ More than in any other disease, the person manages his/her therapy. Any obese or overweight adult diabetic should reduce until he/she attains and maintains normal weight. The person will also do urine testing and keep a chart of results. Skin care, especially foot care, is important. Drug therapy, if necessary, may be with an oral hypoglycemic agent (37).

Acute bacterial prostatitis is an *acute infection of the prostate gland, often caused by the bacteria Escherichia coli*. Symptoms may include lower back and perineum pain that may be referred into the inguinal region and testes. Urinary obstruction symptoms may be present. Sexual intercourse may be painful and sexual desire lost. The man may have fever and nausea. The prostate may be extremely tender and enlarged. Sometimes a penile discharge is present. A urinalysis will usually show both white and red blood cells.

✔ Treatment should include an antibiotic and an analgesic. A sitz bath several times a day may be helpful. The prostate should not be massaged (50).

Prostatitis may become **chronic**, that is, *chronically infected or inflamed*. The symptoms are basically the same as in acute cases, except less severe. Normally there is no fever. The prostate is only slightly tender and enlarged. Ideally prostatic fluid should be obtained for culture. If this is impossible, then a urine specimen should be obtained after prostatic massage and compared to a premassage urine specimen.

✔ Treatment will vary according to findings. Sometimes prostatic massage alone will reduce symptoms of congestion in nonbacterial prostatitis, and increased sexual activity may help reduce congestion. Sitz baths provide comfort, along with analgesics (50).

Lumbosacral strain is said to be experienced at some time by 80 percent of adults, usually in late young adulthood and the middle years. Pain arises from the *strain of ligaments and musculature* and must be distinguished from pain that arises from vertebrae, articular cartilage, and nerve roots. Muscle spasm may be observed over the lumbosacral area, but there should be no radiation of pain to the legs, groin, or testes. Sensory and motor function and reflexes should be intact. There should be no flank pain on percussion and the straight leg raising should be negative. If these additional symptoms are present, immediate medical care is necessary (50).

✔ Usually a muscle relaxant and an analgesic are prescribed if a medical approach is tried. Bed rest is usually part of the regimen. Chiropractic treatment is often successful.

✔ *Back care* is a subject about which education is essential. Proper bending and lifting techniques may prevent problems. Back flexion exercises may be helpful, and a firm mattress of traditional material or a water bed may help reduce an acute problem. Sometimes local heat relieves symptoms, but ice is preferred if strain is only 24 to 48 hours old.

Foot balance, *the ability to alter one's position so that body weight is carried through the foot with minimal effort*, is essential to prevent strain, foot aches and pain. Foot imbalance may result from contracted toes, improper position, size or shape of one or more bones of the foot, weak or rotating ankles, muscle strain, weak ligaments, poor body posture, overweight, arthritis, injuries, and improperly fitted or shaped shoes. Treatment by a podiatrist consists of careful assessment of the posture and balance inlays for insertion into the shoes (120).

A **callus**, *thickening of the outer layers of the skin on the sole of the foot*, is formed in areas of excess pressure and friction. These become painful when congestion and swelling from the callus press on nerve endings and underlying bursa become inflamed.

✔ Foot problems may occur in middle age. Teach the person to observe for the following common signs of need for diagnostic evaluation and possible treatment:

1. Swelling of the feet and ankles.
2. Cramps in the feet and the calf while walking or at night.
3. Inability to keep the feet warm.
4. Loss of the fat tissue on the padded surfaces of the feet.
5. Chronic ulcers on the feet which fail to respond to treatment.
6. Absence of, or bounding pulse in the arteries of the feet.
7. Showing of arteries in the foot on routine x-ray.
8. Burning in the soles of the feet (120).

✔ Teach that the callus or other foot problems should be treated by a podiatrist. If the person scrapes or cuts a callus, there is risk of infection (120).

Abnormal Papanicolaou smear findings in an asymptomatic female are more often Class II, suggesting inflammatory reaction, than any of the other classes. (Class III is somewhat suggestive of malignancy; Class IV is highly suggestive of malignancy; and Class V is "diagnostic" of malignancy [50].) In Class II readings the inflammatory changes should be treated after appropriate workup. A "Pap" smear should be repeated in 6 to 8 weeks after treatment; 90 percent of women with mild dysplasia revert to normal. Class III, IV, or V findings are treated with medication, surgery, or radiation, as indicated, after thorough diagnostic study.

Sexual dysfunction, *severely diminished or absent orgasmic response*, may result from alcoholism, obesity, preoccupation with career or finances, mental or physical fatigue, boredom, fear of failing sexually, or chronic illness related to impaired circulation or neuropathy. For example, in one study of diabetic men, over half of them were impotent, probably because of autonomic neuropathy involving the sacral parasympathetic fibers that supply the penis and bladder. Vascular disease affects potency because a high volume of blood flow is necessary to distend the vascular spaces of erectile tissue. Occlusion of the pudendal arteries or their tributaries may result in impotence. Hypertension, with a blood pressure of 180/110, constitutes a contraindication to coitus because of increased risk of strokes. Antihypertensive drugs, other than diuretics, cause impotence or inhibition of ejaculation. A past myocardial infarction may limit physical activity of any kind, but after a period of recovery most coronary patients resume sexual relations. While hysterectomy does not affect sex drive, oophorectomy may because of the hormonal changes. However, hormone replacement may return sex drive. Adrenalectomy has a negative effect on libido because hormone production is diminished. Most men retain potency after prostatectomy, unless surgical approach has been through the sex-related nerve centers. If the prostate is malignant and surgery more radical, however, the man's possibilities of retaining potency are not as favorable (73). Increased expectations in this age of sexual liberation may also increase sexual as well as other marital problems.

✔ The middle-aged person may subtly, hesitantly, or openly discuss problems of sexual function with you. Listen carefully. Let the person know that such problems are not unusual. You may not know the answers, but your listening can help the person make a decision to seek medical care or counseling, realize the need to change behavior, or assist in attitude and value clarification about sexuality and sexual behavior. Refer the person or couple to a counselor who can help with physical and emotional problems. Your discussion with the physician of the person's problems related to changed libido or impotence can also be helpful. Sometimes a change in medication dosage or modification in treatment regimen can reduce sexual dysfunction.

Psychosocial Concepts

Factors That Influence Research Findings on Cognitive Ability

Because most studies on adult cognition have been cross-sectional, caution is necessary in interpreting the results since many factors are influential. For the middle-aged person especially, amount of education, experiential differences, fixed attitudes, the number of years since formal schooling was completed, and the general health status may negatively influence test scores. Because most intelligence tests are developed for children and adolescents, the kind of subtest given may influence the scores. The middle-ager scores higher on tests that require general information or vocabulary abilities. At age 60, IQ test results are equal to or better than that of young adults. Only arithmetic reasoning shows a plateau through the adult years. Speed requirements of the test may mitigate against the IQ test scores; adults show a peak in speed of performance in the twenties and a gradual decrease in overall speed of performance through the years (100, 110).

In various studies, physically fit and active males were found to have a higher intelligence score than males who engaged in little physical activity (97).

Kangas and Bradway did a 38-year follow-up study of people tested for intelligence as preschoolers, junior high school students, young adults, and in early middle age. They found an increase in IQ across the four testing periods, indicating continued mental growth during middle age and possibly even beyond. Interesting sex differences emerged from these findings. Women whose IQs had been high as children gained less than those with medium or low preadult IQs and less than males with any level of preadult IQ. On the other hand, the higher the level of a male's preadult IQ, the greater his adult gain. These findings have interesting implications in light of the theory that bright women fear success. Women who tested so high as girls may be inhibiting their intellectual potential later in life (57).

Cognitive Processes and Development

Cognitive processes in adulthood include reaction time, perception, memory, learning and problem solving, and creativity.

Reaction time or *speed of performance* is individual and generally stays the same or diminishes during late middle-age. The speed of response is important primarily in test situations, since much of the problem solving necessary in adulthood requires deliberation and accuracy rather than speed. Reaction time is related to complexity of the task, the habitual pattern of response to stimuli, and familiarity with the task. Time for new learning increases with age, but adults in their forties and fifties have the same ability to learn as they did in their twenties and thirties (21).

Memory is maintained through young and middle adulthood; no major age differences are evident. Some quantitative changes may occur. For example, a person in early adulthood who could recite a ten-digit span of numbers as a series of discrete units may recite eight digits grouped or categorized in late middle age. The ability to categorize or group information aids learning. The middle-ager memorizes less readily material which is not well organized and seems to retain less from oral presentation of information than younger students (25). Travis maintains that memory is not reliable in the adult years—or at any age. Most people forget or ignore episodes that do not fit the self-image or that are considered unimportant. People who think they remember an event from childhood or a number of years previously may be making up plausible scenarios, fantasies, or confabulations, based on earlier reports or stories (109).

Learning occurs in adults of all ages. The highly intelligent person becomes even more learned. The capacity for intellectual growth is unimpaired, and is enhanced by interest, motivation, flexibility, a sense of humor, confidence, and maturity attained through experience. Learning means more; it is not just learning for learning's sake. Knowledge is applied; motivation to learn is high for personal reasons. Reluctance to learn occurs if the new material does not appear relevant or does not serve the person as well as current information (110).

Problem-solving abilities remain throughout adulthood. There are no significant differences between 20-, 40-, and 60-year-olds in learning a task. Generally, better educated people perform better than less educated people in any age group. When there is no time limitation, there are no task differences in complex task solutions because young and middle-aged adults use different strategies. Young adults, knowing they can function quickly, may be more likely to use less efficient reasoning strategies such as trial and error. In late middle age, because people know they are becoming slower, they tend to think a problem through first so they can solve it in fewer tries (110).

The middle-ager is able to do all the cognitive strategies of Piaget's *Stage of Formal Operations* described in Chapters 11 and 12. Sometimes the practicality of a situation will call forth use of Concrete Operations; because not all problems in life can be solved by abstract reasoning, the middle-ager does both Operations realistically in problem solving. He/she also uses the fifth stage of cognitive development, problem finding, described in Chapter 11. Societal, occupational, and general life experiences are crucial to cognitive operations of the middle-ager. Thus perceptions about the same situation, problem, or task can vary considerably in a group of middle-agers.

Heath describes cognitive characteristics that are developed in the young adult and used throughout middle age as well. Various patterns mark the development of *intellectual skills*. The mature adult can symbolize experience and behaves in a way that shows organization, integration, stability, and unity in the cognitive process. Representing experience symbolically, as hunches, words, thoughts, or other symbols, is part of becoming mature. The person can reflect on past and current experience and can imagine, anticipate, plan, and hope. The person develops an inner private world that gives him/her resources for happiness and potentialities for anxiety. The person can recall past defeats and triumphs and monitor ongoing thoughts for consistency and logic. When the person solves a problem, he/she can explain how it was solved. Because the mature adult is more imaginatively productive, he/she is capable of producing more images, thoughts, and combinations of ideas, is able to use reflection to gain perspectives about life, and is aware of personal beliefs, values, motives, and powers. The mature person is increasingly interested in other persons and warm, enduring relationships and is adaptable, independent, self-driving, conscientious, enthusiastic, and purposeful. The person can reflect about personal relationships and their sources of strain and satisfaction and concomitantly understand why other persons feel and act as they do (47).

Buhler implies cognitive development as she describes the maintenance and change tendencies in life. Maintenance, through the restitution of deficiencies (need satisfaction) and upholding of the system's internal order, is necessary for cognitive function to occur. Change, involving self-limited adaptation and creative expansion, is part of the cognitive development of the adult. Maintenance and change occur with different emphases in various life stages. The child develops self-limiting adaptation as he/she learns; the adolescent and adult move into creative expansion; after middle age the person assesses the past and self and wants to restore inner order; and in old age the person either continues to follow previous adaptive and creative drives or regresses to need-satisfying tendencies (14).

The intellectually curious have an increased need and ability to spin new syntheses and theories, to make meaningful that which seems meaningless, to coordinate hypotheses formation and testing, to be systematic at problem solving, to seek environmental diversity, and to become more subtle, differentiated, integrated, and complex. The mature person has a progressive integration; that is, he/she is continually open, flexible, curious, and actively engaged. If cognitive efficiency becomes disrupted, a mature person is able to recover from such disorganization more quickly than an immature person, even though the two do not differ in intelligence. The mature person becomes discriminating in decisions based on the facts at hand, can postpone, suppress, or ignore. The person can analyze and judge information, even that which is personally relevant, in terms of demands of the information itself, without being influenced by either personal desires or persuasive opinions of others. Thought becomes objective and judgment independent (47).

Neugarten believes that the person changes cognitively as well as emotionally over time as the result of accumulated experience. The person abstracts from experiences and creates more encompassing and more refined categories for interpreting events. The middle-aged person differs cognitively from the young adult in that he/she was born in a different historical era and thereby has different formative experiences. The middle-ager thus has a greater apperceptive mass or store of past experience by which to evaluate events or make decisions. Through the adult years, perspectives and insights broaden and deepen and attitudes and behaviors change (85).

Although Gould focuses more on personality than cognitive development, he sees adulthood as a time of thoughtful confrontation with the self—letting go of the idealized image, the desire to be perfect, and acknowledging the realistic image of self and personal feelings. The adult continues to gain new beliefs about self and the world. Conflicts between past and present beliefs are resolved (42).

✓ Assist the middle-ager (and others) in understanding the cognitive changes and strengths of cognitive ability. Reinforce a positive self-image related to cognitive abilities.

Creativity. Dennis found an age pattern for creative output. He found that scientists show a peak activity in early and middle adulthood. Unique, original, and inventive productions are more often created in the twenties, thirties, and forties than later in life. The more a creative act depends on accumulated experience, the more likely it is to occur in middle age or later life. People are less productive in total creative output in the twenties than the thirties and forties. Poets, novelists, and scholars gain in productivity in middle and old age, and while quantity may decrease, quality increases as a greater proportion of crystallized intelligence is used. Some creative works cannot be produced without the benefit of years of experience and living, absorbing the wisdom of the culture, and the resultant development of new insights (26).

Creativity is seen not only in famous people. The average middle-ager may have many responsibilities and stresses; however, typically he/she approaches a situation, task, or learning experience in a creative way. To understand better the creative process, read Chapter 5 in *Nursing Concepts for Health Promotion* (82).

✓ You can encourage the middle-ager to pursue creative ideas and activities as well as to approach roles, responsibilities, and tasks in a creative way. Help the middle-ager overcome any self-consciousness about the unique cognitive response to a situation.

With increasing emphasis on continued learning, the middle-aged person is frequently enrolled in refresher courses, continuing education courses, or workshops related to occupation or profession. He/she takes college credit and noncredit courses to deal with specific problems; learn specific content; learn for fun; find an academic program necessary for changing a profession or occupation; gain more personal satisfaction; relieve boredom, loneliness, or an unhappy situation; or broaden the mind, learn for the sake of learning. Rapid technological changes in business or the professions cause obsolescence of knowledge and skills, which also forces middle-agers to continue to learn.

✓ When you are teaching, use methods that capitalize on the learning strengths of mature adults, including active discussion and role play. Deemphasize memorizing and acquisition of large amounts of new information. Assist the learner to develop cognitive strategies that will help him/her synthesize, analyze, integrate, interpret, and apply knowledge. Your major role may be in convincing the middle-ager and others that he/she can learn, since myths to the contrary are prevalent. Further, you can enhance learning by providing a conducive environment—one that considers sensory changes. Your verbal and visual presentations must also consider the sensory changes discussed earlier.

Work and Leisure

Work. Consider that this person grew up under the hardships of the Depression and with the Protestant Ethic. Both stressed the economic and moral importance of work. Thus work came to be respected and sought. To be without a job or to be idle was a harbinger of problems and meant being lazy and worthless. How has the middle-ager adjusted to mechanization, waning of the work ethic, the demise of a full day's work for a full day's pay?

If the person is fortunate enough to be in a business or profession in which he/she works successfully for self or is allowed freedom within a specialized area of work, he/she will feel goal achievement for self, family, and community. He/she will experience the dignity of being productive and will enjoy an increasing self-esteem.

Unfortunately, most middle-agers are not in this position. Most are employed in a system in which the only value is in the production, not the person. Furthermore, only so much production is acceptable; unions have set rules whereby no more than a specified amount can be done within a specified time.

Many middle-aged women work outside of the home, thus they are especially in the middle in terms of the demands of various roles on their time and energy. The middle-aged woman is wife, mother, homemaker, grandmother, worker, and organization member. In one study, 21 percent of the women nationally who were caregivers also had child care responsibility; 9 percent had quit their jobs; 21 percent had work conflict. The middle-aged woman is often in the middle in terms of two competing values: that traditional care of the elderly is a family responsibility, and that women should be free to work outside the home if they wish. Each family member feels the repercussions as the balance of roles and responsibilities change (9). More middle-aged women are working today for a variety of reasons:

1. Inflation and the rising cost of living.
2. Changes in attitudes about gender-appropriate roles as a result of the women's movements.
3. The rising divorce rate that forces the woman to become economically independent.
4. Fewer children in the home.
5. Use of labor-saving devices for the home that results in free time.
6. Increasing educational levels that stimulate career interests.
7. Expectancy of a higher standard of living (9, 53).

✔ Knowing the degree of work stability, extent to which work is satisfying, and the emotional factors that have operated in the person's concept of work and in the self-concept are all important in assessing how well the middle-ager can function as a mentally and physically healthy person. As a professional person, you will have to resolve conflicts related to the work role. Hence, you are in a position to assist the middle-ager in talking about and resolving feelings and values related to work and other activity.

Leadership Role. The middle-ager's cognitive–intellectual stage is in favor of his/her being a designated or an informal leader if other factors are favorable. (Usually middle-aged leaders have developed necessary qualities from childhood on, but occasionally a person does not feel that he/she has this ability until there is a measure of success in the life work.)

The *leader* usually has the following characteristics: (1) adequate socioeconomic resources; (2) higher level of education or success than majority of group to be led; (3) realistic self-concept; (4) realistic goals and ability to encourage others toward those goals; (5) high frustration tolerance; (6) ability to express negative thoughts tactfully; (7) ability to accept success or failure gracefully; (8) ability to delegate authority; (9) understanding of group needs; and (10) flexibility in meeting group needs (25, 47, 60).

The middle-aged person may demonstrate this leadership ability on the job or in community or church organizations. Women who are most successful in leadership careers are those who have little conflict in the multiple roles of career woman, mother, and wife. Their husbands' support and encouragement are major assets (61).

✔ You can encourage or reaffirm the middle-ager in the leadership role. As a nurse, you may also assist the middle-ager in working through feelings or conflicts related to the work setting or the job itself.

Leisure. The middle-aged person, taught little about how to enjoy free time, is now faced with increasing amounts of leisure because of advances in technology, earlier retirement, and increased longevity. The average middle-ager who has moved up the pay scale and whose children may be grown will have more money and more time to take trips or try new hobbies. Yet various factors hinder use of these new opportunities: value of work learned in younger years; cultural emphasis on intellectual pursuits, so that play is considered childish and a poor use of time and talents; conditioning to at least appear busy; fears of regression and not wanting to return to work; lack of previous opportunity to learn creative pursuits or hobbies; and hesitation to try something new because of fear of failure (71).

✔ As a nurse you can help the person avoid feelings of alienation which result from inability to use leisure time. Use the following suggestions with your middle-aged patients/clients:

1. Emphasize that play and recreation are essential to a healthy life.
2. Stress the indispensability of leisure as a part of many activities, whether work or creative endeavors. Leisure is a state of mind as well as use of time away from work. Have the person analyze leisure activities, whether they bring pleasure, work off frustration, make up deficits in life, or create a sense of pressure or competition.
3. Help the person recognize the interplay of physical and intellectual endeavors and the contribution of these to mental health.
4. Differentiate compulsive, competitive, aggressive work and play from healthy, natural work and play. Intrinsic in play are spontaneity, flexibility, creativity, zest, and joy.
5. Recognize the person's creative efforts to encourage further involvement in leisure activities.
6. Educate the person about the importance of preparing for retirement.

7. Inform the person of places, courses, or workshops where he/she can learn new creative skills and use of talents.
8. Encourage the person to enjoy change, to participate in organizations, and initiate stimulating contacts with others.
9. Encourage the person to stop the activity when it no longer meets personal needs (29, 66).

Emotional Development

The middle years, the climacteric, is a period of self-assessment, and greater introspection—a transitional period. In middle age (and beyond), the person perceives life as time left to live rather than time since birth. Time is seen as finite; death is a possibility. Middle-agers clock themselves by their positions in different life contexts—changes in body, family, career—rather than by chronological age. Time is seen in two ways: time to finish what the person wants to do, and how much meaning and pleasure can be obtained in the time that is left (85). The person makes the often agonizing reappraisal of how achievements measure up against goals and of the entire system of values. He/she realizes that the choices of the past have limited present choices. He/she can no longer dream of infinite possibilities. The person is forced to acknowledge that he/she has worked up to or short of personal capabilities. Goals may or may not have been reached; aspirations may have to be modified. The possibility for advancement becomes more remote. The person will have to go on with ever-brighter, ever-younger men and women crowding into the competitive economic, political, and social arena. In the United States, success is highly valued and is measured by prestige, wealth, or power. To be without these by middle age causes stress, and the likelihood of achieving them diminishes with age. Contrary to an earlier trend, however, the middle-ager is again being perceived as a valuable worker because of the experience and knowledge he/she can contribute. Thus he/she is less likely to be replaced on the job by a younger employee just on the basis of age. Federal legislation prohibiting age discrimination contributes to this later trend.

Developmental Crisis. The psychosexual crisis of middle age, according to Erikson, is generativity versus self-absorption and stagnation (32). **Generativity** *is a concern about providing for others that is equal to the concern of providing for the self.* If other developmental stages were managed successfully, the person has a sense of parenthood and creativity; of being vital in establishing and guiding the next generation, the arts, or a profession; of feeling needed and being important to the welfare of humankind. The person can assume the responsibility of parenthood. As a husband or wife, each can see the strengths and weaknesses of the other and combine their energies toward common goals.

A biological parent does not necessarily get to the psychosocial stage of generativity. And the unmarried person or the person without children can be very generative.

The middle-ager who is generative takes on the major work of providing for others, directly or indirectly. There is a sense of enterprise, productivity, mastery, charity, altruism, and perseverance. The greatest bulk of social problems and needs falls on this person, who can handle the responsibilities because of personal strengths, vigor, and experience. There is a strong feeling of care and concern for that which has been produced by love, necessity, or accident. He/she can collaborate with others to do the necessary work. Ideas about personal needs and goals converge with an understanding of the social community, and the ideas guide actions taken on behalf of future generations.

The generative middle-ager may be a mentor to a young adult. A **mentor** *is an experienced adult who befriends and guides a less-experienced and younger adult in the work world or in a social or an educational situation.* The mentor is usually about 10 years older and promotes psychosocial development and success of the younger person in business, management, nursing, or other careers or professions by sponsoring the younger person as an associate, creating a social heir, teaching him/her as much as possible for promotion into a position, or recommending the mentee for advancement (65).

The person's adaptive mechanisms and superego are strong but not rigid. There is an expansion of interests and investment in that for which the person is responsible. Youth and young adults tend to be self-centered. With approaching middle age and the image of one's finite existence faintly in view, the person consciously reappraises and utilizes self. With introspection, the self seems less important and the words *service, love of others,* and *compassion* gain new meaning. These concepts motivate action. In church work, social work, community fund drives, cultural or artistic efforts, the profession, or political work, the person is active and often the leader. The person's goal is to leave the world a better place in which to live. A critical problem, however, is coming to terms with accomplishments and accepting responsibility that comes with achievement. In addition, he/she must come to terms with violations of the moral codes of society, for example, tax loop-holes which are used by some adults, and with superego and ego in balance, develop a constructive philosophy and honest method of operation.

Linden and Courtney believe the most important work of the person begins after parenthood ceases and is cognitive and emotional in nature: preserving culture, maintaining the annals of history, keeping alive human judgment, maintaining human skills, preserving and skillfully contriving the instruments of civilization, and teaching all this to oncoming generations. While the young and middle-aged adult is involved in such functions, these qualities of the human mind are best manifested in the aging person in the late middle years or thereafter (67).

The generative person feels a sense of comfort or ease in lifestyle. There is realistic gratification from a job well done and from what has been given to others. He/she accepts self and the body, realizing that although acceptance of self is originally based on acceptance from others, unless he/she accepts self, he/she cannot really expect acceptance from others.

The mature middle-aged person has tested ways of doing things. He/she can draw on much experience; thus he/she may have deep sincerity, mature judgment, and a sense of empathy. He/she has a sense of values or a philosophy underlying the life, giving a sense of stability and causing him/her to be reflective and cautious. The person recognizes that one of the most generative things he/she can give to society is the life led and the way he/she lives it. Consider the following statement by a 50-year-old man:

> Those were full years—raising the kids with all its joy and frustration. I'm glad they're on their own now. This is a new stage of life. I can go fishing; Mary can go out to lunch. We have more time together for fun, and now we have more time for working at the election polls and in volunteer activities.

The middle years can be wise and felicitous or they can be foolish and frantic, fraught with doubts and despair.

If the developmental task of generativity is not achieved, a sense of **stagnation,** or **self-absorption,** enshrouds the person (32). Thus *he/she regresses to adolescent, or younger, behavior characterized by physical and psychological invalidism.* This person hates the aging body and feels neither secure nor adept at handling self physically or interpersonally. He/she has little to offer even if so inclined. He/she operates on a slim margin and soon burns out. The person is withdrawn, resigned, isolated, introspective, and rebellious, and because of personal preoccupations, he/she is unable to give of self to others. The person becomes like a child, indulging self. Relations with others are impoverished. The fear of old age may cause regression to inappropriate youthfulness in behavior or dress, infidelity, or absence of dignity. Although the person cannot admit the normal physical changes that are occurring, these are apparent to others. He/she fools no one but self.

Certainly the opposite can occur; the middle-aged person can become resigned to inappropriate old age too soon, seeing each physical change to an exaggerated degree. The chronic defeatism and depression which result from feeling too old also isolate the person in self-pity and egocentrism. Consider the following statement by a 50-year-old woman:

> I spent all those years raising the kids and doing housework while Bob moved up the professional ladder. We talked less and less about each other, only about the kids or his job. Now the kids are gone. I should be happy, but I'm lost. I can't carry on a decent conversation with Bob. I don't have any training for a job. And I look terrible! I sit around and eat too much. I wear high collars to hide my wrinkled neck, and no cosmetics will hide the dark circles under my eyes.

When one is self-absorbed, physically, psychologically, and socially, either overpliancy or rigidity in behavior and an intolerant, ruthless, or cynical attitude may develop. This person may lack stamina, self-confidence, and a value system. Immature adults have impaired and less socially organized intellectual skills; their intellectual skills are fused by personal emotions and coordinated in strange and unrealistic ways. The immature person seeks private self-absorption and vicarious immersion in subjective problems of others (47).

Yet the characteristics of the self-absorbed person are health-endeavoring attempts and reparative efforts to cope or adapt. They may or may not work well, depending on the intensity of personality characteristics and the social and physical environment.

Maturity. Because **maturity,** *being fully developed as a person,* is not a quality of life reached at any one age or for all time, the characteristics described as generativity are general guidelines. If the person is doing what is appropriate for age, situation, and culture, then he/she is acting maturely for the age. Attaining feelings of maturity and independence comes later for the professional than for technical workers or laborers because of prolonged education. Also, as the person grows older, the ideal level of maturity and autonomy may recede further into the future and never be fully achieved (47, 52). Maturity is the achievement of efficiently organized psychic growth predicated on integration of experiences of solving environmentally stimulated conflicts. The external environment is a potent force on the person; conflicts are primarily socially incurred. The psychosocial organization in maturity shows a cultural direction. As one ages, the psychic interests broaden and are less selfish. Part of maturity is staying power, the power to see it through, which is different from starting power. Seeing it through is to use faith and persistence, to continue even against great odds. Characteristics of staying power include: (1) integrity of consciousness and personhood, (2) remaining loyal to values, faith, philosophy, beliefs; (3) holding to a cause greater than self, and (4) giving up something worthwhile rather than worrying about present risks.

In adulthood, there is no one set of appropriate personality characteristics or any one characteristic, such as inflexibility or intolerance, that is bad. The great person is inflexible or stands firm in the face of opposition at a crucial moment in history. The great person is intolerant of the evils he/she is trying to combat. Each of us leads a particular life at a particular time, place, circumstance, and with a particular personal history. Success in leading that life depends on a *pattern* of qualities appropriate to that life. No person can lead everyone's life. The mature person is reflective, restructures or processes information in the light of experience, and uses knowledge and expertise in a directed way to achieve desired ends. No one will reach the ideal of self-actualization described by Maslow (Chapter 5, pp. 152–153), yet each can reach his/her own ideal and peak of well-being and functioning relatively free of anxieties, cognitive distortions, and rigid habits and with a sense of the individuality and uniqueness of the self and others (52, 85).

The following are characteristics of positive mental health and maturity:

1. Accepting personal strengths and limits, having a firm sense of identity, and living with the past without guilt.
2. Striving for self-actualization and living up to the highest potential.
3. Developing a philosophy of life and code of ethics, an ability to resist stress and tolerate anxiety, and an equilibrium of intrapsychic forces.
4. Having a sense of autonomy, independence, and ability for self-direction.
5. Having an adequate perception of reality and of factors affecting reality, having a social sensitivity, and treating others as worthy of concern.
6. Mastering the environment: working, playing, solving problems, and adapting to the requirements of life.
7. Valuing human relationships and feeling responsible to others (52).

Personality Development. Emotional or personality development has also been described by the stage theorists Jung (55), Sheehy (101), Gould (41–43), Levinson (65), and Vaillant (113, 114).

Jung divided personality development to correspond to the first and second halves of the life cycle. In the first half—until the age of 35 or 40—the person is in a period of expansion. Maturational forces direct the growth of the ego (the conscious or awareness of self and the external world); capacities unfold for dealing with the external world. The person learns to get along with others and tries to win as many of society's rewards as possible. A career and family are established. To achieve, it is usually necessary for men to overdevelop their masculinity and for women to overemphasize their feminine traits and skills. The young person dedicates self to mastery of the outer world. Being preoccupied with self-doubt, fantasy, and the inner nature is not advantageous to the young adult, for the task is to meet the demands of society confidently and assertively (56, 66, 100).

Jung believed that during the forties the personality begins to undergo a transformation. Earlier goals and ambitions have lost their meaning. The person may feel stagnant, incomplete, depressed, as if something crucial is missing, even if the person has been quite successful, since success has often been achieved at the cost of personality development. The person begins to turn inward, to examine the meaning of life. Separating self from ordinary conformity to the goals and values of mass society and achieving a measure of psychic balance is accomplished through individuation—finding one's individual way (56, 66, 100).

Jung recognized that while middle-aged persons begin to turn inward, they still have much energy and resources for the generativity described by Erikson, as well as for making personal changes. The person may begin new or long-forgotten projects and interests or even change careers. Men and women begin giving expression to their opposite sexual drives. Men become less aggressively ambitious and more concerned with interpersonal relationships. They begin to realize that achievement counts for less and friendship for more. Women tend to become more aggressive and independent. Such changes can create midlife marital problems. While ongoing development may create tension and difficulties, Jung believed that the greatest failures come when adults cling to the goals and values of the first half of life, holding on to the glories and beauty of youth (56, 66, 100).

Neugarten's research (83–85) has found personality characteristics in middle-age similar to those described by Jung (55).

Sheehy (101), Gould (41–43), Levinson (65), and Vaillant (113, 114) also describe midlife stages of development. These stage theorists confirm many of the characteristics already described and emphasize that this is a time of new stability and authenticity.

✔ As you work with the middle-ager, use the concept of generativity versus self-absorption in assessment of the client's developmental level, and promote achievement of this developmental task through your listening, support, encouragement of activities, teaching, and counseling. The self-absorbed person will need referral to a long-term counselor. The generative person or mentor needs to hear that what he/she is doing is indeed a worthwhile contribution. Your own generativity can be a positive model for others. Your reinforcement of another's strengths facilitates further emotional development and maturity.

Changing Body Image

The gradually occurring physical changes described earlier confront the person and are mirrored in others. The climacteric causes realignment of attitudes about the self that cuts into the personality and its definition. Other life stresses cause the person to view self and the body differently. The person not only realizes he/she is looking older but subjectively feels older as well. Work can bring a sense of stress if he/she feels less stamina and vigor to cope with the task at hand. Illness or death of loved ones creates a concern about personal health, sometimes to excess, and thoughts about one's own death are more frequent. The person begins to feel that he/she is coming out second-best to youth, for the previous self-image of the youthful, strong, and healthy body with boundless energy becomes inadequate. Depression, irritability, and anxiety about femininity and masculinity result. In the United States, more so than in European or Asian cultures, youth and vigor are highly valued, a carryover from frontier days. The person's previous personality largely influences the intensity of these feelings and the symptoms associated with body-image changes. Difficulties are also caused by fear of the effects of the climacteric, folklore about sexuality, attitudes toward womanhood, social and advertising pressures in our culture, and emphasis on obsolescence (80).

Whether male or female, the person who lacks self-confidence and who cannot accept the changing body, has a compulsion to try cosmetics, clothes, hair styles, and the other trappings of youth in the hope that the physical attributes of youth will be attained. The person tries to regain a youthful figure and face, perhaps through surgery; tints the hair to cover signs of gray; and turns to hormone creams to restore the skin. These people are patients at times. There is nothing wrong with dressing attractively or changing the color of one's hair. But too few men or women realize that the color and texture of their skin have changed as the color of their hair faded, and that their aging hands contrast considerably with the commercial coloring on the head. Women in the eighteenth century may have had a more realistic self-picture. They used white wigs or powdered their hair instead of dyeing it, perhaps because they recognized that white or gray hair softens the contours and flatters the face as the years go by.

Most people gradually adjust to their slowly changing body and accept the changes as part of maturity. The mature person realizes it is impossible to return to youth. To imitate youth denies the mature person's own past and experience. The excitement of the middle years lies in using adeptly the experience, insights, values, and realism acquired earlier. The person does not need to downgrade or agree continually with everything youth say and do. The middle-ager feels good about self. Healthy signs are that he/she prefers to be this age and has no desire to relive the youthful years.

✔ You can promote integration of a positive body image through your communication skills and teaching. Reaffirm the strengths of being middle-aged to the patient/client, utilizing information presented in this chapter as well as emphasizing the specific strengths of the person.

Adaptive Mechanisms

The adult may use any of the adaptive mechanisms described in previous chapters. **Adult socialization** is *defined as the processes through which an adult learns to perform the roles and behaviors expected of self and by others* and to *remain adaptive in a variety of situations.* The middle-ager is expected and normally considers self to be adaptive. The emphasis is on active, reciprocal participation of the person; little preparation is directed to anticipating, accepting, or coping with failure (1).

The adult, having been rewarded for certain behaviors over the years, has established a wide variety of role-related behaviors, problem-solving techniques, adaptations to stress, and methods for making role transitions; these may not be adaptive to current demands or crises or to increasing role diffusion. There is a continuous need for socialization in adulthood, for a future orientation, for anticipating events, for learning to respond to new demands (1). Ongoing learning of adult roles occurs through observation, imitation, or identification with another, trial and error behavior, the media, books, or fomal education.

Coping or adaptive mechanisms or ego defenses used in response to the emotional stress of the middle years depend on the person's capacity to adapt and satisfy personal needs, sense of identity, nature of interaction with others, sense of usefulness, and interest in the outside world.

The middle-aged adult must be able to channel emotional drives without losing initiative and vigor. During middle age, the person is especially vulnerable to a number of disrupting events: physiological changes and illness in self and loved ones, family stresses, changes in job or role demands or responsibilities, conflict between family generations, and societal changes. The person should be able to cope with ordinary personal upheavals and the frustrations and disappointments in life with only temporary disequilibrium. He/she should be able to participate enthusiastically in adult work and play, as well as have the capacity to experience adequate sexual satisfaction in a stable relationship. The person should be able to express a reasonable amount of aggression, anger, joy, and affection without undue effort, unnecessary guilt, or lack of adequate control (66). Further, the middle-ager is a role model of maturity for the young adult.

The person can retain a sense of balance by recognizing that each age has its unique joys and charms, and the entire life span is valued as equally precious. He/she can appreciate what is past, anticipate the future, and maintain a sense of permanence or stability. The person can adapt successfully to the stresses of middle age by achieving the developmental crisis.

As a nurse, you can help the middle-ager prevent or overcome maladaptive mechanisms. As you extend empathy and reinforce a sense of emotional maturity and health, the person may feel more able to cope with life stressors and perceived failures. You may use principles and techniques of stress management as described in Chapter 12, *Psychiatric/Mental Health Nursing: Giving Emotional Care* (81). You may do teaching or crisis intervention as described in Chapters 5 and 8 of *Nursing Concepts for Health Promotion* (82). If you feel unable to listen to or work with the problems of someone who may be twice your age, refer the person to a counselor.

Midlife Crisis

The midlife crisis was first described by Jung. He believed that at about 40 or 45, the psyche begins to undergo a transformation. The individual feels that the goals and ambitions which once seemed so eternal have lost their meaning. Quite often, the person feels depressed, stagnant, and incomplete, as if something crucial is missing. Jung observed that this happens even among people who have achieved a good measure of social success, for rewards have been won at the cost of a diminution of personality (55). Middle age can be seen as a transition or a crisis.

Midlife crisis *is a major and revolutionary turning point in one's life, involving changes in commitments to career and/or spouse and children and accompanied by significant and ongoing emotional turmoil for both the individual and others.* The term **midlife transition** has a different meaning; it *includes aspects of crisis, process, change, and alternating periods of stability and transition* (55).

For some, midlife is one of the better periods of life: It is a *transition* from youth to later maturity; life expectancy is longer; psychologically and physically, midlife is healthier than ever in history; and parental responsibilities are decreasing. Most people are in their late forties or early fifties when the last child leaves home, leaving a couple of decades for the spouses to be together without the obligations of childrearing. The couple realizes that the myth of decreasing sexual powers is not true. Women in midlife may begin or continue education or a career. Men see midlife as a time of continuing achievement. Experience, assurance, substance, skill, success, and good judgment more than compensate for the disappearance of youthful looks and physical abilities.

Levinson found in his study of men that the period of midlife transition is around ages 40 to 45. For a few the sense of change even in relation to body changes was slight, not particularly painful, and a manageable transition. However, for approximately 80 percent of the men, the early forties evoked tumultuous struggles within the self and with the external world. This period involved for many a profound reappraisal which cannot be an intellectual process. It involves false starts, emotional turmoil, and despair. At least one-third of the male population in the United States between the ages of 40 and 60 years will experience some aspect of midlife crisis (65).

If the person has not resolved the identity crisis of adolescence and achieved mature intimacy in young adulthood, if the person fears the passage of time, physical changes, aging, and mortality, if the person cannot handle the meaning of life's routines and changes, then midlife is seen as a *crisis*.

The person may declare he/she is bored. The nagging feeling that all is not right within the self and with the world can become a way to avoid facing the challenges presented by a deepening self-awareness and to avoid responsibility for personal immaturities or failures. Although many areas of life can be a source of boredom, the two most blamed as tedious and unsatisfying are marriage and work. Leaving either one may be a practical solution to a nagging expediency that was only partially satisfying. Often, however, the joblessness or job change or the affair or the divorce is a headlong flight from aging—an attempt to slow the passage of time by recapturing a lost sense of wholeness, by trying to gain total freedom to explore, by changing goals and becoming a different sort of person. The new freedom may be found to be equally stressful and as full of rejection, competition, loneliness, meaninglessness, and personal dissatisfaction as the old routines. Often the structure and tedium of work or marriage look comfortable, pleasant, and meaningful, only after either situation has been left behind. The identity crisis, when it is over, is seen to have been a denial of reality, not a new level of maturity. The "rational" goal seeking and need to change turns out to be compulsive and meaningless activity.

The psyche itself provides the way out of this crisis. It urges the person to turn inward and examine the meaning of his/her life. This turning inward is prompted by the unconscious, the region in which all the repressed and unlived aspects of the self have grown and now clamor to be heard. The unconscious calls out for recognition in order to bring about psychic balance and harmony (55). This often becomes apparent first in dreams. The unconscious speaks to us primarily through dreams. As middle-aged adults examine their lives and listen to unconscious messages, they sooner or later encounter images of the self, the symbols of wholeness and centeredness. The person must confront the negative aspects of self in order to become whole and find his/her true center (55).

The introspectiveness of middle age can cause a change in perceptions, felt needs, feelings toward others, and a heightened sense of disappointment without the balance of an increased awareness of achievements and positive aspects of life. The person may feel bitter, depressed, and desperate even though he/she has success, wealth, material possessions, and power.

Family experiences are undoubtedly integral to the direction of the midlife crisis. The midlife transition for men, often the husbands of menopausal women, brings new stresses. This period is often accompanied by sexual problems, sometimes leading to affairs, marital disruption, and the abandonment of the wife. Adolescent children may be sexually and aggressively provocative, challenging, or disappointing. Children leaving home for school or marriage change the family balance. Having no children can be a keen disappointment when the man realizes he has no heirs. Some women view their children leaving home and marrying as an extension or expansion of parenting to include the wider interests and loci of their children. Far-flung needs of family members and expanded interests and activities lead to a different kind of parenting. Some women are restored to themselves and to their own development. Restored to themselves does not mean alone: Women depend much more on their relationships for their development—not only for their emotional comfort and security but also to express the acting-on-the-world component of their aggression. The potential for autonomy, changes in relationships, and the development of their occupational skills, contacts, and self-image may start after childbearing is over (90). The woman's new-found autonomy, role changes, and increased interaction with or demands on the husband may be very threatening to the man.

In essence, the midlife crisis involves internal upheaval which may or may not be precipitated by such external events as job crisis, children's maturation, or marital difficulty. Often these are the symptoms, rather than the causes, of the upheaval. Midlife crisis is not always experienced consciously. The feelings of rebellion, meaningless, depression, and need for change may lead instead to altered behavior or attitudes in several life areas, involvement with a variety of causes, or escape into psychosomatic illness, alcoholism, and psychiatric illness (40).

It is healthier in the long range for the person to acknowledge the disruptive feelings and the diffusion of identity, to work through these feelings rather to deny them, and to seek a healthy and constructive outlet for these feelings. Colarusso and Nemeroff describe in detail various issues in midlife for both men and women, related to physical changes, changes in relationships with spouse, family, and children, the relationship of the parent with the same and opposite-sexed child, work relationships and dissatisfactions, and time perspectives (21).

You can be instrumental in assisting the person in working through this crisis. You will use principles of communication and crisis intervention. Refer the person to a counselor who can work with the individual and family. The following guidelines may help the person who feels he/she is in midlife crisis. Share and utilize them as you work with others, or utilize them in your own life.

1. Do not be scared by the midlife crisis. Physical and psychological changes are normal throughout life; see them as opportunities for maturing.
2. Face your feelings and your goals realistically. If you feel confused, see a counselor who can help you sort through your feelings and goals.
3. See your age as a positive asset. Acknowledge your strengths, the benefits of middle age. Take steps to adjust to your liabilities—or to correct them if you can. If a change in hair style or clothes makes you feel better, make that change.
4. Reconcile yourself to the fact that some or many of your hopes and dreams may never be realized and may not be attainable. Remain open to the opportunities that are available; they may exceed your dreams.

5. If the job is not satisfying, consider another job or another field after appraising yourself realistically. Or, be willing to relinquish some responsibility at work.
6. If you dread retirement, plan for it financially, with leisure and other activities.
7. If job pressures are great, seek outlets through recreational activities or other diversions, become involved in community service, renew spiritual study and religious affiliations.
8. Renew old friendships; initiate new ones. Invest in others and in the process enhance personal self-esteem and emotional well-being.
9. Try to be flexible and open-minded, rather than dogmatic or inflexible, in meeting and solving the problems you face.
10. If you are concerned about sexual potency, realize that the problem is typically transient. The more you worry, the worse it gets. Talk about your sexual feelings and concerns with your spouse. The love and concern you have for each other can frequently overcome any impotency. It is important for the woman to perceive sexuality apart from childbearing and menstruation and for the man to perceive sexuality apart from having children and love affairs. If you are so inclined, together read how-to-sex manuals. Seek a marriage counselor if together you cannot work out problems of sexual dysfunction.
11. Share your feelings, concerns, frustrations, and problems with your spouse or confidante so that she/he can understand the changes you are experiencing. Keeping feelings to yourself can increase alienation and the difficulty of repairing the relationship.
12. Examine your attitudes as a parent; strike a balance between care and protection of offspring. Realize their normal need for independence.
13. Realize that frequently the middle-aged woman is becoming more assertive just when the middle-aged man is becoming more passive. Recognizing this as normal and talking about these changes can help the spouses better understand each other's needs and aspirations.
14. Get a physical examination to ensure that physical symptoms are not indicators of physical illness. Do not think that vitamins or health foods alone will cause you to feel differently.
15. Seek counseling for psychological symptoms. The counselor may be a nurse, religious leader, mental health therapist, social worker, marriage counselor, psychologist, or psychiatrist.

✔ You can give some specific suggestions to the spouse of the man in midlife crisis (5):

1. Recognize and acknowledge changes in him, but do not make value judgments. Do not say, "You look awful dressed in that. Who do you think you are, a young swinger?" Say instead, "I notice you're no longer wearing your regular suits and ties. Why is that?"
2. Make it easier for him to talk about his feelings and fears by listening to verbal and nonverbal messages. Avoid telling him how he should feel, dress, or behave.
3. Try not to make him feel guilty by hurling your fears or anger at him. His guilt about your fears will only cause him to withdraw and refuse to discuss his problems with you.
4. Emphasize to him that he does not have to leave to find what he is looking for. Try to find new joint interests, friends, or hobbies. Be willing to see a marriage counselor with him.
5. Focus on changing yourself. Become more alive by taking care of your appearance, keeping informed, and broadening your interests.
6. Avoid threatening his self-concept by appearing too competent in managing all areas of life while he neglects his usual family and home roles. Encourage him to maintain roles. Be prepared to pick up loose ends, however.
7. Try to reestablish the intimacy and closeness that you once shared. Be willing to compromise and change your own attitudes and behavior.
8. Try to maintain a certain spontaneity in your sexual life. Allow a sense of adventure to rekindle the relationship. If you can reestablish an active and satisfying sexual life at this point, you can both be certain that it will continue for many more years.
9. If he is coping with a midlife crisis symptom, focus on his strengths. But do not hand out empty praise. Instead find a real reason to praise him.
10. Do not adopt a motherly role toward him. Whereas sympathy and compassion are constructive, constant mothering and giving advice tend to diminish his sexual interest and ability to relate as husband.
11. Emphasize that the wife should not feel guilty when her husband develops any of the midlife crisis symptoms. It is not her fault. If handled with honesty and intelligence, the midlife crisis in men can be a positive turning point in a marriage, eventually creating a more constructive, satisfying, loving relationship.

Individuals considering midlife career/work changes must be able to assess their current job skills and applicability of them to new careers, explore alternatives within their current job position as well as external counseling services, and examine personal values. Career transition then becomes the response to seeking compatibility between self-image and the world of work (66). How the career change is negotiated depends in part on whether it is forced by external forces, such as job lay-off or technological advances, or voluntarily pursued because of value conflicts or as a means to personal, creative, economic, or social advancement. The person considering career change in life structure needs time, opportunity to talk, and help in working through the various facets of the situation.

Benefits from the midlife crisis include personality growth and deepening maturity because of personal introspection and desire to change behavior to feel better and improve one's life. Further, if the person in crisis can accept assistance, affection, and acceptance from loved ones, he/she can grow closer to them and relationships deepen as a result. Sometimes the changes made in relation to a second career can enhance social status, financial well-being, or a sense of independence. The concern about mortality can motivate the person to take better care of health, to take time to pursue new interests or reinitiate old relationships. The person can experience an invigorating rebirth, generating new energies and new commitments.

Religious and Moral Development

The middle-aged person continues to integrate new concepts from widened sources into a religious philosophy if he/she has gained the religious maturity described in Chapter 12. He/she becomes less dogmatic in his/her beliefs. Faith and trust in God or another source of spiritual strength are increased. Religion offers comfort and happiness. The person is able to deal effectively with the religious aspects of upcoming surgery and its possible effects, illness, death of parents, or unexpected tragedy.

The middle-ager may have become alienated from organized religion in early adulthood or may have drifted away from religious practices and spiritual study because of familial, occupational, and social role responsibilities. As the person becomes more introspective, studies self and life from new perspectives, ponders the meaning of life, and faces crises, he/she is likely to return to study of religious literature, practices of former years, and organized religious groups for strength, comfort, forgiveness, and joy. Spiritual beliefs and religion take on added importance. The middle-ager who becomes "born again" is likely to remain devout and active in his/her faith throughout life. If the person does not deepen spiritual insights, a sense of meaninglessness and despair is likely in old age.

Moral development is advanced whenever the person has an experience of sustained responsibility for the welfare of others. Middle age, if it is lived generatively, provides such an experience. While the cognitive awareness of higher principles of living develops in adolescence, consistent commitment to their ethical applications develops in adulthood after the person has had time and opportunity to meet personal needs and to establish self in the family and community. Further, the level of cognitive development sets the upper limits for moral potential. If the adult remains in the State of Concrete Operations, he/she is unlikely to move beyond the Conventional Level of moral development (law and order reasoning) since the Postconventional Level requires a deep and broad understanding of events and a critical reasoning ability (62).

Although Kohlberg's work on moral development was done on men, women generally come out at Stage 3 of the Conventional Level (Table 13–2), which emphasizes an interpersonal definition of morality rather than a societal definition of morality or an orientation to law and order. Perhaps the stage of moral development often seen in women, with concern for the well-being of others and a willingness to self-sacrifice for others' well-being, is an aspect of Stage 5 of the Post Conventional Level (62).

Loevinger sees middle age as the Autonomous Stage of Ego Development, when the person evolves principles for self apart from the social world. The person deals with the differences between personal needs, principles to live by, and duties demanded by society (69).

Gilligan, whose research centered on moral development in women, found that women define morality in terms of selfishness versus responsibility. Women subjects with high morality scores emphasized the importance of being responsible in behavior, of exercising care with and avoiding hurt to others. Men think more in terms of general justice and fairness; women think in terms of the needs of specific individuals. Gilligan's view of moral development is outlined in Table 13–2 according to three levels and the transition points from Level I to Level II and from Level II to Level III (38).

Developmental Tasks of the Middle-Aged Person

Each period of life differs from the others, offering new experiences and opportunities as well as new tasks to be surmounted. The developmental tasks of middle age have a biological basis in the gradual aging of the physical body, a cultural basis in social pressures and expectations, and an emotional origin in the individual lifestyle and self-concept that the mature adult has developed.

Table 13–2. Moral Development in Women

LEVEL	CHARACTERISTICS
I. *Orientation of Individual Survival*	Concentrates on what is practical and best for self.
Transition 1: *From Selfishness to Responsibility*	Realizes connection to others; thinks of responsible choice in terms of another as well as self.
II. *Goodness as Self-Sacrifice*	Sacrifices personal wishes and needs to fulfill others' wants and to have others think well of her. Feels responsible for others' actions; holds others responsible for her choices. Dependent position. Indirect efforts to control others often turns into manipulation through use of guilt.
Transition 2: *From Goodness to Truth*	Makes decisions on personal intentions and consequences of actions, rather than on how she thinks others will react. Takes into account needs of self and others. Wants to be good to others but also honest by being responsible to self.
III. *Morality of Nonviolence*	Establishes moral equality between self and others; assumes responsibility for choice in moral dilemmas. Follows injunction to hurt no one, including self, in all situations.

✔ The following developmental tasks should be accomplished by middle-aged people (8, 29, 74, 83, 87). Through your care, counsel, and teaching, you can assist your patients/clients to be aware of and to achieve these tasks.

1. Maintain or establish healthful life patterns.
2. Discover and develop new satisfactions as a mate, give support to mate, enjoy joint activities, and develop a sense of unity and abiding intimacy.
3. Help growing and grown children to become happy and responsible adults and relinquish the central position in their affections, free the self from emotional dependence on children, take pride in their accomplishments, stand by to assist as needed, and accept their friends and mates.
4. Create a pleasant, comfortable home, appropriate to values, interests, time, energy, and resources; give, receive, and exchange hospitality; and take pride in accomplishments of self and spouse.
5. Find pleasure in generativity and recognition in work if employed; gain knowledge, proficiency, and wisdom; be able to lead or follow; balance work with other roles; and prepare for eventual retirement.
6. Reverse roles with aging parents and parents-in-law, assist them as needed without domineering, and act as a buffer between demands of aging parents and needs of young adults; prepare emotionally for the eventual death of parents, unless they are already deceased.
7. Maintain a standard of living related to values, needs, and financial resources.
8. Achieve mature social and civic responsibility; be informed as a citizen; give time, energy, and resources to causes beyond self and home. Work cooperatively with others in the common responsibilities of citizenship; encourage others in their citizenship; stand for democratic practices and the welfare of the group as a whole in issues when vested interests may be at stake.
9. Develop or maintain an active organizational membership, deriving from it pleasure and a sense of belonging; refuse conflicting or too burdensome invitations with poise; work through intraorganizational tensions, power systems, and personality problems by becoming a mature statesperson in a diplomatic role, leading when necessary.
10. Accept and adjust to the physical changes of middle age, maintain healthful ways of living, attend to personal grooming, relish maturity.
11. Make an art of friendship; cherish old friends and choose new; enjoy an active social life with friends, including friends of both sexes and of various ages; accept at least a few friends into close sharing of feelings to help avoid self-absorption.
12. Use leisure creatively and with satisfaction without yielding too much to social pressures and styles; learn to do some things well enough to become known for them among family, friends, and associates; enjoy use of talents; share some leisure-time activities with a mate or others and balance leisure activities with active and passive, collective and solitary, service-motivated and self-indulgent pursuits.
13. Continue to formulate a philosophy of life and religious or philosophical affiliation, discovering new depths and meanings in God or a creator that include but also go beyond the fellowship of a particular religious denomination; gain satisfaction from altruistic activities or the concerns of a particular denomination, invest self in significant causes and movements, recognize the finiteness of life.
14. Prepare for retirement with financial arrangements, development of hobbies and leisure activities, and rework philosophy and values.

✔ The single or widowed middle-agers will have basically the same developmental tasks but must find a sense of intimate sharing with friends or relatives.

✔ Peck sees the issues or conflicts that the person must work through in middle age as encompassing the following (93):

1. *Valuing wisdom gained from living and experience versus valuing physical powers and youth.* The person needs to accept his/her age, that youth cannot be regained, and that while physical strength and power may diminish, wisdom may accomplish more than physical strength anyway.
2. *Socializing versus sexualizing in human relationships.* The middle-ager, while still active sexually, now sees and relates to people as humans rather than just on the basis of men or women. The person relates to others without the gender self-consciousness of adolescence or young-young adulthood and sees the intrinsic dignity and worth of all people as social and spiritual beings.
3. *Emotional flexibility versus emotional impoverishment.* The middle-ager, although often accused of being rigid and unable to change, remains accepting of and empathic to others, open to people of different backgrounds, and open to changing personal behavior. The person becomes emotionally impoverished only if he/she withdraws from others, avoids learning from experience, refuses to change, or demonstrates the self-absorption described by Erikson (32).
4. *Mental flexibility versus mental rigidity.* The middle-ager, although accused of being closed to new ideas and excessively cautious, remains open to learning and flexible in problem-solving strategies. The person becomes mentally rigid if he/she avoids new

Table 13–3. Selected Nursing Diagnoses Related to Middle Age[a]

PATTERN 1: EXCHANGING	PATTERN 6: MOVING
Altered Nutrition: More than body requirements	Impaired Physical Mobility
Altered Nutrition: Less than body requirements	Activity Intolerance
Altered Nutrition: Potential for more than body requirements	Fatigue
Potential for Infection	Potential Activity Intolerance
Potential for Injury	Sleep Pattern Disturbance
Potential for Trauma	Diversional Activity Deficit
Potential Impaired Skin Integrity	Impaired Home Maintenance Management
	Altered Health Maintenance
PATTERN 2: COMMUNICATING	PATTERN 7: PERCEIVING
Impaired Verbal Communication	Body Image Disturbance
PATTERN 3: RELATING	Self Esteem Disturbance
Impaired Social Interaction	Chronic Low Self Esteem
Social Isolation	Situational Low Self Esteem
Altered Role Performance	Sensory/Perceptual Alterations
Potential Altered Parenting	Hopelessness
Altered Family Processes	Powerlessness
Parental Role Conflict	PATTERN 8: KNOWING
Altered Sexuality Patterns	Knowledge Deficit
PATTERN 4: VALUING	PATTERN 9: FEELING
Spiritual Distress	Pain
PATTERN 5: CHOOSING	Chronic Pain
Ineffective Individual Coping	Dysfunctional Grieving
Impaired Adjustment	Anticipatory Grieving
Defensive Coping	Potential for Violence: Self-directed or directed at others
Ineffective Denial	Post-Trauma Response
Ineffective Family Coping: Disabling	Anxiety
Ineffective Family Coping: Compromised	Fear
Family Coping: Potential for Growth	
Decisional Conflict	
Health Seeking Behaviors	

[a]Other NANDA nursing diagnoses are applicable to the ill middle-ager.
Source: NANDA Approved Nursing Diagnostic Categories, *Nursing Diagnosis Newsletter*, 15, no. 1 (1988), 1–3.

experiences or learning opportunities or denies social, educational, or technological changes.

✔ NURSING APPLICATIONS

Your role in caring for the middle-aged person and family has been described throughout the chapter. Assessment, utilizing knowledge presented in this chapter, is the basis for formulating *nursing diagnosis.* Nursing diagnoses that may be applicable to the middle-ager are listed in Table 13–3. Interventions may involve health promotion or direct care measures that are described throughout the chapter to assist the person and family in meeting physical, emotional, cognitive, spiritual, and social needs.

Transition to Later Maturity

The middle-ager has developed a sense of the life cycle; through introspection, he/she has gained a heightened sensitivity to the personal position within a complex social environment. Life is no longer seen as an infinite stretch of time into the future. The person anticipates and accepts the inevitable sequence of events that occur as the human matures, ages, and dies. The middle-ager realizes that the course of his/her life will be similar to the lives of others. Gender differences between men and women diminish in reality and perception. Turning points affect all and are inescapable. Personal mortality, achievements and failures, and personal strengths and limits must be faced if the person is to be prepared emotionally and developmentally for later maturity and the personal aging process. The person realizes that the direction in life has been set by prior decisions related to occupation, marriage, family life, and having or not having children. While occupation and lifestyle can be changed, at least to some extent, the results of other earlier decisions cannot be changed. The consequences must be faced and resolved. The middle-ager realizes he/she may not achieve all dreams, but remaining open to opportunities along the way may enable the person to achieve accomplishments never fantasized which are equally meaningful (83–87).

For example, if the young adult woman focused on career and did not marry and have children, at age 50 she may still marry, but having children—or adoption—is less likely. Having no children means not being a grandparent in old age. The need to be a parent, grandparent, or to nurture has to be met in another way. In turn, the single or childless middle-age woman may realize that she has been nurturing a larger number of people than some middle-age women who focused their attention solely on the children.

The person in late midlife realizes that life's developmental markers and crises call forth changes in self-concept and sense of identity, necessitate incorporation of new social roles and behaviors, and precipitate new adaptations. But they do not destroy the sense of continuity within the person from youth to old age. This adaptability and sense of continuity is essential for the achievement of ego integrity in the last years of life.

References

1. Albrecht, G., and H. Gift, Adult Socialization: Ambiguity and Adult Life Crises, in *Life Span Developmental Psychology: Normative Life Crisis,* eds. N. Datan and L. Ginsberg. New York: Academic Press, 1975. 237–251.
2. Angel, Marc, *The Orphaned Adult: Confronting the Death of a Parent,* New York: Human Sciences Press, 1987.
3. Arlin, P. K., Cognitive Development in Adulthood: A Fifth Stage?, *Developmental Psychology,* 11 (1975), 602–606.
4. Atunes, C. M., et al., Endometrial Cancer and Estrogen Use, *New England Journal of Medicine,* 300 (January 4, 1979), 9–13.
5. Balfour, Katharine, Coping With the Male Mid-Life Crisis, *Family Circle,* March 17, 1981, 17.
6. Bates, Barbara, *A Guide to Physical Examination* (3rd ed.). Philadelphia: J. B. Lippincott, 1983.
7. Berglas, Charlotte, *Mid-Life Crisis.* Lancaster, PA: Technomic Publishing, 1987.
8. Blocker, Donald, *Developmental Counseling.* New York: The Ronald Press Company, 1966.
9. Brody, Elaine, Women in the Middle and Family Help to Older People, *The Gerontologist,* 21, no. 5 (1981), 471–480.
10. Brody, Elaine, Parent Care as a Normative Family Stress, *The Gerontologist,* 25, no. 1 (1985), 19–29.
11. Brody, Elaine, et al., Work Status and Parent Care: A Comprehensive Study of Four Groups of Women, *The Gerontologist,* 27, no. 3 (1987), 201–208.
12. Brody, Jacob, Mary Farmer, and Lon White, Absence of Menopausal Effect on Hip Fracture Occurrence in White Females, *American Journal of Public Health,* 74, no. 12 (1984), 1397–1398.
13. Buchaman, Robert, The Widow and the Widower, in *Concerning Death: A Practical Guide for the Living,* ed. Earl Grollman. Boston: Beacon Press, 1974, 287–311.
14. Buhler, Charlotte, The Developmental Structure of Goal Setting in Group and Individual Studies, in *The Course of Human Life,* eds. C. Buhler and F. Massarik. New York: Springer Publishing Company, 1968.
15. Cameron, Paul, Age Parameters of Young Adult, Middle-Aged, Old, and Aged, *Journal of Gerontology,* 24 (1969), 201–202.
16. Cantor, Marjorie, Strain Among Caregivers: A Study of

Experience in the United States, *The Gerontologist*, 23, no. 6 (1983), 597–604.
17. Carlson, Elliot, The Phony War, *Modern Maturity* (February–March, 1987), 34–44.
18. Cicerelli, Victor, A Comparison of Helping Behavior to Elderly Parents of Adult Children with Intact and Disrupted Marriages, *The Gerontologist*, 23, no. 6 (1983), 619–625.
19. Clark, Noreen, and William Rakowski, Family Caregivers of Older Adults: Improving Helping Skills, *The Gerontologist*, 23, no. 6 (1983), 637–641.
20. Cohn, Victor, Estrogen Linked to Lower Death Rates in Women, *The Washington Post*, February 22, 1983, p. 3.
21. Colarusso, Calvin, and Robert Nemeroff, *Adult Development*. New York: Plenum Press, 1981.
22. Collison, Carol, and Sandra Miller, Using Images of the Future in Grief Work, *Image*, 19, no. 1 (1987), 9–11.
23. Coping with the Male Mid-Life Crisis, *Family Circle* (March 17, 1981), 17.
24. Cosby, Bill, *Time Flies*. Garden City, New York: Doubleday, 1987.
25. Cross, K. Patricia, *Adults As Learners*. San Francisco: Jossey-Bass, 1981.
26. Dennis, W., Creative Production Between the Ages of 20 and 80, *Journal of Gerontology*, 21, no. 1 (1966), 8.
27. Diekelman, Nancy, and Karen Galloway, The Middle Years: A Time of Change, *American Journal of Nursing*, 75, no. 6 (June, 1975), 994–996.
28. Dresen, Sheila, The Middle Years: The Sexually Active Middle Adult, *American Journal of Nursing*, 75, no. 6 (June, 1975), 1001–1005.
29. Duvall, Evelyn, and Brent Miller, *Marriage and Family Development* (6th ed.). New York: Harper & Row, 1984.
30. Engel, George, *Psychological Development in Health and Disease*. Philadelphia: W. B. Saunders, 1962.
31. Engel, Nancy, Menopausal Stage, Current Life Change, Attitude Toward Women's Roles, and Perceived Health Status, *Nursing Research*, 36, no. 6 (1987), 353–356.
32. Erikson, Erik, *Childhood and Society* (2nd ed.). New York: W. W. Norton, 1963.
33. Ferguson, Tamara, Decision Making Without a Partner, *Archives of the Foundation of Thanatology*, 2, no. 1 (April, 1970), 21–22.
34. Frank, Ellen, What Are Nurses Doing to Help PMS Patients? *American Journal of Nursing*, 86, no. 2 (1986), 137–140.
35. Friday, Nancy, *My Mother, Myself*. New York: Dell, 1977.
36. George, Linda, and Lisa Gwyther, Caregiver Well Being: A Multidimensional Examination of Family Caregivers of Demented Adults, *The Gerontologist*, 26, no. 3 (1986), 253–259.
37. Getty, Cathleen, and Winifred Humphreys, *Understanding the Family: Stress and Change in American Family Life*. New York: Appleton-Century-Crofts, 1981.
38. Gilligan, C., In a Different Voice: Women's Conceptions of Self and of Mortality, *Harvard Educational Review*, 47, no. 4 (1977), 481–517.
39. Goldstein, Vida, Gretcher Regnery, and Edward Wellin, Caretaker Role Fatigue, *Nursing Outlook*, 29, no. 1 (1981), 24–34.
40. Golan, Naomi, *Passing Through Transitions*. New York: The Free Press, 1981.
41. Gould, Roger, The Phases of Adult Life: A Study in Developmental Psychology, *American Journal of Psychiatry*, 129, no. 5 (1972), 521–531.
42. Gould, Roger, Adult Life Stages: Growth Toward Self-Tolerance, *Psychology Today*, 8, no. 7 (February, 1975), 74–78.
43. Gould, Roger, Transformation in Mid-Life, *New York University Education Quarterly*, 10, no. 2 (1979), 2–9.
44. Grollman, Earl, ed., *Concerning Death: A Practical Guide for the Living*. Boston: Beacon Press, 1974.
45. Guyton, Arthur, *Textbook of Medical Physiology* (7th ed.) Philadelphia: W. B. Saunders, 1986.
46. Hanson, Sandra, William Sauer, and Wayne Seelbach, Racial and Cohort Variations in Filial Responsibility Norms, *The Geronotologist*, 23, no. 6 (1983), 626–631.
47. Heath, D., Model of the Maturing Person, in *Growing Up in College*, ed. D. Heath. San Francisco: Jossey-Bass, 1968, 4–17.
48. Helsing, Knud, Moyses Szklo, and George Comstock, Factors Associated with Mortality After Widowhood, *American Journal of Public Health*, 71, no. 8 (1981), 802–809.
49. Hershel, Jack, Alexander Walker, and Kenneth Rothman, The Epidemic of Endometrial Cancer: A Commentary, *American Journal of Public Health*, 70, no. 2 (1980), 264–267.
50. Hoole, Axalla J., Robert A. Greenberg, and C. Glenn Pickard, *Patient Care Guidelines for Nurse Practitioners* (3rd ed.). Boston: Little, Brown, 1988.
51. Irwin, Theodore. *Male Menopause: Crisis in the Middle Years*. New York: Public Affairs Pamphlets, 1982.
52. Jahoda, Marie, *Current Concepts of Positive Mental Health*. New York: Basic Books, 1958.
53. Jarrett, William, Caregiving Within Kinship Systems: Is Affection Really Necessary? *The Gerontologist*, 25, no. 1 (1985), 5–10.
54. Johnson, Colleen, Dyadic Family Relations and Social Support, *The Gerontologist*, 23, no. 4 (1983), 377–383.
55. Jung, Carl, *Modern Man in Search of a Soul*. New York: Harcourt, Brace, and World, 1933.
56. Kaluger, G., and M. Kaluger, *Human Development: The Life Span* (3rd ed.). St. Louis: C. V. Mosby, 1984.
57. Kangas, J., and K. Bradway, Intelligence at Middle Age: A 38-Year Follow-Up, *Developmental Psychology*, 5, no. 2 (1971), 333–337.
58. Kaplan, Sheila, The New Generation Gap, *Common Cause Magazine* (March–April, 1987), 13–15.

59. Knowles, Malcolm, *The Adult Learner: A Neglected Species* (2nd ed.). Houston: Gulf Publishing, 1978.
60. Knox, Allan, *Adult Development and Learning*. San Francisco: Jossey-Bass, 1978.
61. Kohl, Linda, Husband May Be the Key to His Wife's Career, *St. Louis Globe-Democrat*, January 5, 1977, Sec. A., p. 16.
62. Kohlberg, L. *Recent Research in Moral Development*. New York: Holt, Rinehart & Winston, 1977.
63. LaRocco, Susan, and Denise Polit, Women's Knowledge about the Menopause, *Nursing Research*, 29, no. 1 (1980), 10–13.
64. Lauver, Diane, Irregular Bleeding in Women: Causes and Nursing Interventions, *American Journal of Nursing*, 3, no. 3 (1983), 396–401.
65. Levinson, Daniel, *The Seasons of a Man's Life*. New York: Alfred A. Knopf, 1978.
66. Lidz, Theodore, *The Person: His and Her Development Throughout the Life Cycle* (2nd ed.). New York: Basic Books, 1983.
67. Linden, M., and D. Courtney, The Human Life Cycle and Its Interruptions: A Psychologic Hypothesis—Studies in Gerontologic Human Relations I, *American Journal of Psychiatry*, 109, no. 1 (1953) 906–915.
68. Lindeman, Eric, Symptomology and Management of Acute Grief, *American Journal of Psychiatry*, 101 (1944), 141–148.
69. Loevinger, J., *Ego Development*. San Francisco: Jossey-Bass, 1976.
70. Lowenthal, Marjorie, and David Chiriboga, Transition to the Empty Nest: Crisis, Challenge, or Relief? *Archives of General Psychiatry*, 26, no. 1 (1972), 8–14.
71. Managing the Menopause, *Newsweek* (February 9, 1981), 92–93.
72. Martyn, Pamela, If You Guessed Cardiovascular Disease, Guess Again, *American Journal of Nursing*, 82, no. 7 (1982), 1238–1241.
73. Masters, William, and Virginia Johnson, *Human Sexual Response*. Boston: Little, Brown, 1966.
74. McCoy, Vivian, Adult Life Cycle Tasks/Adult Continuing Education Program Response, *Lifelong Learning in the Adult Years* (October, 1977), 16.
75. Mead, Margaret, *Culture and Commitment: A Study of the Generation Gap*. Garden City, N.Y.: Natural History Press/Doubleday and Company, 1970.
76. Merriam, Sharan, Middle-Age: A Review of the Literature and Its Implications for Educational Intervention, *Adult Education*, 29, no. 1 (1978), 39–54.
77. Miles, Helen, and Dorothea Hays, Widowhood, *American Journal of Nursing*, 75, no. 2 (February, 1975), 280–282.
78. Moshman, David, John Glover, and Roger Bruning, *Developmental Psychology*. Boston: Little, Brown, 1987.
79. Muhlenkamp, Ann, Margaret Waller, and Ann Bourne, Attitudes Toward Women in Menopause: A Vignette Approach, *Nursing Research*, 32, no. 1 (1983), 20–23.
80. Murray, Ruth, Body Image Development in Adulthood, *Nursing Clinics of North America*, 7, no. 4 (1972), 622–624.
81. ——, and M. Marilyn Huelskoetter, *Psychiatric/Mental Health Nursing: Giving Emotional Care* (2nd ed.). Englewood Cliffs, N.J.: Prentice-Hall, 1987.
82. ——, and Judith Zentner, *Nursing Concepts for Health Promotion* (3rd ed.). Englewood Cliffs, N.J.: Prentice-Hall, 1985.
83. Neugarten, Bernice, The Awareness of Middle Age, in *Middle Age*, ed. Roger Owen. London: British Broadcasting Corporation, 1967.
84. ——, Women's Attitudes Toward Menopause, in *Middle Age and Aging*, ed. Bernice Neugarten. Chicago: University of Chicago Press, 1968.
85. ——, Adaptation and the Life Cycle, *The Counseling Psychologist*, 6, no. 1 (1976), 16–20.
86. ——, and Nancy Datan, Sociological Perspectives on the Life Cycle, in *Life Span Developmental Psychology: Personality and Socialization*, eds. P. Bates and K. Schail, New York: Academic Press, 1973, 53–59.
87. ——, and J. Moore, The Changing Age-Status System, in *Middle Age and Aging*, ed. Bernice Neugarten. Chicago: University of Chicago Press, 1968.
88. Nolan, Jo Ellen, Developmental Concern and the Health of Midlife Women, *Nursing Clinics of North America*, 21, no. 1 (1986), 151–159.
89. Nolen, William, Male Menopause: Myth or Mid-Life Reality? *Reader's Digest*, 60, no. 6 (1981), 181–184.
90. Notham, Malkah, Adult Life Cycles: Changing Roles and Changing Hormones, in *The Psychology of Sex Differences and Sex Roles*, ed. J. Parsons. Washington, D.C.: Hemisphere Publishing, 1980.
91. Osteoporosis: Estrogen Connection Clearer, *American Journal of Nursing*, 88, no. 1 (1988), 13.
92. Pearson, Linda, Climacteric, *American Journal of Nursing*, 82, no. 7 (1982), 1098–1102.
93. Peck, R. C., Psychological Developments in the Second Half of Life, in *Middle Age and Aging*, ed. Bernice Neugarten. Chicago: University of Chicago Press, 1968.
94. Peretz, David, Reaction to Loss, in *Loss and Grief: Psychological Management in Medical Practice*, eds. B. Schoenberg, A. Carr, D. Peretz, and A. Kutscher. New York: Columbia University Press, 1970, 20–35.
95. Petersen, Norma, Is the Rebellion Over?, *Parade* (January 31, 1982), 10–11.
96. Pike, Ruth, and Myrtle Brown, *Nutrition: An Integrated Approach* (2nd ed.). New York: John Wiley, 1975.
97. Powell, R., and R. Pohndorf, Comparison of Adult Exercisers and Nonexercisers on Fluid Intelligence and Selected Physiological Variables, *Research Quarterly*, 42, no. 1 (1971), 70–77.
98. Prock, Valencia, The Mid-Stage Woman, *American Journal of Nursing*, 75, no. 6 (June, 1975), 1019–1022.
99. Robinson, Betsy, and Majda Thurnber, Taking Care of

Parents: A Family Circle Transition, *The Gerontologist,* 19, no. 6 (1979), 586–593.
100. Schuster, C., and S. Ashburn, *The Process of Human Development (2nd ed.).* Boston: Little, Brown, 1986.
101. Sheehy, Gail, *Passages.* New York: Bantam Books, 1974.
102. Silverstone, Barbara, and Helen Hyman, *You and Your Aging Parent.* New York: Pantheon Books, 1976.
103. Sinott, J., Everyday Thinking and Piagetian Operativity in Adults, *Human Development,* 18 (1975), 430–433.
104. Sloan, Leonard, What Financial Facts Should a Wife Know? *American Journal of Nursing,* 75, no. 7 (July, 1975), 1202.
105. Soldo, Beth, and Jaana Myllyluoma, Caregivers Who Live With Dependent Elderly, *The Gerontologist,* 23, no. 6 (1983), 1605–1610.
106. Speroff, Leon, PMS—Looking for New Answers to an Old Problem, *Contemporary OB-Gyn,* August, 1983, 102–127.
107. St. George, Joyce, and Barbara Dicicco-Bloom, Using Dramatizations to Train Caregivers for the Elderly, *Nursing Outlook,* 33, no. 5 (1985), 302–304.
108. Toth, Susan, and Andre Toth, Empathic Intervention With the Widow, *American Journal of Nursing,* 80, no. 9 (1980), 1652–1654.
109. Travis, C., The Freedom To Change, *Prime Time* (October, 1980), 27–33.
110. Troll, L., *Early and Middle Adulthood.* Monterey, Calif.: Brooks/Cole, 1975.
111. U.S. Bureau of Census, *Statistical Abstract of the United States: 1981* (102nd ed.). Washington, D.C.: Government Printing Office, 1981.
112. Vaccines for Adult Diseases, *Newsweek* (October 12, 1987), 92–93.
113. Vaillant, G., How the Best and the Brightest Came of Age, *Psychology Today,* 11, no. 9 (1977), 34ff.
114. _____, The Normal Boy in Later Life: How Adaptative Fosters Growth, *Harvard Magazine,* 55, no. 6 (1977), 234–239.
115. Wadsworth, Barry, *Piaget's Theory of Cognitive and Affective Development* (3rd ed.). New York: David McKay, 1984.
116. Warner, Sandra, A Comparative Study of Widows' and Widowers' Perceived Social Support During the Past Year of Bereavement, *Archives of Psychiatric Nursing,* 1, no. 4 (1987), 241–250.
117. Weaver, Terrie, and Richard Millman, Sleep Apnea, *American Journal of Nursing,* 86, no. 2 (1986), 146–150.
118. Weeks, John, and J. Cuellar, The Role of Family Members in the Helping Networks of Older People, *The Gerontologist,* 21, no. 4 (1981), 388–394.
119. Wood, John, Labors of Love, *Modern Maturity* (August–September, 1987), 28ff.
120. *Your Feet After Fifty.* Miami Beach, Florida: Foot Facts Publications, n.d.
121. Zarit, Steven, Pamela Todd, and Judy Zarit, Subjective Burden of Husbands and Wives as Caregivers: A Longitudinal Study, *The Gerontologist,* 26, no. 3 (1986), 260–266.

14

Assesssment and Health Promotion for the Person in Later Maturity

Study of this chapter will enable you to

1. Define terms and theories of aging related to understanding of the person in later maturity.
2. Explore personal and societal attitudes about growing old and your role in promoting positive attitudes.
3. Contrast relationships in the late years with those of other developmental eras, including with spouse, offspring, grandchildren, other family members, friends, pets, and other networks.
4. Contrast the status of either singlehood or widow(er) in later maturity to that status in early and midadulthood.
5. Describe signs and contributing factors to elder abuse and contrast with child and spouse abuse.
6. Describe physiological adaptive mechanisms of aging and influences on sexuality, related health problems, and assessment and intervention to promote and maintain health, comfort, and safety.
7. Discuss the cognitive, emotional, body-image, and spiritual development and characteristics of the aged person, the interrelationship of these, and your role in promoting health and a positive self-concept.
8. Contrast the adaptive mechanisms used by the person in this period with those used in other periods of life.
9. Describe the developmental crisis of later maturity, the relationship to previous developmental crises, and your role in helping the person meet this crisis.
10. List the developmental tasks for this era, and describe your contribution to accomplishments of these.
11. Identify changing home, family, social, and work/leisure situations of this person and your responsibility in helping the person face retirement, loss of loved ones, and changes in roles and living arrangements. Discuss selection of an adequate nursing home or residence for seniors.
12. Describe major federal, state, and local programs to assist the elderly financially, socially, and in health care, and describe your professional and personal responsibility in this regard.
13. Demonstrate remotivation technique and discuss the value, purpose, and use of this and other group processes with the elderly.
14. Summarize the needs of the elderly, standards of nursing care to assist in meeting those needs, and future trends in care of the person in later maturity.
15. Assess and work effectively with a person in later maturity, using the information presented in this chapter, and showing empathy and genuine interest.

I really don't like being labeled a golden-ager. I acknowledge my age and my limits, but I certainly didn't turn incompetent at 65.

When does older maturity begin? The beginning age for this period of the life span is actually dependent upon many individualized factors. However, to make the study of this age group easier, a specific age needs to be identified. Historically, it was the decision to have age 65 as the eligible age for receipt of Social

Key Terms

Aging
Biological age
Social age
Psychosocial age
Senescense
Later maturity
   Young-old
   Old-old
Gerontology
Geriatrics
Ageism
Wear and Tear Theory
Deprivation Theories
Accumulation Theories
Biologic Clock Theories
Immunity Theory
Continuity Theory
Erikson's Epigenetic
   Theory
Peck's Theory
Disengagement Theory
Activity Theory
Lentigo senilis
Presbyopia
Cataracts
Glaucoma
Arcus senilis
Presbycusis
Herpes zoster (shingles)
Parkinson's disease
Alzheimer's disease
Congestive heart failure
Chronic occlusive arterial
   disease
Stasis ulcer
Pitting edema

Brawny edema
Chronic obstructive pulmonary disease
Bronchitis
Bronchoconstriction
Emphysema
Pernicious anemia
Secondary anemia
Chronic lymphocytic leukemia
Hodgkin's disease
Benign prostatic hypertrophy
Osteoporosis
Osteoarthritis
Ego integrity
Despair/self-disgust
Ego differentiation
Body transcendence
Ego transcendence
Regression
Isolation
Compartmentalization
Denial
Rationalization
Somatization
Counterphobia
Rigidity
Sublimation
Crystallized intelligence
Fluid intelligence
Leisure time
Prosumers
Translocation syndrome
Remotivation

Security benefits that helped to establish the beginning age for this age group.

Studies consistently show that most people 65 years and older do not consider themselves old. They consider themselves middle-aged, or even young. However, members of ethnic minorities and lower socioeconomic levels view onset of old age as taking place earlier.

In 1860, 2.7 percent of the population in the United States was over 65 years of age (101). This figure changed dramatically during the next 125 years. By 1985, there were 28.5 million people in this age group, 12 percent of the population. Furthermore, a female reaching age 65 in 1985 had a life expectancy of an additional 18.6 years. A male reaching 65 had a life expectancy of another 14.6 years. With these life expectancies, it is projected that by 2030 there will be about 65 million people or 21.2 percent of the U.S. population who will be 65 years of age or over (161). This continued aging trend of the population requires changes in all aspects of our social structure—employment, housing, education, leisure activities, transportation, industrial development, and health care.

Definitions

Because the terms describing this age group are not clearly defined by the general public nor health care professionals, it is important that we clarify some of the terms to be used in this chapter.

Aging *is a process, which begins at conception and ends at death, of growing old.*

Biological age *is the person's present position with respect to the potential life span, which may be younger or older than chronological age,* and encompasses measures of functional capacities of vital organ systems.

Social age *refers to roles and habits of the person with respect to other members of society, which results from the person's life course through various social institutions.* Social age may be age appropriate, or older or younger, than that of most people in the social group. Social age includes such aspects as the person's type of dress, language, usage, and social deference to people in leadership positions.

Psychological age *refers to behavioral capacity of the person to adapt to changing environmental demands and includes capacities of memory, learning, intelligence, skills, feelings, and motivations for exercising behavioral control or self-regulation.*

Senescence *is the mental and physical decline associated with the aging process.*

Later maturity *is the last major segment of the life span; the stage begins at the age of 65 or 70.* Some authors divide this group into *young-old (65 or 70 to 80 years of age)* and *old-old (older than 80 years of age; a stage often beginning as late as mideighties)* (78).

Gerontology *is the study of the individual in later maturity and the aging process from a physiological, pathological, psychological, sociological, and economic point of view.*

Geriatrics *is a medical specialty concerned with the physiological and pathological changes of the individual in later maturity, and includes study and treatment of the health problems of this age group.*

Later maturity appears to be divided into three sequential segments. The first segment may be regarded as a *social-political* or *cultural-organizational perspective*. Offspring are in a creative period, and the mature adult is in the ruling, protective stance as he/she assumes parental hierarchical leadership over the family of families. The older person becomes concerned with the creation, ordering, and maintenance of a larger society. The second segment is characterized *by a reaffirmation of social, moral, and ethical standards* which are necessary for establishment of pacific relationships among the oncoming generations as they are involved in rendering decisions, planning, erecting social guideposts, and selecting subordinate leaders. The judgmental functions of the mind are most highly developed at this time, created out of actual and vicarious experience with conflict situations and from cultural learning and values. The last segment of psychic maturity involves *retrospective examination*, the need to correlate the present with the past to determine the true nature of accomplishments, errors, and rediscoveries. Cultural vision is at its broadest possible development, embracing one nearly complete life cycle and its interrelatedness with a multitude of other life cycles. The person compares and contrasts his/her values with cultural values and through reasoning and intuition evaluates meaning and purpose and has an increased interest in the history of human development. Values of the adolescent are movement, agility, quantitative productivity, exhibitionistic sexual attractiveness, and artfulness. In contrast, values of the older adult are deliberation, caution, equality, modesty, and loyalty. Whereas the adolescent views self as the ambitious master of a dimly concerned manhood, the older adult views self with real humility as at least a participant in and at most a contributor to the improvement of society (121).

Societal Perspectives

I may be old and wrinkled on the outside but I'm young and vulnerable on the inside.

Ageism *refers to any attitude, action, or institutional structure that discriminates against individuals on the basis of their age.* Ageist attitudes concerning older adults are not new in the United States. Even during colonial days, the elderly were categorized as unnecessary and burdensome (101, 198).

In the United States, old age is frequently characterized as a time of dependence and disease. Negative presentation of the older adults in movies, books, and magazines, in jokes, and on television contribute to negative beliefs and attitudes (68). Society's fear of the changes associated with aging such as gray hair, hearing loss, wrinkles, loss of muscle tone, slowness, and approaching death also contributes to negative attitudes.

There are numerous unproven *myths* and age-related *stereotypes* that pervade American culture.

These myths and stereotypes obscure the truth and may prevent us from achieving our own potential as we grow older. Society stereotypes the older adult as being asexual, unemployable, unintelligent, and socially incompetent. Statements such as "You can't teach old dogs new tricks" and "dirty old men and women" typify the feelings of many. Instead of seeking the truth, most individuals accept myths that have been perpetuated through the years. Some of these myths follow: (1) most older people are institutionalized; (2) old age brings senility or feeblemindedness; (3) old people cannot learn; (4) all old people are similar, and (5) the next generation of older adults will be the same as this generation (53, 184). *Let us consider the reality of each of these myths.*

1. Most older people are institutionalized: *Only about 5 percent* of older adults are actually in institutions. In 1985, the majority (67 percent) of noninstitutionalized older adults lived in a family setting; 30 percent lived alone (161, 184).
2. Old age brings senility or feeblemindedness: Senility is *not* a natural part of the aging process. Senility describes a disease process whose signs and symptoms range from mild confusion and memory loss to severe debilitating emotional disorders. Only 5 percent of older adults show serious mental impairment and only 10 percent demonstrate even mild to moderate memory loss (53).
3. Old people cannot learn: Older adults *can* and *do* learn. However, they may need a longer time period in which to respond to questions and stimuli. When learning problems occur, they are usually associated with a disease process (84).
4. All old people are similar: America's older adults are *quite diverse*. This segment of the life span covers more years than any other segment—sometimes more than 35 years. The older people are, the more varied their physical capabilities, personal style, economic status, and lifestyle preferences.
5. The next generation of older adults will be the same as this generation: The next generation will be better educated, healthier, more mobile, more youthful in appearance, more accustomed to lifestyle change and technology, and more outspoken. The world is changing so quickly that each successive generation is *vastly different* from the ones that came before (53).

Many of the myths and stereotypes associated with aging are culturally determined. The older adult in America lives in a culture oriented to youth, productivity, and rapid pace. Because of this orientation, older Americans may feel that they are not respected, valued, or needed. Cultures and ethnic groups influence the role of the older adult in family relationships and determine health practices. For example, with the Afro-American, aging and death are viewed as natural processes; the older family members are held in esteem. In Asian cultures, the older adults have an important role and the young are expected to respect and care for them. Westernized children may have difficulty accepting this role. Many older adults continue to follow health practices that are linked to their cultural heritage. Respect for these health practices and healing methods must be shown (68, 184).

Theories of Aging

While biological and psychosocial theories of aging have been proposed, the specific cause of aging is unknown.

Biological Theories

Biological theories can be categorized as genetic, nongenetic cellular, and physiological.

Genetic Theories Genetic theories such as *DNA damage theories, random error theory, and somatic mutation by radiation* propose that aging results from change or damage to the genetic information involved in cellular protein formation.

Nongenetic Cellular Theories. These suggest that changes occur in the cellular proteins after their formation. Nongenetic theories include the wear and tear theory, deprivation theories, accumulation theories, free radical theory, and cross-linkage theory. The **Wear and Tear Theory** is associated with the work of Hans Selye. According to this theory, *body systems wear out due to the stress of life*. This theory does not take into consideration the self-repair mechanisms of a living organism. **Deprivation Theories** assume that *aging is caused by deprivation of essential nutrients and oxygen to cells of the body*. **Accumulation Theories** suggest that *substances such as waste materials and lipofuscin accumulate in the cells of living organisms*. These substances interfere with cellular metabolism and ultimately cause cell death.

Physiological Theories. These theories explain aging on the basis of a breakdown of an organ system or impairment in physiological control mechanisms. The **Biological Clock Theory** suggests that *each organism contains genes that control the speed at which metabolic processes are performed. These genes act as a genetic clock*, dictating the occurrence of aging and dying. The **Immunity Theory** proposes that *mutations occur within some cells during the aging process. These mutations result in the formation of proteins that are treated as foreign proteins by the body*. This reaction by the body triggers the formation of autoantibodies which are specific for self-tissue or serum components. In addition to this reaction by the body, the production of antibodies by the immune system diminishes after adolescence (68, 88, 101, 106, 173, 198).

Psychosocial Theories

Just as one biological theory does not adequately address biological aging, one single **psychosocial theory** of aging is not adequate to explain psychological or social aging. The **Continuity Theory** proposes that an *individual's patterns of behavior are the result of a lifetime of experiences, and aging is the continuation of these lifelong adjustments* or personality patterns (26, 172).

Developmental Theories. Several **developmental theories** have addressed psychosocial aging. **Erikson's Epigenetic Theory** suggests that *successful personality development in later life depends on the ability to resolve the psychosocial crises known as integrity versus despair* (58). **Peck's Theory** *hypothesizes that there are three psychological developmental tasks of old age: ego differentiation versus work-role preoccupation, body transcendence versus body preoccupation, and ego transcendence versus ego preoccupation* (154). Robert Havighurst presents several major developmental tasks that must be mastered or achieved in order to meet the developmental needs of later maturity. He uses an eclectic approach that combines previously developed concepts into one theory. According to all developmental theories, the older adult's behavior and response depends on how earlier developmental crises were handled (81).

Sociological Theories. The Disengagement Theory and Activity Theory are both sociological theories. **Disengagement Theory,** proposed by Cumming and Henry, *suggests that all old people and society mutually withdraw, that the withdrawal is biologically and psychologically intrinsic and inevitable, and that it is necessary for aging and beneficial to society*. The Cumming and Henry's Disengagement Theory suggests that society finds ways to minimize the social disruption that results from death of its members. In addition, individuals in a society undergo a self-disengagement process during the middle and later years of life. This process is characterized by a reduction in general energy levels, reduction in societal involvement, and an increased preoccupation with one's own needs and desires (110, 126, 172, 173). Studies do not bear out the Disengagement Theory. The older person may be alone but enjoy the solitude, be mentally alert and responsive socially (117, 126).

Activity Theory, formulated by Havighurst, Maddox, and Palmore to refute Disengagement Theory, is the more popular of the two theories. *Basic concepts of the theory are that most elderly people maintain a level of activity and engagement commensurate with their earlier patterns of activity and past lifestyles and that the maintenance of physical, mental, and social activity is usually necessary for successful aging* (18, 81, 82, 126).

The Activity Theory implies that the older adult has essentially the same psychological and social needs as do middle-aged people. According to this theory, the older adult must compensate for the loss of roles experienced in later maturity. The older adult does not disengage but needs to maintain a moderately active lifestyle (101, 172, 173). In reality, the response to aging by most older adults is a combination of the two theories.

Family Development and Relationships

The changing demographic profile of developed countries has been associated with an increased number of four- and five-generation families. In such families, it is common to have two generations at or near old age, with the oldest person frequently over 75 years. The "generation in the middle" may extend into retirement years in many families. Thus the "young—old," facing the potential of diminished personal resources, may be the group increasingly called upon to give additional support to aged kin.

Several authors have written about aging in different cultures, family relations between generations in different cultures and countries, and how worldwide social changes are affecting the elderly as family members (28, 36, 60, 70, 79, 105, 138, 148, 153, 189, 207, 214).

Relations with Spouse

In later life, responsibilities of parenthood and employment diminish with few formal responsibilities to take their place. There is usually a corresponding decline in social contacts and activities. The factors which affect the social life of the elderly are found in personal social skills and in resources available in the private life. Marital status continues to be a major organizing force for personal life. With children gone and without daily contact with co-workers provided by employment, the elderly lose the basis for social integration. Declining health, limited income, and fewer daily responsibilities may create greater needs for social support. Thus, having a spouse provides increased possibility for increased companionship.

Interestingly, spouses may not increase in their support to each other into late life, perhaps because of increased **interiority** (*introspection*) with aging. Time may erode bases of respect, affection, and compatibility. Sometimes marriages have not been filled with mutual emotional or social support in earlier years, so there is no foundation for increasing mutual emotional support. Women are often the sole support for men; older women tend to feel the husband is not supportive emotionally or in health care. However, women tend to rely on a more extensive network of family and friends for support (50).

For the woman to continually have a spouse in the house or with her, wanting to share in her activities, can be distressing, even though it has been positively anticipated. The loss of privacy and solitude, doing tasks her own way and at her own pace, loss of independence, and loss of contact with friends may all be issues. However, the increased accommodation to meeting husband's needs is offset by increased opportunities for nurturing and being nurtured and for sharing mutual interests.

✒ Your listening and teaching may assist the elderly person in making the necessary adjustments to the spouse.

Relationships with Offspring and Other Family Members

Historical trends toward smaller families, longer life spans, increasing employment of women, and increasingly high mobility of both young and old have important implications for children being a primary resource in old age.

A study by Kivett and Atkinson (108) showed that the number of children is related to the recency with which older parents have seen their child, the amount of assistance older parents receive, and factors influencing older parents' interaction with children. Parents with one child report fewer visits and less help received, especially if the only child is an employed daughter. The middle-aged child, with associated family and career demands and stresses, is not able to spend as much time and effort for the parent. Older parents expect children to assume an appreciable level of responsibility in meeting important health, economic, and emotional needs, regardless of how many offspring there are to share in the assistance. Assistance from children-in-law, grandchildren, siblings and siblings-in-law, and nieces and nephews increases as the number of children decrease. Geographic proximity is a stable prediction of older parent–child interaction, more so than offspring gender or health status of the parent. Daughters who are primarily blue-collar workers provide more assistance to older parents and have more association with parents than corresponding sons. Parents receive more help from offspring as income for the offspring increases (109).

Thomas (193) found that older parents receive and perceive their children's help in several ways. Younger parents receive more help with automobile maintenance and help in the form of gifts. Older parents receive help with shopping and transportation. Parents who most strongly valued family are most desirous of and satisfied with family support. Parents may tend to expect less help from children when they live at a distance or when they work outside the home. Further, they appreciate most the help that keeps them self-reliant or autonomous, maintains social integration, maximizes choice and expressive interactions, and forestalls reliance on more extensive services. Parents with greater degree of ill health express less satisfaction with children's help, possibly because it symbolizes dependency and loss of social integration.

Some elderly people have a limited number of family members; some couples have no children. The childless couple will probably have adapted to childlessness psychologically. However, they are especially vulnerable at crisis points, such as episodes of poor health or death of spouse or housing companion. If those persons/couples cannot drive or have no transportation, they will have greater need for help. It may have a role in strengthening their informal helping networks (109).

✔ Your teaching and referrals may enable the elderly person with few relatives or resources to manage more effectively.

Grandparenthood

The stage of grandparenthood may come to the middle-aged persons, depending upon age of their own childbearing and age of their childrens' childbearing. The relatively young grandparent may not like the connection of age and being a grandparent. Relative youth of grandparents contributes to the complex patterns of help and relationships between the generations. The increasing divorce rate also adds to the complexity of grandparent relationships. The child may have eight sets of grandparents.

Grandparents are often happy with their role, in that they can enjoy the young person and enter into a playful, informal, companion, confidante relationship. The grandchild is seen as a source of leisure activity, someone for whom to purchase items that are also enjoyable to the grandparent. The grandparent typically does not want to get into an authoritarian or disciplinarian role but will, and has the experience to do so, if necessary.

Great-grandparents may wish to be as active in the grandparenting role as they were as grandparents, but advanced age and geographic distance tend to limit their participation. Also, this generation feels removed from the very young, whereas the grandparent generation feels a special tie with the very young.

Social Relationships

Social networks of family, friends, and neighbors provide instrumental and expressive support. They contribute to well-being of the senior by promoting socialization, elevating morale and life satisfaction, buffering the effects of stressful events, and facilitating coping skills and mastery. For example, social supports buffer the effects of stressful life events and represent more than the quantity or proximity of social ties but also the extent to which social ties fulfill needs of the senior. Also, the components of informal support networks—spouses, children, close relatives, distant kin (cousins, aunts, uncles, nieces, nephews), co-workers, close friends, neighbors, and acquaintances—have a variety of functions and vary in importance to the senior. Instrumental help is given in the form of advice, information, financial aid, and assistance with tasks. Socioemotional aid is given in the form of affection, sympathy, understanding, acceptance, esteem, and referral to services (112).

Frequency of use of social networks is not related to physical health. As income decreases, visiting with neighbors declines but visits to close friends or relatives increase, as does the tendency to talk to family members about feelings and to talk to friends about events. The elderly rate helpfulness of children and other family members as important. Lower income increases the senior's reliance on friends and relatives and the value placed on their help. Higher income may provide resources that facilitate social visiting and a broader network of relationships. A higher frequency of social contacts and greater intensity of kin and friend relationships has been found for women in comparison to men. Apparently intimacy or close friendship ties and having a confidant are less important to the male (103, 112).

Supportive ties become smaller and more unstable in old age, and social support may provide burdens for those who provide it to the senior. The closer the bond, the greater the physical, emotional, and financial strains. Burdens and costs may result in being less willing or able to help, physical or psychological distancing, increasing the social isolation of the dependent senior, or becoming enmeshed in the caregiver role to the exclusion of other relationships or roles. Informal networks ideally are integrated with formal support services (112).

An unregulated or informal social welfare system

14 Assessment and Health Promotion for the Person in Later Maturity

naturally exists in the average community or senior residence, which provides more services, security, and hope for the future than is provided by formal agencies. This system of informal assistance through family, friends, and neighbors is the major source of help for the elderly. Among and for seniors, there are three types of neighborhood exchange types: (1) high helpers, who exhibit a more formal quasi-professional style of helping without reciprocation; (2) mutual helpers, who show an interdependent style of give and take; and (3) neighborhood isolates, whose social ties and help sources are primarily outside the neighborhood. High helpers with neighbors are those who also do volunteer work or are active in self-help groups. Often these people have been in the helping professions in their work years; they also had a spiritual/religious orientation with serving others. Mutual helpers have more neighborhood contact and are generally quite outgoing. Isolates have little contact with others and view themselves as quiet people. They may be in poor health and in need of help themselves (71).

Many of the events of later life are exit events, involving continuous threat, stress, and loss, such as widow(er)hood, chronic or poor health, retirement, change in residence, and lower income. Thus coping often becomes problem specific and also involves socialization, learning how to perform new roles, adjusting to changing roles, and relinquishing old roles. Socialization contributes to well-being by lending continuity and structure to the transitions encountered by people (205).

Often you will be able to assist the elderly in asking for and accepting help from others, or in becoming familiar with community resources.

The Caregiver Role

The role of the middle-aged offspring in caring for the elderly parent has been described in Chapter 13. Refer to Chapter 13 and references at the end of that chapter and at the end of this chapter for more information on the caregiver role.

The caregiver in an elderly couple is most frequently the wife, since women live longer than men and are usually younger than the spouse. If the woman is impaired, the husband is often the caregiver. The spouse is the primary source of help for married elderly with impaired capacity, and adult daughters are the major helpers when a spouse is not present or not able to sufficiently help. The probability of relying on friends is highest among impaired elderly who are unmarried and have few family members within an hour's travel. The majority of noninstitutionalized elderly are self-sufficient (43).

When the spouse cannot manage care for the elderly parent, children try to assist. Sons tend to become caregivers only in the absence of an available female sibling and are more likely to rely on their own spouses for support and help. Sons tend to provide less direct care assistance and to be less involved, hence they do not feel as stressed by the caregiving experience (91).

The elderly person who cares for a disabled spouse is a hidden victim, at risk for physical and emotional stresses of caregiving superimposed on stresses of the aging process. He/she is likely to experience a barrage of feelings as well as role overload, including being head of the household. The woman, as the spouse who is the caregiver, may also be chronically ill or disabled. Thus the family caregiver of the noninstitutionalized elderly is in need of help from supportive services. These services for the spouse could include a wives' support group sponsored by a senior center; home health care; adult day care; foster home placement; extended respite care; homemaker, transporter, and repairman services; and visitor or "relief" services.

Several authors discuss the role of the spouse, as the main caregiver, with the disabled elderly (98, 185). Pratt et al. discuss ethical concerns of family members in the caregiver role (159).

Stresses of caring for the elderly person who is physically or cognitively impaired are many. Various authors describe feelings of the middle-aged or elderly caregiver and the family; needs and feelings of the elderly person; issues and conflicts for the family; and ways to manage the caregiving experience (33, 61, 99).

Education and support group programs appear to hold great promise as a means for assisting family caregivers of older relatives. You will have an important role in implementing both of those interventions. Gallagher presents a number of strategies that can be helpful to the caregiver (65).

Widow(er)hood

Because widow(er)hood may occur prior to late life, the feelings, problems, and issues pertinent to the widow(er) have been discussed in Chapter 13. Refer to Chapter 13 and the references at the end of this chapter for additional insights. Megerle also describes the grief/mourning process of the couple and ways the nurse can help (135). Bereavement does not permanently affect health status for most seniors, although the grief reaction may induce physiological symptoms initially. Stress appears to increase as the death approaches, and then health status may deteriorate. Regardless of the predeath mourning done by the survivor, the elderly widow(er) has great increase in psychological distress.

Widow(er)hood disrupts couple-based relationships and obligations to a spouse while introducing emotional and material burdens on those relationships that outlive the marriage. Widow(er)hood may also introduce both a measure of freedom to make new contacts and a stimulus to do so. If the person moves to a smaller dwelling, increased housing density produces a greater increase in social contacts among the widowed than is seen in the married. Without the support that the spouse usually provides, the widowed may turn to friends and relatives as a source of replacement. The widowed may have greater intimacy with their friends than the married. Married people interact more with their spouses (112, 135).

The elderly widowed are not more isolated than elderly married, and elderly women have some advantage over elderly men in their ability to develop or maintain social relationships. Patterns of social relationships established among the married apparently provide the parameters within which social relationships continue among the widowed. Both married and widowed women are more likely to talk to close friends and relatives and to talk to family about worries and to children about crises than are married or widowed men. Loss of spouse allows for expansion or addition of new roles; frequency of contact increases with widow(er)hood. Widow(er)hood results in greater involvement with informal social relationships than marriage (112, 135).

The widow who lives alone in her own home may be in need of a great deal of help. Neighbors often provide this help, especially if children reside out of town. Bryant found that the childless widow, however, may not receive any more help from neighbors than widows with children in spite of greater needs. Perhaps adult children are able to elicit neighbor assistance; such requests for extra help are not forthcoming if there are no children (21).

✔ Your teaching, emotional support, referral to services, and encouragement to continue as active a life as possible are important to the widow(er) as she/he adjusts to losses and new roles.

Divorce and the Elderly

Those who are separated from their spouses and those who are legally divorced total slightly over 5 percent of the population. Both the number of people who were ever divorced, who have been divorced before 65 years, and who are over age 65 when divorce occurs are increasing. Also, the proportion of older persons who have ever experienced a divorce is considerably larger than the proportion who are currently divorced, since many divorced people remarry. In the future, fewer marriages will be terminated by death prior to old age. Also, an increased number of seniors will fall in the ever-divorced and currently divorced categories, since those entering old age in the future will be more accepting of divorce as a solution to an unpleasant marriage. Further, in the future more elderly women will have economic independence because of their years in the work force, and this may encourage higher divorce rates (35, 199).

Being divorced in old age, or in any age, may negatively affect a person's economic position and may increase demands for social welfare support. Typically divorce is associated with a deterioration in the standard of living for women although it has little effect for men. Further, family and kinship relationships are affected by divorce. The children or other relatives who would provide physical help and psychosocial support may not be available to one of the parents in his/her old age. Remarriage also establishes a new set of nuclear family relationships. The experience of being divorced can help the senior cope with bereavement. The person knows survival is possible after a marital relationship ends (34, 199).

✔ Be prepared to give emotional support or crisis intervention to the older person who is encountering divorce or who is reworking the conflicts, dilemmas, and losses of having experienced divorce.

Singlehood

There are a small percentage (about 5 percent of elderly) who are single—never married. They have no spouse or children. They may or may not have living family members. They may or may not live alone. Having lived independently all during adult life, the person may have developed effective adaptive mechanisms and a supportive social network. The assumption is that being married provides social, emotional, and sustenance needs. In fact, the single person who has planned carefully for retirement may be as satisfied with self and life, and as secure in all aspects, as the married person. The single person may be no more lonely than the married person. They do not experience the desolation of widow(er)hood or divorce (204).

Few studies have been done on health status of the single senior. They generally conclude that the well-being of single people tends to be equivalent to that of married persons, while widowed, divorced, and separated persons tend to have lower well-being (205).

Single women tend to have greater education, occupational status, and intellectual ability than married women, suggesting that career orientation makes marriage less attractive for women. Single women are likely to be first-born, which leads to a less romantic view of marriage because of early roles as surrogate parents. Single men do not display the higher educational and occupational attainment found with single women but they are more likely to be only children, suggesting socialization for greater achievement. Psychological integrity and social independence are features of the single personality (204).

The single views fluidity and variety in social relationships, rather than the exclusivity of marriage, as an advantage in promoting opportunities for personal growth, while still protecting autonomy. Lifestyle is geared to preserving personal independence and the development of self, with privacy, self-expression through work, freedom of movement, and preoccupation with expanding experiences, philosophical insights, and imaginative conceptions of life being goals for the person. Single women tend to be happier and better adjusted than single men; marital roles may be less beneficial and more stressful for women than for men. Although single women are happier than single men, they are nevertheless less happy than married women. The characteristic that best explains their relative unhappiness is greater dissatisfaction with family life. The lower well-being of the never married is attributable either to changes accompanying aging which lessen the viability of single lifestyles, or to less support of single living among other older people (204, 205).

⟶ Be alert to special emotional and social needs of the single elderly, to the reticence at times to ask for help, and to the need for information about community resources. You may become a significant confidant as you care for this person.

The Elderly and Pets

Pets are great companions for older people. In 1983, the President signed a law guaranteeing the right to keep pets in government-assisted rental housing for the elderly and handicapped. Several states have adopted laws to allow animals as permanent residents of hospitals and nursing homes.

⟶ The death of a pet can precipitate a deep grief, and mourning will result because of the loss. Crisis counseling, giving the person a helping hand and a shoulder to cry on, may help the person work through the pet's death, or work through feelings related to having to put the pet to sleep. Be aware that the senior who is wanting euthanasia for an apparently healthy pet may be contemplating suicide. Or suicide may follow the death of a pet. For 25 percent of the clients in one counseling service, death of a pet was the last straw in a series of stresses and losses (5).

Elder Abuse

It is estimated that 1,000,000 older Americans are abused annually. The victim is likely to be a Caucasian female over 70 years old with moderate to severe physical or mental impairments. Usually the abuser is a relative (spouse or offspring) residing with the senior (212).

The four main types of abuse are:

① Physical—when the senior is beaten, shoved, slapped, restrained for long periods, or sexually molested.
② Psychological—when the senior is treated like an infant, yelled at, cursed, not included in family activities, or isolated for long periods.
③ Financial—when the senior's resources or money are taken or totally managed by the caregivers without consent, or when the senior is forced to sign over legal title to property.
④ Neglect—when the senior is not given the materials for meeting basic needs, such as food, or when necessary medication, eyeglasses or hearing aids, or medical treatment is withheld.

Hypotheses about the cause of elder abuse include: ① psychopathology in the caregiver, ② stresses of caring for the impaired elder, and ③ dependency of the elder as a trigger for victimizing the person.

Signs and symptoms of the abused elder include:

1. Bruises, fractures, malnourished status.
2. Undue confusion not attributable to physiological consequences of aging.
3. Conflicting explanation about the senior's condition.
4. Unusual fear exhibited by the senior in a presumed safe environment, in the home, or in the presence of the caregiver.
5. A report of the daily routine that has considerable gaps in the sequence.
6. Apparent impaired functioning or abnormal behavior in the caregiver.
7. Indifference or hostility displayed by caregiver in response to questions.

⟶ During assessment of potential abuse, avoid a censuring tone of voice or judgmental expression or stance. Show a willingness to listen to the caregiver's perspective. Solicit the caregiver's early memories of relationships with the senior to learn of long-term conflicts. Most abused seniors are reluctant to report abuse because of ① fear of retaliation, ② exposure of offspring to community censure or legal punishment, and ③ fear of potential removal from their home.

⟶ In planning care and during intervention, be familiar with the reporting laws of your state, and whether the law covers only known abuse or suspected abuse. In most states, professionals who fail to report abuse may be fined, and they are accorded protection from civil and criminal liability if they report abuse.

⟶ Because the abused senior is an adult with full legal

rights, intervention is not possible without the consent of the senior if the person is legally competent. If the client is in a life-threatening situation, is competent, and chooses to remain at home, the nurse must honor that decision after counseling the elder of the danger. If the person is legally incompetent and appears in immediate danger, the nurse should begin appropriate guardianship procedures.

Anderson and Thobadan give a detailed description of this problem and the nurse's role (1). Winter presents an empathic description of the feelings of the abused elder and community action that can be taken (212).

Be aware that advocacy for the abused elder may be difficult; you may receive threats of harm from caregivers who resent the disruption of a previously convenient financial exploitation of an elderly relative. A common situation is when the elder refuses help and desires to remain in an environment that, by your standard, is unacceptable or unsafe. This can be very frustrating. Testifying in court to the nature of specific abusive situations can be anxiety provoking.

Physiological Concepts

Physiological Changes

When we are born, regardless of our genetic background or external influences, we all have one thing in common, the element of aging. From the day of birth, we begin the aging process.

The rapidity and manifestations of aging in each individual depend on heredity, past illnesses, lifestyle, patterns of eating and exercise, presence of chronic illnesses, and level of lifetime stress. However, some generalized physiological changes do occur; these include a decrease in rate of cell mitosis, a deterioration of specialized nondividing cells, an increased rigidity and loss of elasticity in connective tissue, and a loss of reserve functional capacity (88).

Certain other characteristics have been observed about aging:

1. The time of onset, type, and degree of aging differs between men and women and is more distinctive between the sexes in middle life than in the later years.
2. Senescent alterations in one organ, or in the whole organism, can be either premature or delayed in relation to the body's total chronology.
3. The progression of aging in cellular tissues is asymmetrical: In one system the characteristics of old age may be displayed prominently (brain, bone, cardiovascular apparatus, lungs) and be less obvious elsewhere (liver, pancreas, gastrointestinal tract, muscles).
4. Certain pathology is a manifestation of aging.
5. A direct relationship exists between the sum of common aging traits and the length of survival (101).

General Appearance

The general appearance of the older adult is determined in part by the changes that occur in the skin, face, hair, and posture.

Skin. The overall appearance of the skin changes dramatically. It develops creases and furrows and begins to sag. *Irregular areas of dark pigmentation* (**lentigo senilis**) that look like large freckles appear. These are especially common on the dorsum of hands, arms, and face. Some capillaries and small arteries on exposed portions of the skin surface become dilated. The coloring of fair-skinned older adults loses the pinkish flesh tone (88, 209). Berliner's two articles are excellent references and also show pictures of various conditions (9, 10).

Due to changes in the skin cells and cellular elements, there is a loss of skin firmness and resiliency with a decrease in the skin turgor. The elastin fibers in the skin become more brittle and the outer epidermal layer becomes thinner as cells are depleted (209). Normal skin cells in an average 70-year-old live only 46 days as compared to 100 days for a 30-year-old. In addition, skin cells are replaced more slowly in the older adult (107). Because the *sebaceous glands* which normally lubricate the skin with oil decrease activity, the skin becomes dryer and rougher. The inability of the aging skin to retain fluids also contributes to dry, less flexible skin. The skin gradually loses its ability to regulate body temperature. There is a significant reduction in the number of sweat glands. This interferes with the body's ability to sweat freely which can lead to heat exhaustion. Furthermore, the loss of subcutaneous fat which functions as insulation for the body can make the older adult susceptible to the cold. The loss of the subcutaneous fat also accounts for the characteristically emaciated look of old age (88, 106, 209).

Head. Even the appearance of the *face* changes as the nose and ears tend to become longer and broader and the chin line alters (209). Wrinkles on the face are pronounced due to the repeated stress produced by the activity of facial muscles. The predominant mood expressed by the facial muscles of the individual becomes permanently etched on the face in the form of wrinkles (smile or frown lines) above the eyebrows, around lips, over cheeks, and around the outer edges of the eye orbit. Shortening of the platysma muscle produces *neck* wrinkles (173).

➤ Examination of the *mouth* is essential. Ill-fitting dentures cause irritation of oral mucosa, thereby affecting appetite and mastication. Chronic illnesses, such as arthritis, central nervous system disorders, and limited arm movement, may prevent elderly patients/clients from properly carrying out their own oral hygiene. Carcinoma may occur in any portion of the gastrointestinal tract; the aged are especially vulnerable to oral carcinoma.

Gray hair is the universal phenomenon associated with aging, but it is not a reliable indicator of age since some individuals begin graying as early as their teen years. In the older adults, melanin production in the hair follicle diminishes. The hair gradually grays; the exact shade of gray depends on the original hair color. Eventually all the pigmented hair is replaced by nonpigmented hair; gradually the overall hair color turns pure white. Hair loss and thinning due to destruction or regression of the germ center that produces hair follicles occurs. Both males and females are affected. The loss of hair occurs on the scalp, in the pubic and axillary areas, and on the extremities. In most older adults, there is also increased growth of facial hair due to the change in androgen–estrogen ratio (173, 209).

Posture. The posture of the older adult is one of general flexion. The head is tilted forward; hips and knees are slightly flexed. Muscles in the torso are held rigidly. The older adult stands with the feet apart to provide a wide base of support. He/she takes shorter steps which may produce a shuffling gait (173). A shift in the center of gravity occurs as well, which affects movement and balance.

Neurological System

Nervous System Changes. With aging there are major changes in the nervous system that occur normally and that alter the individual's sensory response: (1) nerve transmission is slower; (2) nerve conduction velocity decreases; (3) electrical activity declines; (4) sensory threshold increases, and (5) integration of sensory and motor function declines (88, 173). All of these neurological changes create problems for the older adult. For example, by the age of 70, slower voluntary movement, slower decision making, and slowed startle response are seen; drivers over 65 years of age are involved in a higher percentage of accidents than are younger drivers. The older adult's higher sensory threshold affects pain and tactile perception (88, 173), so more intense stimuli are needed to examine or stimulate the person (4).

Brain. By age 80 the brain weight has decreased by 7 percent. This weight loss is accompanied by a reduction in the cortical area and a decrease in the number of functioning neurons. However, a direct correlation between the brain size and function has *not* been established (106).

Vestibular and Kinesthetic Response. Other changes in the nervous system affect balance and touch. The response to vestibular and kinesthetic stimuli decreases with age. Vestibular sense receptors are located in muscles and tendons; these receptors relay information regarding joint motion and body position in space to the central nervous system. With alteration in these responses, the older adult has decreased equilibrium and coordination (88).

Vision. Visual changes occur. Lacrimal glands produce fewer tears, causing the cornea to become dry and irritated. The lens thicken and yellow; objects take on a yellowish hue; the cells within the lens lose water and shrink. The size of the pupil decreases; it is less responsive to light. Increased lens opacity causes light to scatter, causing sensitivity to glare and difficulty in adjusting from lighted to darker room. These changes interfere with the ability to transmit and refract light. **Presbyopia,** *inability to change lens shape for near vision,* is present in most adults after the age of 45 or 50. Even with corrective lenses the individual may need longer to focus on near objects. Cataract development and glaucoma are frequently found in this age group. With **cataracts** *the lens becomes opaque,* accompanied by diminished vision and increased sensitivity to glare. **Glaucoma** *is caused by damage to the optic nerve from increased intraocular pressure.* These conditions and the other visual changes such as **arcus senilis,** *the accumulation of lipids on the cornea,* can be assessed during periodic eye examinations (4, 88, 106, 123, 173).

Color vision is also altered. For the older adult, colors such as green, blue, and violet are more difficult to see than are red, orange, and yellow. Pastels fade so that they are indistinguishable from each other; monotones, whites, and dark colors are also difficult to see (85). Brighter colors compensate for decline in color discrimination and yellowing and opacity of the lens.

Hearing. Auditory changes of middle age continue through later life. Of all those over 65, 13 percent suffer severe **presbycusis** (*progressive loss of hearing and sound discrimination*). The consonants, especially *s, sh,* and *f,* are examples of high-frequency sounds which produce problems for the individual with presbycusis. The ability to locate the direction from which sound is coming diminishes. Older people have difficulty hearing individuals who speak rapidly or in high tones. Hearing loss may be due to changes in the organ of Corti or loss of nerve cells in the eighth cranial nerve. There is also thickening and less elasticity of the ear drum and decreased production of cerumen. Rate of time for passage of impulses in the auditory nerve increases (4, 85, 88, 173).

Taste and Smell. Both are affected by aging. The number of taste buds are believed to decrease with age. The older adult does experience a decrease in taste sensation and an increased preference for more spices, highly seasoned foods, and more sugar and salt. It is also believed that the sense of smell decreases because the olfactory nerves have fewer cells. This diminished sense of smell combined with the decline in taste sensation may account for the loss of appetite experienced by many older adults. The inability to smell presents hazards for the individual since he/she cannot quickly detect leaking gas, spoiled food, smoke, or burning food.

Cardiovascular System

Although the cardiovascular system undergoes considerable changes with aging, it is still able to maintain the daily cardiac and circulatory functions of the older adult. The cardiovascular system may not be able to meet the needs of the body when a disease process is present or when excess demands caused by stress or excessive exercise occurs.

Structural changes occur within the heart and the vascular system. The cardiac muscle has an increased amount of collagen and fat: the valves become more rigid, and the left ventricle wall increases in thickness. Atherosclerosis is present and its affect on the aorta, coronary arteries, and carotid arteries are especially apparent; large arteries have decreased distensibility and elasticity, and varicose veins are common. Functional changes also occur. The left ventricle is unable to pump large volumes of blood; thus the total cardiac output per minute is lower. Because of the delay in nerve transmission and the thickening of the cardiac muscles, more time is required to complete the cardiac cycle. Since the cardiac output is lower, a greater percentage of the total is sent to the brain and coronary arteries. Muscles and viscera may receive inadequate blood supplies when there is an increased demand for blood flow. Consistent exercise throughout one's lifetime is the best way to maintain adequate cardiac output in later maturity (88, 101, 198, 209).

Respiratory System

The changes produced by aging affect both internal and external respiration. The ability of the body to take oxygen from the outside air and to deliver it to internal organs and tissues is altered.

The lungs and rib cage undergo structural changes; the rib cage becomes less mobile and the elasticity of the lung tissue decreases. There is a gradual decline in the structure and function of the respiratory muscles; these changes decrease the strength of the muscles used in breathing. Due to decreased muscle tone and sensitivity to stimuli, the ability to cough is impaired. In addition, the ciliary mechanism decreases its effectiveness. Both of these factors interfere with effective clearing of the respiratory tract. Less oxygen is delivered from the outside air to the arterial blood; thus the arterial oxygen pressure decreases. The lungs remain hyperinflated even on exhalation, and the proportion of dead air space increases, causing a decrease in the ventilation/perfusion ratio and in the vital capacity (88, 173, 209). Calcification of vertebral cartilages and kyphosis cause more shallow respirations.

Musculoskeletal System

There is a gradual decrease in *height* throughout old age. As the vertebrae collapse from loss of calcium and normal aging, the individual becomes shorter. Height is also affected by curvature of the thoracic spine which frequently occurs in older adults. The older adult may experience a significant *weight* loss around 70 years of age. This is probably due to the decreased number of body cells, the changes in cell composition, and the decrease in the amount of body tissues (173, 209).

The older adult experiences a gradual loss of *muscular strength and endurance*. Muscle cells atrophy, and lean muscle mass is lost. As the elastic fibers in the muscle tissues decrease, the muscles become less flexible and stiffness is noted more frequently. Continued physical activity and proper nutrition can slow muscle atrophy and stiffness (88, 173).

There is also progressive loss of *bone strength* due to loss of bone mineral content. **Osteoporosis** (which will be discussed later) is seen as the extreme version of the universal process of adult bone loss. Active exercise and proper nutrition will decrease the rapidity of bone density loss (209).

Genitourinary System

As with the other body systems, major changes in structure and function are associated with aging. The kidneys, bladder, and ureters are all affected by the aging process.

There is a loss of nephron units in the *kidneys* and the remaining units undergo degenerative changes. This causes a decrease in the filtration rate. By the age of 70 or 80, the glomerular filtration rate is approximately one-half the rate of a 30-year-old. Because of the impaired filtration rate, urea nitrogen, creatinine, uric acid, and even drugs are excreted more slowly. The tubule cells have decreased reabsorption and selection abilities, causing a loss of water and electrolytes. The kidneys respond more slowly to the antidiuretic hormone, decreasing their ability to concentrate urine. The kidneys also need more time to correct alkalosis, acidosis, and/or electrolyte disturbances. When both renal and respiratory functions are impaired, protection against shifts in blood pH is decreased (88, 106, 209).

Some muscle tone loss occurs in the *ureters* and *bladder*. This may cause incomplete emptying of the bladder and increase the risk of retention and bladder infection in the older adult. The bladder capacity gradually decreases, and the older adult experiences frequent urination and nocturia. Older women may develop incontinence when relaxation of the pelvic muscles occurs (88).

Gastrointestinal System

Changes occur throughout the gastrointestinal system.

Mouth. Tooth decay, loss of teeth, degeneration of the jaw bone, progressive gum recession, and increased reabsorption of the dental arch interfere with the older adult's ability to chew food. Saliva becomes more alkaline as the salivary glands secrete less ptyalin and amylase. These changes alter the digestive process at the onset (88, 173).

Gastrointestinal Tract. Because of decreased stimuli from the autonomic nervous system, peristalsis is slowed the entire length of the gastrointestinal tract. There is delayed emptying of the esophagus and stomach. The gastric mucosa shrinks, causing a decreased secretion of pepsinogen and hydrochloric acid. This delays digestion. Digestion is decreased further by the reduction in pancreatic enzymes. Bile tends to be thicker, and the gallbladder empties more slowly. These changes result in a decreased absorption of nutrients and drugs by the gastrointestinal tract. In addition, some older adults do not have enough intrinsic factor and develop pernicious anemia. Malabsorption Syndrome may occur (88).

Elimination of waste products is of equal importance to gastrointestinal function in the aged. Elimination depends on fluid intake, muscle tone, regularity of habits, culture, state of health, and adequate nutrition—all of which interrelate. Alterations in many of these areas occur with aging. Daily routines change, activity may be slowed, illness may have depleted vital reserve, and diet habits may be more erratic. The changes in the cell, and therefore in tissue structure, and the loss of muscle tone may decrease intestinal mobility. Poor nutrition and lack of exercise add to the problem.

In the majority of persons over age 65 there is some degree of immobility—either physical, social, or environmental. Physical changes in the tissues combine with this immobility to produce constipation or fecal impaction, under circumstances that might not so affect a younger person.

✔ Teach the importance of increased fluid intake, of roughage in the diet if possible, and exercise within the person's physical limitations to maintain bowel function. Increasing fluid intake, especially drinking warm water or coffee early in the morning, and having adequate intake of fruits, bulky vegetables, and cereals should be adequate to keep bowel movements normal. Offering daily prune juice and teaching the importance of a regular time for defecation often prevent later problems in the inactive person. If not, the person may try such medications as Metamucil, milk of magnesia, or Colace, but these should be used only until normal bowel function returns. (Note that normal bowel function is defined as the passage of soft stool without difficulty, as opposed to having a bowel movement every day.) Often the older person has self-administered laxatives for years; gastrointestinal muscle tone is then so low that the person may have to take a mild stool softener or laxative daily. Prevention, from early adulthood on, through hydration and eating of bulky foods is important.

Endocrine System

Within the endocrine system, there is no general decrease in hormone secretion, but there is a lack of response to some hormones, especially those of the adrenal and thyroid glands. Thus ability to respond to stress in old age is reduced (7).

Growth hormone, estrogen, and testosterone blood levels do decrease in later maturity. Because of the decrease in estrogen levels after menopause, the breasts of the female have more connective tissue and fat and less glandular tissue. The breast tissues lose elasticity and begin to sag. The lack of estrogen causes the uterus and fallopian tubes to decrease in size. The fallopian tubes also become less motile. The decline of testosterone secretion is not abrupt like that of estrogen. Therefore, the changes are less obvious. However, the gradual decline of hormone does increase the incidence of benign prostatic hypertrophy in the older adult male and affects physical reserves, since testosterone has a nitrogen-conserving effect (88).

Immune System

The older adult has a delayed immune response to infection and a delayed or inadequate response to the stress of an infection. Both of these factors alter the normal inflammatory response, causing altered signs and symptoms to infection. For example, in the older adult, the white blood count does not become as elevated in response to an infection as it does in the middle-aged individual (88).

Hematopoietic System

Although some research suggests minor changes in the blood components of the older adult, the hemoglobin level, red blood cell count, and circulatory blood volume are not significantly changed. Most of the changes that occur are related to specific pathological conditions instead of normal aging (173).

Reproductive System and Changes That Influence Sexual Function

While the male and female experience some common changes as a result of aging, it is well to consider them separately because of certain particular physiological changes relating to sexual response and vigor.

Male Changes. In the male, not only does the production of testosterone continue throughout his lifetime but it is available longer and at a higher level than estrogen in the female. Concentration of the male hormone does diminish with aging, producing a gradual decline in sexual vigor, muscle strength, and active sperm. The testes become smaller and softer and the sperm-producing tubules thicken and thereby inhibit the production of sperm. The prostate gland enlarges, contractions weaken, and the force of ejaculation decreases along with a reduction in the volume and viscosity of seminal fluid (101, 129).

In 1970, Masters and Johnson found that as a sexual partner the older male experiences reduction in the frequency of intercourse, the intensity of sensation, the speed of attaining erection, and the force of ejaculation. Excitement builds more slowly and erection takes longer to attain; with diminished vasoconstriction of the scrotum, there is less elevation of the testes. The plateau phase preceding orgasm lasts longer, the orgasmic phase is of shorter duration, and the expulsion of the seminal fluid is usually completed with one or two contractions as compared to four or more in the young male. In the resolution stage, loss of erection may take seconds as compared to the young man's minutes or hours (129).

Female Changes. The older woman encounters little sexual difficulty if she is in good health, has an open and positive attitude toward sexual relations, and has an available and effective sexual partner. Masters and Johnson recorded effective sexual capacity and performance among women as advanced in age as 78 years (129).

Female sexual performance in later maturity reveals no reduction in sexual desire or excitability with advancing age. Regular sexual stimulation and activity seem to overcome the effects of estrogen starvation. Studies reveal an increase in masturbation for relief of sexual tension in postmenopausal women into their sixth and seventh decades and for men over age 65. There may be an increased level of sexual desire among women after hysterectomies, indicating that there is no connection between fertility and libido. Two studies have indicated that women who have been exclusively homemakers and mothers have a greater difficulty in meeting the advancing physiological changes than women who have combined the role of homemaker with a career (101).

Yet neural and hormonal changes can combine to affect her sexual activity. In coitus, the thinning vaginal walls may make penetration difficult. Burning and frequency of urination may follow intercourse since the atrophic bladder and urethra are not adequately protected. Thus the sex act may become less satisfying and even painful.

Sexuality. It is well known that stress, hormonal activity, general health, and aging can each be assessed according to measurable standards. The data are sufficient to infer that psychological influences can be exerted to produce physiological change in young and old alike. Because of the relationships between the mind and body and the interdependence of all body systems, the societal attitudes regarding the characteristics and needs of older citizens are crucial to their quality of life.

There is no doubt that normal aging of the reproductive system produces a decreased efficiency and a lengthened time for response for both male and female, but unlike other organ systems that perform more specific functions, the reproductive system extends far beyond procreation. It is deeply tied to the need for interpersonal communication, and it involves that warmth and comfort found only in bodily contact. When one is old, the yearning for intimacy, security, and belonging becomes intensified as other privations are felt keenly: loss of friends, job status, active participation in parenting or career, and decision making. Too often the elderly consider themselves members of a third sex, nonpersons whom the functional world passes by.

As our medical technology proliferates and the life span continues to lengthen, we will have an increasing number of elderly, healthy, and alert persons who will demand a greater share of a high quality of life and an opportunity to exercise their capacity for abiding close relationships with the opposite sex in whatever role seems suited to their needs as individuals (101, 106).

Nutrition

Special problems exist in the nutrition of older people. While caloric requirements may be lower than in earlier life, the elderly require somewhat greater amounts of some of the vitamins and trace elements. *Basic to good nutrition* in any age group is an adequate intake of quality protein, fat, and carbohydrate. There must be enough vitamin coenzymes to ensure metabolism of these three nutrients, and absorption of enough bulk elements to maintain a balance of sodium, potassium, calcium, magnesium, and other trace-element cofactors for metabolic needs. Because foods today are subjected to many refinement processes with the loss of some vitamins and essential elements, supplements are often recommended. The Basic 4 food groups are the foundation of a balanced diet for the elderly as in any life stage. Assuring enough protein in the diet each day is probably the greatest dietary problem in meal planning for the elderly person who lives alone, for he or she often wants foods that can be prepared and chewed easily, and he or she may seldom eat meat. Milk products may be poorly tolerated, especially in dark-skinned people, because of decreased lactase, the enzyme for digesting lactose. Fermented products, such as cheese, yogurt, and buttermilk, may be tolerated well and supply needed calcium (24, 73, 156, 206).

The aging process causes an atrophy of olfactory organs and a loss of taste buds. Usually salt and sweet buds are lost first; bitter and sour taste buds remain intact. Two-thirds of taste depends on smell. This may contribute indirectly to abnormalities of absorption, motility, or intermediary metabolism, and a concomitant lack of desire for food. Loss of taste is compounded by gum disease, poor teeth or dentures. Fifty percent of the elderly have lost their teeth; 90 percent who have their natural teeth have periodontal disease. Both loss of teeth and periodontal disease are preventable through good nutrition, oral and dental hygiene, and dental therapy. Food served attractively and at proper temperature is important. The person may find eating each food separately, rather than mixing foods, helps him or her to better taste each food. Food with different textures and aromas should be served in the meal.

Sufficient water or other fluid intake is essential. Fluid intake is often reduced in seniors for several reasons:

1. The aging process reduces the thirst sensation.
2. The senior who has incontinence problems limits fluid intake to reduce output.
3. Fewer meals are eaten; opportunity for fluid intake is less apparent.
4. The senior who takes a diuretic wrongly assumes fluid intake should be reduced.

At least six or seven glasses (8 ounces) of water should be ingested daily to (1) soften stools; (2) maintain kidney function; (3) aid expectoration; (4) moisturize dry skin; and (5) aid absorption of medications, bulk laxatives, and high-fiber foods.

✓ Nursing responsibility begins with the tray that may be served from the kitchen of a person's home or an institution. You can help make mealtime pleasant for the older person. Offer food in a comfortable setting; open cartons and food packets of various sorts and help season the food; and keep the tray attractive, neat, and uncluttered to ensure an appetizing appearance. Make sure dentures and eyeglasses are clean and in place at mealtime instead of in the drawer or in the bedside table. Oral hygiene is important and contributes to a greater enjoyment of food. Mouth care also promotes healthy tissues in the mouth, thereby keeping the first part of the alimentary canal intact and functional.

✓ Adequate treatment of problems at mealtimes is necessary to determine whether or not a poor appetite may be caused by poor-fitting dentures, a sore mouth, individual or cultural preferences in food, or some physical or psychological deterrent to enjoyment of food. The elderly are denied many pleasures, and food should not be one of them. Consult with other members of the health team, especially the dietician and the physician, if there are problems. The family needs to be included, too, and can often be of great help when there are cultural, religious, or ethnic reasons for a poor appetite. Often the most important member of the team, the client/patient, is not consulted enough; he/she should be the first one to be involved in planning nutritional needs, if at all possible. These same principles can be used as a basis for helping the elderly maintain good nutrition in the home, where, as the community health nurse or primary care practitioner, you may need to make careful assessment of the home situation when problems of poor nutrition exist. Determine whether the problem stems from lack of funds, physical handicaps, family structure, cultural barriers, or any combination of similar unmet needs. Often you will be the one who helps the client/patient contact community agencies, family, church, and whatever other means may be available.

▶ Elderly persons living alone and unable to shop or to prepare food may need to have the assistance of a home health aide—available through some community agencies—to shop for them, as well as assist with other routines of living. You might arrange to have meals sent in from agencies designed to give this type of service. These programs are discussed more fully later in this chapter under community planning.

▶ The whole area of patient teaching is affected by the changing needs of the older adult. Adapt your nutrition teaching to these changes and keep in mind the altered responses associated with the aging nervous system.

Rest and Sleep

Rest is of importance. Though older adults may not sleep as many hours as they once did, frequent rest periods and sensible pacing of activities will provide the added energy for a full and active life. Rest may consist of listening to soft music, reading, thinking of happy experiences, napping, or merely lying with eyes closed. Some older adults have several 15- to 60-minute naps during the daylight hours (198).

With so much diversity among the individuals in this age group, it is difficult to state how many hours of *sleep* are recommended. Older adults in reasonably good health probably do not require any more sleep than was required during their middle adulthood.

Aging affects the process of sleep in three areas: length of sleep, distribution of sleep during the 24-hour day, and sleep stage patterns. The older adult requires a somewhat longer period to fall asleep, sleep is lighter, with more frequent awakenings. The total amount of daily sleep declines as the spontaneous interruption of sleep increases. The older adult may actually spend more time in bed but sleep less, waking with the feeling of inadequate sleep. The time spent in Stage IV, the deepest sleep period, and REM (rapid eye movement) decreases. This also contributes to feelings of fatigue (88, 173).

▶ Insomnia is a common problem in the older adult. Many factors may contribute to this. You can determine the person's usual sleeping patterns, the amount and type of daily activity, and the existence of disturbing environmental conditions. Assess the presence of pain, fear, anxiety, lack of exercise, or depression (173).

Exercise and Activity

Culturally imposed ageism tends to discourage the older adult from any type of daily exercise. However, physical activity that is sensibly paced and gradually increased will promote and maintain health. Even if the individual has a decreased exercise tolerance, with supervision a plan can be developed to help him/her achieve higher levels of physical fitness. It is important, however, that the older adult not start an exercise program without consulting the physician who would be aware of any needed limitations.

▶ For the individual who is not especially interested in planned exercise programs, you can suggest walking, bowling, golf, swimming, dancing, games such as shuffleboard and horseshoes, and home and garden chores. All of these activities can improve the well-being of the older adult.

An exercise program regularly followed may bring a dimension of dynamic fitness to life that helps him/her move vigorously and live energetically as long as possible. Histories of vigorous persons in their eighties and nineties, and even over age 100, show that the majority have been physically and mentally active throughout their earlier lives (7, 18, 55).

Health Promotion and Health Problems

Male and female differences in longevity result from hormones, genetic make-up, natural immunity, and lifestyle behavior. Because of the immunity effects of estrogen, women, statistically, develop heart disease 10 years later than men. In the past, lifestyle choices of women also gave them a biological advantage—less drinking of alcoholic beverages, less cigarette smoking, more attention to personal health care, less exposure to risks at work and play. However, as women are changing their lifestyles, there is a narrowing of the gap between the genders in health status and longevity (39).

▶ The focus of health care for individuals in this period of life should be on the prevention of disease and the promotion of health. Although numerous body changes occur with aging, many older adults live active, productive lives.

Immunizations

▶ Since older adults are more susceptible to acute illnesses, they should be encouraged to avail themselves of recommended immunizations against communicable diseases. Individuals who garden and participate in other outdoor activities should receive tetanus immunization as indicated. Immunization for influenza and pneumococcal pneumonia are usually recommended for older adults, especially those with chronic respiratory and cardiovascular diseases (173). Adults at risk for hepatitis should receive hepatitis B vaccination (208).

Safety Promotion and Accident Prevention

Older people have a disproportionate share of accidents that cause bodily injury or death. This is especially true for accidents that occur in the home. Many of these accidents are directly related to physiological changes which result from normal aging.

Visual Changes. Changes in visual acuity produce numerous hazards for the older adult. The older adult's problems with color interpretation, light intensity, and depth perception should be considered in the home and hospital environment. Older adults need a higher light intensity than younger persons. Direct lights, exposed light bulbs, white surfaces, waxed floors, and glossy furniture all produce glare which interferes with the vision of older persons. Lights should be arranged so that they are not directed down from the ceiling. This creates pools of light which may distort the individual's vision. Sharply contrasting colors for door facings and walls, brightly colored doors, stripes of contrasting color along the bottom of a wall, or a yellow or red strip at the edge of each step can help the individual distinguish colors and gauge depths (12, 85).

▹ *The environment should be kept free of hazards*—no articles on the floor, no furniture with sharp edges, no scatter rugs. The baseboards should be painted a darker color than the walls. Signs should be prepared with dark backgrounds and light lettering. Blues and greens on signs should be avoided. Numbers on doors, elevators, and telephones should be large enough for the older adult to see (12, 85). When you are caring for a blind person, follow the guidelines in Table 14–1.

Hearing Impairment. Changes in hearing acuity may predispose the person to accident risks. Many elderly persons have been diagnosed as being mentally ill, whereas in reality they were suffering from a gradual loss of hearing. If one is unable to hear clearly, it is easy to imagine one is being talked about or ignored. This leads to a feeling of depression and behavior is then categorized often as irrational, suspicious, or hostile. This produces isolation and further frustrations and the vicious cycle which ensues may in the end cause real paranoia to develop.

▹ Refer to Table 14–2 for suggestions on effective communication with the hearing impaired person.

Tactile Changes. Changes in *temperature regulation* and the inability to feel pain also produce safety problems. The elderly usually *feel cold* more easily and may require more covering when in bed; a room temperature somewhat higher than usual may be desirable. Most hospitals and nursing homes do not have thermometers that register body temperature below 94°F (35°C). Therefore, statistics are not available on how many elderly persons suffer and often die from hypothermia, but a figure of 25,000 deaths per year has been cited. A nighttime room temperature of 66°F (18.3°C) can be too low for an aged person. The victim may not be aware of the extreme loss of body heat, especially when supine and relatively inactive.

▹ Teach the elderly person the following measures to *prevent hypothermia* in cold weather:

TABLE 14–1. Guidelines for Helping a Blind Person

- Talk to the blind person in a normal tone of voice. The fact that he/she cannot see is no indication that hearing is impaired.
- Be natural when talking with a blind person.
- Accept the normal things that a blind person might do, such as consulting the watch for the correct time, dialing a telephone, or writing his/her name in longhand, without calling attention to them.
- When you offer assistance to a blind person, do so directly. Ask, "May I be of help?" Speak in a normal, friendly tone.
- In guiding a blind person, permit him/her to take your arm. Never grab the blind person's arm, for he/she cannot anticipate your movements.
- In walking with a blind person, proceed at a normal pace. You may hesitate slightly before stepping up or down.
- Be explicit in giving verbal directions to a blind person.
- There is no need to avoid the use of the word *see* when talking with a blind person.
- When assisting a blind person to a chair, simply place his/her hand on the back or arm of the chair. This is enough to give location.
- When leaving the blind person abruptly after conversing with him/her in a crowd or where there is a noise that may obstruct hearing, quietly advise that you are leaving so that he/she will not be embarrassed by talking when no one is listening.
- Never leave a blind person in an open area. Instead, lead him/her to the side of a room, to a chair, or some landmark from which he/she can obtain direction.
- A half-open door is one of the most dangerous obstacles that blind people encounter.
- When serving food to a blind person who is eating without a sighted companion, offer to read the menu, including the price of each item. As you place each item on the table, call attention to food placement by using the numbers of an imaginary clock. ("The green beans are at two o'clock.") If he/she wants you to cut up the food, he/she will tell you.
- Be sure to tell a blind person who the other guests are, so that he/she may know of their presence.

TABLE 14–2. Guidelines for Communicating With the Hearing Impaired Person

- When you meet a person who seems inattentive or slow to understand you, consider the possibility that hearing, rather than manners or intellect, may be at fault. Some hard-of-hearing persons refuse to wear a hearing aid. Others wear aids so inconspicuous or clearly camouflaged that you may not spot them at first glance. Others cannot be helped by a hearing aid.
- Remember the hard-of-hearing may depend to a considerable extent on reading your lips. They do this even though they may be wearing a hearing aid, for no hearing aid can completely restore hearing. You can help by trying *always to speak in a good light* and by facing the person and the light as you speak.
- When in a group which includes a hard-of-hearing person, try to carry on your conversation with others in such a way that he/she can watch your lips. Never take advantage of the disability by carrying on a private conversation in his/her presence in low tones that cannot be heard.
- Speak distinctly but naturally. Shouting does not clarify speech sounds, and mouthing or exaggerating your words, or speaking at a snail's pace, makes you harder to understand. On the other hand, try not to speak too rapidly.
- Do not start to speak to a hard-of-hearing person abruptly. Attract his/her attention first by facing the person and looking straight into the eyes. If necessary, touch the hand or shoulder lightly. Help him/her grasp what you're talking about right away by starting with a key word or phrase, for example, "Let's plan our weekend now," "Speaking of teen-agers. . ." *If he or she does not understand you, do not repeat the same words.* Substitute synonyms: "It's time to make plans for Saturday," and so on.
- If the person to whom you are speaking has one "good" ear, always stand or sit on that side when you address him/her. Do not be afraid to ask a person with an obvious hearing loss whether he/she has a good ear and, if so, which one it is. The person will be grateful that you care enough to find out.
- Facial expressions are important clues to meaning. Remember that an affectionate or amused tone of voice may be lost on a hard-of-hearing person.
- In conversation with a person who is especially hard-of-hearing, do not be afraid occasionally to jot down key words on paper. If he/she is really having difficulty in understanding you, the person will be grateful for the courtesy.
- Many hard-of-hearing persons, especially teen-agers, who hate to be different are unduly sensitive about their disability and will pretend to understand you even when they do not. When you detect this situation, tactfully repeat your meaning in different words until it gets across.
- Teach the family to avoid use of candles. Electric light will give the person a better chance to join the conversation, because he/she can see the lips during conversation. Similarly, in choosing a restaurant or night club, remember that *dim lighting may make lipreading difficult*.
- Teach family members that they do not have to exclude the hard-of-hearing person from all forms of entertainment involving speech or music. Concerts and operas may present problems, but movies, plays, ballets, and dances are often just as enjoyable to people with a hearing loss as to those with normal hearing. (Even profoundly deaf persons can usually feel rhythm, and many are good and eager dancers.) For children, magic shows, pantomimes, and the circus are good choices.
- When sending a telegram to someone who does not hear well, instruct the telegraph company to deliver your message, not telephone it.
- The speech of a person who has been hard-of-hearing for years may be difficult to understand, since natural pitch and inflection are the result of imitating the speech of others. To catch such a person's meaning more easily, watch the face while he/she talks.
- Do not say such things as "Why don't you get a hearing aid?" or "Why don't you see a specialist?" to a person who is hard-of-hearing. Chances are he/she has already explored these possibilities, and there is no need to emphasize the disability.
- *Use common sense* and tact in determining which of these suggestions apply to the particular hard-of-hearing person you meet. Some persons with only a slight loss might feel embarrassed by any special attention you pay them. Others whose loss is greater will be profoundly grateful for it.

---

1. Stay indoors as much as possible, especially on windy, wet, and cold days.
2. Wear layered clothing, and cover the head when outdoors.
3. Eat high energy foods, such as some fats and easily digested carbohydrates, as well as protein daily.
4. Keep at least one room warm.
5. Use extra blankets, caps, socks, and layered clothing in bed.
6. Have contact with someone daily (182).

✓ Perception of and reaction to *painful stimuli* may be decreased with age. Because pain is an important warning device serving the safety of the organism, use caution when applying hot packs or other hot or cold applications. The elderly person may be burned or suffer frostbite before being aware of any discomfort. More accurate assessment of physical signs and symptoms may be necessary to alleviate conditions underlying complaints of pain, such as abdominal discomfort or chest pain, which may be more serious than the older person's perception might indicate.

✓ Dulling of *tactile sensation* occurs because of a decrease in the number of areas of the body responding to all stimuli and in the number and sensitivity of sensory receptors (55). There may be clumsiness or difficulty in identifying objects by touch. The person may not respond to light touch but needs to be touched. Because fewer tactile cues are received from the bottom of the feet, the person may get confused as to position and location. These factors, combined with sensitivity to glare, poorer peripheral vision, and a constricted visual field, may result in disorientation, especially at night when there is little or no light in the room (18). Because the aged person takes longer to recover visual sensitivity when moving from a light to a dark area, night lights and a safe and familiar arrangement of furniture are essential. Sensory alterations may require modification of the home environment and extra orientation to new surroundings. Simple explanations of routines, location of the bathroom, and the way the signal cord works in the hospital are just a few examples of information the older patient needs. Objects in a familiar environment should not be moved. Use touch, if acceptable to the person. Increased hairbrushing or combing, back rubs, hugs, and touch of shoulders, arms, or hands increase tactile sensation.

✔ Understand that some of the changed behavior, discussed later under psychological concepts, is directly related to physical changes in nerve and sensory tissue and influences nursing practice, whether you are giving physical care, establishing a relationship, providing a safe environment, or planning recreational needs. Research indicates that hand, foot, and eye preference becomes more right-sided and ear preference becomes more left-sided with advancing age. Adapt nursing care measures to accommodate these changes (158). The whole area of patient teaching is also affected, because you must understand the altered responses and the changing needs of the elderly before beginning their health education.

Common Health Problems: Prevention and Treatment

The health problems of the older adult may be associated with the aging process, a disease state, or both. You need to consider all of the aspects of aging before deciding on a course of action. As you care for the older adult, refer to Appendices I and II for a schedule of health-screening measures. Refer to a medical-surgical nursing text for in-depth information on all of the following health problems.

Neurologic Diseases. Neurological diseases found in some of the older generation include herpes zoster or shingles, Parkinson's disease, and Alzheimer's disease.

Herpes zoster or **shingles** is thought to be caused by the same virus that causes chicken pox. In this form it causes a *unilateral vesicular eruption which follows the dermatomes of affected nerve roots.* Herpes zoster is thought to attack especially those with altered immune responses such as persons on corticosteroids. Rather severe pain may begin 3 to 5 days before the rash. The rash typically goes through a 1- to 2-week cycle, beginning with macules, progressing to pustules, and finally crusting. Unilateral involvement and the following of the thoracic and cervical nerve roots make diagnosis rather simple.

✔ No drug exists for eradicating this condition. But the drug that is used for herpes II sometimes eases symptoms and shortens the severity of the case. Symptomatic treatment with analgesics for the pain and cool soaks for the lesions are helpful. Underlying immunological problems should be investigated (89).

Parkinson's disease is *a slowly progressive, degenerative disorder* characterized by resting tremor, masklike faces, shuffling gait, forward trunk flexion, and muscle weakness and rigidity. Intellectual impairment is rare. Treatment is symptomatic: Medication is given to correct the imbalance between depleted dopamine and excess acetylcholine. Surgical treatment may reduce tremors and rigidity.

✔ Care involves encouraging the person to remain active and use correct body mechanics as long as possible. Eventually the person may need assistance with hygiene, eating, safety, and activities of daily living (200).

Alzheimer's disease, *presenile dementia* or *neural atrophy which results in cognitive, physical, and emotional deterioration,* begins in the fifties or sixties, but may first become apparent in the sixties, seventies, or eighties. Gradually, the person becomes less able to take care of self and carry out usual roles and responsibilities (123, 200). Both the person and family need considerable assistance and support. Refer to psychiatric nursing texts for more in-depth information.

✔ Beam discusses the concepts, problems, and demoralization of the family when one member develops Alzheimer's disease. The changing behavior of the person may create bewilderment, hurt, and embarrassment. Many practical examples of behavior changes and the aggravating consequences for the family are explained. Ways to manage the person's behavior are discussed to help family members understand that the person's behavior is an attempt of the failing brain to communicate and comprehend. Also, help family members to (1) express their feelings to each other, (2) join with others or a support group in the community who have a similar situation, (3) utilize nonverbal communication techniques with the person, (4) be alert to safety aspects in the home environment in order to prevent accidents, and (5) engage the person in activities that maintain self-esteem and keep the person occupied with adequate sensory input and exercise, without sensory overload or complexity (5).

🗸 Certainly, there needs to be more respite care and day-care services, family support groups, legal aid, and financial assistance to families who care for the Alzheimer patient in their home. The family may also need help in accepting the idea of institutional care and in finding an acceptable facility.

Cardiovascular Disease. Cardiovascular disease is common in the aged. **Congestive heart failure (CHF),** is a condition of *altered cardiac function in which there is not enough cardiac output to meet demands of tissue metabolism, and consequently, sodium and body water are retained.* Often arteriosclerotic heart disease and hypertension are precursors. The person may complain of difficulty with breathing in any position other than sitting or standing, and especially after exertion and at night. There may be ankle swelling, and the person may void much more frequently at night. Fluid retention will show as weight gain. The neck veins may be distended, and rales may be auscultated in the lungs. The heart may beat rapidly and display a "gallop rhythm."

When the diagnosis is established and other conditions are ruled out, the goal is to improve cardiac function and renal excretion. A low-sodium diet is recommended (usually 85 milliequivalents per day). High blood pressure must be corrected with medication if lesser measures do not succeed. Rate and rhythm of heartbeat are regulated with a digitalis preparation, and oral diuretics may be used to increase urinary output. The person should be followed closely until the condition has stabilized (89, 123).

Chronic occlusive arterial disease of the extremities is diagnosed when, because of *partial or complete occlusion of one or more of the peripheral blood vessels,* there is a *decreased blood flow to one or more of the extremities.* Often this condition is associated with diabetes. Depending on the site of the occlusion, the person may experience the following: a cramping pain in the muscles during exercise that is relieved by rest, although cramping may occur at night. The extremity involved may feel cool and pulses may be decreased. The skin may appear shiny with loss of normal skin hair. Appropriate laboratory studies are helpful in ruling out diabetes and blood lipid problems.

🗸 After diagnosis, the person should be evaluated for revascularization. General treatment measures include practicing good skin care, avoiding excess heat or cold, and avoiding smoking and caffeine ingestion. Drugs have not proved beneficial in this condition (89, 123).

Stasis ulcer of the lower extremity results in a *chronic ulcerative skin lesion caused by venous stasis and consequent poor circulation.* In contrast to an arterial problem, the person will have intact peripheral pulses in the extremity involved. There may be **pitting edema** *(induration remains after pushing in skin and tissue with a finger)* or **brawny edema** *(thickened and hardened skin)* around the ulcer site.

🗸 Treatment involves rest and elevation of the involved leg, once or twice daily cleaning with Betadine or hydrogen peroxide solution, and occasionally application of moist heat or Unna's paste boat, a protective device. Healing can be slow and difficult, and the person's extremity must be watched for widening of the lesion and cellulitis (89, 123).

🗸 Directly related to cardiovascular integrity are such concepts as the maintenance of fluid balance, adequate aeration, and relief of undue strain on the aging circulation. These goals can be a basis for planning nursing care in a variety of ways, such as providing enough fluids to ensure sufficient blood volume, guarding against the possibility of circulatory stasis by proper positioning, and encouraging mobility whenever possible. Simple precautions such as not keeping a backrest up too long, thereby preventing pooling of blood in the pelvis or extremities, may be extremely important when the circulation is impaired. Prolonged sitting in a chair should be avoided to prevent dependent edema of the lower extremities. Straining to defecate may cause undue strain on the right side of the heart as the blood is suddenly poured through the vena cava after pressure is decreased in the thorax; therefore, a regimen to ensure easy defecation will indirectly protect the heart from overwork.

🗸 The elderly person is prone to experience orthostatic hypotension and should be assisted out of bed slowly to prevent a sudden drop in the blood supply to the brain with resultant vertigo. Allowing him/her to sit for a moment on the side of the bed before standing up will help circulation to adjust to postural changes. The aged person normally has a higher blood pressure; thus hypotension may occur, even though the blood pressure level appears at the textbook range of normal.

Respiratory Diseases. Respiratory diseases are common in the elderly. Aging changes contribute to the elderly person's susceptibility to both viral and bacterial pneumonia. Other respiratory diseases that afflict many aged are emphysema and chronic obstructive pulmonary disease, and the aged can be more vulnerable to tuberculosis when in fragile health. Lung cancer may also occur.

Chronic Obstructive Pulmonary Disease (COPD) has *three components* to be diagnosed: (1) **bronchitis,** *excessive mucus and sputum production with inflammation of the bronchi;* (2) **bronchoconstriction;** and (3) **emphy-**

sema, *irreversible destruction of distal air space.* Smoking is strongly associated with this complex syndrome. In addition to shortness of breath, sputum production, and wheezing, the person with emphysema will show increasing signs of tachypnea and hyperinflation, have increased anteroposterior chest diameter with decreased diaphragmatic movement, and use increasing accessory chest muscles during respiration. Percussion will produce hyperresonance, while auscultation will produce rhonchi and distant heart sounds. Spirometry is helpful in diagnosing actual lung capacity.

✔ A person with diagnosed COPD should have yearly influenza vaccine and pneumococcal vaccine as indicated. All pulmonary irritants should be avoided, *especially cigarettes.* A bronchodilator is almost always prescribed, and sometimes expectorants. Avoiding sedatives; cold, wet weather, (which increases bronchoconstriction); drinking large amounts of water, and following a routine of postural drainage three or four times daily are all helpful coping mechanisms. If a bacterial infection is suspected, an antibiotic should be given on a short-course basis (89, 123).

✔ Avoidance of smoking and prevention of respiratory infections, along with proper nutrition, rest, and hygiene throughout life, contribute to pulmonary health in old age. If the person has not followed healthful living, then pathological changes are more likely in this system, as well as in the other body systems. Prevention of further pulmonary pathology is essential, whether the person is at home or admitted to a hospital or another institution. For example, postoperative care will be affected and must be modified because of the decrease in pulmonary function. Change the patient's position frequently to stimulate respiration. Assist him/her to breathe deeply and to cough, maintaining position in such a way as to prevent restricted movement of chest muscles. Slumping while on an elevated backrest, poor positioning of the arms while sitting in a chair, or lying in Sim's position may produce pressure that prevents full lung expansion.

✔ Carefully observe and record the respiratory rate and characteristics of the aged person's breathing. Shallow respirations may lead to increased **pCO$_2$** *(carbon dioxide concentration)* and then be followed by a more rapid respiratory rate in an attempt to maintain balance. Auscultation with the stethoscope should be part of the nursing assessment, especially with immobile persons, to determine the character of the breath sounds and to detect rales, which may indicate lung congestion.

✔ These implications for nursing care also relate directly to cardiovascular function, since poor pulmonary function results in altered cardiac response. Thus an understanding of cardiopulmonary relationships is essential for planning adequate care for the aged.

Blood Dyscrasias. Blood dyscrasias in the elderly are pernicious anemia, secondary anemia, and chronic lymphocytic leukemia. Death from Hodgkin's disease is not uncommon.

Pernicious anemia is a *progressive, megaloblastic, macrocytic anemia that results from lack of the intrinsic factor essential for the absorption of vitamin B$_{12}$.* Maturation of red blood cells in bone marrow becomes disordered; white blood cells decrease, and polymorphonuclear leukocytes become multilobed. Symptoms include extreme weakness, numbness and tingling of the extremities, fever, pallor, anorexia, and weight loss. Treatment includes vitamin B$_{12}$ injections and folic acid and iron medications (123, 200).

Secondary anemia is a *reduced hemoglobin, hemotocrit, and red blood cell count* resulting from nutritional deficiency, blood loss, or some condition that causes hemoglobin or red blood cell deficiency. Administration of iron preparation or blood may be necessary (123, 200).

✔ Nursing care for the anemic person, regardless of cause, involves maintaining adequate nutrition, rest to avoid cardiac or respiratory symptoms, safety aspects, preventing infection, and maintaining activities of daily living.

Chronic lymphocytic leukemia is a *neoplasm of blood-forming tissues* characterized by proliferation of small, long-lived lymphocytes, chiefly B-cells, in bone marrow, blood, liver, and lymphoid tissue. **Hodgkin's disease** is a *malignant disorder characterized by painless, progressive enlargement of lymphoid tissue* (200). Indepth information on both of these complex diseases, that, in turn, need multifaceted nursing care, can be found in medical–surgical nursing texts.

Genitourinary Disease. A *common genitourinary disease* of the aging male is **Benign Prostatic Hypertrophy (BPH),** *overall enlargement of the prostate gland via enlargement of the fibrous and muscular tissue.* The aging male will usually complain of difficulty in starting and stopping the urine flow and of a small stream with small amounts voided frequently. Rectal examination will usually reveal a diffuse enlargement of the prostate but with normal landmarks present and no nodules felt. Laboratory studies should rule out other causes of obstructed urinary flow. There is no medical treatment for this condition and the person must be referred to the urologist for surgical evaluation (89).

✔ Cancer of the prostate is a common occurrence at this age. Symptoms are similar to the benign condition. Teach the importance of differential diagnosis and early surgical treatment.

Skeletal Disease. **Osteoporosis** *is the absence of a normal quantity of bone rather than abnormal condition* *of bone*. The process is generalized and involves the entire skeleton. It is expressed as loss of normal cortical thickness; increased porosity in normally compact, cortical bone; and in cancellous bone, thinning, fragmentation, and loss of trabeculae. Postmenopausal and senile osteoporosis are the most common of the metabolic bone diseases and are found to be clinically significant in one-fourth of all Caucasian females in the United States. It is a predisposing cause of 75 percent of fractures of the upper femur. In males at about age 80, the prevalence of osteoporosis is similar but less severe than in women. It is most common among those of northern European extraction. There is a high incidence among Japanese living in the United States, and it is rare among Afro-American males. These differences seem to be related to the amount of normal adult bone mass, since the Black male has the largest initial bone mass and therefore has a greater structural reserve on which to draw.

Some researchers feel that osteoporosis can be prevented or diminished by a daily diet in the young years that is adequate in calcium (800 to 1000 milligrams daily), vitamin D (400 International Units daily), phosphorus, protein, and fluoride (1 part per million in drinking water). Vitamin D and fluoride increase absorption and retention of calcium and thus increase mineralization. Calcium intake in adulthood is often insufficient (73).

Another *common disease*, **osteoarthritis,** related to osteoporosis, is usually restricted to elderly people and is *characterized by both degeneration of articular cartilage and hypertrophy of bone,* usually in the weight-bearing joints and in the dorsal interphalangeal joints of the fingers. Both pain and stiffness are present. The stiffness usually improves with exercise while the pain lessens with rest. Posture changes occur; kyphosis of major joints are common. Center of gravity changes; the person may have difficulty with balance.

✔ Treatment may involve a combination of rest and exercise, application of heat to affected joints, an antipyretic, and, in some cases, physical supports. If the person is overweight or is otherwise traumatizing the affected joints, this should be eliminated (89). Nursing care measures are those described in this section.

✔ Nursing care is influenced by bone resorption in several ways. In the institutional setting you frequently encounter the female patient who has sustained a fractured hip, and since osteoporosis is considered to be a major predisposing cause, planning of care must take this into consideration. These persons will need immediate attention to physical needs as well as preventive care. There will be increased calcium ion concentration in the urine because of extensive resorption not only from the chronic osteoporosis but also from immobility. Care must be taken to ensure adequate hydration or glomerular filtration will decrease and hypercalcemia will result. There is danger of renal calculi forming unless a high urine flow is maintained. Because of osteoporosis, this person also needs gentle handling to avoid a pathological fracture.

✔ Adequate nutrition is important in these people, with sufficient protein, calcium, and phosphorus intake as priorities. Physical therapy, essential for successful treatment, begins at the bedside with range of motion exercises and whatever muscle setting can be done to strengthen back, hips, and thighs for future mobility and rehabilitation (7).

Endocrine–Metabolic Disorders. Hormonal changes are significant to health, since a wide variety of physiological processes are regulated by the endocrine glands. Cellular metabolism, fluid and electrolyte balance, diameter of small blood vessels, and consequently the supply of blood to various tissues are among the body functions mediated by endocrine regulation.

The chemical composition of fluids surrounding body cells must be closely regulated, and when analysis of blood shows alterations in blood volume, acidity, osmotic pressure, or protein and sugar content, older subjects are found to require a longer time to recover internal chemical equilibrium. Insulin, secreted by cells in the pancreas, normally accelerates the removal of sugar from the blood. In older subjects given intravenous insulin with extra glucose, the glucose is removed from their bloodstreams at a slower rate than in younger people because of poorer hormone production. Stress intensifies glucose intolerance. Elderly persons undergoing the stress of surgery, illness, or injury or emotional stress may manifest diabetic symptoms; the elevated blood and urine glucose usually returns to normal when the stressor subsides (7).

Certain physiological changes in the elderly may be caused by these subtle alterations in the chemical composition of body fluids. "Diseases of adaptation" are largely caused by derailments of the stress defense mechanism. Overproduction of the defense hormones in response to bacterial infection, injury, psychological, and other stresses can alter body metabolism enough to have a harmful or even fatal effect on body systems.

Diabetes mellitus is the most common of the endocrine–metabolic disorders in the elderly. It takes its heavy toll because it contributes to inadequately nourished tissues and can lead to retinitis or severe peripheral vascular disease. It patently interferes with normal healing processes and thus precludes optimum recovery from illness or after surgery. This disease has been summarized in other chapters.

Diseases That Affect Sexual Function. Health problems associated with the *sexual changes* of aging are of concern to the older adult. Certain diseases in the elderly female have been linked to estrogen deficiency. There is a statistical rise in atherosclerosis attacking the coronary arteries in aged females (as well as in younger women who have had ovaries removed); women treated with estrogen therapy have had fewer myocardial infarctions. While there is no clear-cut case for a cause-and-effect relationship, the female hormones appear to be crucial to the enzymatic system in the metabolism of fats and proteins.

Factors that contribute to *sexual dysfunction* are essentially the same as those which affect performance at any age: disease or mutilating surgery of the genitourinary tract, diverse systemic diseases, and emotional disturbance coupled with societal attitudes. Treatment of the aged for a physical complaint often contributes to widespread use of drugs. Tranquilizers can give way to excessive use of alcohol or marijuana. These weaken erection, reduce desire, and delay ejaculation. Many of the metabolic disorders are overlooked and go untreated: anemia, diabetes, malnutrition and fatigue may negatively affect the quality of life and cause impotence. Obesity may impose a hazard for cardiac and vascular integrity and at best may be damaging to a healthy self-image.

Many older persons are under the false impression that any sexual activity will increase the danger of illness or even death due to stress on heart or blood pressure. In truth, oxygen consumption, heart rate, and blood pressure increase only moderately during intercourse and may actually afford a distinct therapeutic and preventive measure. In arthritis, for example, the increase in adrenal corticosteroids during sexual activity has been noted to relieve some of the symptoms. The present-day practice of prescribing exercise for cardiac patients attests that sexual intercourse need not be considered dangerous for anyone able to walk about a room.

Radical surgery or dysfunction of the genitourinary tract produces the most devastating effects on sexual capacity and libido. Extensive resectioning due to malignancy may make intercourse difficult if not impossible. Although a decline in desire and capacity for climax may follow hysterectomies, they are by no means inevitable. The loss of childbearing ability and the lack of an ejaculation are for some women and men psychologically traumatic, and these clients may need some support and guidance in adjusting to change.

Nursing care involves first a reexamination of one's own bias regarding sex and sexuality in the aged. Human sexuality covers a wide spectrum and the pattern for each individual is a product of prenatal development and postnatal learning experiences coupled with one's inherent sense of personal identity within a sex classification. This basic pattern is not altered simply by age. It continues to mediate one's capacity for involvement in all life activities.

With this in mind, nursing care planning for the elderly can be made most effective. Realizing the need for sexual expression in some form or other, nurses can be open and nonjudgmental when patients/clients display a desire for warmth, close contact, and companionship. Touch is particularly important to the older person who has been bereft of family ties, perhaps for many years. Some people require more relief from sexual tension than others. If incidents arise that seem unduly unorthodox, such as open masturbation or unusual behavior with the opposite sex, the nurse can be a support person if there is a sincere desire to be available for counseling. An atmosphere of trust must prevail, in which the nurse focuses on the person and not on any specific act.

Exploring alternate lifestyles with persons who are single, alone, and old may be a way for the nurse to be of assistance. Teaching that includes information about therapy available, such as estrogen replacement when there are emotional or physiological problems associated with the climacteric, can help the elderly woman to choose treatment. A thorough knowledge of anatomy and the physiology of normal aging is essential for the nurse who cares for the elderly. Only then can information be accurate and teaching effective. The nurse has a responsibility to communicate also to the families and friends of the older patient/client and to colleagues information that will help in dealing with their inability to understand the sexual needs of the aged.

Intervention can include the following:

1. Becoming better educated about sexuality.
2. Increasing self-awareness.
3. Discussing openly sexuality with peers, staff, and students.
4. Attempting to manipulate the environment of the aged patient/client to provide a healthier milieu in which relationships can be a source of comfort.
5. Evaluating own behavior in terms of intimacy, touch, friendships, and interest in the aged.
6. And above all, accepting the challenge ourselves to live fully and to assist the aged in our care to do the same (48, 106).

Alcoholism. Approximately 10 to 15 percent (over 2 million) of elderly Americans suffer from alcoholism, and contrary to popular opinion, they can be successfully treated. There are two types of elderly alcoholics: those who began alcohol abuse in their youth (about two-thirds of the elderly) and those

Table 14—3 Alcohol Interactions With Medications

ALCOHOL TAKEN WITH MEDICATION	EFFECT ON PERSON
Antidiabetic agents	Increased hypoglycemia; increased alcohol effects
Anticoagulants	Increased effect; possible hemorrhage
Barbiturates	
Tranquilizers	
Narcotics	
Antidepressants	Increased CNS depression, oversedation
Antihistamines	
Anesthetics	
Antibiotics	Inhibits antimicrobial action

whose minimal drinking habits increased in old age as a reaction to and way to cope with various problems and losses. Widowers comprise the largest proportion of late-onset elderly alcoholics.

Because alcohol is a central nervous system (CNS) depressant, there are some adverse effects of alcohol abuse. With low blood levels the person may feel relaxed and comfortable. With increased blood levels, the person may feel a sense of stimulation but in reality the brain centers lose ability to check belligerent or antisocial behavior. Alcohol also interacts with various drugs, either through potentiation of or interference with medication action, as shown in Table 14-3. Other effects cause the person to be accident prone, such as loss of coordination, slower reflex reaction time, slower mental response, which may in turn cause injury of fractures or death. Excess alcohol intake, and as a result poor dietary intake, malabsorption, and progressive liver damage, causes hypomagnesemia and hypocalcemia, resulting in osteoporosis, as well as avitaminosis, causing various deficiency states. Esophagitis, erosive gastritis and ulcer formation, pancreatitis, and liver cirrhosis are serious diseases that may hasten death. Cancer of the mouth, pharynx, and esophagus is more common in the alcoholic. Finally, excess alcohol intake may cause pneumonia, respiratory failure, or cardiac failure, and death.

✔ As a nurse, your acceptance of, listening to, and assessment of the elderly person in various health care sites can be critical for diagnosis and treatment. You are a liaison between the patient/client and other professionals and can facilitate treatment of the alcoholism and prevention or treatment of various complications. Further, your education of and support to the family as well as patient/client can foster their acceptance of the diagnosis and pursuit of treatment.

Psychological Concepts

The psychological and socioeconomic concepts of aging are significant for all who work with the aged, and you will find older people concerned and needing to talk about the many changes they must adjust to. Knowledge of the crises in this life stage is necessary if you are to aid patients/clients and families in the attainment of developmental tasks, in meeting the crises, and in the early or appropriate treatment of these crises.

Cognitive Development

One universal truth that concerns the process of aging is that the onset, the rate, and the pattern are singularly unique for each person. Especially is this true in psychological and mental changes, which generally have a later and more gradual onset than physical aging. Many factors must be considered when assessing the intellectual functioning of older people: (1) sociocultural influences; (2) motivation; (3) interest; (4) sensory impairments that interfere with integration of sensory input into proper perception; (5) educational level; (6) the time since school learning; (7) isolation from others; (8) deliberate caution; (9) using more time to do something, which others may interpret as not knowing; and (10) the adaptive mechanism of conserving time and emotional energy rather than showing assertion. The initial level of ability is important: A bright, 20-year-old will be a bright 70-year-old. Overall, mental ability is incremental (95, 213).

The elder demonstrates **crystallized intelligence,** *knowledge and cognitive ability maintained over the lifetime, dependent on sociocultural influences and life experiences and broad education, which involves the ability to perceive relationships, engaging in formal operations, understanding the intellectual and cultural heritage.* Crystallized intelligence is measured by facility through numbers, verbal comprehension, and general information. It is influenced by the amount the person has learned, the diversity and complexity of the environment, the person's openness to new information, the extent of formal learning opportunities. Self-directed learning opportunities and educational opportunities to gain additional information increase crystallized intelligence after 60 years of age. The loss of biological potential is offset by acquired wisdom, experience, and knowledge. In contrast, **fluid intelligence**, *independent of instruction, social or environmental influences, or acculturation, and dependent on genetic endowment, is less apparent. It consists of ability to perceive complex relationships, use of short-term or rote memory, creation of concepts, and abstract reasoning.* Fluid intelligence is measured by ability to do tasks of memory span, inductive reasoning, and figural relations. (The fluid intelligence actually begins to decrease in middle age. [95].)

Decrease in reaction time or the speed of response is central in origin rather than the result of changes in sensory or motor end organs. The central organization of material, if hurried, will result in decreased quality and quantity of response.

The senior performs certain cognitive tasks more slowly for several reasons: (1) decreased visual and auditory acuity; (2) slower motor response to sensory stimulation, (3) loss of recent memory, and (4) changed motivation. He/she may be less interested in competing in timed intellectual tests. Further, an apparently shorter duration of alpha rhythm in the brain wave affects the timing of response. Reaction time is also slower when the person suffers significant environmental or social losses, is unable to engage in social contact, and is unable to plan daily routines. The person who is ill often endures environmental and social losses by virtue of being in the patient role. Thus he/she may be slower responding to your questions or requests (46, 101, 150, 151).

Studies of intelligence in the aged have shown that although some decline occurs in about the fifth decade of life, persons in later decades show little change when tested. Consequently, general and verbal intelligence, problem solving, coordination of ideas and facts, judgment, creativity, and other well-practiced cognitive skills and wisdom are maintained even into old age if there is no deterioration caused by extensive physical or neurological changes.

Studies indicate that elderly adults are equivalent to young adults in cue utilization, encoding, specificity, decision-making speed, design recognition, spatial memory or awareness of location, and especially when distinctive cues are available. Other studies indicate that cognitive performances of young and old adults are comparable when the task is divided or attention has been interrupted, on assessing contents and products of memory, and on recall and recognition of factual information (80, 130, 177).

In recall of sets of items, the older person usually is less accurate in memory and slower because he/she uses a limited number of strategies for remembering.

However, when the older person deliberately uses memory or encoding strategies, such as rehearsal, he/she does as well as the young adult (215).

Older women excel over men in verbal ability and speed of reaction (151). Older people are able to tolerate very extensive degenerative changes in the central nervous system without serious alteration of behavior if their social environments are sufficiently supportive. If their environment was restricted in early life, however, learning is inhibited in later life. Mental functions do not deteriorate appreciably until 6 to 12 months before death (119, 169).

Usually the capacity to learn, relearn, synthesize, and problem solve continues into old age, even though difficulty in the ordering of time sequences of more recent events and in immediate recall of new learning may exist. Test scores on spatial perception and decoding tasks decrease, possibly because of sensory and coordination changes. Tasks which require making analogies or new classifications and novel situations are more difficult. In addition, older people are apprehensive about new learning, especially in competitive situations, and ask for more details and more specific directions because they anticipate difficulty in learning new tasks.

The older person is favored over the younger person if tasks require redundant information or inference processing (27, 64). Associations between words and events which are logically related and habitual behavior become strengthened throughout life by the continual accumulation of information and adaptation of the person. The person seems more concrete in thinking because he/she strives to be functional or practical. Previously reinforced ways of doing things take precedence over new behavior. But he/she takes longer to react. This slowing of response affects not only learning but contributes as well to accident proneness (42, 150, 151).

Linden and Courtney imply cognition and intellectual development in their definition of maturity. Maturity involves the achievement of an efficiently organized psychic growth predicated on the integration gained from solving environmentally stimulated conflicts and a variety of situations. They believe that it is in the last half of life that the person best draws on cumulative experiences to establish social, moral, and ethical standards, render decisions, assist in planning, erect social guideposts, and establish pacific relationships between oncoming generations. The judgmental functions of the mind are most highly developed after midlife (121).

✔ Adapt such activities as nutrition or preoperative teaching or the learning of new content or techniques, such as insulin injections and colostomy care, to the changes in the aging nervous system, other physiological changes, and cognitive and emotional changes. Consider the aged person's difficulty with fine movement and failing vision when you are using visual aids. Provide adequate lighting without glare; and use sharp colors and large print to offset visual difficulties. Explain procedures and directions for diagnostic tests with the person's possible hearing loss and slowed responses in mind. Use a low-pitched, clear speaking voice. Teach slowly and patiently, with sessions not too long or widely spaced, and with repetition and reinforcement. Material should be short, concise, and concrete. Match your vocabulary to the learner's ability and define terms clearly. Focus on a single topic to promote concentration. Give the aged person time to perceive and respond to stimuli, to learn, to move, to act. This allows for comprehension and appropriate response, and it compensates for decline in perception, memory, and slower formation of associations and concepts.

Emotional Development

Erikson, describing the eight stages of man, states the developmental or psychosexual task of the mature years as ego integrity versus despair (58). A complex set of factors combines to make the attainment of this task difficult for the elderly person.

Ego integrity *is the coming together of all previous phases of the life cycle* (58). Having accomplished the earlier tasks, the person accepts life as his or her own and as the only life for the self. He/she would wish for none other and would defend the meaning and the dignity of the lifestyle. The person has further refined the characteristics of maturity described for the middle ager, achieving both wisdom and an enriched perspective about life and people. Even if earlier development tasks have not been completed, the aged person may overcome these handicaps through association with younger persons and through helping others to resolve their own conflicts.

✔ Use the consultative role to enhance ego integrity. Ask the person's counsel about various situations that relate to him/her personally or to ideas about politics, religion, or activities current in the residence/institution. Although you will not burden the person with your personal problems the senior will be happy to be consulted about various affairs even if his/her advice is not always taken. Acting as a consultant enhances ego integrity. Having the person reminisce also promotes ego integrity.

Without a sense of ego integrity, the person feels a sense of **despair** and **self-disgust**. *Life has been too short, futile. The person wants another chance to redo life.* If life has not been worth the struggle, death is fearsome. The person becomes hypercritical of others, and projects personal self-disgust, inadequacy, and anger onto others. Such feelings are enhanced by society's emphasis on youth, the mass media extolling beauty, and enforced retirement. Ultimately, the people around him/her help the aged person feel either a sense of importance or a feeling of being a burden, too slow, and worthless (58).

✔ Nursing care for the person in despair involves use of therapeutic communication and counseling principles, use of touch, and being a confidant so that the person can work through feelings from the past. The maintenance phase of the nurse–client relationship is important, since the person needs time to resolve old conflicts and learn new patterns of thinking and relating. The person can move to a sense of ego integrity with the ongoing relating of at least one caring person who listens; meets physical needs when the person cannot; nurtures and encourages emotionally; brings in spiritual insights; validates the senior's realistic concerns, fears, or points of anguish; and listens to the review of life, patching together life's experiences. Other references furnish more detail (140).

Personality Development and Characteristics

No specific personality changes occur as a result of aging; values, life orientation, and personality traits remain consistent from at least middle age onward. *The older person becomes more of what he/she was*. The older person continues to develop emotionally and in personality, but adds on characteristics instead of making drastic changes. If he/she were physically active, flexible in personality and participated in social activities in the young years, these characteristics will continue appropriate to physical status and life situation. If the person was hard to live with when younger he/she will be harder to live with in old age. The garrulous, taciturn person becomes more so, and problems of control and dominance are common. Stereotypes describe the older person as rigid, conservative, opinionated, self-centered, and disagreeable to be with. Such characteristics are not likely to be new but rather are an exaggeration of lifelong traits that cannot be expressed or sublimated in another way.

Personality Types. Studies of large samples of seniors reaffirm their uniqueness, but researchers have categorized the variety of their behaviors.

Four personality types were described by Neugarten: the integrated, defended, passive dependent, and disintegrated (144, 145).

The *integrated personality* type is characteristic of most elderly. These people function well and have a complex inner life; intact cognitive abilities, and competent ego. They are flexible, open to new stimuli, and mellow. They adjust to losses and are realistic about the past and present. They have a high sense of life satisfaction. The integrated group is made up of three subtypes: the reorganizers, focused, and disengaged. The *reorganizers* engage in a wide variety of activities; when they lose old roles and related activities they substitute new ones. They are as active after retirement as before. The *focused* are selective in their activities; they devote energy to a few roles that are important to them rather than being involved in many organizations. The *disengaged* are well-integrated persons who have voluntarily moved away from role commitments. Activity level is low, but not because of external losses or physical deficits. They are self-directed, interested in the world, but have chosen the rocking-chair approach to life without guilt. They are calm, aloof, but contented. Thus Neugarten defines the disengaged person differently from Cummings and Henry (144, 145).

The *defended personality* is seen in ambitious, achievement-oriented persons who have always driven themselves hard and who continue to do so. They have a number of defenses against anxiety and a tight control over impulses. This "armored" group has medium to high life satisfaction. The defended group is made up of two subtypes: those who hold on and the constricted. The *holding on* persons have a philosophy of, "I'll work until I drop." So long as they can keep busy, they can control their anxieties and feel worthwhile. The *constricted* are preoccupied with their losses and deficits. They have always shut out new experiences and have had minimal social interactions. Their caution continues as they try to defend themselves against aging. Nevertheless, they are satisfied with life, possibly because they know nothing different (144, 145). Most seniors are resourceful and psychologically healthy.

The *passive-dependent personality* type is divided into two patterns: the succorance-seeking and the apathetic. The *succorance-seeking* have strong dependency needs and seek help and support from others. They manage fairly well as long as they have one or two people to lean on. They have medium levels of activity and medium life satisfaction. The *apathetic* have an extremely passive personality. They engage in few activities and little social interaction. They have little interest in the world around them. They feel that life has been and continues to be hard and that little can be done about it. They have low satisfaction with life (144, 145).

The *disintegrated or disorganized personality* type is found in a small percentage of elderly who show gross defects in psychological functions and deterioration in thought processes. They may be severely neurotic or psychotic. Yet these elderly are not necessarily institutionalized. They may manage to live in the community because of the forbearance or protection of others around them.

Personality and Lifestyle Types. These were categorized extensively for women and men in one longitudinal study. Results of the study showed a diversity of behavior in seniors. No correlations existed between personality and lifestyle, and spouses did not show similar personality types. Health status strongly influenced lifestyle and personality characteristics; healthy people were more active and involved in life roles. Evidence supports the general hypothesis that personality characteristics in old age are highly correlated with early life characteristics. While early adult lifestyles are more likely to continue into old age for men than for women, the early life personality of women is more likely to continue into old age than the early personality type of men (125).

Although the popular stereotype is that women cannot cope effectively, this study revealed that *all* women were higher in ability to cope than in ego disorganization, even those who were more rigid in ego defenses, and women were more adaptable than men. Whenever defensiveness or ego disorganization does occur, it is related to general personality predisposition throughout life, outlook on life, and physical health (125).

Personality problems in old age are related to problems in early life. Even when the younger years are too narrowly lived or painfully overburdened, the later years may offer new opportunities. Different ways of living can be developed as the social environment changes and as the person also changes. Later maturity can provide a second and better chance at life (125).

Authors cite personality trends that are commonly found in the elderly. Some difference is noted between the earlier and later decades of later maturity.

Young-Old Personality. In the *young-old* person (65 to 75 or 80 and sometimes beyond) (119), the personality is frequently flexible, shows characteristics commonly defined as maturity, and is less vulnerable to the harsh reality of aging. The person manifests self-respect without conceit; tolerates personal weakness while using strengths to the fullest; regulates, diverts, or sublimates basic drives and impulses instead of trying to suppress them. He/she is guided by principles but is not a slave to dogma; maintains a steady purpose without pursuing the impossible goal; respects others, even when not agreeing with their behavior; and directs energies and creativity to master the environment and overcome the vicissitudes of life (16, 17, 167).

Motivations change; the senior wants different things from life than he/she did earlier. Concerns about appearance, standards of living, and family change. Stronger incentives, support, and encouragement are needed to do what used to be eagerly anticipated. He/she tends to avoid risks or new challenges and tends to be increasingly introspective and introverted (120, 167).

The elderly are tough; they often endure against great physical and social odds. Experience has taught the senior to be somewhat suspicious, since he/she is likely to be a victim of "borrowings," a fast-sell job for something he/she does not need, thievery, or physical attacks.

Yet generosity is a common trait of the elderly; the person gives of self fully and shares willingly with people who are loved and who seem genuinely interested in him/her.

The elderly person hopes to remain independent and useful as long as possible, to find contentment, and to die without being a burden to others. Increasingly, dependency may undermine self-esteem, especially if the person values independence.

Personality characteristics differ for men and women, especially in relation to assertiveness. The man becomes more dependent, passive, and submissive, and more tolerant of his emerging nurturant and affiliative impulses. The woman becomes more dominant and assertive and less guilty about aggressive and egocentric impulses. Perhaps the reversal in overt behavior is caused by hormonal changes. Perhaps the man can be more open to his long-unfulfilled emotional needs when he is no longer in the role of chief provider and no longer has to compete in the work world. Perhaps the woman reciprocates in an effort to gratify needs for achievement and worth; she expresses more completely the previously hidden conflicts, abilities, or characteristics (145).

Old-Old Personality. Old-old age (80 or 85 years and beyond) (119) is a time for meditation and contemplation, not camaraderie. Camaraderie is for young people who have energy and similarities in background, development, and interest. Old-old people may be friendly and pleasant, but they are also egocentric. Egocentricity is a physiological necessity, a protective mechanism for survival, not selfishness. Life space shrinks. When old-old people get together, certain factors block camaraderie, even if they want to be sociable: varying stages of deafness and blindness, other faulty sense perceptions, and the fact that they may have little in common other than age and past historical era. Old-old people are even more unique in the life pattern than young-old people because they have lived longer. Further, they have less energy to deal with challenging situations, and relating to a group of oldsters can be challenging (16, 167). There is increased interiority in the personality (146).

The person in later maturity, especially in old-old age, may be called childish. Rather, the person is child-like; he/she pays attention to quality in others. He/she senses when another is not genuine or honest—as a person or in activities. The old-old person reacts with sometimes exasperating conduct because he/she sees clearly through the facade and lacks the emotional energy to be as polite as earlier. Self-control, will power, and intellectual response are less effective in advanced age. Many of the negative emotional characteristics ascribed to the elderly may be based on this phenomenon. Only the very simple, those who have not grappled with the complexities of life, or the very ill and regressed will be infantile (167).

The old-old have greater need than ever to hold onto others. They are often perceived as clingy, sticky, demanding, loquacious, and repetitious. This often causes the younger person to want to be rid of the senior, which causes a vicious circle of increased demand and increased rejection.

Preoccupation with the body is a frequent topic of conversation, and other elderly people respond in kind. The behavior is analogous to the collective monologue and parallel play of young children. The talk about the body satisfies narcissistic needs, and it is an attempt to magically relieve anxiety about what is happening. This pattern alienates the young, as well as the young-old, and they tend to avoid or stop conversing with the aged.

Old-old persons intensely appreciate the richness of the moment, the joys or the sorrows. They realize the transience of life and they are more likely to start each day with a feeling of expectancy, not neutrality or boredom. Their future is today. And as a result, they become more tolerant of others' foibles, more thrilled over minor events, and more aware of their own needs, even if they cannot meet them (167).

Irritating behavior of the old-old person is frequently related to the frustration of being dependent on others or helpless and the fear that accompanies dependency and helplessnesss. The tangible issue at hand—coffee too hot or too cold, visitors too early, too late or not at all, or the fast pace of others—is often not really what is irritating, although the person attaches complaints to some thing that others can identify. The irritability is with the self, loss of control, lost powers, and present state of being.

Perhaps the most frequent error in assessing the elderly is the diagnosis of senility. Conditions labeled as such may actually be the result of physiological imbalances, depression, inadequacy feelings, or unmet affectional and dependency needs. Psychological problems in the elderly may often be manifested in disorientation, poor judgment, perceptual motor inaccuracy, intellectual dysfunction, and incontinence. These problems are frequently not chronic and may be very responsive to supportive therapy. Just as few young adults reach complete maturity, few older persons attain an ideal state of personality integration in keeping with their developmental stage.

✓ Nursing needs a strong commitment to assist the elderly in maintaining adaptive mechanisms appropriate to this period of life, although each person will accomplish them in his or her unique way, pertinent to life experiences and cultural background. Cooper's study of concentration camp survivors illustrates the impact of the experience on the person's adaptation (40).

✓ Carry out principles of care previously described to meet emotional and personality needs of the elderly. For further detail about normal emotional development and related nursing functions to maintain emotional health in later maturity, see *Psychiatric/Mental Health Nursing: Giving Emotional Care* (140).

Adaptive Mechanisms

Persons in their older years are capable of changes in behavior but find changing difficult. As new crises develop from social, economic, or family restructuring, new types of ego defenses may be needed. At the same time, the need to change may interfere with developing a sense of ego integrity.

Changing adaptive mechanisms must be developed for successful emotional transition in these later years. Peck lists three developmental stages related to adaptation, and they serve to show not only the tasks involved but also the mechanisms undergoing change as the older personality strives to become integrated (154).

Ego differentiation *versus work-role preoccupation is involved in the adaptation to retirement, and its success depends on the ability to see self as worthwhile not just because of a job but because of the basic person he/she is.* **Body transcendence** *versus body preoccupation requires that happiness and comfort as concepts be redefined to overcome the changes in body structure and function,* and consequently, in body image and the decline of physical strength. The third task is **ego transcendence** *versus ego preoccupation, the task of accepting inevitable death.* Mechanisms for adapting to the task of facing death will be those that protect against loss of inner contentment and which help to develop a constructive impact on surrounding persons (154).

Certain adaptive or defensive mechanisms are used frequently by the aged. **Regression**, *returning to earlier behavior patterns*, should not be considered negative unless it is massive and the person is incapable of self-care. A certain amount of regression is mandatory to survival as the person adapts to decreasing strength, changing body functions and roles, and often increasing frustration. Regression is an adaptive mechanism used by the older adult who is dying, and it is manifested differently than in younger years. The regression is a complex of behaviors not associated solely with a return to former levels of adaptation.

✓ In order to integrate into self-concept and handle the anxiety created by a complex of losses, changes, and adaptations related to aging and dying, the older person behaves in a way that may be confused with senile dementia or drug reactions. Careful assessment is needed, utilizing history of the person's normal patterns and history of illness (190).

✓ The dying elderly person may express regression in any or all of the following behaviors:

1. Massive denial and projection.
2. Misuse of words, confusion about familiar concepts, fragmentation of speech, misinterpretation.
3. Preoccupation with minutiae, impaired ability to deal with simple abstractions.
4. Awkward child-like thinking (190).

✓ The dying elderly person will invest little emotionally into goal setting and care planning. Any goal must be short term. Caregivers, including family, must provide physical and emotional support, recognizing the dying person's need to disengage from self-care and significant others. During the care process, you will need to support the family caregivers and encourage them to talk about perceptions and feelings as well as to explain behavioral changes and needs of the dying person (190).

Other commonly used adaptive mechanisms are described in Table 14–4 (119, 140). McCrae found in a study that controlled for types of stress, that older subjects did not consistently differ from younger subjects in using 26 of 28 coping mechanisms, including rational action, expression of feelings, and seeking help. Middle-aged and older subjects were less likely than younger subjects to use immature and ineffective mechanisms of hostile responses and escapist fantasy. Health threats in all ages elicit wishful thinking, faith, and fatalism (131).

Acute illness at any age influences behavior, affective responses, and cognitive function. These aspects of the person are also effected by chronic illness, but their effects and adaptive mechanisms used are less well known (178).

Body-Image Changes

Physical changes discussed earlier combine to change the appearance and function of the older individual

Table 14-4. Adaptive Mechanisms Utilized by the Older Adult

MECHANISM	DESCRIPTION
Isolation	*By repressing the emotion associated with a situation or idea, while intellectually describing it*, the person can cope with very threatening situations and ideas, such as personal and another's disease, aging, and death, and can begin to resolve the associated fears. Thus the aged can appear relatively calm in the face of crisis.
Compartmentalization	*Narrowing of awareness and focusing on one thing at a time*, so that the aged seem rigid, repetitive, and resistive.
Denial	*Blocking a thought or the inability to accept the situation*, is used selectively when the person is under great stress and aids in maintaining a higher level of personality integration.
Rationalization	*Giving a logical sounding excuse for a situation*, is often used to minimize weakness, symptoms, and various difficulties or to build self-esteem.
Somatization	*Complaints about physical symptoms and preoccupation with the body*, may become an outlet for free-floating anxiety. The person can cope with vague insecurities and rapid life changes by having a tangible physical problem to deal with, especially since others seem more interested and concerned about disease symptoms than feelings about self.
Counterphobia	*Excessive behavior in an area of life to counter or negate fears about that area of life*, is observed in the person who persists at activities, such as calisthenics or youthful grooming or fashion, to retain a youthful appearance.
Rigidity	*Resisting change or not being involved in decision making*, is a common defense to help the person feel in control of self and life. A stubborn self-assertiveness is compensatory behavior for the person who has been insecure, rigid, and irritable.
Sublimation	*Channeling aggressive impulses into sociably acceptable activity*, can be an effective defense to meet old age as a challenge and maintain vigor and creativity. Often the elderly desire to live vicariously through the younger generation, and they become involved with the young through mutual activities, listening, or observing their activities.

and thereby damage the self-image. Loss of muscle strength and tone are reflected through a decline in the ability to perform tasks requiring strength. The elderly person sees self as weakened and less worthwhile as a producer of work either in actual tasks for survival or in the use of energy for recreational activities.

The loss of skin tone, although not serious in itself, causes the aged in a society devoted to youth and beauty to feel stigmatized. Changing body contours accentuate sagging breasts, bulging abdomen, and the dowager's hump caused by osteoporosis. These changes all produce a marked negative effect. This stigma can also affect the sexual response of the older person because of perceived rejection by a partner.

Loss of sensory acuity causes alienation from the environment. Full sensory status cannot be regained once it is lost through aging. Although eyeglasses and better illumination are of great help in fading vision, the elderly recognize their inability to read fine print and to do handwork requiring good vision for small objects. The danger of injury caused by failure to see obstacles in their paths, caused by cataracts, glaucoma, or senile macular degeneration, make the elderly even more insecure about the relationship of their body to their environment. They often seek medical help too late because they do not understand the implications of the diagnosis or the chances for successful correction.

Hearing loss, the result of degeneration of the central and peripheral auditory mechanism and increased rigidity of the basilar membrane, is likely to cause even more negative personality changes in the older person than loss of sight (7). Such behavior as suspiciousness, irritability, and impatience, as well as paranoid tendencies, may develop simply because hearing is impaired. Again the person may fear to admit the problem or to seek treatment, especially if he/she is unaware of the possibilities of help, either through the use of hearing aids or corrective surgery.

Often the elderly view the hearing aid as another threat to body image. Eyeglasses are worn by all age groups and hence are more socially acceptable, but a hearing aid is conceived as overt evidence of advanced age. Adjustment to the hearing aid may be difficult for many people, and if motivation is also low, the idea may be rejected.

✔ Be especially alert as you assess visual and auditory needs of the elderly. One of the modern medical miracles is lens implant surgery for those with cataracts. Seeing the senior presurgery and postsurgery allows you to share the joy of blindness-to-sight as well as to do necessary teaching. Most seniors spend 1 to 2 days in the hospital before returning home.

✔ Hearing needs may not be met as easily, but astute observation can change the situation quickly. Consider the elderly woman who returned to her home after colostomy surgery. Although she had been pleasant and cooperative in the hospital, always nodding "Yes," she had failed to learn her colostomy irrigation routine. The visiting nurse learned, through being in the home and getting information from the family, that the patient was nearly deaf. The patient covered her loss by nodding pleasantly. Slow, distinct instructions allowed her to grasp the irrigation techniques and within several days she was managing well. The nurse also had an opportunity to refer the woman for auditory assessment. Kopac (113) and Hayter (85) give a number of specific ways to modify the environment for sensory impairments.

Jourard speaks of *spirit-titre*. He thinks the way we conceive of our body determines the degree to which our self-structure can be organized for optimum bodily defense against loss of energy. Jourard suggests that the term *spirit* be utilized to express the *titre*, or concentration of purpose, which may be encouraged in the aged to produce a well-integrated "personality-health" (100).

✔ Helping the senior keep an intact, positive body-image will raise his/her *spirit-titre*. Encourage the senior to talk about feelings related to the changing body appearance, structure, and function. Provide a mirror so that he/she can look at self to integrate the overt changes into his/her mental image. Photographs can also be useful in reintegrating a changing appearance. Help the senior to stay well groomed and attractively dressed and compliment efforts in that direction. Touch and tactile sensations are important measures to help the person continue to define body boundaries and integrate structural changes.

Spiritual Development

The elderly person with a mature religious outlook and philosophy still strives to incorporate broadened views of theology and religious action into the thinking. Because the elderly person is a good listener, he/she is usually liked and respected by all ages. While not adopting inappropriate aspects of a younger lifestyle, he/she can contemplate the fresh religious and philosophical views of adolescent thinking, thus trying to understand ideas previously missed or interpreted differently. Similarly, others listen to him/her. The elderly person feels a sense of worth while giving experienced views. Basically he/she is satisfied with living personal beliefs, and they can serve as a great comfort when he/she becomes temporarily despondent over life changes, changes in the family's life, or when confronting the idea of personal death.

The elderly person who has not matured religiously or philosophically may sense a spiritual impoverishment and despair as the drive for professional and economic success wanes. An immature outlook provides no solace, and, if a church member, he/she may become bitter. The person may feel that the church organization, to which he/she gave long and dedicated service, has forgotten since he/she has less stamina for organizational work. The person may feel cast aside in favor of the young who have so many activities planned for them. This person needs help to arrive at an adequate spiritual philosophy and to find some appropriate religious or altruistic activities that will help him/her gain feelings of acceptance, self-esteem, and worth.

✔ *Spiritual Nursing Care.* This includes talking with the elderly, listening to statements that indicate religious beliefs or spiritual needs, and reading scriptures or praying with the person, when indicated or requested. Giving spiritual care to the elderly person may involve prompt physical care to prevent angry outbursts, accepting apologies as the person seeks forgiveness for a fiery temper or sharp tongue. Quoting or reading favorite scripture verses, saying a prayer, providing religious music, or joining with the person in a religious song may calm inner storms. Acknowledging realistic losses, feeling with those who weep, can provide a positive focus and hope. Helping the aged person remain an active participant in church or in Bible study in the nursing home can maintain his/her self-esteem and sense of usefulness. Finally, in dying and near death, the religious person may want to practice beloved rituals and say, or have quoted, familiar religious or scriptural verses.

Developmental Tasks

✔ The following developmental tasks are to be achieved by the aging couple as a family as well as by the aging person living alone. You can assist the elderly person to meet these tasks.

1. Recognize the aging process and define instrumental limitations.
2. Adjust to decreasing physical strength and health changes.
3. Decide where and how to live out the remaining years; redefine physical and social life space.
4. Continue a supportive, close, warm relationship with the spouse, or significant other, including a satisfying sexual relationship.
5. Find a satisfactory home or living arrangement

and establish a safe, comfortable household routine to fit health and economic status.
6. Adjust living standards to retirement income; supplement retirement income if possible with remunerative activity.
7. Maintain maximum level of health; care for self physically and emotionally by getting regular health examinations and needed medical or dental care, eating an adequate diet, and maintaining personal hygiene.
8. Maintain contact with children, grandchildren, and other living relatives, finding emotional satisfaction with them.
9. Establish explicit affiliation with members of own age group.
10. Maintain interest in people outside the family and in social, civic, and political responsibility.
11. Pursue alternate sources of need satisfaction and new interests and maintain former activities to gain status, recognition, and a feeling of being needed.
12. Find meaning in life after retirement and in facing inevitable illness and death of oneself and spouse as well as other loved ones.
13. Work out values, life goals, and a significant philosophy of life, finding comfort in a philosophy or religion.
14. Adjust to the death of spouse and other loved ones (81).

McCoy describes similar developmental tasks for this era (132).

▶ Brown refers to different developmental tasks for the young-old and old-old person, since the changing life situations necessitate different attitudes, efforts, and behaviors. The tasks are listed as follows for each age group (11).

The young-old:

1. Prepare for and adjust to retirement from active involvement in the work arena with its subsequent role change (especially for men).
2. Anticipate and adjust to lower and fixed income after retirement.
3. Establish satisfactory physical living arrangements as a result of role changes.
4. Adjust to new relationships with one's adult children and their offspring.
5. Learn or continue to develop leisure time activities to help in realignment of role losses.
6. Anticipate and adjust to slower physical and slower intellectual responses in the activities of daily living.
7. Deal with the death of parents, spouses, and friends.

The vulnerable old or old-old:

1. Learn to combine new dependency needs with the continuing need for independence.
2. Adapt to living alone in continued independence.
3. Learn to accept and adjust to possible institutional living (nursing and/or proprietary homes).
4. Establish an affiliation with one's age group.
5. Learn to adjust to heightened vulnerability to physical and emotional stress.
6. Adjust to loss of physical strength, illness, and approach of one's death.
7. Adjust to losses of spouse, home, and friends.

▶ These developmental tasks coincide with the Standards for Geriatric Nursing Practice developed by the American Nurses Association. These standards address themselves to the following nursing actions, which summarize those discussed in this chapter.

1. Observing and interpreting signs and symptoms of normal aging as well as pathological changes and intervening appropriately.
2. Differentiating between pathological social behavior and the usual lifestyle of the aged person.
3. Demonstrating an appreciation for the heritage, values, and wisdom of older persons.
4. Supporting and promoting physiological functioning in the aged.
5. Providing protective and safety measures and supporting the aged during stressful situations.
6. Using methods to promote effective communication and socialization of aged persons with individuals, family, and others, thus increasing sensory stimulation.
7. Helping the older person adapt to the physical and psychosocial limitations of the environment, yet fulfill needs.
8. Assisting with the obtaining and use of helpful mechanical devices for improving function.
9. Resolving personal attitudes about aging, dependency, and death to provide assistance in meeting these crises with dignity and comfort (12).

Socioeconomic Concepts

Retirement

As corporations reduce their work force numbers, the older worker is most likely to be released, because of salary and pension costs. Yet, the older worker may be less costly, because of retraining costs and lower absenteeism. Many people are living longer, but working shorter careers, yet, the proportion of young to old people is diminishing. After the turn of the century, it is likely that more older people will be needed in the workplace to relieve the labor shortage (152).

Retirement affects all the other positions the person has held and the relationships with others. Retirement is a demotion in the work system. It will, for most people, mean a sharp reduction in income. Inability to keep up with the former activities of an organization or group may result, and a change in status may require a changing social life (55).

Retirement Planning. Prior planning will help in the transition from worker to retiree. Nurses are often with persons nearing retirement and may be asked directly or through nonverbal cues and disguised statements to help them sort out their feelings as they face this adjustment. While some persons who disliked their jobs, have an adequate income, and participate in a variety of activities eagerly look forward to a pleasurable retirement, many seniors would prefer and are able to work past 65 years.

Despite much work in recent years at both the national and local levels to develop comprehensive programs for the aged, few business organizations have recognized the many ways in which they might assist the potential retiree. Private organizations with large numbers of employees are, for the most part, the only ones having effective retirement preplanning programs. The federal government offers no program in retirement planning for its employees, and this is true for almost all state and local governments as well. Those programs offered usually include lectures and discussions on financial security, health insurance, legal matters, social security benefits, company pension and retirement policies, and health maintenance information.

The retiree may be faced with these questions: Can I face loss of job satisfaction? Will I feel the separation from people close to me at work? If I need continued employment on a part-time basis to supplement social security payments, will the old organization provide it, or must I adjust to a new job? Shall I remain in my present home or seek a different one because of easier maintenance or reduced cost of upkeep? Might a different climate be better and, if so, will I miss my relatives and neighbors?

✒ Whatever the elderly person's need, your role will be supportive. Advocate retirement planning. Recommend agencies that may be useful in making plans, and provide current information on Social Security benefits and Medicare coverage. Unless you are able to discuss these areas of concern and to answer questions, the needs of the person approaching retirement cannot be met. One of the most helpful resources is the large supply of government publications available at little or no cost from the Superintendent of Documents of the Government Printing Office in Washington, D.C. Current lists of material pertinent to health and social programs may be obtained directly from the National Clearing House on Aging, U.S. Department of Health and Human Services, 330 Independence Avenue, S.W., Washington, D.C. 20201.

Use of Leisure. The constructive use of free time is often a problem of aging. What a person does when he/she no longer works is related to past lifestyle, accumulated experiences, and the way in which he/she perceives and reacts to the environment (55).

Leisure time, *having opportunity to pursue activities of interest without a sense of obligation, demand, or urgency,* is an important aspect of life satisfaction. Leisure activity is chosen for its own sake, for the meaning it gives to life, but it involves both physical or mental activity and participation. It is a way to cope with change. Adults value most the leisure activity that involves interaction with others, promotes development, or is expressive, and maintains contact with the broader community. Most people have a core of activity that they enjoy. Use of leisure time by volunteering is rewarding but constrained by household income, education, age (31). Leisure time can also be spent playing with a pet, in essence, a companion.

The elder can contribute in many ways to the community and society following his/her retirement:

1. Through volunteer or part-time work with any hospital, community agencies, or social, welfare, or conservation organization of choice.
2. Through a friendly visitor program to other old or homebound people.
3. Through a telephone reassurance program (calling the same person at the same time each day to determine the status).
4. Through foster grandparent programs in nurseries, preschool or day-care settings, homes for abused or orphaned children, or juvenile detention centers. (Refer to LaRossa's article on foster grandparents in the premature nursery [116].)
5. To homes for battered women or children, providing mothering or fathering skills.
6. To shelters for the homeless, providing counseling, teaching for GED certification, or socializing.
7. To churches and church-related organizations, in many capacities.
8. To Habitat for Humanity, an organization that builds or remodel homes for poor people in various rural and urban areas of the United States, as well as in other underdeveloped nations.
9. As a volunteer for a crisis hot line: suicide, drug use, child care, prayer line.

✒ Table 14–5 lists questions to consider prior to the volunteer role or questions the senior should ask key

Table 14–5. Questions to Consider Before Volunteering

- Do you have the time to give?
- Do you make it a habit to be punctual?
- Do you take responsibility seriously?
- Can you give reasonable advance notice if you must cancel plans or appointments?
- Do you consistently follow through on projects?
- Do you work well with others?
- Do you adhere to an organization's policies and procedures?
- Do you accomplish tasks that have been assigned?
- Would you receive orientation or training you want or need?
- Do you understand and agree with the details of the position and the demands it will place upon you?
- Would you have enough responsibility/authority to challenge you if you desired the challenge?
- Is the organization respected in your community?
- Does the organization respect its volunteers' time?
- Are the current volunteers dedicated to the organization or cause?
- Would you be able to use your experience or educational background?

people in an agency that is being considered for a volunteer role. Explore these with the person.

Because Americans live in a society that has a high work priority, more training for leisure in middle age and earlier or more opportunity for continued employment in old age must be provided through public policy.

The American Association of Retired Persons (AARP) is studying the potential impact upon people as America moves from an industrialized mass society into a more technologically complex but fragmented society in the next 20 years. Older people will be retained as consultants in the work place. All people will need to be educated for a life of ceaseless change, for new activities and new roles with passing years. Older people can lead in creating a better society for all generations (93).

Materialism and productivity have been key American values. As population shifts occur, and society becomes more technologically complex, causing earlier retirement for some workers, the definition of productivity will have to be changed from that which involves exchange of money. Toffler has coined the word **prosumers,** *people who produce goods and services for their families and friends but not for monetary gain.* Family roles are also likely to change, with an older family adopting or nurturing a younger family, giving assistance with child care or other tasks. The elderly will be needed as caregivers across family lines as home care becomes an important aspect of the health care system, and the caregiving role can give added meaning to life (93).

Federal Planning for the Aged in America

The Administration on Aging

In 1958 government interest in the older citizen inspired the formation of the President's Council on Aging, which has since been taken over and expanded by the Administration on Aging (AOA). The AOA was established by the Older Americans Act of 1965 and operates as the central agency for assistance to the aged under the U.S. Department of Health and Human Services (DHHS).

The focus of AOA is to identify the needs, concerns, and interests of older persons and to carry out the programs of the Older Americans Act. It is the principal agency for promoting coordination of the federal resources available to meet the needs of the elderly. Federal grants to state agencies on aging are administered by AOA. The state agencies then act as advocates and assist in the establishment of comprehensive, coordinated service systems for older Americans at the community level. State agencies, in turn, may designate and fund area agencies, county or municipal, which then serve the aged within their own communities. The various social and nutritional services are planned and managed by these local area agencies. Direct grants to Indian tribal organizations may be made by AOA for social and nutritional services to older American Indians. AOA awards grants for research, educational demonstrations, and manpower development projects. It operates the National Information and Resource Clearinghouse for the Aged (30, 117).

The Older Americans Act has promoted research into new approaches, techniques, and methods to improve or expand social or nutritional services or otherwise enhance the well-being of older individuals. It has also supported education of individuals working in aging and related fields, or who may be preparing to do so. Multidisciplinary centers of gerontology established under AOA develop, employ, and disseminate models for teaching and training, conduct research, and operate experimental model service community laboratories in the areas of policy and program significance (30, 115).

Under the amended Domestic Volunteer Service Act of 1973, there are special programs geared to the development of a greater, more significant role in the society for older Americans so that they may participate more fully in the life of their communities and the nation. One of these is the Foster Grandparents Program. It has a dual purpose: (1) to provide part-time volunteer service opportunities for low-income persons age 60 and over, and (2) to give supportive, person-to-person assistance in health, human services, and educational and related agencies to help alleviate the physical, mental, and emotional problems of children having exceptional needs. Through grants, AOA provides the recruitment and training of the volunteers. The participants work 4 hours a day, 5 days a week and receive a stipend equal to the federal minimum hourly wage. Everyone gains in this program: The elderly earn much-needed income along with a sense of dignity and achievement and the children blossom in the warmth of personal attention (30).

The following are examples of projects under this program: work in a juvenile prison helping youth gain education, guidance, and companionship; work with severely burned children in whom the warmth and personal attention seems to promote healing; assisting autistic children with basic tasks and encouraging performance through praise; providing care to infants while unwed mothers attend basic education classes; and helping teen-agers prepare to move out of a mental health institution into a community setting such as a group home or foster home. In Babylon, New York, ten mildly to moderately mentally retarded persons who were formerly institutionalized are now serving as foster grandparents themselves. Not only have they gained a feeling of self-worth, but also the institutional cost to the public has been eliminated.

Another program sponsored by AOA is the Retired Senior Volunteer Program (RSVP). This affords out-of-pocket expenses to persons over 60 who wish to participate in locally organized volunteer projects. The local service organization, the RSVP sponsor, develops a wide variety of service opportunities in the community in hospitals, courts, schools, day-care centers, libraries, and other volunteer settings. Grants are used primarily for travel expenses of the volunteers. The advantage in this program is that many older persons may participate as volunteers whose income might otherwise limit their eligibility (30).

✔ Knowing about the programs available to the elderly will be helpful to nurses in several ways. In counseling, health teaching, and giving support, the nurse may find this knowledge useful as older patients/clients demonstrate a need for guidance in seeking help. Often the answer to loneliness may be participation in a program to help others. In addition, the nurse may have occasion through an employing health agency to apply for federal grant money either for supportive services or for research relevant to aging.

✔ For more information about functions of state and local Area Agencies on Aging, see local AOA representatives.

Social Security

Under the Social Security Act are grouped Old Age Survivors Insurance, Medicare, and Supplemental Security Income for the Elderly.

Old Age Survivors Insurance provides a consistent monthly income to males 65 and older and to females 62 and older. Family payments are made to various dependents: wives 62 and older; dependent children; wives younger than 62 who care for dependent children; dependent husbands or widowers 62 or older; and dependent parents 62 or older after the death of the insured worker. Payments are made also to persons certified to be disabled (69).

The *Supplemental Security Income* program was begun as part of the Social Security Amendments of 1972. It guarantees that the annual income of an older or a disabled person will not fall below a minimum level. This redirected the responsibility for the aged, blind, and disabled poor from the states to the federal government. The program is administered by the Social Security Administration and has one standard for eligibility: low assets and specified low income.

Of public concern in our age is the ultimate viability of the Social Security system. Originally it was assumed that our expanding population and labor force would provide adequately for continued growth as increasing wage base would provide greater taxes. On the contrary, zero population growth, decline of productivity, and inflation threaten the system. The problem is whether or not a diminishing work force of young and middle-aged persons will be willing to support the steadily growing numbers of retired persons. Population aging has created a concern that the projected number of elderly persons in the future will represent a crushing burden on the working population.

The general mandatory retirement age will be raised from 65 years in the future. Federal and some other sectors have already increased mandatory retirement age to 70. According to the Social Security Amendments of 1983, the general retirement age will be gradually raised to 67 from 65 in two stages. A major argument for raising the retirement age is that life expectancy at age 65 has been increasing over the years and is expected to continue to rise in the future. It will be difficult to determine how much to raise the retirement age. Many would consider it unfair to expect that all the years of life expectancy gained should be spent working. At the same time, it is probably unreasonable to expect that all the additional years of life expectancy should be spent in leisure (32). Even if retirement ages are postponed, the number of dependent elderly will continue to increase, and it will do so quite substantially around the end of the first quarter of the twenty-first century.

Although increasing longevity is also a factor, population aging during the first quarter of the next century primarily will result from (1) high birthrates from mid-1940s to mid-1960s, and (2) subsequent declining birthrates in the 1970s and beyond. As fewer children are born, the age structure of the population changes: the young become a smaller, and the old a larger, part of the population. Decreased morbidity accompanies increased longevity: the elderly of the future could remain in or re-enter the work force to compensate for the relatively smaller labor force in the traditional age groups. Then, paying Social Security benefits could be postponed. Changes in the work environment, however, are the prerequisites for keeping older persons in the work force (32).

✔ Understanding the problems that are developing in the Social Security system is important for all who care for the elderly. They will need support when their fears arise and they will benefit from the help of an informed nurse, one who has taken the time, through the use of the media and numerous government publications, to keep abreast of the changing scene regarding Social Security.

Medicare

Our federally financed health insurance program is called Medicare. It provides benefits to persons over age 65 who paid into Social Security, and since 1972 it has extended care to the disabled and some chronically ill persons. There are two parts to Medicare: Part A, hospital insurance, and for those who choose to have a nominal monthly fee deducted from their Social Security checks, Part B, medical insurance.

Under Part A, most hospital costs and costs for a specified period in a skilled nursing facility/home are covered after an annual deductible is met by the insured. Part B of Medicare covers 80 percent of allowable costs for physicians' services and outpatient care. If the charges for services rendered exceed that which Medicare Parts A or B deems reasonable and proper for the particular service, the enrollee must pay the difference. Prospective payment regulations are changing this. Insurance programs specific for supplement to Medicare payments are available.

✔ As with Social Security, the nurse needs to be conversant with current public announcements and other information to be of help and assurance to the elderly who may have great concern when they are ill as to their security and care under this program. The Social Security representative available in all cities and most hospitals can be of help to the nurse in planning for any problems arising in the areas of either Social Security or Medicare. Inform elders, if necessary, of the Medicare Catastrophic Insurance Act, which provides extra coverage.

Federal Role in Health Promotion

The major federal role in the area of health has been that of the Public Health Service, which is now under DHHS. All planning for health care is filtered down through the state, county, and city health departments. Under the U.S. Public Health Service are countless agencies with programs that include health services to veterans, control of food and drugs, construction of health facilities, medical services for retired civil service employees, rent supplements, and provision of public housing.

As part of the ongoing federal concern for the aged, the third decennial White House Conference on Aging was held in Washington, D.C., in November to December of 1981. Whereas the first conference in 1961 produced the concept of Medicare and the second in 1971 helped yield the Older Americans Act, this most recent conference has been more general in its recommendations. The conference served to empower older persons to speak their minds. There was a positive stand taken on residents' rights in nursing homes, the need for staff training, and the upgrading of nursing assistants (38, 191). Although no definitive policy was forthcoming, the conference of 1981 reflects a concern by the elderly for continued improvement and expansion of services, both in long-term care facilities and in the community.

✔ As a nurse, your influence can be felt in these areas through your work, community activities, and in civic affairs by participation in your professional organization.

Community Planning

As people become older, infirm, and less mobile, a battery of community services is needed, not only to provide social activities and a reason to remain interested in life, but also to enable them to live independently. Most of the federal programs operate at the local level in actual practice, but, in addition, there is much that each community can do to provide needed services, which are available through the local Council on Aging. In small communities these services may be limited, but further information may be obtained through any county public health agency.

Community Services

Supportive services may include the following: (1) referral services; (2) visiting and telephone-reassurance programs, sometimes offered through churches or private organizations; (3) services that provide shopping aides; (4) portable meals, sometimes known as "Meals on Wheels" for those who cannot shop for or prepare their own food; (5) transportation and handy-person services; (6) day care or foster home placement for the elderly; (7) recreation facilities geared to the older person; and (8) senior-citizen centers that provide recreation and a place for the lonely to belong. The American Association for Retired People (AARP) is a national organization which has numerous benefits socially and financially through insurance and other programs.

One of the most helpful community services for elders is the senior center. Senior centers are now found in almost all communities, based in a variety of settings. Some are operating in buildings built for this purpose but most are housed in facilities originally planned for other purposes: church halls, community buildings, old schools, mobile-home park clubhouses, and the like. Their programs are federally funded to some extent, but rely heavily on community support. A small staff is maintained and most of the help with programs, maintenance, and materials comes from volunteers among the older persons who attend the center. Programs include such activities such as crafts, social events from cards to dancing, exercise classes, and a full meal served at noon most weekdays. Other services may be daily telephone calls to homebound elderly, information and referral services, home-delivered meals, minor profit-making endeavors, and discount programs in cooperation with local merchants.

Several approaches are being tried in various communities based on the principle that before helping maintain health in the aged or contributing toward restoration of health, those working with community health must understand this age group. Toward this end, many persons enrolled in educational programs for the health professions are carrying out visiting programs with the elderly. Most nursing students are exposed to elderly persons through visits to geriatric centers or by interviewing experiences designed to sharpen communication skills as well as to afford opportunities to gain insight into the needs of older persons.

Group work among the aged has been done with much success in a number of communities and in a variety of settings. Some of these have been initiated in centers operated for the elderly and have been used not only to encourage the individual to participate in a group activity, but also to carry out health teaching. Many types of groups can be developed for the elderly; some are described in reference 140.

As a citizen of the community, you can be active in initiating and supporting local programs such as those described above and in Table 14–6.

Nursing Homes/Extended Care Facilities

The modern-day nursing home, extended care facility, or senior health care center in the United States evolves from the "county poor farms." These farms were a place where the elderly who could not afford better care and who did not have family to care for them lived out their existence. The modernized versions are called *skilled nursing facilities* if certified by DHHS and *intermediate care facilities* if certified by the individual states. The former provide the higher level of care. Ideally, the nursing home will serve as a

Table 14–6. Community Resources for Older People

RESOURCE	SERVICE
Adult Congregate Living Facilities (ACLF)	Room, board, and personal services for elderly who would benefit from living in a group setting but do not require medical services. No nursing or medical services available.
Adult Day Care	Provision of comfortable, safe environment for functionally impaired adults, especially frail elderly, moderately handicapped, or slightly confused, who need care during the day, either because they live alone and cannot manage, or because family needs relief from the care in order to keep the elderly in the home.
Adult Foster Care	Provision for continuous care to a functionally impaired older person in a private home with people who provide all services needed by the elderly individual.
After Care	Posthospitalization rehabilitation, such as cardiac or respiratory rehabilitation, occupational, or physical therapy.
American Association of Retired Persons (AARP)	Nationwide organization for people over 50 which offers discount drug purchases, health and auto insurance, publications, and other activities.

Table 14–6. Community Resources for Older People—Continued

RESOURCE	SERVICE
Area Agency on Aging	Federal agency that provides information, referral services, planning, and coordination, but not direct or health care services, on a regional or county-wide basis.
Congregate Nutrition Sites	Free or low cost meals, social activities, and nutrition or health education provided in local churches or senior centers.
Congregate Living Facility	Apartment complex which provides meals and social programs for older people.
Elderhostel	An on-campus educational experience, living on campus for duration of the course that includes opportunity for new knowledge, travel to various campuses and national and international geographic areas, new experiences, meeting new people.
Foster Care	Placement of nonrelated elderly person in private residence for care.
Foster Grandparents	Federal program paying people with low income, who are over age 60, a modest amount for working over 20 hours a week with mentally or physically handicapped children.
Friendly Visiting	Organized visiting services staffed by volunteers who visit homebound elderly once or twice weekly for companionship purposes if there are no relatives or friends available.
Gray Panthers	Nationwide politically oriented organization that works to raise awareness about issues affecting older people and to advocate and lobby on these issues in local, state, and national government.
Home Health Services	Agency provides intermittent nursing, social work, and physical, occupational, and speech therapies; and other related services in the home, via qualified health care professional or paraprofessionals to home bound person.
Homemaker/Chore Services	Agency provides help with light housekeeping, laundry, home chores, meal preparation, shopping for older people meeting income and other eligibility requirements.
Hospice	A continuum of care systems for persons suffering from terminal disease and for their family, including home care, pain management, respite care, counseling, family support delivered in the home through out-patient and in-patient care—all within the same licensed program. It is medically directed, nurse coordinated, autonomously administered, and provides care for physical, emotional, spiritual and social needs of patient and family using an interdisciplinary team approach.
Long Term Care Ombudsman Committees	Citizen Committees appointed by the Governor who volunteer their time to investigate and resolve grievances or problems of people in nursing homes and ACLFs.
Meals on Wheels	Provision of hot/cold nutritious meals to a homebound elderly person, brought by another person/agency.
Medicaid	Governmental coverage of health care and nursing home costs for older people with limited incomes, who are eligible. People who receive Supplemental Security Income or Aid to Families of Dependent Children are automatically eligible.
Medicare	National health insurance program for people age 65 and older, or disabled, or in some special cases under 65, that is administered by the Social Security Administration. Part A is hospital insurance; Part B covers diagnostic tests, physician fees, outpatient and ambulance costs. Dental, vision, hearing, and preventive services are excluded.
Protective Services	Constellation of social services that assist older, noninstitutionalized people, who manifest at least some incapacity to manage their money or their daily living, or assist those who need protection of life or property.
Respite Care	Agency provides relief for specified hours, a weekend, or a week, for family caregivers, allowing time for the caregiver to shop, have the time for other reasons, or vacation, while care is given to functionally impaired person residing in the home setting.
Senior Center	A program providing a combination of services, designed to be open 3 or more days a week, with meal, recreational, educational, and counseling services available. Sometimes medical services are provided.
Senior Corp of Retired Executives	Agency of retired executives who volunteer their counseling services to small businesses and companies upon request.
Supplemental Security Income—SSI	A minimum monthly income to blind, disabled, and aged persons whose income falls below a specified level. Personal effects, household goods, and home ownership are not counted as assets, although savings, stocks, jewelry, or car would be.
Telephone Reassurance	Daily telephone calls to people who live alone, including the aged and disabled, or telephone crisis and information services provided by an agency.

transitional stop between hospital and home (generally for those over 65); in some cases, however, the stay is permanent.

The goals of the modern-day facility are to provide continuous supervision by a physician, 24-hour nurse coverage, hospital affiliation, written patient care policies and specialized services in dietary, restorative, pharmaceutical, diagnostic, and social services. Unfortunately, these are sometimes hollow goals even though the physical plant is new, licensing is current, and government funds are being used. Often the homes are operated for profit by those outside the nursing or medical profession. The residents are not always physically or mentally able to protest if care is poor, and often families of the residents do not monitor the care. Recent national exposure of blatant neglect in some of the facilities has awakened public and government consciousness, and perhaps this exposure will correct the most glaring problems as well as alert other facilities to their obligation to follow prescribed goals. If standards are met, the nursing home provides an excellent and needed service to our society because the elderly do need to be discharged from expensive acute care hospital beds as soon as possible. Prolonged hospitalization can foster confusion, helplessness, and the hazards of immobility. Further, some elderly cannot care for self.

Selecting a Nursing Home. When you help the family or senior select a nursing home, the following questions should be asked:

1. What type of home is it and what is its licensure status?
2. What are the total costs, and what is included for the money?
3. Is the physical plant adequate, clean, and pleasant? How much space and furniture are allowed for each person?
4. What safety features are evident? Are fire drills held?
5. What types of care are offered (acute as well as chronic)?
6. What is the staff-resident ratio? What are the qualifications of the staff? What are staff attitudes toward the elderly?
7. What are the physician services? Is a complete physical examination given periodically?
8. What therapies are available?
9. Are pharmacy services available?
10. Are meals nutritionally sound and the food tasty? Is eating supervised or assisted?
11. Are visitors welcomed warmly?
12. Do residents appear content and appropriately occupied? (Observe on successive days and at different hours.) Are they treated with dignity and warmth by staff?
13. Has the local Better Business Bureau received any complaints about this facility?
14. Does the administrator have a current state license?
15. Is the home certified to participate in government or other programs that provide financial assistance when needed?

Translocation. The elderly person who is moved to a nursing home or long-term care facility (often rest-of-the-lifetime care facility), or who is moved from one room to another within the same facility, undergoes a crisis called **translocation syndrome,** *physical and emotional deterioration as a result of changes or movement.* A move may be made because of changes in health, in staffing, in the residents, or families desire it. Such a move may be life threatening, however.

People at greatest risk are those who are depressed, highly anxious, severely ill, intermittently confused, or over 85 years of age. People who need structure, who cannot stand changes, or who deny problems or feelings are also more likely to experience difficulty. Reducing relocation's impact begins with enlisting the resident's understanding of the need for the move and participation. The person should be prepared for the move. When he/she can make decisions about the move, and predict what will happen, the person maintains a sense of control, which diminishes the move's impact. Moving to a similar environment also reduces the problems. The ability to express fears, concerns, and anger help. If the person to be moved to an institution is relatively young, had good morale, and had an opportunity to select and then felt satisfied with the new surroundings, the translocation syndrome may be minimal (136).

One way to reduce the crisis of admission to a nursing home or long-term care center or reduce translocation shock is to have preschool or school children visit in the home. Both generations benefit from the exchange of affection. The youngsters bring stimulation to the elderly generation, the older generation can demonstrate stability, wisdom, coping with adversities, and the qualities of ego-integrity (174).

Elderly persons living alone or only with a spouse were, in one study, more likely than those who lived with a child, relative, or friend, to prefer moving to an alternate setting such as a nursing home or senior housing when they were unable to care for self (8).

Taking one's frail loved one to a nursing home is not easy at that point in life when he/she can no longer care for self and home, at that point when the person has lost about everything that was precious and gave life meaning. Neal gives a poignant account of the pain for the elder and for the family, and how the elder works to retain personal integrity and dignity in spite of the emotional assault (142).

Other Living Arrangements

For those elderly who want to live at home but need some degree of care, there are alternatives. A Florida agency is helping more than 10,000 persons stay out of institutions by delivering meals to them at home or shuttling them to community dining centers. Through the program the elderly can hire helpers to wash windows or rake lawns and homemakers to shop or do light housekeeping. Transportation is provided to doctors' offices. Fees are based on ability to pay. The state of Florida estimates it saved 9.5 million dollars in the past year by assisting these persons to live at home.

Senior day-care centers provide another alternative. The charges are reasonable per day, and they cater to persons not as able as those who may avail themselves of the usual senior center.

Some communities have set up centers to match roommates. Two persons may function better than alone, and the costs are shared. A Boston group has sponsored a project that arranges intergenerational living: 14 people ages 30 to 80 share a nineteenth-century townhouse. Everyone takes part in the chores and pays a nominal rent for their own room. Extended families have been created in some cities. A retired hospital administrator with arthritis now shares her four-bedroom home with a young couple and their newborn daughter and each generation learns from the other.

Remotivation

Many health-care workers are doing group work in extended care facilities to combat the effects of institutionalization in the elderly.

Remotivation is one form of group therapy that can be conducted in a hospital, nursing home, or senior center for disengaged or regressed elderly. The training materials for instructing employees in remotivation techniques are available from the American Psychiatric Association's central office in Washington, D.C. Although it originated in the psychiatric setting, the technique is now used nationwide in a variety of settings—old-age facilities, general and chronic-disease hospitals, and in schools for the retarded. The content used is easily adaptable for the type of people in each group.

The goal of this therapy is to remotivate the unwounded areas in the personality of the older adult. The techniques can be used by the average employee—nurse or ancillary—who is closest to the patient or resident for most of the day. It is designed to stimulate self-respect, self-reliance, and self-value in the older person who has become disengaged (67, 140, 194).

Remotivation encourages the person to focus attention on the simple, objective aspects of everyday life. As the patient is helped toward resocialization, the nurse–patient relationship is also strengthened. Staff members display a greater interest in the patient as an individual than they did prior to the use of this technique; they begin to recognize the therapeutic value of their presence in meeting the needs of patients.

The method consists of a series of meetings, usually about 12, led by a person who has received instruction in the technique. No more than 15 patients make up the group, and the sessions last approximately an hour each. The leader guides the group in a discussion through five specific steps:

1. *Creating a climate of acceptance* (5 minutes) through greeting each person by name, expressing pleasure at his/her presence, and making remarks that encourage replies such as comments on the weather, a familiar incident, or the person's apparel.
2. *Creating a bridge to the world* (15 minutes) by relating a current event or referring to a topic of general interest and then encouraging each one to comment. The central topic—a recipe, a familiar quotation, a newspaper item—differs according to the backgrounds of the group members.
3. *Sharing the world we live in* (15 minutes) by expanding step 2 and developing the subject further through the use of appropriate visual aids.
4. *Appreciating the work of the world* (15 minutes) through discussion of jobs, how a certain commodity is produced, how a job may be done quickly and efficiently, or the type of work they have done in the past.
5. *Creating a climate of appreciation* (5 minutes), expressing pleasure in their attendance and their contributions. Plans are made for the next meeting, providing continuity and something to look forward to (163).

You may use this technique as an adjunct to other nursing intervention, for the principles of remotivation technique can be modified for work with other patient groups, to establish initial rapport, or to establish a nurse–patient relationship. Remotivation increases communication and strengthens contact with everyday features of the world for the person who may be advanced in years and perhaps is physically debilitated, but who still has many areas of intact personality.

Group Action Among Older Citizens

Interest in civic, social, political, and economic issues is shown in various action groups that have been organized among older citizens through community projects. The Gray Panthers is a well-known organization, as is AARP, but there are other groups as well.

One example of what older persons can do to help others in their community is explained in a report on a visiting service for isolated elderly persons. The project was initiated by a graduate student in nursing who used epidemiological methods and was planned and executed by a senior citizens' club through a city recreation department. Preparation for the project included a survey of community services to determine which were most and least used, which were inadequate, what changes were needed, and what sort of problems the elderly in the area had to face. The result was the organization of a one-to-one visiting service that brought joy and met needs of the isolated elderly. It also provided the visitors with a sense of independence, social acceptability, recognition, status, and a sense of meaning in their lives at a time when losses of one sort or another had left them vulnerable (3).

Action groups have been formed in many of our major cities in recent years. Their members are elderly persons who are concerned about the needs of their peers and who feel that group action is effective in bringing about legislative change, especially in the area of financial assistance to meet rising costs. Many of these groups have sent representatives to the White House Conference on Aging and have exerted a considerable influence on federal and local planning. Such issues as tax relief, transportation, medical care, and nutrition are of vital interest to many concerned elderly citizens who still feel responsible for themselves and their community.

You may have the opportunity to work with action groups in either an advisory, consultative, or direct participation role.

Retirement Communities

Along with our increased life span and the development of social planning for retirement has come the emergence of a distinct social phenomenon: the retirement apartment complex community.

Apartment complexes are financed privately, by religious organizations, or by the government. The senior must be able to maintain self, although visiting nurse services are acceptable. These complexes may include a central dining room, a nurse and doctor on call, planned social events, transportation services, and religious services. Essentially all living needs are within easy access. Additionally, the seniors have the company of each other if they so desire.

In many cities, hotels have been converted to residence facilities for the elderly. Reminiscent of old-style rooming houses, they provide more supervision and services such as meals, laundry facilities and shopping. In most of these residences, each person is responsible for his or her own room, laundry, and breakfast (197).

Many couples opt for continuous care facilities. An example of this style of living is the type of community that has been built by the Life Care Services Corporation. Since 1961, this nonprofit organization has built 30 retirement communities in 17 states. One or two-bedroom apartments or cottages are available for a one-time endowment and a monthly fee for two persons. Services include one meal a day, maid service, all utilities including local telephone bill, full maintenance, a full recreational and social program, and many extras. The residents have at their disposal a fully equipped health center with 24-hour nursing care service as long as needed in the intermediate or long-term care sections of the nursing home facility.

In many regions of the United States, especially in Florida, the desert Southwest, and California, planned communities have been built that are specifically designed for and restricted to those persons over 55. Some are carefully planned miniature cities of low cost with simply designed homes built around clubhouse activities, golf courses, and swimming and therapy pools. Activities such as bingo games, dance instruction, foreign-language study, crafts, or bridge lessons are offered. Other communities are mobile-home parks where often elaborate coaches cost as much as and are set up as permanent homes.

One sociological aspect of these communities bearing such names as "Sun City," "Leisure World," and "Carefree Village" is the lifestyle adopted by the residents as they try to establish a secure base in a new life that is often far removed from family, former friends, and familiar patterns of living. They show concern for the safety, health, and well-being of each other by watching to see that lights are on at accustomed hours in each other's homes, signifying all is well. Celebration of birthdays with special parties and remembrances, entertaining for visiting friends and relatives of one's neighbors, and visiting the sick members and providing food and transportation to the hospital for the spouse of a sick resident all become part of the new life. The residents participate in activities that are either completely new or have not been indulged in for many years, such as golf, bicycle riding, hiking, and dancing. Even clothes become gayer for both sexes and the popularity of casual dress provides for the members of the "snow-bird" set—those who have moved to a warm climate—a new freedom and a chance to try bright colors and styles they may not have worn in a former setting.

↙ This phenomenon gives you insight into the needs for security, a sense of maximum personal effectiveness and belonging, and a feeling of self-actualization felt by older persons, especially when old patterns are put aside either by choice or because of circumstances mediated by health or socioeconomic conditions. Further, the older adult needs a suitable place to live, supportive relationships, a sense of community, financial security, and a sense of setting and achieving goals.

The Impact of the Able Elderly

The emergence of a population group identified as the well elderly is the result of social and demographic progress in the industrial world. More people are living longer, and poverty, frailty, and dependence are not the common characteristics of most of these older people. In the future, there will be more healthy elderly who are better educated and physically and emotionally capable. Our society can already utilize the elderly population's capabilities; in the future we shall have a rich human resource in larger numbers.

The elderly often give financial support as well as other kinds of assistance to their younger family members; most old people are not a drain on the family. An aging society offers expanding opportunities for family life. Four types of new potentials are present because of recent demographic change: (1) increased complexity of social networks, (2) increased duration of relationships, (3) prolonged opportunities to accumulate experience, and (4) new chances to complete or change role assignments.

The elder's accumulated shared experience builds family bonds, but also helps others deal with a changing historical context. As the elderly leaves certain roles behind, he/she can now pick up new roles—whether it is as a grandparent; in a second career; activity in the political, social, or community arena; being a decision maker; being an advocate for ethical and moral actions; or participating in policy making or creative pursuits in the arts. Hagested and Hudson describe the contributions that well elderly are and will be making to society, and the importance of perceiving the well older person as a contributing resource (76, 92).

Outlook for the Future

↙ The current generation of older persons is where we shall all be one day, and therefore planning for them is planning for all of us. Areas such as health-care delivery, distribution of income over a long life span, sustaining adequate social involvement, coping with organizational systems, and use of leisure are all problems of now and the future. Intervention which seems costly now may be, in the long run, the most economical in terms of tax dollars.

In the face of increasing shortages which raise the cost of living and the change in age and sex distribution by that time, future planning for the elderly will include employment and the attendant problems usually associated with younger persons. Our society will need the experience and wisdom of the senior generation. If persons are employed as late as age 75, health maintenance programs, industrial planning, and awareness of safety needs are just a few of the necessary considerations.

↙ For the older less active persons of the future, Burnside suggests intervening in loneliness through listening, exploring what may be significant to the seniors, and helping them to compensate in some way for personal losses. In addition, she suggests that nurses record the experiences of the elderly for posterity. Day schools for the elderly might encourage research projects, family therapy, and the study of successful aging (18).

↙ Thus you, the nurse of the future, will be challenged to be the innovator. You will be called on to devise and use new treatment methods so that the elderly will function more effectively in society. It is your goal to help them (1) use the potential they have developed throughout life, (2) pass through the years of late maturity with ego intact and satisfying memories, and (3) leave something of their philosophy for posterity.

↙ NURSING APPLICATIONS

Assessment and Nursing Diagnoses

Your role in caring for the elderly person or couple has been described throughout the chapter. Assessment, utilizing knowledge presented about normal aging changing versus pathology in the elderly, provides the basis for *nursing diagnoses*. Nursing diagnoses that may be applicable are listed in Table 14–7.

Interventions

Interventions may involve direct care, the use of verbal and nonverbal skills, availability of self and therapeutic relationship; or support, counseling, education, spiritual care, use of remotivation techniques, or referral as you assist the person in later maturity to meet physical, emotional, cognitive, spiritual, or social needs.

Table 14–7. Selected Nursing Diagnoses Related to Person in Later Maturity[a]

PATTERN 1: EXCHANGING	PATTERN 6: MOVING
Altered Nutrition: More than body requirements	Impaired Physical Mobility
Altered Nutrition: Less than body requirements	Fatigue
Hypothermia	Potential Activity Intolerance
Hyperthermia	Sleep Pattern Disturbance
Stress Incontinence	Diversional Activity Deficit
Potential for Injury	Impaired Home Maintenance Management
Potential for Trauma	Altered Health Maintenance
Potential for Disuse Syndrome	Bathing/Hygiene Self Care Deficit
Potential Impaired Skin Integrity	Dressing/Grooming Self Care Deficit
PATTERN 2: COMMUNICATING	PATTERN 7: PERCEIVING
Impaired Verbal Communication	Body Image Disturbance
PATTERN 3: RELATING	Self Esteem Disturbance
Impaired Social Interaction	Chronic Low Self Esteem
Social Isolation	Situational Low Self Esteem
Altered Role Performance	Sensory/Perceptual Alterations
Sexual Dysfunction	Unilateral Neglect
Altered Family Processes	Hopelessness
Altered Sexuality Patterns	Powerlessness
PATTERN 4: VALUING	PATTERN 8: KNOWING
Spiritual Distress	Knowledge Deficit
PATTERN 5: CHOOSING	Altered Thought Processes
Ineffective Individual Coping	
Impaired Adjustment	PATTERN 9: FEELING
Defensive Coping	Pain
Ineffective Denial	Chronic Pain
Ineffective Family Coping: Disabling	Dysfunctional Grieving
Ineffective Family Coping: Compromised	Anticipatory Grieving
Family Coping: Potential for Growth	Post-Trauma Response
Decisional Conflict	Anxiety
Health Seeking Behaviors	Fear

[a]Other of the NANDA diagnoses related to physiological phenomena are applicable to the ill individual in this group.
Source: NANDA Approved Nursing Diagnostic Categories, *Nursing Diagnosis Newsletter*, 15, no. 1 (Summer, 1988), 1–3.

You represent a whole cluster of psychological potentials for the elderly person; you become the supportive figure, interpreter of the unknown, symbol of the people close to him/her, and possessor of important secrets or privileged information. You become guide and companion. All this occurs if an empathic regard for the elderly person is reflected in your attitude and actions, even though initially your image may have been that of punitive parent. Of prime importance is your willingness to listen, explain, orient, reassure, and comfort the elderly person. Your role is crucial, for you are the one who is most likely to maintain personal contact with the patient either in an institutional setting or in a community agency.

Involve the person's family if possible. The interest of a family member does much to increase motivation on the part of the elderly. Determine family attitudes and evaluate relationships during teaching-learning or visiting sessions where the family is present. This procedure helps the family members alter their attitudes to a more realistic acceptance of their relative's health needs (46).

The cognitive and emotional needs of the elderly person can be met in many ways. Adequate environmental conditions to overcome sensory impairment and clearly defined communication, including explanations of procedures and the necessity for them, are vital. Demonstration and written instructions along with the verbal message, divided into small units, are very effective for teaching skills related to self-care and should be combined with practice sessions. The older person seems to learn more easily when stimuli are logically grouped and sequential, when a larger amount of data is given rather than isolated bits, and when the essential information is relevant to needs, interests, and life experience. He/she is likely to recall this information when necessary. When planning for a new task is overlapped with the execution of a previous one, the older person works slowly and with care. The real situation should be simulated as much as possible so that essential steps of the task can be clearly perceived and the teaching can be adapted to the individual's pattern and ability. Allow the person ample time to respond to a task. Your understanding attitude is important if you are to prevent discouragement and depression.

As in all communication, false assurance can only inhibit the person's ability to develop a trusting attitude and may smack of paternalism. The display of genuine interest and a receptive attitude will show the older person that he/she is not alone and will help immeasurably in allaying fear. Candor helps decrease anxiety, and the person's fear of death, the dark, or the unknown may be overcome to a great degree through your presence.

✔ Encourage the senior to reminisce; it is an effective intervention for many reasons. Reminiscing or life review helps the senior to stay oriented, to be aware of his or her environment, to think in a logical fashion, and to socialize with others. More significantly, as you talk with the person about the past life, you help him/her work through previously unresolved conflicts and to reaffirm the worth of life. He/she gains a new perspective on life and personal accomplishments; self-esteem is elevated and ego integrity is further refined. Ask questions about his/her early years, work experience, family, special events, travel, and hobbies. Listen as the person shares life philosophy and gives counsel. Look at family photographs and treasured objects with him/her. You may wish to establish a group of seniors whose main goal is to reminisce (18, 103).

Loneliness is an outgrowth of psychological changes in the elderly and implies a need to assess carefully situations to determine the signs as described in the following case study:

> An elderly man living alone made no complaint of loneliness, but the astute community health nurse found his home in deplorable untidiness and unsafe clutter, his diet extremely limited, and his personal hygiene poor. After a homemaker was sent in to help him clean the house, sit with him during meals, and provide a chance for a trusting relationship with another person, he became receptive to suggestions for modifying his living habits and eventually began to visit a senior-citizen group regularly and to make new friends. He came to realize that adaptation to isolation had been unsafe. Interest and patience showed by others restored the feeling of being a valued and accepted human being again.

The authors know of other individuals who would not modify living habits but chose to remain (from a health-care viewpoint) in unsafe and unsanitary conditions. Yet instead of giving the person up as a "hopeless case," the nurses continued to foster a relationship of trust, listened to reasons for remaining in the present situation, and helped the person live out the remaining life on his/her own terms.

Helping the elderly person to remain in contact with the environment may be as simple as providing devices such as clocks, watches, and calendars and letting him/her be the one who winds the clock and turns the calendar page each day. If a hearing aid is worn, check its effectiveness. Sudden moves, even within the same institution, increase mortality rates and psychological and physical deterioration. The person should be permitted to remain in familiar territory and with the desired clutter. If a move is essential, he/she should have some choice in the decision, an opportunity to keep valued possessions, and time to adjust to the idea. The person needs to have a personal lounging chair or specific place in the dining room. Room furniture should be arranged for physical safety and emotional security. Privacy must be respected.

Darkness is a cause of confusion. Night lights should be left on, and call bell, tissues, and water placed within easy reach. In the hospital room, contact should be available to the patient through frequent, quietly made rounds at night. Sometimes a patient may remain oriented more easily if the room door is open so that he/she can see the nurses' station and be reassured of not being alone.

The use of touch is very beneficial, for the older person has little physical contact with others. The need for contact comfort is great in the human organism, and you can satisfy this need to a degree, provided you remember that touch is a language and has a special power. In giving medications, physical care, and in doing treatments, touching is a crucial encounter. Often the person will pay close attention to instructions and cooperate more in his/her care when you use touch on the hand or shoulder while speaking. The success of this aid depends on what your hands are saying.

To the elderly, all things connected with food service have psychological implications. Food represents life—it nurtures. Mealtime is thought of as a time of fellowship with others and a sharing of pleasure, and this attitude should be retained as much as possible for older people. Making the food more attractive, talking with the person, comforting and touching, cajoling if need be, may help, especially if food is being refused. Appetizers and special drinks have been successfully used as an aid to therapy (19).

The overall loss of physical capacity, decreased resilience, and lowered capacity to resist stress cause most elderly people to view any illness as a potential major crisis in life. Although it may not be obvious, fear is ever present and death seems to wait in the wings. Unfamiliar surroundings cause apprehension and either temporary or permanent loss of contact with those who could give support—spouse, friends, relatives—may cause anxiety. Such anxiety can reduce recuperative powers and is sometimes more distressing than the illness itself.

During any crisis in which the organism is under stress, there are several alternatives: exhaustion, recuperation through the help of others, or despondency and dependency. Through the second alternative you may work toward resolution of the crisis.

The fine line between independence and dependence is difficult to maintain with patients of any age, but especially in the elderly because of society's view of them. Expectations of those around us generally foster behavior to match. Conflict between independent and dependent feelings can be avoided, usually by first assuming a firm control based on professional competence and then later relaxing and allowing the patient to emancipate self (19).

Working with the elderly person may be very rewarding if you are able to suspend youth-directed attitudes and not measure the person against standards which are inappropriate and perhaps too demanding. As with other age groups and in all our relationships, acceptance of the other person as he/she is, not as you wish him/her to be, is extremely important.

References

1. Anderson, Linda, and Marshelle Thobadan, Clients In Crisis: When Should the Nurse Step In, *Journal of Gerontological Nursing*, 10, no. 2 (1984), 6–10.
2. Armbrecht, James, John Prendergast, and Rodney Coe (eds.), *Nutritional Intervention in the Aging Process*. New York: Springer-Verlag, 1984.
3. Barnes, R., M. Raskind, M. Scott, et al., Problems of Families Caring for Alzheimer's Patients: Use of a Support Group, *Journal of American Geriatric Society*, 29, no. 2 (February 1981), 80–85.
4. Bates, Barbara, *A Guide to Physical Examination* (3rd ed.). Philadelphia: J. B. Lippincott, 1983.
5. Beam, DaMarlene, Helping Families Survive, *American Journal of Nursing*, 84, no. 2 (1984), 229.
6. Beckmann, Linda, and Betsy Houser, The Consequences of Childlessness on the Social-Psychological Well-Being of Older Women, *Journal of Gerontology*, 37, no. 2 (1982), 243–250.
7. Beeson, Paul B., and Walsh McDermott (eds.), *Cecil-Loeb Textbook of Medicine* (16th ed.). Philadelphia: W. B. Saunders, 1982.
8. Beland, Frances, Living Arrangement Preferences Among Elderly People, *The Gerontologist*, 27, no. 6 (1987), 797–803.
9. Berliner, Harriet, Aging Skin, *American Journal of Nursing*, 86, no. 10 (1986), 1138–1141.
10. ———, Aging Skin: Part Two, *American Journal of Nursing*, 86, no. 11 (1986), 1259–1262.
11. Blazer, D., and I. C. Siegler, *A Family Approach to Health Care of The Elderly*. Menlo Park, CA: Addison-Wesley, 1983.
12. Bozian, Marguerite, and Helen Clark, Counteracting Sensory Changes in the Aging, *American Journal of Nursing*, 80, no. 3 (1980), 473–476.
13. Brickfield, Cyril, *Strategies for Good Health*. Washington, D.C.: American Association of Retired Persons, 1986.
14. Brodsky, Ruthan, As Much to Gain as Give: Join the Vital World of Today's Volunteers, *Modern Maturity* (April–May, 1987), 46–50.
15. Brody, Elaine, Pauline Johnson, Mark Fulcomer, et al., Women's Changing Roles and Help to Elderly Parents: Attitudes of Three Generations of Women, *Journal of Gerontology*, 38, no. 5 (1983), 597–607.
16. Brown, Mollie, *Readings in Gerontology*. St. Louis: C. V. Mosby, 1978.
17. Buhler, Charlotte, The Developmental Structure of Goal Setting in Group and Individual Studies, in *The Course of Human Life*, eds. C. Buhler and F. Massarik. New York: Spring, 1968.
18. Burnside, Irene (ed.), *Nursing and the Aged*. New York: McGraw-Hill, 1976.
19. ———, and Dan Blazer, *Handbook of Geriatric Psychiatry*. New York: Van Nostrand Reinhold, 1980.
20. Butler, Robert and Myrna Lewis, *Aging and Mental Health* (2nd ed.). St. Louis: C. V. Mosby, 1977.
21. Bryant, Shirley, Neighbors Support of Older Widows Who Live Alone in Their Own Homes, *The Gerontologist*, 25, no. 3 (1985), 305.
22. Burggraf, Virginia, and Barbara Donlon, Assessing the Elderly, *American Journal of Nursing*, 85, no. 9 (1985), 974–984.
23. Burris, Kathryn, Recommending Adult Day Care Centers, *Nursing and Health Care*, 1, no. 3 (1981), 437–441.
24. Burtis, Grace, Judi Davis, and Sandra Martin, *Applied Nutrition and Diet Therapy*. Philadelphia: W. B. Saunders, 1988.
25. Caldwell, Janice, A Message from the Director, *Gerontology News* (April, 1982), 5.
26. Cameron, Marcia, *Views of Aging*. Ann Arbor, Mich.: The University of Michigan, Institute of Gerontology, 1976.
27. Camp, Cameron, The Use of Fact Retrieval vs. Inference in Young and Elderly Adults, *Journal of Gerontology*, 36, no. 6 (1981), 715–721.
28. Campbell, Ruth, and Elaine Brody, Women's Changing Roles and Help to the Elderly, *The Gerontologist*, 25, no. 6 (1985), 584–592.
29. Caserta, J., Public Policy for Long-Term Care, *Geriatric Nursing*, 4 (1983), 244–247.

30. *Catalogue of Federal and Domestic Assistance.* Washington, D.C.: U.S. Office of Management and Budget, 1981.
31. Chambre, Susan, Is Volunteering a Substitute for Role Loss in Old Age? An Empirical Test of Activity Theory, *The Gerontologist*, 24, no. 3 (1984), 292–298.
32. Chen, Yung Ping, Making Assets Out of Tomorrow's Elderly, *The Gerontologist*, 27, no. 4 (1987), 410–416.
33. Chenoweth, Barbara, and Beth Spencer, Dementia: The Experience of Family Caregivers, *The Gerontologist*, 26, no. 3 (1986), 267–272.
34. Chiriboga, David, Adaptation of Marital Separation in Later and Earlier Life, *Journal of Gerontology*, 37, no. 1 (1982), 109–114.
35. Chiriboga, David, Social Stressors as Antecedents of Change, *Journal of Gerontology*, 39, no. 4 (1984), 468–477.
36. Chow, Nelson Wing-Sun, The Chinese Family and Support of the Elderly in Hong Kong, *The Gerontologist*, 23, no. 6 (1983), 584–588.
37. Clark, Noreen, and William Rakowski, Family Caregivers of Older Adults: Improving Helping Skills, *The Gerontologist*, 23, no. 6 (1983), 637–642.
38. Clemen-Stone, Susan, Diane Eigsti, and Sandra McGuire, *Comprehensive Family and Community Health Nursing* (2nd ed.). New York: McGraw-Hill, 1987.
39. Closing the Gap, *AARP News Bulletin*, 28, no. 12 (November, 1987), 8–9.
40. Cooper, Rhona, Concentration Camp Survivors: A Challenge for Geriatric Nursing, *Nursing Clinics of North America*, 14, no. 4 (1979), 621–627.
41. Cowling, W., and Victor Campbell, Health Concerns of Aging Men, *Nursing Clinics of North America*, 21, no. 1 (1986), 77–84.
42. Cross, K. Patricia, *Adults as Learners*. San Francisco: Jossey-Bass, 1981.
43. Crossman, Linda, Cecelia London, and Clemmie Barry, Older Women Caring for Disabled Spouses: A Model for Supportive Services, *The Gerontologist*, 21, no. 5 (1981), 464–470.
44. Crow, Marjorie, *Pharmacology for the Elderly: The Nurse's Guide to Quality Care*. New York: Teachers College Press, 1984.
45. Crowling, W. Richard, and Victor Campbell, Health Concerns of Aging Men, *Nursing Clinics of North America*, 21, no. 1 (1986), 75–83.
46. Culbert, P., and B. Koos, Aging: Considerations for Health Teaching, *Nursing Clinics of North America*, 6, no. 4 (1971), 605–614.
47. *Cut the Cost/Keep the Care: New Action Steps for 1985–1986*. Washington, D.C.: American Association of Retired Persons, 1986.
48. Damrosch, Shirley Petchel, Nursing Students' Attitudes Toward Sexually Active Older Persons, *Nursing Research*, 31 (1982), 252–255.
49. Delgado, M., and G. Finley, The Spanish Speaking Elderly: A Bibliography, *The Gerontologist*, 18, no. 4 (1978), 387–394.
50. Depner, Charlene, and Berit Ingersoll-Dayton, Conjugal Social Support: Patterns in Later Life, *Journal of Gerontology*, 40, no. 6 (1985), 761–766.
51. Doress, Paula, and Diana Siegel, *Ourselves, Growing Older*. Boston: Simon & Schuster, 1987.
52. Duvall, Evelyn, and Brent Miller, *Marriage and Family Development* (6th ed.). Philadelphia: J. B. Lippincott, 1977.
53. Dychtwald, Ken (ed.), *Wellness and Health Promotion for the Elderly*. Rockville, Maryland: Aspen Publication, 1986.
54. *Eating for Your Health: A Guide to Food for Healthy Diets*. Washington, D.C.: American Association of Retired Persons, 1986.
55. Ebersole, Priscilla, and Patricia Hess, *Toward a Healthy Aging*. St. Louis: C. V. Mosby, 1981.
56. Ekert, David, et al., The Effect of Retirement on Physical Health, *American Journal of Public Health*, 73, no. 7 (1983), 779–783.
57. Ekerdt, David, Raymond Bosse, and Joseph LoCastro, Claims That Retirement Improves Health, *Journal of Gerontology*, 38, no. 2 (1983), 231–236.
58. Erikson, Erik H., *Childhood and Society* (2nd ed.). New York: W. W. Norton, 1963.
59. Estes, Carroll, and Robert Newcomer, *Fiscal Austerity and Aging: Shifting Government Responsibility for the Elderly*. Beverly Hills: Sage Publications, 1983.
60. Fidel-Girgis, Mary, Family Support for the Elderly in Egypt, *The Gerontologist*, 23, no. 6 (1983), 589–592.
61. Fitting, Melinda, et al., Caregivers for Dementia Patients: A Comparison of Husbands and Wives, *The Gerontologist*, 26, no. 3 (1986), 248–252.
62. 5% of People Over 65 Live in Nursing Homes, *The Nation's Health* (July, 1987), 9.
63. Flaste, Richard, Shoddy Portrayal of Aged in Children's Books Decried, *Arizona Daily Star*, 136, no. 35 (February 4, 1977).
64. Fullerton, Audrey, and Anderson Smith, Age-Related Differences in the Use of Redundancy, *Journal of Gerontology*, 35 no. 5 (1980), 729–735.
65. Gallagher, Dolores, Intervention Strategies to Assist Caregivers of Frail Elders: Current Research Status and Future Research Directions, *Annual Review of Gerontology and Geriatrics*, 5 (1985), 249–282.
66. Gelein, Janet, Aged Women and Health, *Nursing Clinics of North America*, 17, no. 1 (1982), 179–185.
67. Gershowitz, Sonya, Adding Life to Years: Remotivating Elderly People in Institutions, *Nursing & Health Care*, 3, no. 3 (1982), 141–145.
68. Gioiella, Evelynn Clark, and Catherine Waechter Bevil, *Nursing Care of the Aging Client: Promoting Healthy Adaptation*. Norwalk, CT: Appleton-Century-Crofts, 1985.

69. Gold, Byron et al., United States Social Policy on Old Age: Present Patterns and Predictions, in *Social Policy, Social Ethics, and the Aging Society*. Rockville Center, MD: National Science Foundation, 1976, 25–35.
70. Goldstein, Melwyn, Sidney Schuler, and James Ross, Social and Economic Forces Affecting Intergenerational Relations in Extended Families in a Third World Country: A Cautionary Tale from South Asia, *Journal of Gerontology*, 38, no. 6 (1983), 716–724.
71. Goodman, Catherine, Natural Helping Among Older Adults, *The Gerontologist*, 24, no. 2 (1984), 138–143.
72. Gordon, Theodore J., The Year 2050: Reflections of a Futurist, *The Lamp*, 63, no. 1 (1981), 26–33.
73. Green, Marilyn, and Joann Harry, *Nutrition in Contemporary Nursing Practice* (2nd ed.). New York: John Wiley, 1987.
74. Gress, L. D., and R. T. Bahr, *The Aging Person: A Holistic Perspective*. St. Louis: C. V. Mosby, 1984.
75. Gunter, Laurie, A New Look at the Older Patient in the Community, *Nursing Forum*, 8, no. 1 (1969), 51–59.
76. Hagestad, Gunkild, Able Elderly in the Family Context: Changes, Chances, and Challenges, *The Gerontologist*, 27, no. 4 (1987), 417–421.
77. Haggerty, Janet, and Anne Juhasz, The Human/Companion Animal Bind: How Nurses Can Use This Therapeutic Resource, *Nursing and Health Care*, 3, no. 11 (1984), 492–501.
78. Hall, E., Acting One's Age: New Rules for Old, *Psychology Today*, 13, no. 11 (1980), 66–80.
79. Hanson, Sandra, William Sauer, and Wayne Seelbach, Racial and Cohort Variations in Filial Responsibility Norms, *The Gerontologist*, 23, no. 6 (1983), 626–631.
80. Harker, Judith, and Walter Riegi, Aging and Delay Effects on Recognition of Words and Designs, *Journal of Gerontology*, 40, no. 5 (1985), 601–604.
81. Havighurst, Robert, *Developmental Tasks and Education* (3rd ed.). New York: David McKay, 1972.
82. ———, A Social-Psychological Perspective on Aging, in *Human Life Cycle*, ed. Wm. Sze. New York: Jason Aronson, 1975, 627–635.
83. ———, W. McDonald, L. Maeulan, and J. Mazel, Male Social Scientists: Lives After Sixty, *The Gerontologist*, 19, no. 1 (1979), 55–60.
84. Hawkins, Joellen, Jessie Igon, Edna Johnson, et al., A Nursing Center for Ambulatory, Well, Older Adults, *Nursing and Health Care*, 5, no. 2 (1984), 209–212.
85. Hayter, Jean, Modifying the Environment to Help Older Persons, *Nursing and Health Care*, 4, no. 5 (1983), 265–269.
86. Hazard, Merle, and Rosemarie Kemp, Keep the Well Elderly Well, *American Journal of Nursing*, 83, no. 4 (1983), 567–569.
87. Henri, J., An Alternative to Institutionalization, *The Gerontologist*, 20, no. 4 (1980), 418–420.
88. Hogstel, Mildred, *Nursing Care of the Older Adult*. New York: John Wiley, 1981.
89. Hoole, Axalla, Robert Greenberg, and C. Glenn Pickard, *Patient Care Guidelines for Nurse Practitioners* (3rd ed.). Boston: Little, Brown, 1988.
90. Horowitz, Amy, Family Caregiving to the Frail Elderly, *Annual Review of Gerontology and Geriatrics*, 5 (1985), 194–246.
91. Horowitz, Amy, Sons and Daughters as Caregivers to Older Parents: Differences in Role Performance and Consequences, *The Gerontologist*, 25, no. 6 (1985), 612–617.
92. Hudson, Robert, Tomorrow's Able Elders: Implications for the State, *The Gerontologist*, 27, no. 4 (1987), 405–409.
93. Imaging the Future, *AARP News Bulletin*, 28, no. 11 (December, 1987), 2, 10.
94. Jackson, J., *Minorities and Aging*. Belmont, Calif.: Wadsworth, 1980.
95. Jackson, Osa (ed.), *Physical Therapy of the Geriatric Patient*. New York: Churchill Livingstone, 1983.
96. Jamieson, Marjorie, and Ida Martinson, Black Nursing: Neighbors Caring for Neighbors, *Nursing Outlook*, 31, no. 15 (1983), 270 ff.
97. Jenkins, Elda Hoke, Homemakers: The Core of Home Health Care, *Geriatric Nursing*, 5, no. 1 (1984), 28–30.
98. Johnson, Colleen, Dyadic Family Relations and Social Support, *The Gerontologist*, 23, no. 4 (1984), 377–383.
99. Johnson, Colleen, and Donald Catalano, A Longitudinal Study of Family Supports to Impaired Elderly, *The Gerontologist*, 23, no. 6 (1983), 612–618.
100. Jourard, Sidney M., *The Transparent Self*. Princeton, N.J.: D. Van Nostrand, 1964.
101. Kaluger, George, and Meriem Kaluger, *Human Development: The Span of Life* (3rd ed.). St. Louis: Times Mirror/Mosby, 1984.
102. Karl, Cherry, The Effect of an Exercise Program on Self-Care Activities for the Institutionalized Elderly, *Journal of Gerontological Nursing*, 8, no. 5 (1982), 282–285.
103. Keith, Pat, et al., Confidants and Well Being: A Note on Male Friendship in Old Age, *The Gerontologist*, 24, no. 3 (1984), 318–320.
104. Kelly, John, Marjorie Steinkamp, and Janice Steinkamp, Late Life Leisure: How They Play in Peoria, *The Gerontologist*, 26, no. 5 (1986), 531–537.
105. Kendig, Hal, and Don Rowland, Family Support of the Australian Aged: A Comparison with the United States, *The Gerontologist*, 23, no. 6 (1983), 643–649.
106. Kenney, Richard, *Physiology of Aging: A Synopsis*. Chicago: Year Book, Medical Publishers, 1982.
107. Kermis, M. D., *The Psychology of Aging: Theory, Research, and Practice*. Boston: Allyn & Boston, 1984.
108. Kivett, Vira, and Maxine Atkinson, Filial Expecta-

tions, Association, and Helping as a Function of Number of Children Among Older Rural-Transitional Parents, *Journal of Gerontology*, 39, no. 4 (1984), 499–503.
109. Kivett, Vira, and Max Learner, Perspectives for the Childless Rural Elderly: A Comparative Analysis, *The Gerontologist*, 20, no. 6 (1980), 708–715.
110. Klaehn, Robin, Entitlement versus Resources: An Ethical Dilemma, *Arizona Nurse*, 35, no. 1 (1982), 1, 10–11.
111. Kobrin, F., Family Extension and the Elderly: Economics, Demographic, and Family Life Cycle, *Journal of Gerontology*, 36, no. 3 (1981), 370–377.
112. Kohen, Janet, Old But Not Alone: Informal Social Supports Among the Elderly by Mental Status and Sex, *The Gerontologist*, 23, no. 1 (1983), 57–63.
113. Kopac, Catherine, Sensory Loss in the Aged: The Role of the Nurse and the Family, *Nursing Clinics of North America*, 18, no. 2 (1983), 373–384.
114. Kra, Siegfried, *Aging Myths: Reversible Causes of Mind and Memory Loss*. New York: McGraw Hill, 1986.
115. Lammers, William, *Public Policy and the Aging*. Washington, D.C.: CQ Press, 1983.
116. LaRossa, Maureen and Josephine Brown, Foster Grandmothers in the Premature Nursery, *American Journal of Nursing*, 82, no. 12, (1982), 1834–1835.
117. Larsen, Reed, Jari Zuzanek, and Roger Mannell, Being Alone Versus Being With People: Disengagement in the Daily Experience of Older Adults, *Journal of Gerontology*, 40, no. 3 (1985), 375–381.
118. Liang, Jersey, Sex Differences in Life Satisfaction Among the Elderly, *Journal of Gerontology*, 34, no. 1 (1982), 100–108.
119. Lidz, Theodore, *The Person: His and Her Development Throughout the Life Cycle* (2nd ed). New York: Basic Books, 1983.
120. Lilja, Paul, Recognizing the Effect of Social Support on Compliance to Medical Regimen in the Elderly Chronically Ill, *Home Healthcare Nurse*, 2, no. 5 (1984), 17–21.
121. Linden, M., and D. Courtney, The Human Life Cycle and its Interruptions: A Psychologic Hypothesis—Studies in Gerontologic Human Relations I, *American Journal of Psychiatry*, 109, no. 1 (1953), 906–915.
122. Lowenthal, Marjorie, Majda Thurnher, and David Chiriboga, *Four Stages of Life*. San Francisco: Jossey-Bass, 1976.
123. Luckmann, Joan, and Karen Sorensen, *Medical-Surgical Nursing: A Psychophysiologic Approach* (3rd ed.). Philadelphia: W. B. Saunders, 1987.
124. Ludeman, K., The Sexuality of the Older Person: Review of the Literature, *The Gerontologist*, 21, no. 2 (1981), 203–208.
125. Maas, Henry, and Joseph Kuypers, *From Thirty to Seventy*. San Francisco: Jossey-Bass, 1974.
126. Maddox, G. L., Disengagement Theory: A Critical Evaluation, *The Gerontologist*, 4, (1974), 80–83.
127. Maeda, Daisaku, Family Care in Japan, *The Gerontologist*, 23, no. 6 (1983), 579–583.
128. Malcolm, Julie, Creative Spiritual Care for the Elderly." *Journal of Christian Nursing*, 4, No. 1 (Winter, 1987), 24–26.
129. Masters, William, and Virginia Johnson, *Human Sexual Response*. Boston: Little, Brown, 1966.
130. McCormack, Peter, Coding of Spatial Information by Young and Elderly Adults, *Journal of Gerontology*, 37, no. 1 (1982), 80–86.
131. McCrae, R., Age Differences in the Use of Coping Mechanisms, *Journal of Gerontology*, 37 (1982), 454–460.
132. McCoy, Vivian, Adult Life Cycle Tasks/Adult Continuing Education Program Response, *Lifelong Learning in the Adult Years* (October, 1977), 16.
133. McCuan, Eloise Rathbone, Elderly Victims of Family Violence and Neglect, *Social Casework: The Journal of Contemporary Social Work*, Family Services Association of America (May, 1980), 296–304.
134. McElmurry, Beverly, and Susan LiBrizzi, The Health of Older Women, *Nursing Clinics of North America*, 21, no. 1 (1986), 161–171.
135. Megerle, Jo-Ann, Surviving, *American Journal of Nursing*, 83, no. 6 (1983), 892–894.
136. Mirotznik, Jerrold, and Asa Ruskin, Inter-Institutional Relocation and Its Effects on Psychosocial Status, *The Gerontologist*, 25, no. 3 (1988), 263–270.
137. Morgan, Leslie, Intergenerational Financial Support: Retirement-Age Males, 1971–1975, *The Gerontologist*, 23, no. 2 (1983), 160–166.
138. Muller, Robert, and Joseph Donnemeyer, Age, Trust, and Perceived Safety from Crime in Rural Areas, *The Gerontologist*, 25, no. 3 (1985), 237–242.
139. Murray, Ruth, Body Image Development in Adulthood, *Nursing Clinics of North America*, 7, no. 4 (1972), 625–630.
140. Murray, Ruth, and Marilyn Huelskoetter, *Psychiatric/Mental Health Nursing: Giving Emotional Care* (2nd ed.). Englewood Cliffs, N.J.: Prentice-Hall, 1987.
141. ____, and Judith Zentner, *Nursing Concepts for Health Promotion* (3rd ed.). Englewood Cliffs, N.J.: Prentice-Hall, 1985.
142. Neal, Patsy, My Grandmother, The Bag Lady, *Newsweek* (February 11, 1985), 14.
143. Neufeld, Anne, and Helen Hobbs, Self-Care in a High-Rise for Seniors, *Nursing Outlook*, 33, no. 4 (1985), 298–301.
144. Neugarten, B., Grow Old Along With Me! The Best Is Yet to Be, *Psychology Today*, 5, no. 7 (1971), 45ff.
145. ____, Adult Personality: A Developmental View, in *Readings in Psychological Development Through Life*,

eds. D. Charles and W. Looft. New York: Holt, Rinehart & Winston, 1973, 356–366.

146. ———, Adaptation and the Life Cycle, *The Counseling Psychologist*, 6, no. 1 (1976), 16–20.

147. Norris, Fran, and Stanley Murrell, Older Adult Family Stress and Adaptation Before and After Bereavement, *Journal of Gerontology*, 42, no. 6 (1987), 606–612.

148. Nydegger, Corinne, Family Ties of the Aged in Cross-Cultural Perspective, *The Gerontologist*, 22, no. 1 (1983), 26–31.

149. Oktay, Julianne, and Patricia Volland, Foster Home Care for the Frail Elderly is an Alternative to Nursing Home Care: An Experimental Evaluation, *American Journal of Public Health*, 77, no. 2 (1987), 1505–1510.

150. Okum, M., and F. DiVesta, Cautiousness in Adulthood as a Function of Age and Instruction, *Journal of Gerontology*, 31, no. 5 (1976), 571–576.

151. ———, I. Siegler, and L. George, Cautiousness and Verbal Learning in Adulthood, *Journal of Gerontology*, 33, no. 1 (1978), 94–97.

152. Older Workers are Bearing Brunt of Most Down-Sizing Programs, *AARP News Bulletin*, 28, no. 11 (December, 1987), 1, 4.

153. Osoko, M., Aging and Family Among Japanese Americans: The Role of Ethnic Tradition in the Adjustment to Old Age, *The Gerontologist*, 19, no. 5 (1979), 448–455.

154. Peck, R. C., Psychological Development in the Second Half of Life, in *Middle Age and Aging*, ed. Bernice Neugarten. Chicago: University of Chicago Press, 1968.

155. Peterson, David, and Rosemary Orgren, Older Adult Learning, *Physical Therapy of the Geriatric Patient*, ed. Osa Jacksen. New York: Churchill Livingstone, 1983.

156. Pike, Ruth, and Myrtle Brown, *Nutrition: An Integrated Approach* (2nd ed.). New York: John Wiley, 1975.

157. Pollick, Martha, Abuse of the Elderly: A Review, *Holistic Nursing Practice*, 1, no. 2 (1987), 43–53.

158. Porac, Clare, Stanley Coven, and Pam Duncan, Life-Span Age Trends in Laterality, *Journal of Gerontology*, 35, no. 3 (1983), 715–721.

159. Pratt, Clara, Vicki Schmall, and Scott Wright, Ethical Concerns of Family Caregivers to Dementia Patients, *The Gerontologist*, 27, no. 5 (1987), 632–638.

160. Price, James, and Patricia Andrews, Alcohol Abuse in the Elderly, *Journal of Gerontological Nursing*, 8, no. 1 (1982), 16–19.

161. Profiles of Centenarians, *Statistical Bulletin*, 68, no. 1 (1987), 2–7.

162. Program Resources Department, *A Profile of Older Americans: 1986*. Washington, D.C.: American Association of Retired Persons and Administration on Aging, 1986.

163. Pullinger, Walter, F., Jr., A History of Remotivation, *Hospital and Community Psychiatry*, 18, no. 1 (1967), 35–39.

164. Rantz, Marilyn, and Kathleen Egan, Reducing Death From Translocation Syndrome, *American Journal of Nursing*, 87, no. 10 (1987), 1351.

165. Register, J., Aging and Race: A Black-White Comparative Analysis, *The Gerontologist*, 21, no. 4 (1981), 438–443.

166. Reinhard, Susan, Financing Long-term Health Care of the Elderly: Dismantling the Medical Model, *Public Health Nursing*, 3, no. 1 (1986), 3–22.

167. Render, Helena, My Old Age, *Nursing Outlook*, 12, no. 11 (1964), 31–33.

168. Resler, Marion, and Gail Tumulty, Glaucoma Update, *American Journal of Nursing*, 83, no. 5 (1983), 752–757.

169. Riegel, Klaus, and Ruth Riegel, Development, Drop, and Death, *Developmental Psychology*, 6, no. 2 (1972), 306–319.

170. Roadburg, A., Perceptions of Work and Leisure Among the Elderly, *The Gerontologist*, 21, no. 2 (1981), 171–176.

171. Sargis, Nancy, Judith Jennrich, and Kathleen Murray, Housing and Health, *Nursing & Health Care*, 8, no. 6 (1987), 334–339.

172. Schiamberg, Lawrence, *Human Development* (2nd ed.). New York: Macmillan, 1985.

173. Schuster, Clara Shaw, and Shirley Smith Ashburn, *The Process of Human Development: A Holistic Life-Span Approach* (2nd ed.). Boston: Little, Brown, 1986.

174. Seefeldt, Carol, The Effects of Preschooler's Visits to a Nursing Home, *The Gerontologist*, 27, no. 2 (1987), 228–232.

175. Shanas, E. The Family as a Social Support System in Old Age, *Gerontologist*, 19 (1979), 169–174.

176. Shanas, E., Social Myth as Hypothesis: The Case of the Family Relations of Old People, *Gerontologist*, 19 (1979), 3–9.

177. Sharp, Matthew, and Eugene Gollin, Aging and Free Recall for Objects Located in Space, *Journals of Gerontology: Psychological Sciences*, 43, no. 1 (1988), P8–P11.

178. Siegler, Ilene, and Paul Costa, Health Behavior Relationships, in *Handbook of the Psychology of Aging* (2nd ed.), eds. James Birren and K. Warner Schaie. New York: Van Nostrand Reinhold, 1985, pp. 144–166.

179. Smeeding, Timothy, and Lavonne Straub, Health Care Financing Among the Elderly: Who Really Pays the Bills? *Journal of Health Politics, Policy and Law*, 12, no. 1 (1987), 35–52.

180. Smith, D. W., E. L. Bierman, and N. M. Robinson (eds.), *The Biologic Ages of Man: From Conception Through Old Age* (2nd ed.). Philadelphia: Saunders, 1978.

181. Sohngen, L., The Experience of Old Age as Depicted in Contemporary Novels: A Supplementary Bibliography, *The Gerontologist*, 21, no. 3 (1981), 303.
182. Some Hypothermia Deaths Tied to Lack of Thermometers, *The AARP News Bulletin*, 23, no. 4 (1982) n.p.
183. Spencer, Gregory, Commentary: Dramatic Growth of Centenarian Population, *Statistical Bulletin*, 68, no. 1 (1987), 8–9.
184. Stanhope, Marcia, and Jeanette Lancaster, *Community Health Nursing: Process and Practice for Promoting Health*. St. Louis: C. V. Mosby, 1984.
185. Stoller, Eleanor, and Lorna Earl, Help with Activities of Everyday Life: Sources of Support for the Noninstitutionalized Elderly, *The Gerontologist*, 32, no. 1 (1983), 68–70.
186. Stone, Robyn, Gail Cafferta, and Judith Sangl, Caregivers of the Frail Elderly: A National Profile, *The Gerontologist*, 27, no. 5 (1987), 616–626.
187. Streib, G., and Shanas, E. (eds.), *Social Structure and the Family*. Englewood Cliffs, N.J.: Prentice-Hall, 1965.
188. Strong, Catherine, Stress and Caring for Elderly Relatives: Interpretations and Coping Strategies in an American Indian and White Sample, *The Gerontologist*, 24, no. 3 (1984), 251–255.
189. Tanner, J. M., *Foetus into Man: Physical Growth from Conception to Maturity*. London: Open Books, 1978.
190. Tatro, Suzanne, and Jan Marshall, Regression: A Defense Mechanism for the Dying Older Adult. *Journal of Gerontological Nursing*, 8, no. 1 (1982), 20–22.
191. The 1981 White House Conference on Aging, *Today's Nursing Home*, 3, no. 2 (1982).
192. Thomas, Ellen, Application of Stress Factors in Gerontologic Nursing, *Nursing Clinics of North America*, 14, no. 4 (1979), 607–619.
193. Thomas, Jeanne, Predictors of Satisfaction with Children's Help for Younger and Older Elderly Parents, *Journal of Gerontology: Social Sciences*, 43, no. 1 (1988), P9–P14.
194. Tolbert, Bennie Mae, Reality Orientation and Remotivation in a Long-Term Care Facility, *Nursing and Health Care*, 5, no. 1 (1984), 40–44.
195. Townsend, P., The Structured Dependency of the Elderly: A Creation of Social Policy in the Twentieth Century, *Aging and Society*, 1, (1981), 5–28.
196. Trends in Longevity after Age 65, *Statistical Bulletin*, 68, no. 1 (1987), 10–17.
197. Trunzo, Candace E., Solving the Age-Old Problem, *Money* (January, 1982), 70,72,76.
198. Turner, Jeffrey, and Donald Helms, *Lifespan Development* (3rd ed.). New York: Holt, Rinehart and Winston, 1987.
199. Uhlenberg, Peter, and Mary Anne Myers, Divorce and the Elderly, *The Gerontologist*, 21, no. 3 (1981), 276–282.
200. Urdang, Lawrence, ed., *Mosby's Medical and Nursing Dictionary*. St. Louis: C. V. Mosby, 1983.
201. U.S. Department of Health and Human Service, New Recommended Schedule for Active Immunization of Normal Infants and Children, *Morbidity and Mortality Weekly Report*. 35, no. 37 (September 19, 1986), 577–579.
202. Vaccines for Adult Diseases, *Newsweek* (October 12, 1987), 92–93.
203. Vitiello, Michael, et al., Circadian Temperature Rhythms in Young Adult and Aged Men, *Neurobiology of Aging*, 7 (1986), 97–100.
204. Ward, Russell, The Never-Married in Later Life, *Journal of Gerontology*, 34, no. 6 (1979), 861–869.
205. Ward, Russell, Informal Networks and Well-Being in Later Life: A Research Agenda, *The Gerontologist*, 25, no. 1 (1985), 55–61.
206. Watkin, Donald, *Handbook of Nutrition, Health, and Aging*. Park Ridge, N.J.: Noyes Publications, 1983.
207. Weihl, Hannah, Three Issues from the Israeli Scene, *The Gerontologist*, 23, no. 6 (1983), 376–378.
208. Wentowski, Gloria, Older Women's Perceptions of Great Grandparenthood, *The Gerontologist*, 25, no. 6 (1985), 593–596.
209. Whitbourne, Susan Krauss, *The Aging Body: Physiological Changes and Psychological Consequences*. New York: Springer-Verlag, 1985.
210. Williams, Sue Rodwell, *Nutrition and Diet Therapy* (5th ed.). St. Louis: Times Mirror/Mosby, 1985.
211. Winski, Joseph, Work Until 70? No Thanks, Most Reply, *Chicago Tribune*, October 22, 1978.
212. Winter, Annette, The Shame of Elder Abuse, *Modern Maturity* (October–November, 1986), 51–57.
213. Witt, Sandra, and Walter Cunningham, Cognitive Speed and Subsequent Intellectual Development: A Longitudinal Investigation, *Journal of Gerontology*, 34, no. 4 (1979), 540–546.
214. Worach-Kardas, Holina, The Polish Family Tradition, *The Gerontologist*, 23, no. 6 (1983), 593–596.
215. Zacks, Rose, Encoding Strategies Used by Young and Elderly Adults in a Keeping Track Task, *Journal of Gerontology*, 37, no. 2 (1982), 203–211.

15

Death, the Last Developmental Stage

Study of this chapter will enable you to

1. Explore personal reactions to active and passive euthanasia and the right-to-die movement versus extraordinary measures to prolong life. Contrast home or hospice care to hospital/nursing home care.
2. Contrast the child's, adolescent's, and adult's concept of death.
3. Discuss personal feelings about death and the dying person.
4. Discuss the stages of awareness and related behavior as the person adapts to the crisis of approaching death.
5. Discuss sequence of reactions when the person and family are aware of terminal illness.
6. Talk with another about how to plan for eventual death.
7. Assess reactions and needs of a dying patient and family members with supervision.
8. Plan and give care, with supervision, to a patient based on understanding of his/her awareness of eventual death, behavioral and emotional reactions, and physical needs.
9. Intervene appropriately to meet needs of family members of a dying person.
10. Evaluate the effectiveness of care given.

Key Terms

Death	Mutual pretense
Closed awareness	Open awareness
Suspicious awareness	Predilection to death

Death has been avoided in name and understanding. There may be no harm in saying "he passed" instead of "he died." There is harm in suddenly facing a patient's death without sufficient emotional preparation.

Issues Related to Dying and Death

Definitions of Death

The aged differ from persons in other life eras in that their concept of future is realistically limited. The younger person may not live many years into the future, but generally thinks of many years of life ahead. The older person knows that, despite medical and technical advances, life is limited.

Death is the last developmental stage. It is more than simply an end process—it can be viewed as a goal and as fulfillment. If the person has spent his/her years unfettered by fear, if he/she has lived richly and productively, if he/she has achieved the developmental task of ego integrity, then he/she can accept the realization that the self will cease to be and that dying has an onset long before the actual death.

If death is considered the last developmental phase, then it is worth the kind of preparation that goes into any developmental phase, perhaps physically, certainly emotionally, socially, philosophically, or spiritually.

Until this century, death usually occurred in the home, but at present over 70 percent of deaths in American cities occur in institutions, so that death has become remote and impersonal.

Because of technological advances, the determination of **death** *is changing from the traditional concept that death occurs when the heart stops beating. Newer definitions of death refer to brain death, established by a flat encephalogram (EEG), usually for a duration of 24 to 48 hours, lack of reflex activity, and pupil dilation.* Vital organs can be kept alive by machines for use in transplants even though the patient is essentially dead, showing no brain activity (65).

The sophisticated machinery has caused some to ask such questions as, "If we declare someone entirely dead when the brain is 'dead' even though most of the body remains alive with the help of life supports, then doesn't that body lose its sanctity and become the object of transplant organ harvesting"? The opposition might answer, "Without the present life-support systems, this person would certainly have been dead. Why not take the opportunity to save another person's life with the needed organ(s)?"

The current issue is not only "When is someone dead?" but "Who decides when to turn off the machines?" Does the patient, medical personnel, a lawyer, the clergy, or the courts?

The family, more than anyone else, will have to live with the memories of their loved ones and the events surrounding death. It is a violation of the family's dignity to rush death. Even though a lesser involved person might say, "Why don't they turn the machines off!," this person should be ignored until all those closely involved with the patient can say with acceptance and assurance, "Now is the time" (36). Increasingly, the *person* is saying that he/she has a right to decide how long machines should maintain personal life or that of a loved one. There are several plausible death concepts: those related to body fluids flow (heart and lung oriented), integrating capacity (whole brain oriented), or experiential and social interaction (neocostically oriented).

✔ Kellmer (44) discusses historical, social, and ethical perspectives of resuscitation and use of life-support technology, and court cases that have set precedents in determining who is declared competent or incompetent to make decisions about right to refuse treatment. She discusses approaches that can be used by hospitals and health care agencies to arrive at decisions about orders not to resuscitate and the importance of policies that have been formulated collaboratively by all departments that are involved in care of patients.

Euthanasia

Euthanasia *is legally defined as the act or practice of painlessly putting to death persons suffering from incurable or distressing diseases.*

✔ While maintaining life beyond all reason is an ethical dilemma for the nurse, an equally taxing ethical dilemma is when the doctor deliberately hastens the patient's death by increasing the dose of a narcotic analgesic, such as morphine, to the point of lethality. The issues and suggested ways to handle them are discussed by a hospital nurse, hospice nurse, pastor, and physician in an article by Janet Fuller (29). Brown (5) also distinguishes between passive and active euthanasia and the moral, ethical, and legal problems with the concept of euthanasia. He emphasizes the need of responsible, moral caregivers who will promote quality of life and right to die with dignity. If each human life is seen as of infinite value, then it will be worth the efforts to ease pain and help the person find meaning in the current situation.

Euthanasia is not new. It was practiced in Greece. African bushmen and North American primitive tribes abandoned their infirm elderly to die; there was insufficient food for anyone who could not produce his/her own food. Eskimo tribal elders cut a hole in the ice and disappeared when they became burdensome.

Most Western countries consider active euthanasia, deliberately hastening death, as first-degree murder. On the other hand, court decisions have been inconsistent about omission of care or inaction to prolong life, which results in passive euthanasia.

The development of Judeo-Christian law from the beliefs of St. Augustine and St. Thomas Aquinas held that suicide was a sin and against natural law. In the past in American institutions, physiological aspects only were considered in prolonging life. Today, sociological and economic aspects are also being considered. The value or quality of life when the person is kept alive by artificial support systems is considered. Costs to patient, family, and society are being considered. Ordinary care is the prevailing standard, not extraordinary means, although what constitutes ordinary care is debated.

Euthanasia is based on two fundamental legal premises: the right to privacy and the right to refuse treatment when informed. The competent patient may decline treatment for religious reasons, fear of pain or suffering, exhaustion of finances, and unlikelihood of recovery. The incompetent patient is not allowed the right to refuse in similar situations for fear of an irrational choice. Medical practice defers to wishes of the family. Those who are disabled, elderly, retarded, or insane may not receive the treatment ordinarily given to others.

Right-to-Die Movement

Another increasingly publicized facet with moral and ethical aspects is the right-to-die movement, first begun in England, Holland, and Scandanavian countries, and which has gained momentum in the United States. Originally the Right-to-Die Society and the movement insisted that people should have the last word about their own lives, either to maintain or discontinue treatment when ill or dying. The District of Columbia and 38 states have adopted living-will laws (also known as right-to-die or natural death laws) that permit mentally competent adults to declare, before they are ill, that they do not want life prolonged artificially or by heroic measures. In states with no formal legislation, living wills have been upheld in courts. Over three dozen states have brain-death laws that allow respirators to be withdrawn when a patient no longer shows signs of brain activity. In the case of a lingering, comatose, incompetent person, the relatives, hospital ethics committee, or the courts have to make decisions about not instituting or withdrawing life-prolonging measures. Or someone designated by the person with durable power of attorney, available in all states, can make decisions about health care, as well as financial and property decisions, in the event of incapacity. Anyone interested in having a living will drawn up can request the free forms appropriate to his/her state from The Society for the Right to Die, Room 323, 250 W. 57th St, New York, NY 10107, or from Concern for Dying, Room 831 at the same address.

Physicians fear indictment for homicide or aiding suicide even when following the living will, although these laws in all states grant immunity to health care professionals who comply with the declaration. Further, in some states there is a penalty if the physician does not comply. Relatives may sue the physician and/or hospital that refuses to follow the patient's wishes reflected in the living will. (Legally, the physician may be charged with battery.)

Nurses are increasingly having to face questions of conscience, ethics, morals, and legalities in relation to what to say to the patient and relatives and what to do in relation to whether to assist with initiating heroic measures when it is known that the patient does not want them, or whether to disconnect life-support machines.

It is now possible to buy manuals on how to commit suicide. These books are becoming increasingly in demand as the public realizes it is illegal for doctors to practice euthanasia, and that often doctors feel forced to prolong life, in whatever condition. The manuals argue against suicide when the problem is a distortion of judgment or a psychiatric disorder, but give a factual guide about the least painful and most effective measures. Violent methods, such as shooting, jumping, or hanging, are counseled against because these are too traumatic for the survivors.

In contrast, the Samaritans, an international suicide prevention group and professionals who work in hospice care, as well as the Medical Association of each country, have been sharply critical of such manuals, believing that they may pressure terminally ill, depressed, or elderly people to exit early because they feel they are a burden and unwanted. It is as if society fosters rejection instead of seeking solutions to the problem (10).

For more information on the types of euthanasia and the moral–ethical issues, see the references at the end of this chapter (3, 27, 36, 38, 39, 45, 50, 51, 68). Many other references are available; much has been written about dying and death. This chapter only gives an overview of the subject.

✔ It is important for you to struggle with the values and issues of death—accidental death, long-term dying, active or passive euthanasia, and right-to-die choices—and consequently the issues and values of life. You will often be queried about your thoughts and beliefs; it is impossible to be value-free but you can be nonjudgmental and accepting of another's values. How you proceed with nursing care of the chronically ill or dying person will be influenced by your beliefs. Do not force your beliefs and values on another, but often the patient/client will appreciate your open sharing of values and beliefs. Such sharing may even give him/her energy to continue to live—with quality of life—against overwhelming odds. *Certainly do all possible so that the person does not face dying and death alone.*

Developmental Concepts of Death

To understand how adults and aged persons perceive death, a review is given here of how the child, adolescent, and adult perceive death. The concept of death is understood differently by persons in the different life eras because of general maturity, experience, ability to form ideas, and understanding of cause and effect.

Children's Concepts of Death

Nagy found three stages in the child's concept of death: (1) death is reversible—until age 5; (2) death is personified—ages 5 to 9; and (3) death is final and inevitable—after age 9 or 10 (57).

The child under 5 sees death as reversible, a temporary departure, like sleep, being less alive, very still, or unable to move. There is much curiosity about what happens to the person after death. The child connects death with funerals, with cemeteries, and absence. He/she thinks dead persons are still capable of growth, that they can breathe and eat and feel, and that they know what is happening on earth. Death is disturbing because it separates people from each other and because life in the grave seems dull and unpleasant. Fear of death in the child of this age may be related to parental expression of anger; presence of intrafamily stress such as arguing and fighting; physical restraints, especially during illness; or punishment for misdeeds. At times the child feels anger toward the parents because of their restrictions and the wish they would go away or be dead. Guilt feelings arising from these thoughts may add to the fear of death (57).

The child from ages 5 to 9 accepts the existence of death as final and not like life. He/she thinks of death as a person, such as an angel, a frightening clown or monster who carries off people, usually bad people, in the night. Personal death can be avoided; he/she will not die if he/she runs faster than Death, locks the door, or tricks death, unless there is bad luck. Parental disciplining techniques inadvertently add to this belief if they threaten that bad things will happen to the child. Traumatic situations also can arouse fear of death (57).

The child after ages 9 or 10 realizes that death is inevitable, final, happens according to certain laws, and will one day happen to him/her. Death is the end of life, like the withering of flowers or falling of leaves, and results from internal processes. Death is associated with being enclosed in a coffin without air, being slowly eaten by bugs, and slow rotting, unless cremation is taught. The child may express thoughts about an afterlife, depending on ideas expressed by parents and other adults and their religious philosophy (57, 66).

Death is an abstract concept and Nagy's stages offer a guide. However, not all children's thinking about death will fit into those stages. Children (and adults) may have a concept of death which contains ideas from all three stages. The ability to think abstractly is acquired slowly and to varying degrees by different people. Usually the child is unable to understand death until he/she is preadolescent or in the chum stage, for until then he/she has not learned to care for someone else as much as for self.

The child's ideas and anxiety about separation and death and the ability to handle loss are influenced by many factors: experiences with rejecting or punitive parents; strong sibling rivalry; violence; loss, illness, or death in the family; the reaction and teaching of adults to separation or death; and ability to conceptualize and assimilate the experience (17).

The child may think of the parent's death as deliberate abandonment for which he/she is responsible, and expect death to get him/her next. The child may fear death is catching and for that reason avoid a friend whose parent has just died. If the child perceives death as sleep, he/she may fear sleep to the point of being unable to go to bed at night or even to nap. He/she may blame the surviving parent for the other parent's death, a feeling which is compounded when the surviving parent is so absorbed in personal grief that little attention is given to the child. The child may use magical thinking, believing that wishing to have the parent return will bring the parent back (17).

The child's fascination with and fear of death may be expressed through the games he/she plays, or concern about sick pets or a dead person. Short-lived pets, such as fish or gerbils, help the child deal with death. Parents should handle these concerns and the related questions in a relaxed, loving manner (69).

Self-Knowledge of Death. Can the sick child realize personal approaching death? Waechter's study showed that despite widespread efforts by adults to shield the sick children from awareness of their diagnosis of cancer and the inevitability of death, the school-aged children in her study knew of their impending death, although they might not say so directly to their parents (72). The evasiveness and false cheerfulness of the adults, either parents or staff, did not hide their real feelings from the child.

Often children know more about death than adults may realize. Children are harmed by what they do not know, by what they are not told, and by their misconceptions. Parents should monitor the child's television viewing carefully, for programs often give an unrealistic impression of death, for example, cartoons and movies that show that death is reversible (or that there is survival or no harmful effects after obviously lethal injuries).

Children's Attendance at Funerals. There are age-based guidelines for a child's involvement in a funeral. Children from 2 to 3 can view the body or be given a brief explanation depending on their level of understanding and relationship to the deceased. But 3- to 6-year-olds benefit from a short private funeral home visit or the service itself. Seven- to 9-year-old children should attend the funeral unless they resist. Eleven- and 12-year-olds should be included in making the arrangements and the funeral service itself. In the teen years, friends of the adolescent should be encouraged to share the grief, and all should be treated as adults.

Suggestions for discussing death with children include the following:

Do not
- Admonish the child not to cry; it is a universal way to show grief and anxiety.
- Tell a mystical story about the loss of the person; it could cause confusion and anxiety.
- Give long, exclusively detailed explanations; beyond the level of understanding.
- Associate death with sleep, which could result in chronic sleep disturbances.
- Force children to attend funerals; ignore signs of grieving in the child.

Do
- Ask the child what he/she is feeling. Bring up the subject of death naturally, in the context of a dead pet, a book character, TV show, movie, or news item.
- Help the child have a funeral for a dead pet.
- Help the child realize he/she is not responsible for the death.
- Tell children what has happened on their level (but not in sordid detail).

- Explain the funeral service briefly beforehand; attendance depends on the child's age and wishes.
- Answer questions honestly, with responses geared to the child's age.
- Remember that expressions of pain, anger, loneliness/aloneness do not constitute symptoms of an illness, but are part of a natural process of grieving.
- Help the child realize that the adults are also grieving and feel upset, anger, despair, and guilt.

Other research is finding similar results about children and the subject of death (11, 27, 28, 30, 31, 46, 52). Although it is not easy for adults to talk with children about death, the book, *Talking About Death: A Dialogue Between Parent and Child*, by Grollman is a helpful reference (37).

Adolescents' Concept of Death

The adolescent is concerned about a personal future and is relatively realistic in thinking, but because of dependency–independency conflicts with parents and efforts to establish individuality, he/she has a low tolerance for accepting death. The healthy young person seldom thinks about death, particularly as something that will happen to the self. He/she fears a lingering death and usually views death in religious or philosophical terms. He/she feels death means lack of fulfillment; there is too much to lose with death (42).

Because of being inexperienced in coping with crisis and the viewpoints of death, the adolescent may not cry at the death of a loved one or parent. Instead he/she may continue to play games, listen to records, withdraw into seclusion or vigorous study, or go about usual activities. If the young person cannot talk, then such activities provide a catharsis. Mastery of feelings sometimes comes through a detailed account of the parent's death to a peer or by displacing grief feelings onto a pet (23). Also, the adolescent may fantasize the dead parent as perfect or feel much the way a child would about loss of a parent. Often the adolescent's behavior hides the fact that he/she is in mourning. Be attuned to the thoughts and feelings of the adolescent who has faced death of a loved one so that you can be approachable and helpful.

Adult Concepts of Death

The adult's attitudes toward and concept about dying and death are influenced by cultural and religious backgrounds. A number of references can provide information (1, 9, 47, 56). The adult's reactions to death are also influenced by whether the death event is sudden or has been anticipated (4). For the adult, the fear of death is often more related to the process of dying than to the fact of death—to mutilation, deformity, isolation, pain, loss of control over body functions and one's life, fear of the unknown, and permanent collapse and disintegration. Premonitions about coming death, sometimes correct, may occur.

Anticipation of Death. There are four responses to viewing death: positivist, negativist, activist, and passivist. Fear of death is less in the person who feels that most of the valued goals have been attained. This person is likely to reflect positively on present activities and death as an aspect of the future and is referred to as a *positivist*. If the person feels that the time left is so short, fears loss of ego integration, wishes that he/she could relive part of life, and fears death, the person is referred to as a *negativist*. A person may perceive death as diminishing the opportunity for continued fulfillment of goals. The achieved goals do not offset the fear of death. Death as a foreclosing of ambition is more distasteful than the prospect of loss of life. A person with such an attitude is referred to as an *activist*. Or the person may not view death with concern or fear, but as a respite from disappointments of life because attempts to attain life goals may have been so overshadowed by failure. Death may be accepted as a positive adjustment to life. Such a person is referred to as a *passivist* (43).

Keith (43) researched changes in four life areas—change in marital status, health, church involvement, and informal family and friend contacts—in relation to perceptions of life and death. In this study, women were more likely to be positivists and men were more likely to be negativists. Persons with lower incomes were more likely to be passivists and negativists than persons with higher incomes. Married men were more likely to be activists and positivists, although change in marital status was not associated with women's perceptions. Men who experienced change in health tended to be negativists, while women whose health had deteriorated were as likely to be positivists as negativists. Women who experienced continuity in health remained positivists. Continuity in church involvement gave no assurance of fostering positive attitudes toward death in men; while women who participated regularly were likely to be positivists, deriving comfort from their religion. Persons with continuous support from social participation more often had positive attitudes toward life. Persons who experienced discontinuity in life were more likely to be negativists or passivists. Women often expressed acceptance of death and less death anxiety than men. Women were more likely to perceive death as another beginning while men perceived death as an end. In the low income family in which care of an ill spouse is undertaken by the family, death may be perceived as a release.

Women are more likely to integrate widowhood than are men, and greater stability of friendships through the life cycle eases adaptation to loss of spouse. The widow is likely to seek intimacy with same-sexed friends, which replace family ties in late life.

The importance of will to live, or lack of it, has been recognized by nurses and others for many years. The person may not be terminally ill, yet because of loss of a loved one, loss of feelings of self-worth and usefulness, boredom or disillusionment with life, may lose the will to live and rapidly decline and die. Often there are few or no causes for death apparent on autopsy. There are some individuals who, despite impending death, maintain hope and endurance, apparently refuse to die and live beyond the time of expected death. A person can program, through unconscious or conscious will, onset of illness, recovery from severe illness, or the time of death. A strong will to live is often associated with the person being interested, involved, or active in life, or having a loved one, spouse, or dependent whom he/she desires to be with or for whom he feels responsible. For some, the death month is related to the birth month, in that some people postpone death in order to witness their birthdays, or another important holiday. The person with excessive fear of death may be unable to die until able to express and work through conscious fears or phobias (43).

Meaning of Death. To the adult facing death because of illness, particularly the elderly, death may have many meanings. Death may convey some positive meanings: a teacher of transcendental truths uncomprehended during life; an adventure; a friend who brings an end to pain and suffering; or an escape from an unbearable situation into a new life without the present difficulties. The great destroyer who is to be fought, punishment and separation, or a means of vengeance to force others to give more affection than they were willing to give in the past are examples of negative meanings (25).

The person who is dying may have suicidal thoughts or attempt suicide. Suicide is a rebellion against death, a way to cheat death's control over him/her.

One woman who had breast cancer spent 15 months planning her suicide. She wrote a book on her right to die when and as she wished, made a videotape, and collected her mementos for preservation after her death. Her last meal before she took a lethal dose of medicine included champagne and special sharing with her husband and son. This approach is repulsive and anti-Christian to some; see *The Illusion of Rational Suicide* published by the Hastings Center Report, December 1982, for a counterattack (10).

Cox writes a poignant account of how one person made a choice about where and how he would die—making his death and the events leading to it a triumph—in a society where society and health care professionals believe that the system is more important than the individual. She writes also of her feelings and beliefs and the ethical decision-making process involved in ensuring that his choice was carried out (13).

The time comes in an illness or in later life when both the person and the survivors-to-be feel death would be better than continuing to suffer. The patient has the conviction that death is inevitable and desirable and works through feelings until finally he/she has little or no anxiety, depression, or conflicts about dying. The body becomes a burden, and death holds a promise. There is little incentive to live.

Recently in the United States the concept of death has been investigated by adults who are not necessarily facing immediate death of themselves or their loved ones. The stigma that formerly caused people to use euphemisms has now been replaced with research involving attitudes toward death and classes on dying and death. For example, one study has concluded that highly creative artists and scientists who feel they have successfully contributed their talents to society have little fear of death (40). Another example involves a religion professor who for several years has taught courses on death at two universities and has had to limit class size because of the subject's popularity. The students face their own concepts and fears about death, study various religious views and myths surrounding death, examine the possible stages of dying, and interview a dying person.

A phenomenon that has gained public interest through Moody's publication *Life After Life* is "coming back to life" after just being declared clinically dead or near dead. The stories (those told to Moody and those heard before and since) have a sameness, although details and interpretation depend on the personality and beliefs of the person (14, 55, 74).

There is more publicity about men and women, of a wide range of age, education, background, religious and nonreligious belief, and temperament, who came close to death or had a near-death experience (NDE), and who recalling what had happened to them upon return to consciousness describe a sense of comfort, beauty, peace, and bliss. The person experienced being outside or separated from the body, communicating with deceased loved ones, gliding down a dark tunnel towards a bright light, reaching a threshold but drawing back because of a sense of responsibility for others. The person longed to remain in this bliss, and the intensity of the experience affected the person's life thereafter in the earthly world. Most were convinced they had been in Paradise or in Heaven, or in the presence of a Supreme and Loving Power and had a glimpse of life to come, regardless of prior religious beliefs. Death is no longer feared. Life is seen as precious and meaningful.

Researchers Michael Sabon, a cardiologist at Emery University, Kenneth Ring, Bruce Greyson, and Ian Stevenson, all psychiatrists, and Fred Shoenmaker, physician in charge of Cardiovascular Services at St. Luke's Hospital in Denver, as well as Dr. Raymond Moody, Jr., have accumulated several thousand case studies to verify near-death experiences. Anesthesia, drugs, hallucinations, or wishful fantasies do not account for these experiences. Clinical death has been recorded by absence of electrical activity in the brain for anywhere from 3 to 30 minutes in hundreds of subjects, although at times adequate brain function continued when heart function stopped. Often the person will describe exactly what happened when the medical team was working to revive him/her, as if the person were looking on from above. See also Orne's article (58).

Papowitz (59) describes near-death experiences that have been recounted by various people. She describes guidelines for caring for the person who is being resuscitated in light of the fact that the person may be able to hear and see what is happening. She describes ways to help the person talk about the near death experience if it is recalled, the importance of listening and taking the necessary time to allow the person to express emotions. Respect that some people view this as a religious experience; some do not. Ask for permission to share the account with family members as a way to enrich their understanding.

This trend toward talking about, investigating, and studying death points to a willingness to confront finally an absolute fact: Each of us will die.

There is evidence of life after death. Each person must integrate this information and come to terms with it in his/her own life.

Behavior and Feelings of the Person Facing Death

When death comes accidentally and swiftly, there is no time to prepare for death. However, death is a normal, expected event to the old, and studies show that most old people anticipate death with equanimity and without fear. The crisis is not death, but where and how the person will die. Studies show that old persons living in their own homes or having adjusted to living in an institution do not fear death. Those who are close to death and are on a waiting list for admission to an institution score the highest for fear of death. The prospect of dying under nonnormal, unexpected circumstances creates the crisis (54).

Widowhood is more expected after age 65; thus, women who are over 65 show less mental or physical illness or immediate mortality than widows who are under 65 years. Mental illness in the widow is associated with self-blame, reports of having missed opportunities and having failed to live up to potentials, and with unexpected death of spouse (54). When the person approaches death gradually by virtue of many years lived or from a terminal illness, he/she will go through a predictable sequence of feelings and behavior.

Awareness of Dying

Glaser and Strauss describe the stages of awareness that the terminally ill or dying person may experience, depending on the behavior of the health team and family, which, in turn, influence interaction with others. He/she may not be aware of prognosis, may respect approaching death, or may be totally aware of diagnosis and prognosis (34).

Closed Awareness. **Closed awareness** *occurs when the person is dying but has neither been informed nor made the discovery.* He/she may not be knowledgeable about the signs of terminal illness, and the health team and family may not want the person to know for fear that "he will go to pieces."

Hospitals are designed to keep information from the patient. Even other patients who know are likely to keep the information from him/her. The doctor and nursing staff spend less time with this patient than other patients; topics of conversation are brief, direct, superficial, and about the present.

Maintaining closed awareness is less likely to occur if the dying person is at home. In the hospital it is maintained primarily to protect the health team and the family; yet the burden of keeping the prognosis a secret from the patient becomes an ever-increasing strain. The only person who is really protected is the doctor, for the nurses who are with this patient throughout the day find being deceitful increasingly difficult. The family may continue to pretend but they are robbed of the opportunity to express openly and share the burden of grief with their loved one and helpful others. The patient and family cannot support each other, nor can the staff fully support the patient. The patient and family have no opportunity to review their lives, plan realistically for the family's future, and close life with the proper rituals. Even legal and business transactions of the patient may suffer as he/she tries to carry on life as usual, starts unrealistic plans, and works less feverishly on unfinished business than he/she would if the prognosis were known.

However, in spite of intentions and efforts of the health team and family, the patient may become increasingly aware. He/she has a lot of time to observe the surroundings even when very ill. Patients no doubt spend more time assessing the personnel and environment than the staff spends assessing them. He/she has time to think about the nonverbal cues and indirect comments from the staff, the inconsistent answers, the new and perplexing symptoms that do not get better in spite of reassurance that they will improve. Privileges that were previously denied are granted, and the patient is subjected to a barrage of diagnostic and treatment procedures. At times the staff may relax their guard when they think he/she does not understand and say something about the prognosis that is understood. All these things help the person formulate the conclusion that he/she is very sick and perhaps even dying. Of course, if the person is kept sedated, as much to relieve the staff from having to face the patient as to relieve the patient's suffering, he/she may be less aware of the external cues.

Suspicious Awareness. **Suspicious awareness** *develops for the reasons previously described. The person may or may not voice suspicions to others, and they are likely to deny his/her verbal suspicions.* A contest for control develops with the patient on the offensive and the staff on the defensive.

The patient watches more closely for signs to confirm suspicions. The changing physical status; the nonverbal and verbal communications of others, with their hidden meanings; the silence; the intensity of or challenges in care; and the briskness of conversation usually will inadvertently tell or imply what he/she suspects.

Now deceitfulness has fully developed. The patient knows that he/she is dying but realizes that others do not know he/she knows.

Mutual Pretense. **Mutual pretense** *occurs when staff and family become aware that the patient knows he/she is dying, but all continue to pretend otherwise.* There is no conversation about impending death unless the patient initiates it, although on occasion staff members may purposely drop cues because they feel the patient has a right to know.

Although the patient now knows and can plan for the remaining life, this measure of dignity is offset because intimate relationships are denied. There is no one to talk with honestly, although all persons involved could benefit. Neither anticipatory grieving nor other preparation for death can be accomplished very well.

Open Awareness. **Open awareness** *exists when the person and family are fully aware of the terminal condition, although neither may realize the nearness nor all the complications of the condition and the mode of death.*

With the certainty of death established, the person may plan to end life in accord with personal ideas about proper dying, finish important work, and make appropriate plans for and farewells with the family. He/she and the family can talk frankly, make plans, share grief, and support each other. The anguish is not reduced but can be faced together.

The health team in the hospital has ideas, although not always verbalized, about how the person ought to die morally and stylistically. These ideas may conflict with or differ from the ideas of the patient and family. The wishes of the patient and the family should always have priority, particularly when they ask that no heroic measures be taken to prolong life. Extra privileges, special requests, or the patient's discharge to the family can be granted. Most people wish to die without pain, with dignity, in privacy, and with loved ones nearby. Often dying in the hospital precludes both privacy and dignity, and the health team should continuously work to provide these rights.

✔ But how? Research physicians, students, and other team members hover over the patient as they attempt to learn more, to develop future treatments. Patients sometimes feel more like experimental animals than dignified human beings. Do you follow orders to prolong life with gadgetry or to hasten death with a lethal dose of medication? How do you decide what the patient's rights are? What if they conflict with the doctor's orders? Does the health team work together on these matters?

✔ One way to work through feelings, clarify ideas, and collaborate with other health-team members would be to suggest a seminar, or series of them, on the topic of death, to be attended by the team. Certain general guidelines could be set, based on the premise that the patient should be granted the right to die as he/she wishes.

Sequence of Reactions to Approaching Death

When the person becomes aware of the diagnosis and prognosis, whether he/she is told directly or learns by advancing through the stages of awareness discussed above, he/she and the family usually go through a predictable sequence of reactions described by Kübler-Ross (48).

Denial and Isolation. These are the initial and natural reactions when the person learns of terminal illness: "It can't be true. I don't believe it's me." The person may go through a number of rituals to support this denial, even to the point of finding another doctor. He/she needs time to mobilize resources. Denial serves as a necessary buffer against overwhelming anxiety.

The person is denying when he/she talks about the future; avoids talking about the illness or the death of self or others; or when he/she persistently pursues cheery topics. Recognize the patient's need, respond to this behavior, and let him/her set the pace in conversation. Later, the person will gradually consider the possibility of the prognosis; anxiety will lessen; and the need to deny will diminish.

Psychological isolation occurs when the patient talks about the illness, death, or mortality intellectually but without emotion, as if these topics were not relevant. Initially, the idea of death is recognized, although the feeling is repressed. Gradually, feelings about death will be less isolated, and the patient will begin to face death but still maintain hope.

✔ If the patient continues to deny for a prolonged time in spite of advancing symptoms, he/she will need much warmth, compassion, and support as death comes closer. Your contacts with the patient may consist of sitting in silence, using touch communication, giving meticulous physical care, conveying acceptance and security, and looking in on him/her frequently. If denial is extensive, he/she cannot grieve or face the inevitable separation. Yet Kübler-Ross found that few persons maintain denial to the end of life (48).

Anger. The second reaction, anger, occurs with acknowledgment of the reality of the prognosis. It is necessary for an eventual acceptance of approaching death. As denial and isolation decrease, anger, envy, and resentment of the living are felt. In America, direct expression of anger is unacceptable, so this stage is difficult for the patient and others. Anger is displaced onto things or people: "The doctor is no good"; "the food is no good"; "the hospital is no good"; "the nurses are neglectful"; and "people don't care." The family also bears the brunt of the anger.

Anger results when the person realizes life will be interrupted before he/she finishes everything planned. Everything reminds the person of life while he/she is dying, and he/she feels soon-to-be-forgotten. He/she may make angry demands, frequently ring the bell, manipulate and control others, and generally make the self heard. He/she is convincing self and others that he/she is not yet dead and forgotten.

✔ Do not take the anger personally. The dying person whose life will soon end needs empathy. The person who is respected, understood, given time and attention will soon lower the angry voice and decrease demands. The person will realize he/she is considered a valuable person who will be cared for and yet allowed to function at maximal potential as long as possible. Your calm approach will lower anxiety and defensive anger.

Bargaining. The third reaction, bargaining, occurs when the person tries to enter into some kind of agreement which may postpone death. He/she may try to be on the best behavior. He/she knows the bargaining procedure and hopes to be granted the special wish—an extension of life, preferably without pain. Although the person will initially ask for no more than one deadline or postponement of death, he/she will continue the good behavior and will promise to devote life to some special cause if he/she lives.

✔ Bargaining may be life promoting. As the person continues to hope for life, to express faith in God's willingness to let him/her live, and to engage actively in positive, health-promoting practices, the body's physical defenses may be enhanced by mental or emotional processes yet unknown. This process may account for those not-so-uncommon cases in which the person has a prolonged, unexpected remission during a malignant disease process. Hope, which is involved in bargaining and which you can support, gives each person a chance for more effective treatment and care as new discoveries are made.

Depression. This is the fourth reaction and occurs when the person gets weaker, needs increasing treatment, and worries about mounting medical costs and even necessities. Role reversal and related problems add to the strain. Depression about past losses and the present condition; feelings of shame about the illness, sometimes interpreted as punishment for past deeds; and hopelessness enshroud the person and extend to the loved ones.

✔ Depression is normal. The family and staff need to encourage the person by giving realistic praise and recognition, letting him/her express feelings of guilt, work through earlier losses, finish mourning, and build self-esteem. You will need to give more physical and emotional help as the person grows weaker. He/she should stay involved with the family as long as possible.

Preparatory Depression. This is the next stage and differs from the previous depression. Now the person realizes the inevitability of death and comes to desire the release from suffering that death can bring. He/she wishes to be a burden no more and recognizes that there is no hope of getting well. The person needs a time of preparatory grief to get ready for the final separation of impending loss—not only are loved ones going to lose him/her but the person is losing all significant objects and relationships. The person reviews the meaning of life and searches for ways to share insights with the people most significant to him/her, sometimes including the staff. Often the fear that he/she cannot share aspects of life or valued material objects with people of his/her own choosing will cause greater concern than the diagnosis of a terminal illness or the knowledge of certain death. As the person thinks of what life has meant, he/she begins to get ready to release life, but not without feelings of grief. Often he/she will talk repetitiously to find a meaning in life.

✔ The family and health team can either inhibit the person during this stage or promote emotional comfort and serene acceptance of death. The first reaction to depressed, grieving behavior and life review is to cheer him/her. This meets your needs but not the patient's. When the person is preparing for the impending loss of all love objects and relationships, behavior should be accepted and not changed. Acceptance of the final separation in life will not be reached unless he/she is allowed to express a life review and sorrow. There may be no need for words if rapport, trust, and a working nurse–patient relationship have been previously established. A touch of the hand and a warm accepting silence is therapeutic. Too much interference with words, sensory stimuli, or burdensome visitors hinders rather than helps emotional preparation for death. If the person is ready to release life and die and others expect him/her to want to continue to live and be concerned about things, the person's own depression, grief, and turmoil are increased. Now he/she wishes quietly and gradually to disengage self from life and all that represents life. He/she may request few or no visitors and modifications in the routines of care and repeatedly request no heroic measures to prolong life.

✔ Honor the patient's requests while at the same time promote optimum physical and emotional comfort and well-being. Explain the feelings and needs of the patient to the family and other members of the health team so that they can better understand his/her behavior. The family should know that this depression is beneficial if the patient is to die peacefully and that it is unrelated to their past or present behavior.

Acceptance. The final reaction, acceptance or a kind of resolution, comes if the person is given enough time, does not have a sudden, unexpected death, and is given some help in working through the previous reactions. He/she will no longer be angry or depressed about the fate and will no longer be envious or resentful of the living. He/she will have mourned the loss of many people and things and will contemplate the end with a certain degree of quiet expectation. Now we see the ultimate of ego integrity described by Erikson (22). Acceptance is difficult and takes time. It depends in part on the patient's being aware of the prognosis of illness so that he/she can plan ahead—religiously, philosophically, financially, socially, and emotionally. This last stage is almost devoid of feeling.

The healthy aged person will also go through some aspects of the reactions discussed above, for as the person grows old he/she contemplates more frequently personal mortality and begins to work through feelings about it.

While Kübler-Ross looks at the dying *person* with the family implied, Giacquinta looks at the *family* with the dying person implied. Table 15–1 outlines the four main stages and the ten phases that the family will experience from the time of diagnosis through the postdeath period (33).

✔ Both the Kübler-Ross (48) and the Giacquinta (33) models are helpful. They are built on observations of hundreds of dying persons and families, but you must not stereotype responses into these stages. Do not assume that everyone is experiencing each stage as the research results describe. Sometimes the person or family will not go through every one of these stages, and the stages will not always follow in this sequence. The person or family may remain in a certain stage or revert to earlier stages. Feelings related to several of the researched stages may exist, the person who has been told he/she has cancer and a limited time to live feels fear, loss of control over destiny, a discontinuity in life goals, a sense of future time being meaningless, and a sense of isolation. A magazine subscription is chosen one year at a time; the 20,000 mile guarantee on tires seems more appropriate than the 40,000 mile guarantee. Friends may react out of fear of disease contagion. Professional colleagues, relatives, and friends avoid talking about the condition, and the person does not bring up the subject out of deference not to burden them. Or that may be all friends or relatives seem to want to talk about. Priorities change; family and close friends become more important. Gradually the person is able to plan for the not-too-far future. Money is less important. Negative friends are avoided. The person must adjust to fatigue, changes in body function or structure, effects of chemotherapy or radiation, the continuing treatment appointments, and the loss of control. Do not convey that the patient or family should be in a certain stage or reacting a certain way. Avoid social and religious clichés. Rather, be a caring, concerned, available person, willing to do nondramatic, simple, but helpful tasks like

TABLE 15–1. The Family's Response to Dying and Death

FOUR MAIN STAGES	THE FAMILY EXPERIENCES:	THE NURSE CAN FOSTER:
Living with Terminal Illness The person learns diagnosis, tries to carry on as usual, undergoes treatment.	*Impact:* Emotional shock, despair, disorganized behavior. *Functional Disruption:* Much time spent at hospital (if traditional surgery-treatment chosen), ignoring of home tasks and emotional needs, weakening of family structure, emotional isolation. *Search for Meaning:* Questioning why this happened. Casting blame on various persons, deity, institutions, habits; realization that "Someday I will die too." *Informing Others (family and friends):* Ascent from isolation, with moral and practical support—or feeling of rejection: others do not understand, do not care, or are afraid. Possible need to retreat again into emotional isolation. *Engaging Emotions:* Beginning grieving, fearing loss of emotional control, assumption of roles once carried by dying person.	Hope as different treatment methods are used, communication, seeking helpful resources, family cohesiveness. Security. Courage, reliable help, understanding of why some people can't help. Problem solving, idea that life will change but will be ongoing.
Living–Dying Interval The person ceases to perform family roles, is cared for either at home or hospital. The person needs to come to terms with accomplishments and failures and to find renewed meaning in life.	*Reorganization:* Firmer division of family tasks. *Framing Memories:* Reviewing life of dying person—what he/she has meant and accomplished, new sense of family history, relinquishment of dependency on dying member.	Cooperation instead of competition, analysis to see if new role distribution is workable. Focus on life review rather than only on what person is now.
Bereavement Death occurs.	*Separation:* Absorption in loneliness of separation as person becomes unconscious. *Mourning:* Guilt, "Could I have done more?"	Intimacy among family members, release of grief as normal. (Refer to Chapter 8 of *Nursing Concepts for Health Promotion* for specific aids during grief and mourning [56].)
Reestablishment	*Expansion of the social network:* Overcoming feelings of alienation and guilt.	Looking back with acceptance and forward to new growth and socialization with a reunited, normally functioning family.

bringing the family member something to drink, watering the flowers sent by a friend, or offering to call a significant person. Equally important will be doing physical care procedures in a thorough but efficient manner so that visiting family members can spend as much time with their dying loved one as possible. Listen to feelings when the person wants to talk but do not probe. Megerle writes a personal account of the difficulties of terminal illness and death for the surviving family members and makes suggestions how health-care professionals can help (54).

Anniversary Reaction and Emotionally Invested Deadlines

The classic anniversary reaction is a psychodynamic pattern in a child who is sensitized by some emotional event—most severely by the death of the parent of the same sex when the child is between the ages of 2 and 16. The specific age of this child at the time of trauma is the key time marker. When the traumatized child grows into adulthood and has a child the same age as he/she was when originally traumatized, the stressful reaction occurs. This reaction also typically involves the age of the parent at the time the event occurred, and the exact date (day, month, year) of the event—these factors function as related emotionally invested markers. For example, a 54-year-old man who suffered a coronary occlusion after apparent good health, revealed that when he was 18 his 54-year-old father had died of a heart attack. He had experienced hostilities toward his father, describing him as having a vicious temper and being responsible for the family's poverty. Now he was 54 and had an 18-year-old son. He blamed his heart attack on the hatred and tension between himself and his relatives. In short, this man had repeated the experience of his father and perhaps subconsciously brought it upon himself through his unresolved feelings toward his father (26).

Emotionally invested deadlines are the result of the emotional investment of the individual into specific dates, events, and anniversaries. When such an emotionally invested date is reached, the person may react with varying degrees of psychological stress ranging from illness to death. Emotionally invested occasions are unique for each person, yet a characteristic in common is that all these dates and events have long-standing emotional meaning for these individuals. The choice of the date or event for the time of death seems fitting to the uniqueness of the person (26). For example, two of the first four presidents died on July 4th, undoubtedly an emotionally invested event for them. The person appears to have psychological vulnerability on an emotionally charged occasion; it is well known and accepted that an emotionally depressed or brooding patient is a poor surgical risk.

While anniversary reaction is classically seen in the middle-aged or aging person, emotionally invested deadlines may be seen at any age. Both phenomena, however, tend to increase with age as one accumulates more and more emotionally charged experiences.

Predilection to Death

The phenomenon of **predilection to death** *is seen in people who, while lacking any signs of emotional conflict, suicidal tendencies, severe depression, or panic, correctly anticipate their own deaths* (13). These persons are firmly convinced of their impending death yet feel no depression or anxiety toward it, regarding it as completely appropriate. Such patients are resigned to death—to fight against it is unthinkable, for death is a release from the burden of their life or body. It is significant that predilection patients experience a lack of close human relationships and emotional isolation from significant others during their terminal period. Death holds more appeal than life because it promises either a reunion with lost love, resolution of long conflict, or respite from anguish. Death is perceived as a release from continuing in a world in which there are no longer any emotional bonds, and thus there is no fear, anxiety, or depression regarding its approach, but rather a distinctly eager and expectant attitude toward its swift occurrence. Research shows that death comes to the predilection patients just as they have anticipated it would, while medically their condition does not warrant such a quick demise, or in some case, any death at all (6, 73).

"Scared to Death" (Death by Autosuggestion)

Unlike the predilection patient, who, convinced of impending death, anticipates it, the scared-to-death individual does not see death as appropriate. He/she believes self to be the victim of a curse or prediction and therefore cannot be saved by anyone or by any means. Psychic death is said to occur when a person is convinced of and accurately predicts his/her own death while no medical cause for death exists. Autosuggestion is the most accurate description for the cause of psychic death; it implies that the person responded in such a way as to convince self of imminent death. A synonym for autosuggestion might be "self-hypnosis." Death without any apparent organic cause has been documented to have occurred as a result of belief in voodoo, curses, predictions (fortune tellers, psychics, clairvoyants), premonitions, and dreams predicting death. There are two types of behavior exhibited by persons who are scared-to-death: (1) in some individuals, following a suggestion of impending death, a panic reaction occurs and they literally die of fright; or (2) the person may take the suggestion calmly, believe it to be useless to resist, give up, and simply die. Death by fright or autosuggestion may occur at any age; Baker cites the case of a 3-year-old boy who died of fright after being caught in a rainstorm (2, 73).

Fear is one of the strongest of emotions and has very definite and demonstrable effects on body homeostasis, particularly the cardiovascular and endocrine systems which prepare the body to physically defend itself or escape. Several physiological causes have been suggested for voodoo and other deaths resulting solely from the conviction of death. Cannon, one of the first researchers of voodoo death, proposed that death was the result of a state of shock due to persistent overactivity of the sympathico-adrenal system, with continuous outpouring of adrenaline and rapid depletion of the adrenal corticosteroid hormones (8, 73).

Cannon (8) reviewed voodoo deaths in primitive cultures in South America, Africa, Australia, New Zealand, Haiti, and some Pacific Islands. He hypothesized that such deaths were the result of prolonged overstimulation of the adrenals by the sympathetic nervous system. Richter (64) and Engel (20) assumed such deaths were the result of complete surrender and loss of hope, the expectation of death, the giving up–given up phenomenon with parasympathetic system failure. Rahe and his associates have correlated illness and death with overwhelming life events (62). Sudden deaths do not occur only in primitive societies. They occur in more developed societies as the result of acute or accumulating stress following rejection, separation, or loss, and the consequent feelings of hopelessness and helplessness. Beliefs may be planted by family or culture during the formative years and later in life as posthypnotic suggestions which are acted out. Removal of support systems and the violation of shared belief systems may cause a sense of rejection, abandonment, and hopelessness, with death as the consequence. Immaturity, suggestibility, infantile dependency, external locus of control, and fatalistic orientation are individual variables observed in relation with sudden death. Sudden death may be the result of a complex of psychological, social, and biological factors (20, 64). Richter proposed that death from autosuggestion resulted from overstimulation of the parasympathetic, rather than the sympathetic, autonomic nervous system and that cardiac arrest had resulted from excessive stimulation of the vagus nerves (64). Rigidity is one of man's first responses to fear; hence, intense panic could lead to a state of body rigidity with cessation of respiration leading to cerebral anoxia, cardiac arrest, and death (2).

✔ Be aware that voodoo, premonitions, dreams, and predictions are taken seriously by some people and practiced as a part of health care in some cultures. Do not discount the impact of such phenomenon. Listen carefully to what the patient/client and family say and do.

Legal Planning for Death

✔ While the person is still healthy and capable of making the many decisions in relation to death, he/she can do much to relieve worries and take the burden of those decisions off others. You are in a position to give the following information to others as indicated.

Although not legally binding, the Living Will is being used by increasing numbers of people. It is a request to be allowed to die rather than to be kept alive by artificial or heroic measures if the person has no reasonable expectation to recover from a physical or mental disability. Copies can be obtained by writing to the Euthanasia Educational Council, in New York.

Representatives from some nursing and funeral homes and cemeteries are educating people to keep a folder, revised periodically, of all information which will be used by those making arrangements at the time of death. Such a folder might include names of advisors such as attorney, banker, life-insurance broker, and accountant. Personal and vital information should be included such as birth certificate, marriage license, military-discharge papers, and copies of wills, including willing of body parts to various organizations. Financial records (or a copy of those held in a safety deposit box), estimated assets and liabilities, and insurance and social security information should be there. Personal requests and wishes, listing who gets what, should be written along with funeral arrangements and cemetery deeds.

Having this information written assumes that the person has made a legal will, has some knowledge of the purposes and functions of probate court, has access to social security information, and has decided on a funeral home and burial plot.

Knowledge of matters such as how to claim survivor's benefits from Social Security and how to claim the government burial allowance for honorably discharged veterans can ease the loved one's confusion at time of death.

These are intellecutal preparations. They cannot ease the sense of loss in the living but they can foster peace of mind, realizing that the deceased's wishes were carried out.

Two books among many that are useful guides for you and those you work with are: *How to Prepare for Death* (16) and *Concerning Death: A Practical Guide for the Living* (9).

✔ NURSING APPLICATIONS

Death is an intensely poignant event, one which causes deep anguish, but one which you may frequently encounter in patient care.

Self-Assessment

Personal assessment, being aware of and coping with your personal feelings about death, is essential to assess accurately or intervene helpfully with the patient, family, or other health workers. How do you protect yourself from anxiety and despair resulting from repeated exposure to personal sufferings? The defenses of isolation, denial, or "professional" behavior are common in an attempt to cope with feelings of helplessness, guilt, frustration, ambivalence about the patient not getting well, or the secret wish for the patient to die. It takes courage and maturity to undergo the experience of death with patients and families and yet remain an open, compassionate human being. You are a product of the culture as much as is the patient and the family and hence will experience many of the same kinds of reactions. Religious, philosophical, educational, and family experiences as well as general maturity also affect your ability to cope with feelings related to death.

You may see, consciously or unconsciously, yourself in the dying person. The more believable the identification with the person or family, the more devastating the experience, as you are forced to recognize personal vulnerability to death. The patient may remind you of your grandfather, aunt, or friend. And you may react to the dying patient as though he/she were that person.

The dying patient may seek an identification and partnership with someone, and often this person is the nurse. You may be unwilling to share the relationship or respond to the dying patient. The sense of guilt which results may be as burdensome as the actual involvement.

Dying in the hospital has become so organized and care so fragmented that you are not necessarily vulnerable to personal involvement in the patient's death. However, you are more likely to be personally affected by and feel a sense of loss from the patient's death if an attachment has been formed to the patient and family because of prolonged hospitalization and if the death is unexpected. Also, if you perform nursing measures which you feel might have contributed to the patient's death, if you have worked hard to save a life, or if the patient's social or personal characteristics are similar to your own, you will feel the loss (7, 11, 21, 34, 35).

Glaser and Strauss describe how the nurse judges a patient's value according to social status and responds accordingly. The patient's death is considered less a social loss, and is therefore less mourned by the nursing staff, if he/she is elderly, comatose, or confused, of a lower socioeconomic class or a minority group, poorly educated, not famous, or unattractive. The dying patient in these categories is likely to get less care or only routine care. The patient with high social value, whose death is mourned, and who receives optimum care by the nursing staff is the person who is young, alert, or likeable, has prominent family status, has a high-status occupation or profession, is from the middle or upper socioeconomic class, or is considered talented or pretty (35).

If the patient's death is very painful or disfiguring, you may avoid the patient because of feelings of guilt or helplessness. In addition, you may be aware of the callous attitudes of other health-team members or of the decision of the family and doctor about prolonging life with heroic measures or not prolonging life. These situations can provoke intense negative reactions if you disapprove of the approaches of other members of the health team.

You must attempt to deal with the various pitfalls of working with the dying: withdrawal from the patient, isolation of emotions, failure to perceive own feelings or feelings of patient and family, displacing own feelings onto other team members, "burning out" from intense emotional involvement, and fearing illness and death.

Support for Nurses. The nurse should be able to say, "I need help in dealing with my feelings about this dying patient" just as easily as she/he would say, "I need help in starting this respirator."

A support system should be available. Specific times should be set aside for staff members to share emotional needs related to a specific dying patient or to learn specifics of the dying process. Often nurses can help each other, but there should also be a specialist with whom to confer: a nurse with additional training, a religious leader, a nun, a psychologist, or a psychiatrist. The specialist should also be available for spontaneous sessions.

The administration may also encourage and sponsor the nurses in taking courses other than in nursing to gain different perspectives (sociology, philosophy, religion), joining professional organizations in which they can share problems or solutions and gain support, changing departments either temporarily or permanently to feel the accomplishment of working with those who recover, and arranging for two primary care nurses (if that is the system) to work together so that they can share emotions and support each other.

If you work with cancer patients exclusively, you may also need special assistance. Although cancer does not always cause death, the American society still equates cancer with death. Optimism and logical thinking are difficult to encourage in the patient and to maintain in yourself. You realize that the cause(s) of cancer is(are) not definitely known, and you may worry about "catching cancer." You may hear many opinions about helpful treatment, both inside and outside the medical establishment; and you may see that some of the established treatments have disastrous side effects. The question comes: Why must the patient endure so much?

If you can think of death as the last stage of life and as fulfillment, you can mature and learn from the patient as he/she comes to terms with personal illness. The meaning of death can serve as an important organizing principle in determining how the person conducts his/her life, and it is as significant for you as for the patient. With time and experience, you will view the role of comforter as being as important as that of promoting care. Then the patient who is dying will be less of a personal threat.

Vachon summarizes some guidelines for the nurse working with dying patients:

1. Individual staff members should be encouraged to gain personal insight and acknowledge their own limits. One's limits vary over time, and extra support or time off may have to be provided when staff members are under a high degree of stress. However, the needs of patients deserve priority; if certain staff members constantly require considerable support, they may be encouraged to seek employment elsewhere.
2. A healthy balance must be maintained between work and an outside life. While this type of work demands considerable personal involvement, there must be times when staff is totally off call and left to pursue own life-affirming activities.
3. The individual must be careful when the "need to be needed" becomes too great and he/she attempts to be everything to everyone. This work is probably best accomplished by a team.
4. The individual must maintain a support system at work and outside the work setting. Hospice units must make provision for ongoing staff support through the use of visitation, psychiatric consultants for the staff, weekly staff support meetings, or other models which seem appropriate to a given unit. In addition, individuals should be encouraged to seek relationships outside the work setting for additional support.
5. For those working in isolation, it may be wise to consider seriously on-going contact with an outside consultant and therapist who can offer guidance as needed and provide support as well (70, 71).

Two books are useful in helping you become aware of and to work through your feelings, either alone or with colleagues (11, 21).

Assessment of Patient and Family

Assessment of the client/patient and family is done according to the standard methods of assessment (56). The total person (the physical, intellectual, emotional, social, and spiritual needs and status) must be assessed to plan effective care. Learn what the patient and family know about the patient's condition and what the doctor has told them, to plan for a consistent approach.

Recognize also that people differ in the way they express feelings about dying and death. Mourning may be private or public. Listen to the topics of conversation the person discusses, observe for rituals in behavior, learn of typical behavior in health from him/her or the family to get clues of what is important. The routines that are important in life may become more important now, and they may assist in preparation for death. Observe family members for pathological responses—physical or emotional—since grief after loss from death increases the risk of mortality for the survivor, especially for the male spouse or relative who is in late middle age or older.

✓ Nursing Diagnosis

Table 15–2 lists nursing diagnoses that may be pertinent to the dying person, related to assessment and need for holistic care.

Intervention with the Family

The family will be comforted as they see compassionate care being given to their loved one. Your attitude is important, for family, as well as clients/patients, are very perceptive about your real feelings, whether you are interested and available, giving false reassurance, or just going about a job. The family often judge your personal relationship with the loved one as more important than your technical skill. Being interested and available takes emotional energy. Without this component in your personality, perhaps you should not be in the profession of nursing.

Try to help the relatives compensate for their feelings of helplessness, frustration, or guilt. Assisting the patient with feeding or grooming or other time-consuming but nontechnical aspects of care can be helpful to them, the patient, and the nursing staff. The family may be acting toward or caring for a patient in a way which seems strange or even nontherapeutic to the nursing staff. Yet these measures or the approach may seem fine to the patient because of the family pattern or ritual. It is not for you to judge or interfere unless what the family is doing is unsafe for the patient's welfare or is clearly annoying to the patient. In turn, recognize when family members are fatigued or anxious and relieve them of responsibility at that point. Encourage the family to take time to rest and to meet their needs adequately. A lounge or other place where the family can alternately rest, and yet be near the patient, is helpful.

Show acceptance of grief. By helping the family express their grief and by giving support to them, you are helping them to, in turn, be supportive to the patient.

Prepare the family for sudden, worsening changes in the patient's condition or appearance to avoid shock and feelings of being overwhelmed.

The crisis of death of the loved one may result in a life crisis for the surviving family members. The problems with changes in daily routines of living, living arrangements, leisure-time activities, role reversal and assuming additional responsibilities, communicating with other family members, or meeting finan-

Table 15–2. Nursing Diagnoses Related to the Dying Person[a]

PATTERN 1: EXCHANGING Altered Nutrition: Less than body requirements Potential for Infection Ineffective Thermoregulation Constipation Diarrhea Bowel Incontinence Altered Patterns of Urinary Elimination Altered (Specify Type) Tissue Perfusion Potential for Injury Impaired Tissue Integrity Impaired Skin Integrity Potential Impaired Skin Integrity PATTERN 2: COMMUNICATING Impaired Verbal Communication PATTERN 3: RELATING Impaired Social Interaction Social Isolation Altered Role Performance Altered Family Processes Altered Sexuality Patterns PATTERN 4: VALUING Spiritual Distress PATTERN 5: CHOOSING Ineffective Individual Coping Impaired Adjustment Defensive Coping Ineffective Denial Ineffective Family Coping: Disabling Ineffective Family Coping: Compromised	Family Coping: Potential for Growth Decisional Conflict Health Seeking Behaviors PATTERN 6: MOVING Impaired Physical Mobility Activity Intolerance Fatigue Potential Activity Intolerance Sleep Pattern Disturbance Diversional Activity Deficit Impaired Home Maintenance Management Altered Health Maintenance Bathing/Hygiene Self Care Deficit Dressing/Grooming Self Care Deficit Toileting Self Care Deficit PATTERN 7: PERCEIVING Body Image Disturbance Self Esteem Disturbance Sensory/Perceptual Alterations Hopelessness Powerlessness PATTERN 8: KNOWING Knowledge Deficit PATTERN 9: FEELING Pain Chronic Pain Anticipatory Grieving Reaction Anxiety Fear

[a] Other NANDA diagnoses are applicable to the dying person.
Source: NANDA Approved Nursing Diagnostic Categories, *Nursing Diagnosis Newsletter*, 15, no. 1 (1988), 1–3.

cial obligations can seem overwhelming. The failure of relatives and friends to help or relatives and friends who insist on giving help that is not needed are equally problematic. Advice from others may add to rather than decrease the burdens. The fatigue that a long illness causes in a family member may remain for some time after the loved one's death and may interfere with adaptive capacities. You can help by being a listener, exploring with the family ways in which to cope with their problems, and by making referrals or encouraging them to seek other persons or agencies for help. Often your willingness to accept and share their feelings of loss and other concerns can be enough to help the family mobilize their strengths and energies to cope with remaining problems.

The most heartbreaking time for the family may be the time when the patient is disengaging from life and from them. The family will need help to understand this process and recognize it as normal behavior. The dying person has found peace. His/her circle of interests has narrowed, and he/she wishes to be left alone and not stirred up by any news of the outside world. Behavior with others may be so withdrawn that he/she seems unreachable and uncooperative. He/she prefers short visits and is not likely to be in a talkative mood. The television set remains off. Communication is primarily nonverbal. This behavior can cause the family to feel rejected, unloved, and guilty about not doing enough for the patient. They should understand that the patient can no longer hold onto former relationships as he/she accepts the inevitability of death. The family needs help in realizing that their silent presence can be a very real comfort and shows that he/she is loved and not forgotten. Concurrently, the family can learn that dying is not a horrible thing to be avoided.

News of impending or actual death is best communicated to a family unit or group rather than to a lone individual, to allow the people involved to give mutual support to each other. This should be done in privacy so they can express grief without the restraints imposed by public observation. Stay and comfort the person facing death, at least until a religious leader or other close friends can come.

Requests by an individual or family to see the dead person should not be denied on the grounds that it would be too upsetting. The person who needs a leave taking to realize the reality of the situation will ask for it; those for whom it would be overwhelming will not request it.

Sometimes the survivor of an accident may ask about people who were with him/her at the time of the accident. The health team should confer on when and how to answer these questions; well-timed honesty is the healthiest approach. Otherwise the person cannot adapt to the reality of the accidental death. The person's initial response of shock, denial, and tears or later grief will neither surprise nor upset the medical team who understand the normal steps in resolving crisis and loss (56). Cutting off the person's questions or keeping him/her sedated may protect the staff, but it does not help the survivor.

The parents who grieve for their dying child need to be respected, to be given the opportunity to minister to the child when indicated, and to be relieved of responsibilities at times. Encourage the parents to share feelings. And work to complement, not compete with, the parents in caring for the child.

Intervention for the Dying Person

Care of the dying patient falls primarily on the nurse. You have sustained contact with the patient, informed by an understanding of dying and of the many needs of the dying person. You know the value of compassionate service of mind and hands. You can protect the vulnerable person and understand some of the distress felt by patient and family. You have an opportunity to help the patient bring life to a satisfactory close, truly to live until he/she dies, and to promote comfort. The patient needs your unqualified interest and response to help decrease loneliness and make the pain and physical care or treatment bearable.

You will encounter frustrations during the care of the dying person for many reasons. There is the challenge of talking with or listening to the patient. Will he/she talk about death? Pain may be constant and difficult to relieve, causing you to feel incompetent. He/she may be demanding, nonconforming to the patient role, or disfigured and offensive to touch or smell. The family may visit so often and long that they interfere with necessary care of the patient. Accusations from the patient or family about neglect may occur or be feared. It is no wonder, then, that in spite of good intentions, religious convictions, and educational programs, you may avoid the dying patient and family. They are left to face the crisis of death alone. As you rework personal feelings about crisis, dying and death and become more comfortable with personal negative feelings and emotional upset, you will be able to serve more spontaneously and openly in situations previously avoided. You will be able to admit, without guilt feelings, personal limits in providing care, to utilize other helpers, and yet to do as much as possible for the patient and family without showing shock or repugnance about the patient's condition.

Physical care of the dying person includes providing for nutrition, hygiene, rest, elimination, and relief of pain or other symptoms. Castles' and Murray's *Dying in an Institution*, "Strategies of Care," also includes care of the mouth, nose, eyes, skin, and peripheral circulation, positioning, and environmental considerations (10). Hospital personnel should not focus exclusively on the patient's complaints of pain or other physical symptoms or needs to avoid the subject of death. Complaints may be a camouflage for anxiety, depression, or other feelings and covertly indicate a desire to talk with someone about the feelings. Analgesics and comfort measures to promote rest can be used along with crisis therapy. Spend sufficient time with the patient to establish a relationship that is supportive. Provide continuity of care. Try to exchange information realistically within the whole medical team, including patient and family, to reduce uncertainty and feelings of neglect.

Thorough, meticulous physical care is essential to promote physical well-being but also to help prevent emotional distress. During the prolonged and close contact which physical care provides, you can listen, counsel, and teach, using principles of effective communication (56). But let the patient sleep often, without sedation if possible. The many physical measures to promote comfort and optimum well-being can be found in texts describing physical-care skills. Nursing care is not less important because the person is dying.

Avoid too strict a routine in care. Let the patient make some decisions about what he/she is going to do as long as safe limits are set. Modify care procedures as necessary for comfort. And through consistent, comprehensive care you tell the patient that you are available and will do everything possible for continued well-being.

During care, conversation should be directed to the patient. Explain nursing procedures, even though the patient is comatose, since hearing is the last sense lost. Response to questions should be simple, encouraging, but as honest as possible. Offer the person opportunities to talk about self and feelings through open-ended questions. When the patient indicates a desire to talk about death, listen. There is no reason to expound your philosophy, beliefs, or opinions. Focus your conversation on the present and the patient. Help the patient maintain the role that is important to him/her. Convey that what he/she says has meaning for you. You can learn by listening to the wisdom shared by the patient, and add to feelings of worth and generativity. Recognize too, when the patient is unable to express feelings verbally, and help him/her reduce tension and depression through other means—physical activity, crying, or sublimative activities.

If the patient has an intense desire to live and is denying or fearful of death, be accepting but help him/her maintain a sense of balance. Do not rob the person of hope or force him/her to talk about death. Follow the conversational lead; if the topics are concerned with life, respond accordingly.

Encourage communication among the doctor, patient, and family. Encourage the patient to ask questions and state needs and feelings instead of doing it for him/her but be an advocate if the person cannot speak for self.

Explore with the family the ways they can communicate with and support the patient. Explain to the family that since the comatose patient can probably understand what is being said, they should talk in ways that promote security and should avoid whispering, which can increase the person's fears and suspicions.

Psychological care includes showing genuine concern, acceptance, understanding, and promoting a sense of trust, dignity, or realistic body image and self-concept. Being an attentive listener and providing for privacy, optimum sensory stimulation, independence, and participation in self-care and decision making are helpful. You will nonverbally provide a feeling of security and trust by looking in frequently on the patient and using touch communication.

Spiritual needs of the dying person, regardless of the spiritual beliefs, can be categorized as follows:

1. Search for meaning and purpose in life and in suffering, including to integrate dying with personal goals and values, to make dying and death less fearful, to affirm the value of life, and to cope with the frustration caused by anticipated death.
2. Sense of forgiveness in the face of guilt about unfulfilled expectations for self, accepting nonfulfillment or incompleteness and making the most of remaining life, acts of omission or acts of commission toward others, resolving human differences.
3. Need for love, through other's words and acts of kindness and silent, compassionate presence. If family and friends are not present, the nurse may be the primary source of love.
4. Need for hope, which connotes the possibility of future good. Concrete hope consists of objects of hope within the person's experience, such as freedom from pain or other symptoms, ability to perform certain tasks, or to travel. Abstract hope or transcendent hope is characterized by distant and abstract goals and incorporates philosophical or religious meanings. Hope may be expressed as belief about afterlife, reunion with deceased loved ones, union with God, a superior alternative to present existence. If there is no belief in the afterlife, hope may be expressed as belief about transfer of physical energy from the deceased body, belief about contributing to another's life through an organ donation, or belief in leaving a legacy in his/her children or community or organizational contributions (12).

You may assist with meeting the person's spiritual needs if requested and if you feel comfortable in doing so. Certainly, you should know whom to contact if you feel inadequate. The religious advisor is a member of the health team. If the patient has no religious affiliation and indicates no desire for one, avoid proselytizing.

Consider the social needs of the patient until he/she is comatose or wishes to be left alone. Visitors, family, or friends can contribute significantly to the patient's welfare when visiting hours are flexible. If possible, help the patient to get dressed appropriately and groomed to receive visitors, to go out of the room to a lounge, to meet and socialize with other patients, or to eat in a patient's dining room or the unit.

Community health nurses have found two distinct attitudes in families of dying patients. The first attitude is, "If he is going to die soon, let's get him to the hospital!" For these families, the thought of watching the actual death is abhorrent. They feel personally unable to handle the situation and feel comforted by the thought of their loved one's dying in a place where qualified professionals can manage all the details. If possible, these families should have their wishes met.

The second attitude is, "I want her to die at home. This is the place she loved. I can do everything that the hospital personnel can do." This attitude can be supported by the visiting nurse. The visiting nurse can usually coordinate community resources so that a home health aide, homemaker services, proper drug and nutrition supplies, and necessary equipment can all be available in the home. Even the comatose patient who requires a hospital bed, tube feedings, catheter change and irrigation, daily bed bath, feces removal, and frequent turning can be cared for in the home if the health team, family, and friends will share efforts.

The families who desire this approach, and who are helped to carry out their wishes, seem to derive a great satisfaction from giving this care.

In one study, one-half of the patients and one-half of the family members interviewed selected the home as the place of care in the terminal stages of disease and as the place to die. Being with family and friends and living in their own home was a high priority for the patient. Home represented the person's life's work and helped to maintain a sense of dignity, identity, and control over dying. They realized at home they would not have to battle extraordinary measures. The family wanted the patient at home because it was his/her wish and because they believed they would desire to be at home if they were dying. In this study, patients and families who chose the hospital as the place of death believed patients would receive better care there. Patients did not want to burden families. Families were concerned about patient's comfort (61).

Age, diagnosis, length of illness, and presence of children in the home were not factors influencing choice of home or hospital in a sample of 441 male patient/female family pairs at a Veterans Administration Hematology-Oncology Clinic. However, the longer the diagnosis had been known, the more likely was the family member to want to keep the patient at home. The older the family member, the more likely she/he was to want to keep the patient in the hospital. The most important anticipated services at home by patients was pain control and the availability of someone to assist day or night if needed. Family members expressed need for equipment, help with the patient's physical care, and assurance that emergency measures could be obtained if necessary (61).

The *hospice* is an institution and a concept that gives the dying person home-like care either at home, with the help of an interdisciplinary team, or in an institution, with a home-like atmosphere and special attention to the needs of the dying and their families. The hospice concept is indeed a "care system" that coexists with a "cure system." In the United States the definition of what constitutes hospice care varies from region to region; the goal, however, is essentially the same. The hospice concept originated in the Middle Ages; St. Christopher's Hospice in England has been the most famous to date. In some hospitals, one unit is designated as the hospice area. A modern, freestanding hospice was opened in 1980 in Branford, Connecticut. Connecticut was the first state to regulate the licensing of hospices. In other states licensing depends on the types of facilities and services a hospice provides (53). More information about hospice care, especially ways that physical pain and other common symptoms can be relieved and ways to work with the psychological aspects of late stage cancer, is found in Geltman and Paige (32) and McPherson (53).

One author describes how a hospice care program enabled an elderly woman to care for her ill husband until his death. A team approach was utilized: (1) a visiting nurse doing multiple interventions, (2) home health aids to do morning household chores, (3) a family physician who made home visits and enabled the patient to have pain control through effective use of medications, (4) a physical therapist who helped the man maintain mobility and who later taught the wife and son to use the Hoyer lift for transfer, (5) a music therapist to bring diversion and suggest exercise to music, (6) the clergy and church choir visits to the home (15).

At times, the patient needs to be alone, either at home or in the hospital, as he/she goes through the preparatory depression discussed by Kübler-Ross and is disengaging self from life, loved ones, and all that has been important to him/her. For you to impose yourself at these times might complicate the emotional tasks near the end of life. You should not, however, abandon the patient; give the necessary care but go at his/her pace in conversation and care.

Although most people who are about to die have made peace with themselves, some bargain or fight to the end. Accept this behavior, but do not encourage the patient to fight for life when the last days are near with no chance for continuing life. Instead, let him/her know that accepting the inevitable is not cowardly. Remember that fear of death is often found more in the living than in the dying, and that this fear is more for the impending separation of intimate relationships than of death itself.

After the death of the patient, your relationship with the family need not end immediately. Explore with them how they will manage. Follow-up intervention in the form of a telephone call or home visit by a nurse, minister, social worker, or nursing-care coordinator would be a way of more gradually terminating a close relationship and performing further crisis intervention as needed. Use this opportunity to evaluate the effectiveness of care given to the family throughout the patient's terminal-care period.

Evaluation

Throughout intervention with the dying patient or his/her family you must continually consider whether your intervention is appropriate and effective, based on their needs rather than yours. Observation alone of their condition or behavior will not provide adequate evaluation. Ask yourself and others how you could be more effective, whether a certain measure was comforting and skillfully administered, and how the patient and family perceived your approach and attitude. Assigning a person unknown to the patient and family to ask these questions will help obtain an objective evaluation. Because of your involvement, you may be told only what people think you want to hear. If you and the patient have established an open, honest communication that encompasses various aspects of dying, and if the patient's condition warrants it, perhaps you will be able to interview the dying to get evaluation answers. You might ask if and how each member of the health team has added physically, intellectually, emotionally, practically, and spiritually to the person's care. You can also ask how each member of the health team has hindered in these areas.

Through careful and objective evaluation you can learn how to be more skillful at intervention in similar situations in the future.

References

1. Aries, Philippe, *Western Attitudes Toward Death.* Baltimore: Johns Hopkins University Press, 1974.
2. Baker, J.C., *Scared to Death, An Examination of Fear—Its Cause and Effects,* London: Frederick Muller 1968.
3. Beauchamp, Joyce, Euthanasia and the Nurse Practitioner, *Nursing Digest,* 4, no. 5 (Winter, 1976), 83–85.
4. Bergman, Abraham, Psychological Aspects of Sudden Unexpected Death in Infants and Children, *Pediatric Clinics of North America,* 21, no. 1 (February, 1974), 115–121.
5. Brown, Harold, Euthanasia: Drawing New Distinctions, *Journal of Christian Nursing,* 3, no. 4 (Fall, 1986), 10–14.
6. Burgess, Karen, The Influence of Will on Life and Death. *Nursing Forum,* 15, no. 3 (1976), 238–258.
7. Burnside, Irene, You Will Cope—Of Course, *American Journal of Nursing,* 71, no. 12 (December, 1971), 2354–2357.
8. Cannon, W., Voodoo Death, *Psychosomatic Medicine,* 19 (1957), 182.
9. Cassini, N., Care of the Dying Person, in *Concerning Death: A Practical Guide for the Living,* ed. Earl Grollman. Boston: Beacon Press, 1974, 13–48.
10. Castles, Mary, and Ruth Murray, *Dying in an Institution: Nurse and Patient Perspectives.* New York: Appleton-Century-Crofts, 1980.
11. Caughill, Rita, ed., *The Dying Patient: A Supportive Approach.* Boston: Little, Brown, 1976.
12. Conrad, Nancy, Spiritual Support for the Dying, *Nursing Clinics of North America,* 20, no. 2 (1985), 415–426.
13. Cox, Cheryl, The Choice, *American Journal of Nursing,* 81, no. 9 (1981), 1627–1628.
14. Davis, A. Jane, Code 45, *American Journal of Nursing,* 77, no. 4 (April, 1977), 627–628.
15. Dobibal, Shirley, Hospice: Enabling a Patient To Die at Home, *American Journal of Nursing,* 80, no. 8 (1980), 1448–1451.
16. Draznin, Yaffa, *How to Prepare for Death.* New York: Hawthorne Books, 1976.
17. Dunton, H. Donald, The Child's Concept of Death, in *Loss and Grief,* eds. B. Schoenberg, A. Carr, D. Peretz, and A. Kutscher. New York: Columbia University Press, 1970, 355–361.
18. Engel, George, A Life Setting Conducive to the Giving-Up, Given-Up Complex, *Annals of Internal Medicine,* 69 (1968), 295–300.
19. Engel, George, Psychological Stress, Vasodepressor (Vasovagal) Syncope, and Sudden Death, *Annals of Internal Medicine,* 89 (1978), 405–412.
20. Engel, George, Sudden and Rapid Death During Psychological Stress: Folklore or Folk Wisdom?, *Annals of Internal Medicine,* 74 (1971), 771–792.
21. Epstein, Charlotte, *Nursing the Dying Patient.* Reston, Va.: Reston, 1975.
22. Erikson, Erik H., *Childhood and Society* (2nd ed.). New York: W. W. Norton, 1963.
23. Evans, Frances, *Psychosocial Nursing: Theory and Practice in Hospital and Community Mental Health.* New York: Macmillan, 1971.
24. Everson, Sally, Sibling Counseling, *American Journal of Nursing,* 77, no. 4 (April, 1977), 644–646
25. Feifel, Herman, ed., *The Meaning of Death.* New York: McGraw-Hill, 1959.
26. Fischer, H.K., and Barney M. Dlin, Man's Determination of His Time of Illness or Death. *Geriatrics,* 26, no. 7 (1971).
27. Foy, N., A Good Birth—A Good Life—Why Not a Good Death?, *Nursing Digest,* 4, no. 2 (1976), 24.
28. Fronn, S., Coping with a Child's Fatal Illness: A Parent's Dilemma, *Nursing Clinics of North America,* 9, no. 1 (March, 1974), 81–87.
29. Fuller, Janet, Lethal Dose: Should a Nurse Resist Doctor's Orders, *Journal of Christian Nursing,* 3, no. 4 (Fall, 1986), 4–8.
30. Gartley, W., and M. Bernascini, The Concept of Death in Children, *Journal of Genetic Psychology,* 110 (1967), 71.
31. Gartner, Claudine, Growing Up to Dying: The Child, The Parents, and The Nurse, in *The Dying Patient: A Supportive Approach,* ed. Rita Caughill. Boston: Little Brown, 1976, 159–190.
32. Geltman, Richard, and Robert Paige, Symptom Management in Hospice Care, *American Journal of Nursing,* 83, no. 1 (1983), 78–85.
33. Giacquinta, Barbara, Helping Families Face the Crises of Cancer, *American Journal of Nursing,* 77, no. 10 (October, 1977), 1585–1588.
34. Glaser, B., and A. Strauss, *Awareness of Dying.* Chicago: Aldine Publishing, 1965.

35. ———, The Social Loss of Dying Patients, *American Journal of Nursing*, 64, no. 6 (1964), 119ff.
36. Griffin, Jerry, Family Decision, *American Journal of Nursing*, 75, no. 5 (May, 1975), 795–796
37. Grollman, Earl, *Talking About Death: A Dialogue Between Parent and Child*. Boston: Beacon Press, 1970.
38. Hendin, David, *Death as a Fact of Life*. New York: Warner Paperback Library Edition, 1973.
39. Herter, Frederic, The Right to Die in Dignity, *Archives of the Foundation of Thanatology*, 1, no. 3 (October, 1969), 93–97.
40. Hoover, Eleanor, Creativity and Fear of Death, *St. Louis Globe-Democrat*, September 25, 1975, Sec. B., p. 4.
41. Kastenbaum, R., and B. Mishara, Premature Death and Self-Injurious Behavior in Old Age, *Geriatrics*, 26, no. 7 (1971).
42. Kastenbaum, Robert, The Kingdom Where Nobody Dies, *Saturday Review: Science*, 55, no. 52 (1972), 33–38.
43. Keith, Pat, Life Changes and Perceptions of Life and Death Among Older Men and Women, *Journal of Gerontology*, 34, no. 6 (1979), 870–878.
44. Kellmer, Dorothy, No Code Orders: Guidelines for Policy, *Nursing Outlook*, 34, no. (1986), 179–183.
45. Kobrzycki, Paula, Dying with Dignity at Home, *American Journal of Nursing*, 75, no. 8 (August, 1975), 1312–1313.
46. Koocher, G., Talking with Children About Death, *American Journal of Orthopsychiatry*, 44, no. 3 (1974), 404–411.
47. Kübler-Ross, Elisabeth, ed., *Death, The Final Stage of Growth*. Englewood Cliffs, N.J.: Prentice-Hall, 1975.
48. ———, *On Death and Dying*. New York: Collier-Macmillan, 1969.
49. Levy, N.B., Self-willed Death. *Lancet* (September 1, 1973).
50. Lieberman, Morton, Social Setting Determines Attitudes of Aged to Death, *Geriatric Focus*, 6, no. 16 (November 1, 1967), 1ff.
51. Maguire, Daniel, *Death by Choice*. Garden City, N.Y.: Doubleday & Co., 1973.
52. McIntire, M., C. Angle, and L. Struempler, The Concept of Death in Midwestern Children and Youth, *American Journal of Diseases of Children*, 123 (June, 1972), 527–532.
53. McPherson, James, Principles of Hospice Care, *Clinical Medicine*, 24, no.1 (1981), 243–250.
54. Megerle, Jo Ann, Surviving, *American Journal of Nursing*, 83, no. 6 (1983), 892–894.
55. Moody, Raymond A., *Life After Life*. New York: Bantam Books, 1975.
56. Murray, Ruth, and Judith Zentner, *Nursing Concepts for Health Promotion*, (3rd ed.). Englewood Cliffs, N.J.: Prentice-Hall, 1985.
57. Nagy, Maria, The Child's View of Death, in *The Meaning of Death*, ed. H. Fiefel. New York: McGraw-Hill, 1959.
58. Orne, Roberta, Nurses' View of NDE, *American Journal of Nursing*, 86, no.4 (1986), 419–420.
59. Papowitz, Louise, Life/Death/Life, *American Journal of Nursing*, 86, no.4 (1986), 416–418.
60. Philips, David P., Deathday and Birthday: An Unexpected Connection, in *Statistics: A Guide to the Unknown*, eds. Judith M. Tanur, et al. San Francisco: Holden-Day, 1972.
61. Putnam, Sandra, et al., Home as a Place to Die, *American Journal of Nursing*, 80, no. 8 (1987), 1451–1453.
62. Rahe, R., and M. Romo, Recent Life Changes and the Onset of Myocardial Infarction and Sudden Death in Helsinki, in *Life, Stress, and Illness*, eds. E. Gunderson and R. Rahe. Springfield, IL: Charles C. Thomas, 1974, 105–120.
63. Rees, W. Dewi, Bereavement and Illness, in *Psychosocial Aspects of Terminal Care*, eds. Bernard Schoenberg, et al. New York: Columbia University Press, 1972.
64. Richter, G., On The Phenomenon of Sudden Death in Animals and Man, *Psychosomatic Medicine*, 19 (1959), 191.
65. Rosner, Fred, The Definition of Death, *Archives of the Foundation of Thanatology*, 1, no. 3 (October, 1969), 105–107.
66. Schoenberg, Bernard, Management of The Dying Patient, in *Loss and Grief*, eds. B. Schoenberg, A. Carr, D. Peretz, and A. Kutscher. New York: Columbia University Press, 1970, 238–260.
67. Schweitzer, Albert, Learning About Dying, *St. Louis Globe-Democrat*, September 11–12, 1976, Sec. A, p. 7.
68. Sherberg, Ellen, Is There a Right to Die?, *St. Louis Post-Dispatch*, June 8, 1977, Sec. H., p. 3.
69. Sugar, M., Normal Adolescent Mourning, *American Journal of Psychotherapy*, 22 (1968), 258–264.
70. Vachon, M. L. S., Motivation and the Stress Experienced by Staff Working with the Terminally Ill, *Death Education*, (Winter, 1978), 12–15.
71. ———, W. Lyall, and S. Freeman, Measurement and Management of Stress in Health Professionals Working with Advanced Cancer Patients, *Death Education*, (Spring, 1978), 10–13.
72. Waechter, Eugenie, Children's Awareness of Fatal Illness, *American Journal of Nursing*, 71, no. 6 (1971), 1168–1172.
73. Weisman, A., and T. Hackett, Predilection to Death, *Psychosomatic Medicine*, 23, no. 3 (1961).
74. Zentner, Reid, personal story of Life After Life, March, 1971.

PART V

Health Promotion Principles and Strategies

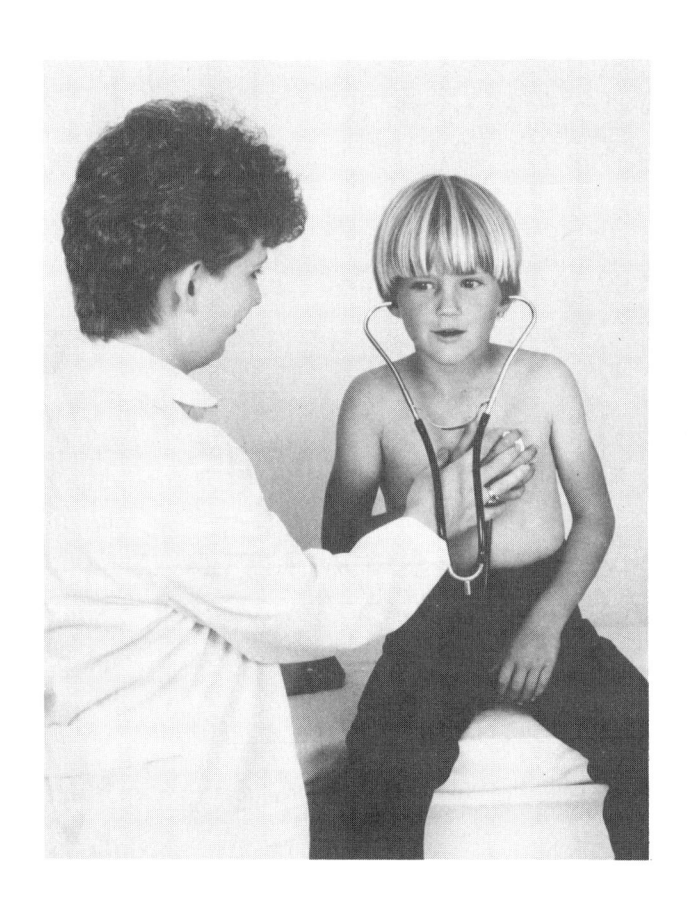

16

Basic Considerations in Health and Illness

Study of this chapter will enable you to

1. Define *health*, *holistic health*, and *illness* and explain the development of these concepts and the meaning of the health–illness continuum.
2. Identify factors that influence development of health and illness.
3. Identify needs that influence behavior and that must be met to maintain health.
4. Describe the external environmental and internal variables that affect behavior and health.
5. Differentiate between stress and anxiety and describe physiological, cognitive, emotional, and behavioral reactions to stress responses in each stage of the General Adaptation Syndrome.
6. Differentiate levels of anxiety and physical, cognitive, emotional, and behavioral manifestations at each level.

"Al, are you ill?"

"No. Why?"

"Your face looks a little puffy."

Al, who thought he was well, suddenly decides he has not had his usual energy for several weeks. He thinks he will make an appointment to see the doctor.

"I wish I knew what you meant by being sick. Sometimes I feel so bad I could curl up and die, but I have to go on because the kids have to be taken care of. Besides, we don't have money for the doctor. Some people can go to bed most anytime with anything, but most of us can't take time to be sick—even when we need to be."

These expressions immediately portray the difficulty in defining health and illness. Each person's definition is affected by cultural concepts, economic level, the value system of self and others, ethnic background, customs, and past experiences.

Key Terms

Wellness
Health–wellness
Disease–illness
Biopsychosocial/holistic health
Health
Behavior
Human needs
    Physiological
    Libidinal
    Ego developmental
Intelligence
Self-concept
Stress
Local Adaptation Syndrome
General Adaptation Syndrome
Alarm Stage
Stage of Resistance
Stage of Exhaustion
Anxiety
Mind–body relationship
Psychosomatic/psychophysiologic
Somatopsychic
Psychoneuroimmunology

✔ As a nurse, your concern, knowledge, and skill are directed to the health needs of persons from many different kinds of backgrounds and in various settings. It is essential, therefore, to understand the physical, mental, emotional, spiritual, and social aspects of wellness and illness; the factors influencing health and illness; and the basic regulatory mechanisms in the human body that normally maintain a state of health. The use of this information will assist you in helping others to maintain as well as regain health.

Definitions of Health and Illness

Working definitions of *health* and *illness*, although generalized, can give perspective. Traditionally they have been defined as opposites. Although *health* and *illness* are subjective and relative terms, Jourard believes that such qualities as hope, purpose, and direction in life can produce and maintain wellness, even in the face of stress. Similarly, demoralization through daily struggle for existence can help produce illness (36).

Wellness *is a process of moving toward greater awareness of and satisfaction from engaging in activities that* *move the person, at any age, with others, toward fitness, a positive nutritional state, positive relations, management of stress, a life purpose, a consistent belief system, commitment to self-care, and environmental sensitivity/ comfort.* The wellness process can be pursued to prevent illness, for rehabilitation, or to enhance the quality of life and maximize potential, whether ill, dying, or overcoming disability, in any setting. Differentiation of self occurs, so that a clear boundary develops between the emotional and intellectual subsystems of a whole person, leading to enhanced problem solving, flexibility in behavior, intimacy in interpersonal relationships, and a higher level of wellness. If the person is not clear about values, a pseudoself exists and is at the whim of the emotional system of others. A solid sense of self increases as consistency between beliefs, feelings, and actions is realized through the value clarification process. Environment is external to the person, it is a changing field that is continuous and contiguous with whole persons. Environment can be modified by, as well as modify, the whole person (11).

Health–wellness and **disease–illness** are now *thought of as complex, dynamic processes on a continuum that includes physical, psychological (emotional, cognitive, and developmental), spiritual, and social components and adaptive behavioral responses to internal and external stimuli.* Health depends on genetic, environmental, sociocultural, and spiritual influences that either help or hinder an individual in actively fulfilling the basic needs and reaching the highest health potential (63). The emotionally healthy person generally shows behavior congruent with events within or around him/her (5, 89). Key concepts in health–wellness include homeostasis, adaptation, dynamic nature of health–illness continuum, influence of internal and external environment, state of harmony with nature and people, comfort, safety, social relationships, and prevention of disease, disability, and social decay.

✔ In nursing, we are concerned about **biopsychosocial** or **holistic health** because the term refers to a *high level and total view of health; the unity of body, mind and spirit, and the person's interrelatedness with others and the environment* (7). **Holistic health** *focuses on acceptance and harmony between one's body, feelings, attitudes, and beliefs; on being open to relationships and change, and on being responsible for one's health and behavior.* A holistic philosophy means viewing people, and their wellness and illness, from every possible perspective and using natural, cultural, or nontraditional methods, as well as medical means, to treat the person—not the disease (46).

✔ Webster (84) describes the need to define health from a holistic view for women and to be sensitive to specific health needs of women in the home, workplace, and health-care setting. It is important to gain an understanding of the woman's personal experience from her, rather than making assumptions or acting on traditional biases. The nurse can assist the woman to feel empowered, to feel that she is capable of responsibility for her health. Interdependence, caring, cooperation, experience as a base for knowledge, and responsibility are valued by women, and the nurse can convey to the woman that these values can be enacted in the health-care system. With social roles in transition, poverty, single parenthood, role conflict, and other sources of stress, the nurse and other members of the health care system must focus on the specific individual/family to provide maximum care possible.

Wellness is a part of holistic health. Ardell defines **wellness** as *an ever-changing process focusing on health enrichment and promotion.* **Wellness** *is the ability to adapt, to relate effectively, to function at near maximum capacity, and includes self-responsibility, nutritional awareness, physical fitness, stress management, environmental sensitivity, productivity, expression of emotions, self-expression in a variety of ways, creativity, personal care, and home and automobile safety* (2).

As used in this book, **health** *is a state of well-being in which the person is able to use purposeful, adaptive responses and processes, physically, mentally, emotionally, spiritually, and socially, in response to internal and external stimuli (stressors) in order to maintain relative stability and comfort and to strive for personal objectives and cultural goals.*

Table 16–1 summarizes a historical review of definitions or concepts of health developed by various theorists, including nursing theorists and leaders.

Factors that Influence the Definitions of Health and Illness

Culture and historical era define health and illness. Thus, there are many definitions of health and illness since each family interprets the culture to the child.

Health is *perceived uniquely by the person* and may vary from day to day and even within a day. According to Third Force theorists, described in Chapter 5, health and illness are defined differently by each person, although the definitions are generally in line with cultural definitions. Health in all of its components is dynamic in that it includes the degree of fitness and adaptation that varies from one time period to another. There is a continual interaction between the physical, mental, spiritual, and social components (45).

Men and women are socialized to define health and illness differently. Statistics show that women in the United States report more illnesses and disabilities, visit the physician more, and are hospitalized more often, including for emotional illnesses. The National

TABLE 16–1. Development of the Concepts/Definitions of Health

ERA/DATE	THEORIST	CONCEPT/DEFINITION
1000 AD		English word, **hoelth,** meaning safe, sound, whole of body. Physical wholeness essential for social acceptance. Persons with malformations or disease ostracized because conditions represented lack of harmony with nature or being unclean.
Late 1800s		Concept of mental health originated as opposed to mental illness, which meant unpredictable, hostile behavior, being a lunatic and thereby ostracized. Causation attributed to evil spirits, satanic powers.
1900		Health—freedom from disease; disease caused by microbes.
1940s		Health included physical and mental status; concept received impetus from experience with psychological trauma in World War II.
		Mental health manifested in ability to withstand environmental stresses; mental illness occurred when person succumbed to life stresses and unable to carry out activities of daily living.
		Dichotomy between physical and mental illness remain.
	Harry Stack Sullivan	**Mental health** is interpersonal adjustive success. The basic or intrinsic direction of the person is forward or toward mental health. **Mental disorder** is a pattern of inadequate or inappropriate interpersonal processes inadequate to the situation, an ineffectiveness of behavior.
1950s	Halbert Dunn	**High level wellness** is integrated functioning oriented to maximizing person's potential, which requires that person maintain a balance, through purposeful activity and direction within the environment. The result is a forward direction toward higher or more mature function throughout the life cycle amid a constantly changing environment.
	L. Aubrey	**Health** is structural wholeness in which sensory processes are intact and function so that balance and adaptability characterize the person. **Mental health** is separate from physical health and is characterized as emotional stability, integration, and adaptation to surroundings so person remains viable in spite of changing conditions. The healthy person experiences contentment, performs functions of human existence and societal living, and manifests cognitive efficiency.
	T. Parsons	**Health** is effective performance of valued roles and tasks for which person has been socialized. Health status determined by ability to currently maintain normal standards of adequacy and future role and task performance.
1960s	René Dubois	**Health** is a state or condition that enables person to adapt to internal and external stresses that arise in the environment. Health is a physical and mental state free of discomfort and pain that permits person to function effectively as long as possible within the environment. Optimum health is a mirage because of an unpredictable environment.
	H. Hayman	**Health** is optimal personal fitness for full creative living; a dynamic process involving interaction of heredity, environment, and behavior to result in vigor, vitality, zest, meaning in life and fulfillment.
1970s	Myra Levine	**Health** is a state characterized by balance between input and output of energy and in which structural, personal, and social integrity exist.
	Dorothea Orem	**Health** is a state characterized by soundness or wholeness of human structures and body and mental functions. **Well-being** is a state characterized by experiences of contentment, pleasure, and happiness, by spiritual experiences, by movement to fulfilling self-ideal, by achieving human potential.
	I. Bermosk and S. Porter	**Health** is an integration of mind, body, spirit, and environment; person is responsible for own health and evolution to greater levels of zest and well-being, to healing self, to expanding consciousness.
	M. Newman	**Health** is the totality of life process, evolving to an expanded consciousness, a fusion of disease and nondisease, a manifestation of a unique pattern, a greater frequency of energy exchange.
1974	World Health Organization	"**Health** is a state of complete physical, mental and social well-being and not merely absence of disease and infirmity." Health is an ideal. Definition reflects person as a total being rather than sum of parts, that health is related to environment, and equated with productive and creative living.

TABLE 16-1. Development of the Concepts/Definitions of Health—Continued

ERA/DATE	THEORIST	CONCEPT/DEFINITION
1980s	Ruth Wu	**Health** is a feeling of well-being, a capacity to perform to the best of one's ability, the flexibility to adjust and adapt to various situations created by subsystems of man or suprasystems in which he exists.
	Dorothy Johnson	**Health** or **wellness** is a balance and stability among the following behavioral systems: affiliative or attachment, dependency, ingestive, eliminative, sexual, aggressive, and achievement, which results in efficient, effective, goal-directed predictable behavior.
	Betty Neuman	**Health** or **wellness** is a condition in which all subsystems—physiological, psychological, and sociocultural—are in balance and in harmony with the whole of man; a state of energy saturation in which the person is free of disruptive needs, forces or noxious stressors that create disharmony and expend energy. The healthy person has considerable resistance to disequilibrium.
	Sister Callista Roy	**Health** is a state and process of successful adaptation through modes that promote being and becoming an integrated whole model, with completeness, unity, and freedom from ineffective coping attempts. The four modes are physiological, self-concept, interdependence, and role performance.
	J.K. Dixon and J.P. Dixon	**Health** is a condition in which positive viability emotions such as acceptance, usefulness, optimism and clarity about life are present and result in psychological comfort, productive behavior, normal physiological function, and self-maintenance behavior. Health is evolutionary and is related to extent to which person contributes to stability and survival of the social group(s).
	T. Tripp-Reimer	**Health** has two dimensions: etic or disease-nondisease state, and emic or wellness-illness, the subjective perception of person or group. Focus on normality or homeostasis as medically defined; some cultures do not focus on medical disease states.
	Nola Pender	**Health** is the actualization of inherent and acquired human potential through goal-directed behavior, knowledgeable and competent self-care, constructive amelioration of barriers to growth, and satisfying interpersonal relationships while adjustments are made to maintain structural integrity, harmony with the environment, and positive change over time.
	L. Wright and M. Leahey	**Family health** is characterized by stability and integrity of structure, adaptability, mastery of developmental tasks leading to progressive differentiation and transformation to meet changing requisites for survival.
	C. Retze	**Family health** is characterized by a functional and productive network, a sense of togetherness that promotes capacity for change, a balance between mutual and independent action among the members, and adaptation to life events.
	G. Smilkstein	**Family health** is characterized by availability of cohesiveness, nurturance, and resources for members growth and sustenance in face of life's challenges.
	Jeanette Goeppinger	**Community health** is the meeting of collective needs through problem identification and management of interactions within the community and between the community and the larger society, considering status, structure, and process dimensions.
	Catherine Tinkham, Elizabeth Voorheis, and N. McCarthy	**Community health** is the process, activities and concerns which are designed to enhance the quality of life and promote well-being of the total population of the community.
	Sarah Archer, C. Kelly, and S. Bisch	**Community health** is characterized by openness to energy exchange, interdependence among community groups, hierarchical organization, self-regulation, dynamic activity, goal-directedness, and synthesizing process of wholeness.

Women's Health Network of Washington, D.C., states that about one-third of the hysterectomies done annually are unnecessary. Some people believe this is an example of male domination of women in the health-care system. Recently, the media has publicized the numbers of unnecessary surgeries being done in the United States. Physicians are also more likely to prescribe drugs for women than for men, especially the mood-changing drugs (31). Often the physician does not take a complete history or learn of underlying problems that can be corrected other than through use of medication. Yet women have longer life expectancies than men and there is no difference between men and women in the incidence of psychosis. Perhaps the seeking of more health care by women reflects: (1) a different perception of illness or disability; (2) different cultural norms about health care behavior for men and women; (3) sex-role conflicts for women, which result in more illness; and (4) differences in diagnostic and treatment services for men and women. All these factors may be operating. The longer life expectancy of women may be the result of early diagnosis and treatment of disease, of inherent sex-linked resistance to disease, or of different exposure or response to noxious physical and social stressors (8, 33, 45).

A person's age influences the definition of health. Children define health as feeling good and being able to participate in desired activities. Children's ideas about health progress from a specific, concrete concern for health practices to future-oriented interests in optimal development and societal problems. Six-year-olds view health as completely different from illness and as a series of specific health practices, such as eating nutritional foods, getting exercise, and keeping clean. Nine-year-olds are less concerned with specific health practices and more concerned with total body states, such as feeling good or being "in shape." To them, health means being physically fit to do the activities of daily living; it is impossible to be partly healthy and partly unhealthy. Twelve-year-olds view health as long-term feeling good, not being sick, participating in desired activities, and as including mental as well as physical components. Some children include a fit environment as part of health. In contrast, adults typically define health as a state enabling them to perform at least minimal daily activities and include physical, mental, spiritual, and social components (47). The adult's perception, as well as life situation, influences the definition of health.

Variables That Affect Behavior and Health

Hall and Allan (26) discuss the importance of the nursing profession focusing on health and not just the disease model. An ecological view, realizing multiple causation in many situations that threaten health, is essential.

Basic Needs

Behavior is *the observable response to environmental stimuli, including verbal reports about emotional state, perceptions, and thoughts*. The primary purpose of behavior is to meet the needs of the person or the group (4).

Human needs are *those aspects of the individual that must be satisfied for life to continue and that can be divided into three broad categories: physiological, libidinal (sensual and affectional), and ego developmental*. **Physiological needs** are *cyclic, perpetual, and imperative for survival. They include the need for oxygen, water, food, elimination, sleep, temperature control or shelter, safety, or movement* (53).

Libidinal needs refer *to sensual-sexual and affectional-emotional needs. Sensual-sexual* needs are not uniformly rhythmic in humans, although hormonal rhythms of the menstrual cycle are correlated with affective and behavioral changes in some women. The basis of sensual-sexual needs is organic, but these needs take on psychologic meanings. *Affectional-emotional* needs are constant and are at the core of normal psychic dependence. The person must be given love, security, approval, respect, support, care, and protection for emotional and physical development (53).

Ego developmental needs refer *to the need for cognitive, perceptual, and memory development (training and education)*. The person must have opportunity for and help with mastery of age-adequate behaviors, including motor coordination; emotional autonomy, independence, and self-identity; social skills; communication skills (speech, reading, writing, nonverbal); adaptive mechanisms; moral development; control of drives; problem solving; work skills; and the opportunity for development of creative and self-actualization behavior (53).

Libidinal and ego developmental needs emerge together; they influence each other and are equally significant for psychic and physical well-being. Ego development proceeds from mastery of simple to complex tasks (53).

Humans are very adaptable in meeting their needs, but adaptive potentials are not unlimited. In prehistoric evolution humans met many stresses, but their genetic constitutions were able to adapt over time. Now humans face threats created by modern technology that have no precedent in their evolutionary past. The rate of biological evolution is too slow to keep up with the effects of technological and social changes (16). Thus certain needs may not be met as well; other needs may be created. Unmet needs affect health status.

In countries where the population continues to increase rapidly, there is a strain on all social and human resources, including economic and educational development, and many people will have unmet needs. In such countries, health promotion is an ideal; preventing starvation and providing shelter are already consuming the resources of many nations. When physiological needs are not met, the other needs previously described cannot be met. It is a challenge to international nursing to foster the meeting of basic needs, disease prevention, and health in the people of all nations (27).

Health in the Third World developing countries could be improved and mortality and morbidity reduced by several not-too-costly measures that are available to developed countries:

1. Measles vaccination to each child (for about the cost of a pack of cigarettes).
2. Proper diet, vitamin/mineral supplementation to prevent blindness, complications from communicable diseases and diarrhea, malnutrition, and death, at cost of pennies per day.
3. Education to local populations about early signs and symptoms of specific diseases and measures to reduce their impact and local resources for help.
4. Education for and assistance with prenatal care to all women.
5. Education about and assistance to local populations in the areas of sanitation and food production (52).

External Environmental Variables

The external environment includes all stimuli, objects, and people impinging on the person.

The *physical environment* contains a wide variety of potential stimuli: gravity, light and sound waves, and meteorological stimuli, such as temperature variation, wind velocity, atmospheric pressure, humidity, solar radiation, air pollutants, ozone, oxygen, carbon dioxide and carbon monoxide levels, electromagnetic fields, day–night and seasonal periodicity, and infectious microorganisms (4). The physical environment, such as housing and sanitation facilities, affects health. Air, food, water, and other pollutants are directly or indirectly the cause of one-half of all cancers. Cigarette smoke is a form of indoor pollution for nonsmokers. Maternal smoking increases the risk of respiratory infection and asthma in the child. Nonsmokers who are chronically exposed to cigarette smoke in the workplace have pulmonary function similar to that of light smokers and poorer than nonsmokers in a smoke-free environment. Lung cancer is increased in nonsmoking wives of heavy smokers (23). Nonsmoking subjects seated adjacent to smoking environments were exposed to similar levels of carbon monoxide and showed similar physiological reactions as the smoker (50). Migrants moving from one environment to another develop the cancer pattern of the new geographic area (28). Mortality rates from cancer, as well as other disease, differ according to geographic region (59).

Meteorological stimuli are mediated primarily by the thermoregulatory centers of the hypothalamus and the autonomic nervous system. Seasonal variations affect every physiological system. In winter, calcium, magnesium, and phosphate blood levels are lowered; thyroid and adrenocorticoid activities are elevated; hemoglobin levels are increased; and gastric acid secretion is high. These changes are gradual and reflect the thermostatic properties of the hypothalamus in conserving heat and energy during cold winter months (42, 82).

Daily variations in *thermal stimuli* simultaneously affect the person. Responses to an approaching cold front include diuresis without increased fluid intake, increased thyrotropin production, elevated leukocyte and thrombocyte levels, elevated hemoglobin, lowered erythrocyte sedimentation rate, and increased fibrinolysis. The opposite changes occur during a heat wave (82). Any extreme fluctuation in environmental conditions results in a temporary disruption of internal environment and requires more energy to restore physiological adaptation.

Sociocultural attributes of climate and weather are reflected in the person's lifestyle, the kind of clothing worn, the food eaten, or the activities engaged in.

Psychological attributes of climate and weather relate to personal preference and symbolic interpretation. Some people have optimal performance in cold weather; others in warm weather. Some people associate fog and rain with depression; to others such weather symbolizes security (24, 82).

Although weather and climatic conditions affect the person in a given geographical setting, the *immediate physical environment* also provides multiple sensory stimuli. Room design and color, combinations of light and sound, and the arrangement of objects and persons in the room all form a *gestalt*, a whole pattern that may be perceived as either pleasant or unpleasant. One is sensitive to the physical and chemical stimuli in the environment that are of sufficient intensity and interest; some stimuli will not be perceived (4).

The *psychological environment* surrounding someone is difficult to ascertain because it has a specific meaning to that person; the person's perception of the environment is a major determinant of behavior. The reactions of others contribute to the development of self-concept and self-esteem, foster support to and involvement with the person, stimulate maturity, and convey limits on behavior (4).

To remain emotionally healthy, it is necessary to be with people who are healthy and in a group climate that contributes to developing one's optimal potential. Emotional health implies the capacity to love, learn, live fully, and share with others in the adventure of life. The emotionally ill person comes from an environment in which there is excessive tension, a barrier to emotional communication, an isolation between people, and in which emotional and social needs are not met. The emotional illness of one person in the family or group spills over so that all members are unhealthy to some degree (45).

Married and unmarried persons differ in their health status. Married men and women have lower morbidity rates for physical illness, use health services less frequently, and live longer than unmarried people. Although married women have a higher incidence of emotional illness than married men, single women have less incidence of emotional illness than single men. Married, employed women exhibit fewer physical and psychiatric symptoms than married, nonemployed women. Single men are at a greater risk for both physical and emotional illness. Sex-role expectations and lifestyle, as well as resultant emotional stress, may be factors behind these statistics (33, 45).

Today, more women, married and unmarried, are employed than ever before. Many working women also bear the major responsibility of child care. Women are exposed to the same physical and emotional hazards of the work environment as men, plus the pressures created by multiple roles and conflicting expectations. The long-term health consequences of these complex changes are generally unknown; however, the National Institute of Health reports increased incidence of stress-related illnesses as a result of these changes (33).

The *sociocultural environment* includes the historical era, family, and other people and groups; social institutions, such as government, schools, and church; all sorts of social events; and shared values and moral, ethical, and religious beliefs. All groups have developed rules and regulations that assist an individual in the specific historical time in the process of becoming a useful and valued member of the group and that serve to constrain certain behaviors. Society helps an individual decide on the rules applicable in a particular situation, but it also grants the privilege of ignoring the rule if he/she so chooses. Punishment will be established for deviancy by the group if the rule is essential for the group's survival. Rules, values, and beliefs are fairly stable and resistant to change, thus giving the person variety with a basis for predicting outcome. Change occurs so rapidly in our society that old values and relationships no longer have the same importance or meaning. Social instability produces conflict and alienation between groups, creates lack of direction for members, and contributes to illness (4, 29).

The family contributes not only to genetic predisposition but also to the actual etiology of specific diseases through lack of hygiene measures, nutritional imbalance, transmission of social values, the socialization process of the child, and the family pattern of daily living and behavior (45). The family may also contribute to long-term health problems in its members through physical or emotional abuse or through sexual assault or incest.

Population density affects social behavior in animal studies and parallels human behavior in crowded conditions. Studies on small mammals show that uncontrolled population growth causes specific behaviors as population density increases: aggression, confusion as the number of social roles in the animal colony decreases, social withdrawal and avoidance of other animals, and loss of interest in tending young (10).

Socioeconomic class, occupation, and social roles influence behavior at various times of the day, preventive health measures practiced, and susceptibility to disease (12). Socioeconomic level influences health care accessibility. More affluent urban people can afford housing, food, and regular medical examinations that can promote health. Yet more affluent people may also be in executive positions or occupations or social roles that are highly stressful or that encourage overeating or social use of drugs or alcohol, thus predisposing the person to chemical dependency. The poorer rural person may not have an annual physical examination but may eat a diet composed primarily of simple carbohydrates, fish, and homegrown fruits and vegetables, which will contribute to health. Social roles are significant to health because they place various demands on the person and call for shifts and flexibility in attitude and behavior, which may be demanding to the point of illness. The occupational role is important. Whether the person is a farmer, nurse, coal miner, physician, executive, or clerk predisposes to different stressors and illnesses. The worker in an industrial plant may be exposed to carcinogenic materials. The miner living in poverty develops respiratory disease; he may realize his work is making him sick, but he is financially unable to change jobs or geographic locations. The middle-class person may work in a clean office, have conveniences to assist with housework, and see the dentist twice yearly for a checkup. The higher the socioeconomic class and occupational position, the greater is the variety of behavioral choices available to specific goals. When availability of resources becomes restricted because of economic or geographical reasons, lifestyle and behavior are restricted (4).

Internal Variables

Genetic inheritance influences the physical characteristics, innate temperament, the activity level, and intellectual potential of the person. Physical characteristics include sex and such features as skin and eye color, hair color and degree of curl, facial structure, and height. The physical characteristics influence the response of others as well as the person's response to the environment. The positive reinforcement and the interaction from the environment that a child or adult with desirable physical characteristics receives affect that person's self-concept development and relationship to others (4).

Intelligence, *the ability to deal with complex, abstract material,* is influenced by inheritance, environment, and sociocultural influences. The test score reflecting intelligence is influenced by many factors: motivation at the time of testing, what the test means to the person, level of anxiety, cultural and social class background of the person, physical environment of the testing situation, and the race and other characteristics of the tester (4).

Circadian and psychobiological rhythms are part of the internal processes of the person, are interdependent with the time–space aspects of the environment, and help to organize behavior. These are discussed further in Chapter 12.

Gender of the person affects disease susceptibility: certain genetic and acquired diseases are more common in one sex than the other. *Sexual identity*, determined embryologically and molded through the influences of sociocultural environment, affects patterns of behavioral responses developed by that person. Crosscultural studies show that division of labor is made on the basis of sex, although not all cultures designate home and child care as female functions. The environment makes distinctions in the expected and valued behaviors for each sex as well as to indicate which sex is more valuable.

Age and developmental level influence illness susceptibility as well as behavior. Response patterns and capabilities are minimal for the first few years of life and near the end of life. The infant has few response patterns available because of two factors: lack of experience and a state of physiological and psychological immaturity. The aged person has limited responses because of declining sensory-perceptual monitoring of the environment and declining physical abilities. The periods of greatest availability of responses to environmental and social demands are in young and middle adulthood; the peak years vary with each person and with occupational groups. Athletes peak earlier than physicians, for example (4).

Race of the person is related to cultural and ethnic experiences, values, and attitudes, as well as the responses of others to the person. Behavioral patterns may vary with the race, as does susceptibility to illness. Descendants of African and Mediterranean people, for instance, are more prone to sickle cell trait and sickle cell anemia (4).

Self-concept is the person's perception of self physically, emotionally, and socially, based on the internalized reactions of others to self. The selfconcept, self-expectations, perceived abilities, values, attitudes, habits, and beliefs affect how that person will handle situations and relate to others. How the person behaves depends on whether he/she feels positively or negatively and on how the person feels others expect him/her to behave in a specific situation. Additionally, the person discloses different aspects of self in various situations, depending on personal needs, what is considered socially acceptable, how others react, and past experience with self-disclosure. Thus the hospitalized patient's behavior may be different from the usual pattern; the person may behave according to others' expectations instead of how he/she desires. These variables also affect health practices and treatment sought. The incidence of cancer has been linked to geographical and environmental factors, for example. In the United States, Seventh Day Adventists have half as much cancer as the national average and rural Mormons in Utah have 60 to 75 percent less, apparently because of their lifestyle, which is related to their religion (28, 43).

The feelings of the person may be related to internal neuroendocrine processes, but they are also related to events in the external environment, including stressful events. A sense of hopelessness, despair, or extreme fear may cause death as well as disease. Many human and animal studies confirm this fact and the death that results from a hex being placed on a member is documented in various societies. When the person becomes an outcast and has nothing to live for, physiological processes stop and death occurs (38).

Feelings are often related to the person's perception of the event. *The Social Readjustment Rating Scale (Life Change Scale)* was devised to assess perceptions of the amount of adjustment required by 43 life events involving personal, social, occupational, and family changes (Table 16–2). Certain life events, especially undesirable ones, are perceived by most people as stressful or as crises because of the amount of change or extent of readjustment required. Because change is stressful, and stress is a causative factor in illness, a relationship exists between the amount of recent change, number of crises encountered, and onset of illness (29, 61). Stressful events may even speed up death (29).

The Stress Response

The Adaptation Syndrome

Stress *is a physical and emotional state always present in the person, one influenced by various environmental, psychological, and social factors but uniquely perceived by the person, and intensified in response when environmental change or threat occurs internally or externally and the person must respond.* The manifestations of stress are both overt and covert, purposeful, initially protective, maintaining equilibrium, productivity, and satisfaction to the extent possible (9, 69).

The person's survival depends on constant mediation between environmental demands and adaptive

TABLE 16–2. Social Readjustment Rating Scale[a]

LIFE EVENT	MEAN VALUE
1. Death of spouse	100
2. Divorce	73
3. Marital separation	65
4. Jail term	63
5. Death of close family member	63
6. Personal injury or illness	53
7. Marriage	50
8. Fired at work	47
9. Marital reconciliation	45
10. Retirement	45
11. Change in health of family member	44
12. Pregnancy	40
13. Sex difficulties	39
14. Gain of new family member	39
15. Business readjustment	39
16. Change in financial state	38
17. Death of close friend	37
18. Change to different line of work	36
19. Change in number of arguments with spouse	35
20. Mortgage over $10,000	31
21. Foreclosure on mortgage or loan	30
22. Change in responsibilities at work	29
23. Son or daughter leaving home	29
24. Trouble with in-laws	29
25. Outstanding personal achievement	28
26. Wife begins or stops work	26
27. Begin or end school	26
28. Change in living conditions	25
29. Change in personal habits	24
30. Trouble with boss	23
31. Change in work hours or conditions	20
32. Change in residence	20
33. Change in schools	20
34. Change in recreation	19
35. Change in church activities	19
36. Change in social activities	18
37. Mortgage or loan less than $10,000	17
38. Change in sleeping habits	16
39. Change in number of family get-togethers	15
40. Change in eating habits	15
41. Vacation	13
42. Christmas	12
43. Minor violations of the law	11

Life Crisis Categories and LCU Scores[a]

No life crisis	0–149
Mild life crisis	150–199
Moderate life crisis	200–299
Major life crisis	300–or more

[a]The LCU score includes those life event items experienced during a 1-year period.

capacities. Various self-regulatory physical and emotional mechanisms are in constant operation, adjusting the body to a changing number and nature of internal and external stressors, agents, or factors causing intensification of the stress state. **Stressors** (*stress agents*) include cold, heat, radiation, infectious organisms, disease processes, mechanical trauma, fever, pain, imagined events, and intense emotional involvement. A moderate amount of stress, when regulatory mechanisms act within limits and few symptoms are observable, is constructive. The exaggerated stress state occurs when stressors are excessive or intense, limits of the steady state are exceeded, and the person cannot cope with the stressor's demands. **Distress** *is negative, noxious, unpleasant, damaging stress* (69, 70).

Responses to stress are both local and general. The **Local Adaptation Syndrome**, typified by the inflammatory response, *is the method used to wall off and control effects of physical stressors locally*. When the stressor cannot be handled locally, *the whole body responds to protect itself and ensure survival in the best way possible through the* **General Adaptation Syndrome**. The general body response augments bodily functions that protect the organism from injury, psychological and physical, and suppresses those functions nonessential to life. The General Adaptation Syndrome is characterized by Alarm and Resistance stages and, when body resistance is not maintained, an end stage, Exhaustion (69, 70).

The General Adaptation Syndrome

The **Alarm Stage** *is an instantaneous, short-term, life-preserving, and total sympathetic-nervous-system response* when the person consciously or unconsciously perceives a stressor and feels helpless, insecure, or biologically uncomfortable. This stage is typified by a "fight-or-flight" reaction (69). Perception of the stressor—the alarm reaction—stimulates the anterior pituitary to increase production of adrenocorticotropic hormone (ACTH). The adrenal cortex is stimulated by ACTH to increase production of glucocorticoids, primarily hydrocortisone, or cortisol, and mineralcorticoids, primarily aldosterone. Catecholamine release triggers increased sympathetic nervous system activity, which stimulates production of epinephrine and norepinephrine by the adrenal medulla and release at the adrenergic nerve endings. The alarm reaction also stimulates the posterior pituitary to release increased antidiuretic hormone (66, 70). Generally the person is prepared to act, is more alert, and is able to adapt.

Physiologically, the responses that occur when the sympathetic nervous system is stimulated are shown in Figure 16–1 (30, 44, 66, 67, 69–71, 77).

Headache from tense neck & shoulder muscles.

Anti-inflammatory responses increase from glucocorticoid production. Defences against inflammation/infection high for short time.

Respiratory rate/depth increased as bronchi dilate, due to increased epinephrine; allows adequate oxygenation.

Hyperglycemia from glucagon secretion in pancreas causing glycogenolysis; for energy demands after initial hypoglycemia, increased glucocorticoid production results in gluconeogenesis in liver; body cells have sufficient glucose for stress response. Protein catabolism due to conversion of protein to glucose.

Gastric glandular acid and volume secretion increased; less essential functions such as digestion and excretion reduced. Intestinal smooth muscles relax, reducing motility. Sphincters contract. Anorexia, constipation, or flatulence may occur.

Salt and water retained by kidneys bolster intravascular blood volume due to increased antidiuretic hormone and aldosterone production and peripheral vasoconstriction; fuller blood pressure, less urinary output, and hemoconcentration result. Sodium chloride in extracellular fluid reduced; potassium levels rise.

Muscle tonus increased by epinephrine production; activities may be better coordinated, or rigidity and tremors may occur. Metabolic alterations in muscles with glycogenolysis and reduced use of glucose. Blood lactate and glucose increase.

Metabolic changes in adipose tissue; lipolysis and release of free fatty acids for use by muscles. Glycerol converted to glucose.

Pupils dilate; use maximum light for vision. Vision initially sharp, later blurred.

Myocardial rate, strength, and output increased by greater epinephrine production; more blood available throughout body as pulse rate and strength increase. Palpitations or arrhythmias may occur.

Blood pressure rises when increased norepinephrine produces peripheral vasoconstriction.

Increased blood clotting due to catecholamine stimulation of increased production of clotting factors. Increased blood viscosity may result in stasis and thrombosis if Alarm Stage persists.

In urinary bladder, detrusor muscle relaxes and trigone sphincter contracts; micturition inhibited. Or person voids only small amounts but feels urgency.

Blood supply shunted to brain, heart, and skeletal muscles rather than to periphery due to peripheral vasoconstriction. Skin pale, ashen, cool. Vasoconstriction stimulated by increased secretion of renin by kidney with reduced blood supply to kidney. Renin secretion stimulates production of plasma angiotensinogen; in turn, production of angiotension I and II causes vasoconstriction and increased blood pressure in vital organs.

Metabolism increased by 150%, providing immediate energy and producing more heat due to catecholamine release. Body temperature may rise. Perspiration. Mild dehydration from increased insensible fluid loss. (Dry lips and mouth occur.) If metabolism remains high, tissue catabolism, insomnia, fatigue, and signs of dehydration such as dry skin, weight loss, and decreased urinary output occur.

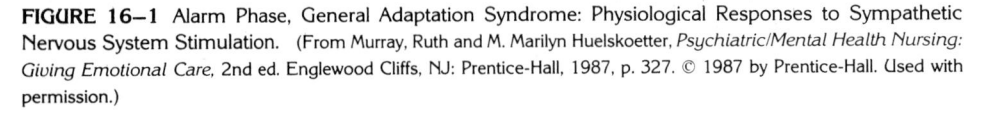

FIGURE 16–1 Alarm Phase, General Adaptation Syndrome: Physiological Responses to Sympathetic Nervous System Stimulation. (From Murray, Ruth and M. Marilyn Huelskoetter, *Psychiatric/Mental Health Nursing: Giving Emotional Care*, 2nd ed. Englewood Cliffs, NJ: Prentice-Hall, 1987, p. 327. © 1987 by Prentice-Hall. Used with permission.)

16 Basic Considerations in Health and Illness **579**

To complicate assessment, there are times when *parts* of the parasympathetic division of the autonomic nervous system are inadvertently stimulated during a stressful state because of proximity of sympathetic and parasympathetic nerve fibers (9). With intensification of stress, opposite behaviors are then observed. They are shown in Figure 16–2 (30, 66–71, 77).

The **Stage of Resistance** *is the body's way of adapting, through an adrenocortical response, to the disequilibrium caused by the stressors of life* (69). Because of the adrenocortical response, increased use of body resources, endurance and strength, tissue anabolism, antibody production, hormonal secretion, and changes in blood sugar levels and blood volume sustain the body's fight for preservation. Body response eventually returns to normal.

If biological, psychological, or social stresses, single or in combination, occur over a long period of time without adequate relief, the stage of resistance is maintained. With continued stressors, the person becomes distressed and manifests objective and subjective emotional, intellectual, and physiological responses, as shown in Figure 16–3 (67–71).

✔ Be aware of these signs and symptoms (Figs. 16–1 to 16–3) in yourself as well as in patients. You will encounter considerable stress in the work of nursing. Identify stressors, especially in situations in which your sense of self is threatened or in which you are

Syncope may result.

Pupil dilation may become fixed causing blurred vision, or constriction may occur, reducing acuity.

Respirations may become difficult because of constricted bronchi. If considerable carbon dioxide has been exhaled earlier with deep respirations, hyperventilation with accompanying tremors, syncope, and dizziness may occur.

Cardiovascular output may diminish causing slow, thready pulse and a drop in blood pressure.

Blood supply does not remain shunted to vital organs but returns to periphery, causing flushed, hot skin and feelings of faintness.

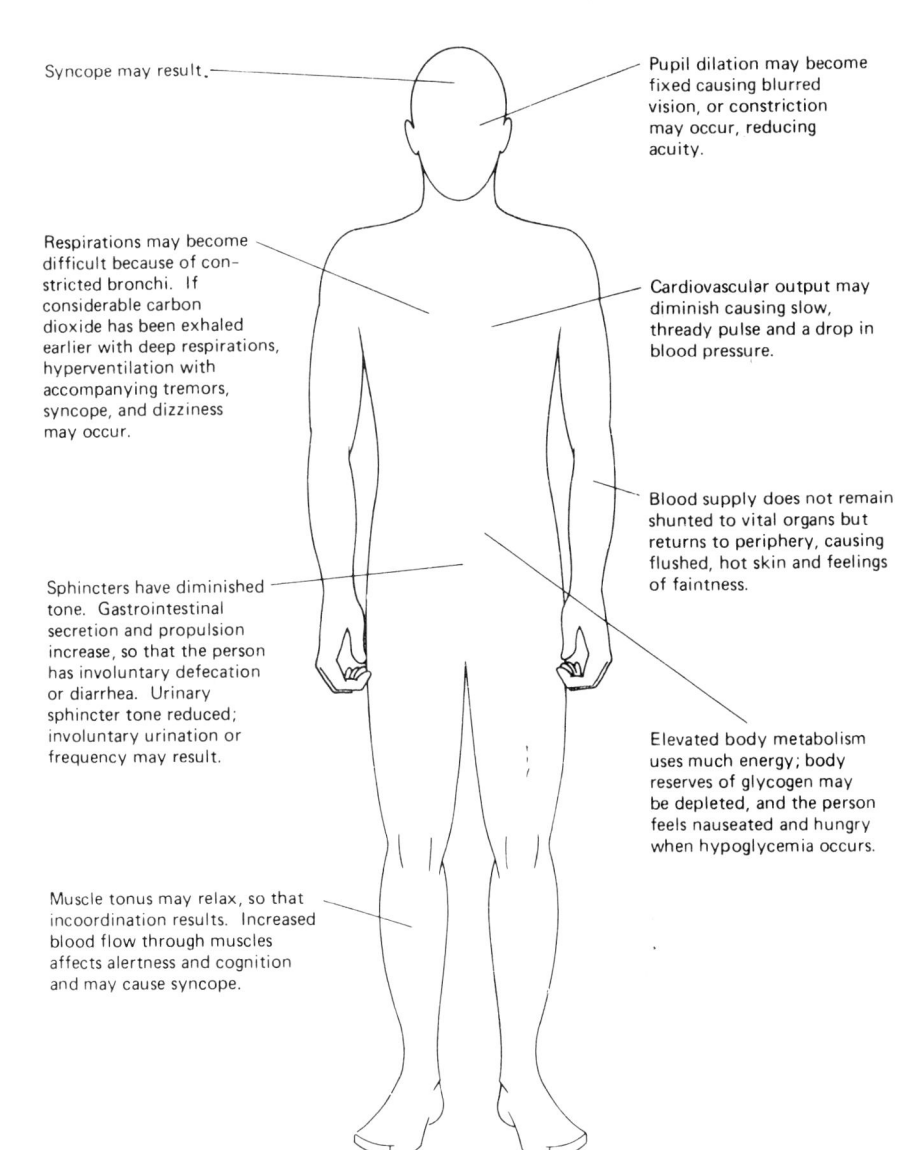

Sphincters have diminished tone. Gastrointestinal secretion and propulsion increase, so that the person has involuntary defecation or diarrhea. Urinary sphincter tone reduced; involuntary urination or frequency may result.

Elevated body metabolism uses much energy; body reserves of glycogen may be depleted, and the person feels nauseated and hungry when hypoglycemia occurs.

Muscle tonus may relax, so that incoordination results. Increased blood flow through muscles affects alertness and cognition and may cause syncope.

FIGURE 16–2 Alarm Phase, General Adaptation Syndrome: Physiological Responses to Parasympathetic Nervous System Stimulation. (From Murray, Ruth, and M. Marilyn Huelskoetter, *Psychiatric/Mental Health Nursing: Giving Emotional Care*, 2nd ed. Englewood Cliffs, NJ: Prentice-Hall, 1987, p. 328. © 1987 by Prentice-Hall. Used with permission.)

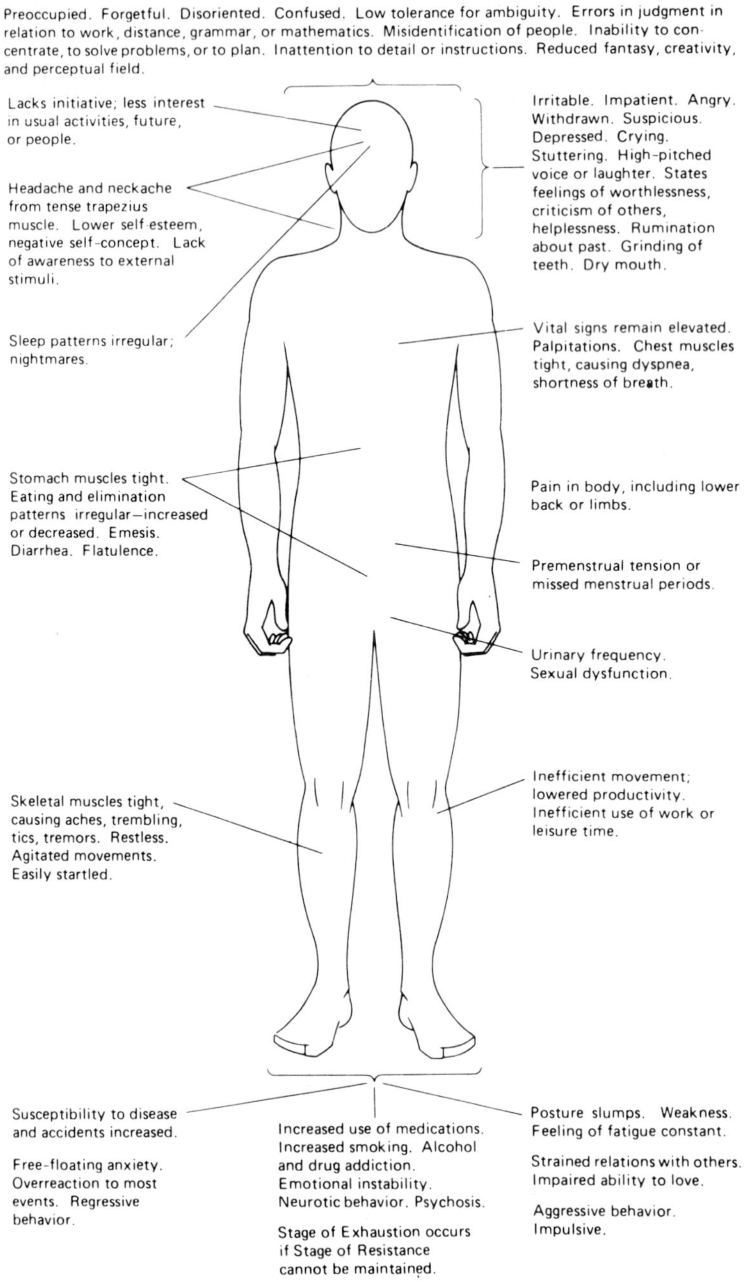

FIGURE 16–3 Stage of Resistance, General Adaptation Syndrome: Signs of Emotional, Intellectual, and Physiological Distress. (From Murray, Ruth and M. Marilyn Huelskoetter, *Psychiatric/Mental Health Nursing: Giving Emotional Care*, 2nd ed. Englewood Cliffs, NJ: Prentice-Hall, 1987, p. 329 © 1987 by Prentice-Hall. Used with permission.)

made to feel incompetent. Share your feelngs and talk about your work experiences with someone whom you trust and who will offer feedback about your coping skills. You will need someone who values you as a person, not just as a worker, who sees you as more than nurse, job, position, or nurturer, and who can help you put stressful work situations into perspective. Strive to develop a sense of being master of your own life and circumstances, a feeling that you can exert some control over what happens to you by the way you view yourself and adjust your behavior. When you can cope with your own work-related and other stressors, then you can help patients and their families to be adaptive.

Stress is additive. The repeated or chronic exposure to stress, even when the stressors are of widely differing kinds, including other people and their feelings, ultimately takes a toll on the individual. Reserves of adaptability are used that cannot be replaced. Some experience with stressors may aid coping with stress and be protective against stress-induced disease. Certain coping methods, feeling in command of the situation, and strong family and social ties can help a person to suffer less deleterious effects of stress. Breaking ties by separating from the group or a loved one, divorce, mobility, or death, and the resultant sense of loss, rejection, and loneliness predispose to disease and death (45, 68, 70).

The **Stage of Exhaustion** *occurs when the person is unable to continue to adapt to internal and external environmental demands.* Physical or psychic disease or death results because the body can no longer compensate for or correct homeostatic imbalances. Manifestations of this stage are similar to those of the Alarm Stage except that all reactions first intensify and then diminish in response and show no ability to return to an effective level of function. Frequent or prolonged General Adaptation Syndrome response triggers disease through adrenocortical hypertrophy, thymolymphatic atrophy, elevated blood glucose, ulceration of the gastrointestinal tract, reduced tone and fibrosis of tissues, and vasoconstriction (69, 70).

✔ Health care workers are concerned with promoting the Resistance Stage and preventing or reversing the Exhaustion Stage, whether through drugs, bedrest, medical treatments, crisis intervention, psychotherapy, or social action. Ideally, you should identify potential stressors that the person might encounter and determine how to alter the stressors or best support the person's adaptive mechanisms and resources physically, emotionally, and socially, for the person will respond as an entity to the stressors. The relationship of stress to life crises or changes must be considered whenever you are doing health promotion measures or intervening with the ill person (45).

Although responses to stressful situations vary, anxiety is a common one. **Anxiety,** *a state of mental discomfort or uneasiness related to a feeling of helplessness or threat to self-image,* occurs in everyone, well or ill. Often there is no objective cause. The ill or hospitalized person may experience anxiety because of environmental changes. The individual exhibits signs of anxiety about the unknown: the outcome of surgery, the stability of job and family income, and possible death. The anxious person may experience the physical and behavioral effects that are described in Table 16–3. Other responses to stress include grief, mourning, and denial. These concepts are referred to in chapter 13. Should the felt mental, emotional, or even physical disequilibrium become severe, mental or physical illness may result. Therefore the health of persons is directly related to and affected by their reactions to both the internal and external environment.

Manifestations of Anxiety

✔ You must be observant of the responses that may indicate psychological stress.

✔ People use various behaviors to cope with anxiety or to attempt to change a stressful situation. Redistribution of energy is often not consciously recognized; thus a person may be unaware of any behavioral shifts, although others notice them. Certain behavioral changes may be the best the person can do at the time, although they seem inadequate to an objective observer.

Table 16–3 summarizes manifestations of the various levels of anxiety (20, 21, 40, 45, 59, 62, 65, 68, 86, 87).

The Mind–Body Relationship

The **mind–body relationship,** *the effect of emotional responses to stress on body function, and the emotional reactions to body conditions,* has been established through research and experience (89). Emotional factors are important in the precipitation or exacerbation of nearly every organic disease and may increase susceptibility to infections. Stress and emotional distress, including depression, may influence function of the immune system via the central nervous system and endocrine mediation, which is related to incidence of cancer, infections, and autoimmune diseases. Apparently adrenal cortical steroid hormones are immunosuppressive. Recurring or chronic emotional stress has a cumulative physiological effect and eventually may produce chronic dysfunction, such as hypertension or gastric ulcers (34). The dynamics involve repression of certain feelings, such as rage or guilt, fooling the mind into thinking the feelings have disappeared. But the body's physiological functions respond to the feelings or perception of the effect (stressor) (69, 72, 75). *When physical or organic symptoms or disease result from feeling states, the process is called* **psychosomatic** *or* **psychophysiologic.** *The opposite process, feeling states of depression or worry in response to physical states, is called* **somatopsychic.**

The new field of **psychoneuroimmunology** *focuses on the links between the mind, brain, and immune system.* This is a newer perspective of the mind and body relationship in psychophysiological causation of illness. Research shows that the immune system responds to the mind. The immune system is a very complex system consisting of about one trillion cells called lymphocytes and about one hundred million trillion molecules called antibodies. The immune system has a special capability that allows it to patrol the body and guard its health (25).

Studies have correlated the levels of one immune

TABLE 16–3. Manifestations and Levels of Anxiety

LEVEL	TYPE	EFFECT
Mild	Physiological	Tension of needs motivates behavior. Adaptive to variety of internal and external stimuli.
	Cognitive	Attentive, alert, perceptive to variety of stimuli, effective problem solving.
	Emotional	No intense feelings; self-concept not threatened. Use of ego adaptive mechanisms minimal, flexible. Behavior appropriate to situation.
Moderate	Physiological	Some symptoms may be present.
	Cognitive	Perceptual field narrows; responds to directions. Tangible problems solved fairly effectively, at least with direction and support. Selective inattention—focus is on stimuli that do not add to anxiety.
	Emotional	Impatient, irritable, forgetful, demanding, crying, angry. Uses any adaptive mechanism, e.g., rationalization, denial, displacement, to protect from feelings and meaning of behavior.
		(Physiological, cognitive, and emotional changes of Alarm and Resistance Stages. Individual functions in normal pattern, but may not feel as healthy physically or emotionally as usual. Illness may result if feeling persists.)
Severe	Physiological	Alarm Stage changes intensify, and Stage of Resistance may progress to Stage of Exhaustion.
	Cognitive	Perceptual field narrows; stimuli distorted, focus is on scattered details. Selective inattention prevails. Learning and problem solving ineffective. Clarification or restatement needed repeatedly. Misinterprets statements. Unable to follow directions or remember main points. Unable to plan or make decisions; needs assistance with details. Disorganized. Consciousness and lucidity reduced.
	Emotional	Self-concept threatened; sense of helplessness; mood changes. Behavior erratic, inappropriate, regressive, inefficient. May be aware of inappropriate behavior but unable to improve. Many ego defense mechanisms used; dissociation and amnesia may be used. Disorientation, confusion, suspicion, hallucinations, and delusions may be present.
		(Psychoses or physical illness or injury may result.)
Panic	Physiological	Severe symptoms of Exhaustion Stage may be ignored.
	Cognitive	Sensory ability and attention reduced so that only object of anxiety noticed. May fail to notice specific object of concern or disastrous event but will be preoccupied with trivial detail.
	Emotional	Self-concept overwhelmed. Ego defense mechanism used, often inappropriately and uncontrollably. Behavior focused on finding relief; may scream, cry, pray, thrash limbs, run, hit others, hurt self. Often easily distracted; cannot attend or concentrate. No learning, problem solving, decision making, or realistic judgments. May become immobilized, assume fetal position, become mute, or be unresponsive to directions. Needs protection.
		(Psychoses may occur.)

substance in saliva (immunoglobulin A [IgA]) and defense against respiratory infection for individuals with different motivational styles. People driven by an inhibited power motivation have lower (IgA) levels than those who form warm, close relationships. Studies show that although not everyone reacts the same consciously to caring and loving, their bodies react by secreting more IgA. Salivary IgA increases even in people who intensely dislike the caring healer. These findings support the premise that it is not necessary to believe in the healer (placebo effect) in order to benefit. At the unconscious level, something in the person will respond to the healer. Increased salivary IgA secretion occurs when the person feels an affiliative connection with the person who is trying to help or is involved in a friendly relationship (25).

Studies also show that type A behavior and an inhibited power motive are connected with the increased secretion of catecholamines, which suppress some aspects of the immune function. Too much of the catecholamine norepinephrine is associated with decline in immunoglobulin A, which makes the body less able to fight off certain viruses (25).

🖎 Psychoneuroimmunology provides a first step toward an affirmative science that makes quality of life as important as traditional sciences have made extension of life possible.

🖎 Simonton, a radiation oncologist, believes that just as we participate in our illness, so we participate in our health. His program involves a frank, honest appraisal of the stresses in life pre-illness, why they were stressful, benefits derived from the illness, and methods to achieve an honest, relatively stress-free, positive attitude about lifestyle and illness. Often the patient finds that prior to illness, the stresses did have the person's full participation. The person may have had a stressor because of failure to confront, to express anger, to grieve, to trust intuitive feelings, or because of unrealistic expectations or lack of courage of personal convictions. Current stressors are analyzed and resolved. An important part of the program is to use mental imagery or visualization, in which natural body defenses are combined with medical treatment to overcome malignant cells by visualizing the body's white cells in overcoming cancer cells. The patient switches from a passive to active role, which enhances the body's immune system. Physical exercise, counseling, and mental imagery are used to overcome feelings about the disease, to set realistic goals, to find an inner advisor to talk and listen to, and to list steps to wellness. The hopelessness and helplessness feelings are removed. The person gains a sense of control by participating actively in the recovery process. Positive, hopeful messages are sent to the limbic system, stimulating the immune system (73).

References

1. Archer, Sarah, C. Kelly, and S. Bisch, *Implementing Change in Communities: A Collaborative Process.* St. Louis: C. V. Mosby, 1984.
2. Ardell, D., *High Level Wellness.* Emmaus, Pa.: Rodale, 1977.
3. Aubrey, L., Health as a Social Concept, *British Journal of Sociology*, 4 (June, 1953), 115.
4. Auger, Jeanine, *Behavioral Systems and Nursing.* Englewood Cliffs, NJ: Prentice-Hall, 1976.
5. Beeson, Gerald, The Health-Illness Spectrum, *American Journal of Public Health*, 57, no. 11 (1967), 1901–1904.
6. Bermosk, I. S., and S. E. Porter, *Women's Health and Human Wholeness.* Norwalk, CT: Appleton-Century-Crofts, 1979.
7. Brallier, L. W., The Nurse as Holistic Health Practitioner, *Nursing Clinics of North America*, 13, no. 4 (1978), 643–655.
8. Briscoe, M., Sex Differences in Perception of Illness and Expressed Life Satisfaction, *Psychological Medicine*, 8, no. 2 (1978), 339–345.
9. Byrne, M., and L. Thompson, *Key Concepts for the Study and Practice of Nursing.* St. Louis: C. V. Mosby, 1972.
10. Calhoun, John, reported by Daniel Rice, *Health Services World*, 8 (1973), 3.
11. Clark, Carolyn, *Wellness Nursing: Concepts, Theory, Research, and Practice.* New York: Springer, 1986.
12. Clemen, Susan, Diane Eigsti, and Sandra McGuire, *Comprehensive Family and Community Health Nursing*, (2nd ed.). New York: McGraw-Hill, 1987.
13. Department of Health and Social Security, *Prevention and Health: Everybody's Business.* Kent, England: Health Departments of Great Britain and Ireland, 1976.
14. Dixon, J. K., and J. P. Dixon, An Evolutionary-Based Model of Health and Viability, *Advances in Nursing Science*, 6, no. 3 (1984), 1–8.
15. Dolfman, M., The Concept of Health: An Historic and Analytic Examination, *Journal of School Health*, 43 (1973), 493.
16. DuBois, Rene. *Man Adapting.* New Haven: Yale University Press, 1965.
17. ———, Man Overadapting, *Psychology Today*, 4, no. 9 (1971), 50 ff.
18. Dunn, Halbert, High Level Wellness for Man and Society, *American Journal of Public Health*, 49, (1959), 789.
19. ———, What High Level Wellness Means, *Canadian Journal of Public Health* (November, 1959), 447.
20. Eisendorfer, Carl, Anxiety in the Aged, in *Phenomenology and Treatment of Anxiety*, eds. W. Fann, et al. New York: Spectrum, 1979, pp. 43–49.
21. Fink, Max, Anxiety, Anxiolytics, and the Human EEG, in *Phenomenology and Treatment of Anxiety*, eds. W. Fann, et al. New York: Spectrum, 1979, 237–250.
22. Goeppinger, Jeanette, Community as Client: Using the Nursing Process to Promote Health, *Community Health Nursing: Process and Practice for Promoting Health*, eds. M. Stanhope and Jeanette Lancaster. St. Louis: C. V. Mosby, 1984.
23. Gortmaker, Steven, et al., Parental Smoking and the Risk of Childhood Asthma, *American Journal of Public Health*, 72, no. 6 (1982), 574–578.
24. Griffith, W., Environmental Effects on Interpersonal Affective Behavior: Ambient Effective Temperature

and Attraction, *Journal of Personality and Social Psychology* (July 1970), 240–244.
25. Guyton, A. C., *Basic Human Physiology: Normal Function and Mechanisms of Defense*, 7th ed. Philadelphia: W. B. Saunders, 1986.
26. Hall, Beverly, and Janet Allan, Sharpening Nursing's Focus by Focusing on Health, 7, no. 6 (1986), 315–320.
27. Hamburg, David, Disease Prevention: The Challenge of the Future, *American Journal of Public Health*, 69, no. 10 (1979), 1026–1033.
28. Higginson, John, A Hazardous Society? Individual Versus Community Responsibility in Cancer Prevention, *American Journal of Public Health*, 66, no. 4 (1976), 359–366.
29. Holmes, T. H., and R. H. Rahe, The Social Readjustment Rating Scale, *Journal of Psychosomatic Research*, 11 (1976), 213–218.
30. Horowitz, Mardi, *Stress Response Syndromes*. New York: Jason Aronson, 1976.
31. Howell, Mary, *National Women's Health Network Newsletter* (Fall 1982), 1–4.
32. Hayman, H., Our Modern Concept of Health, *Journal of School Health* (September, 1962), 253.
33. Ibrahim, Michel, The Changing Health State of Women, *American Journal of Public Health*, 70, no. 2 (1980), 120–121.
34. James, Sherman, and Donald Kleinbaum, Socioecologic Stress and Hypertension Related Mortality Rates in North Carolina, *American Journal of Public Health*, 66, no. 4 (1976), 354–358.
35. Johnson, Dorothy, The Behavioral System Model for Nursing, in *Conceptual Models for Nursing Practice* (2nd ed.), eds. J. Riehl and Callista Roy. New York: Appleton-Century-Crofts, 1980, pp. 207–216.
36. Jourard, Sidney, *The Transparent Self*. New York: D. Van Nostrand, 1971.
37. King, Imogene, *A Theory for Nursing: Systems, Concepts, Processes*. New York: Wiley, 1981.
38. Langone, John, When Hopelessness Kills, *Discover* (October, 1980), 116.
39. Levine, Myra, *Introduction to Clinical Nursing*, 2nd ed. Philadelphia: F. A. Davis, 1973.
40. Lief, Harold, Anxiety, Sexual Dysfunction, and Therapy, in *Phenomenology and Treatment of Anxiety*, eds. W. Fann, et al. New York: Spectrum, 1979, 311–324.
41. Loveland, Cherry D., and S. A. Wilkerson, Dorothy Johnson's Behavioral System Model, in *Conceptual Models of Nursing: Analysis and Application*, eds. J. Fitzpatrick and A. Whall. Bowie, Md.: Robert J. Brady, 1983.
42. Lunar Myth: Fact or Fancy, *West County Citizen Journal*, February 26, 1986, Sec A, pp. 1, 13.
43. Lyon, J., et al., Cancer Incidence in Mormons and NonMormons in Utah, 1966–1970, *New England Journal of Medicine*, 204 (January 15, 1976), 129–133.
44. Marcinek, Margaret, Stress in the Surgical Patient, *American Journal of Nursing*, 77, no. 11 (1977), 1809–1811.
45. Murray, Ruth, M. Marilyn Huelskoetter, and Dorothy O'Driscoll, *Psychiatric/Mental Health Nursing: Giving Emotional Care* (2nd ed.). Englewood Cliffs, NJ: Prentice-Hall, 1987.
46. Narrayan, S. M., and D. J. Joslin, Crisis Theory and Intervention: A Critique of the Medical Model and Proposal of a Holistic Nursing Model, *Advances in Nursing Science*, 2 (1980), 27–39.
47. Natapoff, Janet, Children's View of Health: A Developmental Study, *American Journal of Public Health*, 68, no. 10 (1978), 995–999.
48. Neuman, Betty, *The Neuman System's Model: Application to Nursing Education and Practice*. Norwalk, CT: Appleton-Century-Crofts, 1982.
49. Newman, M., *Theory Development in Nursing*. Philadelphia: F. A. Davis, 19 .
50. Olshansky, Stuart, Is Smoker/Nonsmoker Segregation Effective in Reducing Passive Inhalation Among Nonsmokers, *American Journal of Public Health*, 72, no. 7 (1982), 737–739.
51. Orem, Dorothea, *Nursing: Concepts of Practice*, 3rd ed. New York: McGraw-Hill, 1986.
52. Our New Abilities to Improve World Health, *The Nation's Health* (July, 1985), 11.
53. Parens, Henri, and Leon Saul, *Dependence in Man*. New York: International Universities Press, 1971, 143–151.
54. Parse, R., *Man-Living-Health: A Theory of Nursing*. New York: Wiley & Sons, 1981.
55. Parsons, T., Definitons of Health and Illness in the Light of American Values and Social Structure, in *Patients, Physicians, and Illness*, ed. E. G. Jaco. New York: Free Press, 1958.
56. _____, *Structure and Process in Modern Societies*. Glencoe, IL: The Free Press, 1960.
57. Patterns Found in Regional Cancer Study, *St. Louis Post-Dispatch*, January 9, 1977, Sec. C, p. 38.
58. Pender, Nola, *Health Promotion in Nursing Practice* (2nd ed.). E. Norwalk, CT.: Appleton & Lange, 1987.
59. Peplau, Hildegarde, *Interpersonal Relations in Nursing*. New York: G. P. Putnam's Sons, 1952.
60. Petze, C., Health Promotion for the Well Family, *Nursing Clinics of North America*, 19, no. 2 (1984), 229–237.
61. Rahe, R., and R. Arthur, Life Change Patterns Surrounding Illness Perception, *Journal of Psychosomatic Research*, 11, no. 3 (1968), 341–345.
62. Roessler, Robert, and Jerry Lester, Vocal Patterns in Anxiety, in *Phenomenology and Treatment of Anxiety*, eds. W. Fann et al. New York: Spectrum Publications, 1979, 225–235.
63. Romano, John, Basic Orientation and Education of the Medical Student, *Journal of the American Medical Association*, 143, no. 5 (1950), 411.

64. Roy, Sister Callista, *Introduction to Nursing: An Adaptation Model* (2nd ed.). Englewood Cliffs, N.J.: Prentice-Hall, 1984.
65. Saranson, Irvin, and Barbara Saranson, *Abnormal Psychology: The Problem of Adaptive Behavior* (3rd ed.). Englewood Cliffs, NJ: Prentice-Hall, 1980.
66. Seyle, Hans, Stress Syndrome, *American Journal of Nursing*, 65, no. 3 (1965), 97–99.
67. ———, *Stress without Distress*. Philadelphia: J. B. Lippincott, 1974.
68. ———, Implications of Stress Concept, *New York State Journal of Medicine* (October 1975), 2139–2145.
69. ———, *The Stress of Life* (rev. ed). New York: McGraw-Hill, 1976.
70. ———, Forty Years of Stress Research: Principal Remaining Problems and Misconceptions, *Canadian Medical Association Journal*, 115 (July 3, 1976), 53–56.
71. ———, Stress and the Reduction of Distress, *Primary Cardiology*, 5, no. 8 (1979), 22–30.
72. Shontz, F., Somatopsychology: Concept and Content, *Rehabilitation Psychology*, 12 (1965), 20–27.
73. Simonton, O. Carl, et al., *Getting Well Again*. Los Angeles: J.P. Tarcher, 1978.
74. Smilkstein, G., The Cycle of Family Functions: A Conceptual Model for Family Medicine, *Family Practitioner*, 11 (1980), 223.
75. Solomon, G., A. Amkrant, and P. Kasper, Immunity, Emotions, and Stress, *Annals of Clinical Research*, 6 (1974), 313–322.
76. Sorochan, W., Health Concepts as a Basis for Orthobiosis, in. E. Hart And W. Sechrist (eds.), *The Dynamics of Wellness*. Belmont, Calif.: Wadsworth, 1970.
77. Stephenson, Carol, Stress in Critically Ill Patients, *American Journal of Nursing*, 77, no. 11 (1977), 1806–1809.
78. Sullivan, Harry, *Conceptions of Modern Psychiatry*. Washington, D.C.: The William Alanson White Psychiatric Foundation, 1940.
79. Sullivan, Harry S., *The Interpersonal Theory of Psychiatry*. New York: W. W. Norton, 1953.
80. Tinkham, Catherine, Elizabeth Voorheis, and N. McCarthy, *Community Health Nursing:* Evolution and Process in the Family and Community (3rd ed.). Norwalk, CT: Appleton-Century-Crofts, 1984.
81. Tripp-Reimer, Toni, Reconceptualizing the Concept of Health: Integrating Emic-Etic Perspectives, *Research in Nursing and Health*, 7 (1984), 101–109.
82. Tromp, S. W., Weather, Climate, and Man, in *Handbook of Physiology: Adaptation to the Environment*, eds. D. Dill, E. Adolph, and C. Wilber. Washington, D.C.: American Physiological Society, 1964, 283–293.
83. Under the Weather? *Everyday-St. Louis Post-Dispatch*, February 3, 1985, Sec. D, 1, 14.
84. Webster, Denise, Changing Definitions; Changing Times, *Nursing Clinics of North America*, 21, no. 1 (1986), 87–97.
85. Weiss, S. M., J. Herd, and N. Miller (eds.), *Behavioral Health: A Handbook of Health Enhancement and Disease Prevention*. New York: John Wiley, 1984.
86. Williams, Cindy, and Thomas Holmes, Life Change, Human Adaptation, and Onset of Illness, in *Clinical Practice in Psychosocial Nursing: Assessment and Intervention*, eds. Dianne Longo and Reg Williams. New York: Appleton-Century-Crofts, 1978, pp. 69–85.
87. Williams, R., et al., Disturbed Sleep and Anxiety, in *Phenomenology and Treatment of Anxiety*, eds. W. Fann, et al. New York: Spectrum Publications, 1979, pp. 221–223.
88. Wright, L., and M. Leahey, *Nurses and Families: A Guide to Family Assessment and Intervention*. Philadelphia: F. A. Davis, 1984.
89. Wu, Ruth, *Behavior and Illness*. Englewood Cliffs, NJ: Prentice-Hall, 1973.

17

Health Promotion Strategies

Study of this chapter will help you to

1. Discuss the concept of health promotion and its application to holistic nursing.
2. Define terms related to health promotion and illness prevention.
3. Compare and contrast models of health promotion and illness prevention.
4. Assess health promotion behaviors or lifestyle, utilizing a selected instrument.
5. Differentiate between a social and helpful nurse–client relationship.
6. Describe guidelines for a therapeutic nurse–client relationship.
7. List and describe the phases of the nurse–client relationship and the effect of the nurse's and client's feelings on each phase.
8. Describe methods of therapeutic communication and the rationale for each method.
9. Discuss ways to modify a communication approach to be effective with clients/patients who have communication disorders.
10. Explore how use of effective communication methods is basic to nursing care and contributes to health promotion.
11. Define *health education* and *self-care*.
12. Compare methods of teaching with various ages, including individual and group approaches, and predict when each might be appropriate.
13. Identify the varied opportunities for teaching health promotion.
14. List the characteristics of a medical quack and discuss how you can help people avoid hazards of medical quackery.
15. Describe health screening procedures that should be done at various ages.
16. Describe the importance of and recommendations for adequate nutrition.
17. Describe the benefits of a well-planned exercise schedule and the balance of exercise and rest for health.
18. Review methods to prevent illness and injury, such as immunizations, infection control, safety promotion, control of environmental hazards, and measures to eliminate hazards destructive to life.
19. Describe and practice various methods of relaxation or physical methods for stress management.
20. Discuss stress management measures that will assist the person or family to adapt to or cope with internal or external changes (physical, emotional, social, cultural).
21. Discuss groups in your area whose health promotion needs are not adequately met and ways that could be implemented to improve their health care.
22. Discuss nursing measures that are conducive to health promotion–wellness, considering factors that influence preventive health behavior.

✔ Health promotion and maintenance and disease prevention are not new roles in nursing, although holistic health promotion roles are given increasing emphasis in the nursing process. The knowledge and theories pertinent to health promotion and maintenance are diverse and broad, and relate to physical, psychological, cognitive, social, and spiritual/moral dimensions of the person or family, as shown in Table 17–1.

Key Terms

Health promotion	Learning
Primary prevention	Teaching
Secondary prevention	Education
Tertiary prevention	Health education
Health behavior	Self-care
Illness behavior	Quack
Health Belief Model	Health screening
Health Promotion Model	Progressive relaxation
Resource Model of Preventive Health Behavior	Acupuncture
	Acupressure
	Shiatsu
Human Ecological Model	Reflexology
Model of Multiple Risk Factor Behavior	Biofeedback
	Yoga
Nurse–client relationship	Autogenics
Initial/orientation phase	Thought stopping
	Self-talk
Identification phase	Coping skills training
Working phase	Centering
Maintenance phase	Assertiveness
Termination phase	Guided imagery

✔ Health promotion measures are described in each chapter as appropriate to the content of the chapter. For example, assessment and intervention for health promotion of people of various cultures and religions are described in Chapters 1 and 3, respectively, based on knowledge of cultural and religious/spiritual concepts. Chapter 2 describes health promotion measures in response to environmental contaminants and in the occupational setting. General strategies to promote health of the family unit are described in Chapter 4. The importance of and measures for health promotion for the developing embryo and fetus and for the woman in the prenatal period are described in Chapter 6. Health promotion and safety measures are described for each developmental era, infancy through later maturity, in Chapters 7 through 14. Reference will be made to these various measures or strategies later in this chapter for purposes of integration and synthesis.

✔ Application of knowledge of developmental theories, as described in Chapter 5, facilitate emotional and mental or cognitive health. For example, Erikson's theory can help parents understand normal developmental needs and behavior of their offspring and themselves. Ways to promote a sense of trust, autonomy, initiative, industry, identity, intimacy, generativity, and ego integrity are discussed in Chapters 7 through 14, respectively, and are pertinent to nurses and other health care workers, as well as families and parents. Duvall's theory can help parents understand developmental tasks of offspring and the family unit. With such information they can better contribute to emotional and mental health of offspring, middle-aged and elderly family members, and the total family unit. Understanding of Piaget's theory can assist nurses, teachers, and parents in facilitating intellectual/cognitive development and health of the child. Pia-

Table 17–1. Examples of Health Promotion Strategies Related to Dimensions of the Whole Person

PHYSICAL/PHYSIOLOGICAL	EMOTIONAL	COGNITIVE	SOCIAL	SPIRITUAL/MORAL
• Proper nutrition/fluid balance • Balance of exercise–rest • Immunizations • Safety measures • Temperature control • Prevention of environmental hazards and pollution • Cessation of habits destructive to health (smoking, alcohol or drug abuse, overeating) • Health screening	• Consistent warm, tender, nurturing of offspring • Effective communication • Effective guidance/discipline • Promotion of self-esteem, self-confidence, security • Anxiety reduction measures • Play, use of toys, leisure activities • Crisis resolution	• Promotion of curiosity and learning • Coping methods • Visualization • Imagery • Health education	• Socialization processes • Family, friend, peer relations • Group associations and processes • Maintenance of cultural ties	• Values clarification • Acknowledgement of meaning and purpose of life • Establishment of belief system • Establishment of moral and ethical behaviors

get's theory is discussed in Chapters 7 through 11. Behavioral theories are frequently applied by families in discipline of the child. Understanding the importance of reinforcement and modeling of behavior is useful to nurses, other health care workers, and teachers, as well as to parents and the family unit. Application of behavioral theories are described in Chapters 7 through 14 as appropriate to the developmental era. Behavioral, psychodynamic, family, and humanistic theories all assist in understanding aspects of socialization, social development, and development of language and communication abilities.

This chapter will focus primarily on health promotion strategies not previously described. These strategies are described in more detail in the following sections.

Health Promotion: What Is It?

Hall and Allan discuss the importance of the nursing profession focusing on health and not just the disease model. An ecological view, realizing multiple causation in many situations that threaten health, is essential (45). Further, an ecological view can be useful in health promotion and wellness nursing, resulting in a total or holistic approach and looking at all aspects of the person.

Wellness nursing focuses on joint assessment with the client/patient, including body, mind, and spirit interaction and integration, and historical, social, and cultural factors; application of theory to the specific needs and goals of the person; promoting whole-person healing and self-healing; self-care measures; and evaluation of the movement toward wellness. The person evolves toward wellness by learning: (1) to manage life experiences, (2) to seek challenges, (3) to relate to others flexibly and assertively, (4) to use self-care strategies, (5) to examine and readjust beliefs and practices to maintain goal-directed wholeness, and (6) to develop coping strategies that reduce stress. Clark believes that Wellness Theory is a broad base for practice that can unite nurses in their practice, especially health promotion practice. Wellness Theory can increase cohesiveness among nurses and should reduce arguments about the purpose of nursing. Further, theory on wellness can be explained as a basis for action when members of other disciplines challenge the nurse's practice. Lastly, Wellness Theory can help nurses work with clients/patients to improve their quality of life. From the client's/patient's view, a wellness focus is more in harmony with the perceived needs, sense of autonomy, and lifestyle. A shift in the allocation of governmental funds and services and private insurance programs reinforces the emphasis in use of Wellness Theory and practice and working with the self-care movement (17).

✔ The use of Wellness Theory is applicable to holistic nursing (defined in Chapter 16), which can be practiced in any setting. In holistic nursing you view the client/patient as more than just a collection of body parts. In addition to biological aspects, you also address his/her psychological, social, cultural, and spiritual aspects of care. Nurses and physicians have a complementary relationship. The physician focuses on body system pathology; the nurse focuses on the whole person, well or ill, and the response to illness, in addition to the technology of the specialty. "Caring for a client/patient holistically" means "being part of a team that includes the client/patient and his/her family, nurses, doctors, physical therapists, respiratory therapists, dieticians—anyone who can contribute to the recovery and well-being of the person." For example, in working with persons who have chronic pain, the most important thing is to help them realize that their situation is not hopeless—that in addition to more traditional medical treatments, there are many self-help therapies they can turn to, such as acupressure, exercise, relaxation training, and imagery. A staff of nurses, doctors, psychologists, and physical, occupational, and family therapists work with each person to teach him or her how best to manage the pain and the response to it (71).

Various models are proposed to better understand health promotion and illness prevention behaviors.

Definitions

✔ Until recently most of the focus, and therefore the definitions, in health care was on disease and death. Now more emphasis is being placed on how to achieve, measure, or maintain health. The goal of health promotion is to raise the levels of wellness in individuals, families, and communities. Wellness and illness may exist simultaneously within each of us; you must relate to both aspects of the person

Concepts of health promotion and illness prevention are different although they are used interchangeably. Definitions for health promotion and primary, secondary, and tertiary prevention follow.

Health promotion *consists of activities that increase the levels of health and well-being and actualize or maximize the health potential of individuals, families, groups, communities, and society.* Health promotion is multidimensional in nature: individual–family–community–environment, and society. The person, family, or community moves toward a positively valued state of better health. Avoiding illness is not a significant motive for health promotion behavior. Frequently former patterns of behavior are diminished as new patterns of behavior are learned (84).

Health promotion behaviors focus on prevention or reduction of illness. **Primary prevention** *consists of activities that decrease the probability of occurrence of specific illness or dysfunction in an individual, family, group, or community and reduce incidence of new cases of disorder in the population by combating harmful forces that operate in the community and by strengthening the capacity of people to withstand these forces* (78, 84).

Secondary prevention *consists of early diagnosis and treatment to the pathological process, thereby shortening disease duration and severity and enabling the person to return to normal function as quickly as possible* (84). By shortening the duration of existing cases, the prevalence of disorder is reduced. Early case finding and prompt intervention are emphasized.

Tertiary prevention *focuses on restoring the person to optimal function, through rehabilitation, and within the constraints of the problem, when a defect or disability is fixed, stable or irreversible* (84). *There is a reduction of the rate of residual defects that are sequel to disorder in the affected population.* Tertiary prevention seeks to ensure that people who have recovered from disorders will be hampered as little as possible by their past illness in returning to full participation in the occupational and social life of the community.

Health behaviors *are activities that the person engages in to enhance health, prevent illness, or detect illness.* **Illness behavior** *includes actions an individual who feels ill takes to obtain a diagnosis, prevent complications, and restore health* (84).

Models Related to Health Promotion and Illness Prevention

Health Belief Model

The **Health Belief Model** is a *paradigm used to predict and explain health behavior based on the Value-Expectancy Theory* and *Lewin's Theory. Beliefs, attitudes, values, and knowledge contribute to motivation and underlie any decisions to change behavior.* Lewin conceptualized that some regions of the person's life space have negative value or valence, others have positive valence, others are neutral. Disease has a negative valence and is expected to exert a force to move the person toward health behaviors (84).

The Health Belief Model, developed in the early 1950s by Rosenstock, Hochbaum, and Kegeles, (1) explains why some people who are well take action to avoid illness, while others fail to do so; (2) predicts persons who will use preventive measures; and (3) presents interventions that might increase participation in health-protecting or prevention behaviors (96).

The Health Belief Model states that the client's/patient's perception of health states and risk of disease and the person's probability for taking appropriate health care actions depends on the person's value of health, perceptions about disease, perceived threat of disease, perceptions about the medical team and therapy plans, past experience, contact with risk factors, level of participation in regular health care, life aspirations, and various motivating factors in the environment. The model does not specify which interventions to use to improve the likelihood of someone following health care and preventive actions. The provider and client/patient negotiate which interventions are appropriate (84). Becker (5, 6) modified the model. He believed perceptions about the susceptibility to illness and about seriousness of the illness affect whether the person denies illness, engages in primary prevention, or seeks early treatment. Perceptions are modified by: (1) demographic variables of age, sex, race, and ethnicity; (2) sociopsychological variables of personality, social class, or peer pressure; and (3) structural variables, such as knowledge about the disease and personal contact with the disease. Action to prevent illness and the perceived way to treat disease is also affected by cues to action, including the mass media campaigns, advice from others, reminder postcards from health care professionals, illness of a family member or friend, and newspaper or magazine articles. This model is directed to health protection behavior rather than health promotion. It is assumed that the higher the level of readiness to act, the lower the intensity of cues, internal or external, needed to trigger preventive behaviors. Benefits minus barriers determine the likelihood of taking recommended preventive health action. Beliefs about the effectiveness of recommended preventive actions are also an important determinant of health protecting behaviors. The lower the chance of recovery, the longer people wait before seeking medical attention (3). Barriers such as cost, inconvenience, unpleasantness of procedures, extent of life change required, and fear of pain have great power to prevent the person from engaging in preventive behaviors (16).

Health Promotion Model

The **Health Promotion Model** *developed by Pender derives from Social Learning Theory, which emphasizes the importance of cognitive mediating processes in the regulation of behavior.* Determinants of health promotion behavior are categorized into cognitive–perceptual factors, modifying factors, and variables affecting the likelihood of actions. Cognitive–perceptual factors include: (1) the individual's perceptions, (2) the importance of health, (3) the perceived self-efficacy or conviction that one can carry out behavior to achieve desired outcome, (4) the definition of health, (5) the perceived health status, (6) the perceived benefits of health promoting behavior, and (7) the perceived barriers to health promotion actions. These factors are the primary motivational factors for initiating and maintaining health promotion behavior. Modifying factors that influence health promotion behavior to varying degrees include the following (84):

1. Demographic variables—age, gender, race/ethnicity, education, income.
2. Biological characteristics—weight, size.
3. Interpersonal influences—expectations of significant others, family patterns of health care, interactions with health professionals.
4. Situational factors—access to health promotion services and alternatives, environmental constraints in health behavior.
5. Behavioral factors—previous experience with behaviors that promoted well-being, gaining of necessary knowledge or skill.

Cues to action or variables affecting the likelihood of the person initiating or maintaining health behaviors may be of internal or external origin. Important internal cues are personal awareness of the potential of growth or increased feelings of well-being from beginning health promotion efforts. External cues include conversations with others about their efforts and resulting success; support of significant others; mass media problems about health; family health status; and environmental variables on the level of readiness of the person, family, or group to follow health promotion activity.

Resource Model of Preventive Health Behavior

The **Resource Model of Preventive Health Behavior** *has been proposed by Kulbok. The model hypothesizes that people act in ways to maximize their "stock in health." The greater the social and health resources of the person, the more frequent the performance of preventive behaviors.* Social resources are education level and family income. Health resources are: (1) health status, (2) energy level, (3) concern about health, (4) feelings about independence in caring for self, (5) participation in social groups and religious services, (6) number and closeness of friends and relatives, and (7) general psychological well-being. Preventive health behaviors include diet, physical activity, sleeping, dental hygiene, use of seatbelts, and use of professional services. The model explains some preventive health behaviors (63).

Human Ecological Model

Shaver describes the components of the **Human Ecological Model** in explaining health/wellness status. She uses a biopsychosocial approach. Personal factors that affect health include lifestyle, stress management, affiliation with others, and involvement in healthful activities. Sense of well-being, mood state, and cognitive performance can affect personal behaviors. Environmental factors such as social support, cultural norms, space, time perspectives, energy exchange, and life events affect and are affected by personal behaviors and health status. Host factors, such as personality, gender, age, cognitive ability, and physiological regulation, affect and are affected by personal behaviors and health status. Activities of daily living, signs and symptoms of disease, and sense of personal control influence host factors and environmental factors. Thus, *all biopsychosocial components are interrelated and interdependent.* This integrated, holistic view has considerable implications for the nursing process, and if applied, would contribute to greater service to and with the client/patient (105).

Model of Multiple Risk Factor Behavior

A **Model of Multiple Risk Factor Behavior** proposed by Kar, Schmidtz, and Dyer, *is a multidimensional psychosocial model of determinants of risk-taking behavior.* The model proposes that in populations with comparable ethnicity, socioeconomic, and biological status, risk-taking behavior is dependent on the following variables: (1) behavioral intentions, (2) social support from significant others, (3) accessibility of information and services, (4) personal autonomy, and (5) action situations. The model is based on Systems Theory; behavioral intentions and personal autonomy are internal variables; the other variables are system or external influences. The model has been found to have transcultural applicability (56).

Instruments to Assess Health Promotion and Illness Prevention Behaviors

✓ Various instruments have been developed to assess the behaviors and lifestyles of the person or family, in order to determine intent or activity directed to either health promotion or illness prevention.

✓ Cox has developed the *Health Self-Determinism Index,* which measures motivation in health behavior. Four subscales in the Index are (1) self-determined health judgments, (2) self-determined health behaviors, (3) perceived competency in health matters, and (4) internal–external cue responsiveness. This tool, with further research, should be useful in determining client/patient motivation and how various interventions affect motivation for specific health behaviors (21).

✔ Clark has devised a *Wellness Belief Scale*, based on Rotter's Concepts of Internal Locus of Control, to help clients/patients examine wellness beliefs and their sense of responsibility for wellness (17).

✔ Clark has also developed a self-assessment tool for wellness, which the client/patient uses to determine state of wellness in areas of nutrition, exercise and fitness, coping with stress, relationships with others, and interaction with the environment. The tool also helps the person determine what areas are important and whether or not a change of behavior is desired in a specific aspect of life. Commitment to wellness is also determined (17).

✔ Walker, Sechrist, and Pender developed the *Health Promoting Lifestyle Profile*, which measures six dimensions that indicate a healthy lifestyle: self-actualization, health responsibility, exercise, nutrition, interpersonal support, and stress management. The tool enables researchers to investigate patterns and determinants of a healthy lifestyle and the effects of interventions to alter lifestyle (122).

✔ Pender has designed an extensive assessment tool to help an individual formulate a health protection–promotion plan. The form reviews present physical and stress status, self-care strengths of the person, health goals, areas for self-improvement, family health status, family values, family self-care patterns, family health goals, areas for improvement in family health, and evaluation of progress toward goals (84).

✔ One format for an adult health history is suggested by Pender. The history can be administered by the nurse, or a self-administered questionnaire format that clients/patients can use for self-assessment could be developed. Techniques are also described for both adult and pediatric health histories in *A Guide to Physical Examination* by Barbara Bates (4). Kopf, Salamon, and Charytan (61) describe a preventive health history form designed to obtain medical and psychosocial information for older adults.

✔ Any health history is incomplete if it does not include items concerning sexuality. A sexual history can be obtained most comfortably within the context of a comprehensive health history. In Pender's adult health history form, sexuality questions have been placed in the sections on psychosocial history and review of the genito-reproductive system (84). Information on obtaining a sexual history can also be obtained from Hogan (49).

✔ Sometimes the assessment tool may be very specific, such as the one shown in Figure 17–1, which can be used to gather data about eating habits, as a basis for assessing nutritional status and nutritional health promotion.

Factors That Influence Health Promotion and Illness Prevention Behaviors

Why do some people engage in activities to promote health or prevent illness, while others who appear equally in need for such activities do not? Many forces are in play as a person decides for or against what has been defined as health promotion or illness prevention behavior. Internal (personality), external (environmental), and various knowledge and emotional forces, some unknown to the person, all contribute. *Health behavior* is related to subjective ideas about vulnerability and present health state, the value placed on health and early detection of illness, and the sense of internal versus external control.

Influences on Healthful Behaviors

Understanding the person's perception of health assists in understanding how health behaviors influence appraisal of symptoms, perceived vulnerability, and decisions to seek treatment. Perceptions of health are related to a number of factors already mentioned, plus: (1) cultural norms of activity and inactivity, (2) continuation of rewarding roles and activities, (3) participation in social life, and (4) levels of psychological well-being.

A study by Penders indicated that persons at highest risk for health crises may be the least likely to engage in positive health habits. Subjective personal norms about exercise, weight, or diet affected intention to change behavior more than did health teaching or professional guidance. Behavioral change and continued health behavior was influenced positively by family or group support (84, 85).

In one study, people with high self-esteem who perceived their social support to be very adequate maintained more positive health practices than did those with lower levels of self-esteem and social support. Individuals who take better care of themselves are more likely to attract supportive relationships, and good social support predisposes one to engage in good self-care. Those with more self-esteem would be likely to consider it worthwhile to enhance their health status. Those not needing to expend their time and energy protecting and defending what little self-esteem they have would have more resources available to maintain or improve their health.

There is the direct effect of gender on self-esteem, social support, and lifestyle. The typical woman is more emotionally involved in relationships than is the

---

Record all foods and drinks that you had during the day and during the night.

Day of Week (Circle   Mon   Tues   Wed   Thurs   Fri   Sat   Sun)

Breakfast
  Foods/Amounts (cup, tbsp)   Drinks/Amounts (cup, glass)

Lunch
  Foods/Amounts (cup, tbsp)   Drinks/Amounts (cup, glass)

Dinner
  Foods/Amounts (cup, tbsp)   Drinks/Amounts (cup, glass)

Snacks
  Time   Foods or Drinks   Amount (cup, glass, Tbsp, or pieces)

Do you take vitamin or mineral supplements?   Yes ___ No ___
If yes, please list kind and how many per day.

Do you take any other nutritional supplement? (e.g., yeast, protein bran)
If yes, please list and describe.   Yes ___ No ___

Figure 17–1. Assessment Form for Eating Habits and Nutritional State.

average man. Women generally take better care of themselves than do men. It may be that a way to influence health behaviors is through education about inter- and intrapersonal factors and how these can effect health behaviors. The holistic approach to health care is to blend the social and psychological factors in maintaining the physical self (76).

Findings from Alexy's study (1) suggest that setting goals for illness risk-reduction can be effective in changing behavior. However, results provided no indication that client/patient participation in setting goals was superior to a directive approach. The provider goal-setting group made significant changes in exercise levels, alcohol intake, and seatbelt usage. The control group, which did their own goal-setting, made significant changes in exercise. The provider–client collaborative goal-setting group also changed significantly in exercise and weight reduction. Overall changes in this group were sufficient to make significant differences in life expectancy and potential life expectancy increase. Although significant change occurred in exercise levels and weight reduction in the collaborative group, and change occurred in exercise levels in the provider goal-setting and control groups, such change may be related to the current emphasis on these factors in modern culture. The higher level of success with the provider goal-setting group may indicate that individuals prefer specified programs. Interventions focusing on intermediate behavior change (daily or weekly goals) rather than outcome criteria might represent a more successful strategy with most clients/patients (1).

Prevention Attitudes and Behavior

✔ Sometimes people may be unaware of the illness hazards to which they are exposed, unless you teach and help them pursue alternate behaviors. Sometimes exposure may have unwittingly occurred or is basically unavoidable (40). For example, neurological and endocrine conditions, as well as spontaneous abortions and congenital anomalies, may be increasing as a result of applications of pesticide malathion in the food-growing sectors of the United States. Sometimes exposure to health hazards is the result of unpredictable, unpreventable environmental conditions, such as volcanic eruption or earthquake and are unavoidable. However, increased awareness may encourage action to prevent additional complications or future exposure. Increased awareness may also encourage citizen activity that can change national policy, enforce established standards or create more effective standards, or change practices by the offending parties. A consideration may be the person's/family's perception of the effectiveness of an activity versus the difficulty in implementing it. Your most effective intervention may be to teach and counsel, guide and persuade, so that the difficulty of the preventative care or the necessary medical treatment regimen is perceived as low while the effectiveness of it is perceived as at least moderately, if not highly, effective (104).

Four factors contribute to the perceived seriousness of any given health problems: (1) degree of threat; (2) overt visibility of illness or disability; (3) degree of interference with a person's lifestyle, family, or occupational roles; and (4) communicability of disease to others. The person's concern for the welfare of others may be greater than for personal health. Thus preventive measures are more likely to be followed for communicable disease than for those that affect only the individual (17, 74, 84).

The person chooses the preventive services that are perceived as being most effective in lowering the threat of illness. The higher the educational or socioeconomic levels, the more will people be aware of the entire range of preventive health alternatives available (84).

The person who feels powerless or unable to control the environment is not likely to try preventive health behavior. The person who feels able to control the self internally perceives self as less vulnerable to ill health and usually takes preventive health actions (84).

Four key factors influence the decision to seek preventive care services. First, the person may seek health care because of family encouragement. Second, patterns of using preventive services are learned in the family. The level of the mother's education correlates highly with preventive practices because the mother is often the decision maker in this area. Third, expectations of friends are powerful motivators to seek preventive health care, for parents especially want to fulfill the expectations of peers, neighbors, or friends about what "good parents should do." Fourth, information and respectful care from health professionals also increase the readiness to engage in preventive health behavior, especially if the health professional is seen as knowledgeable and caring. The small-group approach to giving information is more effective than teaching only one person. However, knowing what is healthful is no guarantee that the person will follow healthful patterns of living (84).

Situational determinants that influence the decision to practice preventive measures include cultural values on health and prevention, group norms and pressures, and information from mass media (84).

Yet various barriers impede a person's action even after the decision to take action: high costs, inconvenience, unpleasantness of treatment measures or facilities, pain, fear of findings from early detection measures, inability to decide which course of action would be best, psychological needs that are fulfilled by the illness, or perceived changes in lifestyle that are prescribed as undesirable.

Health-Promoting Relationships

✔ All people need relationships with others in order to remain healthy, physically and psychologically. How you relate to the client/patient will contribute to the health status, and may determine whether the person maintains/continues health practices.

Differences Between a Social and a Helpful Relationship

✔ Establishing a helpful relationship is one of the unique functions separating nursing from other health services.

The **nurse–client relationship** *is a helpful, purposeful interaction over time between an authority in health care, the nurse, and a person or group with health care needs, with the nurse focusing on needs of the client/patient while being empathic and using knowledge.* Through this process the nursing process is put to use, and it must be differentiated from mere association. Social contact with another individual, verbal or nonverbal, may exercise some influence on one of the participants and needs may be met. But inconsistency, nonpredictability, or partial fulfillment of expectations often results. Characteristics of *social relationships* are as follows:

1. The contact is primarily for pleasure and companionship.
2. Neither person is in a position of responsibility for helping the other.
3. No specific skill or knowledge is required.
4. The interaction is between peers, often of the same social status.
5. The people involved can, and often do, pursue an encounter for the satisfaction of personal or selfish interests.
6. There is no explicit formulation of goals.
7. There is no sense of accountability for the other person.
8. Evaluation of interactions does not concern personal effectiveness in the interaction.

✔ A nurse–client relationship is established *when the person's or family's needs are met consistently and unconditionally*. A working nurse–client relationship is, by definition, good, helpful, therapeutic. There is no such thing as a poor nurse–client relationship; there are only poor or unsatisfactory experiences that prevent establishing the relationship. Interactions moving toward a relationship occur whenever direct client/patient care, health teaching, listening, or counseling are done, or when the person's/family's activities are being directed or modified in some way.

The following interactions are *not helpful* to the person because needs are met inconsistently or conditionally:

1. Automatic, in which there is no meaning to either person.
2. Impersonally helpful, in which a service is expertly given but no personal interest or empathy is displayed.
3. Involuntary, in which "carrying out orders" is done as a duty, often the result of the nurse's perception of work as just a job to be done.
4. Inconsistent (that which is conditional in nature)—assisting the patient only when the situation is interesting or when it fulfills the nurse's needs.

✔ The nurse–client relationship is one in which the person's real complaint is uncovered. The focus is on the client's/patient's needs rather than on your own. The person is not a social buddy. There is a giving of self in an objective way to the person and family; yet you do not identify with (feel the same as), pity, or reject the one seeking help. Neither do you feel you are the only person who can help the client/patient. You use the resources that a team can offer whenever doing so is beneficial to the person or family.

The Effect of Feelings on the Relationship

Only through mutual striving for self-awareness and appreciation of the other person's reactions can a nurse–client relationship grow to maturity. Knowing that each person has needs to be met gives meaning to this relationship. You must expect both positive and negative feelings in yourself and in the other, and you must realize that both can be expressed either overtly or covertly.

✔ The client's/patient's positive feelings may be those relating to a sincere desire to cooperate in his/her own care and may include a polite manner toward others. The feelings may be a result of educational, religious, or cultural background, or a combination of these factors. In any event, you are in a position to capitalize on such positive feelings in order to establish rapport and a sense of trust as a foundation for the nurse–client relationship. Additionally, make every effort to learn the person's negative feelings. Insecurity; distrust of unfamiliar persons, routines, and treatments; or helplessness or hostility because of a lack of control over his/her own responses—all may be present.

✔ The positive feelings that you may have toward the client/patient are strongly bound to your commitment to nursing as a way of life. They cannot develop if you are merely doing a job because the negative feelings we all possess can overpower the positive and interfere with the nurse–client relationship. Negative feelings, which may at times be expressed in your reactions, will provoke inappropriate behavior. Talking out your negative feelings with the staff is better than unloading them on the client/patient or family.

The Effect of Behavior on the Relationship

✔ To develop an awareness of the feelings that you take with you to the client/patient, examine your behavior to determine whether it is modified for some people in a helping way and for others in a manner that hinders your effectiveness. Modification of your behavior with, or approach to, different persons is a valuable tool. Surely you would behave differently toward the child than toward the aged person. But behaving differently because a person is rich or poor, Afro-American or Caucasian, quiet or boisterous, grateful or ungrateful, in agreement or disagreement with your value system may prevent you from meeting that person's needs.

✔ Remembering that all behavior has meaning will help you to sharpen and improve those qualities you possess that produce a positive response in others. When inappropriate reactions do occur, analyze them in terms of what preceded them and of what happened after the incident. Search for clues to establish the meaning of feelings. Using the process recording format, you might record the event by writing the conversation and the nonverbal responses of both you and client/patient for closer analysis. Discussing the incident with objective persons may help, perhaps in team conference. Become familiar with your own coping mechanisms; seek to understand their relative value and the ways in which you use them in your approach to nursing care. Take sufficient care of your personal needs outside the nursing setting so that you can give your best professional care to the person or family or group.

✔ Although the relationship with a client/patient is a reciprocal experience, the responsibility for establishing it and for making appropriate changes in it rests with you, not with the client/patient. The relationship is based on each person's perceiving the other as a unique individual without stereotyping. Help the person *not* to see you as the command officer or the "angel in white" and avoid seeing the patient as a "gallbladder" or a room number.

✔ Carrying out the person's planned regimen for health maintenance or restoration will be accomplished more easily because of the nurse–client relationship, for it will naturally foster the tangible as well as the intangible aspects of your care. Above all, keep expectations mutual and remember that the major characteristic of the nurse–client relationship is that *the nursing needs of the individual or family are met in an emotional climate of warmth, support, and mutual trust* (124, 125).

Guidelines for the Nurse–Client Relationship

✔ If you consider your behavior an influence on the person's or family's behavior, you will be in a better position to advise specific approaches for bringing about change. You will want to develop characteristics of a helpful, humanistic relationship. These characteristics include being

1. *Respectful*—Feeling and communicating an attitude of seeing the client as a unique human being, filled with dignity, worth, and strengths, regardless of outward appearance or behavior; being willing to work at communicating with and understanding the client because he/she is in need of emotional care.
2. *Genuine*—Communicating spontaneously, yet tactfully, what is felt and thought, with proper timing and without disturbing the client, rather than using professional jargon, facade, or rigid counselor or nurse role behaviors.
3. *Attentive*—Conveying rapport and an active listening to verbal and nonverbal messages and an attitude of working with the person.
4. *Accepting*—Conveying that the person does not have to put on a facade and that the person will not shock you with his/her statements; enabling the client to change at his/her own pace; acknowledging personal and client's feelings aroused in the encounter; to "be for" the client in a nonsentimental, caring way.
5. *Positive*—Showing warmth, caring, respect, and agape love; being able to reinforce the client for what he/she does well.
6. *Strong*—Maintaining separate identity from the client; withstanding the testing behavior of the client.
7. *Secure*—Permitting the client to remain separate and unique; respecting his/her needs and your own; feeling safe as the client moves emotionally close; feeling no need to exploit the other person.
8. *Knowledgeable*—Having an expertise based on study, experience, and supervision; being able to assist the client in formulating goals.
9. *Sensitive*—Being perceptive to feelings; avoiding threatening behavior, responding to cultural values, customs, norms as they affect behavior; using knowledge that is pertinent to the client's situation.
10. *Empathic*—Looking at the client's world from his/her point of view; being open to his/her values, feelings, beliefs, and verbal statements; stating your understanding of his/her verbal or nonverbal expressions of feelings and experiences.
11. *Nonjudgmental*—Refraining from evaluating the client moralistically or telling the person what to do.
12. *Congruent*—Being natural, relaxed, trustworthy, and dependable, and demonstrating consistency in behavior and between verbal and nonverbal messages.
13. *Unambiguous*—Avoiding contradictory messages; using purposeful communication.
14. *Creative*—Viewing the client as a person in the process of becoming, not being bound by the past, and viewing yourself in the process of becoming or maturing as well (93).

✔ Other features that correlate highly with being effective in a helping relationship are being open instead of closed in interaction with others, perceiving others as friendly and capable instead of unfriendly and incapable, and perceiving a relationship as freeing instead of controlling another (86–88).

Establishing and maintaining a relationship or counseling another does not involve putting on a facade of behavior to match a list of characteristics.

Rather, both you and the client/patient will change and continue to mature. As the helper, you are present as a total person, blending potentials, talents, and skills while assisting him/her to come to grips with needs, conflicts, and self (78, 86–88).

✔ Working with another in a helping relationship is challenging and rewarding. You will not always have all the characteristics just described; at times you will be handling personal stresses that will lower your energy and sense of involvement. You may become irritated and impatient while working with the person. Accept the fact that you are not perfect; remain as aware as possible of your needs and behavior and your effect on the other. Remember that the most important thing you can share with another is your own uniqueness as a person. As you give of yourself, you will in return be given to—rewarded with warmth and sharing from the client/patient.

Phases of the Nurse–Client Relationship

Unless the encounter is brief, the feelings between you and the client/patient and the family and the work jointly done evolve through a sequence of phases. The phases are not sharply demarcated and they vary in duration. They can be compared to human developmental stages because of the degree of dependency–independency and feelings of trust involved: the orientation phase is comparable to infancy, identification to childhood, the working phase to adolescence, and termination to adulthood (86–88).

✔ The **Initial** or **Orientation Phase** *of the relationship begins when you first meet the person or family.* You might carry out intervention measures shortly thereafter, as you function in the role of technical expert, counselor, teacher, referral person, or substitute mother. Your main tasks during this phase, however, are to become oriented to the other's expectations, health needs, and goals through assessment while simultaneously orienting the person to your role and health-care goals and his/her role in the health-care system. You formulate a tentative care plan. Establishing rapport and showing acceptance are vital for assessing and orienting the other person. Be aware of how you are affecting the person and how he/she is affecting you. During this period the person clarifies the health status and its meaning through your exploration of the many factors affecting him/her. Essential to this phase is caring for the person or family in such a way that a sense of trust and confidence in you is established.

✔ The second phase, called the **Identification Phase,** *marks the time when the person has become better acquainted with you, places trust in your decisions and actions, works closely with you, follows your suggestions, and at times imitates your behavior.* He/she sees you as "his/her nurse." You continue the nursing process, actively guiding him/her but also providing opportunities for participation in self-care. You accept dependency without fostering it excessively.

✔ The third, the **Working Phase,** *is the time when the client is becoming more independent, actively using all services and resources offered by the health team.* He/she becomes more assertive and no longer relies so heavily on you. By now he/she is usually regaining physical and emotional health—optimal function—so that behavior begins to change as he/she becomes more involved in decision making about certain aspects of the situation. Although the person seems more independent and even self-centered, you can now work as equal partners in meeting health goals. The client/patient is preparing for convalescence and discharge from your services.

✔ *Maintenance Phase.* Often the nurse who works in an acute care setting does not really experience the rewards of a relationship with the patient. The short stay typical of hospitalization or even the few visits given by a home health nurse allow nothing more than establishing rapport, if that.

The **Maintenance Phase** *in the relationship is only possible in the setting in which a client/patient is followed by the same nurse over a period of time*—for example, in a rehabilitation center, nursing home, senior residence, or psychiatric-mental health agency. Also, the nurse in independent practice or in an ambulatory care clinic may see the same clients/patients over a period of years.

✔ In this phase, termination does not occur for a long time. Often termination only comes with the geographic move or death of the person. The active, working, therapeutic stage goes on until the person has reached his/her potential. In this situation, the person has reached a plateau where support and maintenance are essential for daily living. He/she may live at home, following your directions for health promotion measures, and may call on you for assistance only when chronic illness becomes uncontrolled or when a new condition of pathology or aging arises. Or he/she may be in an institution and need maximal or minimal assistance with daily physical care. What characterizes this phase is that you must actively pursue intervention in order to maintain emotional and social well-being. The reward will be the gratification of seeing a person reassert a will to live, to become creative in coping with problems or making "ends meet," and to remain independent.

✔ The last phase, **Termination,** is *marked by the person's becoming as fully independent as possible, leaving the health care system to return to the community.* Together you plan the management of the health situation after discharge, especially if the client/patient requires any special lifestyle modifications, such as in exercise, hygiene, or diet. This is a time of separation and both you and the person must work through feelings about separation—sometimes past as well as present situations. Mutual attachment develops between you and someone you take care of for a long time and either one or both of you may feel uncertain about the person's ability to manage without you. Together you need to talk about feelings about separation and your confidence in the ability to be independent and remain healthy. Avoid increasing dependency on you at this time to meet your needs. When the client/patient leaves the health care system, each of you should feel no regret about the termination. On the other hand, if there is need for follow-up visits after discharge, your interest and concern in the person or family extend to this ongoing care.

Without the nurse–client relationship, the person's needs are not met and the nursing process is not in force. Mechanical tasks become an end in themselves and the person is not helped to prevent or adapt to his/her illness.

✔ There may be people with whom you cannot form a helpful relationship. There may be situations in which it would be best for the client/patient if someone else were to work with him/her. You need to be aware of your own feelings of discomfort with him/her and you should be able to accept the fact that you cannot work with certain people. Often the reasons will be obscure; you may want to work through the reasons with an instructor or supervisor for your own personal growth (86–88). Reference 78 gives more information on barriers to an effective nurse–client relationship.

Communication to Promote Health

The ability to communicate should not be taken for granted; it is not a simple process but rather a complex system by which the world's work gets done.

Communication is the matrix for all thought and relationships between persons and is bound to the learning process. Early sensory experiences shape subsequent learning abilities in speech, cognition, symbol recognition, and in the capacity for maturing communication. Perception of the self, the world, and one's place in it results from communication. Verbal and nonverbal communication is learned in a cultural setting; if the person does not communicate in the way prescribed by the culture, many difficulties arise, for that person cannot conform to the expectations of society. Disordered thinking, feeling, and actions result, along with mental anguish, and perhaps even physical illness.

✔ Communication is the heart of the nursing process, for it is one of the primary methods used to accomplish specific and general goals with many different kinds of people. It is used in assessing and understanding the client/patient and family as well as in nursing intervention. Communication helps people express thoughts and feelings, clarify problems, receive information, consider alternate ways of coping or adapting, and remain realistic through feedback from the environment. Essentially the client/patient learns something about the self, how to identify health needs, and if and how he/she wishes to meet them.

✔ Analysis of your communication pattern will help you improve your methods. Realize that you cannot become skilled in therapeutic communication without supervised and thoughtful practice. As you talk with another, however, do not get so busy thinking about a list of methods that you forget to focus on the person. Your keen interest in the other person and use of your personal style are essential if you are to be truly effective. To be effective while communicating with the person or family, use simple, clear words geared to the person's intelligence and experience. Develop a well-modulated tone of voice. Be attuned to your nonverbal behavior. Several authors have described principles, attitudes, and methods essential in therapeutic communication that are useful with individual persons as well as with groups (7, 67, 68, 78, 86–89, 124, 125, 133).

Effective Methods

✔ The following methods are basic for conducting purposeful, helpful communication with a person, along with their rationale.

✔ *Using Thoughtful Silence to Encourage the Person to Talk.* Silence gives you and the person time to organize thoughts. It directs the person to the task at hand but allows him/her to set the pace, aids consideration of alternative courses of action and delving into feelings, conserves energy during serious illness, and gives time for contemplation and relaxation. There is a time not to talk. Always focus on the person you are talking with, especially during silence.

✔ *Being Accepting.* This is a difficult task at times. Realize that *all* behavior is motivated and purposeful. Indicate that you are following the person's trend of thought. Encourage the person to continue to talk while you remain nonjudgmental, although not necessarily in agreement.

✔ *Helping the Person Strengthen Self-identification in Relation to Others.* Always use *you, I,* and *we* in their proper context. Do not say "We can take a bath now" but rather "You can take a bath now."

✔ *Suggesting Collaboration and a Cooperative Relationship.* Offer to share and work together with the person; offer to do things *with* and not *for* or *to* him/her. Encourage participation in identifying and appraising problems and involvement as an active partner in treatment. Tell the person you are available to help. "I'll stay with you" or "I'm interested in your comfort" are examples of statements that can help to reassure that you will stay and care regardless of the person's behavior.

✔ *Stating Open-ended, Generalized Leading Questions.* Use these to encourage the person to take the initiative in introducing topics and to think through problems. Examples include: "Is there something you'd like to talk about?" "Tell me about it." "Where would you like to begin?" "Go on." "And what else?" "Would you like to talk about yourself now?" "After that?" Avoid conventional pleasantries after initial greetings because they constrict the person's expression of feelings and ideas. It is important for the person to talk about his/her mental and emotional distress and turmoil and questions, for often he/she cannot cope with feelings until the feelings are stated.

✔ *Stating Related Questions.* Do not let a subject drop until it is adequately explored. Peripheral or side questions help the person work through larger issues and engage in problem solving. Explore by delving further into the subject or idea without seeming to pry. Many clients/patients deal superficially with a topic to test if you are truly interested. Avoid questions that call for a yes or no answer. Explorative questions call for answers that elaborate, thereby helping the person to increase understanding and do further problem solving or clarifying.

✔ *Placing Events Described in Time Sequence.* In order to clarify relationships associated with a given event, determine how it happened, place it in perspective, determine the extent to which one event led to another, and seek to identify recurrent patterns or difficulty or significant cause-and-effect relationships. Ask such questions as "What happened then?" or "What did you do after that?"

✔ *Stating Observations That You Perceive About the Person.* Statements such as "You appear . . . ," "It seems to me that . . . ," "I notice that you are . . . ," and "It makes me uncomfortable when you . . ." encourage mutual understanding of behavior. Such observations offer a basis on which the person can respond without your having to probe, and they call attention to what is happening to help him/her notice or clarify personal behavior. Using this technique, you and the other person can compare observations and you can encourage a description of self-awareness. In addition, when you openly acknowledge that another's efforts at a task or behavior are appropriate to the situation, you reinforce the behavior and add to the person's self-esteem.

✔ *Encouraging Description of Behavior or Observation.* Through statements like "What did you feel?" "Tell me what you now feel," "What does the voice seem to be saying?" and "What is happening?," you can better understand the person when you observe and understand matters as they seem to him/her. There is the need to act out impulses and feelings if the person feels free to state them.

✔ *Restating or Repeating the Main Idea Expressed.* This will convey that it was communicated to you effectively, thereby encouraging the person to continue. Restate the idea until the person does clarify. Reformulating certain statements and using different words bring out related aspects of material that might otherwise have escaped the client's/patient's (or your) attention.

✔ *Reflecting by Paraphrasing Feelings, Questions, Ideas, and Key Words.* This will encourage further talking. Indicate that the person's point of view is important; acknowledge the right to personal opinions and decisions. Encourage the person to accept personal feelings and ideas. Show interest in hearing as much as the person wishes to tell you. Emphasize the word *you* while conversing, as in "*You* feel . . . ," in order to reflect what the person has said. (However, do not just mindlessly parrot his/her words.)

✔ *Verbalizing the Implied.* State the implied or what the person has hinted at or suggested in order to make the discussion less obscure, to clarify the conversation, to show that you are listening and interested, and that you accept what is said. Questions can be used as a subtle form of suggestion. As an example, you might ask, "Have you ever told your wife how you feel?" or "Have you ever asked your boss for a raise?" Regardless of the answer, you have indicated that such an act is conceivable, permissible, and perhaps even expected.

✔ *Attempting to Translate Feelings into Words.* Sometimes what the person says seems meaningless when taken literally. Hidden meanings of verbal expressions, as well as their actual content, must be considered and can be explored by describing the implicit feelings.

✔ *Clarifying.* Clarify when necessary through statements like "I don't understand what is troubling you" or "Could you explain that again?" The person is usually aware if he/she is not being understood and may withdraw or cease to communicate. It is not necessary to understand everything stated as long as you are honest about it and do not pretend to understand when you do not. Attempting to discover what the person is talking about can help him/her become clearer to self.

✔ *Reintroducing Reality.* State reality by voicing doubt or by calmly presenting your own perceptions of the facts in the situation when the person is being unrealistic. Indicate an alternate line of thought for consideration; do not attempt to convince him/her of error by arguing. Such action only provokes resistance and a determination to maintain the idea. Encourage the person to recognize that others do not necessarily perceive events as he/she does or draw the same conclusions. Encourage reconsideration and reevaluation (even though it may not change his/her mind) through statements like "What gives you that impression?" "Isn't that unusual?" and "That's hard to believe." Expressing doubts may reinforce doubts the person already has but has discounted because no one else shared them before. A doubting tone of voice can be as effective as any specific statement.

✔ *Offering Information.* Make facts available whenever the person needs or asks for them. Well-timed teaching builds trust, orients, and gives additional knowledge from which to make decisions or draw realistic conclusions. Inappropriate, excessive, or partial information or advice may cause alarm or needlessly suggest problems to the person. Give the person information about what can be expected and what he/she can do to help self. At times it may be appropriate for you to disclose briefly your own thoughts, feelings, or experiences; do not elaborate on yourself.

✔ *Seeking Consensual Validation.* Search for mutual understanding; words should mean the same thing to both of you. Therapeutic communication cannot take place if both you and the other person attach autistic (private) meanings to the words you both use. Always ask yourself if what you heard could have a meaning other than what you think. As a person defines self for the listener, he/she also clarifies what is meant. Avoid words and phrases that are easily misinterpreted or misunderstood and encourage the person to ask whenever there is doubt about what you mean.

✔ *Encouraging Evaluation of the Situation by the Person.* Help the person to appraise the quality of the experience, to consider people and events in relation to personal and others' values, and to evaluate the way in which people affect him/her personally as well as understand how he/she affects others. A simple query may help the person understand feelings in connection with what happened and refrain from uncritically adopting the opinions and values of others.

✔ *Encouraging Formulation of a Plan of Action.* Do this by asking the person to consider examples of behavior likely to be appropriate in future situations. The person can then plan how to handle future problems or how to carry out necessary self-care.

Summarizing. Summarize important points of discussion and give particular emphasis to progress toward greater understanding. Summarizing encourages both you and the person to part company with the same ideas in mind, provides a sense of closure at the end of discussion, and promotes a grasp of the significance of what was said.

✔ The quality of any response depends on the degree of mutual trust in the relationship. Techniques can be highly successful or they can misfire or be abused, depending on how they are used, your attitude at the time, and the other's interpretation. There must be a feeling of caring, of safety and security in your company, and a feeling that you want to help the person help himself. The more important or highly personal a feeling or idea is, the more difficult it is to say. This situation causes hesitancy in revealing thoughts, feelings, or intimate needs. By using therapeutic principles, such as those previously listed, you will help the person and his/her family identify you as someone to whom ideas and feelings can be safely and productively revealed.

Communicating with the Client/Patient Who Has Communication Difficulties

✔ You will need to gather data from clients/patients with sensory impairments. When you interview a person with hearing impairment, inability to speak the language, or visual impairment, the basic principles still apply, although the specific condition will necessitate some adaptations. The guidelines presented in Tables 14–1 and 14–2 will be helpful. For anyone with a communication disorder, develop rapport and a trust relationship slowly to overcome the reticence or suspicion that might be present. Introduce yourself and your purpose. Use appropriate nonverbal behavior to convey ideas. Use an intermediary, such as a family member or interpreter, if available and necessary, but *not* to the exclusion of talking with the client/patient.

Other Considerations

✔ The first communication problem that you must control is that of personal emotions in the nurse–client–family relationship. Because the main barrier to communication is emotion, you must develop skill in building bridges over this barrier. The basic bridge to effective communication is feeling. Everyone seeks *warmth, security, assurance,* and *appreciation.* When these qualities are present, tough problems can be taken in stride, especially when commitment is combined with skillful use of the methods described in this chapter.

✔ Study yourself to discover those points at which you could be responsible for blocking communication through your own shortcomings. Know your likes and dislikes; recognize them for what they are; and keep them under control. In order to accept another person, you must first accept yourself. You must be aware of your own needs in order to help another meet personal needs.

✔ Cultivate an understanding of the part played by body language in human interactions and be as aware of what you are saying with your body movements as you are of what others say with theirs. Feelings are frequently expressed by gestures, attitudes, gait and body posture, and facial expressions.

✔ In order to make full use of therapeutic communication, the person must feel safe with you, respected by and trusting of you. Revealing one's innermost thoughts and feelings to someone one scarcely knows is difficult for any individual, even when help is needed and expected. Use of communication techniques in counseling makes no attempt to influence the speed or direction of the person's problem-solving efforts; be a facilitator instead of a doer or a teller.

✔ The nurse is in a key position to apply an understanding of the communication process and to carry out therapeutic communication methods in nursing while conducting routine procedures, teaching, and counseling or giving support. Thus you can enable the person and family to achieve optimum wellness and prevent future health problems. In addition, through communication, you will learn of the effectiveness of care you have given.

Application to Daily Living

Although this section has centered around nurse–client–family interaction, the discussions of the communication process, of interviewing, and of techniques and blocks to communication apply equally well to associations with your colleagues and other health team members. In fact, application of all information in this chapter to your everyday relationships with family and friends will promote an increasingly appropriate, harmonious living pattern. The smoother the communication system, the smoother all other systems will function.

✔ Appropriate, realistic, constructive communication between persons is a basic step toward mental, emotional, and, indirectly (but no less significantly), physical health. Communication patterns that block or resist the other person reduce feelings of autonomy and equality and increase feelings of being misunderstood. The resultant emotions—frustration, anger, depression, and the like—will eventually affect the relationship between the persons involved as well as the physiological functioning of the body.

✔ As a nurse, you will find yourself refining your personal pattern of communication, practicing therapeutic communication with others, and teaching others patterns of communication that promote health individually, within the family, and within community social groups.

Health Education

Teaching and learning are important at any stage of the wellness–illness continuum, but recently more emphasis has been placed on health promotion and early prevention.

Definitions

Learning *is the process of acquiring wisdom, knowledge, or skill; an overt change in behavior may be observed.* **Teaching** *is the process of sharing knowledge and insight, or facilitating another to learn knowledge, insight, and skills* (42). These definitions are deceptively simple. Popular magazines, textbooks, and library shelves are full of theories and explanations about how these processes take place. Yet no one can say learning will always take place under certain conditions or teaching will never take place under certain conditions. In spite of myriads of information, people with their unique minds and personalities are always modifying the existing theories.

In actuality, teaching and learning cannot be separated, for while a person is teaching, learning is also taking place, or at least should be. Perhaps the substandard use of learn, as in the sentence "I'm going to learn you something" has more accuracy than people have thought. Both terms connote a lifelong process, an internalization (learning) of thoughts, attitudes, facts, and a consequent externalization (teaching) of those thoughts, attitudes, and facts. Teaching and learning can be conscious and formal, as in the announced situation "Today we are going to learn about the digestive system." Or they can be unconscious and informal, as when a mother frowns and says with a certain tonal emphasis "What is that smell?" The listening and watching child combines a certain smell with a negative mental attitude.

The word **education** *has traditionally meant a process that transmits the culture.* But the word originally came from a Latin word meaning "to draw out." Although we are more familiar with education as a cramming full of facts and information, the other side of the definition is to draw out the mysterious hidden qualities within a person. The amount of education a person has gained and retained has long been measured by IQ (intelligent quotient) tests. But many qualities cannot be measured this way. The IQ test cannot measure how much creative imagination a person has, how much ambition, perserverance, or willingness to cooperate (82). And these qualities are significant, although previously not often considered or given priority. Thus a balanced definition of education is the continuing process of using immeasurable inner resources to gain external information.

Health education *specifically transmits information, motivates the inner resource of the person, and helps people adopt and maintain healthful practices and lifestyles.* It is also concerned with the environment, professional training, and research to maintain and evaluate the process. Traditionally health education focuses on what the professional thinks is good for the patient/client.

Self-care, increasingly popular in recent years, *focuses on what the learner perceives as needs and goals to maintain or enhance health and well-being.* It is generally undertaken prior to illness rather than in response to disease. Health educators should shift their emphasis from pathology that has never been experienced to things the person has done and enjoyed and will be unable to continue to do if more healthy behavior is not implemented.

Assessment

✔ Providing you have a wellness orientation, you still must deal with the client/patient where he/she is—culturally, socially, developmentally, and spiritually. Previously the average lay person did not place health in the same level as did the health worker. The lay person has generally taken action only when he/she believes the susceptibility to a health threat could have serious effects on the person's life, when he/she knows what actions to take to reduce the health threat, and when the health threat is greater than the action threat (95). Therefore, teaching possibilities should be assessed starting at first contact, whether that be in a group meeting, upon admission to the hospital, or in an industrial health work setting. Thereafter, teaching ought to take place at every opportunity, be it mealtime, medicine time, or when talking about family life.

✔ Realistic teaching goals should be set, keeping in mind the basic skills/knowledge you wish to convey. The family should be constantly assessed for its help/hindrance in the process.

Intervention

Some techniques are best suited for teaching on an individual basis whereas others are best for large groups or several subgroups.

✔ ***Individual teaching.*** This can be provided through programmed learning, reading material, audiovisual materials, and one-to-one instruction. *Programmed learning* provides material in carefully planned sequential steps that leads the person to a mastery of the subject. The material is presented through program instruction books or a teaching machine, a simple manually operated machine or a complex computer. One frame of information is presented at a time. The learner then tests his/her grasp of the information in the frame by writing, or in the case of a computer, keying a response to a question, usually a multiple-choice type. The book or machine then gives the correct response. If the learner's response was incorrect, the program then presents (or, in the case of a book, directs him/her to turn to) a repetition of the information or a more detailed explanation, depending on the program and his/her response. The advantages of programmed learning include logical presentation, active learner participation, immediate disclosure of correct response, reinforcement of material and individual pacing (116). For more on using computers to aid learning, see Primarius (91), Cook (20), and Bell (8).

✔ Another method of giving individual instruction is by providing factual material. Many health organizations provide preventive health-teaching *literature* as part of their programs. Evaluating the benefits gained from these materials is difficult because people who receive the material often do not respond to the organization's request for feedback, even when given a stamped answer form. One study tried to determine the effectiveness of a breast self-examination by seeking the reactions of 383 women 1 year after they received teaching kits with filmstrip, teaching notes, and commentary; only 41 percent responded. Women in the upper half of the social scale reacted more favorably: 48 percent of them had established an examination pattern (though not necessarily monthly, as the material suggested) (47). The tendency of upper-class persons to read better and to respond more readily to scientific health teaching than lower-class persons seems evident here.

✔ Other factual reading materials include *autobiographies* of persons with certain disease processes and "how-to" books by persons who have experienced certain health problems directly or indirectly and want to pass along suggestions to others. Fiction also provides valuable insights into physical and mental illness.

✔ With the constant introduction of more sophisticated *audiovisual* equipment into the teaching–learning area, you can get and adapt these devices to individual learning. A recorder and cassettes explaining preventive measures, disease processes, or specific instructions can be loaned to the client. He/she can stop the cassette at any point and replay necessary portions until satisfied with the learning. "Talking Books" is a program that records information for the visually impaired. Closed-circuit television or videotape setups allow the person to hear and view material. You can be involved in producing teaching cassettes and television or VCR programs.

✔ These methods of individual instruction are only individual to a certain point. Only when the client/patient can check learning with a *resource person*, ask further questions as necessary, and have help in making personal applications, will learning become significant. That process involves you. The person does not learn from a machine alone. These discussions with the person need not be long. The important point is to be available when they do have questions and to convey that any question or problem is worthy of your consideration.

✔ *Group Teaching.* This can meet the person's need to achieve status or security through being a group member. Client/patient groups provide a channel through which feelings and needs can be expressed and met, especially if the people have similar problems, such as colostomy or diabetes. Thus you can use the group process to enhance health teaching or for therapy to aid coping with problems. You may also have opportunity to work with a group that has formed to accomplish some specific goal, such as losing weight, promoting research to find a cure for cancer, or providing guidance to parents with mentally retarded children. In some cases, information is not enough. Social support is also necessary, especially when engaging in a lesser-valued activity—like not eating sugar when society says that dessert is the best part of the meal. One study of hospitalized diabetics, some taught individually and some taught in a group by a nurse specialist, showed that the latter demonstrated as much or more knowledge and skill in urine testing as the former (80).

In another study 25 experimental patients participated in a small group session the night before surgery. They discussed their concerns and fears and learned what to expect and how to aid in their convalescence. A randomly selected matched control group of 25 patients who underwent similar surgery but who received only routine care were compared, after surgery, with the first group. Results showed that extra preparation increased patient participation, decreased tension and anxiety, and led to more rapid postoperative recoveries (102). In a similar study patients with preoperative teaching had a hospitalization of 1.3 days fewer than those who received no teaching (90).

One minister who had visited hundreds of patients on the night before surgery said, "Fear of the unknown is what I continually find. I don't necessarily mean about the outcome of the surgery, although that is involved. I mean they don't even know about the recovery room process. Instead of giving spiritual help, I find myself telling them many details which the nursing staff should have taught. With these important details at their command, I can see their anxiety lessen." Small group sessions could reduce these fears.

✔ Explain not only the rather complicated procedures such as surgery and the accompanying routines. Positive results have also been obtained with the explanation of minor procedures. One group, for example, was told what sensations to expect and then had blood pressure cuffs placed on their arms and then the pressure pumped up to 250 mm Hg. Another group was told only of the procedure—that is, "Your blood pressure will be taken." The conclusion was that accurate expectations about sensations do reduce stress, but that patients should be told only about sensations usually experienced, not those rarely experienced (53). Excessively detailed explanations can raise rather than lower anxiety.

✔ If you work with a group, you should initially set a working social climate. People do not automatically start revealing their problems and supporting and helping each other. You must use some introduction technique that focuses on the individual, his/her personality strengths and resources, rather than on a disease or problem. (The person already knows why he/she is there.) Each person can introduce self if the group is small. If the group is large (25 or more), you can break it up into subgroups of 5 each and allow each subgroup at least 20 minutes to plan a presentation. One technique is the inquiring reporter: one person in each group (or subgroup) is chosen to compose a feature story about the personalities and resources of group members. The person then presents the story to the total group in 3 minutes. This method produces immediate ego involvement, creates an atmosphere conducive to participative learning and sharing of problems and resources, and starts the spirit of creative inquiry (60). You can think of other introductory techniques for your particular group situation.

Special Concerns in Client/Patient Teaching

🡆 Most health care agencies post a list of *patient's rights*. You can be instrumental in teaching *clients/patients* about their *right* to health care and rights within a health care agency (see Tables 17–2 and 17–3).

Teaching to Prevent Quackery within the Health-Care System

Standards are set by professional organizations, among them the American Medical Association and the American Nurses Association. However, the "incompetent" or careless doctor has been ignored or "unseen" until recently. Published findings revealing unnecessary operations and fatal reactions from inappropriate antibiotics are making people more aware of their need to use certain standards for choosing and using a doctor. Additionally, self-styled health workers and "quacks" are also offering services. The self-styled health worker may emphasize certain herbs for healing or a special "hand-me-down" formula and does not rely on professionally set standards. A **quack,** *one who makes pretentious claims about the ability to treat others with little or no foundation*, may be found representing any health profession. The quack raises false hopes and causes loss of money and time—often money and time that could be better used for proven treatment.

Why do people go to quacks? Probably the main reason is *fear:* fear of mutilation from surgery, of pain, of dying. Some may go out of ignorance. Some may go to seek a miracle cure. Others may go because they lack patience with the traditional, approved treatment methods. Some have tried everything else—the quack is the "last resort."

🡆 You can help people to avoid quacks by helping them set realistic health goals and by helping them recognize the following typical behaviors of the false practitioner:

1. Claims use of a special or secret formula, diet, or machine.
2. Promises an easy or quick cure.
3. Offers only testimonials as proof of healing power.
4. Claims one product or service is good for a variety of illness.
5. States that he/she is ridiculed or persecuted by traditional health professionals.
6. Promotes products through faithhealers, door-to-door health advisors, or sensational ads.
7. Refuses to accept proven methods of research.
8. Claims the treatment is better than any prescribed by a physician.

🡆 You can identify quackery victims in need of counseling by asking the person the following questions:

1. Is anything taken to combat fatigue, headaches, inability to sleep, bowel or bladder problems, or muscle or backaches? If so, what?
2. Is anything taken to aid digestion, to lose or gain weight, to improve appetite, or a food supplement of any kind?
3. What home remedies are used to alleviate the problem under treatment?
4. Ask about foreign travel and uses of alternate therapies, if the person has cancer; diabetes; arthritis; or other major chronic diseases.

TABLE 17–2. The Patient's Bill of Rights

- The patient has a right to considerate and respectful care. . . .
- The patient has a right to obtain from his physician complete current information about his diagnosis. . . .
- The patient has a right to receive from the physician information necessary to give informed consent to the start of any procedure and/or treatment. . . .
- The patient has a right to refuse treatment to the extent permitted by law. . . .
- The patient has a right to every consideration of privacy concerning personal medical care program. . . .
- The patient has a right to expect that all communications and records pertaining to care should be treated as confidential. . . .
- The patient has a right to expect that within its capacity a hospital must make reasonable responses to the request of a patient for services. . . .
- The patient has a right to obtain information as to any relationship of the hospital to other health care and educational institutions insofar as his/her care is concerned. . . .
- The patient has a right to be advised if the hospital proposes to engage in human experimentation affecting his/her care and the right to refuse to participate in such research projects. . . .
- The patient has a right to expect reasonable continuity of care. . . .
- The patient has the right to examine and receive an explanation of the bill regardless of the source of the payment. . . .
- The patient has the right to know what hospital rules and regulations apply to conduct as a patient.

Reprinted with permission of the American Hospital Association, Copyright 1975.

TABLE 17-3. Teaching Guide for Client's/Patient's Rights

FIVE DOS	FIVE DO NOTS
• When you call the nurse or secretary for an appointment, state your request or problem so that the appropriate appointment time can be scheduled.	• Unless an emergency arises, do not take up extra, unplanned-for time. For example, do not say, "Oh, while I'm here for my ear infection, why don't you do my complete physical."
• Organize thoughts about your present health status or illness and write them down so you can present pertinent facts to the doctor. These will aid him/her in giving a thorough examination or in making a diagnosis.	• Do not lie to yourself or to the doctor. Do not let fear cause you to ignore a situation that may need immediate but minimal treatment.
• Cooperate during the physical examination and allow the doctor to be complete. Do not tell the doctor to skip certain procedures.	• Do not tell the doctor to give you pills. Do not feel cheated if you do not get medication; many illnesses are minor and self-limiting. Your own observance of a health-promotion regimen may be all you need.
• Ask your doctor about proper diet, work load, exercise, and rest to help you maintain maximum health. Ask about realistic limitations. If ill, ask your doctor questions about cost of treatment, medication, diagnosis, causes of condition, chances for recovery, or whatever you want to know related to the situation. If you have more questions after you leave, write them down and call back for answers. If hospitalized, continue to ask questions about drugs and ongoing treatment.	• Do not ask for unnecessary hospitalization for x-rays or tests because the insurance will pay or because grandma is burdensome. Talk with your doctor about alternate plans that will promote long-range health for everyone involved.
• Follow instructions after health promotion plan is established. After time, effort, and money are spent, you are the only loser if you refuse to follow suggestions or directions.	• Do not leave the doctor's office dissatisfied. At least express and explain your feelings. The doctor needs to understand your point of view. Maybe a change can be made or perhaps you need additional information to understand a suggestion or decision.

✔ The following guidelines can be followed if the person asks about quack cures:

1. Answer without sarcasm or antagonism.
2. Explain that promises in the advertisements are not necessarily true.
3. Offer to check with the remedy, if you are not familiar with it, to give more information.
4. Attempt to discredit the false claims by citing studies that disprove the miracle cure.
5. Inform other members of the health team of any alternate therapies or quack methods that are being used by the person.

✔ You should be aware of quackery in your community. Examine the claims of the quack against standard treatment plans. Be willing to compare approaches with the client/patient. Do not ridicule the person who has gone the nontraditional route. Above all, this person needs your listening ear and understanding guidance. Remember that people think in terms of having symptoms and eradicating them. If the latter takes place to their satisfaction, they will place their trust in the health care worker who was responsible for their improvement, regardless of his or her credentials. What you call a *hoax* others may call *hope*.

Use of Health Education Literature

Health care literature is published for consumers in many countries. For example, in the United States many baby formula/food companies, such as Ross Laboratories, print booklets on prenatal, postnatal baby, and child care. In London, England, Domestos Hygiene Advisory Service prints pamphlets under the title *Areas of Risk*, including Baby Hygiene, Home Hygiene, Food Hygiene, Pet Hygiene, Water Sense at Home, Typhoid, and others, such as *The Domestic Safe Houses Book*. The pamphlets are colorful, easy to read, and contain the main health promotion/disease prevention points of the subject. Other literature is also available (50 Upper Brook Street, London).

The journal *Health Link* was first printed in 1985 in the United States. It is published quarterly by the National Center for Health Education, 30 East 29th Street, New York City, 10016, in order to inform and link professionals and volunteers who are engaged in health education. It is written for practitioners in health care, education, public health, social services, and business, and presents timely information as well as current resources.

Health education and promotion is considered important for every country, not just for the United States. In 1976, the Health Departments of Great

Britain and Northern Ireland prepared a booklet, *Prevention and Health, Everybody's Business,* to present a historical discussion on contributions of prevention toward solution of health problems, to suggest ways to advance disease prevention and health promotion, and to present the costs, benefits, and resources available (27).

A text, *Promoting Health: A Practical Guide to Health Education,* published in England in 1985 was at that time the only basic guide in England for professionals that presented theory and practice of health education. More publications will follow, just as more health promotion texts are being published in the United States (32).

✔ At least 20 percent of people in the United States and about 50 percent of health care clients are not able to read materials written at a fourth- or fifth-grade level; they are functionally illiterate. Most patient education materials are written at at least an eighth-grade level. Thus, most health education via the booklet, pamphlet, or written material is not comprehended. Further, Streif's study found that the client's/patient's reading level could not be accurately estimated from their reported last grade completed in school. The Wide Range Achievement Test (WRAT) appears to be an accurate assessment tool to determine comprehension of written materials and could be incorporated into initial assessment. Thus, more appropriate educational aids could be selected, and clients/patients with low reading skills could be encouraged to contact local resources for reading instruction (117).

Evaluation

Evaluation is judging how effective teaching has been. Evaluation is sometimes difficult because clients/patients cannot always be followed long enough to see the results of teaching, and human behavior is so complicated that true changes are hard to measure. However, a starting point is to document everything you teach so that you can recall exactly what you attempted.

✔ Evaluation can be informal or formal. Informal judgments are made constantly. A client/patient compliments or complains. You react to these judgments. You observe how well a client/patient dresses a wound, irrigates a catheter, or cooks a meal after your demonstration. You may write evaluation notes on the learning ability. By questioning the person's understanding, you are evaluating your teaching. If he/she has learned appropriately—can give explanations and can perform the activities that were taught—the teaching has been adequate. Clients/Patients can evaluate their own learning, whether goals were met, and your teaching by using a rating scale or checklist, which further assists your evaluation process.

✔ Every person connected with a teaching-learning program should be involved in evaluating the program. Depending on the specific situation and program, these people might include the participants (patients and teachers); the program director and staff, who can see the program as a whole; the directing committee, who establish objectives and policy; and outside experts, who can be totally objective. Community representatives can supply valuable evaluative information when the teaching is aimed at serving the general public (60).

Health Screening

✔ **Health Screening** *assessing present health status regularly through periodic health examinations,* including dental checkups, and participating in mass screening programs in the community is essential. Learning preventive measures and warning signals of disease, such as those published by the American Cancer Society, The American Heart Association, and the Diabetic Association, assists in keeping up to date. Further, such literature provides useful education for the average citizen.

Regular health assessments are essential for two reasons: (1) The person remains cognizant of practices that will contribute to ensure health and (2) early detection of health problems—potential or actual—is possible.

✔ Refer to the section on physical assessment in Chapters 7 through 14 on how to effectively screen for specific conditions through the life span.

✔ Refer to Appendix I, Review of Systems: Physical Assessment and Health History, which presents health promotion and disease prevention factors to consider for each body system.

✔ Refer to Appendix II, Health Maintenance Procedures, for a list of screening procedures that should be regularly implemented from birth to 17 years, and a list of procedures that should be regularly implemented ages 18 to 80 or beyond years.

✔ Many people engage in self-screening practices; in fact, some types of self-examination practice to detect breast, testicular, skin, or mouth cancer are effective in early detection of disease and thereby prevent serious results or death. However, the person cannot do an accurate Pap smear or rectal examination of self. Self-screening for hypertension requires the right kind of equipment and the correct procedure.

✔ Many kinds of self-examination kits are available. Warn the client/patient that self-screening for some conditions may not be preferable to examination by a nurse practitioner, nurse–midwife, or physician. Many of the self-test kits, whether for diabetes, pregnancy, or blood in the stool, that are bought over-the-counter, have questionable accuracy. Even reliable kits give a false positive or false negative if the procedure is not accurately done.

✔ Risk factors to consider when appraising the person's health status include:

1. Genetic factors.
2. Age.
3. Congenital conditions.
4. Past illness and injury.
5. Family history, such as presence of illness or causes of death in parents, siblings, grandparents or other relatives, history of abuse or incest in family.
6. Environmental threats, such as economic deprivation, occupational hazards, unsafe conditions of home or neighborhood.
7. Lifestyle considerations, such as daily eating and sleeping patterns, work and leisure habits, and use of tobacco, alcohol, or drugs, stress management practices.
8. Personal health habits, such as nutritional practices, mouth and dental care, exercise and sleep patterns, immunizations, periodic physical examinations.
9. Life stresses or changes that have occurred in the past 2 years.

✔ A specific format for risk appraisal for cardiovascular disease, breast, lung, cervical, colorectal, uterine or ovarian, and skin malignancy, automobile accidents, diabetes, and suicide is presented by Pender (84).

✔ Risk appraisal for illness alone is unlikely to result in better health. In fact, even if a risk score is high, that specific person may not develop a specific disease, for uniquely individual reasons, although population studies indicate that statistically, the person has a greater chance of disease development. Further, it is meaningless and unethical to do an appraisal or tell a person of risk without providing education, support, or resources to encourage behavior change that could prevent the risk occurrence. Risk appraisal must be done carefully and with the individual's personality status and needs in mind. The person should indicate a desire for such information prior to your spontaneously giving such information. Weiss has found that predictions about disease occurrence or shortened life expectancy may cause anxiety and depression, a giving-up, and fewer efforts at health promotion, especially in older adults who feel it is too late to change risk status. Or risk predictions may create a sense of guilt and hypochondrial complaints that are not given sufficient attention by the physician, which could further the chance of disease development (130).

Nutritional Recommendations

✔ You have an important role in teaching the client/patient and can act as a role model for healthy nutrition. Encourage the person to maintain essential nutrition and stay within 10 pounds of normal body weight. Nutritionists, in general, agree that the best diet is high in fiber, moderate in protein and fat, and low in sugar and salt. High-fiber foods include bran and other whole grains, raw fruits, and vegetables. These fruits prevent constipation and apparently other gastrointestinal diseases, including cancer. Red meat should not be the main source of protein. Sources of saturated fats, such as red meat, butter, or whole milk, should be limited because they impair the body's ability to reverse cholesterol buildup. Processed foods should not be the mainstay of the diet. Coffee, tea, and cola intake should be limited, for excessive caffeine intake has been linked to feelings of increased stress. Cooking with herbs or using lemon juice, vinegar, or other condiments can decrease the need to use salt as a flavoring.

Maintaining normal nutrition is basic to promoting health. While recommended daily allowances have been established for the average person, it is unknown whether the daily nutritional recommendations are adequate for the man who is 6 foot, 6 inches tall; for the person who weighs 225 pounds; for the person who works hard 16 hours a day; for the athlete; or for the person who is under excessive stress. Extra protein, calories, and fluids are needed for all of these people; it is likely that extra vitamins and minerals are also needed.

Refer to Chapters 7 through 14 for descriptions of nutritional needs and requirements for each age group. Refer also to Appendix III for recommended daily dietary allowances for infants, children, adult males and females, and pregnant and lactating women. Refer to Appendix IV for a list of nutrients, their major sources, and their major functions.

Exercise, Movement, and Rest Recommendations

Refer to Chapters 7 through 14 for information about normal sleep, rest, and exercise needs throughout the life span. Play and leisure as a part of movement and exercise are discussed in each chapter as well. Normal adult sleep cycles are described in Chapter 12.

✔ Encourage the client/patient to maintain a regular, moderate exercise program to enhance physical and emotional health. The exercise should involve large muscle groups in dynamic movement for about 20 minutes 3 or more days a week and should require 60 percent or more of a person's cardiorespiratory capacity. The exertion should be within limits appropriate to the physical status and needs of the person and should also be accompanied by a sense of excitement, flexibility, strength, and energy. At the end of exercise the person should feel replenished rather than bored, burned out, or excessively fatigued (108). Furthermore, the personal need to increase exercise to the point of competitive winning or achievement of maximal physical performance may contribute to eventual anatomical, physiological, and psychological breakdown (52).

There is no evidence that running is better than other aerobic physical exercise, such as fast walking, swimming, bicycling, or dancing. The benefits of running are that it allows for psychomotor expression without the hazards of contact sports and is adaptable to a wide range of weather or geographical conditions, time schedules, personalities, and body types. Running can be social or asocial or organized or unorganized as an activity (52).

Running, or any strenuous physical exercise, also has some hazards. It can become addicting because release of endorphins in the body causes the person to feel euphoric and oblivious to pain or injury while running and very anxious when the exercise is omitted or delayed. The person who engages in intense exercise may engage in other health promotion measures or may feel invulnerable to disease and death. That myth may prevent engaging in other health promotion measures (52). The long-term effects on joints and organs of regular, long-distance running is currently unknown; some orthopedic physicians report musculoskeletal damage resulting from the "pounding" effects. Some physicians also report that breast tissue is damaged if inadequately supported by a brassiere, and pelvic organs in women may suffer prolapse from excessive long-distance running. Other physicians disagree.

✔ Emphasize to clients/patients the importance of avoiding extreme stress, fatigue, or exhaustion, providing for adequate relaxation, rest, and sleep, and using relaxation techniques if necessary. Effectiveness of relaxation techniques has been demonstrated. These techniques are discussed in this chapter.

✔ There are two major obstacles to overcome in undertaking and keeping at an exercise program: making exercise part of a lifestyle and avoiding injury. Suggestions for making exercise a safe part of a lifestyle include the following:

1. Start in small increments and keep it fun.
2. Avoid exercising for 2 hours after a large meal and eating for 1 hour after exercising.
3. Include at least 10 minutes of warm-up and cool-down exercises in an exercise program.
4. Use proper equipment and clothing when exercising.
5. Post goals, pictures of the ideal self, and notes of encouragement in a readily-seen place for self-encouragement.
6. Use visualization daily to picture successful attainment of exercise benefit, e.g., looking toned or graceful, ideal weight.
7. Keep records of weekly measures of weight, blood pressure, and pulse.
8. Focus on the rewards of exercise; keep a record of feelings and compare differences in relaxation, energy, concentration, and sleep patterns.
9. Work with a peer or join a structured exercise class, running club, or fitness center. Spend more time with people dedicated to wellness.
10. Stop exercising or at least slow down and consult with a practitioner if any unusual, unexplainable symptoms occur.
11. Reward self for working toward exercise goals as well as attaining them. For example, after a month in an exercise program, buy a new pair of running shoes or treat yourself to a special wish (17, 24).

Various theories and methods are being proposed to improve health through exercise and movement. These are based on a variety of concepts, including evolutionary development, dance, physical therapy techniques, brain and endocrine function. Nulls and Cohen propose a developmental movement theory that the body teaches the brain; certain movements are proposed to strengthen certain body parts (81). One theory and method is Feldenkrais' Awareness Through Movement Theory (33). His technique is to increase range of motion through increments of small, smooth, slow movements of the body in the direction of balance with gravity, with rhythmic breathing and centering on using imagery with the movement. Kurtz and Prestera proposed body message theory, which focuses on muscular patterns and movements related to feelings. Aerobic exercise, sustained rhythmic activity of large muscle group which entails using large amounts of oxygen, increases heart rate, stroke volume, respiratory rate, and relaxation of blood vessels. Cardiovascular fitness and increased stamina are the goals (64). Body fat is also reduced (13). Aerobic exercises include running, jogging, brisk walking, swimming, aquadynamics, and aerobic dance (64). Correct posture, proper shoes (44), and strengthening abdominal muscles are helpful to enhance effects of aerobic exercise and reduce risks of injury. Increasingly a walk–jog program or brisk walking only is being recommended (136).

Refer to the references by Brown (12), Colt (19), Nulls and Cohen (81), Feldenkrais (33), Kurtz and Prestera (64), Brownell and Stunkard (13), Haag (44), Jones (54), Jordan (55), and Yanker (136) for more information about various exercise techniques and precautions. Clark also furnishes a detailed description of various techniques. Clark also describes exercises for bedridden individuals and for those in a wheelchair (17).

Exercise, such as walking, jogging, or swimming, can reduce anxiety, tension, anger, depression, and pain perception because exercise serves to increase endorphin levels in the body. However, meditation, arts and crafts activities, and diversion have been shown to have similar effects, and these methods could be used with individuals who are antagonistic to an exercise program.

Prevention of Illness and Injury

Immunizations

✔ Teach clients/patients the importance of securing necessary immunizations for the children and adults in the family, especially with outdoor exercise and athletic programs, wide travel, and resurgence of communicable diseases. Refer to Chapters 7 through 14 for information about immunization recommendations for each age group.

Infection Control

✔ Refer to Chapters 7 through 14 for information about common infections for each age group and basic preventive or treatment measures. Teach clients/patients basic hygiene as one way to prevent spread of infection—hand washing, covering mouth when sneezing, avoidance of spitting, avoidance of close contact with others if contagion is possible. Suggest measures that will help him/her to prevent, when possible, and attend to any infection that occurs. First aid measures can be obtained from the Red Cross or can be found in a medical-surgical nursing text. Refer the person to a First Aid Course taught by the Red Cross.

✔ Caring for the body functions, including those factors affecting the skin, mucous membranes, teeth, elimination, and sensory organs, also prevents infection.

Safety Promotion Measures

✔ Teach safety measures to prevent injury and emergency treatment to avoid excessive or unnecessary tissue damage if an accident or illness occurs. A Red Cross course can be useful to the client/patient.

✔ For example, everyone should know how to do the Heimlich Maneuver, named for the physician who developed it. This technique is done if the person is an adult and the airway is blocked by food or an object. First, ask the person if he/she can speak. If not, stand behind the person, place your arms around the waist slightly above the belt line, and make a fist with your right hand. Place your fist, thumb side against the victim's abdomen. Allow the person's head, arms, and upper torso to hang forward on your arm. Grasp your right fist with the other hand and press rapidly and forcefully several times into the victim's abdomen, slightly above the navel and below the rib cage, with a quick upward thrust. This reverse bearing pushes up on the diaphragm, compresses the air in the lungs, and expels the object blocking the respiratory tract. Repeat several times if necessary. If the victim is sitting, stand behind the victim and perform the maneuver in the same way (Figure 17–2).

✔ Other important measures are to use sunscreening lotions, and avoid excessive exposure to sun and heat (to avoid heat exhaustion or heat stroke) or cold weather (to avoid frostbite). Plenty of fluids and cool clothing are important in extreme summer temperatures. Wearing several layers of warm clothing, cover-

FIGURE 17–2. The Heimlich Maneuver

ing the head, and avoiding the vasoconstricting effects of alcohol, nicotine, and fatigue are ways to prevent frostbite.

✔ Many states require the use of seatbelts for the driver and front passengers or all passengers in the car. Reinforce to the client/patient the importance of using safety measures or devices, such as seatbelts in cars, safety equipment in power machines, and sturdy ladders, to prevent injury.

✔ Using principles of body mechanics can prevent injury. When you are moving or lifting objects, do the following to prevent muscle strain or musculoskeletal injury: (1) roll or slide the object rather than lift; (2) move objects on a flat or level surface if possible; (3) keep objects close to the center of gravity in the body; (4) use the largest and strongest muscles to apply force—for instance, thighs, legs, arms, and shoulders; (5) use leverage to apply force or move an object when possible rather than relying on body weight; and (6) reduce friction if possible when using an object. Injury is also prevented by using the proper chair in the workplace. The back of the chair should be high enough to come about 2 inches above the lower tip of the shoulder blades and should tilt backward about 10 degrees. The back of the seat should be 3 degrees higher than the front edge. This will place you forward a bit so that you can lean back to maintain balance, thus putting your body in a good natural position. The depth of the seat should be such that the front edge comes to within 1 inch of the back of your knee, allowing your thighs to rest on it without putting pressure on your knees or calves. Feet should rest on the floor. The person should be advised not to cross knees which interferes with circulation. The aches and strains that develop in workers who sit or stand in poor posture daily can finally result in feeling ill and even in injury. Teach these same body mechanics principles to your clients/patients.

Control of Environmental Hazards

✔ Chapter 2 gives a comprehensive description of environmental hazards to health and control of these hazards. Teach the client/patient about ways to protect self from (1) air pollution (indoor and outdoor); (2) water pollution and soil pollution, including pesticides and herbicides; (3) food contaminants; (4) excess noise; (5) surface pollution; or (6) other hazards related to various occupations. Teach the client/patient and family this information as is applicable.

Cessation of Habits Destructive to Health

Smoking. The hazards of smoking are well publicized; refer to Chapter 2 for description of effects of smoking, and to Chapter 6 for effects of smoking in the fetus. More than 60 carcinogens and tumor initiators have been identified in tobacco and tobacco smoke. Involuntary smokers receive the same chemical mix as smokers, only less of it. Children of smoking parents are more likely to have slower expansion of lungs and more respiratory problems and disease than are children of nonsmoking parents (120). Nonsmoking persons married to smokers have a twofold increased risk of lung cancer. Lung cancer risk in never smokers increased with duration of exposure to a smoking spouse (51).

✔ Nurses often work in a smoke-filled environment, sitting in the nurse's station or lounge, or the supervisor's office, lighting the cigarettes of psychiatric patients, being in the patient's lounge when patients are smoking. Nurses' associations should work with hospitals and other health-care agencies to set up standards that will reduce the amount of tobacco smoke in the environment. Nurses should be leaders in promoting smoking cessation and smoking prevention programs in their communities. Nurses could lead public education campaigns about the hazards of smoking for the smoker and nonsmoker, pregnant women, and children. Nurses who smoke themselves need to engage in smoking cessation programs so that they can serve as role models for others (34).

✔ Table 17–4 provides suggestions for smoking cessation. A recent intervention for smoking cessation is the use of nicotine gum. Although originally thought to be a panacea, recent research shows it is most effective when used in combination with other approaches. Nicotine chewing gum is suggested primarily for smokers who are heavily addicted to nicotine (79, 94, 127).

Alcohol and Drug Abuse. Health teaching and counseling of the client/patient who abuses alcohol and/or drugs could include information from Chapter 6 (effects in fetus and pregnant woman, as well as on the male), from Chapter 11 (effects of drug abuse), from Chapter 12 (effects of alcohol).

The excessive intake of most drugs, alcohol, and food is linked to various diseases. Excessive or inappropriate use of prescribed or over-the-counter drugs frequently has serious consequences. A major problem involves overuse and inappropriate prescription of antibiotics, resulting in resistant strains of microorganisms and inadequate treatment of infections. The excessive and careless prescribing of mood-changing drugs may result in loss of behavioral control and even in physical and psychological addiction. Taking a combination of many prescribed or unprescribed drugs may result in interactive effects that are toxic to the body. Alcohol is a major cause of many accidental injuries and deaths as well as of other diseases. Excessive caffeine consumption has also been linked to breast cancer and other diseases.

TABLE 17-4. Smoking Cessation Suggestions

- Keep a notebook of current and past successes. Use the list as a reminder of your ability to succeed in new ventures.
- Identify a personal reason for quitting smoking other than because "It's bad for me."
- Make a list of things that are personally pleasurable; choose one as a reward (instead of a cigarette) when feeling uncomfortable or bored.
- Make a list of reasons smoking began and compare it with a list of current reasons for smoking.
- Keep a log of each cigarette lit, including the purpose; focus on smoking the cigarette and sensations occurring during and after smoking.
- Put cigarettes in an unfamiliar place.
- Every time a cigarette is reached for, ask "Do I really want this cigarette?," "Do I really need a cigarette?," "What can I do instead of smoking this cigarette?"
- Develop and prepractice responses to peer pressure to smoke, including: "Come on, one won't hurt," "Smoking makes you independent, like an adult," "Here, have one," "Are you a sissy?" Take an assertiveness course if necessary to develop the skill of saying "No."
- Smoke with the opposite hand from the one usually used.
- Buy cigarettes only by the pack, not by the carton.
- Buy different brands of cigarettes and avoid smoking two packs of the same brand in a row.
- Stay away from friends who smoke and from places where people smoke.
- End all meals with foods not associated with smoking, e.g., a glass of milk or half a grapefruit rather than a cup of coffee or a drink.
- Switch to noncaffeinated coffee or tea, or bouillon.
- When using cigarettes as an energizer, substitute six small high-protein meals, sufficient sleep, a glass of milk, a piece of fresh fruit, fruit or vegetable juice, exercise or movement, or a relaxation exercise.
- Have carrot sticks or celery, or sunflower seeds ready to chew instead of smoking a cigarette.
- Eat more foods that leave the body alkaline, such as vegetables, seeds, fruits, and reduce the urge to smoke.
- Write a list of stress enhancers; learn structured relaxation and stress reduction approaches to deal with each stressor.
- Use affirmations, such as, "I no longer smoke," "I can quit," "It's getting easier and easier to quit smoking," or "It's getting easier and easier to think about quitting smoking." Tell six people.
- Use deep breathing or breath for centering when the urge for a cigarette appears.
- Work with a peer who can be called for positive feedback when the urge for a cigarette occurs. Be sure the peer is positive about ability to quit and does not nag or induce guilt.
- Ask friends and co-workers not to leave cigarettes around or offer them.
- When the urge for a cigarette occurs, picture the word "STOP" in big red letters.
- Ask for a hug instead of having a cigarette.
- Choose a time to stop smoking when a peak mental or physical performance is not expected.
- Write a contract and sign it with a trusted person so continuing to smoke will prove embarrassing or will result in great loss.
- Read articles and books by people who have successfully quit smoking or helped others to.
- When feeling depressed, talk with people who have successfully quit smoking and ask for information about why they are glad they quit.

Refer to Chapters 11 and 12 for information about the hazards of obesity.

In summary, you can use the following measures to promote your health as well as the health of others:

1. Basic physical examination every 1 to 3 years.
2. Glaucoma testing for all adults over age 40.
3. Electrocardiograms for all adults over age 40, and then as indicated.
4. Breast examination, digital vaginal examination, and Pap smears for all women over 17 years of age, every 1 to 2 years.
5. Routine screening for cancer of the colon, annual digital prostate examination yearly after age 40; rectal examination, occult blood stool test every year after age 40.
6. Screening for diabetes and hypertension.
7. Appropriate education or behavior modification programs to reduce disease risk or treat the illness.
8. Vision testing annually, and hearing testing every 5 years from age 3 years throughout the life span.
9. Dental screening for caries and preventive care to teeth and gums, from age 2½ to 3 years throughout the life span.
10. Mammogram every 1 or 2 years after mid-thirties.
11. Proctosigmoidoscopy every 3 to 5 years after age 50.
12. Urinalysis, hematocrit, and blood chemistry tests every 1 to 2 years.
13. Tuberculosis test as indicated. Tetanus-Diphtheria (TD) booster every 10 years.
14. Long time smokers—chest x-ray every 1 to 2 years.
15. Walking briskly, reaching 2 steps per second for 20 to 30 minutes at least four times a week, for physical and mental benefits comparable to those of running. Regular flexibility exercises done slowly and gently to maintain range of joint motion.
16. Aerobic exercise to increase pulse rate and induce perspiration but also to boost maximum oxygen utilization and increase the flow of oxygen to the brain.

17. Not smoking.
18. Limiting consumption of alcohol.
19. Practicing moderation in dietary habits and try to maintain an ideal weight.
20. Eating a variety of foods, including whole grain breads and cereals, fruits, vegetables, beans, peas, and nuts, and avoiding saturated fat and cholesterol foods.
21. Limiting salt and sugar, including sucrose intake.
22. Knowing your stress level; avoiding excess stress; seeking involvement with other people and groups.
23. Getting 7 to 8 hours of sleep nightly.

Stress Management

Assessment

Stressful life events have been found to interfere with health promotion and to precede many health problems. Assessment of stress encounters in life, and the potential impact on health, can be done by using several instruments: the *Life-Change Index* developed by Holmes and Rahe (50), the *State-Trait Anxiety Inventory* developed by Spielberger (113), and the *Signs of Distress* developed by Everly and Girdano (31). Modified forms of the Life-Change Index are available for different age and ethnic groups. Holmes and Rahe found that life changes predict the possibility of becoming ill. If enough changes occur within a 2-year period, the chances of becoming ill are increased (50). The State-Trait Anxiety Inventory consists of 20 items that pertain to anxiety the person currently feels (state) and 20 items that pertain to anxiety the person generally feels (trait). A high level of state and trait anxiety indicates that the person may suffer physiological effects of anxiety, which may result in disease (113).

✔ You may have the person do a stress-charting exercise, listing all the stressors presently occurring and the area of life in which the stressor occurs, for example, spouse, children, relatives, friends, work or the profession, personal health effects, finances, social concerns, recreation or leisure, church, other organizational activity, or other areas. Then each stressor should be rated as to the impact it is having, using a scale of 1 to 5, with the number 5 indicating severe impact. Awareness gained from this exercise may motivate the person in use of stress management and relaxation techniques.

✔ Pender has developed the Life Style and Health Habits Assessment, which is divided into ten sections:

1. Competence in self-care.
2. Nutritional practices.
3. Physical or recreational activity.
4. Sleep patterns.
5. Stress management.
6. Self-actualization.
7. Sense of purpose.
8. Relationships with others.
9. Environmental control.
10. Use of health care system.

After the person has completed the form, you can use responses as a basis for health teaching (84).

Intervention

✔ Strategies for adaptation to stressors include biological mechanisms, psychological adaptive mechanisms, and coping behaviors. There are intrapsychic, interpersonal, and system or institutionalized ways of coping with stressors. You will assist clients/patients to develop and use these strategies through (1) direct care, (2) exploration with the person, (3) teaching or counseling of the person, or (4) creating changes in the person, family, group, health care agency, or the client's/patient's environment. Approach intervention from a *holistic* philosophy; mind, body, and culture are a fully unified system. A variety of approaches can be used to prevent or treat illness.

Biological coping mechanisms and responses of the endocrine, neurological, cellular, and biochemical regulatory systems occur in the alarm stage and help the person to maintain the resistance stage, recover from disease, and have the energy level necessary to maintain other adaptive strategies. These responses were described in Chapter 16.

✔ Scandrett and Uecker include self-hypnosis, biofeedback, autogenics, and meditation under the rubric of relaxation therapy and suggest it as an appropriate intervention for the following nursing diagnoses: anxiety, activity intolerance, ineffective breathing pattern, comfort alterations in pain, ineffectual coping, fear, impaired physical mobility, powerlessness, and sleep disturbance.

Physical Methods of Relaxation/Stress Management

✔ *Progressive Relaxation.* **Progressive relaxation** was developed by Jacobson in 1938 and *involves tightening and relaxing muscle groups* of the body for 5 to 7 seconds each, beginning with the hand and moving to the upper and lower arm, the forehead and face, neck, upper back, abdomen, buttocks, thigh, calf, and foot. The person is encouraged to check for relaxation prior to moving to the next major muscle group. In a relaxation session, you and the individual can agree that if he/she is tense, the index finger of the right or left hand will be raised when relaxation is felt (24, 84).

✔ A careful assessment of the person is essential prior to employing relaxation techniques. Baseline and posttreatment vital sign measures will validate physiological changes associated with relaxation. Essential components of the pretreatment interview include assessing:

1. Client's/patient's identification of the most bothersome symptom(s), including onset, duration, and full description.
2. Family history of similar complaints.
3. Client/patient interventions and description of the results, including use of current and recent medications, including over-the-counter drugs.
4. Physical limitations or illnesses.
5. Previous experience with relaxation training.
6. Use of alcohol or mind-altering drugs to relax.
7. Dietary patterns, especially use of caffeine and sugar, and foods that connote relaxation and are eaten at stressful times.
8. Sleep and exercise patterns.
9. Overview of daily routine, including stressors.
10. Psychiatric history, including screening for major depressive or psychotic disorders.
11. Willingness to learn techniques and to practice at home (24).

✔ Although progressive relaxation has proven effective in most studies, precautions should be taken for persons described in the following:

1. Depressed or withdrawn persons: relaxation may cause further withdrawal.
2. Persons who are experiencing hallucinations and delusions: they may lose reality-contact.
3. Persons with cardiac conditions; they should use nontensing relaxation exercises since tightly tensing muscles can increase blood pressure.
4. Persons on medications: the toxic effects of some medications can be increased by the relaxation state.

Acupuncture. **Acupuncture** *is a treatment method based on the Chinese philosophy that all life is a microcosm of a vast, constantly changing flowing circle of energy*, without beginning or end, which flows through the karma (fate) of our lives. This circle is divided into a rising energy, *yang*, seen as positive and male, and a descending energy, *yin*, seen as negative and female. Yet yang and yin are symbolic rather than superior–inferior to each other. The body can reach a balanced state only if both forces are flowing smoothly. The energy of yin and yang together is called qi (chee), and in the body is called true qi. Illness occurs when the flow of true qi around the 12 main channels or meridians of body is impeded or blocked and energy balance becomes disturbed. The 12 meridians are named after 12 organs as defined by Chinese acupuncturists: lung, large intestine, pericardium, bladder, small intestine, triple warmer, stomach, heart, gallbladder, spleen, kidney, and liver (9).

Acupressure. **Acupressure** is the *predecessor of acupuncture. The term is applied to a number of techniques of applying pressure to stimulate acupuncture points on the body.* Acupressure releases tension and relieves pain. It is a preventive treatment used to balance energy by applying pressures to specific points (9).

Shiatsu. **Shiatsu** *is an ancient, simple treatment method, whereby a form of manipulation is administered by the thumbs, fingers, and palms, without any use of instruments*, mechanical or otherwise, to apply pressure to the human skin, correct internal malfunctioning, promote and maintain health, and treat specific disease. Shiatsu is a fusion of the ancient Japanese manipulation therapy, anma, and the Chinese concept of acupuncture; however, no needles are used, only pressure. The philosophy is similar to that of Chinese acupuncture. Illness occurs as a result of excess or deficiency of yin and yang energy or a block of true qi. Gentle pressure along the meridian lines restores the balance (9).

Reflexology. **Reflexology** *is a technique based on the premise that body organs have corresponding reflex points on other parts of the body.* The reflex points are believed to be up to 20 times more sensitive than the corresponding organs. The foot is viewed as one of the scanner screens that records body functions. Working the reflexes in the feet helps rebalance organs by releasing blocks that impede the smooth flow of body energy. There are other areas with reflex points (wrist, hand, ear, neck, abdomen, face, head, arms, legs, nose, and iris), but the feet are the most effective. The act of reflexology is a giving and receiving, a sharing of communication resulting in confidence and mental calming. Together, healer and client/patient call upon the healing energy of the universe to surround, uplift, and permeate; the use of affirmations and the projection of a positive healing environment is a spiritual act of being of service to others (17).

Biofeedback. **Biofeedback** *is a means of receiving feedback or a message from the body about internal physiological processes, using specific techniques or equipment.* It involves use of instruments to develop the ability to read tension in various body systems and to learn ways of releasing the tension when cues of stress response are identified.

Biofeedback permits a person to become familiar

with internal functions, such as a moving index of body temperature or a reading of brain waves. As with externally directed behavior, the person is able with practice to learn how to control internal behavior (17). Most people have experienced the doctor's interpreting for them, in an illness–wellness context, the results of physiological tests. If able to read the same information as it is occurring within you, you are using biofeedback.

Biofeedback has two aspects: the actual use of biomedical devices capable of taking a reading of one's physiological activity, such as temperature or heart rate, and the training in which one learns what to do with the devices. The client/patient is linked to the instruments, which are modified to display the body information as visual or auditory signals, by delicate wires or tubes connected to special sensing materials taped to the skin. The body information is carried back to the devices, which continually read the signals reflecting the constantly changing activity within. As the person continues to work with biofeedback instrumentation, an association develops between changes in body signals and various subjective feelings that are either consciously or subconsciously recognized. The monitor gives information about the degree of success. Dependence on the instrumentation is temporary. Eventually the person should be able to monitor the fluctuations and thereby exercise some conscious control over physiological adaptation. Once learned, control over a physiological function is retained in the person's memory for a long time (17). Biofeedback has been successfully used to treat tension headaches, migraine headaches, hypertension, insomnia, peptic ulcers, colitis, muscle spasms or pain, epilepsy, asthma, anxiety states, panic disorders, phobic reactions, stuttering, and teeth grinding.

A directory of certified feedback practitioners is available from the Biofeedback Society of America, 4301 Owen Street, Wheat Ridge, Colorado, 80030. The following publications also provide information:

1. *Biofeedback Network*
   103 South Groves
   Greensburg, KS 67054
2. *Somatics*
   1516 Grant Avenue, Suite 220
   Novato, CA 94947
3. *Biofeedback and Self Control*
   Aldine Publishing Company
   1323 W. 18th Place
   Chicago, IL 60608

Massage. Massage has had a long and checkered history. It has been alternately extolled and rejected as a therapeutic procedure. We are witnessing an increase in its popularity, as the public is disillusioned with modern depersonalized clinical practices that emphasize surgery and medications rather than personal contact and self-responsibility or preventive maintenance.

✔ The effects of massage are psychological, mechanical, physiological, and reflexive. **Massage** is an art (a unique way of communicating without words and showing caring) and a science; *a systematic manipulation of the body tissue* produces beneficial effects on the nervous and muscular systems, local and general circulation, the skin, viscera, and metabolism.

✔ During massage, the hands stimulate the sensory receptors of the skin and subcutaneous tissues, causing a series of reflex effects, including capillary vasodilation or constriction, relaxation or stimulation of voluntary muscle contraction, and possible sedation or stimulation of pain in an area remote from the area being touched, depending on the type of massage or stroking movements (17).

Yoga. The word **yoga** *means to unite, implying the balance or harmony that can exist within the individual.* Yoga is an Indian philosophical system that emphasizes the practice of special techniques to attain the highest degree of physical, emotional, and spiritual integration. Hatha yoga is the branch that emphasizes physical postures and breathing practices to attain body/mind balance.

Studies of the effects of Hatha yoga have shown it especially beneficial to optimal functioning of the endocrine, circulatory, musculoskeletal, respiratory, and nervous systems. Yoga has been demonstrated to reduce blood pressure, lower pulse rate, reduce serum cholesterol, regulate menstrual flow and thyroid function, increase range of motion in joints, reduce joint pain, and increase feeling of well-being (17).

Autogenics. **Autogenics** *is a form of self-hypnosis that allows the person to induce the feeling of warmth and heaviness associated with a trance state.* The method was developed by Johannes H. Schultz, a Berlin psychiatrist. Autosuggestion with some yoga techniques were developed into a system of autogenic training. The system has been found effective in treatment of disorders of the respiratory and gastrointestinal tracts, the circulatory and endocrine systems, and for anxiety and fatigue. The exercises can be used to increase resistance to stressors, reduce or eliminate sleep disorders, and modify pain reactions. Autogenic therapy is not recommended for children under 5 years old, or for adults who lack motivation or have severe emotional disorders. Those with diabetes, hypoglycemic conditions, or heart conditions should discuss the use of the method with their physicians. Occasionally, a client/

patient may experience a sharp rise or drop in blood pressure when doing the exercises; blood pressure should be taken to ensure the exercises are useful. The exercises can be completed in a comfortable sitting or lying position where the person assumes an attitude of passive concentration. It may take up to 10 months to master the six exercises. Ninety-second sessions five to eight times a day are recommended for mastery. Clark describes in detail the technique to be followed (17).

Krieger's Theory of Therapeutic Touch

Dolores Krieger draws on Eastern beliefs and literature in her Theory of Therapeutic Touch. She theorizes that prana (Sanskrit term for energy) is transferred in the healing act; the source of prana in Eastern thinking is the sun. Eastern thinking contends that well people have an excess of prana; Western physiology texts state there is a great deal of energy in the human body. Krieger pictures the healer as a person with excess prana or energy who has a strong sense of commitment and intention to help people. Healing entails channeling this energy flow by the healer for the well-being of the sick individual. Healers do not become depleted of energy, however, because they are in a constant state of energy input. Healers become depleted of energy only if they draw on their own energy rather than being a channel of energy. Healers are thought to accelerate the healing process by giving the client/patient an extra boost to his/her recuperative system (62).

Krieger presents physiological data to back up her theory. There is evidence that therapeutic touch raises hemoglobin levels and influences EEG patterns. The healer's EEG changes to a high amplitude beta state, indicative of deep concentration similar to meditation, and the person's brain waves are typically low amplitude alpha waves, correlated with a state of calmness and well-being. The person experiences slower, deeper respirations and a sense of warmth and relaxation (62).

According to Krieger, therapeutic touch works well with all stress-related diseases, having a significant effect on the autonomic nervous system, reducing nausea, dyspnea, tachycardia, pallor, and peristalsis. Use of therapeutic touch has also been successful with children and with the terminally ill person (62).

✓ The healer centers and uses the hands (placed 2 to 3 inches from the person's skin) to move quickly over the body, reading signals of illness or blockage of energy flow. The feeling of pressure sensed in the hands when congestion or blockage is present is explained biophysically; as the healer moves the hands over the body, positive ions are picked up. Positive ions are associated with feelings of lethargy, headache, irritability, and inflammations of the mucosal tissues. Negative ions have been noted when the person has a feeling of well-being (62, 92).

✓ Krieger refers to the pressure as a "ruffling in the field"; the healer can move the positive ions by shaking or wiping the hands. When the healer's hands are placed in the area of a "ruffle" and then the hands are moved away from the body in a sweeping gesture, the pressure is reduced and the feeling of energy flow is sensed; this is called "unruffling the field." The unruffling motion can be used to soothe babies or reduce pain and tension. A 2- to 3-minute treatment is sufficient for children or the debilitated. With others the healer stops when the body feels balanced (62, 92).

The object of therapeutic touch is to balance the healer's "field" so that symmetry of energy flow is restored. With practice the hands begin to move toward areas of unbalanced energy flow as they become more sensitive to changes in the field of another person's body. Therapeutic touch has been shown to raise hemoglobin levels, reduce anxiety, relieve headache, as well as promote other physical well-being and healing by redirecting energy fields and enabling the sick person to mobilize personal healing powers (62, 92).

The spiritual implications of therapeutic touch are discussed by two nurses, Wuthnow (135) and Miller (74). Wuthnow believes that the technique can be used by nurses of all faiths who are trained in the technique and that it can be used with or without Christian beliefs (135). Miller believes that Christian nurses cannot use the technique because it represents a wrong relationship with the Holy Spirit and assumes a manipulating role of God (62). (This same argument is used by some Christian nurses against use of guided imagery, visualization, and other cognitive techniques for healing.)

✓ Relaxation techniques can be used with people of any age. Even school age children can learn relaxation training to reduce anxiety and cope with stress which may enhance subsequent stress management (66).

Clark describes in detail various touch and healing interventions that can be used by the nurse, including: (1) behavioral kinesiology interventions, (2) therapeutic touch interventions, (3) yoga interventions, (4) massage interventions, (5) acupressure interventions, and (6) reflexology interventions. A number of books are also available to explain these therapies in detail (17).

Cognitive Methods of Coping, Relaxation, and Stress Management

✓ Both you and your clients/patients need to take time for play, leisure, or diversional activities and spiritual pursuits that are (1) rewarding emotionally,

(2) done voluntarily rather than out of obligation, (3) outside of ordinary life routines, (4) absorbing in attention, (5) are not necessarily productive in earnings, and (6) have definite time and space boundaries. Laughter, pleasant thoughts, and relaxing activities stimulate production of endorphins and enkephalins, chemical pain relievers. Adrenalin and other hormones are also produced, stimulating body function. The body's production of immune cells increases. Arteries and muscles relax, reducing blood pressure (112).

Thought Stopping. **Thought stopping** *is a behavioral modification technique useful when nagging, repetitive thoughts interfere with behavior and wellness.* Unwanted thoughts are interrupted with the command "Stop." An image of the letters of the word stop, a loud noise (such as a buzzer or bell), or a negative stimulus, such as wearing a rubber band around the wrist and snapping it when the unwanted thought occurs is used with the command. Then substitute a thought that is positive, healthful, or desirable. Thought stopping may work because (1) distraction occurs, (2) the interruption behaviors serve as a punishment, (3) an assertive response can be followed by reassuring or self-accepting comments, and (4) a chain of negative and frightening thoughts leading to negative and frightening feelings is interrupted, thus reducing the stress level. Regular practice for 3 to 7 days is necessary for the person to learn to quickly interrupt a negative thought with a positive, constructive alternative thought (17).

Refuting Irrational Ideas. People engage in almost continuous self-talk during waking hours. **Self-talk** *is the internal language used to describe and interpret the world.* When self-talk is accurate and realistic, wellness is enhanced; when irrational and untrue, stress and emotional disturbance occur.

Albert Ellis developed a system to attack irrational ideas or beliefs and replace them with more realistic interpretations and self-talk. Irrational self-talk are statements that "awfulize" experience, make catastrophic, nightmarish interpretations of events. An irrational self-thought leads to unpleasant emotions. Rational self-talk leads to pleasant feelings and a positive interpretation of experiences. Rational thought is based on the idea that events occur and people experience these events (30).

The kinds of statements that Ellis considers irrational include:

1. External events cause most human misery; rather, people simply react as events trigger their emotions.
2. People must always be competent and perfect in all endeavors.
3. Happiness can be achieved by inaction, passivity, and endless leisure.
4. It is easier to avoid than to face life's difficulties and responsibilities.
5. The past determines the present.
6. It is horrible when people and things are not the way you want them to be.
7. Unfamiliar or potentially dangerous situations always lead to fear and anxiety.
8. People are helpless and have no control over what they experience or feel.
9. People are fragile and cannot be told the truth.
10. Rejection and abandonment are the result if one does not always try to please others.
11. There is a perfect love and a perfect relationship.
12. A person's worth is dependent on achievement and production.
13. Anger is bad and destructive.
14. It is bad and wrong to go after what you want and need (30).

Refuting irrational ideas is a skill and requires practice in the following nine steps:

1. Write down the facts of the event, including only the observable behaviors.
2. Write down self-talk about the event, including all subjective value judgments, assumptions, beliefs, predictions, and worries.
3. Note which statements are classified by Ellis as irrational.
4. Focus on the emotional response to the event, using one or two words, such as angry, hopeless, felt worthless, afraid.
5. Select one irrational idea to refute.
6. Write down all evidence that the idea is false.
7. Write down the worst outcome that could happen if what is feared happens or what is desired is not attained.
8. Write down positive results that might occur if what is feared happens or if what is desired is not attained.
9. Substitute alternative self-talk to focus on positive statements (30).

Coping Skills Procedures. **Coping skills training** *grew out of relaxation and systematic desensitization procedures* that were expanded and refined by Meichenbaum and Cameron (72). The procedures include a combination of progressive relaxation and stress-coping self-statements that are used to replace the defeatist self-talk called forth in stressful situations. Coping skill procedures can be used to rehearse via the imagination for real life events deemed stressful. First, a stressful situation is called forth. Next, progressive relaxation is practiced. Finally, coping skills statements are repeated until the situation can be thoroughly completed in rehearsal without feeling stressed. The procedures have been shown effective in the reduction of tension, anxiety, phobias, insomnia, and hypertension. Coping skills procedures can be mastered in approximately 1 week, once progressive relaxation has been learned (30, 39, 72).

✔ *Centering.* **Centering** *refers to separating or differentiating from others so that there is an inner reference or thought of stability, calm, and self-awareness; a sense of self-relatedness, a place of quietude within self where one can feel integrated, unified, and focused.* As a result, you can communicate more openly and listen to self and others more effectively (62).

Centering reduces fatigue, stress, depression, or anger when working with a client/patient. Centering takes little time once the idea is mastered and can be helpful to use prior to any anxiety-provoking situation in the hospital, at home, in social situations, or at work. Centering can also be taught to people to help them gain self-control. Centering can be achieved while standing or sitting, but beginning efforts produce the best results in a sitting position. The method is as follows:

1. Sit in a comfortable chair with feet flat on the floor and hands resting quietly in your lap; close your eyes.
2. Check out your body for tension spots and relax these areas as you exhale.
3. Inhale easily, filling your body with relaxation.
4. Exhale, moving your breathing to your center, about the level of your navel.
5. Continue breathing in this matter until you feel calm, integrated, unified, and focused.
6. (Optional) Picture the body surrounded by a protective shield that allows positive energy in, but keeps negative energy out. The shield may be conceived as a color, light source, or spiritual sense (17).

✔ *Assertive Communication/Behavior.* **Assertiveness** *means to be able to express personal thoughts, feelings, and desires, defining and making known personal rights that are reasonable, while being respectful to the other person and of his/her rights.* Expression of honest feelings, being willing to act on rational thoughts and controlled feelings to achieve a goal, and taking responsibility for consequences are a part of assertive communication and behavior. Stating "I . . ." messages to express feelings and ideas rather than "You make me feel . . ." or "You should . . ." will increase self-confidence, enhance relationships with others, reduce anxiety and stress, and control fear and anger (17).

Assertive communication comes with practice with another, in a group, in front of a mirror, and/or using a tape recorder. Assertiveness includes paying attention to facial expression, voice tone, posture, use of gestures, congruity between words and appearance, in addition to the way statements are phrased.

✔ Various techniques are useful in assertive communication and behavior. You can utilize these in your personal and professional life as well as teach them to clients/patients. A summary of several techniques follows:

1. *Acknowledgment:* When you are criticized, you acknowledge the comment of the other, the feeling implied, and whatever of the criticism is applicable to you. Avoid giving excuses or apologies.

   "Yes, I was late to work this morning. I punched in the time clock 10 minutes after 7:00, so I was 10 minutes late."

   "Yes, I overlooked carrying out the garbage last night, and I can appreciate your sense of frustration."

2. *Clouding:* When you are given a nonconstructive, manipulative criticism that you disagree with, you can stand your ground, implying that there could be other reasons for your action while continuing to listen and communicate. You agree to the part of the criticism that is true without agreeing to any specific action plan.

   a. *Agreeing in Part:*

   Parent: "You always have an excuse to get out of work around home."
   Teen: "I do have a lot of school and church group responsibilities."
   Parent: "You don't seem to care anything about your family."
   Teen: You're right. I guess it does seem that way."

   b. *Agreeing in Probability:*

   Parent: "You're putting on a lot of weight."
   Teen: I may have gained a few extra pounds."
   Parent: "You'd better go on a diet."
   Teen: "Perhaps it is time for starting a diet."

   c. *Agreeing in Principle:*

   Parent: "If you don't study more, you're not going to pass this semester."
   Teen: "You're right. If I don't study, I will fail."

3. Probing: This response can determine whether criticism is constructive or manipulative and clarifies unclear comments. First you isolate the part of the criticism that is most bothersome to the other and then ask what specifically is bothersome about the behavior.

Assertive Probing:

Supervisor: "Your work is not satisfactory."
Nurse: "What about my work bothers you?"
Supervisor: "Everyone else works overtime when necessary; you always leave on time."
Nurse: "What is it about my leaving on time that bothers you?"
Supervisor: "It's not right that you work only by the clock when the rest of us work overtime. None of us like to work overtime, but the work has to be done."
Nurse: "What bothers you about me working by the clock?"
Supervisor: "When you leave, someone else has to finish your work. The rule here is that no one leaves until the shift's work is done."

4. *Broken Record:* This technique can be used when another is not listening to you, when it is necessary to clarify limits about what should be done, or when explanation would provide the other with an opportunity to continue a pointless discussion. The steps are:
   a. Give a short, specific statement about what is desired, without giving excuses.
   b. Using body language that shows you are calm and in control of your feelings, stand or sit erect, maintain eye contact, keep hands and arms quiet at the side.
   c. Calmly and firmly repeat the chosen statement as many times as necessary until the other person realizes there is no negotiation possible. Ignore the other's excuses, ramblings, curses, or false accusations.
   Situation: Driver A pulls out of a parking place, very fast, with a too sharp turn, managing to pull lose the back bumper of the car in the next parking place (Driver B) which is parked right on the line. Driver A pulls forward into the parking place, gets out of the car, and proceeds toward Driver B. Driver B stays in the car. Driver A stands by the car door, yelling how stupid Driver B is to park on the line.

Driver B: Rolling down the window slightly, "Yes, you are right, I am parked on the line."
Driver A: Continues to accuse Driver B, yelling invectives.
Driver B: Maintains eye contact, every 1 minute rolls down the window slightly and says, "When you are ready, I'll talk about what can be done about the bumper." This is repeated for about 10 minutes.
Driver A: Begins to calm down, finally smiles, and says, "OK, what do you want."
Driver B: "I want you to pay for repair of my ripped bumper."
Driver A: "OK." Proceeds to give telephone number, with an adequate down payment (in cash) toward bumper repair, and promise to pay more if cost is greater. "I just don't want my insurance company to get hold of this. Call if it costs more."

5. *Content to Process Shift:* When focus of conversation drifts from the original topic, conversation can be purposefully shifted from the subject (content) being discussed to the feelings between the two speakers (process). The statement should be made with a calm voice and demeanor, defusing anger that has arisen. Attack is avoided.

"We're off the subject, let's get back to what we agreed to discuss."
"I'm feeling uncomfortable about the drift of our conversation, and I notice we both appear tense."
"We seem to be getting into a battle. I sense we are both talking about the same thing, but are coming from a different perspective."

6. *Momentary Delay:* When a situation is compelling or another gives a command or implies an answer right away, it is important not to be swayed by the emotion of the moment. After a deep breath and a moment of delay, the comment could be:

"I'll need more information before I can act." "There may be something to what you say, I need a few minutes to think about this."
"I can understand your feeling. I need a minute to sort out what you are saying."

7. *Time Out:* If the conversation is important, but has reached an impasse because of angry feelings or bias, conversation can be delayed and continued later by setting a near-future time to continue talking, when both parties are more calm.

"We've been talking about this for quite a while, and I don't think we're getting anywhere. I'd like to sleep on it and talk more with you about it tomorrow morning. Let's meet to talk at 8:30 AM."
(Designate a mutually neutral place if possible.)

8. *Joining and Circling the Attacker:* This technique is derived from the martial art of Aiki, in which the attacked person accepts and turns with the attack, then letting the attacker pass on. The focus of the

intervention is to resolve conflict, restore harmony, and problem solve. There are four alternative responses:

a. *Do nothing.* A conscious choice, not a response of fear, when (1) the attack makes no sense, (2) the attacked does not want to dignify the attack by reacting, and (3) more information is needed to determine the reason for the attack.

b. *Use Humor/Deflection:* Give an absurd reason or a surprise line as a reason for not accomplishing something that should have been done.

c. *Joining the Attacker:* The attack is not taken personally and the attacker agrees, then moves to resolve the problem.

> "I don't blame you for feeling the way you do."
> "My job is to work with you. If you think we can work together, I want to hear your complaints."

d. *Parley:* This technique is useful if you have been engaged in a no-win situation; the other person has defined the encounter as a competition or contest.

Guided Imagery

Guided imagery *can be defined as focused attention on an inner, mental picture or a statement of belief of what the individual wants to accomplish by being open to and responding to the language of the unconscious or the deeper body levels.* There are other terms used for imagery, such as imagination, visualization, autosuggestion, mental programming, or self-hypnosis. The term imagination or visualization is not totally descriptive of guided imagery. The term self-hypnosis is frightening to some. Thus, the term that is used in the literature and is effective with clients/patients is guided imagery or imagery, or use of imaging.

Imagery is not new. Some people say, without diminishing God the creator, that the first record of what could be considered a mental image producing results is written in Genesis with the creation. God said, "Light, be," and there was light. There are a number of accounts in the Old and New Testaments of the Bible of how people accomplished what was mentally visualized. For example, records of the fall of the walls of Jericho and the miracles of Jesus convey the power of the mental image. Whenever faith is involved, for example, in the healings of today, the person visualizes what is to be before it comes.

Guided imagery is not the same as a trance, play acting, use of fantasy or denial, the raising of false hope, or the claim to working of miracles. Rather, it is the purposeful use of a technique that requires time and effort to accomplish a purpose.

Physiological Mechanisms Involved in Imagery. Much is still unknown about the private physiological mechanisms that occur during private processes that allow for various results to be manifested.

Imagery is a covert process whose characteristics, while observed, must be inferred. Imaging activity appears to be a complex blend of receptive–perceptual processes and efferent activity. Imagery can be conditioned under certain circumstances; it can show properties of skill learning; it is responsive to motivation; and it has properties of passive receptivity similar to that of reverie, dreams, and hypnosis (106, 107, 110).

Muscle activity changes occur in response to the content of the image. For example, images of lifting an object were associated with increased activity in the arm muscles that would be involved in the actual movement, although the magnitude of the muscular changes are less during imagery than they would be during the overt movement (106, 107, 110). Imagery can reduce muscular tension, as measured by electromyographic recording from the frontalis muscles on the forehead.

Images of moving objects are associated with greater oculomotor activity than images of stationary objects. Skin conduction responses during vividly imagined stressful scenes are more frequent, of greater magnitude, and slower to habituate than are skin conduction responses of nonvivid imagers. Different levels of activity of facial muscles have been measured during imagery of different emotional states, representational of changes that actually occur with different emotional states in real life (106, 107, 110).

Studies employing physiological measures of imagery have used a wide range of measures. These are heart rate, respiration, electroencephalogram (EEG), alpha activity, skin temperature, electromyograph (EMG) activity in a number of different muscle groups, diastolic and systolic blood pressure, salivation, eye movements and pupillary responses, vasomotor responses, and measures of electrodermal activity such as the galvanic skin response (GSR), skin conductance, and skin resistance. Furthermore, significant effects have been reported, at least sometimes, for each measure that has been used. In general, though, it appears that heart rate may be the most sensitive measure in that changes in heart rate associated with imagery have been the most consistently reported. Studies also show an increase in thymosin and white blood count with imagery (107, 110).

Images, especially those without external representation, are apparently processed by the right hemisphere, which has a passive–receptive quality to the type of function it sustains. Right brain hemisphere function is concerned with intuition, visual and spatial events, imagination, and emotion. Receptive, representational, and spatial imagery is linked to right hemisphere functioning. The right hemisphere mediates analogical thinking, perceives the whole experience or "gestalt." In contrast, the left brain is logical and reasoning; it breaks down experience into sequential units, compartmentalizes information and interprets, and deals with verbal images. The right brain is stimulated by and receptive to imagery, and in turn promotes release of chemicals and enzymes in the body that result in relaxation, healing, and well-being. Positive feelings release endorphins, which promote well-being and healing. Brain wave changes occur when the person is in a relaxed state (106, 107, 110). When these physiological changes are facilitated regularly and over time, changes occur in body tissues, individual feelings and reactions, cognition, and life patterns.

The Technique of Guided Imagery. First, a rapport and a climate of trust must be established between the client or patient and you, the nurse or therapist. After initial assessment and exploration of the problem and often after trying other techniques, guided imagery may be proposed to the client/patient as another way to promote healing or change. An explanation is given of what is involved: (1) sitting in a quiet, comfortable environment without distractions; (2) beginning with a technique to obtain total body relaxation; (3) envisioning a peaceful, soothing scene that can maintain relaxation and a positive attitude; (4) focusing attention on what is desired or to be accomplished; (5) telling the therapist what thoughts or feelings come to mind, answering questions, describing the healing; and (6) repeating the process regularly three or four times a day for 15 or 20 minutes. In that way the body learns to respond to the mind.

✔ The nature of the instructions presented to the client/patient appears to have an important impact upon the response. Instructions must be clear, suggestive, and encouraging. Instructions that emphasize involvement of the person in the experience and the goals to be obtained facilitate the process. Imagery works best when the person is motivated to try the technique, when there is confidence in the nurse or therapist, and when there is expectation of success. Some people need more time to become relaxed and to engage in the imagery process. The person should feel it is acceptable if he/she is unable initially to use imagery. However, if you suggest success, the person is likely to be able to image. Use fun imagery exercises initially to help the person realize that he/she can engage in imagery. Then if the person feels that he/she wants to try imagery further as a method, continue with more introduction to and use of the technique.

✔ As the person purposefully sets aside negative or sick images, and images the positive, the healthy, the desired results while in a relaxed state, he/she is told that changes within the body and mind have been activated, which will be seen externally.

✔ It may take some time for the person to gain an image of the desired goal. During that time, have the person talk about the problem as imaged (e.g., physical, emotional, interpersonal, job), the feelings and thoughts that come spontaneously, and then to allow the mind (the deep unconscious) to tell him/her what it would take to correct, heal, or overcome the problem—and thus to reach the goal. It may take a number of sessions to get to this point. At times you may suggest a way for the person to image relief from a symptom.

✔ Before the initial session is ended, emphasize that this technique is totally under the control of the person and therefore can be used in the home or office at will. Encourage regular daily use of imaging, following the same routine each time. The imaging can be combined with prayer, devotional reading, or meditation. This method frees the person to make choices, to accomplish goals, to have a sense of mastery. The person is not under the control of the therapist. One time of full explanation and going through the method with the client/patient may be enough to have the person successfully continue this on his/her own. Or it may take several times. Thus the method may be useful if you have only one contact with the person. Or this method may be repeated in following sessions with the person, especially if there is a deep-seated or long-term problem.

✔ In guided imagery, use of the inner advisor, following relaxation and gaining a comfortable mental peace, can be helpful. It is a way of gaining access to the feelings, anxiety, guilt, and intuitions in the right hemisphere of the brain or the unconscious. The inner advisor is an imaginary creature drawn from the person's subconscious mind, which can be questioned about physical and emotional feelings, and through which a dialogue can be continued which can resolve conflicts and aid decision making. The inner advisor may be expressed as the Holy Spirit or a religious figure; it may be a parent or spouse (living or dead), or it may be a friend, relative, or work colleague. Some people have a pet or favorite animal, such as a squirrel, dog, cat, or pony (41).

✔ Guided imagery can be used alone or with other therapies, whether these therapies involve use of medication, surgery, biofeedback, or individual counseling. Tapes, records, cassettes, discs, and posters and board games that can be used to create a background or an environment for relaxation, meditation, imagery, or just a peaceful mood can be obtained from Music Design, 207 E. Buffalo Street, Milwaukee,

TABLE 17-5. Using Imagery to Promote Health and Healing

SYMPTOM/DISORDER	UNIVERSAL IMAGE	SPECIFIC IMAGE
Sore Throat	Image of cool air or moisture flowing over throat	Image of normally pink throat color, that normal color is overtaking red, inflamed area.
Fever	Image of coolness	Image of cool breeze, waterfall, fountain around self, with overall environment a comfortable temperature; self standing erect and feeling strong, invigorated, comfortable.
Upper Chest Congestion Asthmatic Attack	Image of cool throat and warm chest	Image of cool, normally pink throat and respiratory tree; lung sacs and bronchi are expanding; air flow (seen as arrows, bubbles, streams of clouds) moves in and out. Hold image while breathing in relaxed manner.
Chronic Sinus Problem	Imagine tubes opening and draining	Image sinus compartment as a sink, that you pulled the plug, and that draining is occurring. If persistent congestion, picture self like a plunger at top of sinus compartment, pushing down the drainage through open drain pipe.
Headache	Image hole in head in area of headache, on exhalation, pain goes through hole as a color	Image pain shooting out of top of head, like a volcano, with each exhalation, and a color that denotes calmness setting in and taking over the brain and head area.
Itch or Pain	Image of coolness to area	Image ice cube to the area, as ice melts, itch or pain melts away. Depending on location, may picture pain or itch as sliding off the body area.
Low Back Pain	Image of heavy spine	Image pain dropping down to the floor and walking away from it; image self as erect, strong, active as pain is dropping away.
Tight, Tense Muscle Area	Imagine muscles in area getting wider and longer, unknotting	Image that with deep, slow inhalation, breath is directed to the muscle area, that breath soaks up the tension, and tension is removed with exhalation. Picture muscle stretching and smoothing out. Picture self in a calm, relaxing environment, such as being surrounded by flower beds, the ocean, a lake, and meadow, and that the body is stretched out, a relaxed, happy mood.
Fatigue	Image energy flow entering the body area	Image self as light in weight. Image self surrounded by warmth, color, and music that represents happiness, energy, joy. Picture self as full of joy and dancing, or skipping lightly in a meadow, lane, by the seashore.
Stiff, Painful Joint; Arthritis	Image of warmth	Image of self in warm sunlight at a relaxing place (seashore, field of grass or flowers) and moving freely. Image of rising sun with warm rays aimed at joint or total body. Picture joint as normal in size. Picture self as light, moving at desired pace.
Diarrhea, Colitis	Image of coolness, control	Image of intestine as a tube that is set, firm, not moving and smooth, without bumps, rough areas, irritation. Picture self at activities and being in control. Image intestine as a pipe with plug firmly in place at lower end.
Infection, Cancer	Image white cells carrying off abnormal cells	Image white cells surrounding infectious area or cancer growth, eating up the abnormal area. Image area of infection or growth becoming smaller and smaller. Image antibiotic, chemotherapy, or radiation as an arrow piercing infectious or cancer area, and causing abnormal cells to fall apart and be excreted by body. Image medication like Pac-man, gobbling up the abnormal cells.
Anger, Resentment	Image of peace or harmony	Image feeling as a ball of color, place it in front of you, kick it away. Picture self in control and solving the problem that is creating anger (see Table 17–6). Picture self in an area that was the happiest or most pleasant or most relaxing place you were ever in (vacation area, favorite childhood spot, most comfortable chair in your home, lovely garden area); soak up the calm and beauty and feel anger drain away. Image calming music, see yourself relaxed, light, dancing.

Wisconsin 53202. The catalogue is available on request, and features many artists, and a variety of selections in type of music and instrumentation. Other such catalogues are also available.

Clinical Application of Imagery. If the person believes and participates regularly in the process of guided imagery, there would be a point at which there may be no need for other relaxation therapies.

✔ Guided imagery can be used to promote emotional health by (1) building self-awareness; (2) helping the person to face issues, and facilitating mood change; (3) clarifying the meaning of the situation; (4) assisting in dyadic communication and expression of feelings; (5) promoting a sense of strength and self-control, including overcoming phobias; (6) overcoming negative attitudes about self; and (7) increasing coping resources by releasing unconscious energies (70, 83).

✔ Research increasingly shows that the body responds to our mental picture of it. The body may develop a full-blown infection, remain ill or less functional, or return to a healthy or normally functioning state, depending on the mental image we hold, what we continue to say about the body, to self or others. Imagery can be used to enhance healing either by using a general image or by picturing what the impaired/diseased area would look like if it were normal. Table 17–5 describes universal and specific images that can be used for various conditions after the person becomes relaxed. These are only suggestions. Each person will be able to produce the image that is uniquely applicable and possible to achieve. Both universal and specific images can be held by the person in relation to a body party. Guided imagery can be used to promote physical health by:

1. Reducing the intensity of the stress response.
2. Assisting in control of various bodily symptoms.
3. Reducing and controlling pain symptoms.
4. Promoting weight loss in the obese person.
5. Helping the person to control or stop habits of smoking, alcohol or drug abuse.
6. Promoting healing after surgery or from cancer or various chronic conditions.
7. Increasing mobility and reducing tension, such as in arthritic conditions (70, 83, 101, 106, 107, 109, 110, 114).

✔ Guided imagery can be used to help the person gain cognitive control—to make choices, to make decisions, to change life pattern and behavior, to respond to a situation by imaging and portraying a role, to reduce anxiety and fear, and to reduce depression. Table 17–6 outlines how imagery can be used to cope with or find solutions to a problem. Allow suffi-

TABLE 17–6. Using Imagery to Solve Problems

- Find a quiet place and sit in a relaxed position; close the eyes.
- Clearly and succinctly define the problem, picture telling the problem to a friend.
- Mentally ask, "Am I ready to solve this problem?" If yes is the inner answer, proceed.
- Place the clearly defined problem in a frame or a box.
- Visualize the situation you desire and place it in a frame or box.
- Visualize the steps that will be necessary to achieve the solution. Differentiate each step; continue to think until each step is clearly pictured.
- Any barriers that come to mind in relation to any step of the solution can be looked at and then moved from the pathway to be cast off into space, or to be placed in a locked box. Do this for each barrier that presents itself. Take a deep breath to relax as you do this, so that you feel fully in control of handling barriers.
- Mentally review each step that moves to a solution and picture yourself with the final desired solution. Hold the image.
- Slowly open the eyes.
- In the days or weeks that follow, repeat this process as necessary, with yourself moving toward the goal or solution. See yourself with the solution or goal at hand, in the frame or box. If certain intermediary steps have already been finished, omit them from the mental picture.

Note: Imagery can also be used quickly for an immediate situation with which you must cope or which must be mastered. The preceding method would be done in one sitting.

cient time, free of distractions, to carry out the process (70, 83, 101, 107, 109, 110).

✔ When you have experienced guided imagery and used it with yourself and others, under supervision of someone who knows how to use the technique, and when you believe in the results, you will see results.

✔ You may wish to ask the client/patient to verbalize the process by which healing was enhanced or may allow the person to complete the process without verbalizing unless he/she wishes to. The verbalization does not aid in the process for the client/patient, but can give clues about his/her ability to visualize and further issues with which you can be of assistance.

✔ A major asset of imagery as a nursing intervention is that the person or group member need not expose situations that may be anxiety provoking or embarrassing, or discuss the problem. Additionally, imagery interventions allow you to work with clients/patients who are unable or unwilling to establish an open, working relationship. Imagery works best in nursing situations when the nurse gives the broadest directions, allowing the person to develop his/her own images.

Time Management

✓ Symptoms of inappropriate time management include: chronic rushing, fatigue, listlessness with many slack hours of nonproductive activity, vacillation between unpleasant alternatives, missing of deadlines, insufficient time for rest or personal relationships, and the sense of being overwhelmed by demands and details (24).

✓ Most methods of time management include these steps:

1. Keeping a detailed log of each activity and time spent on each for 5 days.
2. Establish priorities about what is to be accomplished.
3. Eliminate low priority tasks.
4. Write specific goals for 1 month and 1 year.
5. Learn to make and follow through with decisions.

Effective time management has been found effective in minimizing anxiety and job fatigue. To avoid being overwhelmed by goals, priorities, and decisions, work on one at a time (17, 24).

✓ Other rules also help for making time:

1. Learn to say "no"; remind yourself that this is your life and your time to spend as best befits you. Only when your boss asks should you spend time on bottom priority items.
2. Build time into your schedule for unscheduled events, interruptions, and unforeseen occurrences.
3. Set aside several time periods during the day for structured relaxation; being relaxed will allow you to use the time you have more efficiently.
4. Keep a list of tasks that can be done in a few minutes any time you are waiting or are between other tasks.
5. Learn to do two things at once; plan dinner while driving home or organize an important letter or list while waiting in line at the bank.
6. Delegate low priority tasks to others, if possible.
7. Get up 15 to 30 minutes earlier every day than in the past to have a time for meditation or a hobby.
8. Allow no more than 1 hour of television watching for yourself daily. Use it as a reward for accomplishing high-priority items (17, 24).

✓ Part of time management is the ability to make decisions. Procrastination is the great time robber. Procrastination can often be overcome by:

1. Recognizing the unpleasantness of doing a task versus the unpleasantness of putting it off; analyze the cost and risks of delay.
2. Examine the payoffs you receive by procrastinating, e.g., you will not have to do the task; you will not have to face the possibility of failure; you can be taken care of by others; you can gain attention. Examine payoffs for finishing the task. Build a special reward for completing an unpleasant task.
3. Exaggerate whatever you are doing to put off the decision. Keep it up until you are bored and making the decision seems more attractive than procrastination.
4. Take responsibility for your delaying tactics by writing down how long each delay took. Write down how long it took to actually complete the task. Compare.
5. When making unimportant decisions, use a formula to choose: choose south or east over north or west; pick left over right or smooth over rough; pick the easiest, shortest, or closest; pick the one that comes first alphabetically. Then decide a formula for making major decisions.
6. Take small steps toward a major decision. List each step; cross it off the list as it is accomplished.
7. Avoid beginning a new task until you have completed a predecided segment of the current one; allow yourself to fully experience the reward of finishing something (17, 24).

✓ In summary, based on your assessments and related nursing diagnoses, such as those listed in Table 17–7, you can practice some of the following ways to adapt to stress as well as teach these methods to others:

1. Identify stressful aspects of your lifestyle to reduce frequency of the stress response or to avoid stressors when possible.
2. Analyze what is making you tense or anxious and try to lessen the stressfulness of the situation.
3. Develop spiritual and philosophical resources by talking to others who are wiser than you and by using literature and prayer.
4. Keep something as the central core of your life and being, as your shelter or haven—for example, a religious, philosophical, moral, or ethical belief; a special place in your home to relax; a specific time for doing certain pleasurable activities; or a person who is a confidant and friend.
5. Try to slow your hectic pace. Do one thing at a time.
6. Use temporary avoidance of identified stressors at times for regaining strength, energy, and ideas about fun in order to cope.
7. Assume a more passive attitude toward irritating or frustrating events. Consciously work to remain calm or avoid the problem until you are in a better emotional condition to cope with it.
8. Determine ways to enjoy selected stressors as a

challenge by adjusting personal philosophy or behavior patterns.
9. Accept the love and support from others, their encouragement and suggestions: be willing to receive help.
10. Set aside time for relaxation each day. You may want to try relaxation techniques, such as transcendental meditation, yoga, biofeedback, or the relaxation response, or seek sources of joy and humor.
11. Talk about your feelings with friends, family, or a counselor to gain objectivity about the problem, validate ideas and possible solutions, and affirm what you need and want to do.
12. Accept things you cannot change. Do not expect too much from others. Accept your own normal irritation, anger, or crying.
13. Try to correct aspects of your life that cause stress or worry or change a role that does not suit you.
14. Do not push yourself beyond your limits of achievement or expect too much of yourself. Be satisfied with less while you do your best.
15. Use physical exercise and recreation to work off the energy of anxiety and to relieve tension. Find a fulfilling hobby or try doing something helpful for someone. Books and audiotapes are available describing relaxation techniques and recreational activities or hobbies.
16. Use visualization, imagery, or faith to affirm the answer to the problem until the solution is reached.
17. Use conscious cognitive coping responses, such as those described in this chapter.
18. Seek psychotherapy if stress keeps you from functioning at your full capacity.
19. Carry out health promotion measures described in each Chapter.
20. Realize that stressors are inevitable and can be handled and that some are necessary for survival, learning, development, and self-actualization.

Lafferty lists a number of suggestions that will contribute to physical, intellectual, spiritual, emotional, and social health and to a healthy lifestyle (65). In addition to the measures already listed, Lafferty suggests the following measures (65):

1. Intellectual health is stimulated by (a) decreasing the amount of time spent in watching television, except for education or scientific programs, (b) developing a daily routine for study, reading, or adding a vocabulary word, and (c) attending special lectures and programs when available.
2. Spiritual health is promoted through (a) daily meditation, prayer, and devotional reading, (b) discuss-

TABLE 17–7. Selected Nursing Diagnoses Related to Stress Management[a]

PATTERN 1: EXCHANGING
Altered Nutrition: Less than body requirements
Altered Nutrition: Potential for more than body requirements

PATTERN 2: COMMUNICATING
Impaired Verbal Communication

PATTERN 3: RELATING
Impaired Social Interaction
Social Isolation
Potential Altered Parenting
Altered Family Processes
Altered Sexuality Patterns

PATTERN 4: VALUING
Spiritual Distress

PATTERN 5: CHOOSING
Ineffective Individual Coping
Impaired Adjustment
Defensive Coping
Ineffective Denial
Family Coping: Potential for Growth
Decisional Conflict
Health Seeking Behaviors

PATTERN 6: MOVING
Activity Intolerance
Fatigue
Potential Activity Disturbance
Sleep Pattern Disturbance
Diversional Activity Deficit
Impaired Home Maintenance Management
Altered Health Maintenance

PATTERN 7: PERCEIVING
Body Image Disturbance
Self Esteem Disturbance
Sensory/Perceptual Alterations
Hopelessness
Powerlessness

PATTERN 8: KNOWING
Knowledge Deficit
Altered Thought Processes
Pain
Chronic Pain
Dysfunctional Grieving
Post-Trauma Response
Anxiety
Fear

[a]Other NANDA diagnoses may be applicable to the individual.
Source: NANDA Approved Nursing Diagnostic Categories, *Nursing Diagnosis Newsletter*, 15, no. 1 (1988), 1–3.

ing spiritual or religious topics with another person, (c) identifying the weakest personal characteristic in order to work on overcoming it, and (d) reaffirming personal values and strong personal characteristics as a guide to life and behavior.
3. Emotional health is enhanced by (a) recognizing and constructively expressing positive and unhappy or angry feelings, (b) identifying personal strengths and limits and working to overcome limits, (c) dealing appropriately with feelings toward the opposite sex, and (d) seeking professional help with serious adjustment problems or crises.
4. Social health is promoted by (a) showing affection rather than directing criticism to friends and family, (b) working to overcome prejudices or fears of people of another race, the opposite sex, or persons in authority, (c) fulfilling responsibilities to others, and (d) communicating verbally and nonverbally in a way that is honest and clear.

Sites for Health Promotion Nursing

Wellness Programs and Sites

Traditionally the main health concern for employees in the workplace was that of safety and accident prevention. A yearly physical examination was also included in many industries.

Today industries and some hospitals and other work settings are adding programs for their employees that generally include emphasis in four areas: stress reduction, exercise, smoking cessation, and nutritional and weight guidance, particularly for obesity and sodium and cholesterol reduction. Some industries have also established Employee Assistance Programs to help the chemically-dependent employee reduce alcohol or drug intake and remain a safe, dependable worker. Some settings offer day care for workers with young children—to reduce the worker's stress related to child care. Others have stress management programs for their employees as well as their clients/patients. Facilities may boast nearly 24-hour availability of a fully equipped exercise room, gymnasium, handball court, and whirlpool baths, or a rough running track that has been measured out around a furniture factory in rural North Carolina. In some cities the employer uses existing exercise facilities in various clubs or organizations, such as the local chapter of the American Heart Association for screening or teaching programs.

A variety of services can be implemented in housing projects, in nutrition sites or in other sites by a Visiting Nurses Association in order to keep the well-elderly healthy. These services could include a bi-weekly coffee hour to bring free counseling, nutrition and health education, health assessment, referrals, home visits after hospital discharge, and assistance with drug and diet prescriptions. Flexible times for services and easy accessibility would encourage the seniors to come to the nurse-operated health maintenance clinics. That entry into the health-care system is often the way to encourage the senior to obtain necessary medical care as well as to continue health promotion practices.

✔ Various authors propose the following ways to promote and maintain high-level wellness in a community:

1. Improvement of family living and community life conditions.
2. Education to assist the person/family in applying healthful behavior.
3. Education to assist the person/family to apply principles of human relations.
4. Development of high level wellness among individuals in leadership positions, so that they can carry out their roles responsibly and effectively.
5. Maintenance of open information channels and free access to information for intelligent decision making in the community and family.
6. Enhancement of opportunities for creative expression.
7. Promotion of caring relationships and concern for others' welfare.
8. Education about concepts of maturity and its achievement.
9. Extension of the life span, with the mature person sharing potentials for the benefit of society (17, 18, 84).

✔ Health protection or preventive measures in the environment can be used by governmental and other agencies, industries, and communities, to protect people from harm of disease, including implementation of:

1. Toxic agent control.
2. Occupational safety and health measures.
3. Accident prevention and injury control.
4. Water fluoridation and dental health.
5. Surveillance and control of infectious disease.
6. Mass screening programs (84).

The 75th Session of the World Health Organization (WHO) Executive Board, meeting in Geneva in 1985, emphasized the important role which the nursing profession can and must play in the "Health for All" movement. The organization recommended reorientation and training of nurse educators, managers, and nursing leaders in primary health care. Utilizing nursing in the "Health for All" strategy requires a commitment to change on the part of the nursing profession; nurse leaders could serve as activists, stimulating change, and pushing for action. The changing role of nurses in the "Health for All" strategy demands a sound grasp of nursing as well as ability to relate with other health personnel and the community in need of health care. The Director-General of WHO, Dr. Halfdan T. Mahler, said it was evident that the nursing profession was infinitely more ready for change than other professional groups. He pointed out that to practice primary health care one needed love for one's fellow travellers and he considered that nurses had great potential for that kind of love. He stated that it was time that nurses were brought in much more than hitherto as leaders and managers of the primary health care "Health for All" team (132).

New Horizons in Health Promotion: The Nurse Entrepreneur

The nurse entrepreneur spirit is changing the future of health care. Entrepreneurial opportunities are available for those with foresight and a desire to apply nursing skills in a different fashion.

One definition of a **nurse entrepreneur** is someone who has a big enough ego to think that he/she could do anything and a small enough ego to do anything to accomplish that goal, including being financially dependent on parents, spouse, or others.

The health care field does not encourage entrepreneurial behavior, but there are numerous agencies available to assist those with innovative ideas. The Small Business Administration has a packet of information available by mail that will help one to get started. Some community colleges offer courses ranging from 1 day to several weeks. These courses cover various aspects of starting a business. Internal Revenue Service offers a no charge 1-day work-shop quarterly that assists with various government reports such as state, federal tax, and employment security requirements.

In order to become an entrepreneur, one must be motivated by achievement rather than power or affiliation. Some characteristics of an entrepreneur are persistence, optimism, resourcefulness, self-confidence, and not being afraid to follow personal convictions.

There are several special qualities that are essential: positive self-expectancy, self-direction, self-image, self-awareness, self-projection, self-perception, self-control, self-esteem, and self-discipline. An entrepreneur is not one who depends on other sources for any of the above.

Nurses have skills that are applicable to business. Problem-solving skills are taught and nurtured in nursing. Nurses have learned to delegate responsibilities and make excellent use of their time. They know how to motivate, teach, and gain confidence.

In order to do well in business, one must become a part of the business community. Join the local Chamber of Commerce and women's business organizations. Take personal responsibility when things do not work well. Let people know you care. Test your ideas and develop marketing skills. Be alert for business opportunities and learn how to "operate on a shoestring." Learn how to compute cash flow and conduct budget analysis. It is essential to learn how to charge enough, but not too much, for your services or product. You must be convinced that you are the best in your field. Be alert for opportunities. Timing is essential. An entrepreneur is not necessarily a risk taker since he/she is always analyzing the situation and minimizing risks.

Among the factors causing a need for nurse entrepreneurs is the change in the public attitudes and values and growing emphasis on prevention. The present trend of reducing hospital use and curtailment of Medicare and Medicaid are presenting a need for more cost-effective health-care providers. Nurses have been geared to total health care, the best possible care and high quality care regardless of cost. We must now learn how to encompass these ideas with increased productivity and more efficiency and define nursing care as a product.

Nurse entrepreneurs are doing well in several areas. One nurse practitioner in North Carolina has a business providing health care for industries. She employs several part-time RNs, a part-time physician, and a part-time health educator. Another RN is currently attending nurse practitioner school and plans to join the firm. The firm provides whatever is needed in health care from screenings to primary health care and care of chronic problems with a great emphasis on wellness and preventive programs. Another nurse has a business in southern California providing acute hemodialysis service. Yet another nurse started a business in Florida providing a day-care center for children with medical problems.

Due to change and uncertainty, a whole new set of career opportunities are available. The future belongs to those who are able to respond to new demands and who have the courage to follow their convictions.

References

1. Alexy, Betty, Goal Setting and Health Risk Reduction, *Nursing Research*, 34, no. 5 (1985), 283–288.
2. Barrett, Gloria J., Are You A Winner? *Nursing Life*, 7, no. 2 (1987), 23.
3. Bastitella, R., Factors Associated With Delay in the

Initiation of Physician's Care Among Late Adulthood Persons, *American Journal of Public Health,* 61 (1971), 1348.
4. Bates, Barbara, *A Guide to Physical Examination* (3rd ed.). Philadelphia: J. B. Lippincott, 1983.
5. Becker, M. (ed.), *The Health Belief Model and Personal Health Behavior.* Thorofare, N.J.: Charles B. Slack, 1974.
6. Becker, M. et al., Selected Psychosocial Models and Correlates of Individual Health-Related Behaviors, *Medical Care,* 15 (1977), 27–46.
7. Bigham, Gloria, To Communicate with Negro Patients, *American Journal of Nursing,* 64, no. 9 (1964), 113–115.
8. Bell, J. A., The Sale of Microcomputers in Patient Education, *Computer Nursing,* 4, no. 6 (1986), 255–258.
9. Box, Denise, Putting on the Pressure, *Nursing Mirror,* 60, no. 21 (May 22, 1985), 28–29.
10. Briley, Michael, Staying Well: Ten Commandments of Fitness, *Modern Maturity* (February–March 1986), 27–28.
11. Brounson, Ross, Jean Chang, and James Davis, Occupation, Smoking, and Alcohol in Epidemiology of Bladder Cancer, *American Journal of Public Health,* 77, no. 10 (1987), 1298–1300.
12. Brown, R., D. Ramirez, and J. Taub, The Prescription of Exercise for Depression, *Physician Sports Medicine,* 6 (1978), 34–49.
13. Brownell, K., and A. Stunkard, Physical Activity in The Development and Control of Obesity. In A. Stunkard (ed.), *Obesity.* Philadelphia: W.B. Saunders, 1980.
14. Bush, George S., Talking Back to Your Doctor, *Better Homes and Gardens,* (August, 1986), 50–52.
15. ——, Communication Tips: Communicating with Doctors, Lawyers, and Other Experts, *Life Styles* (Spring, 1987), 1.
16. Champion, V., Instrument Development for Health Belief Model Constructs, *Advances in Nursing Science,* 6, no. 3 (1984), 73–85.
17. Clark, Carolyn, *Wellness Nursing: Concepts, Theory, Research, and Practice.* New York: Springer, 1986.
18. Clemen-Stone, Susan, Diane Eigsti, and Sandra McGuire, *Comprehensive Family and Community Health Nursing* (2nd ed.). New York: McGraw-Hill, 1987.
19. Colt, C., S. Wardlow, and A. Frantz, The Effect of Running on Plasma Endorphins, *Life Science,* 28 (1981), 1637–1640.
20. Cook, G. B., A Computer Program for Teaching and Auditing Patients' Knowledge of Diabetes, *Diabetes Education,* 13, no. 3 (1987), 306–308.
21. Cox, Charyl, The Health Self-Determinism Index, *Nursing Research,* 34, no. 3 (1985), 177–183.
22. Davies, Thomas, Is This Test Really Necessary?, *Modern Maturity* (February–March, 1987), 77–82.
23. Davis, B., Health Education, *Nursing Administration Quarterly,* 11, no. 3 (1987), 49.
24. Davis, M., M. McKay, and E. Eshelman, *The Relaxation and Stress Reduction Workbook* (2nd ed.). Oakland, CA: New Harbinger, 1982.
25. Dawson, Deborah, Gerry Henderson, and Barbara Bloom, Trends in Routine Screening Examinations, *American Journal of Public Health,* 77, no. 8 (1987), 1004–1005.
26. Dean, Nadia, Starting An Unusual Day Care Center, *Nursing Life,* 7, no. 4 (1987), 24.
27. Department of Health and Social Security, *Prevention and Health: Everybody's Business.* Kent, England: Health Departments of Great Britain and Northern Ireland, 1976.
28. Durbach, E., et al., Instructional Objectives in Patient Education, *Nursing Outlook,* 35, no. 2 (1987), 82–83, 88.
29. Edelman, Carole, and Carol Lynn Mandle, *Health Promotion Throughout the Lifespan.* St. Louis: C. V. Mosby, 1986.
30. Ellis, Albert, and Harper, R. *A Guide to Rational Living.* North Hollywood, CA: Wilshire Books, 1961.
31. Everly, G., and D. Girdano, *The Stress-Mess Solution.* Bowie, MD: Robert J. Brady, 1980.
32. Ewles, Linda, and Ina Simnett, *Promoting Health: A Practical Guide to Health Education.* Sussex, England. John Wiley, 1985.
33. Feldenkrais, M., *Awareness Through Movement.* New York: Harper & Row, 1977.
34. Feldman, Rosalind, Smoking and the Psych Nurse, *Journal of Psychosocial Nursing,* 22, no. 8 (1984), 13–16.
35. Foltz, Rose G., How One Nurse Turned a Small Business into a Small Fortune, *Nursing Life,* 7, no. 2 (1987), 22–23.
36. ——, Changing the Future of Healthcare: The Nurse Entrepreneur Spirit, *The Tar Heel Nurse,* 49, no. 6 (1987), 3, 13, 18.
37. Friedman, JoAnn, Guiding Patients Through the Labyrinth of Home Health Care Services, *Nursing and Health Care,* 7, no. 6 (1986), 305–306.
38. Girdano, D., and G. Everly. *Controlling Stress and Tension: A Holistic Approach.* Bowie, MD: Robert J. Brady, 1979.
39. Goodman, D., *Emotional Well-Being Through Rational Behavior Training.* Springfield, IL: Charles C. Thomas, 1974.
40. Grether, Judith, et al., Exposure to Aerial Malathion Application and the Occurrence of Congenital Anomalies and Low Birthweight, *American Journal of Public Health,* 77, no. 8 (1987), 1009–1010.
41. Griffin, Margo, In the Mind's Eye, *American Journal of Nursing,* 86, no. 7 (1986), 804–806.
42. Guralnik, David, ed., *Webster's New World Dictionary of the American Language* (2nd college ed.). New York: World Publishing, 1972.

43. Guyton, Arthur, *Textbook of Medical Physiology* (7th ed.). Philadelphia: W.B. Saunders, 1986.
44. Haag, S., Choosing a Running Shoe, *The Minn Wellness Journal* (July, 1981), 1, 4.
45. Hall, Beverly, and Janet Allan, Sharpening Nursing Focus by Focusing on Health, *Nursing and Health Care*, 7, no. 6 (1986), 315–320.
46. Heidt, P., Effect of Therapeutic Touch on Anxiety Level of Hospitalized Patients, *Nursing Research*, 30, no. 1 (1981), 32–37.
47. Hobbs, Patricia, Evaluation of a Teaching Programme of Breast Self-Examination, *International Journal of Health Education*, 14 (1971), 189–195.
48. Hochbaum,, G., Public Participation in Medical Screening Programs: A Sociopsychological Study, *Public Health Service Publication* (No. 572). Washington, D.C.: U.S. Government Printing Office, 1958.
49. Hogan, R. *Human Sexuality: A Nursing Perspective* (2nd ed.). Norwalk, CT.: Appleton-Century-Crofts, 1985.
50. Holmes, J., and R. Rahe, The Social Readjustment Rating Scale, *Journal of Psychosomatic Research*, 11 (1967), 213.
51. Humble, Charles, Jonathon Samet, and Dorothy Pathak, Marriage to a Smoker and Lung Cancer Risk, *American Journal of Public Health*, 77, no. 5 (1987), 598–602.
52. Jarrett, Paul, Some Mental Aspects of Physical Fitness, *Journal of Florida Medical Association*, 67, no. 4 (1980), 378–389.
53. Johnson, Jean E., Effects of Structuring Patients' Expectations on Their Reactions to Threatening Events, *Nursing Research*, 21, no. 6 (1972), 499–503.
54. Jones, D., What's Missing in Aerobic Dance? *The Wellness News*, 6, no. 3 (1985), 2.
55. Jordan, Marsh M., Development of a Tool for Diagnosing Changes in Concern About Exercise: A Means of Enhancing Compliance, *Nursing Research*, 34, no. 2 (1985), 103–107.
56. Kar, S., M. Schmitz, and D. Dyer, A Psychosocial Model of Health Behavior: Implications for Nutrition Education, Research, and Policy, *Health Values: Achieving High Level Wellness*, 7, no. 2 (1983), 29–37.
57. Kegeles, S., et al., Survey of Belief About Cancer Selection and Taking Papanicolaou Tests, *Public Health Reports*, 80 (September, 1965), 815–823.
58. Keller, E., and V. Bzdek, Effects of Therapeutic Touch on Tension Headache Pain, *Nursing Research*, 35, no. 2 (1986), 101–105.
59. Kjervik, Diane, and Ida Martinson, *Women in Health and Illness: Life Experiences and Crisis*. Philadelphia: W.B. Saunders, 1986.
60. Knowles, Malcolm S., Teaching-Learning Teams in Adult Education, in *The Changing College Classoom*, eds. P. Runkel, R. Harrison, and M. Runkel, San Francisco: Jossey-Bass, 1969.
61. Kopf, R., M. Salaman, and P. Charytan, The Preventive Health History Form: A Questionnaire to Use with Older Patient Populations, *Journal of Gerontological Nursing*, 8, no. 9 (1982), 519–523.
62. Krieger, Dolores, *The Therapeutic Touch*. Englewood Cliffs, NJ: Prentice-Hall, 1979.
63. Kulbok, P., Social Resources, Health Resources, and Preventive Health Behaviors: Patterns and Predictions, *Public Health Nursing*, 2, no. 2 (1985), 67–81.
64. Kurtz, R., and H. Prestera, *The Body Reveals*. New York: Harper & Row, 1984.
65. Lafferty, Jerry, A Credo of Wellness, *Health Education* (September–October, 1979), 10–11.
66. Lamontagne, Lynda, Karen Mason, and Joseph Hepworth, Effects of Relaxation on Anxiety in Children: Implications for Coping With Stress, *Nursing Research*, 34, no. 5 (1986), 289–292.
67. Litwack, Lawrence, Janice Litwack, and Mary Ballow, *Health Counseling*. New York: Appleton-Century-Crofts, 1980.
68. MacKinnon, Roger, and Robert Michels, *The Psychiatric Interview in Clinical Practice*. Philadelphia: W. B. Saunders, 1971, pp. 1–64.
69. Marchiondo, K., et al., Establishing a Standardized Patient Education Program, *Critical Care Nursing*, 7, no. 3 (1987), 58, 60–64, 66.
70. Mast, Deborah, Effects of Imagery, *Image*, 8, no. 3 (1986), 118–120.
71. Mayer, Eileen, Nurses Who Care For All of You, *Prevention*, September, 1983, 133–139.
72. Meichenbaum, D., and R. Cameron, Modifying What Clients Say to Themselves, in M. Mahoney and R. Cameron (eds.), *Self-Control Power to the Person*. Monterey, CA: Brooks-Cole Publisher, 1974.
73. Mileo, Nancy, A Framework for Prevention: Changing Health-Damaging to Health-Generating Patterns, *American Journal of Public Health*, 66, no. 5 (1976), 435–439.
74. Miller, Arlene, Should Christian Nurses Practice Therapeutic Touching? No, *Journal of Christian Nursing*, 4, no. 4 (1987), 15 ff.
75. Montague, Karen, Let Like Cure Like, *Nursing Mirror*, 160, no. 21 (May 22, 1985), 30–33.
76. Muhlenkamp, Ann, and Judy Sayles, Self-Esteem, Social Support, and Positive Health Practices, *Nursing Research*, 36, no. 6 (1986), 334–338.
77. Murdough, Carolyn, and Ada Hinshaw, Theoretical Model Testing to Identify Personality Variables Effecting Preventive Behavior, *Nursing Research*, 35, no. 1 (1986), 19–23.
78. Murray, Ruth, and M. Marilyn Huelskoetter, *Psychiatric/Mental Health Nursing: Giving Emotional Care* (2nd ed.). Englewood Cliffs, NJ: Prentice-Hall, 1987.
79. National Institute on Drug Abuse, Life Skills Program, Clearinghouse on Drug Abuse: Kensington, MD, 1984.

80. Nickerson, Donna, Teaching the Hospitalized Diabetic, *American Journal of Nursing*, 72, no. 6 (1972), 935-938.
81. Nulls, M., and B. Cohen, *Developmental Movement Therapy*. Amherst, MA: The School for Body/Mind Centering, 1979.
82. Pardue, Austin, Don't be Frightened by Failure, *Guideposts*, May 1973, 26.
83. Peale, Norman Vincent. *Imaging: The Powerful Way to Change Your Life*. Carmel, NY: Guideposts, 1982.
84. Pender, Nola, *Health Promotion in Nursing Practice* (2nd ed.). E. Norwalk, CT: Appleton and Lange, 1987.
85. Pender, Nola, and Albert Pender, Attitudes, Subjective Norms, and Intentions to Engage in Health Behaviors, *Nursing Research*, 35, no. 1 (1986), 15-18.
86. Peplau, Hildegarde, *Interpersonal Relations in Nursing*. New York: G. P. Putnam's Sons, 1952.
87. ———, *Basic Principles of Patient Counseling* (2nd ed.). Philadelphia: Smith, Kline and French Laboratories, 1969.
88. ———, Talking with Patients, *American Journal of Nursing*, 70, no. 7 (1970) 964-966.
89. Pirandello, L., Language and Thought, *Perspectives in Psychiatric Care*, 8, no. 5 (1970), 230 ff.
90. Preoperative Teaching Found to Shorten Hospitalization, *American Journal of Nursing*, 75, no. 11 (1975), 2078.
91. Primarius, Dobberson K., Computer-Assisted Patient Ed . . . , *American Journal of Nursing*, 87, no. 5 (1987), 697.
92. Quinn, J., Therapeutic Touch as Energy Exchange: Testing the Theory, *Advances in Nursing Science*, 42 (1984), 49.
93. Rogers, Carl, *Client-Centered Therapy*. Boston: Houghton Mifflin, 1951.
94. Rogers, J., *You Can Stop*, New York: Pocket Books, 1977.
95. Rosenstock, Irvin M., What Research in Motivation Suggests for Public Health, *American Journal of Public Health*, 50, no. 3 (1960), 295-302.
96. Rosenstock, J., Why People Use Health Services, *Milbank Memorial Fund Quarterly*, 44 (July, 1966), 94-127.
97. Rotter, J.B., *Social Learning and Clinical Psychology*. Englewood Cliffs, NJ: Prentice-Hall, 1954.
98. Samuels, M., and H. Bennett, *The Well Body Book*. New York: Random House, 1973.
99. Samuels, M., and N. Samuels, *Seeing with the Mind's Eye*. New York: Random House, 1975.
100. Scandrett, S., and S. Uecker, Relaxation Training, in eds. G. Bulechech and M. McCloskey, *Nursing Interventions: Treatment for Nursing Diagnosis*, Philadelphia: W. B. Saunders, 1984.
101. Scarf, M., Images That Heal, *Psychology Today* (September, 1980), 32-46.
102. Schmitt, Florence E., and Powhatan J. Wolldridge, Psychological Preparation of Surgical Patients, *Nursing Research*, 22, no. 2 (1973), 108-115.
103. Schwarz, G. E., Cardiac Responses to Self-Induced Thoughts, *Psychophysiology*, 8 (1971), 462-467.
104. Sennott-Miller, Lee, and Jerry Miller, Difficulty: A Neglected Factor in Health Promotion, *Nursing Research*, 36, no. 5 (1987), 270-272.
105. Shaver, Joan, A Biopsychosocial View of Human Health, *Nursing Outlook*, 33, no. 4 (1985), 186-191.
106. Sheikh, A. A., (ed.), *Imagination and Healing*. New York: Baywood Press, 1984.
107. Shorr, G, E. Sobel, P. Robin, et al. (eds.), *Imagery*. New York: Plenum Press, 1980.
108. Simi, W., "Psychological Benefits of Exercise, *Advances*, 1, no. 4 (1984), 15-29.
109. Simonton, O. C., S. Matthews-Simonton, and J. Creighton, *Getting Well Again*. Los Angeles: J. P. Tarcher, 1978.
110. Singer, Jerome, Towards the Scientific Study of Imagination, in *Imagery (Volume 3): Theoretical and Clinical Applications*, eds. J. Shorr, G. Sobel-Whittington, P. Robin, and J. Connella. New York: Plenum Press, 1983.
111. Smith, Gloria, The New Health Care Economy: Opportunities for Nurse Entrepreneurs, *Nursing Outlook*, 35, no. 4 (1987), 182-184.
112. Snyder, M., Progressive Relaxation as a Nursing Intervention: An Analysis, *Advances in Nursing Science*, 6, no. 3 (1984), 47-58.
113. Spielberger, C. D., R. L. Gorsach, R. Lushens, et al., *Manual for the State-Trait Anxiety Inventory*. Palo Alto, CA: Consulting Psychologists Press, 1983.
114. Squires, Sally, Visions to Boost Immunity, *American Health*, July, 1987, 56-61.
115. Squires, Sally, and Caryl Avery, The Inactive Low: When to Feel, Not Think Things Out, *Self* (June, 1986), 131-133.
116. Stevens, Barbara J., The Teaching-Learning Process, *Nurse Educator*, 1, no. 3 (1976), 9 ff.
117. Streif, Tibert, Can Clients Understand Our Instructions, *Image*, 18, no. 2 (1986), 48-52.
118. Stress and Type A Behavior, *Healthline* (September-October, 1987), 1-2.
119. Suchman, Edward, Preventive Health Behavior: A Model for Research on Community Health Campaigns, *Journal of Health and Social Behavior*, 8, no. 3 (1967), 197-209.
120. Surgeon General's Report Cites Hazards in Passive Smoking, *The Nation's Health* (January, 1987), 1, 13.
121. Taylor, Rosemarie Angela, Making the Most of Your Time for Patient Teaching, *RN*, December, 1987, 20-27.
122. Tiger, L., Optimism: The Biological Roots of Hope, *Psychology Today* (January, 1979).

123. Tornyay, Rheba de, and Martha A. Thompson, *Strategies For Teaching Nursing* (3rd ed..). New York: John Wiley, 1987.
124. Travelbee, Joyce, *Interpersonal Aspects of Nursing*. Philadelphia: F. A. Davis, 1967.
125. Travelbee, Joyce, *Intervention in Psychiatric Nursing*. Philadelphia: F. A. Davis, 1969.
126. Uretsky, Samuel, and Carole Birdsall, Quackery: A Thoroughly Modern Problem, *American Journal of Nursing*, 86, no. 9 (1986), 1030–1032.
127. Van Deusen, D., Kicking the Cigarette Habit: Some Reflections from an Old Pro, *The Wellness Newsletter*, 5, no. 2 (1984), 3–4.
128. Van Hoozer, Helen, et al., *The Teaching Process: Theory and Practice in Nursing*. Norwalk, CT.: Appleton-Century-Crofts, 1987.
129. Walker, Susan, Karen Sechrist, and Nola Pender, The Health-Promoting Lifestyle Profile: Development and Psychometric Characteristics, *Nursing Research*, 36, no. 2 (1987), 76–81.
130. Weiss, S., Health Hazard-Health Risk Appraisals, in *Behavioral Health: A Handbook of Health Enhancement and Disease Prevention* (eds. J.D. Matarazzo, S. M. Weiss, J.A. Herd, and N.E. Miller. New York: Wiley, 1984.
131. Westberg, J., et al., Building a Helpful Relationship: The Foundation of Effective Patient Education, *Diabetes Education*, 12, no. 4 (1986), 374–378.
132. WHO Executive Board Emphasizes Key Role of Nurses in Primary Health Care, *WHO*, January 14, 1985, 1.
133. Wicks, Robert, *Counseling Strategies and Intervention Techniques for the Human Services*. Philadelphia: J. B. Lippincott, 1979.
134. Wilson, M., B. Berger, and E. Bird, Effects of Running and of an Exercise Class on Anxiety, *Perceptual Motor Skills*, 53, (1981), 472–474.
135. Wuthnow, Sara, Should Christian Nurses Practice Therapeutic Touch? Yes, *Journal of Christian Nursing*, 4, no. 4 (1987), 15 ff.
136. Yanker, G. *The Complete Book of Exercisewalking*. Chicago: Contemporary Books, 1983.

APPENDICES

I	Review of Systems: Physical Assessment and Health History	633
II	Health Maintenance Procedures	634
III	Recommended Daily Dietary Allowances, National Academy of Sciences, Revised 1980	638
IV	Major Sources and Functions of Primary Nutrients	639
V	Summary Comparison of Males and Females	645

APPENDIX I

Review of Systems: Physical Assessment and Health History

Constitutional:	Health overall; weight gain or loss; fever; fatigue; repeated infections; ability to carry out activities.
Psychological:	Dreams or nightmares; crying; depression; anxiety; insomnia; diagnosed mental illness.
Integument:	General skin condition and care. Any changes; rash; itch; nail deformity; hair loss; moles; open areas.
Head, Ears, Eyes, Nose, Throat, Teeth:	Head: aches; evidence of trauma or bumps; hair loss. Eyes: eye care; poor eyesight; double or blurred vision; use of corrective lenses or medications. Ears: hearing acuity; reaction to noise level; tinnitus (ringing in ears); presence of infection or pain. Nose and Throat: upper respiratory infections; hoarseness; sore throat; sinusitis; epistaxis (nose bleeds); dysphagia (difficulty swallowing). Teeth: dentures or dental work; caries. Pattern of brushing and use of dental floss. Fluoride application (to 12 years).
Respiratory:	History of respiratory infections; self-treatment of colds. Cough and its duration; last chest x-ray; tuberculin skin test and results; dyspnea (difficulty breathing) and when (night-time, with exertion); wheezing; asthma or bronchitis; hemoptysis (coughing or spitting up blood).
Cardiovascular:	Exercise pattern to maintain cardiovascular health. Edema; varicose veins; heart sounds, including murmur; chest pains; palpitations; hypertension (high blood pressure); electrocardiogram (EKG) and when.
Gastrointestinal:	Dietary pattern; amount of fiber in diet. Heartburn; epigastric pain; abdominal pain; nausea and vomiting; food intolerance; flatulence; diarrhea; constipation; clay-colored, tarry, or bright red stools; hemorrhoids; history of ulcers.
Genitourinary	Nocturia; dysuria; incontinence; resistance; sexual difficulty; venereal disease; history of stones. Men: slow stream; penile discharge; contraceptive use; self-testicular examination (technique and frequency). Women: breast lumps, breast self-examination and how often; menarche; menopause; intermenstrual bleeding; last menstrual period; contraceptive use; last Pap smear.
Musculoskeletal:	Exercise pattern. Neck pain or stiffness; joint pain or swelling; incapacitating back pain; paralysis; deformities.
Neurological:	Syncope; stroke; seizures; paresthesia.
Lymphatic and Hematological:	Enlarged, tender nodes; easy bruising; anemia; bleeding.
Endocrine:	Polydipsia; polyphagia; polyuria; intolerance of heat or cold; weight gain or loss; changes in skin, hair, or nail texture.
Immunological:	Immunization record; what diseases and dates.

APPENDIX II

Health Maintenance Procedures

PROCEDURE	B[b]	MONTHS						YEARS							
		2	4	6	12	15	18	2	3	5	8	11	13	15	17
Complete History	×	×	×	×	×		×	×	×	×	×	×	×	×	×
							(or at first visit)								
Update History		×	×	×	×	×	×	×	×	×	×	×	×	×	×
(including developmental)															
Complete Physical Exam	×	×			×		×	×	×	×	×	×	×	×	×
Height, weight	×	×	×	×	×		×	×		×	×	×	×	×	×
Head circumference	×	×	×	×	×		×								
Blood pressure								×	×	×	×	×	×	×	×
Vision/strabimus[a]		×[a]	×		×[a]		×[a]	×	×	×	×	×	×	×	×
Hearing		×		×	×				×	×	×	×	×	×	×
Hip, feet, spine	×	×											×		
Language screen							×	×	×	×					
Pap—high risk													×	×	×
Immunizations/Screenings															
Phenylketonuria (PKU)	×														
Hypothyroid (T4)	×														
Silver nitrate drops (AgNO)	×														
Vitamin K injection	×														
DTP/TD		×	×	×			×			×			×		
OPV (polio)		×	×				×			×					
MMR (measles, mumps, rubella)					×										
Laboratory															
Tine test					×				×	×		×		×	
Rubella titer (if not vaccinated)												×			
Hematocrit/hemoglobin					×					×			×		
Urine culture (female)									×	×					
Dental/Mouth Check		×	×	×	×		×	×	×	×	×	×	×	×	×
Fluoride Hx		×	×												
Counseling–Health Education															
Safety/accidents	×	×	×	×	×		×	×	×	×	×	×	×	×	×
Poison control		×	×	×	×		×	×	×	×	×	×	×	×	×
Nutrition	×	×	×	×	×		×	×	×	×	×	×	×	×	×
Physical care	×	×	×	×	×		×	×	×	×	×	×	×	×	×
Behavior/psychological/social															
Sex education									×	×	×	×	×	×	×
Tobacco/alcohol use													×	×	×
Safety belt use/ driver education														×	×

[a]Strabismus checked at 2, 12, and 18 months.
[b]B denotes at birth.

	YEARS																								
PROCEDURE	18	19	20	21	22	23	24	25	26	27	28	29	30	31	32	33	34	35	36	37	38	39	40	41	42
Complete History	× or at any beginning point.																								
Update History		×	×	×	×	×	×	×	×	×	×	×	×	×	×	×	×	×	×	×	×	×	×	×	×
Health Hazard Appraisal	× or at any beginning point (optional).																								
Complete Physical Examination	×					×									×					×					
Height/Weight	×	×	×	×	×	×	×	×	×	×	×	×	×	×	×	×	×	×	×	×	×	×	×	×	×
Blood pressure	×	×	×	×	×	×	×	×	×	×	×	×	×	×	×	×	×	×	×	×	×	×	×	×	×
Vision (Snellen)	×			×			×			×			×			×			×			×	×	×	×
tonometry	Influenced by symptoms and family history.																					×			
Hearing (Gross)	×	×	×	×	×	×	×	×	×	×	×	×	×	×	×	×	×	×	×	×	×	×	×	×	×
audiometry	Influenced by circumstances, especially work/noise environment and symptoms.																								
Dental	×	×	×	×	×	×	×	×	×	×	×	×	×	×	×	×	×	×	×	×	×	×	×	×	×
Breast Exam	×	×	×	×	×	×	×	×	×	×	×	×	×	×	×	×	×	×	×	×	×	×	×	×	×
Mammography	Influenced by symptoms and family history.																×		×		×		×		
Pap—high risk	×	×	×	×	×	×	×	×	×	×	×	×	×	×	×	×	×	×	×	×	×	×	×	×	×
Pap—low risk	×	×		×			×			×			×			×			×			×			
Stool guiac		×			×			×			×			×			×			×		×	×	×	×
Testicular exam	×	×	×	×	×	×	×	×	×	×	×	×	×	×	×	×	×	×	×	×	×	×	×	×	×
Prostate Exam	×			×			×			×			×			×						×	×	×	×
Hernia exam	Influenced by work/sports demands—part of complete physical exam.																								
Immunizations																									
TD											×							×							
Influenza	High-risk persons and certain age groups; one time only.																								
Pneumococcal	High-risk persons and certain age groups; one time only.																								
Hepatitis B	High-risk persons.																								
Laboratory																									
Chemistry Panel/CBC	×			×			×			×			×			×			×			×			×
Lipid Panel																		×				×			
Urinalysis	×		×		×		×		×		×		×		×		×		×		×		×		×
Tine Test	× If negative, no need to repeat unless specific situation arises or in high-risk group.																								
Other Tests																									
Pulmonary Function/EKG	Influenced by symptoms.																								
Chest x-ray	Influenced by symptoms; if positive tine test; work hazards; heavy smoking history.																								
Counseling and Health Education	×	×	×	×	×	×	×	×	×	×	×	×	×	×	×	×	×	×	×	×	×	×	×	×	×
Nutritional	×	×	×	×	×	×	×	×	×	×	×	×	×	×	×	×	×	×	×	×	×	×	×	×	×
Behavior/psychological/social	×	×	×	×	×	×	×	×	×	×	×	×	×	×	×	×	×	×	×	×	×	×	×	×	×
Safety/accident	×	×	×	×	×	×	×	×	×	×	×	×	×	×	×	×	×	×	×	×	×	×	×	×	×
Sexuality	×	×	×	×	×	×	×	×	×	×	×	×	×	×	×	×	×	×	×	×	×	×	×	×	×
Tobacco/alcohol/drugs	×	×	×	×	×	×	×	×	×	×	×	×	×	×	×	×	×	×	×	×	×	×	×	×	×

Continued

APPENDIX II. Health Maintenance Procedures—Continued

PROCEDURE	43	44	45	46	47	48	49	50	51	52	53	54	55	56	57	58	59	60	61
Complete History	\multicolumn{19}{l}{At any beginning point.}
Update History	×	×	×	×	×	×	×	×	×	×	×	×	×	×	×	×	×	×	×
Health Hazard Appraisal	\multicolumn{19}{l}{At any beginning point (optional).}
Complete Physical Exam	×				×						×				×				
Height/Weight	×	×	×	×	×	×	×	×	×	×	×	×	×	×	×	×	×	×	×
Blood pressure	×	×	×	×	×	×	×	×	×	×	×	×	×	×	×	×	×	×	
Vision (Snellen)	×			×			×			×			×			×			×
tonometry								×					×					×	×
Hearing (Gross)	×	×	×	×	×	×	×	×	×	×	×	×	×	×	×	×	×	×	×
audiometry	\multicolumn{19}{l}{Influenced by circumstances, especially work/noise environment, and symptoms.}
Dental	×	×	×	×	×	×	×	×	×	×	×	×	×	×	×	×	×	×	×
Breast exam	×	×	×	×	×	×	×	×	×	×	×	×	×	×	×	×	×	×	×
mammography	×	×	×	×	×	×	×	×	×	×	×	×	×	×	×	×	×	×	×
Pap—high risk	×	×	×	×	×	×	×	×	×	×	×	×	×	×	×	×	×	×	×
Pap—low risk	×		×		×			×			×		×			×			×
Stool guiac	×	×	×	×	×	×	×	×	×	×	×	×	×	×	×	×	×	×	×
Sigmoidoscopy		×				×					×				×				
Testicular exam	×	×	×	×	×	×	×	×	×	×	×	×	×	×	×	×	×	×	×
Prostate exam	×	×	×	×	×	×	×	×	×	×	×	×	×	×	×	×	×	×	×
Hernia exam	\multicolumn{19}{l}{Influenced by work/sports demands—part of complete physical exam.}
Immunizations																			
TD			×										×						
Influenza	\multicolumn{19}{l}{High-risk persons and certain age groups.}
Pneumococcal	\multicolumn{19}{l}{High-risk persons and certain age groups; one time only.}
Hepatitis B	\multicolumn{19}{l}{High-risk persons.}
Laboratory																			
Chemistry panel and CBC	×			×			×			×			×			×			×
Lipid panel		×				×				×				×				×	
Urinalysis	×		×		×		×		×		×		×		×		×		
Tine test	\multicolumn{19}{l}{If negative, no need to repeat unless specific situation arises or in high-risk group.}
Other Tests																			
EKG		×	Baseline, then as needed.																
Pulmonary function	\multicolumn{19}{l}{Influenced by symptoms.}
Chest x-ray	\multicolumn{19}{l}{Influenced by symptoms; if positive tine test; work hazards; heavy smoking history.}
Counseling and Health Education																			
Nutritional	×	×	×	×	×	×	×	×	×	×	×	×	×	×	×	×	×	×	×
Behavior/psychological/social	×	×	×	×	×	×	×	×	×	×	×	×	×	×	×	×	×	×	×
Safety/accident	×	×	×	×	×	×	×	×	×	×	×	×	×	×	×	×	×	×	×
Sexuality	×	×	×	×	×	×	×	×	×	×	×	×	×	×	×	×	×	×	×
Tobacco/alcohol/drugs	×	×	×	×	×	×	×	×	×	×	×	×	×	×	×	×	×	×	×

PROCEDURE	\multicolumn{19}{c}{YEARS}
	62	63	64	65	66	67	68	69	70	71	72	73	74	75	76	77	78	79	80
Complete History	At any beginning point.
Update History	×	×	×	×	×	×	×	×	×	×	×	×	×	×	×	×	×	×	×
Health hazard appraisal	At any beginning point (optional).
Complete Physical Exam				×					×				×				×		
Height/Weight	×	×	×	×	×	×	×	×	×	×	×	×	×	×	×	×	×	×	×
Blood pressure	×	×	×	×	×	×	×	×	×	×	×	×	×	×	×	×	×	×	×
Vision (Snellen)			×	×	×	×	×	×	×	×	×	×	×	×	×	×	×	×	×
tonometry				×	×	×	×	×	×	×	×	×	×	×	×	×	×	×	×
Hearing (Gross)	×	×	×	×	×	×	×	×	×	×	×	×	×	×	×	×	×	×	×
audiometry	Influenced by circumstances, especially work/noise environment, and symptoms.
Dental	×	×	×	×	×	×	×	×	×	×	×	×	×	×	×	×	×	×	×
Breast exam	×	×	×	×	×	×	×	×	×	×	×	×	×	×	×	×	×	×	×
mammography	×	×	×	×	×	×	×	×	×	×	×	×	×	×	×	×	×	×	×
Pap—high risk	×	×	×	×	×	×	×	×	×	×	×	×	×	×	×	×	×	×	×
Pap—low risk		×			×			×			×			×			×		
Stool guiac	×	×	×	×	×	×	×	×	×	×	×	×	×	×	×	×	×	×	×
Sigmoidoscopy		×					×					×					×		
Testicular exam	×	×	×	×	×	×	×	×	×	×	×	×	×	×	×	×	×	×	×
Prostate exam	×	×	×	×	×	×	×	×	×	×	×	×	×	×	×	×	×	×	×
Hernia exam	Influenced by work/sports demands—part of complete physical exam.
Immunizations																			
TD					×									×					
Influenza				×	×	×	×	×	×	×	×	×	×	×	×	×	×	×	×
Pneumococcal				×															
Hepatitis B	High-risk persons.
Laboratory																			
Chemistry panel and CBC		×			×				×			×			×			×	
Lipid panel			×																
Urinalysis	×		×		×		×		×		×		×		×		×		×
Tine test																			
Other Tests																			
EKG	Influenced by symptoms.
Pulmonary function	Influenced by symptoms.
Chest x-ray	Influenced by symptoms.
Counseling and Health Education																			
Nutritional	×	×	×	×	×	×	×	×	×	×	×	×	×	×	×	×	×	×	×
Behavior/psychological/social	×	×	×	×	×	×	×	×	×	×	×	×	×	×	×	×	×	×	×
Safety/accident	×	×	×	×	×	×	×	×	×	×	×	×	×	×	×	×	×	×	×
Sexuality	×	×	×	×	×	×	×	×	×	×	×	×	×	×	×	×	×	×	×
Tobacco/alcohol/drugs	×	×	×	×	×	×	×	×	×	×	×	×	×	×	×	×	×	×	×

APPENDIX III

Recommended Daily Dietary Allowances (RDA), National Academy of Sciences, Revised 1980

AGE (years)	WEIGHT (kg)	WEIGHT (lb)	HEIGHT (cm)	HEIGHT (in.)	PROTEIN (g)	VITAMIN A (RE)	VITAMIN D (μg)	VITAMIN E (mg)	VITAMIN C (mg)	THIAMINE (mg)	RIBOFLAVIN (mg)	NIACIN (mg equiv.)	VITAMIN B_6 (mg)	FOLACIN (μg)	VITAMIN B_{12} (μg)	CALCIUM (mg)	PHOSPHORUS (mg)	MAGNESIUM (mg)	IRON (mg)	ZINC (mg)	IODINE (μg)
Infants																					
0.0 to 0.5	6	13	60	24	kg × 2.2	420	10	3	35	0.3	0.4	6	0.3	30	0.5	360	240	50	10	3	40
0.5 to 1.0	9	20	71	28	kg × 2.0	400	10	4	35	0.5	0.6	8	0.6	45	1.5	540	360	70	15	5	50
Children																					
1 to 3	13	29	90	35	23	400	10	5	45	0.7	0.8	9	0.9	100	2.0	800	800	150	15	10	70
4 to 6	20	44	112	44	30	500	10	6	45	0.9	1.0	11	1.3	200	2.5	800	800	200	10	10	90
7 to 10	28	62	132	52	34	700	10	7	45	1.2	1.4	16	1.6	300	3.0	800	800	250	10	10	120
Males																					
11 to 14	45	99	157	62	45	1000	10	8	50	1.4	1.6	18	1.8	400	3.0	1200	1200	350	18	15	150
15 to 18	66	145	176	69	56	1000	10	10	60	1.4	1.7	18	2.0	400	3.0	1200	1200	400	18	15	150
19 to 22	70	154	177	70	56	1000	7.5	10	60	1.5	1.7	19	2.2	400	3.0	800	800	350	10	15	150
23 to 50	70	154	178	70	56	1000	5	10	60	1.4	1.6	18	2.2	400	3.0	800	800	350	10	15	150
51+	70	154	178	70	56	1000	5	10	60	1.2	1.4	16	2.2	400	3.0	800	800	350	10	15	150
Females																					
11 to 14	46	101	157	62	46	800	10	8	50	1.1	1.3	15	1.8	400	3.0	1200	1200	300	18	15	150
15 to 18	55	120	163	64	46	800	10	8	60	1.1	1.3	14	2.0	400	3.0	1200	1200	300	18	15	150
19 to 22	55	120	163	64	44	800	7.5	8	60	1.1	1.3	14	2.0	400	3.0	800	800	300	18	15	150
23 to 50	55	120	163	64	44	800	5	8	60	1.0	1.2	13	2.0	400	3.0	800	800	300	18	15	150
51+	55	120	163	64	44	800	5	8	60	1.0	1.2	13	2.0	400	3.0	800	800	300	10	15	150
Pregnant					+30	+200	+5	+2	+20	+0.4	+0.3	+2	+0.6	+400	+1.0	+400	+400	+150	[a]	+5	+25
Lactating					+20	+400	+5	+3	+40	+0.5	+0.5	+5	+0.5	+100	+1.0	+400	+400	+150	[a]	+10	+50

[a]Supplemental iron (30–60 mg) during pregnancy and for 2 to 3 months after parturition is advised.

APPENDIX IV

Major Sources and Functions of Primary Nutrients

NUTRIENT	MAJOR SOURCES	MAJOR FUNCTIONS
Protein	Meat; poultry, fish; dried beans and peas; eggs; nuts; cheese; milk. Whole grain cereals are incomplete and must be combined with animal protein. Animal and vegetable protein combined increase utilization by body of all amino acids.	Builds, maintains, and repairs body cells; is required for amino acids (8 are essential). Constitutes part of the structure of every cell such as muscle, blood, bones, and ligaments. Supports growth and maintains healthy body cells. Maintains pH balance of blood, acts as buffer system. Regulates osmotic pressure. Constitutes part of enzymes, some hormones, body fluids, antibodies that increase resistance to infection, hemoglobin, plasma proteins. Is source of energy and fuel when inadequate carbohydrate and fat unavailable. Because protein and other nitrogenous compounds are degraded and resynthesized continually, daily intake is needed. Essential for nitrogen balance, excess excreted in urea and urine.
Carbohydrate	Bread; potatoes; pasta; dried beans; corn; rice; fruit; vegetables; sugar; desserts, candy; jam; syrup; honey	Supplies energy and forms ATP so protein can be used for growth maintenance of body cells, and metabolic processes. Maintains body temperature. Supplies fiber in unrefined products—complex carbohydrates in fruits, vegetables, and whole grains—for regular elimination. Assists in fat utilization
Fat	Animal fat; shortening; vegetable oil; butter; margarine; salad dressing; mayonnaise; sausages; lunch meats; whole milk and milk products; nuts. No more than 30% of total calories should be from fat. No more than 10% of fat intake should be saturated fat intake.	Provides concentrated source of energy. Constitutes part of the structure of every cell. Helps control cell permeability. Supplies essential fatty acids. Necessary for absorption of (carrier for) fat-soluble vitamins (A, D, E, and K). Maintains adipose tissue, which insulates and protects inner organs from trauma. Is component of thromboplastin, used in blood clotting. Adds to food taste, texture, and appearance. Provides reserve supply of phosphate ions. Excess animal fat is linked to cancer of gastrointestinal tract and possibly cancer of breast and prostate.

Appendix IV. Major Sources and Functions of Primary Nutrients—Continued

NUTRIENT	MAJOR SOURCES	MAJOR FUNCTIONS
Vitamins		
Vitamin C (ascorbic acid) (water soluble)	Citrus fruits such as orange, grapefruit, lime, lemon, papaya; mango; cantaloupe; pineapple; rose hips; strawberries; raspberries; blackberries; melons; cherries; alfalfa sprouts; watercress; parsley; tomatoes; broccoli; green peppers; raw potatoes; raw leafy vegetables; kale; brussel sprouts; cabbage.	Forms cementing substances, such as collagen, that hold body cells together, thus strengthening blood vessels, hastening healing of wounds and bone fractures, and increasing resistance to infection. Helps develop and maintain healthy bones, teeth, gums; skin, muscles, and blood vessels. Prevents scurvy. Regulates mitochondria and microsomial respiratory cycle. Aids utilization of iron and folic acid metabolism. Normalizes body cholesterol. Decreases risk of cancer of esophagus and stomach. Aspirin prevents absorption.
Thiamine (B_1) (water soluble)	Pork; lean meat; nuts; liver; fish; oysters; crabmeat; dried yeast; milk; whole grains, enriched bread and cereals; pasta; dry beans; peas; lima beans; soybeans; sunflower seeds; brown rice; asparagus; raisins.	Functions as part of coenzyme to promote utilization of carbohydrate and protein and release of energy. Reduces fatigue and weakness. Promotes normal appetite. Contributes to normal functioning of nervous, muscle, and digestive systems. Prevents beriberi.
Riboflavin (B_2) (water soluble)	Liver and other organ meats; ham; poultry; milk and milk products; yogurt; cottage cheese; egg yolk; green leafy vegetables; lean meat; whole grains; soybeans; peas; beans; nuts; enriched bread and cereal; brewer's yeast; blackstrap molasses; sunflower seeds; wheat germ.	Is component of flavoprotein involved in biological oxidation. Is essential for building and maintaining body tissues, antibodies, and red blood cells. Functions as part of a coenzyme in the production of energy within body cells. Promotes carbohydrate, fat, and protein metabolism. Maintains nitrogen balance. Is essential for use of oxygen in cells. Promotes healthy skin, eyes, tongue, lips, mucous membranes. Prevents sensitivity of eyes to light.
Niacin (water soluble)	Liver; meat; rabbit; poultry; fish; peanuts; whole grains; brewer's yeast; fortified cereal and bread products, wheat germ.	Aids utilization of vitamins B_1 and B_2. Is essential for tissue respiration. Functions as part of a coenzyme in fat synthesis, protein utilization, glycolysis and utilization of carbohydrate, and release of energy. Promotes healthy skin, nerves, digestive tract, and blood vessels. Aids digestion and fosters normal appetite. Is required for formation of certain hormones and nerve-regulating substances. Prevents pellagra.
Pyridoxine (B_6) (water soluble)	Liver, meat; fish; poultry; whole grain bread and cereals; wheat germ; brewer's yeast; sunflower seeds; soybeans; nuts; brown rice; bananas; avocado; sweet potato; white potato; corn; white beans; green leafy vegetables.	Is coenzyme in basic reactions of amino acid, fat metabolism, and protein metabolism. Assists antibody hormone, and red blood cell formation. Is involved with function of neurotransmitters. Helps maintain balance of sodium and phosphorus and metabolism of iron and potassium.

NUTRIENT	MAJOR SOURCES	MAJOR FUNCTIONS
Cyanocolabalamin (B_{12}) (water soluble)	Organ meats such as liver, kidney, and heart; lean meat; poultry; fish; oysters; clams; sea vegetables (kelp, dulse, komba); eggs; milk; cheese; brewer's yeast.	Is essential for all blood cell formation. Is coenzyme for synthesis of materials for nucleus of all cells. Is essential for synthesis of nucleic acids, metabolism of certain amino acids, protein, carbohydrate, fat, and generally normal cell function. Converts folic acid to folinic acid. Is especially important for cells of bone marrow, intestinal tract, and central nervous system. Strict vegetarian at risk for deficiency, pernicious anemia.
Folacin (folic acid) (water soluble)	Dark green, leafy vegetables such as collards, mustard greens, turnip greens, kale; organ meats; dried beans; root vegetables; whole grains; brewer's yeast; oysters; salmon; milk; black-eyed peas; lima beans; watermelon; cantaloupe.	Synthesizes nucleic acids and proteins. Acts with B_{12} in making genetic material. Assists metabolism of certain amino acids. Assists in hemoglobin, red blood cell, and protein formation. Is necessary for normal cell division. Prevents anemia.
Vitamin A (retinol) (fat soluble)	Liver; orange-colored fruits; orange, yellow and dark green vegetables such as carrots, winter squash, sweet potatoes, broccoli, and greens; eggs; fortified milk, butter, magarine, cheese.	Assists formation, maintenance, and repair of normal skin, hair, and mucous membranes that line body cavities and tracts, such as nasal passages and intestinal tract, thus increasing resistance to infection. Maintains mitochondrial and liposomal membranes. Functions in visual processes, forms visual purple, thus promoting healthy eye tissue and eye adaptation in dim light or at night. Increases resistance to infection. Decreases risk of cancer of lung, thyroid, esophagus, bladder because it aids in controlling cell differentiation.
Vitamin D (fat soluble)	Fortified milk, butter, margarine; fish liver oil; salmon; tuna; egg yolk; liver; bone meal; sunshine.	Regulates calcium and phosphorus metabolism; promotes intestinal absorption of calcium and phosphorus. Promotes bone mineralization (prevents rickets) and tooth formation.
Vitamin E (fat soluble)	Vegetable oils; liver; wheat germ; whole grain cereals; rice; oats; Brewers yeast; peanuts; foods high in polyunsaturated fatty acids; eggs; molasses; sweet potatoes; leafy vegetables; lettuce; spinach; asparagus; cauliflower, broccoli.	Is essential in cellular respiration. Is antioxidant at tissue level; maintains tissue. Prevents abnormal fat breakdown in tissues. Assists in formation of normal red blood cells and muscle. Functions in reproductive system. Prevents buildup of cholesterol plaque and blood clot formation in blood vessels, thus preventing coronary disease. Protects against exposure to radiation.
Vitamin K (fat soluble)	K_1 is found in lean meat; liver; green plants, green leafy vegetables; tomatoes; cauliflower; peas; carrots; potato; cabbage; soybean and safflower oil; egg yolk; blackstrap molasses; wheat germ. K_3 is synthetic therapeutic form. Half of vitamin K in body synthesized by intestinal bacteria as K_2.	Is essential for synthesis of blood-clotting factors: prothrombin (factor I), factors VII, IX, X. Stimulates coagulation proenzymes II, VII, IX, X.

Appendix IV. Major Sources of Primary Nutrients—Continued

NUTRIENT	MAJOR SOURCES	MAJOR FUNCTIONS
Vitamins (cont.)		
Biotin	Egg yolk; organ meats; fish; brewer's yeast; whole grains; legumes; sardines; most fresh vegetables; lima beans; mushrooms; peanuts; bananas; yogurt.	Is necessary for formation of folic acid. Is necessary for carbohydrate, protein, and fat metabolism. Aids in use of other B vitamins.
Pantothenic acid	Organ meats; lobster; oyster; salmon; brewer's yeast; egg yolk; legumes; whole grains; wheat germ; nuts; soy flour; sunflower and sesame seeds; green leafy vegetables; broccoli; cauliflower; potato.	Aids in formation of some fats, hormones. Aids in metabolism and release of energy from carbohydrates, fats, and proteins. Aids in use of some vitamins. Improves resistance to stress and infection.
Choline	Egg yolk; organ meat; fish; salmon; brewer's yeast; wheat germ; soybeans; legumes.	Aids normal nerve transmission. Aids metabolism and transport of fats.
Inositol	Citrus fruits; whole grains; brewer's yeast; molasses; meat; milk; nuts; vegetables.	Is necessary for formation of lecithin. Aids hair growth.
PABA (Para-aminobenzoic acid)	Organ meats; wheat germ; yogurt; molasses; green leafy vegetables.	Aids bacteria producing folic acid. Acts as a coenzyme in use of proteins. Aids in formation of red blood cells. Acts as sunscreen.
Pangamic acid	Brewer's yeast; brown rice; sunflower, pumpkin, and sesame seeds.	Helps eliminate hypoxia. Promotes protein metabolism. Stimulates nervous and glandular systems.
Minerals		
Calcium	Milk and milk products; chowder, cream soups, puddings made with milk, custards; yogurt; shellfish; salmon; sardines; bone meal; dark green leafy vegetables; egg yolk; whole grains; legumes; nuts; tofu; molasses; broccoli; tomatoes.	Works with phosphorus, magnesium, Vitamin D, other minerals, and protein to build bones and teeth. Assists blood clotting. Is necessary for nerve transmission, heart function, muscle contraction and relaxation, and cell wall permeability. Activates enzyme ATPase. Intestinal absorption of Vitamin D, which decreases with age, necessary for calcium metabolism. Oxylates and phytates in green leafy vegetables and grains interfere with calcium absorption by combining with calcium and creating insoluble compound. Fiber may combine with calcium and limit absorption. Alcohol intake interferes with metabolism. Caffeine and excess salt intake cause calcium excretion.
Phosphorus	Milk and milk products; meat; liver; seafood; whole grains; wheat germ; nuts; egg yolk; legumes; peas; beans; lentils; brown rice; sunflower seeds; brewer's yeast.	Helps formation of nucleic acids. Works with calcium and Vitamin D to build and maintain healthy bones, teeth, and cell membranes. Aids absorption of glucose and glycerol. Transports fatty acids. Acts as buffer system. Aids energy metabolism.
Potassium	Lean meat; whole grains; bananas; oranges; apricots; dried fruits; potato; vegetables; broccoli; spinach; raw cabbage; legumes; sunflower seeds; molasses; wheat germ.	Controls activity of heart, muscles, nervous system, kidneys. Regulates neuromuscular excitability and muscle contraction. Is major intracellular fluid cation. Promotes acid-base balance. Is necessary for glycogen formation and protein synthesis.

NUTRIENT	MAJOR SOURCES	MAJOR FUNCTIONS
Magnesium	Whole grains; cereals; nuts; citrus fruits, figs; green leafy vegetables; swiss chard; dried beans and peas; soybeans; meat; milk; nuts; brown rice; wheatgerm.	Promotes healthy nerve and muscle tissue and function. Is component of bones and teeth. Is activator and coenzyme in carbohydrates, fat, and protein metabolism. Acts as catalyst in use of calcium and phosphorus. Is essential intracellular fluid cation.
Iodine	Iodized salt; seafood; kelp; green leafy vegetables.	Is necessary for thyroid gland to control cell activities and metabolism. Synthesizes thyroxine, the thyroid hormones, which regulates cell oxidation. Promotes growth. Prevents goiter.
Sodium	Table salt; fish; seafood; kelp; baking powder and baking soda; milk; cheese; meat; eggs; celery; carrots; beets; spinach; cucumber; asparagus; turnips; stringbeans; coconut; processed foods and cereals; snack foods such as potato chips, pretzels, or salted nuts.	Maintains normal fluid level and osmotic pressure in cells. Is major extracellular fluid cation. Maintains health of nervous, muscular, blood, and lymph systems. Promotes cell permeability and absorption of glucose. Transmits electrochemical impulse in muscle, resulting in contraction. Promotes acid-base balance. Acts with potassium, magnesium, chlorine. Buffers carbon dioxide and ketones.
Cobalt	Organ meats; oysters; clams; poultry; milk; green leafy vegetables; fruits; supplied by preformed Vitamin B_{12}.	Is component of Vitamin B_{12}. Is essential for red blood cell formation. Activates a number of body enzymes.
Chlorine	Table salt; seafood; meats; liver; fish; ripe olives; rye flour; soybeans; egg yolks; peanuts; wheat germ.	Regulates acid-base balance and chlorine-bicarbonate shift. Is major extracellular fluid anion. Maintains osmotic pressure. Stimulates production of hydrochloric acid. Helps maintain joints and tendons.
Sulfur	Fish; shrimp; eggs; meat; cabbage; Brussels sprouts; asparagus; milk; cheese; nuts; legumes; peas; beans; mustard greens; cauliflower; mashed potatoes.	Is component of amino acids and B vitamins. Is essential for formation of body tissues, collagen, skin, bones, tendons, cartilage. Assists in tissue respiration. Required for oxidation-reduction reactions. Activates enzymes. Aids in detoxification reactions.
Fluorine	Natural supply in water in some areas of United States; fluoridated water; seafood; bone meal; tea.	Is deposited in teeth and bones. May reduce tooth decay by discouraging growth of acid-forming bacteria.
Molybdenum	Legumes; whole grain cereals; milk; liver; dark green vegetables.	Acts in oxidation of fat and aldehydes. Aids in mobilization of iron from liver reserves. Assists in conversion of purine to uric acid.
Vanadium	Fish; whole grains; root vegetables; nuts; vegetable oils.	Inhibits cholesterol formation. May assist in tooth and bone formation.
Trace Minerals		
Iron	Organ and red meats; fish; poultry; beef; pork; lamb; dried and canned beans and peas; enriched whole grain breads and cereals; dark green leafy vegetables; mustard and	Is essential for hemoglobin and myoglobin formation. Helps protein metabolism. Is used by cells as component for oxidation of

Appendix IV. Major Sources of Primary Nutrients—Continued

NUTRIENT	MAJOR SOURCES	MAJOR FUNCTIONS
Trace Minerals (cont.)		
Iron (cont.)	dandelion greens; egg yolk; blackstrap molasses; cherry and prune juice; legumes; nuts; dried fruits.	glucose in production of energy. Aids tissue respiration. Promotes growth. Increases resistance to infection. Is more readily used by body when ascorbic acid, copper, folic acid, and Vitamin B$_{12}$ available. Excess calcium intake interferes with iron absorption.
Zinc	Organ and red meats; sunflower seeds; oysters; herring; seafood; eggs; mushrooms; brewer's yeast; soybeans; wheat germ.	Is component of insulin, serum proteins, reproductive fluid, bone, muscle, eyes, hair, teeth, and liver. Aids digestion and metabolism of phosphorus. Necessary for adequate respiration and digestion. Important for sensory functioning, normal growth, hair, complexion; sexual function, wound healing. Aids healing and resistance to infection, excess of deficiency interfere with immune function.
Copper	Organ and lean meats; seafood; nuts; legumes; molasses; raisins; bone meal; cocoa; food cooked in copperware.	Absorbs and transports iron and aids in formation of red blood cells. Is component of many enzymes, which, in turn, are necessary for development and maintenance of skeletal, cardiovascular, and central nervous systems. Works with Vitamin C to form elastin.
Manganese	Whole grains; green leafy vegetables; legumes; nuts; pineapple; egg yolk; tea; coffee.	Is enzyme activator for urea formation, protein and fat metabolism, glucose oxidation, and synthesis of fatty acids. Is necessary for normal skeletal formation, brain function. Maintains sex hormone production. May protect against pancreatic cancer.
Chromium	Corn oil; clams; whole grain cereals; meat; liver; wheat germ; brewer's yeast; drinking water in some areas of United States.	Stimulates enzymes in metabolism of energy and synthesis of fatty acids, cholesterol, and protein. Increases effectiveness of action of insulin in cell, which improves glucose uptake by body tissues.
Selenium	Seafood; tuna; herring; organ and red meat; brewer's yeast; wheat germ; bran; asparagus; mushrooms; broccoli; whole grains; bread; cereals.	Acts as cofactor in cell oxidation enzyme systems. Is constituent of factor III, which acts with Vitamin E to prevent fatty liver. Preserves tissue elasticity. Protect against heart disease. May prevent liver, colon, breast cancer.
Water	Water; coffee; tea; milk; soup; fruit juices; Jell-O; fruits; vegetables.	Is part of blood, lymph, and body secretions. Aids digestion. Dissolves nutrients and enables them to pass through intestinal wall. Regulates body temperature. Transports body wastes for elimination.

APPENDIX V

Summary Comparison of Males and Females

CHARACTERISTIC	MALE	FEMALE
Physical		
Activity level:		
At birth	Equal to female but more total body movement, difference in types of movement.	Equal to male.
1 wk	More wakeful, fretful, facial grimacing, hand and foot movements.	
Basal metabolism rate	Slightly higher.	Basal temperature increased at ovulation.
Motor ability	Faster reaction time after puberty.	Excels in fine motor coordination and manual dexterity.
Size:		
Height/weight		
At birth	Slightly greater.	
Preschool		Matures more rapidly.
School-age		Matures more rapidly.
Puberty	Exceeds female, but growth spurt comes later than for females.	Growth spurt earlier than in males.
Adulthood	Higher than for average female.	May be similar to male.
Old age	Slight loss in height and weight common.	Loss of 2 to 3 inches of height with thinning intervertebral disks usual; loss of weight similar to male with atrophy of tissues.
Pelvic outlet		Slightly larger.
Muscle mass	Strength similar in both sexes prepuberty. Greater after puberty because of testosterone; 40 percent of body in young adulthood. Atrophy occurs with age and lack of use.	Strength similar in both sexes prepuberty. Similar or greater until puberty; 23 percent of body in young adulthood. Atrophy occurs with age and lack of use.
Adipose tissue	Similar prenatally and until puberty; 15 percent of body in young adulthood.	Similar prenatally and until puberty. Greater after puberty because of estrogen; 25 percent of body in young adulthood. Increased fat gives increased energy supply; better endurance and greater buoyancy.
Heart and lungs	Larger after adolescence; related to total body size.	
Shoulder width; arm length	Greater after puberty; gives greater leverage.	Upper body power one-half to two-thirds of equally well-conditioned male after puberty.
Forearm length and breadth	Greater and larger in comparison to whole arm length or whole body length, which gives greater skill at throwing.	
Blood pressure	Related to age, size, health, and racial background.	Related to age, size, health, and racial background.

Appendix V. Summary Comparison of Males and Females—Continued

CHARACTERISTIC	MALE	FEMALE
Hemoglobin level	Higher; also related to health status.	Lower; also related to health status.
Sensitivity to stimuli:		
Visual	More interested in geometric forms from infancy on.	Greater from infancy on. Female infants show larger area of visual center in right hemisphere than males. At 4 mo recognizes picture of human face; at 6 mo longer attention span for visual stimuli. More interested in people's faces from infancy on. No differences in vision.
Auditory		Better auditory memory; carries tune better. Distinguishes individual voices earlier.
Tactile	Touched less as a child and on fewer areas of body.	Greater from infancy on. Touched more as a child and on more areas of body.
Pain		Slightly increased as birth; less anxiety about from childhood on.
General vulnerability	Statistically significant increase prenatally on through life in genetic disorders, developmental problems, disease, accidental injury, death, suicide. Life span average in 1985: 79.6 yr for Caucasian males, lower for minority males.	Life span average in 1985: 83.6 yr for Caucasian females, lower for minority females.
Onset of puberty	Increase in length of long bones and thickness of cortex. Shoulders wider.	Two years earlier than male. Smaller loss of fat than male. Increase in length of long bones and thickness of cortex. Broader hips. Pelvis structure such that for any given length of stride must rotate pelvis through greater angle than male.
Cognitive		
Overall intelligence	No statistically significant difference. Lower scores after age 60 than for females. Rate of decline same.	No statistically significant difference. Scores slightly higher after 60. Rate of decline same as for males.
Learning of concepts and memory	More learning disability in school age males.	
Information processing		Faster, especially when rapid choice needed.
Verbal language and ability	Similar females in young childhood.	Talks earlier. Better articulation. Excels after age 10 or 11, or earlier. Developed earlier than male. More advanced throughout life.
Quantitative, mathematical ability	Excels after age 11 to 13, possibly related to social expectations.	Same as male until adolescence, possibly related to social expectations.
Curiosity about objects	Greater in young child. Encouraged to explore, manipulate objects from late infancy on.	Encouraged to remain closer to mother, curiosity not encouraged as much.
Analytical ability	No difference when spatial variable controlled. Superior if task involves visual–spatial ability.	No difference when spatial variable controlled. Superior if verbal abilities involved.
Reasoning, problem-solving ability	No difference.	No difference.
Visual–spatial ability	Greater after age 6 to 8. Excels in adolescence and through most of adulthood. No difference after age 60.	Superior to males in preschool years. Uses spatial strategies less effectively and gives up more easily on spatial problems after elementary school. No difference after age 60.

CHARACTERISTIC	MALE	FEMALE
Cognitive (cont.)		
Creativity	Greater if measured by career or professional accomplishment; more male employees receive awards.	Superior if verbal skills used. No difference if nonverbal material used.
Response to Nonverbal Behavior	Uses more dominating nonverbal behavior.	More sensitive to cues; more accurate in interpretation of nonverbal cues. Use of nonverbal behavior differs and facilitates interpersonal closeness. More restricted in demeanor and use of personal space. Touches less and is touched more. More frequent eye contact during conversation. Smiles more.
Verbal Communication Patterns	Adolescent and adult talk for longer periods of time, interrupt others more frequently, control topic of conversation, make more jokes about others, use slang. Discloses more about work and interests. Impedes close interpersonal relations; facilitates interpersonal control.	Adolescent and adult use higher pitch, questioning tone rather than make statements, listen more.
Emotional		
Basic temperament	Unique to individual.	Unique to individual.
Expressiveness	No difference in duration or frequency of crying in infancy. Ages 3 to 5, reacts more to frustrating situation or conflict with adult and fear-inducing situation. Supression and denial used to hide feelings.	No different in duration or frequency of crying in infancy. Ages 3 to 5, responds more to conflict with other children. Reduces total emotional response faster than male.
	Preschool age shows fear more frequently. School age, increasingly inhibits or masks overt fear reaction. From childhood on, shows greater hostility.	Preschool age, no difference in timidity, but reacts more intensely than male.
Self-esteem	Equal to girls; sees self as more powerful.	Equal to males. Greater self-confidence in social competence. Lower sense of efficacy and of confidence to perform well in new tasks by college age.
Dependency	No difference in young child. Child needs nurturance. Receives more contact from mother first 6 mo and more encouragement to leave mother after 12 mo. In childhood, greater need for friend support.	No difference in young child. Child needs nurturance. Receives more contact from mother after 6 mo of age and kept closer to mother after 1 year. Scores same as male on Kessler Passive-Dependency Scale and Succorance Scale, Edwards Personal Preference Schedule.
	In American, western European, and African cultures, ages 7 to 11 more dependent if dependency defined as seeking attention.	In American, western European, and African cultures, ages 3 to 6 more dependent when dependency defined as seeking attention.
Sociability	At 4 mo, reacts as readily to inanimate object as person. Equal in sociability as child; individual differences.	At 4 mo, reacts more readily to people. Smiles earlier than boys and more readily throughout life. Equal in sociability as child; individual differences.
	Late childhood and adolescence has greater number of friends, depends on them more for values and support in case of conflict with adult.	Young female more likely to play alone or relate to nearby adult. Late childhood and adolescence has fewer friends but friendships more intimate or intense. Uses friends as support in personal crisis.

Appendix V. Summary Comparison of Males and Females—Continued

CHARACTERISTIC	MALE	FEMALE
Empathy	No difference; depends on situation and person.	No difference; depends on situation and person.
Affiliation need	No difference in childhood.	No difference in childhood. Possibly greater after adolescence, based on social rewards.
Achievement Motivation	No difference in basic motives. Consistently achieves lower grades in school years. Motivation aroused when achievement, competition, and leadership are emphasized. Rewarded for achieving and succeeding in areas considered sex-role appropriate. Adjusts behavior and cognitions accordingly.	No difference in basic motives. Consistently achieves better grades in school before external impediments to achievement become a serious problem. Motivation aroused when achievement emphasizes social skills. Socially rewarded for avoiding success and for achieving in area considered sex-role appropriate. Adjusts behavior and cognitions accordingly. Visible achievements decrease in females who encounter impediments with traditional wife–mother role. Those career and professionally oriented continue achieving, depending on work setting.
Aggressiveness	Greater in childhood and adulthood. Dependent on definition and socialization. Stimuli that cue aggression may differ. Feels reinforcing relief response after aggressive act. In old age, less assertive and dominant in United States; greater decline in aggressiveness possibly related to decline in testosterone level.	Generally less aggressive, hurtful, assertive, dominant. Dependent on definition and socialization. Stimuli that cue aggression may differ. Feels reinforcing relief response after nonaggressive coping response. In old age, similar to or more assertive and dominant than male.

Results are based on statistical analyses. Be aware that differences that exist between males and females show considerable individual variations in each sex. Males and females fall along a continuum of behavior and test results.

Index

A

Abortion, 367, 444
Abuse:
 of adolescent, 335, 336t
 adult, 425, 438–440
 of aged, 503–504
 characteristics in parent of abuser, 180, 195
 definition, 180
 emotional, 180
 of infant, 194–195
 nurse's role, 180–182
 of preschooler, 269
 of school child, 291t
 sexual, 180
 of toddler, 235, 236t
 types, 180
Accommodation, visual, 237
Accommodative esophoria, 296
Accumulation theory of aging, 498
Acid rain, 48
Acquired Immune Deficiency Syndrome (AIDS), 173, 300–301, 432–434
Acrocyanosis, 199
Activity theory of aging, 499
Acupuncture, 613
Acupressure, 613
Adaptive mechanisms:
 abuse, 335, 336t
 adolescent, 351–352
 definition, 223
 infant, 223–224
 later maturity, 523, 524t
 middle age, 483–484
 preschool child, 282–283
 schoolchild, 321–322
 toddler, 250
 young adult, 418
Addiction, 368
Adolescence:
 career selection 354

Adolescence (cont.):
 definitions, 332–333
 historical perspectives, 332
 stages of, 332–333
 transition to adulthood, 353–354
Adolescent, assessment of:
 adaptive mechanisms, 351–352
 age, 332–333
 body-image development, 349–350
 cognitive development, 344–345
 communication pattern, 345–346
 cultural differences, 338, 351, 364
 developmental tasks, 354–355
 ego functions, 352
 emotional development, 348–349
 exercise needs, 343–344
 family developmental tasks, 333
 family relationships, 333–335, 347–348
 gender comparison, 336, 338, 350–351, 645–648t
 growth, 336
 health problems, 356–361, 362–363t, 363–364, 365–366t, 366–372, 372–375t, 375, 376, 377
 identity sense of, 348–349
 injury, 356–357
 leisure activity, 346–348
 moral-religious development, 352–353, 354
 nutritional needs, 340–343
 peer group relationships, 345–348
 physical characteristics, 335–340
 rest needs, 344
 self-concept development, 349–350
 sexuality development, 336–337, 350–357
Adolescent, intervention with:
 abortion, 367
 alcoholism, 359–361, 376–377
 anorexia nervosa, 341
 contraception, 364, 365–366
 drug abuse, 368–371, 376–377

Adolescent, intervention with (cont.):
 health problems, 355–371, 372–374t
 health promotion, 371, 374–377
 immunizations, 356
 incest, 367–368
 injury prevention, 356
 nutrition, 340–343, 638A
 obesity, 341–343
 physical examination, 339–340
 pregnancy, 343, 364, 366–367
 safety education, 356–357
 sex education, 365–366t, 375
 sexually transmitted diseases, 361, 362–363t, 363–364,
 suicide, 358–359
 teaching family, 333, 334, 339, 341, 343, 344, 345, 346, 347, 348, 349, 350, 351, 352, 353, 354, 355, 356, 357, 359, 360, 371, 374, 375
Adoption, 120–123, 133, 228
 nurse's role, 121, 122t, 133
 phases of relationship, 121t
Adult education, 412, 413, 476–478, 601–604
Adult socialization, 483
Afro-American culture, 4, 16, 24, 33
Age, definitions of, 159, 496
Aged (see also Later maturity):
 community services for, 527, 528, 529, 530, 531, 531–532t
 cultural differences, 498
 family structure, 499–500
 federal planning, 528–530
 financial aid programs, 528–530
 future trends, 536
 group action among, 535
 legislation for, 528–530, 531
 living arrangements, 531, 533–534
 myths, 497
 nursing homes for, 531, 533
 retirement communities, 535–536
 societal aspects, 496, 497–498
 theories of aging, 498–499

Italicized letters following page numbers indicate tables (t), figures (f), and Appendices (A).

649

Ageism, 497
Aging, theories of, 498–499
Agnostic, 92
AIDS (see Acquired Immune Deficiency Syndrome)
Air pollution, 45–48
Alarm Stage, 577, 578f, 579
Alcoholism:
   disease, 359–361, 436, 517–518, 610–611
   Fetal Alcohol Syndrome, 172–173, 360
   prenatal effects, 172–173
Allergic rhinitis, 302
Alzheimer's disease, 513–514
Amblyopia, 208, 269
American Indian/Alaskan Indian Nurses Association, 37
American Indian culture, 4, 6–7, 10–11, 12t, 24, 31, 33, 34, 91–92
Amniocentesis, 425
Anal stage, 145, 247
Androgens, 337
Anemia, 219, 266, 430, 515
Angina pectoris, 474
Animistic, 273
Announcement phase, 424
Anorexia nervosa, 341
Anthropomorphism, 284
Anxiety, 145, 146
   definition, 581
   manifestations, 582t
Appalachian culture, 11, 12t
APGAR score, 199
Arcus senilis, 505
Asian–American culture, 4, 11, 12t, 13t, 14t, 15t, 16t, 23–24, 34–35, 36
Assertive behavior, 617–619
Astigmatism, 242
Attachment behavior:
   assessment, 192–193, 194
   definition, 192
   development of, 192–193, 196–197
   difficulty with, 194–195
   in father, 192–193, 195–197
   infant, 192–193, 194
   nurse's role, 196–197
   toddler, 234–235
Atheistic, 92
Autistic behavior, 197
Autogenics, 614–615
Autonomy, 247

B

Babbling, 221
Baby sitter services, 222–223
Back care, 475

Bad-me, definition of, 249
Baptism:
   adult, 86, 88, 89
   Catholic, 86
   Greek Orthodox, 87
   infant, 86–87
   Mormon, 89
   Protestant, 88
Basic needs, 573
Battered woman, 425, 438–440
Behavior, 159–161, 573
Behavior modification, 143
Benign prostatic hypertrophy, 515
Binding in, definition of, 193
Biochemical factors, 138–139
Biofeedback, 435, 613–614
Biologic oxygen demand, 50–51
Biological clock theory of aging, 498
Biological factors, 138–139
Biological rhythms, 399–402, 406
Biopsychosocial holistic health, 570
Black Nurses Association, 37
Blind, intervention with, 511t
Body-image development:
   adolescent, 349–350
   assessment, 421–422
   definition, 223, 418
   feelings related to, 419–420
   illness, changes in, 421
   infant, 223
   influences on, 418–421
   intervention, 422
   later maturity, 523–524
   middle age, 467, 470–471, 483
   preschool child, 282
   schoolchild, 316–317t, 318, 321
   stereotyped ideas, 420–421
   toddler, 249
   young adult, 418–422
Body mechanics, 610
Body transcendence, 523
Bonding, 192
Brahman, 79
Breastfeeding, 177, 210–212
Bronchitis, 514
Brown fat, definition of, 210
Buddhism, 80–81
Bulimia, 341
Burnout, 406–407
Burns, 268

C

Callus, 495
Caput succadaneum, 199
Carbuncles, 431

Cardiovascular system, 201, 206t, 237, 293–294, 338, 339, 388, 506
Caregiver role, 404, 466, 501
Cataracts, 505
Catholic, Roman, 86–87
Centering, 617
Cephalohematoma, 199
Chaplain, role of, 96–97
Chickenpox, 244
Child:
   adopted, 120–123, 133
   multiple births, 119–120
   only, 118–119
   ordinal position of, 118–120
   step-child, 123–124
Child abuse (see Abuse)
Child socialization, 117
Childbirth:
   anoxia, effect on, 176
   crisis of, 190–91
   delivery, 131
   education for, 130–131, 176
   influences on, 175–177
   medications, effect on, 175–176
   methods, 176
   nurse's role, 130, 191, 192, 226
   preparation for, 130, 190–192
Childrearing practices, 14t, 18–19, 116–127
Chlamydia, 363–364
Closed awareness of death, 551–552
Christian church, 88
Christianity, 86–91
   Amish, 91
   Baptists, 88
   basic beliefs, 489–490
   Catholicism, Roman, 86–87
   Christian Church, 88
   Christian Scientists, 90
   Church of God, 88
   Disciples of Christ, 88
   Episcopal, 88
   Greek Orthodox, 87–88
   Jehovah's Witnesses, 90
   Lutheran, 88
   Mennonite, 91
   Moravians, 91
   Mormon, 89–90
   Neo-Pentecostalism, 91
   Pentecostals, 88, 91
   Presbyterians, 88
   Protestants, 88–91
   Seventh-Day Adventist, 89
   Society of Friends, 90–91
   United Church of Christ, 88
   United Methodist, 88
   Unity School, 90–91
   Waldenses, 91

Italicized letters following page numbers indicate tables (t), figures (f), and Appendices (A).

Index

Christian Scientist, 90
Chronic obstructive pulmonary disease, 514–515
Chronic occlusive arterial disease, 514
Chronopharmacology, 401
Chum stage, 315
Church of Jesus Christ of Latter Day Saints (*see* Mormon)
Circadian rhythms, (*see* Biological rhythms)
Circumcision:
 female, 393–394
 infant, 200
Claiming, definition of, 193
Classification, 305
Cleanliness:
 Buddhism, 81
 Hinduism, 79
 Islam, 83
 Judaism, 84–85
 Shintoism, 81
Client:
 guide to teaching, 605*t*
 rights, 604*t*
Climacteric, 407, 468–469
Cocaine, 370–371
Cognitive conflict, 308
Cognitive development:
 adolescent, 344–345
 definition, 220
 infant, 220–221
 influences on, 411, 412–413, 476, 518, 519
 later maturity, 518–520
 middle age, 476–478
 preschool child, 272–274, 275*t*, 276
 schoolchild, 304–311, 312
 television, effects on, 312–314
 theories of, 148–149, 220, 245, 273–274, 305, 344–345, 476, 477, 478, 518–519
 toddler, 245–246
 young adult, 411–413
Cohabitation, 442
Collaboration, 315
Communication:
 application to daily living, 601
 attitudes in, 600
 assertive, 617–619
 effective methods of, 598–600
 hearing impaired, with, 243, 512*t*
 visually impaired, with, 511*t*
Communication patterns, 197, 204, 221–222, 246–248, 276–277, 278*t*, 312, 345–346
Community services:
 Administration of Aging, 528–529, 532*t*
 for aged, 527, 528–529, 530, 531–532
 American Association for Retired Persons, 528, 531*t*

Community services (*cont.*):
 for battered women, 439–440
 day care centers, 259–261
 family planning, 364, 365–366*t*, 423–425, 426
 Foster Grandparents Program, 529, 532*t*
 for homosexuality, 441
 for infant, 225–226
 infertility, 426
 Meals on Wheels, 531, 532*t*
 nursery schools, 259–261
 for parents, 225–226
 poison control, 242
 for pregnant teen, 376
 Retired Senior Volunteer Program, 529
 for widow(er), 463
Compartmentalization, as adaptivve mechanism, 524*t*
Compensation, as adaptive mechanism, 252
Competition, 315
Compromise, 315
Concrete Operations, 305–306
Conditioning, 142–143
Confucianism, 80, 81–82
Congenital defect, child with, 132–133
Congestive heart failure, 514
Conjunctivitis, 269–270
Conscious, 145
Conservation, 305
Constipation, 219
Continuity theory of aging, 498
Contraception, 364, 365–366*t*
Conversion, (religious), 353
Cooing, definition of, 221
Coping, 615–616
Coping skills training, 616–617
Counterphobia, as adaptive mechanism, 524*t*
Crack (cocaine), 371
Creativity, 478
Crisis, definition of, 189
Critical periods, definition, 160–161, 167
Cultural influences on development, 178–181, 200, 204–205, 238, 263, 293, 294, 304, 309, 319, 324, 338, 351, 364, 393, 394, 429, 434, 463, 466, 498, 576
Cultural relativity, 32
Cults, 92
Culture (*see also* Socioeconomic class; specific religion):
 Afro-American, 4, 16, 24, 33
 aging, influence on, 497–498
 American Indian, 4, 6–7, 10–11, 12*t*, 24, 31, 33, 34, 91–92
 Appalachian, 11, 12*t*, 24
 biological variations, 33–34
 Central America, 4

Culture (*cont.*):
 change, attitude toward, 18*t*
 changes in, 7–8
 characteristics of, 5–9
 childrearing, influence on, 14*t*, 19–20
 communication patterns, 6–7
 comparison of, 11, 24
 components, 8–9
 Cuban, 4
 customs, 8
 Danish, 4
 definition, 4
 Dominican Island, 4
 Dutch, 4, 6
 education, attitude to, 17*t*
 English, 4
 Eskimo, 24, 33, 34
 European, 4, 33
 ethnic, 4
 ethnocentricity, related to, 32
 family, 4, 13*t*, 16, 18–19, 125–127
 Finnish, 4
 French, 4
 German–American, 4, 24
 Greek, 4, 13*t*, 14*t*, 15*t*, 16*t*, 24, 87–88
 group interaction, attitude to, 15*t*
 Gypsy, 24
 health, influence on, 31
 Hispanic, 4, 31
 Icelandic, 4
 influence on development, 178–181
 Irish–American, 4, 24
 Italian–American, 4, 24
 Japanese, 4, 11, 13*t*, 14*t*, 15*t*, 16*t*, 23–24
 Jewish, 24, 33, 84–86
 Latino, 4
 leisure, attitude toward, 17*t*
 Mexican–American, 4, 6, 12*t*, 22–23, 31, 33
 Middle Eastern, 11, 12*t*, 16, 18–21, 24, 34, 36
 Migrant farmer, 24
 Norwegian, 4
 nursing applications, 5, 6, 8, 16, 19, 20, 21, 22, 23, 24, 30, 31–37
 Oriental–American, 11, 12*t*, 24, 33, 34, 35, 36
 Polish–American, 4, 24
 privacy, attitude toward, 15*t*
 Protestant ethic, influence on, 9–10
 Puerto Rican, 4, 24
 regional, 4
 Russian, 4
 Scandanavian, 4
 Scotch, 4
 Slavic, 4
 socioeconomic class, 24–31
 South American, 4
 Southeast Asian, 4, 24

651

Culture (*cont.*):
  Spanish-speaking, 4, 11, 12*t*, 13*t*, 14*t*, 15*t*, 16*t*, 22–23, 24, 36
  time, attitude to, 12*t*, 16*t*,
  United Kingdom, 4
  United States, 4, 7, 9–11, 12*t*, 21–22, 35
  Vietnamese, 24, 34–35
  Welsh, 4
Culture shock, 32
Customs, 8
Cystitis, 432

D

Day care program, 259–261
Death (*see also* Dying person):
  anniversary reaction, 555–556
  autosuggestion, 556–557
  awareness of, 551–552
  beliefs about, 547–548, 549–551
  concepts of:
    adolescent, 549
    adult, 549
    child, 547–549
  definition, 545
  developmental phase, 545
  euthanasia for, 546
  family reactions to, 555*t*
  infant, 228
  legal planning for, 557
  nursing applications, 557–563
  nursing diagnoses related to, 560
  of parents, 466
  predilection to, 556
  preparation for, 79, 80, 81, 82, 83, 84, 85, 87, 89, 551–557
  reactions to approach of, 552–555
  right to, 546–547
  of spouse, 462–463
  teaching related to, 548, 554–555, 557, 563
Decentering, 305
Delivery of child, 131
Denial:
  adaptive mechanism, 290, 524*t*
  of death, 552
  of separation, 235
Dental caries, 429
Deprivation theory of aging, 498
Dermatitis, 219, 303
Despair and self-disgust, 520
Despair, of toddler grief, 235
Desquamation, definition of, 200
Development (*see also* specific developmental era):
  assumptions about, 159–160

Development (*cont.*):
  characteristics of, 157
  childbirth, influence on, 175–177
  definition, 159
  endocrine function, influence on, 438–439, 166–167, 177–178
  family influences, 179–181
  influences on, 138–140, 142, 143–144, 151–152, 162–181
  macroenvironmental influences, 139–140
  norms, 159
  nutrition, influence on, 167–168, 177
  practice, affect of, 177
  prenatal, 162–163, 164–165*t*, 166–175
  prenatal influences on, 162–163, 164–165*t*, 166–175
  principles of, 157–162
  sociocultural influences on, 178–181
  spiritual influences on, 181
  stages of, 145–146,
  stress, affect on, 177
  theory of, 137–153
Developmental tasks:
  adolescent, 354–355
  couple, 115
  definition, 159
  disengagement stage, 116
  establishment stage, 112–113, 115
  expectant stage, 113–114, 424
  infant, 225
  later maturity, 525–526
  middle age, 488–489
  preschooler, 285
  schoolchild, 324–325
  toddler, 252
  young adult, 426, 427*t*
Developmental theories of aging, 498
Devil (Satan) worship, 92
Diabetes, 303, 474–475, 516
Dialects, 6, 30
Diarrhea, 244, 270–271, 431
Dietary habits, religious influence on, 79, 81, 82, 83, 85, 87, 89
Differentiation, definition of, 282
Diplopia, 269
Discipline (*see also* specific developmental era):
  definition, 252
  overpermissive, 280
  permissive, 280
  techniques of, 252, 280–281
Disease–illness, 570
Disengagement stage of parenthood, 116
Disengagement, theory of aging, 498
Displacement, 223
Distress, 577
Divorce, 442–444, 502

Doubt, 248
Drug abuse, 610–611
  definition, 368
  prenatal effects, 170–172
  signs and symptoms, 368–371, 372–374*t*, 436–437, 437*t*,
Drug addiction, 368–371, 372–373*t*
Drug dependence, 368
Dyad, 116
Dying person, assessment of:
  awareness, 546, 547, 551–552
  behavior, 523
  concepts of, 547–551
  crisis of loss, 553
  family reaction to, 555*t*
Dying person, intervention with, 561–563
  crisis intervention, 559
  evaluation of care, 563–564
  family, 555*t*, 559
  home care, 562
  hospice care, 563
  legal planning, 557
  mourning, 554
  nurse's role:
    family, 553–554
    patient, 552–554
    self-assessment, 557
    spiritual needs, 562
    support for self, 556
Dysmenorrhea, 337

E

Early adolescence, 332–333
Eating pattern, 211–215, 239, 265–266, 298–299
Ecological theory, 139–140
Edema, 514
Education (*see also* Health education, specific developmental era):
  client, 601–606
Ego:
  definition, 144–145, 147
  function, 351
  ideal, 145
Ego-developmental needs, 573
Ego differentiation, 523
Ego integrity, 520
Ego-libidinal needs, 573
Ego transcendence, 523
Egocentric, 245, 273
Eight-year-old, assessment of:
  behavior pattern, 316*t*
  body-image development, 320*t*
  cognitive development, 306, 307, 312
  communication pattern, 312
  eating pattern, 298*t*

Italicized letters following page numbers indicate tables (*t*), figures (*f*), and Appendices (*A*).

Index

Eight-year-old, assessment of (cont.):
　physical characteristics 294f, 295
　play activity, 314
Elderly (see also Aged; Later maturity):
　able, impact of, 536
Electra complex, 257
Eleven-year-old assessment of:
　behavior pattern, 316-317t
　body-image development, 320t
　cognitive development, 306
　communication pattern, 312
　eating pattern, 298t
　physical characteristics, 294
　play activity, 314
Emotional abuse, 180
Emotional development:
　adolescent, 348-349
　infant, 222-225
　later maturity, 521-523
　middle age, 480-484
　preschool child, 281-282
　schoolchild, 317-318
　toddler, 247-248, 249-252
　young adult, 413-415, 416
Emphysema, 515-516
Encephalopathy, 269
Endocrine system, 166-167, 208, 237, 336-337, 389, 391, 392, 467-469, 474, 507, 509, 516
Endogenous rhythms, 399
Engrossment, 192
Enuresis, 270
Environment:
　effects on health, 43-70
　legislation affecting, 44-45, 50, 51, 55, 56, 57, 59, 65, 68
　nursing application, 43-44, 47-52, 54-55, 58-59, 61-70
　occupational hazards, 59-61, 62-65t, 66t, 169
　personal responsibility for, 61, 65-66
　pollution, 45-59
　professional reponsibility for, 66-70
　therapeutic, 69-70
Epistaxis, 357
Erickson, E., theory of, 147, 222, 247-248, 281, 317-318, 348-349, 414, 416, 480, 481, 520
Establishment phase, 112-113, 115
Estrogen, 337
Ethic:
　definition, 9
　Puritan (Protestant),9-10
Ethnocentricity, 32
Euthanasia, 546
Exercise, education for, 607-609
Exercise needs, 240, 266, 299-300, 343-344, 395, 410-411, 471-472, 510
Exercise program, 409-410
Exhaustion Stage, 581

Exogenous rhythms, 399
Expectant phase, 113-114, 424

F

Failure to thrive, 181
Family:
　adaptative mechanisms, 111-112
　adoption in, 120-123, 133
　composition, 106, 108
　cultural patterns, 125-127
　definition, 106, 107t
　developmental tasks, 115, 190-193, 196, 235, 262, 292, 333, 387, 466, 467t, 525-526
　extended, 106
　functions, 109-111
　historical perspectives, 126-127
　influences on, 117-118
　interaction, 116-123, 179-180
　matrifocal, 106
　multiple births in, 119-120
　nuclear, 106
　nursing applications, 106, 109, 112, 114, 115-116, 117, 119, 120, 121, 123, 127-133
　only child, 118-119
　ordinal position in , 118-120
　patrifocal, 106
　purposes, 108
　reconstituted, 106
　roles, 107-108t, 109
　size, 119, 125
　stages of development, 112-116
　structure, 123-125, 179
　as a system, 109-111
　tasks, 109
　theories of, 107-108t
Family developmental tasks:
　adolescent, 333
　infant, 115, 190-193, 196
　later maturity, 525-526
　middle age, 466, 467t
　preschooler, 262
　schoolchild, 292
　toddler, 235
　young adult, 387
Family planning, 364, 365-366t
Family relationships (see specific developmental era)
Family size (see Family)
Family structure (see Family)
Family violence, 437-440
Fantasy, 283, 322
Fathering (see also specific developmental era), 126-127, 192-193, 424-425
Fears:
　preschool child, 282-283
　schoolchild, 306

Filial responsibility, 463-464
First Force Theory, 141-143
Five-year-old, assessment of:
　body-image development, 282
　cognitive development, 275t
　nutrition, 263, 265-266, 638A
　physical development, 263, 264-265t
　play activity, 279
　sleep needs, 266
Fluoride mottling, 294
Focusing period, 424
Folklore, 173
Folliculitis, 431
Fontanel, 198
Food additives, 53, 54
Food chain, effect on health, 44f, 49, 50f
Food pollution, 53-54
Foot care, 411, 475
Formal operations, 411-412, 477
Formula preparations, 212, 213t
Four-year-old, assessment of:
　body-image development, 282
　cognitive development, 275t
　nutrition, 263, 265-266, 638A
　physical development, 263, 264-265t
　play activity, 279
　sleep needs, 266
Fourth trimester, care in, 131-132
Frustration, 352
Functional bowel disease, 432
Furuncles, 430-431

G

Gastrointestinal system, 201, 209, 237, 264t, 294, 338, 389, 507
Gender identity (see also Body-image development), 236, 250-251, 257-258, 320-321, 336, 338, 350-351, 410, 411, 412-413, 467-469, 504, 508, 519, 576, 645-648A
Gender role, 389, 645-648A
Generation gap, 458
Generativity, 480
Genetic factors, 138, 575
Genetic theories of aging, 498
Genital stage, 145-146
Geriatrics, definition of (see also Later maturity), 496
Gerontology, definition of (see also Later maturity), 496
Gifted child, 310
Glaucoma, 505
Gonorrhea, 362-363t
Good-me, definition of, 249
Gout, 474
Grandparents, 197-198, 459, 500
Greek culture, 4, 13t, 14t, 15t, 16t, 24, 87-88

654   Index

Grief:
  of parents, 228, 229
  of toddler, 234–235
  of widow, 462–463, 501–502
Growth:
  characteristics of, 157
  definition, 159
  hormone, 177–178
  norms of, 159
  principles, 159, 161–162
  types of, 139
Guided imagery (see Imagery, guided)
Guilt, 281
Gypsy culture, 24

H

Head injury, 268
Headaches, 432
Health, definitions of, 571–572t
Health behaviors:
  definition, 590
  influences on, 572–576, 592–594
Health Belief Model, 590
Health education, 601–606
  assessment for, 602
  childbirth education, 130–131, 176
  definition, 602
  evaluation, 606
  groups, 603–604
  individual, 602–603
  literature, use of, 605–606
  methods, 601–606
  for parents, 133
Health problems (see specific developmental era, assessment)
Health Promoting Lifestyle Profile, 592
Health-promoting relationships, 594–598
Health promotion (see also specific developmental era, intervention):
  assessment tools, 591–592
  cognitive strategies, 588t
  communication for, 598–601
  definition, 589
  emotional strategies, 588t
  influences on, 592–594
  model for, 590
  nurse's role, 570, 579–580, 581, 582, 588, 591–592, 594, 595, 596, 598–601, 602–604, 605, 606–607, 608, 609, 610, 611, 612, 613, 614, 615, 616, 617–619, 619–622, 623–624, 625
  nutritional, 591
  sites for, 625–626
  social strategies, 588t
  spiritual/moral strategies, 588t

Health promotions (cont.):
  strategies for, 588t, 594–612
Health Promotion Model, 590–591
Health screening:
  definition, 606
  risk factors, 607
  tools for, 606, 633A, 634–637A
Health Self-Determinism Index, 591–592
Health teaching (see specific developmental era)
Health-wellness, 570
Hearing, 204, 243, 268, 270, 297, 389, 470, 505–506
Hearing impairment, intervention with, 243, 511, 512t
Heimlich maneuver, 609
Hemangioma, definition of, 199
Hematologic system, 209–210, 237–238, 295, 338, 470, 508
Hepatitis, 357–358, 428
Heredity, 138
Hernia, hiatal, 473
Herpes, 303, 362–363t, 513
Hinduism, 79–80
Hodgkins disease, 515
Holistic care, 36
Holistic health, 570
Homicide, 356
Homosexuality:
  chum stage, 315
  definition, 440
  life-style option, 440–441
Hordeolum, 357
Hormonal changes (see also Endocrine system), 139
Hormone, definition of, 177
Hospice, 563
Hospital wastes, 57–58
Hospitalization:
  of child, 234, 235, 251–252, 271–272, 311
  of dying, 558, 559–561
Human Ecological Model, 591
Human needs, 573
Human sexual response, 392
Hyperopic, 237
Hypertension:
  adult, 474
  juvenile, 244–245

I

Id, 144
Identification:
  binding in, 193
  definitions, 193, 257
  primary, 250
  secondary, 283, 322

Identification phase, nurse–client relationship, 597
Identity diffusion, 349
Identity formation, 348–349
Illness behavior, definition of, 590
Illness, prevention of, 609–612
Imagery, guided:
  clinical applications, 621t
  definition, 619
  nurse's role, 620, 621t, 622
  physiological mechanisms, 619–620, 621t
  problem solving, 622t
  techniques, 620, 621t
Immunity theory of aging, 498
Immunization:
  definition, 217, 266
  schedule:
    adolescent, 356
    adult, 427–428, 510
    infant, 217–218
    preschool child, 266–267
    schoolchild, 300
    toddler, 241
Immunologic system, 209, 237, 295, 508, 581–583
Imperforate anus, 205
Impetigo, 243
Incest, 321, 367–368
Incorporation, as adaptive mechanism, 223
Indoor air pollution, 48
Industry, 318
Infant, assessment of:
  abuse of, 194–195
  activity level, 197
  adaptive mechanisms, 223–224
  age, 190
  appearance, 205
  attachment behavior, 192, 193, 194, 222
  body image development, 223
  cognitive development, 220
  cultural differences, 200, 204–205
  definition, 189
  dehydration, signs of, 212–213
  developmental tasks, 225
  eating pattern, 211–215
  emotional development, 222–225
  family relationships, 189–199, 220–225
  gender comparison, 645–648A
  health problems, 219–220
  injury, 218
  language development, 221
  maternal deprivation, 180–181, 194, 222
  nutritional needs, 200–215, 638A
  physical characteristics, 205, 206–207t, 208–210

Italicized letters following page numbers indicate tables (t), figures (f), and Appendices (A).

Index

Infant assessment of (*cont.*):
    play activity, 213–217
    reflexes, 201, 202t, 203, 206–207t
    separation anxiety, 222
    sexuality development, 224
    sleep pattern, 215–216
Infant, intervention with:
    adoptive baby, 228
    attachment, promotion of, 196–197
    community resources, use of, 225, 226t, 228
    congenitally defective baby, 227–228
    feeding, 211–215
    health promotion, 217–220
    immunizations, 217–218
    infant death, 228
    language development, 221–222
    premature infant, 226–227
    safety measures, 216–217, 218
    sensory development, 203–204, 220–221
    teaching family, 191, 192, 196, 197, 198, 200, 204, 210–211, 212, 213, 214, 215, 216, 217, 218, 219, 220–221, 222, 225, 227, 228
    weaning, 215
Infection control, 609
Infectious mononucleosis, 357
Inferiority, 318
Infertility, 426
Influenza, 427, 428
Initial phase, nurse–client relationship, 597
Initiative, 281
Injury control:
    adolescent, 356
    infant, 216–217, 218
    later maturity, 511–513
    middle age, 472–473
    preschooler, 267–269
    schoolchild, 300–301
    toddler, 241–242
    young adult, 428
Injury, prevention of, 609–612
Insomnia, 405–406, 510
Integration, 282
Intelligence, 220, 518, 519, 575–576
Internal locus of control, 31
Interpersonal theory, 146–147
Intimacy, 414–415
Intrapartal period, 130–131
Introjection, as adaptive mechanism, 283
Irish American culture, 4, 24
Irrational ideas, coping with, 616
Islam, 82–84
Isolation, 322, 416, 524t
Italian–American culture, 4, 24

J

Jainism, 80
Japanese culture, 4, 11, 13t, 14t, 15t, 16t, 23–24

Jaundice, 199–200
Jehovah's Witness, 90
Jewish culture, 24, 33, 84–86
Judaism, 84–86

K

Kindergarten, 259–260
Kohlberg, L., theory of, 149–151, 284, 323–324, 352, 416–417, 487
Kosher food, 85

L

Lactation, nutritional needs, 396
Lacto-ovo-vegetarians, 397–398
Lactose intolerance, 33, 431
Lalling, 221
Language development (*see also* Communication patterns):
    definition, 221
    purposes, 221, 276
    teaching of, 222, 246, 247, 276–277
    types of, 221, 246, 247
Lanugo, 199
Latch-key child, 290
Late adolescence, 333, 353–355
Latency stage, 145
Later maturity, assessment of:
    abuse of aged, 503–504
    adaptive mechanisms, 523, 524t
    age, 496
    alcoholism in, 517–518
    appearance, 504–505
    body image changes, 523–524
    caregiver role, 501
    cognitive changes, 518–520
    death, facing of, 501–502, 520, 523, 550
    developmental tasks, 525–526
    emotional development, 520–523
    exercise needs, 510
    family developmental tasks, 525–526
    family relationships, 499–502, 503–504
    gender comparison, 504, 508, 519, 645–648A
    health problems, 513–518
    mobility, 505–506, 516
    nutritional status, 509–510, 638A
    old-old characteristics, 522–523
    pain, 505, 512
    personality characteristics, 580–584
    physiological characteristics, 504–513
    relationship with pets, 502
    rest needs, 510
    retirement, reaction to, 526–528
    sexuality, 508–509, 517

Later maturity, assessment of (*cont.*):
    social relationships, 500–501
    spiritual development, 525
    spouse relations, 499, 501–502
    stress reactions, 574–575
    transition to, 490
    young-old characteristics, 521–522
Later maturity, intervention with (*see also* Aged; Community services):
    alcoholism, 518
    body image changes, 523–524
    cardiovascular integrity, 514
    cognitive development, 519–520, 537–538
    community involvement, 531, 535–536
    consultative role, 520
    elimination, 516
    emotional needs, 520, 522–523, 536–539
    exercise, 510
    health problems, 511–512t, 637A
    hearing impairment, 511, 512t
    hypothermia, 511–512
    immunizations, 510
    in leisure, 527–528
    mobility, 511, 512–513, 516
    neurological functions, 511, 512, 513–514
    nursing home, selection of, 533
    nutrition, 509–510, 516
    osteoporosis, 516
    reality contact, 522–523, 525, 534
    reminiscence, 538
    remotivation technique, 534
    respiratory function, 514–515
    rest, 510
    retirement, adjustment to, 527–528
    safety measures, 511–513
    sensory perception, 511, 512
    sexuality needs, 517
    skin care, 504, 511–512, 514
    spiritual needs, 525
    standards for care, 526
    structural changes, 505, 506, 516
    teaching, 499, 500, 501, 502, 503, 510, 511, 513, 515, 517, 518, 519–520, 523, 525, 527, 528, 530, 533
    visual impairment, 511t
Lead poisoning, 58–59
Leadership, role, 479
Learning (*see* Cognitive development)
Legal planning for death, 557
Leisure:
    in adolescence, 346–348
    in aged, 527–528
    definition, 527
    influences on, 312–314, 409, 478, 479,
    in middle age, 472, 478–479
    in school child, 311–315
    in young adulthood, 409–410

Lentigo senilis, 504
Leukemia, 515
Life-after-life, 550–551
Life-style options:
  homosexuality, 440–441
    physical illness related to, 361–364, 366–367, 368–371, 431–437, 441
    singlehood, 422–423
    transsexuality, 441–442
    young adulthood, 431–444
Love, 415
Lower class, 16, 448–452
Lumbosacral strain, 475
Lutheran, 88

M

Maintenance phase, nurse–client relationship, 597
Malabsorption syndrome, 243
Male batterer, 438, 439
Malingering, 322
Malnutrition, 239–240
Maltreatment (*see* Abuse)
Marriage, 415–416
Masturbation, 351
Maternal deprivation, 181
Maternal infection, 173–174
Maturational factors, 139
Maturity, 481–482
Measles, 271
Meconium, 201
Medical quackery, 604–605
Medicare, 530, 532*t*
Menarche, 332
Menopause (*see also* Middle age), 467, 468–469
Menstruation, 337
Mentor, 480
Micrograthia, 205
Mid-adolescence, 333
Middle age, assessment of:
  adaptive mechanisms, 483–484
  age, 458
  body-image changes, 467, 470–471, 483
  caregiver role, 464–465
  cognitive development, 476–478
  cultural differences, 463, 466
  developmental tasks, 488–489
  emotional development, 480–483
  empty nest, reaction to, 459, 460
  exercise needs, 471–472
  family developmental tasks, 466, 467*t*
  family relationships, 458–466
  gender comparison, 467–469, 645–648*A*
  health problems, 472–476

Middle age, assessment of (*cont.*):
  leadership ability, 479
  leisure, use of, 479–480
  maturity, 481–482
  midlife crisis, 484–487
  nutritional needs, 471, 638*A*
  personality development, 482–483
  physical characteristics, 467–471
  moral-religious development, 487
  personality development, 482–483
  sexual behavior, 461, 475–476
  sleep needs, 472
  spouse relationships, 460–463
  transition to old age, 490
  widow(er)hood, 462–463
  work, role of, 478–479
Middle age, intervention with:
  estrogen therapy, 469
  health promotion, 473, 636–637*A*
  health teaching, 459, 461, 462, 463, 465, 466, 467, 469, 470, 471, 472, 473, 474, 475, 476, 478, 479, 483, 484, 485–486, 488, 489, 490
  leisure, 479–480
  midlife crisis, 484–487
  nutritional, 471
  safety measures, 472–473
  sexuality, 475–476
  stress, management of, 461–462
  widow(er)hood, 462–463
Middle class, 12*t*, 25–27
Middle East culture, 11, 12*t*, 16, 18–21, 24, 34, 36
Midlife crisis, 484–487
Midlife transition, 484
Migrant workers, 24
Milia, 199
Mind-body relationship:
  definition, 581
  effects, 581–583
Mistrust, 222
Mittleschmerz, 390–391
Model of Multiple Risk Factor Behavior, 591
Modeling, 148
Mongolian spots, 33, 199, 238
Montessori Program, 259
Moral development, 252, 283–285, 323–324, 352–353, 354, 416–418, 487, 525
  super ego development, 257–258, 284–285
  theory of, 149–151, 284, 323–324, 352, 416–417, 487
Morality of constraint, 315
Morality of cooperation, 315
Moratorium period, 424
Mores, 8, 139

Mormon, 89–90
Mother, definition of, 189
Muhammed, 83
Multiplication, 305
Mumps, 303–304
Musculoskeletal chest pain, 356
Musculoskeletal system, 206–207*t*, 209, 237, 264–265*t*, 295, 336, 337–338, 388, 467, 469–470, 505, 506
Mutual pretense, related to death awareness, 552
Multiple births, 119–120
Muslim (*see* Islam)
Myelinization, 236
Myopia, 242

N

National Association of Hispanic Nurses, 37
Near-death experiences, 550–551
Needs, hierarchy of, 152–153
Neglect, 180
Neo-Behaviorists, 142–143
Neonate, assessment of:
  abnormalities, 205
  age, 190
  anoxia, effect of, 176, 199
  APGAR score, 199
  appearance, 198
  chest circumference, 198, 206*t*
  cognitive development, 220
  communication pattern, 204*t*
  cultural differences, 204–205
  feeding pattern, 211
  head circumference, 198–199, 200, 206*t*
  hearing, 204
  length, 200
  meconium, 201
  medications, effects of, 170–173, 175–176
  nutritional needs, 211, 212, 213
  physical assessment, 205
  physical characteristics, 198–205
  prematurity, effect of, 176–177, 226–227
  reflexes, 200*t*, 201, 203
  sensory ability, 203–205
  skin, 199–200
  sleep pattern, 215–216
  vital signs, 201
  weight, 200
Neonate, definition of, 198
Neonate, intervention with:
  parental teaching, 196, 197, 198, 200
  sensory stimulation, 203–204
Neo-Pentecostalism, 91
Nesting, 305

Italicized letters following page numbers indicate tables (*t*), figures (*f*), and Appendices (*A*).

Neurological system, 199t, 201, 202t, 203–205, 208, 236–237, 263, 264–265t, 295, 336, 505–506
Nine-month-old, assessment of:
  cognitive development, 220
  language development, 221
  nutritional needs, 211, 212, 213, 214, 638A
  physical characteristics, 206–207t, 208
  play, 217
  sleep patterns, 216
Nine-year-old, assessment of:
  behavior pattern, 316t
  body image development, 320t
  cognitive development, 306, 307, 312
  communication pattern, 312
  eating pattern, 298t
  physical characteristics, 293, 294f, 295
  play activity, 314
Noise pollution, 54–56
Nongenetic cellular theories of aging, 498
Non-school time, use of, 311–312
Norms, 159
North American Indian religions, 91–92
Not-me, definition of, 249
NREM sleep, 403
Nurse–client relationship:
  definition, 594
  guidelines for, 596–597
  helping relationship, 594–598
  influences on, 595–596
  nontherapeutic relationship, 595
  phases, 597–598
  social relationship, 594–595
Nurse entrepreneur, 626
Nursery school program, 259–261
Nursing diagnosis:
  for adolescent, 355t
  cultural, 35t
  environmental, 68t
  for family, 129t
  for infant, 225t
  for later maturity, 537
  for middle age, 489t
  for preschooler, 285t
  for school child, 324t
  for spiritual care, 96t
  for stress management, 625t
  for young adult, 428t
Nursing homes, 531, 534
Nutrition education, 607
Nutritional assessment form, 593f
Nutritional needs:
  adolescent, 340–343, 638A
  infant, 210–215
  lactation, 396
  later maturity, 506, 509–510, 638A
  middle age, 471, 638A
  prenatal, 167–168
  preschool child, 263, 265–266

Nutritional needs (cont.):
  schoolchild, 297–298, 638A
  toddler, 239–240, 638A
  vegetarians, 215, 265, 397–398
  young adult, 395, 396–397

O

Obesity, 177, 299, 341–343, 397
Occupational hazards, 59–61, 62–65t, 66t, 169
Occupational health assessment 67t
Oedipal complex, 145, 257, 281
One Genus Postulate, 146
One-year-old (see Infant, assessment of: Infant, intervention with; Twelve-month-old)
Only child, 118–119
Open awareness of death, 552
Operant conditioning, 142–143
Oral stage, 145
Ordinal position of child, 118–120
Oriental-American culture, 4, 11, 12t, 13t, 14t, 15t, 16t, 23–24, 33, 34, 35, 36
Orientation phase, nurse–client relationship, 597
Osteoarthritis, 516
Osteoporosis, 506, 515–516
Otitis, 302
Ovulation, 163, 166, 337, 392
Ovulation method, 392

P

Parasympathetic nervous system response, 579
Parataxic mode of experience, 146, 245
Parent, definition of, 189
Parenthood, 114–116
  abusive, 180, 195
  attachment in, 192–193, 194–195
  baby's influence on, 197–198
  crisis of, 190–192
  expectancy phase, 423
  reasons for, 423
  relationship of couple, 190–192
  skills, 191–193, 194, 195–197
Parent education, 133
Parents Anonymous, 194
Parkinson's disease, 513
Patient's rights, 604
Peck's theory of aging, 489, 498, 523
Pediculosis, 303, 432
Peer, definition of, 256, 277
Peer group:
  definition, 277, 345
  dialect, 345–346
  relationship, 277, 345–348

Pentecostals, 88, 91
Perceptual deprivation, 181
Perimenopausal years, 467
Periodontal disease, 429
Person, definitions of, 107t
Pesticides, 51, 53–54
Pets, relation with, 262, 503
Phallic stage, 145
Pharyngitis, 243
Phenylketonuria, 217
Phthirius (lice), 364
Physical assessment (see also Appendices I and II):
  abdomen, 205, 239, 473–474
  APGAR score, 199t
  appearance, 198, 236, 263, 293, 294, 336–337, 388, 467, 504–505
  approach to, 238, 296, 339
  biological rhythms, 399–402
  breasts, 429
  cardiovascular system, 237, 239, 293–294, 297, 338, 339, 388, 430, 470, 474, 506, 514
  chest, 198, 206t
  electrolyte status, 338
  endocrine system function, 166–167, 208, 237, 336–337, 389, 391, 392, 467–469, 474, 507, 509, 516
  extremities, 239
  eye, 205
  gastrointestinal system function, 201, 209, 237, 264, 294, 338, 389, 507
  gender comparison, 645–648A
  genitalia, 205, 239, 336–337, 339–340, 393–394, 429, 475, 508, 515
  girth, 293
  head, 198–199, 200, 205, 206t, 238–239, 294, 473, 504–505, 507
  hearing, 204, 296, 389, 470, 505–506
  height, 200, 205, 206t, 236, 263, 293, 295, 336, 388
  hematologic, 209–210, 237–238, 338, 430, 470, 508, 515
  immunological system function, 237, 295, 508, 581–583
  length, 200
  metabolism rate, 389, 469–470, 474
  motor ability, 206–207t, 237, 263, 264–265, 295,
  muscular, 206t, 209, 236–237, 264–265, 295, 336, 337–338, 388, 467, 469–470, 505, 506
  nervous system function, 208, 236–237, 239, 295, 389, 505–506
  olfactory, 204, 506
  pain, 203, 512
  pelvic, 340, 392, 429, 469
  rectal, 205, 429, 473, 515
  reflexes, 201, 202t, 203, 206t
  renal, 209, 237, 294, 338, 506–507

Physical assessment (cont.):
　　respiratory system function, 208–209, 237, 239, 290, 333, 388–389, 515
　　secondary sex characteristics, 295–296, 336–337
　　skeletal system, 200, 205, 236, 295–296, 297, 336–337, 337–338, 340, 388, 475, 505, 506, 515–516
　　skin, 199–200, 205, 209, 237, 238, 295–296, 336, 338, 339, 388, 430, 431, 475, 504, 514
　　tactile response, 203, 505, 511, 512–513
　　taste, 204, 506
　　technique, 205, 238–239, 296–297, 339–340
　　teeth, 238–239, 294f, 338, 339, 428–429, 470, 507
　　vision, 203, 208, 237, 238, 295, 296, 339, 389, 470, 505, 511
　　vital signs, 201, 206t, 238, 263, 293, 338, 339, 430, 474
　　weight, 200, 206t, 236, 263, 293, 295, 336, 388
Physical development, 198–205, 206–207t, 208–210, 236–239, 263, 264–265t, 293–297, 335–340, 387–389, 467–471, 504–513
Physiological needs, 573
Physiological theories of aging, 498
Piaget, J., theory of, 148–149, 221, 245, 273–274, 305, 315, 324, 344–345, 411–412
Pica, 58, 168
Pinworms, 244
Play:
　　definition, 279–280
　　infant, 216–217
　　preschooler, 277–280
　　purposes, 277–278
　　schoolchild, 314–315
　　toddler, 240, 241t
　　types, 279–280
Pluralistic society, definition, 32
Polarization, definitions of, 193
Polish-American culture, 424
Pollution:
　　air, 45–48
　　food, 53–54
　　lead, 58–59
　　noise, 54–56
　　nurse's responsibility, 43–44, 47–52, 54–55, 58–59, 61–70
　　personal responsibility, 61, 65–66
　　radioactive substances, 47, 48, 49, 54, 57, 69–70
　　soil, 51–53

Pollution (cont.):
　　surface, 54–59
　　water, 48–51
Poor, 28–31
Postpartum, nurse's role, 131–132
Postvention, 359
Poverty, 28
Preadolescent:
　　age, 290
　　chum stage, 315
　　definition, 290
　　physical characteristics, 295–296
Predilection to death, 556
Pregnancy:
　　adolescent, 364, 366–367, 376
　　crisis, 190–191
　　nutrition for, 396, 638A
　　sexual activity during, 393
Prematurity, 132–133, 176–177, 226–227
Premenstrual syndrome, 391–392
Prenatal care, 130
Prenatal development:
　　alcohol, effects on, 172–173
　　drugs, effects on, 170–172
　　endocrine function in, 166–167
　　environmental hazards, 168–174
　　father's health, effects of, 175
　　fetal infection, effects of, 174–175
　　folklore, effects on, 173
　　heredity, related to, 162–163, 166
　　immunologic factors, 175
　　influences on, 166–175
　　maternal age related to, 166
　　maternal emotions, effect of, 175
　　maternal infection, effect of, 173–174
　　maternal nutrition, effect of, 167–168
　　metabolic function in, 166–167
　　nurse's role, 166–180, 181–182
　　nutritional needs, 167–168
　　smoking, effect of, 169–170
　　stages, 164–165t, 166
　　teratogens, 172–173
Presbycusis, 505
Presbyopia, 470, 505
Preschool child, assessment of:
　　abuse, 269
　　adaptive mechanisms, 282–283
　　age, 256
　　body image, 282
　　cognitive development, 272–274, 275t, 276
　　communication pattern, 276–227, 278t
　　developmental tasks, 285
　　eating patterns, 265–266
　　emotional development, 281–283
　　exercise needs, 266
　　family developmental tasks, 262
　　family relationships, 256–258, 274, 276–277, 280–282, 283–285

Preschool child, assessment of (cont.):
　　gender comparison, 257–258, 645–648A
　　health problems, 268–271
　　hospitalization, reaction to, 271–272
　　injury, 267–269
　　language development, 276–277, 278t
　　moral-religious development, 283–285
　　motor development, 264–265t
　　nonfamily relationships, 259–261
　　nutritional needs, 263, 265–266, 638A
　　physical characteristics, 263, 264–265t
　　play, 277–280
　　sexuality development, 257–258, 282
　　sibling relationships, 261–262
　　sleep patterns, 266
　　superego development, 257–258, 284–285
Preschool child, intervention with:
　　body image development, 282
　　communication techniques, 276–277, 280–281
　　day care placement, 259–261
　　education, 259–261, 274, 276
　　guidance, 276–277, 280–281
　　health promotion, 266–270, 634A
　　during hospitalization, 271–272
　　immunization, 266–267
　　nursery school placement, 259–261
　　safety measures, 267–268
　　teaching family, 257, 258, 259, 260, 261–262, 265, 266, 267–268, 270, 271, 272, 276, 280, 281, 282, 283, 284, 285, 286
Prevention:
　　behavior, influences on, 594
　　primary, 590
　　secondary, 590
　　tertiary, 590
Progesterone, 337
Progressive relaxation, 612–613
Projection, as adaptive mechanism, 250, 322
Prostatitis, 475
Prosumers, 528
Protestant, 88–91
Protestant ethic, 9–10
Prototaxic mode of experience, 146
Psychological age, 496
Psychological theory, 140–153
Psychology, definition of, 137
Psychoneuroimmunology, 581–583
Psychosocial development, definition of, 220
Psychosocial theories of aging, 498
Psychosomatic, definition (see also Mind-body relationship), 581
Ptosis, 205

Italicized letters following page numbers indicate tables (t), figures (f), and Appendices (A).

Index

Pubarche, 332
Puberty, 332
Puerto Rican culture, 4, 24
Pyelonephritis, 432

Q

Quackery (see Medical quackery)
Quaker, 90–91

R

Rabies, 304
Radioactive substances, 48, 49, 54, 57, 69–70
Rationalization, 322, 524t
Reaction formation, 250
Recommended Daily Allowances, 638A
Reconstituted family (see also Step-parent family), 123–124
Reflexes, infant, 201, 202t, 203
Reflexology, 613
Regression, as adaptive mechanism, 322, 523
Relaxation, 612–613, 615
Religion, 79–92
  common characteristics, 78–79, 92
  definition, 78
Religious development (see Moral development)
REM sleep, 403–404, 405
Remotivation technique, 534
Renal system, 209, 212, 237, 264t, 294–295, 338, 468, 469, 506
Repression, 283
Resilient children, 179–180
Resistance Stage, 579–581
Resource Model of Preventive Health Behavior, 591
Respiratory system, 208–209, 237, 338, 388–389, 506
Retirement, 526–528, 535–536
Retirement planning, 527–530, 531–532t, 533, 534, 535–536
Reversibility, 305
Reyes syndrome, 244
Rigidity, as defense mechanism, 524t
Ritual, 5
Ritualistic behavior, 321–322
Roles, 5, 16, 18
Roman Catholicism, 86–87
Rubella, 244

S

Safety measures (see Injury control)
Safety promotion, 609–610

School:
  entry, 259–260, 307–308
  experiences, 259–261, 307–311, 319
  hospitalized, child, 311
  nurse's role, 308, 309, 310, 311
  phobia, 308
Schoolchild, assessment of:
  abuse, 291t
  adaptive mechanisms, 321–322
  age, 290
  behavior, 317t
  body image, 318–321
  chum stage, 315
  cognitive development, 304–311
  communication pattern, 312
  cultural differences, 293, 294, 304, 309, 319, 324
  developmental tasks, 324–325
  eating patterns, 298–299
  emotional development, 318–322
  exercise needs, 299–300
  family developmental tasks, 292
  family relationships, 290–292, 298, 308, 309, 311, 314, 317, 318, 319, 321, 322–323
  fears, 306
  gang stage, 315
  gender comparison, 320–321, 645–648A
  health problems, 301–304
  hospitalization, reaction to, 311
  latch-key child, 290
  moral-religious development, 323–324
  nonfamily relationships, 292–293
  nutritional needs, 297–298, 638A
  peer relationships, 314–315
  physical characteristics, 293–297
  play activity, 314
  rest needs, 299
  school experience, 259–261, 307–311, 319
  self-concept development, 317–321
  sexuality development, 295–296, 318–321, 336
  sibling relationships, 291–292
  socialization tasks, 315, 317
  superego development, 317
  teacher relationships, 308, 317, 318, 319
Schoolchild, intervention with:
  during geographic transition, 322–323
  guidance, 317–318
  health promotion, 300–304, 634A
  during hospitalization, 311
  immunization, 300
  safety measure, 300–301
  sexuality education, 321
  teaching family, 291, 292, 293, 296, 298, 299, 300, 301, 304, 306, 307, 308, 309, 310, 311, 313, 314, 315, 317, 318, 319, 321, 322, 325

Science, 9
Scoliosis, 297
Secondary sex characteristics, 295–296, 336–337
Self-actualization, 152–153
Self care:
  definition, 602
  sources of literature, 605–606
Self-concept, 223, 249–250, 282, 318–321, 349–350, 418–422, 467, 470–471, 483, 523–524, 576
Self-esteem, 117
Senescence, 491
Sensory ability, 203, 205, 236–237, 265, 295, 389, 468, 505–506
Separation, response to:
  in infancy, 180–181
  in preschooler, 256, 259
  in schoolchild, 290, 292, 307, 322
  in toddler, 234–235
Seriation, 305
Seven-year-old, assessment of:
  behavior pattern, 316t
  body-image development, 320
  cognitive development, 305, 306, 307, 312
  communication pattern, 312
  eating pattern, 298t
  physical characteristics, 293, 294f, 295
  play activity, 314
Seventh-Day Adventist, 89
Sex education, 224–225, 251, 258–259, 321, 390
Sexual behavior:
  attitudes toward, 361, 375, 389
  cohabitation, 442
  dysfunction, 393, 475, 517
  extramarital, 442
  homosexuality, 433, 440–441
  marital, 415–416
  nursing history of, 394–395
  premarital, 64, 442
  response in, 392
  transsexuality, 441–442
  variations in, 440–442
Sexual dysfunction, 393, 475, 517
Sexual harrassment on job, 408–409
Sexual molestation, 180
Sexuality:
  definition, 224, 339
  education, 224–225, 251, 258–259, 321, 390
  health problems related to,
    abortion, 367, 444
    contraception, 364, 365–366t
    sexually transmitted diseases, 173–174, 361–362, 363t, 363–364
    pregnancy, 364, 366–367, 376, 393
Sexuality development:
  adolescent, 336, 350–351

Sexuality development (*cont.*):
  infant, 224–225
  later maturity, 508–509, 517
  middle age, 461, 475–476
  preschooler, 257–258, 282
  schoolchild, 295–296, 318–321, 336
  toddler, 250–251
  young adult, 289–293
Sexually transmitted disease, 173–174, 361–362, 363*t*, 363–364
Shamanism, 91–92
Shame, 247–248, 251–252
Shiatsu, 613
Shintoism, 80, 81
Shock, cultural, 32
Siblings:
  definition, 261
  relationships, 261–262, 291–292
Sikhism, 80
Singlehood, 422–423, 502–503
Single-parent family, 123, 125, 133, 425–426
Single status, 125
Sinusitis, 473
Silent Unity, 91
Six-month-old, assessment of:
  cognitive development, 220
  language development, 221
  nutritional needs, 211, 213, 214
  physical characteristics, 202*t*, 205, 206–207*t*, 209, 638*A*
  play activity, 216–217
  sleep pattern, 216
Six-year-old, assessment of:
  behavior pattern, 316–317*t*
  body-image development, 320
  cognitive development, 304–305, 307, 312
  communication pattern, 312
  eating pattern, 298*t*
  physical characteristics, 294*f*, 295
  play activity, 314
Skin, 199–200, 237, 268, 293, 295, 296, 336, 338, 388, 430, 467, 469–470, 475, 504
Skinner, B. F., 142–143
Sleep:
  adolescent, 344
  cycle, 402–405
  deprivation, 404–405
  infant, 215–216
  later maturity, 510
  middle age, 472
  preschooler, 226
  promotion of, 405–406
  schoolchild, 299
  toddler, 240–241
  young adult, 402–403

Sleep apnea, 472
Sleep cycle, 402–405
Sleep deprivation, 404–405
Sleep disturbance, 404–405, 510
Smoking, cigarette, 47, 169–170, 304, 437–438
  cessation of, 610, 611*t*
Social age, 496
Social mobility, 458
Social relationship with client, 594–595
Social Security, 529–530
Socialization, 178–179, 315
Sociocultural influences, 3–36
Sociocultural theories of aging, 498–499
Socioeconomic class:
  definition, 4
  influence on behavior and health, 28–31
  lower class, 27–31
  middle class, 12*t*, 25–27
  nurse's role, 24, 30
  upper class, 12*t*, 24–25
Sociopath, 285
Soil pollution, 51–53
Solid wastes, 54–59
Somatization, 524*t*
Somatopsychic, 581
Space, definition of 273
Spanish-speaking culture, 4, 11, 12*t*, 13*t*, 14*t*, 15*t*, 16*t*, 22–23, 24, 36
Speech (*see also* Communication pattern):
  autistic, 246
  definition, 221, 246
Spermatogenesis, 163, 332, 337
Spider nevi, 238
Spina bifida, 205
Spiritual care, 78, 80–92, 93–99, 562–563
Spiritual dimension, 78
Spiritual distress, 96
Spiritual needs (*see also* specific religions):
  assessment, 94–96, 562
  evaluation of care, 99, 563
  intervention in, 96–99, 562
  nursing application, 93
Sprains, 357
Stages I–IV sleep, 403, 404, 405
Standards for geriatric nursing, 526
Stasis ulcer, 514
Step-parent family, 123–124
Strabismus, 242, 269
Strains, 357
Stress:
  definition, 576
  management of, 612–626
  physical, 577, 578*f*, 579–581
  psychological, 581–583
  related to work, 402, 406–409
  Syndrome, 576–581

Stress management:
  assessment, 612
  techniques, 612–626
Stress reactions, 435
Stressors, 577
Subculture, definition of (*see also* Culture: specific religion), 4
Sublimation, 250, 322, 524*t*
Substance abuse, 407 (*see also* Alcohol; Drug abuse)
Suicide, 358–359, 360
Superego: 145, 284–285, 317
Suppression, as adaptive mechanism, 250
Surface pollution, 54–59
Surfactant, 201
Surrogate parent, 426
Suspicious awareness of death, 552
Symbolization, 223
Sympathetic nervous system response, 577, 578*f*, 579
Syntaxic mode, 146, 312
Syphilis, 362–363*t*
Systems theory, 140, 141*t*

T

Taoism, 81–82
Teaching (*see also* Health education; specific developmental era)
  definition, 601
Teaching methods:
  evaluation, 606
  group, 603–604
  individual, 602–603
Teacher–student relationship, 308, 319
Teen, walkaway, 353
Teeth, development of, 207*t*, 213, 215, 236, 267, 294, 339, 389, 396, 470, 505, 507
Television, effects of, 276, 312
Ten-year-old, assessment of:
  behavior pattern, 316*t*
  body-image development, 320*t*
  cognitive development, 306–307, 312
  communication pattern, 312
  eating pattern, 298*t*
  physical characteristics, 294*f*, 295
  play activity, 314, 315
Teratogenic, 68, 168–173
Termination phase, nurse–client relationship, 597–598
Theory:
  of aging, 498–499
  of Bandura, 148
  Behaviorism, 142–143, 246
  biological basis for development, 138–139

Italicized letters following page numbers indicate tables (*t*), figures (*f*), and Appendices (*A*).

Theory (cont.):
   of development, 137–153, 157–162
   ecological, 139–140
   of Erikson, 147, 222, 247–248, 281, 317–318, 348–349, 414, 416, 480, 481, 520
   of family, 107–108t
   First Force, 141–143
   of Freud, 144–146, 247, 250, 257, 283, 284–285, 287
   Hierarchy of Needs, 152–153
   Interpersonal, 146–147
   of Jung, 147–148, 482
   of Kohlberg, 149, 150–151t, 284, 323–324, 352, 416–417, 487
   of Maslow, 152–153
   Neo-Analytic, 146–149
   of Peck, 489, 498, 523
   of Pender, 590–591
   of Piaget, 148–149, 221, 245, 273–274, 305, 315, 324, 344–345, 411–412
   Psychoanalytic, 144–146
   psychological, 140–153
   Second Force, 141, 143–151, 483
   of Skinner, 142–143
   of Sullivan, 146–147, 312, 315
   Systems, 140, 141t
   Third Force, 141, 151–153
   of wellness, 589
Therapeutic communication:
   application to daily living, 601
   effective methods, 598–601
Therapeutic milieu, 69–70
Therapeutic touch, 615
Thought stopping, 616
Three-month-old, assessment of:
   cognitive development, 220
   language development, 221
   nutritional needs, 211, 212, 213, 214, 215, 638A
   physical characteristics, 205, 206–207t, 208, 209
   play, 217
   sleep pattern, 216
Three-year-old:
   body image development, 282
   cognitive development, 225t
   nutritional needs, 263, 265–266, 638A
   physical development, 263, 264–265t
   play activity, 279t
   sleep needs, 266
Time:
   dimensions of, 158–159
   management of, 623
Tinea (ringworm), 303, 357
Toddler, assessment of:
   abuse, 235, 236t
   adaptive mechanisms, 250
   age, 233
   appearance, 236

Toddler, assessment of (cont.):
   attachment behavior, 234–235
   body image development, 249
   cognitive development, 245–246
   cultural differences, 237–238
   developmental tasks, 252
   eating pattern, 259
   emotional development, 247–248, 249–252
   exercise needs, 240
   family developmental tasks, 235
   family relationships, 234–236
   gender differences, 236, 250–251, 645–648A
   health problems, 242–245
   injury, 241–242
   language development, 246–247
   moral development, 252
   negativism, 247, 248, 249
   nutritional needs, 239–240
   physical characteristics, 236–239
   play activity, 240
   self-concept development, 249–250
   separation anxiety, 234–235
   sexuality development, 250–251
   sleep, 240–241
   temper tantrums, 251–252
   toilet training, 248–249
   vision, 237
   vital signs, 237
Toddler, intervention with:
   guidance, 251–252
   hospitalization, 234, 235
   immunizations, 240
   play principles, 241t
   safety measures, 241–242
   teaching family, 234, 235, 239, 240, 243, 244, 245–246, 247, 248, 251–252, 253
   toilet training, 248–249
Toilet training, 248–249
Toys:
   characteristics of, 217, 278–280
   infant, 216–217
   preschooler, 277–280
   schoolchild, 314
   toddler, 240
Transcultural nursing, 32
Transformation, 305
Transition to young adulthood, 353–354
Translocation syndrome, 533
Transsexuality, 441–442
Trust, 222
Twelve-month-old, assessment of:
   cognitive development, 220
   language development, 221
   nutritional needs, 211, 212, 213, 214, 215, 638A
   physical characteristics, 205, 206–207t, 208, 209

Twelve-month-old, assessment of (cont.):
   play, 217
   sleep patterns, 216
Twelve-year-old, assessment of:
   behavior pattern, 316–317t
   body-image development, 320t
   cognitive development, 306, 307, 312
   communication pattern, 312
   eating pattern, 298t
   physical characteristics, 293, 294f, 295
   play activity, 314

U

Ulcer, duodenal/peptic, 473–474
Unconscious, 145, 147
Umbilical cord, 200
Undernutrition, 299
Underweight, 340–341
Undoing, as adaptive mechanisms, 322
United States culture, 4, 7, 9–11, 12t, 21–22, 35
Unity School of Christianity, 90–91
Urinary tract infection, 270

V

Vaginitis, 270, 361, 363
Values (see also Culture; specific religion):
   American Indian, 10–11, 12t
   Appalachian, 11, 12t
   change, 18t
   childrearing, 14t, 19–20
   cleanliness, 19
   education, 17t
   effect of television on, 312–314
   European–American, 11, 12t
   family, 13t, 16, 18–19
   Greek, 11, 13t, 14t, 15t, 16t, 24, 87–88
   health care, 19, 20–24
   interaction, 15t, 19–20
   Japanese, 11, 13t, 14t, 15t, 16t, 23–24
   leisure, 17t
   Mexican, 12t
   Middle Eastern, 11, 12t, 16, 18–21
   nature, 12t
   Oriental, 11, 12t
   Pentecostal, 12t
   privacy, 15t
   social class, 12t, 24–31
   Society of Friends, 12t
   Spanish–American, 11, 12t, 13t, 14t, 15t, 16t, 22–23
   time, 12t, 16t
   United States, 7, 9–11, 12t, 21–22
Value system, 4

Variables affecting behavior, 573–576
Variables affecting health:
　external, 574–575
　internal, 575–576
Vascularization, 410
Vegetarian, 89, 215, 265, 397–398
Vernix caseosa, 199
Vietnamese culture, 24, 34–35
Vision, 203–204, 208, 237, 242, 263, 269–270, 295, 296, 302, 339, 389, 470, 505, 511
Visually impaired, communication with, 511t
Vital signs, 199t, 201, 206t, 237, 238, 263, 293, 338, 388, 470
Voodoo, 93

W

Warts, 303, 364
Water pollution, 48–51
Weaning, 212, 215
Wear and tear theory of aging, 498
Well baby care, 130
Wellness:
　definition, 569–570
　nursing, 589–592
　programs for, 625–626
　theory of, 589
Wellness Belief Scale, 592
Widow(er)hood, 462–463, 501, 502
Work options, 407–409
Working phase, nurse–client relationship, 597
World Health organization, 625, 626

Y

Yoga, 79–80, 614
Young adult, assessment of:
　adaptive mechanisms, 418
　age, 386
　biological rhythms, 399–402
　body image development, 418–422
　cognitive development, 411–413
　developmental tasks, 426, 427t
　emotional development, 413–415, 416
　exercise needs, 395, 409–410
　family developmental tasks, 387
　family relationships, 386–387
　female circumcision, 393–394
　gender comparison, 410, 411, 412–413, 645–648A
　health problems, 427–440
　infertility, 426
　injury, 428
　leisure, use of, 409–410
　lifestyle options, 422–423
　moral-religious development, 416–418
　nutritional needs, 395, 396–397
　parenthood, 423–426
　physical characteristics, 387–389
　premenstrual syndrome, 390–391
　rest needs, 402–403
　self-concept developmment, 418–422
　sexual behavior, 389, 440–442
　sexual dysfunction, 393
　sexual history, 394–395
　sexual response, 392
　sleep cycle, 402–405
　sleep deprivation, 404–405
　stress reactions, 402, 406–409, 577, 578t, 579–583
　work activities, 406–409

Young adult, intervention with:
　abortion, 444
　alcoholism, 407, 436
　battered wife, 425, 437–440
　biofeedback training, 434–435
　for biological rhythms, 401–402
　body image changes, 421–422
　dental problems, 429
　emotional health, 407, 408, 414–415, 416, 421–422, 435, 436, 437, 438, 441, 443, 444
　family relationships, 386–387, 423–425
　　health promotion, 427–440, 635–636A
　　marital problems, 415–416
　　nutritional, 396–399
　　parenthood, 191, 192, 194, 196, 197, 198, 423, 424, 425, 426
　premenstrual syndrome, 391–392
　safety measures, 409–411, 428, 609–610
　self-concept, 419–420, 421–422
　sexuality education, 390, 394
　sleep disturbance, 402, 405–406
　smoking, 437, 610, 611t
　stress management, 612–625
　suicide attempt, 435–436
　teaching, 387, 390, 391, 392, 393, 394, 396, 397, 398–399, 401, 402, 405–406, 409, 411–413, 414–415, 416, 422, 423, 425, 426, 428, 429–430, 431, 434, 435–436, 437, 439, 441, 442

Z

Zen sect, 87
Zoonosis, 54
Zoroastrianism, 83

Italicized letters following page numbers indicate tables (t), figures (f), and Appendices (A).